MW01485784

AFIO's Guide to the Study of Intelligence

Peter C. Oleson, Editor

ISBN-10: 0-9975273-0-7
ISBN-13: 978-0-9975273-0-8

LIBRARY OF CONGRESS CONTROL NUMBER: 2016953150

PUBLISHED BY AFIO, ASSOCIATION OF FORMER INTELLIGENCE OFFICERS
7700 LEESBURG PIKE SUITE 324, FALLS CHURCH, VIRGINIA 22043
WWW.AFIO.COM

NAMES: OLESON, PETER C., 1945 - EDITOR AND AUTHOR | AFIO - ASSOCIATION OF FORMER INTELLI-
GENCE OFFICERS, INC.
TITLE: AFIO's GUIDE TO THE STUDY OF INTELLIGENCE / PETER C. OLESON
DESCRIPTION: FALLS CHURCH, VA: AFIO, [2016]. | SUMMARY: A COLLECTION OF ARTICLES BY EXPERTS
ON MODERN AND HISTORIC NATIONAL SECURITY AND INTELLIGENCE TOPICS. INCLUDES GLOSSARY AND
BIBLIOGRAPHICAL REFERENCES.
IDENTIFIERS: LCCN 2016953150   (PRINT) | ISBN 10: 0-9975273-0-7 (PAPERBACK)
SUBJECTS: LCSH: INTELLIGENCE SERVICE--UNITED STATES HANDBOOKS, MANUALS, ETC.

ASSOCIATION OF FORMER INTELLIGENCE OFFICERS
7700 LEESBURG PIKE, SUITE 324
FALLS CHURCH, VIRGINIA 22043
Web: www.afio.com, Email: afio@afio.com
Tel: 703-790-0320 Fax: 703-991-1278
AFIO is a non-profit tax exempt §501(c)(3) educational association, formed in Maryland
in 1975 and incorporated in Virginia in 1977. AFIO conducts and supports public outreach education programs focusing on the role and importance of US Intelligence for
national security, and providing perspectives on intelligence issues and related events.

First Edition

Front and back cover images © 2016 Shutterstock

Foreword

When I joined the Central Intelligence Agency in 1966, about the only public source of information about the world of intelligence was found in the fiction of John Le Carré and Ian Fleming. For those in the profession, their portrayals were, shall we say, incomplete if not misleading. There were, of course, books published in the 1950s and 1960s about the role of intelligence in World War II but they focused mainly on derring-do operations and offered little about the collection and analysis of intelligence information and virtually nothing about cryptography. Secret intelligence remained largely secret, and neither scholars nor the public had much appreciation for the realities of intelligence work, its many dimensions and complexities, or its role in the decision-making process.

As director of Central Intelligence when the Cold War ended and the Soviet Union collapsed, I believed that public support for a continuing large-scale intelligence effort in the United States would depend upon greater public understanding of the role of intelligence — in how intelligence organizations gather and analyze the military, economic, political and myriad other kinds of information from around the world critical to presidential decision-making and Congressional deliberations, as well as the CIA's role in carrying out covert operations abroad at the direction of the president.

What a difference a quarter of a century makes. During those years, we have seen the emergence of the study of intelligence as a full-fledged and respected field of scholarly research and writing, with teaching curricula, multi-disciplinary conferences and seminars in many colleges and universities. Today, the problem for scholars is not the scarcity of information and documents, but their vast number.

Among the challenges facing many educators is, first, the fact that intelligence is a complex subject, exceeding by far the public perception of what is involved in both intelligence operations and the collection of intelligence information, its verification, analysis, synthesis and relevance for senior policymakers. A second challenge is that so much formerly secret information about intelligence has been declassified in recent years that educators confront a surfeit of books, articles, blog postings and more on the subject.

The goal of this *Guide* is to help deal with both challenges. It addresses the many aspects of the complex intelligence field with focused articles designed to help educators apply the information, insights and knowledge therein to specific course syllabi. And, the *Guide* aims to ease the educator's task by addressing critical topics and providing knowledgeable sources for further reading and exploration.

Intelligence – spying – is often said to be the world's second oldest profession. The *Guide*'s articles on the history of intelligence fill in many missing elements essential to a comprehensive understanding of history, especially in the 20th and 21st centuries. As an example, think how different the course of World War II might have been had the U.S. and U.K. not been able to intercept German message traffic thanks to "Enigma" and Japanese communications due to "Magic." This *Guide* provides information on numerous other instances where intelligence has played a critical – and previously unknown – role. It also provides highly valuable information on the intelligence services of other countries.

The *Guide* is the culmination of a five-year-long effort involving contributions from many experienced intelligence practitioners and noted scholars. It builds on the long-standing mission of public education of the Association of Former Intelligence Officers.

In 1986, as CIA's Deputy Director for Intelligence, I reached an agreement with Professors Ernest May and Richard Neustadt at the John F. Kennedy School of Government to provide them and associated researchers unprecedented access to intelligence analyses and analysts, enabling the preparation of numerous case studies of the role on intelligence in specific policy decisions going back several decades. That scholarly work on the field of intelligence has expanded so broadly since that time is a very welcome development. It is in the best interest of an informed public on this critical subject and, I hope, will as well entice students interested in public service to consider a career in an arena so many of us found stimulating and fulfilling. AFIO's *Guide* renders a great service in facilitating such scholarly work.

Robert M. Gates
5 December 2015

Preface

The *Guide to the Study of Intelligence* grew out of a discussion in 2010 at a board meeting of the Association of Former Intelligence Officers. It was noted that university courses in intelligence were widespread and the relevant literature was blossoming. However, there was little critical guidance available for instructors on what literature was good and what was not so good. The intent of the *Guide* was to provide instructors with an introduction to a topic and relevant research materials that could be used for and in the classroom.

As chairman of the Academic Exchange Committee for AFIO, I had the task of deciding what the Association could do. I recalled an effort of 42 years before, when Professor Allan B. Cole of the Fletcher School of Law and Diplomacy asked me to help him compile a guide for teachers related to the study of Chinese Communism. In 1968, Mao's takeover of Mainland China was not yet twenty years old. Much of the People's Republic and the Chinese version of Communism remained a mystery to scholars. The result was a slim 50-page guide of the current literature.[1]

So an old idea was reborn with a different focus. With the selfless contributions of many intelligence professionals and academics this *Guide to the Study of Intelligence* was born. Soliciting these articles, reading them, and editing them have been a very enjoyable experience. I have learned a great deal about the profession I entered in 1967 and have never left. My hope is that the *Guide* is as useful and enjoyable for others as it has been for me.

Peter C. Oleson, Editor
Galesville, Maryland
October 2015

---

1. Cole, Allan B. and Peter C. Oleson, *Fifty Years of Chinese Communism: Selected Readings with Commentary*, Publication Number 47 (Washington, DC: American Historical Association, Service Center for Teachers of History, 1969).

Acknowledgements

This *Guide* is the result of the collaboration of many people. It would not have been possible except for the contributions of the authors of its many articles. AFIO and the users of this *Guide* owe a debt of gratitude to all of those listed as Contributors. There are others, too numerous to name, who offered suggestions for articles, critiqued various drafts, and recommended recent books and articles applicable to the various topics. My thanks to all of you.

Several individuals contributed valuable guidance at the start of this project. John Lenczowski of the Institute of World Politics helped refine the concept for the *Guide*. Peter Earnest and Mark Stout of the International Spy Museum also helped me focus the effort and avoid some pitfalls. Experienced editor James Bruce offered sage counsel. Professor (emeritus) of History Douglas Wheeler of the University of New Hampshire was a frequent email correspondent and great help. Gene Poteat, president (emeritus) of AFIO, always offered encouragement as well as article contributions.

A special thanks has to go to Elizabeth Bancroft, the Executive Director of AFIO and editor of its journal, The *Intelligencer*. She ushered me through the details of preparing articles for publication, the intricacies of the *Chicago Manual of Style*, obtaining license agreements from all of the authors, and a myriad of other minutiae that are essential to producing a volume such as this. Her artistic sense enhanced many of the *Guide's* articles published in The *Intelligencer*.

My wife, Luuk, deserves an extended hug and kiss for all the time I spent over the computer lost in thought. Her patience is one of the pillars upon which this *Guide* was constructed.

Peter C. Oleson

Dedication

To those who have educated me about world affairs
and the field of intelligence,
and continue to do so.

Table of Contents

PART I – INTRODUCTION TO THE TOPIC

PART II – HISTORY OF INTELLIGENCE

PART IV – ESPIONAGE, COUNTERINTELLIGENCE, AND COVERT ACTION

PART V – POLICY, OVERSIGHT, AND ISSUES

PART VI – INTELLIGENCE ABROAD

PART VII – MISCELLANY

Introduction

The "many studies of policy-making in East and West which fail to take intelligence into account are at best incomplete, at worst distorted."
— Christopher Andrew, Historian[1]

The goal of the *Guide to the Study of Intelligence* is to help instructors teach about the field of intelligence. This includes secondary school teachers of American History, Civics, or current events and undergraduate and graduate professors of History, Political Science, International Relations, Security Studies, and related topics, especially those with no or limited professional experience in the field. The assumption is that none of the secondary school teachers or undergraduate instructors is an expert in the topic of intelligence. Even those who are former practitioners are likely to have only a limited knowledge of the very broad field of intelligence, as most spend their careers in one or two agencies at most and may have focused only on collection or analysis of intelligence or support to those activities.

In each of the articles the intent is to identify the important learning points for students and the materials that an instructor can use to teach. This includes books, articles, and web sites that meet certain criteria, such as:

- Balance. A recommended book or article should address more than one side of a subject. If it does not, then a book or article representing the opposing point of view should be referenced also. The Guide is intended as an apolitical, non-partisan effort.

- Completeness. If a recommended book or article covers only a small portion of the topic, article authors were encouraged to include others that address other portions.

- Supportable. It is unhelpful to present to teachers materials that are assertive but not supported by any evidence. Article authors were requested to clearly identify opinion pieces, including the authors' biases, if known or discernible.

---

1. Christopher Andrew (2010), "Intelligence in the Cold War," in M.P. Leffler & O.A. Westad (Eds.) *The Cambridge History of the Cold War*. Cambridge: Cambridge University Press, p 417.

Different authors have taken different approaches to their topics. Some have addressed how to construct a course; others have been more narrative; and others have recounted their experiences in the White House, State Department, and CIA. Some of the recommended readings are in foreign languages.

Some of the languages needed by the Intelligence Community: Arabic, Dari, Farsi, Hausa and other sub-Saharan languages, Hebrew, Indonesian, Korean, Kurdish, Mandarin, Pashto, Punjabi, Russian, Somali, Swahili, Turkish, Urdu.

In order to ensure that the *Guide* is useful and not overwhelming each article is relatively brief. Of course, this means that the topics addressed in the *Guide* are not comprehensive. However, some addressing complex subjects, such as reconnaissance from space, intelligence in World War II, and the history of espionage cases, are somewhat lengthy.

The *Guide* is organized into seven parts. Part I includes four introductory articles. Part II is on the history of intelligence from antiquity to the post-Cold War world. Part III examines the intelligence disciplines, applications, and support to various missions. Part IV relates to teaching about espionage, counterintelligence, and covert action. Part V addresses some of the major issues related to intelligence policy and oversight. While most of the *Guide* is US-centric, Part VI focuses on intelligence organizations in other countries. Part VII includes three articles on how to stay informed and the literature of intelligence.

The *Guide* is published in both pdf and hardcopy formats. The pdf version appears on the AFIO website (*http://www.afio.com*) and is electronically searchable. All articles are downloadable and free to copy and use. The printed version is available via AFIO.[2] See the AFIO website for price and cost of mailing.

The subject of intelligence evokes various reactions often depending upon one's political persuasion. We expect that some readers will differ with the content of some of the articles. Each article reflects the views of its author(s) and not necessarily the views of AFIO. AFIO encourages feedback on the *Guide* and any of its articles. Email *guide@afio.com*.

"Intelligence goes to war every day." – John Hamre[3]

---

2. Absent an index, readers of the printed volume are directed to the pdf version, which is electronically searchable.
3. Comment by John Hamre, former Deputy Secretary of Defense, to the Association of Former Intelligence Officers, May 2, 2014.

Glossary

Abbreviations, acronyms, and terms used in *Guide* articles

This Glossary is limited. Readers are encouraged to use the following glossaries, which are far more comprehensive:

- Defense Intelligence Agency, Terms and Definitions of Interest for Counterintelligence Professionals, 9 June 2014, available at *https://fas.org/irp/eprint/ci-glossary.pdf*.

- Goldman, Jan, *Words of Intelligence: An Intelligence Professional's Lexicon for Domestic and Foreign Threats*, Second Edition (Lanham, MD: Scarecrow Press, 2011). This is a 300-page dictionary of terms, abbreviations, and acronyms covering both the intelligence and homeland security fields. Its entries are drawn from multiple government sources, plus NATO documents, legal papers, and scholarly volumes. It includes a useful topical index. It is quite comprehensive.

A

A-11 OXCART – CIA-developed predecessor to the better known US Air Force SR-71 high altitude Mach 3 reconnaissance aircraft.

ABM – Anti-ballistic missile.

Abwehr – German military intelligence (1920 – 1945).

ACIC – Aeronautical Charting and Information Center (US Air Force).

ADDNI – Assistant Deputy Director of National Intelligence.

AFMIC – Armed Forces Medical Intelligence Center, now NCMI.

AFSA – Armed Forces Security Agency. Predecessor to NSA.

AGI – Advanced geospatial intelligence.

AIVD – Dutch General Intelligence and Security Service.

All-source – Analysis that relies on all of the collection disciplines.

AO – Area of operations.

ASD(SOLIC) – Assistant Secretary of Defense (Special Operations and Low

Intensity Conflict).

ASW – Anti-submarine warfare.

ATF – See BATF.

B

BATF – Bureau of Alcohol, Tobacco, Firearms, and Explosives, US Department of Justice.

BBC – British Broadcasting Corporation.

B-Dienst (Beobachtungsdienst) – The codebreaking department of German naval intelligence in World War II.

BI – (1) Business intelligence. (2) Background investigation. (3) Bureau of Investigation (predecessor to the FBI).

Bigot list – list of individuals who are authorized access to exceptionally sensitive information.

Black Chamber – US SIGINT organization (1919 – 1929).

Black program – Highly secret program, the existence of which is not acknowledged.

Black site – Secret location. Usually associated with CIA.

BND –Bundesnachrichtendienst, German foreign intelligence service.

BOP – Bureau of Prisons, US Department of Justice.

BOTNET – Robotic network. A computer network controlled by other than its owner.

BSC – British Security Coordination.

C

CA – Covert action.

Cambridge Five – British Communist sympathizers recruited by Soviet intelligence (Donald Maclean, Guy Burgess, Kim Philby, Anthony Blunt, and John Caincross).

Cast – US Navy SIGINT site in the Philippines.

CBME – Combined Bureau Middle East, British intelligence organization in Cairo during World War II.

CBRNE – Chemical, biological, radiological, nuclear, and explosives.

CCP – Consolidated Cryptologic Program. Budget for national SIGINT activities.

CDC – Centers for Disease Control and Prevention (Department of Health and Human Services).

CEO – Chief Executive Officer.

Cheka – All-Russian Extraordinary Committee to Combat Counterrevolution and Sabotage. Bolshevik secret police (1917 – 1922).

CI – (1) Counterintelligence. (2) Confidential informant, law enforcement term for a human source. (3) Competitive intelligence (private sector).

CIA – Central Intelligence Agency.

CIAP – CIA Program. Budget for the CIA.

CIFA – Counterintelligence Field Activity (DoD).

Cipher – An algorithm used to transform words, numbers, letters, or symbols for the purposes of disguising a message's content.

CISEN – Centro de Investigación y Seguridad Nacional, the "Mexican CIA."

CJCS – Chairman, Joint Chiefs of Staff.

Clandestine – Something done secretly without the knowledge of others not involved.

CMA – Community Management Account. Budget for the DNI's office.

CNA – Computer network attack. Cyber attack to disrupt a computer network.

CND – Computer network defense.

CNE – Computer network exploitation (subset of cyber intelligence).

CNO – Computer network operations (includes CNA, CND, and CNE).

Code – A system of words, numbers, letters, or symbols substituted for others for the purposes of disguising a message's content.

Codeword – a word chosen to identify along with a level of classification particularly sensitive information.

COIN – Counter insurgency.

COMINT – Communications intelligence (subset of SIGINT).

Comintern – Communist International, a Soviet sponsored international organization (1919 – 1943) promoting Communism. Also a front for Soviet intelligence operations.

COMSEC – Communications security.

CORONA – program name for the US's first imagery reconnaissance satellites.

Counterproliferation – Efforts to impede the spread of WMD.

Covert – Not openly acknowledged by the actor.

CPB – Bureau of Customs and Border Protection, Department of Homeland Security.

CRITIC – Critical intelligence communication.

CRS – Congressional Research Service.

CRT – Cathode ray tube.

CSEC – Communications Security Establishment Canada.

CSIS – Canadian Security Intelligence Service.

CWC – Chemical Weapons Convention.

Cyber – Relating to computers and networks, information technology, and virtual reality.

Cyber intelligence – sometimes considered a subset of SIGINT.

D

DARPA – Defense Advanced Research Projects Agency.

DCI – Director of Central Intelligence (1947 – 2004).

DCIA – Director Central Intelligence Agency.

D&D – Denial and deception. Also CD&D for concealment, denial and deception.

D-Day – Term used for the initiation date of a major military operation.

DDCI – Deputy Director of Central Intelligence.

DCRI – Direction centrale du renseignement intérieur. French domestic intelligence agency (2008 – 2014).

DDO – Deputy Director of Operations (CIA's clandestine HUMINT directorate).

DDOS – Distributed denial of service, a form of cyber attack.

DDP – Deputy Director for Plans (CIA), later DDO – Deputy Director for Operations.

DEA – Drug Enforcement Administration, US Department of Justice.

DF – Direction finding (a SIGINT technique). Also D/F.

DGI – Dirección General de Inteligencia, Cuba's intelligence service.

DGSE – Direction Générale de la Sécurité Extérieure, French foreign intelligence agency.

DGSI — Direction générale du renseignement intérieur. French domestic intelligence service since 2014.

Disinformation – false or misleading information.

DHS – Department of Homeland Security (US).

DI – Defence Intelligence (UK Ministry of Defence).

DIA – Defense Intelligence Agency.

DIAC – Defense Intelligence Analysis Center.

DMA – Defense Mapping Agency.

DNA – Deoxyribonucleic acid.

DNI – Director of National Intelligence (2004...).

DoD – Department of Defense (US). Also DOD.

DoJ – Department of Justice.

Double agent – Intelligence agent secretly working for the target nation and against the nation employing him/her.

DST — Direction de la surveillance du territoire. Previous French domestic intelligence agency.

DTRA – Defense Threat Reduction Agency.

E

ELINT – Electronic intelligence (subset of SIGINT).

Enigma – Sophisticated German enciphering machine introduced in the 1920s. Also refers to the German Morse Code cipher used during World War II.

EO – (1) Executive Order. (2) Electro-optical.

ESM – Electronic surveillance measures. Often confused with ELINT.

EU – European Union.

EW – Electronic warfare.

F

FAA – Federal Aviation Administrations, Department of Transportation.

FBI – Federal Bureau of Investigation, US Department of Justice.

FBIS – Foreign Broadcast Information Service (CIA).

FBMS – Foreign Broadcast Monitoring Service (1941 – 1947).

FEMA – Federal Emergency Management Administration, Department of Homeland Security.

FIS – Foreign instrumentation signals (subset of SIGINT). Also FISINT or

TELINT, telemetry intelligence.

FISA – Foreign Intelligence Surveillance Act.

FISC – Foreign Intelligence Surveillance Court.

Fish – German radio-teletype printer system decrypted by the Allies in World War II.

Five Eyes – SIGINT agreement linking the US, UK, Canada, Australia, and New Zealand.

FORTITUDE – Codename for deception operations related to Operation Overlord, the Normandy invasion on June 6, 1944.

FMV – Full motion video. A type of IMINT.

FRD – Federal Research Division (Library of Congress).

FSB – Federal Security Service of the Russian Federation (1991 ...).

FSO – Federal Protective Service (Russia) (1991 ...).

FRUMEL – Fleet Radio Unit – Melbourne. Joint US Navy-Australian SIGINT unit in World War II.

FUSAG – First US Army Group – the fictional unit commanded by General George Patton. Part of the FORTITUDE deception operations.

FYDP – Future Years Defense Program.

G

GAO – Government Accountability Office (US).

GCCS – Government Code and Cipher School, the British code breaking organization at Bletchley Park. Now GCHQ.

GCHQ – Government Communications Headquarters (UK), Britain's signals intelligence organization.

GDIP – General Defense Intelligence Program.

GEOINT – Geospatial intelligence. The correlation of imagery, geospatial and other information.

Gestapo – Nazi Germany's secret police organization (1933 – 1945).

Global Hawk – High altitude long endurance unmanned aerial vehicle.

GPS – Global Positioning System.

GRU – Soviet/Russian military intelligence organization of the General Staff.

Gulag – Soviet prison camps.

H

Hagelin – Enciphering machine used by Italy in World War II and broken by the Allies.

HAC – House Appropriations Committee.

HASC – House Armed Services Committee.

HFDF – High Frequency Direction Finding.

HIDTA – High Intensity Drug Trafficking Area. Counter-drug law enforcement task force.

HPSCI – House Permanent Select Committee on Intelligence.

HSI – Homeland security intelligence.

HUMINT – Human source intelligence.
HVT – High value target.
Hypo – US Navy SIGINT site at Pearl Harbor, Hawaii.

I

IA – Information Assurance.
IAEA – International Atomic Energy Agency, element of the United Nations.
I&A – Intelligence and Analysis (Department of Homeland Security).
IAFIE – International Association for Intelligence Education.
IC – Intelligence Community (US).
ICs – Integrated circuits.
ICBM – Intercontinental ballistic missile.
ICD – Intelligence Community Directive.
ICE – Bureau of Immigration and Customs Enforcement, Department of Homeland Security.
ICJ – International Court of Justice.
IED – Improvised explosive device.
Illegal – an intelligence officer operating under a false identity and not connected ostensibly with his/her sponsoring country.
IMINT – Imagery intelligence.
Imperial General Staff – Japanese high command in World War II.
In-Q-Tel – CIA's venture capital technology investment organization.
INFOSEC – Information security.
INR – Bureau of Intelligence and Research (Department of State).
INT – Intelligence discipline, normally a collection discipline (e.g., HUMINT, SIGINT, IMINT, OSINT, MASINT).
IOB – Intelligence Oversight Board (subset of PIAB).
IP – Intellectual property.
IPB – Intelligence preparation of the battlefield.
IRTPA – Intelligence Reform and Terrorism Prevention Act (2004).
ISC – Intelligence and Security Committee (UK Parliamentary body).
ISG – Iraq Survey Group.
ISR – Intelligence, surveillance, reconnaissance.
IT – Information technology. Also ICT, Information and communication technology.

J

JCS – Joint Chiefs of Staff (US).
JITF-CT – Joint Intelligence Task Force – Counterterrorism (DIA element).
JMIC – Joint Military Intelligence College (now National Intelligence University).
JN-25 – Japanese Navy operational code in World War II.
JIC – Joint Intelligence Committee (UK).
JIO – Joint Intelligence Organization (UK).
JSPS – Joint Strategic Planning System (US).

JSTARS – Joint Surveillance Target Attack Radar [aircraft].
JTAC – Joint Terrorism Analysis Center (UK).
JTTF – Joint Terrorism Task Force (FBI-led interagency groups).
JWICS – Joint Worldwide Intelligence Communications System.

K

KGB – Committee for State Security. Soviet (later Russian) intelligence service (1954 – 1991).
KH – Keyhole. Designation for US imagery reconnaissance satellites.

L

LASD – Los Angeles Sheriff's Department.
LE – Law Enforcement.
LIDAR – Light (or laser) detection and ranging.
Line X – KGB's technology espionage group.
Luftwaffe – German Air Force during World War II.

M

M&A – Mergers and acquisitions.
MAD – Mutual Assured Destruction.
MAGIC – Codename for intelligence from breaking Japanese codes.
MASINT – Measurement and signatures intelligence.
MGB – Ministry of State Security (USSR) (1946 – 1953).
MI – Military intelligence (US).
MI5 – British Security Service.
MI6 – British Secret Intelligence Service.
MI8 – British Radio Security Service in World War II that, inter alia, ran the Y-Service.
MICE – Money, ideology, compromise/coercion, ego, motivations for committing espionage.
MIP – Military Intelligence Program. Budget for tactical intelligence activities in DoD.
MOVINT – Movement intelligence. A concept involving imagery and time.
MP – (1) Member of Parliament (UK). (2) Military Police.
MPS – Ministry of Public Security (Peoples Republic of China).
MSS – Ministry of State Security (Peoples Republic of China) (1983 …).
Multi-INT – Analysis that uses more than a single source of intelligence. Less comprehensive than all-source.
MVD – Ministry of Internal Affairs (USSR) (1953 – 1954).

N

NASA – National Aeronautics and Atmospheric Administration.
NATO – North Atlantic Treaty Organization.
NCIX – National Counterintelligence Executive.
NCMI – National Center for Medical Intelligence (DIA), formerly AFMIC.
NCPC – National Counterproliferation Center.
NCS – National Clandestine Service (US).
NCTC – National Counterterrorism Center.
NGA – National Geospatial-Intelligence Agency.
NGP – National Geospatial-Intelligence Program. Budget for NGA.
NIE – National Intelligence Estimate.
NIP – National Intelligence Program. Formerly the NFIP – National Foreign Intelligence Program. Overall budget for national intelligence activities.
NIU – National Intelligence University.
NKGB — Peoples' Commissariat for State Security. Soviet intelligence and security service (1941 – 1946).
NKVD – Peoples' Commissariat for Internal Affairs. Soviet intelligence service (1922).
NMEC – National Media Exploitation Center (DIA).
NIMA – National Imagery and Mapping Agency (1996 – 2003). Renamed as NGA.
NPIC – National Photographic Interpretation Center (CIA/DIA element).
NRL – Naval Research Laboratory.
NRO – National Reconnaissance Office.
NRP – National Reconnaissance Program. Budget for the NRO.
NSA – National Security Agency.
NSC – National Security Council.
NTIS – National Technical Information Service (US Department of Commerce).
NTM – National Technical Means.
NYPD – New York (City) Police Department.

O

OB – Order of Battle.
OFAC – Office of Foreign Assets Control (US Department of the Treasury).
OGPU – All Union State Political Directorate, the Soviet secret police (1923-1934).
Okhrana – Tsarist secret police (1882 – 1917).
OKW – Oberkommando der Wehrmacht. German High Command in World War II.
OMB – Office of Management and Budget (Executive Office of the President).
ONI – Office of Naval Intelligence (US).
OPCW – Organization for the Prohibition of Chemical Weapons.
OPEC – Organization of Petroleum Exporting Countries.
OSC – Open Source Center (at CIA).
OPELINT – Operational ELINT.

OSINT – Open source intelligence.
OSS – Office of Strategic Services.
OVERLORD – Codename for the Normandy invasion in World War II.
OXCART – See A-11 OXCART.

P

PC – Personal computer.
PCC – Policy Coordinating Committee. NSC committee in George W. Bush Administration.
PDB – President's Daily Brief.
PIAB – President's Intelligence Advisory Board. Formerly PFIAB, President's Foreign Intelligence Advisory Board.
PGM – Precision guided munitions.
PI – Photo interpreter.
PLA – Peoples Liberation Army (Peoples Republic of China).
2PLA – Second Department of the PLA General Staff. HUMINT, SIGINT, IMINT, and counterintelligence organization of Chinese military intelligence.
PM – Program manager.
POW – Prisoner of war.
POW-MIA – Prisoner of War-Missing in Action. (DIA analytical cell.)
PPBE – Planning, programming, budgeting and execution [system], DoD's financial planning and management system.
PRC – Peoples Republic of China.
Predator – Medium altitude unmanned aerial vehicle.
Principals Committee – Senior most committee in the NSC structure.
PSI – Proliferation Security Initiative, international effort to inhibit the spread of WMD.
PURPLE – Japanese diplomatic code broken by the US Army's SIS in September 1940.

Q

QDR – Quadrennial Defense Review.

R

Radar – Radio [frequency] detection and ranging.
RADINT – Radar intelligence.
RAF – Royal Air Force (UK).
R&D Research and development.
RCMP – Royal Canadian Mounted Police.
RF – Radio frequency.
RN – Royal Navy (UK).
RPV – Remotely piloted vehicle. See also UAV.

S

SAC – (1) Strategic Air Command (US Air Force). (2) Senate Appropriations Committee.

SACO – Sino-American Cooperative Organization. US Navy element in China during World War II engaged in weather intelligence, coast watching, and sabotage.

SALT – Strategic Arms Limitation Talks.

Säpo – Säkerhetspolisen, Swedish security police (Ministry of Justice).

SASC – Senate Armed Services Committee.

SCI – Sensitive compartmented information.

SCIP – Strategic and Competitive Intelligence Professionals (formerly Society for Competitive Intelligence Professionals).

SD – Sicherheitsdeinst. Intelligence agency of the SS and Nazi Party responsible for internal security.

SDECE — Service de documentation extérieure et de contre-espionnage. French foreign intelligence service (1945 – 1981).

SEAL – Sea, air, land. US Navy special operations.

SIGINT – Signals intelligence.

SIOP – Single Integrated Operations Plan (US nuclear war plan).

SIS – (1) British Secret Intelligence Service (also known as MI6). (2) US Army Secret Intelligence Service, the code breaking arm of Army intelligence in World War II. (3) FBI Special Intelligence Service, the FBI's intelligence organization in Latin America during World War II.

Sit Room – White House Situation Room.

SOE – Special Operations Executive, British infiltration and sabotage organization in World War II.

SOF – Special operations forces.

Spetznaz – Soviet/Russian special operations forces.

SS – Shutzstaffel, Nazi paramilitary organization under Himmler. The Waffen (armed) SS was a separate military force from the Wehrmacht.

SSCI – Senate Select Committee on Intelligence.

START – Strategic Arms Reduction Talks.

Stasi – Ministry of State Security. East German secret police and intelligence service.

SUV – Sports Utility Vehicle.

SVR – Russian foreign intelligence service (1991...).

T

TEMPEST – Program to shield electronic machines from emitting electromagnetic and acoustic information that can compromise information.

Tradecraft – Techniques and tools used in all aspects of intelligence collection and analysis.

TRIPLEX – British clandestine thefts from diplomatic pouches during World War II.

TSA – Transportation Security Administration, Department of Homeland Security.

TUNNY – Allied codename for decipherment of the German Fish communications.

U

U-2 – CIA-developed high altitude reconnaissance aircraft.

UAV – Unmanned serial vehicle. Also UAS, unmanned aerial system. Often called "drones."

UBL – Usama Bin Laden. Also OBL – Osama Bin Laden.

U-boat – German submarine in World Wars I and II.

UFAC – Underground Facilities Analysis Center (DIA).

UK – United Kingdom.

ULTRA – Codeword used to designate intelligence gathered from decryption of German ciphers, such as Enigma and Fish.

UN – United Nations.

USAID – US Agency for International Development.

USCG – US Coast Guard, Department of Homeland Security.

USD(C) – Under Secretary of Defense (Comptroller). DoD chief financial officer.

USD(I) – Under Secretary of Defense (Intelligence).

USGS – US Geological Survey (Department of the Interior).

USSOCOM – US Special Operations Command.

USMS – US Marshals Service, US Department of Justice.

USSR – Union of Soviet Socialist Republics (1922 – 1991)

USSS – United States Secret Service, Department of Homeland Security.

V

VENONA – Codeword for the breaking of Soviet diplomatic and intelligence codes in the late 1940s.

Vet – the process of critically examining the veracity and accuracy of a HUMINT source or the accuracy and completeness of intelligence information.

VoIP – Voice over Internet protocol.

W

Wehrmacht – German army in World War II.

Wig-wag – Late 1800s system of messaging using one flag or light. Similar to Morse code dots and dashes.

WMD – Weapons of mass destruction.

WW I – World War One (1914 – 1918).

WW II – World War Two (1939 – 1945).

X

X-2 – Counterintelligence element of the OSS in Europe in World War II.

XX Committee – "Double Cross" Committee that managed British double agent operations against the Axis in World War II.

Y

Y-Service – British tactical signals intelligence organization focused on direction-finding and breaking low-level codes.

Contributors

STEWART BAKER, J.D. is a partner in the law firm of Steptoe & Johnson in Washington, D.C., with a law practice that covers homeland security, international trade, cybersecurity, data protection, and travel and foreign investment regulation. He was General Counsel of the Silberman-Robb WMD Commission in 2004-2005. From 2005 to 2009, he was the first Assistant Secretary for Policy at the Department of Homeland Security. Mr. Baker has also been General Counsel of the National Security Agency and is the author of *Skating on Stilts* (Stanford: Hoover Institution Press, 2010), a book (and blog) on terrorism, cybersecurity, and other technology issues. He is a member of the board of AFIO.

JOSHUA BART is an operations research specialist and intelligence analyst for The Inter-Sec Group in San Antonio, Texas. He is an alumnus of The University of Texas at San Antonio (UTSA) where he studied Political Science, International Studies, and Global Analysis. Mr. Bart is pursuing a Master's certification in Geographic Information Systems from UTSA.

Eleni Braat, Ph.D. is Assistant Professor in the History Department of Utrecht University, the Netherlands. Her research and teaching include 20th century intelligence, international and political history. She specializes in the tensions between secrecy and democracy in the field of intelligence and diplomacy in 20th century Europe. Her most recent book, published in her capacity as the official historian of the Dutch General Intelligence and Security Service (AIVD) (2008-2014), is: *Van oude jongens, de dingen die voorbij gaan. Een sociale geschiedenis van de Binnenlandse Veiligheidsdienst, 1945-1998 (Old boys and the things that pass. A social history of the Dutch Security Service, 1945-1998).*

JAMES B. BRUCE, PH.D. is a Senior Political Scientist at the RAND Corporation. He retired from CIA in 2005 after serving nearly 24 years as Deputy National Intelligence Officer for Science and Technology and as Vice Chairman of the DCI (now DNI) Foreign Denial and Deception Committee. Formerly a senior fellow at CIA's Sherman Kent School for Intelligence Analysis, he has held management positions in CIA's Directorates of Intelligence and Operations. He also served as a senior staff member on the Commission on the Intelligence Capabilities of the United States Regarding Weapons of Mass Destruction (Silberman-Robb WMD Commission). He has authored numerous classified studies including National Intelligence Estimates. His unclassified publications have appeared in *Studies in Intelligence*, the *Defense Intelligence Journal*, *World Politics*, and several anthologies. He co-edited, with Roger George, *Analyzing Intelligence: National Security Practitioners' Perspectives*, 2nd ed. (Georgetown University Press, 2014). Formerly a faculty member at the National War College, he is an adjunct professor at Georgetown University and previously at Columbia and American Universities. He is a member of the boards of directors of AFIO and the National Strategy Information Center (NSIC).

RONALD L. BURGESS, JR., LTG, US ARMY (R), M.S., was the 17th Director of the Defense Intelligence Agency, serving from 18 March 2009 to 24 July 2012. He has served as Director of Intelligence, J-2, at the Joint Special Operations Command (JSOC), US Southern Command, and the Joint Staff. From August 2005 to February 2009 he was the Deputy Director of National Intelligence for Customer Outcomes and later the Director of the Intelligence Staff. He twice served as the Acting Principal Deputy Director of National Intelligence. He retired in September 2012 after 38 years in the US Army.

STEPHEN H. CAMPBELL, B.SC., M.A.L.D., is a security consultant specializing in non-state threats. He is President of Non-State Threat Intelligence, LLC, and Strategy Adviser to Eosedge Legal. He has held roles as a researcher, analyst, consultant, educator, and marketing strategist. He earned a B.Sc. Honors First Class in Physics from the University of Glasgow, a Masters in Law and Diplomacy from the Fletcher School of Law and Diplomacy, and is currently studying for a Masters of Science in Cyber Security at the University of Fairfax.

DAVID L. CHARNEY, M.D., is Medical Director of Roundhouse Square Psychiatric Center, Alexandria, Virginia. He has been a consultant and therapist to Intelligence Community personnel for many years. He has worked on the defense teams for several accused spies, including Earl Pitts, Robert Hanssen, and Brian Regan. Many common assumptions about spy motivation have been brought into question by Dr. Charney's work.

ROBERT M. CLARK, PH.D., J.D., is a consultant for the US Intelligence Community, a faculty member of the Intelligence and Security Academy, and adjunct professor of intelligence studies at the University of Maryland University College and Johns Hopkins University. Dr. Clark served in the United States Air Force as an electronics warfare officer and intelligence officer. At CIA, he was a senior analyst and group chief managing analytic methodologies. He subsequently was President and CEO of the Scientific and Technical Analysis Corporation. Dr. Clark has published three books: *Intelligence Analysis: A Target-centric Approach*, now in its fourth edition; *The Technical Collection of Intelligence*, published in 2010; and *Intelligence Collection*, published in 2013. He is co-author of *Target-Centric Network Modeling*, and co-editor of *The 5 Disciplines of Intelligence Collection*, both published in 2015.

JONATHAN D. CLEMENTE, M.D., is a physician in Charlotte, North Carolina. He is Chief of the Department of Radiology at Carolinas Medical Center and has an adjunct faculty appointment with the University of North Carolina – Chapel Hill School of Medicine. He is writing a scholarly history of medical and psychological support for the Intelligence Community and a history of the US medical intelligence program from World War II to the present.

ELBRIDGE COLBY, J.D., is a fellow at the Center for a New American Security, where he focuses on issues of strategy, nuclear weapons, and intelligence and serves as a consultant or advisor to a number of US Government entities. He previously served for over five years in the US Government in a number of intelligence and nuclear policy positions, including on the Silberman-Robb WMD Commission and with the Office of the Director of National Intelligence. He is a graduate of Harvard College and Yale Law School.

JOSÉ MEDINA GONZÁLEZ DÁVILA, PH.D., has a B.A. in International Relations from the Monterrey Superior Studies Institute of Technology (ITESM) (Mexico); an M.A. in International Studies from the Graduate School of Public Policy and Public Administration of the ITESM, specializing in foreign, Soviet and Russian intelligence; and a Ph.D. in Social Anthropology from the Universidad Iberoamericana, specializing in ethnology and military anthropology. He is a professor at the Naval Superior Studies Center of the Mexican Navy, and the Anahuac University (Mexico-North). He has also been an intelligence consultant for different government organizations. His lines of research are Strategic and International Intelligence, Military Anthropology, and National Security.

LAWRENCE D. DIETZ, M.A., M.B.A., J.D., LL.M., is chief legal officer of TAL Global and has over 30 years of military and commercial intelligence and security experience. As an Adjunct Professor for American Military University, he teaches about intelligence and security. He retired as a Colonel in the US Army Reserve. His degrees include B.S. in Business Administration, Northeastern University; M.B.A. (with distinction), Babson College; J.D., Suffolk University Law School; LL.M. in European Law, University of Leicester, United Kingdom; and MS in Strategic Studies, US Army War College. He is the author of a blog on Psychological Operations (PSYOP) at http://psyopregiment.blogspot.com.

ROBERT E. DUPRÉ, M.B.A., is a retired Air Force officer with over forty years of military and civilian engineering experience in intelligence analysis and the development and operation of intelligence collection and communications systems. He recently retired as a consultant to Air Force development activities at the Electronic Systems Center, Hanscom Air Force Base, Massachusetts, and as an adjunct instructor of business studies at Southern New Hampshire University. He was formerly an Assistant Professor at the University of Massachusetts, Lowell, Massachusetts.

HUW DYLAN, PH.D., is Lecturer in Intelligence and International Security at the Department of War Studies, King's College London, where he leads the program in Intelligence and International Security. His research is focused on British and US intelligence in the early Cold War and the relationship between intelligence and deception. He is a regular commentator on intelligence and security issues on the BBC. His book *Defence Intelligence and the Cold War* is published by Oxford University Press.

THOMAS FINGAR, PH.D., is a Distinguished Fellow at Stanford University's Freeman Spogli Institute for International Studies. From 2005 through 2008, he served as the first Deputy Director of National Intelligence for Analysis and, concurrently, as Chairman of the National Intelligence Council. He was previously Assistant Secretary of State for Intelligence and Research. Dr. Fingar received his B.A. (Government and History) from Cornell, and his M.A. and Ph.D. degrees (Political Science) from Stanford. He taught and held a number of research positions at Stanford from 1975 to 1986. He is a career member of the Senior Executive Service and a recipient of the Presidential Rank Award for Distinguished Senior Professionals and the National Intelligence Distinguished Service Medal.

ROWENA REGE FISCHER, M.P.H., M.S., J.D., earned a B.S. in Microbiology and Molecular Genetics, a Masters in Public Health in Epidemiology, and a M.S. in Chemistry for which she designed and built an instrument for near single molecule detection. She taught college chemistry and then left the sciences for law school where she authored two papers on how export control laws apply to researchers at US universities. After law school, she was a Presidential Management Fellow and gained broad experience in how the US Government administers its export control laws. She currently works as an attorney for the government.

JENNIFER H. FISHER, M.A., spent 18 years at CIA as an analyst, operations officer and Chief of Station. She joined Motorola in 1995, and held a number of senior level positions in competitive intelligence, strategy, risk management and human resources. In 2010 she founded Clear Talent LLC, which provides security and recruiting services to small businesses supporting the intelligence community. Since 2013 Jenny has served as Vice President of Administration for UI LABS, a not-for-profit, independent research, training, and commercialization engine that curates partnerships that bring together innovative industrial partners and best-in-class technical capabilities and resources to tackle grand challenges.

CARL FORD, M.A., served for over 40 years in a variety of military, intelligence, policy and academic positions. As an army officer he served two tours in Vietnam – the first at MACV and the second, after a branch transfer to intelligence, as a case officer in the Central Highlands. On his return he was assigned to the Defense Intelligence Agency as a China analyst. He joined CIA's Office of Strategic Research in 1974. In 1978 he was a Congressional Foreign Affairs Fellow for Senator John Glenn focusing on arms control and foreign policy. The following year he became a professional staff member of the Senate Foreign Relations Committee. He returned to CIA as the National Intelligence Officer for East Asia in 1985. In 1989 he was seconded to the Department of Defense to be the Principal Deputy Assistant Secretary for International Security Affairs. Upon retiring from CIA in 1993 he consulted until appointed by the President in 2001 as the Assistant Secretary of State for Intelligence and Research. He retired from the Department of State in October 2003. He has since taught at Georgetown University's School of Foreign Service, George Mason University, and National Park College. He has a B.A. in Asian Studies and a M.A. in East Asian Studies from Florida State University.

MICHAEL FREDHOLM has written extensively on the history, defense strategies, security policies, intelligence services, and energy sector developments of Eurasia. He is affiliated with the Stockholm International Program for Central Asian Studies (SIPCAS) which, since 2012, is based at the Swedish Research Institute in Istanbul, Turkey. At SIPCAS, he has made a special study of Central Asian geopolitics, Afghanistan, Islamic extremism, and the causes of and defense strategies against terrorism. He has worked as an independent advisor to governmental, inter-governmental, and non-governmental bodies for more than two decades. He has lectured at numerous institutions and universities around the world, including Ankara, Istanbul, Madrid, New Delhi, Oslo, Shanghai, Tashkent, Vienna, and Vilnius.

ARTHUR E. GERRINGER is the President/CEO of The Inter-Sec Group, which provides anti-terrorism, intelligence, security and training services to the US Government and military. He is a 40-year veteran of the military intelligence and law enforcement communities. He has been an intelligence analyst, counterintelligence agent, interrogator, physical security specialist, college adjunct professor, investigator, and trainer. Mr. Gerringer holds numerous certifications and college degrees in political science and criminal justice.

TOBIAS T. GIBSON, PH.D., is an Associate Professor of Political Science and the Security Studies Program coordinator at Westminster College in Fulton, MO. He is a non-resident fellow at the National Security Network and a contributor for The Hill. His areas of expertise include the American executive and judicial branches, constitutional law and security. Dr. Gibson earned his Ph.D. at Washington University in St. Louis.

EDWARD J. GLANTZ, M.B.A., PH.D., P.E., completed his Ph.D. in cognitive science, and is currently a Senior Lecturer in the College of Information Sciences and Technology at Pennsylvania State University, where he teaches courses in Security, Risk and Analysis. Dr. Glantz earned an M.B.A. from the

Wharton School of Business and undergraduate degrees in both Mechanical Engineering and General Arts and Sciences.

JAN GOLDMAN, ED.D. is Professor of Intelligence and National Security at Tiffin University. He is the founding editor of the International Journal of Intelligence and Ethics, has organized six international conferences, and is a co-founder of a non-profit association focusing on intelligence and ethics. His recent publications include The Central Intelligence Agency: An Encyclopedia of Covert Operations, Intelligence Gathering, and Spies, 2 vols.; Intelligence and Information Policy for National Security: Key Concepts and Terms and War on Terror Encyclopedia: From the Rise of Al Qaeda to 9/11 and Beyond.

MICHAEL S. GOODMAN, M.A., PH.D. is Professor of Intelligence and International Affairs in the Department of War Studies, King's College London. He has published widely in the field of intelligence history, including Spying on the Nuclear Bear: Anglo-American Intelligence and the Soviet Bomb (Stanford University Press, 2008); Spinning Intelligence: Why Intelligence Needs the Media, Why the Media Needs Intelligence (Columbia: Columbia University Press, 2009); Learning from the Secret Past: Cases in British Intelligence History (Georgetown University Press, 2011); The Routledge Companion to Intelligence Studies (Routledge, 2014); Spying on the World: The Declassified Documents of the Joint Intelligence Committee, 1936-2013 (Edinburgh University Press, 2014); and The Official History of the Joint Intelligence Committee, Volume I: From the Approach of the Second World War to the Suez Crisis (Routledge, 2014). He is seconded to the Cabinet Office as the Official Historian of the Joint Intelligence Committee.

KARL HAIGLER, M.A., is a retired Military Intelligence officer having served in the intelligence division of the Joint Staff and as an analyst in the Defense Intelligence Agency's Soviet Ground Forces Division. He was the Director of Adult Education in the US Department of Education and a member of the Senior Executive Service. He also served as special advisor to the Governor of Mississippi on literacy and workforce development issues. He has been a secondary school teacher and an instructor in post-secondary education. He is president of Haigler Enterprises International, Inc., a management consulting firm.

PHILIPPE HAYEZ, a graduate of Sciences Po Paris [The Paris Institute of Political Studies] and École nationale d'administration, is an adjunct professor at the Paris School of International Affairs, Sciences Po Paris. As a civil servant, he was a member of the French Ministry of Defense's Policy Planning Staff (Délégation aux Affaires stratégiques) and took managing positions in the French DGSE between 2000 and 2006. He publishes occasional papers on intelligence and security.

JAN P. HERRING, a well-recognized expert in the Business Intelligence field, is a charter member of the Society of Competitive Intelligence Professionals, a SCIP Fellow, and 1993 recipient of the Society's Meritorious Award. His professional experience includes developing Motorola's highly acclaimed intelligence program, co-founding the Academy of Competitive Intelligence, and setting up the US Government's first business intelligence program. Before his Business Intelligence career, Mr. Herring served 20 years with the CIA as an analyst, field collector and a manager. His assignments covered a wide range of intelligence activities, including: weapons systems and threat analysis for the National Reconnaissance Program; managing the IC's National Technical Assessment program for DoD; and leading IC efforts in a wide variety of international affairs, including strategic arms limitation negotiations; export control implementation; and the opening of US-China trade relations. During his government career, he served as Chairman of the DCI's Scientific & Technical Intelligence Committee and as the first Chairman of the Inter-Agency Technology Transfer Intelligence Committee. Mr. Herring's last government assignment was as the first National Intelligence Officer (NIO) for Science & Technology. Upon leaving CIA, he was awarded the Agency's highest honor, the Medal of Distinction, and received letters of commendation from President Ronald Reagan, Attorney General William F. Smith, and Director of the FBI, William H. Webster, for his contributions to national security, and federal law enforcement. He is the author of numerous articles and several book chapters on intelligence in the private-sector and co-edited a two-volume series entitled *The Art and Science of Business Intelligence Analysis* (Greenwich, CT, JAI Press, 1996.) Mr. Herring has a bachelor's degree in physics from the University of Missouri.

G. PHILIP HUGHES, M.A., M.A.L.D., M.P.A., currently Senior Director of the White House Writers Group (a Washington, DC corporate communications consulting firm), has served as US Ambassador to Barbados and the Eastern Caribbean; Executive Secretary (and, earlier, Director for Latin American Affairs) of the National Security Council; Assistant Secretary of Commerce for Export Enforcement; Deputy Assistant Secretary of State for Politico-Military Affairs; and Deputy Assistant for National Security Affairs to Vice President George H.W. Bush. He currently serves as Chairman of the Association for Diplomatic Studies and Training; as Senior Vice President and Secretary of the Council of American Ambassadors; and as Adjunct Professor of Diplomacy at the Institute of World Politics. Ambassador Hughes is a graduate of the University of Dayton and holds graduate degrees from the Fletcher School of Law and Diplomacy and Harvard University.

JOHN ALAN IRVIN spent 14 years in the US Army and 10 with the Central Intelligence Agency. He has been an artillery, paratroop, and psychological operations officer. At the CIA he served in the Clandestine Service as both a collection management and case officer as well as in managerial positions.

Stéphane Lefebvre, M.A., has worked for three Canadian intelligence organizations. When this article was written, he was Defence Scientist-in-Residence at the Canadian Centre for Intelligence and Security Studies, Norman Paterson School of International Affairs of Carleton University. He is now pursuing a Ph.D. in the Department of Law at Carleton University.

Jeremy (Jez) Littlewood, Ph.D., is the Director, Canadian Centre for Intelligence and Security Studies and an Assistant Professor at the Norman Paterson School of International Affairs of Carleton University. He previously worked at the University of Southampton (UK), and has served on secondment to the UK Foreign and Commonwealth Office, at the United Nations Department for Disarmament Affairs in Geneva, and with H.M. Forces (Army) in the UK.

Mark M. Lowenthal, Ph.D., is President and CEO of the Intelligence & Security Academy. He served as the Assistant Director of Central Intelligence for Analysis and Production; Vice Chairman for Evaluation on the National Intelligence Council; staff director of the House Permanent Select Committee on Intelligence; office director and as a Deputy Assistant Secretary of State in the State Department's Bureau of Intelligence and Research (INR); and Senior Specialist in US Foreign Policy at the Congressional Research Service, Library of Congress. He has written eight books, including the standard text on intelligence, *Intelligence: From Secrets to Policy*, and over 90 articles or studies on intelligence and national security issues. Dr. Lowenthal received his B.A. from Brooklyn College and his Ph.D. in history from Harvard University. He is an Adjunct Professor at the Johns Hopkins University; he was an adjunct at Columbia University from 1993-2007. In 2005, Dr. Lowenthal was awarded the National Intelligence Distinguished Service Medal. In 1988, he was the Grand Champion on "Jeopardy!," the television quiz show.

N. John MacGaffin, III, served 31 years as CIA officer, including four assignments overseas as Chief of Station, primarily in Middle East, and at CIA HQs, including Head of Strategic Planning and Evaluation, Chief of the Central Eurasian operational division, and associate DDO. After CIA, he was senior adviser to the Director of the FBI, responsible for long-range enhancement of CIA/FBI relationships and development of the FBI Five-Year Strategic Plan. In 1998, he chaired a commission for the Secretary of Defense, the DCI, and the Director of FBI to restructure the national counterintelligence system – known as "CI-21," implemented by the Bush administration. In 2009, he co-chaired, with former FBI Director Louis Freeh, a second national level review of the US Counterintelligence Program. He is a member of the Board of Visitors of National Intelligence University and a board member of AFIO.

DAVID G. MAJOR, a graduate of Syracuse University, served five years in the US Army before becoming a FBI Special Agent. During his 24-year career he served in numerous field offices as well as FBI Headquarters in the SCI Security Office, the Counterintelligence Division, and the Inspection Division. He was the first FBI Special Agent detailed to the National Security Council as the director of counterintelligence programs in the Reagan administration. He worked foreign counterintelligence his entire career. Upon retiring, he founded the Centre for Counterintelligence and Security Studies (CI Centre), which provides counterintelligence, counterterrorism and security training for both government and the corporate sector. He is a member of the board of AFIO, a national board member for the Espionage Research Institute International (ERII) and a member of the Society of former Special Agents of the FBI (SOCXFBI).

STEPHEN MARRIN, PH.D., is an associate professor teaching in the Intelligence Analysis program at James Madison University. Before his academic career began, he spent five years as an analyst with the CIA and the US Government Accountability Office (GAO). Holder of a B.A. from Colgate University and M.A. and Ph.D. degrees from the University of Virginia, he is Chair of the Intelligence Studies Section of the International Studies Association and was previously on the Board of the International Association for Intelligence Education. A prolific author on aspects of intelligence analysis and analytical theory, he is on the editorial advisory board of the International Journal of Intelligence and Counterintelligence. His books published by Routledge have been *Intelligence Theory: Key Questions and Debates* (2008), *Improving Intelligence Analysis: Bridging the Gap between Scholarship and Practice* (2011), and *Revisiting Intelligence and Policy: Problems with Politicization and Receptivity* (2013).

HEDWIGE REGNAULT DE MAULMIN, M.A., is a 2015 graduate in international affairs from the Paris School of International Affairs, Sciences Po Paris, France.

ROBERT A. MCDONALD, PH.D., is the Director of the Center for the Study of National Reconnaissance at the National Reconnaissance Office. He is a career CIA officer in the Senior Intelligence Service, and has served in a variety of CIA positions, including the Executive Secretary of the Director of Central Intelligence's (DCI's) Committee on Imagery Requirements & Exploitation, and the Representative of the DCI to the National War College where he also served as a professor of national security policy and psychology. His has a B.A. and M.A. in Political Science from New York University; M.S. in national security strategy from the National Defense University; and Ph.D. in the field of developmental psychology from the University of Maryland.

JOHN J. MCGONAGLE, JR. is the Managing Partner of The Helicon Group, a global competitive intelligence research and analysis firm. He is co-author of eight books on competitive intelligence including *Protecting Your Firm Against Competitive Intelligence*, and *Bottom Line Competitive Intelligence*. He has presented competitive intelligence workshops, seminars and training sessions on six continents and has served as an expert witness on competitive intelligence and related topics. He has served in adjunct undergraduate and graduate positions with Lehigh University, DeSales University, and Kutztown University. He received the prestigious Fellows Award in 1998 from SCIP and its Meritorious Award, SCIP's highest award, in 2007. He has been a featured presenter at numerous international conferences on competitive intelligence and corporate strategy.

EDWARD F. MICKOLUS, PH.D., did his undergraduate work at Georgetown University and earned his M.A., M.Phil., and Ph.D. at Yale University. He served for 33 years with CIA as an analyst, operations officer, manager, recruiter, and public affairs officer. He is the author of 30 books and scores of scholarly journal articles on intelligence, international terrorism, international organizations, African politics, psychology, law, education, and humor. He later taught with Washington-area contracting firms at various Intelligence Community organizations. He is the Deborah M. Hixon Professor of Intelligence Tradecraft at the Daniel Morgan Academy in Washington, DC and also teaches at the University of North Florida. He is the founder and President of Vinyard Software, Inc., which produces computer-readable chronologies of terrorist events and biographies of terrorists.

ROBERT A. MIRABELLO, COL. USAF (R), M.A., has forty years of experience in military and national intelligence training and education. Currently a senior faculty member of the Intelligence and Security Academy, he is also an adjunct at the National Intelligence University and University of Maryland University College. From 1990 to 2007 he served at the National Intelligence University, including as dean of the School of Intelligence Studies. Since retiring from federal service, he has managed or advised professional development programs for the Director of National Intelligence and at the Department of Homeland Security.

PHILIP MUDD, M.A., is Director of Global Risk at SouthernSun Asset Management, in Memphis, Tennessee. He served as Senior Intelligence Adviser at the FBI until 2010, and he was Deputy Director of CIA's Counterterrorist Center during 2003-05.

WILLIAM M. NOLTE, PH.D., is a 30-year veteran of the US Intelligence Community. He is the former director of education and training in the office of the Director of National Intelligence and Chancellor of the National Intelligence University. He is a former Deputy Assistant Director of Central Intelligence. He was Director of Training, Chief of Legislative Affairs, and Senior Intelligence Advisor at NSA. He also served as Deputy National Intelligence Officer for the Near East and South Asia during the Gulf War. He has taught at several Washington area universities, is on the board of CIA's Studies in Intelligence, and directed the Intelligence Fellows Program. He holds a B.A. from La Salle University and a Ph.D. from the University of Maryland.

ROBERT A. NORTON, PH.D., is a Professor at Auburn University and an Adjunct at the Air Command and Staff College. He teaches Open Source Intelligence and Informational Analysis. A Veterinary Microbiologist and biological weapons expert, Dr. Norton is a long-time researcher and professional consultant to many federal agencies on national security issues and the use of OSINT. He was awarded the FBI Director's Community Leadership Award for research on the US food production system and agricultural security.

PETER C. OLESON, M.A., is a former associate professor of intelligence studies in the Graduate School of Management and Technology of the University of Maryland University College. He spent a 48-year career in the discipline, as a senior executive in the Office of the Secretary of Defense and Defense Intelligence Agency, managing director of an aerospace firm's think tank, CEO of an intelligence and technology-oriented management consulting firm, and an educator. He has served on the faculties of the National Defense Intelligence College and CIA University. He is a member of the AFIO board of directors, chairman of the academic outreach committee, and editor of AFIO's *Guide to the Study of Intelligence*.

STEFANIA PALADINI, B. (HONS), M.A., M.SC., LL.M, PH.D., is an Associate Professor at Coventry University, UK, where she is also in charge of a European Commission project researching Chinese investments in Europe. Before joining academia, she worked several years for the Italian central government, seven of which were spent in East Asia as trade commissioner. She obtained her Ph.D. in International Relations and Security Studies from City University of Hong Kong.

MIRIELLE M. PETITJEAN, MAJ., US AIR FORCE, is a student at the National Defense Intelligence College. She has served as the intelligence, surveillance, reconnaissance (ISR) Operations Team Chief in the 612th Air and Space Operations Center, Davis-Monthan Air Force Base, and in 12th Air Force (Southern Command) and Special Operations Command Directorates of Intelligence. She was chief of intelligence for the 41st Rescue Squadron.

S. EUGENE (GENE) POTEAT, LL.D. (HON.), is President Emeritus of the Association of Former Intelligence Officers and a retired CIA Senior Scientific Intelligence Officer. Gene is an electrical engineer and physicist, holds a Master's degree in National Security and Intelligence Studies and an honorary doctorate from the Institute of World Politics, a graduate school in Washington, where he lectures on technology, intelligence, and national security. He began his career with the Bell Telephone Laboratories in New Jersey and Cape Canaveral, Florida. His CIA career included work on the U-2, A-12 Oxcart, various space and underwater systems. His CIA assignments included the Directorate of Science and Technology, management of CIA's worldwide network of SIGINT sites, the National Reconnaissance Office, Technical Director of the Navy's Special Programs Office and Executive Director of the Intelligence Research and Development Council. He served abroad in London, Scandinavia, and the Middle East.

DOUGLAS R. PRICE, M.S., has worked in cyber intelligence since 1974 when he first worked for NSA's Computer Security Division within its Office of COMSEC Applications. He later joined System Development Corporation where he led red team security studies, performed penetration tests, and designed encryption systems for computer networks. From 1983 until 2011 he worked for SPARTA, Inc. developing cyber intelligence tools and techniques. He is currently a member of the Board of AFIO.

ROBERT W. PRINGLE, PH.D., received his degree in Russian history from the University of Virginia. After service as an Army intelligence officer in Vietnam, he was a Foreign Service Officer from 1974 to 1983 in southern Africa and Moscow. He joined the CIA in 1983 as an intelligence analyst and manager. Following his retirement, he taught at the University of Kentucky, Georgetown College (KY), and Virginia Military Institute. The second edition of his *Historical Dictionary of the Russian Intelligence* has just been published. He has also written widely on the military and intelligence history of the Soviet Union.

EDWARD M. ROCHE, PH.D., J.D., was educated at The Johns Hopkins School of Advanced International Studies in Washington, DC, Concord Law School, and Columbia University in the City of New York. In his overseas work, he has organized research projects on national technology policies for microelectronics, information technology, and telecommunications in Brazil, Japan, Korea, Russia, China and Europe. He is the author of *Corporate Spy: Industrial Espionage and Counterintelligence in the Multinational Enterprise* and *Snake Fish: The Chi Mak Spy Ring*. He teaches business intelligence, international law, and technology intelligence at the Grenoble École de Management, Grenoble, France.

F.W. RUSTMANN, JR. is a 24-year veteran of the National Clandestine Service, retiring as a member of the Senior Intelligence Service. He is the founder and Chairman of CTC International Group, Inc. of West Palm Beach, Florida, a leading provider of business intelligence, legal support and analysis. Among other assignments, he was an instructor at the CIA's covert training facility known as "The Farm." He is the author of *CIA, Inc.: Espionage and the Craft of Business Intelligence* (Brassey's, 2002).

ERNESTO J. SANCHEZ is an attorney, who focuses his practice on international law, and senior analyst at Wikistrat, Inc. The American Bar Association has published his book, *The Foreign Sovereign Immunities Act Deskbook*, on the law governing lawsuits against foreign governments in US courts.

JOHN R. SANO, M.A., is currently Vice President of AFIO. He was formerly the Deputy Director of the CIA's National Clandestine Service from 2005-2007. He holds a B.A. in Political Science and an M.A. in Asian Studies from St. John's University in NY and a Masters in International Affairs from Columbia University, NY.

FLORIAN SCHAURER, PH.D., is working as a political scientist for the German Armed Forces. He holds a Ph.D., M.A., in political philosophy from the University of Zurich, a Master's degree in political science, philosophy and religious studies from the University of Heidelberg, and a Master's in human rights law from the University of Oxford.

DAVID SHEDD, M.A., is the retired acting director of the Defense Intelligence Agency. A career CIA official he has served overseas, in CIA headquarters, and on the National Security Council staff as Senior Director and Special Assistant to the President for Intelligence Programs and Reform. He has also served as the chief of staff to the Director of National Intelligence and as the Deputy DNI for Policy, Plans, and Requirements. He earned his masters degree from Georgetown University.

ROSE MARY SHELDON, COLONEL, PH.D., is holder of the Burgwyn Chair in Military History at the Virginia Military Institute. She received her Ph.D. in ancient history from the University of Michigan and has specialized in ancient intelligence history. She is on the editorial boards of the *International Journal of Intelligence and Counterintelligence* and *Small Wars and Insurgencies* and has served on the board of the *Journal of Military History*. She has authored more than three dozen articles on aspects of ancient intelligence and several books including *Espionage in the Ancient World: An Annotated Bibliography* (McFarland, 2003), *Intelligence Activities in Ancient Rome: Trust in the Gods, But Verify*, (Frank Cass, 2005), *Spies in the Bible* (Greenhill Books, 2007), *Operation Messiah: St. Paul, Roman Intelligence and the Birth of Christianity*, (Vallentine-Mitchell, 2008), *Rome's Wars in Parthia: Blood in the Sand* (Vallentine-Mitchell, 2009), and *Ambush! Surprise Attack in Ancient Greek Warfare* (London: Frontline Books).

ROBERT A. SMITH, M.S.S.I., is President of ProtectionMetrics LLC and an Adjunct Associate Professor, University of Maryland University College (UMUC) in the Graduate School's Intelligence Management Program. He is a 25-year veteran of the US Secret Service, retiring in 2001 as Special Agent in Charge, Office of Protective Operations. He later served as the Deputy Assistant Director of the Federal Law Enforcement Training Center (FLETC). He has a B.A. in Criminal Justice and Criminology from the University of Maryland and a Master of Science of Strategic Intelligence from the Joint Military Intelligence College. He also serves on the Board of the International Association for Intelligence Education and is a member of the Maryland Chiefs Association of Police Training Committee.

THOMAS R. SPENCER, J.D., is a Miami lawyer and Fellow, Chartered Institute of Arbitrators, London. He concentrates in the areas of international and domestic business law and national security law. He is the co-author of *Recent Trends in National Security Law*, 2015 (Aspatore Books, Thomson-Reuters Publications). He regularly represents officers of the National Clandestine Service.

WILLIAM C. SPRACHER, ED.D., is a contracted faculty member at the National Intelligence University, teaching courses on social analysis, globalization, intelligence leadership & management, peacekeeping & stability operations, and Latin America. A retired US Army colonel, he served for over 30 years in Armor, Military Intelligence, and the Foreign Area Officer program. He was Army Attaché to Peru and Defense Attaché to Colombia prior to his final assignment as military professor at the Center for Hemispheric Defense Studies, National Defense University. Earlier he taught US government, comparative political systems, and intelligence & public policy in the Social Sciences Department at the US Military Academy, from which he graduated in 1970. He has a master's degree in international relations from Yale University, a master's in political-military studies from the US Army Command & General Staff College, and a doctorate in education from George Washington University. He serves on the boards of directors of the International Association for Intelligence Education (IAFIE) and the National Military Intelligence Association (NMIA); for the latter, he is editor of its publication, the *American Intelligence Journal*.

JAMES STEINER, PH.D., is Public Service Professor (Intelligence Studies) and Program Coordinator, Homeland Security, Cyber Security, and Emergency Management at Rockefeller College, SUNY Albany. He is a retired CIA officer and has taught intelligence analysis at the FBI Academy. He has served as a senior consultant to both the Undersecretary for Intelligence at DHS and the New York State Homeland Security Advisor.

JAN STÖRGER, M.A., is an information security expert. He holds master level degrees from the University of Mannheim (Dept. of Economics) and the Panthéon-Sorbonne University in Paris (Dept. of Law).

MARK STOUT, PH.D., is the Director of the M.A. in Global Security Studies and the Certificate in Intelligence programs at Johns Hopkins University's Krieger School of Arts and Sciences, Advanced Academic Programs in Washington, DC. He has degrees from Stanford and Harvard Universities and a Ph.D. in history from the University of Leeds. He has served in the CIA and the State Department's Bureau of Intelligence and Research and for three years was the

Historian of the International Spy Museum.

MICHAEL J. SULICK, PH.D., a career intelligence officer, was director of CIA's National Clandestine Service (2007-2010) responsible for managing global covert operations on major threats to national security. He was also chief of CIA counterintelligence (2002-2004). Since his retirement, he has written *Spying in America* and *American Spies*, a two-volume history on Americans spying against the US from the Revolutionary War to the present. He is a member of the board of AFIO.

JOHN F. SULLIVAN was a polygraph examiner with the CIA for 31 years (1968-1999). Since retiring in 1999, he has written two books about polygraphs in the CIA, lectured extensively, served as a consultant and expert witness in lawsuits involving polygraph issues.

ADAM D.M. SVENDSEN, PH.D., is an intelligence and defense strategist, educator and researcher, and a Consultant at the Copenhagen Institute for Futures Studies (CIFS). He has been a Visiting Scholar at Georgetown University, held a post-doctoral fellowship at the University of Copenhagen, taught at the University of Nottingham, and worked at Chatham House on the International Security Programme and at the International Institute of Strategic Studies (IISS), London. He has authored three books: *Intelligence Cooperation and the War on Terror: Anglo-American Security Relations after 9/11* (London: Routledge/Studies in Intelligence Series, 2010); *Understanding the Globalization of Intelligence* and *The Professionalization of Intelligence Cooperation: Fashioning Method out of Mayhem*, both (Basingstoke: Palgrave Macmillan, 2012).

MICHELLE K. VAN CLEAVE, J.D., served as the National Counterintelligence Executive under President George W. Bush. As the head of US counterintelligence, she was responsible for directing and integrating FBI, CIA, Defense and other counterintelligence activities across the federal government. She has also held senior staff positions in the Senate and House of Representatives, the Pentagon, and in the White House Science Office, where she served as Assistant Director and General Counsel under Presidents Ronald Reagan and George H.W. Bush. A lawyer and consultant in private life, she is a Senior Fellow at George Washington University and a principal with the Jack Kemp Foundation. She is a member of the board of AFIO.

CARL ANTHONY WEGE, M.S., is a Professor of Political Science at the College of Coastal Georgia. He has traveled in Asia, Latin America, Africa, and Israel and published a variety of articles discussing terrorism and security relationships involving Hezbollah, Syria, and Iran.

GARY E. WEIR, PH.D., is Chief Historian at the National Geospatial-Intelligence Agency, a guest investigator with the Woods Hole Oceanographic Institution, and teaches for the University of Maryland. His works include "Fish,

Family, and Profit: Piracy and the Horn of Africa," part of *Piracy and Maritime Crime*, the Naval War College's Newport Paper Number 35 (2010). Sponsored by a lessons-learned grant from the Director of National Intelligence, Dr. Weir also examined the development of hyperspectral science as an intelligence tool (2011) and then for NGA explored the evolution of Activity-Based Intelligence (2013). His present work focuses on the history of geo-positioning at NGA.

DOUGLAS L. WHEELER, PH.D., is Professor of History Emeritus, University of New Hampshire. He holds an A.B. from Dartmouth College, and an M.A. and Ph.D., from Boston University. He was a Fulbright grantee, served in the US Army (1963-65), was an instructor at the US Army's Intelligence School, and has been a consultant on foreign affairs. Since 1969 he has taught an undergraduate course, "Espionage and History," at the University of New Hampshire. In 1984-85, he was the Richard Welch Research Fellow in the advanced history of intelligence, Center for International Affairs, Harvard University. He lectures widely on intelligence history.

JON A. WIANT, PH.D., is a retired intelligence officer. During his 36 years with the government, Mr. Wiant served in senior positions at Departments of State and Defense, Central Intelligence Agency and the White House. He was twice Deputy Assistant Secretary of State for Intelligence and also was Director for Intelligence Policy, National Security Council. He graduated from the University of Colorado and was a Danforth Fellow at Cornell University. He was awarded the National Intelligence Distinguished Service Medal and is a decorated Vietnam combat veteran. In retirement Mr. Wiant was Professor of Intelligence History at the National Defense Intelligence College and is currently an Adjunct Professor of George Washington University's Elliott School of International Affairs.

Part I – Introduction to the Topic

The definition of "intelligence" is a fluid one. Some define it as knowledge, others as a process, a product, an organization, or an activity. In the first instance, intelligence equates to knowledge. Former Assistant Director of Central Intelligence for Analysis and Production, **Dr. Mark Lowenthal**, differentiates intelligence from information, a lower order category.

"Information is anything that can be known, regardless of how it is discovered. Intelligence refers to information that meets the stated or understood needs of policy makers and has been collected, processed, and narrowed to meet those needs."[1]

"Narrowed" refers to the synthesis and analysis of information to make it relevant to policy maker's needs. Criminal justice professor **David L. Carter** of Michigan State University in Law Enforcement Intelligence: A Guide, states "It is clear ... that information must be analyzed before it is classified as intelligence." Some reduce this to the formula: intelligence = information + analysis.[2] One can conceptualize a ladder with "data" at the bottom, "information" at higher rungs, and "intelligence" at the top.

In a report for the UK's Security Sector Development Advisory Team, a RAND-Europe study stated: "Intelligence is a special kind of knowledge, a specialised subset of information that has been put through a systematic analytical process in order to support a state's decision and policy makers. It exists because some states or actors seek to hide information from other states or actors, who in turn seek to discover hidden information by secret or covert means."[3] Thus the concept of what intelligence is transcends the Atlantic.

Perhaps the most comprehensive definition of intelligence comes from Australian author **Don McDowell** who writes:

Information is essential to the intelligence process. Intelligence, on the other hand, is not simply an amalgam of collected information. It is instead the result

---

1. Lowenthal, Mark M. *Intelligence From Secrets to Policy*, 6th Edition (Los Angeles: SAGE CQ Press, 2015): 2.
2. Carter, D. L. *Law Enforcement Intelligence: A Guide for State, Local, and Tribal Law Enforcement Agencies*, 2nd Edition (Washington, DC: U.S. Department of Justice, Office of Community Oriented Policing Services). https://intellprogram.msu.edu/resources/publications.php
3. Hannah, Greg, Kevin A. O'Brien, Andrew Rathmell. *Intelligence and Security Legislation for Security Sector Reform* (Santa Monica, CA: RAND Corporation, 2009).

of taking information relevant to a specific issue and subjecting it to a process of integration, evaluation, and analysis with the specific purpose of projecting future events and actions, and estimating and predicting outcomes.[4]

This introductory section to the Guide to the Study of Intelligence contains four articles. The first, by **John MacGaffin** and **Peter C. Oleson**, explores the philosophy of why intelligence is important. The authors provide historical examples of where intelligence had decisive influence on critical decisions and address the necessary elements of intelligence for gaining advantage and confidence. **Dr. Stephen Marrin**, a professor of intelligence studies at James Madison University, and a former intelligence analyst, in his article "Why Teach About Intelligence" discusses the evolution of intelligence studies and how such studies contribute to more traditional courses on civics, comparative government, history, and other fields. For those new to intelligence, Professor Oleson's article, "Getting Started: Initial Readings for Instructors of Intelligence," is a starting point.

Finally in this section is Professor **Peter Oleson's** examination of how intelligence has spread far beyond the traditional national security community and is used by federal, state, and local entities focused on homeland security and law enforcement. Intelligence is also employed extensively in the global business community.

---

4. McDowell, Don. *Strategic Intelligence: a Handbook for Practitioners, Managers, and Users*, Revised Edition (Lanham, MD: The Scarecrow Press, 2009): 53.

GUIDE TO STUDY OF INTELLIGENCE

Decision Advantage, Decision Confidence

The Why of Intelligence

John MacGaffin and Peter Oleson

Why have an intelligence service? If one believes that intelligence is the world's second oldest profession, obviously the need for intelligence has long been recognized. One should note that many rely on intelligence for various reasons. Nations have used intelligence since ancient times.[1] But others do too.[2] Intelligence is important to law enforcement and the private sector. It is also important to revolutionaries, terrorists, drug cartels, and other criminal organizations.

For nations, intelligence has provided warning of attack. As historian John Keegan has noted "[t]he intelligence services of all states originated ... in the efforts to avert an enemy's achieving a military advantage [and] to achieve military advantage in return."[3] Additionally, intelligence has given nations understanding of an adversary's intentions and covertly advanced policy implementation. For companies, intelligence has assisted strategic planning, risk assessments, market decisions, R&D, and investments. For criminals, intelligence has provided forewarning of law enforcement actions, aided unlawful enterprises — including the subversion of police and politicians — and allowed intimidation of witnesses. Of course, there are many other uses.

---

1. See Col. Rose Mary Sheldon, PhD., "A Guide to Intelligence from Antiquity to Rome," *The Intelligencer*18 (1), Summer/Fall 2011; and other historical articles in the *Guide to the Study of Intelligence* at *http://www.afio.com/40_guide.htm*.
2. See Peter C. Oleson, "Who Are the Customers for Intelligence?" *Guide to the Study of Intelligence*, *http://www.afio.com/40_guide.htm*.
3. John Keegan, *Intelligence in War: Knowledge of the Enemy from Napoleon to Al-Qaeda* (New York: Alfred A. Knopf, 2003), 4.

At its most fundamental, intelligence is intended to provide decisionmakers with an advantage. This is true whether the decisionmaker is a head of state making critical choices in foreign policy, a combatant commander planning details of offense or defense, a drug smuggler looking for an opening in the border, or a financial official making decisions about long term investments. Certainly, some decisions must be made without any contribution from intelligence, in which case the decisionmaker could be blind. But if significant intelligence is available in support of decision making, it can provide a *decision advantage* so the decision-maker is better informed and understands more aspects of an issue in ways that would not be possible without the intelligence. This decision advantage can be especially critical when adversaries or competitors do not possess the same insights or do not know what the opposing decisionmaker does.

It is also important to recognize that the decision advantage that comes as a result of pertinent, accurate intelligence is always accompanied by a corresponding *disadvantage* to an adversary, competitor, or others involved. The advantage-disadvantage dynamic represents a zero-sum situation. The offsetting disadvantage may sometimes be unintended, but most often it is at the heart and intent of the matter, e.g., one negotiator possessing intelligence about the negotiating strategies and plans of the opposing party is in a stronger position both during the negotiating process and in the ultimate outcome. A targeteer knowing the location of an unsuspecting enemy is another example. That is why resources were expended and risks taken to collect and analyze the information in the first place.

Decision Advantages

Probably the most significant example of decision advantage occurred during World War II with the Allies' breaking of the German Enigma and Japanese diplomatic and naval operational codes. The ability to read the German radio traffic gave the Allied planners an enormous strategic advantage for the Normandy landings and operational commanders an ability to counter Nazi attacks and exploit their weaknesses. British historian Sir F. H. Hinsley has said that the war in Europe would have lasted two, three, or four years longer had it not been for breaking the German codes.[4] And US Army Chief of Staff Marshall reported:

> *Operations in the Pacific are largely guided by the information we obtain of Japanese deployments. We know their strength in various garrisons, the rations and other stores continuing [sic] available to them, and what is of vast importance, we*

---

4. F. H. Hinsley. "The Influence of ULTRA in the Second World War," address to the Security Group seminar at Babbage Lecture Theatre, Cambridge University Computer Laboratory, October 19, 1993. http://www.cix.co.uk/~klockstone/hinsley.htm.

check their fleet movements and the movements of their convoys. The heavy losses reported from time to time which they sustain by reason of our submarine action largely results from the fact that we have the sailing dates and routes of their convoys and can notify our submarines to lay in wait at the proper point.[5]

Breaking of the Japanese codes proved crucial in Pacific naval warfare and provided President Truman critical intelligence influencing his decision to employ the atomic bomb.[6]

In more recent history, the 1962 Cuba missile crisis is a good example of intelligence giving decision advantage to President Kennedy despite the fact that the latest National Intelligence Estimate discounted the possibility of Khrushchev placing missiles on the island. Tipped by SIGINT and some disturbing HUMINT reports, a U-2 spy plane mission collected photography revealing the existence of offensive missiles on the island, without the Soviets knowing about the discovery. This clandestine discovery, which took place a fortnight before the missiles were to become operational, provided the President and his advisors the advantage of time (albeit not a lot of time) to come up with an effective yet prudent response avoiding a nuclear war. President Kennedy's reading of the situation was strengthened by the US's prior intelligence on Soviet missile systems that had been provided by Russian Col. Oleg Penkovsky, one of the most important CIA human sources of the Cold War.

In 1995, the use of geospatial intelligence provided US negotiators an important advantage in the Dayton Peace Accords for the Bosnian war. As Dr. Gary Weir explained, the rapid construction of detailed maps reflected the "territorial dispositions negotiated less than thirty minutes earlier." Based on satellite imagery and other geographical and intelligence information, these maps and three-dimensional imagery used by the US negotiators "guaranteed accuracy, consistency, and reliability" that "in one instance... proved crucial in persuading Yugoslav President Slobodan Milosevic to compromise on a disputed area."[7]

US intelligence capabilities have given US and allied negotiators an advantage in various arms control negotiations. Satellite imagery, SIGINT, and on-site inspection capabilities (both human and technical) have allowed various US administrations to reach agreement on limiting both nuclear and

---

5. Marshall to Dewey, September 25, 1944, SRH-043, cited in Christopher Andrew, *For the President's Eyes Only* (New York: Harper, 1996), 142-3.

6. Peter C. Oleson, "From Axis Surprises to Allied Victories: The Impact of Intelligence in World War II," *Guide to the Study of Intelligence*, http://www.afio.com/40_guide.htm; Douglas J. MacEachin. *The Final Months of the War with Japan: Signals Intelligence, US Invasion Planning, and the A-Bomb Decision.* (Washington, DC: Central Intelligence Agency, Center for the Study of Intelligence, 1998). https://www.cia.gov/ library/center-for-the-study-of-intelligence/csi-publications/books-and-monographs/the-final-months-of-the-war-with-japan-signals-intelligence-u-s-invasion-planning-and-the-a-bomb-decision/csi9810001.html#rtoc2.

7. Gary E. Weir. "The Evolution of Geospatial Intelligence and the National Geospatial-Intelligence Agency," in the *Guide to the Study of Intelligence*, http://www.afio.com/40_guide.htm.

conventional arms.

There are also examples of when a nation was at significant disadvantage because of a lack of intelligence or poor analysis of the intelligence that was available. In World War I, a lack of intelligence about the target area of Gallipoli contributed to the debacle suffered by the combined British-Australian-New Zealand-French forces at the hands of the Ottoman Empire. For the US, the surprises of the 1941 Japanese attack on Pearl Harbor and of Al-Qaida's September 11, 2001 terrorist attacks were both attributed to a failure of intelligence collection and analysis. The US may also have missed warnings before the North's June 1950 invasion of South Korea due to spying by William Wiseband, a Soviet NKVD agent in the US Army's SIGINT organization, who told the Soviets that the US had broken its codes. "US SIGINT went deaf when the Soviets changed codes."[8]

The US was at a disadvantage due to a lack of intelligence, poor tradecraft, and faulty analysis in deciding on war with Iraq in 2003. The US had no vetted and controlled agents of its own inside Saddam's Iraq, relying on technical collection, access to UN inspection teams, defectors, and exile groups. The most compelling defector, Curveball, was controlled by a foreign intelligence service, the German Federal Intelligence Service (*Bundesnachrichtendienst*, BND), which refused to give the US access or even his true name until well after the war. He turned out to be a skilled fabricator; his claims of mobile biological weapons proved to be wholly false. The exile Iraqi National Congress persuaded US lawmakers and senior policymakers in the White House and Defense Department of Saddam's weapons of mass destruction (WMD) program. Saddam had a WMD program prior to 1991 that was shielded by an active and very capable deception and denial program. After 1991, for deterrence purposes, Saddam had an effective deception effort to convince his regional enemies that he still had extensive WMD capabilities. His harassment of UN inspectors suggested he had something to hide. The US was hoodwinked. What US intelligence analysts lacked was current intelligence from both technical and human sources that were controlled and vetted as reliable and up-to-date. The result was a long and costly conflict.[9]

Intelligence can also aid decisionmakers to know whether past policy or operational decisions are being successful or failures. During the Vietnam conflict, CIA's evaluations of intelligence about the enemy were often in conflict with the Pentagon's more optimistic operational assessments. This use of intelligence has often led to clashes between intelligence professionals and policymakers vested in a particular policy.[10]

---

8. David G. Major and Peter C. Oleson. "Espionage Against America," *Guide to the Study of Intelligence*, http://www.afio.com/40_guide.htm. See footnote 25.

9. This analysis is based on private correspondence between David Kay, chief of the Iraqi Survey Group, and co-author John MacGaffin.

10. An interesting case study related to this point is recounted in James J. Wirtz's article, "Intelligence

Decision Confidence

Intelligence provides more than decision advantage. Less evident – but absolutely critical and generally unrecognized – is that it can provide decision-makers with *decision confidence*. It is simply in the nature of the world that adversaries or competitors often try to confuse and deceive their opponent's decision-making processes and, at times, succeed. Foreign intelligence services are principal instruments to undertake denial and deception programs. They discretely position *information* intended to lead others to make erroneous or flawed decisions, the consequences of which serve their interests. By their nature, the elements of such denial, deception, and perception management programs appear authentic. Intelligence collection and analysis or policy decisions, therefore, which are based on such information, can be seriously flawed.

One job of counterintelligence is to expose for decisionmakers the fact and nature of hostile denial, deception, or perception management efforts. Put another way, collection and analysis, which are not informed by a serious counterintelligence lens, can significantly mislead the very decisionmaker whom it intended to support. Successful intelligence collection and analysis, accompanied by counterintelligence, is necessary to provide decisionmakers not only decision advantage but also decision confidence.

While the importance of identifying hostile denial and deception is easy to understand, there are other more subtle aspects of counterintelligencethat also provide clear decision confidence. Consider, for example, the confidence in his choices that a decisionmaker can have when counterintelligence provides not only an important foreign government secret, but also the knowledge that the foreign government is operating on the understanding that its adversary/competitor does not know that secret. Or consider how much better a decisionmaker can understand all the nuances of a nation's foreign policies when he has visibility into the secret instructions and direction that that nation's leadership has given to its own intelligence service. Beyond denial and deception, a well-placed agent in a hostile intelligence service can provide insights into that government's secret plans and intentions that run directly contrary to its public pronouncements or its private assurances to the US.

Knowing whether a foreign intelligence or law enforcement service has or does not have secret sources within one's own service or organization can also provide confidence. This comes from one's own intelligence service penetrating an opponent's intelligence service. By betraying the US's human sources within the KGB and GRU, Aldrich Ames gave the Soviets confidence in their own counterintelligence. The KGB went to great lengths to protect its own penetrations of both the CIA and FBI (Robert Hanssen) to maintain

---

to Please? The order of battle controversy during the Vietnam War," *Political Science Quarterly* 106 (2), Summer 1991 239-263. *http://www.jstor.org/stable/2152228.*

their confidence in knowing about US counterintelligence operations. Pablo Escobar's Medellin drug cartel focused an intense counterintelligence effort against both Colombian government elements and the US to determine how secure his operations were.

Another aspect of counterintelligence, which is critical and not generally understood, is the mitigation of covert threats. Military force and diplomacy are asked to mitigate overt threats to national security by use of kinetic force or negotiation. Likewise, counterintelligence can provide decisionmakers with a mitigation tool for use when faced by sub rosa threats posed by foreign intelligence services.

A prime example of mitigation is the early 1980s covert action to frustrate Soviet illegal acquisition of Western technologies. A Soviet defector provided the French with over 4,000 documents detailing the goals, achievements, and unfilled objectives of the KGB's Line X technology officers. The documents identified the Line X officers, how they obtained various technologies, from which companies in what countries, and often who provided the restricted technologies. President Mitterrand shared this counterintelligence information, codenamed the Farewell Dossier, with President Reagan at the Ottawa economic summit in July 1981. Rather than stopping the hemorrhaging by exposing the Line X personnel – the normal counterintelligence reaction – which would have been only temporary, President Reagan approved a covert action to provide the Soviets with desired technologies that had been "improved" with "extra ingredients" in their hardware and software. The covert action involved multiple US Government agencies, many private companies, and allied nations. With the advantage of knowing the KGB shopping list, CIA fed back — through controlled channels — items on the list that were designed to pass acceptance testing but had hidden Trojan Horses,[11] which would cause them to fail randomly in service. The Soviets were provided flawed stealth technology, defective turbines,factory plans, convincing but flawed ideas for a space shuttle and combat aircraft, and corrupted industrial control software. "Every microchip [the Soviets] stole would run fine for 10 million cycles, and then it would go into some other mode. It would break down; it would start delivering false signals and go to a different logic."[12] This caused severe setbacks for major segments of Soviet industry.

The most dramatic consequence of the Farewell covert action impacted the Soviet natural gas industry. A critical element of the economy that earned hard currency from the West, the Soviets needed advanced pipeline control technology for the new trans-Siberian pipeline. When export control restric-

---

11. A Trojan Horse is a few lines of software, buried within a normal program, that will cause a system to go berserk at some future date or upon receipt of an external command.

12. Thomas C. Reed, former National Security Council staff member and secretary of the Air Force, interview with Steve Ketterman, March 26, 2004.

tions prevented its purchase, Line X officers tried to steal it from a Canadian company. They succeeded, but once in the USSR, the computers and software ran the pipeline beautifully – for a while. Then the software commanded a covert pipeline pressure test. "We expected that the pipeline would spring leaks all the way from Siberia to Germany, but that wasn't what happened. Instead the welds all blew apart."[13] The result was the most monumental non-nuclear explosion and fire ever seen from space[14] and severe damage to the Soviet economy. The Soviet defector, Lt. Colonel Vladimir Vetrov, murdered his mistress and carelessly admitted his spying in late 1982 and was executed. In 1984-85, the US and allied countries mitigated the Line X threat, expelling approximately 250 Soviet "diplomats": 41 from the UK; 55 from the US; and others from France, Italy, Germany, Belgium, Netherlands, Canada, and Japan.[15]

Necessary Elements of Intelligence for Advantage and Confidence

Like a three-legged stool, there are three essential elements of intelligence needed for solid decision advantage or confidence:collection, analysis, and counterintelligence.

Collection can be a very difficult business. In the SIGINT realm, there is a constant struggle between successful collection measures and countermeasures, such as encryption. Disclosures of techniques, such as those by Edward Snowden, inevitably result in loss of collection.[16] For HUMINT, finding worthwhile agents in a state that terrorizes its citizens (e.g., Iraq under Saddam before the invasion of 2003) is not an easy thing. Even more difficult is the penetration of terrorist cells or ethnically homogeneous groups. That is why liaison and collaboration with foreign intelligence and security services and law enforcement organizations are an important, complex, and sometimes controversial part not only of HUMINT, but of the other intelligence disciplines as well. Liaison contacts are often the most secret and sensitive elements of bilateral relations and, in many countries, intelligence service leaders are also policy and power players. For example, since 1983, CIA maintained a discreet relationship with the KGB, intended primarily to provide a venue for informal airing of potentially contentious issues, known as the "Gavrilov channel." [17]

---

13. Reed, Ketterman interview.
14. Thomas C. Reed. *At the Abyss: An Insider's History of the Cold War* (New York: Presidio Press, 2004).
15. The Farewell episode is explained by Gus W. Weiss, the principal architect of the covert action, "The Farewell Dossier," *Studies in Intelligence* 39 (5), 1996, at https:\\www.cia.gov/csi/studies/96unclass and, from a French perspective, by Yves Bonnet, *Contre-espionage: Memoires d'un patron de la DST* [Counterintelligence: Memoirs of former head of the DST – the French internal security service of the time] (Paris: Calman-Lévy, 2000).
16. Peter C. Oleson, "Assessing Edward Snowden: Whistleblower, Traitor, or Spy?" *The Intelligencer* 21 (2), Spring-Summer 2015, 15.
17. Milt Bearden & James Risen, *The Main Enemy: The Inside Story of the CIA's Final Showdown with the*

Fed by collection, analysis is difficult. "In many cases ... collection is incomplete or inconclusive and analysts must work from fragments, some of which are contradictory, in order to assess what is going on or is likely to happen."[18] This can limit the confidence policymakers have in intelligence. Former Deputy Director of National Intelligence for Analysis Thomas Fingar has noted: "Perhaps the most important reasons all-source analysis is essential are the complexity of the issues the Intelligence Community is expected to address, the volume of information that might be germane to understanding those issues, the often short timelines within which analytic input is required if it is to be useful, and the consequentiality of many decisions made by the United States government."[19] Conveying intelligence to a policymaker to give him decision confidence "can be very difficult because the language that is used is often conditional or hedged."

Yet, as former CIA Assistant Director for Analysis and Production Mark Lowenthal notes: "Wise policymakers understand that they cannot know all of the possible outcomes of the decisions they face. Intelligence analysis serves to bound their uncertainty, to give policymakers a better sense of what might or might not happen, based on known conditions, the actors involved, and the decisions made. It is important to understand that 'bounding uncertainty' is not the same as telling someone what will happen."[20]

Critical aspects of analysis occur long before the final assessments are made on the bits and pieces of collected information. Vetting (i.e., the careful and critical examination) of one's source can be difficult. Vetting applies not only to human sources but technical sources as well. The failure of the vetting process can have significant consequences, as illustrated by Curveball.[21] The Abwehr's failure to vet its agents in Britain during World War II allowed British counterintelligence to undertake extensive deception operations on numerous occasions with disastrous consequences for the German military.[22] Counterintelligence vetting and vulnerability evaluations are critical to having confidence in planning operations and making fundamental policy decisions.

Like a three-legged stool, take away one element and decision advantage and confidence suffer. While collection and analysis are well understood, counterintelligence often is not and is the least valued of the three. Partly this comes

---

KGB (New York: Random House, 2003): 189. See also "Dangerous Liaisons: Post-September 11 Intelligence Alliances," *Harvard International Review* 24 (3), September 2002, 49-54.

18. Mark Lowenthal. "Intelligence Analysis, Guide to its Study," *The Intelligencer*, Summer-Fall 2011, 61. http://www.afio.com/40_guide.htm.

19. Thomas Fingar. "A Guide to All-Source Analysis," *The Intelligencer*, Winter-Spring 2012, 63. *http://www.afio.com/40_guide.htm.*

20. Lowenthal. "Intelligence Analysis," 61.

21. "The Record on CURVEBALL: *Declassified Documents and Key Participants Show the Importance of Phony Intelligence in the Origins of the Iraq War.*" National Security Archive, The George Washington University, 2007.

22. See Thaddeus Holt, *The Deceivers: Allied Military Deception in the Second World War* (New York: Scribner, 2004).

from the view, particularly among intelligence analysts and policymakers, that counterintelligence equals counterespionage – the catching of spies, but nothing more. Given that limited perspective, it is understandable that their bias is that counterintelligence has little, if anything, to offer the analytic and policy process. A very senior National Intelligence Council member once told one of the authors that there was no role for counterintelligence in his analyses. "There is nothing that we or policymakers need from counterintelligence," he said; that decision was overturned several years later.

Counterintelligence can often inform both analysts and policymakers. The realization that an adversary seeks or has obtained our secrets or evaded our laws can, in fact, tell us important things about the adversary. An example is the extensive clandestine attempts by Iran to evade US export controls.

Another invidious reason for resisting counterintelligence is that analysts and policymakers have experienced counterintelligence information that undercuts firmly held analytic views, policies, and plans. An adversary's denial and deception, once uncovered, might reveal that the adversary had actually planted the "dots" on which a policy or an act was premised, resulting in egg on the face if the government had already taken action based on a flawed premise. Counterintelligence often adds tension and difficulties to the policymaking process, which, given natural tendencies, often makes it very difficult to bring the counterintelligence perspective to the table. In contrast to the narrow view of the National Intelligence Council official cited above, a former national security advisor told one of the authors that the full insights that counterintelligence can provide were critical to the policy-making process but were not vigorously sought out by analysts and policymakers as a matter of course. As Iraqi Survey Group Chief David Kay concluded, "clandestine collection and information validation is essential to intelligence and required to provide effective support to policymakers...."[23]

Only with all three elements of intelligence – collection, analysis, and counterintelligence – can decisionmakers have decision advantage and decision confidence. And this is why we have an intelligence community.

READINGS FOR INSTRUCTORS

Many books on crises and conflicts provide examples of how intelligence has provided decision advantages and confidence to leaders and commanders. The two texts below are relevant to this topic.

Allison, Graham and Philip Zelikow. *Essence of Decision: Explaining the Cuban Missile Crisis*, 2nd Edition, (New York: Longman, 1999). This book examines various decision models of the world's most dangerous nuclear crisis.

---

23. David Kay private correspondence with co-author John MacGaffin.

May, Ernest R. (editor). *Knowing One's Enemies: Intelligence Assessment Before the Two World Wars*, (Princeton: Princeton University Press, 1984). A very thought-provoking series of articles on intelligence and the intelligence failings on all sides that often resulted in flawed strategic decisions.

N. John MacGaffin, III, served 31 years as a CIA officer, including four assignments overseas as chief of station, primarily in the Middle East, and at CIA HQs, including head of strategic planning and evaluation, chief of the Central Eurasian operational division, and associate deputy director of operations (DDO). After CIA, he was a senior adviser to the FBI director and deputy director, responsible for long-range enhancement of CIA/FBI relationships and development of the FBI Five-Year Strategic Plan. In 1998, he chaired a commission for the secretary of defense, the DCI, and the FBI director to restructure the national counterintelligence system – known as CI-21 – implemented by the Bush administration. In 2009, he co-chaired, with former FBI Director Louis Freeh, a second national-level review of the US Counterintelligence Program. He is a member of the of National Intelligence University Board of Visitors and is an AFIO board member.

Peter C. Oleson is the editor of *AFIO's Guide to the Study of Intelligence*, a member of the AFIO board, and chairman of its academic outreach. Previously he was director for intelligence and space policy for the secretary of defense and assistant director for plans and policy of the Defense Intelligence Agency. He was founder and CEO of Potomac Strategies & Analysis, Inc., a consulting firm on technology and intelligence, and an associate professor in the University of Maryland University College graduate school.

GUIDE TO THE STUDY OF INTELLIGENCE

Why Teach About Intelligence

Stephen Marrin, Ph.D.

Intelligence studies gain a lot of attention because of the links to spies and spying. The subject influences popular culture through action-packed books, television shows, and movies; consequently, people become curious about the real world of intelligence. The success of the International Spy Museum in Washington, DC, demonstrates the overlap between myth and reality. Teaching about intelligence provides an opportunity to bring James Bond and Jack Ryan into the classroom, but the actual substance of intelligence studies can be much, much more than what Hollywood depicts.

While the literature about teaching intelligence has been getting more attention recently, its foundations began many decades ago.[1] In 1957, Washington Platt recommended that intelligence organizations adapt "formal education followed by practical experience" for those who wanted to enter, and suggested that the best way to do so was through "more advanced courses, comparable to graduate courses in other professions."[2] In 1960, Peter Dorando recommended that academic colleges or universities create "a basic course of study in the meaning of intelligence, its significance as the foundation for policy planning and a guide for operations, how it plays those roles, and the principles and processes by which it is produced and formulated. Such a course should ... develop broad principles applicable in all fields."[3]

The field of intelligence education took many more years to develop fully. By the 1980s, the literature on teaching intelligence consisted of field surveys[4]

---

1. For more about teaching intelligence, see chapter titled "Improving Intelligence Analysis Through Training and Education" in Stephen Marrin. *Improving Intelligence Analysis: Bridging the Gap between Scholarship and Practice,* (Routledge, 2011).
2. Washington Platt's "Strategic Intelligence Production: Basic Principles," (Praeger, 1957), 256-258.
3. Peter J. Dorando. "For College Courses in Intelligence." *Studies in Intelligence* 4 (3), 1960, A15-A19.
4. Marjorie W. Cline (ed). *Teaching Intelligence in the mid-1980s: A Survey of College and University Courses on the Subject of Intelligence* (Washington, DC: National Intelligence Study Center, 1985); Hayden

supplemented by efforts on the part of government organizations to support the teaching of intelligence.[5] But as a wide variety of intelligence education programs sprung up after the 9/11 terrorist attacks to meet the demand for more focused education and training in this area, the literature on teaching intelligence has expanded even further. Contributions now provide an overview of the value of intelligence education, and critique its somewhat haphazard implementation.[6] With the creation of the International Association for Intelligence Education (IAFIE) in 2004, more research and writing has been done on various aspects of teaching intelligence, some of which have ended up in the literature.[7] All of this work has shown that those who teach intelligence do so for a number of different purposes and from a number of different perspectives.

One purpose in teaching intelligence is to explain how the US Government is structured and what it does. Most of the students who take courses on intelligence in political science departments around the country acquire this kind of knowledge. This can also lead to discussion of how intelligence organizations are subject to the checks and balances of the political system; and how the executive, legislative, and judicial branches are each involved in the process of governance. As such, it normalizes the intelligence function as part of the machinery of government. When the instructor focuses on the branches of government or case studies on the role of intelligence in supporting foreign policy, the goal is to provide the student with a broad foundation of knowledge in order to contextualize the more focused study of intelligence in the making and execution of foreign or national security policy.

A variation of this approach to teaching intelligence can be used in comparative politics courses: those that compare different kinds of political systems. For example, during the Cold War, there was an effort to understand the different kinds of intelligence services based on the political system of the respective government (democratic, communist, dictatorship) and what that meant in terms of the strengths and weaknesses of the various intelligence

---

Peake. *The Reader's Guide to Intelligence Periodicals* (Washington, DC: National Intelligence Book Center, 1989).

5. Central Intelligence Agency. *Symposium on Teaching Intelligence, October 1-2, 1993.* (Washington, DC: Center for the Study of Intelligence, 1994); US Joint Military Intelligence College. *Teaching Intelligence at Colleges and Universities. Conference Proceedings.* Washington DC; Center for Strategic Intelligence Research, 18 June 1999; US Joint Military Intelligence College. *A Flourishing Craft: Teaching Intelligence Studies* (ed. Russell G. Swenson), Papers Prepared for the 18 June 1999 JMIC Conference on Teaching Intelligence Studies at Colleges and Universities (Washington DC: Center for Strategic Intelligence Research, June 1999).

6. Martin Rudner, "Intelligence Studies in Higher Education: Capacity-Building to Meet Societal Demand," *International Journal of Intelligence and Counterintelligence* 22 (1), Spring 2009, 110-130. Peter Monaghan, Intelligence Studies, *The Chronicle of Higher Education,* 20 March 2009; William Spracher, "Teaching Intelligence in the United States, the United Kingdom, and Canada," *International Studies Encyclopedia.* (ed. Robert A. Denemark), (Malden, MA: Wiley-Blackwell, 2010), 6779-6800; Stephen Campbell. "A Survey of the U.S. Market for Intelligence Education." *International Journal of Intelligence and Counterintelligence* 24 (2), Summer 2011, 307-337.

7. Mark Lowenthal. "Intelligence as a Profession: IAFIE Sets Its Sights," *American Intelligence Journal,* Summer 2006: 41–42.

systems.[8] More recent efforts take differences between different countries and compare how the systems of intelligence fit within the overall machinery of government.[9] Studying and teaching intelligence in this way provides the student with an opportunity to explore the theoretical constructs that predominate in comparative politics using intelligence-related cases and illustrations.[10]

Variations to this political science approach can also be taken in world politics, area studies, or international relations courses using varied frames of reference, depending on the knowledge and expertise of the instructor. Inevitably, the most accessible cases to use would be those related to security studies or international security. For example, one could teach intelligence in context of particular kinds of national security threats including regional actors (North Korea, Iran), areas of instability (Syria, Egypt), areas of conflict (Afghanistan, Syria), the proliferation of WMD materials, and various non-state actors (terrorism, narco-trafficking, money laundering, piracy). The intelligence studies portion of the course would then examine the role of intelligence in helping governments understand the threat (separating out capabilities and intentions) by addressing what it does in order to collect and evaluate information on these kinds of targets. The security studies portion of the course could address how intelligence helps governments know what the threat is (description), why it developed (explanation), its significance (evaluation), and how it is likely to change in the future (forecasting), and use that as an opportunity to discuss the various kinds of intelligence products.

Another purpose for teaching intelligence is to understand American or world history. Taking the historian's perspective can lead to discussions of the involvement of intelligence organizations in various episodes in American history, from the Revolutionary War up to recent modern history. The historian's approach can help students understand what happened in the past that led the world to be as it is. Intelligence has played a role in the rise and fall of civilizations, the winning and losing of both battles and wars, and—just as significant—the prevention of conflict as part of a broader conception of national security. Incorporating intelligence into the study of history provides a more detailed and nuanced understanding of the real world of foreign policy and policymaking.

---

8. Roy Godson (ed). *Comparing Foreign Intelligence: The U.S., the USSR, the U.K. and the Third World* (Washington, DC: Pergamon-Brassey's, 1988).

9. Philip H.J. Davies. *Intelligence and Government in Britain and the United States: A Comparative Perspective* (ABC-Clio/Praeger, 2012); Peter Gill, Mark Phythian, Stuart Farson, and Shlomo Shpiro (eds), *Handbook of Global Security and Intelligence National Approaches* (Westport, CT: Praeger Security International, 2008).

10. Peter Gill. "Knowing the Self, Knowing the Other: The Comparative Analysis of Security Intelligence" in Loch Johnson (ed.) *Handbook of Intelligence Studies* (Routledge, 2007), 82-90.; Kevin O'Connell. "Thinking about Intelligence Comparatively." *The Brown Journal of World Affairs* 11 (1), 2004, 189–202.

Editors' Note: Understanding History

Dr. Mark Stout, the former historian of the International Spy Museum, and currently a Johns Hopkins University professor, has noted that our understanding of history has changed once intelligence files were declassified or revealed. Some of his examples are illustrative:

The Normandy landings and many of the Allied victories in Europe during World War II were the consequence of good intelligence and derivative deceptions of the Nazis (Sicily, Normandy). In the Battle of the Atlantic, Allied victory over German U-boats was dependent largely upon signals intelligence.

In the Pacific, the Battle of Midway was the canonical example of the contributions of SIGINT to having foreknowledge of an enemy's plans and countering them successfully.

Cold War controversies, such as the guilt or innocence of the Rosenbergs and Alger Hiss, were really only settled with the release of VENONA decrypts of Soviet GRU and KGB communications indicating both were controlled Soviet agents.

Was Senator Joseph McCarthy right in his charges about communists in the US Government? With the release of VENONA and old investigative files, we now know that he mostly wasn't.

The nature of the Communist Party of the USA: was it deeply involved in espionage or were simply a few of its members spies for the USSR? We know the answer to this thanks to the work of scholars like John Earl Haynes and Harvey Klehr working with the VENONA decrypts, the Mitrokhin files, the Vassiliev materials, and other revelations that have dribbled out of KGB archives.

The outcome of the pivotal 1948 Italian elections in which the CIA ran its first covert action supporting the democrats; the KGB was even more heavily subsidizing the Italian Communist Party.

The 1922 Washington Naval Treaty; the US side was greatly helped by the SIGINT work of Herbert Yardley's *American Black Chamber*.

Christopher Andrew argues compellingly in *The World Was Going Our Way* (Basic Books, 2005) that KGB operations were central to – not peripheral to – the conduct of Soviet foreign policy.

In addition, Dr. Stout has noted some major historical events are intrinsically intelligence stories. The following are some major historical incidents that one cannot comprehend fully without assessing their related intelligence issues.

- The Battle of Gettysburg
- The Zimmerman Telegram
- The attack on Pearl Harbor
- The Cuban Missile Crisis
- The 1968 Tet Offensive
- The 1973 coup against Allende in Chile
- The Soviet war in Afghanistan
- The US war in Afghanistan

- The 2003 Iraq War
- Understanding the nature of the East German state.

In variation to the disciplinary approach, one can also study intelligence as a subset of other academic fields: anthropology, sociology, communications, media studies, film, literature, and others. Each academic discipline will have its own way of orienting the student to the subject and providing contextualizing approaches for critical thought and evaluation. Some of these approaches will use a similar social scientific lens but shift the emphasis to different kinds of questions. Others will abandon social science altogether and focus on different kinds of theories and modes of understanding. For example, former CIA case officer and inspector general Fred Hitz's course at Princeton University on "The Myth and Reality of Espionage: The Spy Novel" provided an opportunity to explore other aspects of the business, including legality and morality.[11]

An additional purpose for teaching intelligence is to prepare the student for a career in intelligence. This can be done at the course or programmatic level. Sometimes entire programs or degrees are built on this purpose. Those that do so are like other graduate-level public policy schools who prepare students for careers in government by providing them with knowledge about the field as well as some of the skills associated with it. These are "intelligence schools" that serve a similar function for the intelligence profession as do medical schools for medicine or journalism schools for journalism. In this case, however, most of these practitioner-oriented schools tend to emphasize intelligence analysis because it is the analytic skill-set that is most easily developed in the academic context.[12] As more programs are created that do this, more resources are becoming available for those who want to teach students what intelligence analysis entails.

In addition to the conventional teaching methods of readings, lecture, and discussion, sometimes teaching in different ways can help in the learning process. For example, teaching intelligence in historical context can also have a more practical or applied focus: learning the lessons of history. A number of instructors have recommended the case study approach to teaching intelligence, and have written a variety of case studies to help in that process. Others use interactive simulations as well. An approach used in some of these kinds of courses is the practical simulation or exercise related to intelligence analysis and production: the crisis simulation or exercise in producing a National Intelligence Estimate. Some of these simulations take place entirely in an academic context; others include outside actors playing roles of senior decisionmakers. The CIA has supported some of these exercises, getting involved both in their creation as well as their implementation. The value of this kind of exercise is that it shifts

---

11. Ken Howard. "Myth and Reality of Espionage: Former CIA Inspector General Leads Freshman Seminar Based on Life Experience," *Princeton Weekly Bulletin.* Vol 89 No 13, January 10, 2000. *http://www. princeton.edu/pr/pwb/00/0110/p/espionage*.shtml.
12. Stephen Marrin. "Training and Educating US Intelligence Analysts. *International Journal of Intelligence and Counterintelligence* 22 (1), Winter 2008-2009, 131-146; James Breckenridge. "Designing Effective Teaching and Learning Environments for a New Generation of Analysts," *International Journal of Intelligence and Counterintelligence* 23 (2), Summer 2010, 307-323; Michael Landon-Murray. "Social Science and Intelligence Analysis: The Role of Intelligence Education," *Journal of Applied Security Research* 6 (4), 2011:, 491-528.

the learning emphasis from the normal "reading, thinking, writing" approach to one of "learning by doing." The intent is for one kind of learning to reinforce the other, to provide real world examples of issues or difficulties involved in the production of intelligence.

Readings for Instructors

There are a couple of overview books, which have become predominant in terms of teaching introductory intelligence courses:

> Andrew, Christopher. *For the President's Eyes Only*. Harper Perennial, 1996.

> Lowenthal, Mark. *Intelligence: From Secrets to Policy*. CQ Press College, 5th edition, 2011.

Much of the intelligence literature is produced in article form, so access to the journals in the field should supplement content from books. The three primary academic journals are:

> (1) the *International Journal of Intelligence and Counterintelligence*,

> (2) *Intelligence and National Security*, and

> (3) CIA's *Studies in Intelligence*.[13]

> The best place to go to find a breakdown of this literature by topic is J. Ransom Clark's online annotated bibliography of the intelligence literature, found here: *http://intellit.muskingum.edu/*.

There are also books that have compiled a thematic "best of" from previously published works. These can be good overviews for courses on intelligence and national security:

> Andrew, Christopher, Richard J. Aldrich, and Wesley K. Wark (eds.). *Secret Intelligence: A Reader* (New York and London: Routledge, 2009).

> George, Roger Z. and Robert D. Kline (eds). *Intelligence and the National Security Strategist: Enduring Issues and Challenges*. Rowman and Littlefield Publishers, 2006.

> Johnson, Loch K. and James J. Wirtz (eds.). *Intelligence and National Security: The Secret World of Spies*. (New York/Oxford. Oxford University Press, 2nd edition, 2008).

Another option would be books that have acquired a range of articles on different subject matter—not previously published—that could be used to supplement other books or articles:

> Bruce, James and Roger George (eds.). *Analyzing Intelligence: Origins, Obstacles,*

---

13. The Association of Former Intelligence Officers (AFIO), Naval Intelligence Professionals (NIP), and the National Military Intelligence Association (NMIA) publish journals with articles about the intelligence profession. AFIO's *Intelligencer* is published in print three times per year. On-line-only are the journals by NIP – *Naval Intelligence Professionals Quarterly* – and NMIA's *American Intelligence Journal,* which appear on-line once a year. All of these journals tend to emphasize practitioner-authors rather than academic researchers.

and Innovations (Georgetown University Press, 2008).

Gill, Peter, Stephen Marrin, and Mark Phythian (eds.). Intelligence Theory: Key Questions and Debates. Routledge, 2008.Johnson, Loch (ed.). Handbook of Intelligence Studies (Routledge, 2006), 199-210.

Resources to support the use of case studies in teaching intelligence include:

May, Ernest R. and Philip D. Zelikow (eds.). Dealing with Dictators: Dilemmas of U.S. Diplomacy and Intelligence Analysis, 1945–1990, BCSIA Studies in International Security. (Cambridge, MA: The MIT Press, 2006).

Shreeve, Thomas W.. Experiences to Go: Teaching with Intelligence Case Studies. (Washington, DC: Joint Military Intelligence College, September 2004.

Walton, Timothy. Challenges in Intelligence Analysis: Lessons from 1300 BCE to the Present. (New York: Cambridge University Press, 2010).

Resources to support intelligence school analytic skills and simulations include:

Central Intelligence Agency. A Tradecraft Primer: Structured Analytic Techniques for Improving Intelligence Analysis (Washington, DC: US Government, March 2009). Available online at https://www.cia.gov/library/center-for-the-study-of-intelligence/csi-publications/books-and-monographs/Tradecraft%20Primer-apr09.pdf

Heuer, Richards J. Jr., and Randolph H. Pherson. Structured Analytic Techniques for Intelligence Analysis. (Washington, DC: CQ, 2010).

Major, James. Communicating with Intelligence: Writing and Briefing in the Intelligence and National Security Communities. (Lanham, MD. Scarecrow, 2008).

Wheaton, Kristan J.. "Teaching Strategic Intelligence Through Games." International Journal of Intelligence and Counterintelligence 24 (2), Summer 2011: 367-382.

Dr. Stephen Marrin is an associate professor teaching intelligence analysis (IA) in the James Madison University Department of Integrated Science and Technology (ISAT) in Harrisonburg, Virginia. Before that, he taught intelligence in the Brunel University Department of Politics and History in London, England. Before that, he taught in the Mercyhurst University Intelligence Studies Department at in Erie, PA. Previously, he was a CIA and US Government Accountability Office (GAO) analyst. Holder of a Ph.D. from the University of Virginia, he is program chair of the International Studies Association Intelligence Studies Section and was previously on the Board of the International Association for Intelligence Education. A prolific author on aspects of intelligence analysis and analytical theory, the National Journal in 2004 profiled him as one of the 10 leading experts on the subject of intelligence reform.

Getting Started

Initial Readings
for Instructors of Intelligence

Peter C. Oleson

his article, the first for AFIO's Guide to the Study of Intelligence, is intended to provide a starting place for educators interested in the subject of intelligence but who may not have had practical experience or exposure to the field.

The subject of intelligence is complex. In addressing national security decision-making, of which intelligence is a significant component, former national security advisor, Lt. Gen. Brent Scowcroft, wrote:

> Today the problem is much harder than it was during the Cold War. Then, we faced a single overriding challenger, a reality that shaped the world and our policies ... that world is gone. Today's world is anything but tidy. In some respects it is the exact opposite of the Cold War. There is no place on earth that cannot become tomorrow's crisis. Globalization is eroding borders and individual state's abilities to manage transnational challenges such as financial crises, environmental damage, networked terrorists, and international crime, to name a few.[1]

The White House and others expect the intelligence community to forewarn of impending threats and long-term strategic challenges. Failure to do so elicits almost instantaneous criticism of an "intelligence failure." What is often under-appreciated are the difficulties in collecting, verifying, processing, collating, and analyzing the enormous flood of information that is available to produce useful intelligence.

---

1. Roger Z. George and Harvey Rishikov (eds.). *The National Security Enterprise: Navigating the Labyrinth* (Georgetown University Press, 2011), xi.

Defining "Intelligence"

Some define "intelligence" as knowledge; others as a process, a product, an organization; or an activity. In his textbook, former CIA Deputy Director for Analysis and Production Mark Lowenthal differentiates intelligence from information, a lower order category: "Information is anything that can be known, regardless of how it is discovered. Intelligence refers to information that meets the stated or unstated needs of policymakers and has been collected, processed, and narrowed to meet those needs."[2] Perhaps the most comprehensive definition of intelligence comes from Australian author Don McDowell who writes:

> Information is essential to the intelligence process. Intelligence, on the other hand, is not simply an amalgam of collected information. Instead, it is the result of taking information relevant to a specific issue and subjecting it to a process of integration, evaluation, and analysis with the specific purpose of projecting future events and actions, and estimating and predicting outcomes.[3]

As McDowell points out, the primary focus of intelligence is prospective.

Today intelligence is used for many purposes. Besides the traditional tracking of foreign military capabilities and scrutiny of foreign government intentions, intelligence is used for the "new problems of the twenty-first century – nuclear proliferation, terrorism, failing states, cyber threats, global warming, and the international economic reshuffle."[4] Intelligence supports national security planning, diplomacy, homeland security, and enforcement of our laws. Furthermore, businesses employ intelligence techniques, often learned from former intelligence officers, for the purposes of strategic planning, understanding their marketplace and competitors, and protecting their products and physical and intellectual assets. Later articles in this series will address many of these uses.

Intelligence Communities

Best known is the nation's intelligence community, a grouping of 16 federal agencies, not including the Office of the Director of National Intelligence. See http://www.intelligence.gov or http://www.dni.gov/faq_intel.htm for listings of the organizations of the national intelligence community.

Since the attacks of 9/11, other intelligence communities have emerged in the US. Senior officials of the Department of Homeland Security refer to "homeland security intelligence" and the "homeland security intelligence community" as something distinct from the national intelligence community. This homeland security intelligence community includes governmental elements

---

2. Mark M. Lowenthal. *Intelligence: From Secrets to Policy*, 4th Ed., (CQ Press, 2009), 9.
3. Don McDowell. *Strategic intelligence: a Handbook for Practitioners, Managers, and Users*, Revised Edition, (Scarecrow Press, 2009), 53.
4. George and Rishikov, 7.

COMPARATIVE TERMS USED IN THE NATIONAL
AND LAW ENFORCEMENT INTELLIGENCE COMMUNITIES

National Intelligence Terminology	Law Enforcement Terminology
HUMINT Informant (willing source) Agent (controlled source)	Witness Confidential Informant (CI) Surveillance Dumpster diving Undercover
SIGINT COMINT (communications) ELINT (electronic transmissions) FIS (foreign instrumentation signals – telemetry) CNE (computer network exploitation)	Pen register (record of dialed numbers) Trap & trace (incoming "Caller ID") Wiretap (content, transcript)
IMINT* Photograph Electro-optical imagery Multi – or hyper-spectral imagery Infrared (thermal) imagery Radar imagery	Surveillance photographs Closed circuit TV video
OSINT Print Broadcast (radio, TV) Internet Online data bases Gray literature (limited availability)	Travel records Bank records Document evidence
MASINT Heat Vibration Magnetism Chemistry Radiation Energy Acoustics	Forensics

* IMINT is often combined with other geographic and environmental information to produce "geospatial intelligence (GEOINT)."

not included in the national intelligence community, such as the intelligence entities within the Department of Homeland Security Bureaus of Immigration and Customs Enforcement, Customs and Border Protection, the Transportation Security Administration, the US Secret Service, as well as the 70-plus state and regional intelligence fusion centers throughout the US. There is overlap in organizations and missions between the national intelligence community and the homeland security intelligence community.

Similarly, with the adoption of the concept of "intelligence-led policing" since 2000, there has been a growing law enforcement intelligence community. The FBI uses intelligence for more than counterterrorism and counterespionage investigations, as do many of the other members of this intelligence community. Elements of the law enforcement intelligence community include the Drug Enforcement Administration (DEA); the Bureau of Alcohol, Tobacco, Firearms, and Explosives (BATF); the US Marshals Service (USMS); the Bureau of Prisons (BOP); and state, local, and tribal law enforcement agencies. Both the Los Angeles Sheriff's Department and the New York Police Department maintain sizable intelligence elements. As with the homeland security intelligence community, there is organizational and mission overlap. For example, the FBI is a member of all three intelligence communities, and DEA is a member of the national and law enforcement intelligence communities.

Terminology

There are similarities between these various communities, but also significant differences in mission, culture, and language. Each community has developed its own terminology to describe its techniques. For example, in the national intelligence community, there are various disciplines that describe how information is collected. These are human source intelligence (HUMINT), signals (SIGINT), imagery (IMINT), open source (OSINT), and measurement and signatures (MASINT). The law enforcement intelligence community, reflecting its traditional investigative heritage, uses more precise descriptors of how it collects information. The table above lists the comparative terms of both communities.[5]

READINGS FOR INSTRUCTORS

The increasing number of books and articles about intelligence pose a challenge to anyone new to the field. Because of popular myths fostered by novels, movies, and television, much written about the intelligence field is inaccurate or sensationalized to enhance sales. Many written by former intelligence officers are prescriptions for reform largely based on personal experiences. The sources described here are this author's choices for those who want reliable information on which to base course materials for their students.

Widely used in universities is Mark Lowenthal's *Intelligence: From Secrets to Policy*, now in its sixth edition, covers the basics of the intelligence field, recounts the central themes of the evolution of the US national intelligence community, and explains its current layout. His treatment of law enforcement intelligence, however, is sparse. Chapters address the processes of collecting and analyzing intelligence, support to national policymakers, and the specialized topics of counterintelligence and covert action. He identifies many of the transnational issues of interest to intelligence as well as challenging ethical issues. Easily read, this book also contains many

---

5. Law enforcement terminology is taken from David L. Carter, *Law Enforcement Intelligence: A Guide for State, Local, and Tribal Law Enforcement Agencies*, 2nd Ed. (2009). US Department of Justice, on-line at *https://intellprogram.msu.edu/resources/publications.php*.

amusing asides and insight. Lowenthal has extensive experience in intelligence having worked for the director of central intelligence, the House Intelligence Committee, the State Department, and the Congressional Research Service. If one is to obtain only one book about intelligence, this is that book.

British author Christopher Andrew's 1995 *For the President's Eyes Only* remains one of the best published.[6] The book traces the major developments in American intelligence from the Revolutionary War through the administration of George H. W. Bush ending in 1993. Well written and researched by an established intelligence scholar, this book's extensive bibliography will also serve as a departure point for historical research. One hopes for an updated edition that addresses the past decade and a half.

Scientific writer and journalist David Owen has written *Hidden Secrets: A Complete History of Espionage and the Technology Used to Support It*, an interesting illustrated book that addresses many aspects of intelligence.[7] Despite its hyped subtitle (it is by no means a "complete" history), the book provides a brief overview of most intelligence collection disciplines. Of value to educators are the anecdotes and sidebars (often with the inflated label "case studies") that address the impact of intelligence in history. Some famous, as well as lesser known, successes and failures in espionage are described. Owen's inclusion of foreign examples and explanation of how intelligence aided important wartime deceptions adds to the educational value of the book. There are some minor technical errors, but they are not significant. The book is a useful source for extracting interesting historical points and examples for students, especially at the secondary level.

One of the best spy stories ever written is *A Secret Life* by journalist Benjamin Weiser.[8] With extensive inside assistance from the Central Intelligence Agency, Weiser writes the story of Polish Colonel Ryszard Kuklinski, who for almost a decade funneled the most sensitive of secrets concerning the Soviet Union and Warsaw Pact to the West. He revealed Moscow's offensive strategy and plans against Europe and the secret locations of wartime headquarters. Kuklinski was such a sensitive source that dissemination of his intelligence was severely restricted within CIA and the national intelligence community. His revelations prompted a fundamental change in US nuclear targeting policy and provided forewarning of the Communist regime's and Moscow's moves against the Polish Solidarity movement. Weiser's book is extraordinary in its detailed description of the spy tradecraft employed by CIA. This is the tale of a remarkable intelligence success that survived in secret for nine years from August 1972 until November 1981, when the CIA secreted Kuklinski out of Poland.

CIA's covert paramilitary operations are of considerable interest to students. There are many publications addressing this aspect of CIA's mission, but few can equal Gary Schroen's first-person account of leading a CIA team

---

6. Christopher Andrew. *For the President's Eyes Only: Secret Intelligence and the American Presidency from Washington to Bush.* (Harper Perennial, 1995).

7. David Owen, *Hidden Secrets: A Complete History of Espionage and the Technology Used to Support It.* Firefly Books, 2002 (pbk).

8. Benjamin Weiser. *A Secret Life: The Polish Officer, His Covert Mission, and the Price He Paid to Save His Country,* (Public Affairs, 2004 (pbk).

into the Panjshir Valley of Afghanistan in late September 2001 to spear-head the war against the Afghan Taliban and its Al-Qaida allies.[9] He details how the CIA team worked with the indigenous Northern Alliance, whose charismatic leader, Ahmed Shah Masood, was assassinated on Osama Bin Laden's orders on September 9, 2011. A former CIA station chief in Kabul and about to retire when he was tapped to head Operation Jawbreaker, Schroen is explicit about the difficulties his team faced getting into the Panjshir, then working with competing Afghan factions, and coordinating with the subsequent arrival of US Special Forces and the Air Force-managed air campaign, all the while enduring chronic health problems. First In is a primer on how CIA operates in a paramilitary operation.

Intelligence judgments and operations seem to stir constant controversy in the nation's capital. The press contains fragmented news items and editorials almost daily on intelligence. Keeping track of issues from an academic perspective is difficult. Fortunately, the Congressional Research Service (CRS) produces periodic studies for Congress on many intelligence topics. These unclassified reports can most easily be found on the web site of the Federation of American Scientists (http://www.fas.org/sgp/crs/intel/index.html). Congress does not make CRS reports readily available to the public. CRS national defense specialist Richard A. Best, Jr. produces annually Intelligence Issues for Congress. This study summarizes intelligence-related legislation and reports, reviews on-going congressional concerns, and identifies potential issues that the current Congress is likely to address. Intelligence Issues for Congress is important reading for any serious educator.

In the last few years, the government has created informative and relatively comprehensive web sites related to intelligence. The web site for the Office of the Director of National Intelligence (http://www.dni.gov) provides a wealth of background information on the national intelligence community as well as news releases, speeches, reports, testimony to Congress, management directives, and other publications. One section explains the 2004 Intelligence Reform and Terrorism Prevention Act and efforts at reforms. The site links to all of the member agencies of the intelligence community. Of particular interest at CIA's web site is the link to the Center for the Study of Intelligence (https://www.cia.gov/library/center-for-the-study-of-intelligence/csi-publications/csi-studies/index.html), which is CIA's in-house academic research center. The Center's site has an extensive list of declassified studies, unclassified extracts from Studies in Intelligence, CIA's periodic scholarly journal, and publications.

Lastly, instructors should explore the AFIO website for educational materials appropriate to their objectives. At http://www.afio.com/12_academic.htm are links to universities that teach about intelligence and selected course syllabi. At http://www.afio.com/27_worldwideweb.htm are links to government organizations and other sites of interest.

Peter C. Oleson is an associate professor of intelligence studies in the University of Maryland University College Graduate School of Management and Technology. He spent 40 years in the discipline, as a senior executive in the Office of

---

9. Gary Schroen. First In: An Insider's Account of How the CIA Spearheaded the War on Terror in Afghanistan (Presidio Press, 2005).

the Secretary of Defense and Defense Intelligence Agency, managing director of an aerospace firm's think tank, chief executive officer of an intelligence and technology-oriented management consulting firm, and an educator. He has served on the faculties of the National Defense Intelligence College and CIA University. He is a member of the AFIO Board of Directors, chairman of the academic outreach committee, and coordinator for *The Guide to the Study of Intelligence*.

GUIDE TO THE STUDY OF INTELLIGENCE

Who Are the Customers for Intelligence?

Peter C. Oleson

Who uses intelligence and why? The short answer is almost everyone and to gain an advantage. While nation-states are most closely identified with intelligence, private corporations and criminal entities also invest in gathering and analyzing information to advance their goals. Thus the intelligence process is a service function, or as Australian intelligence expert Don McDowell describes it,

> Information is essential to the intelligence process. Intelligence... is not simply an amalgam of collected information. It is instead the result of taking information relevant to a specific issue and subjecting it to a process of integration, evaluation, and analysis with the specific purpose of projecting future events and actions, and estimating and predicting outcomes.[1]

It is important to note that intelligence is prospective, or future oriented (in contrast to investigations that focus on events that have already occurred).

As intelligence is a service, it follows that it has customers for its products. McDowell differentiates between "clients" and "customers" for intelligence. The former are those who commission an intelligence effort and are the principal recipients of the resulting intelligence product. The latter are those who have an interest in the intelligence product and could use it for their own purposes.[2] Most scholars of intelligence do not make this distinction. However, it can be an important one as there is an implied priority associated with a client over a customer.

---

1. Don McDowell. *Strategic Intelligence: A handbook for practitioners, managers, and users*, Rev. Ed., (Lanham, Maryland: The Scarecrow Press, Inc., 2009), 53.
2. McDowell, 85.

Intelligence Communities (plural)

There are four communities that use intelligence: the national security community, the homeland security community, the law enforcement community, and the private sector.

When thinking about intelligence, often the first thought one has is of the *national* intelligence community. This is the grouping of 16 agencies (not including the Office of the Director of National Intelligence and its several centers) that are involved in intelligence support to national security, foreign and defense policy, military support, and counterespionage.[3]

The clients and customers of national security intelligence include the President and his national security team. While the President and members of the National Security Council represent the apex of this team, the national security team extends across many departments and agencies of the federal government and geographically to the commanders of the combatant commands and their subordinates.[4]

Since the attacks of 9/11, other intelligence communities have evolved in the U.S. Senior officials of the Department of Homeland Security (DHS) refer to "homeland security intelligence" (HIS) and the "homeland security intelligence community" as something distinct from the national intelligence community.[5] This homeland security intelligence community includes governmental elements not included in the national intelligence community, including the intelligence entities within the DHS Immigration and Customs Enforcement Bureau, the Customs and Border Protection Bureau, the Transportation Security Administration, the US Secret Service, and state and regional intelligence fusion centers throughout the US. There is some overlap between the national intelligence community and the homeland security intelligence community, as the Department of Homeland Security Office of Intelligence and Analysis and the US Coast Guard are members of both communities.[6] According to a former head of DHS intelligence, homeland security intelligence

"...needs to be more than just counterterrorism. Instead HSI needs to be a strategic effort based on creating a new tradecraft rather than focusing on traditional formulas in terms of intelligence collection."[7]

Customers for homeland security intelligence include some of the same as above. The President, the secretary of homeland security, and the attorney

---

3. See *http://www.odni.gov* for the listing of the organizations of the national intelligence community.
4. See the chart "Who Are the Customers for U.S. Intelligence?"
5. Remarks of Charlie Allen, former DHS undersecretary for intelligence to the International Association for Intelligence Education, Washington Chapter, September 14, 2010, from the notes of the author.
6. For a detailed overview of the HSI enterprise, see Mark A. Randol 2009, *The department of homeland security intelligence enterprise: operational overview and oversight challenges for congress*, Congressional Research Service 7-5700, (2009) http://www.crs.gov, R40602.
7. *INSA Insider*, November 23, 2010. This is an e-mail sent periodically to Intelligence and National Security Alliance association members.

general are all principal customers for such intelligence. But so are governors and other officials at the state, local, and tribal levels of government. Under the US political system, if an incident occurs in a state, the governor of that state is the principal in charge of responding. The federal government plays a supporting role. The establishment of intelligence fusion centers[8] in many states represents a significant customer base for homeland security intelligence. These fusion centers are managed by state officials or a consortium of regional and local law enforcement officials. One example is the regional fusion center in the Cleveland, Ohio area, which is manned by state and local police agencies and DHS assignees. Other fusion centers serve an entire state. [9]

While there is a strategic aspect to HSI, the great emphasis is on operational and tactical intelligence that will allow prevention of a terrorist incident. Principal customers for this level of homeland security intelligence include the enforcement arms of the DHS, the Department of Justice, state and local police departments, and other first responders.[10] Special mechanisms have been created to allow the sharing of classified national intelligence with often uncleared state, local, and tribal police.[11]

Similarly, with the adoption of the "intelligence-led policing" concept since 2000, there has been a growing law enforcement intelligence community. The FBI uses intelligence for more than counterterrorism and counterespionage investigations, as do many of the other members of this intelligence community. Elements of the law enforcement intelligence community include the Drug Enforcement Administration (DEA); the Bureau of Alcohol, Tobacco, Firearms, and Explosives; the US Marshals Service, the Bureau of Prisons; and state, local, and tribal law enforcement agencies. Both the Los Angeles Sheriff's Department and the New York Police Department maintain sizable intelligence elements. As with the homeland security intelligence community, there is overlap. For example, the FBI is a member of all three intelligence communities, and DEA is a member of the national and law enforcement intelligence communities.

Law enforcement intelligence has many of the same customers that homeland security intelligence does. At the federal level, principal customers would be the attorney general and the secretaries of the Treasury and homeland security, and the enforcement arms of their departments. Principal customers at the state level include the state police organization and local jurisdictions,

---

8. "State and major urban area fusion centers serve as focal points within the state and local environment for the receipt, analysis, gathering, and sharing of threat-related information between the Federal Government and state, local, tribal, territorial, and private sector partners." US National Intelligence: An Overview 2013, at http://www.ODNI.gov.

9. Briefing by the Cleveland fusion center to the annual AFIO conference in 2011.

10. See Chapter 2 of Carter, D. L. (2009). Law enforcement intelligence: A guide for state, local, and tribal law enforcement agencies (2nd ed.). Washington, DC: U.S. Department of Justice, Office of Community Oriented Policing Services. Retrieved from https://intellprogram.msu.edu/resources/publications.php.

11. The Interagency Threat Assessment and Coordination Group (ITACG) was created to help DHS, the FBI and the NCTC produce terrorism and related products tailored to the needs of state, local and tribal police as well as private sector partners.

including tribal police. Many of the state intelligence fusion centers are "all threat" centers. This term means that they focus on criminal activity other than terrorist activity, such as drug production and smuggling and gang activity.

Intelligence is no longer the exclusive purview of the government. Intelligence techniques have been adopted by private businesses seeking to be competitive in an increasingly global marketplace. Many major corporations now employ analysts that utilize the intelligence skills and techniques traditionally identified with the national intelligence community. These include market analysis for business planning and investment, the protection of critical infrastructures against criminals and others who would exploit them, and identification and pursuit of counterfeiters of a company's goods.

WHO ARE THE US CUSTOMERS FOR INTELLIGENCE?

DEPARTMENT / AGENCY	PRINCIPAL USES FOR INTELLIGENCE
President & Vice President	Threat understanding; policy determinations
Congress	Legislation & government oversight
NATIONAL SECURITY COMMUNITY	
National Security Advisor	Threat understanding; foreign & defense policies coordination
Secretary of State	Foreign policy advice, negotiations, security of diplomatic posts
Secretary of the Treasury	Financial policy, enforcement of sanctions
Secretary of Defense	Defense policy advice, command & control of military forces, weapons systems R&D
Chairman, Joint Chiefs of Staff (CJCS)	Military advice; command & control of military forces
Combatant Commanders	Command & control of military forces
Subordinate Military Commanders	Command & control of military forces
Attorney General	Legal advice, direction of the FBI and prosecutions
Secretary of Homeland Security / Director, Secret Service	Protection of the President, vice president & foreign dignitaries
Secretary of Energy	Nuclear weapons R&D
Director of National Intelligence (DNI)	Threat understanding; intelligence advice
National Counterterrorism Center (NCTC)	Counterterrorism strategies & plans
National Counterproliferation Center (NCPC)	Counterproliferation strategies
National Counterintelligence Executive (NCIX)	Coordination of counterintelligence activities
HOMELAND SECURITY COMMUNITY	
Secretary of Homeland Security	Homeland security policy advice
Customs and Border Protection (CPB)	Anti-smuggling, WMD detection, illegal entry
Immigration & Customs Enforcement (ICE)	Visa / immigrant identity fraud
US Coast Guard (USCG)	Water borders & port security, anti-smuggling
Transportation Security Administration (TSA)	Airport, rail, and bus security
Attorney General	Oversight of FBI operations

Director, Federal Bureau of Investigation (FBI)	Counterintelligence & counterterrorism investigations; intelligence operations
State, Local & Tribal law enforcement agencies	Counterterrorism planning & operations
Fusion Centers	Terrorism threat understanding
Law Enforcement Community	
Attorney General	Department of Justice management
Director, Federal Bureau of Investigation (FBI)	Counterintelligence, counterterrorism, criminal activity investigations
Director, Drug Enforcement Administration (DEA)	International drug smuggling; domestic abuse of controlled substances
US Attorneys	Prosecutions
Bureau of Alcohol, Tobacco & Firearms (ATF)	Investigation of firearms smuggling & explosives
Bureau of Prisons	Control of gangs
Secretary of Homeland Security	Oversight of subordinate elements
Subordinate DHS elements (USSS, CBP, ICE, USCG)	Investigation of selected crimes (e.g., threats to the President, financial cyber crimes, smuggling, fraud)
State, Local & Tribal law enforcement agencies (e.g., NYPD, LASD)	All types of criminal investigations
OTHER FEDERAL AGENCIES	
Secretary of Commerce	Enforcement of export controls
US Trade Representative	Negotiation of trade pacts
Federal Trade Commission	Violations of US laws
Securities and Exchange Commission	Market manipulation, fraud, etc.
Secretary of Transportation	Aviation policy
Federal Aviation Administration (FAA)	Security of airlines
Federal Emergency Management Agency (FEMA)	Disaster and terrorism event mitigation planning & operations
Federal Reserve	Integrity of the US dollar
INTERNATIONAL ENTITIES	
United Nations	
International Atomic Energy Agency (IAEA)	International nuclear industry & treaty compliance monitoring
Allies (e.g., NATO)	Coalition defense, counterterrorism, international crime & many other purposes
"Nontraditional Allies" or "Issue-Specific Allies" (e.g., Russia, China, Others)	Counterterrorism, international crime, cooperative operations (e.g., anti-piracy patrols)
PRIVATE SECTOR (ILLUSTRATIVE EXAMPLES)	
Technology Firms	Technology trends, competitor activities, market understanding, etc.
Natural Resources Firms (e.g., Oil Exploration Companies)	Strategic planning, investment, risk assessments, other
Financial Sector (e.g., Banks, Investment Firms, Reinsurance Companies, etc.)	Financial markets understanding, financial risk assessments, opportunity identification
Pharmaceutical Firms	Product counterfeiters

Uses of Intelligence

Intelligence has no intrinsic value. Intelligence collected, analyzed, and put on the shelf is worthless. It is wasteful of expensive and often dangerous efforts. Intelligence is a service, and should be evaluated as such. Its *raison d'être* is to assist others in the accomplishment of their goals. This could be a national policymaker, a district police commander, or the board of directors of a company contemplating a major industrial investment. Intelligence is a specialized function that adds value to a larger enterprise. If it does not, it cannot be justified. In some cases the value of intelligence may be measured in increased efficiency, but most often it is for increased effectiveness.

Intelligence can be used for strategic, operational, and/or tactical purposes. McDowell notes that

> Strategic intelligence analysis can be considered a specific form of research that addresses any issue at the level of breadth and detail necessary to describe threats, risks, and opportunities in a way that helps determine programs and policies." As such "strategic intelligence is a manager's tool." Whereas, "intelligence that services the daily needs of supervisors and line managers and focuses on immediate, routine, and on-going activities of the organization – the frontline functions, as it were – may be called tactical or operational intelligence....[12] [T]he most practical, intimate application of intelligence to identifying and dealing with target individuals and organizations has always been termed tactical. Activities involving operations against multiple targets of like or related character, where coordination of effort is the key, is called operational, and the intelligence designed to support it is operational intelligence.[13]

Strategic intelligence is used in many ways by many entities, but principally for policymaking and resource planning. At its most fundamental, intelligence is used for strategic warning. It has been the failure of providing strategic warning that has led to the most in-depth examinations of the national intelligence community and calls for reform. The prime examples are the failures to warn of the 1941 Japanese attack on Pearl Harbor and the 9/11 2001 Al-Qaida attacks on the US.[14] At the national level, strategic intelligence studies are often used for educational purposes by policymakers.[15] This is especially true early in a new administration when policymakers are adjusting to their new positions and responsibilities. Intelligence analysis underlies most policy planning efforts that address foreign or defense issues. A more controversial use of intelligence is for the evaluation of existing policies and whether they are successful or not. This use of intelligence has often led to clashes between intelligence profes-

---

12. McDowell, 5, 7.
13. McDowell, 13.
14. See Thomas H. Hammond, "Intelligence organizations and the organization of intelligence," *International Journal of Intelligence and Counterintelligence* 23 (4), 680-722.
15. Of interest is former CIA official Jack Davis's article, "Insightful interviews: A policymaker's perspective on intelligence analysis," *Studies in Intelligence* 38 (5), 1995, 7-15.

sionals and policymakers who are vested in a particular policy.[16]

Another use of strategic intelligence is for treaty monitoring. The 1979 ratification of the Strategic Arms Limitation Talks (SALT II) treaty was held up in the US Senate when concerns were expressed that the US could not monitor Soviet compliance with the treaty's terms. Not until Secretary of Defense Harold Brown testified in detail in executive session about US intelligence capabilities against the Soviet Union were these concerns allayed.[17]

Intelligence is critical to national defense resource planning and investment. President Eisenhower supported the development of the U-2 reconnaissance aircraft and of programs to develop satellite-based imagery and signals collection in order to learn about the size and capabilities of the strategic forces of the Soviet Union. Imagery from U-2 over flights of the Soviet Union (up until May 1960, when a Soviet surface-to-air missile downed Francis Gary Power's U-2) revealed that the estimated strength of the Soviet long-range aviation bomber force and intercontinental missile force were exaggerated. This permitted the President to avoid unnecessary investments in US strategic weapons programs at that time. Intelligence estimates are used to support investment decisions in the annual defense budget process. The sizing of US forces is justified in terms of the threats faced by the United States. During the Cold War, the intelligence community developed lengthy and detailed National Intelligence Estimates on Soviet strategic nuclear forces, conventional forces, and other strategic topics, which were used by US force planners to justify investments in military systems. The acquisition plans for major weapons systems are also based on intelligence estimates. Each planned major weapon system is supposed to respond to a validated intelligence threat assessment.[18] The underlying philosophy in both the sizing of forces and design of advanced weapons is to gain an advantage over a potential adversary.

Operational and tactical intelligence is used for various purposes. Warning or alerting of impending attack or commission of a crime is critical to operational commanders in the military, homeland security, or law enforcement communities. Intelligence also helps them decide how to deploy their forces in anticipation of an operation or response to a target's activities. Intelligence can also identify new targets or individuals previously unknown to military and law enforcement operators.

In the business intelligence field, intelligence is used also for gaining an advantage over competitors and influences the development of corporate

---

16. An interesting case study related to this point is recounted in James J. Wirtz's article, "Intelligence to Please? The order of battle controversy during the Vietnam War," *Political Science Quarterly* 106 (2), Summer 1991, 239-263. http://www.jstor.org/stable/2152228.

17. Personal experience of the author who helped write portions of Secretary Brown's testimony when on the staff of the Office of the Secretary of Defense.

18. See Department of Defense Instruction 5000.02, *Operation of the defense acquisition system*, December 8, 2008, and Defense Intelligence Agency Directive 5000.200, *"Intelligence threat support for major defense acquisition programs,"* January 19, 2005.

strategies, marketing campaigns, and investments for new products.[19]

In all of the communities identified the clients and customers for intelligence vary according to the subject, their mission and responsibilities, and circumstances. What is notable is how far the intelligence profession has spread since the early days of World War II to involve today so many governmental, private and international organizations.

READINGS FOR INSTRUCTORS

Don McDowell's *Strategic Intelligence: A handbook for practitioners, managers, and users*, Rev. Ed., (Lanham, Maryland: The Scarecrow Press, Inc., 2009) is an excellent guide to how to conduct intelligence analyses for different purposes.

The website of the Office of the Director of National Intelligence (*http://www.dni.gov*) has many reference publications useful for understanding the applications of intelligence.

The Congressional Research Service (CRS) periodically updates a paper entitled "Intelligence Issues for Congress." It contains non-partisan discussion of contemporary issues related to intelligence. It is available via the website of the Federation of American Scientists (*http://www.fas.org*). Also available at this website are other intelligence related government documents useful for classroom instruction.

Peter C. Oleson is a former member of the staff of the secretary of defense and assistant director of the Defense Intelligence Agency. He has taught about intelligence matters at the National Defense Intelligence College (now National Intelligence University), CIA University, and the University of Maryland University College. He was a member of the AFIO Board of Directors and is director of its academic outreach committee.

---

19. See Stephanie Hughes, "Competitive intelligence as competitive advantage: The theoretical link between competitive intelligence, strategy and firm performance," especially Figure 1, p 7. *Journal of Competitive Intelligence and Management*, 3 (3), 2005, 3-18.

Part II – History of Intelligence

Intelligence is often called the world's second oldest profession. Certainly it has been around for all of recorded history. In this section various authors trace the history of intelligence from antiquity to modern times. Much that has been written about intelligence is speculative, inaccurate, or reflects a philosophical bias. The first article provides a cautionary note. In his "A Note About Historiography," Professor of History (emeritus) at the University of New Hampshire, **Dr. Douglas Wheeler**, alerts readers to the inherent limitations of intelligence histories and emphasizes the need to distinguish between fact and opinion and truth and fiction.

In her "A Guide to Intelligence from Antiquity to Rome" **Col. Rose Mary Sheldon, PhD**, a history professor at Virginia Military Institute, gives substance to the adage that intelligence is the world's second oldest profession.

Professor Douglas Wheeler in "A Guide to the History of Intelligence in the Age of Empires, 1500-1800" addresses the use of intelligence by England, France, and Prussia. He also provides historical insights on the international evolution of intelligence in his "Guide to the History of Intelligence: 1800-1918," which addresses the age of industrialization and the establishment of nation-states' permanent intelligence organizations.

Penn State professor, **Dr. Edward J. Glantz, P.E.**, outlines the use of intelligence in the American Civil War. His "Guide to Civil War Intelligence" addresses human agents on both sides and the growth of signals intercepts and technical means (i.e., balloons) for intelligence gathering.

Historian **Mark Stout, PhD**, explains how World War I witnessed the birth of modern intelligence. His recommended readings for instructors covers most of the major belligerents.

Professor Wheeler provides further historical insights with his "Intelligence Between the World Wars, 1919-1939 – A World Made Safe For Deaths of Democracy."

Intelligence reached a zenith in World War II. **Peter Oleson's** lengthy examination of the impact of intelligence in World War II details how the Allies, whose pre-war intelligence capabilities were minimal, suffered from Axis surprises but eventually prevailed by breaking Axis codes and ciphers and building an international intelligence behemoth.

Dr. Michael Sulick, former director of the National Clandestine Service, reviews various aspects of intelligence during the Cold War. He identifies the major spies on each side that had significant impact, the impact of advances in technical intelligence collection, especially satellite collection, and the use of covert action. He further addresses the relationship of politics and intelligence analysis and the shortcomings in analysis, especially by the KGB.

In response initially to the Cold War CIA became a center for innovative scientific collection of intelligence unavailable by other means. Former senior scientific intelligence officer, **Gene Poteat** recollects some of CIA's efforts in his article "Scientific and Technical Intelligence: A Memoir by a S&T Intelligence Officer."

Stephen H. Campbell, while a Research Associate in the International Security Studies Program at the Fletcher School of Law and Diplomacy, Tufts University, has written about intelligence in the post-Cold War period. His first article, entitled "Guide to Intelligence in the Post-Cold War Period, Part I – The Changed Environment," explores how and why intelligence has changed so significantly. In his second article, "Guide to Intelligence in the Post-Cold War Period, Part II – The Impact of Technology," he surveys the enormous impact of a variety of technologies on the field of intelligence, in some cases revolutionizing collection, processing, and analysis.

GUIDE TO THE STUDY OF INTELLIGENCE

A Note About Intelligence Historiography

Douglas L. Wheeler, PhD

Historians face a challenge. The history of intelligence and its impact on world affairs has only been addressed recently by scholars. Not until after World War I did journalists, former spies, and a few academics begin to publish about secret intelligence. American writer Richard Wilmot Rowan, one of the rare students of intelligence history, in his encyclopedic 1937 book, *The Story of Secret Service*, wrote that historians had ignored the history of espionage. Spying, he observed, had had a greater impact on history than on historians.

The extent to which spying has influenced the course of history remains a debatable topic, but in the last 40 years, more historians have focused on intelligence. Today, there is substantial intelligence literature available to students, especially for the period beginning with World War I. In the 1970s, pioneering scholars of intelligence history declared that the subject was the "missing dimension" of diplomatic history. The same could be said for military and political history.

Understanding intelligence history and the influence of intelligence on history presents interesting challenges. The subject's very terminology is confusing. Take the word "intelligence," which in its English military-political connotation (not its educational definition as "the ability to think") has at least three different meanings. Intelligence is a special kind of information, a process of obtaining it, and an organization that does this work. Then there is the deceptive, secretive nature of the subject, the routine denial of public access to intelligence records, the debatable quality of intelligence produced, and a plethora of myths and legends that distort public understanding. Other complicating factors include the fact that, in the public mind, there has long been a stigma attached to espionage, an occupational hazard that can discourage recruitment for this work and confounded some scholars who considered studying the fraught topic. A further difficulty in writing intelligence history is that even if a student discovers what intelligence was available to a commander in battle, it is not always clear what the commander knew and when. And finally, it is the victors and commanders of battles that usually write the histories; rarely do the spies and spymasters.

Even with these challenges, instructors and students can take advantage of the ongoing electronic revolution and consult a growing intelligence literature in print as well as online. Conditions for studying the subject have markedly improved, but even so, one confronts the historian's traditional dilemmas: how to distinguish between fact and opinion, between truth and fiction, and how to measure the impact of intelligence on history.

GUIDE TO THE STUDY OF INTELLIGENCE

A Guide to Intelligence From Antiquity to Rome

Col. Rose Mary Sheldon, PhD

People have always spied on each other. There is no period in which we cannot search for intelligence history, as long as there are texts that survive. One reason that people do not know about intelligence in the ancient world is that the information is scattered in specialty journals. Another is the information is in languages other than English. Fortunately, this situation has begun to change. Books and articles in English on intelligence in the ancient world have increased over the last 25 years. Francis Dvornik's textbook and my bibliography on ancient espionage serve as introductory guides to the subject.[1]

Other studies have focused on specific cultures. Two major studies have appeared on the intelligence activities of ancient Rome[2] and several more have been published on the ancient Greeks.[3]

What I refer to as intelligence activities, in fact, includes a whole range of subjects that are only loosely bound by the fact that modern intelligence services practice them. Besides intelligence gathering, counterintelligence, covert action, and clandestine operations, there are tradecraft techniques such as the use of codes and ciphers, political assassination, escape and evasion,

---

1. Dvornik, Francis, *The Origins of Intelligence Services*, New Brunswick, NJ: Rutgers University Press, 1974, and Rose Mary Sheldon, *Espionage in the Ancient World: An Annotated Bibliography*, Jefferson: North Carolina, McFarland, 2003.

2. Austin, N. J. E. and N.B. Rankov, *Exploration: Military and Political Intelligence in the Roman World from the Second Punic War to the Battle of Adrianople*. New York: Routledge, 1995, and R.M. Sheldon, *Intelligence Activities in Ancient Rome: Trust in the Gods, but Verify*, London: Frank Cass, 2005.

3. Starr, Chester G., *Political Intelligence in Classical Greece*, Brill Leiden, *Mnemosyne* Supplement 31, 1974; J.A. Richmond, "Spies in Ancient Greece," G&R 45 (1998), pp. 1-18; R. M. Sheldon, "Tradecraft in Ancient Greece," *Studies in Intelligence* 30, 1 (1986), pp. 39-47. Revised version with notes in *International Journal of Intelligence and Counterintelligence* 2, 2 (1988), pp. 189-202; Frank Santi Russell, *Information Gathering in Classical Greece*, Ann Arbor: University of Michigan Press, 1999; R.M. Sheldon, *Ambush! Surprise Attack in Ancient Greek Warfare*, Frontline Books, London. (Forthcoming); Andre Gerolymatos, *Espionage and Treason. A Study of the Proxenia in Political and Military Intelligence Gathering in Classical Greece*, Amsterdam, 1986.

disguises, disappearing ink, breaking into other people's mail ("flaps and seals"), and even "fluttering" (lie detection). These all occurred, in some form, in the ancient world.

Targeting an enemy and collecting intelligence must go hand in hand with the ability to transmit the information to those who need it most. Texts of the ancient writers like Aeneas Tacticus, Polybius, Polyaenus, Sextus Julius Africanus, and Vegetius[4] all contain snippets of information on ancient signaling. There are more than 50 references from all of antiquity, most are Greek; others are Roman. David Woolliscroft collected them in his book Roman Military Signalling, where he lists all the references and demonstrates how Roman frontier systems worked.[5]

Disguising one's written messages was also a skill known to the ancients.[6] The bibliography on one of the most enigmatic and unsolved cryptograms in antiquity is collected in my Cryptologia article "The Sator Rebus. An Unsolved Cryptogram?"[7] Governments classifying documents was also a practice known to the ancients.[8]

No ancient author tells us more about sending secret messages than Aeneas Tacticus. He provides the first instructional text on communications security and describes in detail 18 different methods of sending messages, some of them using ciphers. The best translation with commentary is still by David Whitehead.[9] Another article on secret communication is Albert Leighton's "Secret Communications Among the Greeks and Romans."[10]

Ancient tricks for collecting information and concealing messages seem amusing to us because of their quaintness and simplicity by modern technology standards. Ancient cryptograms would hardly deceive a modern military censor, but could well have fooled a simple-minded gatekeeper or a barbarian policeman in an age when reading and writing were uncommon. Tricks with vowels and consonants, for example, were unheard of even among educated people. Like other elements of great inventions now part of our thought and

---

4. Aeneas Tacticus in the 4th century BC wrote several treatises on the art of war. Polybius was a Greek military and political historian. Polyaenus, a Macedonian, wrote "Stratagems in War." Sextus Julius Africanus was a 3rd century Christian historian and one-time soldier. Vegetius (Publius Flavius Vegetius Renatus) wrote "De Re Militari," which was much translated and concerned military organization and how to manage troops and military situations.

5. Woolliscraft, David. Roman Military Signalling (Stroud, Gloucestershire: Tempus, 2001).

6. Texts on cryptography and secret writing include: Leighton, Albert C., "Secret Communications among the Greeks and Romans," Technology and Culture 10 (2), April 1969, 139-154; Reinke, Edgar C., "Classical Cryptography," Classical Journal 50, October 1962-May 1963,113-121; Dodge, Louise, "Cipher in Cicero's Letters to Atticus," American Journal of Philology 22 (1901), 439-41; and Ezov, Amiram, "The 'Missing Dimension' of C. Julius Caesar," Historia 45 (1996),. 64-94.

7. Sheldon, R. M., "The Sator Rebus. An Unsolved Cryptogram?" Cryptologia 27 (3), July, 2003, 233-287.

8. Sheldon, R. M., "Spying in Mesopotamia: The World's Oldest Classified Documents," Studies in Intelligence 33 (1), Spring, 1989, 7-12.

9. Aeneas Tacticus, Aineias the Tactician, D. Whitehead trans. with commentary (Oxford: The Clarendon Press, 1990).

10. Leighton, Albert C., "Secret Communications among the Greeks and Romans," Technology and Culture 10 (2), April 1969, 139-154.

action, the ideas behind these ancient practices still apply. Other ancient tradecraft techniques are described in the texts in the footnote.[11]

Intelligence failures resulted in disasters much as they do today. Several Roman debacles might have been prevented with better intelligence gathering. Whether it be the slaughter of Varus' three legions in Germany's Teutoburg Forest,[12] Trajan's dubious foray into Parthia (modern day Iran),[13] or Caesar's near disaster in Britain.[14] Intelligence gathering was an integral part of what happened. Every ambush in antiquity relied on advanced intelligence on the enemy's whereabouts so the trap could be sprung.[15]

The study of intelligence activities cuts across all chronological and cultural barriers, but its study presents historians with certain problems. Intelligence activities are supposed to be clandestine; they are not routinely recorded. For this reason, studying intelligence has become, in the words of one writer, "the missing dimension" of much political and diplomatic history.[16] Ancient spies, unlike their modern counterparts, did not retire and write memoirs. The ancient intelligence officer, if he were not successful, might draw the historian's notice indirectly, because his failure meant his execution or a major military disaster. On the other hand, when an ancient intelligence officer succeeded, he remained unheralded and faded into obscurity, unnamed and unrewarded, at least publicly.

The history of intelligence should start at the beginning, and incorporating ancient examples is no longer so difficult. With a little bit of digging into the ancient sources we find that enough evidence remains to show that the ancients understood that intelligence activities have always been an integral part of statecraft and warfare, and no one could have run a city-state or an empire without some attention being paid to intelligence gathering. In order to control their populations, to keep abreast of political developments abroad, and for

---

11. Millar, C. H. M., "Some Escapes and Escapers in the Ancient World," Greece and Rome 5 (1958), 57-61; Mayor, Adrienne, Greek Fire, Poison Arrows & Scorpion Bombs: Biological and Chemical Warfare in the Ancient World (Overlook 2003); and Mayor, Adrienne, The Poison King: The Life and Legend of Mithradates, Rome's Deadliest Enemy (Princeton University Press 2009).

12. Sheldon, R. M., "Slaughter in the Forest" Small Wars and Insurgencies 12 (3), Autumn, 2001, 1-38.

13. Sheldon, R. M., "Trajan's Parthian Adventure: With Some Modern Caveats," in Eunan O'Halpin, Robert Armstrong, and Jane Ohlmeyer (eds.), Intelligence, Statecraft and International Power, Historical Studies XXV. Papers read before the 27th Irish Conference of Historians Held at Trinity College, Dublin, 2005, 153-174; and Sheldon, R. M., Rome's Wars in Parthia: Blood in the Sand (London: Vallentine Mitchell, 2010).

14. Sheldon, R. M., "To the Ends of the Earth: Caesar, Intelligence and Ancient Britain," International Journal of Intelligence and Counterintelligence 15 (1), Spring 2002, 77-100; Belfiglio, Valentine J., "Roman Amphibious Operations against Britain in 55 B.C.," Military and Naval History Journal, March, 1998, 3-13; and Belfiglio, Valentine J., "The Roman Amphibious Assault against Britain in 54 B.C.," Military and Naval History Journal, March 2000, 15-21.

15. Sheldon, R. M., "The Odysseus Syndrome: Ambush and Surprise in Ancient Greek Warfare," in European History: Lessons for the 21st Century, Essays from the 3rd International Conference on European History, Edited by Gregory T. Papanikos and Nicholas C.J. Pappas (Athens: ATINER, 2007), ch. 8.

16. Andrew, Christopher and David Dilks (eds.). The Missing Dimension: Governments and Intelligence Communities in the Twentieth Century (University of Illinois Press, 1985).

the internal security of their own regimes, they needed a means to collect the intelligence that enabled them to make informed decisions.

Colonel Rose Mary Sheldon is a history professor at the Virginia Military Institute. She received her PhD in ancient history from the University of Michigan and has specialized in ancient intelligence history. She is on the editorial boards of the *International Journal of Intelligence and Counterintelligence* and *Small Wars and Insurgencies*, and has served on the board of the *Journal of Military History*. She has authored more than three dozen articles on aspects of ancient intelligence and several books, including *Espionage in the Ancient World: An Annotated Bibliography* (McFarland, 2003), *Intelligence Activities in Ancient Rome: Trust in the Gods, But Verify*, (Frank Cass, 2005), *Spies in the Bible* (London: Greenhill Books, 2007), *Operation Messiah: St. Paul, Roman Intelligence and the Birth of Christianity*, (Elstree, Hertfordshire, England: Vallentine-Mitchell, 2008), *Rome's Wars in Parthia: Blood in the Sand* (Elstree, Hertfordshire, England: Vallentine-Mitchell, 2010), and *Ambush! Surprise Attack in Ancient Greek Warfare* (London: Frontline Books, 2012).

GUIDE TO THE STUDY OF INTELLIGENCE

The History of Intelligence in the Age of Empires, 1500–1800

Douglas L. Wheeler, PhD

Although spying is older than war, the systematic employment of spies and permanent intelligence services came only after 1850. Before the technological and political revolutions of the 1800's transformed the world, leaders and commanders sought intelligence for traditional purposes and in traditional ways: in times of peace, banks, insurance companies, and merchants sought information to protect or expand their investments; in war, scouts probed the enemy and soldiers and sailors intercepted messages, interrogated prisoners, found documents, and sent out spies to discover the enemy's strength and plans. Like chess players, diplomats sought warning of their adversaries' strategies and next moves. Kings and princes dispatched spies to protect their royal lives and kingdoms.

The period of 1500-1800 was a time of transition from the late Renaissance to early modern history, from the age of sail to coal-powered steamships. In 1500 in the West, while monarchs and diplomats employed spies, there were no permanent intelligence services. By 1800, as the West entered early stages of the industrial revolution, warfare underwent important changes in tactics, weaponry, and planning; and armed forces and foreign ministries toyed with the notion of creating permanent intelligence units.

The secret arts of spying were nurtured more extensively and had an ancient history in the East, especially in India and China. In India's Moghul Empire, during its zenith from the 1550's to 1750, for example, emperors used intelligence services widely both in war and peace. Moghul emperors such as Akbar; Jahangir; Shah Jahan, creator of the Taj Mahal; and Aurangzeb, sponsored personal spy corps with networks of scavengers, mendicants, merchants, and ascetics who reported on conspiracies and plots.

During the Renaissance and later as the Ottoman Empire reached its apogee in the 16th and 17th centuries, various developments led to a greater emphasis on intelligence. These included the beginnings of residential diplomacy,[1] the formation of nation-states with record-keeping bureaucracies, overseas empires with national trading companies, the birth of international insurance companies such as Lloyd's of London, religious conflicts within Christianity as well as between Christianity and Islam, the modernization of warfare, and industrialization. All were of interest to competing major powers.

A classic example of intelligence that influenced the course of history is during the Anglo-Spanish conflict of the 1580's and 1590's, when a weaker Elizabethan England stood up against the world power, Spain, under King Phillip II. Elizabeth I had many domestic and foreign enemies, but was fortunate to have several clever secretaries of state, most famous of which was the well-travelled and educated Sir Francis Walsingham, who established networks of spies in Scotland, France, The Netherlands, Italy, Spain, and England.

By placing spies in the Spanish court, Walsingham learned of conspiracies to assassinate the queen and of Phillip's plans to invade England with the Armada. An especially helpful correspondent-spy was the ambassador from the city-state of Florence, Giovanni Figliazzi. England's intelligence efforts, though some agents were amateurish, others duplicitous, and the spying was not well-financed, were superior to Spain's. Providence in 1588 took a hand in the fate of the Spanish Armada when a great storm in the English Channel wrecked and scattered the fleet before it could land its invasion force.

Intelligence networks of that time were transitory and rarely survived the monarchs or the terms of their officers. However, intelligence practices were developed that are still used today. One was the availability of "secret funds" for spying, bribery, and propaganda used by England, France, Austria, and other European states. George Washington, during the revolution and as president, used secret funds provided by Congress. Another was the establishment of special offices or *Cabinets noires* ("Black Chambers") to intercept the mail of foreign diplomats and others. Such Black Chambers included experts in cryptanalysis (the reading of secret writing), technicians who could open and restore undetected mail seals, and linguists to translate foreign languages. Beginning as early as the late 16th century in France, such activities were located in the

---

1. Residential diplomacy was a new practice among both city-states and emerging nation-states in Europe that presented opportunities for more spying. The practice replaced the pre-Renaissance itinerant diplomacy, when ambassadors did not reside for any length of time in the countries to which they were accredited but moved from place to place. At least one Italian city-state introduced residential diplomacy in the 13th century, but the Republic of Venice in the 14th and 15th centuries was a principal pioneer of residential diplomacy. Venetian diplomats submitted regular, detailed reports on their observations abroad. Although ambassadors were not supposed to spy, diplomats' collection of intelligence could include the use of spies. A 17th century Spanish ambassador resident in England remarked that in his day ambassadors were little more than "public spies." Others labeled such diplomats as "honorable spies," who, it was assumed, were all gathering intelligence for their countries.

foreign ministry and in post offices.

Cardinal Richelieu (1586-1642), chief minister of French King Louis XIII, placed as great an emphasis on spying on his domestic enemies as against foreign powers. Richelieu initiated the practice of keeping police files on the king's subjects. In the 1639 siege of a Spanish fortress, the French intercepted enemy messages, enabling the deception of the Spanish by sending a falsified messagethat ordered the fortress to surrender. It did.

By 1700, the French were reputed to be clever spymasters. It was no coincidence that the English intelligence vocabulary is dominated by words adopted from French, such as reconnaissance, reconnoiter, surveillance, spy, and spying. At the end of the century, during the wars of French Revolution, the potent new French word, *espionnage*, entered English common usage as "espionage."

Whatever the truth of the notion that the French led in such secret arts (certainly the English writer and secret agent Daniel Defoe assumed this to be the case), the French spy networks played significant roles in French efforts to surpass its imperial rival, Britain, dominate European politics, and to build an overseas empire.

One of the most bizarre cases of a diplomat carrying out espionage was that of Chevalier Charles d'Eon (1728-1810), French soldier, swordsman, diplomat, and spy, who spent half his life as a man and half as a woman. D'Eon carried out important diplomatic missions for King Louis XV and was a member of the so-called "King's Secret," a clandestine group not known to most of France's Government. Among d'Eon's successful diplomatic missions was spying in England as well as in Catherine the Great's Russia. D'Eon is interesting not only for the gender question but because after dismissal, he (she?) kept secret documents about a French invasion plan and the secret unit he had been part of and sought to blackmail the king to be reinstated.

The great Prussian monarch, Frederick the Great (1712–1786) took great pains to collect intelligence before campaigns and battles. His classic military writings address the methods of employing military spies. His typology of military spies was inspired by hard-won experience, a practical sense, and current French spy doctrine. Four types of spies, he observed, were hired to discover enemy secrets: common spies, from the common people in the specific combat theater; double spies, where renegades spied for pay; spies of consequence from the "better classes"; and coerced spies, who could include prosperous burghers who spied for Prussia because they had been threatened with loss of property or feared the fate of their hostage families. The patriot-spy, who spied because of national loyalty, was not in the typology. Such motivation would not become common until years later with the emergence of nationalism sparked by the American and French Revolutions. Frederick once quipped that a commander he had faced in battle was preceded in the field with a hundred cooks while he was preceded by a hundred spies.

By the late 18th century, as the sun was setting on the French and Spanish Empires and rising on the British, intelligence work reflected continuity as well as change. Before invention of the telegraph, signal flags on land and at sea speeded the sending of messages, and diplomats increasingly used secret writing in their correspondence. Code names for spies were adopted and the use of invisible ink, to hide messages in letters, became more sophisticated. Private companies, such as Lloyd's of London and the Rothschild banks, had efficient intelligence-collection systems, which relayed news from abroad sometimes more rapidly than government agencies. For example, news sent by private carrier pigeon of the outcome of important battles in the late 18th and early 19th centuries reached private companies in London before the British Government.

Intelligence activities during the American Revolutionary War (1775-1783) were significant, but it is difficult to conclude that Washington's intelligence successes provided the margin of victory. The Americans held a natural advantage as locals in knowing the country better than the invaders, but the British had more experience in military and naval intelligence and were superior in naval power. The most celebrated American spy of the Revolution was a young teacher and volunteer in the Continental Army, the patriot-spy-martyr Nathan Hale (1755-1776), who volunteered to spy for General Washington. Left out of textbooks' brief mention of Hale is the fact that Hale's fellow Connecticut soldiers, when they learned that he had volunteered to spy for General Washington, sought to talk him out of the mission, because they considered spying immoral and dishonorable work. Hale justified what he described as a "peculiar service" as being necessary to the patriots' cause, and since no one else had volunteered, he would. Disguised as a Dutch schoolmaster seeking a job, Hale was discovered and executed. Despite his minor clandestine role, Hale is celebrated as a hero and the symbol of selfless patriotism. No fewer than 10 statues commemorate Hale's patriotic sacrifice, including one at the CIA and another at Yale University, his *alma mater*.

An important advantage for the American revolutionary forces was that George Washington himself was the main spymaster and analyst and had a keen appreciation of the importance of secret intelligence. Even though Washington had to pay spies out of his own pocket, his espionage system was more focused, centralized, and efficient, than that of the British.[2]

The French, beginning in 1778, used their expertise in deceptive arts to disguise their assistance to the Americans. The French secret agent, Pierre-Augustin Caron de Beaumarchais (1732-1799), author of *The Marriage of Figaro*, developed a novel method of clandestine assistance to an ally. Organizing what might have been the first dummy or front company, "Rodrigue, Hortalez and Company," Beaumarchais expedited the dispatch of French arms, munitions,

---

2. Congress reimbursed Washington $17,000 after the war for intelligence expenses.

and provisions from French ports to the American rebels.

During the French Revolution and its subsequent Terror (1789-1794), the revolutionary Foreign Ministry developed an intelligence organization that presaged those later found in Bolshevik Russia, the Soviet Union, and Nazi Germany. This unit spied, countered foreign spies, carried out mail and press censorship, sabotage, assassinations, and produced disinformation and propaganda to bolster revolutionary France against both internal and external enemies.

The period of 1500-1800 saw intelligence grow in importance in war as well as in peacetime. Military and political espionage became more sophisticated and complex. The diversity of spies increased. Secret messages became more complex and required the employment of mathematicians and linguists. Military manuals discussed the use of spies in warfare. Deception by means of false messages and use of dummy commercial companies for secret assistance foreshadowed intelligence activities in later wars. Intelligence operations by the French after 1789 foreshadowed the aggressive intelligence services of the totalitarian powers in the 20th century.

READINGS FOR INSTRUCTORS

There is no single volume of the intelligence history of the 1500-1800 period, but two references are recommended. First is Richard W. Rowan's eccentric, but witty, and fascinating narrative of intelligence history from ancient times, *The Story of Secret Service* (New York: Literary Guild, 1937). It is dated in its analysis, sketchily documented, and lacks an index, but for pre-1800 history it remains unique. A revised edition of this book, with an added index, appeared in 1967, but with some pre-1800 material cut: Richard W. Rowan and Robert G. Deindorfer, *Secret Service: Thirty-three Centuries of Espionage* (New York: Hawthorn, 1967). Second, highly recommended, but a door-stopper of a book is David Kahn, *The Codebreakers: The Story of Secret Writing* (2nd rev. edition, New York: Scribner, 1996). At 1,181 pages, it is encyclopedic but quite simply the greatest history ever written of secret writing, cryptology, and intelligence in any language.

An accessible, concise account of spying during Queen Elizabeth I's reign is in Alan Haynes, *Invisible Power: The Elizabethan Secret Services 1570-1603* (Stroud, UK: Alan Sutton, 1992; 1994 paper ed.). A rare, comparative analysis of spies' motives in Elizabethan and Cold War Britain was written by Michael Burn, *The Debatable Land. A Study of the Motives of Spies in Two Ages* (London: Hamish Hamilton, 1970). Despite its age, the most succinct history of spying and diplomacy from 1500 to 1815 remains James Westfall Thompson and Saul K. Padover's *Secret Diplomacy, Espionage and Cryptography 1500-1815* (New York: Frederick Ungar, 1937, 1st ed.; reprinted 1963, 1965).

The best documented work on British intelligence in the 18th century, with an emphasis on late 18th century naval intelligence, is Steven E. Maffeo's *Most Secret and Confidential: Intelligence in the Age of Nelson* (Annapolis, MD:

Naval Institute Press, 2000). Also recommended is a work by distinguished military historian John Keegan, *Intelligence in War: The Value – and Limitations – Of What the Military Can Learn About the Enemy* (New York: Vintage, 2002; paper ed., 2004). Recommended for pre-1800 intelligence history and trenchant analysis especially are his "Introduction" and Chapter One, "Knowledge of the Enemy," pp. 3-25.

Douglas L. Wheeler is professor emeritus of history at the University of New Hampshire. He holds an AB from Dartmouth College, and an MA and PhD from Boston University. He was a Fulbright grantee, served in the US Army (1963-1965), was an instructor at the US Army's Intelligence School, and has been a consultant on foreign affairs. Since 1969, he has taught an undergraduate course, "Espionage and History," at the University of New Hampshire. In 1984-1985, he was the Richard Welch Research Fellow in the advanced history of intelligence at the Harvard University Center for International Affairs.

GUIDE TO THE STUDY OF INTELLIGENCE

A Guide to the History of Intelligence, 1800-1918

Douglas L. Wheeler, PhD

Wisdom is better than weapons of war.

—— Ecclesiastes 9:18, cited by
William Reginald "Blinker" Hall,
Royal Navy Admiral,
Director of Naval Intelligence, 1914-1918.

During the 19th century, an age of industrialization, military and diplomatic intelligence evolved greatly over the course of the many armed conflicts in the West, including the Napoleonic Wars (1795-1815), the Crimean War (1854-56), the American Civil War (1861-1865), the Austro-Prussian (1866) and Franco-Prussian (1870-71) Wars, many colonial wars including the Spanish-American War (1898), the Anglo-Boer War (1899-1902), and the Russo-Japanese War (1904-05). New developments affecting intelligence included technological innovations; rapid communication and transportation enabling speedier collection and dissemination of secret information; the introduction of the military attaché system in foreign countries to collect intelligence; the creation of permanent intelligence services in Western armies and navies; the creation of the first spy schools for training intelligence agents in Germany, Austria, France, and Britain; as well as the introduction of the first laws penalizing leaks of military secrets to the press or the public.

The Age of Industrialization and Intelligence (1800-1914)

The first Duke of Wellington (1769-1852) once made a simple observation about battlefield intelligence. As the British Army's field commander, he wanted to know what was "on the other side of the hill." In his day, cavalry scouts, spies or messengers collected such intelligence and reported in person to the commander or to one of his key subordinates. Spies' capabilities to collect and deliver intelligence improved after 1830 with the inventions of photography, the typewriter, the telegraph, improved secret writing, superior optics for telescopes and binoculars, observation balloons, railroads and the fast steamship.

As warfare became more complex and the size of armies grew, Western armed forces developed war plans, anticipating scenarios and planning for contingencies. Intelligence services, seeking knowledge of enemy plans and intentions, were presented with a new target. Obtaining enemy war plans became a major focus.

Despite the improvements in intelligence methods, during the late 1800's, most states were poorly prepared for war, and their intelligence services often were surprised. Examples include Austria in 1866 and France in 1870, both of whom were surprised by Prussia. Notable exceptions, however, were Prussia, whose military intelligence in the Austro-Prussian War of 1866 and in the Franco-Prussian War of 1870-1871 was effective; and the Japanese, whose military intelligence contributed to its stunning victory in the Russo-Japanese War, 1904-1905. Contributing factors were the employment of "saturation" spying techniques and leaders who heeded what their spies discovered and acted upon it.

Industrial espionage, the theft of trade and manufacturing secrets, became more prevalent and complex. Nations competed economically. Private companies had long protected their correspondence by the use of secret writing and by keeping their employees under surveillance. The British Government protected its textile industry by forbidding the immigration of textile workers. This was not entirely successful. Francis Cabot Lowell (1775-1817), a wealthy Bostonian merchant-trader-entrepreneur, was allowed to visit new textile mills in England and Scotland in 1810. Lowell admired what he saw but was unable to obtain drawings or models of the new power looms. Instead he memorized the designs of the looms, and, by 1814, had engineered the first up-to-date cotton mills in Waltham, Massachusetts. After his death, the new industrial city of Lowell, Massachusetts, was named in his honor. The Lowell case demonstrates those qualities a successful industrial spy required: resourcefulness, an extraordinary memory, sure knowledge of the subject at hand, and a keen attention to detail.

Industrialization, urbanization, and the increase in literacy in the West prompted the development of modern mass-circulated daily newspapers. The modern newspaper contained not only news but, at times, useful "intelligence." A foreshadowing of a now familiar conflict between freedom of the press and security of military information came during the Crimean War (1854-1856). The British press covered the war in detail and dispatched foreign correspondents who reported from the battlefields. *The Times of London* provided readers with detailed information on the British forces' makeup, command structure, and strength — in other words, the British order of battle. Russian officers began to read such reports from mailed copies of *The Times*. The Russian czar was not joking entirely when he later claimed that now he had no need for spies as he only had to read *The Times*. Three decades later, in 1889, responding to another leak of military secrets to the public, British Parliament passed its first Official Secrets Act, which penalized both the possession and the use of government information by "unauthorized persons."

In the 19th century, permanent intelligence services were established among the European powers, the United States, Russia, and Japan, as shown in Figure 1.

Year	Country	Name of Service	Type of Intelligence
1804	France	Sureté	Political intelligence & counterintelligence
1850	Austro-Hungarian Empire	Evidenzbureau	Military intelligence & counterintelligence
1860	Germany	Section IIIb, General Staff	Military intelligence
1875	France	Deuxieme Bureau, Army General Staff	Military intelligence
1881	Japan	Kempei Tai	Army counterintelligence
1881	Russia	Okhrana	Political secret police
1883	United States	Office of Naval Intelligence	Navy intelligence
1885	United States	Bureau of Military Information	Army intelligence
1887	Britain	Department of Naval Intelligence	Navy intelligence
1908	United States	Bureau of Investigation	Criminal investigation (after 1917, counter-espionage)
1909	Britain	MO-6 (later MI-6)	Foreign intelligence
1911	Britain	MO-5 (later MI-5)	Counterintelligence

Figure I. The founding of permanent intelligence services

Following the Crimean War, European powers inaugurated the military attaché system, a complement to the existing residential diplomacy, a practice the United States adopted in the 1880's. Following the theory that sharing information on armed forces among the powers would encourage peaceful mediation of international conflicts and prevent wars, army and navy officers abroad were expected to collect military information. By protocol the attachés were not supposed to spy, but, in fact, quite a few became involved in espionage.

Europe's most sensational spy scandal, the Dreyfus case, which lasted from 1894 to 1906, originated with the German military attaché in Paris. Colonel Max Von Schwarzkoppen hired spies to acquire French secrets, including war plans and weaponry data. After French military counterintelligence discovered that a spy had sent a message to this attaché, they arrested Captain Alfred Dreyfus (1859-1935), an artillery and General Staff officer, assigned to intelligence. Dreyfus, an Alsatian Jew, underwent a closed military trial in which his defense counsel was denied access to the main evidence. Thus framed, Dreyfus was convicted of treason. He was to serve a life sentence on Devil's Island, a remote French island off South America. After a long, bitter campaign carried out in the press, the courts, the barracks, and the government, Dreyfus was finally acquitted and rehabilitated.

The case typified the pervasive fear of spies in an era of intensifying nationalism, economic rivalries, imperialism, arms races, and militarism. The Dreyfus affair polarized French politics and strengthened the war fever, which gripped pre-1914 Europe. The Dreyfus case was also a case of anti-Semitism, a miscarriage of military justice, a military and political scandal that polarized French politics for decades, and a case of the politicization of an ineffective intelligence service.

The Redl affair in Austria was another spy scandal involving secret war plans. Colonel Alfred Redl (1864-1913), an Austrian General Staff officer, rose to be deputy head, Austrian Army Intelligence. After 1900, he became a double agent who sold Austria's top secrets to Russia, including the identities of Austrian spies and its war plan for attacking Serbia. His principal motive was money to maintain an extravagant lifestyle. In 1913, Redl's treason was discovered when his successors in Austrian intelligence applied Redl's own innovative counterintelligence surveillance methods for mail opening. When confronted by authorities, Redl committed suicide in a Vienna hotel room. Despite Austria's efforts to keep his treason secret and to avoid a spy trial, Austrian newspapers discovered some of the facts. The resulting scandal shook the Austrian establishment. The significance of Russia's possession of Austria's war plans may be debatable, but there is no doubt that the Redl case added to the spy scares and paranoia that preceded World War I.

World War I and Intelligence (1914-1918)

The August 1914 outbreak of World War I represented a huge strategic intelligence failure of European intelligence services. They not only failed to predict the cascading effects of treaties that dragged many European powers into the conflict, they failed to foresee the bloody trench warfare stalemate resulting from new, deadly, defensive firepower.

World War I was the first total war in which the production capabilities on the home front were as vital as the military on the battlefront. Both the Allied and Central Powers employed their intelligence services to carry out missions of sabotage and psychological warfare with the aim of undermining civilian morale on the home front along with the viability of the enemy's armies at the front. In the case of Germany, it sowed revolution in Russia to eliminate an enemy. In total war, the home front constituted a new battlefront.

Two new methods for intelligence collection emerged as the result of technological advances: the use of aerial photography to discern enemy locations and activities and the interception of enemy radio messages and telegrams. Exploitation of intercepted Russian radio signals contributed to the significant German victory at Tannenberg in August 1914.

Agent operations contributed to Allied efforts on the Western front. A Belgian spy group, known as "the White Lady" and supported by British

Sources of 19th Century Spies' Message Texts

One way to make intelligence history come alive in the classroom is to present texts of spies' secret messages and encourage discussion by having students "read the secret message." This adds realism and specificity to the study of this topic and illustrates an important lesson that successful intelligence work is a complex process. Highlighting selected spy messages in their historical contexts demonstrates that intelligence work does not cease when a spy acquires a secret and sends a relevant message. An intelligence success requires more: the message must be useful and useable, and the recipient needs to act on this intelligence in a timely and appropriate manner. Recommended are two spies' message texts from 19th Century American wars — the War of 1812 and the Civil War. The first message is an 1814 letter to President James Madison from an anonymous correspondent, most likely an impressed American sailor on a Royal Navy vessel in the Chesapeake Bay. The letter warned the president of a British plan to invade and attack the capital. The timely warning was ignored and the White House was burned. The second is an 1864 message to General Burnside from the most successful federal spy, Miss Elizabeth Van Lew, a resident of Richmond, Virginia. These texts are available in two books: the 1814 message appears in Walter Lord's *The Dawn's Early Light* (New York: Norton, 1969), p. 213. The text of Van Lew's message is in Elizabeth R. Varon's *Southern Lady, Yankee Spy: The True Story of Elizabeth Van Lew, A Union Agent in the Heart of the Confederacy* (New York: Oxford University Press, 2003), p. 114.

intelligence, tracked Germany troop trains *en route* to the front. One of its unheralded successes gave several days of warning of a massive March 1918 German offensive, which the Germans hoped would throw back the Allied armies and win the war.

Intelligence supported the British economic blockade of Germany. Spy networks in the neutral Netherlands detected points at which Germany was breaching the blockade and provided British intelligence the information needed to plug those points through diplomatic pressure or through Royal Navy action. The blockage of Germany, which led to severe food deprivation on the home front and famine conditions by late 1918, played an important role in the eventual collapse of the German armies' will to fight, political instability in Germany, and the domestic revolution against Germany's ruling group.

The Zimmermann Telegram saga is a tale of British intelligence effectiveness. On January 16, 1917, German Foreign Secretary Zimmermann sent an encoded telegram via underwater cable to Germany's ambassador in Mexico with a bizarre proposal that if Mexico would join Germany in the war, in return it would receive German support and get back the lost territory comprising the states of Texas, Arizona, and New Mexico. In the same telegram, the Germans announced that they would renew unrestricted submarine warfare against the Allies. The day the war began, British naval vessels cut Germany's trans-Atlantic submarine cables. Germany was forced to use foreign telegraph cable systems for its diplomatic messages. British Admiral William Reginald "Blinker" Hall (1870-1943), the director of Naval Intelligence, had spies in telegraph offices in key locations and obtained copies of the Zimmerman message, which was then decrypted in Room 40, the Admiralty's cryptanalytic cell. Hall understood that he had a potential bombshell. However, the British spymaster understood that if he revealed the telegram's text, Britain risked losing an invaluable source of intelligence. Furthermore, Britain risked alienating both neutral Sweden and the US. Instead, Hall decided to reveal the intercepted telegram to the American Embassy in London, convince the American diplomats that the text was genuine, without revealing how it was obtained. When he read the telegram, President Wilson ordered the Department of State to leak it to the American newspapers. This helped shift American public opinion against Germany. The Zimmermann Telegram demonstrated how the course of a war could be changed by effective intelligence operations off the battlefield.

READINGS FOR INSTRUCTORS

There is a much larger literature on the history of intelligence from 1800 to World War I than there is for the pre-1800 eras. While a global perspective on intelligence history is lacking, the two encyclopedic works recommended in the 1500-1800 intelligence history article also remain helpful to the instructor for the later era: Richard W. Rowan, *The Story of Secret Service* (1937), for after 1800, see pp. 168-663; and David Kahn, *The Codebreakers* (2nd ed., 1996), refer to pp. 187-350. Kahn's essay on the cryptologic story of the Zimmermann Telegram is definitive.

Much of the historical literature on this period focuses on spymasters, intelligence organizations, specific incidents, or on one power's intelligence efforts. Two books by Christopher Andrew, a British historian of intelligence, are highly recommended — a lively history of British intelligence after 1800, *Her Majesty's Secret Service: The Making of the British Intelligence Community* (New York: Viking, 1985) and how American Presidents used intelligence — For *The President's Eyes Only: Secret Intelligence and the American Presidency from Washington to Bush* (New York: Viking, 1995), see especially pp. 12-64. For an excellent survey of French intelligence history, see Douglas Porch, *The French Secret Services: From the Dreyfus Affair to the Gulf War* (New York: Farrar, Straus, Giroux, 1995), refer to pp. 3-114.

For intelligence aspects of the Napoleonic Wars from a British perspective, see Mark Urban, *The Man Who Broke Napoleon's Codes* (New York: Harper/Collins, 2001), which studies the codebreaking of George Scovell, one of Wellington's staff officers who served in Spain. A classic article on 1861-1865 American intelligence is by the dean of American Civil War intelligence historians, Edwin Fishel, "[Civil War Intelligence] Myths That Never Die," *International Journal of Intelligence and Counterintelligence* 2 (1), Spring 1988, pp. 27-58. For American intelligence from 1800 to 1918, see G. P. A. O'Toole, *Honorable Treachery. A History of U.S. Intelligence, Espionage and Covert Action from the American Revolution to The CIA* (New York: Atlantic Monthly Press, 1991), see pp. 82-310.

The best single book on the Zimmermann Telegram remains Barbara Tuchman's *The Zimmermann Telegram* (New York: Ballantine, 1958; 1966). For an enduring analysis of the intelligence assessment failures of both the Allied and Central Powers' intelligence services, see the classic pioneering study by Ernest R. May (ed.), *Knowing One's Enemies: Intelligence Assessment Before the Two World Wars* (Princeton, NJ: Princeton University Press, 1984), refer to Part One, "The First World War," pp. 11-233.

Douglas L. Wheeler is professor emeritus of history at the University of New Hampshire. He holds an AB from Dartmouth College, and an MA and PhD from Boston University. He was a Fulbright grantee, served in the US Army (1963-1965), was an instructor at the US Army's Intelligence School, and has been a consultant on foreign affairs. Since 1969, he has taught an undergraduate course, "Espionage and History," at the University of New Hampshire. In 1984-1985, he was the Richard Welch Research Fellow in the advanced history of intelligence at the Harvard University Center for International Affairs.

GUIDE TO THE STUDY OF INTELLIGENCE

Civil War Intelligence

Dr. Edward J. Glantz, P.E.

When the American Civil War began in 1861, there was no precedent for having an organization dedicated to intelligence. As a result, intelligence activities of the Union and Confederacy were decentralized. Information was gathered and used at local levels by opportunists seeking to support their cause, or battlefield commanders seeking an advantage. The term "intelligence" was not used; instead, "secret service" described intelligence activities as well as detective work. The risks of spying then were great. A suspect caught in disguise (i.e. not a regular army uniform) gathering or distributing information could be hanged. This was the fate of Confederate Will Talbot left behind by his unit to spy in Gettysburg. Captured in June 1863, Brigadier Geneneral John Buford ordered Talbot to be hanged.

American officers learned about intelligence from studying military history. "It is pardonable to be defeated, but not to be taken by surprise," wrote Frederick the Great. And French Marshal Saxe is credited with stating "Too much attention cannot be given to spies and guides ... they are as necessary to a general as the eyes are to the head."[1]

Careful attention to the collection of information, its timely analysis, and use was not always followed during the Civil War. On December 13, 1862, army commander Ambrose Burnside chose not to change his battle plan at Fredericksburg, even though a captured Rebel had offered "full information of the position and defenses of the enemy." The result was a federal disaster.

Both sides tried to obtain information by intercepting enemy documents and mail, decoding messages, and interrogating prisoners. Commanders on both sides served as their own intelligence officers, including Confederate generals Thomas "Stonewall" Jackson, who directly supervised the mapping

---

1. Edwin C. Fishel, *The Secret War for the Union: The Untold Story of Military Intelligence in the Civil War.*

of the Shenandoah Valley, and James A. Longstreet, who personally debriefed a spy reporting on Union Army movements toward Gettysburg.

Below is a sampling of Civil War spies and scouts for both sides, although the majority of the intelligence was probably provided by the observations of anonymous agents and "false deserters," who also spread false information.

Union Spies and Scouts

It is believed the Union was better at spying on the enemy and detecting its own information leaks.[2]

CHARLES POMEROY STONE was appointed inspector general of the District of Columbia militia at the beginning of the war by Lieutenant General Winfield Scott, then commander-in-chief of the US Army. With most of the US Army deployed in Indian country, Stone's detectives worked undercover with groups volunteering to disclose secessionists and their plots. His work resulted in disbanding the National Volunteers for Southern Sympathies and purging the National Rifles of secessionists who were planning to storm the Treasury building. Stone also performed classic intelligence analysis comparing detective and independent reports to confirm a plan to assassinate President Abraham Lincoln.

ALLEN PINKERTON formed the nation's first detective agency in Chicago 10 years before the Civil War. He developed modern investigative techniques, such as "shadowing" a suspect (i.e. surveillance) and working undercover. In 1861, he guarded Lincoln on the way to his inauguration, possibly foiling an assassination attempt. Early in the war, Pinkerton worked for General George McClellan, occasionally undercover using the alias Major E. J. Allen. Working counterintelligence, Pinkerton's operatives arrested Rose Greenhow, whose spy network had funneled information to the Confederates from the nation's capital. Pinkerton resigned in 1862 after overestimating Confederate forces in Richmond. That judgment encouraged McClellan to delay his attack, and Lincoln fired him.

LAFAYETTE BAKER began his service working for General Winfield Scott. Baker claimed that he, under the alias Sam Munson, had gathered information on Southern military installations by pretending to photograph high-raking Confederate officers. Later, Baker was responsible for tracking the conspirators responsible for the assassination of President Lincoln.

GEORGE SHARPE, a lawyer, headed the Bureau of Military Information formed in 1863 for Major General Joseph Hooker, the first organized federal unit dedicated to the gathering and analysis of intelligence. It gathered information

---

2. CIA Center for the Study of Intelligence, *Spies Like Us: History of American Intelligence*, Center for the Study of Intelligence, (Central Intelligence Agency, 2007).

from agents, prisoners of war, refugees, Southern newspapers, and documents retrieved from battlefield corpses. Sharpe's spies counted tents to estimate troop numbers, approximate cannon numbers by the length of the artillery train, and counted guards at forts and ammunition dumps. In May 1863, with information from Sharpe's agents and informants, Hooker exploited a gap in the rear of Lee's Fredericksburg lines that threatened the Army of Northern Virginia. Sharpe used Elizabeth Van Lew in the Richmond underground to recruit Samuel Ruth to spy. As superintendent of the Richmond, Fredericksburg, and Potomac railroad, Ruth provided information about Confederate Army movements and also slowed bridge repair and supply shipments to Richmond. As a result, a Confederate War Department clerk wrote, "The enemy are kept fully informed of everything transpiring here."[3]

ELIZABETH VAN LEW used her status and connections to operate an extensive spy ring in Richmond. She brought food, clothing, and writing paper to Union soldiers held in Libby Prison. She passed prisoner information on troop levels and movements back to Union commanders. She also operated a spy ring that included War and Navy Department clerks. After the war, President Lincoln met her for tea and said, "You have sent me the most valuable information received from Richmond during the war."[4]

GRENVILLE M. DODGE was told by General Ulysses S. Grant, "You have a much more important command than that of a division in the field."[5] Dodge used intelligence to gather information from runaway slaves, spies – including women – working in the South, and a trained Corps of Scouts. Dodge taught scouts to estimate enemy numbers by measuring the length of road taken up by a column of soldiers. He also used a pro-Union cavalry unit made up of Southerners. To prevent interception, his coded messages were sent by rider, not telegraph. Dodge was so discreet that little is known about his operations or the names of most of his agents. At the beginning of the war, Dodge was appointed colonel of the 4th Iowa Volunteer Infantry Regiment and was wounded commanding the 1st Brigade, 4th Division, at the 1862 Battle of Pea Ridge, after which he was appointed brigadier general of volunteers and placed in command of the District of the Mississippi.

Confederate Spies and Scouts

The Confederacy's intelligence was even less organized than the Union's, although the South was more effective at conducting covert (i.e. "secret")

3. Thomas Allen, *The Bureau of Military Information: Intelligence in the Civil War* (Central Intelligence Agency, 2010).
4. Elizabeth R Varon, *Southern lady, Yankee spy; the true story of Elizabeth Van Lew, a Union agent in the heart of the Confederacy*, (Oxford University Press, 2003).
5. Thomas Allen, *ibid*.

operations, such as sabotage. Southern agents fueled antiwar feelings and encouraged succession from the Union in Indiana, Illinois, and Ohio. Confederates also set fires in New York City to disrupt Northern-manufacturing hubs. The Confederacy's signal corps included a covert agency, the Secret Service Bureau. Scouts, cavalry, and guerrilla units, such as Colonel John Mosby's Partisan Rangers, discovered federal secrets through direct observation, capturing Union officers' personal papers in baggage trains and waylaying federal messengers.

Famous agents for the South include J. E. B. Stuart, Rose Greenhow, Isabella Marie Boyd, Nancy Hart Douglas, George "Lightning" Ellsworth, and John Wilkes Booth.

MAJ. GEN. JAMES EWELL BROWN STUART'S cavalry's reconnoitering provided effective intelligence for the South that the North did not have at the war's beginning. At Gettysburg, when Stuart chose to raid towns and not scout, he deprived Lee of critical information.

ROSE GREENHOW traveled in Washington political circles and used friendships with presidents, generals, senators, and high-ranking military officers to gather information for the Confederacy at the start of the war. During the July 1861 Bull Run campaign, Maj. Gen. Pierre Beauregard used information from Greenhow to provide early warning of Union movements. In 1861, Pinkerton, finding maps of Washington fortifications and notes on military movements, arrested Greenhow. She continued sending messages to the South from prison until deported to Richmond in 1863. She received a full military burial in Oakdale Cemetery, Wilmington, North Carolina, where her epitaph reads: "Mrs. Rose O'N. Greenhow, a bearer of dispatches to the Confederate Government."

ISABELLA MARIE BOYD spied from her father's hotel in Front Royal, Virginia, providing valuable information to General Stonewall Jackson. She was caught and threatened with death – a punishment unusual for women captives. She survived and continued spying. In a closet, she eavesdropped and learned of the reduced Union strength at Front Royal. When the Confederates arrived, she braved enemy fire to tell the rebels to tell Jackson "the Yankee force is very small. Tell him to charge right down and he will catch them all." Jackson was successful and penned a note of gratitude: "I thank you, for myself and for the army, for the immense service that you have rendered your country today." For her contributions, she was awarded the Southern Cross of Honor and given captain and honorary aide-de-camp positions by Jackson.[6]

NANCY HART DOUGLAS became expert with firearms and horses on her family farm. During the war, she joined the Confederate Moccasin Rangers in present-day West Virginia where she served as guide and spy. Hart became so

---

6. Thomas Robson Hay. "Boyd, Belle" Notable American Women. Vol. 1, (Belknap Press of Harvard University Press, 1975).

famous that Union forces in West Virginia offered a reward for her capture in 1862. Although captured shortly thereafter, she managed to escape.

GEORGE "LIGHTNING" ELLSWORTH was a Canadian telegrapher who served in the Confederate cavalry under Brig. Gen. John Hunt Morgan. Morgan recruited Ellsworth to telegraph "disinformation" (false or misleading information) to the Union. He earned his nickname "Lightning" in Morgan's first Kentucky Raid in July 1862 after sending a telegram in knee-high water during a thunderstorm. Ellsworth developed the ability to imitate the distinctive style, or "fist," of other telegraphers, including several Union telegraphers based in Kentucky and Tennessee. England's The Times declared the use of the telegraph to spread disinformation as the greatest innovation to come out of the war.[7]

JOHN WILKES BOOTH used his skills as an actor to escape detection while spying for the South. He gained notoriety in April 1865 as President Lincoln's assassin.

Intelligence Technology of the Civil War

The American Civil War highlighted the industrial revolution's innovations of iron-making, telegraphy, and steam engines. Intelligence benefitted from new technology, including tethered balloons and signal messaging.

Intelligence Signaling

In the Civil War, significant developments were made in military telecommunications, which created unique intelligence gathering opportunities. In 1863, the Army Signal Corps contributed to intelligence gathering from its troops posted on the high ground. Both sides could intercept the opponent's "wig-wag" messages and telegraph signals. Wig-wag messaging, or "wig-wagging," was invented in the 1850's by US Army Major Albert J. Myer, and used by Signal Corps troops on both sides during the Civil War. Different than semaphore, only one flag, lantern, or torch was used to communicate similar to Morse code dots and dashes. Intercept operations, cryptanalysis, and cryptography came into their own in the Civil War.

Civil War Encryption

Cryptography – the writing of codes and ciphers – is an ancient art, and the cryptographic techniques used in the Civil War were not new. What was new was the telegraph, which enabled quickly sending messages far and wide. "Wiretapping" the telegraph lines, of course, followed. Hence, both sides used

---

7. Wikipedia contributors. "George Ellsworth." Wikipedia, The Free Encyclopedia. Wikipedia, The Free Encyclopedia, September 23, 2010. Web. February 11, 2011.

codes and ciphers to hide the real "plaintext" message in encrypted "ciphertext." Opponents used "cryptanalysis" to decrypt the intercepted ciphertext. Civil war cryptography techniques were mostly ciphers based on substitution and transposition. Substitution means exchanging the original letter with a known substitute. A simple substitution example, the "Caesar shift," offsets the original letter a certain number of spaces in the alphabet. The sender and receiver would agree on the "key" used to encode and decode the message. For example, using a key that shifts three-places, the word "CAT" would be rewritten as "FDW" in the ciphertext. The receiver uses the key in reverse to translate ciphertext "FDW" back to plaintext "CAT." Transposition means rearranging the letters in a certain pattern, creating an "anagram." The "rail fence cipher" is an example. If a two-line key is used, every other letter is dropped to a second line. The message is re-written starting with the letters remaining on the first line, followed by those on the second line. The letters are not changed; they just appear out of order. For example, plaintext "GATE" would now appear as "GTAE" in ciphertext. At the time of the Civil War, the words "code" and "cipher" were used interchangeably.

In 1864, Confederate telegraph operator Charles Gaston tapped into communications between U. S. Grant's headquarters and Washington on a wooded area east of Petersburg, Virginia. With scouts pretending to be woodcutters, he listened to high-level Union Army telegraph communications. Colonel George H. Sharpe, head of the Union Army of the Potomac's counterintelligence service, was aware of the interception, but did not interfere since the communications traffic was not interrupted. For two months, the intercepted Union messages were sent to Richmond, possibly to skilled cryptologist Edward Porter Alexander.

It is not known whether the South decoded any of the intercepted Union messages. Gaston did intercept a valuable message sent unencrypted, describing 3,000 head of cattle being delivered to Grant's headquarters at Coggin's Point, near Richmond. At dawn of September 16, 1864, a Confederate raiding force under Major General Wade Hampton overran Union pickets and made off with the cattle.

Confederate President Jefferson Davis used a dictionary code to communicate with General Albert Sidney Johnston. Each word in the message was replaced by its location in a specific dictionary possessed by both men. For example, the word "division" would be written as "265-2-10," referring to page 265, column 2, and word 10 of this dictionary. Johnston then communicated to his second-in-command, General Pierre G. T. Beauregard, using the Caesar cipher. Eventually, both the Union and Confederates standardized communications by adopting a more advanced form of the Caesar cipher from 1587 called the Vigenère.

Battlefield Balloons

In the summer of 1861, Professor Thaddeus S. C. Lowe used his hot-air balloon, the "Enterprise," to support the Union Army's map-making. At the first Battle of Bull Run, Lowe used flag signals to direct gunners on the ground to fire at unseen targets. In April 1862, Union Major General Fitz John Porter floated untethered to observe Confederate positions, before veering back to Union lines and crashing safely. Eventually Lowe built seven balloons for military use. A key innovation was development of gas generating equipment that allowed balloons to be inflated and maintained in the field. Besides mapping and forward artillery observation, the balloons monitored troop movements. However, by mid-1863, threats of bad weather and enemy artillery fire brought an end to use of balloons. The balloon foreshadowed today's overhead reconnaissance from spy planes and satellites.

Civilian Intelligence

Intelligence on Confederate forces provided by "Negroes" was referred to as "Black Dispatches" by Union military men. This information was both prolific and productive. For instance, a Virginia slave told at least one Union officer that Confederate forces would evacuate Yorktown before they did on May 3, 1862. In 1862, Frederick Douglass wrote:

> The true history of this war will show that the loyal army found no friends at the South so faithful, active, and daring in their efforts to sustain the government as the Negroes. Negroes have repeatedly threaded their way through the lines of the rebels exposing themselves to bullets to convey important information to the loyal army of the Potomac.[8]

In addition, civilians used coded messages to protect important information for the Underground Railroad.

As it was illegal to teach slaves to read or write, dance, spirituals, code words (e.g., "Hope" for Cleveland, "Midnight" for Detroit), phrases, and memorized symbols were used by slaves to communicate secretly. Secret messages may have been hidden in quilt patterns to help slaves escape.[9] Each pattern had a different meaning, such as the "Monkey Wrench" (prepare to leave), "Star" (follow the North Star), "Crossroads" (major city ahead), and "Wagon Wheel" (pack essential provisions). The messages could be visible in quilts hung over a fence or windowsill to air. Following the code of secrecy, however, many of these covert communications were never documented.

---

8. P. K. Rose. *Black Dispatches Black American Contributions to Union Intelligence During the Civil War*, CIA Center for the Study of Intelligence (Central Intelligence Agency, 1999).
9. Jacqueline L. Tobin and Raymond G. Dobard, *Hidden in Plain View: A Secret Story of Quilts and the Underground Railroad* (Anchor Books, 2000).

Conclusion

"The art of war is simple enough," Grant wrote. "Find out where your enemy is. Get at him as soon as you can. Strike him as hard as you can and as often as you can, and keep moving on."[10] The need to "find out where" called for good intelligence.

Readings for Instructors

The following are recommended readings for instructors on Civil War intelligence —

Antonucci, Michael, "Code Crackers: Cryptanalysis in the Civil War," *Civil War Times Illustrated*, July-August, 1995. *http://www.eiaonline.com/history/codecrackers.htm*. This is a very nice introduction to the use of cryptology in general, and cryptanalysis in particular, during the Civil War.

Caesar Shift: http://www.simonsingh.net/The_Black_Chamber/caesar.html.

Center for the Study of Intelligence, "Intelligence in the Civil War," (Central Intelligence Agency, 1999). *https://www.cia.gov/library/publications/additional-publications/civil-war/index.html*. This PDF available from the CIA publications library provides a good overview of many aspects of Civil War intelligence.

Either, Eric, "Intelligence: The Secret War Within America's Civil War," *Civil War Times*, June 26, 2007, *http://www.historynet.com/intelligence-the-secret-war-within-americas-civil-war.htm*. The Wider History Group, publisher of 10 history magazines, introduces aerial intelligence from balloons in the Civil War.

Feis, William B. *Grant's Secret Service*, (University of Nebraska Press, 2004).

Fishel, Edwin C. *The Secret War for the Union: The Untold Story of Military Intelligence in the Civil War*, (Houghton Mifflin Co., 2005). Fishel was a pioneer in discovering and writing about the relatively unknown use of intelligence in the Civil War.

Varon, Elizabeth R. *Southern Lady, Yankee Spy*. (Oxford University Press, 2003. Varon is a professor of history at Wellesley. In this book, she describes in detail the activities of Union spy Elizabeth Van Lew in Richmond.

Winkler, H. Donald, *Stealing secrets; how a few daring women deceived generals, impacted battles, and altered the course of the Civil War*, (Cumberland House Publishing, 2010). An overview of 36 women who spied for the Confederacy and the Union.

Dr. Edward J. Glantz, P.E. completed his PhD in cognitive science and is currently a professor of practice at the Pennsylvania State University College of Information Sciences and Technology, where he teaches courses in security, risk, and analysis. Dr. Glantz earned an MBA from the Wharton School of Business and undergraduate degrees in mechanical engineering and general arts and sciences. Dr. Glantz is a Civil War re-enactor (*http://www.148thpvi.org/*) along with his wife, Lisa, and three children.

---

10. William B. Feis. *Grant's Secret Service*. (University of Nebraska Press, 2002).

GUIDE TO THE STUDY OF INTELLIGENCE

Intelligence in World War I

1914-1918

Mark Stout, Ph.D.

All the major powers entered World War I ill-prepared for what was to come. This was true with regard to the societies, the fighting forces themselves, and certainly the intelligence services. The war was a struggle not just of armies and navies but of entire empires and economies. Not surprisingly then, it saw a vast expansion of intelligence organizations, an influx of new intelligence collection technologies, a flood of data, and the penetration of intelligence services into the lives of everyday people.

When the war started in the late summer of 1914, the few military intelligence personnel who existed still thought about intelligence and reconnaissance in ways more reminiscent of the Franco-Prussian War or the American wars on the Great Plains than of modern realities. The decision by the editors of the US Army's Infantry Journal to publish a two-part translation of a French military work entitled The Service of Information: A Practical Study starting in the July-August 1914 issue illustrates this point. The article noted that "the spy reveals himself by ... his great politeness ... his calculated self-effacement, his habit of looking at or hearing things without appearing to do so" and mentioned cavalry but not the airplane, and signaling with fires and smoke but not by radio or telephone.[1] Meanwhile, national intelligence services, such as Britain's MI-5 and MI-6 (as they later became known) were tiny outfits, where they existed at all.

The United Kingdom and France, among other World War I belligerents, underwent spy scares in the years before the war. For instance, in France, it was widely believed that roadside advertising signs for the popular Kub brand

---

1. De Rudeval, J. Raoult, "The Service of Information: A Practical Study," *Infantry Journal* 11 (1), July-August, 1914, 88-114; and 11 (2), September-October, 1914, 264-288.

bouillon cubes contained coded information from German spies that would be used by invading armies. Such fears only proliferated after the start of the war. Once the United States entered the war in 1917, it aimed domestic surveillance at anyone who had ties real or imagined to Germany or other Central Powers or who had gripes with the United States Government. Hence, there was widespread surveillance of the Lutheran Church, the International Workers of the World, African-Americans, and others. The 1917 case of an American naval officer who was investigated because his housekeeper "looked German," was not atypical.[2]

Though most spy mania was ill founded, there was legitimate reason for governments to be concerned. What we now call covert action or influence operations played a bigger role in World War I than in any previous war. For example, the United States and the other Entente allies tried to play on ethnic divisions within the Austro-Hungarian Empire, and Germany mounted an extensive sabotage campaign in the United States from 1914 to 1917 to stem the flow of munitions and supplies from this country to the Allies.[3] Germany and the Ottoman Empire, home to the caliph, also tried to inspire Muslims to launch a military jihad against their imperial overlords in London, Paris, and St. Petersburg.

World War I saw significant changes in espionage. While many espionage operations—notably the Allied train-watching networks in Belgium and Germany—continued to rely on physical observation, espionage also entailed more and more the theft of secrets from inside foreign bureaucracies.

Even greater evolution took place in technical intelligence collection. World War I saw the creation of sizeable staffs both in the field and in national capitals to make and break code and cipher systems. The competition between makers and breakers of systems became so intense that mathematically one could calculate how much time would pass from the first use of a new codebook until the enemy would be able to read messages sent using it. Traffic analysis—the derivation of intelligence information from the patterns of message distribution rather than the contents of the messages—also dates to World War I.

There was similar growth in aerial reconnaissance. In many ways, the day-to-day workhorse of aerial reconnaissance was the tethered balloon, but the newfangled airplane was the up and coming technology. By the end of the war, observation planes were equipped with cameras and radios. Fighter planes existed largely to attack balloons and observation planes. Frank Luke,

---

2. Dorwart, Jeffery M. *The Office of Naval Intelligence: The Birth of America's First Intelligence Agency, 1865-1918* (Annapolis: Naval Institute Press, 1979), 119.

3. In World War I, the Central Powers consisted of the German Empire, the Austro-Hungarian Empire, the Ottoman Empire, and Bulgaria. The Entente Powers, or Allies, encompassed the French Republic, the British Empire, the Russian Empire, Japan, Belgium, Serbia, Greece, Montenegro, Romania, Italy, and the United States, though the last preferred to refer to itself as an "associated" rather than an Allied power.

the second-ranked American fighter ace of the war, specialized in shooting down German observation balloons. In effect, he was a counterintelligence officer. The flourishing of aerial reconnaissance led to the development of photo interpretation, which, in turn, led to the flourishing art of camouflage.

The vast amounts of data available to commanders and decision makers were useful at all levels from the front line trenches to national considerations of grand strategy. Extensive intelligence collection and analysis was a critical component of the British naval blockade against Germany. It also enabled the first glimmerings of what became strategic bombing. When the American delegation went to the Paris Peace Talks in 1919, it made sure to arrange for intelligence support.

World War I saw the birth of modern intelligence

The intelligence services of all the powers that survived the war were sharply scaled back as part of the post-war demobilizations,[4] but the intelligence business was irrevocably changed. Intelligence personnel of 1918 would have readily understood the work of their counterparts in World War II or even the Cold War. The examples of World War I intelligence officers Allen Dulles and cryptanalysts Dillwyn (Dilly) Knox and William Friedman illustrate the point. Dulles ultimately rose to become the director of central intelligence for Presidents Eisenhower and Kennedy. Knox was one of the most important members of the Government Code & Cipher School (GC&CS) at Bletchley Park, Britain's codebreaking organization, until his death in 1943 and Friedman made comparably important contributions to American SIGINT during World War II and eventually retired from the National Security Agency in 1955. In short, World War I saw the birth of modern intelligence.

READINGS FOR INSTRUCTORS

World War I may have been "The Great War," but the amount of scholarly literature devoted to intelligence in that war is not great. In fact, it is dwarfed by the literature of intelligence in World War II. The scholarly neglect of WW I intelligence is illustrated by the fact that a single bibliographic essay published in 2012 by Daniel Larsen[5] was able to capture almost everything worthwhile on the subject in English and French while even including a few items in German and Italian. For the sake of concision, this article focuses on book-length treatments, but Larsen's review will be of interest to those seeking to dive deeper

---

4. The exception might be the newly established Bolshevik Soviet Union, which in 1917 rapidly grew a new secret service, the Cheka, under Felix Dzerzhinsky.
5. Larsen, Daniel, "Intelligence in the First World War: The State of the Field," *Intelligence and National Security* 29 (2), 2012.

or into more obscure corners of the topic.

Strategic Assessment

Ernest May's edited volume Knowing One's Enemies: Intelligence Assessment Before the Two World Wars (Princeton: Princeton University Press, 1984) is a classic of intelligence literature. There is no comparable work.

British Intelligence

Christopher Andrew's Her Majesty's Secret Service: The Making of the British Intelligence Community (New York: Penguin, 1987) contains the best broad view of the state of British intelligence on the eve of the Great War and how it developed during the war from London to the front lines.

Andrew's Defend the Realm: The Authorized History of MI5 (New York: Vintage Books, 2010) contains an indispensable treatment of British domestic intelligence during the War. Richard Popplewell's Intelligence and Imperial Defence: British Intelligence and the Defence of the Indian Empire, 1904-1924 (London: Frank Cass, 1995) looks at British counterintelligence operations in the Empire.

Keith Jeffery's The Secret History of MI6 (New York: Penguin, 2010), also an authorized history, contains the best overall account of British espionage operations abroad during the War. World War I spy memoirs are not notable for their rigid devotion to truth. Two that are worthwhile, however, are All's Fair: The Story of the British Secret Service behind the German Lines (New York: G. P. Putnam's Sons, 1934) by South African Henry Landau, who conducted important operations out of The Netherlands, including overseeing the famous Dame Blanche spy network and Compton Mackenzie's Greek Memories (London: Cassell, 1932), which netted him a prosecution for violating the British Official Secrets Act. Robin Bruce Lockhart's Reilly: Ace of Spies should be avoided at all cost. For a reliable account of British intelligence operations in Russia, see instead Michael Occleshaw's Dances in Deep Shadow: Britain's Clandestine War in Russia, 1917-1920 (London: Constable, 2006).

The performance of the British Expeditionary Force (BEF) intelligence arm has long been the subject of criticism, perhaps as a corollary of the now-discredited "lions led by donkeys" myth. Jim Beach's Haig's Intelligence: GHQ and the German Army, 1916-1918 (Cambridge: Cambridge University Press, 2013) goes a long way toward rehabilitating BEF intelligence and its leader, General John Charteris. Two excellent works cover British military intelligence in the Middle East: Polly Mohs' Military Intelligence and the Arab Revolt: The First Modern Intelligence War (New York: Routledge, 2007) and Yigal Sheffy's British Intelligence in the Palestine Campaign 1914-1918 (London: Frank Cass, 1998).

Patrick Beesly's Room 40: British Naval Intelligence 1914-1918 (Oxford: Oxford University Press, 1984) is the best work overall work on the subject. Thomas Boghardt's recent The Zimmermann Telegram: Intelligence, Diplomacy, and America's Entry into World War I (Annapolis: Naval Institute Press, 2012) gives a first rate account of the interception and decryption by Room 40 of the infamous telegram and how Britain used it as part of its campaign to bring the United States into the war. Boghardt finds that the telegram played less of a role in America's actual march toward war than has previously been thought.

American Intelligence

Christopher Andrew's For the President's Eyes Only: Secret Intelligence and the American Presidency from Washington to Bush (New York: HarperCollins, 1995) has an excellent chapter on Woodrow Wilson and intelligence. The Archaeologist Was a Spy: Sylvanus G. Morley and the Office of Naval Intelligence (Albuquerque: University of New Mexico Press, 2003) by Charles H. Harris III and Louis R. Sadler contains a good overview of the American intelligence services during World War I. It also provides a fascinating case study of how the Office of Naval Intelligence conducted human intelligence in Latin America, a major field of interest for the Navy and War Departments at the time.

Jeffrey Dorwart's Office of Naval Intelligence: The Birth of America's First Intelligence Agency, 1882-1918 (Annapolis: Naval Institute Press, 1979) does a lot well in a relatively few pages. James L. Gilbert's World War I and the Origins of U.S. Military Intelligence (Lanham: Scarecrow Press, 2012) is a workmanlike treatment of its subject, covering both War Department intelligence in the United States and the intelligence components of the American Expeditionary Forces in France. Bruce Bidwell's History of the Military Intelligence Division, Department of the Army General Staff: 1775-1941 (Frederick: University Publications of America, 1986) is a thorough but dry official history covering both foreign and domestic operations.

Herbert O. Yardley's American Black Chamber (Annapolis: Naval Institute Press, 2004) is a spirited account of code making and breaking in the War and State Departments from 1917 to the late 1920s. A scandalous bestseller in its day, it should be treated with caution because it takes more than a few liberties with the truth, usually to inflate Yardley's role and genius. Nevertheless, it is a classic of intelligence literature, not least because it inspired literally generations of Americans to join the intelligence services or to study the intelligence services. It should be read in conjunction with David Kahn's The Reader of Gentlemen's Mail: Herbert O. Yardley and the Birth of American Codebreaking (New Haven: Yale University Press, 2004).

Roy Talbert's Negative Intelligence: The Army and the American Left, 1917-1941 (Jackson: University Press of Mississippi, 1991) and Joan M. Jensen's Army Surveillance in America, 1775-1980 (New Haven: Yale University Press, 1991) are excellent treatments of American domestic intelligence. Jensen also wrote what is still the best work on the quasi-official American Protective League (APL), a 250,000 man volunteer counterintelligence force: The Price of Vigilance (Chicago: Rand McNally, 1969). The APL's quasi-official history The Web (Chicago: Reilly & Lee Co., 1919) written by Emerson Hough is a fascinating and occasionally frightening artifact of the time. Mark Ellis' Race, War and Surveillance: African Americans and the United States Government during World War I (Bloomington: Indiana University Press, 2001) is a good introduction to surveillance of African-Americans during the War.

German Intelligence

There is a great lack of literature available on German intelligence during World War I. The most famous German spy of that war was, of course, Mata Hari. However, time spent studying her is time wasted, unless the purpose is to consider how someone so inconsequential became so prominent. Thomas Boghardt's *Spies of the Kaiser: German Covert Operations in Great Britain during the First World War Era* (New York: Palgrave Macmillan, 2004) is a fine guide to German intelligence operations in Britain. German covert operations in the United States are covered in Reinhard Doerries' *Imperial Challenge: Ambassador Count Bernstorff and German-American Relations, 1908-1917* (Chapel Hill: University of North Carolina Press, 1989). Sean McMeekin's *The Berlin-Baghdad Express: The Ottoman Empire and Germany's Bid for World Power* (Cambridge: Belknap Press, 2010) has a good account of the effort to turn Muslims against the Allies. The memoirs of the German military intelligence head, Major Walter Nicolai, are available in English as *The German Secret Service* (London: S. Paul, 1924).

Other Countries

As little as there is on German intelligence, there is even less on the other belligerents. Douglas Porch's *The French Secret Services: From the Dreyfus Affair to the Gulf War* (New York: Farrar, Straus, and Giroux, 1995) is useful for France. The military intelligence efforts of the Austro-Hungarian Empire are generally agreed to have been first-rate. Sadly, there is nothing book-length (and precious little of any length) in English on the subject. The situation is comparable for Russian, Italian, and Turkish intelligence.

Technical Intelligence Collection

David Kahn's monumental *The Codebreakers: The Story of Secret Writing* (New York: Scribner, 1996) contains an excellent discussion of the cryptologic efforts of all major belligerents in World War I. Terrance Finnegan's *Shooting the Front: Allied Aerial Reconnaissance in the First World War* (Stroud: Spellmount, 2011) is beautifully illustrated and will leave the reader with a comprehensive understanding of the topic.

Women in Intelligence

In *Female Intelligence: Women and Espionage in the First World War* (New York: New York University, 2003), Tammy Proctor estimates that some 6,000 women served British intelligence in some capacity during World War I in capacity. She effectively debunks the seductress stereotype of the female spy.

Mark Stout is the director of the MA program in Global Security Studies at Johns Hopkins University in Washington, DC. He has degrees from Stanford and Harvard Universities and a PhD in history from the University of Leeds. He has served in the CIA and the State Department Bureau of Intelligence and Research, and, for three years, was the historian of the International Spy Museum.

GUIDE TO THE STUDY OF INTELLIGENCE

Intelligence Between the World Wars, 1919-1939

"A World Made Safe for Deaths of Democracy"

— The final chapter title
of Richard W. Rowan's 1937 book,
The Story of Secret Service (p. 664)

Douglas L. Wheeler, PhD

Between the end of World War I and the onset of World War II, many intelligence services grew in size, budget, and function; and their roles in military, diplomatic, and political affairs assumed increasingly greater importance. The exception was during the early and mid-1920s, when intelligence services reduced budgets and personnel numbers. For example, at the end of World War I, the US Office of Naval Intelligence (ONI) had about 300 personnel, but by early 1924, its personnel strength had been reduced to 40.This period was marked by numerous small, short armed conflicts, and witnessed revolutionary innovations in intelligence-related technologies.

Out of the lingering Great Depression and international conflicts emerged the principal totalitarian states of the 20th century: Nazi Germany, Stalinist Soviet Union, and militarist Japan. Each created a "police state," a term describing the use of intelligence and police services for the repression of domestic opposition including exiled opponents abroad. The totalitarian intelligence services also produced propaganda boasting of military prowess to intimidate weaker states. Their intelligence services' operations abroad were often for economic penetration. Especially good at this were Japan and the Soviet Union. A favored method was saturation by infiltrating both "legal" (with diplomatic cover) and "illegal" spies. The three Soviet secret services (OGPU, GRU, and Comintern) were active worldwide. The Soviets favored targeting Western industrial zones and heavily trafficked ports as well as principal economic centers from Berlin to Stockholm to Paris to London to New York and beyond. Despite the propaganda and the post-1934 dispatch of German "tourists" to several continents, the Third Reich's secret services were less effective in this work than their Japanese and Soviet counterparts.

The 1920s: International Intrigue and Small Wars

The terms of the June 1919 Versailles peace treaty shaped requirements for the intelligence services of Britain and France, which sought to determine if Germany was disarming as required. Germany's extensive rearmament program, which from 1922 to 1933 was carried out in secret in conspiracy with the Soviet Union, was a major collection target for Western governments, investigative newspapers, and German and other European organizations, which viewed German rearmament as a threat to peace. One sensational scandal in 1935 resulted from a private exposé of the sub rosa German rearmament program by investigative journalist and Nazi oppositionist Berthold Jacob Solomon, a German Jew, who the Gestapo kidnapped in Switzerland and incarcerated in a German prison. The international outrage and Swiss diplomatic pressure forced the Nazi regime to release him, and he left Germany for exile.

European newspapers reported on numerous spy incidents during this period. One of the more curious cases involved

Popular Perceptions

From popular culture of the time emerged some long lasting images of spies. Out of World War I came the Mata Hari story, which purported to typify the seductive role of women in spying. Today's use of "sexpionage" perpetuates that myth. By the 1930s, the image of the real life spy conducting surveillance out-of-doors in a trench coat, a garb first designed by a London clothier for British officers to wear over their uniforms in trench warfare, became an almost universal depiction of the spy. The term "Fifth Column," originated in the Spanish Civil War (1936-1939) during the siege of Madrid. It meant that an organized underground of agents behind the battlefront would rise up and undermine the defense against external attack.

Polish Major Jerzy Sosnowski, who in 1926 was sent to Berlin to uncover the plans and intentions of the post-war Weimar Republic. With a well-funded cover as a wealthy, aristocratic Polish war hero, playboy, racehorse owner, and businessman, Sosnowski built a spy ring, which penetrated Germany's War Ministry. He was arrested in Berlin in 1934 and put on trial as a spy. Several of the aristocratic German women spies he had recruited, who were also his lovers, were also put on trial. Unlike Sosnowski, who was released and returned to Poland as part of a German-Polish spy exchange, the women were executed by beheading. Upon his return to Poland, Sosnowski was arrested and accused of having been "turned" by Germany and was given a 15-year prison sentence. The twists and turns of the Sosnowski case illustrate the extent to which deception had become a common practice in the European espionage wars.

CONFLICTS IN THE INTER-WAR PERIOD (1919-1939)

Europe	
1917-1921	Ukrainian War of Independence
1918-1921	Russian Civil War (Bolsheviks)
1918-1920	Latvian War of Independence
1918-1920	Hungarian–Romanian War
1919-1921	Anglo-Irish War
1919	Estonian War of Independence
1919-1920	Lithuanian War of Independence
1919	Czechoslovak-Polish War
1920	Russo-Polish War
1920	Vlora War (Italy-Albania)
1920	Polish-Lithuanian War
1934	Austrian Civil Strife
1936-1939	Spanish Civil War
1939	Slovak-Hungarian War
Middle East	
1919-1922	Turkish War of Independence
1919-1922	Greco-Turkish War
1920-1921	Franco-Turkish War (Cilicia)
1920	Iraqi Revolt/War
1926-1928	French suppression of Syrian Revolt
1936-1939	British Palestine sectarian strife
Africa	
1920-1927	Franco-Spanish pacification of Morocco
1922	South African pacification of SW Africa
1925-1935	Italian aggression in Libya
1930	Gugsa Welle's rebellion, Ethiopia
1935-1936	Italo-Ethiopian War
Asia	
1919	3rd Anglo-Afghan War (NW frontier)
1920s	British pacification of Burma, India
1927-1937	Chinese Civil War
1931	Japanese invasion of Manchuria
1932	Japanese attack on Shanghai
1937-1945	Sino-Japanese War
1939	Russo-Japanese Border War (Outer Mongolia)
Latin America	
1920-1935	US interventions – Nicaragua, Haiti, Dominican Republic, and Honduras
1927-1929	Cristero War (Mexico)
1932-1935	Chaco War (Bolivia – Paraguay)

The end of World War I and the peace settlements did not bring an end to conflict in Europe or elsewhere. Numerous conflicts ensued: wars of independence, nationalist resistance to European colonialism, frontier readjustments of the new Eastern European states created in the aftermath of the peace treaties, brutal civil wars in Russia and Spain, and territorial aggression by Japan and Italy in Asia and Africa. Consequently, the European states' intelligence services were busy.

For more than half of the interwar period, British and French intelligence services focused on the emerging Soviet Union, which despite its efforts to foster communist revolutions either by invading a neighbor (Poland, 1920) or by fomenting internal uprisings of communist workers, sailors, and soldiers (Germany, Hungary, and Austria), remained the only country that practiced Communism. After the Russian Civil War ended in 1920-21 with the Bolshevik victory, a secret war proceeded, which pitted the British and French secret services against the Soviet Union's expanding services. From the Bolshevik's initial secret police, the CHEKA (Emergency Committee), grew a larger service with various acronyms such as OGPU (the Joint State Political Directorate) and NKVD (People's Commissariat for Internal Affairs). Even though the OGPU (1923-1934), for example, dominated the intelligence field and was much larger and better funded, it was not the sole secret service: there was also Soviet military intelligence, renamed the GRU in 1942, as well as departments of the Communist International (Comintern), which employed agents at home and abroad.[1] The Soviet Union remained diplomatically isolated throughout much of the 1920s. It was not recognized diplomatically until the late 1920s (and not until 1933 by the United States) and did not join the League of Nations until 1934. Its foreign and defense policies functioned with the presumption that the main Western capitalist states, which had worked to defeat the Bolsheviks, remained hostile.

Soviet intelligence services sought to discover the military plans and intentions of adversaries such as Britain, France, Germany, and the United States, as well as Japan, to which it had lost the 1904 Russo-Japanese War and continued to have territorial disputes in the Far East. In addition, Soviet spies sought to obtain Western industrial and economic secrets to industrialize and compete with Western powers and strengthen the Soviet Armed Forces.

The Soviets employed different types of spies: "legals," who used diplomatic cover at Soviet consulates and embassies; and "illegals," who used all manner of cover, including Soviet press and trade associations established in foreign capitals, as well as a variety of philosophically sympathetic agents who infiltrated workers' unions, defense industries, and merchant marine crews. The targeting of workers and merchant seamen in major ports in Germany, the Low Countries, and Scandinavia had the dual purpose of encouraging the overthrow of capitalism through paralyzing strikes and sabotage in the event of war with the Soviet Union.

Stalin used the long arm of Soviet intelligence to neutralize and murder exiled White Russians (the side that lost the Russian Civil War) and other USSR enemies wherever they resided abroad. Such tactics became public knowledge in Paris, a major sanctuary for thousands of White Russians, after 1919 when newspapers wrote stories about opponents or defectors being kidnapped from Paris streets or murdered in Switzerland. Most famously, Stalin's principal rival, Leon Trotsky, was exiled in 1929 and assassinated in Mexico in 1940 by a Soviet agent recruited and trained by the NKVD during the Spanish Civil War (1936-1939).

Two intelligence-related technologies, which were new in World War I, were further developed in the 1920s: signals intelligence, which grew out of the contest between cryptography and cryptanalysis with the use of two-way

---

1. For a history of Soviet and Russian secret services, see Robert W. Pringle, "Guide to Soviet and Russian Intelligence Services," *Intelligencer* 18 (2), Winter/Spring 2011, 51 – 54. Also on-line at *http://www.afio.com/guide.*

radios in addition to telegraphy and photography, used from airplanes to locate enemy forces and weaponry. Various intelligence services throughout the world tried to exploit the protected communications of other states. Germany enjoyed some success against British naval signals between the wars. Germany introduced a sophisticated cryptographic machine in the 1920s called Enigma. Polish and French codebreakers began to solve Enigma codes, which became a key advantage for Allied intelligence in World War II. In addition, spies and counterintelligence agents employed concealable cameras with which to photograph purloined documents as well as industrial and military equipment. Furthermore, secret agents could now use portable equipment for recording voices without the subjects' knowledge or for tapping telephone lines. These technologies became common tools in future international secret wars, although even major powers could not always afford to equip their agents with such devices. As of September 1939, for example, Britain's spies abroad still did not have two-way radios.

Hitler, Mussolini, and Stalin were Spies

Hitler, Mussolini and Stalin each had minor intelligence service credentials. Though they were but tiny cogs in the intelligence wheel, they were participants: Hitler was a spy and propagandist for the German army in the early years of the ill-fated Weimar Republic; Mussolini late in World War I acted as a French secret agent, and Stalin before the 1917 Revolution had been an informant in Czarist Russia's secret police, the Okhrana.

In the 1920s, US intelligence focus was largely domestic. The anarchist and communist threats at home were the principal focus. Foreign intelligence collection was accomplished by a limited number of military and naval attachés posted in selected European and Asian countries. However, the US developed a significant signals intelligence capacity between the wars, despite setbacks and modest budgets. When World War I ended, Department of State codebreaking pioneer, Herbert O. Yardley, moved the Cipher Bureau, commonly known as the Black Chamber, to New York City and was financed by the Department of State and the Navy. In 1921, at the Washington Naval Arms Limitation Treaty Conference, Yardley's reading of the Japanese delegates' secret diplomatic messages gave an advantage to American diplomats and enabled the United States to constrain Japan's naval construction allowance in the final treaty. But in 1929, Secretary of State Stimson shut down Yardley's New York signal intelligence unit, later describing the event with the now legendary comment, "Gentlemen do not read each other's mail." That same year, nevertheless, the US Army Signal Intelligence Service (SIS) was established and used Yardley's unit's old files. SIS was headed by codebreaking genius William Friedman, who by 1939-1940 had achieved successes in reading high-level diplomatic traffic from the new Japanese encoding "Red" machine. Meanwhile, in 1924, the US Navy established a codebreaking unit in the Office of Naval Intelligence and began to work on Japanese diplomatic and naval traffic. In signals intelligence, there was competition between the Army and Navy units.

The 1930s: The Not-So-Secret March to World War II

The totalitarian states built-up their secret intelligence services during the 1930s. Nazi Germany and Japan, in particular, initiated aggressive subversion on an unprecedented scale. Japanese intelligence played an active role in the territorial expansion into Manchuria (1931) and Mainland China (1937), which marked the beginning of World War II in the Far East. Japan's services conducted subversion, deception, and provocations to justify military intervention.

While Italy's takeover of Libya and conquest of Ethiopia (Abyssinia, 1935-1936), were sideshows, the Spanish Civil War (1936-1939), which began as a domestic conflict and caused at least 600,000 deaths and uncounted injuries and destruction, is viewed by many historians as the prelude and rehearsal for World War II in Europe. The Soviet Union supported the loyalists of the Spanish Republic; while the Fascist powers, Germany and Italy, supported General Franco's Nationalists. One legacy was the Soviet enlistment of Spanish spies, saboteurs, and assassins who, after the Republic fell, participated in Stalin's underground activities, including infiltrating various countries and carrying out revenge missions abroad.

One of the most talented secret agents of all was Richard Sorge, a spy for Soviet military intelligence (GRU) who served in the Far East. Sorge's father was German, his mother Russian. Sorge was in China and then Japan under cover as a newspaper reporter. His principal mission was to discover Japan's plans toward the Soviet Union, but by posing as a German and gaining access to the German Embassy in Tokyo, he also collected information on the Third Reich's strength, plans, and intentions. His warning of Germany's intentions appear to have been ignored by Stalin, but his intelligence on Japan's intention not to invade the Soviet Far East allowed Stalin to reposition significant forces from Siberia to face west.

In the 1930s, the number of arrests of spies and spy trials rapidly grew in Europe. Typically, spy scares heightened concerns about security and trials stirred patriotic feelings. After 1930 in most states, espionage during peacetime could result in capital punishment.

By the time World War II began with the September 1, 1939 German invasion of Poland, most of the intelligence services were far larger and better equipped than they had been in 1914. However, assessments of potential enemies in the late 1930s were often wide of the mark. Many states' assessments were more accurate in terms of counting numbers of enemy forces and resources, but less accurate in plotting plans and intentions. Britain's intelligence system overestimated Nazi Germany's Air Force strength by almost 50%, yet came closer in estimating ground forces' numbers, if not their military prowess.

In the US, the Justice Department's Federal Bureau of Investigation, beginning in 1936, was given presidential authority to devote greater resources against subversives, including foreign spies, especially Nazi and Japanese agents and, to a lesser extent, Soviet spies. With the September 1939 outbreak of war in Europe, the intelligence efforts of the Army, Navy, and FBI began to grow rapidly.

READINGS FOR INSTRUCTORS

No comprehensive intelligence history exists of the period between the world wars. Most coverage is by individual country or regime.

Great Britain

For an introduction to British intelligence after 1918, there is Christopher Andrew's *Her Majesty's Secret Service: The Making of the British Intelligence Community* (New York: Viking, 1986; originally published in 1985 as *Secret Service: The Making of the British Intelligence Community*, updated in paperback in 1998 by Viking), but it should be noted that in the late 1990s official histories of MI-6 and MI-5 were published and include materials that cover this era. See Keith Jeffery, *The Secret History of MI6, 1909-1949* (New York: Penguin, 2010), and Christopher Andrew, *Defend The Realm. The Authorized History of MI5* (New York: Knopf, 2009).

France

For spies, international crime and intrigue in interwar France, Michael Miller's *Shanghai on the Métro* (Berkeley: University of California Press, 1994) utilizes police files and popular spy literature. For a larger perspective on France's intelligence history, Douglas Porch's *The French Secret Services* (New York: Farrar, Straus, Giroux, 1995) remains indispensable. The classic anthology related to intelligence assessments in the 1920s and 1930s (as well as pre-1914) in Britain, Germany, Russia, France, Italy, Japan, and the United States, is Ernest R. May (ed), *Knowing One's Enemies* (Princeton, NJ: Princeton University Press, 1984) based in large part on government archives.

USSR

Studies of Soviet intelligence to 1939 represent a field unto itself and includes biographies and autobiographies of spies, early Soviet defectors, and underground agents. A good biography of master spy Richard Sorge, is Robert Whymant, *Stalin's Spy* (New York: St. Martin's Press, 1998). A classic anatomy of Soviet spying into the early Cold War years by a Russian-born historian is David Dallin's *Soviet Espionage* (New Haven, CT: Yale University Press, 1955). Biographies of early Soviet defectors, several of whom were intelligence officers, are in Gordon Brook-Shepherd, *The Storm Petrels* (New York: Ballantine Books, 1978).

Japan

For information on pre-1940 Japanese intelligence (besides a chapter in Ernest May's book cited above), see the chapter by J. W. M. Chapman, "Japanese Intelligence, 1918-1945: A Suitable Case for Treatment" in Christopher Andrew and James Noakes (eds.), *Intelligence and International Relations* (1900-1945) (Exeter, UK: Exeter University Publications, 1987).

America

Useful material on American intelligence services between the world wars is in an archive-based study by Robert G. Angevin, "Gentlemen Do Read Each Other's Mail: American Intelligence in the Interwar Era," *Intelligence and National Security* 7 (2), 1992, 1-29. G. J. A. O'Toole's general survey of American intelligence history has useful chapters (25-29) on 1918 to 1939: *Honorable Treachery* (New York: Atlantic Monthly Press, 1991). The Office of the National Counterintelligence Executive has posted on its website a loosely edited but interesting and detailed multivolume history of US counterintelligence. See *http://www.ncsc.gov/publications/ci_references/index.html*.

Douglas L. Wheeler is professor emeritus of history at the University of New Hampshire and a previous contributor to the *Guide to the Study of Intelligence*. See his articles "A Guide to the History of Intelligence in the Age of Empires, 1500-1800," *Intelligencer* 18 (3), Summer/Fall 2011; "A Guide to the History of Intelligence, 1800-1918," *Intelligencer*, 19 (1), Winter/Spring 2012; and "A Note About Intelligence Historiography," *Intelligencer* 18 (3), Summer/Fall 2011.

GUIDE TO THE STUDY OF INTELLIGENCE

From Axis Surprises to Allied Victories

The Impact of Intelligence in World War II

Peter C. Oleson

As governments declassify old files and scholars examine the details of World War II, it is apparent that intelligence had an important impact on many battles and the length and cost of this catastrophic conflict. As Nigel West noted, "[c]hanges in American, British, and even Soviet official attitudes to declassification in the 1980s allowed thousands of secret documents to be made available for public examination, and the result was extensive revisionism of the conventional histories of the conflict."[1] More so than any time in history, intelligence played a central role in World War II. Historians F. H. Hinsley and David Kahn have suggested that the Allies' success at breaking the German codes shortened the war in Europe by years and helped turn the tide in the Pacific.[2] The Allies did not enter World War II with good intelligence; rather, initial Allied losses and failures were often the result of poor or unconvincing intelligence or no intelligence at all. A war that started with Axis military successes in its early phases (1939 – 1942), based partially on their intelligence preparations, was brought to a conclusion aided by Allied intelligence successes (1942 – 1945).

The Bleak Years: 1939 – Mid-1942

The Axis powers repeatedly surprised Poland, Britain, France, and others,

---

1. Nigel West, *Historical Dictionary of World War II Intelligence*, series Historical Dictionaries of Intelligence and Counterintelligence No. 7, Lanham, MD: The Scarecrow Press, Inc., 2008, xx.
2. F. H. Hinsley. "The Influence of ULTRA in the Second World War," lecture to the Security Group seminar at Babbage Lecture Theatre, Cambridge University Computer Laboratory, October 19, 1993. *http://www.cix.co.uk/~klockstone/hinsley.htm*. See also David Kahn, *Hitler's Spies: German Military Intelligence in World War II* (New York: Macmillan Publishing Company, 1978).

who were often blinded by preconceptions and biases, in both a strategic and tactical sense. When war broke out on September 1, 1939, the Polish leadership, ignoring their own intelligence, lacked an appreciation of German military capabilities: their cavalry horses were no match for German Panzers. British Prime Minister Neville Chamberlain misread Hitler's intentions, unwilling to accept the evidence at hand. This was the consequence of the low priority given to British intelligence in the period between wars.[3]

Near the end of the "Phony War" (September 3, 1939 – May 10, 1940) in the West, the Germans engineered strategic, tactical, and technological surprises. The first came in Scandinavia in early April 1940.

Norway

The April 9 German invasion of Norway (and Denmark) was a strategic surprise for the Norwegians and British. The Norwegians had concerns about British intervention interrupting its ore trade with Germany. Not wanting the British to box them in, as occurred in World War I, the Germans wanted naval and air bases in Norway. German Grand Admiral (Großadmiral) Erich Raeder planned an unconventional move depending on surprise. According to him, the planned Operation Weserübung "goes against all rules of naval warfare. According to those rules the operation could only be carried out if we had superiority at sea. This we did not have: On the contrary, we shall be carrying out the operations in the face of the clearly superior British fleet."[4] The British mindset was that the superior Royal Navy would deter any such German move. The Norwegians had little intelligence capability, British intelligence had few tested and believed human sources inside Germany, and Enigma decrypts were nonexistent at the time. Dutch intelligence warnings were received skeptically. Britain's signals intelligence (SIGINT) organization, the Government Communications and Cipher School (GC&CS) alerted the Admiralty to a revealing decrypted German naval hand cipher, which the Admiralty ignored. Bad weather limited aerial reconnaissance. Aerial photos of the German port of Bremen had shown many assembled ships, but their significance was not understood as aerial reconnaissance was not routine.[5] Lacking intelligence sources, ignoring some warnings, and with tight German security, the invasion succeeded at little cost.

Disaster was a teacher for Britain. On June 3, the Admiralty again ignored

---

3. Basil Collier, *Hidden Weapons: Allied Secret or Undercover Services in World War II* (Barnsley: Pen & Sword Books Ltd., 1982), xiii.

4. Olav Riste, "Intelligence and the 'Mindset': The German Invasion of Norway in 1940." *Intelligence and National Security* 22 (4) (August 2007), 534, footnote 34.

5. Riste, ibid.; F. H. Hinsley, *British Intelligence in the Second World War*, Abridged Edition (London: HMSO, 1993), 12; Stephen Budiansky, *Battle of Wits: The Complete Story of Codebreaking in World War II* (New York: The Free Press, 2000), 140; and R.V. Jones, *Most Secret War: British Scientific Intelligence, 1939-1945* (London: Penguin Books, 1979, 2009).

a SIGINT warning of unusual naval activity, and the German battle cruiser SMS Gneisenau sank the British carrier HMS Glorious with 1,500 hands. After this, newly installed Prime Minister Winston Churchill asked to see all new Enigma decrypts,[6] prompting senior officers to request Enigma briefings in response.[7] GC&CS had begun to break German Enigma codes in March-April 1940, and, by June, was starting to extract useful intelligence from this new source.

Attack in the West

The Norwegian surprise was followed by another a month later. Without declaring war to alert its neutral neighbors, Germany invaded Luxembourg, Holland, and Belgium. The initial seizure of the crucial Belgian fort at Eben Emael on May 10-11, 1940, entailed both tactical and technological surprise. The use of only 85 glider-borne troops, who landed on top of the fort's 750 defenders, bypassed the extensive Belgian defense network intended to prevent the Germans from crossing the strategic Albert Canal bridges. Prior to the operation, the Germans employed extensive denial, deception, and security measures to hide the training of paratroops and glider assault forces. The preciseness of their attack demonstrated excellent foreknowledge of the objective. The silent gliders defeated the Belgian's warning system based on aircraft engine sound detectors. As British author James Lucas observed, a technological "military revolution occurred with the adding of a vertical flank to battlefield dispositions."[8] The use of airlifted troops, paratroops, and glider-borne soldiers was a surprising innovation first demonstrated in the Norwegian invasion that caught Dutch and Belgian defenders unprepared. German paratroops leapt over the Dutch strongholds and unexpectedly seized Dutch bridges and the airfield near Rotterdam into which reinforcements were flown. Seaplanes flew in other reinforcements on the River Maas. The last Dutch

The Enigma Machine

Enigma was a German developed enciphering machine introduced in the late 1920s. It was an electro-mechanical device using both a plug board and multiple 26-position rotors. Early versions used three rotors, later versions, five. "The greatest selling point was even if the machine fell into enemy hands it would still be useless. The secret of the machine lay in its rotors.... [U]nless one knew which rotor went where, and what position each rotor started in, the Enigma machine was useless.... At the time of its use it was the epitome of ciphering machines" for Morse transmissions.* The German armed forces, paramilitary Protection Squadron (*Schutzstaffel*, SS), police, railroads, and others used more than 200 versions of Enigma codes. Each had to be decrypted separately.

_____

* Charles Cooper, "The Enigma Machine," notes for Probabilities and Statistics (US Naval Academy, April 16, 2002), retrieved from *http://www.usna.edu/Users/ math/wdj/sm230_cooper_ enigma.html.*

---

6. Hinsley, *British Intelligence*, 18-26.

7. Budiansky, *Battle of Wits*, 149.

8. James Lucas, *Storming Eagles: German Airborne Forces in World War II* (London: Cassell & Co., 1988), 43.

resistance ended on May 14, and Belgium surrendered on May 28.[9]

Initially, the Poles broke early pre-war versions of Enigma and shared their success with the French and British. With the fall of Poland and France, the effort against Enigma fell to the British. On May 22, 1940, GC&CS broke the German *Luftwaffe* Enigma code, which it read more or less without interruption for the rest of the war. Luftwaffe messages provided a lot of intelligence on ground and naval operations and plans, as well as its own activities.[10] But this was too late to affect the German offensive.

From a well-placed American Nazi sympathizer, Tyler Kent, the Germans knew the Allies were unprepared for operations on the Western Front in the winter of 1939-1940, and used the time to prepare a western campaign.[11] Despite reports from Belgian, French, and Swiss intelligence, the timing and direction of the June 5, 1940 German attack into France again achieved tactical surprise. "For the French it was axiomatic that the Ardennes were impassable. The British deferred to this conviction." [12] The British ignored the warnings from Paul Thümmel, a high-ranking Abwehr (German military intelligence) officer[13] that the attack would come through the Ardennes. German intelligence on the Allies was good.[14] From British documents captured in Norway, photoreconnaissance, and reading some high-grade French ciphers, the Germans knew of the plans, dispositions, and quality of French and British forces facing theirs. The Maginot Line fortresses were flanked and attacked from the rear. The French Army, much of the best of which was decimated in Belgium and around Dunkirk, was again surprised by the combined arms tactics of the German Blitzkrieg.[15] France surrendered on June 22, 1940. With the fall of France, the focus of the war in Europe shifted to Britain, the Mediterranean, and the Atlantic.

Battle of Britain and the Blitz

The following month marked the beginning of the Battle of Britain. Radar became an important British source of intelligence, although from the end of 1939, tactical SIGINT from the Royal Air Force's (RAF) Y-Service helped Britain's Fighter Command detect takeoffs and direction of Luftwaffe planes before

9. Ibid, 40–3, 48, 51.

10. Collier, *Hidden Weapons*, 92.

11. Kent was a disaffected code clerk in the American Embassy in London. Peter Rand, *Conspiracy of One: Tyler Kent's Secret Plot Against FDR, Churchill, and the Allied War Effort* (Guilford, CT: Lyons Press, 2013).

12. Robert J. Young, "French Military Intelligence and Nazi Germany, 1938-1939," in Ernest R. May (Ed.), *Knowing One's Enemies: Intelligence Assessment Before the Two World Wars* (Princeton: Princeton University Press, 1984).

13. Thümmel, known as A-54, was an asset of Czech intelligence, which, after Germany seized Czechoslovakia, moved to London. The Czechs provided A-54's reports to both the British and Soviets. Hinsley, *British Intelligence*, 12, 26-30.

14. Ibid, 26.

15. Luftwaffe close air support of the Wehrmacht was a tactical surprise. Collier, *Hidden Weapons*, 88.

their detection by radar. The outnumbered Fighter Command, thus guided, inflicted heavy losses on the Luftwaffe, causing it in mid-November to revert to nighttime raids. The RAF Y-Service focused on tactical SIGINT and low-level codes and was not privy to the highly sensitive Enigma decrypts at this time.[16]

Anti-Nazi Spies Who Helped the Allies

The Allies were aided by several anti-Nazi sources within Germany who knowingly leaked information. In November 1939, Hans Ferdinand Mayer, an anti-Nazi mathematician and physicist, wrote a seven-page report on German weapons advances, many of which were unknown to the British. Given anonymously to the British naval attaché in Oslo, the "Oslo report" revealed how the Junker 88 was to be used as a dive bomber; that the German Navy had a radio-controlled anti-ship rocket-driven glider (HS-293)* that was being tested at the Peenemünde weapons research site; British bombers could be detected by radar at 120 kilometers, and Germany had another parabolic dish radar, the *Würzburg*, operating at 50-centimeters wavelength; the Luftwaffe could detect its own bombers via a system operating at 6-meters wavelength; and the Navy had two new torpedoes that were radio and acoustic controlled and were magnetically fused. British ministries largely ignored this intelligence until R.V. Jones became the head of scientific intelligence for both the Air Ministry and MI6.**
Paul Thümmel, "a high ranking officer in the Abwehr, ... had originally offered his services to the Czechs, who referred to him as A-54. He supplied not only good information about the equipment, the order of battle and the mobilization plans of the German Army and Air Force, but also advance notice of the German plans for action against Czechoslovakia from the spring of 1938, for the seizure of Prague in the spring of 1939 and, from that spring, for the attack on Poland."***
"The Poles had achieved this success [in breaking Enigma] with brilliant mathematical ingenuity, by methods they would have been unable to devise but for the fact that the French Secret Service had supplied them with material obtained from Hans-Thilo Schmidt, a German employee of the cipher branch of the German Army...."#
Fritz Kolbe was an anti-Nazi courier for the German Foreign Ministry. From 1943, he provided more than 2,600 documents with significant intelligence to Allen Dulles, Office of Strategic Services (OSS) chief in Switzerland, including on morale in Berlin, German expectations for the Allied invasion, the V-1 and V-2 rocket programs, and advanced jet aircraft, and exposed the German spy "Cicero" in the British Embassy in Istanbul. ##

---

* One sunk the troopship HMT *Rohna* on November 26, 1942 in the Mediterranean with the loss of 1,138 killed, mostly US troops. James G. Bennett. The Rohna Disaster (Xlibris,1999).
** Collier, *Hidden Weapons*, 60; R.V. Jones, *Most Secret War*, 67-71.
*** Hinsley, *British Intelligence*, 12.
# Ibid, 14.
Tony Patterson, "Germany finally honours the 'traitor' spy who gave Nazi secrets to America," *The Independent*, 25 September 2004; Anthony Quibble, "Alias George Wood." *Studies in Intelligence* 10, No. 1 (Winter 1966).

Battle of the Beams. In June 1940, an Enigma decrypt revealed the Luftwaffe was using a navigational beam called Knickebein to guide its bombers over Britain. Confirmed by prisoner-of-war interrogations and captured documents from downed German aircraft, the British developed masking beacons ("meacons"), which by September were having an effect. "The early detection and partial frustration of Knickebein – a feat then known to only a few – was an early and major British victory in the Battle of Britain."[17] When the Germans introduced improved bombing beams, the British rapidly

---

16. Hinsley, *British Intelligence*, 17, 38-40.
17. Brigadier General Telford Taylor, Columbia University law professor, assigned to Bletchley in WW II, in *The Breaking Wave: The Second World War in the Summer of 1940* (New York: Simon and Schuster, 1967), cited in R. V. Jones, *Most Secret War,* 110.

countered them. The improved Y-Gerät navigational beam was introduced in January 1941; the British had operational countermeasures by February that significantly lowered German bombing accuracy.[18] "By February 1941 the Battle of the Beams was as good as won."[19] The last large Luftwaffe raid on London occurred on May 10-11. In May, most German bombers redeployed to the Eastern Front.

War at Sea

"[I]t was quickly realized by strategists on both sides that the war would be won or lost on the question of whichever side successfully dominated the Atlantic Ocean."[20] In August 1940, Germany began unrestricted submarine warfare with the goal of isolating Britain and starving it into submission. "The Battle of the Atlantic was the dominating factor all through the war," according to Churchill.[21] Except for agents reporting the departure of U-boats from their base at Brest, France, and direction finding (DF) on radio transmissions, there was no intelligence on U-boats. By the end of 1938, the Germans were reading one of the Royal Navy's codes. By late 1941, the naval cryptanalytic service, the B-Dienst, was also reading British Naval Ciphers #2 and #3 used for Anglo-Canadian-American convoys and directing U-boats to intercept the convoys.

At GC&CS in early 1941, cryptanalytic efforts against the naval versions of Enigma were aided by the captures of a German armed trawler, two weather ships, and U-110, which provided an Enigma machine, additional rotors, and settings tables. GC&CS was able to break the German Navy's home waters and dockyards codes and began to read other naval traffic. Through Enigma decrypts, the Royal Navy was able to eliminate eight clandestine German Navy support ships in the Atlantic,[22] and by June had reduced the U-boats' successes against convoys.[23]

When the German battleship DKM Bismarck forayed from Norway into the north Atlantic in May 1941, British DF and traffic analysis proved decisive in tracking her after she sank HMS Hood, damaged Prince of Wales, and escaped.[24] A decrypted Luftwaffe message revealed her destination was Brest, and, on May 26, Bismarck was intercepted and sunk.

When the US entered the war, U-boat commander Admiral Raeder turned

---

18. Hinsley, *British Intelligence*, 47-48.

19. R. V. Jones, *Most Secret War*, 179.

20. Peter Scott Roberts, review of John R. Bruning, *Battle for the North Atlantic: The Strategic Naval Campaign that Won World War II in Europe* (London: Zenith Press, 2013) in *Intelligence and National Security* 29 (6), 2014, at http://dx.doi.org/10.1080/02684527.2013.858517.

21. David Kahn. "Intelligence in World War II," *Journal of Intelligence History* 1 (1), (Summer 2001), 12.

22. Hinsley, *British Intelligence*, 50-58.

23. Hinsley, Cambridge address.

24. Budiansky, *Battle of Wits*, 189.

his attention to the US East Coast. In the first six months of 1942, almost 500 ships were sunk off the North American coast.[25] U-boat sinkings of merchant vessels far exceeded Britain's shipbuilding capacity.[26]

In 1942, the Germans came to realize the scope of supplies reaching the USSR[27] and turned to intercepting convoys bound for Murmansk. A low point for the Allies came in three days in July 1942, when Convoy PQ-17 lost 23 out of 36 ships to U-boats and Luftwaffe aircraft from northern Norway.[28] Fearing that the German battleship KMS Tirpitz was at sea, despite a lack of SIGINT, First Sea Lord Sir Dudley Pound ordered PQ-17 to scatter. "... [N]ot for the first nor the last time, [SIGINT] was unable to provide that last and vital clue to the intentions of the enemy...."[29]

Southeast Europe, the Mediterranean, and North Africa

On June 11, 1940, Italy entered the war. Its invasion of Albania was a surprise.[30] However, GC&CS decrypts gave a month's warning of Italy's September attack from Libya on Egypt. Counterattacking in early December, the 30,000-man British force captured half of Italy's 250,000-man invasion force.[31] Geographically, Italian East Africa posed a threat to the Suez Canal and Egypt's security. Britain's Combined Bureau Middle East (CBME), a GC&CS outpost, was deciphering 90% of Italian radio messages in East Africa, which was a major aid in defeating Italy's forces there; unfortunately, the Secret Intelligence Service (MI6) had a lack of human sources in the Italian territories.[32]

North Africa. Despite Enigma decrypts (now identified by the codeword "ULTRA") and Y-Service intercepts of the introduction of Luftwaffe units into North Africa in December 1940, the British were reluctant to believe German Army forces were in North Africa until Field Marshall Erwin Rommel's initial offensive on February 22, 1941.[33] The Germans used ground and air reconnaissance well, and its field SIGINT unit exploited the poor British communications security. Rommel's signals battalion warned of Britain's May and June counterattacks, which stalled when they ran into superior German armor and anti-tank guns for which there was no forewarning. British field intelligence was weak.[34]

---

25. Roberts, review, 2.
26. Hinsley, *British Intelligence*, 308.
27. Ibid, 154.
28. Patrick Beesly. "Convoy PQ 17: A Study of Intelligence and Decision-making." *Intelligence and National Security* 5 (2), (1990), 292-322.
29. Ibid, 319.
30. Collier, *Hidden Weapons*, 114.
31. Budiansky, *Battle of Wits*, 182.
32. Thaddeus Holt, *The Deceivers: Allied Military Deception in the Second World War* (New York: Scribner, 2004); also Collier, *Hidden Weapons*, 134.
33. Hinsley, *British Intelligence*, 66.
34. Ibid, 77-79.

From 1941 through mid-1942, Rommel enjoyed a significant SIGINT advantage over the British in North Africa.[35] In January 1942, the Germans began to read the cipher of the US Army attaché in Cairo, Colonel Frank Fellers, who reported in detail on British Army conditions and plans. Feller's messages were a great advantage to the Germans. He inadvertently tipped off the Germans to convoys planning to relieve the British-held island of Malta between Italy and Libya in June 1942, and to the precursor commando raids against nine Axis airfields in Libya and Crete. British and Free French commandos were slaughtered. Only two out of the six ships of the Gibraltar convoy reached Malta; the Alexandria 11-ship convoy turned back under heavy air attack with serious losses.[36] The timing and direction of Rommel's May 1942 assault was based on what he learned from SIGINT. By the end of June, Rommel had driven the British out of Libya and advanced to within 90 miles of Alexandria, Egypt.[37]

Yugoslavia, Greece, and Crete. On April 6, 1941, the German Army invaded Yugoslavia, after a British encouraged coup d'etat and, along with Italian forces, entered Greece. Alerted by a human intelligence (HUMINT) source, the British pulled troops from North Africa and sent them to Greece. However, with no photoreconnaissance capability and poor field intelligence, British forces were no match for the Wehrmacht and, by late April, were evacuated. SIGINT, however, helped reduce the scale of the calamity."[38]

On May 20, German airborne forces invaded Crete. GC&CS had "deciphered the complete German invasion plans for Crete at least three weeks in advance of their intended date of operations."[39] But the Allied commander, Lieutenant General Sir Bernard Freyberg, was convinced it would be a seaborne invasion and had poorly positioned the island's defenders. Some historians point to Freyberg's bias as paralyzing his actions in light of the intelligence he received.[40] The British also overestimated the size of the attacking force. By the end of the month, the Allies abandoned the island. It was a Pyrrhic victory as the Germans badly underestimated the size of the defending force. German casualties were considerable and "left them with a crippled airborne arm" that was not used again in the west for the remainder of the war.[41]

Elsewhere in the region, Axis intelligence and propaganda fueled anti-British sentiment in the Middle East, prompting the British to divert troops to Syria

---

35. Wil Deac. "Intercepted Communications for Field Marshall Erwin Rommel," originally published in *World War II Magazine*, at *http://www.historynet.com/intercepted-communications-for-field-marshal-erwin-rommel.htm/1.*

36. Hinsley, *British Intelligence*, 198, and Deac,"Intercepted Communications."

37. Ibid.

38. Hinsley, *British Intelligence*, 73.

39. R.V. Jones, *Most Secret War*, 204.

40. See Saul David, *Military Blunders: The How and Why of Military Failure* (New York: Carroll & Graf Publishers, Inc., 1997), 333-48.

41. Hinsley, *British Intelligence*, 84.

and Iraq from North Africa.[42]

Barbarossa

On June 22, 1941, Germany invaded the Soviet Union. Despite many intelligence indicators and warnings, Stalin and Soviet forces were caught by surprise.[43]

"Richard Sorge [a Soviet military intelligence (GRU) asset in Tokyo] ... receive[d] solid information about a planned Nazi surprise attack against the Soviet Union. Joseph Stalin, who had signed a non-aggression pact with Hitler two years before, refused to believe the Nazi ruler would have the audacity to violate the treaty."[44] The Soviet's Alexander Rado GRU espionage ring in Switzerland provided warnings, as did the Soviet military attaché's agents in Berlin, the Yugoslav military attaché, and Swedish sources. It became known that the Abwehr (military intelligence) was recruiting specialists on the Ukraine, Crimea, and the Caucasus.[45] In preparation, the Germans entered Romania in October 1940. Reports of German plans from agent Thümmel were ignored.[46] After breaking the Japanese diplomatic code (Purple) in late 1940, the US provided GC&CS with the results of its cryptanalysis and copies of the decryption machines. On June 4, 1941, the decryption of a Japanese diplomatic message from Berlin to Tokyo revealed that Hitler had decided Communist Russia must be eliminated.[47] A week later, the British foreign secretary gave the Russian ambassador full details of British intelligence on the German build-up.[48] In March 1941, GC&CS broke the German railroad Enigma codes, which revealed the widespread movement of German forces to opposite Russia.[49]

Two weeks after the German invasion, London started to provide the Soviets regular intelligence summaries about the Eastern Front via the British Military Mission in Moscow. However, not everything was shared. As Stalin

---

42. See Commander Youssef H. Aboul-Enein & Basil H. Aboul-Enein. *The Secret War for the Middle East: The Influence of Axis and Allied Intelligence Operations During World War II* (Annapolis, MD: US Naval Institute Press, 2013).

43. See David E. Murphy, *What Stalin Knew: The Enigma of Barbarossa* (New Haven, CT: Yale University Press, 2005). Murphy "presents a mosaic of Soviet intelligence reporting found in no other work of Western scholarship." Some of the information provided "is truly enlightening, and changes scholarly understanding of German disinformation and how it influenced Soviet policy." Review by Robert Pringle, *International Journal of Intelligence & Counterintelligence* 19 (4), (Winter 2006-2007). In his book, *Operation Barbarossa* (Cambridge, MA: MIT Press, 1974), Barton Whaley details 84 warnings the USSR received of German attack plans. See also John Erickson, "Threat Identification and Strategic Appraisal by the Soviet Union, 1930-1941" in Ernest R. May (Ed.), *Knowing One's Enemies*, 375-423.

44. Sulick, *Spying in America*, 35. Sorge's major source was Hotsumi Ozaki, an advisor to Japanese Prime Minister Konoe. Ken Kotani. *Japanese Intelligence in World War II* (Oxford: Osprey Publishing, 2009), 68.

45. Collier, *Hidden Weapons*, 186-190.

46. Hinsley, *British Intelligence*, 90-91.

47. Ibid, 115.

48. Ibid, 109.

49. Budiansky, *Battle of Wits*, 186.

severely limited intelligence sharing with Allies, British knowledge of Soviet order of battle (OB) was based on German assessments revealed through ULTRA. ULTRA also indicated that the Germans were reading Soviet ciphers, But this intelligence was not passed to the USSR.[50]

Of great strategic significance, "[w]ithin a few weeks of the German invasion of Russia, [Sorge] was able to tell Moscow, on the highest authority, that the Japanese government had no immediate intention of attacking the Soviet Union and that its eyes were fixed on Indo-China and the Netherlands East Indies.... On the strength of [Sorge's information] the Soviet High Command further reduced its forces in the Far East by moving to European Russia substantial formations which arrived in time to take part in the defence of Moscow and the Soviet counter-offensive in the winter of 1941-42."[51] The October 1941 – January 1942 Battle of Moscow frustrated Hitler's priority objective.

Beginning in the spring of 1942, GC&CS could read both German police ciphers and the SS's Enigma key. ULTRA revealed SS treatment of people in the captured territories and the exterminations of Jews.[52]

In September 1941, the Deutsche Reichspost, the German telephone and telegraph organization, broke the American A-3 voice encoder (vocoder). Through a site on the Dutch coast, it had "become adept at intercepting and breaking A-3 [telephone] calls between President Franklin Roosevelt and other prominent political and military leaders, including Prime Minister Winston Churchill."[53] US Army Chief of Staff George Marshall never trusted the A-3. In July 1943, SIGSALY (X System, Project X, Ciphony I, Green Hornet) replaced the A-3.[54]

Surprises in the Pacific

As a member of the World War I Entente Powers, Japan was given the League of Nations mandate over former German territories in the Pacific and the German concession in Shandong Province, China.[55] In 1931, Japan invaded Manchuria, a resource rich area of China, and created the puppet state of Manchukuo in 1932. In the face of Western criticism of its actions and atrocities, Japan withdrew from the League of Nations. By 1934, Japan had instituted an aggressive espionage campaign against the US.[56] By 1941, through various spies,

---

50. Hinsley, *British Intelligence*, 115.
51. Collier, *Hidden Weapons*, 206.
52. Budiansky, *Battle of Wits*, 198.
53. Patrick D. Weadon, *Sigsaly Story*, 2000. *https://www.nsa.gov/about/cryptologic_heritage/ center_crypt_ history/publications/wwii.shtml.*
54. Ibid, and David Kahn, *The Codebreakers*, Second Edition (Scribner, New York, 1996), 555-556
55. Mark R. Peattie, *Nanyo: the Rise and Fall of the Japanese in Micronesia, 1885-1945*, Pacific Islands Monograph Series, No. 4. (Honolulu: University of Hawaii Press, 1988), 43.
56. Tony Matthews, *Shadows Dancing: Japanese Espionage Against the West, 1939-1945* (London: Hale, 1993; New York: St. Martin's, 1994). Matthews tells of the Japanese using Spanish diplomatic missions

it compiled a 200-page encyclopedia on US Navy capabilities.[57] A spy ring in Honolulu reported on Pearl Harbor, and DF from Japanese-controlled Kwajalein Island tracked air patrols out of Hawai'i. This DF intelligence was valuable in planning the Japanese fleet's approach to Hawai'i in December 1941. The spy ring's reports on the depth of Pearl Harbor prompted the Japanese to modify shallow water torpedoes (Koku Gyorai Type 91, modification 2) that were used with devastating effect on December 7, 1941.[58] The Japanese apparently also had broken US and British diplomatic codes.[59]

Pearl Harbor. "Prior to Pearl Harbor ... US policymakers held assumptions and expectations – that it would be impossible for Japan to attack a well defended and distant naval base – that contributed to the lack of warning and preparedness."[60] From the Japanese perspective, a preemptive strike against the US fleet in Hawai'i was a necessary prelude to any move in force into Southeast Asia and its needed natural resources. In 1941, before the US imposed an oil embargo, Japan received 85% of its petroleum from US sources.[61]

The US had little insight into Japanese military moves at the time of the attack. US intelligence was fragmented, "disorganized and under-resourced." [62] President "Roosevelt had already set up his own private network of spies because the traditional intelligence system left him so much in the dark on what was happening overseas...." "The primitive and parochial intelligence units in the Army, Navy, and State Department were underfunded and undermanned dumping grounds for poor performers."[63] Most of Roosevelt's focus, however, was on Europe.

In 1936, the US Army Signal Intelligence Service (SIS) cracked the main Japanese diplomatic code, "Red." In March 1939, the code was changed and named "Purple." Purple was finally broken on September 20, 1940. The code-name "Magic" stuck after SIS analysts were deemed "magicians" for breaking Purple. The Army's success in breaking the Japanese diplomatic code[64] led

---

for its intelligence work.

57. Budiansky, *Battle of Wits*, 167. For details on Japanese espionage, see David Major & Peter Oleson, "Espionage Against America" *Guide to the Study of Intelligence*, http://www.afio.com/40_guide.htm.

58. Kotani. *Japanese Intelligence.*

59. Valerie Reitman. "Japan Broke U.S. Code Before Pearl Harbor, Researcher Finds," *Los Angeles Times*, December 7, 2001. http://articles.latimes.com/2001/dec/07/news/mn-12562.

60. Kent Center, *Occasional Papers: Making Sense of Transnational Threats*, 3, No. 1 (Central Intelligence Agency, Center for the Study of Intelligence, October 2004), 5.

61. Pearl Harbor Review – International Agreements. http://www.nsa.gov/about/cryptologic_ heritage/ center_cryptologic_history. Charles Meachling, "Pearl Harbor: The First Energy War," *History Today*, 50, December 2000.

62. Christopher Andrew. *For the President's Eyes Only: Secret Intelligence and the American Presidency from Washington to Bush* (New York: Harper, 1996), 75. Michael Warner, *The Office of Strategic Services: America's First Intelligence Agency* (Monograph), (Central Intelligence Agency: Center for the Study of Intelligence, 2000), 2, at https://www.cia.gov/library/publications/intelligence-history/oss/.

63. Douglas Waller, *Wild Bill Donovan: The Spymaster Who Created the OSS and Modern American Espionage* (New York: Free Press, 2011), 70.

64. Andrew, *President's Eyes Only*, 105. In the late 1930s, the Soviets broke Japan's diplomatic codes. Kōzō Izumi, a Japanese diplomat whose Russian wife was an NKVD [Soviet secret service] asset, pro-

to competitive friction with the US Navy over responsibilities for decryption and reporting.[65] The "success … in breaking the Japanese diplomatic code … had the ironic effect of distracting attention" from the more important naval operational code, JN-25.[66] Some success was made against JN-25 in 1940, but a variant, JN-25b, was introduced in December 1940. "A detailed study by the … NSA, later concluded that the failure to break JN25b was due solely to a shortage of resources." "… [I]t was only the lack of manpower – and machine power – that prevented the Navy from reading JN-25 in the critical months before Pearl Harbor." From 1939, usually only two people worked on the problem, sometimes five. By late 1941, the number increased to eight. When later broken, JN-25b had many indicators of a surprise attack by six carriers on a fleet in the "north Pacific." This reflected Navy Department "myopia" of the significance of SIGINT.[67]

US Navy SIGINT personnel were following Japanese naval movements by traffic analysis. The Pacific DF net consisted of stations at Corregidor, Guam, Pearl Harbor, Dutch Harbor in the Aleutians, Samoa, and Midway Island. However, in November and December 1941, traffic analysis reports were sent to Washington by mail and were running two, sometimes three weeks behind.[68] Realizing that the Americans were monitoring their communications, the Japanese had radio operators generating dummy traffic to mislead the eavesdroppers into thinking that some of the ships sailing through the north Pacific to attack Pearl Harbor were still in home waters.[69]

US decision makers underestimated the Japanese Navy's abilities. The shallow water torpedoes were one example. The Japanese had studied the November 1940 British attack on the Italian fleet in Taranto that used such torpedoes. Ironically, in early 1941, senior US Navy officers had envisioned an aerial torpedo attack on Pearl Harbor launched from aircraft carriers, but they had no impact on increasing readiness. The Pearl Harbor attack represented a strategic, tactical, and technological surprise[70] for the US.

Philippines and Southeast Asia. Little is published in English from Japanese sources on Japan's intelligence successes in World War II.[71] Japan's turn toward Southeast Asia was predicated by the need for resources. It attacked the Philippines and Malaya on December 8. Despite several hours of warning that

---

vided Japan's codebooks and keys to the Soviets. Hiroaki Juromiya & Andrej Peplonski. "Kōzō Izumi and the Soviet Break of Imperial Japanese Diplomatic Codes." *Intelligence and National Security*, 28 (6), 2013, 769-84.

65. Budiansky, *Battle of Wits*, 167.

66. Ibid, 5-6.

67. Ibid, 217. Andrew, *President's Eyes Only*, 120-122.

68. Pearl Harbor Review, *http://www.nsa.gov/about/cryptologic_heritage/ center_cryptologic_history*.

69. Ibid.

70. Frans B. Bax. "Intelligence Lessons from Pearl Harbor." *Studies in Intelligence* (November 2002), 1-9, cited in the Kent Center Occasional Papers: *Making Sense of Transnational Threats*, 3, No. 1. (Central Intelligence Agency: Center for the Study of Intelligence, October 2004).

71. See Kotani, *Japanese Intelligence*.

the Japanese had attacked Pearl Harbor, confusion hampered American actions in the Philippines. "MacArthur was convinced that Japan would not attack until April 1942. He claimed that by then the Army's defensive preparations in the Philippines would be complete...."[72] "MacArthur's irresponsible optimism" contrasted sharply with US Asiatic Fleet commander Admiral Thomas "Hart's stark realism."[73] Half of the Army Air Force's aircraft were destroyed in the initial Japanese air raids.

Japanese forces invaded British Malaya at the same time. The Japanese War Ministry's espionage Unit 82 had discovered that all of Singapore's defenses faced the sea and the "impregnable fortress" was largely unguarded toward the land. The British had badly assessed Japanese capabilities and, blinded by their biases, ignored what intelligence provided.[74] Britain's strategic plan for Singapore's defense depended upon strategic warning in time to allow the Royal Navy to reinforce the Far East from Europe. On December 10, 1941, Japanese aircraft sank HMS Prince of Wales and HMS Repulse off Malaya. Admiral Sir Tom Phillips adhered to the Admiralty view that capital ships could not be sunk by aircraft, despite contrary evidence from US Brigadier General Billy Mitchell's controversial 1921 tests. Singapore fell by February 15 and the Dutch East Indies fell by March 9.

South Pacific. In January 1942, the Japanese moved on the Australian-administered South Pacific islands beginning with an assault on Rabaul, New Britain. From here, the Japanese advanced on northern New Guinea and into the Solomon Islands to cut the supply lines from the US to Australia and New Zealand.

Turning of the Tide: 1942 – 1943

In January 1942, faced with multiple fronts in the war, the US and Britain agreed on a complete exchange of military intelligence at all levels. By that autumn, a division of labor was agreed concerning SIGINT: Britain would take the lead against Germany and Italy, the US against Japan. Canada joined the Atlantic intelligence effort against the U-boats; and by June, GC&CS was sharing decrypts of U-boat messages. In the Pacific, Australia and the US joined forces in a combined SIGINT effort.[75]

---

72. John Gordon. *Fighting for MacArthur: The Navy and Marine Corps' Desperate Defense of the Philippines* (Annapolis, MD: Naval Institute Press, 2011), 21.

73. Ibid, 23.

74. David, *Military Blunders*, 65. There was also a racist element in viewing the Japanese and their abilities. Collier, *Hidden Weapons*, 247.

75. Hinsley, *British Intelligence*, 115-116.

Mediterranean and North Africa

Despite the multiple defeats suffered in 1941, British forces dealt significant blows to the Axis that year. Intelligence contributed to all of them.

Battle of Cape Matapan. In late March, tipped by SIGINT, the Royal Navy intercepted the Italian fleet south of Crete and sank three cruisers and two destroyers and damaged a battleship. Directing airborne reconnaissance to disguise the true source as sensitive ULTRA intelligence, "...it was the first naval battle in which carrier-based aircraft played a decisive role, and the first battle of any kind in the Second World War in which the timely use of signals intelligence played the decisive role."[76] The Italian fleet withdrew and the battle "consolidated British naval control of the eastern Mediterranean."[77]

Malta. British-held Malta was a constant thorn in the side of the Axis sitting astride the supply lines to North Africa. By June 1941, GC&CS had broken many of the Italian codes; Italian codes based on the Hagelin C38 machine were "a baby compared to Enigma" and were easily broken.[78] A single intercept allowed British destroyers from Malta on April 16, 1941 to sink an entire convoy (five merchant ships and three destroyers) carrying elements of the 15th Panzer Division.[79] Decrypts provided advance notice of every supply convoy from Italy to Libya and allowed British destroyers and aircraft in late 1941 to sink 48 ships resupplying North Africa, stopping reinforcements, and starving the Afrika Korps of fuel.[80]

El Alamein. Rommel's advance deep into Egypt, slowed by British defensive actions, stalled in early July 1942 due to supply shortages and exhaustion. On July 10, he suffered several intelligence-related strategic losses. One was when Australian troops overran his field SIGINT unit, Radio Intercept Company 621. Its capture revealed how successful German SIGINT had been.[81] That same month, the British broke the Wehrmacht's medium-grade field cipher used in North Africa.[82] GC&CS already could read almost daily the Luftwaffe's Enigma for North Africa.[83] The British also informed the US that its diplomatic code used by Colonel Fellers in Cairo was compromised, ending Rommel's "gute Quelle" (good source).[84]

Coupled with the loss of intelligence sources, planted British disinformation as to the Eighth Army's readiness deceived Rommel.[85] Via doubled Axis

---

76. Budiansky, *Battle of Wits*, 186.
77. Hinsley, *British Intelligence*, 73.
78. Hinsley, Cambridge address.
79. Hinsley, *British Intelligence*, 80.
80. Ibid, 182, 194, 237.
81. Ibid, 229 footnote.
82. Ibid, 184.
83. Ibid, 180.
84. Deac, "Intercepted Communications."
85. The British cut their teeth on deception operations in the Middle East. Holt, *The Deceivers*, 240, 244.

agents, a special deception unit fed false OB information to German intelligence. The October 23 British attack on El Alamein surprised the Germans. Rommel was away in Germany. Montgomery was well informed of German reactions via aerial reconnaissance, Enigma decrypts, and the Army Y-Service's tactical SIGINT, which had improved greatly. During battle, Y-Service intercepts and DF were more valuable than Enigma in reflecting unit movements and conditions.[86] RAF reconnaissance and Y-Service intercepts frustrated Rommel's October 28 attempt to counterattack. This "defeat was the turning point of the battle."[87] "The deception operation for Montgomery's offensive [at El Alamein] was one of the great success stories of the war."[88] From then on, Rommel was on the defensive, retreating across Egypt, Libya, and Tunisia.

Operation Torch and Allied Victory in North Africa. On November 8, 1942, Allied forces landed at Casablanca, Oran, and Algiers, in French North Africa, creating a second front for the Afrika Korps. Human and diplomatic sources had helped prepare for Torch.[89] Coordinator of Information William Donovan "... sent a dozen officers to work as 'vice consuls' in several North African ports, where they established networks and acquired information to guide the Allied landings..." Topographical intelligence was good,[90] and the British could read French Air Force codes.[91] Despite the fact that German naval intelligence had broken Allied convoy codes[92] and the Luftwaffe had sighted the Torch convoys entering the Mediterranean five times, 340 ships passed through Gibraltar without loss.[93] Increasingly bold British deception operations were employed as well as deceptive tactical communications. British employed deceptive radio transmissions similar to those of previous Malta relief convoys. German U-boats were ordered to withdraw eastward in reaction and were out of position for the landings.[94] Using doubled Abwehr agents, the British suggested there would be simultaneous attacks against Norway and northern France and a major relief operation for Malta.[95]

Despite the initial success of the Torch landings, once the seasoned Wehrmacht directly opposed the untested US Army, the poor state of US tactical intelligence and command and control was exposed. Poor maps, which led to

---

86. Hinsley, *British Intelligence*, 248.
87. Ibid, 243.
88. Holt, *The Deceivers*, 240, 244.
89. Collier, *Hidden Weapons*, 266; Warner, *Office of Strategic Services*, 8.
90. Hinsley, *British Intelligence*, 260.
91. Ibid, 261.
92. The B-Dienst did not discover the Torch convoys bound for North Africa. "Only twenty-three of the more than one thousand transits to North Africa were intercepted and sunk by U-boats." *http://worldwar2database.com/html/atlantic43_45.htm*. The Germans did not believe the US could carry troops directly from America to North Africa. Collier, Hidden Weapons, 266.
93. Hinsley, *British Intelligence*, 260
94. Ibid, 260.
95. Ben Macintyre, *Double Cross: The True Story of the D-Day Spies* (New York: Crown Publishers, 2012), 126-127.

units getting mixed up, contributed to the February 1943 disaster at Kasserine Pass. Despite intelligence warnings, US II Corps Commander Major General Lloyd Fredendall failed to prepare adequate defenses. US forces were also surprised by the new German Tiger tanks, against which American 37-mm guns had little effect.[96]

With sea lanes from Italy largely cut, German forces relied on Luftwaffe air transport for reinforcements and critical supplies. In April 1943, SIGINT prompted Allied air attacks on concentrated Luftwaffe transports in Tunisia, destroying over 100 transport aircraft, representing almost 25% of the Luftwaffe's transport capacity.[97] These losses, coupled with the transport losses at Stalingrad, crippled Luftwaffe air transport for the rest of the war. On May 8, 1943, the North African campaign ended with the surrender of remaining Axis forces in Tunisia.

Eastern Front

Battle of Stalingrad. From July 1942 to February 1943, the Wehrmacht and the Red Army were locked in the most monumental strategic battle of World War II.[98] Hitler underestimated the capabilities of Russian troops and armor. The Soviet T-34 tank proved to be the equal or superior to German armor until the introduction of the heavier Panther and Tiger tanks later in the war.[99] The mid-November Soviet counteroffensive annihilated the German Sixth Army. By the time of the Casablanca Conference at the end of January 1943, the Allies' strategic situation had changed.

The British Joint Intelligence Committee assessed that the Wehrmacht had lost 40 divisions, 14 at Stalingrad alone.[100] British assessments were aided by a further SIGINT success: the breaking of the German "Fish" radio-teleprinter ciphers, which tied the German High Command (OKW) to major German headquarters. Codenamed "Tunny," Fish intercepts "[t]hough less voluminous than Enigma, and more difficult to decrypt ... made a valuable contribution to Whitehall's knowledge of the strategic situation on the Russian front: it revealed the planning, the [German assessments of the situation] and the supply difficulties of the German commands."[101]

Little is published in English on Soviet intelligence successes in World War II and understanding of Soviet SIGINT is poor. In Stalin's purges of the late 1930s, the "GRU [military intelligence] was smashed to pieces." "... [I] ntelligence officers and undercover agents were recalled in the hundreds and

---

96. David, *Military Blunders*, 348-364.
97. Hinsley, *British Intelligence*, 290.
98. Ibid, 125.
99. David, *Military Blunders*, 197-208.
100. Hinsley, *British Intelligence*, 323.
101. Hinsley, Cambridge address; and Hinsley, *British Intelligence*, 323.

put to death." Consequently, the impact of "the purges makes any rational accounting of the [Soviet] assessment process almost impossible."[102] Distrustful of Britain, after a honeymoon period in 1941, Anglo-Soviet intelligence exchanges diminished.[103]

Battle of Kursk. The British tipped Moscow to the upcoming German offensive, which started on July 4, 1943, although Soviet intelligence probably already had a good idea of the planned German offensive from its own sources. Soviet intelligence had improved significantly by the time of the battle. Aerial reconnaissance of German forces was good, which added to Enigma-based reports from the British Military Mission, reports from the Lucy spy ring,[104] and probably also from Soviet SIGINT. Unknown to London at this time, a "Cambridge Five" Soviet agent within GC&CS, John Cairncross, provided the Soviets verbatim transcripts of Tunny decrypts, thereby confirming that the British had broken German codes.[105] The Soviet counterattack eight days later resulted in the largest tank battle ever fought. Losses at Kursk on both sides were enormous but more significant for Germany. This was the last German strategic offensive on the Eastern Front, and the Soviets had the initiative for the rest of the war.

Turnaround in the Pacific

Battles of the Coral Sea and Midway. A major intelligence breakthrough for the US took place in February 1942 when Navy cryptanalysts began to read Japanese messages sent in the JN-25b naval general-purpose code.[106] In mid-April, SIGINT intercepts revealed that a large Japanese convoy was to enter the Coral Sea in early May. The May 8-9 Battle of the Coral Sea revealed that US tactical intelligence was lacking. Japanese air reconnaissance found the US fleet first, but aerial counterattacks stopped the invasion force headed for Port

---

102. John Erickson, "Soviet Union, 1930-1941," 402-403.

103. Ryan E. Bock. "Anglo-Soviet Intelligence Cooperation, 1941-45: Normative Insights from the Dyadic Democratic Peace Literature," *Intelligence and National Security* 30 (6), 2015, published online (May 21, 2014) *http://dx.doi.org/10.1080/02684527.2014.900267*. Also Robert W. Stephan has written about Soviet military counterintelligence and deceptions operations against the Nazis. See *Stalin's Secret War: Soviet Counterintelligence Against the Nazis, 1941-1945* (Lawrence, KS: University of Kansas Press, 2004).

104. Collier, *Hidden Weapons*, 208-209. The Lucy spy ring had several high-ranking German sources, including Major General Hans Oster, chief of staff to Admiral Wilhelm Canaris, head of the Abwehr. See *The Rote Kapelle* (Central Intelligence Agency, 1984) and Anthony Read and David Fisher. *Operation Lucy: Most Secret Spy Ring of the Second World War* (New York: Coward, McCann, 1981). *Rote Kapelle* ("Red Orchestra") was the German name for the Lucy spy ring. By November 1942, the Soviets also had broken Enigma. Zdzislaw J. Kapera."Summary Report of the State of the Soviet Military Sigint in November 1942 Noticing 'Enigma,'" *Cryptologia* 35 (3), July 2001, 247-56.

105. Cairncross was uncovered as a spy in 1951.

106. Frederick D. Parker, "A Priceless Advantage: US Navy Communications Intelligence and the Battles of Coral Sea, Midway, and the Aleutians," *United States Cryptologic History*, Series IV, World War II, Volume 5 (National Security Agency: Center for Cryptologic History, CH-E32-93-01, 1993), 20.

Moresby on New Guinea's southern coast.[107]

Less than a month later, SIGINT would contribute to a strategic defeat of the Imperial Navy. Admiral Isoruku Yamamoto's decision to attack Midway Island was partially based on the erroneous belief that Doolittle's April 18 raid on Tokyo came from Hawai'i via Midway, not from the carrier Hornet. Doolittle's B-25 bombers were Army Air Corps land-based aircraft and not perceived as capable of taking off from Navy carriers. "The Americans had no inkling of the effect the Doolittle raid had had on the Japanese sense of honour." This led the Japanese to conclude it had to take Hawai'i and Midway was the first step.[108] In July 1940, Congress had passed the "Two Ocean Navy" bill and the US Navy was building 15 battleships, 11 carriers, 54 cruisers, 191 destroyers, and 73 submarines. [109]This led to the Japanese belief it had to destroy the US Pacific fleet early in 1942 before the US' industrial might could become a factor. Yamamoto, therefore, sought a decisive battle against the US Navy.[110]

On May 14, 1942, Fleet Radio Unit Pacific (FRUPAC, Station Hypo), the US naval cryptographic unit in Hawai'i, decrypted a message about an "invasion force" for "AF." "AF" was unknown and within the Navy there were arguments over the Japanese designation "AF" and the Japanese objective. Using a ruse about a water shortage on Midway, subsequent decrypts confirmed that "AF" was Midway Island and gave the timing of attack — June 3 or 4.[111] Due to SIGINT, the US, although outnumbered, was "able to concentrate its forces for a slight advantage where it counted the most, at the scene of the battle." US Admiral Chester Nimitz knew the Japanese objectives, OB, organization, timetable, and direction of attack. "This situation was in sharp contrast to the Battle of the Coral Sea only a few weeks before, when CINCPAC was virtually blind to unfolding events."[112] The result was a stunning victory for the US, four of the first-line Japanese carriers were sunk, their pilots lost. After Midway, the Imperial Navy remained on the defensive for the rest of the war.

"Midway moved code breaking and signals intelligence from an arcane, little understood, and usually unappreciated specialty to the very center of military operations."[113] "Midway, Nimitz said later, 'was essentially a victory of intelligence.'"[114]

Despite the SIGINT revelations, there were intelligence failures that were costly for the Allies in the Pacific. The August 7, 1942 Guadalcanal landings by

---

107. Collier, *Hidden Weapons*, 303-304.
108. Budiansky, *Battle of Wits*, 2.
109. PL 757, Chapter 644, 76th Congress, July 19, 1940.
110. Parker, "Priceless Advantage," 37; Patrick D. Weadon, The Battle of Midway: How Cryptology enabled the United States to turn the tide in the Pacific War (National Security Agency brochure), *http://www.nsa.gov/about/cryptologic_heritage/center_crypt_history/publications/battle_midway.shtml*
111. Budiansky, *Battle of Wits*, 19.
112. Parker, "Priceless Advantage," 61.
113. Budiansky, *Battle of Wits*, 21.
114. Andrew, *President's Eyes Only*, 125.

US Marines caught the Japanese by surprise, but Imperial forces reacted quickly. In the Battle of Savo Island on the night of August 8-9, 1942, a Japanese surface fleet attacked, and poor Allied tactical intelligence and command and control contributed to the loss of one Australian and three US cruisers. Coastwatchers had provided 80 minutes of warning of Japanese air attacks on Guadalcanal during the day but were ineffective at night when the Japanese fleet attacked.[115]

The Counterintelligence War

When war broke out in 1939, Britain was consumed with fear of fifth columnists. The British Security Service (MI5) "managed to neutralize an extensive network of Nazi sympathizers in the United Kingdom by pretending to represent the German government...." John Bingham, aka Jack King, "the British agent was handling six senior-level pro-Nazi operatives — five of them British subjects — who were regularly supplying him with British state secrets believing he was passing them on to the Gestapo. The archives show that, between 1942 and 1945, 'King' helped MI5 identify "scores ... and probably ... hundreds" of devoted Nazi sympathizers in the UK."[116]

SIGINT played an important role in counterintelligence operations. The British Radio Security Service (also known as MI8, which ran the Y-Service) decrypted hasty Abwehr preparations to introduce agents into Britain. With this advanced knowledge, all but one of the 25 sent to England between September and November 1940 were captured. Of the 24 captured, one committed suicide, five were executed, 15 imprisoned, and four became double agents for the British.[117]

Of concern, in early 1940, GC&CS intercepted "Nazi traffic indicating the German ambassador in Italy was receiving messages from the US Embassy in London, including Roosevelt-Churchill correspondence."[118] On May 18, MI5 arrested Tyler Kent, a US Embassy code clerk, for spying. Kent was a "virulent isolationist and a Nazi sympathizer"[119] [120]

By December 1940, GC&CS had broken the codes used between Abwehr headquarters and its stations. By the second half of 1941, the British had so complete a knowledge of the Abwehr's organization and operations throughout Europe, Latin America, and the Middle East that it posed little threat from

---

115. Collier, *Hidden Weapons*, 312-313.

116. "British spies infiltrated Nazi sympathizer groups, wartime files show," *IntelNews.org*, February 28, 2014, *http://intelnews.org/2014/02/28/01-1427/* and BBC News, February 27, 2014, *http://www.bbc.com/news/uk-26365085*.

117. Macintyre, *Double Cross*, 36.

118. Sulick, *Spying in America*, 151.

119. ibid, 149

120. Peter Rand, *Kent's Secret Plot Against FDR, Churchill, and the Allied War Effort* (Lyons Press, Guilford, CT, 2013), 113, 218.

then on.[121]

Using captured Abwehr agents who had been doubled, and recruiting others, the British began to feed the Abwehr false intelligence. An original purpose was to demonstrate that the agents sent were productive and it was unnecessary to send more. However, reading Abwehr Enigma traffic, the British began to see the value of turned agents for strategic deceptions.[122] In January 1941, the British established the Twenty Committee – better known by its Roman numeral designation: XX, or double-cross, to coordinate controlled double agents worldwide. Almost all Axis agents in the Middle East and in the India Theater feeding the Germans in Kabul were under British control.[123] "MI5 ran a double-cross system of labyrinthine complexity...."[124] Before the war, 70 German agents infiltrated into Britain. There were another 220 during the war hidden in the 7,000-9,000 refugees that entered Britain each year. Only three are known to have evaded detection.[125] About the XX system, Churchill wrote: "Tangle within tangle, plot and counter-plot, ruse and treachery, cross and double-cross, true agent, false agent, double agent, gold and steel, the bomb, the dagger and the firing party, were interwoven in many a texture so intricate as to be incredible and yet true."[126]

One of the more interesting double agents was Juan Pujol, who arrived in England in the summer of 1942. A fabricator recruited by MI5 as Agent GARBO, by 1943, Pujol had established a network of 27 mythical sub-agents and sources of information for the Abwehr. He had a "remarkable talent for duplicity" and got the Abwehr to pay for his mythical subagents. He made the XX system self-financing. Project MIDAS "would prove to be one of the most profitable and least known operations of the war." GARBO later would become an important deception vehicle for the Allies.[127]

The British used every means possible in its counterintelligence operations. For example, TRIPLEX was material the British surreptitiously took from foreign diplomatic pouches, often using an attractive woman as a "honey pot." Ironically, the effort was run by Anthony Blunt, a homosexual MI5 officer who was also an NKVD spy.[128] As the war progressed, the British brought the US into its fold. The Office of Strategic Services (OSS) Counterintelligence Branch (X-2) set up at the urging of British officials, was privy to ULTRA materials that the US Army and Navy denied OSS, and developed a close relationship with MI5. In

---

121. Hinsley, *British Intelligence*, 118-119.
122. Hinsley, *British Intelligence*, 119.
123. Holt, *The Deceivers*, 308.
124. Nigel West, *Historical Dictionary of World War II Intelligence*, xxv.
125. Keegan, *Intelligence in War*, 289.
126. Winston S. Churchill, *Thoughts and Adventures* (London, 1991), 55.
127. Macintyre, *Double Cross*, 89, 116.
128. Nigel West & Oleg Tsarev, eds. *TRIPLEX: Secrets from the Cambridge Spies* (New Haven: Yale University Press, 2009).

1943, X-2 was included in the Double Cross System.[129] The end result was that German intelligence, largely dependent upon human agents, was emasculated.

German counterespionage severely hampered Britain's Secret Intelligence Service (MI6).[130] Britain's first attempt to insert spies into France failed. "A high proportion of the Special Operations Executive (SOE) agents in France ... were discovered by German radio counter-intelligence...." All agents dropped into Holland were captured.[131] "Despite its weaknesses, the Abwehr's counterintelligence performed well [early in the war]. Working with the Gestapo it broke the Soviet 'Rote Kapelle' spy ring, penetrated major resistance networks in France, seriously damaged British clandestine operations in Belgium, and controlled and doubled back those in Holland."[132]

In 1939, President Roosevelt assigned to the FBI the principal counterespionage investigative responsibility, with the Army and Navy keeping responsibility for counterintelligence within their services and industrial contractors. In 1937, the Abwehr had acquired the revolutionary Norden bombsight from a German immigrant and sympathizer. It also got the proprietary data for synthetic rubber.[133] Through a double-agent operation (the Sebold case) at the end of July 1941, the FBI rolled up all 33 Nazi agents in one night. Historian G. J. A. O'Toole credits the Sebold case and British information on German operations in the Western Hemisphere with helping convince President Roosevelt to cooperate with British Security Coordination.[134]

The FBI was active throughout Latin America. The German spy ring in Brazil was quickly rounded up after Brazil's August 1942 declaration of war on Germany. However, Axis spies in Argentina "flourished for much of the war," but did not help the German war effort.[135]

In June 1942, the Abwehr landed a sabotage team on Long Island, New York, that a Coast Guard beach patrol discovered; and four more near Vero Beach, Florida. All were caught within weeks. The last spy attempt occurred in November 1944 when a U-boat put ashore two spies in Maine .[136] The British torpedoed the U-boat that landed them and alerted the FBI. Named Operation Pastorius, the saboteurs were sent by the Sicherheitsdienst (SD), the intelligence arm of the SS and Nazi Party, not by the Abwehr. Two of the poorly trained

---

129. Andrew, *President's Eyes Only*, 139-40. Denial of cryptographic intelligence to OSS poisoned later relationships between the newly established CIA and NSA. See [Author's name redacted], "A Fixation on Moles: James J. Angleton, Anatoliy Golitsyn, and the 'Monster Plot': Their Impact on CIA Personnel and Operations." *Studies in Intelligence*, 55, No. 4, December 2011, declassified April 2013.

130. Hinsley, *British Intelligence*, 118.

131. Keegan, *Intelligence in War*, 24.

132. Holt, *The Deceivers*, 108.

133. Major & Oleson, "Espionage Against America," footnote 12.

134. Peter Duffy, *Double Agent* (New York, Scribner, 2014) and G. J. A. O'Toole, *Honorable Treachery: A History of US Intelligence, Espionage, and Covert Action from the American Revolution to the CIA* (New York: The Atlantic Monthly Press, 1991 - reissued in 2015 as paperback), 351.

135. Kahn, "Intelligence in World War II," 15-16.

136. Sulick, *Spying in America*, 144-146.

team, George Dasch and Edward Kerling, "defected" and told the FBI about the operation.

GC&CS SUCCESSES AGAINST ENIGMA AND ITALIAN CIPHERS*

Spring 1940	Initial Luftwaffe Enigma Morse code ciphers decrypted (Red key).
September 1940	Additional Luftwaffe Enigma key broken (Brown).
Winter 1940-41	Enigma decrypts grow from 50 to 250 per day.
February 1941	Luftwaffe Light Blue Enigma key broken (Luftwaffe operations in North Africa).
June 1941	German Navy home waters Enigma broken (Dolphin key).
June 1941	Wehrmacht Enigma key used on the Eastern Front broken (Vulture).
June 1941	Luftwaffe's SIGINT service's Enigma key broken.
June 1941	Enigma decrypts grow to 1,300 per day.
June 1941	Italian C-38m code broken revealing port activity and convoy movements in the Mediterranean to North Africa.
Mid-September to November 1941	Afrika Korps operational Enigma keys broken.
December 1941	Abwehr (German military intelligence) Enigma broken.
January 1942	All new Luftwaffe Enigma keys broken as soon as introduced.
Summer 1942	GC&CS was solving 30 Enigma keys out of 50 in use.
December 1942	GC&CS began to read the new, four-rotor, naval Enigma key (Shark) after a blackout beginning in February 1942.
Early 1943	GC&CS broke "Fish" radio-teleprinter transmissions linking German high command with subordinate armies and army groups.
Mid-1943	Enigma decrypts grow to between 3,000 and 4,000 per day. Italian C-38 and Japanese PURPLE (diplomatic) codes in addition. GC&CS eventually identified over 200 different Enigma keys.
March 1944	The "Fish" link from Berlin to Field Marshal von Rundstedt, commander of forces in France, broken, three months before the Normandy landings.

* Hinsley, *British Intelligence*, 14, 116-7, 439.

Intelligence contributions to Allied Victories

By mid-1943, the tide of battle had turned in the Allies favor in both Europe and the Pacific. Intelligence was playing an increasingly important role in the air war over Germany, the Battle of the Atlantic, Allied invasions in southern Europe, on the Eastern Front, and in the Pacific. Strategic and tactical SIGINT became the backbone of intelligence.

Air War Against Germany

By early 1943, British intercepts of Enigma messages, aircraft radio-telephony, navigational beams, and low-level codes provided a good understanding of Luftwaffe operations and defensive systems as well as providing several hours warning of most air attacks and probable targets. Enigma revealed intelligence on German radars. The February 27-28, 1942 Bruneval Raid obtained key pieces of the Würzburg flak control radar from the French coast and captured a radar technician. Analysis of German radar led to the development of "Window" or chaff, although it was not used for many months for fear of reciprocal action by the Luftwaffe negating Allied air defenses.[137]

Long neglected before the war, the British greatly increased their photoreconnaissance capabilities and established a Central Interpretation Unit (CIU). Intelligence, however, had little impact on British strategic bombing policy before 1943, largely due to the personal predilection of the chief of Bomber Command, Air Chief Marshal Sir Arthur Harris, for nighttime strategic bombing of German cities. The US Eighth Air Force, however, developed a target intelligence organization at High Wycombe to support its daytime operations. The OSS Research & Analysis Branch (R&A) "made one of its biggest contributions in its support to the Allied bombing campaign in Europe." Its Enemy Objectives Unit identified German fighter aircraft factories and synthetic oil production facilities. "When American bombers began hitting synthetic fuel plants, ULTRA intercepts quickly confirmed that the strikes had nearly panicked the German high command." "[S]carcity of aviation fuel all but grounded Hitler's Luftwaffe and, by the end of [1944], diesel and gasoline production had also plummeted, immobilizing thousands of German tanks and trucks."[138] OSS R&A special studies on the German ball bearing industry and synthetic oil production industries aided strategic target priorities.[139]

Battle of the Atlantic

"...[T]he battle ... in the Atlantic between December 1942 and May 1943 was the most prolonged and complex battle in the history of naval warfare.... "[T]he very fact that the struggle was so prolonged and so finely balanced suggests that the ability to read [German] communications must have been an asset of crucial importance to the Allies." "Early warning of U-boat sailings was usually obtained from Home Waters Enigma."[140] "From characteristics such as length, call signs and format, the Allies could on many occasions tell if a radio message from a U-boat was a passage, sinking, sighting, weather, contact, or position report."[141] But by June 1941, GC&CS began to read the U-boat Enigma, which eventually "transformed the situation."[142] Allied convoys were rerouted

---

137. Hinsley, *British Intelligence*, 141, 164-165, 170, and R. V. Jones, 40-1, 239-249.

138. Ibid, 171, 412. See also Richard Overy. *The Bombers and the Bombed: Allied Air War over Europe, 1940-1945* (New York: Viking Penguin, 2013). Warner, *Office of Strategic Services*, 12.

139. O'Toole, *Honorable Treachery*, 414-415.

140. Hinsley, *British Intelligence*, 307, 381.

141. David Syrett, "The Infrastructure of Communications Intelligence: the Allied D/F Network and the Battle of the Atlantic." *Intelligence and National Security* 17 (3), Autumn 2002, 169.

142. Hinsley, *British Intelligence*, 129.

around U-boat wolf pack concentrations. Furthermore, the centralized command and control of U-boats resulted in frequent radio communication that was vulnerable to radio direction finding. "... [O]n many occasions D/F was the only timely communications intelligence available to the Allies on the activities of U-boats." As there were periods when the Naval Enigma was unreadable, there were always delays in decrypting messages – in August 1941, for example, of six to seven days.[143] On February 1, 1942, the German Navy added a fourth wheel to its Enigma machines, greatly complicating it. GC&CS could not solve it for 11 months.[144]

In early 1943, the British learned that the B-Dienst was reading its ciphers and providing U-boats accurate intelligence on convoy movements. March 1943 marked the high point for U-boat sinkings of Allied ships. In mid-March 1943, convoys SC112 and HX229 ran into U-boat wolf packs. "The battle around SC112 and HX229 ... was the costliest of the war." Of 90 merchant ships and 20 warships, 22 were sunk with loss of only two U-boats.[145] In June 1943, Royal Naval Cipher #3 was replaced, which the Germans never broke.[146]

Also by early 1943, GC&CS was reading the naval Enigma key. "Shark" was the designator for the four-rotor naval Enigma machine. "Not only was it believed by the Germans that their codes were so complex that the Allies could never decrypt an encoded radio message in time to be of operational use, but it was also a firmly-held conviction by the [German navy U-boat headquarters] that it would be nearly impossible for the Allies to D/F, systematically and accurately, extremely short high-frequency radio transmission."[147] This was a major German intelligence failure.

At the same time, the British introduced a new anti-surface vessel radar for patrol aircraft. Up until the end of 1942, the British "original [anti-surface vessel] radar had worked ... [but] it was now becoming useless because the Germans equipped their U-boats with receivers to detect it, and thus the approach of our aircraft long before they themselves could detect the U-boat." The new radar operated on a different frequency that U-boats could not detect.[148]

The Royal and US Navies carried out a unified anti-submarine warfare program. "They operated virtually as a single organization." On May 20, 1943, the US Tenth Fleet was established to be a centralized clearing house for all aspects of anti-submarine warfare (ASW), including ULTRA, SIGINT, HFDF, Operations Research, convoy routing, and R&D. Prior to the Tenth Fleet's establishment, the Allies sank an average of four U-boats per month. In the month after its establishment, the Allies sank 41 and an average of 23 per

143. Syrett, "D/F Network," 163, 165.
144. Hinsley, *British Intelligence*, 134.
145. Keegan, *Intelligence in War*, 240.
146. Hinsley, *British Intelligence*, 308-10; Budiansky, *Battle of Wits*, 293.
147. Syrett, "D/F Network," 164.
148. R.V. Jones, *Most Secret War*, 319.

month thereafter. This outstripped the rate of U-boat production for which air reconnaissance provided an accurate estimate.[149] "Germany had a total of 842 U-boats that saw battle. Of these, the Allies sank 781 and captured two...,"[150] with U-boat crews suffering a 70% mortality rate.[151] In late May, U-boats were withdrawn from the mid-Atlantic. In July, a decrypted Japanese diplomatic message (Purple) confirmed the withdrawal and Hitler's hopes for new types of U-boats equipped with better flak, search receivers, and acoustic torpedoes.[152] The U-boat attack on two convoys on September 20, 1943 marked "... their last substantial success in the Battle of the Atlantic."[153]

The Battle of the Atlantic was the longest battle of World War II: 2,073 days. "Without success in the battle of the Atlantic ... there would have been no epic victories at El Alamein or in Burma – and there would have been no 'Crusade in Europe,' launched via the Normandy landings of June 1944."[154]

Invasions of Sicily and Italy

Sicily. Allied deceptions played a major role in Operation Husky, the invasion of Sicily. Field Marshal Wilhelm Keitel, chief of the German Supreme Command of the Armed Forces (Oberkommando der Wehrmacht, OKW), believed the Allied OB was twice its actual from false information fed through British controlled agents.[155] On April 30, 1943, in Operation Mincemeat, a British submarine set ashore off Spain a body, purported to be Royal Marines Major William Martin. He was carrying dispatches and high-level correspondence suggesting the Allies' targets were Sardinia and the Balkans. Mincemeat played to a known Hitler fear of a Balkans invasion. ULTRA of May 12 indicated that the Germans bought the deception.[156] Additionally, Operation Solo was a deception threatening an attack against Norway. Solo played to Hitler's obsession with Norway known through ULTRA. "Throughout 1943, the Germans kept twelve divisions idle in Norway that would have been far more useful in Italy or the Ukraine."[157] "At Husky D-Day [July 9-10] there were only two German divisions in Sicily in addition to the Italian forces there."[158] SIGINT and photo-reconnaissance were used to plan pre-landing attacks on Luftwaffe bases that

---

149. Andrew, *President's Eyes Only*, 136; US Navy, United States Tenth Fleet: From Anti-submarine Warfare to Cyberspace, *http://www.public.navy.mil/fcc-c10f/Pages/ustenthfleethistory.aspx)*. Kahn, "Intelligence in World War II," 8.
150. US Navy, Tenth Fleet.
151. Roberts, review, 2.
152. Hinsley, *British Intelligence*, 319, 379.
153. Ibid, 383-384.
154. US Navy, Tenth Fleet.
155. Holt, *The Deceivers*, 379.
156. Hinsley, *British Intelligence*, 341.
157. Holt, *The Deceivers*, 493.
158. Ibid, 379.

disrupted its ability to react.[159]

Italy. SIGINT and photoreconnaissance provided good intelligence on German OB and defenses before the September 9, 1943 American landing at Salerno, a week after the British Eighth Army landed, largely uncontested, on the boot of Italy at Calabria. Faced with stiff German resistance that stalled the Allied advance, the Allies outflanked the Germans by landing up the coast at Anzio, south of Rome, on January 22, 1944. Battlefield intelligence and an ULTRA intercept revealed Field Marshal Albert Kesselring's plan to attack the US Army struggling to expand the Anzio beachhead, which was frustrated by superior Allied firepower. The February 19, 1944 Allied counterattack caught Kesselring by surprise. On June 4, the Allies entered Rome. ULTRA showed Hitler was reluctant to give up Italian territory despite his generals' recommendations.[160] However, in "the day-to-day fighting the Army Y-Service [tactical intercepts] yielded even more intelligence than high-grade SIGINT, and it was no doubt more valuable to the operational authorities."[161]

The Pacific

"By early 1943 ... naval cryptanalysts had mastered the JN25 system so thoroughly that they were able to decrypt all of its variants almost without interruption for the remainder of the war."[162]

US Submarine Warfare. "Regular reading of the Japanese convoy codes gave American submarines an almost total mastery over the Japanese supply lines...."[163] In June 1943, the US broke the codes of the Japanese Army water transport organization – the Army's navy.[164] The Office of Naval Intelligence apparently stole codes from Japanese Consulates in New York City and San Francisco. The record of this is fragmentary, largely based on a June 8, 1942 memorandum from Commander Alvin Kramer. Before the war, the Navy was admonished not to undertake clandestine operations against Japanese diplomatic facilities by the Army, which was fearful of compromising its success against the Purple code. NSA historian Robert Benson concludes the Japanese merchant shipping and attaché codes were obtained through these means.[165]

As Army Chief of Staff Marshall reported: "Operations in the Pacific are

---

159. Hinsley, *British Intelligence*, 339-347.

160. Ibid, 526.

161. Ibid, 378.

162. Andrew, *President's Eyes Only*, 125.

163. Budiansky, *Battle of Wits*, 319.

164. Ibid, 325.

165. Robert Louis Benson, *A History of US Communications Intelligence during World War II: Policy and Administration, Volume 8*, World War II, Series IV, United States Cryptologic History (National Security Agency: Center for Cryptologic History, 1997), 46. "The Flag Officers Code was never solved by the Americans." NSA, Pearl Harbor Review – JN25. *https://www.nsa.gov/about/cryptologic_heritage/center_crypt_history/pearl_harbor_review/jn25.shtml*.

largely guided by the information we obtain of Japanese deployments. We know their strength in various garrisons, the rations and other stores continuing [sic] available to them, and what is of vast importance, we check their fleet movements and the movements of their convoys. The heavy losses reported from time to time which they sustain by reason of our submarine action largely results from the fact that we have the sailing dates and routes of their convoys and can notify our submarines to lay in wait at the proper point."[166]

Pacific Campaigns. At the end of January 1942, the Navy's SIGINT site at Cavite ("Cast") in the Philippines was evacuated to Java and then to Australia, where it was reconstituted as Fleet Radio Unit – Melbourne (FRUMEL), a joint US-Australian effort. On August 7, 1942, US Marines landed on Guadalcanal and found a buried copy of the newly instituted JN-25c9 code and cipher books. It was finally read in November 1942. On April 14, 1943, a decrypt revealed Imperial Navy Commander Yamamoto planned to visit Bougainville, Solomon Islands. Four days later, 18 long-range US P-38 fighters shot down his plane. [167]

By mid-1943, American naval and air power had forced the Japanese largely onto the defensive. In May, the Alaskan islands were recaptured, as was Tarawa in the Gilbert Islands in the central Pacific. By November, US forces had invaded Bougainville, part of the Japanese defensive perimeter for its major base at Rabaul, New Britain. SIGINT tipped off the Navy to a planned Japanese reinforcement of New Guinea. The subsequent March 2-4 Battle of the Bismarck Sea, in which Allied air forces and PT boats sank all eight transports and five escorts, ended Japanese attempts to reinforce Lae, a major New Guinea port, by sea.

"No cryptologic continuity on Japanese [Army] communications had been built up before Pearl Harbor, principally because of the impossibility of intercepting the existing Japanese military nets either in the home islands or on the mainland of East Asia. It was not until April 1943 that an initial entry was made into one of the principal Japanese Army systems."[168]

General Douglas MacArthur, commander of the Southwest Pacific, however, did not embrace SIGINT or the OSS. "General Douglas MacArthur in the South Pacific and Admiral Chester Nimitz in the Central Pacific saw little use for OSS."[169] MacArthur's preference was clearly slanted toward visual reconnaissance, including both aerial and coast watcher sources; he seldom passed on SIGINT-related intelligence received from FRUMEL.[170] Nonetheless, SIGINT played an important role in his campaigns. A watershed occurred when the

---

166. Marshall to Dewey, September 25, 1944, SRH-043, cited in Andrew, *President's Eyes Only*, 142-143.

167. Budiansky, *Battle of Wits*, 325.

168. John Patrick Finnegan & Romana Danysh, Military Intelligence, Army Lineage Series, Center of Military History, (Washington, DC: United States Army, 1998), 78, *http://www.history.army.mil/html/books/060/60-13-1/cmhPub_60-13-1.pdf*.

169. Warner, *Office of Strategic Services*, 8.

170. Parker, "Priceless Advantage," footnote 42, 19.

Australians captured the Japanese Twentieth Division's entire cryptologic library in January 1944 at Sio, New Guinea. "From the time of the capture of the Sio material until the end of the war, the Allies read approximately 2,000 messages a day."[171] SIGINT's greatest contribution to the New Guinea campaign was the discovery of a Japanese convoy carrying reinforcements. In late April and early May 1944, US submarines sank the convoy, causing the Japanese to lose all of the equipment and 4,000 troops frustrating the Japanese plan to reinforce western New Guinea and allowing MacArthur to speed up his western New Guinea offensive.[172]

Geography of the Pacific helped Allied SIGINT. Isolated on islands, the Japanese had to communicate over the air code change instructions in the old code, which gave Allied cryptographers the instructions at the same time.[173]

China. "At least a dozen American intelligence units operated in China over the course of the war, all of them competing for sources, access, and resources...."[174] The US Navy enjoyed a better relationship with the Chinese than did either the British, who the Chinese suspected of having further colonial ambitions, or the OSS. US naval intelligence placed personnel in China to provide essential weather information to the Pacific fleet. Under the Sino-American Cooperative Organization (SACO), coast watchers also provided information on Japanese movements and conducted sabotage in conjunction with Nationalist Chinese guerillas.[175] "Tai Li [head of the Nationalist Chinese intelligence service] demanded that American intelligence operations in China be run—wherever possible—by the office of Capt. Milton E. Miles, the commander of [SACO]." "Gen. Claire L. Chennault, creator of the famous 'Flying Tigers' and chief of US air power in China, needed accurate target intelligence. OSS filled his need through an 'Air and Ground Forces Resources Technical Staff.'"[176]

Japanese intelligence was "uncoordinated, unsophisticated, and inept." The Imperial General Staff had no intelligence organization. Strategic decisions were made by a committee unaffected by intelligence. There were separate Army and Navy intelligence offices, plus other intelligence related organizations in the Foreign Ministry and Greater East Asia Ministry, which disseminated their reports separately. The Japanese relied heavily on espionage and fifth column reports, although it enjoyed extensive SIGINT success against Chinese codes and limited success against British and US codes. Japanese HUMINT collapsed

171. Sharon A. Maneki, "The Quiet Heroes of the Southwest Pacific Theater: An Oral History of the Men and Women of CBB and FRUMEL," *United States Cryptologic History*, Series IV, World War II, Volume 7 (National Security Agency: Center for Cryptologic History, reprinted 2007), 23, 28.
172. Ibid, vii.
173. Ibid, 38.
174. Warner, *Office of Strategic Services*, 37.
175. Linda Kush, *The Rice Paddy Navy: US Sailors Undercover in China; Espionage and Sabotage Behind Japanese Lines During World War II* (Oxford: Osprey Publishing, 2013, Kindle edition); Warner, *Office of Strategic Services*, 37.
176. Warner, *Office of Strategic Services*, 37.

in the US with the FBI arrests after Pearl Harbor, and the FBI's efforts limited Japanese collection activities in Latin America. The geography of the Pacific with American control of the sea and air "meant in the later stages of the war the Japanese ... were forced to rely on intelligence reports from Berlin and neutral capitals, plus radio traffic analysis and inferences from American sea and air activity."[177]

The Great Deception: "Fortitude"
and the Normandy Landings – 1944

The Normandy landings ("Overlord") were a daring and risky Allied undertaking the Nazi defenders fully expected. The invasion's success can be attributed to good Allied intelligence and intelligence-enabled deception. "Most secret sources" (i.e., ULTRA intercepts) and "special means" (i.e., controlled enemy agents) were the two most powerful tools of the trade and were the keys to Allied success with deception. There had been extensive Allied deception operations in all theaters of the war. In 1942-1943, the strategic aim was to keep as many Axis forces as possible away from the Eastern and Mediterranean Fronts. In 1944, the aim was to encourage the Nazis to hold back as many forces as possible to repel a future attack at the Pas de Calais.[178] In June 1943, Thomas "Tar" Robertson, operational chief of the XX program, reached the startling conclusion that every single German agent in Britain was actually under his control. The XX system was, in fact, a weapon.[179]

In November 1943, the Japanese military attaché in Berlin sent a 32-part report to Tokyo on the Western Wall defenses, which "... gave a detailed account of the numbers and sites of every element in the coastal defense system, from the heaviest coastal battery down to grenade throwers...."[180] In the second half of the war, the Japanese Embassies in Europe were to prove of immense intelligence value because they were repeating back to Tokyo their versions of German assessments and their knowledge of German intentions. The MAGIC intercepts were almost as valuable on some subjects (such as the Normandy landings) as were the direct ULTRA intercepts from the German horse's mouth.[181] Little did the Japanese know they were sharing this detailed intelligence with the Allied invasion planners.

"Fortitude South" was the deception plan for the Normandy landings. Its strategic aim was to disguise the date of attack, exact location, and its nature – to raise in the Germans' minds whether it was the "real" invasion or a pre-

---

177. Holt, *The Deceivers*, 61, 109-112.
178. Ibid, 98.
179. Macintyre, *Double Cross*, 1, 4.
180. Hinsley, *British Intelligence*, 436-437.
181. Hinsley, Cambridge address.

liminary feint. "Fortitude North" was related to a potential invasion of Norway from northern Britain, playing to a known fear of Hitler. Operation Copperhead used a look-alike actor to imitate Field Marshal Bernard Montgomery who was paraded before a known German agent in Gibraltar just before D-Day, suggesting an invasion was not imminent. Operation Ironside threatened an attack in the Bordeaux region of southwestern France from southern Britain and the US.[182]

SIGINT revealed that the "Germans greatly exaggerated Allied strength in Britain in 1943."[183] Allied deception planning played to this misperception. Deception planners created the First US Army Group (FUSAG) under then Lieutenant General George Patton, believed by the Germans to be one of the Allies best combat generals, with 150,000 men in southeastern England. A "[h]uge effort went into physical deception, camouflage, and signals traffic, but the Germans were not really paying attention. And why would they? They had numerous spies on the ground providing copious evidence of exactly what was going on." Principal among the deception agents were Roman Garby-Czerniawski (Brutus), a Polish captive, recruited by the Abwehr and sent to Britain who then volunteered to the British; and Pujol (Garbo), who ran a fictional network of sub-agents.[184] German aerial reconnaissance over Britain was very limited. Thus much of the visual and SIGINT deception efforts were wasted.

In March 1944, GC&CS broke the Fish radio-teletype link between Field Marshal Karl von Rundstedt, commander of German forces in the west, and Berlin.[185] This new SIGINT source provided high-level German plans and intentions and estimates of the invasion threat. "The Allied deception plan that would prove crucial in the success of D-Day owes a great debt to Bletchley Park's breaking of the German teletype machine."[186]

On April 20, 1944, a Japanese naval attaché message reported that the Germans expected the invasion would be centered on Boulogne and revealed Rommel's strategy to defeat the landings on the beach.[187] On May 27, nine days before D-Day, Japanese Ambassador Baron Hiroshi Ōshima lunched with Hitler. On June 1, Ōshima's intercepted message to Tokyo confirmed that Allied deceptions had led the Germans to overestimate Allied strength and that Hitler believed the major assault would be at the Pas de Calais.[188] Enigma decrypts revealed that "... the Germans did not believe in the few days before D-Day that the landings were imminent, and they remained uncertain of their destination." Meanwhile Allied SIGINT, photoreconnaissance, and resistance

---

182. Macintyre, *Double Cross*, 235.
183. Holt, *The Deceivers*, 481
184. Macintyre, *Double Cross*, 227.
185. Hinsley, *British Intelligence*, 439.
186. Budiansky, *Battle of Wits*, 315.
187. Hinsley, *British Intelligence*, 448, 460.
188. Macintyre, *Double Cross*: 309; Hinsley, *British Intelligence*, 449.

reports "enabled the Allies to make an all but totally accurate assessment of the German order of battle in the Overlord area on D-Day ..."[189] and to cripple heavy defenses. Photoreconnaissance was used extensively to target German batteries. On D-day, only four batteries were active in the assault area; 21 had been damaged or destroyed.[190]

Appreciating the importance of intelligence, on D-Day, the Allies bombed the German's jammers and knocked out the headquarters of the Luftwaffe's SIGINT service and large portions of their radar network.[191] Bombing and jamming reduced German radar coverage to 5%.[192] Knocking out the Luftwaffe's SIGINT capabilities contributed to the lack of air attacks against the D-Day forces. As the Germans had lost their meteorological ships, they did not expect landings in such bad weather as there was on June 4/5.[193] Enigma decrypts and intercepted ship-to-ship tactical communications allowed the Allies to map the German minefields off the beaches "which proved to be of crucial importance for the success of the landings." Air attacks crippled German mine-laying boats.[194]

While Overlord was a tactical success, the German forces positioned near the Pas de Calais posed an existential threat to the Allied armies in Normandy. Allied deception efforts continued after the Normandy landings emphasizing the mythical threat from Patton's FUSAG. "German troops could be redeployed from Calais to Normandy in a matter of days: every hour the deception held firm would be measured in thousands of lives saved; if it failed, the butcher's bill would soar." "Allied casualty rates averaged 6,674 a day for the seventy-seven days of the Normandy campaign. Those numbers would have been far higher, had it not been for..." the XX operators.[195]

In early July, Japanese diplomatic messages revealed that the Germans still believed Patton's FUSAG would land at the Pas de Calais with 23 divisions. A July 7 Japanese naval mission message reported there were 30 divisions in England waiting to land. And a July 10 Japanese ambassadorial message to Tokyo reaffirmed that belief.[196] The continued deception delayed a massive German reaction for over a month allowing the Allies to greatly build their strength.

Post mortem studies of the D-Day landings "attributed [its] remarkable success ... at so little cost in large measure to the excellence of the intelligence on the defences and the topography of the invasion area."[197] This was in

---

189. Ibid, 450-453.
190. Ibid, 466.
191. R.V. Jones, *Most Secret War*, 411-412.
192. Hinsley, *British Intelligence*, 467.
193. Ibid, 468.
194. Ibid, 461-2.
195. Macintyre, *Double Cross*, 6.
196. Hinsley, *British Intelligence*, 496, 500.
197. Ibid, 471. Not to be overlooked were the contributions in Normandy of the French Resistance and the 93 Jedburgh teams operated by the OSS and SOE. Warner, *Office of Strategic Services*, 16.

sharp contrast to the intelligence of the August 1942 Dieppe raid. The Naval commander ignored warnings based on SIGINT of German ships in the area and many landing craft were caught offshore and the Dieppe defenders were alerted to the landing. Poor topographical intelligence resulted in the Allied tanks being unable to scale the rocky beach. Of the 5,000 raiders involved, 70% were killed, wounded, or captured in the debacle.[198] One failing in Normandy, however, was not foreseeing the challenge of the countryside's hedgerows. The Allies' advance was stalled several days until tanks could be outfitted with plows to break through these obstacles.[199]

Six weeks after the Normandy landings, on August 15, 1944, the Allied landings ("Dragoon") in southern France achieved total surprise. OSS agents provided detailed intelligence on troop dispositions, defense, fortifications, and minefields. The 7th Army G-2, Colonel William Quinn, later said "We knew everything ... and where every German was. And we clobbered them."[200] The Germans were concerned about a landing at Genoa, Italy, another Allied deception story.[201]

The Drive Across France

Trapped between the advancing Allied armies and hounded by the French resistance, aided by joint British SOE-Free French-American OSS Jedburgh teams, the deterioration of the German position in Normandy resulted in much increased Enigma traffic and intercepted tactical communications.[202] By the time of the Third Army's breakout (Operation Cobra) Patton (no longer the "commander" of the mythical FUSAG in Britain) had become an astute consumer of SIGINT. ULTRA provided extremely accurate OB information, often having exact figures down to the man and the gun for German units facing the Third Army. "An army has never moved as fast and as far as the Third Army in its drive across France, and ULTRA was invaluable every mile of the way." It is unclear whether Patton had much knowledge of communications intelligence (COMINT) or exposure to it during the North African or Sicilian campaigns, but he learned its worth in the drive across Western Europe after the D-Day landings.[203] Tactical SIGINT was welcomed when it disclosed specific enemy intentions (e.g. a maneuver or attack) in time for commanders to prepare an effective response. It was highly valued if it revealed specific vulnerabilities (e.g., shortages in either fuel or certain ammunition) of enemy units within reach that

---

198. David, *Military Blunders*, 103, 115.
199. Observation of General James A. Van Fleet, then a colonel commanding the 8th Infantry Regiment on D-Day, as told to Joseph Goulden. Private e-mail in author's library.
200. Waller, *Wild Bill Donovan*, 265.
201. Holt, *The Deceivers*, 619-620.
202. Hinsley, *British Intelligence*, 506.
203. Based upon a contemporary report written by Major Warrack Wallace, "General Patton and COMINT" *http://www.nsa.gov/about/cryptologic_heritage/center_crypt_ history/almanac/index.shtml#article3.*

a commander could then exploit. But by far, the bulk of SIGINT that mattered to ground forces consisted of enemy unit identifications and DF fixes.[204] The Jedburgh teams often provided vital topographical and OB intelligence to rapidly advancing Allied forces that outran their map and intelligence support.[205]

From SIGINT, the Allies learned that German ground troops were abandoning southern and southwestern France and were returning to defend the Fatherland.[206] ULTRA also revealed German stay-behind agents. OSS X-2 and Allied agents captured most and some turned into additional "special means."[207] But with the collapsing German Army, strategic deception opportunities dwindled.

Eastern Front

Two weeks after the Normandy landings, the Red Army opened a coordinated major offensive in the center of the Eastern Front, taking Minsk, and giving the Germans a defeat on the scale of Stalingrad. By mid-July, the Soviets launched two more major attacks. By mid-August, the Germans abandoned Estonia and Latvia on the Baltic coast. The southern offensive resulted in the collapse of Germany's allies, Romania and Bulgaria; and, by the end of September, the Soviets entered Yugoslavia. Budapest was captured in mid-February. Soviet intelligence had improved greatly during the war – the Soviet Air Force had expanded its photoreconnaissance capabilities and Moscow was reading German communications – and contributed to effective deception operations against the Wehrmacht.[208]

The Soviets had a large number of GRU and NKVD agents inserted with Tito's Yugoslav partisans and other teams in Hungary. Tito's partisans fought both the Germans and their Chetnik collaborators. GC&CS SIGINT and reports from the SOE teams in Yugoslavia provided the British with details of the partisan infighting.[209] Hungarian counterintelligence left the SOE operations largely alone and cooperated with MI6 against the USSR in the conflict's later stages.[210]

---

204. George F. Howe, "American Signal Intelligence in Northwest Africa and Western Europe," *United States Cryptologic History*, Series IV, Volume I (Center for Cryptologic History, National Security Agency, 2010, completed in 1980, declassified in 2010), 170.

205. Will Irwin, *The Jedburghs: The Secret History of the Allied Special Forces, France 1944* (New York: Public Affairs, 2005).

206. Howe, "American Signal Intelligence," 187.

207. Holt, *The Deceivers*, 648.

208. The. Zdzislaw J. Kapera, "Summary Report of the State of the Soviet Military Sigint in November 1942 Noticing 'ENIGMA.'" *Cryptologia* 35, No. 3 (July 2011), 247-56. See also Robert W. Stephan's *Stalin's Secret War: Soviet Counterintelligence Against the Nazis, 1941-1945* (Lawrence, KS: University of Kansas Press, 2003). Reviews at *http://intellit.muskingum.edu/russia_folder/russiawwii_folder/russiawwii-genk-z.html*.

209. Hinsley, *British Intelligence*, 357.

210. Author's notes from lecture by Dr. Laszlo Ritter, Hungarian Academy of Sciences, at the Cryptologic History Symposium, Johns Hopkins Applied Physics Laboratory, 2013.

Final Surprises and Allied Victory in Europe: 1944 – 1945

Despite Allied successes, German military resistance remained formidable. Hitler hoped for new weapons to reverse the tide of war. And despite overwhelming material resources and insight into German plans and intentions, intelligence failures contributed to costly Allied reverses.

V-Weapons: British intelligence received hints of new long-range Nazi weapons from the initial Oslo report in 1939. In December 1942, a Danish chemical engineer reported to MI6 that rockets with a 200-kilometer range were being developed at Peenemünde, Usedom Island, on the Baltic coast. Bugging of two German general officer POWs mention a 200-kilometer rocket program.[211] In April 1943, the first photoreconnaissance of Peenemünde in almost a year revealed a "torpedo-line" object. A June Enigma decrypt referred to winged rockets and London as a target. One of Allen Dulles' covert agents in the Abwehr provided confirmation of the V-1 and V-2 programs.[212] The accumulating intelligence prompted a heavy bomber raid on Peenemünde on the night of August 17/18 that delayed the rocket program up to six months.[213] Days later, a V-1 winged drone crashed on Sweden's Bornholm Island, and the Swedes provided intelligence about the wreckage to the British. In September 1943, R. V. Jones, the chief of scientific intelligence for the Air Ministry and MI6, warned of the construction of rocket launch sites in Belgium and northern France, on which the French Resistance provided much of the intelligence..[214] The first V-1 attacks began a week after the Normandy landings.

Tactical SIGINT gave British air defenses advanced notice of most of the V-1 launches, often 70 minutes before acquisition by radar. The XX Committee employed doubled agents' reports to deceive the Germans as to the accuracy of the V-1s. From January 1941 to September 10, 1944, there was no Luftwaffe aerial reconnaissance of London, so the Germans were reliant on the false agent reports. From September to December 1944, of the 1,300 V-1s launched, only 66 reached London. Air defenses, tipped off by SIGINT and aided by radar, destroyed 60% of those crossing the English Channel.[215]

There was very little intelligence on the V-2.[216] An Enigma decrypt indicated one test flew over 160 miles (250 kilometers) and impacted in Sidlice, Poland. In June 1944, an errant V-2 fell on Sweden. The Swedes provided the British pieces in exchange for jammers and the results of British analysis. But there ensued a technical debate within the British establishment over the range, warhead, and accuracy of V-2s. Some did not believe such a weapon was possible. Certainly the

---

211. For insight into how the British tapped high-ranking German POWs see Sönke Neitzel (ed.), *Tapping Hitler's Generals: Transcripts of Secret Conversations, 1942-45* (London: Frontline Books, 2013).
212. Kahn, "Intelligence in World War II," 18.
213. R. V. Jones, *Most Secret War*, 360-361.
214. Ibid, 364.
215. Ibid, 421-2. Hinsley, *British Intelligence*, 567-570.
216. Ibid, 571.

British had never attempted such a weapon.[217] On September 8, 1944, the first V-2 landed on London. Their launch pads were hard to detect in aerial photos. Radar gave only a few minutes warning. Of the 1,190 V-2s launched against Britain, 1,054 landed in the country, half on London.[218]

Market Garden: Despite its successes in France, Allied intelligence was fallible. A failure to heed intelligence warnings contributed to the disastrous September 1944 airborne invasion of the Netherlands. Enigma decrypts, Dutch underground reports, and aerial reconnaissance all indicated elements of four German divisions, including two Panzer, in the target area of Arnhem. One Enigma message indicated that the Germans believed Arnhem to be the Allies' objective.[219] Field Marshal Montgomery, the British commander, believing that the Germans would not put up a fight, dismissed the intelligence. Operation Market Garden, launched on September 17, was a failure. After heavy losses, the British and American airborne forces retreated on September 25. The Market Garden disaster is a case when bias reigned over evidence. The British corps intelligence officer was dismissed for insisting that the intelligence was accurate.[220]

Battle of the Bulge: On December 16, 1944, under heavy overcast, the Wehrmacht launched a massive counterattack against the thinly held Allied line in the Ardennes Forest of Belgium and Luxembourg. Preoccupied by its own offensive against the Siegfried Line,[221] the Allies were caught by surprise. Ignored intelligence indicators and mistaken judgments, coupled with good German security, contributed to the Allied surprise.

Decrypted Japanese diplomatic messages from Berlin forewarned of a planned German offensive as early as late August. By the end of September, British intelligence was aware of a major German mobilization of up to 60 divisions. SIGINT revealed plans for a major Luftwaffe deployment to the west of close support aircraft. POW interrogations and civilian eyewitness reports indicated a forthcoming offensive.[222] In October, the Abwehr and SD changed cipher procedures; their messages were not recovered until December, too late for any warning.[223] Also, the Germans practiced strict radio discipline in early December, often an indicator of a coming offensive. But British assessments underestimated German strengths and plans and did not imagine the risks Hitler would take.[224] Recent revelations suggest that Hitler was a heavy user of drugs, including methamphetamines that give a feeling of euphoria but are

217. R.V. Jones, *Most Secret War*, 430-461.
218. Ibid, 459; Hinsley, *British Intelligence*, 571.
219. Ibid, 544.
220. David, *Military Blunders*, 117-132.
221. From mid-September, the US and Germany were locked in a struggle of attrition in the Hurtgen Forest area south of Aachen and north of the Ardennes.
222. Hinsley, *British Intelligence*, 550-66 and Collier, *Hidden Weapons*, 297-299.
223. Holt, *The Deceivers*, 126-127.
224. Hinsley, *British Intelligence*, 550-66.

mentally destructive. How this may have affected his risk-taking in the Battle of the Bulge is open to speculation. Evidence of this is contained in a US military intelligence dossier, but the source(s) of the intelligence are not public.[225] Furthermore, Allied euphoria at the collapsing German Army reinforced old habits of ignoring intelligence.

By December 19, SIGINT revealed to the Allies that the Wehrmacht was headed for the Meuse River and the port of Antwerp. Allied ground and air counterattacks and German supply difficulties finally stalled the offensive. The battle, the biggest and bloodiest battle fought by the US during the war, lasted until the end of January 1945; 19,000 GIs were killed and 70,000 wounded.[226] SIGINT was not decisive in the Battle of the Bulge, but did give the Allies an advantage.[227] Allied attempts at deception, however, were "defeated by the [Allied Military Police] radio net, which ... handed the true information to the Germans 'on a silver platter.'" German tactical SIGINT was good.[228]

The results of Hitler's Ardennes offensive were even worse than his generals had feared. Although it had delayed Eisenhower's planned drive into Germany by about six weeks, it had resulted in well over 100,000 German casualties, over 600 ruined armored vehicles, and a loss of over 1,000 aircraft. German resources had been largely wasted, and that meant that when the Russians and the Western Allies renewed their attacks, both would be able to advance more rapidly. The tying-up of the German reserves in the Ardennes offensive proved a godsend for the Red Army, which opened its winter offensive on the Eastern Front on January 12, 1945, eventually enabling it to reach its principal objective, Berlin, before the Western Allies.[229]

In the final months of the war, OSS recruited "volunteer" agents from Axis POWs and inserted more than 200 into Germany. "[T]he data they collected on industrial and military targets significantly aided the final Allied air and ground assaults on Germany.[230] In the spring of 1945, high-ranking German officials began to explore secret peace arrangements. OSS Switzerland chief Allen Dulles brokered the surrender of German forces in Italy in April, saving many lives.[231]

In the final weeks of the war, "[t]he Allies had obtained good tactical intelligence during these advances from [photoreconnaissance], POW, and especially from Y [operational tactical SIGINT], the enemy's VHF links supplying a

225. The Independent, "Hitler was 'a regular user of crystal meth,' American Military Intelligence dossier reveals," October 25, 2014. For a physician's perspective see D. Doyle, "Adolf Hitler's Medical Care," *Journal of the Royal College of Physicians of Edinburgh* 35 (1), 75-82.
226. Stephen E. Ambrose, *Americans at War* (Oxford, MS: University Press of Mississippi, 1997), 52.
227. Hinsley, *British Intelligence*, 550-566.
228. Holt, *The Deceivers*, 658.
229. Franz Kurowski, "Dietrich and Manteuffel," in Correlli Barnett (ed.), *Hitler's Generals* (New York: Grove Weidenfeld, 1989), 432.
230. Warner, *Office of Strategic Services*, 22.
231. Ibid.

steady flow of information in plain language."[232] By late April, the speed of the Allied advance and overwhelming superiority made operational intelligence largely superfluous.[233] Germany surrendered on May 8, 1945.

Post Conflict Lingering Concerns. As the war drew to a close, two topics of great interest prompted formation of separate intelligence task forces. One was ALSOS, the other was TICOM.

The ALSOS (Greek for "grove") mission focused on capturing German scientific and technical knowledge, especially information on German R&D on atomic weapons and biological research. Its ostensible medical mission was to camouflage and divert attention from the primary objective of atomic intelligence.[234]

The technological superiority of German tanks, jet aircraft, and rockets had caused the Allies great concern.[235] The Target Intelligence Committee (TICOM) mission also included capturing German cryptographic information and equipment. One revelation was the discovery of a hitherto unknown Nazi Party SIGINT unit separate from all others under the control of Hermann Göring. Another was a German machine for breaking Soviet codes.[236]

Victory in the Pacific

By late 1944, overwhelming American naval and air power forced the Japanese onto the defensive on most fronts. In June 1944, US Marines captured the islands of Saipan, Guam, and Tinian in the Marianas campaign, which became B-29 bases for the strategic bombing of the Japanese homeland islands. SIGINT allowed the Army Air Forces to exact a high price on Japanese ships and men going to Leyte Island, Philippines. The October 23-26 Battle of Leyte Gulf, the largest naval battle in history, broke the back of the remaining Japanese fleet, assuring Allied naval and air superiority in the Pacific. After this, the Japanese had to abandon large garrisons that they could no longer resupply.[237]

In the Philippines, guerillas controlled almost half of the country and provided MacArthur with much of his intelligence on the Japanese. In Decem-

---

232. VHF is very high frequency, referring to tactical radios. Hinsley, *British Intelligence*, 610.

233. Ibid, 611.

234. From a captive "...we obtained the first substantial picture of German BW activities. It was a totally amateurish profile and allowed us pretty well to exclude any danger from the use of such weapons in the final phase of the conflict. This essentially coincided with the findings of our physicist colleagues concerning nuclear developments." "An analysis of the assembled documents confirmed our earlier judgment that German interest in BW had been short-lived and amateurish." Carlo Henze, M.D. "Recollections of a Medical Intelligence Officer in World War II." *Bulletin of the New York Academy of Medicine* 49 (11), November 1973, 966, 970-971, 973.

235. TICOM Archive: *Secret Intelligence in Nazi Germany*. http://www.ticomarchive.com/ home/origin-of-ticom

236. https://www.nsa.gov/public_info/_files/european_axis_sigint/Volume_7_goerings_ research_bureau. pdf. Review of James Bamford's book *Body of Secrets*, *Cryptologia* XI (3), 129-141 (July 1987). See also http://www.ticomarchive.com/iv-case-studies/russian-fish.

237. Maneki, *Quiet Heroes*, 38.

ber, the main island of Luzon was invaded; fighting continued until the end of the war.

Intelligence proved fallible with the February 19, 1945 invasion of Iwo Jima when it did not discover a change in Japanese defense strategy. The extensive Japanese tunneling and defense in depth, not at the beach as previously encountered, belied the intelligence estimate that the island would fall within a week. It did so finally on March 26.[238]

On April 1, Okinawa was invaded. The ferocious fighting and kamikaze ("divine wind") attacks, which took a heavy toll of an estimated 65,000 Allied killed and wounded, lasted until mid-June. The level of casualties was to have a significant influence on later Allied strategy toward Japan. The last major naval engagement took place on April 7, 1945, when tipped by SIGINT, US submarines on reconnaissance patrol spotted 10 Japanese warships, including the large battleship Yamato, sailing toward Okinawa. Navy aircraft sank the Yamato, one cruiser, and four destroyers.[239]

Allied intelligence[240] enjoyed a significant advantage over Japanese intelligence. Japanese codebreakers were decentralized and fragmented. Although the Japanese could read Chinese military and diplomatic codes, some British weather and merchant codes, and American aircraft movement codes, especially in MacArthur's Southwest Pacific Theater, a post-war Japanese assessment stated:

> Our [Japanese] navy was not able to break the American military's code(s); our intelligence appreciations and strategic estimates were primarily based on communications intelligence which was derived from enemy traffic analysis, call sign identification, direction-finding bearings, and interception of plain language transmissions (particularly those of aviators when airborne)... only a few of our many intelligence estimates based on communications intelligence really 'hit the mark,' and our navy's confidence in them was, therefore, relatively low.[241]

B-29 operations became a priority target for Japanese SIGINT, which could exploit open air-to-air communications and do traffic analysis. Japanese SIGINT broke call signs for the B-29s in 1944 and would alert radar stations and interceptor aircraft. In early August 1945, a US intercept revealed that Japanese COMINT was following the unusual operations of the 509th Bomb Group, which was conducting trials for the atomic bomb.[242]

---

238. Jeff M. Moore, "The High Cost of Faulty Intel," Naval History, February 2005. http://www.military.com/NewContent/0,13190,NH_0205_Intel-P1,00.html
239. William H. Garzke & Robert O. Dulin, Battleships: Axis and Neutral Battleships in World War II (Annapolis, Maryland: Naval Institute Press, 1985), 60.
240. By this time in the war, the US and Australia enjoyed a close SIGINT partnership.
241. Edwin T. Layton (translator), "America Deciphered Our Code," Proceedings, June 1979, 98-100, derived from Volume 43 of the Japanese War History Series, Chapter 14, Section 3, 591-592.
242. Author's notes from the 2013 Cryptologic History Symposium.

Invasion of Japan and the A-Bomb Decision

The Army and Navy disagreed over the strategy to defeat the Japanese in their home islands. The Navy preferred a strategy of blockade and bombardment to weaken the Japanese military. MacArthur, by this time the overall land and air forces commander in the Pacific, pushed for an amphibious invasion of Kyūshū ("Nine Provinces"), the southernmost home island, and later attacking Honshū ("Main Island") near Tokyo.[243] The debate was unsettled when President Roosevelt died on April 12, 1945.

Also being debated at political levels was the meaning of "unconditional surrender" contained in the July 26 Potsdam Declaration. Assistant Secretary of State Joseph C. Grew, the leading Japan expert in the State Department, proposed keeping the Emperor even with unconditional surrender.[244] On July 13, while President Truman was en route to the European victors' conference at Potsdam, SIGINT revealed the Japanese had approached Russia to negotiate a peace. But SIGINT also revealed divided opinions of Japanese leaders.[245]

Previously, in May, while fighting still raged on Okinawa, the Joint Chiefs of Staff (JCS) agreed on Project "Downfall," the invasion of the Japanese home islands. However, SIGINT was providing indications of what invading forces would face. The original estimates were for 246,000 defenders on Kyūshū. Anticipated US casualties were projected at 193,000. As SIGINT accumulated, the estimate grew to over 1,100,000 defenders with many kamikaze forces. MacArthur and Army Chief of Staff Marshall differed on the estimates. "MacArthur's practice was to not allow intelligence to interfere with his aims, and his history of complaints about [his intelligence chief] Willoughby's reports resulted mainly from their contradiction of his own estimates and preferred courses of action."[246] MacArthur challenged the accuracy of intelligence estimates. In a cable to Marshall, MacArthur stated:

> Throughout the Southwest Pacific Area campaigns, as we have neared an operation, intelligence has invariably pointed to greatly increased enemy forces. Without exception, this buildup has been found to be erroneous.[247]

However, "[in] those instances during MacArthur's Pacific campaign when

---

243. Douglas J. MacEachin, *The Final Months of the War With Japan: Signals Intelligence, US Invasion Planning, and the A-Bomb Decision* (Central Intelligence Agency: Center for the Study of Intelligence). https://www.cia.gov/library/center-for-the-study-of-intelligence/csi-publications/books-and-monographs/the-final-months-of-the-war-with-japan-signals-intelligence-u-s-invasion-planning-and-the-a-bomb-decision/csi9810001.html, 3-4.

244. Richard B. Frank, *Downfall: The End of the Imperial Japanese Empire.* (New York: Penguin, 1999), 214.

245. Andrew, *President's Eyes Only*, 152-3; and Frank, *Downfall*, 238.

246. Douglas J. MacEachin, *Final Months*, 223; and Thomas B. Allen & Norman Polmar, *Codename Downfall: The Secret Plan to Invade Japan — and Why Truman Dropped the Bomb.* (New York: Simon and Schuster, 1995), 224.

247. MacEachin, *Final Months*, 35, footnote 86, citing Message C31897, MacArthur to Marshall: CINCAFPAC to WARCOS, 9 August 1945. Naval Historical Center and MacArthur Bureau of Memorial Archives, WD1106.

the ULTRA-derived assessments were not entirely accurate, the errors tended to be on the low side."[248]

President Truman's concern with casualties was conditioned by the bloody battle for Okinawa, in which Japanese civilians as well as the military fought US forces. Kamikaze attacks had taken a heavy toll of Navy ships, sinking approximately 50 US and Canadian ships.[249] Marshall told the President that casualties would probably exceed the official number to be approximately 250,000. That and "[d]ecrypted messages from Tokyo [that] indicated that the Japanese would not surrender even if the Allies launched an all-out land invasion of the country ... played a role in ... Truman's decision to drop the atomic bomb on the country."[250] On August 6, the first atomic bomb was dropped on Hiroshima. Three days later, the second destroyed Nagasaki. On August 14,[251] Japan agreed to unconditional surrender. The last hostilities ended a month later when Japanese forces in Burma surrendered.

Conclusions

Historian John Keegan has written "[w]ithout our knowledge of Ultra and Magic, it would be impossible to write the war's history; and, indeed, all history of the war written before 1974, when the Ultra secret was revealed for the first time, is flawed by reason of that gap."[252]

Intelligence played a far more prominent role in World War II than in any previous conflict. After a while, it became a strategic advantage for the Allies. In 1939, Allied intelligence was ill-prepared for the conflict. German and Japanese intelligence had been active for years preparing for war.

Before the war, US intelligence was fragmented between the War and Navy Departments and the FBI. All were underfunded and engaged in interagency bickering. The Army and Navy fought over the collection, production, and reporting of SIGINT. The FBI pushed for its own role and carved out Latin America as its own sphere. All opposed the creation of the OSS, and the Army, Navy, and JCS denied OSS access to SIGINT.[253] Each had independent agreements with the British regarding intelligence exchange and cooperation.

The British were the senior partners in Allied intelligence activities, especially their application to deception efforts against the Nazis. Suspicion of the Americans, especially concerning security, evaporated slowly. "London insisted that the Americans imitate British security practices to protect the

---

248. Ibid, footnote 87.
249. Denis and Peggy Warner, *The Sacred Warriors: Japan's Suicide Legions* (Aarhus, DK: Van Nostrand Reinholt, 1982).
250. Sulick, *Spying in America*, 162.
251. August 15 in Japan.
252. Keegan, *Intelligence in War*, 322.
253. [Author's name redacted], "CIA-NSA Partnership: A Brave New World [Redacted]," Declassified "Secret//X1," *Studies in Intelligence* 48 (2), (Summer 2004).

vital ULTRA secret from unauthorized disclosures." "This British caution kept the Americans in the awkward status of junior partners for much of the war, particularly during the planning for covert action in support of the D-Day landings in Normandy in 1944."[254]

SIGINT was the most important source for strategic intelligence. Historian David Kahn notes "... codebreaking ... with its associated sorceries, such as direction-finding and traffic analysis, was by far the most important source of intelligence in World War II for both sides."[255] "[A]ll the intelligence the OSS produced never matched the value of the Ultra electronic intercepts in Europe and Magic in the Pacific."[256] In the early years, many Allied commanders were not knowledgeable or trusting of SIGINT, which led to many disasters, e.g., the fall of Crete, surprise in the Philippines even after learning of the attack on Pearl Harbor, and the destruction of convoy PQ-17. Bias often overruled intelligence as evidenced by the surprise over the invasion of Norway; the loss of Royal Navy capital ships to Japanese aircraft off Malaya; the unexpected German forces refitting at Arnhem, the Market Garden objective; and MacArthur's persistent disagreements with intelligence assessments, especially regarding the invasion of the Japanese home islands.

ULTRA – Enigma and Fish – and JN-25 and MAGIC (the decryption of Japanese diplomatic and attaché codes) were "the best intelligence available to British and American commanders." Then CIA historian Michael Warner wrote "[w]ithout ULTRA and MAGIC, the war might have been lost."[257] British historian F. H. Hinsley opined that "we wouldn't in fact have been able to do the Normandy Landings ... until at the earliest 1946, probably a bit later. It would have then taken much longer to break through in France.... And altogether therefore the war would have been something like two years longer, perhaps three years longer, possibly four years longer than it was."[258] SIGINT proved vital in specific battles for both the Axis, e.g., in North Africa and the Atlantic; and the Allies, e.g., the Atlantic U-boat campaign and at Midway.

Ironically, MAGIC intercepts were very important in understanding Nazi thinking as Ambassador Hiroshi Ōshima reported in detail to Tokyo on his discussions with Hitler and others. Chief of Staff Marshall stated that Japanese messages from Berlin were "our main basis of information regarding Hitler's intentions in Europe."[259]

As valuable as strategic SIGINT was, operational or tactical SIGINT was most important for combat commanders, who also relied on more traditional

---

254. Warner, *Office of Strategic Services*, 29, 8-9.
255. Kahn, "Intelligence in World War II," 7.
256. Waller, *Wild Bill Donovan*, 389.
257. Warner, *Office of Strategic Services*, 29. Most historians would qualify this statement, preferring a judgment that the war would have lasted longer.
258. Hinsley, Cambridge address.
259. Kahn, "Intelligence in World War II," 12.

intelligence sources – reconnaissance patrols, POW interrogations, and captured documents and equipment, especially cryptologic materials. The capture of Rommel's SIGINT unit in North Africa had strategic significance by thereafter denying him his advantage. Captured radar components from downed aircraft and the Bruneval raid helped the British scientists develop effective countermeasures to Luftwaffe bombing of Britain.

Born in World War I, photoreconnaissance became vital for the air war and identifying strategic targets, especially German war industries and oil production. By mid-war, it had become an intelligence discipline of its own. The British were the pioneers in knitting together the various elements of intelligence (SIGINT, HUMINT, POW interrogations, reconnaissance, radar, etc.) for the purpose of supporting operations.[260]

Counterintelligence and subsequent double agent operations proved critical for deceptions. Much of this also depended on ULTRA decrypts. The surprise of the Normandy landings is perhaps the greatest wartime deception in history. Certainly, it was one of the most complex deception operations ever.

"Germany lost the intelligence war," historian David Kahn notes. "At every one of the strategic turning points of World War II, her intelligence failed. It underestimated Russia, it blacked out before the North African invasion, awaited the Sicily landing in the Balkans, and fell for thinking the Normandy landing a feint."[261] German intelligence was "disorganized and unregimented" with various elements competing. Intelligence "... findings streamed together only in the mind of Adolf Hitler."[262] The greatest failing may have been in strategic analysis, which should have illuminated to the Germans the fact that it alone could not compete against the combined economic and potential military strengths of the Allies.[263]

The Japanese were not heavily invested in intelligence, which played a subordinate role in strategic decisions. Japanese policymakers and war planners were not interested in intelligence. Operations planners thought their judgments were superior to the intelligence departments in the Navy and Army.[264] Japanese intelligence, which was "overwhelmingly military," focused almost exclusively on collecting short-term operational intelligence.[265] Like Germany, Japanese strategic intelligence failed. Japanese leaders "engaged in 'best case' analysis" concerning their enemies, especially the recuperative powers and industrial might of the US."[266] "Any intelligence findings which indicated

260. Comments of Dr. Michael Warner, US Cyber Command historian at the AFIO Symposium, May 1-3, 2014. Author's notes.
261. Kahn, *Hitler's Spies*, 539.
262. Ibid, 42.
263. Ibid, 526.
264. Kotani, *Japanese Intelligence in World War II*, 160.
265. Michael A. Barnhart, "Japanese Intelligence Before the Second World War: 'Best Case' Analysis" in Ernest R. May (Ed.), *Knowing One's Enemies*, 424-426.
266. Ibid, 424.

that America would fight back could not be accepted by the policy-makers in Tokyo. Nor would they examine evidence that the economic disparity between the United States and the Japanese Empire was so great that their defeat was certain."[267]

Historian Ernest May has noted that "... intelligence estimates are useful only if acceptable to the people who have to act on them."[268] In many cases, both Axis and Allied decision makers and commanders ignored or rejected intelligence. May also noted that "... widely accepted presumptions [before and during the war] were often quite wrong" and resistant to being even questioned even in the face of intelligence.[269]

Allied success in World War II is often credited to American industrial might. At the 1943 Teheran conference, Stalin toasted "To American production, without which this war would have been lost."[270] But the enormous manpower sacrifice of the USSR and British fortitude were other crucial factors. These were aided by extraordinary Allied intelligence. As historian Thaddeus Holt concludes "The Western Allies in the Second World War beat their enemies by valor in full measure. But that valor was aided by guile on a level never before seen; the most systematic and skillful deception ever practiced in warfare."[271] And it was Allied intelligence that enabled that guile. "What effect did intelligence have on the war? It cannot be said to have won it. The war was won by the greater material and human forces of the Allies and by the bravery and spirit of the men and women in combat and in support. But intelligence shortened the war, thus contributing to victory. It saved lives – on both sides."[272]

By the end of the war, Britain and the US had built an intelligence behemoth. SIGINT cooperation continued almost without interruption after hostilities. Cooperation in other intelligence disciplines was rapidly renewed after the descending of the Iron Curtain and the 1947 passage in the US of the National Security Act but with a different focus – the Soviet Union, a former but temporary ally.

The major intelligence legacy of the war for the US was a commitment not to be so surprised by an adversary nation again, hence the establishment of a Central Intelligence Agency and creation of the "Five Eyes" SIGINT community of the US, the United Kingdom, Canada, Australia, and New Zealand.

---

267. Ibid, 454.
268. Ernest R. May, "Capabilities and Proclivities," in Ernest R. May (Ed.), *Knowing One's Enemies*, 504.
269. Ibid, 540.
270. Budiansky, *Battle of Wits*, 243.
271. Holt, *The Deceivers*, xi.
272. Kahn, "Intelligence in World War II," 20.

READINGS FOR INSTRUCTORS

Much remains unknown about intelligence activities during World War II. While many of the wartime documents of the British and Americans have been declassified, those of the Soviet Union largely have not. Many Japanese records were destroyed at the end of the war before they could be secured and preserved. Many topics, even large theaters of operations (e.g., China-Burma-India and Latin America), have been omitted in this article due to space and time limitations. Instructors will profit greatly from the intelligence bibliography at *http://intellit. muskingum.edu/ maintoc.html*. The footnotes contain many useful references. Recommended below are books that give a broad overview of intelligence during World War II.

Andrew, Christopher. *For the President's Eyes Only: Secret Intelligence and the American Presidency from Washington to Bush* (New York: Harper, 1996). See Chapter 3 – Franklin D. Roosevelt: The Path to Pearl Harbor, Chapter 4 – Roosevelt at War (1941 – 1945), and Chapter 5 – Harry S. Truman (1945 – 1953).

Budiansky, Stephen. *Battle of Wits: The Complete Story of Codebreaking in World War II* (New York: The Free Press), 2000. Budiansky provides a comprehensive explanation of what Axis and Allied codes and ciphers were broken. The layman can understand the technical explanations of the cryptanalytic processes. Most significantly, the author explains the consequences of the cryptanalytic efforts and how they affected battles and Allied strategies from Cape Matapan, Midway, El Alamein, the Atlantic, through and after the Normandy invasion.

Collier, Basil. *Hidden Weapons: Allied Secret or Undercover Services in World War II* (Barnsley: Pen & Sword Books Ltd., 1982). Collier is one of the officially accredited British World War II historians. Knowledgeable of ULTRA from his experience as an RAF Fighter Command headquarters intelligence officer, he offers a comprehensive view of the "use and misuse,"[273] failings and successes of Allied intelligence in Europe and the Far East throughout World War II. While Collier does not go into great detail in all aspects of intelligence, his overview is a good introduction to the topics and guide for further readings.

Hinsley, F. H. *British Intelligence in the Second World War* (Abridged Edition) (London: HMSO, 1993). Hinsley was the official historian for MI6. The original official history is in six volumes, appropriate for research scholars, but overwhelming for others. The abridged edition at over 600 pages is still quite detailed.

Holt, Thaddeus. *The Deceivers: Allied Military Deception in the Second World War* (New York: Scribner, 2004). Holt details the expanding efforts at deception throughout the war. He provides excellent appendices and a list of relevant abbreviations.

Jones, R. V. *Most Secret War: British Scientific Intelligence, 1939-1945* (London: Penguin Books, 1979, 2009). This is a classic discussion of scientific intel-

---

273. R. V. Jones in Foreword: vii.

ligence and its contributions to the Allied war effort.

Kahn, David. Hitler's Spies: German Military Intelligence in World War II (New York: Macmillan Publishing Company, 1978).

— "Intelligence in World War II," Journal of Intelligence History 1 (1), Summer 2001.

Keegan, John. Intelligence in War: Knowledge of the Enemy from Napoleon to Al-Qaeda (New York: Alfred A. Knopf, 2003).

Kotani, Ken. Japanese Intelligence in World War II (Oxford, UK: Osprey Publishing, 2009). This is one of the few sources in English on this topic.

May, Ernest R. (ed.). Knowing One's Enemies: Intelligence Assessment Before the Two World Wars (Princeton: Princeton University Press, 1984). A very thought-provoking series of articles on intelligence and the failings on all sides.

MacEachin, Douglas J. The Final Months of the War with Japan: Signals Intelligence, US Invasion Planning, and the A-Bomb Decision (Central Intelligence Agency: Center for the Study of Intelligence, 1998). https://www.cia.gov/ library/center-for-the-study-of-intelligence/csi-publications/books-and-monographs/the-final-months-of-the-war-with-japan-signals-intelligence-u-s-invasion-planning-and-the-a-bomb-decision /csi9810001.html#rtoc2. This is an excellent examination of the SIGINT that influenced the atom bomb decision.

Macintyre, Ben. Double Cross: The True Story of the D-Day Spies (New York: Crown Publishers, 2012).

— Operation Mincemeat: How a Dead Man and a Bizarre Plan Fooled the Nazis and Assured an Allied Victory (New York: Crown Publishers, 2011). A deception operation made famous by the 1956 movie The Man Who Never Was.

Masterman, J.C. The Double-Cross System: The Incredible Story of How Nazi Spies Were Turned into Double Agents (Guilford, CT: Lyons Press, 2012).

Sulick, Michael J. Spying in America: Espionage from the Revolutionary War to the Dawn of the Cold War (Washington, DC: Georgetown University Press, 2012). Sulick addresses most of the significant spy cases in American history.

Warner, Michael. The Office of Strategic Services: America's First Intelligence Agency (Monograph) (Central Intelligence Agency: Center for the Study of Intelligence, 2000). https://www.cia.gov/library/publications/intelligence-history/ oss/. This concise history of OSS covers its myriad missions and activities.

Wohlstetter, Roberta. Pearl Harbor: Warning and Decision (Stanford: Stanford University Press, 1962). This is a classic study of why the US was surprised at Pearl Harbor. However, other historians argue with her conclusions.

Many useful research materials are available over the Internet. CIA's Center for the Study of Intelligence (https://www.cia.gov/library/publications) contains many monographs, Studies in Intelligence articles, and declassified documents providing rich detail on many relevant aspects of World War II intelligence. NSA's Center for Cryptologic History (https://www.nsa.gov/about/ cryptologic_heritage/ center_crypt_history/index.shtml) also contains many useful articles and volumes related to World War II SIGINT.

Peter C. Oleson is the editor of the Association of Former Intelligence Officers

(AFIO)'s Guide to the Study of Intelligence, a member of the AFIO board, and chairman of its academic outreach. Previously, he was the director for intelligence and space policy for the secretary of defense and assistant director for plans and policy of the Defense Intelligence Agency. He was founder and CEO of Potomac Strategies & Analysis, Inc., a consulting firm on technology and intelligence and an associate professor in the University of Maryland University College graduate school.

The author wishes to acknowledge the recommendations and assistance he has received from Emeritus Professor Douglas Wheeler of the University of New Hampshire, the contributor of several articles to the Guide. Thanks also to Dr. Robert Clark, Joe Goulden, Michael Sulick, Robert MacDonald, Richard Florence, and Hayden Peake for their critiques of the draft and helpful recommendations.

GUIDE TO STUDY OF INTELLIGENCE

Intelligence in the Cold War

Michael J. Sulick, PhD

A "Cold War" by definition is an intense conflict that stops short of full-scale war. In the Cold War between the US and USSR, the superpowers and their allies relied heavily on intelligence to avert a full-scale war, which, in the nuclear age, could have led to catastrophic destruction. Because of its prominent role, intelligence became a topic of heightened interest in popular culture, scholarly research and investigative journalism.

The secrecy shrouding intelligence operations and the varying reliability of sources has complicated the study of Cold War intelligence, but in the past two decades, the publication of volumes of declassified material affords new opportunities for instructors and students. Works by intelligence officers on both sides provide first-hand accounts of high-level policy deliberations as well as details of specific operations. More importantly, the continuing declassification of documents by the US and other governments now allow more informed research on Cold War period intelligence.

Documents of the CIA and other Intelligence Community agencies are available at the National Records and Archives Administration (NARA), the libraries of US Presidents during the Cold War, and various other websites such as the Wilson Center's Cold War International History Project (CWIHP) and George Washington University's National Security Archive.[1] The websites of US Intelligence Community agencies also include official organizational histories that cover the Cold War period. Documents from foreign archives, including those of the USSR and Soviet bloc, are also available, a welcome development since most Cold War intelligence history has been written by Westerners reliant on primarily Western sources.

---

1. Cold War International History Project, Wilson Center *http://www.wilsoncenter.org/program/cold-war-international-history-project*; GWU's National Security Archive, *http://www2.gwu.edu/~nsarchiv/*

Considering the vast amount of material now available, this guide is but a starting point and touches briefly on some unique aspects that distinguish intelligence in the Cold War: the role of individual spies and Western failures of counterintelligence; the significant impact of technology on intelligence; the substantial use of covert action by the superpowers; and intelligence analysis.

Spy vs. Spy

Most HUMINT, i.e. intelligence from human spies, is fragmentary, gleaned from a host of sources with varying degrees of access, and must be connected together like pieces of a jigsaw puzzle to clarify enemy capabilities and intentions. Few spies singlehandedly have a major impact on national security, but Cold War intelligence was characterized by some rare cases on both sides in which information from individual spies proved vital during crises or could have changed the balance of power.

Early in the Cold War, the superpowers were unevenly matched in espionage. The Soviet intelligence services, the KGB (Komitet gosudarstvennoy bezopasnoti, the Committee of State Security) and GRU (Glavnoe razvedyvatel'noe upravlenie, Soviet Armed Forces General Staff Main Intelligence Directorate), inherited a spying tradition that dated back centuries.[2] Spying on one's neighbors, colleagues, and even family was as ingrained in the Russian soul as privacy rights and free speech are in America. The Soviets had thoroughly penetrated the US Government in the 1930s-1940's and their acquisition of America's atom bomb secrets leveled the superpower playing field at the Cold War's outset.[3] From the counterintelligence perspective, the Soviets guarded their secrets by pervasive monitoring of foreigners in the USSR, restricting foreign contact with its citizens, especially those with access to secrets, and recruiting spies in Western intelligence services.

Except in wartime, the US had no institutions or expertise in intelligence collection or counterintelligence through most of its history. The US did not establish a central authority to find spies until President Roosevelt, worried about looming involvement in a world war, assigned the task to the FBI in 1939. With the advent of the Cold War, the nation realized the need for a centralized intelligence capability and established the CIA in 1947.[4] In spite of these efforts,

---

2. Recommended readings: William R. Corson and Robert T. Crowley, *The New KGB: Engine of Soviet Power* (New York: Morrow, 1985) and John Dziak, *Chekisty: The History of KGB* (Lexington MA: Lexington Books, 1988).

3. Recently released documents from the Mitrokhin archive include a list of about 1,000 KGB agents in the US over several decades. http://www.huffingtonpost.com/2014/07/06/soviet-spy-secrets-kgb-documents_n_5562147.html.

4. Recommended readings: John Ranelagh, *The Agency* (New York: Simon and Schuster, 1986). A more recent historical look is by Timothy Weiner, *Legacy of Ashes: The History of CIA* (New York: Doubleday, 2007), a scathingly critical diatribe, which covers the CIA from its inception to 2007. As some reviewers have noted, Weiner's book is laced with factual errors and a strongly anti-CIA bias (Nicholas Dujmovic, "Review of Legacy of Ashes," *https://www.cia.gov/library/center-for-the-study-of-intelligence/csi-publica-*

the US would founder in its initial attempts to collect intelligence on the Soviet Union and would suffer serious counterintelligence failures from spies in its ranks throughout the Cold War.

The US may have been an easy intelligence target, but the British, French, West Germans, and others were penetrated by the Soviets as well, sometimes at the top levels of government. Because of the close cooperation between the US and United Kingdom, Soviet spies in the UK were able to betray the secrets of both nations in the early days of the Cold War.[5] In Berlin, one of the US' first technical operations, the building of a tunnel to tap into Soviet military communications, was compromised by George Blake, a spy in British intelligence.

The Soviets and its allies failed to recruit spies at the top levels of the US Government as they had in the 1930s-1940's. As the Cold War progressed, however, they found American spies whose information could have drastically changed the precarious balance of power. Thanks to one Cold War spy, naval communications officer John Walker, the Soviets knew every move of America's nuclear ballistic missile submarine fleet, which was considered the most invulnerable leg of the nation's land, air and sea defense triad.[6] As Naval Intelligence Director William Studeman noted, Walker's betrayal could have had "war winning implications for the Soviet side."[7] If the superpowers had only engaged in a conventional war in Europe, the Soviets would also have enjoyed a distinct advantage — a spy in the US Army, Sergeant Clyde Conrad, had given their surrogates, the Hungarian service, NATO's complete defense plans for the continent.[8] Even America's intelligence and counterintelligence agencies were penetrated by the Soviets. Aldrich Ames, an officer in CIA's Directorate of Operations Soviet Division, betrayed over 20 major spies along with other information about agency operations, and FBI Special Agent Robert Hanssen compromised sources and a host of sensitive intelligence community operations.

The revelation after the Ames arrest that the CIA had over 20 sources inside the USSR was startling considering its difficulties in acquiring Soviet Bloc sources in the Cold War's early days. Eventually, the US acquired Soviet Bloc sources, some of whom singlehandedly provided information that had significant influence on foreign policy.

---

tions/csi-studies/studies/vol51no3/legacy-of-ashes-the-history-of-cia.html).
5. Recommended readings on British intelligence in general, which include treatment of the "Cambridge Spy ring," are Keith Jeffery, *The Secret History of MI-6: 1909-1949* (New York: Penguin, 2010), based on access to the foreign intelligence service's official archives; and Christopher Andrew, *Defence of the Realm: The Authorized History of MI-5* (New York: Knopf, 2009), which in turn is based on similar access to the internal security service's files.
6. Pete Earley, *Family of Spies: Inside the John Walker Spy Ring* (New York: Bantam, 1988).
7. Admiral William Studemann statement cited in George Church, "Justice for the Principal Agent," *Time*, September 8, 1986.
8. Stuart Herrington, *Spies Among Us: Inside the Spycatcher's World*. Colonel Herrington headed the Army investigation that led to the identification of Conrad as a spy for Hungary.

Among the first was Dmitriy Polyakov, who rose through the ranks to become a GRU major general, the highest-ranking spy the US ever had inside the Soviet Government. Polyakov's information on the increasing split between the Soviet Union and China played a critical role in President Nixon's decision to open diplomatic relations with China in 1972. Adolph Tolkachev, an electronics engineer at a highly classified research institute, provided Soviet military secrets for over eight years that "saved the US billions of dollars in defense expenditures in the 1980s."[9] Polish Army Colonel Ryszard Kuklinski kept the US apprised of plans to impose martial law in Poland in 1981 and Soviet deliberations to suppress rising opposition to the communist regime. US allies contributed their share of vital intelligence from Soviet spies. Perhaps the most significant of all was GRU colonel Oleg Penkovskiy, who passed to the CIA and British MI-6 manuals on Soviet missile systems that would play a critical role in the 1962 Cuban missile crisis.[10]

Technical Intelligence

The unprecedented twentieth century advances in technology revolutionized intelligence and had an enormous impact on foreign policy. Penkovskiy's information, while crucial, was complemented by intelligence gleaned from new technical collection. The manuals Penkovskiy provided served to clarify imagery from reconnaissance flights over Cuba that indicated the construction of Soviet ballistic missile sites. The integration of HUMINT, overhead reconnaissance, and the National Security Agency's (NSA) monitoring of communications confirmed Khrushchev's maneuvering and ultimately prevented a nuclear confrontation.[11]

In the early days of the Cold War, the US had few sources of information on Soviet strategic weapons capabilities. US aerial reconnaissance flights intercepted military communications and photographed military facilities, but could only sniff around the edges of Soviet territory without risking being shot down. At President Eisenhower's initiative, the CIA developed the U-2, a high-altitude aircraft that could penetrate deep into Soviet territory.[12] Eisenhower ended CIA U-2 overflights of the USSR in 1960 after pilot Francis Gary Powers was shot down and paraded before the world media. The U-2 incident proved to be a major diplomatic embarrassment for Eisenhower, the first of

9. Barry G. Royden, "Tolkachev, A Worthy Successor to Penkovsky," *Studies in Intelligence* 47 (3), 5-33.

10. Jerrold Schechter and Peter Deriabin, *The Spy Who Saved the World: How a Soviet Colonel Changed the Course of the Cold War* (New York: Scribner, 1992).

11. Recommended readings: Laurence Chang and Peter Kornbluh, *Cuban Missile Crisis, 1962: A National Security Archive Documents Reader* (New York: New Press, 1998) and Mary S. McAuliffe (ed.), *CIA Documents on the Cuban Missile Crisis 1962* (Washington, DC: Central Intelligence Agency, 1992).

12. C. K. Ruffner, *Corona: America's First Satellite Program* (Washington DC: CIA Center for the Study of Intelligence, 1995) and *The CIA and the U2 Program, 1954-1974* (Washington, DC: CIA Center for the Study of Intelligence, 1998).

many that US Presidents would confront because of intelligence activities.

Despite the incident, the U-2 saved the US billions of dollars in unnecessary expenditures on bombers and missiles, located Soviet targets, mapped air defenses, and provided the US with the ability to discount bluffs by Soviet leaders exaggerating the size and strength of their strategic arsenal. The U-2 shoot down was also unfortunate since the program was about to be replaced because of a significant development in aerial reconnaissance. The 1957 Soviet launch of Sputnik sparked a huge investment in scientific research, especially on space technology, and one of its most significant achievements was the Corona program that developed a photoreconnaissance capability from space.

The US reconnaissance satellite effort played a critical role in preventing nuclear war. Successive generations of spy satellites relayed photos back to earth in real time, especially useful in monitoring quick-developing crises around the globe, and produced increasingly higher resolution imagery for more accurate assessments of Soviet weapons capabilities. Developments in space communications led to similar advances in NSA's monitoring capabilities.

Once the Soviets developed their own reconnaissance satellites, both sides dramatically increased their knowledge of each other's arsenals. Overhead reconnaissance became an essential key to the conclusion of strategic arms treaties between the superpowers during the Cold War since imagery aided the superpowers' ability to monitor compliance.

While overhead reconnaissance was the most important technological development of the Cold War, technological advances produced other innovative operations. In 1974, the CIA contracted the secret construction and deployment of the Glomar Explorer to salvage a sunken Soviet submarine from the Pacific Ocean floor. Sophisticated technology on the Glomar enabled the painstaking removal of sections of the submarine underwater, hidden from detection by aircraft or spy satellites.[13]

Covert Action

Throughout history, intelligence services have not only collected secrets but conducted other covert activities to further their nations' interests. In the Cold War, these covert activities were essential instruments of Soviet policy to expand communism around the globe and US policy to counter and reverse that expansion. These covert activities entailed a variety of measures, including disinformation, propaganda, psychological warfare, and the arming and support of governments or insurgent groups. The KGB dubbed such activities "active measures" while the US termed its efforts "covert action," activities run by the CIA to further US national interests while hiding the American hand.

---

13. Matthew Aid and Thomas Blandon, "Project Azorian: The CIA's Declassified History of the Glomar Explorer," National Security Archive, *http://www2.gwu.edu/~nsarchiv/nukevault/ebb305/index.htm*.

US policymakers viewed covert action as a middle option between diplomacy and military action, which might have escalated into a nuclear confrontation.[14] Every US President sanctioned covert action to some degree, and the foreign policy legacies of many were tainted by those that failed.

At the outset of the Cold War, the Soviets used subversion as one of their tools to occupy Eastern Europe. US fears of Soviet encroachment in Western Europe prompted the use of covert influence to prevent a communist victory in the 1948 elections in Italy. Buoyed by this victory, the Eisenhower administration embraced covert action to overthrow the prime minister of Iran in 1953 and, a year later, the leftist-leaning president of Guatemala.

The euphoria over covert action as a panacea to reverse Soviet expansion ended with the 1961 Bay of Pigs fiasco, the US covert action that is the most discussed in intelligence literature. Although covert action is intended to hide American involvement, information about the Cuban exiles' training leaked to the media, and Castro's intelligence service riddled the force with spies. The exiles were easily defeated and the operation caused another diplomatic embarrassment for the US.[15]

The Bay of Pigs did not deter future Presidents from resorting to covert action. Many of the most publicized operations tarnished the Presidents' reputations and the US' image at home and abroad. During the Johnson Administration, the CIA's involvement in Operation Phoenix in Vietnam, a counterinsurgency program to root out the Vietcong, was reviled when revelations surfaced about South Vietnamese indiscriminate torture and assassination. President Nixon's covert attempts to unseat Chile's Marxist leader, Salvador Allende, also failed and were denounced as proof of the US' imperialist ambitions.

Covert action survived intense Congressional scrutiny of Intelligence Community activities in the mid-1970s. An internal CIA report compiled a litany of agency violations of its charter, including illegal wiretapping and surveillance of American citizens, human experimentation with hallucinogens, and involvement in plots to assassinate foreign leaders. Both houses of Congress formed special committees to review the full range of activities by the CIA and other agencies, which led to the establishment of permanent Congressional committees on intelligence.[16]

---

14. Recommended readings: Roy Godson, *Dirty Tricks or Trump Cards: US Covert Action and Counterintelligence* (Washington DC: Brassey's, 1995) and John Prados, *Presidents' Secret Wars: CIA and Pentagon Covert Operations from World War II through the Persian Gulf*, Rev. ed. (Chicago: Ivan R. Dee, 1996).

15. Lyman b. Kirkpatrick, inspector general, CIA and Pentagon covert operations from documents, nsarchiv.gwu.edu/NSAEBB.NSAEBB341/Grpt1.pdf; and Jim Rasenberger, *The Brilliant Disaster: JFK, Castro, and America's Doomed Invasion of Cuba's Bay of Pigs* (New York: Scribner, 2011).

16. See the report of the Senate Select Committee to Study Government Operations with Respect to Intelligence Activities (known as the "Church Committee") at http://www.intelligence.senate.gov/churchcommittee.html. Also see Gerald Haines' article about the unauthorized publication of the House's parallel investigation at https://www.cia.gov/library/center-for-the-study-of-intelligence/csi-publications/csi-studies/studies/winter98_99/art07.html. The internal CIA report on unauthorized activities is available at http://www2.gwu.edu/~nsarchiv/NSAEBB/NSAEBB222/family_jewels_full.pdf.

Although Presidents still employed covert action, an emboldened Congress began to exercise a more direct role. In 1982, Congress defunded President Reagan's program to overthrow the Sandinista regime in Nicaragua. Reagan's CIA Director William Casey and others circumvented the ban by facilitating the sale of arms to Iran in exchange for Western hostages and used the proceeds to fund the Nicaraguan rebels. The secret deal eventually surfaced and led to various investigations and a black eye for the administration.[17]

While many covert action programs were criticized as failures, some were judged more positively. As one example, another Reagan-era covert action program dealt one of the final blows to the Soviets' dream of worldwide communism and to the USSR itself. The December 1979 Soviet invasion of Afghanistan to ensure the survival of a friendly communist regime was confronted with increasing resistance by the "*mujaheddin*," multi-national Moslem insurgent groups. Reagan's provision of arms and funding to the mujaheddin, particularly the "Stinger," an advanced portable anti-aircraft missile, ultimately contributed to forcing the Soviet withdrawal.

Ironically, the most publicity and the most studies of US Cold War intelligence focus on CIA's covert action more than its primary role of producing intelligence. Despite the volumes written on CIA covert action, most of them harshly critical, there is still a rich mine of history to come for the student of Cold War intelligence. The passage of time and declassification of government documents has led in some cases to more dispassionate re-examinations of the programs. In recent years, scholars have suggested that internal political dynamics played a more important role in the 1953 Iran coup than the CIA, a key point since US involvement has been touted as a cause of the Islamic regime's current anti-Americanism.[18] Similarly, assessments of Operation Phoenix have been tempered by extensive document declassification and an internal history of the CIA's role in Vietnam.[19] Release of documents on the Chile covert action has also prompted scholars to reconsider some aspects of the Nixon Administration's program to oust Allende.[20]

Intelligence Analysis

The sophistication of intelligence analysis, primarily in US and Western

---

17. The 1986 Tower Commission was followed in 1987 by Congressional hearings into the Iran-Contra Affair. See *http://www.presidency.ucsb.edu/PS157/assignment%20files%20public/TOWER%20EXCERPTS. htm* and *http://archive.org/stream/reportofcongress87unit#page/n7/mode/2up*.

18. Darioush Bayandor, *Iran and the CIA: The Fall of Mosaddeq Revisited* (London: Palgrave/Macmillan, 2010) and Mark Gasiorowski, "Why Did Mosaddeq Fall?" in Mark Gasiorowski and Malcom Byrne (eds.), *Mohammed Mosaddeq and the 1953 Coup in Iran* (Syracuse, NY: Syracuse University Press, 2004), 262–80.

19. Thomas L. Ahern, *Vietnam Declassified: the CIA and Counterinsurgency* (Lexington KY: University Press of Kentucky, 2009).

20. Kristian Gustafson, *Hostile Intent: US Covert Operations in Chile, 1964-1974* (Dulles VA: Potomac, 2007).

services, developed significantly during the Cold War. Analysts became more adept at integrating information from all available sources: human spies, technical intelligence, and overt sources. A new phenomenon that emerged during the Cold War was intense public debate over intelligence estimates.

The analyst's goal is to present the most objective assessment to aid policymakers' decisions. Maintaining objectivity became a daunting challenge during the Cold War when estimates were often publicly praised or vilified in partisan political debate. Bureaucratic politics also affected estimates as different agencies would base their own analysis on the equities of their institution.

The priority task of intelligence during the Cold War was warning of potential military confrontation with the Soviet Union, and thus the assessment of Soviet strategic weapon capabilities and intentions became the most controversial topic of US intelligence analyses.[21] In the early decades of the Cold War, the US military raised alarms that the Soviets were surpassing the US in those capabilities to justify budget requests for additional weaponry. The specter of a "bomber gap" and then "missile gap" fueled increased defense spending despite CIA analyses that disagreed with the military's more alarming estimate.

The issue also illustrated the impact of intelligence analysis on US domestic politics throughout the Cold War. In his 1960 presidential campaign, Kennedy exploited the supposed bomber gap to attack the Republicans as weak on national security. Eventually, the advent of overhead reconnaissance led to more accurate assessments that showed the gaps did not exist. The Soviet military capabilities debate, however, continued throughout the rest of the Cold War.

During the Vietnam conflict, CIA analysts were also at odds with the military as well as with the Johnson Administration. Pessimistic about the President's bombing of North Vietnam, CIA argued that the campaign would not reduce the will or ability of the communists to fight on. CIA analysts also disputed military estimates of North Vietnamese troop strength and were proved right by the 1968 massive Tet Offensive.[22]

In the 1970s, the military, supported by hawkish Republicans, again argued that CIA analysts were underestimating the Soviet threat. In 1976, then CIA Director George H. W. Bush assembled a "Team A" of CIA analysts and "Team B," outside experts in three specific areas, to conduct a competitive analysis of the topic. The Team B experts working on Soviet strategic objectives were firmly convinced that the Soviets would do anything, even engage in nuclear war, to achieve world hegemony. The hardliners' assessment was leaked to the media, and the CIA was pressed to reflect the more hawkish views in its estimate.

---

21. John Prados, *The Soviet Estimate: US Intelligence and Russian Military Strength* (New York: Dial, 1982).

22. Sam Adams, *War of Numbers: An Intelligence Memoir* (South Royalton VT: Steerforth Press, 1994). Adams was the CIA analyst who developed the controversial estimate.

Some critics believe the collapse of the Soviet Union blindsided the CIA and the entire Intelligence Community. Senior CIA officials have admitted that analysts were slow to realize the imminent collapse, but note that they were alerting policymakers for years about the stagnating Soviet economy.[23] Also, from early 1989, the CIA had been warning policymakers of a festering crisis brewing in the USSR because of its increasingly declining economy.

The Soviet Union itself was blind to its own deteriorating situation. That blindness was also evident in its intelligence analysis. Based on defector Vasili Mitrokhin's information, British scholar Christopher Andrew noted that Soviet intelligence analysis was always poor in contrast to their collection of secrets from spies.[24] While a certain amount of politicization enters assessments in Western intelligence services, it was endemic in the KGB, which tailored its analysis to endorse the regime's policies. Gorbachev mandated more objective assessments once he came to power, but by then it was too late for the KGB's ingrained culture of communist political correctness to overcome old habits. As in the past, KGB assessments, such as they were, blamed Soviet policy failures on the evil machinations of the West.

Conclusion

Markus Wolf, East Germany's notorious foreign intelligence chief during the Cold War, claimed in his memoirs that "the intelligence services contributed to a half century of peace ... by giving statesmen some security that they would not be surprised by the other side."[25] While Wolf's comments are undoubtedly self-serving, others also believe that intelligence ultimately provided the superpowers with the knowledge and confidence to avoid a devastating nuclear war. The contribution of intelligence, its successes, failures, costs, and consequences, are still debatable; and the continuing release of new archival material will afford students of the Cold War with increasing opportunities to examine a host of issues in the conflict that shaped the world order for over four decades.

READINGS FOR INSTRUCTORS

Andrew, Christopher. *For the President's Eyes Only: Secret intelligence and the American Presidency from Washington to Bush* (New York: Harper Perennial, 1995). Andrew's study, which focuses primarily on the Cold War, is the

---

23. Bruce Berkowitz, "US Intelligence Estimates of the Soviet Collapse: Reality and Perception" in *Ronald Reagan: Intelligence and the End of the Cold War* (Washington DC: CIA Center for the Study of Intelligence, 2011).
24. Christopher Andrew, *The Sword and the Shield: The Mitrokhin Archives and the History of the KGB* (New York: Basic Books, 1999), 429.
25. Markus Wolf and Anne McElvoy, *Man Without a Face: The Autobiography of Communism's Greatest Spymaster* (New York: Public Affairs, 1997), 382.

most comprehensive treatment of the role of intelligence in Presidential decision-making.

Weiser, Benjamin. *A Secret Life* (New York: Public Affairs, 2004). This is the story of Polish Colonel Ryszard Kuklinski. Based partly on access to CIA files and the officers involved, the book provides an excellent introduction to the tradecraft used to keep spies safe and the psychological strains of espionage.

Vertefeuille, Jeanne and Sandra Grimes. *Circle of Treason: A CIA Account of Traitor Aldrich Ames and the Men He Betrayed* (Annapolis, MD: Naval Institute Press, 2012). The authors were directly involved in the hunt for a Soviet mole and the unmasking of Ames, the most notable CIA spy of the Cold War. The book not only illustrates the difficulties of espionage investigations and the damage caused by spies but also provides the best account of Dmitriy Polyakov, one of those betrayed by Ames and the highest ranking Soviet spy of the Cold War.

Andrew, Christopher and Oleg Gordievskiy. *The KGB: the Inside Story of its Foreign Operations from Lenin to Gorbachev* (London: Sceptre, 1991). Russia's declassification of Cold War intelligence documents is meager compared to that of Western governments but this book and the following more than compensate. Gordievskiy was a senior KGB officer who spied for British intelligence.

Andrew, Christopher and Vassili Mitrokhin. *The Sword and the Shield: The Mitrokhin Archives and the History of the KGB* (New York: Basic Books, 1999). Mitrokhin was a KGB archivist who smuggled out voluminous KGB files and defected to British intelligence.

Wallace, Bob and Keith Melton. *Spycraft: the Secret History of CIA Spytechs, From Communism to Al Qaeda* (New York: Dutton, 2008). While this book only deals tangentially with major technical developments such as overhead reconnaissance and electronic eavesdropping, it is the most comprehensive and detailed study of technical support to spy tradecraft.

George, Roger Z. and James B. Bruce (eds.). *Analyzing Intelligence: Origins, Obstacles and Innovations* (Washington, DC: Georgetown University Press, 2008). Understanding the debate on US estimates during the Cold War requires knowledge of the unique challenges analysts faced and this study is one of the best introductions for the student.

A career intelligence officer, Michael Sulick was director of CIA's National Clandestine Service (2007-2010) responsible for managing global covert operations on major threats to national security. He was also chief of CIA counterintelligence (2002-2004). Since his retirement, he has written *Spying in America: Espionage from the Revolutionary War to the Dawn of the Cold War* (Georgetown University Press, 2012) and *American Spies: Espionage Against the United States From the Cold War to the Present (Georgetown University Press, 2013)*, a two-volume history on Americans spying against the US from the Revolutionary War to the present. He currently serves on the board of the Association of Former Intelligence Officers.

GUIDE TO THE STUDY OF INTELLIGENCE

Scientific and Technical Intelligence

A Memoir by a S&T Intelligence Officer

S. Eugene Poteat, LLD(Hon.)

EDITOR's Introduction

The first Soviet atomic bomb test on 29 August 1949 caught the US by surprise. Aided by a long-term and successful espionage operation against the Manhattan Project, the detonation highlighted the lack of US intelligence on the USSR. The next year, UN forces in Korea began encountering advanced Soviet-made fighters (MiG-15, some flown sub rosa by Russian pilots) that were superior to America's aircraft. Clearly the US needed more and better intelligence about its adversaries and their weapons capabilities to develop appropriate countermeasures and its own weapons systems. Existing signals intelligence (SIGINT) and technical sensors proved inadequate, calling for a new generation of scientific and technical collection systems to support the development of ever more sophisticated US countermeasures and advanced weapons systems.

The CIA took the lead in the development of new, highly sophisticated approaches to scientific and technical intelligence collection. While much of what CIA undertook remains cloaked behind a curtain of secrecy, the following reminiscences of a senior CIA scientific and technical intelligence officer gives insight into how the CIA responded to the challenge.

A Memoir

Long before I joined CIA, its analysts had been unable to answer President Eisenhower's critical "bomber and missile gap" questions. The president called in the nation's leading scientists for advice on what technology might be brought to bear on the issues. This advisory group became known as the "Land Panel," after one the group's more innovative and active members, Edwin "Den" H. Land, president of the Polaroid Corporation. The panel quickly came up with solutions to the "bomber and missile gap" and other intelligence questions as well: 1) get spies inside the Soviet Union, 2) use high-altitude aerial reconnaissance to see what missiles and bombers the Soviets have, and 3) begin the development of reconnaissance satellites since aerial reconnaissance will eventually be vulnerable to improving Soviet antiaircraft missile defenses. Surprisingly, Eisenhower directed the CIA to take the lead in developing and operating both the U-2 aerial reconnaissance and the reconnaissance satellite efforts with support from the US Air Force. Then Director of Central Intelligence Allen Dulles objected, saying the CIA was not in the business of developing such high-technology systems. Eisenhower's response was, "Well, you are in that business now, because it has to be done in secret."[1] President Eisenhower approved the Land Panel findings in November 1954. The U-2 flew its first mission over the USSR on July 4, 1956, continuing until the May 1, 1960 shoot-down of Francis Gary Powers. As a testament to the developers of the U-2, it is still in service with the Air Force and NASA today. The first successful photographic reconnaissance satellite mission occurred on August 10, 1960.

I was recruited into the CIA from Cape Canaveral, Florida in 1959 and initially underwent the requisite indoctrination into the principals of intelligence and espionage. Contrary to the widely held perception that intelligence is the purloining of secret information from foreign countries, which is then used for advantage in wartime and as an aid to diplomacy, and the catching of foreign spies, or counterintelligence, I learned that intelligence serves a number of other purposes, such as technology development in support of other intelligence programs; support to treaty negotiations and monitoring, arms control; and more. Until the recent scholarly literature on the subject, published materials on intelligence primarily focused on intelligence disasters, such as the Bay of Pigs or the shoot-down of Gary Powers' U-2 over the Soviet city of Sverdlovsk. The story of American intelligence is much fuller. Recounted here are some of the challenges and successes CIA faced to answer critical national security questions.

Americans were shocked when Khrushchev publicly humiliated President Eisenhower over the U-2 affair. Not widely known was that the U-2's photographs had disproved Khrushchev's boast that Soviet missiles were "being cranked out like sausages," that American fears of a severe bomber and ballistic missile gap with the Soviets were unfounded, or that its intelligence was a key ingredient in American diplomacy that permitted President Kennedy to call

---

1. See Richard Garwin, CORONA: America's First Reconnaissance Satellite System. A View from the Land Panel, Notes for Presentation George Washington University, May 23, 1995, at http://www.fas.org/rlg/052295CRNA%20CORONA%201-7.pdf; Gregory Pedlow and Donald Welzenbach, The CIA and the U2 Program, 1998, at https://www.cia.gov/library/center-for-the-study-of-intelligence/csi-publications/books-and-monographs/the-cia-and-the-u-2-program-1954-1974/; and David Robarge, Archangel: CIA's Supersonic A-12 Reconnaissance Aircraft, 2012, at https://www.cia.gov/library/center-for-the-study-of-intelligence/csi-publications/books-and-monographs/a-12/index.html.

Khrushchev's bluffs during the 1961 Berlin crisis and the 1962 Cuban missile crisis.

At the time of the U-2 shoot-down, the CIA was already well along in developing the U-2's replacement, the A-11 OXCART reconnaissance aircraft, at Lockheed's Skunk Works in Burbank, California. The OXCART was to fly at over 90,000 feet at Mach 3.3. The original aircraft was designated the A-11 and later the A-12. It would become the predecessor to the Air Force's better-known SR-71 Blackbird. The CIA and Air Force jointly had the CORONA photographic satellite well under way in a parallel development that would eventually replace all aircraft over-flights of the Soviet Union.

Concerns about the vulnerability of the yet-to-fly OXCART to the Soviet air defense radar network were the basis for the project's most sensitive aspect. The OXCART was to be invisible to the Soviet radars—the first-ever stealth aircraft. The engineering approach to stealth was to create an airplane that would result in a deceptively small blip on enemy radar screens by shaping the airplane with razor-sharp edges, or chines, by tilting the rudders inboard to reduce radar reflections, and by using as much composite radar-absorbing material as possible. But how small a radar target was stealthy enough? That depended on how good the Soviet air defense radars were.

But for policymakers, there were more questions about the Soviet air defense radars than there were answers. President Eisenhower, having been badly burned over the U-2 incident, nonetheless endorsed continued development of OXCART, but made it clear that there would be no overflights of the Soviet Union unless the CIA could prove, absolutely, that it would be invisible to their air defense radars.

The Intelligence Community (IC) had no hard information about the transmitter power of Soviet radars, their receiver sensitivity, the spatial coverage of their beams, or even how widespread they were deployed, much less anything about their counter stealth capabilities. The CIA's clandestine service could offer no help since it did not have a single case officer inside the Soviet Union at the time. This was because US Ambassador in Moscow Llewellyn Thompson would not permit such risky, "dirty" business as intelligence to jeopardize his sensitive diplomatic position during his initial term (1955-1957).[2]

American electronic intelligence (ELINT) had virtually nothing to offer about Soviet radar capabilities against stealth. The only option seemed to fall back on making the best possible intelligence estimate with regard to Soviet radar capabilities for dealing with a high and fast airplane with a very small radar cross section. In the words of other intelligence veterans, "Estimating is what you do when you don't know and cannot find out."

But there were several problems with the IC's estimates. There was often insufficient information available to produce even a guess, much less a rea-

---

2. Thompson again served in Moscow from 1967-1969.

sonable estimate, on such esoteric topics as a radar's ability to detect stealthy aircraft. When available, communications intelligence (COMINT) and photography (PHOTINT) were considered the most credible sources of relevant intelligence, and provided the bulk of the technical contributions to National Intelligence estimates (NIEs). ELINT's contribution was virtually nil, and intelligence analysts considered it next to useless. One prominent CIA operations officer said that his clandestine service considered ELINT the only five-letter cuss word, that he viewed ELINT as worthless, and that only his agents could be relied on for worthwhile information. He was right in that ELINT provided little information about Soviet radars other than their identification and general location—even when they were within line-of-sight of our ELINT receivers. Most Soviet radars, however, were well beyond the line-of-sight of ELINT.

This was the scene when I joined the CIA's Office of Scientific Intelligence as a new engineer. I was soon cleared into the OXCART project and into its stealth aspect. The OXCART mission planners were especially concerned about just how widespread the Soviet early warning radars were and where they were located. It seemed impossible, however, to determine the number, exact location, or any other technical information on those radars. I recalled an occasion at Cape Canaveral in the early 1950s, when the signal from a ground-based radar located a thousand miles beyond our horizon was picked up at the Cape—the signal had been reflected off a Thor missile during a test flight. A plan was made to exploit this same phenomenon (later called "bi-static intercept") to intercept high-powered radars well over the horizon by pointing ELINT antennas at Soviet ballistic missiles during their flight testing and using the missile's radio beacon for pointing, or simply programming the ELINT antennas to follow the missile's predicted trajectory. Previously, the common practice had been to point the antennas at the horizon, in the direction of the target radars. There was little wonder no distant signals were ever intercepted.

Project MELODY

CIA management approved Project MELODY. There were no computers in those days, so our feasibility studies and engineering calculations involved solving spherical trigonometry equations using slide rules, tables of logarithms, and hand-cranked calculators. MELODY was installed at a CIA monitoring site on the shores of the Caspian Sea in northern Iran in late 1960. Over the ensuing years, MELODY produced bi-static intercepts of virtually all the Soviet missile tracking radars, including some located at a test range nearly a thousand miles away. The fixed location of MELODY and limited trajectories of the Soviet missiles being tracked, however, still did not provide the locations of all the air defense radars throughout the Soviet Union that were needed by the OXCART mission planners.

A new powerful Soviet air defense early warning radar, called TALL KING, began to appear about this time, which, if deployed widely, appeared to improve significantly the Soviets' air defenses. TALL KING radar quickly became the OXCART's nemesis. MELODY's success with the high-powered, missile-related radars led to the idea of using the moon as a distant bi-static reflector to locate the Soviet TALL KING radars deployed in the Soviet Union.

Stretching the bi-static concept as far as we could, we attached sensitive ELINT receivers, tuned to the TALL KING frequency, to the giant 60-foot RCA radar antenna just off the New Jersey Turnpike near Moorestown, and pointed at the moon. Over time, as the Earth and moon revolved and rotated, all the Soviet radars came into view one at a time and their precise geographic locations plotted. The extremely large number of radars that were found and their extensive coverage of the Soviet Union was disturbing news for the OXCART Program Office—and for the US Air Force's Strategic Air Command (SAC), which had to plan wartime bomber penetrations routes.

Now assigned to the OXCART Program Office, I was given the job of trying to obtain the hard technical data needed to resolve the stealth vulnerability issue. In looking at the Soviet air defense radars, particularly TALL KING, and, to a lesser degree, the radars associated with anti-aircraft missile systems, we knew we had to get answers that could stand the most stringent scrutiny from the policymakers that would be involved in approving future OXCART overflights. I assembled a small group of engineers and scientists who were known for their innovation, their understanding of the Soviet air defense system, and a nose for running one-of-a-kind field operations anywhere in the world. We outfitted a C-97 cargo aircraft that operated in the air corridors from West Germany to Berlin—which had line-of-sight access to East German-based Soviet radars—with laboratory precision measurement instruments. There was a similarly equipped Air Force RB-47 reconnaissance aircraft that operated around the periphery of the Soviet Union. This effort led to a series of airborne ELINT systems that could measure a radar's spatial coverage and radiated power with extreme precision. The system could also measure other important radar signal parameters, including radio frequency coherence, polarization, and internal and external signal structure—details that provided even further insight into a radar's performance that would be vital to designers and builders of electronic jammers.

The precise dimensions of the TALL KING's antenna were also needed for our calculations. One US Army military attaché got close-in ground photographs of the radar in East Germany. The antenna was mounted on a small brick base, and we asked for the dimensions of one of the bricks. It turned out the bricks were from the nearby Pritzwalk Brick Factory and easily acquired. When we asked our clandestine service to filch a Pritzwalk brick, we dared not admit it was for an ELINT project. We were happy with their impression that it was to be hollowed out and used for an agent's dead drop.

Our special systems were installed in a series of Air Force planes, starting with the C-97 and RB-47, then C-130s, and finally ever more modern aircraft.[3] Missions were flown around the world, along the periphery of all Communist countries and in the Berlin air corridors. Technical reports on the mission results were published by CIA and distributed throughout defense and intelligence communities, as well as to the defense industry's electronic countermeasures designers. These reports were eventually distributed to allied countries as well.

One revelation of this accurately measured air defense coverage was that the Soviet's low-altitude radar coverage was far better than our analysts' earlier estimates, and the SAC quickly changed its wartime plans to penetrate at much lower and survivable altitudes. The projects also answered the analysts' question of whether the TALL KING radar also had a height-finding capability for determining an aircraft's altitude as well as its bearing and range. One of our RB-47s, towing a special antenna nearly a mile behind the aircraft over the Sea of Japan, abruptly descended 5,000 feet and then quickly climbed back to cruise altitude. A nearby National Security Agency (NSA) monitoring site confirmed that the Soviets' had in fact observed and reported the change in altitude.

Project PALLADIUM

We now knew the Soviet air defense radars' power and spatial coverage, but that was only half the answer to the OXCART's stealth—and health. We also needed to know the sensitivity of the Soviets' radar receivers and the proficiency of their operators. The CIA had a stable of top outside scientists to draw on, and with their help and suggestions, I came up with an electronic scheme to generate and inject carefully calibrated false targets into the Soviet radars, deceiving them into seeing and tracking "ghost" aircraft.

We could simulate a false target including its range and speed. Our project was dubbed PALLADIUM. Basically, we received the radar's signal and fed it into a variable delay line before transmitting the signal back to the radar. By smoothly varying the length of the delay line, knowing the radar's power and spatial coverage from the aircraft precision measurements, we could now simulate an aircraft of any radar cross section, from an invisible stealth airplane to one that made a large blip on Soviet radar screens—and anything in between, at any speed and altitude, and fly it along any prescribed path. The real trick was to find some way of discovering which of our blips the Soviets could see on their radar screens—the smallest size blip being a measure of the sensitivity of the Soviets' radars and the skill of their operators. We began looking at a number

---

3. The US Air Force now operates two specialized RC-135 Combat Sent airborne technical ELINT collectors to obtain precise measurements on radars of interest in many countries.

of possible Soviet reactions that might give us clues as to whether our ghost aircraft was seen. We finally discovered that certain Soviet communications links could be monitored to reveal Soviet detection and tracking of our ghost.

Every PALLADIUM operation consisted of a CIA team with its ghost aircraft system, a NSA team to monitor the communications links, and a military operational support team. Covert PALLADIUM operations were carried out against a variety of Soviet radars around the world, from ground bases, naval ships, and submarines.

When the Soviets covertly moved into Cuba in an attempt to checkmate US military superiority, it presented a golden opportunity to measure their SA-2 anti-aircraft missile radar system's sensitivity. One memorable operation, conducted during the Cuban Missile Crisis, had the PALLADIUM system mounted on a Navy destroyer out of Key West. The destroyer lay well off the Cuban coast, out of sight of the Soviet radars near Havana, but with our PALLADIUM antenna just breaking the horizon. A false aircraft was made to appear to be a US fighter plane about to overfly Cuba. The idea was for the early warning radar to track our electronic aircraft and then for a Navy submarine, that had covertly slipped into Havana Bay, to surface and release a series of calibrated metallic balloon-borne spheres of different sizes that would rise into the path of the oncoming false aircraft. It took a bit of coordination and timing to keep the destroyer, submarine, and false aircraft all in line between the Havana radar and Key West. We expected the Soviets would track and report the intruding aircraft and then switch on their SA-2 radars in preparation for firing their missiles—and would also report seeing the other strange targets, our spheres, as well. The NSA team, with its skilled team of Russian and Spanish linguists and their monitoring systems on board the destroyer, would provide feedback. The smallest spheres reported seen by the SA-2 radar operators would correspond to the size, or smallest radar cross section aircraft, that could be detected and tracked.

While we got the answers we went after, it was not without some excitement—and entertainment. Cuban fighter planes had fired on a Liberian registered freighter the day before. This led us to expect that the Cubans and Soviets would not hesitate to attack a US-flagged vessel. In the middle of the operation, Cuban fighter planes were dispatched to intercept the intruder. We had no trouble in manipulating the PALLADIUM system to keep our ghost aircraft just ahead of the pursuing Cuban fighters. When the NSA team heard the Cuban pilot radio his controllers that he had the intruding aircraft in sight and was about to make a firing pass to shoot it down, we all had the same idea at the same instant. The engineer moved his finger to the switch, I nodded yes, and he switched off the PALLADIUM system.

Important Achievements

By now, we felt we knew at least as much about the Soviets' radars as they did. We also knew that their radars were excellent, state of the art, and their operators were proficient. We had finished our special mission, concluding that as soon as the OXCART came over the horizon, Soviet air defense radars would immediately see and track it. At the same time, however, we had established realistic stealth radar cross section goals that, if met by the next generation of stealth aircraft, would allow the aircraft to fly with impunity right through the Soviet radar beams. The F-117 stealth fighter would eventually be the first aircraft to meet these goals—with the help of other CIA engineers and scientists.

Even before we had finished our projects, it had become obvious that, if the OXCART could not fly stealthily, it could in the meantime fly safely, relying on its superior performance to out-fly anti-aircraft missiles. But we would need a stable of effective electronic countermeasures systems in the future. Our small group had already spun off two other groups, one to take on the job of developing electronic jammers and warning receivers for the OXCART, SR-71, and the U-2s that were still flying, and a second group to continue investigating revolutionary techniques to improve stealth technology.[4]

President Eisenhower had personally approved the initial development of the OXCART program, and Kennedy had supported its continued secret development—but made it clear there would be no overflights of the Soviet Union unless its stealthiness and invulnerability were guaranteed, which was not to be. In one of President Johnson's first speeches, he announced the existence of this unique aircraft, effectively declassifying the project. Shortly thereafter the Soviets began development and testing a new surface-to-air missile, the SA-5, clearly designed to intercept such extremely high-altitude, high-speed aircraft as the OXCART.

During the years that our small group of engineers was in existence, we would occasionally discuss just how far we could go in terms of probing, spoofing, and injecting false targets, signals and information into an enemy's electronic or communications networks to covertly learn more about his hidden, concealed, or secret capabilities and intentions. We also brainstormed about what responses or secondary reactions, observables, or seemingly unrelated

---

4. The CIA's electronic countermeasures expertise would eventually benefit the Air Force. One of the U-2 missile warning receivers developed was modified and installed in an Air force fighter plane and became the basis of a later system called WILD WEASEL, used to locate and destroy SA-2 missile sites in North Vietnam. WILD WEASEL became the stuff of great stories and legends about the derring-do of the pilots who hunted down the SA-2 sites, launched their radar-killing missiles in close, and dodged the missiles fired at them during these encounters. Mike Nastasi, *The Wild Weasels: Daredevils in the Sky, Military History* Online at http://www.militaryhistoryonline.com/vietnam/airpower/wildweasel. aspx and W. A. Hewitt, *Planting the Seeds of SEAD: The Wild Weasels in Vietnam*, School of Advanced Airpower Studies, Air University, Maxwell Air Force Base, Alabama, PhD Thesis, May 1992. http://www. au.af.mil.

responses to our probing we might look for when radiation security, encryption and deception were used. The process had no name at that time, but in retrospect, we were unwitting participants in the beginnings of what is now known as information warfare.

Caught Cheating

One of MELODY's more significant contributions would come about during negotiations with the Soviets on the 1972 Anti-ballistic Missile (ABM) treaty—which included an obligation not to give non-ABM systems, such as the new Soviet SA-5 anti-aircraft missile, capabilities to counter strategic ballistic missiles—and not to test them in an ABM mode. In preparing a NIE, intelligence analysts were debating whether the SA-5 anti-aircraft missile could be upgraded to become an ABM and whether the Soviets might try to so test it covertly.

After nearly a year of trying to come up with an estimate of SA-5 capabilities and Soviet intentions, many analysts believed that the Soviets would never dare cheat on such an important treaty. I suggested that we assume that the Soviets, based on their history, should be expected to cheat by testing their SA-5 against one of their own ballistic missiles, and that we need only find a way to catch them at it. Much to the chagrin of the some analysts, MELODY answered the question within a few weeks. MELODY was modified by adding a special ELINT receiver tuned to the SA-5's ground-based target-tracking radar frequency—which was known by then. We relied on an Air Force's surveillance radar in another country for a tip-off of Soviet missile launches. MELODY, pointing its antenna at the Soviet missiles in flight from the Sary Shagan missile test range nearly 1,000 miles away, readily intercepted the SA-5 target tracking radar signals in the forbidden ABM role. During one of the ensuing Geneva negotiating sessions, Dr. Henry Kissinger, using intelligence derived from the MELODY intercepts, looked his Soviet counterpart in the eye and read him the dates and time they had cheated on the treaty. The cheating immediately ceased, and the Soviets began a mole-hunt for the spy in their midst that most surely had tipped us off.

Counting Enemy Troops

During the Vietnam War, CIA's special task force engaged in a heated debate with the Army and Secretary of Defense McNamara's office over the infiltration rate of North Vietnamese soldiers. CIA estimates were much larger than those of the Department of Defense (DOD), and if they could be validated, did not bode well for the outcome of the war. A quick study revealed that the Air Force had airdropped acoustic sensors along the Ho Chi Minh Trail in an attempt to detect and count infiltrators.[5] Both the Air Force and Navy also had SIGINT aircraft, EC-47s, EC-130s, and EC-121s, orbiting off the Vietnamese coast to intercept and count the number of small radios carried by the infiltrating groups, always traveling in fixed numbers, on their trek south on the trail. A good estimate was obtained by multiplying the radios by the number of men per group. The problem was that the orbiting SIGINT airplanes could not fly high enough to intercept all the radios on the very long trail.

Our solution was simply to get an airplane that could fly high enough to intercept all the radios simultaneously for an accurate count. The Air Force quickly found a special radio receiver, installed it in a U-2, and had the operation underway in about a month. A U-2 could stay aloft for 12 hours; two could provide 24-hour coverage. The infiltration rate turned out to be more like a flood. The DOD would finally accede to the higher CIA numbers.

Looking Back Over a Career
Some Thoughts

Presidents turned to CIA to answer vital questions. CIA evolved and invested in its technical capabilities to respond as required. President Eisenhower valued and understood intelligence from his wartime experiences, supported the U-2 program, and used its intelligence effectively. Kennedy, new to his office, while badly burned by the Bay of Pigs debacle, was always a quick learner, and effectively used U-2 collected intelligence in defusing both the Berlin and Cuban missile crises. Other presidents were not so friendly to intelligence. President Reagan had a predilection for using intelligence to counter the Communists. He encouraged many high-technology programs, such as the Strategic Defense Initiative (SDI)—disparagingly labeled Star Wars by the media—against which the Soviets had no hope of competing. Reagan's intelligence services, with his personal knowledge, would then foil the KGB's extensive efforts to steal American computers and communications know-how, which the USSR needed to match the SDI technology and improve its lethargic industries. [6]

Having learned the value of intelligence from his job as Nixon's national security advisor, Secretary of State Henry Kissinger became a voracious con-

---

5. For a history of the Igloo White sensor program see Philip D. Caine, Igloo White, July 1968 to December 1969, Headquarters PACAF, January 1970, declassified and available via http://en.wikipedia.org/wiki/Operation_Igloo_White. The Vietnam order of battle controversy is examined by Naval Postgraduate School professor James Wirtz, "Intelligence to Please? The order of battle controversy during the Vietnam War," Political Science Quarterly 106 (2), Summer 1991, 239-263. http://www.jstor.org/stable/2152228.
6. The fascinating story of the covert action to respond to the extensive Soviet pilfering of US and Western technologies is told by Gus W. Weiss, "The Farewell Dossier," Studies in Intelligence, at https://www.cia.gov/library/center-for-the-study-of-intelligence/csi-publications/csi-studies/studies/96unclass/farewell.htm.

sumer and user of intelligence. Not only did he use it effectively to reduce Soviet cheating on the ABM treaty, he cut off the supply of CIA satellite photography to an ally, Britain, until he gained their agreement allowing the U-2 to operate from the British air base in Cyprus during the ceasefire in the 1974 Arab-Israeli war. On those occasions when we were briefing a high-level panel on a planned CIA operation, to obtain the requisite approval before proceeding, Kissinger was, more often than not, the panel member that thoroughly grilled us on every detail of the planned operation, including background, ramifications if things went wrong, and whether other options were considered.

History is replete with examples of the use, and abuse, of intelligence and intelligence organizations. Strong-willed leaders often think they know best, especially if the intelligence is soft or only an imprecise estimate. Even if the intelligence is hard, they still may choose to ignore it, depending on their own political agendas. Presidents and other policy makers seem more likely to use, abuse, or ignore intelligence, depending on their predilection or prejudice toward the subject. Intelligence is an esoteric and often misunderstood subject, and a busy President or other policymaker, if he has no prior reading or understanding of the subject, will find difficulty in acquiring it. A policymaker with an unreasoned prejudice against intelligence, along with a lack of understanding of its historical value, can do as much, if not more harm to the national interest as can one with a predilection toward intelligence and a belief that it can do more than it actually can.

The CIA's ever-more advanced high-tech intelligence collection systems, with a new generation of ultra-high tech satellites, the operation to recover a Soviet missile submarine from the floor of the Pacific Ocean, and the many other classified collection systems, has led to CIA's reputation as one of the nation's leading R&D establishments. Besides development of pioneering aircraft such as the U-2 and A-11 OXCART, CIA scientists and engineers have developed space-based systems for imagery and SIGINT collection, and digital systems which formed the foundations for today's GEOINT capabilities. Project AZORIAN was a multi-year effort to recover the Soviet submarine K-129, which sank in April 1968. In the summer of 1974, the specially built ship, Glomar Explorer, recovered part of the submarine.[7] Project GTTAW was a covert tap on an underground cable in Moscow that connected the Soviet nuclear weapons R&D complex with the Defense Ministry. For six years, CIA officers accessed the recorders on the cable revealing much about Soviet weapons capabilities and developments.[8]

---

7. Project Azorian: The CIA's Declassified History of the Glomar Explorer at http://www2.gwu.edu/~nsarchiv/nukevault/ebb305/.
8. Milt Bearden and James Risen, The Main Enemy: The Inside Story of the CIA's Final Showdown with the KGB, New York: Ballantine Books, 2003.

READINGS FOR INSTRUCTORS

Each year more and more materials are declassified and released about US intelligence efforts to obtain the information needed for policymaking and defense planning. Recommended are the following:

Garwin, Richard. CORONA: America's First Reconnaissance Satellite System. A View from the Land Panel, Notes for Presentation George Washington University, May 23, 1995, at *http://www.fas.org/rlg/052295CRNA%20 CORONA%201-7.pdf.*

Pedlow, Gregory and Donald Welzenbach, The CIA and the U2 Program, 1998, at *https://www.cia.gov/library/center-for-the-study-of-intelligence/csi-publications/ books-and-monographs/the-cia-and-the-u-2-program-1954-1974/.*

Robarge, David. Archangel: CIA's Supersonic A-12 Reconnaissance Aircraft, 2012, at *https://www.cia.gov/library/center-for-the-study-of-intelligence/csi-pub-lications/books-and-monographs/a-12/index.html.*

In The Wizards of Langley: Inside the CIA's Directorate of Science and Technology, Boulder, CO: Westview Press, 2002, researcher Jeffrey T. Richelson writes "Several of the most important collection systems the United States operates today are direct descendents of earlier CIA programs."

Many CIA technical efforts are discussed in Robert Wallace and H. Keith Melton Spycraft: The Secret History of CIA's Spytechs, from Communism to Al-Qaida by. London: Penguin Books, 2008. Wallace was the former chief of CIA's Office of Technical Services.

Gene Poteat was president of the Association of Former Intelligence Officers and is a retired CIA senior scientific intelligence officer. He presently writes and lectures on intelligence and national security issues.

GUIDE TO THE STUDY OF INTELLIGENCE

Intelligence in the Post-Cold War Period

— Part I —
The Changed Environment

Stephen H. Campbell, B.Sc., M.A.L.D.

The role of intelligence has undergone fundamental shifts since the end of the Cold War. Intelligence is no longer the purview of a few high-level decisionmakers, it is now everybody's business. Within conflict zones, intelligence is collected, analyzed, and used at lower and lower levels of command. Within the tranquility of domestic life, local law enforcement and even ordinary citizens have become producers and consumers of intelligence. Publics expect their security and intelligence agencies to be more proactive and collaborative at home and abroad to preempt security threats. At the same time, they expect their governments to uphold their civil liberties.

This article explores the causes and nature of these shifts. The approach is more thematic than chronological. Intelligence does not operate in a vacuum. It is shaped by the nature of the threats that it must confront and the environment within which it operates. The collapse of the Soviet Empire led to a proliferation of new states and left power gaps that others were quick to fill. New threats emerged from sub-state actors. It also removed the largest impediment to global capitalism. As great power conflict became a distant memory, economic espionage increased, the criminal underworld feasted on the rewards of a deregulated global economy, and intelligence agencies increasingly turned to a burgeoning commercial sector for help.

The Collapse of the Soviet Union

After the fall of the Berlin Wall in 1989, the East German secret police, the

Stasi, collapsed.[1] Civil activists occupied offices of the Ministerium für Staats-sicherheit (Ministry of State Security, MfS, Stasi) and revealed a vast network of informants that had spied on neighbors, friends, and family. With 91,015 staff and 189,000 informants ("Inoffizielle Mitarbeiter," unofficial employees), 1 in 50 of the population had ties to the Stasi.The CIA managed to obtain copies of the Stasi's foreign files, which revealed that the Stasi controlled almost all the CIA's agents in the GDR in 1988-1989.[2] The files were used to prosecute Americans and West German citizens for treason.[3] Motivated to gain membership in NATO and the European Union (EU), the services of other Eastern European states were quick to purge their ranks of agents who had ties to serious corruption, organized crime or previous human rights abuses.[4] A similar transition to democratically accountable intelligence soon occurred in South Africa when apartheid collapsed in 1994.[5] Nearly two decades later, repressive security services in the Middle East would implode following the popular revolts of the Arab Spring. For example, Egypt's notorious State Security Investigation Service was disbanded on March 15, 2001, and replaced on May 3, 2001, by the new National Security Service.[6]

Like the Communist Party and the USSR itself, the KGB became a major casualty of the failed 1991 coup to oust Mikhail Gorbachev.[7] Almost all of the leadership were implicated. The KGB was broken up into five services,[8] but, in contrast to East Germany, only a limited effort was made to open the KGB archives.[9] Although thousands of former KGB professionals left the services in the 1990s, some of the most effective Russian assets remained in place. In 1995, the CIA discovered that Aldrich Ames had been spying for the Russians for 10 years. A few years later, Robert Hanssen, an FBI special agent, was arrested, having spied for the Russians for 20 years.[10] By the first decade of the 21st cen-

---

1. Thomas Wegener Friis, Kristie Macrakis, and Helmut Mueller-Enbergs (eds.). *East German Foreign Intelligence. Myth, Reality and Controversy* (New York: Routledge, 2010), 3.
2. Ibid, 4-5, 7; Robert Gerald Livingston, "Rosenholz. Mischa's Files, CIA's Booty," in ibid, 74-75.
3. Livingston, "Rosenholz:" 79-80.
4. Thomas C. Bruneau and Florina Cristiana (Cris) Matei, "Intelligence in the Developing Democracies: The Quest for Transparency and Effectiveness," in Loch Johnson (ed.), *The Oxford Handbook of National Security Intelligence* (Oxford: Oxford University Press, 2010).
5. Paul Todd and Jonathan Bloch, *Global Intelligence: The World's Secret Services Today*, (London: Zed Books, 2003), Chapter 7, "Intelligence in the South."
6. "Egyptians Doubtful About New Secret Service," *Hiiraan Online*, May 9, 2011.
7. Todd and Bloch, *Global Intelligence*, Chapter 5, "From KGB to FSB and Back Again?"
8. The five agencies are the SVR (foreign intelligence), FSB (internal security), FAPSI (communications), FSO (federal protection), and GUSP (special programs). The GRU (military intelligence) was left largely untouched. Robert W. Pringle, "The Intelligence Services of Russia," in Loch Johnson (Ed.), *The Oxford Handbook of National Security Intelligence*, (Oxford: Oxford University Press, 2010). See also Robert Pringle's article "Guide to Soviet and Russian Intelligence Services" in The *Intelligencer 18 (2)*, Winter-Spring 2011.
9. It was not until the 1992 defection of KGB archivist Vasili Mitrokhin to Great Britain that many of the KGB's Cold War secrets were revealed. See Christopher Andrew and Vasili Mitrohkin, *The Sword and the Shield: The Mitrohkin Archive and the Secret History of the KGB* (New York: Basic Books, 1999), and *The World Was Going Our Way: the KGB and the Battle for the Third World* (New York: Basic Books, 2005).
10. Todd and Bloch, 74-75. The 1995 Aspin-Brown Commission concluded that Ames had ruined the

tury, Russian espionage efforts against the US were back at "Cold War levels"[11] and the Federal Security Service (FSB) was demonstrating the ruthlessness of its predecessor. Incidents include the FSB storming of the Nord-Ost Theater in 2002 and the Beslan School in 2004, in which many hostages were killed, and the assassinations of defector Aleksandr Litvinenko and journalist Anna Politkovskaya in 2006.[12] This resurgence reflected the priorities of President Putin, a former KGB officer, who took over from Yeltsin in 1999, and brought former KGB members, dubbed "siloviki" ("person of force") into government and industry. One study found that 78% of the top thousand leaders in Putin's Russia belonged to a former security agency or had ties to it.[13]

Western intelligence agencies were downsized after the Cold War. The Dutch foreign ntelligence service was for a short time actually abolished, and some suggested there was no longer need for the German Federal Intelligence Service) (Bundesnachrichtendienst, BND). But cooler heads prevailed. The Dutch service was hurriedly re-established and the National Intelligence and Security Agency (BND) retained[14] Across the board, human intelligence took the largest hit. In the US, a "peace dividend" of around 30% was implemented by the end of the 1990s and the CIA's budget was slashed by 23%.[15]

One important outgrowth of security sector reform and downsizing was the rise of private corporations, such as Sandline International, Executive Outcomes, and MPRI, offering security and intelligence services.[16] These found a market in developing countries whose fragile regimes could no longer count on the support of the superpowers,[17] and in the developed world, where the hiring freezes of the 1990s, the expanding global economy, and the increased tempo after 9/11 combined to turn them into major players in the world of intelligence. Companies such as Booz Allen Hamilton, Lockheed Martin, SAIC, L3 Communications, CACI International, and IBM are now full partners with the CIA, the NSA, and the Pentagon in their most sensitive operations. By one estimate, in 2008, the outsourcing of intelligence activities in the US was a $50B

CIA's ability to spy against the Soviets during the Cold War's final years. As a result of his treachery, at least 10 Agency assets inside the Soviet Government in Moscow were executed. Among the secrets that Hanssen revealed was how American officials planned to continue governance if a nuclear war broke out with Russia. Loch K. Johnson, *National Security Intelligence: Secret Operations in Defense of the Democracies* (Cambridge, UK: Polity Press, 2012), 116-118.

11. Mary Louise Kelly, "U.S. Official: Russian Espionage at 'Cold War Levels'," *NPR*, June 6, 2007.

12. Pringle, "The Intelligence Services of Russia."

13. Ibid.

14. Richard J. Aldrich, "Beyond the Vigilant State: Globalization and Intelligence," *Review of International Studies* 35 (4), 2009; Wolfgang Krieger, "The German Bundesnachrichtendienst (BND): Evolution and Current Policy Issues," in Johnson (ed.), *Oxford Handbook of National Security Intelligence*.

15. Todd and Bloch, 4, 38.

16. P.W. Singer, *Corporate Warriors: The Rise of the Privitized Military Industry* (Ithaca, NY: Cornell University Press, 2003); Robert Young Pelton, *Licensed to Kill: Hired Guns in the War on Terror* (New York: Crown Publishers, 2006).

17. Elke Krahmann, "Private Security and Military Actors," in Robert A. Denemark (ed.), The International Studies Encyclopedia (Blackwell Publishing, 2010), Blackwell Reference Online.

a year business consuming 70% of the intelligence budget.[18]

The Emergence of New Threats

During the Cold War, the core intelligence task of Western agencies was to monitor the USSR's strategic and military posture, which meant gathering intelligence on missile deployments, Soviet troop movements, and military plans.[19] When the Soviet Empire collapsed, this task assumed a much lower priority; compared to 58% in 1980, in 1993, only 13% of the US intelligence budget was aimed at Russia.[20]

Economics became the new battleground. The Clinton administration asked the CIA to improve intelligence in three areas: supporting trade negotiations, tracking legal and illegal tactics that other countries were using to win business, and spotting financial troubles that could become foreign policy crises. To handle economic intelligence, it set up an Office of Intelligence Liaison in the Commerce Departmen.[21]

But it was not long before new security challenges emerged. Iraq invaded Kuwait and "low intensity conflicts" broke out in the Balkans, the Horn of Africa, and Afghanistan.[22] The reordering of the system following the end of the Cold War altered cost-benefit calculations and led to increased contestations for power in many parts of the world, requiring a dramatic increase in the number of UN peacekeeping operations. Since 1988, the UN has conducted 53 peacekeeping operations, to such places as Namibia, Cambodia, El Salvador, Mozambique, Somalia, Liberia, Sierra Leone, Haiti, Congo, East Timor, and Sudan.[23]

At the same time, criminals took advantage of deregulation and globalization.[24] In Russia, the failure to provide a regulatory framework for

---

18. Tim Shorrock, *Spies for Hire: The Secret World of Intelligence Outsourcing* (New York: Simon and Schuster, 2008); Aldrich, "Beyond the Vigilant State"; Krahmann, "Private Security and Military Actors."

19. Andrew Rathmell, "Towards Postmodern Intelligence," *Intelligence and National Security*, 17 (3), 2002, 87-104.

20. James Bamford, *Body of Secrets: Anatomy of the Ultra-Secret National Security Agency* (New York: Doubleday, 2001), 553.

21. David E. Sanger and Tim Weiner, "Emerging Role for the CIA: Economic Spy," *The New York Times*, October 15, 1995; Todd and Bloch, 55.

22. Anne L. Clunan and Harold A. Trinkunas (eds.), *Ungoverned Spaces. Alternatives to State Authority in an Era of Softened Sovereignty*, (Stanford, CA: Stanford University Press, 2010), 22.

23. Ibid; Phil Williams, "Here Be Dragons. Dangerous Spaces and International Security," in Clunan and Trinkunas (eds.), *Ungoverned Spaces*; See http://www.un.org/en/peacekeeping/documents/operationslist.pdf, accessed March 6, 2012.

24. The term "'globalization" was barely used before 1989 but has since been deployed to explain the notion that boundaries are being rendered increasingly porous – almost meaningless – by the sheer volume of cross-border activity. Michael Cox, "From the cold war to the world economic crisis," in John Baylis, Steve Smith, and Patricia Owens, *The Globalization of World Politics. An Introduction to International Relations* (Oxford: Oxford University Press, 2011). For a more anecdotal account see, Thomas L. Friedman's highly readable *Lexus and the Olive Tree* (New York: Anchor Books, 2000) and its sequel, *The World is Flat* (New York: Picador, 2007).

business encouraged organized crime to become a surrogate for government. Once-disconnected gangs of thugs, thieves, and former intelligence officers hijacked the nation's economy and penetrated deep into Russian business and state enterprises. They offered protection, contract enforcement, arbitration and debt collection. Protection rackets ("kryshi") and their associated street gangs ("gruppirovki") became the midwives of capitalism.[25] As the number of weakly governed areas around the globe increased, crime went global. Asymmetries in regulation and governance created incentives for engaging in "jurisdictional arbitrage," as transnational criminals simply sought out those areas with the most distracted, inept or corruptible authority structures.[26] The spread of liberal economic reforms, the emergence of instantaneous forms of communication and the growth of émigré communities were major drivers. Country after country in the 1990s lowered the barriers to trade, eliminated regulations inhibiting foreign investment, and removed exchange controls to permit the free buying and selling of currencies. The wire transfer and ATM markets reached global scope, financial capital began to move unimpeded, and money launderers found themselves in paradise.[27] The market for trafficked counterfeit goods, narcotics, weapons, and humans grew as high as 20% of world GDP, according to some estimates. The Big Five organized criminal groups from China, Columbia, Italy, Japan, and Russia – the Chinese Triads, the Colombian Cartels, the Italian Mafia, the Japanese Yakuza, and the Russian Mob – expanded their overseas operations, while new criminal activity emerged in places such as Albania, Nigeria, Mexico, and the Gulf of Aden.[28]

Although leftist terrorism receded as communism collapsed, the 1990s saw an increased frequency of terrorist attacks around the world, in Bombay, Calcutta, New York, Khobar, Nairobi, and Dar es Salaam.[29] While these events garnered increased attention,[30] it was the 1995 sarin gas attack in Tokyo, and especially the use of fuel-filled jets as missiles in the US on September 11, 2001, that revealed the power of religiously motivated terrorism in the post-Cold War world.[31] The conventional wisdom that terrorists "want a lot of people watching"

25. Williams, "Here Be Dragons"; John Kerry, *The New War: The Web of Crime That Threatens America's Security* (New York: Simon & Schuster, 1997), 22; Misha Glenny, *McMafia: A Journey Through the Global Criminal Underworld*, (New York: Alfred A. Knopf), 2008, 54-55.
26. Clunan and Trinkunas, 9; Robert Mandel, *Dark Logic: Transnational Criminal Tactics and Global Security*, (Stanford, CA: Stanford University Press, 2011), 30.
27. Mandel, 21-25, 68, 72. Moisés Naím, *Illicit: How Smugglers, Traffickers, and Copycats are Hijacking the Global Economy*, (New York, Anchor Books, 2005), 17-24.
28. Mande, 15-18, and Chapter 4, "Major Transnational Criminal Organizations."
29. Paul R. Pillar, "Dealing with Transnational Threats," in *US Department of Commerce, Directorate of Intelligence 1952-2002: Fifty Years of Informing Policy* (Springfield, VA: National Technical Information Service, 2002); Todd and Bloch, 183.
30. Pillar, "Dealing with Transnational Threats."
31. Bruce Hoffman, "CBRN Terrorism Post-9/11," in Russell D. Howard and James J.F. Forest, *Weapons of Mass Destruction and Terrorism* (New York: McGraw-Hill, 2012).

but "not a lot of people dead"[32] no longer held. Powerful non-state actors were now capable of wreaking havoc on a global scale and posing a tier 1 threat to international security without the direction of states.[33]

The possibility that weapons of mass destruction would fall into the hands of terrorist groups now haunted Western security establishments. Globalization was making it easier for countries to set up quasi-governmental organizations and front companies to buy and sell dual-use nuclear technologies.[34] Having stolen nuclear secrets while working in the Netherlands, A.Q. Khan succeeded in fathering the bomb in Pakistan, and reoriented his purchasing network into the world's first nuclear supermarket. Khan found willing customers in Iran, Iraq, North Korea (the "axis of evil"), and Libya.[35] To add to the post-9/11 angst, the October 2001 anthrax attacks fueled fear of a mass biological attack.

The post-Cold War security environment was a far cry from the "perpetual peace" predicted by advocates of the "End of History" thesis.[36] The long-term decline of the Westphalian state articulated by Robert Kaplan in his vision of the "Coming Anarchy"[37] was creating a new era in which authority was dispersed and a medieval power structure was emerging.[38] Clinton's DCI, James Woolsey, captured the nature of the new threats well when he warned that a "garden of snakes had replaced the single dragon."[39]

Intelligence Agencies Adapt

The new threats forced intelligence agencies to adapt. In contrast to the large, slow-moving, clearly bounded, observable targets of the Cold War, the new targets were small, agile, amorphous, and hidden.[40] In the Cold War, enemies were easy to find and observe, but difficult to neutralize. Now the opposite was true. The new enemies were relatively easy to neutralize once found. Finding and observing them was the problem.[41] Obscurity was their

---

32. Brian M. Jenkins, "International Terrorism: A New Mode of Conflict," in David Carlton and Carlo Schaerf (eds.), *International Terrorism and World Security* (London: Croom Helm, 1975), 15.

33. Richard H. Shultz, Douglas Farah, and Itamara V. Lochard, "Armed Groups: A Tier-One Security Priority," *US Air Force Institute for National Security Studies*, Occasional Paper 57, September 2004.

34. James A. Russell, "Peering into the Abyss," *The Nonproliferation Review*, 13:3, 2006.

35. See, for example, Gordon Corera, *Shopping for Bombs: Nuclear Proliferation, Global Insecurity, and the Rise and Fall of the A.Q. Khan Network* (Oxford: Oxford University Press, 2006).

36. Francis Fukuyama, *The End of History and the Last Man*, (New York: Free Press, 1992).

37. Robert D. Kaplan, "The Coming Anarchy," *The Atlantic Monthly*, February 1994.

38. Williams, "Here Be Dragons"; see also Andrew Linklater, "Globalization and the Transformation of Political Community," in Baylis, Smith and Owens, *The Globalization of World Politics*.

39. Testimony before the US Senate Select Committee on Intelligence (SSCI), 2 February 1993. Douglas F. Garthoff, *Directors of Central Intelligence as Leaders of the U.S. Intelligence Community 1946-2005* (Washington, DC: Center for the Study of Intelligence, 2005), 221.

40. Gregory F. Treverton, *Intelligence for an Age of Terror* (New York: Cambridge University Press, 2009), Chapter 2, "The Changed Target."

41. Neal Pollard, "On Counter-Terrorism and Intelligence," in Gregory F. Treverton and Wilhelm Agrell. *National Intelligence Systems: Current Research and Future Prospects* (New York: Cambridge University Press, 2009).

greatest asset. They exhibited small "signatures," low "signal-to-noise" ratios and indicators that lacked the uniqueness needed for effective warning intelligence. Example indicators were the surveillance of targets and the purchase of dual-use technologies.[42]

In the Cold War, most intelligence consumers were located at the apex of national-security decision-making.[43] Now the number of consumers was mushrooming to include state and local officials, managers of infrastructure, and even private individuals. An airport security officer or a public health doctor might now have a more urgent "need to know" about a threat than the US President because he or she might be in a more immediate position to thwart it.[44] Similarly, intelligence in conventional wars was typically collected by upper echelon intelligence sections and passed to subordinate units to facilitate action. Now Western militaries were fighting counterinsurgencies in which platoons and companies were both collecting and acting upon intelligence. Intelligence flows were becoming more bottoms-up than top-down.[45]

These changed realities demanded a new approach to information. For half a century, intelligence agencies had developed a labyrinth of classifications and compartments to minimize the threat of espionage.[46] But this system was now preventing the information sharing needed to address new dispersed enemies with no respect for boundaries. Intelligence agencies now had to balance their traditional need for exclusion with the new need to form horizontal knowledge networks. These networks had to span foreign/domestic, public/private, and national/local boundaries.[47] Instead of a linear problem-solving approach the time-sensitive and fragmented nature of the new targets demanded a continuous, recursive dialogue amongst collectors, analysts, and consumers.[48]

Intelligence agencies around the world adapted with varying speeds to these non-state threats. Unconstrained regimes in the Middle East were swift to clamp down. Egypt's Mukhabarat, for example, dismantled much of the Al-Jihad terrorist group in the early 1990s using a legion of informants – street kids, merchants, doormen, hotel employees, civil servants, and taxi drivers.[49]

---

42. Daniel Byman, *The Five Front War: The Better Way to Fight Global Jihad* (Hoboken, NJ: John Wiley and Sons, 2008), Chapter 3, 'Tracking Down and Disrupting Terrorists"; Treverton, "The Changed Target."
43. Treverton, "The Changed Target."
44. Ibid.
45. Christopher C.E. McGarry, *Inverting the Army Intelligence Pyramid* (Fort Leavenworth: School of Advanced Military Studies, US Army Command and Staff College, 2011).
46. Michael Herman, "Counter-Terrorism, Information Technology and Intelligence Change," *Intelligence and National Security* 18 (4), 2003.
47. Andrew Rathmell, "Towards Postmodern Intelligence"; William J. Lahneman, "The Need for a New Intelligence Paradigm," *International Journal of Intelligence and Counterintelligence* 23 (2), 2010.
48. Robert M. Clark, *Intelligence Analysis. A Target-Centric Approach*, Chapter 1, "The Intelligence Process"; Treverton, "The Changed Target."
49. Owen L. Sirrs, *A History of the Egyptian Intelligence Service: A history of the mukhabarat, 1910-2009* (London: Routledge, 2010).

The repressive practices of Middle Eastern security agencies would drive Islamist extremists abroad and cause them to shift their focus from the "near enemy" to the "far enemy."[50]

For liberal democracies, the struggle would be long and protracted. The small, highly secretive British and Ulster intelligence agencies learned, with some exceptions,[51] to use force against the Provisional Irish Republican Army (PIRA) in a constrained and legitimate manner.[52] They also learned the importance of inter-agency collaboration,[53] so that, by 1994, the MI5, Special Branch, and regional police forces throughout the UK were frustrating three out of every four attempted terrorist attacks.[54] This experience would serve the British well when confronting the growing threat of Islamist militants in the following decade.

The huge US intelligence community (IC), "flawed by design" according to Amy Zegart,[55] was the slowest to adapt. In the 1990s the IC resisted the recommendations of several commissions to revamp its information practices.[56] After 9/11, Congress passed legislation that helped to remove the "wall" between law enforcement and foreign civilian intelligence. The Patriot Act legalized "joint-purpose surveillance," permitting agents conducting espionage investigations to furnish information to law enforcement personnel.[57] While remaining "allergic" to the prospect of a standalone domestic intelligence agency,[58] Congress did accept commitments from the FBI to transform itself into an "agency that can prevent terrorist acts, rather than react to them as crimes."[59] It responded to the perennial urge to "fix the machine"[60] by creating a new Department of Homeland Security in 2002 and a new position of director of national intelligence in 2004. New centers for counterterrorism, counter-

---

50. Fawaz Gerges, *The Far Enemy: Why Jihad Went Global* (New York: Cambridge University Press, 2005).
51. These included collaboration with loyalist paramilitaries and turning a blind eye to human rights abuses by their most valued informers. Tony Geraghty, *The Irish War: The Hidden Conflict between the IRA and British Intelligence* (London: Johns Hopkins University Press, 2000); Martin Ingram and Greg Harkin, *Stakeknife: Britain's Secret Agents in Ireland* (Madison, WI: University of Wisconsin Press, 2004).
52. Martin Dillon, *The Dirty War: Covert Strategies and Tactics Used in Political Conflicts*, New York: Routledge, 1990.
53. This lesson was manifested in the establishment of the Irish Joint Section and "tasking and co-ordination groups" in the 1970s. Brian A. Jackson, "Counterinsurgency in a Long War. The British Experience in Northern Ireland," *Military Review*, January-February 2007.
54. Stella Rimington, Richard Dimbleby Lecture, *Security and Democracy* (London: BBC Educational Developments, 1994), 9.
55. Amy B. Zegart, *Flawed by Design: The Evolution of the CIA, JCS, and NSC*, Stanford, CA; Stanford University Press, 2000.
56. Amy B. Zegart, *Spying Blind: The CIA, the FBI, and the Origins of 9/11* (Princeton, NJ: Princeton University Press, 1997), Chapter 2, "Canaries in the Coal Mine. The Case for Failed Adaptation."
57. *The USA Patriot Act: Guide to the Issues* (Washington, DC: The Century Foundation, 2004).
58. Jennifer E. Sims and Burton L. Gerber, *Transforming U.S. Intelligence*, Washington, DC: Georgetown University Press, 2005: 206.
59. Alfred Cumming and Todd Masse, *FBI Intelligence Reform Since September 11, 2001: Issues and Options for Congress*, Washington, D.C.: Congressional Research Service, RL32336, 2004.
60. Richard K. Betts, "Fixing Intelligence," *Foreign Affairs* 81 (1), January-February 2002.

proliferation, and counterintelligence were established under the new Office of the Director of National Intelligence (ODNI).[61]

US military intelligence was quicker to adapt. The concept of joint intelligence was already firmly established,[62] so it was not a huge leap for the Department of Defense (DOD) to work with national agencies to form National Intelligence Support Teams in the 1990s and Joint Intelligence Operations Centers in the new century.[63] To prosecute fleeting targets, intelligence and air operations became increasingly coordinated,[64] and special forces honed the process of "find, fix, finish, exploit, analyze" (F3EA) down to a science.[65]

US paramilitary forces came into their own after 9/11, in contrast to the struggle they had finding their footing in the 1990s. CIA covert action in the 1990s was marked by a half-hearted campaign to work with opposition groups in Iraq to topple Saddam Hussein, but Saddam's intelligence apparatus proved too adept at uncovering assassination plots and executing conspirators. In Guatemala, the CIA's contribution to fighting the "war on drugs" was colored by accusations of human rights abuse.[66] In the winter of 2001, however, CIA covert teams worked with special operations and indigenous forces to overthrow the Taliban in a matter of weeks.[67] By 2004, US Special Operations Command (USSOCOM) had become the lead command in "global operations against terrorist networks." Its role was outlined in the classified "Unified Command Plan." After the ouster of the Taliban, Donald Rumsfeld fought for special operations forces to take the lead in the fight against Al-Qaeda. In 2002, he commissioned an influential review by the Defense Science Board, which recommended an increased emphasis on covert action to gain "close target access" and a greater role for special operations forces in "intelligence

61. Gregory F. Treverton, *Intelligence for an Age of Terror* (New York, Cambridge University Press, 2009), Chapter 4, "The Imperative of Change."

62. The concept was born in World War II and came of age in 1986 with the Goldwater-Nicholls reforms, which also created US Special Operations Command. James D. Marchio, "Days of Future Past. Joint Intelligence in World War II," *Joint Forces Quarterly*, Spring 1996; Charles Cogan, "Hunters not Gatherers: Intelligence in the Twenty-First Century," *Intelligence and National Security* 19 (2), 2004.

63. James M. Lose, "Fulfilling a Crucial Role. National Intelligence Support Teams," CIA Center for the Study of Intelligence, *Studies in Intelligence*, Winter 1999-2000; Federal Document Clearing House, "DoD To Set Up Joint Intelligence Operations Centers Worldwide," *Regulatory Intelligence Data*, April 12, 2006.

64. Raymond T. Odierno, "ISR Evolution in the Iraqi Theater," *Joint Force Quarterly*, July 2008.

65. Michael T. Flynn, Rich Juergens, and Thomas L. Cantrell, "Employing ISR. SOF Best Practices," *Joint Forces Quarterly* 50, 3rd quarter 2008; Mark Urban, *Task Force Black: The Explosive True Story of the SAS and the Secret War in Iraq* (London: Little, Brown, 2010).

66. Robert Baer, *See No Evil: The True Story of a Ground Soldier in the CIA's War on Terrorism* (New York: Three Rivers Press, 2002); John Prados, *Safe for Democracy: The Secret Wars of the CIA* (Chicago: Ivan R. Dee, 2006), 597-612.

67. Henry A. Crumpton, "Intelligence and War: Afghanistan, 2001-2002," in Jennifer E. Sims and Burton Gerber, *Transforming U.S. Intelligence* (Washington, DC: Georgetown University Press, 2005). For anecdotal accounts, see Gary C. Schroen, *First In: An Insider's Account of How the CIA Spearheaded the War on Terror in Afghanistan* (New York: Balantine Books, 2005) and Gary Berntsen and Ralph Pezzullo, *Jawbreaker: The Attack on Bin Laden and Al-Qaeda: A Personal Account by the CIA's Key Field Commander* (New York: Crown Publishers, 2005).

preparation of the battlefield" (IPB).[68] Thousands of raids later, the May 2011 takedown of Osama bin Laden[69] showed that the Pentagon's covert capabilities had come a long way since the ill-fated 1980 mission to rescue the American hostages in the embassy in Teheran.

The "exploit" part of the new F3EA cycle was the key to launching follow-on operations and creating a spiral of success. US operations against Al-Qaeda after 9/11 were modeled in part on the "kingpin" strategy used successfully between 1989 and 1996 to bring down the leaders of the Medellin and Cali cocaine cartels in Colombia. The 1991 Operation Cornerstone, for example, produced a spiral of raids that led to numerous arrests and convictions.[70] Some raids conducted in the post-9/11 counterinsurgency campaigns netted a treasure trove of intelligence from "site exploitation." Computers and hard drives seized during a US raid in Taji, Iraq, led to the discovery of huge arms caches and high-value leaders of Al-Qaeda in Iraq (AQI). Documents found in Tuzliyah, Iraq, and on a hard drive in Julaybah, Iraq, in 2007 gave coalition forces unprecedented insight into AQI organization and financial structures. Documents and hard drives captured by US Special Forces in Sinjar, Iraq, offered unrivaled insight into the foreign fighters entering Iraq. Follow-on actions reduced the flow from 120 a month to 10 to 20 a month. Out of such raids, the new discipline of "document and media exploitation" was born, and a national center and repository were set up.[71]

But the bulk of intelligence came from detainees. In sharp contrast to the Cold War, when the most useful intelligence was willingly revealed by defectors, the challenge now was extracting timely intelligence from detainees unwilling to talk.[72] The exposure of mass detentions at Guantanamo Bay, "harsh interrogations" at Abu Ghraib, the practice of "extraordinary rendition," and the existence of secret CIA prisons generated huge anti-US sentiment around the world.[73] It also led to considerable soul-searching and debate within the US,[74]

68. *United States Special Operations Command History* (MacDill AFB, FL: USSOCOM History and Research Office, 2007), 16; Cogan, "Hunters not Gatherers: Intelligence in the Twenty-First Century"; Defense Science Board, DSB Summer Study on Special Operations and Joint Forces in Support of Countering Terrorism, August 16, 2002.

69. Chuck Pfarrer, *Seal Target Geronimo: The Inside Story of the Mission to Kill Osama bin Laden* (New York: St. Martin's Press, 2011).

70. Ed Blanche, "Hunting Bin Laden," *The Middle East*, January, 2009; Ron Chepesiuk, *The Bullet or the Bribe: Taking Down Colombia's Cali Drug Cartel* (Westport, CT: Praeger, 2003), Part III, "The Fall."

71. Renny McPherson, "Inside Al Qaeda's Hard Drives," *Boston Globe*, July 17, 2011; Eric Schmitt & Thom Shanker, *Counterstrike: The Untold Story of America's Secret Campaign Against Al Qaeda* (New York: Times Books, 2011), Chapter 3, "The Exploitation of Intelligence"; Office of the Director of National Intelligence, "Document and Media Exploitation," Intelligence Community Directive 302, July 6, 2007.

72. Frederick Hitz, "The Importance and Future of Espionage," in Loch K. Johnson, *Strategic Intelligence, Volume 2, The Intelligence Cycle* (Westport, CT: Praeger Security International, 2007).

73. Peter L. Bergen, *The Longest War. The Enduring Conflict Between America and Al-Qaeda* (New York: Free Press, 2011), Chapter 7, "The Gloves Come Off."

74. After 9/11, early positions taken by the US Government by the Office of Legal Counsel that the Geneva Conventions do not apply to captured Al Qaeda or Taliban operatives were overturned by the

as Europe largely stood by in dismay. Most countries in Europe had already grappled with these issues and had incorporated the European Convention on Human Rights into their domestic laws in the 1990s. Even in the UK, despite the special relationship, there was political and intellectual consensus that torture remained anathema. Britain had learned from the Troubles that "inhuman and degrading treatment" was largely counter-productive in the long-term.[75]

The "find" part of the F3EA cycle was also dependent upon human intelligence. But HUMINT from spy runners recruited at Oxford or Yale and taught to frequent the embassy cocktail circuit was of little use in tracking down terrorists.[76] In contrast to the need for a few highly placed agents inside the closed systems of the Cold War, the emphasis was now on a plethora of access agents who could lead the agency to clandestine terrorist cells. This meant recruiting unassociated observers in shops and mosques, and penetrating support networks of financial donors, arms suppliers, and money launderers.[77] Security agencies built huge networks of informants to preempt the threat of terrorism. In Israel, one estimate from June 2003 suggested that as many as 80% of potential terrorist attacks were being foiled through intelligence from informants. In the US, an estimate from October 2011 put the number of FBI informants at around 15,000. The DEA had their own network of 5,000 registered informants and 10,000 sub-sources.[78] In the decade after 9/11, with a handful of exceptions, the FBI thwarted high-profile domestic terror plots in the US through informants and sting operations.[79] A critical ingredient was cooperation with state and local law enforcement through Joint Terrorism Task Forces.[80]

It was another story abroad. One of the most salient features of intelligence in the post-Cold War period has been the explosive growth in foreign

---

US Supreme Court, which ruled in summer of 2006 in "Hamdan v Rumsfeld" that unlawful combatant detainees of the US military held in DoD custody must be afforded the protections of Article 3 of the Geneva Conventions prohibiting cruel and inhumane treatment. The McCain Amendment, which became law in Dec. 2005 as part of the Detainee Treatment Act, and applies also to US intelligence agencies, forbids US personnel in US facilities from using coercive interrogation techniques not set forth in the US Army interrogation manual. Frederick P. Hitz, *Why Spy? Espionage in an Age of Uncertainty* (New York: St. Martin's Press, 2008), 56, 164.

75. Len Scott and R. Gerald Hughes, "Intelligence in the Twenty-First Century: Change and Continuity or Crisis and Transformation?" *Intelligence and National Security* 24 (1), 2009.

76. Reuel Marc Gerecht, "The New Clandestine Service: The Case for Creative Destruction," in Peter Berkowitz (ed.), *The Future of American Intelligence* (Stanford, CA: Hoover Institute Press, 2005).

77. Michael Butler, "Killing Cells: Retooling Human Intelligence Collection for Global Decentralized Terrorism," International Studies Association Annual Convention, 2009.

78. Steve Hewitt, *Snitch: A History of the Modern Intelligence Informer* (London: Continuum International, 2010), 127; Trevor Aaronson, "The Informants," Mother Jones, October 2011; Robert K. Ackerman, "Intelligence Key to Counterdrug Efforts," *Signal Magazine*, October 2010.

79. Exceptions included Major Nidal Hasan, Faisal Shahzad, Najibullah Zazi, and Hesham Mohamed Hadayet. Aaronson, "The Informants."

80. Robert Mueller and Matthew Olsen, "FBI Counterterrorism and Intelligence Operations," Hearing before the House Permanent Select Committee on Intelligence, Oct 6, 2011.

intelligence liaison, especially with domestic security services.[81] To preempt terrorist plots being hatched in the remote camps of Pakistan or the apartments of Hamburg,[82] the internal services of foreign countries proved invaluable. After 9/11, the FBI and even the NYPD increased the number of counterterrorism liaison officers abroad, while the CIA set up Counterterrorist Intelligence Centers modeled on its counternarcotics centers in Latin America and Asia.[83] They knew their country, and their powers exceeded anything the FBI could do.[84] By 2005, the CIA reported to Congress that "virtually every capture or killing of a suspected terrorist outside Iraq since the Sept. 11, 2001, attacks – more than 3,000 in all – was a result of foreign intelligence services' work alongside the agency."[85] Just as money launderers and accountants led to the king-pins of the Cali Cartel in the early 1990s,[86] spiritual advisers and couriers led intelligence agencies to senior Al-Qaeda leaders after 9/11. In 2006, tracking of spiritual adviser Sheikh Abd Al-Rahman led to the killing of Abu Musab al-Zarqawi. In 2011 surveillance of courier Ibrahim Saeed Ahmed, whose nom de guerre was Abu Ahmed al-Kuwaiti, led to the killing of Osama bin Laden.[87] Attempts to recruit ideologically motivated insiders proved to be less successful and highly risky, as demonstrated by the tragic deaths of seven CIA officers at Forward Operating Base Chapman in December 2009, in a suicide attack by extremist Humam al-Balawi, whom they believed Jordanian intelligence had "turned."[88]

Intelligence liaison also became important in multilateral peacekeeping missions[89] and in dismantling transnational proliferation networks. In 1998, cooperation between British and American intelligence revealed A.Q. Khan's plans to assist Libya in building nuclear weapons. The CIA then recruited informers within Khan's network who tipped them off in 2003 to a shipment

---

81. Aldrich, "Beyond the Vigilant State.

82. Paul Pillar, "Fighting International Terrorism: Beyond September 11th," *Defense Intelligence Journal*, Winter 2002.

83. Adam Svendsen, "The globalization of intelligence since 9/11: frameworks and operational parameters," *Cambridge Review of International Affairs* 21 (1), August 13, 2008; Dana Priest, "Foreign Network at Front of CIA's Terror Fight: Joint Facilities in Two Dozen Countries Account for Bulk of Agency's Post-9/11 Successes," *Washington Post*, November 18, 2005.

84. Aldrich, "Beyond the Vigilant State."

85. Ibid.

86. Ron Chepesiuk, *The Bullet or the Bribe*.

87. Sean D. Naylor, "Inside the Zarqawi Takedown. Persistent Surveillance Helps End 3-Year Manhunt," *Defense News* 21 (4), June 12, 2006; Peter L. Bergen, *Manhunt: The Ten-year Search for bin Laden from 9/11 to Abbottabad* (New York: Crown Publishers, 2012).

88. Joby Warrick, *The Triple Agent: The Al-Qaeda Mole Who Infiltrated the CIA* (New York: Doubleday, 2011).

89. A review of UN peace operations in 2000 known as the Brahimi Report convinced the organization that its long-standing aversion to intelligence was no longer tenable. It concluded that UN peacekeepers needed "field intelligence and other capabilities" to "mount a defense against violent challengers." The UN also needed intelligence to monitor ceasefires and agreements on the decommissioning of weapons, and to investigate war crimes. Simon Chesterman, "Does the UN have intelligence?" *Survival* 48 (3), August 3, 2006; Richard J. Aldrich, "Intelligence and International Security," *International Studies Encyclopedia*, Denmark, Blackwell Publishing, 2010; Hugh Smith, "Intelligence and UN Peacekeeping," *Survival* 36 (3), Autumn 1994.

of centrifuge parts to Libya. The October interception of the German-owned ship BBC China by Italy delivered enough evidence both to convince Qaddafi to renounce his WMD programs and to persuade President Musharraf to shut down the Khan network in an unprecedented series of intelligence-led negotiations.[90]

Intelligence liaison, however, had its risks. The inflated judgments about Iraq's WMD programs in the infamous 2002 National Intelligence Estimate used to justify the invasion of Iraq were based in part on intelligence from foreign agencies that turned out to be fabricated. After Saddam was removed from power in 2003, the Iraq Survey Group found no evidence that Iraq had attempted to reconstitute its nuclear or biological programs.[91] This included the testimony of an Iraqi chemical engineer codenamed "Curveball" who was feeding falsities to his German handlers,[92] and a forged document passed by Italian intelligence purporting to show Iraqi purchases of yellowcake in Niger.[93] The US IC responded to these failures by requiring that information concerning the reliability of sources be included in all future analytic products. Intelligence Community Directive 206, an outcome of the initiative "Analytic Transformation" headed by Thomas Fingar, requires that analysts provide "consistent and structured sourcing information." It encourages analysts to acquire from collectors insight into the nature and reliability of sources.[94]

READINGS FOR INSTRUCTORS

Conferences. A series of conferences organized by the University of Wales over the past decade help explain the changing nature of intelligence. See special editions of *Intelligence and National Security* 19 (2), Summer 2004; 21 (5), October 2006; and 24 (1), February 2009. In 2002, The Netherlands Intelligence Studies Association in The Hague organized a conference resulting in a collection by Ben de Jon, Wies Platje, and Robert David Steele,

---

90. Catherine Collins and Douglas Frantz, *Fallout: The True Story of the CIA's Secret War on Nuclear Trafficking* (New York: Free Press, 2011); Gordon Corera, *Shopping for Bombs: Nuclear Proliferation, Global Insecurity, and the Rise and Fall of the A.Q. Khan Network* (Oxford: Oxford University Press, 2006); David Albright, *Peddling Peril: How the Secret Nuclear Trade Arms America's Enemies* (New York: Free Press, 2010).

91. Duelfer Report of September 30, 2004, available at https://www.cia.gov/library/reports/general-reports-1/iraq_wmd_2004/index.html, accessed March 18, 2012.

92. The German BND adopted poor interrogation practices when debriefing the Iraqi defector, Rafid Ahmed al-Janabi, who was able to manipulate his handlers to gain political asylum. Bob Drogin, *Curveball: Spies, Lies, and the Con Man Who Caused a War* (New York: Random House, 2007); Paddy Allen, Jo Blason, Helen Pidd and Martin Chulov, "Life and Times of Rafid Ahmed Alwan al-Janabi, AKA Curveball," *The Guardian*, February 15, 2011.

93. Peter Eisner, "How Bogus Letter Became a Case for War," *The Washington Post*, April 3, 2007.

94. See Office of the Director of National Intelligence, Intelligence Community Directive Number 206. Sourcing Requirements for Disseminated Analytic Products, October 17, 2007; Richard H. Immerman, "Transforming Analysis: The Intelligence Community's Best Kept Secret," *Intelligence and National Security* 26 (2-3), May 20, 2011; Tom Fingar, "All Source Analysis" in the *The Intelligencer 19 (1)*, Winter-Spring 2012: 63-66.

Peacekeeping Intelligence: Emerging Concepts for the Future (Oakton, VA: OSS International Press, 2003). In 2003, CIA and RAND teamed up on a series of workshops and published findings in *Making Sense of Transnational Threats*, CIA Kent Center Occasional Paper 3 (1), 2004. One of the paper's authors, Gregory Treverton, used these findings as the basis for his excellent *Intelligence for an Age of Terror* (New York, Cambridge University Press, 2009).

Agency Histories. John Diamond's *The CIA and the Culture of Failure: U.S. Intelligence from the End of the Cold War to the Invasion of Iraq* (Palo Alto, CA: Stanford University Press, 2008) is a comprehensive study of the interplay of intelligence and policy. John Prados' *Safe for Democracy: The Secret Wars of the CIA* (Chicago: Ivan R. Dee, 2006) details CIA covert action. Garrett M. Graff's *The Threat Matrix: The FBI at War in the Age of Global Terror* (New York: Little Brown and Company, 2011) documents the transformation of the FBI since 9/11. Historian Christopher Andrew's *The Defence of the Realm: The Authorized History of MI5* (London: Penguin Books, 2009) relates the evolution of British domestic intelligence.

Intelligence and Terror. See the seminal *9/11 Commission Report* (New York: Barnes & Noble, 2006); the Washington insider account by Eric Schmitt & Thom Shanker, *Counterstrike: The Untold Story of America's Secret Campaign Against Al Qaeda* (New York: Times Books, 2011); the comprehensive, on-the-ground chronicle by Seth G. Jones, *Hunting in the Shadows: The Pursuit of al Qa'ida since 9/11* (New York: W. W. Norton, 2012); and the thought-provoking Jan Goldman (ed.), *Ethics of Spying: A Reader for the Intelligence Professional* (Lanham, MD: The Scarecrow Press, 2006).

Stephen H. Campbell is a research associate in the Tufts University Fletcher School of Law and Diplomacy International Security Studies Program, where he specializes in intelligence and non-state armed groups. His career has included positions as analyst, consultant, educator, and marketing strategist in the information technology industry. Mr. Campbell earned a B.Sc. honors first class in physics from the University of Glasgow and a masters in law and diplomacy from the Fletcher School. He can be reached at *stephen.campbell@tufts.edu*.

GUIDE TO THE STUDY OF INTELLIGENCE

Intelligence in the Post-Cold War Period

— Part II —
The Impact of Technology

Stephen H. Campbell, B.Sc., M.A.L.D.

The first part of this article explored how changes in geopolitics and economics have affected intelligence since the end of the Cold War. The implosion of the world's second superpower and the forces of globalization, however, have only so much explanatory power. In the two decades since the end of the Cold War, advances in technology have played a significant role in transforming the world of intelligence both externally (the threat environment) and internally (the intelligence process).

Technology has empowered adversaries with the ability to form virtual communities that erode state power. It has enabled the theft of secrets and the proliferation of dangerous knowledge over vast distances. Governments no longer have a monopoly over information. Secrets are harder to keep than ever before. At the same time, technology has made the dream of near real-time fusion of intelligence come true. It has revolutionized tradecraft. And it continues to hold out the promise of being able to detect dangerous substances.

This article explores these changes thematically, by examining the fields of imagery and geospatial technology, materials and weapons science, and information and communication technology, respectively.

Imagery and Geospatial Technology

Advances in technology have enabled imagery to play a crucial role in tactical battlefield support, in contrast to the largely strategic role it played during the Cold War.[1] At the same time, the fusion of real-time imagery, GPS

---

1. Imagery intelligence (IMINT) was critical to keeping the Cold War "cold." It kept a close eye on the

data, and digital maps into geographic information systems has forged a new discipline – geospatial intelligence – thereby revolutionizing military command and control.[2]

The 1991 Gulf War heralded these changes with the use of unmanned aerial vehicles (UAVs) for reconnaissance, the first large-scale use of precision-guided munitions (PGMs), and the tactical use of radar from satellites and new JSTARS aircraft. PGMs accounted for 9% of weapons deployed in Desert Storm (Iraq, 1991). This increased to 29% in Allied Force (Kosovo, 1999) and to 70% in Enduring Freedom (Afghanistan, 2001).[3] The war had a profound impact. Adversaries could not tackle the US on its own terms.

US airpower drove Chinese war planners to put Command, Control, Communications, Computers, Intelligence, Surveillance and Reconnaissance (C4ISR) at the heart of their military modernization strategy. For the Chinese, the Gulf War "changed the world." There would be no repeat of the Red Army victories of the 1950s. People's Liberation Army strategy evolved to combine network and electronic warfare against an adversary's information systems at the start of any conflict.[4] The People's Republic of China (PRC) and others began to move their weapons of mass destruction (WMD), missiles, and military leadership underground.[5]

Compared to the Cold War, when satellites tracked targets such as airfields and warships, post-Cold War foes were low-contrast.[6] Satellites had trouble identifying an arms deal in a village square, a small fast-moving convoy of terrorists in the desert, or a training camp consisting of little more than tents and rifle ranges.[7] Military commanders turned to aerial surveillance, increasingly unmanned, relying on satellites more for navigation and secure communication.

There are large, medium, and small UAVs. Large UAVs, such as the Global Hawk, are designed for long-term surveillance and are launched from air force bases. Medium UAVs, such as the Predator and Reaper, are designed for tactical surveillance and reconnaissance and require a runway for launch. Small UAVs,

---

stockpiles of Soviet missiles, helped to dispel the bomber and missile "gaps," and enabled the verification of arms control treaties. John M. Diamond, "Re-examining Problems and Prospects in U.S. Imagery Intelligence," *International Journal of Intelligence and Counterintelligence* 14 (1), Spring 2001.

2. Mark W. Corson and Eugene J. Palka, "Geotechnology, the U.S. Military, and War," in Brunn, Cutter and Harrington (Eds.), *Geography and Technology*, (Dordrecht: Kluwer Academic Publishers, 2004).

3. Ibid; Benjamin S. Lambeth, *Air Power Against Terror. America's Conduct of Operation Enduring Freedom*, (Santa Monica, CA: RAND, 2005), xxii.

4. Joel Brenner, *America the Vulnerable. Inside the New Threat Matrix of Digital Espionage, Crime, and Warfare*, (New York: Penguin Press, 2011), 120, 135; Bryan Krekel, Patton Adams, and George Bakos, *Occupying the Information High Ground: Chinese Capabilities for Computer Network Operations and Cyber Espionage*(Washington, DC: US-China Economic and Security Review Commission, 2012).

5. Jeffrey T. Richelson, "Unearthing Secrets," *C4ISR Journal*, August 1, 2008; W. Happer et. al., *Characterization of Underground Facilities*, (McLean, VA: Mitre Corporation, 1999).

6. Michael T. Flynn, Rich Juergens, and Thomas L. Cantrell, "Employing ISR. SOF Best Practices," *Joint Forces Quarterly* 50, 3rd quarter 2008.

7. Patrick Radden Keefe, "A Shortsighted Eye in the Sky," *The New York Times*, February 5, 2005.

such as the Raven, are designed for tactical, over-the-hill visibility and can be launched by hand.[8] Full-motion video sensors were introduced on UAVs in the Balkans in 1995, bringing improved spatiotemporal awareness.[9] A decade later, this capability was honed in the US Army's "Constant Hawk" program to enable forensic backtracking of IED attacks in Iraq.[10]

A major development has been the arming of UAVs. Frustrated by the ineffectiveness of cruise missile strikes in retaliation for the 1998 Al-Qaeda bombings in East Africa, the CIA and US Air Force cooperated after 9/11 to arm the Predator UAV with Hellfire missiles.[11] Armed UAVs remove the "organizational blink" between sensors and shooters.[12] Primed by laser designators, armed UAVs reduced the sensor-shooter-cycle to an average of 20 minutes in Operation Enduring Freedom.[13] By the end of the decade drones had killed many of the CIA's most wanted high-value individuals.[14]

Materials and Weapons Science

Officially recognized by the US intelligence community (IC) in 1986,[15] "measurement and signatures intelligence" (MASINT) is the "CSI" of intelligence. MASINT is based on "technically-derived measurements of physical phenomenon intrinsic to an object or event."[16] Like imagery intelligence, advances in technology have enabled MASINT to play a much more tactical role than it played during the Cold War. Typical Cold War targets were submarines (acoustic) and nuclear tests (seismic). Most MASINT analysis required sophisticated database lookups and signature matching that took too long for use in tactical settings.[17] Newer sensors equipped with miniaturized on-board processors and signature databases now enable near-instantaneous identification of battlefield entities.[18] Positive identification occurs at the sensor location, not

---

8. Richard Best, Jr., *ISR Acquisition: Issues for Congress*, Washington, DC: Congressional Research Service, 2010.

9. Timothy R. Uecker, *Full Motion Video (FMV): The New Dimension of Imagery* (Maxwell AFB, AL: Air University, 2005).

10. Evan C. Dertien and Eric J. Felt, *Persistent Surveillance: Maximizing Airpower Effectiveness in Irregular Warfare* (Maxwell AFB, AL: Air University, 2007),: 11.

11. Jeffrey T. Richelson, "Technical Collection in the Post-September 11 World," in Gregory F. Treverton, and Wilhelm Agrell, *National Intelligence Systems: Current Research and Future Prospects* (New York: Cambridge University Press, 2009).

12. Flynn, Juergens, and Cantrell, "Employing ISR. SOF Best Practices."

13. Anthony H. Cordesman, *The Lessons of Afghanistan: War Fighting, Intelligence, and Force Transformation* (Washington, DC: CSIS, 2002), 66.

14. Peter Bergen and Katherine Tiedemann, *The Year of the Drone. An Analysis of U.S. Drone Strikes in Pakistan, 2004-2010* (Washington, DC: New America Foundation, 2010).

15. John D. Macartney, "John, How Should We Explain MASINT?" *The Intelligencer* 12, Summer 2001.

16. David Bunker, Air Force Institute of Technology, *What is MASINT?*, March 2009; DoD Instruction 5105.58, *Measurement and Signature Intelligence* (MASINT), April 22, 2009.

17. John Macartney, "How Should We Explain MASINT?."

18. William K. Moore, "MASINT: New Eyes in the Battlespace," *Military Intelligence* 29, Jan-Mar 2003.

in a laboratory thousands of miles from the operation.[19]

There have been particular advances in "imagery-derived MASINT, sometimes called "advanced geospatial intelligence.""[20] Hyper-spectral remote sensing, developed in the 1980s,[21] has become important in supporting special operations, and in countering camouflage, narcotics, and proliferation.[22] Night-vision technology has given advantage to regular forces during desert operations and to special forces during raids. The technology was advantageous to US forces operating in the desert during the Gulf War. It has been pivotal in night raids against terrorists and insurgents since 9/11. Advances included improved image intensification and resolution using gallium arsenide photocathodes.[23] And laser intelligence has become integral to the US Air Force's "kill chain."[24] In particular, the use of laser designators by forward air controllers to "paint" targets for laser-seeking missiles has had a profound effect on air-ground warfare in the new century. During Operation Enduring Freedom, the invisible laser beams emanating from the Special Operations Forces Laser Acquisition Marker (SOFLAM) became known to Taliban and Al-Qaeda forces as the "Death Ray."[25]

However, despite significant research, the promise of new methods of unambiguously detecting and characterizing lethal chemical, biological, radiological, nuclear, and explosives (CBRNE) materials has not yet been realized. Controversy ensues when force is used preemptively, such as the 1998 US bombing of a pharmaceuticals factory in Sudan, based on seemingly incomplete intelligence. A soil sample taken near the factory by a CIA agent was found to contain trace amounts of a chemical used in the production of VX nerve gas. Media reports suggested that the chemical could be the byproduct of the breakdown of an agricultural insecticide.[26] The identity of perpetrators, for example of the October 2001 anthrax attacks in the US, remains inconclusive. Following the attacks, the FBI launched one of the most expensive and manpower-intensive investigations in its history. Although it was able to match

---

19. Ibid.
20. National Geospatial Intelligence Agency, *National System for Geospatial Intelligence. Geospatial Intelligence (GEOINT) Basic Doctrine*, September 2006, 45.
21. The technology was pioneered by the Jet Propulsion Laboratory and enables collection from 200 or more spectral regions. James B. Campbell and Randolph H. Wayne, *Introduction to Remote Sensing*, Fifth Edition (New York, Guildford Press, 2011), 15-16.
22. Jeffrey T. Richelson, "MASINT The New Kid in Town," *International Journal of Intelligence and Counterintelligence* 14 (2), Summer 2001.
23. US Army Night Vision and Electronic Sensors Directorate, *History*, http://www.nvl.army.mil, accessed May 8, 2012; Mark Urban, *Task Force Black. The Explosive True Story of the SAS and the Secret War in Iraq* (London: Little Brown, 2010).
24. Lambeth, *Air Power Against Terror*.
25. Robin Moore, *The Hunt for Bin Laden. Task Force Dagger. On the Ground with the Special Forces in Afghanistan*, (New York: Ballantine Books, 2003), 2-5; Stephen Biddle, *Afghanistan and the Future of Warfare: Implications for Army and Defense Policy* (Carlisle, PA: Strategic Studies Institute, 2002).
26. Gregory Koblentz, "Countering Dual-Use Facilities: Lessons from Iraq and Sudan," *Jane's intelligence Review* 11 (3), March 1, 1999.

the anthrax to cultures in a flask belonging to US Army scientist Bruce Ivins, the FBI's genetic analysis "did not definitively demonstrate" that the mailed anthrax spores were grown from Dr. Ivins' flask, according to a review by the National Academy of Sciences.[27]

New detectors at borders have been withdrawn for being too slow or producing too many false alarms. The Obama administration quietly cancelled programs promoting the Advanced Spectroscopic Portal and the Cargo Advanced Automated Radiography System. In Los Angeles, there were hundreds of false alarms per day, set off by Chinese toilets, granite countertops, and bananas.[28] Advances in cosmic ray and particle physics have yet to be incorporated into nuclear detectors. For example, scientists are working on a transportable high energy linear accelerator that is apparently able to stimulate fission and detect "special nuclear material" from distances of 200 meters or more; "muon radiography" promises to penetrate shielding and detect dense, fissile material without being hazardous to human beings; and new superconducting "transition-edge" sensors are reputed to be so sensitive that they are able to overcome the false alarm problem. To bring these technologies from the lab into the field, engineers will need to overcome problems of size, cost, safety and power consumption.[29] And with the exception of robotics,[30] none of the exotic new technologies has yet been able to deliver standoff detection of improvised explosive devices. Despite investment in an array of new approaches, both trace detection (e.g. laser-induced breakdown spectroscopy, Raman spectroscopy, and differential reflection spectroscopy) and bulk detection (e.g. neutron, nuclear quadrupole resonance, and millimeter/terahertz sensors), few standoff techniques are able to detect explosives unambiguously and consistently at a distance of more than 10 meters. Detection at distances of 100 meters or more is beyond current science and technology concepts. Thus anomaly detection is still performed by visual observation, radar, infrared or canine detection (the most effective). [31]

Some incremental improvements have been made. Polymerase chain reac-

27. Scott Shane, "Colleague Disputes Case Against Anthrax Suspect," *The New York Times*, April 22, 2010; Scott Shane, "Expert Panel is Critical of F.B.I. Work in Investigating Anthrax Letters," *The New York Times*, February 15, 2011.

28. David E. Sanger, "Nuclear-Detection Effort is Halted as Ineffective," *The New York Times*, July 29, 2011; Mickey McCarter, "DHS Cancels Next Generation Radiation Portal for Cargo Screening," *Homeland Security Today*, July 27, 2011.

29. Jonathan Medalia, CRS, *Detection of Nuclear Weapons and Materials: Science, Technologies, Observations*, June 4, 2010; Kent D. Irwin, "Seeing with Superconductors," *Scientific American*, November 2006.

30. Robots used in Iraq and Afghanistan, such as the "PackBot," have come a long way since British forces first used a converted lawnmower in Ireland in the 1970s to defuse bombs. P.W. Singer, "War of the Machines," *Scientific American*, July, 2010; David Dugan, *Bomb Squad*, PBS Documentary, October 1997.

31. John E. Parmeter, "The Challenge of Standoff Explosives Detection," *Proceedings of the 38th Annual International Carnahan Conference on Security Technology*, October 2004; Maurice Marshall and Jimmie C. Oxley (eds.), Aspects of Explosives Detection, (Amsterdam: Elsevier, 2009); Rowan Scarborough, "Pentagon may trim IED detector budget," *Washington Times*, September 7, 2010.

tion (PCR) technology, invented in 1983,[32] has become the standard method for detecting biological agents.[33] UN inspectors adopted the technique in 1996 to overcome Iraqi denial of its anthrax program,[34] and has since evolved to enable near "real-time" identification of pathogens.[35] Nevertheless, most biological agents are colorless, odorless, do not exhibit a signature that can be remotely sensed,[36] and can easily be hidden.[37] Planners, therefore, regard pre-attack surveillance as unrealistic, and have instead designed systems such as BioWatch to provide warning of an attack in progress.[38]

While not officially a MASINT discipline, the science of identifying individuals has evolved significantly in the past 20 years. Before the introduction of digitized biometrics, criminals, terrorists, and insurgents could hide behind a web of multiple identities when they traveled. For example, the 19 hijackers from 9/11 used 364 aliases in their forms of identification, including different spellings of their names and "noms de guerres." At the time, visa screening systems at consular offices was based on simple name checks.[39] The introduction of digital photographs and fingerprinting in programs such as US-VISIT has made such dissemblance much harder.[40] Similarly, the introduction of handheld systems for collecting biometrics has proven vital to holding territory gained in counterinsurgencies. For example, in 2003 the Department of Defense began to collect biometrics in Iraq using systems such as the Biometric Automated Toolset and the Handheld Interagency Identity Detection Equipment. After the US Marine Corps captured the town of Fallujah, they issued identity cards with iris scans to the population, effectively walling off the city and making it difficult for insurgents to reestablish themselves.[41]

Correlation of fingerprints collected abroad with databases used by US immigration has exposed high-profile terrorists and prevented enemies of

---

32. John M. S. Bartlett and David Sterling, "A Short History of the Polymerase Chain Reaction," *Methods in Molecular Biology, PCR Protocols* 226, 2003.

33. Simon Labov and Tom Slezak, "The Indispensable Technology: Detectors for Nuclear, Biological, and Chemical WMD," in Stephen M. Maurer, *WMD Terrorism. Science and Policy Choices*(Cambridge, MA: MIT Press, 2009).

34. Using PCR, inspectors found anthrax on equipment that had previously tested negative. Gregory Koblentz, *Living Weapons. Biological Warfare and International Security*, (Ithaca, NY: Cornell University Press, 2009), 98.

35. A process that used to take 6 to 12 hours in the laboratory now takes 20 to 40 minutes using portable DoD field kits. Jonathan Beard, "Overview of DARPA's Biological Warfare Defense Programs," in DARPA, *DARPA: 50 Years of Bridging the Gap*, (Arlington, VA: DARPA, 2008); Zygmunt F. Dembek (ed.), *Medical Aspects of Biological Warfare*, (Washington, DC: Borden Institute, 2007), 404.

36. Robert M. Clark, *The Technical Collection of Intelligence* (Washington, DC; CQ Press, 2011), 13.

37. Labov and Slezak, "The Indispensable Technology."

38. BioWatch is a program operated by the Department of Homeland Security (DHS) in 30 cities in the United States designed to detect a biological attack. Ibid.

39. National Commission on Terrorist Attacks Upon the United States, *Monograph on 9/11 and Terrorist Travel*, August 2004.

40. Rey Koslowski, *Real Challenges for Virtual Borders: The Implementation of US-VISIT*(Washington, DC: Migration Policy Institute, 2005).

41. Jody Kieffer and Kevin Trissell, "DOD Biometrics – Lifting the Veil of Insurgent Identity," *US Army Acquisition, Logistics & Technology*, April-June 2010.

the US from entering the country. For example, Mohamed al Kahtani was identified as the possible "20th hijacker" after he was captured in Afghanistan in December 2011. His fingerprints matched those of a man who was denied entry on August 3, at Orlando International Airport, where cameras captured Mohamed Atta, apparently waiting to pick him up. Hundreds of Iraqis have been denied US visas when their fingerprints have turned up in the DoD database of known insurgents.[42] Forensic scientists have used "latent fingerprints" to track down bombmakers. Increasingly, counterinsurgents perform the job of police investigators to collect evidence essential to the prosecution of captured personnel. The FBI set up the Terrorist Explosives Device Analytical Center in 2003 to handle the analysis of "latent fingerprints" found on IEDs. Within its first five years, the center identified 56 bomb makers. [43]

DNA profiling, invented in 1983, has had a big impact on forensics, enabling the resolution of thousands of criminal cases.[44] Even without a precise match, "ancestral typing" and "familial DNA testing" have been used to track down serial killers and rapists. In 2003, for example, the Baton Rouge serial killer was tracked down with the help of genetic ancestral typing. In 2006, the Deare Valley shoe rapist in Yorkshire, England, was tracked down through familial DNA testing via his sister, who had a drunk driving conviction,[45] DNA has been used to identify both the perpetrators and the victims of terrorist attacks. For example, starting in the late 1980s, the Royal Ulster Constabulary Special Branch was able to use DNA from hair follicles at bombing scenes to track down and incriminate members of the Provisional IRA. And as of February 1, 2009, 1,654 remains of those killed at the World Trade Center on 9/11 had been linked by DNA to known individuals.[46] It has also been used to confirm the identities of high value individuals killed in "targeted killings." The most famous example was the use of DNA to confirm the death of Osama bin Laden.[47]

Information and Communication Technology

At its core, intelligence is about acquiring and processing information,

---

42. John D. Woodward, Jr., "Using Biometrics to Achieve Identity Dominance in the Global War on Terrorism," *Military Review*, Sept-Oct, 2005; Ellen Nakashima, "Post-9/11 Dragnet Turns Up Surprises," *The Washington Post*, July 6, 2008.
43. Alan T. Ivy and Kenneth J. Hurst, *Formalizing Law Enforcement Procedures for DoD Units Conducting Combat Operations*(Quantico, VA: Marine Corps War College, 2008);
44. English geneticist Alex Jeffreys first used DNA in 1983 as a means of establishing personal identity. Sheldon Rimsky and Tania Simoncelli, *Genetic Justice. DNA Data Banks, Criminal Investigations, and Civil Liberties*(New York: Columbia University Press, 2011), 48.
45. Ibid, 66-67, 92-93; Dov Fox, "The Second Generation of Racial Profiling," *American Journal of Criminal Law* 38, 2010.
46. Tony Geraghty, *The Irish War*, 2000, 83-89; Office of the Chief Medical Examiner, New York, *Update on the Results of DNA Testing of Remains Recovered at the World Trade Center Site and Surrounding Area*, February 1, 2009.
47. Peter L. Bergen, *Manhunt. The Ten-Year Search for bin Laden from 9/11 to Abbottabad*(New York: Crown Publishers, 2012), 227, 242.

much of it from communication, so the revolution in information and communication technology (ICT) has had a most profound effect on the intelligence world.

The External Impact of ICT

The internet has added a new "cyber" domain to the existing contested spaces of air, space, land, and sea.[48] This seemingly benign communications medium[49] has altered the threat environment in several ways. Firstly, it has enabled a new form of sabotage. Cyber weapons can disrupt the command and control systems of decisionmakers, as the Russian attacks on Estonia and Georgia in 2007 and 2008 demonstrated. The Russian attacks used a brute force method called "distributed denial of service" (DDOS). Hackers used DDOS in 2007 to shut down government ministries and banks after the Estonians announced plans to move a WWII memorial to their Russian "liberators." The following year, the Russians used DDOS again to bring down Georgia's communications network to confuse the leadership as Russian troops entered the country.[50] Or they can disrupt industrial control systems, as the sophisticated "Stuxnet" attacks on Iranian centrifuges by the US and Israel revealed in 2010. The attack took out nearly 1,000 centrifuges through alternate acceleration and deceleration. It sent signals to the Natanz control room indicating normal operation. The result was a delay in the Iranian nuclear program of at least a year and a half. Spearheaded by US Strategic Command, the operation was called "Olympic Games." It was approved by President Bush in 2006 and continued by President Obama in 2008. The National Security Agency (NSA) designed the code in cooperation with Israeli intelligence, including Unit 8200. Due to a programming error, it leaked onto the internet in 2010.[51]

Secondly, the new domain has enabled the mobilization of de-territorialized communities capable of challenging state and religious authority.[52] Thirdly, cyberspace has become a virtual sanctuary for terrorists and insurgents, a place where they can raise funds, recruit and educate members, plan and launch attacks, and publicize the results with impunity.[53] And lastly, it has created a

---

48. Rebecca Grant, *Victory in Cyberspace* (Arlington, VA: Air Force Association, 2007).

49. Frederick L. Wettering, "The Internet and the Spy Business," *International Journal of Intelligence and Counterintelligence* 14 (3), 2001.

50. Joel Brenner, *America the Vulnerable. Inside the New Threat Matrix of Digital Espionage, Crime, and Warfare* (New York: Penguin Press, 2011), 39-40.

51. David E. Sanger, "Obama Order Sped Up Wave of Cyberattacks Against Iran," *The New York Times*, June 1, 2012.

52. For a general discussion see the trilogy by Manuel Castells, *The Information Age: Economy, Society and Culture* (Malden, MA: Blackwell Publishing, 2009-2010); for the impact of migration and the internet on political Islam see Olivier Roy, *Globalized Islam. The Search for a New Ummah* (New York: Columbia University Press, 2004) and Gary R. Bunt, *Islam in the Digital Age. E-Jihad, Online Fatwas and Cyber Islamic Environments* (London: Pluto Press, 2003).

53. Magnus Ranstorp, "The Virtual Sanctuary of Al-Qaeda and Terrorism in an Age of Globalization,"

"spy heaven" for malicious actors who steal massive quantities of data while remaining anonymous and hard to detect.[54]

The cyber domain has created an enormous target for criminals. The US, for example, spends in excess of $400B annually on R&D, the largest by far in the developed world.[55] Since much of the intellectual property from this investment is now stored on networked computers, US competitive advantage gained from years of research can vanish instantly. Intellectual property has become a critical "factor of production" in post-industrial economies.[56] The internet has enabled sophisticated remote theft. Individual computers, of course, have always been subject to physical theft or borrowing (so-called "black jobs"). What makes internet espionage so effective is that the theft is achieved by "recruiting" operating systems, word processors or even firewalls with access to the information needed.[57] Data can be acquired through pre-installed "trapdoors," "Trojan Horse" attacks, or direct "hacking" that exploits known system vulnerabilities.[58]

In the post-Cold War period, Chinese actors have become "the world's most active and persistent perpetrators of economic espionage," and have amassed an impressive array of US defense technologies through espionage. Although many of the perpetrators are not government agencies, the PRC is clearly involved. State Department cables published by WikiLeaks in 2010 revealed that "Operation Aurora" had been directed by a senior member of the Politburo. The operation involved the cyber-theft of intellectual property from Google and thousands of other well-known US and European companies.[59] China's triumphs include acquisition of design blueprints for the US built B-1 bomber, Northrop Grumman's B-2 stealth bomber, the US Navy's Quiet Electric

---

in Johan Eriksson and Giampiero Giacomello (eds.), *International Relations and Security in the Digital Age* (New York: Routledge, 2007); Gabriel Weimann, *Terror on the Internet. The New Arena, the New Challenges* (Washington, DC: US IOP, 2006).

54. Wettering, "The Internet and the Spy Business"; Office of the Counterintelligence Executive, *Foreign Spies Stealing US Economic Secrets in Cyberspace. Report to Congress on Foreign Economic Collection and Industrial Espionage, 2009 – 2011*, October 2011.

55. National Science Board, *Science and Engineering Indicators 2012* (Arlington, VA: National Science Foundation), 4-41.

56. Susan W. Brenner and Anthony C. Crescenzi, "State-Sponsored Crime: the Futility of the Economic Espionage Act," *Houston Journal of International Law* 389, 2006; Andrew Rathmell, "Towards Postmodern Intelligence," *Intelligence and National Security* 17 (3), 2002.

57. Wettering, "The Internet and the Spy Business"; James R. Gosler, "The Digital Dimension," in Jennifer E. Sims and Burton Gerber (eds.), *Transforming U.S. Intelligence* (Washington, DC: Georgetown University Press, 2005).

58. Ibid. For an introduction to cyber-theft see Joel McNamara, *Secrets of Computer Espionage: Tactics and Countermeasures* (Indianapolis, IN: Wiley Publishing, 2003); for a more advanced up-to-date survey see Stuart McClure, Joel Scambray, and George Kurtz, *Hacking Exposed 7 Network Security Secrets & Solutions* (Emeryville, CA: McGraw-Hill Osborne Media, 2012).

59. Office of the Counterintelligence Executive, *Foreign Spies Stealing US Economic Secrets in Cyberspace*; Kim Zetter, "Report Details Hacks Targeting Google, Others," *Wired Magazine*, February 3, 2010; James Glanz and John Markoff, "Cables Discuss Vast Hacking by a China Fearful of the Web," *New York Times*, December 4, 2010; both cited in Brenner, *America the Vulnerable*, Chapter 3, "Bleeding Wealth."

Drive system and the W-88 miniature nuclear warhead.[60] Chinese success is due to long-term planning, extensive grant-funded research, and a huge pool of recruits. Until the 1980s, the Chinese regime's spying was largely domestic in nature. But in the post-1980s era, as China increased its economic activity abroad, its Ministry of State Security (MSS) began to focus on foreign commercial secrets, while the People's Liberation Army started acquiring foreign technology, much of it for weapons and military systems. The PRC uses at least five national grant programs to fund research related to information warfare: the 863 National High Technology R&D Program, the 973 National Key Research Program, the National 242 Information Security Program, the MSS 115 Program, and the National 219 Information Security Application Demonstration Project.[61] While the Chinese rely on their network of émigrés for much of their military espionage,[62] they have increasingly turned to cyberspace for economic espionage. A 2009 report determined that electronic media were involved in all 10 recent cases involving foreign economic espionage that led to indictments, mostly involving Chinese companies.[63]

Information technology has eroded the monopoly that government agencies once enjoyed over intelligence. Public access to internet, database, and search engine technology means that government analysts now have to compete with the media, academics, and NGOs. Policymakers are no longer living in an age of information scarcity. They no longer require their intelligence service to tell them what is going on in the world or how to interpret events, and they can no longer assume that proprietary intelligence is superior to open sources. For example, NGOs offering open source intelligence (OSINT) assessments include UK-based Oxford Analytica, Jane's Information Group, the International Institute for Strategic Studies, and Stratfor.[64]

Of course, satellite and internet technologies from their earliest days have been exploited for commercial gain. The US launched the CORONA imagery and GRAB electronic intelligence satellites in 1960. AT&T followed by launching the first commercially funded communications satellite called "Telstar" in 1962.[65]

60. Joseph Fitsanakis, "Is China the New Spy Superpower?," *Intel News*, December 16, 2011.
61. "China's Growing Spy Threat," *The Diplomat*, September 19, 2011; Peter Mattis, "Assessing the Foreign Policy Influence of the Ministry of State Security," *China Brief* 11 (1), January 14, 2011; Bill Gertz, "Chinese Spy Who Defected Tells All," *The Washington Times*, March 19, 2009; Bryan Krekel, Patton Adams, and George Bakos, *Occupying the Information High Ground: Chinese Capabilities for Computer Network Operations and Cyber Espionage* (Washington, DC: US-China Economic and Security Review Commission, 2012), 59-63.
62. Paul D. Moore, "How China Plays the Ethnic Card," *The Los Angeles Times*, June 24, 1999.
63. Derrick Spooner, Dawn M. Cappelli, Andrew P. Moore, and Randall F. Trzceciak, *Spotlight on Insider Theft of Intellectual Property Inside the U.S. Involving Foreign Governments or Organizations* (Pittsburgh, PA: Carnegie Mellon University CERT Program, 2009).
64. Wesley K. Wark, "Learning to Live with Intelligence," *Intelligence and National Security* 18 (4), December 2003; Carmen A. Medina "What to Do When Traditional Models Fail. The Coming Revolution in Intelligence Analysis," *Studies in Intelligence* 46 (3), 2002; Alan Dupont, "Intelligence for the Twenty-First Century," *Intelligence and National Security* 18 (4), 2003.
65. Robert A. McDonald and Sharon K. Morena, *Raising the Periscope. Grab and Poppy: America's Early*

What is remarkable in the post-Cold War period is that commercial forces have driven the democratization of specific technologies such as satellite imagery and encryption hitherto reserved exclusively for the secret world of intelligence. In the early 1990s, the US Congress passed legislation permitting private companies to operate satellites and sell high-resolution images on the global market. In the late 1990s, Western intelligence and law enforcement agencies also lost a complex battle in which high-grade encryption became available to private organizations and individuals.[66] While such deregulations benefit millions, terrorists can now make full use of Google Earth and encrypted Voice over Internet Protocol (VoIP) to mount attacks. In January 2008, Al-Qaeda's Global Islamic Media Front announced support for the Advanced Encryption Standard (AES) with its Mujahideen Secrets 2.0. That November, Lashkar-e-Taiba planned and executed a successful terrorist attack in Mumbai, India, using Google Earth and secure VoIP communication.[67]

ICT democratization has increased transparency, making secrets harder to keep and intelligence agencies less effective. Vast amounts of information can now be transferred and made instantly accessible to a global audience via the internet.[68] In 2010, a young US Army intelligence analyst working in Baghdad downloaded more than a quarter of a million US diplomatic cables and passed them to the whistle-blowing group WikiLeaks.[69] This incident, possibly the most massive unauthorized disclosure of classified documents in American history, illustrates the degree to which technology has turbocharged espionage.[70]

To be sure, technology has not been the only driver of transparency. Higher expectations concerning accountability,[71] and the need to preempt today's threats force agencies into the open.[72] When transatlantic flights are cancelled or armed police storm a private residence, liberal democratic publics want an

---

ELINT Satellites (Chantilly, VA: NRO, 2005); Air Command and Staff College, *AU-18 Space Primer* (Maxwell AFB, AL: Air University Press, 2009).

66. John C. Baker, *Trading Away Security? The Clinton Administration's 1994 Decision on Satellite Imaging Exports*(Washington, DC: Institute for the Study for Diplomacy, 1997); Aldrich, "Beyond the Vigilant State," *Review of International Studies* 35 (4), 2009; Whitfield Diffie and Susan Landau, *Privacy on the Line. The Politics of Wiretapping and Encryption* (Cambridge, MA: MIT Press, 2007).

67. Ellen Messmer, "Al-Qaeda group claims to have strengthened its encryption security," *Network World*, January 23, 2008; John Bumgarner and Michael Mylrea, "Jihad in Cyberspace," *The Counter Terrorist*, March 12, 2010.

68. Sir David Omand, "Can we have the Pleasure of the Grin without Seeing the Cat? Must the Effectiveness of Secret Agencies Inevitably Fade on Exposure to the Light?," *Intelligence and National Security* 23 (5), October 2008.

69. Gabriel Liulevicius, *Espionage and Covert Operations: A Global History. Course Guidebook* (Chantilly, VA: The Great Courses, 2011), 186.

70. Ibid.

71. A. Denis Clift, "The Coin of Intelligence Accountability," Loch K. Johnson (Ed.), *Strategic Intelligence, Volume 5, Intelligence and Accountability. Safeguards Against the Abuse of Power* (Westport, CT: Praeger Security International, 2007).

72. David Omand, "Intelligence Secrets and Media Spotlights. Balancing Illumination and Dark Corners," in Dover and Goodman, *Spinning Intelligence. Why Intelligence Needs the Media, Why the Media Needs Intelligence* (New York: Columbia University Press, 2009).

explanation.[73] International politicians must also justify the preemptive use of force by revealing intelligence. Colin Powell's dramatic February 2002 presentation at the UN was simply a global example of the public use of intelligence in a post-9/11 world.[74]

The Internal Impact of ICT

ICT has fundamentally reshaped the intelligence process. Advocates in the late 1990s suggested replacing the industrial-age assembly line model with a new information-age network approach. The way to become an "agile intelligence enterprise" was to adopt the private sector's "virtual corporation."[75] The key was to embrace the open architectures, publish and subscribe protocols, and distributed database capabilities of the information revolution.[76] These aspirations were given fresh impetus in the aftermath of 9/11 when it became clear that the CIA and FBI had failed to disseminate information on the run-up to the attacks.[77] Ten years later, despite ongoing bureaucratic resistance, the Markle Foundation president reported significant progress.[78] The disruption of several terrorist plots over the past decade demonstrates clear improvements in inter-agency information sharing. The Markle testimony cites the Najibullah Zazi plot. Zazi was arrested in September 2009 in connection with an al Qaeda plot to bomb the New York subway system. The plot was disrupted due to the collaborative efforts of the FBI, the DHS and the New York and Denver police. The sharing of information via state and local fusion centers and Joint Terrorism Task Forces was instrumental.[79]

Others are less convinced that information sharing has made America safer. Paul Redmond, who led the investigation to find Aldrich Ames, warns that a blind focus on information sharing will inevitably ease the work of enemy spies and make the work of identifying them and neutralizing them more difficult. Redmond fears that the interconnection of more and more networks will lead to a breakdown in compartmentation. Similarly, Loch Johnson fears the possibility of a future Ames or Hanssen who not only steals from his own corner of the IC but has access to the full network of the IC's computers. Information experts counter that the solution is to apply policy-driven technologies

---

73. Ibid.

74. Wark, "Learning to Live with Intelligence."

75. Bruce D. Berkowitz, "Information Technology and Intelligence Reform," *Orbis*, Winter 1997; Bruce D. Berkowitz and Allan E. Goodman, *Best Truth. Intelligence in the Information Age* (New Haven, CT: Yale University Press, 2000).

76. Ibid.

77. National Commission on Terrorist Attacks Upon the United States, *9/11 Commission Report* (New York: Barnes & Noble, 2006).

78. Zoe Baird Budinger and Jeffrey H. Smith, "A Lesson of 9/11: Washington Can Work," *The Washington Post*, August 26, 2011.

79. Zoe Baird Budinger and Jeffrey H. Smith, *Ten Years After 9/11: A Status Report on Information Sharing*, Senate Committee on Homeland Security & Governmental Affairs, October 12, 2011.

to control, discover, access, and use information, even as capabilities to share information are improved (admittedly an enormous task for an intelligence community the size of the US IC). Intelligence Community Directive 501, issued in 2009, describes the types of policies required.[80] The general increase in transparency has made other aspects of counterintelligence difficult. Creating deep and effective cover through "backstopping" that will stand up to intense electronic scrutiny is more difficult than ever. Identity information such as address, profession, and association membership are immediately verifiable using search tools. Because so much personal information is available online, it is almost impossible to remake a person's life history including records of education, credit cards, residence, family, children's schools, library cards, and driver's licenses.[81] And in an age of persistent surveillance, concealing sponsorship of covert operations is also getting harder, as demonstrated by the remarkable Dubai videos of the Mossad assassination of Hamas paramilitary Mahmoud al-Mabhouh in 2010.[82]

The flipside is that ICT has made spy handling and tradecraft easier and safer. Individuals with potential access to secrets can be "spotted" and their vulnerabilities identified by mining social networks, chat rooms, credit histories, and spending habits. Numerous data services will disclose a person's credit rating, mortgage payment, magazine subscriptions, grocery purchases, car payments, society memberships, etc.[83] Spy handlers no longer need to meet their spies face-to-face in safe houses but can meet virtually using secure video casting.[84] The secret documents that were photographed and dead-dropped during the Cold War are now likely to be imaged and transmitted electronically.[85] Easily concealed memory cards reduce the need for compromising devices to hide film or secret writing material.[86] And a Cold War covert communication (covcom) plan involving dangerous brush passes, car tosses, or dead drops can now be completed safely in seconds over the internet. Digital dead drops are made by saving uncompleted e-mails on providers' hard drives, anonymous remailers and peer-to-peer services that bypass service provider hubs are used to communicate with sources, and messages are made secure with encryption

---

80. Paul J. Redmond, "The Challenges of Counterintelligence," in Loch K. Johnson, *The Oxford Handbook of National Security Intelligence* (New York: Oxford University Press, 2010); Loch K. Johnson, *National Security Intelligence. Secret Operations in Defense of the Democracies* (Cambridge, UK: Polity Press, 2012), 127-128; Budinger and Smith, *Ten Years After 9/11*.

81. Robert Wallace and H. Keith Melton, *Spycraft. The Secret History of the CIA's Spytechs, from Communism to Al-Qaeda* (New York: Penguin Group, 2009), Chapter 25, 'Spies and the Age of Information"; Brenner, *America the Vulnerable*, 190.

82. Brenner, *America the Vulnerable*, 157-163.

83. Robert Wallace, "A Time for Counterespionage," in Jennifer E. Sims and Burton Gerber (Eds.), *Vaults, Mirrors, and Masks. Rediscovering U.S. Counterintelligence* (Washington, DC: Georgetown University Press, 2009); Wettering, "The Internet and the Spy Business."

84. Wallace, "A Time for Counterespionage."

85. Wallace and Melton, "Spies and the Age of Information."

86. Ibid.

and invisible with steganography or "chaffing" (the sender embeds bogus bits into the message and the receiver "winnows" out the chaff to reveal the message). Portable covert operating systems on USB sticks ensure that no traces of encrypted messages are left behind.[87]

On balance, however, ICT has not made analysis any easier. The information explosion makes it tougher to distinguish true signals from ambient noise.[88] Analysts simply cannot keep up with the flood of imagery intelligence collected by UAVs. According to Marine Corps General James Cartwright, it will require 2,000 analysts to process video feeds from a single Predator with next generation sensors.[89] The problem is particularly acute in signals intelligence. By 1995, the NSA was vacuuming up the equivalent of the Library of Congress every three hours.[90] By 2007, the amount that NSA analysts were able to process had fallen below 1%.[91] In addition to rebuilding their collection infrastructures to cope with the revolution in fiber optics,[92] UKUSA agencies are scrambling to find a solution to the volume problem. *A priori* intelligence covert teams[93] can collect targeted close-in SIGINT. With an identifier, they can use triangulation to geo-locate the source of signals from radios, satellite, or cellular phones.[94] With a voiceprint, they can home in on a suspect's communication. US SIGINT technicians were able to develop a voiceprint of 9/11 mastermind Khalid Sheikh Mohammad (KSM) from a recording of an interview conducted by *Al-Jazeera* reporter Yosri Fouda in June 2002. The voiceprint was used to narrow the search for KSM, which ended in Rawalpindi on March 3, 2003.[95] Or with a phone captured from a raid, they can use "call chaining" or "link analysis" to track down accomplices.[96]

Without a lead, however, agencies have to turn to data mining, raising

---

87. Wallace and Melton, "Spies and the Age of Information;" Wettering, "The Internet and the Spy Business."

88. Wark, "Learning to Live with Intelligence."

89. Eli Lake, "Drone Footage Overwhelms Analysts," *The Washington Times*, November 9, 2010.

90. Matthew M. Aid, "All Glory is Fleeting: SIGINT and the Fight Against International Terrorism," *Intelligence and National Security* 18 (4), 2003.

91. Tim Shorrock, *Spies for Hire: The Secret World of Intelligence Outsourcing* (New York, Simon and Schuster, 2008), 218.

92. The radome protected antennae of the global "Echelon" network have almost become redundant as companies like Global Crossing funnel the world's communication through optical fibers. By one estimate, the volume of international communications transmitted over subsea cables increased from 2% in 1988 to 80% in 2000. To intercept the new cable traffic, national SIGINT agencies have installed black boxes in the offices of international telecommunication carriers. Domestic agencies have solicited the same cooperation from ISPs. James Bamford, *The Shadow Factory. The Ultra-Secret NSA from 9/11 to the Eavesdropping on America* (New York: Anchor Books, 2008), "Book III: Cooperation."

93. Such as the US Army's Intelligence Support Activity or the CIA's Special Collection Service. Matthew M. Aid, "All Glory is Fleeting."

94. There are numerous examples. See, for example, "Suspect Tracked by Phone Calls," *B.B.C. News*, August 1, 2008.

95. Robert N. Wesley, "Capturing Khalid Sheikh Mohammad," in James J. F. Forest (ed.), *Countering Terrorism and Insurgency in the 21st Century, Volume 3: Lessons from the Fight Against Terrorism* (Westport, CT: Praeger Security International, 2007).

96. Bamford, *The Shadow Factory*, 149.

civil liberty concerns. In the past decade the US and the UK have had to cancel and replace Orwellian government projects, designed to capture and store private citizen data, with smaller, more private-sector initiatives. In the US, the ambitious DARPA project, "Total Information Awareness," was swiftly killed by Congress in 2003, while the NSA's "Trailblazer" was broken down into smaller projects in 2005. In the UK, the equally ambitious Government Communications Headquarters (GCHQ) "Intercept Modernization Program" was revamped in 2009 to avoid a "single central store" by allowing government access to data stored by the communication providers themselves.[97] In 2009, the Christmas Day bomber reminded the public of the need for advanced analytic tools, which are now popular with analysts in law enforcement and the military. Nigerian Umar Farouk Abdulmutallab attempted to detonate a concealed explosive device on Northwest Airlines Flight 253 over Detroit on December 25, 2009. His name was already in the US Terrorist Identities Datamart Environment (TIDE) and a UK watch list, he had been refused a visa by Great Britain, his father had warned the US Embassy in Nigeria that his son had become radicalized and had disowned his family, he had paid cash for his flight ticket, and he had boarded the plane with no luggage.[98] New tools to conduct "digital forensics" have also been developed to cope with the explosion of digital information being seized by investigators. After the 2005 London bombings, the UK passed legislation extending the time that terrorism suspects could be held without being charged, in part because they needed more time to analyze the computer hard drives and CCTV systems seized after the attacks. Contemporary forensic tools include "EnCase" and "Forensic Toolkit."[99]

READINGS FOR INSTRUCTORS

Agencies and Corporations

For a balanced look at the NSA after the Cold War, see Matthew M. Aid, *The Secret Sentry. The Untold History of the National Security Agency*(New York: Bloomsbury Press, 2009). For a more critical take, see James Bamford, *The Shadow Factory. The Ultra-Secret NSA from 9/11 to the Eavesdropping on America*(New York: Anchor Books, 2008) or the companion 2009 PBS film *The Spy*

---

97. Tim Shorrock, *Spies for Hire*, Chapter 6: "The NSA, 9/11, and the Business of Data Mining"; Siobhan Gorman, "NSA's Domestic Spying Grows As Agency Sweeps Up Data," *The Wall Street Journal*, March 10, 2008; Richard J. Aldrich, *GCHQ. The Uncensored Story of Britain's Most Secret Intelligence Agency*(London: HarperPress, 2010), 543-548; "Jacqui Smith Scraps Plan For Email Database," *The Telegraph*, April 27, 2009.
98. Norbert E. Luongo, "Watchlists in United States and Canada: An Intricate Web," *Air and Space Law*, 34:3, Jan 10, 2010; Ashlee Vance and Brad Stone, "Palantir, the War on Terror's Secret Weapon," *Bloomberg Businessweek*, November 22, 2011.
99. Simon L. Garfinkel, 'Document and Media Exploitation," *ACM Queue*, Nov-Dec 2007; Mark Pollitt, "A History of Digital Forensics," Chapter 1 in K.P.Chow, S. Shenoi (eds.), *Advances in Digital Forensics VI, IFIP Advances in Information and Computer Technology* 337, 2010.

Factory. For a history of UK SIGINT, see Richard Aldrich, GCHQ. *The Uncensored Story of Britain's Most Secret Intelligence Agency*(London: HarperPress, 2010).

The official history of the National Geospatial-Intelligence Agency (NGA) and predecessors is *Advent of the National Geospatial-Intelligence Agency*, September 2011, by the Office of the NGA Historian, available at *http://www.nga1.mil*. The agency's *Pathfinder* magazine provides technical details. For a history of CIA's Office of Technical Services, see Robert Wallace and H. Keith Melton, *Spycraft. The Secret History of the CIA's Spytechs, from Communism to Al-Qaeda*(New York: Penguin Group, 2009). For the rise of the US intelligence-industrial complex, see Tim Shorrock's *Spies for Hire: The Secret World of Intelligence Outsourcing*(New York: Simon and Schuster, 2008).

Imagery and Geospatial Technology

For a technical dive into imagery intelligence, see James B. Campbell and Randolph H. Wayne, *Introduction to Remote Sensing*, Fifth Edition(New York, Guildford Press, 2011). One way to make the topic more accessible is to use short videos, such as Penn State's The Geospatial Revolution, available at *http://geospatialrevolution.psu.edu*.

Materials and Weapons Science

The best book on MASINT is Robert M. Clark's *The Technical Collection of Intelligence*(Washington, DC: CQ Press, 2011). Teachers can use TV shows like *24*, *Spooks* (MI5), or *CSI* to contrast "Spytainment"[100] and the real world.[101]

For an understanding of the science of weapons, see Stephen M. Maurer, *WMD Terrorism: Science and Policy Choices*(Cambridge, MA: MIT Press, 2009); Gregory D. Koblentz, *Living Weapons: Biological Warfare and International Security*(Ithaca, NY: Cornell University Press, 2009); and Maurice Marshall and Jimmie C. Oxley (eds.), *Aspects of Explosives Detection*(Amsterdam: Elsevier, 2009).

Information and Communications Technology

For a short analysis of the impact of ICT, see Bruce D. Berkowitz and Allan E. Goodman, *Best Truth: Intelligence in the Information Age*(New Haven, CT: Yale University Press, 2000). For the impact of the media, see Robert Dover and Michael S. Goodman (eds.), *Spinning Intelligence: Why Intelligence Needs the Media, Why the Media Needs Intelligence*(New York: Columbia University Press, 2009).

For communication and cyber intelligence, see Ross Anderson, *Security Engineering: A Guide to Building Dependable Distributed Systems*(Indianapolis, IN: Wiley, 2008). For surveillance technologies, see the 2011 PBS film *Are We Safer*.[102] The rise of cyber-espionage is documented by Joel Brenner in *Amer-*

---

100. Amy Zegart, "Spytainment: The Real Influence of Fake Spies," *International Journal of Intelligence and Counterintelligence*, 24 (3), June 2011.

101. Robert Dover, "From Vauxhall with Love. Intelligence in Popular Culture," in Dover and Goodman, *Spinning Intelligence*.

102. The film is based upon investigations published by Dana Priest and William M. Arkin in *The Wash-*

ica the Vulnerable: Inside the New Threat Matrix of Digital Espionage, Crime, and Warfare(New York: Penguin Press, 2011). Post-Cold War Chinese espionage is covered by David Wise's *Tiger Trap: America's Secret Spy War with China*(New York: Houghton Mifflin Harcourt, 2011).

Stephen H. Campbell is a research associate in the Tufts University Fletcher School of Law and Diplomacy International Security Studies Program, where he specializes in intelligence and non-state armed groups. His career has included positions as analyst, consultant, educator, and marketing strategist in the information technology industry. Mr. Campbell earned a B.Sc. honors first class in physics from the University of Glasgow and a masters in law and diplomacy from the Fletcher School. He can be reached at *stephen.campbell@tufts.edu*.

ington Post, and encapsulated in *Top Secret America: The Rise of the New American Security State* (New York: Little, Brown and Company, 2011).

Part III – Intelligence Disciplines, Applications, and Missions

In the intelligence field there are various disciplines related to how intelligence is collected. The five disciplines related to how intelligence is collected include:

- Open Source intelligence (OSINT) – this includes broadcast and printed materials that are openly available, including radio, TV, Internet, newspapers, magazines, and books. It also includes limited distribution materials, such as conference reports and letters, that are not protected, called "gray materials."

- Human source intelligence (HUMINT) – this includes the classic spy and law enforcement's confidential informant. It also includes information from witnesses, diplomats, attachés, journalists, government officials, academics, and others. It further includes liaison with other intelligence services.

- Imagery intelligence (IMINT) – sources include film-based and electro-optical sensors, video, and synthetic aperture radar (SAR) whether taken from the ground, aircraft, unmanned aerial systems, or satellites.

- Signals intelligence (SIGINT) – has three components: communications intelligence (COMINT), which includes the content of telephonic, telegraphic, radio, or computer communications and associated metadata; electronic intelligence (ELINT), which includes the emanations from non-communications emitters, such as radars; and foreign instrumentation signals (FISINT), which are the telemetry associated most often with testing of systems under development. Cyber intelligence is usually considered to be part of COMINT.

- Measurement and Signatures intelligence (MASINT) – involves data from various sub-disciplines, including electro-optical, radar, radiofrequency, geophysical, nuclear radiation, and material sampling. Various aspects of MASINT overlap with both SIGINT and IMINT.

In addition, Geospatial intelligence (GEOINT) is a hybrid discipline combining collection and analysis to create geographically and temporally relevant intelligence. GEOINT incorporates IMINT with geographical information and other data to produce intelligence, maps, charts, geodetic information, and derived reports, such as safety-related notices to airmen and mariners as well as intelligence consumers.[1]

Dr. Robert Clark has contributed four of the fundamental textbooks on intelligence analysis and collection. His article, "Perspectives on Intelligence Collection," examines how collectors and analysts perceive the intelligence disciplines (INTs), why "stovepipes" came about, and the often-confusing and conflicting terminology used in the Intelligence Community. His article is fundamental to understanding how the complex processes of collection and analysis of intelligence function.

Appreciating signals intelligence can be difficult for students. In "A Guide to Teaching Signals Intelligence," **Lawrence Dietz** presents different approaches for teaching the topic and practical exercises for students.

The "Guide to Imagery Intelligence (IMINT)" by retired Air Force imagery specialist **Robert E. Dupré** covers the growth of imagery intelligence from the invention of photography in the 1830s through the world wars to today's multispectral and radar imagery and commercial imagery satellites.

Professor Robert Norton provides an introduction to the use of openly available information for intelligence purposes in his "Guide to Open Source Intelligence." His detailed footnotes and bibliography provide many avenues for further research and reading. **Florian Schauer** and **Jan Störger** provide a European viewpoint regarding the growth and challenges of open source intelligence.

John Sano, the former deputy director of the National Clandestine Service, addresses the generational and technological changes that challenge HUMINT managers in his article, "The Changing Shape of HUMINT."

Everything occurs somewhere on the earth. The synthesis of imagery with cartography and many other sources of information is the foundation of geospatial intelligence. **Dr. Gary Weir**, the chief historian for the National Geospatial-Intelligence Agency (NGA), recounts the history of how GEOINT evolved and how it has been used for many widely varying purposes.

Numerous books have been written about the Central Intelligence Agency (CIA) and National Security Agency (NSA); far fewer about their community counterpart, the Defense Intelligence Agency (DIA). In "The History of the Defense Intelligence Agency" its 17th director, **Lieutenant General Ronald Burgess**, US Army (Ret.), recounts the development and evolution of the organization.

The gathering of intelligence from space is no longer the hush-hush topic it once was. In his article, "I Can See It From Afar; I Can Hear It From Afar," **Dr. Robert McDonald**, director of the Center for the Study of National

---

1. For a detailed explanation of the various intelligence disciplines see Lowenthal, Mark M. and Robert M. Clark, The 5 Disciplines of Intelligence Collection (Los Angeles: SAGE CQ Press, 2016)

Reconnaissance at the National Reconnaissance Office (NRO), describes the origins and evolution of space-based reconnaissance and its contributions to intelligence and national security.

Cyber espionage has become a daily news topic. But how did this come about? **Doug Price** in his article on "The Evolution of Cyber Intelligence" traces how computers became intelligence targets and how the methods used to access them evolved along with the spread of the Internet. He also discusses the subject of cyber counterintelligence.

World War II was the first conflict in which deaths from disease were fewer than combat casualties. Medical intelligence came into its own at the start of the war and contributed to lessening disease-related casualties. **Jonathan Clemente, M.D.,** writes about the evolution of medical intelligence in the Army and the Intelligence Community and the roles of today's National Center for Medical Intelligence.

"Analysis is the most important aspect of intelligence," writes former Assistant DCI for Analysis and Production, **Dr. Mark Lowenthal** in his Intelligence Analysis, Guide to Its Study. He highlights the analytical process and its challenges.

Dr. Tom Fingar was the first Deputy Director of National Intelligence for Analysis. Many of the current Intelligence Community initiatives for analysis began on his watch. His article, "All-Source Analysis," provides a snapshot of the current state of national intelligence analysis, addresses the many modern challenges, and the rationale underlying today's analytical transformation.

Intelligence analysis changed dramatically after the Al-Qaida attacks of 9/11. The mission of identifying and tracking individual terrorists and their networks required a more tactical focus by intelligence analysts and the collection of new forms of information. To do this required the fusion of information from many agencies both within the US and in war zones overseas. **Philip Mudd**, the former deputy director of CIA's Counter Terrorist Center (CTC) and senior intelligence advisor to the FBI, describes the many changes in his article "Understanding Terrorism Analysis."

Preventing the spread of weapons of mass destruction (WMD) is a central focus of the Intelligence Community. In her article on counterproliferation, **Rowena Rege Fischer** details the international regime constructed to counter the proliferation of WMD, which intelligence supports, and the challenges faced.

Arthur E. Gerringer and **Josh Bart** examine law enforcement intelligence in their article, "A Guide to Law Enforcement Intelligence," and explain some of the similarities and differences with national security intelligence. In addition, former Secret Service agent **Robert Smith**'s article on the evolution of law enforcement intelligence addresses how it is very much a part of national security strategy today. He documents national policy on information sharing and the scope of intelligence-led policing at the federal, state, and local levels today.

In "Intelligence Support for Military Operations," former Military Intelligence officer and Defense Intelligence Agency analyst, **Karl Haigler** addresses the complex topic of intelligence support for military operations. He addresses today's challenges of intelligence support to counterinsurgency and cyber threats.

Since the attacks on 9/11 our traditional definitions of intelligence have evolved. National intelligence now encompasses both foreign and domestic aspects due to the cross border characteristic of modern terrorism. National Intelligence University professor **Dr. William Spracher** addresses some of the issues that have arisen in his article: "Homeland Security and Intelligence: Fusing Sometimes Incompatible Missions." In a related article, retired CIA officer and SUNY Albany professor **James Steiner** evaluates the need for education and training of first responders and others in "Homeland Security Intelligence" and how it can help them with their missions.

An interesting contrast to Haigler's article is **Air Force Major Petitjean**'s discussion of how intelligence has been used in humanitarian operations and for disaster relief. She highlights Hurricane Katrina and the 2010 Haitian earthquake.

The use of intelligence techniques has spread far beyond the national security and law enforcement communities. Increasingly the private sector is employing intelligence techniques to support organizational goals and operations. **John McGonagle** recounts the growth of *competitive intelligence*, how it is employed, and some of the issues associated with it in the private sector. A good example of how one corporation embraced business intelligence efforts to help guide its strategic planning, investment, marketing, and other efforts is the case study of Motorola Corporation by former CIA analyst and later leader of Motorola's Corporate Competitive Intelligence group, **Jenny Fisher**.

Intelligence liaison is an age-old practice between nations and intelligence services. European scholar, **Adam Svendsen**, who has studied this practice extensively, explains the historical evolution of liaison and the many demands that drive it the 21st Century.

GUIDE TO THE STUDY OF INTELLIGENCE

Perspectives on Intelligence Collection

Robert M. Clark, PhD

Introduction

Intelligence is collected in many ways: from spies, eavesdropping, technical sources, and openly available materials. The various means are traditionally described as "intelligence disciplines" or, in shorthand, "INTs." The term "INT," however, has also been applied to a few specialized analysis disciplines, resulting in some confusion: is a concept having an "INT" suffix a collection INT or an analytic method?

How you view the intelligence collection INTs depends on where you sit. Collectors have a specific view of the collection function, structure, and process. And for them, it makes sense. It follows the US Intelligence Community (IC) organization. To do their jobs most effectively, analysts need to take a different perspective, one that is not closely tied to the existing functional or structural divisions. Let's examine those views, starting with function.

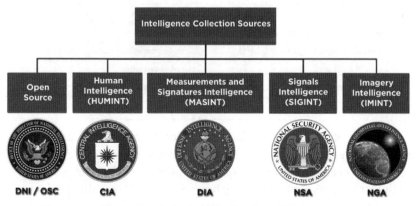

Figure 1: Collector's Functional View of Intelligence Collection

Functional View: the collector's and analyst's perspectives

The traditional and easiest to understand view of collection divides the sources up by following the existing organizational structure. For the US, this results in the breakout shown in Figure 1. For a collection manager, Figure 1 is the simplest and most logical way to view the functions performed by collection. So we have large collection organizations such as the National Geospatial-Intelligence Agency (NGA), responsible for imagery (IMINT) collection; and the National Security Agency (NSA), responsible for signals intelligence (SIGINT). These are the *stovepipes* that intelligence professionals know well. Though they make collaboration difficult, stovepipes serve a number of essential purposes.

Collectors sometimes refer to these as "cylinders of excellence," which provides a clue as to how the divisions developed historically and a reason to functionally view them through that lens. Each stovepipe has built a critical mass of expertise, an elite force that its members consider to be the best in the world at what they do. Another reason that the stovepipe structure works well for collectors is that it identifies the *functional managers* of the major collection INTs. Functional managers have the job of protecting equities. They must plan for collection and define the areas of responsibility for the various INTs.

Primarily, functional managers must ensure that the entire collection process is effectively and efficiently managed, and they must argue their case for budget dollars each year.

As Figure 1 is the simplest and most logical way to view the functions performed by collection, there is another way to view collection functionally, shown in Figure 2. It is important to understand the difference, because it shapes how analysts can best collaborate with collectors and deal with customers.

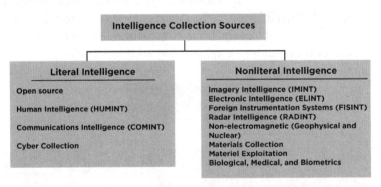

Figure 2: Analyst's Functional View of Intelligence Collection

One type of collection produces *literal* information. It is the form that we use for everyday communication. Analysts understand how literal intelligence is collected and used. It requires no special exploitation after the processing step (usually just language translation) to be understood. It literally speaks for itself.

Nonliteral information, in contrast, usually requires expertise in special processing and exploitation for analysts to make use of it. Most customers don't understand it. British author Michael Herman has written that there are two basic types of collection. He describes the types on the left as "Access to human thought processes" and the types on the right as "Observations and measurements of things."[1]

There are at least a few reasons for thinking this way about collection as an analyst. First, analysts request the types of collection that they need, without a focus on where the collection actually comes from or which specific organization it resides in. Though Figure 1 identifies the functional manager for each type of collection, it doesn't accurately describe where collection actually occurs. The Defense Intelligence Agency (DIA) and the military services collect more human intelligence (HUMINT) than CIA does, and the State Department is a key HUMINT provider (although diplomatic reports are not officially termed "intelligence"). NSA collects measurement and signature intelligence (MASINT) signals. All the organizations in Figure 1, and several others, collect open source.

Both literal and non-literal collection are essential, of course. But, a second reason analysts use this functional delineation is that the two have to be judged differently. For example, literal intelligence can help determine intent and do predictive analysis, while non-literal collection usually cannot. A weakness of literal collection, though, is that people are less reliable than the scientific measurements collected non-literally. People may be misinformed or lie. During World War II, General Rommel lied to Berlin about being short of supplies. The British, intercepting Rommel's communications, mistakenly believed him and attacked. Saddam Hussein's generals routinely lied to him about their capabilities, and he in turn lied to them about having weapons of mass destruction (WMD).

Third, when making an assessment, analysts have to be wary of literal and non-literal specific biases. In literal collection, they must rely on translators. For non-literal, they must rely on the processor or exploiter's judgment. Customers sometimes receive and tend to act on raw literal collection, because they can readily grasp it. That is not necessarily a good thing, because they are not trained analysts. But this functional view helps them see where they may be able to give input and where they may not challenge the collection. Interpreting a hyperspectral image or an electronic intelligence (ELINT) recording isn't usually within a customer's skill set.

Two Views of the Process

The intelligence collection process is typically portrayed as a one cycle

---

1. Michael Herman, *Intelligence Services in the Information Age* (New York: Frank Cass Publishers, 2001), 82.

loop: question in, answer out. Figure 3 illustrates what the inside of a stovepipe looks like. It makes a nice picture but does not convey what is actually happening. Instead, collection is a highly iterative and continuous process. Collectors jump around a lot in the diagram of Figure 3.

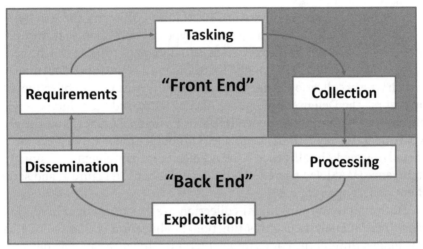

Figure 3: Collector's Process View

Collectors often refer to the "front end" and "back end" of the process, as indicated. Figure 3 also illustrates what they mean. In this view, the "cycle" divides into three distinct stages: requirements and tasking are the "front end"; collection is the middle action; and processing, exploitation, and dissemination are referred to as the "back end." In an ideal system, you'd then identify the gaps in knowledge, revise the requirements, and the process begins anew.

It is easy to think of it as a straight line process with a beginning and an end, rather than a cycle. That's how it works in practice. How you get from dissemination to requirements is almost an unknown for collectors. That's because they typically have no control over that step. Someone else has to do it. Usually, that's the job of an analyst.

There's another way to think about both collection structure and process, as shown in Figure 4, that is more useful for analysts. This view treats collection as many separate stovepipes, each having a specialized variant of the process shown in Figure 3, and each producing a different type of intelligence product, therefore, having a different function. It also has two distinctly different products.

Much of collection is high volume, with automated processing and of a mass of material which then is disseminated widely. In the field, you get a lot of open source (OSINT), imagery intelligence (IMINT), and SIGINT without having to ask for it.

The other kind is often called targeted collection; I often describe it as "boutique" collection. Think of the contrast between a mass-market store such as Wal-Mart, and a boutique such as Tiffany's that caters to a select customer set. Targeted collection is usually expensive, produced in small quantity for a few customers. It requires extensive processing and exploitation.

The collection INTs shown in blue are targeted. Those shown in gold-or-ange are usually mass collection, but sometimes are targeted. ELINT is an example: it can be either (operational ELINT is mass collection, technical ELINT is targeted). Cyber collection often is targeted, but much of it is mass collection.

Why is this important for analysts? Because they handle collection requests quite differently, depending on which type they are dealing with. Mass collection typically has a formal requirements structure. Imagery collection, for example, may have massive target decks. A target deck is a list of existing intelligence targeting requests and the target related data. Getting your target into those decks means navigating a formal requirements structure. In contrast, targeted collection tends to be focused on a single event, facility, or individual. Think here of the hunt for Osama bin Laden or of collection against a North Korean ballistic missile test. Analysts tend to become much more directly involved in targeted collection than in mass collection.

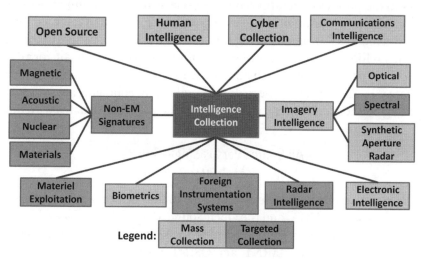

Figure 4: Analyst's Process View

It's also valuable for both analysts and collectors to view collection struc-turally as Figure 4 shows it, because the cultures are different within each box shown in the figure. ELINT, foreign instrumentation signals intelligence (FISINT), and communications intelligence (COMINT) are lumped within the category "SIGINT" in Figure 1. However, these three INTs have distinctly different cultures, different technical disciplines, and different security com-partmentation practices. The same is true for the three IMINT subcategories shown in Figure 4. When working with collectors in all of these disciplines, it is essential to realize that fact and to understand that they cannot be treated simply as "SIGINT collectors" or "imagery analysts."

Boundary Issues
and the "Name Game"

General Michael Hayden, former Director of the National Security Agency and Central Intelligence Agency, has said that when he was an ROTC instructor he would quote this line from Confucius to his new students: "The rectification of names is the most important business of government. If names are not correct, language will not be in accordance with the truth of things."[2]

We often deal with boundaries (areas of responsibility) in the IC by choosing names for collection or analysis that emphasize the importance of our mission. After all, we prefer to work for an elite and respected organization and we want to believe that what we're doing is of value for national security. Also, we like to go into budget negotiations with a strong negotiating position. So, violating Confucius' edict, we choose names and their definitions that suit our bureaucratic purposes. For example, most of the intelligence community refers to the pilotless aircraft used in reconnaissance as an unmanned aerial vehicle (UAV). In US Air Force circles, it is an article of faith to call it a remotely piloted vehicle (RPV), emphasizing the need for a pilot somewhere in the loop.

In intelligence, the misuse of names often results in confusion for all parties: collectors, analysts, and customers. It also results in the naming of many things as "INTs" that have little to do with collection. Following are some of the resulting boundary issues and competing terms that are associated with them.

All Source Versus Single Source
Versus Multi-INT Analysis

National intelligence collection organizations perform what is called single source analysis. NSA, NGA, and the Open Source Center (OSC), for example, all do single source analysis: their job is to process, exploit, and analyze material collected from COMINT, IMINT, and OSINT, respectively. They often make use of material from other INTs, and refer to such material as collateral intelligence. So, if an imagery analyst uses COMINT, she would refer to the COMINT as "collateral." And a COMINT analyst using imagery would call the imagery "collateral."

A number of national agencies and military service units are charged with producing all source analysis. For example, CIA, DIA, Department of Homeland

---

2. Michael Hayden, "The Future of Things 'Cyber'," *Strategic Studies Quarterly*, Spring 2011, accessed 28 June 2013 at *http://www.masonbay.com/clients/dev2/chertoff-html/articles-the-future-of-things-cyber.php.*

Security (DHS), and the State Department all have the responsibility to provide all-source analysis at the national level.

Supposedly, a boundary exists between these two analysis types. It is a boundary that is often ignored. Single source analysis groups want to produce all-source intelligence, and because intelligence is shared among collection organizations, they usually are able to do so. Michael Herman observed that "The single-source agencies now are not pure collectors of 'raw intelligence'; they are also institutionalized analysts, selectors, and interpreters"; and on the distinction between the two, that it is "intellectually artificial to chop up into parts what is in reality a continuous search for the truth."[3]

There are good reasons to encourage, rather than discourage, the proclivity of single-source analysts to do all-source analysis (which, playing the name game, they prefer to call "multi-INT fusion"). If it can be done effectively, the single-source analyst can pick up some of the workload of producing intelligence, so that the heavily loaded all-source analyst gets some help. And the whole idea of competitive analysis is built around the idea of a fresh and different perspective looking at the raw material. A different set of eyes on the material can often surface something important.

On the other hand, the single-source analyst simply doesn't have the same breadth of access to sources, and usually doesn't have the same depth of experience or expertise in dealing with the topic, nor the close access to the customer that the all-source analyst has. So the single source analyst producing all-source intelligence can provide a poor assessment (which the customer might just use). Another pitfall is that the single-source analyst can fail to do his/her primary job on the single source because of a focus on the all-source problem.

Operational Information
Versus Intelligence

In the course of combat operations, friendly units are constantly observing the enemy actions visually and also using imagery and electronic means. This could be considered intelligence collection, or simply operational information. Depending on which side you sit organizationally, you're likely to have different names for it. A few examples:

- A Predator video could be considered either intelligence or operational information. If the video is used for on-the-spot targeting, it logically would be operational information. If it is retained and analyzed for future use, it more likely is intelligence. But intelligence officers are prone to call the product "movement intelligence" (MOVEINT), while operational staff simply call it full motion video (FMV), avoiding the word "intelligence."

---

3. Herman, *Intelligence Services*, pp. 192-93.

- ELINT intercepts that are used to geolocate enemy radars are referred to as operational ELINT (or OPELINT) in intelligence circles. But the US military uses the term electronic support measures (ESM) for OPELINT that is used to support electronic and physical attacks on a target. The term ESM was coined specifically to keep the product out of intelligence budgets and away from intelligence management.

- A battlefield radar detects opposing forces' aircraft and helicopter movements. This usually would be considered operational information. But the product might have intelligence value, and would then be referred to as "radar intelligence" or RADINT.

As the examples suggest, there may be boundaries, but they are fuzzy ones. The difference becomes important primarily when the US goes through its annual funding exercise. A collection system that provides operational information goes into the Defense budget and requires different approvals than one that is deemed for intelligence use in the National Intelligence Program budget.

Naming New Collection Methods

When a new collection method becomes important for customers, and it doesn't fit cleanly into the existing structure, we often see a battle of names for it. Following are a few that have developed over the last 10 years, including some that are still being argued.

GEOINT, AGI, and
Imagery-Derived MASINT

Figure 1 shows NGA as the functional manager for IMINT. Most taxonomies replace IMINT with the term geospatial intelligence (GEOINT). According to NGA doctrine, GEOINT is the product of integrating imagery, imagery intelligence, and geospatial information. But since geospatial information also is collected via OSINT, SIGINT, HUMINT, and MASINT, the GEOINT product would seem to result from either all-source analysis or multi-INT fusion, depending on your preferred terminology. GEOINT arguably is not a collection INT – no collection system collects GEOINT.

NGA has defined a special type of GEOINT called advanced geospatial intelligence (AGI). The definition calls AGI "technical, geospatial, and intelligence information derived through interpretation or analysis using advanced processing of all data collected by imagery or imagery-related collection systems." Presumably, this refers to infrared, spectral, and radar imagery. DIA, with functional responsibility for MASINT, prefers to call it "imagery-derived MASINT."

Cyber Collection

Perhaps one of the most important sources of raw intelligence today, cyber collection does not fit cleanly into any of the traditional five INTs. It has some aspects of open source (since it relies heavily on the Web). It arguably is a type of SIGINT, since it can require intercepting internet communications. But how do you characterize placing a Trojan or worm on a victim computer, downloading the hard drive, and activating the victim's video camera? Such a process does not involve intercepting a deliberately transmitted signal. And how to characterize a HUMINT operation that downloads files from a single computer, one that never connects to the internet?

The result of these complexities is another naming contest. Those in the SIGINT business have coined the term "SIGINT at rest" to argue that cyber collection is a SIGINT activity. Those who find that terminology somewhat strained, especially when applied to standalone computers, argue that "HUMINT-enabled" cyber collection is more appropriate.

Identity Intelligence

Biometrics has become an important source of intelligence as the focus of much collection, especially in Iraq and Afghanistan, has been on identifying and tracking individuals. The result has been the creation of a new "INT," called *identity intelligence*. While biometrics is about collection, and logically a type of MASINT, the term "identity intelligence" would seem to describe the product of all-source analysis, much like GEOINT.

Conclusion

The US Intelligence Community has developed, over time, an incredibly complex system for collecting and processing raw intelligence. It is effective, far from perfect, but the best in the world in providing intelligence to support a broad range of customers. It succeeds despite the challenges of collaborating across the stovepipes and the tensions created by budget competition. Collectors and analysts are best served when each understands the other's perspectives of function and process. Sound assessments depend on this understanding.

READINGS FOR INSTRUCTORS

Clark, Robert M. *Intelligence Collection* (Washington DC: Sage/CQ Press, 2014) (available in August 2013). Takes a systems approach to collection, explaining the structure, function, and process of all of the INTs listed in Figure 2.

Crumpton, Henry A. *The Art of Intelligence* (New York: Penguin Press, 2012). This is perhaps the best available explanation in print of how a clandestine service actually functions.

Kahn, David. *The Codebreakers: The Comprehensive History of Secret Communication from Ancient Times to the Internet* (New York: Scribner, 1996). A classic, this is the standard reference on cryptology and its history.

US Commission on the Roles and Capabilities of the United States Intelligence Community. *IC21: The Intelligence Community in the 21st Century*. (Washington, DC: GPO, 1996). Accessed at *http://www.access.gpo.gov/congress/house/intel/ic21/index.html*. Though 17 years old, this report provides a good summary of the major INTs.

NATO Open Source Intelligence Handbook, 2001, accessed at *http://www.oss.net/dynamaster/file_archive/030201/ca5fb66734f540fbb4f8f6ef759b258c/NATO%20OSINT%20Handbook%20v1.2%20-%20Jan%202002.pdf*. This book, along with, the NATO Open Source Intelligence Reader and the NATO Intelligence Exploitation of the Internet, provides a comprehensive view of open source collection.

Robert M. Clark currently is an independent consultant for the US Intelligence Community. He is also a faculty member of the Intelligence and Security Academy and a professor of intelligence studies at the University of Maryland University College.

Dr. Clark served in the US Air Force as an electronics warfare officer and intelligence officer, reaching the rank of lieutenant colonel. At CIA, he was a senior analyst and group chief responsible for managing analytic methodologies. He subsequently was president and CEO of the Scientific and Technical Analysis Corporation, directing intelligence collection and analysis support efforts and the creation of new collection and analysis methodologies.

As a consultant, Dr. Clark helped develop the DNI's Intelligence Community Officers' Course and served as a faculty member from 2001 to 2008. From 2008 to 2009, he was the course director of the DNI's "Introduction to the Intelligence Community" course.

Clark holds an SB from MIT, a PhD in electrical engineering from the University of Illinois, and a JD from George Washington University. He is a presidential interchange executive, a member of the Virginia state bar, and a patent attorney.

Dr. Clark's *Intelligence Analysis: A Target-centric Approach* is now in its fourth edition. His second book, *The Technical Collection of Intelligence*, was published in 2010. His third book, *Intelligence Collection*, was published in 2013.

GUIDE TO THE STUDY OF INTELLIGENCE

A Guide to Teaching Signals Intelligence

Lawrence D. Dietz

If you ever made a call on a cell phone, or sent a text message, or posted on a blog, you may have wondered if anyone else was listening in on your communications. You watch crime thrillers only to learn that the federal government finally was able to arrest organized crime gangsters by tapping their phones. What you may not have known is that these are examples of how signals intelligence (SIGINT) can be employed.

Definition

According to the National Security Agency (NSA), "SIGINT ... encompasses any intelligence ... collected over the electromagnetic spectrum. SIGINT derives intelligence from transmissions associated with communications, radars, and weapons systems.... It complements other forms of intelligence....[1]

It is important to point out that SIGINT is just one of several intelligence disciplines. Another is human intelligence (HUMINT), familiar to most people thanks to James Bond and others of his ilk. Imagery intelligence (IMINT), which can be thought of as Google Earth where pictures of areas and buildings taken from satellites, combined with other data, are used to develop a profile of a target. Open source intelligence (OSINT), such as everything available in the public library, is another. Lastly, measurement and signatures intelligence (MASINT) is best compared to the forensic tests shown in the *CSI* television series. In practice, intelligence analysts use all the "Int's" in concert as it is accepted practice not to rely on a single source, but to confirm information through several sources.

Prior to proposing some approaches for instructors to teach about SIGINT,

---

1. http://www.nsa.gov/sigint/index.shtml

it is useful to consider and define the components of SIGINT. Most generally accepted definitions say that SIGINT is composed of:

- Communications intelligence (COMINT), deriving intelligence from communications such as radios or telephones.
- Electronic intelligence (ELINT), deriving intelligence from noncommunications emitters, such as radar.
- Foreign instrument signals (FIS, FISINT), deriving from foreign telemetry signals, such as from satellites.
- The newest component is computer network exploitation (CNE), which encompasses exploiting computer networks and the internet for useful intelligence.

Approaches to Teaching SIGINT

Three alternative and complementary approaches are feasible for the teaching of SIGINT: the historical, the technical, and via practical exercises.

Historical Approach. Intercepting the secrets of one's enemies has been a proven tactic for thousands of years. SIGINT often depends on breaking an enemy's codes. Consequently, the study of SIGINT is not complete without the study of cryptography, the coding and decoding of secret messages.[2]

There are several famous, and some not so famous, instances of when SIGINT turned the tide of war or public opinion. One is the January 1917 Zimmermann Telegram, ably chronicled in Barbara Tuchman's book (see "Readings for Instructors"). The Zimmermann Telegram was a major reason President Wilson acquiesced to entering World War I. In an intercepted diplomatic note, the Germans and Japanese promised Mexico it could regain some of its territory the US "stole" in the War of 1846-48 if Mexico would join Germany in war against the US.

Another historical incident that is good to study is the January 1968 capture of the US Navy's SIGINT ship *Pueblo* by the North Koreans and the subsequent imprisonment of the crew. Students should explore the relationships between those entrusted with the secret codes and the role of the ship's captain, who was not. The *Pueblo* can also be used to debate how much effort should be given to protecting SIGINT sources, which often are fragile and therefore sensitive.

An interesting topic is the controversy of whether or not FDR had foreknowledge that the Japanese were going to attack Pearl Harbor because the US had broken the Japanese Purple Code used to encrypt its diplomatic traffic. (See Wohlstetter in "Readings for Instructors.")

An unusual scenario that combines history, Native American culture, and SIGINT is the story of the Navajo Code Talkers of World War II. In those days,

---

2. http://www.wordcentral.com/cgi-bin/student?book=Student&va=cryptography

radio transmissions were sent in the clear, meaning they weren't encrypted and, therefore, heard by anyone on the same frequency. To befuddle the Japanese, the US Marine Corps employed Navajo speakers who used their native language with which the Japanese were totally unfamiliar.

Technical Approach. A technical approach is best suited for students who excel in math and logic. Under this approach, an instructor shows how basic code systems work. There are extensive resources available. For example, the NSA has cryptograms on-line at: *http://www.nsa.gov/kids/games/games00002.shtml.*

Instructors can develop basic handouts using substitution codes where one letter is substituted for another. Other simple techniques are described by the University of Illinois (Chicago) at *http://cryptoclub.math.uic.edu/indexmain. html.* These include the Caesar (shift) Cipher, Affine Cipher, Vigenere Cipher, Multiplicative Cipher, using numbers for letters, and the Substitution Cipher. This resource also introduces the concept of frequency analysis as a tool used to break substitution codes. Frequency analysis is based on the fact that some letters, like vowels — especially "e," are used frequently while other letters are used less frequently. Consider breaking your class into two groups. One would be using the code to communicate while the other would be trying to crack the code. Or you could divide the class into teams with a prize for the team that cracks the code first.

Another option is to develop an alphabet of symbols and use that alphabet to encode and decode simple messages.

Practical Exercises. There are several practical exercises that can be used to teach about SIGINT.

"Radio Silence" In the first phase of this exercise, students refrain from using their cell phones, tablets, and computers for a fixed time period. No cell calls, no texting, no e-mails. To be effective, the time frame has to be long enough to be more than a minor inconvenience. While radio silence prevents the interception of messages by unauthorized persons, the associated inability to communicate has other effects. These are interesting to explore.

In the subsequent phase of this exercise, the instructor explains the concept of "sneaker-net," whereby students put their e-mails or messages on a thumb drive and another student sends his communications out for them. This is the method employed for years by Osama bin Laden (OBL) as a means to avoid detection by SIGINT. His computer was not connected to the internet. Rather, he wrote his e-mails and messages and created his audio and video presentations and loaded them on a portable drive. One of his trusted couriers then took the drive to another location where it was plugged into the internet and the traffic sent.

Current Event Analysis   Students are encouraged to analyze a major current event, such as the Libyan conflict. They have to assess how the parties involved are communicating and design a plan to intercept and analyze those communications. Students can be given a copy of US Army Field Manual 2.0 on Intelligence (http://www.fas.org/irp/doddir/army/fm2-0.pdf). Depending on the nature of the class, this exercise can be supplemented with maps and students asked to "plot" key locations of people and/or places and indicate those that might be fruitful sources of intelligence. Instructors could expand the scope of the exercise by encouraging the use of Google Earth as means of providing IMINT as well.

Conclusion

Signals intelligence has had a profound impact on conflicts and diplomacy throughout history. Today's reliance on electronic communications over smart phones and tablets and the ubiquitous nature of the internet means that SIGINT will remain a major source of intelligence in the future.

READINGS FOR INSTRUCTORS

James Bamford has written extensively on NSA and signals intelligence. His *The Puzzle Palace: Inside America's Most Secret Intelligence Organization* (Penguin Group, 1982) was at that time a controversial exposé. His later books were *Body of Secrets* (Anchor Books, 2001) and *The Shadow Factory: The NSA from 9/11 to Eavesdropping on America* (Anchor Books, 2009). A recent comprehensive history and examination of NSA is by Matthew Aid, *Secret Sentry: the Untold History of the National Security Agency* (Bloomsbury Press, 2010).

Other recommended books include Barbara Tuchman, *The Zimmermann Telegram* (Ballantine Books, 1958); Simon Singh, *The Code Book: The Science of Secrecy from Ancient Egypt to Quantum Cryptology* (Anchor Books, 1999); and Mitchell B. Lerner, *The Pueblo Incident: A spy Ship and the Failure of American Foreign Policy* (Modern War Studies, University of Kansas Press, 2002). *The Zimmermann Telegram* is an easy read and might seem to be more of a thriller than a historical commentary. Singh's book is an excellent primer for anyone who is interested in cryptography.

Two widely acclaimed books, fundamental for SIGINT students, are David Kahn's massive *The Codebreakers: The Comprehensive History of Secret Communications from Ancient Times to the Internet* (Scribner, 1967) and Roberta Wohlstetter's seminal analysis of the warning failure at Pearl Harbor, *Pearl Harbor: Warning and Decision* (Stanford University Press, 1962). *The Codebreakers* is a classic, but due to its length and technical content, not for the timid.

Several websites are valuable for teaching about SIGINT. Most titles are descriptive enough.

http://www.nsa.gov — The NSA website is quite authoritative. A visit to the National Cryptologic Museum next to NSA at Fort Meade, MD, is also worthwhile.

http://www.nsa.gov/about/_files/cryptologic_heritage/publications/coldwar/venona_story.pdf —Venona was the codeword associated with the breaking of the Soviet codes used by its spies in the United States during and just after World War II.

http://www.crows.org/ —This is the site of the trade association of electronic warfare and information operations vendors and professionals. It takes its name from the "Ravens," who were the mascots of WWII radar operators. The Old Crows provide a wealth of information on electronic warfare, computer network operations and have also become a respected source of resources for information operations (IO).

http://www.usspueblo.org/ — for materials on the Pueblo incident.

COMINT and the Battle of Midway: http://ibiblio.org/hyperwar/PTO/Magic/COMINT-Midway.html — (a site of the National Archives and Records Administration).

Pearl Harbor Revisited; Navy Communications 1924–1941; http://www.history.navy.mil/books/comint/ComInt-Biblio.html — (US Navy, Naval Historical Center)

1990 Army War College Paper on the History of COMINT; http://www.dtic.mil/cgi-bin/GetTRDoc?AD=ADA237861&Location=U2&doc=GetTRDoc.pdf

1996 Presentation about Ultra at Bletchley Park by Harry Hinsley, the official historian of British intelligence in World War II. Ultra was the codeword associated with the breaking of the Nazi codes during World War II. http://www.cl.cam.ac.uk/research/security/Historical/hinsley.html

An on-line record of experiences by a former member of the Air Force's SIGINT organization. http://vivausafss.org/Kivett.htm

Breakdown: How America's Intelligence Failures Led to September 11, by Bill Gertz, (Washington, DC: Regnery, 2002), http://www.crows.org/ Gertz is an investigative journalist with Washington Times newspaper.

"Intelligence Failures in Vietnam," http://academic.brooklyn.cuny.edu/history/johnson/65vn-5.htm

"National Security Agency Releases History of Cold War Intelligence": http://www.gwu.edu/~nsarchiv/NSAEBB/NSAEBB260/index.htm

"A Brief Look at ELINT at NSA," http://ftp.fas.org/irp/nsa/almanac-elint.pdf

Army Security Agency (ASA) COMSEC site: http://www.davehatfield.com/davehatfield/ASACOMSEC.html

Article on space-based SIGINT and satellites of many countries, http://en.citizendium.org/wiki/SIGINT_space-based_platforms

Lawrence Dietz is chief legal officer of TAL Global and has over 30 years of military and commercial intelligence and security experience. As an adjunct professor for American Military University, he teaches about intelligence and security. He retired as a colonel in the US Army Reserve. His degrees include BS in business administration, Northeastern University; MBA (with distinction), Babson College; JD, Suffolk University Law School; LLM in European law, University of Leicester, United Kingdom; and MS in strategic studies, US Army

War College. He is the author of a blog on psychological operations (PSYOP) at http://psyopregiment.blogspot.com.

GUIDE TO THE STUDY OF INTELLIGENCE

Imagery Intelligence

Robert E. Dupré

I magery intelligence (IMINT) is a valued and often essential element of the entire intelligence picture. A perusal of the US Intelligence Community (IC) website at http://www.intelligence.gov provides an insight into its importance and displays where imagery fits into the overall intelligence picture. Imagery can take many forms with the most well-known being conventional film (e.g., 35 mm camera), electro-optical (e.g., digital camera), and video (e.g., camcorder). More esoteric imagery forms are also of intelligence use and examples of such are infrared photography and radar imagery. Regardless of type, trained imagery experts interpret (analyze) images to yield useful intelligence data.

In the US, intelligence imagery analysis is conducted at centers such as the National Geospatial Intelligence Agency in Springfield, Maryland (*https://www1. nga.mil*), or at the National Air and Space Intelligence Center at Wright-Patterson Air Force Base in Dayton, Ohio (*http://www.afisr.af.mil/units/nasic/index. asp*). These facilities are key elements in photographic analysis supporting US Government operations.

Brief History of IMINT

The use of imagery for intelligence applications has a long and rich history. Prior to the invention of photography, scouts would deliver tales of their observations to military commanders. They might draw pictures and maps in the dirt to illustrate what they had observed. They would use word pictures to convey information, but the military commander would always have to create a mind picture of the scout's descriptions. This all began to change with the advent of photography in the 1830's. This new invention was used to document battles and occasionally to view an enemy's positions from high ground to record the positions of enemy combatants. Pioneering photographer Matthew Brady created an important historical record of the American Civil War with his photographs. Manned balloons were used during the Civil War to observe enemy positions and activities, and on at least one occasion, photographs obtained from a balloon vantage point were used to support military operations. The need for relatively long exposure times to take 1860's vintage photographs caused blurring because of balloon motion and limited the utility of these early intelligence products. Experiments continued through the late 1880's in places like Germany with photographs taken from balloons, kites, and early rockets, but without much success.

The advance of camera and film technology (smaller cameras, shorter exposure times, more efficient lenses), when tied to the invention of the aircraft, created the opportunity for true imagery support for intelligence and military operations. A brief history of the first aerial observation activity of World War I may be found in the "Aviation History" area of *http://www.pilotfriend.com*. Additional information may be found in *Shooting the Front*, which is listed in the "Readings for Instructors" section.

IMINT in World Wars One and Two

The primary use of aerial photography in WWI was to support frontline tactical operations. As the sophistication of both aircraft and photography increased, it became possible to expand the usefulness of aerial photography. Longer range aircraft, aircraft dedicated to photographic missions, more capable cameras, and trained photo interpreters combined to allow aerial photography to broaden in application. It became possible to collect information that served longer-range analyses of an adversary's future plan. Information about factories, shipyards, harbors, airfields, etc. could be used for both near-term targeting and long-term strategic planning.

In WWII, even low technology efforts yielded useful intelligence imagery data when photographs, known as Aunt Minnies, taken by commercial photographers, journalists, or tourists, showed areas of interest or intelligence targets. These were mostly ground-level photos made available to an intelligence agency of a location of particular interest. They were called Aunt Minnies because someone's aunt (or grandmother, etc.) was often in the photos along with the location of interest. During WWII, the Office of Strategic Services (a predecessor of the CIA) checked thousands of antique shops for Aunt Minnie postcards in addition to checking magazine publisher's files to discover photos of interest areas.

WWII also saw vast technological advances in the use of photography to support military applications and featured the conversion of various combat aircraft, such as the B-17 or British Mosquito, for use as aerial photographic reconnaissance platforms. The book, *Evidence in Camera*, describes the WWII use of aerial reconnaissance from the British perspective. Many of the histories of WWII devote sections to the aerial collection of photography and the military successes resulting from the data.

The Korean War brought the development of aircraft that were specifically designed for photography collection. An example would be the RF-80, a variant of the F-80 Shooting Star Fighter/Bomber. Previously, fighter or bomber aircraft had only been modified to serve a photo collection role rather than being initially designed for that purpose.

The Cold War Years

During the Cold War, the buildup of Soviet strategic capability drove US intelligence collection needs and resulted in the development of strategic platforms such as the U-2 and the SR-71 reconnaissance aircraft. These high-altitude, manned collection platforms were specifically designed to provide access to denied territory primarily for photographic collection. Developed in secrecy, the U-2 was used to obtain information about the emerging Soviet strategic systems. President Eisenhower proposed in 1955 an "Open Skies" policy for the world where arms agreements could be verified by mutual inspection. When the Soviet Union rejected this policy, U-2 overflights of the Soviet Union were initiated in 1956. The loss of one of these aircraft over the Soviet Union in 1960 created an international incident. That story is told by the pilot, Francis Gary Powers, in his book *Operation Overflight*.

The U-2 aircraft also played a prominent role in the Cuban Missile Crisis. The more capable SR-71, originally developed as the A-12 under a CIA program (see *"Archangel: CIA's Supersonic A-12 Reconnaissance Aircraft"* in the "Readings for Instructors" section) reached operational capability in the 1960s and was used during the Vietnam War and in other areas of the world to collect valuable imagery until its retirement in the 1990s.

The development of space-borne photographic collection systems is documented in texts such as *Eye in the Sky, Corona: America's First Satellite Program*, and *The Wizards of Langley*.

The use of spacecraft to obtain imagery from denied areas eliminated the danger of attack on airborne systems but created a much more complex, costly, and less flexible collection system. Spacecraft are restricted to very predictable and not easily changed orbits. One can initially optimize an orbit to maximize coverage (daytime passage over an area of interest, for example), but changing the spacecraft's orbit to accommodate a different threat is extremely difficult, or in some cases impossible, because of the laws of physics. An aircraft can maneuver or delay its departure in response to bad weather, but a spacecraft is restricted to its pre-determined orbital path. Also, many a photograph taken from space has shown nothing but cloud cover or has had a cloud obscuring the target of interest. Early space photographs also suffered from poor quality compared to aircraft coverage, but advancing technology has skillfully addressed and resolved that issue. Details about the types of satellites used and their operations may be found in the book *Deep Black*.

The Modern Era of UAVs and SAR

By the 1990s, new systems had been developed that improved photographic intelligence. Electro-optic sensors (think digital cameras) entered into common use. The unmanned aerial vehicle (UAV) was developed and could send video in real time back to battlefield commanders, who could then observe an engagement in progress. By the time of the Second Gulf War, the Predator UAV was outfitted with ordinance (Hellfire missiles) and was capable of not only observing action but of attacking targets of opportunity. The development of synthetic aperture radar (SAR) imagery now allows surveillance of targets of interest at night and through clouds. SAR images can reveal to imagery interpreters intelligence not available in conventional images.

The 1990s also witnessed the growth of international and commercial satellite imaging. While the former Soviet Union had maintained a robust Cosmos imagery program, the first civil imagery satellite, Landsat, was launched in 1972, and the French launched their SPOT remote sensing satellite in 1986. The first of the privately funded earth imaging satellites was launched in 1999. Ikonos was managed by Space Imaging, Inc., a spin-off of Lockheed, a company well-versed in imagery systems. By 2003, competitor imagery satellite systems had been orbited (QuickBird and OrbView), one (EROS-A1) by an Israeli company. Canada developed RadarSat 1, a SAR system, and India continued with its IRS program, which had its first launch in 1995. To date, 13 countries have orbited satellite imaging systems. The US commercial systems were based on digital imaging technology developed for the IC. Recent systems collect imagery in from 3 to 10 spectral bands with a resolution as good as 0.5 meters. The geospatial information (imagery plus other geographical information) collected is used for many purposes, including disaster monitoring, urban planning, agriculture, environmental protection, law enforcement, and resource monitoring.

Future Trends in IMINT

The most recent trend in IMINT is the optimization of advanced communications capabilities to enable the delivery of quality imagery to highly automated processing centers. The rapid interpretation of images, fused with other intelligence material, has resulted in the ability to deliver finished integrated intelligence analyses to decision makers in a timely fashion.

Imagery collection and processing have improved by leaps and bounds since the American Civil War. The timeline from collection to delivery of actionable information to a decisionmaker has been reduced from days/hours to minutes/seconds. Image resolution quality has been improved so that decision makers can now often discern the "what" of an image without explanations by an interpreter.

About 500 B.C., the great Chinese military thinker, Sun Tzu, wrote a treatise on war in which he said: "If you know the enemy and know yourself you need not fear a hundred battles. If you know yourself and not the enemy, for every victory you will suffer a defeat. If you know neither yourself nor the enemy, you are a fool and will meet defeat in every battle." Imagery intelligence data is a key element in "knowing one's enemy." It is expected that this will remain true for the foreseeable future.

READINGS FOR INSTRUCTORS

Babington-Smith, Constance. *Evidence in Camera: The Story of Photographic Intelligence*, (Sutton Publishing, 2004), ISBN: 0750936487

Article author's description: This book documents the exploits of Babington-Smith, who, with her colleagues in the Allied Central Interpretation Unit, were the first to identify the German V-1 launch site at Peenemünde, thus discovering the evidence of Hitler's V-weapons program.

Burrows, William E. *Deep Black*, (Random House, 1986), ISBN: 0-394-54124-3

Article author's description: Burrows provides insight into the US Government's space-based intelligence collection capabilities with an emphasis on imagery collection.

Day, Dwayne A. Brian Latell, and John M. Logsdon (eds.) *Eye in the Sky: The Story of the Corona Spy Satellites* (Smithsonian Institution Press, 1999), ISBN: 1560987731.

Article author's description: This Smithsonian History of Aviation Series book presents the story of the Corona spy satellite program documenting one of the most important breakthroughs in twentieth-century intelligence gathering.

Finnegan, Terrence J. *Shooting the Front*, (National Defense Intelligence College, 2007), available through the Government Printing Office bookstore (http://tinyurl.com/6kq7kkp).

GPO description: Provides a pioneering study of the impact of aerial photography on America's fledgling air force during its baptism of fire above the trenches of the Western Front. This comprehensive history from the Defense Intelligence Agency highlights aerial photography's ability to command the high ground and provide a concise view of a battle area, both tactically and strategically. It is an authoritative account of aerial reconnaissance and the interpretation of photographs as they evolved into the most important sources of intelligence along the entire Western Front during World War 1.

Pedlow Gregory and Donald E. Welzenbach. "The CIA and the U-2 Program 1954-1974," (Central Intelligence Agency: Center for the Study of Intelligence, 1998), available at *https://www.cia.gov/library/center-for-the-study-of-intelligence/csi-publications/books-and-monographs/the-cia-and-the-u-2-program-1954-1974/index.htm.*

Article author's description: This book describes the history of the U-2 program from the CIA perspective and showcases the key contributions of designer "Kelly" Johnson to US imagery collection capability.

Powers, Francis Gary. *Operation Overflight,* (Holt, Rinehart and Winston, 1970), ISBN: 03-083045-1.

Article author's description: Power's book is a personal memoir that describes his selection and training to fly the U-2; his final mission over the Soviet Union; his capture, trial, and incarceration; and finally his return to the United States.

Richelson, Jeffrey T. *The Wizards of Langley,* (Westview Press, 2002), ISBN: 978-0-8133-4059-3.

Article author's description: Richelson provides a detailed description of the operations of the CIA Directorate of Science and Technology, which had oversight over the development of the most sophisticated airborne and spaceborne imagery collection assets of the US.

Robarge, David. *Archangel: CIA's Supersonic A-12 Reconnaissance Aircraft* (Central Intelligence Agency: Center for the Study of Intelligence, 2007), available at *https://www.cia.gov/library/center-for-the-study-of-intelligence/csi-publications/books-and-monographs/a-12/index.html.*

Article author's description: This monograph provides important insight into the clandestine development of this important reconnaissance aircraft at the Lockheed "Skunk Works" facility in California.

Ruffner, Kevin C. (ed.). *Corona: America's First Satellite Program,* (Central Intelligence Agency: Center for the Study of Intelligence, 1995), available at *https://www.cia.gov/library/center-for-the-study-of-intelligence/csi-publications/books-and-monographs/index.html.*

Article author's description: This PDF file is a compendium of declassified CIA documents that delivers a detailed description of the Corona satellite system development and operations. It includes original intelligence analyses and photography from the actual missions.

Stoney, W. E. *Guide to Land Imaging Satellites* (American Society for Photogrammetry and Remote Sensing, 2005; *http://www.asprs.org*).

Disclaimer: The opinions stated in this article are those of the author and not those of AFIO or of the US Government.

Robert E. Dupré is a retired US Air Force officer with over 40 years of military and civilian engineering experience in intelligence analysis and the development/operation of intelligence collection and communications systems. He is currently a consultant to Air Force development activities at the Electronic Systems Center, Hanscom AFB, MA, and an adjunct instructor of business studies at Southern New Hampshire University. Mr. Dupré is an AFIO member.

GUIDE TO THE STUDY OF INTELLIGENCE

Open Source Intelligence

A Growing Window Into the World

R. A. Norton, Ph.D.

Open Source Intelligence (OSINT) utilizes information that is openly available to all. The world overflows with information – facts and figures, writing and descriptions, pictures, videos, and audio recordings. Some of it is secured (or "classified"). Most is not but is disorganized and thereby hard to find. OSINT collection attempts to find nuggets of information, which can then be collated, synthesized, and analyzed. What does the latest Chinese stealth fighter plane look like? This was discovered through OSINT. What did Ayman al-Zawahiri, Osama Bin Laden's deputy say about Al-Qa'ida's intentions? Again, this is learned through OSINT.

Properly used, OSINT becomes the foundation upon which the other types of intelligence (human intelligence, HUMINT; imagery intelligence, IMINT; signals intelligence, SIGINT; and measurement and signatures intelligence, MASINT) rest.[1] OSINT complements traditional methods of gathering intelligence providing context and confirmation.

OSINT is ancient, used since before biblical times. In revolutionary America, George Washington[2] kept abreast of British troop strengths and movements through spies that among other things gathered newspapers, publically available information and pamphlets. During the 1863 Gettysburg Campaign, General Lee's intelligence officers monitored Northern troop move-

---

1. A quick description of the various INTs, including OSINT is available at: *https://www.cia.gov/library/ publications/additional-publications/the-work-of-a-nation/work-of-the-cia.html*.
2. Many historians consider George Washington to have been "America's First Military Intelligence Director." For further information see: *https://www.cia.gov/news-information/featured-story-ar- chive/2007-featured-story-archive/george-washington.html*.

ments through the accounts of Northern newspapers.[3] During the 1899-1902 Philippine War, US military planners had to rely on intelligence reports that were little more than copied encyclopedia articles.[4] During both world wars, military intelligence examined books and newspapers for valuable information. In their dash across France, General Patton's troops used Michelin maps collected from gas stations. Publically available maps are good examples of OSINT, still used today for geospatial understanding.

In the wake of World War II, the government realized that a more formalized process was necessary to gather information, including that which was publically available. Thus, when the Central Intelligence Agency (CIA) was founded in 1947, it assumed primary responsibility for OSINT as well as HUMINT collection. Huge amounts of publically available information were gathered by CIA's Foreign Broadcast Information Service (FBIS) and Foreign Document Division. During the Cold War, the Office of Strategic Research gained information about foreign nuclear capabilities from public statements by foreign officials and published reports by scientists (focused particularly on the USSR and China but also on other countries like France).[5] During this same period the Office of Economic Research exploited public information concerning OPEC oil production, Soviet grain production, and the strength of foreign currencies and foreign company acquisitions.[6] Developments in the Soviet space program were also monitored by CIA and US Air Force via technical literature.[7]

The need for more complete information on more subjects was identified by the 9-11 Commission. Part of the 2004 reorganization of the Intelligence Community (IC) included the establishment of an Open Source Center at CIA by renaming FBIS.[8] A similar capability exists at the Defense Intelligence Agency

---

3. A fascinating account of intelligence-related problems experienced by both the North and South during the Gettysburg Campaign is provided by *The Gettysburg Campaign – A Study in Command* by Edwin B. Coddington (Charles Scribner's Sons, 1968). The author points out that utilization of Northern newspapers by Southern commanders caused problems due to the sometimes unreliable information [deliberately or inadvertently] provided (19). Vetting and validation of OSINT reliability continues to be a challenge to this day.

4. Encyclopedia articles are but one early example of OSINT. Military planners were severely hampered by the lack of intelligence throughout the Philippine War. Detailed accounts of the problems can be found in *The Philippine War: 1899-1902*, by Brian McAllister Linn (University Press of Kansas, 2000).

5. See: *The U.S. Intelligence Community* by Stafford T. Thomas (University Press of America, 1983, 58-60) for a contemporary review of the Cold War intelligence apparatus, which included in its priorities the collection of technical documents and foreign publications by the Office of Strategic Research.

6. A review of OSINT collection and utilization history during the Cold War era can be found in Jeffrey T. Richelson's interesting volumes, The U.S. Intelligence Community, Fourth Edition, (Chapter 12) (Westview Press, 1999) and *The Wizards of Langley – Inside the CIA's Directorate of Science and Technology* (Westview Press, 2002) .

7. One of the best reviews of OSINT history and current use is Stephen C. Mercado's article, Sailing the Sea of OSINT in the Information Age, available at *https://www.cia.gov/library/center-for-the-study-of-intelligence/csi-publications/csi-studies/studies/vol48no3/article05.html*.

8. Additional information on the Open Source Center can be found at *https://www.cia.gov/news-information/press-releases-statements/press-release-archive-2005/pr11082005.html* and *https://www.cia.gov/library/publications/additional-publications/the-work-of-a-nation/cia-director-and-principles/centers-in-the-*

(DIA),[9] where military-relevant OSINT is produced for decisionmakers in the Department of Defense.

With the myriad of today's technical collection capabilities, reasonable questions to ask are, "Why OSINT?" and "Why now?" The answer is quite straight forward, as OSINT's characteristics include the speed with which it can be collected; the available quantity, quality, and clarity of information; its ease of use; and the comparative low cost of its collection.[10] Information is expanding exponentially. Much of it is on the Worldwide Web. Without efficient means for retrieval and organization, much of it would remain undiscovered. Search strategies and software are being developed by the Intelligence Community to make open source information discovery easier and its organization more efficient.

OSINT is challenging because of its volume and because each piece of information must be verified or "vetted," often in unique ways. Vetting is important for any intelligence process. If a newspaper or cable news source reports that an individual said something, how does the OSINT analyst know that the reported statement is accurate? The newspaper may be controlled by a repressive government or aligned with a political party. Deception techniques are common. Our adversaries know we are watching and listening and often try to fool us with spurious information, which can spread quickly throughout the Internet. In the case of OSINT analysis, multiple independent sources providing the same or confirmatory reports are a requirement for validating the information. This is a never ending process as new information is continually collected.

One of the most important tools for the OSINT analyst is large commercial search engines, such as Google or Yahoo, to name but two. Search engines increase access efficiencies through indexing and search algorithms that can process rapidly millions of pages of data and documents. Search engines can be very specific, focusing on specific countries or domains, published books, or specialized scientific literature. An experienced OSINT analyst knows where the best information is likely to be found. Large scale or limited searches can be made using specific strategies so that only the most relevant information is extracted. Then the "analytic process" begins.

In the analysis process, the analyst identifies "findings" (i.e., facts that he knows and can verify) and gaps (things he knows he does not know). For example, with the Al-Zawahiri statement, the analyst can locate the video and

---

cia.html.

9. A brief introduction to the purposes and practices of Military Intelligence, including the use of OSINT is available at *http://www.dia.mil/history/*.

10. A detailed discussion of OSINT utility is provided by Stephen C. Mercado's article, "Reexamining the Distinction Between Open Information and Secrets," available at *https://www.cia.gov/library/center-for-the-study-of-intelligence/csi-publications/csi-studies/studies/Vol49no2/reexamining_the_distinction_3.htm*.

confirm the information. While he knows some characteristics of the new Chinese stealth fighter from the photograph, gaps in knowledge remain of the technical specifications and aerodynamic capabilities. Both findings and gaps are used to determine requirements for additional collection, perhaps through other INTs. In the case of the stealth fighter, a requirement might be to obtain specific information about the aircraft's wings, which could in turn provide indications about its aerodynamic capabilities. These requirements might be fulfilled through OSINT, or overhead IMINT, or SIGINT, or HUMINT.

OSINT is often used in conjunction with other INTS. Information from multiple sources and means are synthesized by all-source analysts, who take the sum of the different types of information to construct a comprehensive answer to the requirement and in a timely and accurate manner. The process is repetitive, since with each new finding and gap new questions arise.

Good OSINT analysts are problem solvers who possess specific technical knowledge, such as specialized language skills, cultural, and/or scientific expertise as well as cognitive skills.[11] OSINT analysts who monitor native language websites and blogs and have language and dialect fluency, particularly related to problem regions of the world are highly desirable. The wars in Afghanistan and Iraq have verified the importance of language and cultural knowledge. Intelligence analyst position applicants possessing detailed knowledge of regional language, dialects, and slang are highly sought out in current recruiting programs. Subject matter experts in many technical areas like chemistry, physics, and engineering are also considered high priority by many IC agencies.[12] Requirements for specialized OSINT skills are likely to increase in the future, as the web continues its expansion and the quantity of information continues its explosion.

Though not a panacea for all intelligence problems, OSINT is a very powerful toolthat can provide a needed understanding of the world around us and of potential threats that we face.

READINGS FOR INSTRUCTORS

The following are recommended readings for instructors on Open Source

---

11. An excellent and detailed summary of the cognitive aspects of intelligence analysis, applicable to OSINT, is provided in *Thinking and Writing – Cognitive Science and Intelligence Analysis*, by Robert S. Sinclair, available on-line at *https://www.cia.gov/library/center-for-the-study-of-intelligence/csi-publications/books-and-monographs/thinking-and-writing.html*. Some of the pitfalls encountered in the cognitive process are found in the classic text, *Psychology of Intelligence Analysis* by Richards J. Heuer, Jr., also on-line at *https://www.cia.gov/library/center-for-the-study-of-intelligence/csi-publications/books=and-monographs/psychology-of-intelligence-analysis/index.html*.
12. Specific recruiting priorities for the Intelligence Community are available at *http://www.usajobs.opm.gov/*.

Intelligence:

De Borchgrave, Arnaud Thomas Sanderson, and John Macgaffin. *The Missing Dimension of Intelligence* (Center for Strategic and International Studies, 2006).

Students wishing to know more about the emerging subspecialty of OSINT called "sociocultural intelligence" should read the excellent volume, *Sociocultural Intelligence – A New Discipline in Intelligence Studies*, by Kerry Patton (Continuum International Publishing Group, Bloomsbury Academic, 2010).

Recommended introductory texts (which include discussions on OSINT) are:

Clauser, Jerome, *An Introduction to Intelligence Research and Analysis*, (The Scarecrow Press, Inc., 2008).

Hall, Wayne Michael and Gary Citrenbaum. *Intelligence Analysis: How to Think in Complex Environments*, (2009).

Robert A. Norton, PhD, is a professor at Auburn University and an adjunct at the Air Command and Staff College. He teaches open source intelligence and informational analysis. A veterinary microbiologist and biological weapons expert, Dr. Norton is a long-time researcher and professional consultant to many federal agencies on national security issues and the use of OSINT. He was awarded the FBI Director's Community Leadership Award for research on the US food production system and agricultural security.

GUIDE TO THE STUDY OF INTELLIGENCE

The Evolution of Open Source Intelligence (OSINT)

Florian Schaurer and Jan Störger

This article presents the views on open source intelligence
by two European authors and practitioners.

Introduction

Here, the term OSINT is defined as the collection, processing, analysis, production, classification, and dissemination of information derived from sources and by means openly available and legally accessible and employable by the public in response to official national security requirements. This article addresses OSINT's genesis as an intelligence discipline, arguing that it should rather be referred to as tradecraft, as well as its contributions to an integrated, all-source knowledge management process within the intelligence enterprise.

History of OSINT

The history of exploiting open information reaches back to the emergence of intelligence as an instrument supporting a government's decisions and actions. Yet, it was not a methodical effort until the United States pioneered the institutionalization and professionalization of a stand-alone capacity for monitoring foreign media, with the establishment of the Foreign Broadcast Monitoring Service (FBMS), which grew out of a research initiative at Princeton University. The FBMS rapidly gained momentum after the Japanese attack on Pearl Harbor. In 1947, it was renamed the Foreign Broadcast Information Service (FBIS) and put under the newly established CIA. In 2005, following the attacks of 9/11 and the passage of the Intelligence Reform and Terrorism Prevention Act, FBIS – with other research elements – was transformed into the Office of the Director of National Intelligence's Open Source Center (OSC). Since its establishment, the OSINT effort has been responsible for filtering, transcribing, translating (thus interpreting), and archiving news items and information from all types of foreign media sources.

In 1939, the British Government asked the British Broadcasting Corporation (BBC) to launch a civilian, and later commercial, service scrutinizing foreign print journalism and radio broadcasting with its *Digest of Foreign Broadcasts*, later entitled the *Summary of World Broadcasts* (SWB), and now known as BBC Monitoring. As a 1940 BBC handbook has it, the aim was to erect a "modern Tower of Babel, where, with exemplary concentration, they listen to the voices of friend and foe alike." By mid-1943, the BBC monitored 1.25 million broadcast words daily. A formal partnership between the BBC and its US counterpart was instituted in 1947/48 with agreement on the full exchange of output. Also in 1948, the research arm of the US Library of Congress was established out of the Aeronautical Research Unit to provide customized research and analytical services using the vast holdings of the library. It is now known as the Federal Research Division (FRD).

During the Cold War, countries on both sides of the Iron Curtain created open source collection capacities, often embedded in their clandestine intelligence services. Open sources not only "constituted a major part of all intelligence," according to CIA analyst Stephen Mercado, but eventually became "the leading source" of information about the adversaries' military capabilities and political intentions, including early warning and threat forecasting. For example, the East German Ministry for State Security (MfS, the Stasi) analyzed 1,000 Western magazines and 100 books a month, while also summarizing more than 100 newspapers and 12 hours of West German radio and TV broadcasting daily.

Open sources during the Cold War were already a well-established resource of information, often the first resort for targeting other collection efforts, or "the outer pieces of the jigsaw puzzle," as Joseph Nye put it.[1] With internet technology, publicly available information has had a tremendous impact on every aspect of modern-day political, social, and economic life. One needs to be aware, though, that the internet itself is not a source (except for its metadata); rather it is a means to transport information and a virtual location.

Most intelligence communities were slow in appreciating the internet's value for two reasons: (1) Intelligence agencies seek an informational advantage through covertly dealing with secrets. Relying on open information and its respective copyright restrictions runs counter to that idea. (2) In most cases, it is more difficult, risky, and expensive to apply clandestine methods to acquire secret sources, thus giving the impression that those sources must be of higher value than open sources, confusing the method with the product or mistaking secrecy for knowledge.

After the Soviet Union's collapse, Western intelligence agencies redirected

---

1. . Committee on Homeland Security. *Giving a Voice to Open Source Stakeholders* (Washington, DC: Committee on Homeland Security, 2008) *http://chsdemocrats.house.gov/SiteDocuments/OpenSourceReport.pdf*.

their operations to new geographic and thematic priorities, such as Africa and Asia, non-state actors, low-intensity conflict in expeditionary environments, political and religious terrorism, the proliferation of weapons of mass destruction (WMD), and the vulnerabilities of computer networks, which resulted in a greater emphasis on open sources. The US military first coined the term OSINT in the late 1980s, arguing that a reform of intelligence was necessary to cope with the dynamic nature of informational requirements, especially at the tactical level on the battlefield. In 1992, the Intelligence Reorganization Act defined the objectives of information gathering as "providing timely, objective intelligence, free of bias, based upon all sources available to the US Intelligence Community, public and non-public." In 1994, the Community Open Source Program Office (COSPO) was established within the CIA. In 1996, the Commission on the Roles and Capabilities of the US Intelligence Community (more commonly known as the Aspin-Brown Commission) concluded "a greater effort also should be made to harness the vast universe of information now available from open sources." Parallel efforts by NATO to generate a framework for the use of OSINT led to the publication of several handbooks, primers and practical manuals of varying quality. With the European Media Monitor (EMM) and an OSINT Suite, among other tools and projects, the European Union (EU) Commission's Joint Research Centre (JRC), is developing its own instruments for tackling the challenges that the ever-growing flood of information poses.

The 9/11 event proved to be a watershed for OSINT, with the National Commission on Terrorist Attacks upon the United States (9/11 Commission) in 2004 recommending the creation of an open source agency without further comment or detail. This concept was picked up in 2005 – along with respective recommendations by the Commission on the Intelligence Capabilities of the United States Regarding Weapons of Mass Destruction (WMD Commission) – when the director of national intelligence (DNI) established the OSC, absorbing the CIA's FBIS with the World News Connection (WNC) under the supervision of the National Technical Information Service (NTIS). The OSC presents itself as the "US Government's premier provider of foreign open source intelligence [and] provides information on foreign political, military, economic, and technical issues beyond the usual media from an ever expanding universe of open sources." At the same time, an assistant deputy director of national intelligence for open source (ADDNI/OS) was appointed, increasing the visibility of the national open source enterprise. With the development of regional fusion centers, which are focused on homeland security and law enforcement issues, OSINT is a major source in merging and consolidating relevant intelligence into actionable products.

OSINT and the Private Sector

In economic terms, national security as a public good is provided efficiently only by the government or under state supervision. Despite its substantial value, OSINT requires no special permissions. Because non-state contractors may be superior regarding their capabilities and resources for delivering OSINT, they can contribute to a better provision of national security. Intelligence derived from sources or using means that are openly available, but illegal, should not be considered OSINT, e.g. leaks of classified information, the legal status of which is in question, or proprietary information. CIA's venture capital firm In-Q-Tel's investment in Recorded Future, a web-monitoring predictive analysis tool, proves former CIA Director Michael Hayden's statement that "secret information isn't always the brass ring in our profession."[2]

A crucial point in government-private sector partnerships for OSINT is the need for non-disclosure regulations to protect national security. Sometimes, an intelligence product based solely on openly available information must be classified to protect the government's interest from being revealed. Intelligence agencies must integrate and control outreach activities and contractors' efforts to prevent jeopardizing operational and national security. Partnerships with academia avoid potential conflicts between the state and profit-oriented players. Universities are a fertile ground for capturing expertise that exists within the public sphere and can be ideal partners for intelligence agencies.

The fact that open sources often provide the majority of intelligence input makes OSINT an essential part of an all-source intelligence effort. Every intelligence professional should be knowledgeable of OSINT sources and methods, especially as analysis and collection are increasingly merging with each other. Nevertheless, outreach activities and open source exploitation have to be supported by specialized elements to ensure that analysts keep up with emerging technologies and the market. Specialized OSINT experts are most qualified to identify potential capability gaps and to assess where contractors can be of use. One good way to integrate the knowledge and skills of the private sector into the Intelligence Community is an OSINT certification program, currently being introduced in the US, for example.

Challenges Facing OSINT

Because of its open nature, OSINT can facilitate sharing. But the means for sharing need to be improved for OSINT as well as for more restrictive categories of intelligence. This need exists not only in the national security community, but also with those charged with domestic security and enforcement of laws. Thus, a vertically and horizontally consistent sharing and safeguarding system

---

2. Noah Shachtman. "Google, CIA Invest in 'Future' of Web Monitoring" July 28, 2010. *http://www.wired.com/dangerroom/2010/07/exclusive-google-cia/*.

must be established.

Openness is important for governments' credibility and justifying their decisions to the public and international allies. However, there is an inherent vulnerability if an adversary uses open sources to undermine the state's national security. OSINT can be used for vulnerability evaluations of one's own nation.

Adversarial states will also manipulate open sources for deceptive purposes. In today's world, however, with vast amounts of information openly available, such deceptive schemes become more difficult.

Although the fast pace of developing information technology is an important challenge, the human factor should not be underestimated. Ultimately, it is always human expertise that makes the difference in intelligence tradecraft. Collectors and analysts therefore need both legal and practical training, the appropriate literacy, and first-class technical capabilities (such as data mining, network analysis, and translation solutions) to put disparate pieces of raw OSINT data into context and make sense of them. With the advent of new internet-based media, the variety, volume, and velocity of information multiply. Today's challenge is no longer "connecting the dots," but organizing the information flow, distinguishing between signals and noise, and by validating sources in a timely manner to support both government decision makers and the war fighter.

READINGS FOR INSTRUCTORS

An excellent overview of the Open Source Center's policies, procedures, and products is in Hamilton Bean, "The DNI's Open Source Center – An Organizational Communication Perspective" in *International Journal of Intelligence and Counter-Intelligence* 20 (2), 2007.

Magdalena Adriana Duvenage, a South African scholar, provides a solid examination of the impact of the information revolution on intelligence analysis and knowledge management in *Intelligence Analysis in the Knowledge Age* (2010), available at *http://scholar.sun.ac.za/bitstream/handle/10019.1/3087/Duvenage,%20M.A.pdf?sequence=1*.

Stevyn Gibson, in his publication "Open Source Intelligence – An Intelligence Lifeline" (2004), gives a brief synopsis OSINT's emerging role, drawing together the contextual influences that are bringing about its potentially starring role. Available at *http://www.rusi.org/downloads/assets/JA00365.pdf*.

Arthur S. Hulnick, a professor at Boston University and former CIA officer, has written, "The Dilemma of Open Source Intelligence – Is OSINT really intelligence?" in Loch K. Johnson (ed.), *The Oxford Handbook of National Security Intelligence* (2010) This is a scholarly article on OSINT's role in and for the private sector, OSINT and intelligence reform, and OSINT's counterintelligence aspects.

William J. Lahneman's article, "The Need for a New Intelligence Paradigm," in the *International Journal of Intelligence and Counter-Intelligence* 23 (2), 2010, is an important text on the intelligence community's organizational culture that emphasize secrecy, not knowledge sharing, arguing that facilitating both kinds of information flows require a new approach to the intelligence enterprise.

An insightful public discussion about the government's practical needs for OSINT is the LexisNexis "Open Source Intelligence Roundtable: OSINT 2020 – The Future of Open Source Intelligence," available at *http://www.dni.gov/speeches/Speech_OSINT_Roundtable_20100617.pdf*.

Other reference items related to OSINT include the following

Harris Minas: "Can the Open Source Intelligence Emerge as an Indispensable Discipline for the Intelligence Community in the 21st Century?" (2010), at *http://rieas.gr/images/rieas139.pdf*. This is an academic thesis addressing OSINT as an issue of research for critical intelligence studies.

NATO *Open Source Intelligence Handbook* (2001), Available at *http://blogs.ethz.ch/osint/files/2010/08/nato-osint-handbook-v12-jan-2002.pdf* This is a rather outdated guidance for NATO staff on open source exploitation with the internet being the default C4I architecture, arguing that a robust OSINT capability enables intelligence staffs to address many intelligence needs with internal resources.

Brian Rotheray, A History of BBC Monitoring (2010), *http://www.monitor.bbc.co.uk/about_us/BBCMhistory%20revisions%20x.pdf*. This book celebrates the first 70 years of BBC Monitoring and covers the main political, technological, and social aspects of its history.

Stephen C. Mercado, "Sailing the Sea of OSINT in the Information Age" *Studies in Intelligence* 48 (3), 2004, *https://www.cia.gov/library/center-for-the-study-of-intelligence/csi-publications/csi-studies/studies/vol48no3/article05.html*. This is a classical account of OSINT expanding into the areas of human intelligence, imagery intelligence, and signals intelligence, thereby demanding a sustained approach by the IC to open sources.

These several directives directly or indirectly address OSINT policies and applications

United States Department of the Army, *Open Source Intelligence* FMI 2-22.9 (2008). Available at *http://ftp.fas.org/irp/doddir/army/fmi2-22-9.pdf*. This is the US Army's interim doctrine, serving as a catalyst for analysis and development of OSINT training, concepts, materiel, and force structure.

United States Department of Defense Instruction No. 3115.12: *Open Source Intelligence* (2010) *http://www.dtic.mil/whs/directives/corres/pdf/311512p.pdf*. This directive establishes policy, assigns responsibilities, and prescribes procedures for OSINT operations within the US Department of Defense.

United States Intelligence Community Directives No. 301 (2006), No. 205 (2008), No. 304 (2008), No. 623 (2008), No. 612 (2009). Available at *http://www.fas.org/irp/dni/icd/*.

United States Open Source Center (OSC), History. (2009) *https://www.opensource.gov/public/content/login/attachments/202244099/255164545.pdf*. This is a one-page history of OSC.

Kurt Werren, Kian Fartab, *All Source Collection* – Kernstück eines leistungsfähigen Nachrichtendienstes (2010). Available at *http://www.asmz.ch/fileadmin/asmz/ASMZ_aktuell/2010_04/All_Sources_Collection_Deutsch_1_.pdf*. This is an important contribution to the improvement of all-source collection, analysis, and production (in German).

Florian Schaurer is as an open source intelligence specialist at the International Relations and Security Network at ETH Zurich, Switzerland. He is a reserve officer at the German General Staff Command College and holds a master's degree in political science, philosophy, and religious studies from the University of Heidelberg and a PhD in political philosophy from the University of Zurich.

Jan Störger is a consultant focusing on security-related issues for various countries. He holds a master's degree in European governance and administration from the University of Potsdam, a master of law from the Panthéon-Sorbonne University in Paris, and a master in economics degree from the University of Mannheim.

GUIDE TO THE STUDY OF INTELLIGENCE

The Changing Shape of HUMINT

John R. Sano

A lthough often described as the world's second oldest profession, spying – and specifically human intelligence (HUMINT) – continues to evolve. While the basic tenets of human espionage remain constant, there are a variety of factors, which over time have impacted both the tenets and the parameters of spying. It is not just the "how" of HUMINT, but also the motivations and the methodologies employed. Demographics, technology and cultural expectations all play a role in the shaping of a clandestine service officer.

Demographics

The majority of officers serving today in America's Intelligence Community (IC), be it the Central Intelligence Agency (CIA) National Clandestine Service (NCS), or in any of the other 16 organizations that comprises our IC, have joined post – 9/11. Despite the attendant controversies that have plagued the IC over the years prior to, and especially after, the traumatic events of September 11, 2001, today's IC member remains highly motivated, patriotic, and professional. One significant difference, however, is their "career expectancy." In years past, clandestine service officers, often joined with the general expectation that they would serve 20 or more years. This was reflective of the general trend at the time – and not just in the intelligence world – of the "cradle to grave" syndrome, where an employee could expect to spend an entire career in one company or organization. Today's employees – be it in the public or private sector – expect to have several careers over the course of their employable lifespan. Some perhaps view an IC stint as a stepping-stone to something else, others perhaps as a culmination of a career progression; although given the age restrictions for entry into the IC, this is less likely. This presents a challenge to management as how to utilize their talents – for whatever period of time they serve.

As former National Security Agency (NSA) and CIA director US Air Force (ret.) General Michael Hayden, when asked about attrition and the retention of highly trained officers, remarked "... managers need to motivate their workforce as best as possible, keep them challenged, but don't hide from them the pros and cons of working in the Intelligence Community and above all, when they do leave, make sure they leave with your best wishes. They may come back, and/ or recommend the organization to others."[1]

Managing this younger, more technically astute, workforce can be problematic for a number of reasons – not the least of which is the dramatic generational difference when it comes to learning. Today's workforce thinks and processes information significantly differently from its predecessors. As Dr. Bruce Perry of Baylor College of Medicine has stated, "Different kinds of experiences lead to different brain structures."[2] As such, today's workforce receives information much faster than their predecessors. And while reception does not always equal comprehension, it does present an issue for managers as well as for IC instructors. Education within the world of HUMINT is in large measure "anecdotally based," with instruction incorporating legacy-based scenarios, or "tribal memories," to emphasize key points. While useful, it is often a technique that many younger practitioners of espionage find unfamiliar, even ineffective.

Growing up on a regular diet of technology-driven information, today's clandestine officer is better connected and more adept at multi-tasking and networking than previous generations. Adjusting to this significant divide is often difficult, for most instructors view education in much the same way as they themselves were taught – via lectures, step-by-step logic and "tell-test" instruction. Today's officers are more comfortable with procedures that they grew up with – TV, internet, video cams, cell phones, and all the other accoutrements associated with the digital age.

What does this mean? Aside from the way today's officers want to learn, it also impacts expectations. Today's clandestine service officer expects to access any information, anytime, anywhere, and on any device. Aside from the obvious security aspects, there is also the problem of managing these expectations – attempting to inculcate the proper balance of security vs. expediency, not to mention patience within an increasingly impatient workforce – is no easy task, but, nonetheless, a critical aspect of any clandestine activity.

In essence, this "digital divide" differentiates the current generation of officers from their predecessors, the former being "digital natives," while the latter are relegated to the status of "digital immigrants." This is not merely a semantic distinction: today's college graduate has spent more time watching TV

---

1. Private conversation between the author and Gen. Hayden in July 1999, reprinted with the general's permission.
2. Bruce Perry. *The Memories of States: How the Brain Stores and Retrieves Traumatic Experience* (Baylor College Press, 1997).

and in front of a computer screen than reading books or attending lectures. As such, the thinking patterns they use to learn are markedly different from those of their predecessors. They learn, *inter alia*, via networking, random access (e.g. hypertext), and preferring video game scenarios to regimented lectures, and all forms of social media (e.g., blogs) over repetitive and often outdated texts.

This digital divide extends to HUMINT operations in terms of both the officers engaged and their targets. If, for the sake of argument, we restrict our discussion to traditional espionage — i.e., the spotting, assessing, developing, and eventual recruiting of human targets – then targets and targeteers (i.e., the HUMINT operations officer) can often be at variance. Avenues of approach can prove problematic. If the target is, like the targeteer, a digital native, then access and eventual development is often symbiotic. If, however, the target is a digital immigrant, the differences can create difficulties; not insurmountable, but which have to be addressed as part of the recruitment cycle.

HUMINT Defined

Human intelligence encapsulates a wide range of skills – from traditional diplomatic dialogue, to manipulation, to deceit. At its core is the ability to recruit an individual to conduct espionage, to "spy." Ancillary skill sets include counterintelligence, surveillance, liaison exploitation, the use of "cover" – either commercial, or more likely official – and false flag operations (the ability to pose as a representative of a country other than the United States).

The acquisition of an individual(s) to spy at our behest is commonly referred to as the *recruitment cycle*, which includes – in sequential order:

- **Spot** – the ability to identify an individual who has access to information that we want;
- **Assess** – identifying the individual's vulnerabilities and determining whether he/she may be susceptible to a recruitment "pitch;"
- **Develop** – manipulating the individual's vulnerabilities with the intent of making them more amenable to agreeing to your proposal, which is defined as the
- **Recruitment** – the formality of securing an individual's cooperation to steal secrets.

HUMINT complements, and can be bolstered by, other "INTs" – predominantly signals intelligence (SIGINT); geographical-spatial intelligence (GEOINT); measurement and signature intelligence (MASINT); and increasingly open source intelligence (OSINT), a fairly recent development as an INT, but one which generates a near overwhelming amount of information that can be used for myriad intelligence efforts. As one example, the bulk of SIGINT operations are often HUMINT enabled, i.e., a human source initiates the penetration of a system, either through the provision of technical information then further exploited by NSA, or via the introduction of technical devices (switches, or other electronic mechanisms) into foreign databases or electronic infrastructures.

As the country's national HUMINT manager – the CIA, and specifically the NCS, also engages in cooperative relationships with other intelligence as well as law enforcement entities – both domestic and especially foreign intelligence and security organizations. The CIA, by statute, is also tasked with undertaking covert action (CA) which is "… an activity or activities of the United States Government to influence political, economic, or military conditions abroad, where it is intended that *the role of the United States Government will not be apparent or acknowledged publicly*...." HUMINT operatives conduct all CA activity.

Technology

Today's clandestine service officers have grown up in a world of digital expediency, if not dependency, and while schooled in the nuances of conducting traditional espionage, rely increasingly on technical assistance in the application of their tradecraft. This is a good thing, as technology has increased efficiency and in many instances shortened timelines. Yet with improvements in efficiency and speed comes vulnerabilities as well – vulnerabilities that often cannot be foreseen readily or assessed accurately.

The digital revolution has made our day-to-day lives easier, albeit for digital immigrants perhaps a bit more confusing and frustrating at times. What is equally true is that with these efficiencies have come additional responsibilities and risks for the tradecraft of espionage. Learning about potential targets or adversaries and crafting an approach via technical means – whether it is via e-mail or a social blog, or through more elaborate and esoteric mechanisms such as avatars, or similar methods – might well be expeditious, but highly insecure. Further, communicating via these mechanisms further complicates matters for the same security issues. While the longstanding (and clearly digital immigrant) *modus operandi* of "chance encounters," cryptic telephonic codes, and clandestine meetings in a safehouse or rolling car may appear antiquated, they have proven generally more reliable from a security perspective, but certainly more time consuming. This is not to say that technology does not play an important role in approaches and maintaining contact with an agent, but only when used in – for lack of a better term – "moderation." Too often espionage operations are over-reliant on the "ease" of utilizing technical means to communicate, which is vulnerable to hostile counterintelligence activities.

Aside from the security issues attendant in the over-reliance on technology, there are also the cultural changes that have accrued over time. In the not-so-distant past, communicating with headquarters was not nearly as quick as today's near-instantaneous speeds nor offering as many alternatives. In today's world, the previous time lag in headquarters' responses to the field have diminished from days, to hours or minutes. While coordination has become more efficient and timely, it has resulted in the transfer of greater decision-making responsibility to headquarters, vice the field. Given the dearth of experience of many field operatives – a byproduct of the 1990s "peace dividend,"[3] and while not risk averse, it has promoted a penchant to defer operational decisions to managers who are perceived as having more experience.

Cultural Expectations

During the Cold War, intelligence targets were clearly defined – the Soviet Union being the primary (if not almost exclusive) focus. In today's post-9/11 environment, the targets are more diverse and elusive. Non-state terrorist targets pose unique and unprecedented challenges. While today's operations officers face many of the same ethical and moral challenges their predecessors did when working against more traditional targets, the continuing political controversies over whether US (specifically CIA and military) actions during the continuing war on terrorism have further complicated the situation. Whether combating terrorism on legal and moral grounds was and is justified calls into question whether such activities warrant continuing in any form. Espionage has always faced moral quandaries, yet in years past, HUMINT operations were often rationalized in terms of the "end justifying the means." In most cases, this was the containment, if not disruption of the aggressive Russian intelligence services, the KGB (now the SVR) and GRU.[4] While one could make the same case for the terrorist target, the fundamental difference between these targets (e.g. KGB vs. Al-Qa'ida, or other affiliated groups) is that the former was politically based while the latter is more religiously focused. Today's operations officers may be less inclined to adopt an "end justifies the means" mentality than their predecessors.

The Future

The IC will continue to undergo change, influenced as much by domestic politics as developments beyond our borders. Despite technological advances, HUMINT will continue to occupy a critical role in providing intelligence to US policymakers. Discerning plans and intentions can only come from the recruitment of human sources. Even information stored digitally often requires

3. Through budget cuts, Congress severely restricted hiring of IC personnel during much of the 1990s. The political rationale was that the US should enjoy a "peace dividend" from the dissolution of the Soviet Union, the newly independent Eastern European nations, and the end of the Cold War. The consequence was that few were hired during this period resulting in a paucity of experienced middle managers over the ensuing two decades.
4. For a brief history of Soviet/Russian intelligence services see Robert W. Pringle, "Guide to Soviet and Russian Intelligence Services," *The Intelligencer* 18 (2), Winter/Spring 2011.

human access; and even with data that is extracted electronically, there is still the requirement to interpret those documents and how they fit into the larger context. Human beings are essential to all processes and operations – whether they are public or private based. As such they are the first and last line of security. They are also the first and last entry points into the intelligence arena.

As we continue to advance technologically, in essence making our world smaller, the potential threats posed by these advancements will make both protecting and exploiting real secrets exponentially more difficult. In addition, as these challenges continue to grow, those tasked with addressing them will need to adjust at a much more rapid rate. This applies both to field operatives as well as to their managers. As described above, the differences in experience and cultural expectations will continue to exacerbate the relationship, but only temporarily as the "old guard," or "digital immigrants" gradually gives way to the "new guard," or "digital natives." Traditional approaches to espionage – while forming the bedrock for HUMINT – will have to be further augmented. The next generation of operatives and their managers will need to be more familiar with, if not adept at, technological augmentation. Augmentation, not replacement. While the tendency to rely increasingly on technology to make HUMINT collection more efficient is commendable, adherence to the core principals will ensure that human operations remain as secure as possible.

Constrained budgets, while often cyclical in nature, will likely remain flat, if not decreased, over the next several years or longer. The IC, for many years immune to the exigencies of financial debate within Congress – particularly during times of crises – is no longer exempt. While the old adage, "there will always be money for good operations" will remain fairly constant, what constitutes "good operations" may likely shift – dependent upon the prevailing political winds and the prioritization of competing requirements (both operational and structural/administrative). In addition, hiring and promotions within the IC are contingent to a significant degree on the availability of funds. While both will continue – hiring dependent on attrition rates and promotions on performance metrics – the availability of both will be diminished.

The impact on the future generation of officers cannot be underestimated. With a workforce that can be expected to remain, on average seven years, any limitations on advancement could have a deleterious effect on morale as well as retention. Today's IC officers are, however, exceptionally adaptive, and resilient. Though they may stay for a shorter period of time than their predecessors, their accomplishments and dedication to the mission are of equal measure and will serve the IC well in the years ahead.

READINGS FOR INSTRUCTORS

Mark Lowenthal. *Intelligence. From Secrets to Policy*, 4th edition. (Washington, DC: CQ Press, 2009).

Jennifer Sims and Burton Gerber. *Transforming U.S. Intelligence* (Washington, DC: Georgetown University Press, 2005).

Loch Johnson. *National Security Intelligence* (Cambridge, UK: Polity Press, 2012).

Jeffrey Richelson. *The U.S. Intelligence Community*, 5th edition. (Boulder, CO: Westview Press, 2008).

James Olson. *Fair Play* (Sterling, VA: Potomac Books, 2006).

Allen Dulles. *The Craft of Intelligence* (Guilford, CT: The Lyons Press, 2006).

Loch Johnson. *Secret Agencies, U.S. Intelligence in a Hostile World* (New Haven, CT: Yale University Press, 1996).

John Sano is currently AFIO vice president. From 2005 to 2007, he was deputy director of the CIA's National Clandestine Service. He holds a BA in political science and an MA in Asian studies from St. John's University, New York. and an MS in international affairs from Columbia University, NY.

GUIDE TO THE STUDY OF INTELLIGENCE

The Evolution of Geospatial Intelligence and the National Geospatial-Intelligence Agency

Dr. Gary E. Weir

Something Happened in Dayton

On November 1, 1995, President William Clinton called on the warring factions in Bosnia to end the conflict that had cost over 300,000 Serb, Croat, and Muslim lives since 1991. He invited their representatives to come to Wright-Patterson Air Force Base in Dayton, Ohio, to negotiate an end to the ethnic discord.

At Dayton, the US delegation relied on a technical team led by the Defense Mapping Agency (DMA) and the US Army Topographic Engineer Center. These agencies drew together a support team of over 50 individuals who digitally mapped the disputed Balkan areas in near real-time to assist the diplomats in their deliberations. The digital renderings included up-to-date terrain visualizations with overlaid cultural and economic data relating to potential boundaries.

Using automated cartography, computer-assisted map tailoring, and spatial statistical analysis, the team regularly furnished fresh maps reflecting territorial dispositions negotiated less than 30 minutes earlier. The digital technique guaranteed accuracy, consistency, and reliability.

The power and flexibility of the technology and the technicians gave the political decisionmakers the confidence needed to reach agreement. Three-dimensional visual imagery of the disputed areas permitted cartographers to walk negotiators through disputed terrain, giving them a vivid and virtual experience of the space. In at least one instance, this three-dimensional experience proved crucial in persuading Yugoslav President Slobodan Milosevic to compromise on a disputed area.

These hard-working cartographers and analysts collectively contributed to the Dayton Peace Accords, leading to a temporary, but significant, suspension of regional violence. In this case, the professional lesson did not go unlearned. Combining people and talent from eight agencies and offices the following year into the National Imagery and Mapping Agency (NIMA) reflected initiatives underway, but also spoke to the wisdom of asking those involved in defense imagery and mapping, including DMA, to emulate the Dayton success on a more permanent basis.

Of course, the agency's enabling legislation simply brought people together and initially could do nothing more. For many months after the creation of NIMA, imagery analysis and geospatial information services within the agency remained in separate and culturally distinct worlds. Seeing the potential in integration, a number of senior leaders recommended strongly that the agency integrate the talents assembled under the NIMA umbrella. Strong cultural identities on all sides at times made the idea of cartographers and other geospatial specialists regularly emulating the Dayton experience a very difficult and almost unlikely prospect.

Recognizing possibilities in the combination, several people stepped forward to bridge the gap. In one case, a DMA veteran and senior cartographer felt that she might help. Having worked for a time in private industry on one of the first automobile navigation system studies, the need to integrate skills and personnel to achieve a goal seemed natural. Working with the NIMA Production Cell at the Washington Navy Yard, she gained approval for a plan to blend the analytical skills applied to imagery with those of the geospatial arts and sciences. In 1999, she began to hire cartographers, geographers, and other geospatial professionals for placement in some of NIMA's imagery analysis offices.

In the process, all concerned began to appreciate more fully the cultural divide between the world of maps and imagery. Speaking with some old hands at the imagery effort, this former DMA veteran received responses to her plan that ranged from "What am I going to do with one of them?" to "We would not recruit from that university." In an exchange with one imagery analyst, she asked, "Where do you get your requirements from?" To that point in time, cartographers lived by the routine of a production schedule, discrete well-defined projects each with a neat beginning, middle, and end. Instead of an answer characteristic of her professional world, she learned that the imagery people just knew what to do. In short, they "owned" their areas of specialty, their tasks, their analysis, and the process of reporting. They thought out loud, collaborated regularly, and directed their own work to serve the mission at hand. The DMA veteran recently recalled, "I was immediately jealous." She wanted that ownership, the freedom and responsibility it offered, and the same flexibility for people in her own field in collaboration with the imagery world.

The bloody conflict in Chechnya presented the perfect opportunity. Driven for a time by this civil war, NIMA's Eurasian Branch turned potential into practice. In 2000, those leading the integration initiative asked a Bethesda-based cartographer to join the Eurasia group to merge his talent with their imagery analysis. The newcomer to the Eurasia Branch had only recently joined NIMA via Rand McNally, and a senior colleague felt that he had "a sense for cartography. He had a sense for displaying information in a thematic context, and wove it into a story."

Once augmented by a geospatial professional, the Eurasia group managed to set cultural barriers aside, listened, shared, and proceeded to issue intelligence products that had their customers immediately clamoring for more, frequently describing the output as "phenomenal." As one senior NIMA manager remembered it, Eurasia's new cartographer "was a rock star": he provided the magic ingredient that brought the effort and the output to another level. Intellectual insight into a crisis situation expressed in a tight, complementary symphony of image and idea quickly set a new standard for professional achievement. This pioneering group, one among many, arrayed their early products on a display surface at the Navy Yard that quickly became known as the "Wall of Fame." In a visit to NIMA during this period, Director of Central Intelligence George Tenet lingered for a considerable time over the intelligence on the Wall of Fame, viewing this imagery enhanced by geospatial context with the distinct feeling that the future lay before him. Starting with eight embedded geospatial specialists, within six months those leading the integration initiative had little trouble placing eighteen more in various imagery offices in NIMA.

The success of the Navy Yard Eurasia Branch eroded cultural barriers and promoted professional integration. Coming together as NIMA certainly created the critical mass of talent and insight, but people willing to trust, collaborate, and experiment provided the catalyst. NIMA's customers understood the crisis in Chechnya as never before, through a new lens called geospatial intelligence (GEOINT). Intelligence had entered a new era.

GEOINT Evolutionary Benchmarks

The Vietnam War

Long before the United States became engaged in the Vietnam conflict, the Army Map Service (AMS), the St. Louis Aeronautical Chart and Information Center (ACIC), the National Photo Interpretation Center (NPIC), and the Navy Hydrographic Office, all NGA predecessors, collected data and prepared aeronautical and maritime charts, maps, and analyses for that region.

During a tense summer in 1954, for a moment the United States seriously considered intervention to help the French after their defeat at Dien Bien Phu. The AMS provided analyses of the terrain around the cities of Hanoi and Saigon to provide American policymakers with critical intelligence on the challenges of intervention. Division of the country followed the 1954 French defeat. However, in the late 1950s and into the 1960s, contractors and survey parties provided the AMS with aerial photographs permitting the first complete and accurate maps of Vietnam.

In 1959, President Dwight Eisenhower requested U-2 missions over Vietnam and the surrounding region, and tasked NPIC with an evaluation of the results. NPIC analysts also visited the region to estimate the needs generated by the growing conflict between North and South Vietnam. By 1962, NPIC analysts had already begun conducting bomb-damage assessments, identifying possible targets, and producing intelligence products.

As demands for targeting information grew, along with American involvement on the side of South Vietnam, the ACIC deployed a new database targeting system, which enabled American and allied pilots to evade Communist air defenses more effectively and to place their ordnance on target more accurately. Exploiting photography from the new SR-71 Blackbird, analysts could identify the exact coordinates of newly found targets and send that information to allied forces for action.

With the beginning of American ground combat in Vietnam, experiences during 1965 and 1966 quickly demonstrated the inadequacy of coastal charts based largely upon World War II data. In particular, the Army's appreciation of the river deltas fell far short. Consequently, over the next three years, the Naval Oceanographic Office (NOO) completed comprehensive geodetic, coastal, and harbor surveys of that complex coastline using a series of survey vessels. In addition, during December 1966, the NOO established a branch in Saigon to provide updated maritime charts and publications for use by local fleet and Marine Corps units in their blockade, interdiction, and naval air support actions.

Increasing American military involvement required accurate information about the names of natural and cultural features in Vietnam and adjoining countries, for application to maps and charts and for operational purposes. The US Interior Department Geological Survey Board on Geographic Names provided guidelines for standardizing names. The AMS survey parties collected name data in the field for topographic maps of Vietnam and other countries, and similar staffs at the NOO and ACIC provided names for maritime and aeronautical charts, respectively.

The Cuban Missile Crisis

In late August 1962, NPIC, using data from U-2 flights, identified the installation of Soviet missile sites in Cuba. just 90 miles off the coast of Florida. On October 15, President John F. Kennedy and his civilian and military advisors learned that photos taken the day before revealed the presence of six long, canvas-covered objects initially called unidentified military equipment. Further analysis branded the objects as Soviet medium-range ballistic missiles. Photographs also revealed missile installations in a significant state of readiness with supporting transporters, command and control quarters, cables, and launch erectors. In the seven weeks since late August, when NPIC analysts made the first photo identification of the surface-to-air missile sites in Cuba, the Soviets had managed to ship and assemble an arsenal of offensive weapons with nuclear capability.

Using irrefutable photographic evidence, and with confidence in the analysis, President Kennedy and his closest advisors developed a strategy that gave the United States the moral high ground and incomparable situational awareness in the ensuing public confrontation with the Soviet Union. In a nationally televised address, the President revealed publicly the existence of Soviet offensive weapons capable of striking deep into the United States. He called for their immediate removal, and he declared a "strict quarantine" on all shipments by air or sea to Cuba. Intense diplomatic exchanges followed, in both official and unofficial channels.

Tensions mounted as Soviet ships steamed toward Cuba in the days immediately after the speech. On October 24, half of the 25 Soviet vessels en route to Cuba either turned back or altered course to avoid the US Navy's positions around the island. Meanwhile, President Kennedy and Soviet Premier Nikita Khrushchev exchanged diplomatic notes that resolved the conflict. On October

28, Premier Khrushchev announced that the Soviet Union would withdraw all missiles and related equipment from Cuba in exchange for a pledge from the United States not to invade the island. Only in the 1990s, with the opening of documents related to Soviet policy, did the world learn that the Soviet military in Cuba actually did have nuclear warheads at their disposal on the island and that the commanders in the area had the authority to use them.[1] Not publicized at the time was President Kennedy's agreement to remove similar missiles from Turkey, situated geographically as close to the Soviet Union as Cuba was to the United States.

Aerial surveillance photography had not only revealed the initial build-up of Soviet missiles in Cuba; it also revealed the missiles' state of readiness and, during the quarantine, the nature of cargo carried by Soviet ships. Photographic interpreters once again clearly established the critical value of their craft.

September 11

On September 11, 2001, radical Islamic terrorists hijacked four commercial airliners and flew one of them into the Pentagon and two others into the twin towers of the World Trade Center in lower Manhattan. The fourth crashed in Pennsylvania when the passengers resisted and fought their hijackers. In all, some 3,000 innocent individuals lost their lives. President George W. Bush declared a global war on terrorism.

Two days later, NIMA welcomed retired Air Force Lieutenant General James R. Clapper Jr. as its second (and first civilian) director, succeeding geospatial pioneer Army Lieutenant General James C. King. Soon after his arrival, the new director began to promote products that emerged from a variety of new initiatives, like NIMA's work on Chechnya in 2000. This ambitious synthesis of source and image emerged during General King's tenure and became known simply as GEOINT. Among his newly created list of offices was the Office of Geospatial-Intelligence Management. Its mission was to provide the director, in his role as the geospatial intelligence functional manager for the Intelligence Community (IC), with the plans and policies to manage geospatial intelligence resources and a new system to be known as the National System for Geospatial Intelligence (NSG). The first task of the new office was to develop and publish a series of formal communications that would comprise the doctrine of GEOINT. The first of these, Geospatial Intelligence Basic Doctrine, appeared in July 2004.[2]

The global war on terrorism dramatically changed the nature of NIMA's priorities and products. Recognizing that new threats could occur at any time or place, Director Clapper decided both to make regional analytic overviews more

---

1. Dino Brugioni, *Eyeball to Eyeball: The Inside Story of the Cuban Missile Crisis* (New York: Random House, 1991); Gary E. Weir, *Rising Tide* (New York: Basic Books, 2003).

2. James R. Clapper Jr., *Geospatial Intelligence (GEOINT) Basic Doctrine No.1*, (Washington, DC: NGA, 2004).

robust, and to embed NIMA analysts throughout the Defense Department's military commands and the IC. His concept of a unifying discipline and doctrine evolved into a new agency name — the National Geospatial-Intelligence Agency (NGA). The new name represented the maturation of a new discipline and the increased unification of NIMA's parts.

The House-Senate Intelligence Committee report investigating the September 11, 2001 attacks recommended creating a director of national intelligence as the principal intelligence adviser to the President and the statutory intelligence advisor to the National Security Council. This cabinet-level official would coordinate all 15 components of the IC, a task that previously fell to the CIA director. On February 17, 2005, President George W. Bush named John Negroponte, former UN ambassador and US ambassador to Iraq, to the post. By April, Congress confirmed the director of national intelligence, and within months a new National Intelligence Strategy drove NGA operations.

NIMA Becomes NGA

NIMA officially became the NGA with the November 24, 2003 signing of the fiscal 2004 Defense Authorization Bill.

The passage of the Homeland Security Act a year earlier clarified the agency's role in supporting its national customers and helped strengthen NIMA's relationship with other domestic agencies. After September 11, 2001, the agency quickly began to utilize tactics, techniques, procedures, and solutions it had long used overseas, only now applying them to domestic situations with congressional approval. Some of these new tasks included surveying the World Trade Center site as an aid to reconstruction efforts, and supporting the counterterrorism activities of the CIA. NGA also played a significant role in site examination and response planning for major national and international events, working with domestic and overseas authorities to provide maps and geospatial intelligence for training and security at the Winter Olympics in Salt Lake City (2002) and Turin (2006), and the summer games in Athens (2004). The same period saw more involvement in newly intensified efforts to protect the US President, the vice president, and other high-ranking officials, and to provide better security for US military and other government facilities.

Operation Enduring Freedom

The swift military response to the 2001 terrorist attacks on New York City and Washington, DC, christened Operation Enduring Freedom (OEF), began on 7 October, and NIMA's new product, GEOINT, followed American forces. OEF's objectives, as articulated by President George W. Bush, included the destruction of terrorist training camps and infrastructure within Afghanistan, the capture of Al–Qa'ida leaders, and the cessation of in-country terrorist activities. In addition to American participation, the coalition included more than 68 nations, with 27 having representatives at US Central Command headquarters in Tampa, Florida.

As OEF began, the Taliban controlled more than 80 percent of Afghanistan and seemed poised to overwhelm their domestic opponents. By mid-March 2002, the coalition removed the Taliban from power in Afghanistan. Assisted by special maps, aeronautical navigation data, and geospatial intelligence products supplied by NIMA, US Transportation Command addressed all force positioning and most logistical needs in theater by air.

With a combination of overwhelming firepower, delivery systems, and ever more accurate targeting information from NIMA, the ratio of sorties to successful strikes improved dramatically, from an average of 10-aircraft-per-target during Desert Storm in 1991 to two-targets-per-aircraft during OEF. US airmen and aircraft, some operating from western Missouri and assisted by both NIMA navigational aids and on-site support, flew the longest combat missions in US history, some taking more than 15 hours, and broke another duration record for surveillance missions at 26 hours. The agency also supported extensive use of unmanned aerial vehicles, which permitted around-the-clock surveillance of critical sites, facilities, and troop concentrations.

Directed from Tampa by Central Command, which provided real-time connectivity to forces operating 7,000 miles away, the OEF effort drew support from 267 bases. The coalition operated from 30 locations in 15 countries and regularly overflew 46 nations. In every case, NIMA's ability to represent the battlefield literally and virtually at each location provided unprecedented insight into each mission.

Operation Iraqi Freedom

On March 19, 2003, the United States, United Kingdom, and other coalition forces began conducting military operations designed to depose Saddam Hussein and deprive the state of Iraq of any weapons of mass destruction it might possess. During Operation Iraqi Freedom (OIF), imagery from reliable commercial satellites supplemented NGA's own assets to supply the necessary imagery in support of diplomatic initiatives, humanitarian relief, and reconstruction efforts. Commercial imagery aided in defining deployment locations for Patriot missile and air defense batteries, assisted in mission planning for the seizure of Kirkuk in northern Iraq, and helped locate and characterize minefields along the border between Iraq and Iran. It demonstrated that coalition forces did not ignite the Baghdad oil fires, and provided context for decisions to strike or pass on select Iraqi industrial targets.

The military and humanitarian efforts in Afghanistan and Iraq occasioned the largest overseas deployment of NGA and NIMA personnel in the agency's history. To facilitate arrangements for their overseas tours and ensure efficiency, NIMA established the Office of Global Support, initially called the Office of

Deployed and Externally Assigned Personnel, in August 2003.

Beyond a Name

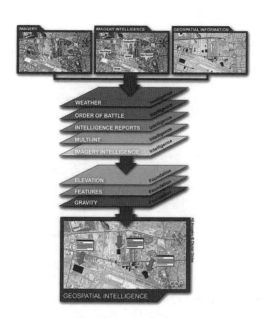

Well before the tragedy of September 11, 2001, intelligence that depended upon the Earth's physical attributes, as well as the art and science of interpreting that information, changed quietly but fundamentally. Combining most of the nation's capable imagery and geospatial intelligence assets within NIMA in 1996 went beyond simply addressing problems of efficiency and economy. Rather, NIMA suddenly provided a critical mass of skills and technologies under a single mission umbrella that soon enabled the IC to realize a significant step in the evolution of its craft and product. Creating NGA acknowledged, in name and in practice, the confluence of every possible sort of imagery with geospatial, human, signals, electronic, and open source intelligence. This confluence created the innovative, sophisticated, and powerful product NGA Director James Clapper formally christened GEOINT. The change of name from NIMA to NGA had little to do with semantics. The nature of intelligence had changed forever.

GEOINT demonstrated its unique ability to illuminate critical situations in ways that permitted both intelligent policy decisions and timely action. GEOINT confirmed ethnic cleansing atrocities in Kosovo through the latest in imaging and geospatial technology enhanced by an incomparable knowledge of culture and context. From the cities hosting the Olympics to the disaster of Hurricane Katrina in New Orleans, NGA provided timely GEOINT products that allowed American authorities at every level to improve the quality and the timing of their security and emergency response. Even the 2006 White House report, in reviewing the Katrina disaster response and offering recommendations for improvement, applauded NGA timeliness during the crisis. GEOINT offered a preliminary version of the same total picture for responders that the administration proceeded to recommend for the entire nation as a part of a standard plan to address major disasters.

While firmly rooted in a past that extends back to surveyors like the young George Washington and President Thomas Jefferson's explorers Lewis and Clark, GEOINT has only recently emerged as a new synthesis of extraordinary technologies and valuable personal skills. The NGA has the dual responsibility to learn daily from past GEOINT achievements and to practice, for the greater good, the powerful combination of technology and art it has created.

Readings for Instructors

Books and Monographs:

Allyn, Bruce J., James G. Blight, and David A. Welch (eds.). *Back to the Brink: Proceedings of the Moscow Conference on the Cuban Missile Crisis, January 27–28, 1989* (Cambridge, MA: Center for Science and International Affairs, Harvard University; Lanham, MD: University Press of America, 1991).

Babington-Smith, Constance. *Air Spy: The Story of Photo Intelligence in World War II* (New York: Harper, 1957; Reprint, Falls Church, Virginia: American Society for Photogrammetry and Remote Sensing, 1985).

Brugioni, Dino. *Eyeball to Eyeball: The Inside Story of the Cuban Missile Crisis* (New York: Random House, 1991).

Buisseret, David (ed.). *From Sea Charts to Satellite Images: Interpreting North American History Through Maps* (Chicago: University of Chicago Press, 1990).

Crouch, Tom D. *The Eagle Aloft: Two Centuries of the Balloon in America* (Washington, DC: Smithsonian Institution Press, 1983).

Finnegan, Terrence J. *Shooting the Front: Allied Aerial Reconnaissance and Photographic Interpretation on the Western Front—World War I* (Washington, DC: National Defense Intelligence College, 2006).

Fischer, Irene K. *Geodesy? What's That?: My Personal Involvement in the Age-Old Quest for the Size and Shape of the Earth* (New York: iUniverse, 2005).

Goss, John. *The Mapmaker's Art: An Illustrated History of Cartography* (London: Studio Editions, 1993).

Haydon, Frederick Stansbury. *Military Ballooning During the Early Civil War* (Baltimore, M.D.: John Hopkins University Press, 2000).

Kahn, David. *The Codebreakers: The Story of Secret Writing* (New York: Mac-Millan Publishing Company, Inc., 1967).

Keegan, John. *Intelligence in War: Knowledge of the Enemy from Napoleon to Al-Qaeda*. New York: Random House, 2003.

Maury, Matthew Fontaine, John Leighly (ed.). *Physical Geography of the Sea and Its Meteorology* (Cambridge: Harvard University Press, 1963).

McAuliffe, Mary S. (ed.). *CIA Documents on the Cuban Missile Crisis, 1962*. (Washington, DC: History Staff, Central Intelligence Agency, 1992).

McDonald, Robert A. *Corona—Between the Earth and the Sun: The First NRO Reconnaissance Eye in Space* (Bethesda, MD: American Society for Photogrammetry and Remote Sensing, 1997).

Pedlow, Gregory W. and Donald E. Welzenbach. *The CIA and the U-2 Program, 1954–1974* (Washington, DC: Central Intelligence Agency, 1998). *[https://www.cia.gov/csi/books/U2/]*.

Pinsel, Marc I. *150 Years of Service on the Seas: A Pictorial History of the U.S. Naval Oceanographic Office from 1830 to 1980. Vol. 1, 1830–1946* (Washington, DC: GPO, 1982).

Richelson, Jeffrey T. *America's Secret Eyes in Space: The U.S. Keyhole Spy Satellite Program* (New York: Harper Collins, 1990).

Robarge, David. *Intelligence in the War for Independence* (Washington, DC: Center for the Study of Intelligence, 1997).

Ruffner, Kevin C., ed. *CORONA: America's First Satellite Program* (Washington, DC: Central Intelligence Agency, 1995).

Stanton, William. *The Great United States Exploring Expedition of 1838–1842* (Berkeley: University of California Press, 1975).

Weber, Gustavus A. *The Hydrographic Office: Its History, Activities, and Organization* (Baltimore: Johns Hopkins Press, 1926; Reprint, Washington, DC: AMS Press, 1974).

Wilford, John Noble. *The Mapmakers: The Story of the Great Pioneers in Cartography—from Antiquity to the Space Age*, 2d ed. (New York: Knopf, 2000).

Periodicals:

Brugioni, Dino. "Aerial Photography: Reading the Past, Revealing the Future." *Smithsonian* 14 (12), December 1984, 150–161.

Brugioni, Dino, and Robert Poirier. "The Holocaust Revisited: A Retrospective Analysis of the Auschwitz-Birkenau Extermination Complex." *Studies in Intelligence* 22 (4), Winter 1978, 11–29.

Doll, John G. "Cloth Maps of World War II." *Western Association of Map Libraries* 20 (1), November 1988, 24–35.

Hall, R. Cargill. "From Concept to National Policy: Strategic Reconnaissance in the Cold War." *Prologue* 28, (2), Summer 1996, 113.

Hall, R. Cargill. "Origins and Development of the Vanguard and Explorer Satellite Programs." *Air Power Historian* 9, October 1964, 102–108.

Hall, R. Cargill, and Donald E. Hillman. "Overflight: Strategic Reconnaissance of the USSR." *Air Power Historian* 43 (1), Spring 1996, 28–39.

Hudson, Alice, and Mary McMichael Ritzlin. "Introduction to the Preliminary Checklist of Pre-Twentieth-Century Women in Cartography." *Cartographica* 37 (3), Fall 2000.

Luvaas, Jay. "The Role of Intelligence in the Chancellorsville Campaign, April–May 1963." *Intelligence and National Security* 5 (2), April 1990, 99-115.

Richelson, Jeffrey T. "The Keyhole Satellite Program." *Journal of Strategic Studies* 7 (2), 1984, 121–153.

Sayle, Edward F. "George Washington, Manager of Intelligence." *Studies in Intelligence* 27 (4), Winter 1983, 1–10.

Schultz, Mark E. "The Power of Geospatial Intelligence." *Defense Intelligence Journal* 14 (1), 2005,79–87.

Tyner, Judith. "The Hidden Cartographers: Women in Mapmaking," *Mercator's World* 2 (6), November – December 1997, 46–51.

Dr. Gary E. Weir is chief historian at the National Geospatial-Intelligence Agency, a guest investigator with the Woods Hole Oceanographic Institution, and teaches for the University of Maryland. His works include "Fish, Family, and Profit: Piracy and the Horn of Africa," part of *Piracy and Maritime Crime*, the Naval War College's Newport Paper Number 35 (2010). Sponsored by a lessons-learned grant from the director of national intelligence, Dr. Weir also examined the development of hyperspectral science as an intelligence tool (2011) and then for NGA explored the evolution of activity-based intelligence (2013). His present work focuses on the history of geo-positioning at NGA.

GUIDE TO THE STUDY OF INTELLIGENCE

History of the
Defense Intelligence Agency

Lieutenant General Ronald L. Burgess, Jr.

[Editor's Note: Numerous books have been written about the Central Intelligence Agency and National Security Agency, far fewer about their community counterpart, the Defense Intelligence Agency (DIA). This article in AFIO's *Guide to the Study of Intelligence* series recounts the DIA's development and evolution.]

D IA's story begins at the height of the Cold War, when Secretary of Defense Robert McNamara established the agency on 1 October 1961. McNamara's action instituted a longstanding recommendation originally found in the 1946 Congressional Joint Committee on the Investigation of the Pearl Harbor Attack, which recommended the integration of all Army and Navy intelligence organizations. "Operational and intelligence work required centralization of authority and clear-cut allocation of responsibility," the committee wrote.[1] At the time of DIA's creation, which brought defense intelligence into conformance with the Department of Defense Reorganization Act of 1958, the Joint Chiefs of Staff wrote, "national intelligence and military intelligence are indivisible in practice." Since its humble origins, DIA has become a central player in both the defense and national intelligence arenas, reflecting this judgment.

DIA achieved early recognition in September 1962, when its photo interpreters noticed in the initial U-2 imagery that surface-to-air missile sites in Cuba were arranged in a pattern similar to those in the Soviet Union around intercontinental ballistic missile facilities. This photo analysis, combined with human intelligence, claiming the Soviets were putting missiles in Cuba, led DIA's first director, US Air Force Lieutenant General Joseph Carroll, to call for more U-2 reconnaissance flights over Cuba. The subsequent U-2 mission on 14 October 1962—its flight path based on DIA's analysis—photographed a convoy

---

1. Origins of the Defense Intelligence Agency. http://www.dia.mil/history/features/origins.

of Soviet medium-range ballistic missiles just before it pulled off the road under a canopy of trees. After the Cuban Missile Crisis abated and the Soviets removed their missiles and bombers, President Kennedy asked DIA to brief the nation. John Hughes, who was a special assistant to Lieutenant General Carroll, took the stage in the State Department auditorium on 6 February 1963. Introduced by Secretary McNamara, Hughes used many of the slides and U-2 photos that President Kennedy had ordered declassified.[2]

The war in Vietnam dominated the last half of the 1960s. DIA provided current and long-term analyses to commanders and defense policymakers on the strength of the Viet Cong and North Vietnamese, their logistics, and air defense capabilities. Estimates of enemy strength in Vietnam became controversial with disagreements between DIA and the CIA.[3] DIA deployed people into the theater, including experts to translate and exploit captured enemy documents. DIA also collected and analyzed intelligence on US prisoners of war and military members missing in action. DIA provided intelligence for the 1970 raid to free American POWs held at the Son Tay prison camp west of Hanoi, including information from a human source in Hanoi who claimed two days before the raid that the prisoners had been moved. The raid went forward on the chance the source was wrong or that the captives had been returned. As it turned out, the source had been correct, the Son Tay camp, flooded by monsoon rains, held no POWs.

During the same period, DIA's long-term strategic analyses focused on preventing strategic surprise by assessing potential adversaries' capabilities. In 1965, DIA assumed responsibility for managing the new Defense Attaché System, consolidating the individual services' attaché systems.

In the 1970s, DIA became involved in the collection and production of intelligence to support strategic arms control negotiations with the Soviet Union – including the Strategic Arms Limitation Talks (SALT I, SALT II) and the anti-ballistic missile treaties. Later that focus expanded to provide intelligence needed for the new nuclear deterrence strategy set forth in President Carter's Presidential Directive 59. This was a radical shift in US policy, from focusing on massive retaliation to a deterrent strategy of selected options targeting. When it came time to develop an operational nuclear war plan, the Joint Chiefs of Staff relied on DIA to provide the intelligence foundation supporting the new US nuclear strategy.

The late December 1979 Soviet invasion of Afghanistan signaled a new level of Soviet adventurism, and Western concerns grew about the pace and scale of the Soviet military build-up. Following President Reagan's 1980 elec-

---

2. Video footage from that briefing can be viewed on DIA's public website: http://www.dia.mil/history/features/cuban-missile-crisis.
3. James J. Wirtz, Intelligence to Please? The Order of Battle Controversy During the Vietnam War, 2004 . (On the web at http://www.jstor.org/stable/2152228.)

tion, Secretary of Defense Caspar Weinberger briefed North Atlantic Treaty Organization (NATO) allies on Soviet military developments. Eager to educate their citizens about Moscow's intentions and growing capabilities, a number of NATO ministers asked Secretary Weinberger if there were a way to declassify his briefing, pictures, and charts. The secretary turned to DIA, and the resulting 10 annual unclassified publications, the *Soviet Military Power* series, which chronicled Soviet military capabilities and intentions, had enormous impact on the public in Europe and elsewhere.

DIA underwent rapid change in the 1980s. In 1984, the new Defense Intelligence Analysis Center (DIAC) opened at Bolling Air Force Base (now called Joint Base Anacostia-Bolling) in Washington, DC, allowing the Agency to consolidate many of its functions in one location. Today, an expanded DIAC building serves as—and is called—the DIA headquarters.

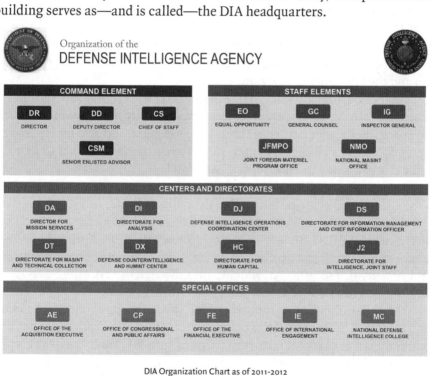

DIA Organization Chart as of 2011-2012

The year 1985 became known as the "Year of the Terrorist" with the highly publicized hijackings of the Italian cruise ship *Achille Lauro*, Trans World Airlines Flight 847, attacks on airports in Rome and Vienna, and other deadly acts. DIA provided analytic and collection support during these crises, and provided intelligence related to the conflicts in Central America, Operation EL DORADO CANYON (the 1986 retaliatory airstrike on Qaddafi's Libya), and the nation's growing counternarcotics efforts. DIA's Central America Joint Intelligence Team (CAJIT) was the first national-level intelligence fusion center and became a model for similar elements within the Intelligence Community in later years.

In 1986, Congress passed landmark legislation known as the Goldwater-Nichols Act, which reorganized the US military, strengthening the roles of the chairman, Joint Chiefs of Staff, and the combatant commands. Intended to enhance joint efforts across the military, the Goldwater-Nichols Act also designated DIA as a "combat support agency," denoting increased responsibilities to provide timely operational intelligence support to the unified and specified commanders around the world. In this capacity, DIA led the departmentwide effort to develop joint intelligence doctrine and strengthen the infrastructure needed for timely intelligence support of military operations.

As the 1980s transitioned into the 1990s, a succession of crises—from the fall of the Berlin Wall, to Operation JUST CAUSE in Panama, to the 1991 collapse of the Soviet Union, and to Operations DESERT SHIELD and DESERT STORM in the Persian Gulf— required DIA often to shift its focus. DIA organized and led an integrated effort to provide intelligence to US and coalition forces deployed in Saudi Arabia to support the initial aerial campaign against Iraq and the later ground invasion.[4]

The period after DESERT SHIELD and DESERT STORM saw significant change for DIA. In 1992, DIA was given responsibility for the Army's Missile and Space Intelligence Center in Huntsville, Alabama, and also for the Armed Forces Medical Intelligence Center, now known as the National Center for Medical Intelligence, at Fort Detrick, Maryland.

During the mid-1990s, DIA provided intelligence support during reactions to the military-led coup in Haiti and to the Balkans Crisis. In 1995, consistent with the trend for consolidating similar activities within the separate services, the Defense HUMINT Service[5] was established within the Agency to oversee human source intelligence collection. In 2008, the separate Counterintelligence Field Activity (CIFA) was consolidated into the Defense HUMINT Service to form the Defense Counterintelligence and HUMINT Center.

The post-Cold War environment of the 1990s abruptly ended on September 11, 2001. The impact of the terrorist attacks was so significant that it is common to refer to recent history in terms of "pre-9/11" and "post-9/11" eras.

Prior to the 11 September attacks, DIA had taken steps to ramp up its counterterrorism efforts. After the Al-Qaida suicide bombers' October 2000 attack on the USS *Cole*, DIA reorganized its counterterrorism office into the Joint Terrorism Analysis Center (JTAC). After the 11 September attacks, the JTAC mission was expanded and sharpened, and the organization was christened

---

4. The DIA website contains a detailed history of intelligence support efforts prior to, during, and after DESERT SHIELD / DESERT STORM. It illustrates the scope and complexity of the intelligence effort to support a modern military campaign. See http://www.dia.mil/history/features/gulf-war/.

5. HUMINT stands for human source intelligence, which includes overt human collectors, such as defense attachés, and covert sources, including controlled agents and cooperating foreign military intelligence liaison services.

the Joint Intelligence Task Force-Combating Terrorism (JITF-CT).[6] JITF-CT has provided enhanced analysis and production to support worldwide efforts to counter terrorism. JITF-CT analysts produced daily assessments of possible terrorist threats to defense personnel, facilities, and interests.[7] The JITF-CT Weapons Branch is recognized for starting the counter – improvised explosive device (IED) effort in Iraq.[8] JITF-CT remains at the center of DIA's anti-terrorism efforts today.

The Defense Intelligence Analysis Center (DIAC) which opened in 1984 at Bolling Air Force Base (now Joint Base Anacostia-Bolling), Washington, DC.

In the months after the 9/11 attacks, the US and coalition partners embarked on Operation ENDURING FREEDOM, toppling the Taliban regime in Afghanistan. Antiterrorist initiatives took place in other parts of the world as well, including in the Philippines and the Horn of Africa. In March 2003, the US and coalition forces launched Operation IRAQI FREEDOM. In each of these operations, DIA provided intelligence on enemy troop dispositions, weaponry, and damage assessments from airstrikes. The agency also helped locate high-value targets and assessed insurgent capabilities, intentions, and potential. DIA produced fine-grain tactical and operational intelligence for combat forces as well as strategic estimates for policy and decisionmakers. The agency also supported the Iraq Survey Group (ISG), an interagency body tasked with searching Iraq for weapons of mass destruction.[9]

DIA's work is not limited to antiterrorism and counterinsurgency. In addition to its protracted commitments in Iraq, Afghanistan, and elsewhere,

6. http://www.dia.mil/history/.

7. https://www.cia.gov/library/reports/archived-reports-1/Ann_Rpt_2001/smo.html.

8. Stephen Philips, "The Birth of the Combined Explosives Exploitation Cell," Small Wars Journal, see http://www.smallwarsjournal.com/mag/docs-temp/52-phillips.pdf.

9. http://www.dia.mil/history/.

Multiple Responsibilities

- In addition to overseeing Defense Intelligence Agency (DIA)'s operations, the DIA director also has a number of other responsibilities, including:
- Program manager for the General Defense Intelligence Program (GDIP), which funds important intelligence activities at the nine combatant commands and the military services
- Program manager for all Department of Defense (DOD) human intelligence
- Director of the Defense Attaché System
- Program manager for DOD counterintelligence
- Functional manager for all measurement and signature intelligence (MASINT)
- Oversight of all-source analysis conducted throughout the DOD, including work conducted at the combatant commands, the military services, and their service centers: the Army National Ground Intelligence Center, the Office of Naval Intelligence, the Marine Corps Intelligence Activity, and the Air Force National Air and Space Intelligence Center.

the agency monitors North Korean missile launches and tracks the development of Iran's nuclear program. It is also heavily engaged in supporting efforts to counter the proliferation of weapons of mass destruction, interdict narcotics trafficking, conduct global information operations (cyber), and assess foreign military capabilities in space and cyber-space. In 2004 and 2005, DIA also provided an unprecedented level of support to foreign and domestic humanitarian missions, especially the Indian Ocean tsunami and Hurricane Katrina.

While DIA deployed personnel forward during Vietnam, DESERT STORM, and Haiti, the Agency's deployments in the post-9/11 era have increased by an order of magnitude. Since DIA absorbed the civilian intelligence professionals at the nine combatant commands, the majority of DIA employees now work outside of the Washington area. Some have observed that DIA has gone from a Washington-based agency with small numbers of deployed personnel to a forward-deployed agency, supported by a headquarters in Washington. This is a significant change in DIA's culture. Today, DIA, with 16,500 civilian and military personnel, is approximately twice the size it was before 9/11. Approximately 800 personnel are forward deployed temporarily to Afghanistan and elsewhere worldwide. Hundreds more reside at the combatant commands, and others are stationed at overseas regional support centers that operate and maintain classified networks. Still others are assigned to liaison offices in Ottawa, London, Canberra, Auckland, and elsewhere.

Today DIA's responsibilities are focused on four core operational capabilities: all-source analysis, human intelligence (HUMINT), counterintelligence, and measurement and signature intelligence (MASINT). In addition, DIA manages the nation's premier worldwide top secret communications network – the Joint Worldwide Intelligence Communications System (JWICS). DIA also is the executive agent for a number of director of national intelligence (DNI) centers and activities that serve the entire intelligence community. These include the Underground Facility Analysis Center (UFAC), the National Center for Medical Intelligence (NCMI), the National Media Exploitation Center (NMEC), the Prisoner of War-Missing in Action (POW-MIA) Analytic Cell, and the National Intelligence University (NIU).

Today, DIA is truly a global agency, operating 24/7 wherever US forces are engaged and at every echelon of the chain of command, providing the daily intelligence updates for the unified and specified combatant commands, the secretary of defense and the chairman of the Joint Chiefs of Staff. DIA analysts also write for the *President's Daily Brief*, prepare target packages for national-level special operations units conducting raids against high-value targets, and provide strategic assessments for commanders in combat zones. The story of DIA's evolution is one that finds the agency serving as the hub of the defense intelligence wheel and simultaneously as the engine integrating national and military intelligence.

READINGS FOR INSTRUCTORS

The following titles are recommended for a more in-depth understanding of intelligence successes and failures, lessons on leadership and organizational change, and optimizing performance:

Betts, Richard K. and Thomas G. Mahnken. (eds.) *Paradoxes of Strategic Intelligence: Essays in Honor of Michael I. Handel* (London: Frank Cass, 2005). This collection of essays covers a variety of salient topics, including intelligence and combat leadership, intelligence failure, surprise, and politicization of intelligence.

Drucker, Peter F. *The Five Most Important Questions You Will Ever Ask About Your Organization* (San Francisco: Jossey-Bass, Inc., 1997). This book challenges readers to take a close look at the very heart of their organizations and what drives them. It provides a simple tool for self-assessment and transformation.

Grabo, Cynthia M. *Anticipating Surprise: Analysis of Strategic Warning* (Lanham, MD: University Press of America, 2004). This is a seminal study of the warning discipline from a leading practitioner.

Jervis, Robert. *Why Intelligence Fails: Lessons from the Iranian Revolution and the Iraq War* (New York: Cornell University Press, 2010). This is an unblinking look at intelligence failure leading up to the Iranian revolution in 1979 and the Iraq weapons of mass destruction (WMD) debacle.

Kam, Ephraim. *Surprise Attack: The Victim's Perspective* (Tel Aviv: Tel Aviv University, 1988). Kam's book has been called a definitive examination of strategic surprise. The author delves into the psychological factors that may contribute to an inability to assess accurately indications and warning of an impending attack.

Nagl, John A. *Learning to Eat Soup with a Knife: Counterinsurgency Lessons from Malaya and Vietnam* (Westport, CT: Praeger, 2002). This book focuses on counter-insurgency lessons from the 1950s war in Malaya and from the Vietnam War, and addresses how institutions learn when confronted with change.

Sinek, Simon. *Start with Why: How Great Leaders Inspire Everyone to Take Action* (London: Penguin, 2009). All too often, individuals and organizations focus first on WHAT and do not have a clear WHY. The author finds that great leaders lead with WHY and personify a sense of purpose that inspires peers, subordinates, and seniors alike.

Useem, Michael. *Leading Up: How to Lead Your Boss So You Both Win* (New York: Crown Business, 2003). This book effectively uses historical examples to discuss how leaders have built successful organizations. It discusses organizational communications and leadership challenges related to building a common purpose within a group that everyone then works to achieve.

DIA maintains an extensive website (*http://www.dia.mil*) useful for further information about DIA. Of particular interest is the 2012-2017 DIA Strategic Plan at *http://www.dia.mil/about/strategic-plan*, DIA's history at *http://www.dia.mil/history/*, and articles at *http://www.dia.mil/history/features/*. Also worth exploring are the websites for the DIA-hosted National Intelligence University (*http://www.ni-u.edu*) and its associated press (*http://www.ni-u.edu/ni_press/press.html*), which has many on-line resources.

US Army Lieutenant General Ronald L. Burgess, Jr. was the 17th director of the Defense Intelligence Agency, serving from 18 March 2009 to 24 July 2012. He served previously as director of intelligence (J-2), Joint Special Operations Command (JSOC); J-2, US Southern Command; and J-2, the Joint Staff. From August 2005 to February 2009, Burgess was the deputy director of national intelligence for customer outcomes, later transitioning to director of the Intelligence Staff. During this period, he twice served as the acting principal deputy director of national intelligence. In September 2012, he retired after 38 years in the US Army.

GUIDE TO STUDY OF INTELLIGENCE

I Can See It From Afar;
I Can Hear It From Afar

Intelligence From Space[1]

Robert A. McDonald, Ph.D.

The middle of the 20th century witnessed a revolution in intelligence gathering, one that gave the world a new perspective—from afar. With the launch of America's Grab electronic reconnaissance (ELINT) satellite in June 1960 and the launch of America's Corona imagery reconnaissance (IMINT) satellite two months later, the US Intelligence Community (IC) marked the beginning of what would be a growing capability to see and hear intelligence targets of interest from space, hundreds of miles above the Earth's surface. The discipline of national reconnaissance was born.

The perspective from space changed the practice of intelligence gathering. It gave intelligence officers the ability to monitor denied areas; regular access to remote targets of interest, the means for collecting large quantities of data, and the perspective of a synoptic view. It also gave those collecting intelligence the security of distance from the target. Operating from space has made observation very different.

Understanding Collection of Intelligence From Space

What defines space? In its simplest definition from a geocentric perspective, space is what is beyond the Earth's atmosphere and extends into the universe. For the purposes of collecting intelligence from satellite platforms, space

---

1. Editor's Note: The author wrote this article in an unofficial capacity as an independent activity, and it represents his personal assessment and views. The content of the article does not reflect the official position of the National Reconnaissance Office (NRO) or any other US Government entity. It has been approved for public release.

can be considered to begin somewhere in the upper atmosphere at the point where a satellite is able to orbit the earth. This generally is at 62.1 miles (100 kilometers) above Earth's mean sea level, an altitude known as the Kármán line.[2]

Terminology for National Reconnaissance

National Reconnaissance is the term for the discipline and practice of space-based intelligence collection and associated activities. It comprises technical intelligence collection funded by the National Reconnaissance Program and conducted by the National Reconnaissance Office (NRO) under its mission to conduct research, development, acquisition, launch, and operation of satellite reconnaissance systems and other missions as directed, to include the NRO communications infrastructure. The most common terminology for national reconnaissance is "satellite reconnaissance."

Over the years, for security reasons, there have been euphemisms used in place of the term "satellite reconnaissance." During 18 years of its early history, the mere "fact of satellite reconnaissance" was classified, and the term "overhead" came into use—an ideal term because of both its ambiguity and its application to national imagery and signals intelligence (SIGINT) operations with either high-altitude aircraft (i.e., the U-2 and SR-71) or satellites (i.e., Grab, Corona, and their follow-on systems). It was only after President Carter declassified the "fact of photoreconnaissance satellites" in 1978, during his policy discussions related to Strategic Arms Limitation Talks (SALT) II, that there could be open acknowledgement of space borne intelligence.

The phrase "National Technical Means" or "NTM" also has been used for space-based reconnaissance activities. This usage was derived from language in the 1972 SALT I Interim Agreement and Protocol on Limitation of Strategic Offensive Weapons. At that time, the US and USSR agreed to use this euphemism because of the then sensitivities associated with public acknowledgment of satellite reconnaissance. The treaty avoided the term "satellite reconnaissance" and merely stated, "... each Party shall use national technical means of verification at its disposal in a manner consistent with generally recognized principles of international law."

Because of its use in an international treaty, the terminology, "national technical means," has a narrower, specialized, diplomatic meaning linked to the language in the treaty; however, it has become convenient to use national technical means (and its acronym, NTM) as shorthand for national reconnaissance. Because of the treaty context, the terminology actually has broader meaning than merely "national reconnaissance." NTM would include not only collection via satellites, but also via aircraft, seismic and electronic sensors, and other technical means designed to monitor a state's activities related to treaty compliance.

The expression "national reconnaissance" is the more precise terminology for use when referring to nationally controlled space-based intelligence collection and related activities.

The environment of space is hazardous and unfriendly, putting intelligence operations at risk. Space is a near vacuum with pressure nearly at zero. It is extremely cold with temperatures dropping to absolute zero. Gravity at the altitude of where satellites orbit the earth is much less than on the surface of Earth. At 200 miles (321.8 km) altitude, gravity is about 90% of what it would be at sea level; however, spacecraft in orbit constantly are falling toward the Earth in a circular motion that creates the orbit, and any objects in a spacecraft would be in a microgravity environment while in this "free fall."[3] There are

---

2. The Kármán line is named for Theodore Von Kármán, who in the 1950s identified the dividing line between aeronautics and astronautics. Aeronautics depended on the atmosphere; astronautics depended on the absence of an atmosphere. Note that the USAF and NASA define space as beginning at an altitude of 80.5 km/50 mi, the altitude at which anyone who reaches it is awarded astronaut wings. Montgomery, J. and St. John, A., *Space Environment, Aerospace Dimensions*, Module 5. 2nd Edition (Maxwell AFB, AL: Civil Air Patrol, 2010).
3. This "free fall" would be like riding in an elevator after the cable breaks (Montgomery and St. John, *Space Environment*.

also radiation belts with very high energy particles that have the potential to interfere with satellite operations. Electromagnetic energy (e.g., x-rays, ultraviolet, gamma rays, microwaves, radio waves), along with meteoroids and the charged particles of cosmic rays all are present in space. The very high energy particles can pass through the skin of a satellite, be absorbed by its electrical components and directly affect the electronics of the satellite, as well as have adverse effects on the data in any on-board memory. The harsh environment of space, with its threatening temperature, vacuum conditions, radiation belts, and solar storms, all are important operational threats that designers of reconnaissance satellites and the operators of satellite reconnaissance missions must take into consideration as they deal with the physics of space missions.[4]

The designers and operators of satellite reconnaissance missions face the practical realities of the physics of space missions — the challenges of leaving earth and circling it, i.e., launch operations and orbital motion.

Launch Operation. The first challenge is getting into space—launching a satellite so it has enough power or thrust to counteract the force of gravity. The spacecraft's weight, payload, and launch vehicle are major factors in determining the energy necessary to achieve orbital altitude. Weight, therefore, is a significant consideration in the design and construction of satellites. The launch initially will be vertical to move the spacecraft through the dense part of the atmosphere at a speed that is low enough to keep it from burning up. Once the vehicle is at the appropriate altitude, it then is put into orbit.[5]

Orbital Motion. The second challenge is getting into orbit— pitching the spacecraft over horizontally and accelerating to orbital speed. After the spacecraft is beyond the densest part of the atmosphere, it is given sufficient horizontal velocity so that its curved path does not intersect the surface of the Earth. That motion parallel to the surface of the Earth will keep the spacecraft in orbit. Selecting and inserting the satellite into the right orbit is critical to the success of the reconnaissance mission. The eccentricity, altitude, inclination, period, and resultant ground trace collectively describe the nature of the satellite's orbit and its potential applicability to a particular reconnaissance mission.[6] These various orbital characteristics are fundamental to defining such mission requirements as the field of view and frequency of access that the reconnaissance satellite would have over any intelligence target on the Earth's surface. The nature of the orbit both provides opportunities and places limitations on the intelligence gathering capabilities of any particular reconnaissance satellite. For each reconnaissance mission, the planners and operators must

---

4. T. Damon, *Introduction to Space: The Science of Spaceflight* (Malabar, FL: Orbit Book Co., 1990), 45-60; and Montgomery and St. John, *Space Environment*.
5. Damon, Introduction to Space, 27-44.
6. Eccentricity refers to the shape of the orbit, which is most often elliptical. Inclination is the angle of the orbit, e.g., 90 degrees is a polar orbit; zero is an equatorial orbit. Period is the time to complete one orbit. Ground trace is the track over the Earth's surface.

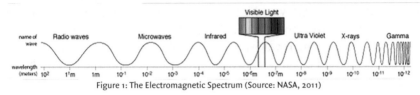

Figure 1: The Electromagnetic Spectrum (Source: NASA, 2011)

tailor the orbit to the mission of the reconnaissance satellite.[7]

Different Earth orbits offer satellites varying perspectives, and each type of orbit is valuable for a different purpose. Some orbits appear to hover over a single spot, providing a constant view of one portion of the Earth, while others may circle Earth, passing over many different locations in a day, providing frequent revisits. Some orbital maneuvering is possible to adjust the orbit, but this takes energy, and energy requires fuel. An orbit can be modified by applying thrust at the proper time and in the proper direction. The orbit can be increased in size by applying energy opposite to the direction of motion; the orbit can be decreased in size by applying energy (or retrofiring) in the direction of motion. The orbit's eccentricity also can be changed. An orbit can be circularized by applying a particular amount of energy at apogee.[8]

After a reconnaissance satellite is in the appropriate orbit, the focus turns to the collection of data, and these data are in the form of electromagnetic radiation. This is the essence of intelligence from space: collecting radiation along the electromagnetic spectrum.

TYPES OF EM RADIATION	WAVELENGTH
Radio Waves	1011 micrometers
Radar	105 micrometers
Infrared	102 micrometers
Visible Spectrum	1 micrometer
Ultraviolet	10-1 micrometers
X-Rays	10-2 micrometers
Gamma Rays	10-4 micrometers

Table 1. Types of radiation in the electromagnetic (EM) spectrum (Damon, 1990, 49, 75).

The Electromagnetic Spectrum. All matter on Earth radiates energy either as particle energy, such as the alpha particles from uranium, or as pure energy, such as in the electromagnetic spectrum. Astrophysicists will tell you that all objects in the universe emit electromagnetic radiation. (See Figure 1.) Electromagnetic radiation can be viewed as a stream of photons, which are mass-less particles. Each photon contains a certain amount of energy and travels at the speed of light in a wave-like pattern. The type of radiation is determined by the energy in its photons. Radio waves have low-energy photons;

---

7. Damon, Introduction to Space, 27-44; and H. Riebeek, "Catalog of Earth Satellite Orbits," Earth Observatory, 2009. Retrieved from http://earthobservatory.nasa.gov/Features/OrbitsCatalog/ (accessed 29 Jun 2014).
8. Damon, Introduction to Space, 27-44; and Riebeek, "Catalog of Orbits."

Figure 3. Example of space-based radar image showing Point Reyes, CA, 1964. The arrows point to dense rain squalls where visibility was less than ¼ mile. (Source: NRO experimental Quill program; courtesy of CSNR Reference Collection as published by CSNR in Trailblazer 1964: The Quill Experimental Radar Imagery Satellite Compendium, edited by J. Outzen.)

Figure 2: Example of visual spectrum image, Shea Stadium, Queens, New York City, 1980 (Source: NRO Hexagon KH-9 image prepared by CIA's NPIC; courtesy of CSNR Reference Collection)*

* The CSNR Reference Collection is a part of the Center for the Study of National Reconnaissance (CSNR), the NRO's independent social science research body that conducts research into the discipline, practice, and history of national reconnaissance — explaining the discipline of national reconnaissance, identifying lessons from its practice, and documenting its historical experience. This, and other similarly identified photographs and images included in this guide are from that collection.

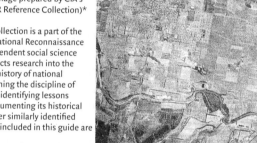

Figure 4. Example of infrared image acquired as part of an experimental mission by the Corona film-return system in 1968. (Source: An NRO image prepared by CIA's NPIC; as published in 1997 by the American Society for Photogrammetry & Remote Sensing in Corona Between the Earth and the Sun.)

microwave photons have a little more energy, and as you move along the spectrum, the amount of energy increases with gamma-rays having the most energy.

The visible part of the electromagnetic spectrum consists of the colors that are in a rainbow – from reds and oranges, through blues and violets. The waves in the electromagnetic spectrum vary in size from very long radio waves the size of buildings, to very short gamma rays smaller than the size of the nucleus of an atom (see Table 1). Objects of higher temperature radiate shorter waves; objects of lower temperature radiate longer waves.[9] All matter that has a temperature above absolute zero emits electromagnetic radiation over a continuum of wavelengths. Green vegetation reflects green light from the sun; transmitters on the Earth's surface emanate radio waves; even the human body, a living organism with a temperature of 98.6° F, emits radiation in the form of infrared. These, and all other objects on the Earth's surface, absorb

9. Damon, Introduction to Space, 75. NASA, "The Electromagnetic Spectrum," 2011, http://science.hq.nasa.gov/kids/imagers/ems/index.html. NASA, "Electromagnetic Spectrum – Introduction," 2014, NASA Goddard Space Flight Center. http://imagine.gsfc.nasa.gov/docs/science/know_l1/ emspectrum.html.

and reflect other ambient radiation in the environment.[10]

With all matter being either direct or indirect sources of electromagnetic radiation, any radiation that is not otherwise absorbed, but emanated or reflected, can be collected by sensors on reconnaissance satellites.[11]

Objects and scenes on the Earth's surface have properties that determine how and what kind of radiation they emanate, absorb, and reflect. These properties provide the basis for analyzing the collected electromagnetic radiation, the results of which become intelligence from space, or the intelligence products of what has become "national reconnaissance."

Sometimes national reconnaissance satellites might target electromagnetic radiation from the visible spectrum and produce literal pictures that will become IMINT; in other cases, the reconnaissance satellites might target radiation such as radio waves and electronic signals that will become electronic intelligence (ELINT); and in still other cases, reconnaissance satellites might target radiation that, after analysis, might become more esoteric kinds of intelligence.

Reconnaissance satellites have the potential—although not always the capability—to carry a range of sensors that potentially could detect and collect the available radiation across the entire electromagnetic spectrum. (See FIGURES 2, 3, and 4 for examples of historic visible, radar, and infrared collection.)

In its most basic sense, intelligence from space is nothing more than expanding the capabilities of the human senses across the electromagnetic spectrum through the use of innovative technology as sensors, and by raising into space the altitude of observation. But this is a capability that was not always available to human observers and intelligence analysts. It only became a reality with the 1960s space-age revolution in intelligence collection.[12]

The Growth & Origin of National Reconnaissance From Space

Space reconnaissance grew out of the airborne strategic reconnaissance missions at the end of World War II. It is a story of how humans, trying to see more and hear more than their senses could acquire and process, were able to sense the radiation of the world in ever-evolving, increasingly sophisticated, and dramatically technical ways. Over time, pioneering innovation and imag-

---

10. Environmental Protection Agency (EPA), "Uranium," 2012. *http://www.epa.gov/radiation/radionu-clides/uranium.html#properties*; NASA, "The Electromagnetic Spectrum"; Nuclear Regulatory Commission (NRC), (2013). "Radiation Basics," 2013, *http://www.nrc.gov/about-nrc/radiation/health-effects/radiation-basics.html*.

11. EPA, "Uranium"; NASA, "The Electromagnetic Spectrum"; USNRC, "Radiation Basics."

12. The CSNR Reference Collection is a part of the Center for the Study of National Reconnaissance (CSNR), the NRO's independent social science research body that conducts research into the discipline, practice, and history of national reconnaissance—explaining the discipline of national reconnaissance, identifying lessons from its practice, and documenting its historical experience. This, and other similarly identified photographs and images included in this guide are from that collection.

ination developed sensors to detect various forms of radiation. It required four revolutions over centuries to bring about the 1960s space-based revolution and the discipline of national reconnaissance.

The first revolution (which took place between the 9th century BC and the 17th century AD) extended the sensory range through the use of lenses for vision and funnels for hearing; the second revolution (which took place in the air during the mid-19th century) looked upward in altitude and used balloons for reconnaissance platforms; the third revolution (which took place during the early 20th century) used the increased altitude of aircraft and their speed as new platforms for observation.

The Fourth Revolution: Emergence of Space Intelligence. The fourth revolution, in the middle of the 20th century, raised the platform for overhead remote sensing beyond the atmosphere, providing a synoptic view of the world. In 1960, the US IC brought the world its first capability to listen from space by acquiring—from antennas on an orbiting satellite—electromagnetic signals emanating from transmitters on the Earth's surface, and to see from space by acquiring—from film on an orbiting satellite—images of the earth's geospatial surface. The earliest national reconnaissance satellites—the first a signals intelligence (SIGINT) satellite, and the second an IMINT satellite—set the standard for all national reconnaissance programs that were to follow. Understanding their stories is fundamental to understanding the discipline of national reconnaissance.

The First SIGINT Reconnaissance Satellite: Grab. The world's first intelligence collector from space was the Galactic Radiation and Background (Grab) satellite. Grab was the unclassified name for project Dyno, the classified name for this SIGINT satellite program. As part of the Grab cover, a legitimate scientific payload, the solar radiation (SolRad) measurement mission package was launched on Grab.[13] The Naval Research Laboratory (NRL) designed Grab to be an ELINT search and technical intelligence collector against air and ballistic missile defense systems in the Soviet Union. It collected radio frequency (RF) pulses from Soviet air defense radars and transponded the data to huts at ground stations that encircled the Soviet Union. Personnel at the ground stations recorded the data from the satellite and then dispatched tapes with these data, initially to NRL, and then to the National Security Agency (NSA) and the US Air Force Strategic Air Command (SAC), where analysts exploited the data and developed technical intelligence about Soviet radar.[14]

---

13. National Reconnaissance Office, History of the Poppy Satellite System. Draft Program C manuscript in the CSNR Reference Collection, 1978. Formerly a classified Top Secret/SCI document approved for release 6 June 2012. Wilhelm, P. (2002). "Cutting Edge Work at the Naval Research Laboratory" in R. A. McDonald (ed.), *Beyond Expectations—Building an American National Reconnaissance Capability: Recollections of the Pioneers and Founders of National Reconnaissance* (Bethesda, MD: American Society for Photogrammetry and Remote Sensing, 2002),155-161.
14. McDonald, R. A. & Moreno, S., *Raising the Periscope – Grab and Poppy – America's Early Elint Satellites* (Chantilly, VA: Center for the Study of National Reconnaissance, 2005); Potts R. L. *U.S. Navy/*

The Grab series of ELINT satellites had five missions between June 1960 and April 1962 (see FIGURE 5). There were launch failures and problems attaining orbit. These kinds of mishaps should be expected in the development of innovative, complex, first-of-a-kind programs. The second launch, in November 1960, experienced a failure on launch. The Thor rocket burned out 12 seconds early, and range safety destroyed the vehicle.[15] Only two missions were successful. Nevertheless, Grab 1, launched in June 1960, was operational for nearly three months. The intelligence collected fundamentally changed the US National Intelligence Estimates (NIEs) on the Soviet Union's capability to defend against a US strategic nuclear strike. While estimates suggested that the Soviets had a minimal capability to defend itself, the Grab intelligence made it clear that the Soviets could detect and defend itself against a US nuclear attack.[16]

Corona: The First IMINT Reconnaissance Satellite.

The world's second intelligence collector from space was the Corona IMINT satellite that the CIA and Air Force made a success, even though many earlier believed it was highly improbable that a photo reconnaissance system could return film from space.[17] Corona was the classified name for the project. For its initial period of development and operation, the CIA and the Air Force conducted its activities under the cover of the Discoverer flight series. Corona's initial failed attempts seemed to validate this view. The Corona program experienced 12 unsuccessful attempts before having a successful mission. Finally, Corona Mission 9009 (cover named Discoverer Mission XIV) returned some 3,000 feet of film providing more than 1,650,000 square miles of coverage of the Soviet Union.[18]

Figure 5. The Grab satellite, approximately 20 inches in diameter and weighing 40 lbs. (Source: NRL; CSNR Reference Collection)

NRO Program C Electronic Intelligence Satellites (1958-1977). Draft manuscript in the CSNR Reference Collection, 3 Sep 1998. Formerly a classified Secret/SCI document approved for release 13 June 2012.; Wilhelm, Naval Research Laboratory.

15. (NRO, History of Poppy.)

16. R. A. McDonald. & S. Moreno, *Raising the Periscope*, (Potts, *NRO Program C*).

17. While Corona was the first operationally successful photosatellite reconnaissance system, there were a series of predecessor developmental satellite activities that included the Military Satellite System, known as Weapon System 117L (WS 117L). The WS 117L was a family of separate subsystems that were to carry out different missions. By 1959, WS 117L had evolved into three separate programs: Missile Defense Alarm System (MIDAS), the basis for later satellite-borne missile warning systems; the Satellite and Missile Observation System (Samos), a family of read-out and film-return photo reconnaissance satellites, later to be cancelled; and the soon-to-be-operational Discoverer Program, which was a cover for the clandestine Corona program. Perry, R L. *A History of Satellite Reconnaissance: The Robert L. Perry Histories.* CSNR Classics Series,) (Washington, DC: Center for the Study of National Reconnaissance, 2012). This is the edited, published version of a series of formerly classified, draft manuscripts prepared from 1964-1974.; US Air Force Space and Missile Systems Center. *Historical Overview of the Space and Missile Systems Center, 1954-2003* (Los Angeles Air Force Base: History Office, Space and Missile Systems Center, 2004), "Chapter V Satellite Systems," 33-54 *http://www.losangeles. af.mil/shared/media/document/AFD-060912-025.pdf* (accessed 21 Sep 2014).

18. McDonald, "Introduction: Models for Success—Recollections of Accomplishments," in R. A. McDonald (ed.), *Beyond Expectations—Building an American National Reconnaissance Capability: Rec-*

Corona was an IMINT system that used traditional film, ejected it from orbit, and recovered the film capsule as it re-entered the atmosphere. After processing at Kodak, the film was available to photo interpreters at the CIA's National Photographic Interpretation Center (NPIC) in Washington, DC; NPIC subsequently was incorporated into what initially was the National Imagery and Mapping Agency (NIMA) and then the National Geospatial-Intelligence Agency (NGA) in 2003.[19] The first mission had limited resolution and cloud cover, but it provided enough information to locate major airfields and military installations, as well as identify the types of aircraft. It also helped interpreters develop signatures for what Soviet installations looked like, something that would guide identifications in future missions.[20]

After Corona's third mission in June 1961, the NPIC interpreters had clear imagery over the western Soviet Union and saw the first intercontinental ballistic missiles (ICBMs) and medium-range missile bases. What they saw gave them the evidence to conclude that even though the Soviets had started to build missile bases and production facilities, the Soviets had almost no operational missiles. NIEs at the time had concluded that there was a missile gap and that the Soviets could launch ICBMs in an initial attack against many US targets. This information gap had created the perception of this "missile gap."[21] Corona imagery provided the evidence that the Soviets did not have an operational capability for strategic missiles. Space intelligence had debunked the so-called "missile gap."

Continued Evolution of Intelligence From Space. Throughout the early development of national reconnaissance in space, the Grab and Corona programs had difficulties, but they had the support of the President. President Eisenhower personally approved the Grab and Corona programs, and it was Eisenhower who was willing to support them even when they seemed to be failing. Eisenhower's military assistant, Army General Andrew Goodpaster told Ed Miller, a pioneering engineer on Corona's recovery system, that Eisenhower was an "intelligence junkie" and always wanted to know what was "over the top of the next hill." In spite of repeated failures in the Corona program, Eisenhower told Goodpaster, "They'll get it right. They'll get it right." And of course they did get it right, and have gotten it right many times more.[22]

ollections of the Pioneers and Founders of National Reconnaissance (Bethesda, MD: American Society for Photogrammetry and Remote Sensing, 2002), xxiii-xxxvii.

19. McDonald "Introduction." In R. A. McDonald (Ed.), Intelligence Revolution 1960: Retrieving the Corona Imagery That Helped Win the Cold War (Chantilly, VA: Center for the Study of National Reconnaissance, 2012), 1-13.

20. D. S. Doyle, "Photo Interpreter Challenge," in I. Clausen, E. A. Miller, R. A. McDonald, & C. V. Hastings, Intelligence Revolution 1960: Retrieving the Corona Imagery that Helped Win the Cold War (Chantilly, VA: Center for the Study of National Reconnaissance, 2012), Chap. 8, 65-69.

21. The McDonald, "Corona's Imagery: A Revolution in Intelligence and Buckets of Gold for National Security," in McDonald (ed.), Corona Between the Sun & the Earth: The First NRO Reconnaissance Eye in Space (Bethesda, MD: American Society for Photogrammetry and Remote Sensing).

22. E. A. Miller, "Satellite Recovery Vehicle Challenge," in I.Clausen, E. A. Miller, R. A. McDonald, & C.

The Grab and Corona programs were only the beginning of national reconnaissance in space. The Grab program transitioned into the follow-on Poppy program and multiple other follow-on SIGINT programs. Corona operated from 1960 until 1972—well beyond its planned two years. But the National Reconnaissance Office (NRO) launched Corona's replacements, the first of its high-resolution Gambit imagery systems, in 1963; and then, in 1971, the broad-area search Hexagon imagery system. As early as 1978, the NRO began its transition from these film-return systems to near-real-time digital imagery collection. All of these follow-on national reconnaissance systems over the years provided the nation with invaluable information from space, not only in the area of national security, but also for many civil applications.

This fourth revolution has been an amazing transformation from the collection of comparatively limited, poor quality imagery and limited narrow intercepts of signals to the timely collection and processing of large volumes of data from across a growing range of the electromagnetic spectrum.

Intelligence From Space Over the Years

Since the 1960s, the NRO has perfected its space-borne collection systems and expanded their range of applications. In its collection activities, the NRO has interactively worked with all the intelligence collection disciplines—IMINT, SIGINT, HUMINT, measurement and signature intelligence (MASINT), open source (OSINT), and the like—tipping off other collection capabilities. For example, a SIGINT collector might identify a radar signal, and that would tip off an IMINT collector to look at a particular location to both confirm the "find" and collect imagery for detailed analysis.

Cold War photoreconnaissance missions worked interactively, conducting search and surveillance activities against specific targets. The Hexagon KH-9 broad-area search system would search large geographic areas for new Soviet threats and identify intelligence targets of interest. In subsequent operations, the NRO would precisely point the Gambit KH-8 high-resolution imaging system at the target to collect high-quality images that would provide a higher level of detail for more in-depth analyses. (FIGURE 6 shows a naval target acquired during a broad-area search KH-9 mission; FIGURE 7 shows another naval target acquired during a high-resolution KH-8 surveillance mission).

The national security applications of space-based intelligence have been broad and many. Some of the more significant applications include monitoring and assessing strategic threats, mapping, target planning, influencing arms control policy, monitoring nuclear proliferation, contributing to scientific and technical intelligence analyses, supporting military operations, as well as civil

---

V. Hastings, *Intelligence Revolution 1960: Retrieving the Corona Imagery that Helped win the Cold War* (Chantilly, VA: Center for the Study of National Reconnaissance, 2012), Chap. 5, 41-48.

Figure 6. Broad-area search coverage of a Naval Intelligence Target of Interest, Severodvinsk, former Soviet Union, 1982 (Source: NRO KH-9 image prepared by CIA's NPIC; courtesy of CSNR Reference Collection)

interests.

Monitoring and Assessing Strategic Threats. One of the earliest national security applications has been monitoring and assessing strategic threats, especially the threat from the former Soviet Union. National reconnaissance answered questions such as: How many strategic bombers and ballistic missiles did the Soviet Union have, how were these systems deployed, what were their capabilities, what other weapons systems were the Soviets developing, and what were their capabilities likely to be? National reconnaissance is ideal to answer these questions because its platforms can monitor vast areas of terrain and search for changes that might be of interest. FIGURE 8 shows coverage of Yurya, some 500 miles east of Moscow, where the NRO had been collecting imagery in 1961. At that time, there were no intelligence targets of interest in the highlighted area. The NRO, however, continued to collect imagery of this and other areas. One year later, NRO assets acquired coverage in which analysts identified the first evidence of a Soviet deployment of an intercontinental ballistic missile (ICBM) launch complex. (FIGURE 9)

Figure 7. High-resolution surveillance coverage of a Naval Intelligence Target of Interest at Mykolayiv, former Soviet Union, 1984 (Source: NRO KH-8 image prepared by CIA's NPIC; courtesy of CSNR Reference Collection)

The NRO also would monitor the Soviet Union for research and development activities such as missile testing to assess the USSR's progress in weapons development that might impact on the strategic threat. (See FIGURE 10 for an example of a Soviet missile test facility.)

Mapping. Mapping is a valuable application of national reconnaissance data where satellites can obtain significant image coverage and geodetic data in support of US military requirements. Imaging satellites provide photogrammetric control data with the required geometric accuracy to assist cartographers

Figure 9. Yurya ICBM Complex showing construction of an SS-7 launch site, almost 1 year after the date of the reconnaissance image in Figure 8, June 1962 (Source: NRO KH-4 imager prepared by CIA's NPIC; courtesy of CSNR Reference Collection)

Figure 8. Cold War image of the USSR at the future site of an ICBM launch site, future site of Yurya ICBM Complex June 1961.

Figure 10. Tyuratam Missile Test Range, former USSR, August 1984. (Source: NRO KH-9 panoramic camera image prepared by CIA's NPIC; courtesy of CSNR Reference Collection

in constructing accurate maps.[23]

Prior to the advent of the digital age, the NRO relied on its film-return systems for mapping imagery. The Hexagon satellite, in particular, had a dedicated mapping camera. (See Figure 11 for an example of this kind of mapping image.)

With the advent of the digital age, both the collection of imagery and the preparation of mapping products turned to the digital world. As a consequence of that transition, intelligence and mapping information have become comingled into new products called geospatial intelligence products.

Even though the primary mission of national reconnaissance imaging systems has been for national security purposes—both mapping and intelligence, there have been extensive applications for domestic mapping. During the Cold War, even though 95% of the total coverage was directed at acquiring imagery of foreign areas, the NRO acquired at least 5% of its imagery coverage for domestic purposes, primarily mapping.[24]

Even during the early days of the

23. McDonald, "Corona, Argon, and Lanyard: A Revolution for US Overhead Reconnaissance," in R. A. McDonald (ed.), *Corona – Between the Earth and the Sun: The First NRO Reconnaissance Eye in Space* (Bethesda, MD: American Society for Photogrammetry and Remote Sensing, 1997), 61-74.
24. DoD Instruction 5000.56, Programming Geospatial-Intelligence (GEOINT), Geospatial Information and Services (GI&S), and Geodesy Requirements for Developing Systems (Jul 9, 2010); CJCS Instruction CJCSI 3110.08D, Geospatial Information and Services Supplemental Instruction to Joint Strategic Capabilities, Plan (JSCP) (Dec 10, 2010); Joint Publication 2-03, Geospatial Intelligence in Joint Operations (Oct 31, 2012; Digital Nautical Chart, NGA Products & Services, *https://www1.nga.mil/ ProductsServices/NauticalHydrographicBathymetricProduct/Pages/DigitalNauticalChart.aspx*; (accessed Oct 11 2014).

Figure 11. Hexagon KH-9 mapping camera imagery of Kubinka Airfield (near Moscow), former Soviet Union, 1979, at 20X magnification. (Source: NRO image as prepared by NPIC, courtesy of CSNR Reference Collection.)

From Maps to Geospatial Intelligence*

The 20th century cartographic agencies— such as the Army Map Service, Air Force's Aeronautical Chart and Information Center, the oceanographic and charting services of U.S. Naval Hydrographic Office, the U.S. Geological Survey, and the Defense Mapping Agency—used satellite reconnaissance imagery to produce basic maps.

The digital age and the precise geo-location of 21st century national reconnaissance data changed that with satellite reconnaissance imagery being one component of what has come to be a more sophisticated and integrated product—a geospatial intelligence (GEOINT) product.

GEOINT is an integrating intelligence discipline that exploits and analyzes imagery, along with a range of other geospatial-related information, such as geodetic, geomagnetic, gravimetric, aeronautical, topographic, hydrographic, littoral, cultural, and toponymic data. The integration of these data results in the production of visual depictions and descriptions of physical features along with any other geospatial data—all referenced to precise locations on the Earth's surface.

The technology of the 21st century saw the transition from map products to geospatial intelligence products.

*DoD Instruction 5000.56, Programming Geospatial-Intelligence (GEOINT), Geospatial Information and Services (GI&S), and Geodesy Requirements for Developing Systems, July 9, 2010; CJCS Instruction CJCSI 3110.08D, Geospatial Information and Services Supplemental Instruction to Joint Strategic Capabilities, Plan (JSCP), 10 Dec. 2010; Joint Publication 2-03, Geospatial Intelligence in Joint Operations, 31 Oct 2012; Digital Nautical Chart, NGA Products & Services, https://www1.nga.mil/ProductsServices/NauticalHydrographicBathymetricProduct/Pages/DigitalNauticalChart.aspx; (accessed 11 October 2014).

Cold War, when national reconnaissance imagery was highly classified, the IC had established arrangements with the US Geological Survey (USGS) where the USGS would use imagery from the classified national reconnaissance systems—in special facilities—for domestic map production. See Figure 12 for a map prod-

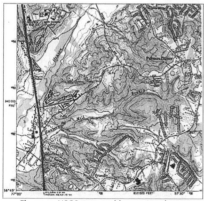

Figure 12. USGS topographic map (southwest corner of 1965 Anacostia Quadrangle), 7.5 minute series. (Source: USGS; courtesy of CSNR Reference Collection)

uct where the USGS had used national reconnaissance data to update the map (indicated by the purple overprinting).

Target Planning. National reconnaissance supported military targeting from its beginning. The first Grab SIGINT satellite mission collected technical data useful for targeting. Figure 13 is a pictorial depiction of the raw data that the Grab sensors collected. Though initially difficult to interpret, analysts were able

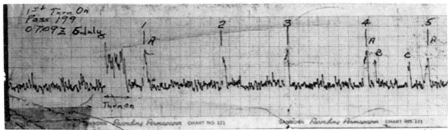

Figure 13. Example of raw data transmitted by the Grab satellite. (Source: Naval Research Laboratory, courtesy of the CSNR Reference Collection.)

to extrapolate from these data the type of radar that was emitting the signal, where it was located, and what its effective range was. Among the signals that analysts identified in the Grab data were those of Soviet early warning, height-finding, and ship-borne type radar.

The volume of data from the Grab's first mission had been very large, a major surprise to analysts at the time. In reviewing the tapes, the analysts were able to determine the magnitude of the Soviet air defense system, an intelligence issue of high interest to US Cold War target planning. With the data, the NSA analysts changed their estimates and Air Force analysts determined the Soviet radar sites' location and capabilities and the associated Soviet air defense weapons. The analysts put these kinds of data together with other intelligence information to produce products similar to the one depicted in Figure 14.[25]

These intelligence products were particularly valuable to the SAC target planners, whose bombers would have to encounter Soviet air defense forces in any nuclear confrontation. Because of this, the follow-on SIGINT satellites, along with NRO's IMINT satellites—which also provided photographs of the actual targets—became critical intelligence sources for SAC to use in building the single integrated operations plan (SIOP), the US general nuclear war plan. National reconnaissance data has continued to play an important role in the planning of wide range of specific military operations that have included bombing missions and special operations actions.[26]

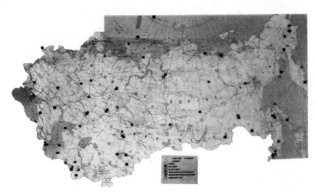

Figure 14. A "map plot" of selected signals that the Grab satellite collected over the former Soviet Union and transmitted to the ground stations (Source: NRL, courtesy of the CSNR Reference Collection.)

---

25. McDonald & Moreno, *Raising the Periscope*; Potts, Program C.
26. McDonald & Moreno, *Raising the Periscope*; Potts, Program C.

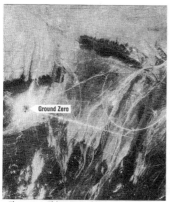

Figure 15. Chinese nuclear test site at Lop Nor showing ground zero four days after the nuclear test, 1964. (Source: NRO KH-4 image as prepared by CIA's NPIC; courtesy of CSNR Reference Collection).

Monitoring Nuclear Proliferation. By virtue of being "on station" at all times, national reconnaissance systems are in a position to monitor activities that prepare for and test nuclear weapons. In this way, these systems are ideal to support the requirement to monitor and detect the testing of nuclear weapons. (Figure 15 is an example of a nuclear test in China during the Cold War.)

Influencing Foreign Policy. National reconnaissance has played a major role over the years in supporting many foreign policy objectives. One of the most important Cold War examples is how national reconnaissance gave US policymakers both the data and the confidence to enter into arms control agreements. It was national reconnaissance systems (under the "National Technical Means" euphemism) that provided concrete data on Soviet strategic systems and became the primary means for subsequent treaty verification. For example, it was national reconnaissance imagery that made it clear that the Soviets were constructing the SS-7 ICBM at Yurya (see Figure 9). And then, to comply with the subsequent 1972 SALT I Interim Agreement on Strategic Missiles, the Soviets deactivated the SS-7 ICBM system, and destroyed its launch facilities. Since then, national reconnaissance systems have had a long history in building arms control confidence and treaty verification.[27]

Figure 16. Comparative images showing appearance mass burial Site Near Izbica, Kosovo (Source: Image released by DoD and State Department, April and May 1999; courtesy of CSNR Reference Collection).

National reconnaissance also has influenced and been an instrument in addressing human rights violations. The State Department used reconnaissance imagery to publicly document violations such as ethnic cleansing. The two images of Izbica (in former Yugoslavia) in Figure 16 show the appearance of mass grave sites of a Serbian massacre of the Kosovar Albanians. The State Department used the imagery to corroborate earlier reports from refugees and other evidence.[28]

---

27. McDonald, "Corona, Argon, and Lanyard: A Revolution for US Overhead Reconnaissance," in R. A. McDonald (ed.), *Corona – Between the Earth and the Sun: The First NRO Reconnaissance Eye in Space* (Bethesda, MD: American Society for Photogrammetry and Remote Sensing, 1997), 61-74.
28. McDonald, "NRO's Satellite Imaging Reconnaissance: Moving From the Cold War Threat to Post-Cold War." *Defense Intelligence Journal 8 (1)*, Summer 1999.

Figure 17. A high-resolution Cold War image of a Soviet aircraft carrier under construction, Mykolayiv, former USSR, 4 Jul 1984 (Source: An NRO Gambit KH-8 image with annotation by NPIC; courtesy of the CSNR Reference Collection.)

Contributing to Scientific & Technical Intelligence Analyses. National reconnaissance can provide the IC with information to do detailed scientific and technical analysis of foreign weapons systems. Figure 17, of a Soviet aircraft carrier, is an example of a high-resolution image that was used for that purpose.

Playing a Role in Military Operations. National reconnaissance can be a significant contributor to a wide range of military activities and operations. These have included maintaining order of battle information, monitoring the operational deployment of adversary submarines and other weapons systems, applying knowledge learned from scientific and technical assessment of space intelligence to the development of US weapons. Of particular interest is national reconnaissance's historic role in planning and evaluating military operations. FIGURE 18 is an example of one such image that Department of Defense (DoD) used in planning a 1998 attack on the Zhawar Kili Support Complex, a suspected terrorist training facility in Afghanistan. The coverage captures in one image, all of the natural, cultural,

Figure 18. Image of Zhawar Kili Support Complex, Afghanistan. (Source: Released by DoD, 20 August 1998; courtesy of CSNR Reference Collection.)

and terrorist-related activities in that scene.[29]

The digital age has introduced additional dynamic tools to use with national reconnaissance data for mission planning, especially with regard to manipulating and displaying large volumes of spatial and temporal data in geospatial products. One example is the use of displayed visualization of large volumes of multi-source data to detect changes that reflect

29. JCS Chairman Henry Shelton held a press conference after US missile strikes against terrorist-related targets associated with the then Al–Qa'ida leader, Osama Bin Ladin. He pointed out how planners had concluded this site was a terrorist training camp. McDonald, "Imaging Reconnaissance."

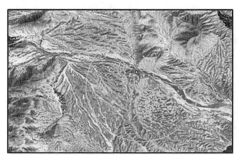

Figure 19. Millions of data elements from multi-intelligence sources as temporally and geospatially displayed on an overhead image. (Source: Unidentified overhead image; courtesy of CSNR Reference Collection.)

patterns of human activity. These geospatial patterns, when temporally displayed, are not only valuable for military mission planning, but also for battlefield forensics. When the geospatial display, which can render millions of data elements, is given temporal motion (i.e., reflects changes over time), patterns emerge that suggest specific activities, such as communications patterns, that can explain battlefield activities. (See FIGURE 19 with a static image annotated with points of activity.)

Bomb Damage Assessment. FIGURE 20 is an example of national reconnaissance imagery from Operation Desert Fox[30] where military analysts compared the pre – and post-strike status of the Directorate of Military Intelligence Headquarters building in Baghdad and how it had been reduced to rubble in the post-strike coverage.[31]

Supporting Civil Requirements. Space-based intelligence can acquire information that not only is useful for national security purposes, but also useful to satisfy civilian requirements, which can include monitoring changes on the Earth's surface (e.g., surveying glaciers and bodies of water), assessing the impact on natural resources (e.g., environmental monitoring, assessing mining activities), assessing natural disasters (e.g., evaluating tornado damage), and conducting scientific research (e.g., the

Figure 20. Pre- and post-strike comparative imagery of the Baghdad Directorate of Military Intelligence Headquarters, Iraq, 1998, (Source: Image released by DoD, 17 December 1998; courtesy of CSNR Reference Collection.)

study of geology and archeology). In the late 1980s and early 1990s, the director of central intelligence's Committee on Imagery Requirements and Exploitation (COMIREX) had been exploring the feasibility of declassifying the Corona program and much of its film. This coincided with early 1990s interests within the scientific and environmental communities for unclassified access to early satellite reconnaissance imagery for scientific purposes. President Clinton's

---

30. Operation Desert Fox was the 1998 military operation executed when Iraq refused to permit unrestricted UN inspection for weapons of mass destruction.
31. US DOD, Pentagon press briefing with US Navy Vice Admiral Scott A. Fry, director, J-3, Joint Staff and Rear Admiral Thomas R. Wilson, director, J-2, Joint Staff, Dec 18, 1998, *http://www.defense.gov/photos/newsphoto.aspx?newsphotoid=1722*; McDonald, "Imaging Reconnaissance."

Figure 21. Portion of a KH-4B frame at contact scale with the area around the U.S. Merchant Marine Academy in Great Neck, Long Island, highlighted in a box, 1970. (Source: NRO Corona imagery as prepared by CIA's NPIC; courtesy of CSNR Reference Collection)

Figure 22. An approximate 30X enlargement of the US Merchant Marine Academy at Kings Point on the Great Neck Peninsula, 1970. (Source: NRO Corona image as prepared by CIA's NPIC; courtesy of CSNR Reference Collection)

1997 Executive Order to declassify Corona film made the imagery broadly available for use by the scientific community, as well as for the wide range of other civil purposes.[32]

The Value of Intelligence From Space

Intelligence collection from space represents the birth of the discipline of national reconnaissance—the fourth revolution in reconnaissance, which has provided a way to observe and collect a broad range of electromagnetic radiation from above the Earth's surface.[33] This revolutionary capability has a number of characteristics that make it exceptionally valuable to the IC. First, it provides unique access to the world's surface. It can listen and look into areas of the Earth where access is denied for political reasons or military and environmental threats. Second, and perhaps equally important, is the fact that the very nature of national reconnaissance—i. e.,

Figure 23. Graphic depiction of the ground area in a single Hexagon KH-9 panoramic camera frame for its coverage of the 370 nautical miles between Cincinnati, OH and Washington, DC (Source: CSNR Reference Collection)

32. McDonald, "Corona, Argon, and Lanyard," 61-74.
33. Historically, the early NRO was heavily involved in airborne national reconnaissance through its Program D. The NRO mission as stated in DoD directives is to be "...responsible for research and development (R&D), acquisition, launch, deployment, and operation of overhead reconnaissance systems, and related data-processing facilities to collect intelligence and information to support national and DoD missions and other United States Government (USG) needs.... " (DoD Directive 5105.23, "National Reconnaissance Office (NRO)," June 28, 2011).

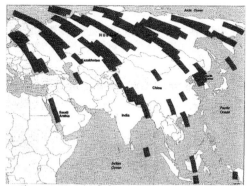

Figure 24. Example of a four-day coverage of the Eurasian land mass during the 1965 Corona Mission 1017. (Source: Map prepared by CIA's NPIC; courtesy of CSNR Reference Collection.)

its view from space—offers a synoptic perspective of the terrain of interest. And finally, it can provide a broad, simultaneous view of the electromagnetic radiation emanating from a large area of targets of interest, wherever the radiation may be on the electromagnetic spectrum.

An example of the capability of national reconnaissance to collect "big data" is how a single frame of a space image can offer a wide view of the landscape. Figure 21 shows extensive coverage of terrain in the New York City area at contact scale on a partial frame. It captures coverage that extends from Long Island to New Jersey. The power of the information content is such that a small portion of that frame can be enlarged 30X to display specific details of the relatively small area of the US Merchant Marine Academy (Figure 22).

The follow-on Hexagon KH-9 camera would capture an even greater swath of the Earth's surface, a footprint of 370 nautical miles wide (Figure 23). This simultaneous collection of electromagnetic radiation from large areas of the Earth's surface gives intelligence officers an opportunity to "see it all."[34]

The SIGINT and IMINT national reconnaissance platforms have the capability to provide persistent and predictable coverage of the Earth's terrain. The map at Figure 24 offers an early example of this. It portrays a typical Corona KH-4A coverage of the Eurasian land mass over a four-day period. Impressive, when compared with what a single aircraft with a camera could acquire during the same period. The map does not indicate which areas were cloud covered, but on most early missions, about 50 percent of the imagery was obscured by clouds.[35]

The comprehensive intelligence that national reconnaissance missions acquired during the 20th century played a critical role in ending the Cold War, and then went on into the 21st century to contribute to the success of almost all military and intelligence operations since then. We know from those experiences the tactical advantage—and often strategic survival—that came to the US because of the benefits from the intelligence collected by the space-based sensors.

Two US Presidents publicly have underscored its great value. In 1967, President Lyndon B. Johnson remarked:

34. McDonald, "Corona, Argon, and Lanyard."
35. McDonald, "Corona, Argon, and Lanyard."

"We've spent $35 or $40 billion on the space program. And if nothing else had come out of it except the knowledge that we gained from space photography, it would be worth ten times what the whole program has cost. Because tonight we know how many missiles the enemy has ... "[36]

In 1978, President Jimmy Carter, while building support for the SALT II treaty, also highlighted the value of space-borne imagery intelligence in maintaining peace:

"Photoreconnaissance satellites have become an important stabilizing factor in world affairs in the monitoring of arms control agreements. They make an immense contribution to the security of all nations. We will continue to develop them."[37]

And since the late 1970s, the US has continued to develop and refine its national reconnaissance capability. The capability has become so common that, in the 21st century, many began to take space-based data collection and its associated technology for granted. Each new improvement often is seen to be routine.

The business of national reconnaissance is far from routine. The development and refinement of national reconnaissance has taken place over an extended period of time. All of its advances took imagination, pioneering innovation, and perseverance, often through many trials and errors that are inevitable in the development of untested technology. The creation of the US national reconnaissance capability also took a significant investment in time and funding. But the benefits since the latter half of the 20th century and into the 21st century unquestionably are invaluable.

The legacy of national reconnaissance has been one that has changed the way we view the world. It has created breakthroughs in the engineering and management of aerospace technology; it has revolutionized the technology and operation—not only of intelligence—but also of military and commercial activities. This revolution of national reconnaissance gave the world a new perspective on all natural and cultural features on the surface of the Earth—the ability to view and listen to events and activities on the Earth's surface from the safety and exceptional vantage point of space.

READINGS FOR INSTRUCTORS

Berkowitz, B. & Suk, M. *The National Reconnaissance Office at 50 Years: A Brief History*. 2nd Edition. (Washington, DC: Center for the Study of National Reconnaissance, 2014).

---

36. President Lyndon. B. Johnson, remarks to educators in Nashville, TN, March 16 1967.
37. President Jimmy Carter remarks at the Congressional Space Medal of Honor Awards Ceremony, Kennedy Space Center, FL, October 1, 1978.

Burnett, M. Hexagon (KH-9) *Mapping Camera Program and Evolution*. CSNR Classics Series. (Washington, DC: Center for the Study of National Reconnaissance, 2012). This is a redacted, unclassified edition. The former NRO Program A published the original classified version in 1982.

Center for the Study of National Reconnaissance, *National Reconnaissance Almanac* (Chantilly, VA: Center for the Study of National Reconnaissance, 2011).

Chester, R. J. A *History of the Hexagon Program*. CSNR Classics Series. (Washington, DC: Center for the Study of National Reconnaissance, 2012). This is a redacted, unclassified edition. It is the Hexagon story from the perspective of the Perkin-Elmer Corporation and originally published as a classified history in 1985.

Clausen, L.; Miller, E. A.; McDonald, R. A.; & Hastings, C. V. *Intelligence Revolution 1960: Retrieving the Imagery That Helped Win the Cold War*. CSNR's *In the Words of Those Who Served* series. (Washington, DC: Center for the Study of National Reconnaissance, 2012).

McDonald, R. A. *Beyond Expectations-Building an American National Reconnaissance Capability: Recollections of the Pioneers and Founders of National Reconnaissance*. (Bethesda, MD: American Society for Photogrammetry and Remote Sensing, 2002).

McDonald, R. A. *Corona Between the Sun & the Earth—The First NRO Reconnaissance Eye in Space*. (Bethesda, MD: American Society for Photogrammetry and Remote Sensing, 1997).

McDonald, R. A. & Moreno, S. K. *Raising the Periscope—Grab and Poppy: America's Early ELINT Satellites*. Second Printing (Chantilly, VA: Center of the Study of National Reconnaissance, 2005).

Oder, C. E.; Fitzpatrick, J. C.; & Worthman, P. E. *The Gambit Story*. CSNR Classics Series. (Washington, DC: Center for the Study of National Reconnaissance, 2012) . This is a redacted, unclassified edition that includes new front matter and three new appendices with declassified KH-8 images and briefing material. The former NRO Program A published the original classified version in 1991.

Oder, C. E.; Worthman, P. E.; et al. *The Hexagon Story*. CSNR Classics Series. (Washington, DC: Center for the Study of National Reconnaissance, 2012). This is a redacted, unclassified edition. The former NRO Program A published the original classified version in 1992.

Outzen, J. O. *Critical to US Security: The Gambit and Hexagon Satellite Reconnaissance Systems Compendium* (Washington, DC: Center for the Study of National Reconnaissance, 2012). This is a collection of primary source documents with an introduction by NRO Historian James Outzen.

Robert A. McDonald is the director of the NRO Center for the Study of National Reconnaissance. He is a career CIA officer in the Senior Intelligence Service, and has served in a variety of CIA positions, including executive secretary of the director of central intelligence's (DCI's) Committee on Imagery Requirements & Exploitation, and the DCI representative to the National War College, where he also was a professor of national security policy and psychology. He has a BA and MA in political science from New York University; MS in national security strategy from the National Defense University; and PhD. in developmental psychology from the University of Maryland.

GUIDE TO THE STUDY OF INTELLIGENCE

A Guide to Cyber Intelligence

Douglas R. Price

The Evolution of Cyber Intelligence

Computers came into widespread use in the late 1960s and were used typically for large scientific studies, military planning, and large-scale business applications, such as personnel records, payroll, accounting, and data storage. Since such computers often contained information of interest, they became an intelligence target. The focus of early intelligence activities was often on recruiting people who had access to the computers of interest and supplying them with tools that would enable access to the information of interest. Computer systems administrators focused on trying to understand their system's vulnerabilities through various systems analyses and penetration testing. Those seeking unauthorized access looked at exploiting these vulnerabilities to bypass the computers' rudimentary protection mechanisms to gains access to other users' data.

As Rand Corporation's Willis Ware noted in 1967:

> Espionage attempts to obtain military or defense information regularly appear in the news. Computer systems are now widely used in military and defense installations, and deliberate attempts to penetrate such computer systems must be anticipated.[1]

Ware described a wide range of attacks against computers, ranging from humans (programmers, maintenance staff, etc.); to faulty software; to implanted hardware bugs; to wiretaps, crosstalk, and unintended radiation of

---

1. Willis H. Ware, "Security and privacy in computer systems," AFIPS Spring Joint Computer Conference Proceedings (1967), vol. 30, pp. 287-290, available at *http://www.rand.org/content/ dam/rand/pubs/ papers/2005/P3544.pdf*.

signals from the computer equipment.

In the 1970s, timesharing systems became common and allowed several people to use a single computer simultaneously, often from remote locations using modems[2] over telephone lines. As this occurred, cyber efforts broadened to include modem intercepts and techniques for stealing passwords to gain access to the systems.

During the 1980s, as computers started to be connected into networks, access to each computer was granted to a much wider community, often worldwide. This presented intelligence services new opportunities for clandestinely accessing computers remotely via a network. An early example was the KGB-sponsored German hackers who penetrated several hundred computer systems connected to the US Military's MILNET networks.[3]

Another event that occurred during the 1980s and greatly affected the cyber espionage world was the introduction of the personal computer (PC). IBM introduced their floppy disk-based PC in 1981, followed by the PC XT in 1983, which came with a hard disk drive. Intel introduced the 32-bit 386 microprocessor in 1985, and a number of vendors cropped up to produce a wide variety of "IBM compatible" personal computer systems. These PCs were incredibly useful for storing information, and came with word processing software that facilitated the production of nicely formatted reports, some of which were of obvious interest to the world's intelligence services.

In the 1980s and 1990s, the PC itself was often the target of an intelligence operation. Typically, an unattended PC in a home, hotel room, or office setting would be physically accessed and the data clandestinely copied. Sometimes, a software bug would be installed (e.g., a keystroke logger, which clandestinely records every typed character) or an electronic transmitter would be planted.[4]

Some intelligence services had the ability to detect from a distance the radio waves emitted by PC electronics and the high voltage cathode ray tube (CRT) computer monitors, which led to the design of TEMPEST shielding and the location of PCs inside specially prepared electromagnetic screen rooms, particularly in embassies and other sensitive working spaces.[5] As discussed by Ryan Singel in a *Wired Magazine* article:

> The principal of the TEMPEST attack is deceptively simple. Any machine that processes information — be it a photocopier, an electric typewriter or a laptop —

---

2. Acronym for modulator/demodulator, a device for transmitting data over telephone wires by modulating the data into an audio signal to send it and demodulating an audio signal into data to receive it. dictionary.search.yahoo.com.

3. Cliff Stoll in The Cuckoo's Egg: Tracking a Spy Through the Maze of Computer Espionage, (New York: Pocket, 1995).

4. See Robert Wallace and H. Keith Melton, SPYCRAFT: The Secret History of the CIA's Spytechs from Communism to Al-Qaeda, (New York: Dutton, 2008); and Ronald Kessler, The Secrets of the FBI, (New York: Crown Publishing, 2011).

5. "TEMPEST: A Signal Problem," NSA Cryptologic Spectrum, 1972, available at http://www.nsa.gov/public_info/_files/cryptologic_spectrum/tempest.pdf.

has parts inside that emit electromagnetic and acoustic energy that radiates out, as if they were tiny radio stations. The waves can even be picked up and amplified by nearby power lines, telephone cables and even water pipes, carrying them even further. A sophisticated attacker can capture the right frequency, analyze the data for patterns and recover the raw information the devices were processing or even the private encryption keys inside the machine.[6]

In the late 1980s, the first BOTNETs (robotic networks) began to appear.[7] BOTNETs spread throughout a network in search of vulnerable computers, which they turn into unwitting agents that execute actions at the direction of the BOTNET controller. Infected computers can be programmed to carry out espionage and covert actions. In fact, many of the methods used in cyber intelligence are derived from the methods used in classical human intelligence (HUMINT) operations. BOTNETs recruit agents (vulnerable computers), communicate with them covertly using a variety of data concealment techniques and dead drops (controlled web servers), and command these agents to do various tasks (disseminate messages, steal or corrupt data, etc.). Today there are armies of these "sleeper agents" embedded as malicious software (malware) on infected computers ready to respond to commands from those who enter instructions from their surreptitiously linked command and control centers.

In the 1990s, two other trends emerged: smart phones started incorporating computing capability, and computing devices such as laptops and tablets started incorporating radios for two-way communication with cell phone towers and network routers. Smart phones and tablets, such as the iPad, combine a computer with a cell phone and a wireless internet radio, and are thus subject to a variety of intelligence operations that exploit the devices' computer software, communications, and geospatial characteristics.

As we moved into the 21st century, there was an accelerated trend of using the internet as a universal connection medium, for which the term "Internet of Things" has been coined. There are already stories appearing about smart refrigerators being hacked to send out spam e-mails.[8] From a cyber intelligence standpoint, the Internet of Things provides a larger and more diverse set of targets for recruitment.

Tools, Techniques, and Tradecraft

Tools and techniques refer to the basic building blocks of an intelligence capability, such as malicious web servers that install a wide variety of malware

6. Ryan Singel, "Declassified NSA Document Reveals the Secret History of TEMPEST," *Wired Magazine*, 29 Apr 2008, available at http://www.wired.com/threatlevel/2008/04/nsa-releases-se/.
7. Timothy B. Lee, "How a grad student trying to build the first botnet brought the Internet to its knees," *The Switch/Washington Post*, November 1, 2103, available at http://www.washingtonpost.com/blogs/the-switch/wp/2013/11/01/how-a-grad-student-trying-to-build-the-first-botnet-brought-the-internet-to-its-knees/.
8. *Science News*, United Press International, "Smart refrigerator hacked to send out spam emails," 17 Jan 2014.

on unprotected computer systems. Tradecraft refers to the integrated use of these tools and techniques as part of carefully crafted operations. It is tradecraft that separates a professional intelligence organization from the thousands of hackers that troll the internet looking for people who naively believe that somebody in Nigeria is going to send them a million dollars. The tradecraft used in cyber intelligence operations parallels the tradecraft used in HUMINT operations, but with the use of automated methods to implement the tradecraft.

The HUMINT activities in Table 1 on the next page are taken from Maloy Krishna Dhar's book, *Intelligence Tradecraft*. As can be seen in the table, there are analogous activities in the cyber intelligence realm.[9]

Kim Zetter, writing for *Wired Magazine*, describes one such product called Remote Control System from the Italian firm Hacking Team, which controls software that can be clandestinely installed on a variety of smart phones and computers; the total number of these software agents is not mentioned, but they are controlled from 320 command and control servers located in 40 countries worldwide.

The new components target Android, iOS, Windows Mobile, and BlackBerry users and are part of Hacking Team's larger suite of tools used for targeting desktop computers and laptops. They allow, for example, for covert collection of emails, text messages, call history and address books, and they can be used to log keystrokes and obtain search history data. They can take screenshots, record audio from the phones to monitor calls or ambient conversations, hijack the phone's camera to snap pictures or piggyback on the phone's GPS system to monitor the user's location.[10]

Even the computer hardware can be used for espionage purposes. During the 1980s, the Soviets intercepted a number of electronic typewriters headed to the US Embassy in Moscow and modified their electronics. An NSA report describes the tampering with these systems.

... found that this implant represented a major Soviet technological improvement over their previous efforts. The bug could be rapidly and easily installed by nontechnical personnel; it resisted detection by conventional methods; and it was wireless and remotely controlled. Search by disassembly and visual inspection, when conducted by any but the best trained technicians, would normally be unproductive... The first goal of the GUNMAN Project, to replace all of the electronic equipment in the U.S. embassy in Moscow with signaturized equipment, was a daunting challenge. Electronic equipment included teletype machines, printers, computers, cryptographic devices, and copiers – in short, almost anything that plugged into a wall socket."[11]

---

9. Maloy Krishna Dhar, *Intelligence Tradecraft, Secrets of Spy Warfare*, (New Delhi, India: Manas Publications, 2011); and Joel McNamara, *Secrets of Computer Espionage: Tactics and Countermeasures*, (Indianapolis: Wiley, 2003).
10. Kim Zetter, *Wired Magazine*, 24 Jun 2014, "Researchers Find and Decode the Spy Tools Governments Use to Hijack Phones," available at http://www.wired.com/2014/06/remote-control-system-phone-surveillance/.
11. Sharon Maneki, *Learning from the Enemy: The GUNMAN Project*, 2009, (declassified) Center for Cryptologic History, available at http://www.nsa.gov/public_info/_files/cryptologic_histories/ learning_from_the_enemy.pdf.

TABLE 1. COMPARING HUMINT AND CYBER INTELLIGENCE ACTIVITIES†

HUMINT Activity	Analogous Cyber Intelligence Activity
Spotting and assessing a person	Targeting a computer for malware
Recruiting a source	Spear phishing a computer user
Agent validation (Vetting)	Detection of honeypots
Cover	Useful looking software (with backdoor functions)
Disguise	Benign file names of malware
Sleeper agents	Latent malware on infected computers
Covert communications (COVCOM) to agent	Data hiding for concealment of BOTNET command and control, and data exfiltration
Dead drops	Web servers under BOTNET control
Countersurveillance	Avoiding detection by anti-virus software

† "Spear Phishing" is the practice of sending fraudulent messages to a recipient to deceive him into revealing sensitive information such as personal passwords. A "honeypot" is a computer system on the internet that is expressly set up to attract and trap people who attempt to penetrate other people's computer systems. "Backdoor" refers to a clandestine entry into a computer's software. A "sleeper agent" remains hidden until called to service by his controllers. A "dead drop" is a secret place where spies hide their documents for their controllers to later retrieve.

That was 30 years ago. Today's computer systems are filled with integrated circuits (ICs) from all over the world; a typical PC has a dozen or more microprocessors for computing, graphics, keyboard processing, peripheral interfaces, hard disk controllers, DVD and CD ROM controllers, printer controllers, etc. These ICs are relied upon, or "trusted," to perform their expected actions and no more, but there is some concern about having to trust such chips for critical applications. The Defense Advanced Research Projects Agency (DARPA), the Pentagon's R&D wing, has released details about a three-year initiative it calls the Trust in Integrated Circuits program, to address the concern of backdoor functions being built into commercial chips.[12]

Elements of a Cyber Intelligence Program

The intelligence function is typically described as having a set of functional areas, e.g., collection, covert action, intelligence analysis, and counterintelligence. These areas also apply to cyber intelligence.

Cyber Collection

The tools, techniques, and tradecraft described above can be applied to a collection operation whose goal is the clandestine acquisition of data from a target computer system. James Gosler, former director of the Clandestine Information Technology Office at CIA, wrote:

---

12. Sally Adee, "The Hunt for the Kill Switch," IEEE Spectrum, May 2008.

Intelligence targets are increasingly using computer networks as the repositories for their secrets. As a result, clandestine photography is rapidly yielding to sophisticated technical operations that exploit these networks. ... Clandestine technical collection no longer requires physical proximity to the target. U.S. information systems can be remotely targeted and their secrets collected and exfiltrated to any part of the world.[13]

Many governments have active cyber espionage programs. The Chinese in particular are reported to have a very large and aggressive program of cyber espionage. A recent report by the Mandiant Corporation describes the Chinese cyber espionage organization in detail.[14]

Cyber Covert Action

Cyber intelligence techniques can also be used to support covert actions, such as disinformation, influence operations, election tampering, sabotage, etc. The Russian adventures in Estonia, Georgia, Ukraine, and elsewhere provide examples of disinformation campaigns being conducted with the help of cyber means, such as hacked web sites.

In 2010, the Iranians discovered that their uranium enrichment program was degraded because the centrifuges in their nuclear facility had malfunctioned. It was discovered that the industrial control system that supervised the centrifuges was corrupted by a specially crafted software package that has come to be known as STUXNET.[15]

Election tampering has long been a focus of covert action by many nations. Researchers have noted that many of the electronic voting machines used to tally votes are vulnerable to tampering. As Joseph Stalin might have said, "It's not who votes that counts, it's who counts the votes." A cyber attack against the voting machines, the systems that read the votes from the machines, the systems used to generate or maintain the software, or a network that interconnects the machines could be used to carry out this type of covert action.[16]

Cyber Intelligence Analysis

A cyber intelligence program must have a strong analytic capability, with multiple levels of analysis. In the initial analysis, closest to the collected data,

---

13. James R. Gosler, "The Digital Dimension," in Jennifer Sims and Burton Gerber (eds.). *Transforming U.S. Intelligence* (Washington, DC: Georgetown University Press, 2005).

14. Mandiant Corporation, *APT1: Exposing One of China's Cyber Espionage Units*, 2013, available at *http://intelreport.mandiant.com/*.

15. David Kushner, "The Real Story of STUXNET," *IEEE Spectrum*, March 2013, available at *http://spectrum.ieee.org/telecom/security/the-real-story-of-stuxnet*.

16. Johns Hopkins University. "Electronic Voting System Is Vulnerable To Tampering: Computer Researchers Find Critical Flaws In Popular Software Produced For US Elections." *ScienceDaily*, 28 July 2003. *www.sciencedaily.com/releases/2003/07/030725081820.htm*.

significant processing and analysis is required to make sense of collected data. The collection product tends to be raw files, without the overall design. The same is true for collected data packets from a network; extensive analysis is required to put these into a form for higher levels of analysis.

One aspect of cyber intelligence analysis is the study of vulnerabilities. If you're going to study vulnerabilities, whether for purpose of defending against them or using them offensively, you need a way to organize them. The National Geospatial Intelligence Agency has been pioneering the use of Activity Based Intelligence as a means for conducting cyber intelligence analysis. Geospatial refers to developing information about who or what is, was, or will be, where and when. As NGA Director Letitia Long remarked:

> General Keith Alexander, the head of CYBERCOM and the Director of NSA, has challenged NGA to "visualize" cyber. We have accepted that challenge and are using advanced multi-INT fusion and GEOINT techniques – called activity based intelligence – ABI – to answer the General's call and give CYBER COMMAND deeper insights for their strategic, operational, and tactical planning. We are depicting cyber in the physical domain and connecting the "bits and the bytes" with the "bricks and mortar.[17]

Cyber Counterintelligence

The United States faces a cyber intelligence threat of immense proportions. The defensive (security) community tends to focus on protective features (gates, guards, and guns) and on identifying attackers for prosecution.

On the other hand, counterintelligence focuses on understanding the threat: who are the actors, what are their motivations and methods, and how can proven counterintelligence methods counter these threats. In his book, computer security expert Bruce Schneier presents an excellent methodology for conducting risk assessments using attack trees to model the decision making process of the attacker.[18]

One of the counterintelligence challenges with regard to cyber operations is that of attribution. Often, the details of how an attack occurred can be discovered, but it is difficult to determine who is behind the attack. Given the nature of the internet, where traffic between points A and B can flow through many nodes located in multiple countries, and the presumed end points can be functioning as relays to repackage, process and forward traffic to yet other nodes, it is difficult to state definitively where the commands originated or data ends up.

Weaknesses in tradecraft can be exploited. Reuse of the same methods in multiple operations can be disastrous when breaks into one network can

---

17. Letitia A. Long, Prepared Remarks delivered at INSA Leadership Dinner, April 30, 2013, available at https://www.nga.mil/MediaRoom/ SpeechesRemarks/Pages/INSALeadershipDinner.aspx.
18. Bruce Schneier, *Secrets and Lies: Digital Security in a Networked World* (Indianapolis: Wiley, 2004).

be used to detect and defeat other networks of agents. The technical flaw in the production of one-time pads used by Soviet intelligence in the 1940's was compounded by the fact that these pads were used to report on nearly all Soviet intelligence operations operating in the US at that time. The cryptographic break of this system allowed multiple independent networks of spies to be detected, monitored, and neutralized.[19] One could imagine what would happen if all agents in a given country used the same dead drop, or the same method of communication, or the same disguise, or anything that allows a foreign security service to detect spies via their use of some compromised technique. A similar phenomenon exists in the cyber world. The STUXNET code referred to previously had several variants (e.g., STUXNET, FLAME, DUQU, GAUSS), which have been published by the anti-virus community. If another variant of this code were to show up in the future, it is likely it will be detected quickly.

There is a lot that can be learned from counterintelligence history. During World War II, both the allies and the Germans successfully turned networks of agents against their masters. The British Double Cross operation and its German counterpart provide examples of how networks of agents can be turned.[20] A similar situation exists in the cyber world, in which BOTNETs of automated agents can be turned by a good CI program to deceive the adversary intelligence service.

The Chinese are mounting a massive economic intelligence operation against the US and others. We could examine history to get some ideas for how to counter this espionage. When the Soviets were conducting economic espionage against the US in the 1970s, the Reagan administration responded by using a CI-based covert action program to send a message: We know what you're doing, we don't like it, and we're going to put a stop to it. The FAREWELL case tells how we did this, and it could be applied to the cyber world.[21]

A common mistake by counterintelligence services is to assume that the adversary would operate using the same methods that they use against the adversary. This phenomenon is known as mirroring, viewing the adversary by looking in a mirror at how one's own operations are conducted. In reality, each nation is different in terms of how they conduct intelligence operations due to differences in goals and objectives, available resources, "home turf" advantages, etc. In his book Tower of Secrets, Victor Sheymov provides an example of mirroring in which Soviet counterintelligence spent months looking for electronic bugs in its Beijing embassy, only to discover later that the Chinese were using ancient,

---

19. Nigel West, *Venona: The Greatest Secret of the Cold War* (London: Trafalgar Square March 2001).
20. John C. Masterman, *The Double Cross System*, (New Haven: Yale University Press, 1972); Philippe Ganier-Raymond, *Tangled Web: The Shocking and Still Unsolved Story of One of the Greatest Failures of Allied Espionage During World War II* (New York: Pantheon, 1968).
21. Sergei Kostin and Eric Raynaud, *FAREWELL, The Greatest Spy Story of the Twentieth Century* (Las Vegas: AmazonCrossing, 2011).

but effective, methods involving passive acoustic chambers.[22]

Summary

Cyber intelligence has come a long way since the 1960s and has echoed the evolution of computing and networking technologies. The use of cyber intelligence techniques for clandestine information collection, covert action, and counterintelligence has become commonplace. As the technology world continues to evolve, one can expect the cyber intelligence discipline to keep pace.

SUGGESTED READINGS FOR INSTRUCTORS

A good overall view of the tools and techniques used in cyber operations can be found in Joel McNamara, *Secrets of Computer Espionage: Tactics and Countermeasures* (Indianapolis: Wiley Publishing, 2003).

An excellent overview of HUMINT tradecraft is provided in *Spycraft: The Secret History of the CIA's Spytechs, from Communism to Al-Qaeda* by Robert Wallace and H. Keith Melton, (New York: Plume, 2009).

For an Air Force perspective, in which cyber is viewed in the context of a military conflict, see Jason Healey (ed.), *A Fierce Domain: Conflict in Cyberspace, 1986 to 2012*, (Cyber Conflict Studies Association, 2013) (http://www.cyberconflict.org/blog/2013/7/23/a-fierce-domain-launches.html).

For examples of how cyber can be used to support covert operations, see David E. Sanger, *Confront and Conceal, Obama's Secret Wars and Surprising Use of American Power* (New York: Crown Publishers, 2012).

Doug Price began his career in 1974 as an engineer for NSA's Office of COMSEC Applications Computer Security Division. In 1978, he joined System Development Corporation, where he performed penetration testing, led red team security studies, and designed encryption systems for computer networks. From 1983 until his retirement in 2011, he worked for SPARTA, Inc., developing cyber intelligence tools and techniques. Mr. Price is currently a member of the Board of AFIO.

---

22. Victor Sheymov, *Tower of Secrets, A Real Life Spy Thriller*, (Annapolis: Naval Institute Press, 1993).

GUIDE TO THE STUDY OF INTELLIGENCE

Medical Intelligence

Jonathan D. Clemente, MD

The Beginnings

The intersection of medicine, intelligence, and national security dates from the early days of World War II. Alarmed by the rise of totalitarianism in Europe and Japan in the late 1930s, the intelligence elements in the FBI and the Departments of State, War, and Navy stepped up collection of information on foreign military and political developments. In September 1940, the War Department, desiring a comprehensive military intelligence program, directed the chiefs of each of the Army technical services to establish their own intelligence section. By 1940, the traditional Army technical services, in order of seniority, were the Quartermaster Corps, the Corps of Engineers, the Medical Department, the Ordnance Department, the Signal Corps, and the Chemical Warfare Service. These bureaus were responsible for providing supplies, equipment, training, and service in their particular area of expertise.[1] These "technical intelligence" sections served as clearinghouses for foreign technical information between their branch and the War Department's Military Intelligence Division. At the start of World War II, the Military Intelligence Division (MID) was part of the War Department, General Staff broadly responsible for formulating policy and plans related to Army intelligence activities and coordinating with Naval and Army Air Corps Intelligence and the FBI.

With the threat of war, medical officers in the Army Surgeon General's Preventive Medicine Subdivision were tasked to write about public health in occupied territories for inclusion in an Army field manual on military government. These officers also conducted sanitary surveys of proposed military bases in Newfoundland, Central and South America, and the West Indies deemed

---

1. Bruce W. Bidwell. *History of the Military Intelligence Division, Department of the Army General Staff, 1775-1941* (Frederick, Maryland: University Publications of America, 1986), 305.

essential for Western Hemisphere defense.[2] In June 1941, the US Army Surgeon General established a separate "Medical Intelligence Subdivision."

Like most of the military, the Medical Intelligence Subdivision was unprepared for war in December 1941. But over the next three years, the small staff of medical intelligence physician-analysts contributed the "health and sanitation" chapter for more than 120 Joint Army – Navy Intelligence Studies (JANIS) used for planning Allied military operations.

Initially "medical intelligence" was disseminated to field commanders and military surgeons through a series of Technical Bulletins called TB-MEDs. The typical TB-MED detailed public health and sanitation in a particular country, local medical facilities, medical practitioners, and social services. Each TB-MED included an extensive list of diseases of military significance, other serious diseases likely to affect smaller numbers of troops, and diseases causing high morbidity and mortality among the native population. It concluded with recommendations for public health measures designed to mitigate the impact of disease on military operations. World War II was the first war in American history where the number of combat casualties exceeded those from disease and non-battle injuries.

As the war progressed, the scope of medical intelligence activities expanded. Captured enemy medical equipment and drugs were examined to improve Allied medical care. Enemy medical personnel were interrogated on medical problems within their ranks. Specially briefed medical officers assigned to the Office of Strategic Services (OSS) were tasked with collecting intelligence on German biological warfare plans and capabilities and on medical conditions inside occupied territory. While lines drawn on military maps might have separated the combatants, nothing prevented the spread of deadly wartime diseases, like epidemic louse-borne typhus, across frontlines.

The medical intelligence program rapidly dissipated at the end of the war as part of demobilization, but remained a function of the Army Surgeon General. In 1947, the nascent CIA began producing medical intelligence reports focused on Communist Bloc medical capabilities and research trends. During the Korean War, the US Intelligence Community reorganized scientific and technical intelligence activities to clarify lines of responsibility and avoid unnecessary duplication. On August 14, 1952, Director of Central Intelligence Directive DCID-3/4 codified dividing the scientific and medical intelligence programs into military and civilian spheres.[3]

---

2. The United States secured the rights to these areas from Britain on September 2, 1940, in exchange for fifty mothballed American destroyers.

3. The Armed Services were assigned responsibility for intelligence production on foreign weapon systems and equipment, *military medicine* and biological warfare defense. The CIA was given primary responsibility for intelligence production on foreign basic science research, applied research and development, and *civilian medicine* and public health. Montague, Ludwell Lee. 1992. *General Walter Bedell Smith as Director of Central Intelligence, October 1950-February 1953.* University Park, Pa: Pennsylvania State University Press, pg. 179.

The US Army Medical Intelligence and Information Agency (USAMIIA) carried the weight of the military medical intelligence program. In 1963, DoD intelligence functions, including medical intelligence, were consolidated under the Defense Intelligence Agency (DIA). However, DIA disbanded its Medical Intelligence Division in 1972 as part of the post-Vietnam War reduction in force. The Army Surgeon General resumed primary responsibility for military medical intelligence, In 1979, USAMIIA was relocated from the Forrestal Building in Washington, DC, to Fort Detrick, Maryland. Fort Detrick has deep ties to the military medicine community. From 1943 to 1969, Fort Detrick was the center for US biological warfare research. Historical tenant's organizations include the US Army Medical Materiel Agency and the US Army Medical Research Institute of Infectious Diseases. Today, it hosts the National Center for Medical Intelligence.[4]

Responding to criticism that USAMIIA focused more on "information collection" than "intelligence analysis," Congress briefly eliminated all funding for the agency in 1981. DIA managers appealed to Congress and reached a compromise to re-establish the medical intelligence unit as a tri-service (Army-Navy-Air Force) intelligence activity. In 1982, USAMIIA was renamed the "Armed Forces Medical Intelligence Center" (AFMIC) under executive direction of the Army surgeon general and deputy chief of staff for intelligence. In January 1992, Congress authorized the permanent transfer of AFMIC to DIA.[5] AFMIC prepared intelligence assessments and forecasts on foreign military and civilian medical systems, infectious disease and environmental health risks, and biomedical research. These informed military planners and national security policymakers of health risks and foreign health-care capabilities before deploying US forces overseas.[6]

Throughout the 1990s, there was growing concern among senior US leaders over global infectious diseases. The spread of infectious disease was facilitated by a dramatic rise in drug-resistant organisms, a lag in development of antibiotics, environmental degradation, insufficient healthcare infrastructure in developing areas, and the ease of international travel.

The September 11, 2001 attacks and anthrax attacks a month later heightened fears that infectious diseases could be weaponized. These events reaffirmed the role that medical intelligence could play in safeguarding the nation's health by identifying potential man-made biological threats, but also by providing early warning of naturally occurring foreign diseases from

---

4. Schumeyer, Gerard [COL/USA].. "Medical Intelligence ... Making a Difference." *American Intelligence Journal*, 17 (1&2), 1996, 11-15.

5. *Ibid*, Schumeyer.

6. Colonel Anthony M. Rizzo, director, National Center for Medical Intelligence: "Meeting Emerging and Constantly Changing Health Threats with a Central Point of Information and Intelligence," *Military Medical/CBRN Technology* 12(5), August 2008, http://www.military-medical-technology.com/mmt-archives/24-mmt-2008-volume-12-issue-5/146-national-center-for-medical-intelligence.html, accessed 4 August 2013.

imported food, livestock, immigrants, and returning US troops.

September 11th led to sweeping changes in the US Intelligence Community (IC), including the creation of a director of national intelligence. Within days of the attack, the Department of Homeland Security (DHS) was established to coordinate a comprehensive strategy to protect the country from a variety of threats and develop an effective response to attacks and natural disasters. In 2006, AFMIC expanded its support to homeland security by providing intelligence assessments in areas of biological terrorism, biological warfare, counterterrorism, and counterproliferation.[7]

On July 2, 2008, the AFMIC was designated the National Center for Medical Intelligence (NCMI), to reflect the organization's wider audience to include those in the White House, Department of State, DHS, other domestic customers, and foreign partners.[8] Presently, the NCMI serves as the lead Department of Defense (DoD) activity for the production of medical intelligence responsible for coordinating and preparing "integrated, all-source intelligence for the Department of Defense and other government and international organizations on foreign health threats and other medical issues to protect U.S. interests worldwide."[9]

Teaching about the role of medical intelligence

Historically, warfighters and national security policymakers have used finished medical intelligence at the strategic, operational, and tactical levels of war. At the strategic level, the objective of medical intelligence is to identify broad trends in foreign military and civilian biomedical research and development that could present a threat to national security, such as life science technologies that can be used for either legitimate medical purposes or bioterrorism. While medical intelligence analysis has focused on traditional nation-state adversaries such as China, North Korea, Russia, and Iran, highly capable non-state and sub-state actors, such as Hizballah, play a key role in public health in developing areas. Transnational terrorism poses a persistent threat to American national security. In particular, the medical threat from terrorists' use of low-tech weaponry such as so-called radiological "dirty bombs" must be properly understood.

At the operational and tactical level, the objective of medical intelligence is to detect threats to deployed personnel from infectious diseases, environmen-

---

7. Rizzo, *ibid.*
8. "AFMIC Expands Mission," *DIAA Log*, November 2008. *http://www.diaalumni.org/images/DIAA_Nov08_Log2.pdf*, accessed 4 August 2013. Foreign partners include NATO, UK, Canada, and Australia.
9. DoD Instruction 6420.01, March 20, 2009, National Center for Medical Intelligence (NCMI), *http://www.dtic.mil/whs/directives/corres/pdf/642001p.pdf*, accessed 4 August 2004. Joshua Michaud, "National Center for Medical Intelligence," in Katz, Rebecca, and Raymond A. Zilinskas.. *Encyclopedia of Bioterrorism Defense* (Oxford: Wiley-Blackwell, 2011).

tal hazards, biowarfare agents, and food and animal borne diseases. Military personnel and aid workers serve overseas in areas where often they have little, if any, natural immunity to endemic diseases like malaria or dengue fever. Stability operations require a high degree of cultural and social interaction, such as sharing of food, lodging, and recreational facilities for extended periods of time, which increases the exposure to diseases. Such operations frequently occur in areas with significantly degraded public health infrastructure, poor sanitation, and general civil unrest; factors that increase the likelihood of the outbreak of communicable disease. Medical countermeasures can be taken at an early stage to conserve the health of friendly forces and non-combatants.

Through identification and characterization of select highly virulent biological agents and toxins, and of foreign facilities and personnel capable of handling and modifying those agents, medical intelligence analysis can help assure that such potential biowarfare agents are not accidentally released or transferred to unlicensed facilities or hostile non-state actors. Analysis of foreign medical capabilities informs military planners of the levels of host nation support, and optimal locations to construct medical facilities. Careful analysis can identify critical vulnerabilities in an adversary's medical supply chain, important medical causes of combat ineffectiveness among enemy troops, and diminished operational readiness.

One approach to studying medical intelligence is to examine the role of each of the current major organizational divisions of the National Center for Medical Intelligence.

The NCMI has four major divisions: Infectious Disease, Environmental Health, Global Health Systems, and Medical Science and Technology. Its staff of approximately 150 personnel (including analysts on-site from other federal agencies such as the National Security Agency and National Geospatial-Intelligence Agency) has substantial expertise in a wide range of biomedical, public health, and engineering related fields.

NCMI's Infectious Disease Division forecasts, tracks, and analyzes the occurrence of infectious diseases with high pandemic potential, such as the 2009 H1N1 influenza pandemic, highly pathogenic H5N1 avian influenza, and the endemic infectious diseases of every country in the world. Baseline data on endemic diseases helps identify the emergence of naturally occurring pathogens and to distinguish them from biological terrorism. Infectious *Disease Risk Assessments* utilize "a unique methodology that estimates disease risk in terms of its operational impact, including realistic projections of potential days lost on deployments in the absence of appropriate countermeasures."[10]

NCMI collaborates on strategic bio-surveillance with the Centers for Disease Control and Prevention (CDC), DHS, and other federal agencies to share data and analyses regarding possible biological events that could threaten

---

10. Michaud, *ibid.*

national security. NCMI's access to multiple sources of classified intelligence is significant since some foreign governments do not report accurate public health data to the press or international health organizations. An April 2009 NCMI intelligence assessment predicted the pandemic potential of H1N1 two months prior to the official declaration by the World Health Organization (WHO) and the CDC.[11] According to one analyst, this assessment "brought valuable planning time and 'thinking space' to the US authorities well before the WHO announced its pandemic ratings."[12] National security policymakers are concerned over the impact of climate change on worldwide infectious disease rates in the developing world. Warmer temperatures can lead to the spread of insect-borne infectious diseases in susceptible populations. The public health infrastructure in impoverished areas is often inadequate to detect disease outbreaks early. A serious outbreak of disease in such an area could quickly overwhelm the local government and result in destabilizing mass migrations across international borders.[13]

NCMI's Environmental Health Division assesses environmental risks to military health readiness from air, water, soil, and food contamination in an area of operation. The division analyzes industrial chemical facility hazards, long-term forecasts on trends in foreign environmental health, and prepares "predictive hazard area models" detailing the possible effects of a large-scale release of toxic chemicals or radioactive material.[14] During disaster relief operations, the division has prepared spot assessments of emerging environmental threats to aid workers such as from particulate matter, asbestos, or volcanic ash. NCMI has studied the threat of chlorine gas in improvised explosive devices in Iraq and potential radiation exposure hazards to military personnel from North Korea's nuclear testing.[15]

NCMI's Global Health Systems Division evaluates the medical capabilities of countries around the world. It maintains the DoD database on foreign military and civilian medical infrastructures including all medical facilities, laboratories, blood banks, and pharmaceutical plants.[16] Such information is used to recommend suitable medical facilities to treat US personnel deployed overseas in emergency situations or to assist military planners in avoiding collateral damage to medical sites. *Medical Capabilities Assessments* help determine

11. Cheryl Pellerin, "Medical Intelligence Center Monitors Health Threats," *Armed Forces Press Service*, 10 October 2012, *http://www.defense.gov/news/newsarticle.aspx?id=118163*, accessed 4 August 2013.

12. Miller D. "The US Defense Intelligence Agency's National Center for Medical Intelligence," *Journal of the Royal Naval Medical Service*. 95 (2), 2009, 89-91.

13. Jessica Q. Chen, "Climate change reveals disease as a national security threat," *The Washington Post*, January 30, 2011, Section, A03; Jessica Q. Chen, *http://www.washingtonpost.com*, accessed 4 August 2013.

14. *Op Cit.*, Michaud; *Op. Cit.*, Damien K.

15. Peter Buxbaum, "Military medical intelligence center gets a new name," *Government Health/IT News*, 7 July 2008, *http://www.govhealthit.com/news/military-medical-intelligence-center-gets-new-name*, accessed 5 August 2013.

16. Pellerin, *Op. Cit.*.

the combat readiness of foreign armies, the ability of host nations to support deployed US troops, and existing medical infrastructure that might be used in disaster or humanitarian relief operations.[17] This type of medical intelligence has implications for 'strategic warning' because it considers key logistical preparations for combat operations. Foreign armies preparing for war need to mobilize their medical support system and this may provide a specific warning of impending offensive operations.

NCMI's Medical Science and Technology Division examines foreign civilian and military biomedical research and development, including human performance modification, vaccinations, drugs, and emerging threats from bio-engineered disease-causing microbes, naturally occurring emerging infectious diseases, and drug-resistant pathogens. Identifying the medical threat posed by foreign weapons systems facilitates the development of suitable countermeasures. The study of foreign medical countermeasures against nuclear, chemical, and biological agents may provide information on adversary intentions.[18] If a foreign military begins inoculating its soldiers against a specific infectious agent, it could indicate that they are developing a biological warfare capability, planning an attack against a country that already possesses that capability, or merely addressing a legitimate public health concern. Assessments of baseline capabilities and biomedical R&D trends may help discern between these alternatives.

Conclusions

The National Center for Medical Intelligence "provides timely warning and projection of significant infectious disease and environmental health risks to U.S. personnel abroad and within the United States; analysis of foreign developments in life science technology and countermeasure development; and analysis on health trends, foreign health diplomacy, military and civilian health system capabilities, and biosafety and biosecurity policies."[19] As demonstrated by the 2003 SARS outbreak, the 2009 influenza pandemic, and the spread of multi-drug resistant tuberculosis, infectious diseases are not constrained by international borders. Left unchecked, such outbreaks can spread rapidly across the globe with significant adverse impact on economic and social stability. With its unique mission, NCMI produces biomedical and environmental related assessments that are critical to military force and homeland health protection.

Instructors teaching about medical intelligence may ask their students to consider how various public health, environmental, and social factors

---

17. Michaud, *Op. Cit.*. The Medical Capabilities Assessments are the descendants of the World War II Technical Bulletin-Medical series.
18. Michaud, *Op. Cit.*.
19. DoD Directive 6490.02E, Comprehensive Health Surveillance, 8 February 2012, *http://www.dtic.mil/whs/directives/corres/pdf/649002e.pdf*, accessed 4 August 2013

might impact military operations, disaster relief, or broader national security interests.

READINGS FOR INSTRUCTORS

The literature on the role and mission of medical intelligence is unfortunately scant. Study of the subject should begin with the US Army Medical Department's official history of medical intelligence during World War II written by the Division's wartime chief, Dr. Gaylord Anderson. (in US Army Medical Department, *Preventive Medicine in World War II*, Volume IX, Special Fields, Chapter V, "Medical Intelligence," Washington, DC: Department of the Army, Office of the Surgeon General, 1969.) Although dense, the chapter provides an exceptional overview of the conceptual origins and early development of the US medical intelligence program in response to the wartime demands of the first truly global conflict. For a ground-level view of medical intelligence activities during World War II, see Henze, Carlo. "Recollections of a Medical Intelligence Officer in World War II." *Bulletin of the New York Academy of Medicine* 49.(11), Nov 1973, 960-973; or Jarcho., Saul. "Historical Perspectives of Medical Intelligence" *Bulletin of the New York Academy of Medicine* 67 (5), Sep-Oct 1991, 501-506.

For a discussion of the post-war organization of US medical intelligence and an historical overview of the role of medical intelligence at the strategic, operational, and tactical levels during the Cold War, the reader is referred to my own article: Clemente, Jonathan D. "The Fate of an Orphan: The Hawley Board and the Debates over the Postwar Organization of Medical Intelligence," *Intelligence and National Security* 20 (2), Jun. 2005, 264-287.

Several declassified articles from the CIA's in-house journal, Studies in Intelligence, discuss aspects of medical and life science support to the IC. These are available on the CIA website at *https://www.cia.gov/library/center-for-the-study-of-intelligence/kent-csi*.

Carey, Warren F. and Myles Maxfield, "Intelligence Implications of Disease," *Studies in Intelligence* 16 (2), Spring 1972,71-78) illustrates the problems of monitoring the public health situation in denied areas.

Petro, James B. "Intelligence Support to the Life Science Community: Mitigating Threats from Bioterrorism," *Studies in Intelligence* 48 (3), 2004,57-68).

Former AFMIC health analyst Denis C. Kaufman has written an insightful analysis of the role and mission of medical intelligence from the perspective of the late 1990s: *Medical Intelligence: A Theater Engagement Tool*. Report No. A360983. (Carlisle Barracks, PA: US Army War College), 21 Feb. 2001, *http://www.dtic.mil/dtic/tr/fulltext/u2/a389063.pdf*, accessed 6 August 2013.

For a broad view of the national security implications of global disease see: Johnson, Loch K. *Bombs, Bugs, Drugs, and Thugs: Intelligence and America's Quest for Security* (New York, London: New York University Press, 2002).

For a discussion of the role of medical intelligence in the 1982 "Yellow Rain" controversy – the allegations that the former Soviet Union used tricothecene mycotoxins as a biological weapon in Laos and Afghanistan see:

Barton, Rod. *The Weapons Detective: The Inside Story of Australia's Top Weapons*

Inspector. (Melbourne: Black Inc. Agenda, 2006).

Pribbenow, Merle L. "'Yellow Rain': Lessons from an Earlier WMD Controversy" *International Journal of Intelligence and CounterIntelligence.* 19 (4), 2006, 737-745.

A number of National Intelligence Council assessments dealing with global health issues can be found on The Office of the Director of National Intelligence (ODNI) website *http://www.dni.gov/index.php/about/organization/national-intelligence-council-nic-publications,* including:

Global Trends 2030: Alternative Worlds

2008: Strategic Implications of Global Health

2003: SARS: Down But Still a Threat

2002: The Next Wave of HIV/AIDS: Nigeria, Ethiopia, Russia, India, and China

2000: The Global Infectious Disease Threat and Its Implications for the United States

Examples of declassified AFMIC medical intelligence assessments, such as "Health Services Assessment: Iraq, March 2002," can be found on DIA's FOIA Electronic Reading Room, *http://www.dia.mil/public-affairs/foia/reading-room/.*

Examples of more recent unclassified NCMI assessments such as "Worldwide: New 2009-H1N1 Influenza Virus Poses Potential Threat to U.S. Forces," 1 May 2009, can be found posted on *http://www.globalsecurity.org.*

An example of an unclassified NCMI Environmental Health Risk Assessment "Haiti: Environmental Health Risk," 14 January 2010, can be found at *http://www.med.navy.mil/sites/nmcp/Clinics/nepmu2/Documents/DIA%20Haiti_Environmental%20Health%20Risk.pdf.*

Examples of AFMIC-era Medical Capabilities Studies for Iran and the former Soviet Union can be found on the Digital National Security Archive Collection, The U.S. intelligence community organization, operations and management, 1947-1989. *http://nsarchive.chadwyck.com.* The DNSA is a paid electronic database available through many academic libraries.

Jonathan D. Clemente, M.D., is a physician in Charlotte, North Carolina. He serves as vice chief of the Carolinas Medical Center Department of Radiology and has a faculty appointment with the University of North Carolina – Chapel Hill School of Medicine. He is writing a scholarly history of medical and psychological support for the US Intelligence Community and a history of the US medical intelligence program from World War II to the present.

GUIDE TO THE STUDY OF INTELLIGENCE

Intelligence Analysis

A Guide to its Study

Mark Lowenthal, PhD

"It is very difficult to make predictions, especially about the future."
—Lawrence Peter ("Yogi") Berra

The first intelligence analyst was probably the caveman from one cave who came back and gave an assessment of the strength of a neighboring cave: how many warriors, what weapons (rocks, clubs, spears) they had, how many women, and the nature of the intervening terrain. He was then asked for an assessment of either the success of an attack by his clan, or the likelihood of the other clan attacking. The means of collection and the scope of the problem were limited but the question was life or death in nature.

Analysis is the most important aspect of intelligence: providing assessed judgments to policy makers that they can use to help them make decisions. Every other part of intelligence feeds into analysis, even operations. (The reverse flow, from analysis to operations, is also true, but operations are less frequent than the daily output of analysis.) Wise policymakers understand that they cannot know all of the possible outcomes of the decisions they face. Intelligence analysis serves to bound their uncertainty, to give policymakers a better sense of what might or might not happen, based on known conditions, the actors involved, and the decisions made. It is important to understand that "bounding uncertainty" is not the same as telling someone what will happen. If one looked at a verbal scale of probability, the opposite ends would be "Always" and "Never." These two conditions are of no interest to intelligence analysts. After all, if we know with certainty that something will or will not happen, why do we need analysts? We do not. Analysts live and work further in from those two poles. As the National Intelligence Council explains it, the boundaries are "Remote" and "Almost Certainly." This discussion of likelihood can now be found in every National Intelligence Estimate (NIE), each of which includes a page entitled, "What We Mean When We Say: An Explanation of Estimative Language."[1]

Analysis is difficult for several reasons. First, it is about human beings who act and react for a variety of reasons, some of which may appear irrational (to the observer). Humans can always change direction as well. Second, every state seeks to keep secret some of what it does, what it has, what it lacks, and what it plans from other states. Secrets are the essence of intelligence: trying to discern these hidden factors. If we are lucky, good collection may reveal what we want to know. In many cases, however, collection is incomplete or inconclusive and analysts must work from fragments, some of which are contradictory, in order to assess what is going on or is likely to happen. It is important here to distinguish between secrets and mysteries. Secrets are known but hidden: someone somewhere knows what is happening at the Iran nuclear facility at Natanz. Our goal is to find that person. Mysteries may or may not be knowable: who built Stonehenge? Intelligence is in the business of discovering secrets, not solving mysteries.

Analysis is not about predictions, that is, something that can be foreseen. Intelligence is about estimates: a more tentative judgment based on varying degrees of intelligence, not all of which is equally reliable – indeed, the reliability of some of it may not be known at all. Conveying this to a policymaker can be very difficult because the language that is used is often conditional or hedged. Here a gulf develops: analysts write this way to convey the limits of what is known reliably but policy makers sometimes see this as analysts being pusillanimous. The best way to avoid this gulf is for analysts to explain to policymakers, preferably at the outset of their relationship, the nature of what they do and how they express themselves.

It is also important to understand that intelligence collection is an imperfect process and will rarely be able to provide analysts with everything they need to know. Therefore, analysts are trained to extrapolate what they do not know from what they do know, as the Duke of Wellington once put it.[2] This becomes another reason for the imperfection of analysis.

Analysis is also an open-ended process in that most of the issues being addressed do not have closure. This is a major difference between intelligence analysis and scientific research or legal proceedings. Experiments have conclusions, they either work or they do not. Court cases have verdicts. But intelli-

---

1. See, for example, "Prospects for Iraq's Stability: A Challenging Road Ahead," January 2007, p. 5, at http://www.dni.gov/press_releases/20070202_release.pdf.
2. Among the places where this quote is cited is the UK Defence Ministry website (http://www.mod.uk/DefenceInternet/AboutDefence/People/Speeches/MinAF/20110110TransformingDefence.htm), in this case citing a speech by Armed Forces Minister Nick Harvey, MP, January 10, 2011. The original citation is apparently in remarks the Duke of Wellington made to John Croker and is quoted in Louis J. Jennings (ed.), The Croker Papers: The Correspondence and Diaries of the Late Right Honourable John Wilson Croker, LL.Dm F.R.S, Secretary of the Admiralty from 1809 to 1830 (1884), Vol.III, 276.

gence issues continue. They may morph – the Soviet Union collapses but then we worry about Russian stability – but they do not end. This makes it more difficult to judge how well analysis is doing because we may have indications on a short-term basis but we are less likely to see it on a strategic basis. The Soviet Union is a perfect example. From 1946 on, the US was committed to the "containment" policy, containing Soviet expansion until they either relented or collapsed. Intelligence analysis had both successes and failures against the Soviet Union, but almost no way to judge whether the goals of containment were actually being met – until they collapsed.

A central issue in analysis is the question of how right, how often, on which issues. Clearly, analysis cannot be correct all of the time. Indeed, there is no number or batting average that can be given. Much depends on the nature of the question being asked. If it is a straightforward or fairly factual question (how many strategic missiles does Russia have, with what number of warheads) then analysis should be correct most of the time. But if it is a more complex, more far-reaching question (what is Kim Jongil likely to do next), then the error rate will go up. Regrettably, in the aftermath of 9/11 and the Iraq weapons of mass destruction (WMD) estimate, there seems to be a growing expectation that intelligence can and should be correct most of the time – if they just work harder and share more, then the answer will be there. This is, from an analyst's point of view, unrealistic and places an added burden on the analysts. Indeed, it may have the perverse effect of making analysts gun shy and hedging their analysis more than they normally would.

In pursuit of this goal of increased accuracy, we have seen both the Intelligence Community (IC) and Congress fiddle with various issues, primarily improved intelligence sharing and an emphasis on more alternative analyses. But they have not made any changes that are likely to improve substantially the IC's "batting average" because that goal is much more elusive and is probably not responsive to reforms imposed from without, if it is responsive at all.

Nothing underscores this mindset of expectations more than the insidious and wholly inapt and demeaning phrase, "connecting the dots." Nothing could be further from the reality of analysis. In "connect the dots," the child only gets the dots he needs – no extra dots, no missing dots. And they are numbered and there are drawings within the dots to help discern the overall picture. In reality, analysts are asked to make coherent patterns from constantly shifting pieces of information, a much more difficult task.

All sorts of interesting intellectual traps can creep into analysis and it is the job of the analysts and the supervisors to be alert to them and to weed them out mercilessly. Some of the more common ones are:

Mirror-imaging: assuming that the actor or state being analyzed reacts in the same way as the analyst or his state would. ("They're just like us," is a typical formulation.)

Premature closure: leaping on the first hypothesis as the correct answer and failing to probe for other hypotheses that might also be plausible.

Groupthink: everyone agreeing to conclusions for social reasons, not analytical ones.

Mindsets: fitting new intelligence into already formed conclusions.

Another recurring critique has been that intelligence analysis has showed a lack of imagination or is risk averse. The sub-text here is quite consistent with other critiques: if the analysts only think hard enough, long enough, and inventively enough, they should come up with more accurate analysis. Certainly, we want analysts to be imaginative, to think of alternative outcomes. But we do not want them to give equal credence to every possible outcome or to create laundry lists of outcomes. After all, policymakers can do that for themselves. Indeed, what the policymakers look to the intelligence analysts to do is winnow down the laundry list of possible outcomes, to indicate which ones are more or less likely. Also, there is – or should be – a *quid pro quo* here as well: if we want analysts to be imaginative and to take risks in their analysis, then we have to give them the right to be wrong some of the time. We cannot ask the analysts to be imaginative and correct all of the time. Also, no amount of more imaginative analysis will eliminate all intelligence surprise. For example, there is no reason to expect that any analyst could have posited that the self-immolation of a Tunisian fruit seller would ignite revolts across the Arab world. The intellectual model for US intelligence analysis is "competitive analysis." This means that we want to bring to bear many different analysts with many different skill sets and many different backgrounds on a given issue. The assumption is that this will foster a more rigorous debate about the intelligence and is more likely to reveal areas of disagreement – which can be crucial for the analysts and the policy makers. Competitive analysis also imposes certain costs. The most obvious one is that it requires a larger analytic cadre, many of whom may be writing about the same issues as analysts in other agencies. This can appear to an outsider to be redundancy but there is no other way to foster competitive analysis. Another cost is the possibility that, as analysts argue about differing views on an issue, there may be an occasional tendency to accept "lowest common denominator" analysis, that is, to find intellectual mid-points in arguments and settle on that rather than continue to fight it out. This is obviously unsatisfactory intellectually and in terms of the utility of the analysis itself. The fact that analysis is competitive also means that there are winners and losers in the analytic process. Some analysts' careers prosper as their papers go forward and other's careers do not because their views did not prevail.

One of the bedrock rules of intelligence in the US (and among our Commonwealth partners) is that intelligence does not make policy. What this means is that intelligence will go through all of the plusses and minuses of a given situation or of a potential decision but they will not then offer which choice to make. This rule exists for two reasons. First, the government belongs to the policymakers – elected officials and their appointees. Intelligence is a service. Second, this rule helps intelligence preserve its objectivity – a crucial attribute. If intelligence officers make policy recommendations, they may then be tempted to produce new analysis that supports the wisdom of their advice. Even though intelligence analysts may be concerned about the outcome, by eschewing an advisory role, they can maintain their professional objectivity.

This leads us to the issue of politicization, the cardinal sin for all analysts. Simply put, politicization is writing analysis to please the reader, regardless of the variance from sound analysis. Politicization can happen in one of two ways: policymakers can order it; or analysts will do it either wittingly or not simply to please or appease policymakers. Either way it is wrong. Intelligence analysts spend a great deal of time being alert for and worrying about politicization, but it does not appear to occur that often.

It is crucial to remember that intelligence analysis is an intellectual process. We can establish rules and standards, we can try out new analytic tools and methodologies. But it all comes down to knowledgeable analysts thinking interesting thoughts that they can express clearly in writing. For example, at the behest of Congress, the Office of the Director of National Intelligence came up with a set of Standards of Analytic Tradecraft. The first seven are all reasonable standards, but following each of them to the letter will not automatically lead the analyst to the eighth standard: "Accurate judgments; assessments." Intelligence analysis is not a recipe or a construction manual that will produce the same result each time. We seem to have lost any appreciation for the sheer difficulty of coming up with correct analytic judgments on challenging issues on a consistent basis.

READINGS FOR INSTRUCTORS

What should one read to become more conversant with the key issues in intelligence analysis? The list of available books and articles is long and growing. Here are a few that I have found most useful.

Roger George and James Bruce, two veteran analysts, edited *Analyzing Intelligence: Origins, Obstacles and Innovations* (Georgetown University Press, 2008), which covers the entire range of analytical issues in articles written by seasoned intelligence and policy veterans.

Richards Heuer's *The Psychology of Intelligence Analysis* (Central Intelligence Agency: Center for the Study of Intelligence, 1999), available at *https://www.cia.gov/library/center-for-the-study-of-intelligence/csi-publications/books-and-monographs/index.html* is a now classic treatment of the various intellectual traps and pitfalls that can bedevil analysts.

An insight into how intelligence professional view some of their problems can be found in *A Tradecraft Primer: Structural Analytic Techniques for Improving Intelligence Analysis*, (Central Intelligence Agency: March 2009), at *https://www.cia.gov/library/center-for-the-study-of-intelligence/csi-publications/books-and-monographs/Tradecraft%20Primer-apr09.pdf*.

Robert Jervis, an academic who was written extensively on analysis, has written *Why Intelligence Fails* (Cornell University Press, 2010), which looks at two key analytic cases: Iran's 1978 revolution and Iraqi WMD.

Finally, my own *Intelligence: From Secrets to Policy* (CQ Press, 2009, 4th edition) deals with a range of analytical issues and also devotes attention to the importance of the policy maker in the analytical process.

Dr. Mark Lowenthal is the president and CEO of the Intelligence & Security Academy and has served as the assistant director of central intelligence for analysis and production; vice chairman for evaluation on the National Intelligence Council; staff director of the House Permanent Select Committee on Intelligence; office director and a deputy assistant secretary of state in the State Department Bureau of Intelligence and Research (INR); and senior specialist in US foreign policy at the Library of Congress Congressional Research Service. He has written five books and over 90 articles or studies on intelligence and national security issues. Dr. Lowenthal received his BA from Brooklyn College and his PhD in history from Harvard University. From 1993 to 2007, he was an adjunct professor at Columbia University. He is an adjunct professor at the Johns Hopkins University. In 2005, Dr. Lowenthal was awarded the National Intelligence Distinguished Service Medal. In 1988, he was the Grand Champion on *Jeopardy!*, the television quiz show.

GUIDE TO THE STUDY OF INTELLIGENCE

A Guide to All-Source Analysis

Thomas Fingar, PhD

The meaning of "all-source analysis" has evolved over time in ways that reflect important changes in the way the Intelligence Community (IC) operates and analysts perform their jobs. Books and articles on intelligence written more than a few years ago often drew a distinction between "all-source analysis," which integrated information from multiple types of sources (such as human intelligence or HUMINT and signals intelligence or SIGINT), and analysis that utilized or focused on a single type of information (such as imagery or IMINT).

This now-outmoded typology was intended to distinguish between specialists with particular expertise in interpreting photographs, discovering the true meaning of words used in deliberately obscured communications (for example, use of "wedding" as a substitute for "terrorist attack"), and other "technical" specialties, and analysts who worked on complicated problems and puzzles requiring the integration of many types of information. Unfortunately, the distinction often was conflated in ways that implied status differences akin to those between blue – and white-collar workers. These status differences sometimes were applied to agencies as well as individual analysts. Thus, for example, the Central Intelligence Agency (CIA), the Defense Intelligence Agency (DIA), and the State Department's Bureau of Intelligence and Research (INR) were described as all-source analytic agencies; the National Security Agency (NSA) and the National Geospatial Intelligence Agency (NGA) were characterized as single-source or single-INT agencies.[1]

The distinction was never as clear in practice as it was in the typology, but

---

1. See, for example, Mark M. Lowenthal, *Intelligence: From Secrets to Policy, Fourth Edition (Washington, DC: CQ Press, 2009), 38, 125, 139;* and Richard L. Russell, "*Achieving All-Source Fusion in the Intelligence Community*" in Loch K. Johnson (ed.), *Handbook of Intelligence (New York: Routledge, 2009), 189-198.*

to the extent that it actually had an impact on the way the IC operates, it impeded the ability of analysts (and sometimes entire agencies) to access certain types of information and to integrate insights from multiple intelligence disciplines. It was, in effect, a situation that sometimes compelled analysts to work difficult problems without being able to collaborate with counterparts in other agencies. That was never desirable, and good analysts and responsible managers often found ways to overcome the inherent strictures of the distinction. But in the fast-paced, information-rich, and highly demanding environment of the 21st century, sharing information and capturing the insights of informed colleagues cannot be a function of individual initiative and creative workarounds.[2]

The potential perils of bureaucratic and behavioral impediments to information sharing, all-source analysis, and collaboration among analysts with complementary skills were tragically revealed by the events of September 11, 2001 and the 9/11 Commission's post-mortem analysis.[3] Few consequences of failure to access and incorporate information from all available sources will be as dramatic or tragic as were the events of 9/11, but the purpose of intelligence analysis is to help decisionmakers anticipate, understand, and manage developments with the potential to affect the security of our nation, the safety of or citizens, and the interests of our country. They deserve and demand nothing less than the best possible analytic support. That, in turn, requires tapping all available sources of information, integrating the insights of numerous specialists, and applying high standards of analytic tradecraft.

The 2004 Intelligence Reform and Terrorism Prevention Act was designed, among other goals, to break down obstacles to information sharing and to facilitate collaboration and "all-source analysis" of the wide and expanding range of national security issues.[4] To meet the challenges of the 21st century, we can no longer tolerate false distinctions between "all-source" and "single-INT" analysts or agencies. Stated another way, providing high-quality analysis and enhancing policymaker understanding of complex developments require utilizing all types of information and the insights of everyone who can contribute. Information sharing and collaboration are now essential attributes of intelligence analysis. For example, imagery analysts need (and have) access to SIGINT and HUMINT that could help them to determine the purpose of a construction project. Diplomatic reporting and SIGINT are useful to determine the veracity or biases of a clandestine HUMINT source. Freely available unclassified materials (open source intelligence or OSINT) provides context

---

2. For more on what is expected of the IC, see Thomas Fingar, Reducing Uncertainty: Intelligence Analysis and National Security (Stanford, CA: Stanford University Press, 2011), chapters 1-2.

3. The National Commission on Terrorist Attacks upon the United States, The 9/11 Commission Report (Washington, DC: US Government Printing Office, 2004); and Amy Zegart, Spying Blind: The CIA, the FBI, and the Origins of 9/11 (Princeton, NJ: Princeton University Press, 2007).

4. See Intelligence Reform and Terrorism Prevention Act of 2004, Public Law 108-458—Dec. 17, 2004, Sec 102(b) at http://www.dni.gov/history.htm.

for all kinds of other reporting. In other words, all analysts are—and must be—all-source analysts.

All-source analysis entails more than simply making more intelligence available to more analysts. Probably the most important attribute is the systematic way that it utilizes information from multiple and varied sources to assess, interpret, and explain a development, discovery, or policy conundrum. Step one is to identify or define what it is that needs to be explained. Unless an analytic challenge is defined with reasonable precision, it is impossible to know what kinds of information might help to clarify what has occurred, why it happened, where developments appear to be headed, and other critical dimensions of the problem. Stated another way, unless one can specify with reasonable precision what needs to be explained, it is hard to know where to look for answers or what types of information and expertise might be most helpful. Simply amassing information on the assumption that "the answer must be in there somewhere" is seldom an effective strategy and can be highly counterproductive.

Defining and redefining the core question is often an iterative process but the ideal starting point should be, "What question, if it can be answered, will provide the most useful insight into the phenomenon being studied?" This will typically be followed by subsequent questions such as, "What kinds of information are most likely to help me to answer the core question?" and "Where might I obtain that kind of information?" Some core questions can be answered using publicly available information (OSINT), others can best be addressed using IMINT or SIGINT. Most analysts prefer to have multiple sources that can be used to corroborate or raise questions about what has been reported or revealed by other sources. Generally speaking, one can have higher confidence in information that comes from multiple sources and/or types of sources but, as every analyst must learn, sometimes information truly is "too good to be true" because its purpose is to mislead. This is what is known in the intelligence business as disinformation. Distinguishing disinformation from reliable intelligence requires both skill and familiarity with the characteristics of individual types of sources and how the same or related information is reflected in other sources.

Refining the key question to be examined benefits from, and often requires, obtaining and integrating information from colleagues who are familiar with the subject matter but may—and preferably do—approach the subject from different directions and utilize different types of information. The structure of the US IC—16 agencies plus the Office of the Director of National Intelligence supporting dozens of bureaucratic organizations and missions and hundreds of customers—assures the existence of multiple perspectives on almost every issue.[5] Although it makes for untidy organization charts and

---

5. For more information, see Thomas Fingar, "Analysis in the U.S. Intelligence Community: Missions,

invites suspicion and accusations of duplication of effort, the structure of the IC creates strengths as well as weaknesses. The primary reason for the existence of multiple agencies is to optimize abilities to support specific missions and customers. One-size-fits-all intelligence is not very useful to anyone; to be useful, intelligence must be tailored to the needs of specific customers. Simply put, the secretary of state requires different types of intelligence and intelligence support than do the secretary of defense, the attorney general, or the commander of US Forces in Korea.

Each agency has assembled people with different types of expertise and trained them to focus on using what they know and what they can discover to support the missions of their primary customers. The result is a considerable amount of complementary expertise and independently developed analyses that can be integrated to achieve more holistic understanding of difficult problems. The structure and different missions also facilitate specialization and divisions of labor that enable the IC as a whole to cover more issues more effectively than would otherwise be the case. The existence of multiple agencies reporting to different cabinet-level superiors also has a downside in that it fosters and perpetuates organizational pathologies found in all large enterprises (e.g., unhealthy rivalries, reluctance to trust "competitors," and other impediments to collaboration).[6]

Although many structural elements of the US IC are conducive to collaboration across agency boundaries and among analysts with complementary experience and expertise (including in the use of particular types of sources), the amount of collaboration—and all-source analysis—were long-constrained by bureaucratic rivalries and incentives to work problems without substantial input from other agencies or analysts. The 9/11 Commission and other studies critical of impediments to "information sharing" captured a portion of this malady but impeded access to information from "all sources" was only part of the problem and was probably the easiest to address. The more important dimension of the problem was that too many analysts could not easily seek or obtain analytic insights from colleagues elsewhere in the Community.

Perhaps the most important reasons all-source analysis is essential are the complexity of the issues the IC is expected to address, the volume of information that might be germane to understanding those issues, the often short timelines within which analytic input is required if it is to be useful, and the consequentiality of many decisions made by the US Government. In other words, the problems are hard; there is lots of information, albeit never as much as one desires and often of uneven quality; deadlines are short; and decisions

Masters, and Methods," in National Research Council, Intelligence Analysis: Behavioral and Social Science Foundations (Washington, DC: The National Academies Press, 2011), 3-27.
6. See, for example, Catherine H. Tinsley, "Social Categorization and Intergroup Dynamics," in National Research Council, 199-223.

affecting US interests can be very important to our nation and our relationships with other countries. Because the decisions matter, it is imperative that they be as well informed as possible. It is the IC's responsibility to ensure that they are.

The first requisite for analytic collaboration/all-source analysis is ready access to information and ease of sharing and discussing information with colleagues everywhere in the IC. "Need to know" has been replaced by "responsibility to provide" because "collectors" and other information stewards cannot possibly know the full range of analysts who might find a given piece of intelligence helpful or, if queried about the information in a given report, might be able to provide insights helpful to others. There are, and must be, some restrictions on access, but the working criterion is—and must be—that "all" information, of whatever source or type, must be accessible to all analysts with the clearances required for access to all but a small percentage of all intelligence.[7] Universal access facilitates collaboration and all-source analysis because analysts no longer have to guess whether a particular colleague, especially one that is not known to him or her, has access to a particular report or stream of reporting.

A second requisite is to be able to tap expertise wherever it exists, certainly anywhere in the IC and, sometimes, anywhere inside or outside the US Government. This entails being able to discover and consider the perspectives of experts who utilize different types of information and interpret it using criteria appropriate to the missions they support (i.e., the different perspectives that result from the IC structure). Sometimes this entails soliciting information, insights, and advice from colleagues with whom one has worked previously and may take the form of "Do you have any information that would help me to understand this puzzle?" or "Which of these alternative hypotheses do you think best fits the data we have on this subject?" At other times, the analyst seeking help from colleagues can post a general inquiry within "A-Space" or on *Intellipedia* asking whether anyone has information or insights that might clarify the question he or she is trying to answer.[8] Such inquiries, and "publicly" posted exchanges among analysts who may not know one another, are the most "all-source" of all because they have the potential to tap different sources and types of information, different analytic perspectives, and the expertise of people in other organizations with whom the requesting analyst has had no previous contact.

A third requisite for all-source analysis is transparency in the analytic

---

7. See Bob Brewin, "Now It's 'Responsibility to Provide,'" Government Executive, April 7, 2009 at *http://www.govexec.com/dailyfed/0408/040708wb.htm*; and Intelligence Community Directive 501: Discovery and Dissemination or Retrieval of Information within the Intelligence Community (January 21, 2009) at *http://www.dni.gov/electronic_reading_room/ICD_501.pdf*.

8. A-Space is the name of a digital collaborative workspace open to all IC analysts with required security clearances. Intellipedia is a classified Wiki modeled on Wikipedia utilized by IC analysts, collectors, and many other US Government employees. For more information, see "A-Space," Wikipedia at *http://en.wikipedia.org/wiki/A-Space*; and "Intellipedia," Wikipedia at *http://en.wikipedia.org/wiki/Intellipedia*.

process: analysts must "show their homework" and anyone who looks at the analytic process should be able to determine without difficulty what sources were used, the degree of confidence in the sources, whether there is intelligence that contradicts or is inconsistent with that used to reach analytic judgments and, if so, why it was considered less reliable, what assumptions were used to close information gaps, why sources were evaluated and weighted as they were, and so on. In other words, the analytic tradecraft must be as transparent as possible.[9] This applies to "single INT" as well as all-source judgments. For example, an imagery analyst who determines that the crate sitting on a dock contains a particular type of missile from a specific country must explain why he or she came to that conclusion. Most of the time, the explanation will derive from information gleaned from multiple sources and types of analysis.

The primary missions of intelligence analysis are to reduce uncertainty, provide warning, and identify opportunities for intervention to change the course of events. Achieving these missions cannot be accomplished by passively waiting to see what types of information dribble into the electronic in-box. To provide the timely, targeted, and consequential support desired and demanded by those who rely on the IC, analysts must formulate questions designed to provide insight, give guidance to collectors on where to look for information that might help answer the question, and enlist the help of colleagues with complementary expertise, better knowledge of specific information streams, or alternative perspectives on the problem. Seeking help wherever it might be available, from whoever might have something to contribute is the essence of all-source analysis. In a growing number of cases, it is also the only practical way to provide the kinds of support required by the US national security enterprise.

READINGS FOR INSTRUCTORS

The readings recommended here provide additional detail and perspectives on the roles and characteristics of all-source intelligence analysis.

Mark M. Lowenthal's *Intelligence: From Secrets to Policy*, Fourth Edition, (Washington, DC: CQ Press, 2009) provides brief descriptions of different types of intelligence analysis and how they fit into the broader universe of intelligence activities and national security decisions.

Thomas Fingar, *Reducing Uncertainty: Intelligence Analysis and National Security* (Stanford, CA: Stanford University Press, 2011) describes the scope, escalating requirements, and different types of all-source analysis.

---

9. See Intelligence Community Directive 203: Analytic Standards (June 21, 2007) at http://www.dni.gov/electronic_reading_room/ICD_203.pdf; and Intelligence Community Directive 206: Sourcing Requirements for Disseminated Analytic Products (October 17, 2007) at http://www.dni.gov/electronic_reading_room/ICD_206.pdf.

Books containing short articles, many written by intelligence analysts, on the relationship of analysis to specific intelligence and policymaking arenas, include...

George, Roger Z. and James B. Bruce (ed.). *Analyzing Intelligence: Origins, Obstacles, and Innovations* (Washington, DC: Georgetown University Press, 2008)

Sims, Jennifer E. and Burton Gerber (ed.). *Transforming U.S. Intelligence* (Washington, DC: Georgetown University Press, 2005).

Excellent books on intelligence analysis by academics include:

Betts, Richard K. *Enemies of Intelligence: Knowledge & Power in American National Security* (New York: Columbia University Press, 2007)

Jervis, Robert. *Why Intelligence Fails* (Ithaca, NY: Cornell University Press, 2010).

Two volumes recently published by the National Research Council examine similarities and differences between intelligence analysis and the challenges of working complex problems in other organizational contexts. They are:

Intelligence Analysis: Behavioral and Social Scientific Foundations (Washington, DC: The National Academies Press, 2011)

Intelligence Analysis for Tomorrow: Advances from the Behavioral and Social Sciences (Washington, DC: The National Academies Press, 2011).

Dr. Thomas Fingar is the Oksenberg-Rohlen Distinguished Fellow at Stanford University's Freeman Spogli Institute for International Studies. From 2005 to 2008, he served as the first deputy director of national intelligence for analysis and, concurrently, as chairman of the National Intelligence Council. He was previously assistant secretary of state for intelligence and research, principal deputy assistant secretary of state for intelligence research. Dr. Fingar received his BA (government and history) from Cornell, and his MA and PhD degrees (political science) from Stanford. He taught and held a number of research positions at Stanford from 1975 to 1986. He is a career member of the Senior Executive Service and recipient of the Presidential Rank Award for Distinguished Senior Professionals and the National Intelligence Distinguished Service Medal.

GUIDE TO THE STUDY OF INTELLIGENCE

Understanding Terrorism Analysis

Philip Mudd

Intelligence and law enforcement analysis has changed dramatically since 9/11 with dramatically increased interagency fusion of information from a wide variety of sources. Intelligence Community (IC) analysts supporting the pursuit of individual Al-Qa'ida members and cells have developed tactical skills to supplement their traditional analytical tradecraft focused on strategic assessments of nation states. This change in focus, with its requirement to sort through massive new data sets — from phone and e-mail information to content on social media sites – has led analysts to grow the discipline of network analysis. Analysts adapt rapidly emerging software tools to help make sense of what has become known as "big data." This tactically focused analysis, often referred to as "targeting" analysis," was in its inception before the 9/11 attacks. Targeting analysis uses sophisticated methods to map within a network either potential terrorists or, occasionally, to identify potential sources and their access for recruitment. It is now a core analytic function.

Other post-9/11 changes in the analytic profession are proving equally profound. IC analysts who previously focused on overseas targets now work with federal, state, and local law enforcement professionals to confront Al-Qa'ida-inspired actors within the US. As the push for information sharing domestically among federal, state, and local entities took shape, cooperation overseas among disparate US agencies also mushroomed. In the war zones of Iraq and Afghanistan, tactical fusion centers, which combine intelligence, military, and law enforcement analysts and operators, undertook data-intensive analyses of networks of foreign fighters and specific terrorist groups on a day-to-day basis. These fusion centers enabled 24-hour raid cycles by the US military, its allies and partners that became a hallmark of real-time efforts to disrupt adversary networks.

Changed Focus of Intelligence

The impetus for this revolution in intelligence analysis, with its emphasis on tactical support; domestic partnerships; and global, real-time fusion among US agencies, reaches beyond the global counterterrorism campaign. At the core of this tactical intelligence work has been the effort to understand sub-national entities and individuals — from foreign fighters funneling suicide bombers into Iraq to Al-Shabaab fundraisers in the US — and the networks in which they participate. As a result of the emergence of the kinds of digital data that emanate from everyday life in the 21st century — from individuals' financial transactions and travel data to the electronic feeds from the ubiquitous communications devices people everywhere now carry — analysts can accelerate mapping people geographically and within networks by rapidly arraying the digital trails they leave. Targeting analysis is here to stay. It has applications that clearly apply to criminal cartels, human traffickers, and gangs. Further, the tools and methodologies that proved increasingly effective in foreign battlefields seem likely to become common practice as analysts confront new networks in the US and overseas.

This data-intensive analysis, based on new tools to automate the understanding of networks, also has led to changes in analytic culture, with far more analysts embedded with, or supporting, field operators than in previous decades. The need for rapid analysis to feed rapid reaction operations led to more deployments of analysts overseas; closer partnerships between analysts and operators in headquarters units; and the growth of an entire cadre of analyst "targeteers," who built not only careers but also a new analytic profession out of the capability to sort information quickly enough to find, fix, and finish a rapidly moving target in a battlefield environment.

Tactical Fusion of Intelligence Drives Operations

The fusion model was critical on the battlefield, where 24-hour operations centers, manned by analysts and operators from a wide range of US federal agencies and the military, combined signals intelligence (SIGINT), tactical and strategic human intelligence (HUMINT), imagery, detainee interrogation reports, and a vast array of data collected in raids (e.g., hard drives, thumb drives, e-mail, and phone numbers) to piece together a steadily changing picture of networks of foreign fighters, facilitators, and insurgent factions. By feeding in and then assessing new information every day, analysts could chart and then re-chart fluid network analyses of networks, prioritizing targets for a next round of raid operations after adjusting the network picture to account for the previous night's operations and the intelligence gained. This tactical analysis proved critical in supporting operators conducting raids against Al-Qa'ida and foreign fighter cells around the world.

The fusion model also fed the maturing intelligence architecture surrounding the use of unmanned aerial vehicles (UAV – commonly referred to as "drones") that allowed for enhanced collection against Al-Qa'ida targets. The authorization of UAV use for intelligence-led strikes against Al-Qa'ida targets in areas such as Pakistan, Afghanistan, Yemen, and Somalia changed the battlefield. Using standoff weapons that did not require US personnel on the ground, drone operations decimated the Al-Qa'ida organization and eliminated leaders with unprecedented precision.

Cross Agency and Foreign Partnerships

Strategic analyses in Washington also evolved as a result of the requirement to fuse a wider variety of data sources. The post-9/11 emphasis on "information sharing" among agencies was instantiated by combining analysts and data from across the US Government in the new National Counterterrorism Center (NCTC). A variety of study groups after 9/11, particularly the 9/11 Commission, highlighted the fractured, stovepiped nature of the US IC, with its separate data pools and chains of command at major components including Central Intelligence Agency (CIA), Defense Intelligence Agency, National Security Agency (NSA), State Department, the Federal Bureau of Investigation (FBI), and the various intelligence-generating components of what would become Department of Homeland Security (DHS; including intelligence drawn from customs, immigration, transportation, and border control agencies). In the past, analyses that reflected the combined work of analysts from across the IC were infrequent, with interagency assessments from the joint National Intelligence Council (assessments such as all-agency National Intelligence Estimates) forming the backbone of episodic and largely strategic interagency cooperation. Today, NCTC produces not only the core US Government appraisals of Al-Qa'ida's overall strength but tactical assessments of emerging threats or even new persons of interest who appear to be affiliated with Al-Qa'ida.

These cross-agency partnerships today also include agencies outside the defined post-World War II IC. The nature of the terrorism target itself drove these partnership changes. In the past, law enforcement might have faced criminal threats in major US cities while intelligence professionals focused on foreign militaries and stability in far-flung capitals. The globalization of threats to reach across borders, so that Al-Qa'ida operators in the tribal areas of Pakistan might be communicating with a trainee in a European or North American city, meant that threats simultaneously involving both federal intelligence professionals and US federal, state, and local law enforcement officers became commonplace. Evidence of this mixture of foreign and domestic threats is now spread across the US intelligence landscape, with the rapid growth in FBI-led Joint Terrorism Task Forces (JTTF), which combine a wide variety of agencies, to the posting of NYPD officials in major cities overseas to partner with foreign police services.

The prominence of the US homeland in plots of Al-Qa'ida and its affiliates, and, more generally, the political push to involve new entities in the US intelligence infrastructure, from state and local police to US companies and federal agencies responsible for missions such as transportation, border, port, and coastline control, and customs — also led to the DHS' creation. This new constellation of agencies, under one roof, is still in the midst of building a capability to partner more with corporations and law enforcement outside the traditional Washington orbit of federal bureaucracies.

Old intelligence partnerships grew as well, with the pace and depth of US engagement with foreign security services expanding in tandem with the spread of the Al-Qa'ida ideology to affiliates around the world. During much of the post-war history, the traditional responsibilities of US intelligence was collecting, reporting, analyzing, and disseminating intelligence information on issues ranging from the Soviet nuclear threat to Latin American instability. With the intensification of counterterror operations worldwide, however, US intelligence focused on identifying, capturing, and detaining terror suspects. In this, the partnering and support for foreign security services proved crucial. These services not only provided substantial support in the global counter-terror campaign – and often unique intelligence from surveillance against terror targets in their countries and human sources (HUMINT) inside terror organizations — they also grew substantial capabilities internally, sometimes with financial, technical, and training support from US agencies.

Detainee information mushroomed during the post-9/11 period, including both tactical information from fighters detained on the battlefield, in Iraq and Afghanistan, and the intelligence provided by "high-value" Al-Qa'ida members held at "black sites" — secret facilities overseas — maintained by the CIA to hold prisoners that it and partner security services had captured in overseas raids. As the number of senior al-Qa'ida members in detention increased, detainee information, coupled with traditional HUMINT, SIGINT, and intelligence provided by friendly security services, provided a rapidly clarifying picture of the Al-Qa'ida network, and the damage the core group suffered as its leaders tried to recreate their group in the tribal areas of Pakistan.

In another twist in the secret world of intelligence, US industry became a key consumer of intelligence information and analysis, and various US agencies built mechanisms to foster contacts and information sharing between the federal government and US companies. Terrorists looking for iconic targets, from aircraft to major oil facilities, hotels, and retail outlets, drove industry to grow its own internal threat units, and to reach out to government to learn more about how terrorists might target the private sector.

The Changing Threat From Al-Qa'ida

This drive to share information nationally, among federal, state, and local agencies that had not been close partners, grew out of the changed threat facing the United States. From intelligence operations in Vietnam in the 1960s through the continuation of the Cold War through the 1970s and 1980s to the later focus on "rogue" states (e.g., Iran, North Korea, and Iraq), the US IC had focused on large foreign threats operating overseas. There was not much need to work with state and local partners, nor to target collection against potential threats domestically. Historically, in the world of terrorism, the domestic and the international worlds did not overlap: domestic terrorism in the United States during the 1970s was high, but groups lacked an international nexus. Conversely, Palestinian groups in the 1970s and beyond, and state sponsors of terrorism (most prominently Iran, sometimes working through its ally Lebanese Hizballah), typically operated overseas.

The advent of Al-Qa'ida and its affiliates in countries from the Philippines through South Asia, the Middle East, Africa, and Western Europe, bridged the gap between domestic and foreign terror. Al-Qa'idist ideology emphasizes the importance of attacking the "far enemy" (including the United States) rather than expending energy on the "near enemy" (local governments such as those in North Africa and the Arabian Peninsula). The theory is simple: if Al-Qa'ida attacks can inflict enough casualties to persuade the US to withdraw its forces from Muslim countries (as it did in Lebanon and Somalia), the corrupt leaders of those countries then would lose US backing and thereby become more vulnerable to Islamist overthrow. So Al-Qa'ida brought attacks to the US homeland, under the assumption that the US would not have the will to maintain an overseas presence in Islamic countries after taking casualties in terror attacks.

This melding of domestic and overseas threats became more complex as the decade of the 2000's progressed. In the wake of the 2001 attacks, the primary intelligence focus remained overseas, penetrating the core Al-Qa'ida leadership in Pakistan to try to stop plots emanating from that tight group. As the decade passed, though, more affiliated organizations — groups that adopted Al-Qa'ida's ideology but retained some independence of action — cropped up, expanding the potential threat to US interests overseas and raising the specter that these new affiliates would take the initiative from the embattled Al-Qa'ida core to stage attacks in the US. Faisal Shahzad's failed attempt to detonate a vehicle-borne improvised explosive device in Times Square on May 1, 2010 underscored this emerging threat from affiliates: a Pakistani militant organization, Tehrik-e Taliban Pakistan (TTP), which was affiliated with, but not a part of, the Al-Qa'ida organization, sponsored Shahzad's plot.

Controversies

The change in threat and the US counterterror response has not been without controversy. The blurring of domestic and international lines, in the age of globalized terror organizations, led to changes in the intelligence business, and questions about what the government should collect in a digital world. The revelations of former NSA contractor Edward Snowden about the extent of NSA collection of information, such as domestic phone and e-mail data, has led to a national debate — along with Congressional scrutiny and legislative changes — about how much data the government collects on its own citizens. The collection itself stemmed from the government's interest in combing through these new, vast data collections to find linkages within the US as new plots, and new players, emerged. This data allowed for an unprecedented ability for government analysts to automate how they map networks, and to make connections across vast data warehouses that would have been unthinkable in the previous century.

The CIA's operation of "black sites" and harsh interrogation techniques on detainees have also been controversial both in the US and in other countries.

The use of UAVs armed with weapons also ignited debates, about the use of lethal force outside war zones and the future of US intervention against targets in ungoverned spaces, such as extremist-inhabited areas of Africa. The traditional American definition of a war zone does not fit well with modern globalized terrorism. The concept of a war zone, historically defined by geographical boundaries, figures prominently in legal arguments on the use of force. Terrorists, however, move across national boundaries.

The Future

While the attraction of Al-Qa'ida has declined in the group's key recruiting and fundraising areas during the past decade, from Indonesia to Saudi Arabia and the United Kingdom, the persistence of its now-globalized ideology will challenge security services, including those in Europe and the United States, to remain focused on Al-Qa'ida spinoffs for years to come. Al-Qa'ida hotbeds remain in key areas, from the Sunni extremist groups in Iraq to Al-Qa'ida's sympathizers in Pakistan, Yemen, and North Africa. Further, Syria now serves as a magnet for foreign fighters, including hundreds from Europe, raising the prospect that those fighters will gain contacts and experience that they will transfer west when that campaign dies down.

The success or failure of governments to control these battlegrounds — and to limit the chances that Al-Qa'ida offshoots will find safe havens that will allow them to plot against the West, as groups in Yemen and Somalia have done in recent years — will hinge on the question of whether governments show the will and capability to disrupt safe havens. In Somalia and Yemen, for example, government forces' sustained operations against entrenched Al-Qa'ida affiliates have resulted in significant pressure on extremist groups and their leaders. They then are forced to spend their time and resources defending local territory, with less time to develop foreign-focused terrorist wings.

Counterterrorism analysis will remain a requirement for years to come. While the large, centralized Al-Qa'ida adversary has declined, newer spinoffs have adopted the group's globalist ideology. The threat from these groups has ebbed and flowed during the past decade, with hotspots moving from Indonesia and Saudi Arabia to Iraq, Western Europe, Somalia, Yemen, northern Nigeria, and the Sahel. The threat will continue the need for interagency analysis and tactical support for operations. The models developed to counter Al-Qa'ida might well serve as templates for the intelligence-led fight against adversaries of the future, such as cartels, human trafficking groups, or cyber criminals. For all the questions as these new intelligence approaches and tools have raised, though, the US IC is facing new, still-unresolved, questions about the nature and extent of intelligence operations in America.

The analytic approaches developed for counterterrorism, though, also are driving the public debates about the role of intelligence in democratic societies. The extent of data collection, in an age when individuals around the world freely expose more and more personal information on the internet, is raising questions about how the digital age will redefine privacy. Unlike the debate about physical privacy — we expect searches in airports, but we would resist a similar search in a grocery store — debates about cyber privacy have not reached the stage where culture has defined boundaries. Camera footage on a public street has become an accepted source of intelligence; personal information on a Facebook page is more questionable. These debates will not slow. Intelligence agencies seeking to identify new threat networks will turn to whatever data is available as the fastest way to map connections among individuals.

Expanding public and political expectations for intelligence and law enforcement also will drive policy and controversy in this era of tactical, data-driven analysis. Preemption has become the standard for intelligence and law enforcement today: public expectations have evolved quickly, and investigating a terror cell after an attack, rather than uncovering the cell beforehand, is seen as a failure. This pressure to develop preventive intelligence will drive law enforcement agencies to use technical and human intelligence to uncover conspiracies before they fully develop, and questions about preemptive investigative techniques, such as human sources who help to advance a plot, will continue in parallel with the emphasis on preemption.

READINGS FOR INSTRUCTORS

The website for the director of national intelligence (DNI – http://www.dni.gov)

describes the National Counterterrorism Center's mission, functions, and history. The NCTC's own homepage (*http://www.nctc.gov*) lists the various partner agencies that man this interagency entity (although some aspects of this website are out of date).

Michael Bayer, the former head of the Department of State (DOS) Diplomatic Security Service transnational criminal investigative section, addresses the issues of partnerships between law enforcement and intelligence. He critiques the primacy of the US military approach to counterterror operations over international law enforcement. See Michael D. Bayer, *The Blue Planet: Informal International Police Networks and National Intelligence* (Washington, DC: National Defense Intelligence College Press, February 2010).

For a wide-ranging review of legal issues related to counterterrorism, see Lynne K. Zusman (ed.), *The Law of Counterterrorism* (Washington, DC: American Bar Association, 2011). Of particular note is Chapter VII, "Intelligence and the Law: Introduction to the Legal and Policy Framework Governing Intelligence Community Counterterrorism Efforts," by W. George Jameson, former CIA general counsel.

Annual country reports on terrorism can be found on the DOS website (*http://www.state.gov/j/ct/*).

The US Military Academy at West Point maintains the Center for Combating Terrorism. Its journal, *Sentinel*, includes articles on terrorism, counterterrorism, homeland security, and internal conflict.

Georgetown University Professor Bruce Hoffman's *Inside Terrorism* (revised edition) (New York: Columbia University Press, 2006) remains one of the fundamental texts on the subject.

John Horgan, director of the Pennsylvania State University International Center for the Study of Terrorism from 2007 to 2013, and Kurt Braddock have edited a series of articles on terrorism and counterterrorism in their *Terrorism Studies: A Reader* (New York: Routeledge, 2012) that provide a wide-ranging look at the topic.

A number of institutions maintain databases on terror incidents. These include the University of Maryland (*http://www.start.umd.edu/gtd/*), which is supported by the DHS; the RAND Corporation (*http://www.rand.org/nsrd/projects/terrorism-incidents.html*), and others.

Philip Mudd is director of global risk at SouthernSun Asset Management, in Memphis, Tennessee. He served as senior intelligence adviser at the FBI until 2010, and he was deputy director of the CIA Counterterrorist Center during 2003-2005.

GUIDE TO THE STUDY OF INTELLIGENCE

Counterproliferation

Rowena Rege Fischer

C ounterproliferation is a nebulous term. Simplistically, it is that which is done to counter proliferation. According to the *Oxford Dictionary*, counterproliferation is defined as an "action intended to prevent an increase or spread in the possession of nuclear weapons."[1] But, is it limited to nuclear weapons? What about biological or chemical weapons? According to the National Counterproliferation Center, counterproliferation seeks to "eliminate or reduce the threats caused by the development and spread of WMD."[2] The CIA, FBI, and the Department of Homeland Security (DHS) Immigration and Customs Enforcement (ICE) agency all include weapons of mass destruction (WMDs) technology under counterproliferation.[3] The term weapons of mass destruction (WMD) is often used to reference nuclear weapons, but chemical and biological weapons also fall within this definition. This article on countering the spread of WMDs focuses on nuclear weapons, but the reader should understand that similar principles apply to chemical and biological weapons.

Why does one seek to counter the proliferation of WMDs? The international community seeks to categorize the use of WMDs as *jus cogens*[4] – i.e., the acts are so against the fundamental values of the international community that they cannot be tolerated and may not be disregarded.[5] Flowing from this is an

---

1. *http://www.oxforddictionaries.com/us/definition/american_english/counterproliferation.*
2. *http://www.counterwmd.gov/.*
3. See *https://www.cia.gov/news-information/press-releases-statements/press-release-2010/cia-launches-new-counterproliferation-center.html, http://www.fbi.gov/about-us/nsb/fbi-counterproliferation-center,* and *http://www.ice.gov/counter-proliferation-investigations/* discussing how each agency views counterproliferation. It is interesting to note that FBI and ICE definition also includes non-WMD technology under counterproliferation.
4. *http://www.law.cornell.edu/wex/jus_cogens.*
5. International Court of Justice summary of the Advisory Opinion on the Legality of the Use by a State of Nuclear Weapons in Armed Conflict ("the threat or use of nuclear weapons would generally be contrary to the ... principles and rules of humanitarian law" (*http://www.icj-cij.org/docket/files/95/7497.pdf.*

obligation to prevent additional nations from obtaining WMDs.[6] As countries historically developed their WMD programs indigenously[7] or acquired the WMD as whole part(s), the international community historically focused on promoting dismantling of these programs by restricting the use and stockpiling of WMDs.[8] An example of this was when the Soviet Union dissolved, a large concern was that whole nuclear weapons would be acquired by other countries seeking such weapons. But, as the world has gotten more global and parts are manufactured in multiple countries and then shipped to yet other countries for assembly for use in a totally different country, rogue nations desiring illicit WMD programs have been able to capitalize on this global market in order to develop these programs. So, now, the proliferation concern to be countered is not only the suitcase containing the whole nuclear weapon being shipped to the neighboring country,[9] but also the multiple parts being shipped from multiple nations that can later be assembled to make the whole nuclear weapon.

But, how does one obtain these parts? Does one go to the local grocery store or the local shopping mall? Almost, apparently. In January 2004, the then-International Atomic Energy Agency (IAEA) director general stated that

---

6. See United Nations Security Council Resolution (UNSCR) 1540, which states that the proliferation of WMDs and their means of delivery are a threat to international peace and security. UNSCR 1540 also obligates the states to implement procedures to prevent such proliferation, and cooperate with other States to accomplish the goal of preventing proliferation. (*http://www.un.org/en/sc/1540/*.

7. Although the United States mostly developed its nuclear weapons program during World War II indigenously, many of the scientists were brought to the United States from Europe, including Germany. For example, Enrico Fermi. (*http://www.atomicheritage.org/mediawiki/index.php /Enrico_Fermi*); Emilio Segre (*http://www.atomicheritage.org/mediawiki/index.php/Emilio_Segre*); Hans Bethe (*http://www. atomicheritage.org/mediawiki/index.php/Hans_Bethe*) and Niels Bohr (*http://www.atomicheritage.org/ mediawiki/index.php/Niels_Bohr*).

8. See for example the Protocol for the Prohibition of the Use in War of Asphyxiating, Poisonous or other Gases, and of Bacteriological Methods of Warfare (aka, the 1925 Geneva Protocol) which prohibited the use of chemical and biological weapons in international armed conflicts (*http://www.un.org/disarmament/WMD/Bio/1925GenevaProtocol.shtml*); the Convention on the Prohibition of the Development, Production and Stockpiling of Bacteriological (Biological) and Toxin Weapons and on their Destruction (aka, Biological Weapons Convention), opened for signature in 1972 (*http://www.un.org/disarmament/ WMD/Bio/*); the Hague Convention of 1899, a multilateral treaty which inter alia prevented the signatories from discharging projectiles "the sole object of which is the diffusion of asphyxiating or deleterious gases" in a war between signatory States (*http://en.wikipedia.org/wiki/Hague_Convention_of_1899*); the Convention on the Prohibition of the Development, Production, Stockpiling and Use of Chemical Weapons and on their Destruction (aka, Chemical Weapons Convention), adopted in 1992 (*http://www. opcw.org/chemical-weapons-convention/*); the Convention on the Physical Protection of Nuclear Material, adopted in 1979, renamed in 2005 the Convention on the Physical Protection of Nuclear Materials and Nuclear Facilities, mandates that the signatory States protect domestic nuclear facilities and material, provides for expanded cooperation between the States related to smuggled nuclear material and mitigation of radiological consequences due to sabotage (*http://www.iaea.org/ Publications/Documents/ Conventions/cppnm.html*); and the Treaty on the Non-Proliferation of Nuclear Weapons (aka Non-Proliferation Treaty (NPT), opened for signature in 1968, which seeks to prevent the spread of nuclear weapons and technology, promotes cooperation in peaceful uses of nuclear energy and seeks disarmament (*http://www.un.org/disarmament/WMD/ Nuclear/NPT.shtml*). As of 2013, 190 countries have joined the treaty. North Korea withdrew from the NPT. India, Israel, Pakistan and South Sudan never joined. *http://en.wikipedia.org/wiki/ Treaty_on_the_Non-Proliferation_of_Nuclear_Weapons*.

9. The transport of the suitcase containing the nuclear weapon is also a counterterrorism concern. Counterproliferation looks to understand how nations and international terrorists are developing indigenous WMD programs and the status of each.

shopping for nuclear weapons in the international black market was as easy as going to Wal-Mart.[10] The man credited as being the father of this global network of nuclear weapons parts is A. Q. Khan. To understand how this global market developed and how to counter the threat of this global illicit market, one must first learn about Khan's history.

Khan was a Pakistani scientist who studied metallurgy in The Netherlands and then worked in Europe where he gained further knowledge of civilian nuclear uranium enrichment process.[11] His employer permitted him more access than he was authorized and vetted for; although not possessing the appropriate security clearances, the Anglo-Dutch company, URENCO, asked Khan to translate secret centrifuge plans.[12] His employer also had lax security rules,[13] which Khan exploited. He was known to take classified documents home; he would walk through URENCO buildings taking notes in his native Urdu, which he would claim were letters to his family; and he would take readily available, but discarded, centrifuge prototype parts home. None of this would have been an international concern if not for Khan's desire to help his country, Pakistan, develop a nuclear weapon. Unbeknownst to his employer, Khan had offered his services to then Pakistan Prime Minister Zulfikar Bhutto,[14] which was apparently accepted. In hindsight, it appears that Khan exploited his job, the lax security measures of his employer, and utilized his and the Pakistan Government's resources to assist Pakistan's nascent nuclear weapons program.[15] And, then in 1975, Khan returned to Pakistan, where he was legitimately employed in Pakistan's weapons program. He was eventually promoted to Pakistan's Engineering Research Laboratory (ERL), which was later re-named in his honor. While in Pakistan, he was able to exploit his contacts in Europe by collaborating and consulting with them. In addition to his knowledge and his contacts, Khan's other key take-aways from his work in Europe were the names and contact information for manufacturers and distributors of supplies for nuclear applications.[16] With that knowledge and with the Pakistan Government's shopping list, he was able to advance Pakistan's nuclear weapons program until Pakistan joined the select list of nations with nuclear weapons in 1998. What then for the man who came up with all this? It should not surprise anyone that in addition to his assistance to Pakistan's nuclear weapons

10. David E. Sanger, "The Struggle for Iraq: Weapons Inspectors," New York Times, January 24, 2004, A12, column 4.

11. "Any state with enrichment facilities [to produce enriched uranium] or reprocessing facilities would therefore already be skilled in ... the most difficult part of building a nuclear weapon: obtaining the necessary fissile material." http://www.wired.com/dangerroom/2007/12/a-week-after-it/.

12. William Langewiesche, "The Wrath of Khan," The Atlantic, November 2005. http://www.theatlantic.com/magazine/archive/2005/11/the-wrath-of-khan/304333/.

13. Ibid.

14. Ibid.

15. Ibid.

16. Ibid.

program, Khan is also credited with assisting China, North Korea, Libya, and Iran in their nuclear weapons programs over several years.

In utilizing open markets, Khan rarely went to the manufacturer; rather he went through middlemen working through front companies and utilized false end-destinations for the items.[17] In this respect, Pakistan, using Khan, was the first country to use open markets, albeit covertly and using subterfuge, to develop its nuclear weapons program. Historically, countries had utilized indigenous development, acquisition of scientists, acquisition from another country, diversion from a civilian nuclear program, and espionage.[18] By changing tactics, Khan made it easier to acquire the technology and simultaneously made countering proliferation more difficult because he made it harder to identify. If all that a nation or a terrorist needs to acquire a WMD is to acquire the parts and put them together, and if the intelligence services of the licit countries cannot identify the purchasers, the purchases, the middlemen, and the front companies used to acquire the parts for these illicit WMD programs, the risk of getting caught is dramatically reduced for the illicit nations.[19]

Given this global marketplace for nuclear weapon parts and ambitious scientists who could gain tremendous accolades from their home nation, how do licit countries fulfill their obligations under jus cogens to the proliferation of WMDs?

Prosecution is one tool, but that usually occurs after the dirty deed is done – i.e., after the nation has acquired the part or has attempted to acquire the part by taking substantial steps toward the goal thereby paving the way for the next person. Additionally, how does a licit country prosecute someone from a procurement network for a country illicitly seeking WMD technology? Are these procurement agents within the boundaries of the licit country? Prosecutions in absentia are occasionally possible,[20] but how much of a deterrent is such a prosecution when the country lacked in personum jurisdiction over the defendant? The Department of Justice has a fact sheet of recent federal prosecutions for export violations.[21] Many of these summaries discuss extraditing the defendants from third countries. But, what if that is not successful? How can one have a prosecution if the defendant is savvy and does not travel to a country willing to extradite them,[22] and their home country treats them as a

---

17. William Langewiesche, "The Point of No Return," The Atlantic, January 2006. *http://www.theatlantic.com/magazine/archive/2006/01/the-point-of-no-return/304500/*.
18. *http://www.iiss.org/en/publications/strategic%20dossiers/issues/nuclear-black-markets—pakistan—a-q—khan-and-the-rise-of-proliferation-networks—-a-net-assessmen-23e1/nbm-chapter-02-5303*.
19. For example, the US Intelligence Community had not detected India's preparation for their 1988 nuclear bomb tests. *http://en.wikipedia.org/wiki/Pokhran-II#Movement_and_logistics*.
20. See for example the in absentia trial and sentencing of A.Q. Khan in The Netherlands for attempted espionage. This was overturned later on a legal technicality. *http://en.wikipedia.org/wiki/Abdul_Qadeer_Khan#Research_in_Europe*.
21. *http://www.justice.gov/nsd/docs/export-case-fact-sheet-201311.pdf*. DOJ Fact Sheet.
22. An example of which is Milad Jafari, who was indicted in 2010 on multiple export violations but is not listed as having been sentenced. See DOJ Fact Sheet and *http://www.isisnucleariran.org/assets/pdf/*

national hero akin to how Pakistan treats A. Q. Khan? Pakistan renamed their national research institute after him; provided him with a military escort for years when he travelled; he received Pakistan's highest civilian award; although he confessed to proliferating, he was placed under house arrest in one of the largest houses in Pakistan and no one from the international community was allowed to question him. He was later pardoned.[23]

Interdicting the shipment en-route is another tool and the Proliferation Security Initiative (PSI) is an example of a regime designed for this end-goal.[24] According to the Department of State (DOS), PSI seeks to stem the proliferation of WMDs *inter alia* by "interdicting the transfer or transport of WMD, their delivery systems and related materials to and from states and non-state actors of proliferation concern"; and improve procedures for exchange of information [i.e., intelligence] relevant to proliferation activity. But this, too, has the flaw of paving the way for the next person. Additionally, how does one know which global shipment to stop? The answer to that is intelligence.[25] When there is "solid" intelligence, PSI is a mechanism for sharing it.[26] And, PSI has been successful. For example, according to the DOS, in part due to intelligence, in January 2004, US and British agents seized a German-flagged ship carrying centrifuges and other parts used to create enriched uranium as it traveled from "a Persian Gulf country" to Libya."[27] Another example is in June 2011, when US naval forces intercepted a shipment suspected of containing ballistic missile technology from North Korea to Myanmar.[28]

Part of knowing which shipment to stop, one must know which parts or technology should be restricted from the nations and terrorists seeking illicit WMD programs. The multinational groups and agreements that assist with this discussion are the Nuclear Suppliers Group; the Australia Group; the Convention on the Prohibition of the Development, Production, Stockpiling, and Use of Chemical Weapons and on their Destruction (Chemical Weapons Convention); Convention on the Prohibition of the Development, Production, and Stockpiling of Bacteriological (Biological) and Toxin Weapons and on their Destruction (Biological Weapons Convention); and the Wassenaar Arrangement on Export Controls for Conventional Arms and Dual-Use Goods and Technologies (Wassenaar Arrangement). These multinational agreements are then incorporated into the export laws of the nations, which in turn enables

Jafari_10Feb2011.pdf.

23. *http://en.wikipedia.org/wiki/Abdul_Qadeer_Khan#Pardon.2C_IAEA_calls.2C_and_aftermath,* http:// *www.theatlantic.com/magazine/archive/2005/11/the-wrath-of-khan/304333/,* http://www.theatlantic. com/magazine/archive/2006/01/the-point-of-no-return/304500/?single_page=true and *http://www.wash-ingtonpost.com/wp-dyn/content/article/2009/02/06/AR2009020603730.html.*

24. *http://www.state.gov/t/isn/c27726.htm.*

25. *http://2001-2009.state.gov/t/isn/rls/fs/46839.htm.*

26. *Ibid.*

27. *http://www.dw.de/german-ship-seized-with-uranium-making-parts-for-libya/a-1075724.*

28. *http://www.armscontrol.org/factsheets/PSI.*

prosecutions of violators.

US export control laws also include economic sanctions, which seek to stem the money flow enabling the illicit purchases.[29] The Non-Proliferation Sanctions also block the property of those engaged in proliferation activity. "Blocking" means title is retained by the target, but the target may not exercise ownership rights without permission of the Treasury Department Office of Foreign Assets Control (OFAC).[30] In other words, the owner may not sell or otherwise trade the item or transfer blocked funds from bank accounts.[31] Additionally, banks have paid record fines for violating these laws.[32]

Most of the discussion thus far has been on the proliferation of WMD parts and pieces. What about the whole WMD? What is in place to prevent the transport of, say, the whole nuclear weapon to an illicit country or terrorist group? This can be accomplished by reducing the number of WMDs available for transport or by enhancing the protection of the WMDs. Many of the multinational agreements and treaties were discussed earlier in this paper. The US also has programs designed to prevent the illicit transfer of the whole WMD. The Department of Defense Defense Threat Reduction Agency (DTRA) is responsible under the Nunn-Lugar Cooperative Threat Reduction Program for working with other nations and international organizations to secure and dismantle WMDs and related infrastructure from the former Soviet Union states.[33] According to DTRA "the program has deactivated more than 7,500 nuclear warheads, neutralized chemical weapons, safeguarded [nuclear material], converted weapons facilities for peaceful use, mitigated bio-threats, and redirected the work of former weapons scientists and engineers."[34]

How does the world know which countries have illicit WMDs and which ones do not? International organizations such as the International Atomic Energy Agency (IAEA) and the Organization for the Prohibition of Chemical Weapons (OPCW)[35] monitor the WMD programs per country. IAEA inspectors visit the sites of suspected illicit nuclear weapons. Of course, this requires the cooperation of the country developing the illicit nuclear weapon. Iraq's success in the 1990s in hiding its illicit development of nuclear weapons is outlined in the book by Dr. Mahdi Obeidi, the scientist in charge of developing the

---

29. http://www.treasury.gov/resource-center/sanctions/Programs/Pages/Programs.aspx.

30. http://www.treasury.gov/resource-center/faqs/Sanctions/Pages/answer.aspx.

31. http://www.treasury.gov/resource-center/faqs/Sanctions/Pages/answer.aspx.

32. See http://online.wsj.com/news/articles/SB10001424052702303901504577462512713336378, which discusses ING Bank's record $619 million fine in 2013. The article also discusses the previous record fines paid by Switzerland's Credit Suisse Group AG and the UK's Lloyds Banking Group PLC. See also http://online.wsj.com/article/SB12306759616688285.html, a 2009 article which discusses how even the New York County District Attorney was looking into illegal transactions by ten banks.

33. http://en.wikipedia.org/wiki/Nunn–Lugar_Cooperative_Threat_Reduction and http://www.dtra.mil/Missions/nunn-lugar/nunn-lugar-home.aspx.

34. http://www.dtra.mil/Missions/Nunn-Lugar/GlobalCooperationInitiative.aspx.

35. http://www.opcw.org/our-work/non-proliferation/.

program.[36] Iran recently agreed to give IAEA inspectors greater access to its nuclear facilities.[37]

But, how do these international organizations know which countries are attempting to build illicit WMD programs and where? The information can come from the countries trying to prevent the illicit proliferation of WMDs, as Colin Powell noted during his 2003 speech to the UN regarding Iraq's WMD program.[38] During this speech, he said that the US had intelligence based on technical sources such as intercepted telephone calls and human sources who "risked their lives" to provide this information.[39] But, the intelligence community must be careful about knowing the reliability of each piece of intelligence. For example, years after Powell's UN speech, it came out that much of the most critical intelligence he referenced was based on one human source, Curveball, who was believed to be unreliable and who later admitted to lying about Iraq's WMDs.[40] The intelligence can also come from the inspections done by international organizations.[41]

As one can see, the systems in place for countering the WMD proliferation are complicated. Is there a sheriff in charge? For the US, the answer is "somewhat." The Office of the Director of National Intelligence (ODNI) National Counterproliferation Center (NCPC) aids the US in countering the worldwide WMD threat.[42] NCPC develops strategies to counter WMD proliferation, works with policymakers within and outside government, and seeks to eliminate intelligence gaps relating to the proliferation of WMDs.[43] NCPC's mission is related to WMD. As noted earlier, although the CIA limits counterproliferation efforts to WMD, the FBI and ICE include the proliferation of non-WMD technology also within their definition.[44] An interesting dichotomy is with FBI versus ICE. FBI investigates these under its National Security Branch, which is headed by an individual whose appointment and removal requires ODNI concurrence.[45] In other words, FBI's Counterproliferation Center (CPC) inter alia reports to ODNI and is within the intelligence community. However, ICE is not an IC member,[46] and, therefore, the ICE Counter-Proliferation Investigative

36. Mahdi Obeidi. *The Bomb in My Garden: The Secrets of Saddam's Nuclear Mastermind* (John Wiley & Sons, 2005).
37. *http://www.washingtonpost.com/world/middle_east/irans-signs-agreement-with-iaea-to-allow-broader-inspections-of-nuclear-sites/2013/11/11/fef81002-4ad5-11e3-ac54-aa84301ced81_story.html*.
38. *http://www.theguardian.com/world/2003/feb/05/iraq.usa*.
39. Ibid.
40. *http://www.newsmax.com/Headline/colin-powell-iraq-wmd/2011/02/16/id/386373*.
41. Obeidi, *The Bomb in My Garden.*
42. *http://www.dni.gov/index.php/about/organization/national-counterproliferation-center-who-we-are.*
43. *http://www.counterwmd.gov/howwedoit.htm.*
44. See footnote 3 supra.
45. 50 USC 3041(b)(2)(H) and Executive Order 12333, as amended.
46. See for example Executive Order 12333, as amended, which does not list ICE as a member of the USIC.

Unit does not report to ODNI. Although NCPC lists the DHS[47] as a partner, it is unclear which DHS sections are at NCPC.[48]

Conclusion

In this game of cat-and-mouse, nations covertly seek WMD programs while the international community seeks to counter their efforts. The international community works through the UN, and through multilateral agreements and partnerships. Additionally, individual licit countries work through their laws and policies to aid in these efforts. This results in a multi-level domestic and international system to counter proliferation – i.e., acts which are considered *jus cogens*.

READINGS FOR INSTRUCTORS

Cirincione, Joseph, Jon B. Wolfsthal, and Miriam Rajkumar. *Deadly Arsenals: Nuclear, Biological, and Chemical Threats* (Washington, DC: Carnegie Endowment for International Peace, 2005).

Cooper, David A. *Competing Western Strategies against the Proliferation of Weapons of Mass Destruction: Comparing the United States to a Close Ally* (Westport, CT: Praeger, 2002).

Laqueur, Walter. *The New Terrorism: Fanaticism and the Arms of Mass Destruction* (Oxford: Oxford University Press, 1999).

Smith, Derek. *Deterring America: Rogue States and the Proliferation of Weapons of Mass Destruction* (New York: Cambridge University Press, 2006).

Turner, Stansfield. *Caging the Genies: A Workable Solution for Nuclear, Chemical, and Biological Weapons* (Boulder, CO: Westview Press, 1999, 2nd edition).

Rowena Rege Fischer earned a BS in microbiology and molecular genetics; a Masters in Public Health in epidemiology; and a MS in chemistry, where she designed and built an instrument for near-single-molecule detection. While in law school, she authored two legal papers on how export control laws apply to researchers at US universities. After receiving her JD, she was a Presidential Management Fellow (PMF) who used her fellowship to gain broad experience in how the US Government administers its export control laws. She is currently a government attorney. The opinions and thoughts expressed in this paper are hers alone and are not endorsed by the US Government.

---

47. The Office of Intelligence and Analysis in DHS is part of the USIC. EO 12333, as amended.
48. *http://www.counterwmd.gov/partners.htm.*

Guide to the Study of Intelligence

Law Enforcement Intelligence

Arthur E. Gerringer and Josh Bart

Amerian society, with its strong sense of civil liberties, has long held in disdain the conduct of intelligence operations within the US against its own citizens. Yet the intelligence gathered by law enforcement agencies has played an important role in preventing criminal activity and acts of terrorism. Intelligence gathered by law enforcement is often overlooked by those who narrowly view the Intelligence Community (IC) as just the military and those three letter agencies, such as the CIA or NSA. While the FBI and Drug Enforcement Administration (DEA) are listed as IC members, a comprehensive list of contributing agencies of intelligence must also include the Justice Department Bureau of Alcohol, Tobacco, Firearms, and Explosives (ATF); Department of Homeland Security (DHS) Immigration and Customs Enforcement (ICE), Secret Service (USSS), and Customs and Border Protection (CPB); and all state and local law enforcement agencies. In actuality, the state and local agencies often are greater producers of tactical or operational intelligence than federal agencies, due to their familiarity with their areas of jurisdiction and life on the street.

The goals of law enforcement intelligence are to save lives, protect property, and preempt crime. The concept of "intelligence-led policing" stresses the use of intelligence to effectively and efficiently allocate policing resources. Additionally, law enforcement agencies regularly use their intelligence to support investigations and contribute to prosecutions. The critical difference between investigations and intelligence is that investigations are retrospective and focus on an event that has occurred, while intelligence is prospective and attempts to predict likely future events. Investigations produce evidence that can be used for prosecutions. Intelligence produces judgments based on an incomplete picture of the future. Evidence from investigations must be made public under our system of jurisprudence. To do so with intelligence would negate its value.

The intelligence cycle for law enforcement is a fluid one, but not dissimilar to the traditional intelligence cycle. The first step is to determine the requirements and direction for the collection process. As collected information is gathered from a wide array of open, human, and technical sources, it must be collated and processed before exploitation takes place. Certain information must be translated from foreign languages, and all information must be evaluated for reliability and relevancy. Once this raw intelligence is deemed appropriate, the analyst evaluates and interprets its significance and disseminates it to authorized consumers. Feedback occurs throughout the entire process and involves revising requirements or guidelines based on policymakers' decisions as to how to proceed using the processed intelligence.

Law enforcement agencies employ similar collection methods to the national intelligence community, but they vary in scale and scope and terminology. For example, one term used by civilian and US Army law enforcement officials is "criminal intelligence" (CRIMINT). CRIMINT describes longer-term crime data and behaviors of organizations and groups. Open sources (OSINT) for law enforcement intelligence include publicly available information as well as data, such as travel records and financial statements, that may require a warrant to obtain. The use of witnesses, undercover agents, confidential informants, surveillance, and dumpster diving (picking through discarded trash) is akin to human intelligence (HUMINT). Wiretaps, call traces, forensics, surveillance photos, and closed circuit TV video are means of technical law enforcement intelligence collection.

Regardless of their differing nomenclatures, each of these types of intelligence provides valuable insights and indicators of potential future criminal activities. Historically, the sharing of law enforcement intelligence has been limited. Assessments of intelligence failures have revealed that important indicators were often available but overlooked or not used. For instance, one indicator of potential terrorist activity that was not appreciated until after the 9/11 attacks was the enrollment of certain individuals in flight training schools.[1]

To be effective, law enforcement intelligence analysts must be accurate, timely, and predictive. Analysts must be aware of what is known, what is unknown or unclear, and what is presumed. Understanding this assists in both

---

1. See the *9/11 Commission Report*.

the feedback and the planning stages of the intelligence process. During the analytical phase of the cycle, analysts employ a number of different methods and models to predict both possible and probable results. These techniques range from comparing current situations with relevant historical events, to designing probability matrices and timelines, and development of social network models. There are a number of computer modeling and analytical software that are used such as *Analyst's Notebook*, *Orion*, and *Black Oak*. Additionally, in many cases, the use of "red-teaming" and "devil's-advocacy analysis" is highly beneficial when attempting to analyze the target organization. Of importance in an often "politically correct" environment is that intelligence analysts must (1) be willing to make judgments and not rely solely on computer-produced data and (2) be willing to stick their professional necks out and take a chance on a position that may not be popular. In recent years, emphasis has been placed on the professional training of law enforcement intelligence analysts. According to the International Association of Law Enforcement Intelligence Analysts (IALEIA) and the Department of Justice (DOJ), it is preferred that law enforcement intelligence analysts have a four-year college degree or a minimum of five years' experience.[2] Further, it is important for analysts to continue their educations through additional training throughout their careers.

Prior to September 11, 2001, law enforcement agencies typically consisted of units designed to deal with major narcotics trafficking, gangs, organized crime, and, occasionally, dignitary protection. In a post-9/11 America, however, many law enforcement agencies now have terrorism divisions, especially those operating within large metropolitan areas, particularly Houston, Los Angeles, and New York. Many have their own specialized Counterterrorism and Criminal Intelligence Bureaus.

Over the past decade, cooperation and coordination between law enforcement and the IC has been emphasized, resulting in the expansion of task-oriented units such as the Joint Terrorism Task Forces (JTTF) led by the DOJ and the FBI. JTTF units "are small cells of highly trained, locally based, passionately committed investigators, analysts, linguists, SWAT experts, and other specialists from dozens of US law enforcement and intelligence agencies."[3] The first JTTF was an FBI and NYPD cooperative initiative created in 1980. In 2002, the National JTTF was established to coordinate communication with localized JTTFs. There are currently over 100 JTTFs across the country. Another example of a multi-agency intelligence task force is the High Intensity Drug Trafficking Area (HIDTA) fusion centers. HIDTA fusion centers house federal, state, and local law enforcement intelligence personnel to coordinate anti-drug trafficking efforts.

In addition to JTTFs, regional and local joint fusion centers serve as terror-

---

2. *Law Enforcement Analytic Standards* handbook.
3. Department of Justice.

ism prevention and emergency response centers. These were created through a joint project by the DOJ and the DHS between 2003 and 2007. These fusion centers are funded by state and local police departments, and many house federal homeland security analysts. Their charters differ depending upon the jurisdiction, and some address all types of criminal activity, not just terrorism.

In 2003, the National Criminal Intelligence Sharing Plan (NCISP) was produced to serve as a model for local, state, tribal, and federal law enforcement agencies to enhance sharing of critical information. According to the Institute for Intergovernmental Research, the NCISP proposes a "nationwide communications capability that will link together all levels of law enforcement personnel, including officers on the streets, intelligence analysts, unit commanders, and police executives for the purpose of sharing critical data." There is a plethora of intelligence – and investigatory-related data bases and communications systems used for sharing data. For sensitive intelligence the Homeland Security Information Network (HSIN) is a principal mode for pushing national intelligence to law enforcement agencies and for sharing sensitive data between agencies.[4]

Despite these sharing initiatives, law enforcement intelligence agencies and divisions are not without limitations. In many instances, the budgets for law enforcement agencies are too constrained to allow for sufficient intelligence capabilities. Law enforcement intelligence units often cannot analyze collected data because of their limited personnel. Differing federal, state, and local laws and overlapping jurisdictions can inhibit the effective sharing of law enforcement intelligence between the tiers of agencies. Furthermore, as often depicted in popular television shows, organizational and personal jealousies can have negative effects and will never be completely expunged. The inherent secrecy that cloaks intelligence also fosters suspicions of improper behavior by law enforcement and infringements of civil liberties. The political reaction to even perceived violations often constrains law enforcement intelligence activities.

Despite limitations that exist, law enforcement's use of intelligence is expanding. Intelligence has become a major focus for some traditional law enforcement agencies, such as the FBI, and is a vital tool for urban police departments, such as the NYPD, that are targets of international terrorists. The walls to sharing vital law enforcement intelligence are crumbling, but progress is often constrained by legal issues. Nonetheless, intelligence-led policing will remain as a central strategy for law enforcement.

---

4. See http://www.dhs.gov/files/programs/gc_1156888108137.shtm for a description of HSIN.

READINGS FOR INSTRUCTORS

Those students who take an interest in this subject should educate themselves in all aspects of the field — the criminal mind; modus operandi of criminals; the planning, training, financing, and support functions for criminal organizations; and the available tools and resources that allow law enforcement intelligence personnel to delve deeply into criminals' psychological and cultural makeup. More and more academic institutions are offering criminal justice degrees and certificates, but a caution must be exercised against relying solely on the output of technology. Technology only manipulates what humans input. Law enforcement intelligence analysts must learn to think critically to apply effectively the intelligence they produce in support of the law enforcement mission.

The following are recommended readings for instructors and interested students:

Carter, David L. *Law Enforcement Intelligence Operations: An Overview of Concepts, Issues and Terms* (Tallahassee, FL: SMC Sciences Inc., 1990).

Carter, David L. *Law enforcement intelligence: A guide for state, local, and tribal law enforcement agencies* (2nd ed.). (Washington, DC: US Department of Justice Office of Community Oriented Policing Services, 2009). Retrieved from https://intellprogram.msu.edu/resources/publications.php.

Harris, Don R. et al. *The Basic Elements of Intelligence Revised* (Washington, DC: US Department of Justice Law Enforcement Assistance Administration, 1971).

International Association of Chiefs of Police. *Criminal Intelligence: Concepts and Issues Paper* (IACP National Law Enforcement Policy Center, 1998, updated in 2003).

Maguire, Mike "Policing by risks and targets: Some dimensions and implications of intelligence-led crime control," in *Policy and Society: An International Journal of Research and Policy* 9 (4), 2000.

Peterson, Marilyn B. *Applications in Criminal Analysis: A Sourcebook* (Westport, CT: Greenwood Press, 1994).

US Department of Justice. *Intelligence-Led Policing: The New Intelligence Architecture.* (Washington, DC: Bureau of Justice Assistance, 2009).

Wright, Richard, Bob Morehouse, Marilyn B. Peterson, and Lisa Palmieri (eds.). *Criminal Intelligence for the 21st Century* (Association of Law Enforcement Intelligence Units and the International Association of Law Enforcement Intelligence Analysts, 2011).

Joshua Bart is an operations research specialist and intelligence analyst for The Inter-Sec Group in San Antonio, Texas. He is an alumnus of The University of Texas at San Antonio (UTSA), where he studied political science, international studies, and global analysis. Mr. Bart is pursuing a master's certification in geographic information systems from UTSA.

Arthur E Gerringer is the president/CEO of The Inter-Sec Group, which provides antiterrorism, intelligence, security, and training services to the US Government and military. Mr. Gerringer is a 40-year veteran of the military intelligence and law enforcement communities. He has been an intelligence analyst, counter-intelligence agent, interrogator, physical security specialist, college adjunct professor, investigator, and trainer. Mr. Gerringer holds numerous certifications and three college degrees.

GUIDE TO THE STUDY OF INTELLIGENCE

Law Enforcement Intelligence

Its Evolution and Scope Today

Robert A. Smith

S
ocieties rely on intelligence to reduce uncertainty and support decisions affecting their security and survival.[1] Both national security intelligence and law enforcement intelligence have assumed greater importance in our globalized and interconnected world where threats can be measured in terms of hours, minutes and seconds. These two categories of intelligence overlap and often are indistinguishable from one another.

The National Strategy for Homeland Security[2] calls for "a common framework" to (1) prevent and disrupt terrorists' attacks; (2) protect the American people, our critical infrastructure, and key resources; (3) respond to and recover from incidents that do occur; and (4) continue to strengthen the foundation to ensure our long-term success. The strategy also states: "the law enforcement community, along with the intelligence community, must work to develop and implement national information requirements – develop a process for identifying information gaps, determining critical information requirements, and meeting those requirements collaboratively. We also encourage the implementation of *Intelligence-Led Policing* by state, local, and tribal law enforcement." [Emphasis added][3]

What Is Law Enforcement Intelligence?

The definition of law enforcement intelligence is "The end product (output)

1. T. Fingar, . *Reducing Uncertainty: Intelligence Analysis and National Security* (Stanford, CA: Stanford University Press, 2011),35.
2. *Office of the President of the United States, National Strategy for Homeland Security*. (Washington, DC,),1.
3. Ibid, 20.

of an analytic process that collects and assesses information about crimes and/or criminal enterprises with the purpose of making judgments and inferences about community conditions, potential problems, and criminal activity with the intent to pursue criminal prosecution or project crime trends to support informed decision making by [law enforcement] management."[4] The current definition of law enforcement intelligence incorporates the additional roles law enforcement agencies acquired in post 9/11 legislation that required all levels of law enforcement to detect, deter, prevent, respond to, and mitigate criminal and terrorist activities. These additional requirements encompass homeland security infrastructure protection, transnational organized crime, cybercrime, counterterrorism, weapons of mass destruction, contingency planning for both hometown and the *National Response Framework* and *National Incident Management System*, as well as intelligence support for order maintenance associated with public demonstrations, major event planning and National Special Security Events, such as Super Bowls or political conventions.

Law enforcement organizations' mission statements reflect two primary responsibilities: (1) to protect life, property, and constitutional guarantees;[5] and (2) preserve order by preventing crime, pursuing and apprehending offenders, and obtaining evidence for criminal prosecution and convictions."[6]

Reevaluation
6
Planning and Direction
1
Collection 2
Dissemination
5
4
3
Processing/ Collation
Analysis

Source: U.S. Department of Justice. (2005), The National Criminal Intelligence Sharing Plan (NCISP), Washington, DC; Department of Justice Global Justice Information Sharing Initiative, p. 3.

Law enforcement "methods of investigation"[7] are similar to the "intelligence cycle/process" in that the criminal investigator collects information and uses critical thinking and reasoning skills to determine what, when, where, by whom, why, and how a crime occurred. Key to this process is analysis, converting information into evidence, to prove or disprove hypotheses that a person or group perpetrated a crime or is about to perpetrate a crime. Criminal

4. US Department of Justice Bureau of Justice Assistance Global Justice Information Sharing Initiative. *Minimum Criminal Intelligence Training Standards for Law Enforcement and Other Criminal Justice Agencies in the United States*, Appendix – Criminal Intelligence Glossary of Terms – October 2007, "Law Enforcement Intelligence" (Washington, DC, 2007), 4;. as well as D. L. Carter . *Law Enforcement Intelligence: A Guide for State, Local, Tribal Law Enforcement Agencies* (Washington, DC: US Department of Justice Office of Community Oriented Policing Services, 2009), 445.

5. H. Goldstein. *Policing a Free Society* (Cambridge, MA: Ballinger, 1977), 35.

6. International Association of Chiefs of Police National Law Enforcement Policy Center, "Criminal Intelligence: Concepts and Issues Paper" (Alexandria, VA: IACP, 2003), 2.

7. C. E. O'Hara . *Fundamentals of Criminal Investigation*, 3d. ed. (Springfield, Il, Charles Thomas Publisher, 1973), 5-21.

investigators in the US are required to meet legal standards of proof in our courts of law. Additionally, both law enforcement intelligence units and investigators must operate within the framework of the US Constitution, federal Rules of Criminal Procedures, and statutory and case law to ensure citizens' civil liberties and rights are protected.[8] Violations of civil liberties are subject to both civil and criminal liability for federal agents and for state and local law officers.

Even though law enforcement agencies and the Intelligence Community (IC) operate under different sets of legal authorities, jurisdictions, mandates, and methods, both use the intelligence cycle/process and similar "tradecraft" as tools to satisfy their respective mission requirements. However, being largely prospective, national security intelligence rarely meets the standards of proof necessary for the courtroom.

The law enforcement and IC occasionally find themselves mutually affected by a criminal case, especially as when a defendant seeks access to classified information to assist the defense [Rule 16 of the Federal Rules of Criminal Procedures – Discovery and Inspection]. When this occurs, an issue of major concern to both communities is the protection of sensitive intelligence sources and methods. This protection is governed by the Classified Information Procedures Act [Public Law 96-456] and by the intelligence agencies placing restrictions on access to the information or by including special warning and caveats that restrict the use of the information.[9] An example is the presidential "state secrets" privilege [Reynolds v U.S.][10] Many critics are quick to assume that as all information obtained in a criminal investigation is subject to public scrutiny and review by courts of law and defendants this also applies to intelligence. However, the requirement for disclosure or discovery in court is only applicable to intelligence the law enforcement agency or prosecutor presents as evidence. The investigator or prosecutor can decide not to use intelligence that may reveal sensitive information regarding operational, tactical, and strategic law enforcement operations, informant identities, or operationally sensitive sources and methods.

The law enforcement community tries to prevent crime by identifying and prosecuting persons who are conspiring to commit – or have committed – crimes, as well as maintaining public order by monitoring criminal enterprises and extremist activities. Law enforcement intelligence supports operational and tactical decision-making as well as prosecutions. By contrast, the national security IC informs policymakers of threats and trends important for national defense, foreign relations, economics, counterintelligence, and transnational crime suppression including that associated with organized criminal organi-

---

8. C. H. Black . *Black's Law Dictionary*, 3d. ed. "Proof," (St. Paul, MN. West Publishing Co., 1991), 385 and 844-845.
9. Ibid
10. Ibid

zations and terrorist groups.[11] National security intelligence produce judgments (including National Intelligence Estimates) "based on a sizeable body of fact – but the facts are never so complete as to remove all uncertainty from the judgment."[12] – [or] "chiseled in stone – 'facts' that can be established like evidence in a courtroom trial."[13]

The Evolution of Law Enforcement Intelligence in the US

The use of intelligence for law enforcement purposes has paralleled political and social crises in the US. As early as the 1870's, law enforcement intelligence activities were utilized to prevent and control crime and violence.[14] By 1880, the New York City Police Department (NYPD) had an intelligence capability, when "intelligence gathering became an organized enterprise" [in the Detective Bureau].[15]

Since the 1970s, the law enforcement community has endeavored to establish standards and guidelines to provide better crime analysis and criminal intelligence functions while protecting citizens' civil liberties. Organizations such as the Law Enforcement Intelligence Unit, the Association of Law Enforcement Intelligence Analysts, Association of Crime Analysts, and the Departments of Justice and Homeland Security have developed and implemented criminal intelligence standards and professionalization training and certification of law enforcement intelligence analysts[16] and officers.[17]

Scope of Law Enforcement Intelligence in the United States Today

Law enforcement in America is "highly diverse and decentralized."[18] There are over 12,500 local police agencies and more than 809,000 state and

---

11. US Department of Justice. *United States Attorneys' Manual*. Washington, DC: Department of Justice, Section 9-90 (Washington, DC: Department of Justice, 2003), 210. Retrieved from *http://www.justice. gov/usao/eousa/foia_reading_room/usam/title9/90mcrm.htm*.

12. J. McLaughlin . "NIE Is Not as Decisive as it May Seem." CNN, December 10, 2007, Retrieved from *http://edition.cnn.com/2007/Politics/12/10/mclaughlin.commentary/index.html?iref=allsearch*.

13. Fingar. *Reducing Uncertainty*, 70.

14. W. Bowen, and H. Neal, H. *The United States Secret Service* (Philadelphia, PA, Chilton Co., 1960), 149-151.

15. J. Lardner and T. Reppetto. *NYPD: A City and Its Police* (New York, NY: Henry Holt and Co. LLC., 2000), 81.

16. US Department of Justice and International Association of Law Enforcement Intelligence Analysts. *Law Enforcement Analytic Standards*. 2d ed. (Washington, DC: Department of Justice, Global Justice Information, 2012).

17. U.S Department of Justice Bureau of Justice Assistance, Global Justice Information Sharing Initiative. *Minimum Criminal Intelligence Training Standards for Law Enforcement and Other Criminal Justice Agencies in the United States*. (Washington, DC: US Department of Justice Office of Community Oriented Policing Services, 2007).

18. Wesley Skogan and Kathleen Frydl (eds.). *Fairness and Effectiveness in Policing: The Evidence*. Committee to Review Research on Police Policy and Practices. (Washington, DC: National Academies Press, 2004), 2, 47.

local sworn officers. At the federal level, there are 73 agencies that account for 120,348 personnel plus 33 Inspector General Offices with law enforcement powers.[19] The four largest federal agencies, two in the Department of Homeland Security (DHS) and two in the Department of Justice (DOJ), employ two-thirds of all federal officers. The largest federal agency is the DHS US Customs and Border Protection (CBP) with 36,863 federal officers/investigators. The DHS US Immigration and Customs Enforcement (ICE) is the fourth largest federal agency with 12,466 federal officers/investigators. The DOJ employs about a third of federal officers in 2008, the Bureau of Prisons being the largest with 16,835 officers and the FBI being the second largest with 12,760 officers and special agents.[20] Approximately 75 percent of law enforcement agencies in the US have less than 24 sworn officers, and more often than not, do not have full-time analysts and intelligence officers.[21]

Prior to the 9/11 attacks on the US, many large urban police departments had intelligence units to analyze and map crime (often referred to as "Comp-Stat"). Intelligence analysis underpinned intelligence led policing efforts. Following the 9/11 attacks, the *Intelligence Reform and Terrorism Prevention Act of 2004* (IRTPA) mandated a national Information Sharing Environment (ISE). Subsequently, the *National Criminal Intelligence Sharing Plan* (NCISP) was developed. The NCISP was designed to ensure all law enforcement agencies, regardless of size or jurisdiction, have an intelligence capability.[22] Today state and local law enforcement agencies receive shared intelligence through a multitude of information sharing networks. These include the National Law Enforcement Telecommunications System (NLETS), the National Criminal Information System (NCIC), the Regional Information Sharing system (RISS), and the FBI and High Intensity Drug Trafficking Area (HIDTA) centers. The NCISP further recommended nationwide implementation of intelligence-led policing and the establishment of the Criminal Intelligence Coordinating Council to advise on implementation and provide guidance to the attorney general.[23]

The IRTPA also authorized the establishment of 78 state and urban intelligence fusion centers to work in conjunction with the 110 Joint Terrorism Task Forces (JTTF). Fusion centers and JTTFs serve distinct, but complementary roles: fusion centers are operated by state and local entities to share all crimes and all hazards threat information; the FBI-led JTTFs focus on terrorism-related investigations. The DOJ and DHS collaborated to develop state and urban area

19. US Department of Justice. *Federal Law Enforcement Officers, 2008*, NCJ238250 (Washington, DC: Department of Justice Office of Justice Programs Bureau of Justice Statistics, June 2012), 1, 11.
20. Ibid, 2-3.
21. US Department of Justice Bureau of Justice Assistance, Global Justice Information Sharing Initiative, The National Criminal Intelligence Sharing Plan (NCISP) (Washington, DC; Department of Justice Global Justice Information Sharing Initiative, 2003): iii.
22. US Department of Justice, The National Criminal Intelligence Sharing Plan (NCISP), iv.
23. US Department of Justice . "Criminal Intelligence Coordinating Council" (Tallahassee, FL: Institute for Intergovernmental Research, 2004). Retrieved from *http://www.iir.com/giwg/council.htm*

fusion center standards and guidelines, as well as national Suspicious Activities Reporting (SARs) and privacy and civil liberties standards and guidelines.[24]

Conclusion

The 2010 *National Security Strategy* states: "to prevent acts of terrorism on American soil, we must enlist all of our intelligence, law enforcement, and homeland security capabilities. We will continue to integrate and leverage state and major urban area fusion centers that have the capability to share classified information; establish a nationwide framework for reporting suspicious activity; and implement an integrated approach to our counterterrorism information systems to ensure that the analyst, agents, and officers who protect us have access to all relevant intelligence throughout the government."[25]

FBI Director Robert S. Mueller III, stated on March 12, 2012, during his testimony before the US Senate Select Committee on Intelligence, "The ability of the criminal justice system to produce intelligence is often overlooked and underestimated ... the ultimate goal in criminal cases is to obtain the cooperation of individuals who during plea agreements provide valuable information" that becomes actionable intelligence for both law enforcement and national security intelligence agencies.[26]

"The terrorist attacks of 9/11 served as a catalyst for dramatic changes to the United States national security enterprise," wrote Director of National Intelligence James Clapper. "Among those changes is the recognition that our local, state, and tribal law enforcement agencies make critical contributions not only to the protection of our communities but to the security of the United States at large.... The progress we have made to improve coordination between the intelligence community and law enforcement since 9/11 has been phenomenal."[27]

---

24. US Department of Homeland Security. "National Network of Fusion Centers Fact Sheet" (2013). Retrieved from *http://www.dhs.gov/national-network-fusion-centers-fact-sheet*.

25. Office of the President of the United States, *National Security Strategy* (Washington, DC, May 2010), 20. Retrieved from *http://www.whitehouse.gov/sites/default/files/rss_viewer/National_Security_Strategy.pdf*.

26. R. S. Mueller, III. US Senate Intelligence Committee Hearing, "Worldwide Threats to the U.S.," March 12, 2013, Retrieved from CSPAN http://www.c-span.org/events/senate-intelligence-comte-hearing-on-worldwide-threats-to-the-us/10737438688-1/

27. J. R. Clapper . "Effective Intelligence Must Remain a Top Priority." *The Police Chief.* (Alexandria, VA: The International Association of Chiefs of Police, 2012), 12. Retrieved from *http://naylornetwork.com/iac-nxt*

READINGS FOR INSTRUCTORS

Besides the sources identified in the footnotes, the following are recommended for further reading.

A comprehensive history of law enforcement intelligence in America can be found in D. L. Carter. *Law Enforcement Intelligence: A Guide for State, Local, and Tribal Law Enforcement Agencies, 2d ed.* (Washington, DC: US Department of Justice Community Oriented Policing Services, 2009). This is available on the Web at *http://it.ojp.gov/docdownloader.aspx?ddad=1133*.

Current law enforcement intelligence analyst guidance for best practices provided in *Criminal Intelligence For the 21st Century* (Richmond, VA: Association of Law Enforcement Intelligence Units and International Association of Law Enforcement Intelligence Analysts, 2011).

Contemporary guidance to assist law enforcement first responders in accessing and understanding federal intelligence reporting and to encourage the sharing of information outlined in the *Interagency Threat Assessment and Coordination Group, Intelligence Guide for First Responders, 2nd Ed.* (Washington, DC: Interagency Threat Assessment and Coordination Group, 2011). This is on the web at *http://www.nctc.gov/docs/ITALG_Guide_For_First_Responders_2011.pdf*)

Robert A. Smith is president of ProtectionMetrics LLC and an adjunct associate professor, University of Maryland University College (UMUC) in the Graduate School's Intelligence Management Program. Mr. Smith is a 25-year veteran of the US Secret Service retiring in 2001 as special agent charge of the Office of Protective Operations. He later served as deputy assistant director of the Federal Law Enforcement Training Center (FLETC). Mr. Smith has a BA in criminal justice and criminology from the University of Maryland and a MS in strategic intelligence from the Joint Military Intelligence College. Mr. Smith also serves on the Board of the International Association for Intelligence Education and is a member of the Maryland Chiefs Association of Police Training Committee.

GUIDE TO THE STUDY OF INTELLIGENCE

Guide to Intelligence Support for Military Operations

Karl Haigler

The importance of timely and accurate intelligence to support frontline troops can hardly be exaggerated. For the wars in Afghanistan, Iraq, and the ongoing worldwide campaign against terrorists, military commanders and civilian policy makers rely on intelligence professionals to piece together information from a variety of sources on an adversary's capabilities and intent.

One should understand the different contexts of defense intelligence: strategic, operational, and tactical. Intelligence support of military policy-making and strategy development is "strategic intelligence;" support to planning operations at the national or regional level is referred to as "operational intelligence;" and intelligence that is required to execute local operations or react to an adversary's actions is "tactical intelligence."[1]

Strategic intelligence is defined as "the product of gathering information about foreign military capabilities, intentions, plans, dispositions, and equipment; analyzing the contents of that information; and disseminating the findings to decision makers, combat troops, and other recipients."[2] The Department of Defense's 2010 Quadrennial Defense Review (QDR) identifies a variety of threats and issues of global security of strategic intelligence concern. Specific focus is given, for instance, to weapons of mass destruction (WMD): "The instability or collapse of a WMD-armed state is among our most troubling concerns. Such an occurrence could lead to rapid proliferation of WMD material, weapons, and technology, and could quickly become a global crisis posing

---

1. John Keegan's *Intelligence in War* (2003) provides many historical cases that illustrate the differences between tactical and strategic intelligence, such as in Operation Desert Storm (p. 314).
2. http://www.dia.mil/history

a direct physical threat to the United States and all other nations." A National Intelligence Estimate (NIE) is the Intelligence Community's product related to such a high-priority strategic issue. Underscoring the defense intelligence interest in such a threat, the undersecretary of defense for intelligence (USD(I)) wrote in 2008: "The Defense Intelligence Enterprise must combat this threat through focused intelligence that identifies potential threat sources, methodologies, and threat-based protective measures. It must also develop accurate and timely risk assessments for military and civilian planning, decision making, and potential operational use."[3]

According to the Department of Defense (DoD), operational intelligence is required "for planning and conducting campaigns and major operations to accomplish strategic objectives within theaters or areas of operations." Over the past decade, counterinsurgency (COIN) operations have presented challenges to traditional approaches to operational intelligence. In Iraq and Afghanistan, adaptations to traditional operational intelligence doctrine, such as developing close relationships with indigenous populations, have been critical to success. Urban combat in Iraq required new ways of organizing the collection and exploitation of intelligence. One example comes from the 1st Armored Division 2d Brigade Combat Team. The brigade commander's account of how his unit developed indigenous human sources, exploited captured insurgent technology, and aligned the information gained from these sources with the brigade's special intelligence requirements (SIR) provides valuable lessons learned in COIN operations.[4]

"Tactical intelligence is ... required for planning and conducting ... military operations at the local level. It concerns information about the enemy that is designed to help locate the enemy and decide which tactics, units, and weapons will most likely contribute to victory in an assigned area, and when properly applied, it can be a significant force multiplier."[5] The tactical analyst in ground warfare evaluates information gathered from a variety of sources to support his Commander's Critical Information Requirements (CCIR). Fundamental to this task is the analyst's ability to help the commander visualize the threats that his forces could face in his area of operations (AO) as part of the Intelligence Preparation of the Battlefield (IPB).[6] One of the most prominent tactical threats faced today is the improvised explosive device (IED). The evolution of this asymmetric warfare tactic over the past two years in Afghanistan now includes the use of crude bombs that have no metal parts. The analyst needs to identify the sources and nature of these devices, including the many forms they

3. Office of the undersecretary of defense for intelligence, "The Defense Intelligence Enterprise": 16.
4. .Ralph O. Baker, "HUMINT-Centric Operations: Developing Actionable Intelligence in the Urban Counterinsurgency Environment," *Military Review* 87, March-April 2007), 12-21. (*http://findarticles.com/p/articles/mi_m0PBZ/is_2_87/ai_n27175922/*)
5. http://www.dia.mil/history
6. *US Army Field Manual 2-0,* "All-Source Intelligence," Chapter 5, Paragraph 5.5.

may take—from roadside bombs to vehicle-borne and body-borne explosives. Tactical intelligence supports attacks on the human networks that make and deploy IEDs as well as defeating the devices themselves. For example, airborne electronic warfare (EW) assets have been used to remotely detonate IEDs before they pose a threat to friendly forces. Imagery from unmanned aerial systems is used to detect the planting of IEDs. Video is used to track individuals to their hiding places and bomb factories.

The military intelligence analyst receives information from a variety of technical means, each of which makes a unique contribution, as well as human sources. Signals intelligence (SIGINT), exploiting an adversary's use of the electromagnetic spectrum, has been used to provide early warning of pending enemy attacks or the disposition his forces. One historical example, when SIGINT was a crucial source, is the Battle of the North Atlantic, when the U-boat threat during World War II threatened England's survival. In modern times SIGINT on enemy air defense radars provides targeting intelligence for an air campaign to establish air superiority. Used in combination with other forms of intelligence, SIGINT can reveal telltale signatures of specific military units or equipment operating in an area of interest for the purposes of identification, tracking, and targeting.

Imagery intelligence (IMINT) is used in many ways to assist both military forces and civilian decision makers. Imagery forms the basis for Geospatial Intelligence (GEOINT), which is the "exploitation and analysis of imagery and geospatial information to describe, assess, and visually depict physical features and geographically referenced activities on the Earth."[7] IMINT is collected via satellites, unmanned aerial vehicles (e.g., the Predator), reconnaissance aircraft (e.g., the U-2), and ground systems. IMINT is "the only intelligence system that allows [ground force] commanders to visualize their area of operations in near real time as the operation progresses."[8] IMINT is also critical in planning and intelligence preparation of the battlefield (IPB). Perhaps the most famous public example of IMINT was the publication of aerial photos of Soviet missiles during the Cuban Missile Crisis. Given the gravity of the situation, President Kennedy's release of IMINT to make the diplomatic case at the United Nations and convince the American people of the need for military action provided a precedent for the public use of IMINT.[9]

Human intelligence (HUMINT) collection operations focus on "determining the capabilities, threat characteristics, vulnerabilities, and intentions of threat and potential threat forces" and involve screening, interrogation, debriefing (e.g., of friendly forces), and liaison operations with friendly foreign

---

7. http://www.nga.mil
8. *US Army Field Manual 2-0*, "Imagery Intelligence," Chapter 9, paragraph 4.
9. http://www.fas.org/irp/imint/cubakent.htm

militaries and intelligence services.[10] HUMINT includes acquiring documents and media sources, such as computers and hard drives. The 2d Brigade Combat Team's account in Iraq details the identification and training of informants and the exploitation of their information for both force protection and developing actionable intelligence. HUMINT also contributes to a greater understanding of the culture and "the nuances of local demographics" such as different ethnic, sectarian, political, and tribal groups.[11] HUMINT can be crucial for military purposes. For instance, during the Cuban Missile Crisis, the CIA-Secret Intelligence Service asset, Oleg Penkovskiy, a Soviet General Staff military intelligence colonel, provided critical intelligence on the Soviet strategic rocket forces readiness and capabilities. Anti-Castro sources in Cuba also helped pinpoint the location of missile sites in western Cuba.[12]

"Measurement and Signature Intelligence [MASINT] is ... derived from specific technical sensors for the purpose of identifying ... distinctive features associated with [a target.]"[13] Among intelligence scholars there is some controversy, as noted by Lowenthal, as to whether MASINT constitutes a separate technical discipline or whether it represents a hybrid of other disciplines.[14] Nevertheless, the contributions of MASINT in detecting WMD, monitoring potential weapons development sites, and countering an adversary's tactics of denial and deception can be significant. In addition, by identifying the electronic, physical, thermal, acoustic, and other signatures of an adversary's weapons system, MASINT contributes to the library of threat models used for subsequent threat assessments and tactical scenarios.

Open-source intelligence [OSINT] produces intelligence derived from the analysis of publicly available information. It supplements and supports other intelligence gathering activities by providing background cultural or biographical information, for instance, relevant to a commander's requirements. Analysis of information from unclassified sources can be used effectively to reduce the need for more complex classified data gathering. In addition to its supporting and potential cost-saving role, OSINT provides valuable insights of its own. In a March 26, 2001 interview on National Public Radio, Lieutenant Colonel Reid Sawyer, an Army intelligence officer and head of West Point's Combating Terrorism Center, said: "I think that open source provides a critical lens into understanding the world around us in a much more dynamic way than traditional intelligence sources can provide."

Reliance on any single source of intelligence information can bias an analyst's judgments or blind him to a threat. The intent of "all-source analysis" is for

---

10. *US Army Field Manual 2-0*, "Human Intelligence," Chapter 7, paragraph 5.
11. Baker, 17.
12. Lowenthal, Mark, *Intelligence: From Secrets to Policy*: 4th Edition, (CQ Press, Washington, D.C., 2009), 72.
13. *US Army Field Manual 2-0*, "Measurement and Signature Intelligence," Chapter 10, Paragraph 1.
14. Lowenthal, 96.

the analyst to draw upon a variety of sources and means. The analyst needs to be alert to an adversary's potential use of deception, especially in exploiting the US's well-known reliance on technology-based data collection. Technological advancements in intelligence, as has been noted in assessments of Operation Desert Storm, should not be viewed as making a nation "deception-proof."[15] Deception detection, then, can be one of the valuable insights that intelligence can make regarding an adversary's intent, operational vulnerabilities, or tactical predilections.[16]

"Intelligence, Surveillance, and Reconnaissance (ISR)" is the term used by the military to describe the systems, processes, and products associated with all of the information gathering capabilities of the military. ISR plays a critical role supporting the planning of operations. An interesting recent example is the raid on Osama Bin Laden's compound in Pakistan. The National Geospatial-Intelligence Agency (NGA), the Intelligence Community's experts on IMINT and GEOINT, employed both IMINT and MASINT capabilities, to do the following:

- Create a three-dimensional rendering of Bin Laden's Abbottabad compound using imagery and laser-based sensing devices—laser radar, or ladar;
- Analyze data from a sophisticated next-generation unmanned aerial vehicle that kept watch on the compound before, during, and after the raid;
- Help the Joint Special Operations Command create precise mission simulators for the pilots who flew the helicopters to practice before the raid; and
- Provide the CIA and others assessments of the number of people who lived inside the compound, their heights and genders.[17]

The role of the NGA in the Bin Laden raid is a classic example of the value of ISR for time-sensitive decision-making where "ISR visualization helps the commander ... identify fleeting opportunities for intelligence collection or strike operations against adversary time-sensitive targets that may warrant dynamic re-tasking of collection platforms or re-targeting of strike assets."[18]

The shorter the time frame that the intelligence is needed and the closer the analyst works to the tactical level, the greater the reliance is on those assets providing the most timely, accurate information and those assets that are within the analyst's ability to "task" or access easily. This is particularly true where the location of a high-value target (HVT) of immediate interest may emerge from information that is time-sensitive. In such a case, the analyst must coor-

---

15. http://www.au.af.mil/info-ops/index.htm.
16. .John B. Sheldon, "Deciphering Cyberpower: Strategic Purpose in Peace and War, *Strategic Studies Quarterly*, Summer 2011, 104.
17. Marc Ambinder, "In Raid on Bin Laden, Little-Known Geospatial Agency Played Vital Role," *National Journal*, May 5, 2011 (http://www.nationaljournal.com/whitehouse/in-raid-on-bin-laden-little-known-geospatial-agency-played-vital-role-20110505?page=1)
18. Joint and National Intelligence Support to Military Operations, Joint Publication 2-01, Chapter III, 28

dinate with assets that can provide target acquisition. This form of "combat information," data gained from ISR assets, may be shared with commanders prior to analysis depending on the urgency of the data for current operations.[19]

In cyber warfare, operations and intelligence functions blur. This is illustrated by the commander of the US Cyber Command being the same person as the director of the National Security Agency (NSA), the Intelligence Community's SIGINT organization. A recent article noted that the use of cyber viruses by the military can include "studying the cyber-capabilities of adversaries or examining power plants or [how] other networks operate."[20] In combating WMD proliferation, the use of cyber-weapons against vital computer operating systems can disrupt and delay a target nation's ability to produce weapons-grade material, for instance, as has been speculated with introduction of the Stuxnet virus in Iranian nuclear facilities.[21]

The strategic importance of intelligence to cyber warfare is a high-priority topic, as cyber warfare can contribute to one's "ability in peace and war to manipulate the strategic environment to one's advantage while at the same time degrading the ability of an adversary to comprehend that same environment."[22] At the tactical level cyber warfare can: "disrupt and sabotage adversary cyber-dependent activities and communications; steal information that is valuable to the adversary; monitor and spy on adversary activities through cyberspace; and deceive cyber-dependent adversaries into making decisions (or not making decisions) that are favorable to the perpetrator through the manipulation of adversary information...."[23] Given the microsecond speed of cyber warfare, intelligence preparation of the cyber battlefield is essential.

Conclusion

The critical nature of intelligence's role in supporting military operations will not decrease over time. In fact, given the likely role of counterinsurgency warfare and the threats from non-state actors in asymmetric warfare, the foreseeable future underscores the importance of intelligence for success on the battlefield—to include "non-kinetic" warfare in cyberspace. The variety of technical means, for collection and analysis, can present challenges in and of itself for "all-source" analysts. The role of human judgment, in not being overwhelmed by the deluge of data and maintaining a sensitivity to deception, makes the education and training of analysts a high priority for the Intelligence

19. Joint Publication 2-01, Chapter III, 2-3.
20. Nakashima, Ellen, "List of Cyber-Weapons Developed by Pentagon to Streamline Computer Warfare," *Washington Post*, May 31, 2011. (*http://www.washingtonpost.com/national/list-of-cyber-weapons-developed-by-pentagon-to-streamline-computer-warfare/2011/05/31/AGSubIFH_story.html*)
21. Sheldon, 104.
22. Sheldon, 103.
23. Sheldon, 104.

Community. The role of the analyst supporting future military operations highlights the need to exploit "lessons learned" in current operations: an analyst's prioritizing the need for greater cultural understanding against the insatiable demands for "real time" displays of the battle area is likely to get more attention in the allocation of resources for non-traditional warfare. A well-balanced approach to the preparation of emerging analytical talent and development of the current intelligence workforce should reflect the evolving nature of the threats to the nation's security and should anticipate the implications of these threats to the needs of military commander and civilian policy maker alike.

READINGS FOR INSTRUCTORS

The following books, articles, and documents are suggested for a greater understanding of military intelligence.

Baker, Ralph. "HUMINT-Centric Operations: Developing Actionable Intelligence in the Urban Counterinsurgency Environment," *Military Review*, 87 (March-April 2007), 12-21.

Jones, R. V. *Reflections on Intelligence* (London: Mandarin Paperbacks, 1990). See especially Chapters 5, 6, and 10.

Kahn, David. *The Codebreakers: The Comprehensive History of Secret Communication from Ancient Times to the Internet* (New York: Scribner, 1996).

Keegan, John. *Intelligence in War: Knowledge of the Enemy from Napolean to Al-Qaeda* (New York: Alfred A. Knopf, 2003). See especially Chapters 1, 3, 6, 8, and Conclusion.

Lowenthal, Mark. *Intelligence: From Secrets to Policy: 4th Edition*, (Washington, DC: CQ Press, 2009). See especially Chapters 5 and 6.

Sheldon, John B. "Deciphering Cyberpower: Strategic Purpose in Peace and War," *Strategic Studies Quarterly*, Summer 2011.

Warner, Michael. *The Office of Strategic Services: America's First Intelligence Agency*, (Washington, DC: CIA Center for the Study of Intelligence, 2000).

ORIGINAL SOURCES IN INTELLIGENCE:

Office of the Secretary of Defense, Department of Defense, "Quadrennial Defense Review," February, 2010. *http://defense.gov/qdr*

Office of Undersecretary of Defense (Intelligence), Department of Defense, "The Defense Intelligence Enterprise," 2008. Source document can be found at the Naval Postgraduate School's Homeland Security Digital Library, *http://www.hsdl.org*

Headquarters, Department of the Army, *US Army Field Manual 2-0 Intelligence*, 2010

Joint Chiefs of Staff, Department of Defense, *Joint and National Intelligence Support to Military Operations*, Joint Publication 2-01, 2004. *http://www.fas.org/irp/dod/jp2_01.pdf*

THE WEB SITES LISTED BELOW ARE VALUABLE SOURCES FOR UNDERSTANDING INTELLIGENCE IN SUPPORT OF MILITARY OPERATIONS.

http://www.fas.org: This is the website for the Federation of American Scientists. Its intelligence project has archived many historically relevant documents related to intelligence.

https://www.cia.gov: This is the CIA's website. The link to the Center for the Study of Intelligence admits the researcher to a wealth of published and declassified studies related to intelligence.

http://www.dia.mil/About/History/: This site provides a succinct account of definitions, concepts, and the intelligence analysis process.

https://www.hsdl.org/c/: A searchable database that provides access to strategic, executive-level documents related to issues of intelligence located on site of Naval Postgraduate School.

https://www.nga.mil/Pages/Default.aspx: This is the website of the National Geospatial-Intelligence Agency.

http://www.au.af.mil/info-ops/index.htm: An extremely comprehensive database that contains web sites and other resources of strategic, operational, and tactical intelligence interest. See the Intelligence Gateway to get started.

http://www.acronymfinder.com: Along with http://www.answers.com this is a good resource for getting information on acronyms and other esoteric intelligence terminology for beginners.

http://www.carlisle.army.mil: This is the site for the Army's War College.

Karl Haigler is a retired military intelligence officer. He served in the US Army Reserve, the intelligence division of the Joint Staff, and as an analyst in the Defense Intelligence Agency's Soviet Ground Forces Division. He was the director of adult education in the US Department of Education and a member of the Senior Executive Service. He also served as special advisor to the governor of Mississippi on literacy and workforce development issues. He has been a secondary school teacher and an instructor in post-secondary education.

The author wishes to thank Jeff Holcomb, David Campbell, Terry Clark, Mike Gillies, and Tom Brister for their insights and contributions on the theory and practice of intelligence. He also wants to recognize students at Wake Forest University and Forsyth Country Day School (Lewisville, NC) for their keen participation in intelligence analysis simulations.

GUIDE TO THE STUDY OF INTELLIGENCE

Homeland Security and Intelligence

Fusing Sometimes Incompatible Missions

William C. Spracher, Ed.D.

One purpose of the *Guide to the Study of Intelligence* is to offer "suggestions for instructors teaching various topics for which intelligence is an important component."[1] As a National Intelligence University faculty member, I can attest that many courses are taught on intelligence per se, and somewhat fewer on homeland security, the latter usually by rotating faculty "chairs" from the Department of Homeland Security (DHS), the Federal Bureau of Investigation (FBI), and the US Coast Guard (USCG).[2] At times, however, the students hailing from all the armed services and most of the civilian agencies of the Intelligence Community (IC) view these subjects as separate and distinct. One is outward-looking, focused primarily on what we used to carefully define as "foreign intelligence," the other inward-looking, focused on "domestic intelligence."

The multiple terrorist attacks of September 11, 2001 prompted a critical relook of the boundaries between foreign and domestic intelligence gathering as it became painfully obvious that threats are all around us and in our midst. The Homeland Security Act of 2002 created DHS, formally established March 1, 2003, combining assets from 22 different departments and agencies and more than 85,000 personnel previously performing related but separate duties.[3] The USA PATRIOT Act of 2001 also changed the way intelligence and homeland security are viewed, as did the Intelligence Reform and Terrorism Prevention Act of 2004, which in part mandated the establishment of the Office of the Director of National Intelligence (ODNI) and called for the creation of a

---

1. AFIO website, http://www.afio.com/40_guide.htm.
2. *Catalog, 2014-2015*, National Intelligence University, 4.
3. DHS website, http://www.dhs.gov/history.

National Intelligence University (NIU). Other key documents which influenced the development of the US national security establishment since then have included the 9/11 *Commission Report* and the *WMD Commission Report*.[4]

Several years ago, when NIU was operating under one of its previous names, the Joint Military Intelligence College (JMIC), I was asked to contribute an article on how homeland security relates to intelligence. The result was "Homeland Security and Intelligence: Can Oil Mix with Water in an Open Society?"[5] In that piece, I argued that one of the most controversial aspects in the process of developing DHS, and refining the concept of homeland security overall, is the role of intelligence in gathering information on the terrorist threat and analyzing it for key decisionmakers.[6] I explored the intelligence challenges for homeland security, to include the problems of merging disparate cultures—law enforcement vice intelligence; civilian actors vice military; federal efforts vice those at the state, local, and tribal levels; and a domestic focus vice the foreign perspective. At play is the traditional tradeoff between the rights of ordinary US citizens to their privacy and the national security imperatives of the country at large, a delicate balancing act that has taxed the patience and sensitivities of the American people, and the more time that has elapsed since a major attack inside the borders of the US the more outraged some people seem to become. Witness the huge reaction to revelations of domestic and diplomatic spying by the PFC Bradley Manning, "WikiLeaks," and Edward Snowden sagas that still fill the headlines of our newspapers.[7]

"Homeland security" is a relatively new term in the American lexicon. We have long dealt with law enforcement, counterintelligence, and internal security (plus a term that Americans tend to recoil at hearing, but citizens of many other countries have routinely practiced—countersubversion), and we tend to separate those inward-looking exercises from the more outward-looking foreign intelligence. The FBI traditionally was responsible for counterintelligence (CI) within the borders of the US while the Central Intelligence Agency (CIA) had purview over CI overseas, and that is still the case, though the FBI maintains legal attachés overseas at a number of US Embassies, in particular those in countries with a large number of US citizens. The armed forces, especially the US Army, got into a great deal of trouble in the late 1960s-early 1970s

---

4. The former, promulgated on July 22, 2004, is officially known as *The Final Report of the National Commission on Terrorist Attacks Upon the United States*; and the latter, promulgated on December 3, 2008, is officially known as *World at Risk: Commission on Prevention of Weapons of Mass Destruction, Proliferation, and Terrorism*.

5. William C. Spracher, "Homeland Security and Intelligence: Can Oil Mix with Water in an Open Society?" in *Learning with Professionals: Selected Works from the Joint Military Intelligence College* (Washington, DC: Joint Military Intelligence College, 2005), 139-140. Originally published in *Low Intensity Conflict & Law Enforcement* 11 (1), Spring 2002, 29-54.

6. Ibid, 145.

7. Julie Tate, "Bradley Manning Sentenced to 35 Years in WikiLeaks Case," *The Washington Post*, August 21, 2013; Barton Gellman, "Edward Snowden, after Months of NSA Revelations, Says His Mission's Accomplished," *The Washington Post*, December 23, 2013.

when they were pulled by various Presidential administrations into collecting information on domestic actors, and particularly those assessed as somehow tied to communism and/or posing a threat to our national security.

Most of the existing intelligence oversight mechanisms the US utilizes today came about in the 1970s as a result of tightening controls against such abuses. We now have in Congress the Senate Select Committee on Intelligence (SSCI) and the House Permanent Select Committee on Intelligence (HPSCI), which oversee intelligence activities of the various components of the Executive Branch that formerly tended to get their guidance only from the President and the National Security Council. After 9/11, there were created a White House Homeland Security Council and Homeland Security Committees in both houses of Congress.[8] Needless to say, some of the latter's duties overlap with those of the intelligence select committees. Furthermore, DHS probably receives more oversight than any entity in the Executive Branch. I have seen mind-boggling charts showing how many different committees and subcommittees routinely oversee one function or another of the vast and complex Cabinet department known as DHS.[9] To complicate matters even more, the Department of Defense (DOD) exercises a function known as "homeland defense."[10] There is an assistant secretary for homeland defense and Americas' security affairs overseeing this function, and, of course, that senior official collaborates closely with the various entities responsible for homeland security and also those responsible for intelligence.

At about the time the homeland security/homeland defense lash-up was being worked out institutionally and statutorily, an excellent article on this issue was published in the National Defense University's premier publication, *Joint Force Quarterly*. Here is an excerpt from the article, titled "The DOD Role in Homeland Security":

> To date the Secretary of Defense has specifically referred to DOD involvement as homeland defense rather than homeland security—signifying more than a semantic difference. Defense implies deterrence and/or response whereas security is more comprehensive; defense is part of security but not the only part. This distinction avoids having the Pentagon become embroiled in an ill-defined mission as capstone agency for Federal, state, and local police and first response agencies. The Department of Defense is not prepared, willing, or in some cases constitutionally permitted to play that role. Yet because agencies that must respond to the consequences of an attack using weapons of mass destruction need resources now instead of after another terrorist attack, the DOD mission must be expanded from just defending the

---

8. Mark M. Lowenthal, *Intelligence: From Secrets to Policy*, 5th ed. (Washington, DC: CQ Press, 2012), 31.

9. "Untangling the Web: Congressional Oversight and the Department of Homeland Security," *CSIS Business Executives for National Security*, December 10, 2004, 6. It should be noted that the White House Homeland Security Council has now been folded into the National Security Council.

10. M. E. Krause, "Homeland Defense and Security," *Joint Force Quarterly* 40, January 2006. See also "DOD Releases Strategy for Homeland Defense and Defense Support for Civil Authorities," *DOD News Release* 172-13, March 22, 2013.

homeland to supporting homeland security, especially since a future attack could inflict more casualties than were suffered on 9/11.[11]

Another part of the Pentagon is also tied in closely with the intelligence organs, and that is under the control of the assistant secretary for special operations and low intensity conflict (ASD SO/LIC).[12]

The DHS is now a full-fledged member of the 16-agency IC through its Office of Intelligence and Analysis (I&A). Interestingly, when the department was first stood up, that entity was known as the Directorate of Information Analysis and Infrastructure Protection. However, growing pains and some confusion as to the scope of its mission soon led to splitting out the intelligence and infrastructure protection functions.[13] There was a fairly rapid turnover of I&A directors too as the department struggled to find its proper niche in the IC and sort out clearly defined roles and missions. The department still suffers from rapid turnover of key billets and slowness in recruiting high-level talent, which even when found often takes months to get through the US Senate confirmation process.[14] Protection of critical infrastructure is key in an era when the terrorist threat inside our national borders is palpable. Some would not define it as an intelligence mission per se but cannot dispute that it is at least closely related to intelligence. For example, a few academic entities that look at these subjects—without inserting the word "intelligence" into their names—include the George Washington University Homeland Security Policy Institute, the Naval Postgraduate School Center for Homeland Defense and Security, the George Mason University (GMU) School of Law Center for Infrastructure Protection and Homeland Security, and the US Military Academy (USMA) Department of Social Sciences Combating Terrorism Center. The GMU center produces an excellent monthly CIP Report and the USMA center a monthly CTC Sentinel, which are highly commended to instructors looking for current teaching materials.

The CIP Report, produced digitally on a monthly basis, can be accessed at http://cip.gmu.edu. Each issue is introduced by the center director, a retired US Army lieutenant general whom this author knew when he was director of the Army Staff and later deputy undersecretary of the army for international affairs. The "Report" focuses on a different theme each month. For example,

---

11. Adrian A. Erckenbrack and Aaron Scholer, "The DOD Role in Homeland Security," *Joint Force Quarterly* 35, Summer 2003, 1.

12. "Assistant Secretary for Special Operations/Low-Intensity Conflict," Fact Sheet, undersecretary of defense for policy, undated, accessed at http://policy.defense.gov/solic, November 25, 2014.

13. Office of the Inspector General, Department of Homeland Security, *Survey of the Information Analysis and Infrastructure Protection Directorate*, undated. See also James Burch, "The Domestic Intelligence Gap: Progress Since 9/11?" in Proceedings of the 2008 Center Homeland Defense & Security Annual Conference, *Homeland Security Affairs*, online journal of the Center for Homeland Defense and Security, Naval Postgraduate School, 2008.

14. Jerry Markon, "Top-Level Turnover Makes It Harder for DHS to Stay on Top of Evolving Threats," *The Washington Post*, September 21, 2014, accessed September 30, 2014, at http://www.washington-post.com/politics/top-level-turnover-makes-it-harder-for-dhs-to-stay.

in July 2014, it was "State and Tribal"; in August 2014, "Water and Water Infrastructure"; in September 2014, "Risk and Risk Management"; and in October 2014, "Cybersecurity." As the director points out in his cover introduction to the latest issue, partnerships are critical in the homeland security field—e.g., a cybersecurity research partnership among GMU, IBM Corporation, and the National Science Foundation.[15] The center's associate director served as a panelist during a one-day workshop this author organized in November 2012 with the theme "Intelligence Education and Training."[16] Many of these same issues are discussed via a LinkedIn group known as "The Intelligence and Homeland Security Alliance," which interested parties can access through LinkedIn, the popular social media site used widely within the US Government and commercial entities.[17] Another excellent resource is a news compilation of articles dealing with homeland security and intelligence, known as the "CABLE-Gram," disseminated to select members by the National Military Intelligence Association (NMIA).[18]

There is no shortage of books that deal with homeland security, and many of them examine the role of intelligence in generating information of value that assists our national, state, local, and tribal entities in keeping us safe. Michael Chertoff, DHS secretary in the George W. Bush administration and now head of his own influential consulting firm, The Chertoff Group, in 2009 published *Homeland Security: Assessing the First Five Years*. The foreword was penned by former Representative Lee H. Hamilton, who is now president of the Woodrow Wilson International Center for Scholars in Washington, DC. Hamilton stated that "both during and after my tenure as vice chairman of the 9/11 Commission, I witnessed striking changes, ranging from the restructuring of our intelligence agencies to the creation of the Department of Homeland Security. ... The FBI had made counterterrorism a top priority, fundamentally changing the law enforcement culture and direction of the Bureau. An integrated terrorist watch is now complete."[19] In other words, the FBI is one of those IC agencies where counterterrorism, intelligence, and homeland security all come together and are fused.

In the intelligence business, we often say our job is to minimize uncertainty, though we cannot eliminate it entirely. Similarly, Chertoff observes that in the homeland security effort "it is neither possible nor desirable to pursue

15. Mick Kicklighter, director, George Mason University School of Law CIP/HS, *The CIP Report* (13) (3), October 2014,1.
16. William C. Spracher, "Editor's Desk," *American Intelligence Journal*, Vol. 31, No. 2, 2013, with theme "Intelligence Education and Training," pp. 3-5.
17. "Intelligence and Homeland Security Alliance," LinkedIn.
18. For more information see http://www.nmia.org.
19. Lee H. Hamilton, in Foreword to Michael Chertoff, *Homeland Security: Assessing the First Five Years* (Philadelphia: University of Pennsylvania Press, 2009), vii. See also *Today's FBI: Facts & Figures, 2013-2014* (Washington, DC: US Department of Justice, 2014).

a risk elimination strategy."[20] DHS does what it can to minimize risk, but it cannot eliminate it. Intelligence and homeland security share that dilemma, i.e., how to enhance security, knowing that the world is a dangerous place with countless bad actors wishing us harm, but without unduly stepping on the individual rights and liberties that our citizens are guaranteed by the US Constitution. It is a fragile balance, and one in which past misdeeds and over-reaches have produced a plethora of scandals and legal battles.[21]

Former Secretary Chertoff insists, "We must use every tool in the security toolbox, and in the coming years we will have to invent a few tools that do not yet exist."[22] At the same time, he concedes, "Governments must continue to use old-fashioned counter-intelligence: working to prevent people from committing espionage, stealing data or passwords, or implementing trapdoors in systems."[23] Cybersecurity seems to be the hot-button issue of the early 21st century, and cyber warfare has apparently supplanted conventional, much less nuclear, warfare as the method of choice for our wily adversaries. Both the intelligence and homeland security communities are heavily involved in the cyber effort. Witness the fact that the director of the National Security Agency (NSA), one of the largest, most expensive, and most secret of the IC, has been dual-hatted since 2010 as the commander of US Cyber Command, a subordinate element of US Strategic Command. For its part, DHS is responsible for coordinating cybersecurity with the non-governmental sector, to include private corporations. Intelligence and homeland security both are intricately intertwined with the cyber world. According to Chertoff, "In the wake of September 11, the United States moved decisively and effectively to create a new Department of Homeland Security, remove some of the barriers between intelligence agencies, hunt for Al Qaeda leaders overseas, and institute numerous measures to prevent or reduce our vulnerability to further attacks."[24]

Intelligence is even essential to some aspects of homeland security that may not be immediately obvious, such as public safety and public health. Chertoff suggests, "In a very real way, intelligence is a critical element in promoting public health in the twenty-first century. The value of this kind of intelligence was vividly demonstrated in London in spring 2008, and at the trial of those suspected of plotting to blow up transatlantic airliners in 2006. Based on diligent intelligence gathering, we learned about the elaborate efforts made to manufacture explosive devices concealed in sport drink bottles. There simply is no adequate substitute for good intelligence that can help us detect the ini-

---

20. Chertoff, 6.
21. See, for example, discussion of the 1920 Palmer raids in David Major and Peter Oleson, "Espionage Against America," in the *Guide to the Study of Intelligence*, at hrrp://www.afio.com/publications/MAJOR%20OLESON%20Espionage%20DRAFT%20ver%202014Nov10.pdf.
22. Ibid, 54.
23. Ibid, 100-101.
24. Ibid, 125.

tial emergence of dangerous biological pathogens or their appearance in our country."[25] It is not surprising, then, that one of the increasingly important subordinate analytical production centers of the Defense Intelligence Agency (DIA) is the National Center for Medical Intelligence (NCMI), formerly known as the Armed Forces Medical Intelligence Center (AFMIC), located at Fort Detrick in Frederick, Maryland.[26] With the Ebola epidemic sweeping through west Africa in 2014, and people worldwide frightened that it will spread, US homeland security has a new threat to deal with, and the President has involved US military forces in helping to contain the situation. Though the bulk of them are performing logistical tasks not in the immediate vicinity of infected patients, it would not be surprising if some of them are working in intelligence specialties. Speaking of DIA, it maintains close coordination with DHS. For example, as previously mentioned, there is a DHS chair on the NIU faculty. In addition, a member of the DIA senior executive service is presently serving on a joint duty assignment with DHS as chief, cyber intelligence integration.[27]

A couple of other books come to mind that in part examine the overlap of homeland security and intelligence. Looking at the former in an international context, and how it affects alliances and partnerships, is *North American Homeland Security: Back to Bilateralism?* by three authors who insist DHS was established as "the central agency in the largest overhaul since World War II to keep not only the United States safe, but also revive a wider security community."[28] The book focuses on the three North American nations of the United States, Canada, and Mexico, and evaluates how well each can protect its citizens while dealing bilaterally and trilaterally with its neighbors. Looking at "trilateralism" and "intelligence instincts" after 9/11, the authors observe, "Intelligence becomes meaningless in a vacuum or if tardy.... Forging partnerships may be useful, as between Canada and the United States, but integrating the disparate agencies demands more attention and resources than any of the countries can offer, or show interest in."[29] As the continuing debate in the US on immigration reform demonstrates, not only is unilateral action by one branch of one government of concern, but unilateral action by one nation without coordination or consultation with neighboring nations can lead to problematic spillover effects and unintended consequences. Just as intelligence sharing and collaboration are challenges for international relations, homeland security must take into consideration differing "homelands," perspectives on how to protect them, and legal frameworks that often clash.

---

25. Ibid, p. 137.
26. See Jonathan D. Clemente, MD, "Medical Intelligence," *The Intelligencer* 21 (1), Fall/Winter 2013, http://www.afio.com/40_guide.htm.
27. DIA internal communications on personnel assignments.
28. Imtiaz Hussain, Satya R. Pattnayak, and Anil Hira, Preface, *North American Homeland Security: Back to Bilateralism?* (Westport, CT: Praeger Security International, 2008), vi.
29. Ibid, 236-237.

Finally, Jonathan White's book, *Defending the Homeland: Domestic Intelligence, Law Enforcement, and Security*, though now a bit dated, is well worth examining. The author opines that "organizational conflict between the intelligence and law enforcement communities is a managerial issue, but it also impacts the Constitution."[30] He quotes from *The National Strategy for Homeland Security*, which calls for increased information sharing among law enforcement agencies.[31] Similarly, there is a *National Intelligence Strategy*, promulgated by the DNI, most recently in 2014. In that document, Director James Clapper lists the IC's "Mission Objectives" as strategic intelligence, anticipatory intelligence, current operations, cyber intelligence, counterterrorism, counterproliferation, and counterintelligence.[32] These very same objectives translate nicely to areas the homeland security community must be concerned about. In a section of his book titled "The Inevitable Failure of Intelligence," White confesses that "despite the best intentions and the creation of better systems, intelligence will fail at certain points," a fact that has been examined in the past by such eminent scholars as Richard Betts of Columbia University.[33] "Intelligence is competitive, and our enemies are trying to beat us. Terrorists only need to be successful one time. .. The best system cannot stop every attack. When prevention and interdiction can do no more, state and local law enforcement will be called to the scene to manage a crisis. In terms of homeland security, the mission will shift from offense to defense."[34]

It is often argued that one of the main reasons intelligence and law enforcement cannot be compatible is the differing goals of the two. While law enforcement aims to arrest perpetrators of a crime (a retrospective focus) and obtain a conviction, intelligence (with a prospective focus) often prefers to gain information about trends and patterns without rolling up the sources of that information too soon. To do this, sometimes a low-level perpetrator of a crime, or an enemy combatant, will be monitored but not apprehended for a time in the interest of finding the high-level orchestrator of the crime or the military action planned. In other words, short-term, tactical success might be sacrificed for long-term, strategic success. In the latter case, the overall threat is what counts, not individual actors doing malicious things.

As just one example, a Department of Justice (DOJ) Drug Enforcement Administration (DEA) agent or a DHS Immigration and Customs Enforcement (ICE) agent may desire to make an arrest, yet the intelligence information utilized has to be managed in such a way that it can be used as evidence in a

---

30. Jonathan White, *Defending the Homeland: Domestic Intelligence, Law Enforcement, and Security* (Belmont, CA: Wadsworth, Cengage Learning, 2004), 19.

31. Ibid, 74.

32. *The National Intelligence Strategy of the United States of America* (Washington, DC, 2014), 2.

33. Richard K. Betts, "Analysis, War, and Decision: Why Intelligence Failures Are Inevitable," in *World Politics* 31 (1), October 1978, 61-89, http://www.jstor.org/stable/2009967.

34. White, op. cit., 76.

trial. This often runs counter to what an intelligence officer's aims are, which are more likely to develop comprehensive, confirmed information to support a policymaker, combatant commander, or decisionmaker of some sort. The type of information needed to accomplish that objective—and how it is protected, exploited, and released—may be radically different. Still, in the high-threat environment of the present century post-9/11, where transnational actors often are not sponsored by states and pay no attention to borders, international law, or the norms of human decency, intelligence agencies and law enforcement/ homeland security agencies must work together. Elements from both play a key role in keeping our citizens safe and our governments at all levels functioning effectively for the well-being of all.

READINGS FOR INSTRUCTORS

Chertoff, Michael. *Homeland Security: Assessing the First Five Years* (Philadelphia: University of Pennsylvania Press, 2009).

Hussain, Imtiaz, Satya R. Pattnayak, and Anil Hira. *North American Homeland Security: Back to Bilateralism?* (Westport, CT: Praeger Security International, 2008).

Logan, Keith G. *Homeland Security and Intelligence* (Westport, CT: Praeger), 2010.

Lowenthal, Mark M. *Intelligence: From Secrets to Policy.* 5th ed. (Washington, DC: CQ Press, 2012).

Spracher, William C. "Homeland Security and Intelligence: Can Oil Mix with Water in an Open Society?" *Learning with Professionals: Selected Works from the Joint Military Intelligence College* (Washington, DC: Joint Military Intelligence College, 2005).

US Army War College. "Homeland Security: A Selected Bibliography." Carlisle, PA: US Army War College Library, April 2011.

US Department of Justice Federal Bureau of Investigation. *Today's FBI: Facts & Figures, 2013-2014* (Washington, DC: Government Printing Office, 2014).

US Office of the Director of National Intelligence. *The National Intelligence Strategy of the United States of America* (Washington, DC: Government Printing Office, 2014).

White, Jonathan. *Defending the Homeland: Domestic Intelligence, Law Enforcement, and Security* (Belmont, CA: Wadsworth, Cengage Learning, 2004).

William C. Spracher is a contracted faculty member at the National Intelligence University, teaching courses on social analysis, globalization, peacekeeping & stability operations, and Latin America. He is a retired US Army colonel who served for over 30 years in armor, military intelligence, and the Foreign Area Officer program. He was Army attaché to Peru and defense attaché to Colombia prior to his final assignment as military professor at the National Defense University Center for Hemispheric Defense Studies. Earlier, he taught political science at the US Military Academy, from which he graduated in 1970. He has a master's degree in international relations from Yale University, a master's in political-military studies from the US Army Command & General Staff College, and a doctorate in education from George Washington University. He serves on the boards of directors of the International Association for Intelligence Education (IAFIE) and the National Military Intelligence Association (NMIA); for the latter, he is editor of its principal publication, the *American Intelligence Journal*.

GUIDE TO THE STUDY OF INTELLIGENCE

Evaluating and Teaching
Homeland Security Intelligence[1]

James Steiner, PhD

When he was Department of Homeland Security (DHS) undersecretary for intelligence, Charlie Allen was fond of saying that virtually all homeland security programs that address threats require intelligence support to be successful. The local firefighter, police officer, and emergency room medical personnel in Boston are just as legitimate intelligence customers as those working overseas for the Federal Bureau of Investigation (FBI), military, and State Department. Unfortunately, even 14 years after 9/11 these newer, nontraditional customers remain underserved, especially compared to long-term national security intelligence customers.

This deficiency is a major reason why intelligence is a priority area for homeland security education and training. The potential student population is massive, including not only undergraduate and graduate students and intelligence professionals but the over 10 million homeland security practitioners, many of whom are still learning what intelligence is and how to use it. Given the size and diversity of this customer set, intelligence education and training is most effective when structured on a customer and mission basis. This helps each student see the potential of intelligence to help them accomplish their specific mission.

Evaluating Homeland Security Intelligence

Intelligence support to federal counterterrorism customers since 9/11 has enabled military, diplomatic, covert action, and law enforcement officers

---

1. Much of this paper is drawn from the author's textbook, *Homeland Security Intelligence* (Thousand Oaks, CA: CQ Press/SAGE, 2015).

to be successful. The fundamental reason for this strong record is that federal departments and agencies with the lead roles in counterterrorism have decades of experience producing and using intelligence. These customers control their own (relatively) well-funded, well-trained departmental intelligence organizations; have direct input into prioritizing intelligence collection through the Intelligence Community (IC); and are themselves knowledgeable customers who trust and act on the intelligence provided them. As written in texts from the time of Sun Tzu,[2] war fighters, diplomats, and covert action officers all need to acquire and use specific, tailored intelligence to achieve victory consistently.

This criticality of intelligence also applies to success in domestic law enforcement operations. Even before 9/11, the FBI, Drug Enforcement Administration, Immigration and Customs Enforcement, and other federal law enforcement elements had extensive experience in intelligence driven operations ranging from FBI counterintelligence programs to the takedown of mafia leaders and drug trafficking organizations. State and local law enforcement are supported with national level intelligence through the FBI sponsored Joint Terrorism Task Force (JTTF) system[3] and the DHS–sponsored (but locally owned) fusion centers.[4] These police forces are valued by the FBI as massive and reliable intelligence collectors and, in the case of imminent threats, operational partners.

A handful of state and local law enforcement agencies (with the New York Police Department at the pinnacle) have substantial independent counterterrorism intelligence and operational capabilities because they face the greatest domestic threat. All state and local law enforcement have benefited from a trend toward intelligence led policing, begun in the United Kingdom but was well established and growing in the US long before 9/11.[5]

The US' homeland security enterprise can be proud of the fact that, with the exception of the attacks at Fort Hood and in Boston, there has not been a successful major terrorist attack within the US since 9/11, although there have been a total of 65 terrorist plots uncovered to date.[6] But this success also means that first responders (and associated government and private sector executives) have rarely been tested by major terrorist attacks, and it is not clear whether they receive sufficient intelligence support to be prepared if and when such

---

2. See Sun Tzu, *The Art of War* (New York: Penguin Books, 2002), 95; and Erik J. Dahl, *Intelligence and Surprise Attack: Failure and Success from Pearl Harbor to 9/11 and Beyond* (Washington, DC: Georgetown University Press, 2013),184. This is the primary thesis of Dahl's book.

3. Federal Bureau of Investigation, "Protecting America from Terrorist Attack: Our Joint Terrorism Task Forces," *http://www.fbi.gov/aboutus/investigate/terrorism/terrorism_jttfs*.

4. See *2011 National Network of Fusion Centers: Final Report*, May 2012, *https://www.dhs.gov/sites/default/files/publications/2011nationalnetwork fusioncentersfinalreport.pdf*.

5. See Marilyn Peterson, *Intelligence Led Policing: The New Intelligence Architecture* (Washington, DC: US Department of Justice Office of Justice Programs Bureau of Justice Assistance, September 2005), *https://www.ncjrs.gov/pdffiles1/bja/210681.pdf*.

6. April 2015. See *http://www.heritage.org/research/reports/2015/04/65thislamistterroristplotorattacksince-911persistentterrorismrequiresconstantvigilance*.

attacks might occur. First responders have been very effective to date, but with only two terrorist successes, we should not reduce our focus on providing first responders with more and better intelligence support.

First responders deal with emergencies every day but almost never come up against a terrorist situation. On the other hand, the consequences of many terrorist attacks are similar to the consequences of criminal activity, and the procedures and capabilities for response are quite similar. For example, the protocols for responding to an active shooter are the same no matter who is shooting—whether a Major Nidal Hasan at Fort Hood or a James Holmes at the Century 16 movie theater in Aurora, Colorado. However, first responders need intelligence both for situational awareness in the event of an actual attack and for ensuring realism in planning, training, and exercises. This is especially true in training for situations where first responders could become targets.

The use of the terrorism-related planning scenarios derived from the *Strategic National Risk Assessment*[7] provides the intelligence input needed to make training and exercises realistic and to ensure development of response capabilities. However, it is not clear that the first-responder community is receiving sufficient intelligence support for situational awareness. Most first responders, especially volunteer firefighters, emergency medical personnel, public works departments, and hospital emergency rooms, do not receive intelligence reports on a regular basis. First response is led at the local level, and determining how much time and treasure to spend on preparing to respond to a terrorist incident remains a local decision. Threat intelligence should be provided to state and local government executives—and even the private sector—so they can make difficult risk management and resource allocation decisions.

With the exception of law enforcement and the National Guard, first responders do not own their primary intelligence providers, have no direct impact on national level intelligence collection, and have only recently begun gaining experience using intelligence – arguably three of the most important characteristics of successful intelligence support to the federal and law enforcement customers.

The DHS undersecretary for intelligence has the fundamental responsibility for providing intelligence support to first responders and the governors, mayors, and other elected officials that direct them. There is a clear conduit for producing and providing situational awareness intelligence to these customer sets. The material is produced by the IC (primarily at the National Counterterrorism Center and its Interagency Threat Assessment and Coordination Group, FBI, and DHS), sent to the state or local fusion centers, and then disseminated to state and local government leaders and first responders. Arguably, fusion

---

7. US Department of Homeland Security, The Strategic National Risk Assessment in Support of PPD 8: A Comprehensive RiskBased Approach Toward a Secure and Resilient Nation (December 2011), *http:// www.dhs.gov/xlibrary/assets/rmastrategicnational riskassessmentppd8.pdf.*

center analysts are ideally placed to discern what state and local intelligence customers need to know from these national level intelligence products. They can provide unique added value by tailoring the federal intelligence to their own customer set. For example, at every fusion center, intelligence analysts should routinely add to all federally produced intelligence products a section called "Implications for My City/State," before disseminating them to leaders and first responders.

Today, intelligence support to the owners and operators of the US' critical infrastructure is mixed. DHS has compiled and monitors a list of the roughly two thousand of the most important physical facilities of our critical infrastructure. Because of their size and importance to the economy, these priority facilities receive special attention and support from DHS and their sector specific agencies (SSAs),[8] including t h e granting to selected personnel of security clearances and access to the actual operational and tactical threat intelligence. Not surprisingly, the highest caliber of support goes to those facilities that have an SSA that is also associated with the IC. The defense industry is supported by the Defense Intelligence Agency and port security personnel receive intelligence support from their SSA, the US Coast Guard.

However, it is a mixed bag in other areas. For example, in the commercial facilities sector, large firms such as Wal-Mart have their own corporate intelligence/security programs and work closely with DHS. But what about owners and operators of independent stores and small shopping malls? Recent graduate research concludes that most facilities in the retail sector and other critical infrastructure sectors receive no intelligence on terrorist threats.

In some cases, fusion centers and state and local governments attempt to fill the gaps in providing intelligence (information) support to private facilities, and often provide sanitized versions of operational and tactical threat "information" (rather than classified intelligence) to facility owners and managers. But the effort at the state and local level is mixed, at best. At the federal level, intelligence organizations push the intelligence product to the customer; but also knowledgeable customers pull intelligence from producers by demanding sophisticated support. This is rarely the case in the private sector or even at the state and local level. Islands of excellent intelligence support can be found in areas that face high threats, but these are the exceptions. The homeland security intelligence enterprise must provide better intelligence to the private sector to improve critical infrastructure protection and especially with cyber security.

The Homeland Security Intelligence Education Mandate

The demand for homeland security intelligence comes from both intelli-

---

8. US Department of Homeland Security, "Critical Infrastructure Sector Partnerships," *http://www.dhs. gov/criticalinfrastructuresectorpartnerships*.

gence producers and homeland security customers. A recent mixed methods research paper on designing a graduate curriculum for homeland security ranked "intelligence" as the third most important area of emphasis (out of 11 required areas).[9] Many of the 355 academic institutions[10] that offer degrees and/or certificates in homeland security already include one or more courses in intelligence.

Not surprisingly, most of these courses are traditional surveys and focus on the internals of the intelligence production process: the intelligence cycle and the members of the US IC. Most textbooks for overview courses on intelligence are structured in a similar fashion. A recommended goto book for teaching courses on the internals of intelligence is Mark Lowenthal's *Intelligence: From Secrets to Policy*,[11] which follows this structure and works well for teaching traditional courses.

But there is a different paradigm – one structured around the intelligence customer and his/her mission rather than on the intelligence production process – that can help current or potential homeland security practitioners. Taking an example from another field, if we were teaching MBA students about the automotive sector, the industrial process focus (analogous to the intelligence production cycle) would work well. We would study the research, development, production, marketing, and sales of vehicles, and examine the materials, labor, engineering, styling, manufacturing, and sales distribution network of the auto industry. Such a course would be of great interest to those who want a career working in the automotive industry — but it would be less useful to those whose primary responsibility is to actually purchase cars and trucks for their company.

Alternatively, these students are better served by a course that focuses on motor vehicles as products. One could begin by identifying and categorizing the different customer sets and their distinct transportation needs, such as retail delivery, long haul commercial transport, commuting, and recreation. After analyzing such needs of specific customer sets, this study would focus on the most appropriate product lines for each customer, such as trucks versus SUVs versus automobiles, not to mention product subsets such as subcompact, compact, full size, and luxury. This course would be useful to customers of, as well as marketers in, the automotive industry.

Homeland security intelligence courses structured in an analogous fashion put the focus on the customer and his/her mission—the homeland

---

9. John M. Persyn and Cheryl J. Polson, "Understanding Homeland Security Education Graduate Program Core Content Priorities: A Mixed Methods Research-based Approach," 8th Annual Homeland Defense and Security Education Summit, Colorado Springs, CO., October 910, 2014.

10. Based on the number of academic and research institutions in the University and Agency Partnership Initiative, Center for Homeland Defense and Security, Naval Postgraduate School, Monterey, CA. *https://www.chds.us/?special/info@pgm=Partner.*

11. Mark Lowenthal, *Intelligence: From Secrets to Policy*, 6th ed. (Thousand Oaks, CA: CQ Press/SAGE, 2014).

security practitioner who receives and uses the intelligence product to achieve a specific goal.

A Homeland Security Intelligence Course Approach[12]

To set the stage, a homeland security intelligence course normally would begin with an overview of the broad range of players in the homeland security and intelligence enterprises.[13]

Next, after describing the intelligence cycle, the traditional "customer" box is expanded to show the full range of homeland security missions or functions as shown below.

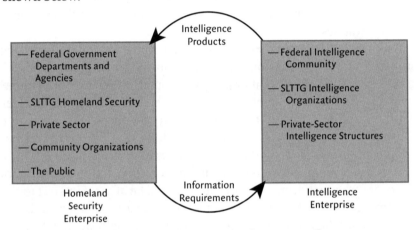

FIGURE 1: HOMELAND SECURITY ENTERPRISE — INFORMATION REQUIREMENTS

Once this foundation is in place, the course could delve into each specific homeland security mission, identifying and discussing the major actors, and looking at how intelligence supports them. Individual lectures should cover the range of programs. Two lectures might be required for the "prevent" mission: one for intelligence support to counterterrorism programs overseas and one focused on support to domestic efforts. Three lectures could address intelligence support to our diverse "protect" programs: first, programs protecting US borders and airspace; second, activities protecting critical infrastructure and key resources; and finally, a whole-of-the-nation effort to protect the cyber infrastructure and information. On the other hand, intelligence support to our "respond" and "recover" missions could be covered in one lecture, with the bulk of the discussion devoted to emergency response, treating the recovery efforts as the final step in response.

Using this paradigm, most professionals can identify their specific jobs

---

12. This section and the course structure follow the structure of my textbook. See Steiner (2015).
13. Steiner 2015, 3. SLTTG is State, Local, Tribal, and Territorial Governments.

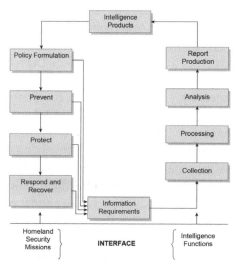

FIGURE 2: INTELLIGENCE SUPPORT TO HOMELAND
SECURITY — MISSIONS

as included in at least one of these missions, but only a handful will be familiar with the intelligence dimension of other homeland security missions. Unclassified and/or declassified intelligence products can help students look at the full range of intelligence needed and used by the entire homeland security enterprise.

For example, in dealing with our overseas "prevent" programs, three declassified intelligence reports can be parsed by the students. The first, a CIA intelligence report[14] assesses the threat posed by terrorist/insurgent groups in Peru in the early 1990s and can be used strategically to help decide if the US should take action to disrupt, dismantle, and/or destroy the threat; whether such action should use diplomacy, covert action, or military force; and whether the US should act unilaterally or with the Peruvian Government. Next, going down the military track, the Army intelligence handbook on Peru[15] can be used by defense and military planners

Missions		Prevent			Protect		Respond + Recover
Homeland Security Actors	Policy Formulation	Overseas	Domestic	Borders + Airspace	Critical Infra-structure	Cyber Assets	
Federal Government	✔	✔	✔	✔	✔	✔	✔
State + Local Government	✔		✔		✔	✔	✔
Private Sector	✔				✔	✔	✔
Community Organizations						✔	✔
Public						✔	✔

FIGURE 3: SECURING THE HOMELAND — MAJOR ROLES AND RESPONSIBILITIES

---

14. Directorate of Intelligence, Central Intelligence Agency, Tupac Amaru Revolutionary Movement: Growing Threat to US Interests in Peru (March 28, 1991), *http://www.foia.cia.gov/sites/default/files/document_conversions/89801/DOC_0000393913.pdf.*
15. Army Country Profile: Peru *http://www.gwu.edu/~nsarchiv/NSAEBB/NSAEBB64/peru32.pdf.*

to construct an operational plan. Finally, a tactical intelligence product[16] from the 470th Military Intelligence Brigade can be used that reports on a sighting of a band of insurgents, with specifics on how many and where, and which direction they were heading. This is the near-realtime intelligence that our troops on the ground need to attack the enemy.

When addressing a domestic emergency, the response to the Boston Marathon bombing in 2013 is a useful example. In this example, students can see how specialized training and exercises for first responders and hospital emergency room personnel familiarized them with an attack involving an improvised explosive device (IED). Their preparedness actions included creating the procedures and acquiring the capabilities that enabled them to deal effectively with the aftermath of the attack. That specialized training and those exercises, of course, were designed using extensive intelligence on terrorist tactics, practices, and procedures involving IEDs around the world, and, in fact, the attack itself was very similar to one of the intelligence intensive national planning scenarios (#12)[17] developed as part of the preparedness cycle. Other lectures could provide more examples of strategic, operational, and tactical intelligence and how they are used.

By the end of such a course, students should have a strong appreciation for the categories of intelligence needed by the broad range of homeland security practitioners. Hopefully, they would be better prepared not only to receive intelligence products, but also to demand intelligence support tailored to their needs. In fact, perhaps the single most important theme in this education/training is that intelligence must be tailored to the needs of each specific client in the diverse homeland security customer set. Implicit in this theme is the assertion that in meeting this imperative, the intelligence product will be significantly different depending on the mission of the customer.

For example, consider the characteristics of the intelligence product produced for the New York governor to help him and his staff in the risk analysis and management process leading to appropriate funding levels in the New York State budget for cyber security as opposed to funding for counterterrorism. Now think about the intelligence product required by the federal immigration officer at a port of entry trying to spot an Al-Qa'ida operative attempting to enter the US. Clearly, these two customers (one strategic, one tactical), whose positions require them to address very different dimensions of homeland security (resource allocation, border protection), demand and deserve very different intelligence products.

---

16. The full (declassified) tactical report, produced by the 470th Military Intelligence Brigade is available at *http://www.gwu.edu/~nsarchiv/NSAEBB/NSAEBB64/peru31.pdf*

17. US Department of Homeland Security, National Planning Scenarios (March 2006), *https://publicintelligence.net/nationalplanningscenariosversion2132006final draft/*, 121.

READINGS FOR INSTRUCTORS

There are only a few texts, listed below, that address the relationship between homeland security and intelligence. Most homeland security texts fail to address the intelligence relationship and many intelligence texts do not address specifically the homeland security mission.

Hulnick, Arthur S. *Keeping Us Safe: Secret Intelligence and Homeland Security* (Westport Connecticut: Praeger, 2004). Boston University professor and former CIA officer Hulnick was the first to take a targeted look at intelligence and homeland security. Eleven of his 12 chapters are on intelligence support to the preventers. His text is now dated and there have been significant organizational changes since. There is very little discussion of the role of state and local elements of the homeland security establishment, much less their intelligence requirements.

Logan, Keith (ed.). *Homeland Security and Intelligence* (Santa Barbara, California: Praeger, 2010). This book of readings has some chapters that are quite good, but others poorly conceptualized and written. It has little to offer on the role of state and local government as intelligence producers and consumers.

O'Sullivan, Terry M. (ed.). *Department of Homeland Security Intelligence Enterprise: Overview and Issues* (Hauppauge, NY: Nova Publisher, 2011). This book uses publically available US Government documents. The first two chapters come from a GAO study "The Department of Homeland Security Intelligence Enterprise: Operational Overview and Oversight Challenges for Congress." The remainder of the book contains transcripts from congressional hearings. The sole focus is on intelligence produced and consumed by DHS.

Steiner, James. *Homeland Security Intelligence* (Thousand Oaks, CA: CQ Press/ SAGE, 2015). Much of this article is derived from this text.

Taylor, Robert and Charles Swanson. *Terrorism, Intelligence, and Homeland Security* (New York: Prentice Hall, 2015). Although this book has "intelligence" in the title, it is a criminal justice textbook and is limited to the law enforcement customer.

James Steiner is public service professor (Intelligence Studies) and program coordinator, homeland security, cyber security, and emergency management at Rockefeller College, SUNY Albany. He is a retired CIA officer and has taught intelligence analysis at the FBI Academy. He has served as a senior consultant to both the DHS undersecretary for intelligence and the New York State homeland security advisor.

GUIDE TO THE STUDY OF INTELLIGENCE

Intelligence Support to Disaster Relief and Humanitarian Assistance

Major Mirielle M. Petitjean, USAF

In the last few years, intelligence, surveillance, and reconnaissance (ISR) capabilities — technical systems that can collect multiple types of intelligence data that are normally classified — have played an important role in humanitarian assistance and disaster relief. Due to changes in law and policies that allow for more flexibility in the use of intelligence systems within the United States and the dissemination of intelligence products at lower classification levels, ISR assets help identify for first responders, federal civil agencies, and government and private aid organizations, areas where relief efforts should be focused and what kind of supplies and aid victims need. This article highlights ISR usage for humanitarian assistance and disaster relief over the last decade.

Hurricane Katrina

The value of intelligence for situational awareness has been known for decades. The National Geospatial Intelligence Agency (NGA), the US Government's imagery intelligence (IMINT) manager, has supported disaster relief operations in the US since 1992. Hurricane Katrina in 2005, however, was the first time that classified national capabilities, Air Force, Air National Guard, and Department of Homeland Security ISR assets were all deployed in support of domestic national disaster relief operations.[1] Changes in law after the 2001 terrorist attacks on the US allowed for increased flexibility in the use of ISR assets to complement and improve major domestic emergency and disaster response operations.[2]

---

1. Kevin Buddelmeyer, "Lessons Learned From Hurricane Katrina" (masters thesis, Air Command and Staff College, 2007), 5-10.
2. Ibid.

A sample graphic created by the National Geospatial Agency in Support of Hurricane Katrina relief efforts (source: NGA Fact Sheet retrieved from https://www1.nga.mil/Newsroom/PressKit/Documents/hurricane_factsheet.pdf)

IMINT played the largest role in helping tailor response efforts. Most of the contributing organizations provided images, maps, full motion video, and terrain analyses that were used to create damage assessments and monitor the affected areas for stranded survivors and potential dangers. NGA had begun imaging critical infrastructure, such as roads and ports, around the Gulf of Mexico prior to the hurricane hitting.[3] It also pre-deployed teams of analysts and systems experts to the Gulf Coast region, which enabled the creation of the first holistic damage assessment after the hurricane struck.[4]

The Air Force employed the U-2 "Dragon Lady," the venerable high-altitude aircraft that has been in operation since 1956, which flew within a few days after the hurricane struck.[5] Other aircraft used included the OC-135 "Open Skies," a military version of the Boeing 707 equipped with a high-resolution camera; the Air National Guard's RC-26, a twin turboprop reconnaissance aircraft with a full motion video capability; and Lockheed C-130 "Scathe View," which has an infrared and electro-optical (also known as panchromatic) sensor.[6] The aircraft provided high-resolution imagery that analysts uploaded into a library for federal and state agencies to access.

Signals intelligence (SIGINT) also played a role in post-Katrina operations. Because of classification and the laws prohibiting electronic surveillance within the US without a warrant, SIGINT typically does not play as large a role in disaster relief. However, during the aftermath of the hurricane, the National Security Agency (NSA), which serves as the lead US agency for SIGINT, helped reconnect families that had been separated by the storm.[7] Because of NSA's efforts, the Federal Response to Hurricane Katrina Lessons Learned Report, recommended increasing NSA's role in domestic emergency response.[8]

3. The White House. *The Federal Response to Hurricane Katrina: Lessons Learned Report.* (Washington DC: The White House, 2006), 126.

4. Ibid. As a result of its work, NGA was one of the few federal agencies lauded in the US government's after action report on its response to Hurricane Katrina. (National Geospatial Agency, "What We Do" National Geospatial Agency On-Line. https://www1.nga.mil/ABOUT/WHATWEDO/Pages/default.aspx (accessed February 20, 2011).

5. George Cloutier, "U-2 Aids in Katrina Relief," US Air Force On-Line (September 13, 2005). http://www.af.mil/news/story.asp?id=123011772 (accessed February 22, 2011).

6. Bob Dashman, "RC-26 'Eye in the Sky' Rapidly Deploys," Air National Guard On-Line (July 29, 2008). http://www.ang.af.mil/news/story.asp?id=123108569 (accessed February 20, 2011).

7. The White House, 94.

8. Ibid.

The use of different ISR capabilities before, during, and after Hurricane Katrina set a precedent for subsequent disasters. In Hurricane Dolly in 2008, RC-26 crews alerted rescue teams of people stranded in their vehicle.[9] In 2007, NGA and U-2s collected imagery showing the status of wildfires burning in California.[10] Most recently, ISR aircraft and NGA analysts aided cleanup efforts in the Gulf of Mexico after the April 2010 oil leak. NGA obtained national and commercial satellite imagery and created 3-D models to track the oil leak.[11] Imagery was used to identify surface slicks to direct cleaning crews to the areas requiring attention.[12]

Haiti Earthquake

One of the best examples of the use of ISR assets in humanitarian operations occurred on January 12, 2010, when a 7.0 magnitude earthquake struck Haiti, killing 230,000 and leaving widespread destruction in the capital of Port au Prince and rural areas. The US Agency for International Development (USAID) took the lead for disaster relief and on January 13 the US military received orders to assist relief efforts.[13] USAID and military personnel needed to know how much and what kind of damage the earthquake caused.[14]

US Government planners relied on two primary intelligence disciplines: open source intelligence (OSINT) and IMINT to assess the damage. OSINT sources included news reports and information posted on social media networks describing the damage.[15] This information provided insights into the local situation and needs of the people living in the country. Imagery was collected by Navy P-3 "Orion" aircraft and the new RQ-4 "Global Hawk" unmanned aerial vehicle (UAV) as well as imagery satellites.[16] These platforms provided full motion video and still imagery that was key to understanding the status of roads, bridges, air and sea ports, and Haitian government buildings.[17] This

---

9. Ibid.

10. 9th Reconnaissance Wing Public Affairs, "Beale Airmen, ISR Assets Support California Wildfires," *US Air Force On-line* (October 26, 2007). *http://www.af.mil/news/story.asp?id=123073471* (accessed February 20, 2011).

11. Christina H., "NSG Extends GEOINT Reach to Unclassified Communities," *Pathfinder: The Geospatial Intelligence Magazine* On-Line 8, no.6 (November/December 2010): 10-11. *https://www1.nga.mil/Newsroom/Pathfinder/novdec10/Documents/novdec2010.pdf* (accessed February 14, 2011).

12. Susan Romano, "Deepwater Horizon Airspace Activity Now Coordinated at 601st AOC," *US Air Force On-Line* (July 13, 2010). *http://www.1af.acc.af.mil/news/story.asp?id=123213296* (accessed February 15, 2011).

13. John Ryan, Russ Goerhing, and Robert Hulslander, "USSOUTHCOM and Joint Task Force-Haiti … Some Challenges and Considerations in Forming a Joint Task Force," *Joint Center for Operational Analysis Journal* XII, no. 2, (Summer 2010): 1.

14. Ibid., 2.

15. Ibid., 2-3.

16. Ibid., 3.

17. Douglas Fraser and Wendell Hertzelle, "Haiti Relief: An International Effort Enabled through Air, Space and Cyberspace," *Air and Space Power Journal* XXIV, no. 4 (Winter 2010): 9.

information helped planners determine how to get relief workers and supplies into Haiti and how to transport those people and supplies once they were in country.

As relief operations continued, the US deployed human intelligence (HUMINT) teams to gather information on the ground and additional aircraft, including the U-2, RQ-1 "Predator" UAV, RC-26s, and an experimental airborne laser imaging (LIDAR) research test bed aircraft.[18] The RQ-1s' and RC-26s' full motion video helped determine the accessibility of roads for aid distribution and enabled aid workers to avoid hostile situations.[19] The U-2s contributed high-resolution imagery that expedited damage assessments.[20] Despite being experimental, the LIDAR provided very high-resolution 3-D graphics that, when analyzed by NGA experts, revealed the growth rates of refugee camps springing up and debris and vertical obstructions blocking travel routes.[21] LIDAR was also used to identify potential flood areas and areas vulnerable to mud slides during the forthcoming rainy season.[22]

NGA coordinated the acquisition of and analyzed imagery from satellites. US Government, foreign government, and commercial satellites all provided images of Haiti after the earthquake.[23] Japan, France, and Canada tasked their satellites to collect radar and electro-optical images of Haiti as well.[24] Commercial imagery satellites included GeoEye, Ikonos, Quickbird, and Worldview.[25] All of these sources also provided pre-earthquake images of Haiti for comparison with post-earthquake pictures.

Although IMINT provided a large amount of valuable information, additional information from HUMINT was needed to create a holistic picture of what was happening inside the country. For instance, while images of hospitals could show the condition of the building, they could not show what was happening inside the building.[26] This meant that planners and aid workers did not know if the hospital could receive patients. To help overcome this and other similar problems, HUMINT teams conducted ground reconnaissance in Port au Prince and areas outside the capital to determine the status of critical infrastructure and local government offices.[27] Eventually these reports were combined with imagery to create a common operational graphic, which enabled better inte-

---

18. Ryan, Goerhing, and Hulslander, 3.
19. Laura Lundin and Jay Krasnow, "Support Teams Essential to Haiti Earthquake Response," *NGA's Pathfinder* On-Line (March/April 2010), 5. *https://www1.nga.mil/Newsroom/Pathfinder/mar_apr_10/Pages/SupportTeamsEssentialtoHaitiEartquakeResponse.aspx* (accessed February 15, 2011).
20. Fraser and Hertzelle, 9.
21. Lundin and Krasnow, 4.
22. Ibid.
23. Fraser and Hertzelle, 9.
24. Stephen Clark, "Satellite Images Show Haiti Earthquake Catastrophe," *Spaceflight Now* (January 14, 2010). *http://spaceflightnow.com/news/n1001/14haiti/* (accessed February 14, 2011).
25. Ibid.
26. Ryan, Goerhing, and Hulslander, 3.
27. Ibid., 3-4.

A LIDAR image of a neighborhood in Port au Prince.
(Retrieved from: http://www.opentopography.org/index.php/blog/detail/a_quick_look_at_
nga_lidar_from_haiti/, original source: NGA)

gration between the disparate organizations providing aid.[28]

Despite the accomplishments described above, there were many challenges that had to be overcome. The biggest challenge in Katrina and Haiti was distribution of the large amount of information to a wide range of recipients in a timely manner.[29] Another challenge was that the US possesses a limited number of ISR assets and the professionals needed to process, analyze, and disseminate intelligence from these assets. With multiple concurrent missions to support, ISR planners have to balance assets against the different customers that need ISR.

These challenges are frequently recognized and highlighted in after-action and lessons learned reports.[30] In Haiti, previous lessons learned contributed to the early push to get intelligence products posted on an open network.[31] This helped the government avoid the information sharing problems that had slowed down other response efforts.[32]

ISR has proven its worth in humanitarian assistance and disaster relief operations several times over the last decade. All of the intelligence disciplines contributed to damage assessments, the protection of relief workers and the delivery of supplies to where they were needed most. Most importantly, these efforts helped ease human suffering. Because of this, and despite the challenges that remain, ISR's role in these operations will likely increase in the future.

READINGS FOR INSTRUCTORS

There is little academic research that has focused on this relatively new area of ISR operations. NGA's website, https://www1.nga.mil/Pages/Default.aspx, is a good place to learn more about imagery intelligence and intelligence operations supporting different contingencies. The US Government frequently uses the All Partners Access Network (APAN) Website, https://community.apan.org/ as a

---

28. Ibid., 4.
29. Buddelmeyer, 21-22; *The White House*, 94; and Ryan, Goehring, and Hulslander, 4.
30. Ibid.
31. Ryan, Goehring, and Hulslander, 4.
32. Ibid.

collaboration network during crises.

Buddelmeyer, Kevin. "Lessons Learned From Hurricane Katrina." Masters Thesis. (Air Command and Staff College, 2007).

Clark, Stephen. "Satellite Images Show Haiti Earthquake Catastrophe." Spaceflight Now, (January 14, 2010). http://spaceflightnow.com/news/n1001/14haiti/ (accessed February 14, 2011).

Cloutier, George. "U-2 Aids in Katrina Relief." US Air Force On-Line, (September 13, 2005). http://www.af.mil/news/story.asp?id=123011772 (accessed February 22, 2011).

Dashman, Bob. "RC-26 'Eye in the Sky' Rapidly Deploys." Air National Guard On-Line, (July 29, 2008). http://www.ang.af.mil/news/story.asp?id=123108569 (accessed February 20, 2011).

Fraser, Douglas and Wendell Hertzelle. "Haiti Relief: An International Effort Enabled through Air, Space and Cyberspace." Air and Space Power Journal XXIV 4, Winter 2010, 5-11.

H., Christina. "NSG Extends GEOINT Reach to Unclassified Communities." Pathfinder: The Geospatial Intelligence Magazine On-Line 8 (6), November/December 2010, 10-11. https://www1.nga.mil/Newsroom/Pathfinder/novdec10/Documents/novdec2010.pdf (accessed February 14, 2011).

Haviland, Mark. "After Katrina: ACC's Intel Team Applies Lessons Learned." Air Force On-Line (August 31, 2006). http://www.acc.af.mil/news/story.asp?id=123026271 (accessed February 21, 2011).

Lundin, Laura and Jay Krasnow. "Support Teams Essential to Haiti Earthquake Response." Pathfinder: The Geospatial Intelligence Magazine On-Line 8 (2), March/April 2010, 3-5. https://www1.nga.mil/Newsroom/Pathfinder/mar_apr_10/Pages/SupportTeamsEssentialtoHaitiEartquakeResponse.aspx (accessed February 15, 2011).

Meisner, Susan. "NGA Supports Haiti Earthquake Recovery Efforts." Pathfinder: The Geospatial Intelligence Magazine On-Line 8 (1), January/February 2010, 4. https://www1.nga.mil/Newsroom/Pathfinder/jan_feb_10/Pages/NGASupportsHaitiEarthquakeRecoveryEfforts.aspx (accessed February 15, 2010).

9th Reconnaissance Wing Public Affairs. "Beale Airmen, ISR Assets Support California Wildfires." US Air Force On-line (October 26, 2007). http://www.af.mil/news/story.asp?id=123073471 (accessed February 20, 2011).

Robinson, Amy. "FAA Authorizes Predators to Seek for Survivors." US Air Force On-Line (August 2, 2006). http://www.af.mil/news/story.asp?storyID=123024467 (accessed February 22, 2011).

Romano, Susan. "Deepwater Horizon airspace activity now coordinated at 601st AOC." US Air Force On-Line (July 13, 2010). http://www.1af.acc.af.mil/news/story.asp?id=123213296 (accessed February 15, 2011).

Ryan, John, Russ Goerhing, and Robert Hulslander. "USSOUTHCOM and Joint Task Force-Haiti...Some Challenges and Considerations in Forming a Joint Task Force." Joint Center for Operational Analysis Journal XII, no. 2, (Summer 2010): 1-16.

The White House. The Federal Response to Hurricane Katrina: Lessons Learned Report. (Washington DC: The White House, 2006).

Major Mirielle M. Petitjean, USAF, is a student at the National Defense Intelligence College. She has served as the ISR Operations Team chief in the 612th Air and Space Operations Center, Davis-Monthan Air Force Base, and in 12th Air Force (Southern Command) and Special Operations Command Directorates of Intelligence. She was chief of intelligence for the 41st Rescue Squadron. This article does not represent the views of the US Government.

GUIDE TO THE STUDY OF INTELLIGENCE

Competitive Intelligence

John J. McGonagle

Competitive intelligence (CI) principally involves the private sector.[1] It goes by a variety of names. Its definition remains somewhat fluid. For example, CI is:

- The use of lawful and ethical procedures to collect data and then analyze it to assist an enterprise, profit, non-profit, or governmental, to compete better.

- A way to help an enterprise obtain and then maintain a competitive advantage.

- Actionable intelligence, on the entire competitive environment, which includes an enterprise's competitors, suppliers, customers, and potential competitors, as well as its regulatory and political environment.

Other terms describe elements of competitive intelligence.[2] Competitive intelligence is not espionage or spying; both are unlawful. Business intelligence is an older term for competitive intelligence[3]. It has fallen out of use as a synonym for CI, since it has also been adopted by those involved with knowledge management and data mining[4], which are internally-focused, not externally-focused, processes.

---

1. In the context of governmental intelligence, "CI" often refers to counterintelligence. In this article it only means competitive intelligence.

2. See Table 1.

3. Compare, for example, the titles over time from the same author: Kirk W.M. Tyson, *Business Intelligence*, Merced, CA: Leading Edge Publications, 1986 and Kirk M. W. Tyson, *The Complete Guide to Competitive Intelligence (Fifth Edition)*, Merced, CA: Leading Edge Publications, 2010.

4. The process of sifting through massive amounts of data (in computer readable form) to reveal intelligence, hidden trends, and relationships between customers and products and storing the data for easy retrieval. Knowledge Management is the combination of Data Warehousing and Data Mining, aimed at exploiting all data in a company's possession.

Where did competitive intelligence come from?

CI traces its origins to Professor Michael E. Porter's[5] seminal 1980 work, *Competitive Strategy: Techniques for Analyzing Industries and Competitors*, in which he describes creating a competitor analysis system[6]. Also, there's some evidence that the retirement of US government intelligence community officials at the same time also served to introduce the concept of competitive intelligence to corporations.

Motorola is recognized as the home of one of the first full-time modern competitive intelligence units:

[Jan Herring[7]] "Although I started my intelligence career in 1963, I became a private sector competitive intelligence professional in 1983 when I joined Motorola. [Robert Galvin[8], then CEO of Motorola] wanted a business intelligence program very much like the ones he had observed in government....My approach was [to apply] government principles, theory, and practices using my own professional skill."[9]

[Robert Galvin] "[Jan Herring] oversaw [Motorola's] development of a pioneering business intelligence system based on national security principles.[10]"

Since that time,

Table 1. Some Competitive Intelligence Terminology

Competitive Benchmarking: Involves using CI techniques to develop data on competitors, which is then used for benchmarking. Differs from other forms of benchmarking in that the target, a competitor, is not cooperating in the project, and, in fact, is unaware of the project at all. Also known as Shadow Benchmarking.

Competitor Analysis: An assessment of the strengths and of the weaknesses of current and potential competitors. This aims at bringing all of the relevant sources of competitive analysis into one framework to support effective strategy creation, execution, monitoring and adjustment.

Environmental Scanning: Study and interpretation of political, economic, social and technological events/trends that influence a business, an industry or the market.

Gaming: An exercise that has people either acting as themselves or playing roles in an environment that can be real or simulated. Games can be repeated but cannot be replicated, as is the case with simulations and models. Also known as War Gaming or Scenario Playing.

Market Intelligence: Intelligence developed on the most current activities in the marketplace.

Reverse Engineering: Discovering the technological principles of a device, object, or system through analysis of its structure, function, and operation. It often involves taking something apart.

Strategic Intelligence: Competitive intelligence provided in support of strategic, as distinguished from tactical, decision-making.

---

5. Porter is Bishop William Lawrence University Professor at the Harvard Business School.

6. Michael E. Porter, "Appendix B: How to Conduct an Industry Analysis," *Competitive Strategy: Techniques for Analyzing Industries and Competitors*, New York: The Free Press, 1980, pp. 368-82.

7. Jan Herring was former director of intelligence at Motorola, and before that a career intelligence officer at the CIA. See also Jenny Fisher, "Competitive Intelligence: A Case Study of Motorola's Corporate Competitive Intelligence Group, 1983-2009," in the *Guide to the Study of Intelligence, The Intelligencer*, the Association of Former Intelligence Officers, Vol. 20, No. 3, Spring/Summer 2014. Available on the web at *http://www.afio.com/40_guide.htm*.

8. Galvin had served on the US President's Foreign Intelligence Advisory Board.

9. "Symposium: Lessons Learned and the Road Ahead," *Competitive Intelligence Review*, 8:1, pp. 7, 8-9 (1997).

10. Robert W. Galvin, "Competitive Intelligence at Motorola," *Competitive Intelligence Review*, 8:1, pp. 3, 4 (1997).

CI has been adopted by numerous private organizations, as well as included in university-level courses, and has been nurtured by numerous professional organizations, including the Strategic and Competitive Intelligence Professionals (SCIP, formerly the Society of Competitive Intelligence Professionals) and the International Association for Intelligence Education (IAFIE).[11]

Where is CI today?

Emerging today are two types of CI, varying by the perspective of the end-user. Over the past 30 years, most CI has been provided by individual CI analysts to another person or another unit within a business, or to their end-user (customer). Within the last 10 years, an alternative has developed whereby the individual manager develops CI for his or her own use and there is no one dedicated full-time to the CI process. For these people, CI is an additional management tool just as are directing personnel, undertaking strategic planning, coping with six Sigma, doing budgeting, etc.

There are multiple forms of competitive intelligence, depending on focus:

- Competitor intelligence – focused only on competitors.
- Strategic intelligence – supporting the development and execution of corporate strategy and strategic planning.
- Marketing intelligence – supporting sales and marketing.
- Environmental scanning – studying and interpreting political, economic, social and technological events/trends that influence a business, an industry or the market.
- Technology intelligence or competitive technical intelligence – activities that allow a firm to respond to competitive challenges or identify and exploit opportunities resulting from technical and scientific change.
- Competitive benchmarking – techniques to benchmark a competitor, without its involvement.

Is there a CI Cycle?

CI traditionally is viewed as following a cycle[12], not unlike the intelligence cycle found in the literature of government intelligence operations[13]. That cycle usually starts with the determination of need, followed by research, then

---

11. For more on this, see Larry Kahaner, *Competitive Intelligence*, Simon & Schuster, New York, 1996, pp.15-19.

12. *See, e.g.,* Kenneth Sawka, "Your Company's New Foray into Competitive Intelligence: Factors for Success," in *Starting a Competitive Intelligence Function* (Kenneth Sawka and Bonnie Hohhof, eds.), Competitive Intelligence Foundation, Alexandria, VA 2008, p.4.

13. *See, e.g.,* Robert M. Clark, *Intelligence Analysis: A Target-Centric Approach* (Second Edition), CQ Press, Washington, DC, 2008, p. 10; John Nolan, *Confidential*, HarperBusiness, New York, 1999, pp. 7 *et seq.,* and Kahaner, *op. cit.* at 43 *et seq.* This reflects the significant influence of former government intelligence analysts who have joined companies as CI analysts.

analysis, then communication to the customer and its utilization. In the case of the individual doing it himself or herself, this cycle really does not exist; rather, this is merely an approximation of the thought processes that individual goes through. Increasingly CI professionals are recognizing that the feedback necessary at every step in the CI cycle to every other step the cycle means that the CI cycle, as it operates for the classic CI professionals, also is more of a theoretical description.[14]

Is CI useful?

Actually the question should be "Where would it not be useful?"

The most common uses for CI are in the development and execution of corporate strategy, in support of sales and marketing operations, in product development, and risk management. It is also used in many other places ranging from human resources to customer profiling and from reverse engineering to patent mapping[15]. But in all cases, the goal is to understand where a competitor, or supplier or customer, is, what they are doing and what they are capable of doing. Then sound analysis can often predict what they are likely to do. But CI is not strictly predictive, it is also an analytical discipline.

Establishing the monetary value of CI is not an easy proposition[16], in part because most businesses do not employ any objective measurement methods[17], or are very reluctant to release it when they do. However, there is some evidence that clearly show its utility and value:

- In a rare disclosure, in 1994, NutraSweet's CEO publicly valued CI to NutraSweet at $50 million ($80 million today). That figure, he said, was based on a combination of revenues gained and revenues which were "not lost" to competitive activity.[18]

- A mid-1990s study of the packaged food, telecommunications and pharmaceutical industries, reported that organizations that engaged in high levels of CI activity show 37% higher levels of product quality, which is, in turn associated with a 68% increase in business performance. It also reported that organizations that engaged in high levels of CI activity show

---

14. For a more detailed critique, see John McGonagle, "An Examination of the 'Classic' CI Model," *Journal of Competitive intelligence and Management*, 4:2, 2007, pp 71-86.

15. "Patent mapping is essentially the visualization of the results of statistical analyses and text mining processes applied to patent documents. Patent mapping allows the creation of a visual representation of information from and about patent documents in a way that is easy to understand. Using bibliographic data one can identify which technical fields particular applicants are active in, and how their filing patterns and IP portfolios change over time. It is also possible to find out which countries lead in which fields." *http://www.epo.org/searching/essentials/business/stats/faq.html*

16. *See, e.g.*, John J. McGonagle and Carolyn M. Vella, *Bottom Line Competitive Intelligence*, Quorum Books, Westport, CT, 2002, pp. 11-20.

17. Dale Fehringer, Bonnie Hohhof, and Ted Johnson, *State of the Art: Competitive Intelligence* – Executive Summary, Competitive Intelligence Foundation, Alexandria, VA, 2006, p. 13.

18. Robert Flynn, "NutraSweet Faces Competition: The Critical Role of Competitive Intelligence," *Competitive Intelligence Review*, Vol. 5:4 (Winter 1994) 4-7.

36% higher levels of quality in strategic planning. And, high confidence levels in strategic plans are, in turn, associated with a 48% increase in business performance.[19]

- Several years after that, it was reported that CI's participation in the value extraction process of intellectual asset management alone has financial impacts ranging from millions of dollars (patent maintenance & filings), to tens of millions of dollars (licensing), to hundreds of millions of dollars (R&D) to billions of dollars (M&A).[20]

In most cases, however, the situation is as noted by IBM:

"IBM is not sure that [calculating a return on investment for the intelligence function] is possible within its organization, nor would the calculated value be accepted by the organization. The calculated value would likely be much greater than others expect given the high-level strategic decisions linked to competitive intelligence."[21]

Management Issues

Because of its nature there are management issues associated with CI. One is its relationship to market research[22]. One way to look at this relationship is to understand the fundamentals that drive market research versus CI. It is only a slight overstatement to say that market research is primarily quantitative, forward-looking, and often of a relatively short time horizon. CI on the other hand, is largely qualitative (in most cases), involves retrospective as well as prospective views, and, particularly in the case of supporting strategy, can span periods of years in the future. In cases where CI is part of a business early warning system, CI may be looking forward 5, 10 even 20 years. Developing, using and supporting such activities requires corporate management dedication and patience. But the payback can be significant.[23]

For example, Professor Ben Gilad has described the case of the then-aerospace division of Daimler-Benz which operated in an industry "where product cycles last twenty-five years"[24]. During its operations, before the division was sold, it provided an early warning on the 1998 economic crisis in Asia as well as

---

19. Bernard Jaworski and Liang Chee Wee, *Competitive Intelligence: Creating Value for the Organiza-tion* – Final Report on SCIP Sponsored Research, Vienna, VA, The Society of Competitive Intelligence Professionals, 1993.

20. Paul Germeraad, "Intellectual Asset Management: The New Strategic Weapon of Corporation America," in SCIP, *14th Annual International Conference and Exhibit — Proceedings* (SCIP, April-May 1999) pp. 47-62.

21. "IBM Corp." in APQC International Benchmarking Clearinghouse, *User-Drive Competitive Intelli-gence: Crafting the Value Proposition*, APQC, Houston, 2003, p. 95.

22. For more on this, see Alf H. Walle, III, *Qualitative Research in Intelligence and Marketing*, Quorum Books, Westport, CT, 2001, pp. 1-45.

23. For more on this, see Alessandro Comai and Joaquin Tena Millan, *Mapping & Anticipating the Competitive Landscape*, EMECOM Ediciones, Barcelona, Spain, 2006 and Ben Gilad, *Early Warning*, AMACOM, New York, 2004.

24. Gilad, *op.cit.*, p. 183.

the later take-over of one large key competitor, McDonnell Douglas, by another large competitor, Boeing[25]. As the then-head of the process later dryly reported, because of the early warning process, the division was "not surprised...and was equipped to respond quickly" to these radical changes.[26]

Ethical and Legal Issues

With respect to ethical and legal issues, the late Professor Stevan Dedijer, a CI pioneer, once opined:

> "Intelligence today is about using the collective knowledge of the organization to reach an advantageous position in industry. Spying is dying – only idiots resort to these kinds of shady activities. Only companies with an inadequate intelligence capability and with inferior knowledge-acquisition strategies seek to obtain information by illegal or unethical means."[27]

A major perceptual issue is that to some CI is associated with spying. Spying (or, more correctly espionage) is a crime in every state and most nations. If properly conducted CI does not engage in any criminal activity.[28]

Given that, what are the usual ethical limits on CI collection activities? There are two types: formal and unwritten (or informal).

Most well-run corporate CI programs have a written ethics policy. Many companies just adopt the "SCIP Code of Ethics for CI Professionals"[29]:

- "To continually strive to increase the recognition and respect of the profession.
- To comply with all applicable laws, domestic and international.
- To accurately disclose all relevant information, including one's identity and organization, prior to all interviews.
- To avoid conflicts of interest in fulfilling one's duties.
- To provide honest and realistic recommendations and conclusions in the execution of one's duties.
- To promote this code of ethics within one's company, with third-party contractors and within the entire profession.
- To faithfully adhere to and abide by one's company policies, objectives and guidelines."

The SCIP Code is aimed at its own members, containing elements that should be limited to the Society's members. While it is a good place to start, a better way to proceed is to develop a formal policy statement, reflecting a

---

25. Gilad, *op. cit.*, pp. 187-91.
26. As quoted in Gilad, *op. cit.*, p. 189
27. David Bloom, "Stevan Dedijer," *The Guardian*, August 11, 2004, *http://www.guardian.co.uk/news/2004/sep/01/guardianobituaries.obituaries* Access date, 29 September 2011.
28. It must be noted, however, that not all nations and cultures abide by the legal constraints and ethical standards generally governing CI activities in the United States.
29. *https://www.scip.org/CodeOfEthics.php.*

firm's unique situation and competitive environment. It should be drafted in cooperation with the legal department, be simple and direct, and provide guidance (not merely tell employees to contact someone if they have a question)[30].

The unwritten rules can be the most important. What underlies most of them is fear of embarrassment. CI analysts must not do something that could cause concern for their employer or bring unwanted attention to it. One rule of thumb is "*Never do anything that one would not want to see reported the next day in the local newspaper.*" Whether or not there is a written policy, the cold facts are that taking some action that hurts an employer's reputation can put one's job at immediate risk.

The potential consequences of unethical behavior can be illustrated by the following actual case:

- Several years ago one of the largest consumer goods firms in the US (Procter & Gamble), which had a well-regarded CI unit, authorized a research project against a global competitor, Unilever. The details are not precisely clear, but it appears that the first CI firm with which Procter & Gamble contracted then brought in a second group of firms as subcontractors, and some of these subcontractors may, in turn, sub-subcontracted some work to yet other groups. That meant that some individuals working on the assignment were three levels away from the Procter & Gamble and its direct supervision.

- The results were predictably catastrophic: one subcontractor was accused by Unilever of attempting to obtain its trash to go through later. There was no indication that the CI firm had actually acted illegally.

- Events then moved rather quickly. Procter & Gamble's CEO flew across the Atlantic to meet with Unilever's CEO, at his "request." Procter & Gamble paid a rather substantial price for its management failures: first was a substantial cash settlement, believed to be at least US $10 million; second, Procter & Gamble agreed that it would not enter a certain market niche for a period of years, the very niche that was the focus of the CI assignment; third, at Procter & Gamble headquarters, several CI personnel were terminated and a senior CI manager "retired" quickly thereafter; and fourth, Procter & Gamble purged its approved contractor list, removing every firm that was involved in this case, even a CI firm which claimed that it blew the whistle on the misdeeds of others.[31]

Most legal limits on CI address how information is collected. Foremost are the usual legal limits against stealing materials from a

---

30. For examples of good and bad policies, as well as guidance on drafting a policy, see McGonagle and Vella, *The Manager's Guide to Competitive Intelligence*, op. cit., 72-86.

31. Richard Conniff, "Mr. Clean: John Pepper used to run Procter & Gamble. Now he's revamping Yale's administration. Can Fortune 500 culture work in the Ivy League?," *Yale Alumni News*, March/April 2005, *http://archives.yalealumnimagazine.com/issues/2005_03/pepper.html*; Andy Sewer, "P&G's Covert Operation An intelligence-gathering campaign against Unilever went way too far." *Fortune Magazine*, Sept. 17, 2001, *http://archive.fortune.com/magazines/fortune/fortune_archive/2001/09/17/310274/index.htm*; and confidential interviews by the author.

competitor. The US Economic Espionage Act of 1996[32] deals specifically with the theft of trade secrets. While there have been many headlines on alleged theft of US firm's business information by Chinese nationals, the US courts had seen only a handful of prosecutions under EEA, with most of them apparently involving Chinese nationals or businesses.[33]

More broadly, there are state[34] trade secrets laws that have relevance to CI in that they deal with the protection of corporate trade secrets and the consequences for anyone who improperly obtains and uses a trade secret. However, trade secret laws require that the person or company who claims something is a trade secret has a legal obligation to take significant steps to protect it. To put it another way, just because someone puts a stamp on a document that says "trade secret," that does not make that document a trade secret, if the individual then hands out several hundred copies of the document at a tradeshow. If legal and ethical CI activities enable a company to recreate independently what a competitor claims is a trade secret, there is not a violation the law.

Conclusion

In its first 30 years, CI has emerged as a powerful force, providing guidance to businesses and non-profits at both the tactical and strategic levels. As it has grown, it has also changed – moving from a tool of specialists to part of the tool-box of generalists. In so doing, it has moved well beyond its governmental intelligence origins.

Readings for Instructors

On competitive intelligence in general:

> John J. McGonagle and Carolyn M. Vella, Proactive Intelligence: the Successful Executive's Guide to Intelligence, London: Springer, 2012. Written for business people who do not spend full time producing CI.

---

32. 18 USC sec. 1831 et seq.

33. Robin L. Kuntz, "How Not to Catch a Thief: Why the Economic Espionage Act Fails to Protect American Trade Secrets," 2013, p. 1, http://btlj.org/data/articles/28_AR/0901-0934_Kuntz_081413_Web.pdf and Trade Secrets Institute, Brooklyn Law School, "Cases from the Economic Espionage Act," http://tsi.brooklaw.edu/category/legal-basis-trade-secret-claims/economic-espionage-act.

34. The state laws are usually based on the Uniform Trade Secrets Act, a model law, drafted by the National Conference of Commissioners on Uniform State Laws, dealing with the civil penalties for misappropriation of trade secrets. It has been passed, in one form or another, in forty-seven states, Puerto Rico, and the US Virgin Islands. For additional information, see http://www.uniformlaws.org/Act.aspx?title=Trade%20Secrets%20Act (accessed July 31, 2014).

Herbert E. Meyer, Real-World Intelligence: Organized Information for Executives, Friday Harbor, WA: Storm King Press 1991 (New Edition). A classic look at CI, easy to read and digest.

On analysis:

Babette E. Bensoussan and Craig S. Fleisher, Analysis without Paralysis: 10 Tools to Make Better Strategic Decisions, Upper Saddle River, NJ: FT Press, 2008. An excellent book on analytical methods, written for the practitioner.

Anne P. Mintz (ed.), Web of Deception: Misinformation on the Internet, Medford, NJ: CyberAge Books, 2002. A well-done look at why the Internet is not a real source of useful data.

On using competitive intelligence:

Ben Gilad, Early Warning: Using Competitive Intelligence to Anticipate Market Shifts, Control Risk, and Create Powerful Strategies, New York: AMACOM, 2004. A classic on using CI for long-range planning.

Larry Kahaner, Competitive Intelligence: From Black Ops to Boardrooms – How Businesses Gather, Analyze, and Use Information to Succeed in the Global Marketplace, New York: Simon & Schuster, 1996. A business reporter's look at CI in action, using real names and real cases.

John J. McGonagle, Jr. is the Managing Partner of The Helicon Group, a global competitive intelligence research and analysis firm. He is co-author of eight books on competitive intelligence including *Protecting Your Firm Against Competitive Intelligence*, and *Bottom Line Competitive Intelligence*. John has presented competitive intelligence workshops, seminars and training sessions on 6 continents and has served as an expert witness on competitive intelligence and related topics. He has served in adjunct undergraduate and graduate positions with Lehigh University, DeSales University, and Kutztown University. Mr. McGonagle received the prestigious Fellows Award in 1998 from SCIP and its Meritorious Award, SCIP's highest award, in 2007. He has been a featured presenter at numerous international conferences on competitive intelligence and corporate strategy.

GUIDE TO THE STUDY OF INTELLIGENCE

Competitive Intelligence

A Case Study of Motorola's
Corporate Competitive Intelligence Group, 1983-2009

Jennifer H. Fisher

For 30 years during the 16th century, the wealthy Fugger family of Germany published a newsletter containing firsthand information from their agents in Europe, Africa, Asia, and the Americas on events potentially impacting the family's far-flung businesses, including price of goods, competitor activities, political events, street crimes, and wars. Thus marks one of the earliest documented uses of competitor and market intelligence to support decision making in a commercial enterprise.

History is replete with stories of industrial espionage, but competitive intelligence as a recognized discipline and tool in the US for corporate decision making has its origins in the early 1970s. US industry giants in such wide-ranging industries as oil, photography, bicycles, disposable diapers, baby food, and electronics gathered, analyzed, and acted on information regarding their competitors to gain market advantage in rapidly changing industries. In 1980, Michael Porter introduced the "five factors analysis" as a means of understanding competitors and choosing appropriate competitive strategic responses in a publication widely viewed as the foundation of modern competitive intelligence. In the mid-1980s, many large US corporations – Exxon Mobil, Proctor and Gamble, Abbot, Johnson and Johnson, and Motorola – installed formal competitive intelligence organizations designed not only to support tactical marketing and product development decisions but also to help guide high level strategy.

The term competitive intelligence is broadly defined as the defining, gathering, analyzing, and distributing intelligence about the products, customers, competitor, and environmental factors needed to support business executives in their decision making. Further refinements in this definition are found in the plethora of publications on competitive intelligence techniques dating to the early 1980s. In particular, a number of studies have been published on the distinction between illegal corporate espionage and competitive intelligence, with extensive guidelines on how to legally and ethically collect, analyze and act upon competitor information.

As demonstrated in this case study of Motorola, the corporate competitive intelligence organization's vitality directly correlates to its ability to provide critical decision-making support through market shifts, organizational structure, leadership changes, and strategic redirections.

The 26-Year Evolution of Motorola Competitive Intelligence

Founded in 1983 by then CEO and Chairman Bob Galvin, the Motorola Corporate Competitive Intelligence (CI) group thrived as an integral part of senior decision making for 26 years, until being disbanded in late 2009 as preparations began to separate Motorola into two independent companies. Throughout its storied history, Motorola Corporate CI produced a steady stream of well-sourced intelligence analyses on competitors' moves, industry and market evolution, and technology trends, and responded to thousands of inquiries in support of decisions impacting the growth and direction of this multi-billion dollar global company.

As a member of the President's Foreign Intelligence Advisory Board (PFIAB) during the 1980s, Bob Galvin observed the key role that the Intelligence Community played in supporting the nation's vital decisions. He recognized that intelligence professionals were experts in collecting information. They sensed indicators, they prepared estimates, and they made net assessments, along with alternate estimates and assessments.[1] He immediately saw value in importing this type of capability into Motorola.

In designing the group, Galvin insisted that it be led by a former US Government intelligence officer. He argued that even corporate intelligence should be best left to intelligence professionals. He reached out to Jan Herring, a 20-year CIA veteran and former national intelligence officer for science and technology, to lead the group. A succession of six former CIA professionals followed Jan, setting Motorola CI apart from other companies with corporate intelligence functions. This distinguishing design element also gave the group a unique aura within Motorola, and immediately raised its acceptance level among key business heads in a highly decentralized company culture with a healthy suspicion of corporate initiatives.

---

1. John E. Prescott and Stephen H. Miller. *Proven Strategies in Competitive Intelligence* (John Wiley and Sons, Inc, 2001).

The CI group was positioned at a very senior level of the corporation, reporting to the head of corporate strategy, who was part of the CEO's senior leadership team. At this senior level, the group was privy to the ever-changing intelligence needs of senior decisionmakers, assuring that its focus and reporting was never out of step with the key needs of corporate leaders. It also assured that the group was intricately involved and actively contributing to strategic planning cycles of the corporation. Throughout its history, Motorola CI remained at this senior level, with the head of the CI group as a member of the company's most senior strategic planning team, providing direct support to a succession of CEO's and numerous heads of strategy.

Bob Galvin also assured its success by publicly endorsing the group with the Motorola senior executives, commissioning its members to be "sufficiently annoying" in presenting well sourced, fine-tuned analysis especially when reporting ran contrary to prevailing opinion.

Mission and Performance Evaluation

The new corporate group's mission was to provide relevant, actionable, and timely strategic intelligence. It focused "beyond the headlights" to collect, analyze, and provide insight to Motorola senior executives regarding competitors' anticipated moves, technology evolution, and market and industry trends. While the CI group remained small throughout its history, growing to 10 members at its height, its budget was evaluated yearly on five key performance measures, which remained constant throughout the group's history:

- Evidence of impact on business decisions
- Early warning of competitors' moves
- Identification, analysis, and recommendations on new growth opportunities
- Influence and impact on strategic planning – short – and long-term
- Counterintelligence and security awareness in global markets

In addition, most of Motorola's businesses retained their own intelligence teams dedicated to serving the business' specific product, technical, sales, and strategy requirements. Corporate CI knitted these decentralized groups together, providing assistance and support and, on occasion, providing external validation when internal intelligence groups found it difficult to get traction on issues. This virtual intelligence organization's members shared leads, and served as independent sounding boards for each other's intelligence analyses.

Providing Value

The CI group's value lay not only in its ability to collect and produce large volumes of information, but also in the skill of its members to take multi-sourced inputs, seek alternate opinions, analyze trends and patterns, and produce independent analyses that both considered implications to Motorola and provided options for action. As illustrated in the graphic below,[2] the team focused the bulk of time and resources on these higher-value activities. Intelligence publications always identified the "so what" to the reader and presented options for action, ever conscious of maintaining objectivity. This conscientious attention to the value of its product to key decisionmakers is likely the single most important factor in the CI group's longevity.

To achieve this focus on high-value activity, team members became expert at staying abreast of the company's strategic shifts. They learned how to produce intelligence reports "just in time" to support critical decisions. They became intimately familiar with the corporate calendar, and which agenda items were up for discussion, particularly at strategic planning sessions. They proactively sought candid feedback on intelligence they produced, and used this feedback as a foundation for new requirements.

In contrast, in cases when CI group members failed to connect with decisionmakers on a relational level, they quickly found themselves out of step with how those executives received and processed intelligence information. As a result, they missed opportunities to use intelligence to its maximum effect.

Under constant budget constraint, the team learned to focus and weed out the "nice to have" requests for information. By asking the key question, "What problem are you trying to solve?" the CI group often rerouted the requestor to readily available sources of information. Other times it allowed the CI group to pinpoint the real question, thus assuring more accuracy in their response. Topics introduced as possible intelligence projects had to pass the "so what" test by other team members in lively production meetings. Through this process of continual reprioritization, the CI group successfully branded its publications as "must read now" for all executives on the distribution list.

---

2. "The Intelligence of BI" presentation to the Conference Board, June 2005.

Data and leads flowed in from the group's ever-growing network. Team members were evaluated on the quantity and quality of intelligence produced as well as their ability to identify new network members who not only could provide leads and insights but also unbiased and thoughtful feedback. This network consisted of Motorola engineers with close ties to industry associations and standards bodies, market researchers; trade show attendees, sales executives, and competitive intelligence professionals in the businesses, as well as external industry analysts and technical experts within academia and international associations.

In partnership with Motorola's Legal Department, the CI group established a rigorous code of ethics, closely aligned to the code of ethics espoused by the Society of Competitive Intelligence Professionals (SCIP, now known as the Strategic and Competitive Intelligence Professionals). This code mirrored Motorola's strong ethical culture. The CI team led mandatory ethics training throughout the corporation, as well as within the SCIP community as a whole. In 2000, the group also completed a year-long process to create and institutionalize an intelligence career management system for Motorola. This program defined the qualities and functional characteristics of a CI professional for advancement along a career ladder. This was shared with the greater SCIP and the US Government Intelligence Community.

Responding to Challenges

The CI group took a hard look at its role in any poor decision making at the company. In some cases, there was insufficient, well-sourced intelligence to counterbalance the prevailing sentiment toward a particular decision. In other instances, the intelligence was ample but members of the CI group assumed that information was already known, and did not take the initiative to assure that it got into the right hands. At times, the team opted for the "good enough" answer that assured broad acceptance. But in most cases that were attributed to intelligence failures, CI team members simply lacked the confidence or seniority to challenge prevailing sentiment even when intelligence was well sourced.

Throughout its history, Motorola's Corporate CI group encountered many of the same challenges facing government intelligence organizations: changes in leadership, shifts in strategic direction, reorganizations from decentralized to centralized and back again, and constant budget pressure.

Team composition changed throughout the years in response to shifting requirements. As Motorola grew globally, team members joined in Asia, Latin America, and Europe. A native Korean speaker with strong analytical skills provided vastly greater insight into emerging competitors Samsung and LGE. And, to understand the impact of financial markets and mergers and acquisition activity in the telecommunications industry in the late 1990s, the team recruited several members with experience in interpreting financial statements.

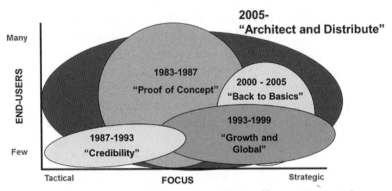

Each New Motorola Executive Saw Different Potential
for Motorola CI

From an initial focus on "no surprises," the group shifted to broader analysis of technology and industry trends in the 1990s. In 2000-2002, priority shifted to understanding the impact to Motorola of frenetic merger and acquisition activity in the related industries. As an integral part of Motorola's centrally driven strategy team, the CI group provided market and competitor analysis to support growth initiatives championed by then CEO Chris Galvin. Starting in 2006, the group mirrored the decentralization trends in the corporation. In contrast to its centralized collection, analysis, and distribution role of the past, focus turned more to architecting and distributing intelligence programs across Motorola's far flung business intelligence organizations. The CI group remained as the "glue" for decentralized intelligence teams in the corporation until 2009.

Conclusion

Perhaps Bob Galvin captured the essence of Motorola Corporate CI most clearly during a 1996 SCIP roundtable on competitive intelligence: "[A]n intelligence department can be seen as a professional entity that supports, or stimulates, or once in a while hits home runs, or most of the time gets some pretty good bunts in to help move along the more fundamental culture and character of the institution."[3] Whether by getting some good bunts and occasionally hitting a home run, the CI group served as an integral contributor for 26 years to the growth of Motorola as a global company.

---

3. John E. Prescott and Stephen H. Miller. *Proven Strategies in Competitive Intelligence,* (Hoboken, NJ: John Wiley and Sons, Inc, 2001).

READINGS FOR INSTRUCTORS

The following publications are recommended for a further understanding of the discipline of competitive intelligence:

Corporate Executive Board, "Structure and Role of the Competitive Intelligence Function," *The Corporate Executive Board* (Washington, DC, 2002).

Corporate Strategy Board, "Strategic Intelligence: Providing Critical Information for Strategic Decisions," *The Corporate Strategy Board*, (Washington, DC, 2000).

Fleisher, Craig S. and Babette E. Benoussan, *Strategic and Competitive Analysis: Methods and Techniques for Analyzing Business Competition* (Upper Saddle River, NJ: Prentice Hall, 2003).

Fuld, Leonard M., *Competitor Intelligence: How to Get It, How to Use It* (New York: Wiley, 1985).

Gilad, Ben, *Early Warning: Using Competitive Intelligence to Anticipate Market Shifts, Control Risk, and Create Powerful Strategies* (American Management Association, 2003).

Herring, Jan, *Measuring the Effectiveness of Competitive Intelligence: Assessing and Communicating CI's Value to Your Organization* (Alexandria, VA: Society of Competitive Intelligence Professionals, 1996).

Porter, Michael E., *Competitive Strategy: Techniques for Analyzing Industries and Competitors* (New York: The Free Press, 1980).

Porter, Michael E., *Cases in Competitive Strategy* (New York: The Free Press, 1983).

Prescott, John E. and Stephen Miller, *Proven Strategies in Competitive Intelligence* (Hoboken, NJ: John Wiley and Sons, Inc, 2001).

Jenny Fisher spent 18 years at CIA as an analyst, operations officer, and chief of station. She joined Motorola in 1995 and is the fifth in a line of former CIA officers to lead the Motorola CI group. In 2010, Jenny founded Clear Talent LLC, which provides security and recruiting services to small businesses supporting the intelligence community.

GUIDE TO THE STUDY OF INTELLIGENCE

Intelligence Liaison

Adam D.M. Svendsen, PhD

requently known as "intelligence cooperation," intelligence liaison has evolved substantially over the years. This article, written from a British-European perspective, identifies several challenges intelligence liaison has confronted during its evolution, particularly in the context of international affairs.

The British were pioneers in intelligence liaison.[1] Confronting the many challenges of empire required its frequent and highly pragmatic use. Intelligence liaison varies considerably in its directness, being bilateral and also multilateral and plurilateral, involving many different participants. However, bilateral remains the most common and viable form.[2]

Some History

Intelligence liaison – in its broadest definition – has been underway for centuries.[3] However, it has only been recognized as a particular intelligence topic since the early 1940s. Examples of intelligence liaison can be found in some early texts, such as Thucydides' *History of the Peloponnesian War*, dating from 431 BC, in which he penned that: "*information had been conveyed to Hippias by their accomplices.*"[4] From very early days, intelligence liaison could have

1. See also R. Dover and M.S. Goodman (eds), *Learning from the Secret Past: Cases in British Intelligence History* (Washington, DC: Georgetown University Press, 2011).
2. A.D.M. Svendsen, *Understanding the Globalization of Intelligence* (Basingstoke: Palgrave Macmillan, 2012), p.93.
3. A.D.M. Svendsen, *The Professionalization of Intelligence Cooperation: Fashioning Method out of Mayhem* (Basingstoke: Palgrave Macmillan, 2012), p.36; also P. Knightley, *The Second Oldest Profession* (London: Deutsch, 1986).
4. Chapter 1 of 'The First Book' of Thucydides (431BC/2009AD), *History of the Peloponnesian War*, via: http://classics.mit.edu/Thucydides/pelopwar.html (accessed: 2015 [emphasis added]); H. Sidebottom, *Ancient Warfare* (Oxford: Oxford University Press, 2004).

decisive impact; its value as a useful tool for influencing developments and event navigation is apparent across the globe,[5] overlapping with the Chinese strategist Sun Tzu's insights that: 'All warfare is based on deception.'[6] As US Strategy Professor Michael Handel has noted: 'Sun Tzu's definition of deception is very broad...', including 'both active and passive measures, from elaborate deception plans, simple baits, and diversion, to secrecy and concealment...', and intelligence liaison work for communication purposes was no exception to that long list of tasks.[7] Handel observed: "It is the role of intelligence and the ability to obtain reliable information in real time that has changed the most since the classical works on strategy and war were written."[8]

Later practitioners reaped greater benefits from increasingly optimized intelligence liaison. Queen Elizabeth I's renowned "spymaster," Sir Francis Walsingham (c.1530-90), was very much involved in such activities. Through his networks he developed "a complex system of espionage at home and abroad, enabling him to reveal the plots of Throckmorton and Babington against the Queen."[9]

In earlier years, intelligence cooperation tended to pivot around particular noteworthy individuals, such as Walsingham, and be conducted on a temporary or ad hoc, case-by-case basis. For instance, the Duke of Wellington for his intelligence gathering relied on the scout-like qualities of 'Exploring Officers' at the decisive Battle of Waterloo (1815), rounding off the Napoleonic Wars (1803-15). Notable amongst those officers were Lt. Col. Colquhoun-Grant and George Scovell, in his capacity as Wellington's 'code breaker', while Prussian General Von Müffling, amongst others, was Wellington's liaison with his allied forces. However, as before, once peace arrived the military intelligence organizations were essentially disbanded, as they were no longer required.[10]

Notably, "The phenomenon of 'liaison' entered the intelligence context via the... military and diplomatic worlds ... This includes the word "liaison" itself coming from French, the nineteenth-century language of mainstream military and diplomatic business... Indeed, from its outset, liaison has been closely associated with the history and professionalization of intelligence and

---

5. See also A.D.M. Svendsen, "Intelligence Liaison: An essential navigation tool," in J. Schroefl, B.M. Rajaee and D. Muhr (eds), Hybrid and Cyber War as Consequences of the Asymmetry (Frankfurt a.M.: Peter Lang International Publishers, 2011); C.S. Gray, 'Thucydides was right: Defining the future threat', http://www.StrategicStudiesInstitute.army.mil (2015).

6. As quoted in M.I. Handel, "Deception, Surprise, and Intelligence," ch.15 in his, Masters of War: Classical Strategic Thought (London: Routledge, 2001 [3rd rev. and expanded ed.]), p.215; see also Sun Tzu (translated by Lionel Giles, 1910), The Art of War (US: Filiquarian Publishing 2006); A.D.M. Svendsen, "Strategy and Disproportionality in Contemporary Conflicts," Journal of Strategic Studies, 33, 3 (2010), pp.383-385.

7. Handel, Masters of War, p. 217.

8. Handel, Masters of War, p.216.

9. Entry on 'Sir Francis Walsingham' in D. Crystal (ed.), The Cambridge Biographical Encyclopedia (Cambridge: Cambridge University Press, 1998 [2ed.]), p.973.

10. "History of The Intelligence Corps," British Army (London: UK Ministry of Defence, 2010), p.1.

its institutions – for instance, being strongly linked to the functions of military attachés, where conducting liaison remains a central role."[11] In the case of the UK, "early developments in the realm of liaison appear to owe much to security and intelligence cooperation against anti-colonial agitators and against the revolutionaries of the late nineteenth century."[12] As further observed:

> The continued gradual growth and regularization of British intelligence liaison generally during the late nineteenth and twentieth centuries can be associated with three key developments: firstly, the institutionalization and professionalization of intelligence...; secondly, the proliferation of European 'grand alliances' or blocs, their associated politics and the inauguration of the UK alliance 'commitment' tradition – to which the UK still adheres today, most notably with the UK–US alliance; and thirdly, the growth of formal and informal global (British) Empire management requirements, where having a global hegemony of intelligence power was, and continues to be (as the US has subsequently found and China is learning), essential for primacy in domestic and international affairs. Over time, natural, as well as 'man-made', disasters and crises have similarly had an important impact...[13]

Nineteenth Century Adventures

From the Victorian era onwards, empire management requirements were an important driver for British intelligence liaison. While the Empire rapidly expanded during the latter part of the eighteenth and nineteenth centuries, that expansion brought with it many challenges of both an intra – and extra-Empire nature. Noteworthy examples include the North American competition with France and the later colonial revolution,[14] the frequently European-linked subversive "anarchist terrorism ... the Irish-Fenian terrorism and the developments associated with the Indian-Sikh rebellion and the Indian revolutionary movement."[15]

Much formal and informal, behind-the-scenes, security communication occurred across the globe, and contributed towards the negotiation of those problems. As British historian Richard Popplewell later found from his research on the UK's Imperial Defence work, "the British were able to defeat the Indian revolutionaries only by developing a complex intelligence network on a global scale..." Their covert means against terrorism was why they were unwilling to publicize their successes.[16]

---

11. Svendsen, *The Professionalization of Intelligence Cooperation*, p.16.
12. *Ibid.*, p.18.
13. *Ibid.*, p.37; see also C. Andrew, *Secret Service: The Making of the British Intelligence Community* (London: Heinemann, 1985), and his, *The Defence of the Realm* (London: Allen Lane, 2009); K. Jeffery, *The Secret History of MI6* (New York: Penguin, 2010).
14. F. Anderson, *Crucible of War: The Seven Year's War and the Fate of Empire in British North America, 1754-1766* (New York: Vintage Books, 2000). The Seven Year's War was known as the French and Indian Wars in US history.
15. Svendsen, *The Professionalization of Intelligence Cooperation*, p.39.
16. R.J. Popplewell, *Intelligence and Imperial Defence: British Intelligence and the Defence of the*

From the late nineteenth century, the UK was involved in the "Scramble for Africa" in direct competition with the other European imperial powers. Greater political attention and strategic management was required from London,[17] and intelligence liaison performed an important supporting role, being employed for tactical and operational, as well as strategic ends, underpinning both military and diplomatic initiatives. By 1884-1885, the Scramble for Africa was at full speed when thirteen European countries and the United States met in Berlin to agree on the rules of African colonization. From 1884 to 1914, the continent continued to undergo much upheaval with direct implications for intelligence functions.[18] According to an official British Army history of the UK military Intelligence Corps:

> Prior to the [(second)] Boer War [(1899-1902)] the British Army tended to form ad hoc intelligence organisations during campaigns in order to provide the commander with the necessary information and intelligence ... John Churchill, the first Duke of Marlborough, stated that "no war can be conducted successfully without early and good intelligence"... By the end of the [(Boer)] war, the intelligence element of the British Forces increased from 2 officers to 132 officers and 2,321 soldiers.[19]

This showed growing numbers involved in intelligence and liaison-related activities.

For the UK, Pax Britannica was becoming increasingly difficult to maintain. By the beginning of the twentieth century, "perceived imperial overstretch was not far from being at the forefront of British decision-makers' minds."[20] Overlapping alliance obligations were growing as the UK became increasingly committed to a range of agreements. This was to help bolster and sustain its current high international standing, both diplomatically and militarily, and to be able to secure and maintain a seat at the top-table of world politics, enabling the UK to "punch above its weight" in foreign affairs.

Alliance commitments

During the modern historical era, alliances assumed prominence in Western international relations. From the end of the nineteenth century to the beginning of the twentieth century, European states committed themselves to various alliance arrangements such as, in 1879, the "Dual Alliance" between Germany and

---

Indian Empire, 1904–24 (London: Frank Cass, 1995), p.5; see also J. Paxman, Empire (London: Viking, 2011).

17. See T. Pakenham, The Scramble for Africa (London: Abacus, 1991).

18. "The Scramble for Africa," St. John's College Library, Cambridge, UK (accessed: 2015).

19. "History of The Intelligence Corps," p.1.

20. Svendsen, The Professionalization of Intelligence Cooperation, p.38; see also J. Charmley, 'Splendid Isolation'? Britain and the Balance of Power 1874–1914 (London: Hodder & Stoughton, 1999); D. Reiter, Crucible of Beliefs: Learning, Alliances and World Wars (Ithaca, NY: Cornell University Press, 1996).

Austria-Hungary, later in 1882 becoming the "Triple Alliance" when Italy joined. Further alliance commitments were witnessed in 1894 when the Franco-Russian Alliance came into effect.[21]

These alliances' formation "occurred in a climate of intense international imperial competition between the European Powers, which extended beyond merely the shaping of the modern European Continent" to involving the imperialist-inspired African adventures.[22]

Ultimately, however, due to its empire commitments and other interests demands, increasingly the UK "started tentatively committing itself to the European alliance system – for example, through the Anglo-French Entente in 1904, and then in 1907 to an Anglo-Russian Convention."[23] By the time of the First World War (1914-18), some – albeit limited –exchanges of military-relevant intelligence were taking place between the newly-fashioned allies of the UK, France and Russia.[24] Acting as forges, the crucibles of the early twentieth century wars were to have significant impact on intelligence liaison trends.

Twentieth Century Wars and their Cold War aftermath

The immediate demands of the First World War spurred greater intelligence work, with a rapid increase in manpower, and increased exchange of intelligence.[25]

By the time of the Second World War (1939-1945), intelligence liaison witnessed rapid growth and greater internationalization – including the number and diversity of actors (or parties) involved. Some of this liaison resulted in significant developments. The Poles sharing their cryptanalytic efforts against the German Enigma cipher with the French and British led eventually to the Allies' intelligence dominance over Nazi Germany.[26] By 1942, British and American signals intelligence was largely integrated.[27] Following British Prime Minister Sir Winston Churchill's famous edict to "set Europe ablaze!," this also included the coordinated conduct of covert or direct action activities and other special operations, involving the British, French, and Americans of the Special Operations Executive (SOE) and Office of Strategic Services (OSS).[28] In

---

21. Svendsen, *The Professionalization of Intelligence Cooperation*, p.37.

22. *Ibid.*; see also, e.g., M. Howard, *The Franco-Prussian War: The German Invasion of France 1870-1871* (London: Routledge, 2001).

23. Svendsen, *The Professionalization of Intelligence Cooperation*, pp.37-38.

24. M. Herman, *Intelligence Power in Peace and War* (Cambridge: Cambridge University Press/Chatham House – Royal Institute of International Affairs – RIIA, 1996), pp.200–201; "History of The Intelligence Corps," pp.2-3.

25. See also, on UK intelligence work during the First World War, e.g., J. Beach, *Haig's Intelligence: GHQ and the German Army, 1916–1918* (Cambridge: Cambridge University Press, 2013).

26. F.H. Hinsley, *British Intelligence in the Second World War* (Abridged edition) (London, HMSO, 1993), p. 14.

27. Hinsley, *British Intelligence*, pp.442-467.

28. M.R.D. Foot, *SOE in France* (London: HMSO, 1966 [1968 rev. ed.]); C.J. Murphy, *Security and Special*

November 1944, OSS director Donovan wrote in a memorandum to US President Franklin D. Roosevelt, that: "Your correspondent suggests that OSS has been penetrated by the English Intelligence Service. If by penetration is meant that we have worked closely together with that Service in the spirit of cooperation that you have urged upon us, then the statement is true; but if more than that is meant, the statement is not true and on the contrary we have greatly profited by our working with the British and at the same time we have maintained the integrity of our organization."[29]

The joint Allied breaking and exploitation of the codes of their Axis enemies, most notably ULTRA (Germany) and MAGIC (Japan), resulted from close liaison. Prominent wartime liaison agreements were struck, notably the 1943 BRUSA (Britain–USA) pact that enabled SIGINT to "became increasingly 'pooled' and 'shared,' especially between the UK, the USA and the other English-speaking countries..."[30] Other wartime agreements relating to defense and military intelligence, including imagery intelligence (IMINT), concluded in parallel, quickly demonstrated their value. This was despite the obvious counterintelligence-associated risks, such as sources and methods compromise, that might potentially be involved from their outset.[31]

The contemporary intelligence historian can point to other important trends relating to intelligence liaison around the early 1940s. To handle the exchange of intelligence as workloads grew rapidly – both in terms of the volume of exchanges and the quality exploitation of product – intelligence liaison officers (ILOs) increasingly came into being.

At the start of the Second World War, British Security Coordination (BSC) was established to handle the management of UK intelligence, counterintelligence, and influence operations in the US. The BSC was headquartered in the International Building of the Rockefeller Center, conveniently located in central New York. Facilitating UK-US intelligence liaison, in particular with the OSS, BSC was led by Canadian businessman Sir William Stephenson – 'call-sign' Intrepid.[32] The value of conducting intelligence liaison work continued on a growth trajectory during the war, involving all domains of intelligence activity.

The wartime BRUSA liaison extended into peacetime and grew as the Cold

---

Operations: SOE and MI5 During the Second World War (Basingstoke: Palgrave Macmillan, 2006); "History of The Intelligence Corps," p.3; Douglas Waller, Wild Bill Donovan: The Spymaster Who Created the OSS and Modern American Espionage (New York, Free Press, 2011).

29. Quoted in Svendsen, Understanding the Globalization of Intelligence, p.27; see also P.H. Hansen, Second to None: US Intelligence Activities in Northern Europe, 1943–46 (Dordrecht, NL: Republic of Letters, 2011).

30. Svendsen, The Professionalization of Intelligence Cooperation, p.18.

31. Ibid., pp.19-20; see also R.J. Aldrich, Intelligence and the War against Japan: Britain, America and the Politics of Secret Service (Cambridge: Cambridge University Press, 2000); "History of The Intelligence Corps," pp.3-4.

32. H. Montgomery Hyde, The Quiet Canadian The Secret Service Story of Sir William Stephenson (London: Constable, 1989) and his, Room 3603: The Incredible True Story of Secret Intelligence Operations During World War II (Guildford, CT: The Lyons Press/The Globe Pequot Press, 1962).

War began to burgeon. An official US liaison office was opened in London, and "[b]etween 1946 and 1948, with some periodic updates since, a range of agreements, overall forming the UKUSA arrangement, were negotiated and signed." Importantly, "[s]till in operation today, the UKUSA arrangement includes the 'Five Eyes' of the UK, the USA, Australia, Canada and New Zealand."[33]

Related liaison "teething-problems" were not too far behind, however, with "[p]erhaps the most (in)famous British ILO [being] Harold 'Kim' Philby, who was posted to Washington in October 1949 and was later exposed as one of the 'Cambridge Five' Soviet spies."[34] Such episodes of betrayal, including several involving North Atlantic Treaty Organization (NATO) liaison, pointed to there being risks relating to intelligence liaison blowback.[35]

Risk management techniques were apparent within liaison domains. Indeed, contained within the appendices of the – now declassified – documents relating to UKUSA in particular (and highlighted here as an example), officials had already written into the agreements damage-limitation procedures to act as safeguards to prevent, or at least mitigate, instances of intelligence compromise. The documents noted: "In addition to the ... regularly assigned [liaison] personnel, visits by selected personnel for short periods of time to deal with special problems will be encouraged."[36]

Despite the occasional shocks to the system, the increased intelligence-sharing process generally continued on both bilateral and multilateral bases. Intelligence liaison was expanded to include high-level strategic exchanges, often for important political reasons. The need for extensive liaison was "further enhanced by the advent of nuclear weapons and the need for joint early warning systems to defend against potentially catastrophic nuclear strikes subject to the deterrence threat of mutually assured destruction (MAD)."[37] Sharing responsibilities and geographic specialization provided broader incentives

33. Svendsen, The Professionalization of Intelligence Cooperation, p.19; see also A.D.M. Svendsen, "Buffeted not Busted: The UKUSA 'Five Eyes' after Snowden," e-ir.info (8 January 2014) – via: < http://www.e-ir.info/2014/01/08/buffeted-not-busted-the-ukusa-five-eyes-after-snowden/ > (accessed: March 2015); R.J. Aldrich, The Hidden Hand: Britain, America and Cold War Secret Intelligence (London: John Murray, 2001).

34. Svendsen, The Professionalization of Intelligence Cooperation, p.19; see also C.R. Moran, Classified: Secrecy and the State in Modern Britain (Cambridge: Cambridge University Press, 2013); R.J. Aldrich, "The Secret State," ch.19 in P. Addison and H. Jones (eds), A Companion to Contemporary Britain 1939-2000 (London: The Historical Association/Blackwell Publishing, 2005).

35. Svendsen, Understanding the Globalization of Intelligence, p.235, col.2.

36. 'Liaison Personnel' in "Appendix I – Sheet 1: Liaison and Methods of Exchange," 1 June 1951, p.85, para.5, HW/80/9 – UK National Archives (declassified June 2010).

37. Svendsen, The Professionalization of Intelligence Cooperation, p.19; J.L. Gaddis, The Cold War (London: Penguin, 2005), p.326; H. Dylan, Defence Intelligence and the Cold War: Britain's Joint Intelligence Bureau 1945-1964 (Oxford: Oxford University Press, 2014); M.S. Goodman, The Official History of the Joint Intelligence Committee: Volume I: From the Approach of the Second World War to the Suez Crisis (London: Routledge Government Official History Series, 2014) and his Spying on The Nuclear Bear: Anglo-American Intelligence and the Soviet Bomb (Stanford, CA: Stanford University Press, 2007); L. Scott, Macmillan, Kennedy & the Cuban Missile Crisis: Political, Military and Intelligence Aspects (Basingstoke: Palgrave/Macmillan, 1999).

for maintaining intelligence liaison initiatives.[38]

Wrecked by the high financial and material costs of the two world wars, the UK began a retreat from empire, termed the "End of Empire." Gradually, "Pax Britannica painfully waned and fitfully passed on the mantle to Pax Americana during the Cold War and beyond," especially after the Suez Crisis of 1956.[39] But, resisting decline, the UK simultaneously "continued its intelligence liaison links with many of its former colonies and the Commonwealth countries....",[40] notably Canada, Australia, New Zealand and several in Africa.

Throughout the Twentieth Century and into the Twenty-First, UK-US intelligence liaison remained central, albeit at times played out hidden from public view in the shadows of secrecy.[41] This included during the 1982 Falklands War, when Western Hemisphere countries – such as the US and Chile – struck a fine balance in their interactions with the UK. For instance, adopting that path was necessitated as they provided a valuable mixture of both direct and indirect assistance in helping the UK recapture the Falkland Islands from Argentina after its armed invasion.[42]

The UK Intelligence Corps recounted in 2010, "Since the second world war, the Corps has deployed with the British Amy on all its major deployments – Palestine, Cyprus, Korea, Suez, Brunei, Indonesia, Dhofar, Northern Ireland, Falkland Islands, the Gulf, Africa and the former Yugoslavia, Sierra Leone, Iraq and Afghanistan...",[43] demonstrating a substantial roll-call of deployments for the UK also requiring much intelligence input, including enhanced international liaison interactions with, amongst other partners, host countries.

Remaining highly intriguing alongside equally noteworthy episodes of its absence and/or perversion, intelligence liaison overall played a growing role in multilateral operations in modern times. Examples include NATO's intelligence cooperation during the Cold War, in the Balkans conflicts, and in Afghanistan.

---

38. M.M. Aid and C. Wiebes (eds), *Secrets of Signals Intelligence During the Cold War and Beyond* (London: Routledge, 2001); R.J. Aldrich, "British intelligence and the Anglo-American 'Special Relationship' during the Cold War," *Review of International Studies*, 24, 3 (1998); L.C. Jenssen and O. Riste (ed.), *Intelligence in the Cold War: Organisation, Role and International Cooperation* (Oslo: Norwegian Institute for Defence Studies, 2001).

39. W. Scott Lucas, *Divided We Stand: Britain, the US and the Suez Crisis* (London: Hodder and Stoughton, 1995).

40. Svendsen, *The Professionalization of Intelligence Cooperation*, pp.39-40; see also C. Walton, *Empire of Secrets: British Intelligence, the Cold War and the Twilight of Empire* (London: HarperPress, 2013); R. Cormac, *Confronting the Colonies: British Intelligence and Counterinsurgency* (Oxford: Oxford University Press, 2014); R.J. Aldrich, "The UK–US Intelligence Alliance in 1975: Economies, Evaluations and Explanations," *Intelligence and National Security*, 21, 4 (August 2006); D. Stafford and R. Jeffreys-Jones (eds), *American-British-Canadian Intelligence Relations 1939-2000* (London: Frank Cass, 2000).

41. R.J. Aldrich, *The Hidden Hand: Britain, America and Cold War Secret Intelligence* (London: John Murray, 2001).

42. J. Borger, "US feared Falklands war would be 'close-run thing,' documents reveal," *The Guardian* (1 April 2012); "Reagan On The Falkland/Malvinas," *The National Security Archive* (Washington, DC: 1 April 2012); H. Alexander, "'Without Chile's help, we would have lost the Falklands'", *The Daily Telegraph* (7 July 2014); L. Freedman, *The Official History of the Falklands Campaign: War and Diplomacy: v. 2* (London: Routledge, Government Official History Series, 2007).

43. "History of The Intelligence Corps," p.4.

Liaison was also a prime instrument in the 1990-1991 coalition war against Iraq (Desert Shield / Desert Storm), the 2003 invasion of Iraq (Operations Iraqi Freedom), and in the multi-national anti-piracy campaign in the Indian Ocean.[44]

Twenty-First Century Demands

Today, we can reasonably claim that we are "substantially 'back to the future'" when it comes to the use of intelligence liaison for both offensive and defensive purposes. With the global rise of terrorism and the attendant demands of other multi-functional operations, such as counter-insurgency (COIN) work, liaison has continued utility for the contemporary intelligence and security practitioner.[45,46] With wide-ranging international cooperation after the 11 September 2001 terror attacks in the US and during the so-called 'War on Terror' or 'Long War' (c.2001-present), liaison plays a crucial role, especially with a growing Special Forces dimension.[47]

Today, many demands drive intelligence liaison activities, including such tasks as: crisis management, United Nations-sponsored peacekeeping and humanitarian operations, cyber attacks, counter-insurgency, counter-terrorism, counter-proliferation, and the countering of transnational organized crimes, and so forth. Adroitly balancing these collective challenges sits very much at the top of ever-expanding contemporary intelligence, defense

---

44. For beginning insights, see references in and across related texts such as Svendsen, *Intelligence Cooperation and the War on Terror, Understanding the Globalization of Intelligence*, and *The Professionalization of Intelligence Cooperation*.

45. R.J. Aldrich, "Dangerous Liaisons: Post-September 11 Intelligence Alliances," *Harvard International Review*, 24, 3 (Fall, 2002); see also A.D.M. Svendsen, "Exemplary 'friends and allies'? Unpacking UK-US relations in the early Twenty-First Century," *Journal of Transatlantic Studies*, 9, 4 (December 2011), pp.342-361; A.D.M. Svendsen, "'*Flectas Non Frangas*': Revisiting early Twenty-First Century UK-US defence relations (2000-05) after five years," *Defense & Security Analysis*, 28, 3 (September 2012), pp.234-246; A.D.M. Svendsen, "The Federal Bureau of Investigation and Change: Addressing US domestic counter-terrorism intelligence," *Intelligence and National Security*, 27, 3 (June 2012), pp.371-397.

46. Svendsen, *The Professionalization of Intelligence Cooperation*, p.41; see also A.D.M. Svendsen, *Intelligence Cooperation and the War on Terror: Anglo-American Security Relations after 9/11* (London: Routledge/Studies in Intelligence Series, 2010); R.J. Aldrich, R. Cormac, and M.S. Goodman (eds), *Spying on the World: The Declassified Documents of the Joint Intelligence Committee, 1936-2013* (Edinburgh, Scotland: Edinburgh University Press, 2014).

47. For in-depth case studies, see on counter-terrorism interactions: Svendsen, *Intelligence Cooperation and the War on Terror*, esp. pp.39-100, and Svendsen, *Understanding the Globalization of Intelligence*, esp. pp.27-56; for WMD counter-proliferation interactions: Svendsen, *Intelligence Cooperation and the War on Terror*, esp. pp.101-164, and Svendsen, *Understanding the Globalization of Intelligence*, esp. pp.56-73; see also R.J. Aldrich, "Transatlantic Intelligence and Security Cooperation," *International Affairs*, 80, 4 (2004); W. Rees and R.J. Aldrich, "Contending cultures of counterterrorism: transatlantic divergence or convergence?," *International Affairs*, 81, 5 (2005); A.D.M. Svendsen, "Re-fashioning risk: Comparing UK, US and Canadian security and intelligence efforts against terrorism," *Defence Studies*, 10, 3 (September 2010), pp.307-335; A.D.M. Svendsen, "Special Issue on The CIA and US Foreign Relations Since 1947: Reforms, Reflections and Reappraisals," *Intelligence and National Security* 2-3 (April-June 2011) – Section I: "Challenges and Reform," *H-Diplo/ISSF Roundtable Reviews*, III, 6 (December 2011), pp.26-43; A. Finlan, *Special Forces, Strategy and the War on Terror* (London: Routledge, 2009); A.D.M. Svendsen, "Sharpening SOF tools, their strategic use and direction: Optimising the command of special operations amid wider contemporary defence transformation and military cuts," *Defence Studies*, 14, 3 (2014), pp.284-309.

(including military), security and law enforcement (including police) agendas. As termed by security analyst Glen Segell, today's complex landscape of information exchange consists of being "M4IS2: multiagency, multinational, multidisciplinary, multi-domain information sharing and sense making; and the eight entities that do M4IS2 are commerce, academia, government, civil society, media, law enforcement, military and non-government/non-profit."[48] Therein lies the broad range of contemporary intelligence liaison challenges.

Showing that they are not divorced from the wider contexts in which they are intimately embedded, the intelligence liaison trends "rode on the back of the exponentially accelerating communications, information and technology revolutions experienced during the twentieth century and beyond, including the computer, digital and Internet/cyber revolutions...," and "[i]ntimately associated with all of these related developments is the rise of the increasingly sophisticated COMSEC and INFOSEC dimension..."[49], today known as 'information assurance'. Fusion activities and their supporting structures, such as fusion centers to facilitate the different forms intelligence liaison takes, have gained in significance, as recent developments in the US – for example, relating to cyber threat intelligence sharing – can attest.[50]

In recent times, "[a]longside the aforementioned significant developments has been the flourishing of "private" and "business intelligence" ... These developments also include "private intelligence" burgeoning in other areas – for instance, commercially, and with regard to surveillance and monitoring activities. Today, digital and social media, such as Twitter and Facebook are included in the intelligence purview... phenomena such as "Collective Intelligence" (or COLINT) are increasingly harnessed by both private and public sector intelligence and military communities."[51] The use of Twitter by NATO

---

48. G. Segell, "BOOK REVIEW: International Intelligence Cooperation and Accountability...," *Political Studies Review*, 10, 3 (September 2012), p.411; see also Svendsen, *Understanding the Globalization of Intelligence*, pp.54-55, p.93.

49. Svendsen, *The Professionalization of Intelligence Cooperation*, p.20; Svendsen, *Understanding the Globalization of Intelligence*, esp. p.79; J. van Buuren, "Analysing international intelligence cooperation: institutions or intelligence assemblages?" ch.7 in I. Duyvesteyn, B. de Jong and J. van Reijn (eds), *The Future of Intelligence: Challenges in the 21st century* (London: Routledge, 2014); "'Cyber attack war games' to be staged by UK and US," *BBC News* (16 January 2015).

50. See, e.g., E. Nakashima, "New agency to sniff out threats in cyberspace," *The Washington Post*, and P. Leary, "New US Cyber Hub Won't 'Collect Intelligence,'" *Defense News* (10 February 2015); T. McCarthy, "CIA to make sweeping structural changes with focus on cyber operations," *The Guardian* (6 March 2015); C. Kavanagh, "A Global Consensus on Cyber Security Is Gaining Momentum," *Defense One* (13 April 2015).

51. Svendsen, *The Professionalization of Intelligence Cooperation*, p.20; see also A.D.M. Svendsen, "Collective Intelligence" entry in G. Moore (ed.), *Encyclopedia of U.S. Intelligence* (EUSI) (New York: Taylor & Francis/CRC Press, 2014); C. Moesgaard, "Private Military and Security Companies – From Mercenaries to Intelligence Providers," *DIIS Working Paper*, 09 (Copenhagen: DIIS, 2013); K.L. Petersen, *Corporate Risk and National Security Redefined* (London: Routledge, 2012); K.L. Petersen, "The corporate security professional: A hybrid agent between corporate and national security," *Security Journal*, 26, 3 (2013), pp.222–235; P.R. Keefe, "Privatized Spying: The Emerging Intelligence Industry," chapter 18 in L.K. Johnson (ed.) *The Oxford Handbook of National Security Intelligence* (Oxford: Oxford University Press, 2010); A.D. Clift, "The Evolution of International Collaboration in the Global Intelligence Era,"

for targeting information during its campaign in Libya during 2011 stands out as a foremost example of harnessing "new" technology for intelligence liaison purposes.[52]

The more recent (2014-2015) international campaign against Islamic State or ISIS/ISIL has again demonstrated the value of international intelligence liaison, including with a multitude of highly diverse partners with different, albeit suitably overlapping, agendas. This is particularly relevant for many intelligence, surveillance and reconnaissance (ISR) missions conducted primarily for the purposes of precision targeting of adversaries;[53] and for many other problems, including the "foreign fighters" or "returnees" issues from conflicts in the Middle East, Afghanistan, Africa, Chechnya and elsewhere.[54]

Intelligence liaison blowback remains a risk, as evidenced by the revelations of Edward Snowden, which exposed intelligence cooperation between many countries and which ignited fierce political criticism in some, with associated debates remaining lively.[55]

Conclusions

In regard to intelligence liaison, several common threads become apparent over the course of time. Intelligence liaison has risen in importance. This has occurred in both quantitative (the volume of its use) and in qualitative (the different forms in which it takes place) terms, with intelligence liaison

ch.13 in Johnson (ed.), *The Oxford Handbook of National Security Intelligence*; T.E. Nissen, *#TheWeaponizationOfSocialMedia: @Characteristics_of_ Contemporary_Conflicts* (Copenhagen, Denmark: Royal Danish Defence College – RDDC/FAK, 2015).

52. Svendsen, *The Professionalization of Intelligence Cooperation*, p.21; see also A.D.M. Svendsen, 'NATO, Libya operations and intelligence co-operation – a step forward?', *Baltic Security & Defence Review*, 13, 2 (December 2011), pp.51-68; M. Urban, 'Inside story of the UK's secret mission to beat Gaddafi', *BBC Newsnight* (19 January 2012); see also W.R. Curtis, 'A "Special Relationship": Bridging the NATO Intelligence Gap', *MA Thesis* (Monterey, CA: US Naval Postgraduate School, June 2013).

53. See, for example, "US-led coalition providing tactical support in Tikrit offensive against Isis," *Associated Press* (24 March 2015).

54. See, for instance, R. Mason, "Cameron says UK and Turkey working hand in glove to stop Isis fighters," *The Guardian* (9 December 2014); R. Coolsaet, "Will the foreign fighters issue ever end?" *European Geostrategy* (19 April 2015); "Australia and Iran will share intelligence to fight IS," *BBC News* (20 April 2015); see also M. Hosenball, P. Stewart and W. Strobel, "Exclusive – U.S. expands intelligence sharing with Saudis in Yemen operation," *Reuters* (11 April 2015); D. DePetris, "What Did Saudi Arabia Achieve in Yemen?" *Defense One* (28 April 2015); A. Baron, "Everyone Is Losing Yemen's War," *Foreign Policy* (28 April 2015); S. Blank, "European geopolitical dilemmas," *European Geostrategy* (29 April 2015); "OSCE Troika urges advancement in political process aimed at solving crisis in Ukraine," *Organization for Security and Co-operation in Europe – Press Release* (28 April 2015).

55. See as discussed in Svendsen, "Buffeted not Busted: The UKUSA 'Five Eyes' after Snowden;" see also the cautions raised earlier in 2012, before Snowden's leaks from June 2013, in Svendsen, *Understanding the Globalization of Intelligence*, pp.87-89. For further background, S. Chesterman, "Privacy and Surveillance in the Age of Terror," *Survival*, 52, 5 (2010), pp.31–46, and his book, *One Nation under Surveillance* (Oxford: OUP, 2011); D. Lyon, *Surveillance Studies* (Cambridge: Polity, 2007); S. Landau, *Surveillance or Security?* (Cambridge, MA: MIT Press, 2011); V. Mayer-Schönberger and K. Cukier, *Big Data: A Revolution That will Transform How We Live, Work and Think* (London: John Murray, 2013) and their "The Rise of Big Data: How It's Changing the Way We Think About the World," *Foreign Affairs* (May/June 2013).

also becoming more centrally involved in overall political and international affairs.[56] Intelligence liaison has experienced episodes of – what might be characterized as – disruption and frustration, from which it has been forced to (more or less) successfully adapt. These include, for example, the 'insider betrayals', shown especially by the case of Philby, and/or 'intelligence liaison blowback', demonstrated particularly by the case of Snowden.

While this article has largely focused on 'Anglo-American' and especially UK intelligence liaison and its long history, many others have also engaged in similar activities.[57] Intelligence liaison remains a vital tool for several different entities around the globe.

Adam D.M. Svendsen, PhD (Warwick, UK) is an intelligence and defense strategist, educator and researcher, and a Consultant at the Copenhagen Institute for Futures Studies (CIFS). He has been a Visiting Scholar at Georgetown University, held a post-doctoral fellowship at the University of Copenhagen, taught at the University of Nottingham, and worked at Chatham House on the International Security Programme and at the International Institute of Strategic Studies (IISS), London. He has authored three books: *Intelligence Cooperation and the War on Terror: Anglo-American Security Relations after 9/11* (London: Routledge/Studies in Intelligence Series, 2010 [Pbk 2012]); *Understanding the Globalization of Intelligence* and *The Professionalization of Intelligence Cooperation: Fashioning Method out of Mayhem*, both (Basingstoke: Palgrave Macmillan, 2012).

56. Also see as discussed in detail throughout Svendsen, *Understanding the Globalization of Intelligence*; Svendsen, "Strategy and Disproportionality in Contemporary Conflicts;" essays in H. Born, I. Leigh and A. Wills (eds), *International Intelligence Co-operation and Accountability* (London: Routledge/Studies in Intelligence Series, 2011); J. McGruddy, "Multilateral Intelligence Collaboration and International Oversight," *Journal of Strategic Security* (2013); J. van Buuren, "From Oversight to Undersight: the Internationalization of Intelligence," *Security and Human Rights* (2014), pp.239–252.

57. For a focus beyond merely Anglo-American intelligence and security worlds, see, e.g., A.D.M. Svendsen, "On 'a continuum with expansion'? Intelligence co-operation in Europe in the early Twenty-first Century," ch.8 in C. Kaunert and S. Leonard (eds), *European Security, Terrorism, and Intelligence: Tackling New Security Challenges in Europe* (Basingstoke: Palgrave Macmillan/Palgrave Studies in European Union Politics Series, 2013); R.J. Aldrich and J. Kasuku, "Escaping from American intelligence: culture, ethnocentrism and the Anglosphere," *International Affairs*, 88, 5 (September 2012), and P.H.J. Davies and K.C. Gustafson (eds), *Intelligence Elsewhere: Spies and Espionage Outside the Anglosphere* (Washington, DC: Georgetown University Press, 2013); Z. Shiraz, "Drugs and Dirty Wars: intelligence cooperation in the global South," *Third World Quarterly*, 34, 10 (2013); C. Hillebrand, *Counter-Terrorism Networks in the European Union: Maintaining Democratic Legitimacy after 9/11* (Oxford: OUP, 2012); M. Tierney, "Past, Present, and Future: The Evolution of Canadian Foreign Intelligence in a Globalized World," *Canadian Military Journal*, 15, 2 (Spring 2015), pp.44-54. For what can be learnt from fiction or "spy-fi" sources, see, e.g., A.D.M. Svendsen, "Painting rather than photography: Exploring spy fiction as a legitimate source concerning UK-US intelligence co-operation," *Journal of Transatlantic Studies*, 7, 1 (March 2009), pp.1-22; F.P. Hitz, *The Great Game: The Myth and Reality of Espionage* (New York: Knopf, 2005); C.R. Moran and R. Johnson, "Of Novels, Intelligence and Policymaking: In the Service of Empire: Imperialism and the British Spy Thriller 1901–1914," *CIA Studies in Intelligence*, 54, 2 (June 2010), pp.1-22.

Part IV – Espionage, Counterintelligence, and Covert Action

Former National Counterintelligence Executive **Michelle Van Cleave** explains the complex world of counterintelligence, what it is and is not, in her article "What is Counterintelligence?" As an instrument of statecraft she explains its defensive and offensive characteristics and identifies many of the failures when US national secrets were stolen by foreign intelligence services as well as successes. She emphasizes how critical the analysis of foreign intelligence services is and explains the close relationship between counterintelligence and deception operations.

After World War I, the US became a major target for foreign espionage. Former FBI counterintelligence supervisory special agent **David Major** and co-author **Peter Oleson** trace the modern history of foreign espionage against America and highlight many of the major counterintelligence cases that have occurred.

Industrial espionage has grown significantly to where it has become a priority national concern. The theft of American technology and trade secrets has enhanced adversaries and weakened US industries. **Edward M. Roche, PhD, JD**, explains the dimensions of industrial espionage today and provides many examples and explanations of the underlying motivations, often by insiders.

Former CIA Scientific Intelligence Officer **Gene Poteat's** article "Counterintelligence, Homeland Security and Domestic Intelligence" provides many insights into the history of counterintelligence in the US, some of its successes and many of its failures. It is sobering to consider some of the potential consequences he identifies. As such Poteat's article complements Michelle Van Cleave's explanation of what counterintelligence is.

What motivated people like Aldridge Ames, Robert Hanssen, or Edward Snowden to betray their country? As psychiatrist **David Charney, M.D.**, and co-author and former CIA case officer **John Irvin** explain, the answers are complex and individual. Their "Guide to the Psychology of Espionage" details attempts to understand such motivations.

Former CIA polygrapher **John Sullivan** writes about the use of the polygraph in the CIA. He surveys the evolution of its use and the reasons for its controversial reputation.

Covert action is what captures students' and the public's imagination when discussing intelligence. Long time operative, diplomat, policymaker, and academic **Jon A. Wiant** demystifies the subject with his article "A Guide to Teaching About Covert Action." He explains the link of covert action to national security policy, much of its history, governing policies, and presents a rich reading list for the interested.

GUIDE TO THE STUDY OF INTELLIGENCE

What is Counterintelligence?

A Guide to Thinking
and Teaching About CI

Michelle K. Van Cleave

Why study counterintelligence?

The study of "counterintelligence" (CI) is rare in academia. While modern courses on international relations often include intelligence, they usually fail to consider how countering foreign intelligence activities is also an instrument of state power. No inquiry into intelligence theory or practice is complete without addressing the meaning and scope of counterintelligence.[1] What is the value of intelligence if you cannot assess its reliability or truth?

CI is intertwined with our history, laws, and ethics, and major espionage cases have affected American society and politics from German saboteurs and communist movements to terrorist cells today.[2] The CI mission that supports and is governed by our Constitution and democratic institutions is utterly different from that practiced by security states such as the former Soviet Union (and its successor).

Also, the counterintelligence "mindset," its puzzles, and intellectual challenges, stretch the imagination and provide insight into how we think. How do we know what we perceive is correct? How do we measure what an adversary knows about us? How do we determine whether or not we are successful in keeping our secrets and projecting the image we wish to project? How do we

---

1. John Ehrman, "Toward a Theory of CI: What are We Talking About When We Talk about Counterintelligence?" *Studies in Intelligence 53, (2),* at *https://www.cia.gov/library/center-for-the-study-of-intelligence/csi-publications/csi-studies/studies/vol53no2/toward-a-theory-of-ci.html.*
2. Michael J. Sulick, *Spying in America: Espionage from the Revolutionary War to the Dawn of the Cold War* (Washington DC: Georgetown University Press, 2012).

know what and whom to trust? Consider for example the deception paradox: "Alertness to deception presumably prompts a more careful and systematic review of the evidence. But anticipation of deception also leads the analyst to be more skeptical of all of the evidence, and to the extent that evidence is deemed unreliable, the analyst's preconceptions must play a greater role in determining which evidence to believe. This leads to a paradox: The more alert we are to deception, the more likely we are to be deceived."[3]

This article is a short cut to some basic concepts about counterintelligence: what it is and is not. Educators in history, government, political science, ethics, law, and cognitive psychology should consider whether and how CI lessons might enrich their courses. Recommended additional readings are suggested in the footnotes.

A general introductory course on US CI should have five key learning objectives:

1 Understanding the meaning of counterintelligence, its place within intelligence studies, and its role in international relations as an instrument of statecraft.[4]

2 Understanding the difference between tactical and strategic CI,[5] the difference between CI and security,[6] and the range of foreign intelligence activities from targeting national security secrets and proprietary corporate information to conducting operations to influence our policymakers and public attitudes.

3 Exploring the history of CI in the United States, the roles and missions of government CI organizations, and how CI functions as an input and tool for

---

3. Michael I. Handel, "Intelligence and Deception" in Roger Z. George and Robert D. Kline (eds.), *Intelligence and the National Security Strategist: Enduring Issues and Challenges* (Washington, DC: National Defense University Press, 2004), 379, quoting Richards Heuer, "Strategic Deception: A Psychological Perspective" a paper presented at the 21st Annual Convention of the International Studies Association, Los Angeles, California, March 1980, 17, 28. Handel's article is a nice primer on deception: how to do it and how to avoid it.

4. "Counterintelligence for National Security" *Studies in Intelligence* 2 (4), at *https://www.cia.gov/library/center-for-the-study-of-intelligence/kent-csi/vol2no4/html/v02i4a10p_0001.htm*.

5. Michelle Van Cleave, "The Question of Strategic Counterintelligence: What is it, and what should we do about it?" *Studies in Intelligence* 51 (2), at *https://www.cia.gov/library/center-for-the-study-of-intelligence/csi-publications/csi-studies/studies/vol51no2/strategic-counterintelligence.html*.

6. Counterintelligence complements but should not be confused with security. Center for the Study of Intelligence, "Counterintelligence for National Security," *Studies in Intelligence* Vol. 2, No 4, see esp. section entitled "Counterintelligence as Activity." *https://www.cia.gov/library/center-for-the-study-of-intelligence/kent-csi/vol2no4/html/v02i4a10p_0001.htm*. The practical objectives of CI and security are not always in concert – which Christopher Felix (TN James McCargar) called "one of the classic conflicts of secret operations." As he explains, "[CI] operations are offensive operations which depend for their existence as well as success on constant, if controlled, contact with the enemy. Security, on the other hand, is a defensive operation which seeks to destroy the enemy's operations and to cut off all contact with him as dangerous." Christopher Felix, *A Short Course in the Secret War*, 4th ed, (Lanham, Maryland: Madison Books, 2001), 126. The interdependency between CI and the security disciplines has led to some long-playing theoretical discussions about which – if either – may be said to encompass the other; in practice, at a minimum, the two must be closely linked.

national security policymaking and execution.[7]

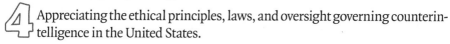 Appreciating the ethical principles, laws, and oversight governing counterintelligence in the United States.

Identifying the sub-disciplines of both offensive and defensive CI and the concepts of deception operations and analysis, double agents, and asset validation.[8]

What is Counterintelligence?

It is both an intelligence discipline and a national security mission and involves:

- catching spies and putting them in jail;
- a set of tactical activities to protect and enable successful intelligence operations;
- the national security function that supplies insights into foreign intelligence threats to the United States, including options to defeat them as national policy may direct; and
- "an intellectual exercise of almost mathematical complexity"[9]

Counterintelligence is perhaps the least understood of the intelligence disciplines.[10] The popular notion is that of catching spies and putting them in jail, but spy catching is only the most visible part of a far more complex concept that encompasses all of the above. CI is arguably also the most essential of the intelligence disciplines. Why? Because even if you were able to collect vast quantities of secret information and produce exquisite analysis, without effective counterintelligence you could not have confidence in any of it.

With both a national security and homeland security mission, CI has defensive and offensive components. It is an instrument of statecraft, just as intelligence is serving to advance the objectives of nation states. When successful, CI contributes to national security by serving both as a shield (guarding

---

7. Michelle Van Cleave, *Counterintelligence and National Security* (Washington DC: National Defense University Press, 2007). The current article draws heavily from this source.

8. Asset validation is "the process used to determine the asset authenticity, reliability, utility, suitability and degree of control the case officer and others have." (US Department of Defense Joint Publication 2.01.2) For an understanding of the importance of asset validation and especially what can go wrong if it isn't done right, see the example of "Curveball" and the Iraq war, examined by the Commission on the Intelligence Capabilities of the United States Regarding Weapons of Mass Destruction ("WMD Commission") Laurence H. Silberman and Charles S. Robb (Co-Chairmen) *Report to the President of the United States, March 31, 2005*, Chapter 7; for insight into broader reforms needed in U.S. counterintelligence, see Chapter 11, available at *http://www.fas.org/irp/offdocs/wmdcomm.html*.

9. Felix, *op cit.*

10. For excellent overviews of US counterintelligence by two former heads of CIA's counterintelligence, see James Olson, "The Ten Commandments of Counterintelligence" *Studies in Intelligence*, Winter-Spring 2001, at *https://www.cia.gov/library/center-for-the-study-of-intelligence/csi-publications/csi-studies/studies/fall_winter_2001/article08.html*; and Paul Redmond, "The Challenges of Counterintelligence," in *The Oxford Handbook of National Security Intelligence*, Loch Johnson, ed. (New York: Oxford University Press, 2010), 537-554.

against penetrations of our government and our allies and alerting security) and a sword (conducting offensive CI operations that shape foreign perceptions and degrade foreign intelligence capabilities).[11]

The first clue to understanding counterintelligence is in the word itself. What is it that counterintelligence is "counter" to or against? If you answered "foreign intelligence threats," you are correct.[12] But what does that mean? By statute...

> The term "counterintelligence" means information gathered, and activities conducted, to protect against espionage, other intelligence activities, sabotage, or assassinations conducted by or on behalf of foreign governments or elements thereof, foreign organizations, or foreign persons, or international terrorist activities. (50 USC 401a)

Counterintelligence encompasses both "information" and "activities." When we collect intelligence on what foreign intelligence services are doing that intelligence is called "counterintelligence information." For example, who are their spies? Where and how do they operate? Who are their sources? What are their means of collection and communication? What are their vulnerabilities? When we conduct activities to stop, disrupt, or exploit foreign intelligence operations, those actions are counterintelligence operations. They may include both defensive activities (such as technical countermeasures to protect sources and methods of collection) as well as offensive operations (such as passing "feed material" through a double agent that helps persuade an adversary to take the action you want him to take).

Counterintelligence may also refer to the mission or organizations that gather the information and conduct the activities to counter foreign intelligence activities; for example, "I work for counterintelligence." In the United States, operational counterintelligence responsibilities are split in gross terms between the needs of domestic security against foreign agents (FBI), and the operational needs of intelligence collection (CIA) and military actions abroad. The FBI, responsible for enforcing US espionage laws, has the lion's share of US counterintelligence duties. CIA's counterintelligence role is to protect our spies and ensure that we are not misled by foreign deception or denial. Department of Defense (DOD) counterintelligence elements protect its warfighting components against enemy intelligence operations.[13] To tie it all together, the National

---

11. For purposes of simplicity and richness of insights, this guide is written from the perspective of US counterintelligence. Other nation states have different counterintelligence practices and histories.

12. A note on terminology: You may hear the oxymoron "counterintelligence threat." This is incorrect in the same way one does not speak of a "counterterrorist threat" or a "counterproliferation threat;" rather they are terrorist or proliferation threats, respectively. The correct terminology is a foreign intelligence threat to which counterintelligence is the response. (Strictly speaking there is such a thing as a CI threat but that refers to the narrow case in which the intelligence operation itself must contend with the CI activities of its target or within its theater of operations.)

13. In addition to the operational elements (FBI, CIA, and the three military services), other departments and agencies that are particular targets of foreign interest have constituted CI offices to meet their individual needs for analytic support or to address insider threat concerns. Key examples include

Counterintelligence Executive serves as head of US counterintelligence.[14]

What are foreign intelligence threats?

To understand counterintelligence, we must first ask how foreign governments and other entities employ intelligence capabilities against us. You might think, well, isn't that obvious? Don't they use their spy services just like the US does – to collect secret information of value? Yes, but that is not the complete story.

Espionage. Foreign adversaries use their intelligence capabilities to penetrate, collect, and compromise US national security secrets (plans, intentions, and capabilities vital to protecting our security and well-being and that of our friends and allies) in order to advance their interests and defeat U.S. objectives. They also target critical technologies and other sensitive proprietary information to achieve economic advantage over US business and industry (*economic espionage*). This includes intelligence collected from human sources (HUMINT) as well as from technical means including signals intelligence and computer network exploitation (*cyber espionage*).

Deception/Perception Management. Adversaries seek to manipulate and distort the picture of reality upon which policymakers plan and implement national security strategies, R&D and other programs, and economic policies. These foreign intelligence activities include corrupting the intelligence we gather through deception or denial, and conducting influence operations aimed at decision-makers.

Other intelligence operations. Finally, adversaries may use intelligence activities to disrupt and counter our operations (e.g., covert action, special operations, and other sensitive military and diplomatic activities).

In short, foreign governments as well as terrorist organizations and criminal cartels use intelligence to achieve advantage. "Every intelligence operation has a political object," Lenin once instructed. Counterintelligence helps find what that objective is and provides options to defeat it.

The Functions of Counterintelligence

America's defense has long depended on strategic secrets — the locations of our hidden retaliatory forces; the codes by which we protect our military and

---

the CI offices within the Department of Energy and the National Nuclear Security Administration, the CI offices within the several intelligence agencies (e.g., the National Reconnaissance Office, National Security Agency, National Geo-Spatial Intelligence Agency, Defense Intelligence Agency), and other departments and agencies with intelligence missions (Treasury Department, the Coast Guard), a number of DoD entities engaged in classified R&D (e.g., the Defense Threat Reduction Agency, the Ballistic Missile Defense Office) and the important CI support functions at the State Department and the Department of Homeland Security.

14. Counterintelligence Enhancement Act of 2002 (50 USC 401 *et seq*).

diplomatic communications, intelligence sources and methods that give us warning and permit us to understand the threats and opportunities we face, and the sensitive technologies that give us military and commercial advantage. To survive with our values intact, the United States needs a clear appreciation of which secrets and other strengths we must protect, and the will do to so.

It is the job of US counterintelligence to 1. *identify*, 2. *assess*, 3. *neutralize*, and 4. *exploit* the foreign intelligence activities directed against us.

Identify: Most Americans would be astonished by the extent to which foreign intelligence services have stolen our nation's secrets, often with impunity. With the possible exception of the Coast Guard, hostile intelligence services have penetrated every department and agency with sensitive national security responsibilities, most more than once. The former Soviet Union was especially successful in stealing US secrets, a tradition that continues unabated under Vladimir Putin's Russia. The Russian intelligence presence in the United States is now equal to its Cold War levels, a sizing decision presumably indicative of the return on investment.[15] But the Russians are far from alone; other hostile services have literally gone to school on the old KGB's practices. And then there is China. As reported a decade ago by a special Congressional Commission, the Chinese stole all US nuclear weapons design secrets enabling them to leapfrog generations of technology development.[16] To this day, we do not know how China acquired those volumes of supremely guarded national security information; but we do know that Chinese intelligence is still at work, aggressively targeting not only America's defense secrets but our industry's valuable proprietary information as well for commercial advantage.

Counterintelligence's first priority is to identify the foreign intelligence activities directed against the United States and our interests so that action can be taken. This includes answering such questions as: Who are they (which governments, entities, services, individuals)? What are they doing (e.g., recruiting sources, stealing documents, setting up front companies)? Where/against what targets are they operating (e.g., American businessmen travelling abroad, national security laboratories, military computers or communications systems, CIA stations in third countries, company x)? This threat data triggers protective security measures (personnel screening, information handling, computer security, physical security) and operational security efforts for intelligence collection, military activities, and other sensitive national security operations.

The activities of foreign intelligence services can be an indicator of emerg-

---

15. A compelling perspective on contemporary Russian intelligence operations in the United States – and to a lesser extent, US *naïveté* – can be found in Pete Early, *Comrade J: The Untold Story of Russia's Master Spy in America After the End of the Cold War* (New York: Putnam's Sons, 2008). As summed up on the book's front cover: "When the Soviet Union disappeared, the spies did not."

16. Report of the Select Committee on U.S. National Security and Military/Commercial Concerns with the People's Republic of China ("Cox Commission"), 105th Congress, 2nd session, 1999; Report 105-851, at *http://www.house.gov/coxreport/pref/preface.html*.

ing threats. Intelligence activities are classic precursors to attack. During the Cold War, when NATO was concerned about a possible Warsaw Pact attack through the Fulda Gap, US intelligence kept watch for missile and aircraft readiness stages and forward movements of armor and personnel. Warning of attack today is more subtle; but intelligence preparation is a necessary pre-condition even for terrorist attacks. As the Defense Science Board pointed out, "No observation is more important in countering terrorism than to understand that would-be perpetrators, to succeed, must participate in the gathering and application of intelligence."[17]

All intelligence services practice deception, from the mundane practices of lying and falsifying documents to elaborate double and triple agent operations to the exploitation of channels of communications known to be compromised. Adversaries (and even friends[18]) attempt to mislead US intelligence and to sway decisionmakers. And the more they know about US intelligence, the greater their chances for success.

Successful penetrations have netted an enormous amount of US classified information, enabling enemies to hide from or deceive US intelligence. One of the greatest bargains in espionage history was the Soviets' purchase in 1977 of the technical manual for the new KH-11 reconnaissance satellite from former CIA employee (now convicted spy) William Kampiles, for a paltry $3,000. As a result of this and other compromises, US intelligence must assume as a matter of course that overhead imagery and other technical collection will be met by denial and deception efforts.

There is a continuing market for stolen US secrets, which may be sold or bartered to third parties. The knowledge gained of US sources and methods – through spies, unauthorized disclosures, and even some authorized disclo-sures – has aided extensive concealment and denial programs that increase our uncertainty about foreign capabilities and intentions, and more effective foreign deception operations. India's nuclear tests in 1998 – which came as a shock to US intelligence – were a prime example. Many nations have learned how to present a false picture of reality. These foreign denial and deception practices by denying vital information or distorting analysis can lead to faulty judgments. The danger is that useless or deceptive information – whether from human or technical collection – may be integrated into reports to policymakers,

17. Defense Science Board, Task Force on Strategic Intelligence Needs for Homeland Defense, Report to the Secretary of Defense, No. 308 (Fall, 2001).
18. For an accounting of British influence operations against the US in the lead-up to America's entry into World War II, see Thomas E. Mahl, *Desperate Deception: British Covert Operations in the United States, 1939-1944* (London: Brassey's Inc., 1998). Among other things, Mahl recounts how the Secret Intelligence Service (SIS, MI-6), under William Stephenson's direction, counterfeited and passed to the US Government a Nazi map that purported to show Hitler's designs on the Western Hemisphere. The fake map was a featured exhibit by the unwitting President Roosevelt in his 1941 Navy Day speech calling for the repeal of the remaining neutrality legislation. The original map and the other deception material may be found in the official history by Nigel West, *British Security Coordination: The secret history of British intelligence in the Americas*, (London: St Ermin's Press, 1998).

weapons designers, war-fighters, or the warning community as if it were true. Modern technology compounds the avenues for deception, but the problem is one known to the ancients. The notion that "all warfare is based on deception" dates from the 6th century BC writings of Sun Tzu, who devotes the closing pages of *The Art of War* to the classes and value of spies, how to convert enemy spies to one's own service, and how to use "doomed spies" as double agents "to carry false tidings to the enemy." To these instructions to the successful general he adds the strong caution that the use of spies to deceive and mislead is a two-way street, and that "without subtle ingenuity of mind, one cannot make certain of the truth of their reports."

The possibility of deception is ever-present in intelligence work. Like intelligence, scientific inquiry seeks knowledge about the unknown. The difference is that microbes under a microscope are not purposefully trying to hide and deceive the biologist, intelligence adversaries are. Deception analysis focuses on providing a quality check on the information gathered about foreign nations in order to uncover the purposeful falsehoods sent out by others.

Assess: Analysis of the intelligence activities of adversaries or allies, competitors or partners, provides a window into their interests, purposes, and plans, and options for defeating them. In practice, CI tasks must be prioritized by a sophisticated assessment of threats, which proceeds from an understanding of how others' intelligence capabilities are used to advance their objectives.[19] CI operations have positive intelligence requirements, which include answering such questions as:

- What is the "American targets" capability of the adversary service? (Foreign intelligence services have a set cadre of personnel trained to go after American targets; US counterintelligence needs to understand who they are and how they operate.)
- What is the doctrine by which the service deploys?
- What are its budget, training, and personnel records?
- What are its liaison relationships? And what are their resources, their targets?
- What are the critical nodes of foreign collection against us?
- What are the signatures of the intelligence precursors to an attack?
- What is their leadership structure?
- How and by whom are they tasked?

This analytic work, in turn, should lead to refined collection requirements to fill in the blanks in US knowledge and to support operational planning to

---

19. Over the course of 70 years, US and British intelligence acquired many insights into KGB operations. See for example Wayne Lambridge "A Note on KGB Style: methods, habits and consequences" *Studies in Intelligence*, 11, Summer 1967, 65-75, at *https://www.cia.gov/library/center-for-the-study-of-intelligence/kent-csi/vol15no1/html/v15i1a08p_0001.htm*.

exploit foreign intelligence vulnerabilities.

The intelligence activities of adversaries and friends are important factors to consider as part of sound national security policymaking. Each of the major challenges confronting America – defeating global terrorism, countering weapons of mass destruction, ensuring the security of the homeland, transforming defense capabilities, fostering cooperation with other global powers, promoting global economic growth — has an embedded counterintelligence imperative. For instance, our insights into the intelligence activities of the other main centers of global power may confirm or otherwise shape prospects for cooperative action. US policy toward Russia is a case in point.[20] Consider the case of China's intelligence activities, which increasingly rival those of Russia as a US counterintelligence concern. We know that the most likely conflict between the United States and China would be over Taiwan and that such a conflict would likely involve naval engagements. There are specific dimensions to those engagements, which would shape Chinese intelligence collection objectives against US targets, within Taiwan, and globally. Scenario-driven logic trees of this kind can yield a taxonomy for prioritizing CI analytic efforts and drive collection to support that analysis.

Assessments of foreign intelligence capabilities can shape policy deliberations and frame options for actions, answering questions as:

- If confronted with the prospect of war with Iran, what operations will Iranian intelligence conduct against the United States and what are our options to neutralize those operations?

- If North Korea attempts to sell and deliver a nuclear device or nuclear materials, what contribution can our counterintelligence forces make in the efforts to detect and intercept such activities?

- What hostile intelligence activities directed against the United States might neutralize our capacity to exercise effective control of outer space?

- To what extent are the intelligence elements of South Korea and Taiwan susceptible to deception by their adversaries and can we discern that and guard against efforts to misdirect us?

- What role do Cuban intelligence personnel play in Venezuela, and what influence does Havana exercise over that government?

---

20. Much of the old KGB's Cold War activities are recounted by Christopher Andrew and Vasili Mitrokhin in in *The Sword and the Shield: The Mitrokhin Archive and the Secret History of the KGB* (New York: Basic Books, 1999). Drawing on unprecedented access to over 25,000 pages of KGB files, the book documents the breadth and audacity of the former Soviet intelligence attack on the US – including notably its extensive active measures and disinformation campaign, which as it turns out would appear to have met even the most conspiracy-minded suspicions of the anti-communist American right wing. As one observer points out, the real importance of the book is "the sheer weight of accumulated detail which reveals a madly compulsive Soviet over-reliance on clandestine means for conducting its foreign policy, maintaining security and ideological control at home, and acquiring the technological infrastructure of a modern state." Thomas Powers, *Intelligence Wars: American Secret History from Hitler to Al-Qaeda* (New York: NY Review of Books, 2002), 96.

- What efforts might undermine the effectiveness of our ballistic missile defense system? How effective are our security preparations in protecting against these actions?

Neutralize: Counterintelligence has a positive intelligence role in identifying threats and assessing foreign intelligence capabilities, but that is only the beginning. The most distinguishing feature of counterintelligence is that it is an operational function protecting intelligence collection and analysis and other national security activities. "For the intelligence-minded man, to know about the opposition and his installations is the whole goal; for counterintelligence, knowing is only the beginning of the road – something has to be done about the information."[21] The emphasis on doing extends beyond the intelligence community to include law enforcement. When a spy is arrested, or a pseudo "diplomat" caught in *flagrante delicto* and expelled, or an asset discredited as working for the other side, the CI elements that neutralized the foreign intelligence operation have done their job.

The neutralization of foreign intelligence threats is an essential part of protecting secrets. Sound security measures such as locks, guards and gates, background investigations and polygraphs, computer firewalls and document controls are unquestionably vital, but they can only protect so far. One can pile on so much security that no one can move and still there will be a purposeful adversary looking for ways to get at what it wants. Counterintelligence goes after the adversary.

Campaigns to neutralize enemy intelligence capabilities have long been an essential part of war planning. In preparation for the Iraq War, for example, US counterintelligence's project code-named "Imminent Horizon" mapped Iraqi intelligence operations worldwide to render them ineffective. Such plans also have a place in national security strategy in times of peace.

One of the best examples of strategic CI operations was the effort in the early 1980s to stop the Soviets' illicit acquisition of advanced technologies. The Nixon Administration's *détente* policies had opened the flood gates to Soviet intelligence in their clandestine efforts to obtain scientific knowledge and technologies from the West.

---

21. C.N. Geschwind, "Wanted: An Integrated Counterintelligence" *Studies in Intelligence*, Summer 1963, 15, at *https://www.cia.gov/library/center-for-the-study-of-intelligence/kent-csi/vol7no3/html/ v07i3a02p_0001.htm*. This article, while very dated, offers some interesting insights into the differing tradecraft of clandestine HUMINT collectors and CI operations: "It is the job of intelligence to collect and analyze information. Espionage for this purpose, insofar as it is aggressive, acts only with the objective of getting past the opposing counterintelligence and security forces as uneventfully as possible. Since the gathering of intelligence is a secret preparatory function, agents doing it are not supposed to undertake executive action, agitate, or otherwise risk attracting attention. Counterintelligence, on the other hand, is engaged in covert war, all-out and immediate. It has to take action—at home by investigating, arresting, interrogating, doubling, and prosecuting Communist operatives, and abroad by carrying out recruitment, neutralization, harassment, diversionary, and psywar operations against their secret service system. These diverse concepts of responsibility for action not only are fundamentally incompatible but call for agents of fundamentally different temperament and attitudes."

This effort was suspected by a few U.S. Government officials but not documented until 1981, when French intelligence obtained the services of Col. Vladimir I. Vetrov, [codenamed] Farewell, who photographed and supplied 4,000 KGB documents on the program. In the summer of 1981, President Mitterrand told President Reagan of the source, and, when the material was supplied, it led to a potent counterintelligence response by CIA and the NATO intelligence services.[22]

Farewell provided detailed information on Soviet technology acquisition efforts, including how it was run by Line X of the KGB and exactly what it was after. It set off a far-reaching technology control effort, including export control enforcement actions and effective international cooperation in interdicting unlawful transfers. US intelligence developed new sources to expose end users and gain insights into Soviet activities. The ensuing CI operations to disrupt Soviet technology collection were broad and thorough. Within the US, and jointly with NATO governments in Western Europe and others, some 200 Soviet intelligence officers were expelled and their sources compromised. Line X was effectively out of business.[23] In the fall of 1986, another 80 Soviet intelligence officers, assigned under diplomatic cover in New York, San Francisco and Washington, were ordered to leave the country — the culmination of a series of diplomatic and CI moves to curtail Soviet intelligence operations in the United States.[24]

Importantly, this CI campaign was part of the broad Reagan Administration strategy toward the former Soviet Union. Embodied in National Security Decision Directive 75, the central objective was to "contain and over time reverse Soviet expansionism by competing effectively on a sustained basis with the Soviet Union in all international arenas."[25] The US defense buildup of the 1980s was the strategy's centerpiece. When Farewell walked through the door, the United States was just beginning its military modernization effort. R&D efforts supporting the Strategic Defense Initiative, and new composite materials enabling stealth capabilities, and breakthroughs in supercomputing and other extraordinary information technologies, among many, many other marvels of engineering and design, were all at stake and targeted by the KGB.

Exploit: By exploiting insights into foreign intelligence activities, counter-

22. Gus W. Weiss, "The Farewell Dossier" *Studies in Intelligence* 39 (5), 1996) 121-126. *https://www.cia.gov/library/center-for-the-study-of-intelligence/csi-publications/csi-studies/studies/96unclass/farewell.htm.*
23. Ibid.
24. David Major, "Operation 'Famish,'" *Defense Intelligence Journal* (Spring 1995).
25. "The contest would range from buildups in nuclear and conventional weaponry through new and openly discussed war-fighting strategies, economic sanctions, the aggressive promotion of human rights, overt and covert support for anti-Soviet resistance movements in Eastern Europe and Afghanistan as well as for opponents of Marxist regimes in Angola, Ethiopia, and Nicaragua, and the vigorous employment of rhetoric as an instrument of psychological warfare, a trend which culminated in the President's March, 1983, claim that the Soviet Union was 'the focus of evil in the modern world.'" John Lewis Gaddis, "Strategies of Containment: Post-Cold War Reconsiderations," lecture presented at The Elliott School of International Affairs, George Washington University, April 15, 2004.

intelligence can help turn events to our advantage. For example, Morris Childs was deputy head of the Communist Party of the USA and trusted confidant of his former instructors, Yuri Andropov (later head of the KGB and the Soviet Union) and Mikhail Suslov (later the Politburo's chief ideologist). Childs was also working for the FBI — a highly successful double agent operation called "Operation Solo" that continued for 23 years.[26]

How does an intelligence service know when it has the upper hand? Or when it is being played or misled by the other side? It needs a feedback mechanism, e.g., sources inside the adversary's intelligence apparatus that can provide a check on their perceptions, doubts or beliefs. The ultimate goal of offensive CI

> ...is to penetrate the opposition's own secret operations apparatus: to become, obviously without the opposition's knowledge, an integral and functioning part of their calculations and operations... [A successful CI penetration] puts you at the very heart of his actions and intentions towards you.... Most importantly, you are in a position to control his actions, since you can, by tailoring intelligence for him to your purposes, by influencing his evaluation, mislead him as to his decisions and consequent actions.[27]

As described above, Farewell gave US counterintelligence the keys to neutralize the KGB's campaign to piggyback on US technology investments. But that was not all. Having the Line X shopping list also meant that it might be possible to control some part of their collection, to "turn the tables on the KGB and conduct economic warfare of our own." As the late Gus Weiss tells the story,

> I met with Director of Central Intelligence William Casey on an afternoon in January 1982. I proposed using the Farewell material to feed or play back the products sought by Line X, but these would come from our own sources and would have been "improved," that is, designed so that on arrival in the Soviet Union they would appear genuine but would later fail. U.S. intelligence would match Line X requirements supplied through Vetrov with our version of those items, ones that would hardly meet the expectations of that vast Soviet apparatus deployed to collect them.
>
> If some double agent told the KGB the Americans were alert to Line X and were interfering with their collection by subverting, if not sabotaging, the effort, I believed the United States still could not lose. The Soviets, being a suspicious lot, would be likely to question and reject everything Line X collected. If so, this would be a rarity in the world of espionage, an operation that would succeed even if compromised. Casey liked the proposal.
>
> As was later reported in Aviation Week and Space Technology, CIA and the Defense Department, in partnership with the FBI, set up a program to do just

---

26. John Barron, *Operation Solo: The FBI's Man in the Kremlin* (Washington DC: Regnery Publishing, 1996).
27. Felix, *op cit*, 121.

what we had discussed: modified products were devised and "made available" to Line X collection channels.[28]

Golden opportunities of the kind *Farewell* provided do not come knocking every day. The national CI enterprise needs to seek out high value insights into foreign intelligence activities, recognize gold when it appears (and fools' gold for what it is), and be creative and agile and competent enough to seize the moment.

The world of offensive counterintelligence is most familiar in its supporting role to military operations. The finest historic example, of course, is Operation Overlord, the Allied landing at Normandy. D-Day was a huge risk, which succeeded because of masterful planning, including the most sweeping deception in military history. The Allies could not hope to hide the fact that they intended a cross-Channel invasion; but through the use of elaborate decoys and ruses, misleading communications, finely orchestrated double agent operations,[29] and a host of other inventive measures, they led the Germans to believe the landing site would be at Pas de Calais. The surprise was total.[30]

The use of strategic deception in peacetime presents its own set of special considerations. Actions taken to manipulate, distort or falsify information to mislead the enemy may have the unintended consequences of deceiving the public, calling into question core democratic values. The law is unclear and the ethical questions even more challenging when deception may work to save lives and advance freedom; the practical questions concerning the design and employment of deception are no less complex for national security decision makers, as well as for members of the press.[31]

For deception to be successful, "two things are imperative: First, the enemy must be kept totally in the dark about what you don't want him to know, and second, you must know everything he is thinking all the time, especially when he's confronted with what you want him to believe." In any deception

---

28. Weiss, op cit, 124.

29. The use of double agents, which figured so prominently in WWII deception operations under the code name "Double-cross," is a complex and sophisticated counterintelligence technique. "A double agent is a person who engages in clandestine activity for two intelligence or security services (or more in joint operations), who provides information about one or about each to the other, and who wittingly withholds significant information from one on the instructions of the other or is unwittingly manipulated by one so that significant facts are withheld from the adversary... The double agent serves also as a controlled channel through which information can be passed to the other service, either to build up the agent in its estimation or for purposes of deception" (as was the case with Overlord). F.M. Begoum, "Observations on the Double Agent" *Studies in Intelligence,* Winter 1962, at *https://www.cia.gov/library/center-for-the-study-of-intelligence/kent-csi/vol6no1/html/v06i1a05p_0001.htm.*

30. For the full story see Ben Macintyre, *Double Cross* (New York, Crown Publishers, 2012). Concerning British counterintelligence and its role in supporting deception for Operation Overlord and other actions in World War II, see Basil Collier, *Hidden Weapons: Allied Secret or Undercover Services in World War II* (London: Sword Books Ltd., 1982, 2006).

31. For a discussion of these and other matters see U.S. Army War College and Triangle Institute for Security Studies, Conference Brief "Strategic Deception in Modern Democracies: Ethical, Legal, and Policy Challenges" compiled by Dr. Carolyn Pumphrey and LtCol Antulio Echevarria II (2003), accessible over the internet at *http://www.pubpol.duke.edu/centers/tiss/pubs/Summary.html.*

campaign, the feedback loop is all-important. Cambridge University World War II historian F. H. Hinsley continues,

> We were able to locate, early on, the entire German espionage network in Britain, eliminate parts of it and use others to feed Hitler disinformation. We were also able to learn Hitler's thinking about where and when the invasion would eventually come, play to his prejudices and hunches, and learn when and whether he took our bait. We were reading his mind all the time.[32]

Offensive CI seeks to influence the adversary's decision makers by manipulating the intelligence product that informs their decisions, "luring your opponent into doing voluntarily and by choice what you want him to do."[33] This was the role counterintelligence played in Operation Overlord, luring the Germans to mass their forces in the wrong place.

In peacetime too, US counterintelligence needs to think offensively — How does the foreign intelligence service operate? What are its vulnerabilities? How can they be exploited? What are the indicators that might give warning of intelligence operations against us? Are there tripwires we can design to give us an edge? Are there CI avenues available to influence foreign decision making to help achieve larger U.S. national security objectives?[34]

The Future of Counterintelligence

The litany of spies inside the US Government – from the British agents in the Revolutionary War to those stealing atomic secrets in World War II to traitors now in jail (such as former CIA officer Rick Ames and former FBI Special Agent Robert Hanssen) – spans our history and tells many stories: Who would spy against their own country? For whom, and why? What did they steal, and how? How were they caught? And what does the future hold?

At the start of the 21st century, there are many more highly capable foreign intelligence services in the world than ever before, and we are only just beginning to understand their potentials. Today, these foreign services can also take advantage of the self-appointed revealers of Western secrets (like the stateless organization Wikileaks or former NSA contractor Edward Snowden, now living in exile in Russia) who at best have no way of knowing what harm their actions may cause. Furthermore, modern technologies, such as biometrics for identification and "big data" search and retrieval, offer US and foreign CI

---

32. Quoted in "The Masters of Deception: At England's Bletchley Park, Recalling the Code-Breakers and Illusion-Makers" *The Washington Post*, May 31, 1999, C-1.

33. Felix, *op cit*, 128.

34. Office of the National Counterintelligence Executive, "The National Counterintelligence Strategy of the United States" (Washington, DC: NCIX Publication No. 2005-10007, March 2005) *http://www.ncix. gov/publications/strategy/docs/FinalCIStrategyforWebMarch21.pdf*. This was the first national strategy developed to guide US counterintelligence; it also set out for the first time the offensive dimension of counterintelligence at the strategic level. See also subsequent iterations of the national CI strategy, available on the webpage of the Office of Director of National Intelligence (*http://www.dni.gov/*).

organizations new tools, often difficult to counter. The future of counterintelligence may be even more challenging than its past.

A member of AFIO's Board, Michelle Van Cleave served as the National Counterintelligence Executive under President George W. Bush. As the head of US counterintelligence, she was responsible for directing and integrating FBI, CIA, Defense, and other counterintelligence activities across the federal government. She has also held senior staff positions in the Senate and House of Representatives, the Pentagon, and in the White House Science Office, where she served as assistant director and general counsel under Presidents Ronald Reagan and George H.W. Bush. A lawyer and consultant in private life, she is a senior fellow at George Washington University and a principal with the Jack Kemp Foundation.

GUIDE TO THE STUDY OF INTELLIGENCE

Espionage Against America

David G. Major and Peter C. Oleson

At the beginning of the 20th century, the United States transcended from being an isolated nation separated by vast oceans and engaged in world events, to becoming a prime espionage target for military, political, intelligence, and economic information.

America: The Target

America's pivotal role in World War I altered its position in the international arena. No longer a distant country, America's industrial power and the outbreak of the war made it of interest to Europe's intrigues. Even before the US entered the war, the German Intelligence Service in 1914 began sending its officers to the US.

Today, the US is a major target of espionage for more than 140 foreign intelligence services.[1] Why? Because it has the most advanced technologically enabled military the world has ever witnessed with a global footprint, is involved with every significant world event, and has the strongest and most advanced economy. It is also the world's financial center. More than any other nation, the US is the creator of ideas. It leads the world in research papers, patents issued, and expenditures by industry and government for research and development.[2] The US is the center of higher education for the world, especially the developing world, including China.[3]

---

1. In a March 29, 2007 speech before the ABA Standing Committee on Law and National Security, National Counterintelligence Executive (NCIX) Joel Brenner stated "there are now 140 foreign intelligence services that try to penetrate the United States or US organizations abroad, and for many of them, we are their number one target." Cited by Michael Sulick. *Spying in America: Espionage from the Revolutionary War to the Dawn of the Cold War* (Washington, DC: Georgetown University Press, 2012), 271.
2. *Scientific American*, October 2012, 44.
3. Seventeen of the top 20 universities are in the United States according to the 2013 academic ranking

Foreign intelligence collectors seek US classified information and technology, especially those with military applications. However, today anything of value is a highly prized target for economic espionage, including proprietary information, trade secrets, and R&D data. Prime private sector targets are industries in the information technology, manufacturing, financial, and pharmaceutical fields. But consumer companies, biological, and medical institutions, and the service sector are increasingly targeted.

Russia, Cuba, and the Peoples Republic of China (PRC), are — and have been — the most aggressive in targeting US national security information. Since the Economic Espionage Law of 1996 was passed, 85% of all the economic espionage cases resulting in criminal charges have involved spies from Asian countries including the PRC, Taiwan, South Korea, and India, with the PRC being the most active. The number one country behind the illegal export of restricted technology is Iran, with the PRC the next largest diverter of technology.[4]

US Counterintelligence

Counterintelligence (CI) is a strategic discipline whose mission has been redefined many times in the past 100 years. Its primary focus has been, and continues to be, to identify nations, organizations, and individuals involved in intelligence collection activities directed against US Government institutions, private sector organizations, individuals (including the media), and to take action to neutralize those efforts. According to Executive Order 12333, as amended by EO 13470 signed August 2008, counterintelligence is defined as:

information gathered and activities conducted to identify, deceive, exploit, disrupt, or protect against espionage, other intelligence activities, sabotage, or assassinations conducted for or on behalf of foreign powers, organizations, or persons, or their agents, or international terrorist organizations or activities.

As such, counterintelligence includes the disciplines of security counter-measures, operations security, counterterrorism, and countering offensive actions directed against the US. The CI discipline is a secondary decision by the state. The decision to conduct intelligence operations against a state or organization is a "primary" decision. Thus, if no efforts are made to "counter" an intelligence activity, it becomes easier for the collector. Therefore, one

---

of world universities by Shanghai Jiad Tong University. They are Harvard, Stanford, University of California at Berkeley, Massachusetts Institute of Technology, CalTech, Princeton, Columbia, University of Chicago, Yale, University of California at Los Angeles, Cornell, University of California at San Diego, University of Washington, Johns Hopkins, University of California at San Francisco, University of Wisconsin – Madison. Non-US universities cited were Cambridge University, Oxford University, and the Swiss Federal Institute of Technology – Zurich. *Foreign Policy* magazine, July/August 2014, 63.

4. CI Centre analysis of publicly revealed espionage and trade diversion cases. *http://www.cicentre.com*.

"cannot *not* do counterintelligence" because the decision to collect against you has already been made.

The intelligence collection threats to the US and its CI responses have evolved. For most of its early history, the US Government had no intelligence or CI organizations. When threatened, the US temporized and then disbanded its *ad hoc* capabilities at the conclusion of hostilities.[5]

The Anarchist threat in the early 20th century finally spurred the US Government to action. Attorney General Charles Bonaparte in 1908 created the Bureau of Investigation (the predecessor of today's FBI), largely to counter this threat that was viewed as originating from overseas. Thus the FBI, from its origins, was primarily a counterintelligence — vice law enforcement — organization.

Espionage History

World War I. With the outbreak of World War I, the German General Intelligence Staff immediately targeted the neutral US with a focus on sabotaging, preventing, or disrupting shipment of war materials to Germany's enemies. Starting in 1914, their agents sabotaged US munitions and chemical plants, and planted bombs on munitions ships crossing the Atlantic Ocean, causing fires and sinkings. The Germans also undertook biological warfare by infecting mules and horses being shipped to the war in Europe. The massive July 30, 1916 explosion on Black Tom's Island in Jersey City harbor, which killed two, injured hundreds, and blew out windows in Manhattan across the Hudson River, was caused by German agents and led to the passage of the Espionage Act of 1917. No individuals were arrested for the Black Tom's Island sabotage.

Post World War I. In 1919, Anarchists sent letter bombs to 36 Americans, including Attorney General A. Mitchell Palmer. One Italian Anarchist accidentally blew himself up on the doorstep of Palmer's Washington, DC, home. The Department of Justice misunderstood the difference between an anarchist and a communist. Communist activity was growing in the US as a response to the 1917 communist revolution in Russia. In this environment, Congress passed an amendment to the Espionage Law (the Sedition Act of 1918), which made it a crime to advocate the overthrow of the US if you were an alien, punishable by deportation, but not a crime if you were a US citizen. Arrests could be made without warrants. In January 1920, Palmer directed the Bureau of Investigation along with local police to detain over 10,000 people, with 3,000 of those arrested. Using the Sedition Act, 556 foreigners were deported to Europe. Initially this action was supported by the public and media. Palmer became

---

5. See Sulick (2012) for the history of how counterintelligence was handled by John Jay's Committee on Detecting and Defeating Conspiracies during the Revolutionary War, the exploits of Pinkerton and Baker during the Civil War, and during the Spanish-American War.

a leading candidate for president. In 1920, however, he predicted communist riots, which did not materialize. Legal experts and the media began criticizing Palmer and the Bureau's alleged heavy-handed methods, which led to congressional hearings in 1921. This led to a public rebuke of CI activities, which were viewed by some as persecution of individuals' political beliefs. US Government efficacy to investigate political beliefs has been, and continues to be, a contentious issue. It boils down to the question "does belief lead to action?" and if it does, should the government investigate belief to prevent action that could damage the state?

When J. Edgar Hoover was appointed director of the Bureau of Investigation in 1924, he directed that the Bureau only investigate violations of law. With this decision, the US discontinued all CI activities. Some local police departments established intelligence squads to continue to investigate communist organizations and individuals in their cities.

Also in 1924, the first Soviet military intelligence (Army Staff Second Directorate, renamed GRU in 1926) officers arrived in the US establishing an illegals *residency*. In 1928, the first Joint State Political Directorate (OGPU)[6] illegals[7] arrived. Since the US had no active CI organization, it was unaware of the presence of these intelligence collectors. Over the next two decades, the Soviets grew multiple espionage networks in the US in conjunction with domestic communist movements. They were involved in recruiting and/or handling individuals who volunteered to be espionage agents — most of whom were ideologically sympathetic members of the Communist Party of the US and, in the Depression era, believers of Soviet propaganda.

World War II. With the rise of the Nazis in 1933, there was a growth of pro-Nazi sympathy of the German-American Bund. President Franklin Roosevelt directed the FBI to begin investigating the Bund in 1938, and Congress provided special funding to jump-start this CI effort. By 1939, the president directed the FBI — along with US Army Intelligence (MI) and the US Navy Office of Naval Intelligence (ONI) — to undertake responsibility for counterintelligence, counter-espionage, and subversive investigations in the US.

In the 1930's, Nazi Germany and Imperial Japan began conducting aggressive espionage activity against the US (as did the Soviet Union). The FBI was successful in identifying, penetrating, and neutralizing the majority of the collection activities of Germany and Japan before the start of WWII, but not of the Soviet Union. German military intelligence(Abwehr) had some success targeting US industrial secrets. From sympathizers in 1937, the Abwehr obtained the formula for synthetic rubber, which proved essential for its military during

---

6. OGPU was the name of the Soviet secret police from 1922 to 1934. For a history of Soviet and Russian secret services, see Robert Pringle, "Guide to Soviet and Russian Intelligence Services," *The Intelligencer* 18 (2), Winter/Spring 2011.

7. An "illegal" is an intelligence officer who operates under either his true name or a false identity and is not connected ostensibly with a facility associated with the illegal's sponsoring country.

the war, and the highly classified Norden bombsight. The Germans, however, were unable to manufacture the bombsight.[8] In 1939, William Sebold, a naturalized immigrant in the 1920's, returned to Germany to visit his parents. The Nazi security police, the Gestapo, blackmailed him to spy, and then turned him over to the Abwehr. Sebold alerted US authorities while still in Germany and volunteered as a double agent for the FBI. When he returned to the US in 1941, Sebold became the Abwehr's radio operator for every German agent operating in the US. This enabled the FBI to arrest all 33 members of the Abwehr's network. A year later, the Germans landed four agents on Long Island and four in Vero Beach, Florida, by submarine. When one of the potential saboteurs turned himself in to the FBI, all were arrested within two weeks. Six of the eight were executed in Washington DC in August of the same year. Thus, Nazi Germany had no *bona fide* agents in the US. The subsequent ones they tried to operate were all controlled FBI double agents. Britain's MI-5 (Security Service) and the FBI cooperated in running double agents against German intelligence during World War II.[9] In early 1942, diplomatic relations were broken and the US Army detained all German diplomats and businessmen in the US at The Greenbrier — a luxurious resort in the West Virginia mountains — and later deported to Germany.

Japan also had some espionage success against the US prior to the attack on Pearl Harbor. Before the war, several Japanese spies were arrested and prosecuted, including: former naval officer John Semer Farnsworth (who spied from 1933 to 1937), who compromised the gunnery capabilities of every US ship; Otto and Friedel Kuehn, of Honolulu, who provided intelligence on Pearl Harbor from 1936 to 1941; US Army Captain Rufo Caingat Romero (who spied from 1939 to 1940), who attempted to sell for $25,000 ($291,000 in 1999 dollars) classified maps of Bataan and Corregidor to an individual with Japanese intelligence connections — he was sentenced to 15 years in a federal penitentiary; and Harry Thomas Thompson, a former US Navy yeoman, who spied for Japan in 1934–1935. Thompson was arrested in March 1936, convicted, and sentenced to 15 years. Via its espionage by 1941, the Japanese had compiled a 200-page guidebook to the US Navy and its capabilities.

The FBI and Office of Naval Intelligence (ONI) attempted a double agent CI operation against the Japanese. Between March and June 1941, the CI operation targeted a Japanese intelligence ring that had 13 agents on the West Coast and in Hawaii. A critical tip came in March 1941, when Al Blake told the ONI in Los Angeles an old acquaintance, Torachi Kono, had asked him to spy for Japan. Operated as a double agent by ONI and the FBI, the Japanese tasked Blake to collect intelligence on Pearl Harbor. Kono was arrested in June 1940 along with

---

8. Sulick (2012), 134-6.
9. Thaddeus Holt, *The Deceivers: Allied Military Deception in the Second World War* (New York: Scribner, 2004).

Itaru Tachibana, who ran a ring of agents, and another intelligence officer. Following their arrests and Tokyo's threat to arrest American military officers in Japan, the State Department requested the US attorney in Los Angeles not to prosecute. All were allowed to leave the US for Japan without being prosecuted. The well-funded Japanese espionage efforts that had operated in America for several years before the war passed a high volume of intelligence to Tokyo.

Japan attacked the US using intelligence collected by their agents and by a Japanese intelligence officer in Hawaii assigned to the consulate – Navy Lieutenant Takeo Yoshikawa. As with the Germans, in early 1942, the Army detained all Japanese diplomats and businessmen in the US, placing them under house arrest at The Homestead — a resort in Hot Springs, Virginia — and later deported to Japan via Mozambique, eliminating wartime intelligence collection against the US. Based on previous investigations, the FBI arrested 3,346 individuals identified as German, Italian, or Japanese enemy aliens within the first 72 hours after Pearl Harbor. These arrests were based on information indicating each individual represented a genuine national security threat to the nation. There was at least one Japanese agent in the US during World War II. Between 1935 and 1944, Velvalee Dickinson, who owned and managed a doll shop in New York City, used correspondence about dolls to conceal information about US Naval forces, which she was attempting to convey to the Japanese via South America. Wartime censors identified her.

Treasury Secretary Henry Morgenthau proposed in December 1941 the relocation of all Japanese-Americans away from the West Coast and the freezing of Japanese assets and businesses. Morgenthau asked FBI Director Hoover if this could be done. Hoover referred the request to Attorney General Frank Biddle and advised that he opposed such a move, stating "arrests of enemy aliens had already been made ... that factual cases had been prepared on each of them and their arrests approved by the Attorney General ... that of course, citizens of the United States were not being included in any arrests, unless there were specific actions upon which criminal complaints could be filed...." By E.O. 9066, Roosevelt tasked the Army with the responsibility to relocate more than 120,000 Japanese-Americans, the majority from the West Coast. No Japanese-Americans were detained in Hawaii.

Soviet Espionage. Soviet spies had deeply penetrated the FDR Administration. Subsequent research of primary sources[10] identified 541 clandestine Soviet agents in the US during the 1940-1950 period. Further revelations from KGB files smuggled out by retired KGB officer Vasili Mitrokhin indicate that the Soviets had as many as 1,000 sources in the US.[11] Almost all of these indi-

---

10. These sources include the KGB files smuggled out of the USSR by KGB archivist Vasili Mitrokhin in 1991; former KGB officer Alexander Vassiliev emigrated to the UK in 1996 and co-authored two books based on KGB files; and VENONA, the Army, later NSA, effort to decrypt Soviet transmissions, which revealed extensive espionage against the US and by name the identities of 349 agents.
11. "Soviet Defector's trove of KGB secrets made public," *Associated Press*, July 6, 2014. *http://apnews*.

viduals were either members of the US Communist Party or were sympathetic to communist objectives. The Soviets had so many agents and so few intelligence officers in the US that American agents ran other American agents. During WWII, the Soviet intelligence services (NKVD and GRU) had only 18 professional intelligence officers in the US to control this large number of agents. By the end of World War II, Soviet spies had penetrated every agency in the US Government except the FBI and ONI. By 1947, at the start of the Cold War, the US had essentially no political, military, or industrial secrets uncompromised by Soviet intelligence.

> In the 1940's the Soviets ran "the most colossal espionage operation against the United States in its history."[1]
>
> 1. Sulick (2012), 3.

FIGURE 1. EXAMPLES OF A FEW OF THE MANY SOVIET SPIES IN THE US GOVERNMENT 1930S – 1950

Name	Spied for	Impact / Significance
Harry Dexter White Assistant Secretary of Treasury	NKVD 1934-45	A top Soviet spy of the 1930s and 1940s.[†] Provided sensitive Treasury documents to Soviets. Also provided engraving plates for Allied military marks allowing Soviets to print occupation currency. Called to testify in front of Congress in 1948 about his espionage activity, he testified for one hour and that week died of a heart attack.
Alger Hiss Director, Office of Special Political Affairs, Department of State	GRU 1935-45	Delegate to Yalta Conference. Provided information that allowed Stalin to insist on having veto power in the proposed UN Security Council. Acting secretary general at UN founding conference. Only convicted of perjury. Served 44 months in prison.
Lauchlin Currie White House economic advisor	NKVD Mid-1930s to 1945	Longest-serving special assistant to FDR. Provided detailed information on presidential decisions. Revealed existence of the VENONA program to Soviets. Currie was one of those blamed for losing China to the Communists by the actions he took in Treasury and the White House. Used his position to influence efforts to cover up the Amerasia magazine espionage in 1945. Denied espionage when he testified to Congress in 1948 and moved to Colombia.[††]
Duncan Lee Confidential Assistant to Office of Strategic Services (OSS) Director Major General William Donovan	NKVD 1942-44	Revealed "anti-Soviet" activities by OSS including support to Eastern European groups that wanted to keep the Soviets out of their countries. Also revealed activities at Oak Ridge, part of the Manhattan Project. Denied espionage when he testified to Congress in 1948, moved to the Caribbean and later to Canada.

† Sulick (2012), 206
†† A June 1945 FBI raid on the *Amerasia* magazine offices discovered 1,700 classified State Department, Navy, OSS, and Office of War Information documents. Three staff were indicted, but only two were fined. The "Amerasia Affair" became a cause célèbre for anti-communists, including Senator Joseph McCarthy.

excite.com/article/20140707/eu—britain-spy_archive-0a92e12efb.html.

William Weisband Army's Secret Intelligence Service	NKVD 1934-50	Revealed US had broken high-grade codes used by Soviet military, police, NKVD and nuclear development program (Project BOURBON). Also revealed VENONA project was decrypting Soviet intelligence and military communications. US SIGINT went deaf when Soviets changed codes. Only sentenced to one year for contempt of court.†
Laurence Duggan Chief of Latin American Division, State Department	NKVD 1934-48	Provided Soviets copies of cables from US ambassador in Moscow to State Department. On December 15, 1948, 10 days after being questioned by the FBI about whether he had had contacts with Soviet intelligence, Duggan fell to his death from his office at the Institute of International Education, on the 16th floor of a building in midtown Manhattan.
Judith Coplon Department of Justice	NKVD-MGB 1945-49	Worked in foreign agents registration section and then in counterintelligence with access to FBI files. Passed sensitive documents to her Soviet handler. Convicted in 1950 but released on bail in 1952, her conviction was overturned on a technicality.
Charles Kramer Senate Subcommittee of War Mobilization	NKVD 1944-45	Tried to recruit Robert Oppenheimer, the Los Alamos chief of development for the Manhattan Project. Kramer had been for more than two years one of the principal subjects of an FBI investigation of Soviet espionage launched in early November 1945, following the defection of Elizabeth Bentley to the FBI. Bentley claimed that Kramer was a leading member of an espionage ring headed by Victor Perlo. FBI agents interviewed Kramer on August 27, 1947, but "refused to discuss his activities during the period when he was employed by the US Government." In the summer of 1948, Bentley and Whittaker Chambers, another defector from the Soviet cause, publicly identified Kramer as a member of the Communist and Soviet underground in the 1930s and during World War II. When called to testify before the House Committee on Un-American Activities (HUAC), Kramer refused to answer any questions about his Communist background. He continued to work for the Progressive Party until it disbanded in 1955, after which he moved to Oregon.
Klaus Fuchs Manhattan Project	GRU, later NKVD 1941-50	A member of the British Atomic Energy Research Establishment, Fuchs was sent from London to the US to work on the Manhattan Project, assigned to Oak Ridge and Los Alamos. Gave Soviet sketches of the atomic bomb and its components and research on ignition systems and the bomb core – two critical components. Also revealed British atomic research secrets. Sentenced to 14 years. Moved to East Germany after release in 1959.

† Some believe Weisband's 1948 revelations about Project BOURBON caused the US to miss warnings about Stalin's approval of North Korea's 1950 invasion of South Korea, a conflict that resulted in 4 million casualties including over 36,000 American dead. Historians Harvey Klehr, John Haynes, and Alexander Vassiliev wrote [Weisband] "did incalculable damage to American interests and likely changed the course of the early Cold War." *Spies: The Rise and Fall of the KGB in America* (New Haven: Yale University Press, 2009), 398.

Julius & Ethel Rosenberg Manhattan Project	NKVD 1942-50	Ran ring of eight agents that provided more than 20,000 documents and much information on the atomic bomb as well as more than 100 other weapons programs. Convicted and executed in 1953.
Theodore Hall Manhattan Project	NKVD then MGB 1944-53	Revealed secrets of the plutonium bomb and the use of a polonium trigger. The first Soviet bomb test in 1949 employed plutonium with a polonium trigger. Maybe the most important of all of the atomic spies.[†] He was never arrested or publically identified as a Soviet spy until the 1990s.
George Koval Manhattan Project	GRU illegal 1940-48	American born, emigrated to USSR in 1932 with his parents. The GRU recruited him to be an illegal. Returned to US in 1940, and joined the Army in 1943. Deputy GRU illegal rezident in New York and later penetrated Oak Ridge. Provided the Soviet Union information about the production processes and volumes of the polonium, plutonium, and uranium used in American atomic weaponry, and descriptions of the weapon production sites. Vanished in 1948 after being warned by the GRU and returned to USSR.

† Sulick (2012), 243-251.

Soviet penetration of British intelligence also impacted US national security. The US shared much intelligence with Britain after the war. Soviet spies in Britain's wartime Government Communications and Cipher School (GC&CS) provided Moscow with details of intelligence gained from the Enigma decryptions as well as other cryptographic information. Kim Philby, the wartime head of the Secret Intelligence Service's (SIS's; also known as MI-6) offensive CI branch, was a Soviet spy. His posting to Washington, DC, in 1949 provided him with access to VENONA decrypts. In 1951, Philby warned his fellow "Cambridge Five" conspirator Donald Maclean that he had been identified as a Soviet agent and was about to be arrested. Given this warning, Maclean, accompanied by fellow spy Guy Burgess, escaped to Moscow.

The FDR Administration had been warned in 1939 that there were hundreds of Soviet agents within the administration. Undersecretary of State Adolph Berle told FDR of information provided by disaffected communist, GRU and OGPU agent Whittaker Chambers and NKVD illegal defector Walter Krivitsky. FDR dismissed the warnings as "absurd." In 1949, the three-year old VENONA project, designed to read Soviet wartime diplomatic codes and encrypted cables, produced intelligence on Soviet espionage in the US. As WWII ended, a few of the "true believers" who were GRU and NKVD clandestine agents revealed their espionage activities. This included Whittaker Chambers, who serviced a spy ring within the State and Treasury Departments; and Elizabeth Bentley, a NKVD courier, who revealed to the FBI in August 1945 more than 80 Soviet intelligence agents, 27 of whom worked in the government. VENONA added to the revelations from Igor Gouzenko, a Soviet code clerk, who defected in 1945 in Ottawa, taking more than 100 documents about Soviet espionage in Canada and the US. When the FBI advised the British Secret Service of Bentley's defection and the details of Soviet agents, Kim Philby immediately warned the NKVD. The NKVD quickly put its entire agent network "on ice." As the FBI began to investigate the individuals Bentley identified, none were actively engaged in espionage because of Philby's disclosure. This explains why so few Soviet spies of this era were arrested. Chambers and Bentley testified before Congress in 1948, but were ridiculed by many in the media and Congress. At a press conference, President Truman authorized the following direct quotation about Congress: "They are using these hearings simply as a red herring, to keep from doing what they ought to do." Eleanor Roosevelt described Elizabeth Bentley's testimony as "the fantastic story of this evidently neurotic lady."

Senator Joseph McCarthy seized upon reports about the lax security within the FDR Administration during WWII as well as the 1948 House hearings. He held repeated Senate hearings from 1952 through 1954, questioned government officials, and made unsupported allegations. While the basis of McCarthy's charges are now known to be true, his methods, inaccuracies, and excesses negatively impacted CI efforts, causing them to be viewed with disrepute by the public and media.

After WWII, the Soviet NKVD (later MGB/KGB) and GRU decided against using anyone as espionage agents who had communist connections, because American CI was aggressively targeting the Communist Party or communist sympathizers. In fact, Congress had outlawed the Communist Party in 1940 with the passage of the "The Alien Registration Act" known as "The Smith Act" (18 USC § 2385). It stated that whoever with intent to cause or advocate the overthrow or destruction the government in the United States by force or violence has committed a felony. Since the Community Party advocated this objective, it became *de facto* illegal to be a member of the Party.

> Americans have always disbelieved that one of their own would spy against the country. "This disbelief spawned a 'national capacity for naiveté,' as former CIA counterintelligence chief Paul Redmond dubbed it, which surfaced as early as the American Revolution."[1]
>
> ---
>
> 1. Sulick (2012), 2, citing former CIA chief of counterintelligence, Paul Redmond, "America Pays the Price for Openness," *Wall Street Journal*, June 2000.

In 1957, William Fisher (alias Rudolf Abel), who came to the US as an illegal in 1948, was arrested and convicted with considerable publicity. Fisher was sentenced to 30 years in prison but was exchanged in 1962 for U-2 pilot Francis Gary Powers. Between 1945 and 1965, 50 individuals were charged with espionage-related charges in the US, 43 of who were Soviet spies.

During the period 1945 to 1992, US CI programs concentrated on countries that were considered hostile to the US, which included all Warsaw Pact countries. This was the "criteria country list." A few countries allied with the US were identified as also conducting espionage and, after repeated warnings, were added to the "criteria country list." The vast majority of US CI efforts, however, were directed toward the Soviet Union.

The "Dark Ages." Some refer to the period of 1965 to 1975 as the "Dark Ages" for US CI. The first Soviet intelligence officer to become a CIA recruitment-in-place was GRU Lieutenant Colonel Pyotr Popov, who volunteered in Vienna, Austria, in 1953. The KGB arrested him in 1959. The CIA did not know how he had been compromised. When KGB Major Anatoly Golitsyn defected to the CIA in Helsinki in 1961, he advised that the CIA was penetrated by a "mole" (code name "Sasha") and that the KGB was planning a massive deception operation supported by false defectors and agents. James Angleton, head of CIA's CI, became obsessed with the concept and of the existence of moles in the CIA. When another KGB officer, Yuri Nosenko, defected to the CIA in 1964, claiming that the KGB had never recruited former US Marine Lee Harvey Oswald (who had defected to the USSR and returned and assassinated President JFK), Angleton became convinced Nosenko was a false defector, a part of the deception plan outlined by Golitsyn. In 1964, CIA imprisoned Nosenko for three years.[12]

Before Angleton's tenure, US intelligence had 13 Soviet intelligence officers as "recruitments–in-place"; beginning in 1966, CIA's offensive HUMINT operations against the USSR came to a halt. No new sources were recruited or walk-ins accepted by the CIA since CIA's CI managers considered all potential new Soviet sources controlled by the KGB as part of a massive deception operation.

Between 1966 and 1974, US military CI arrested 13 individuals in the US military for espionage for the Soviet Union. The FBI arrested only one individual for espionage during this period.

On the domestic front, to the detriment of foreign CI, the FBI's primary CI focus was on domestic groups opposing the Vietnam War and the US racial conflict. This included such groups as the Students for a Democratic Society (SDS), the Weathermen, Jewish Defense League (JDL), Black Panthers, Ku Klux Klan (KKK), Republic of New Africa, and others implicated in violence and/ or bombings, including of the US Capitol. During the years 1972 to 1975, the nation's politics were diverted by the Watergate break-in, the investigation of the President's cover-up actions, and pending impeachment, including media assertions of alleged misdeeds by the Intelligence Community (IC). In 1975, the Senate convened an investigatory committee (Senate Select Committee to Study Government Operations With Respect to Intelligence Activities, also

---

12. The Nosenko affair remains controversial. Divided opinions as to his *bona fides* and how CIA handled his case and who was responsible remain. See Sam Halpern and Hayden Peake, "Did Angleton Jail Nosenko?," *International Journal of Intelligence and Counterintelligence*, Vol. 3, No. 4, pp 451-64, and David Wise, *Molehunt*, New York, Random House, 1992, especially Chapter 11, "AEFOXTROT."

known as the Church Committee), and the House of Representatives (Pike Committee) conducted a similar investigation of the US IC. While much criticism was leveled at various intelligence agencies, including the FBI's domestic intelligence program against communist and hate groups, the FBI's foreign counterintelligence program was largely exonerated. The Church Committee agreed to keep the FBI's national double agent operations secret, and out of its reports, and did not define double agents as a "covert action" requiring Congress be advised of these operations as it is for other covert action programs.

The "Golden Age" – 1975 to 1992. Following the "Dark Ages," a new "Golden Age" emerged for CI. In 1975, CIA Director William Colby forced Angleton to retire. Nosenko was deemed a real *bona fide* defector, and much of Golitsyn's information was determined to be untrue and/or embellishments. In the period 1975 to 1992, US CI arrested or filed charges against 125 individuals as clandestine agents, of which 62 were working for Soviet intelligence. One of the reasons for this success was the number of Soviet intelligence officers "recruited" by the FBI (10) and by CIA (10). In addition, previous concerns about holding public trials for espionage, which could compromise intelligence sources and methods, were tempered with the passage in 1980 of the Classified Information Procedures Act (18 USC App. III § 1-16) that allowed use of classified materials without public disclosure.

Time magazine labeled 1985 "The Year of the Spy" due to the number of espionage cases revealed. Eighteen individuals were arrested and 10 identified as Soviet agents. Those arrested included Navy Warrant Officer John Walker and his ring of three,[13] Ronald Pelton from the National Security Agency (NSA), and Army Warrant Officer James Hall (all Soviet spies); Navy Middle East analyst Jonathan Pollard (an Israeli spy); and Larry Wu-Tai Chin, a CIA translator and later China analyst (the longest active PRC spy against the US). By providing cryptographic materials to the Soviets, "Walker and his fellow spies alone had upset the balance of nuclear defense in the Soviet's favor." Former KGB Major General "Oleg Kalugin called Walker 'the number one agent' in the history of the KGB..... Vitaliy Yurchenko echoed Kalugin's assessment.... [T]he Walker case was the greatest in KGB history and even surpassed the atomic bomb spies." During the decade of the 1980's, 92 Americans were arrested for spying, 47 for the USSR.

The fall of the Berlin Wall opened up new sources of counterespionage information for the CIA and FBI. CIA obtained the files of East Germany's secret police (Stasi) and foreign intelligence service (HVA) in 1990, including the identities of its spies.[14] As the Soviet Union began to break-up, another new source became available. In 1992, Vasili Mitrokhin, a retired KGB officer and archi-

---

13. Sulick (2012), 105.
14. "CIA buys East German spy files," *The Baltimore Sun*, January 3, 1999. http://articles.baltimoresun.com/1999-01-03/topic/9904280930_1_stasi-hva-espionage).

vist at the KGB Centre, who had secretly copied thousands of pages of official KGB files, defected to Britain and provided this information to British and US intelligence, the most important CI source since VENONA. Mitrokhin brought 25,000 pages of notes of Soviet espionage against the West dating back to the 1930's. In 1996, former KGB officer Alexander Vassilieva exploited KGB archives and authored books with Western historians revealing details of Soviet era espionage before the archives were again closed.

At the direction of President George H. W. Bush in 1990, the IC did a comprehensive study to identify all the countries conducting intelligence collection against the US: over 70 were identified. In 1992, the FBI restructured its approach to CI and adopted the National Security Threat List (NSTL), which categorized countries as either aggressively targeting the US and representing a military threat or those conducting some level of collection and exploiting the US. Espionage related to "the proliferation of chemical, biological, and nuclear weapons; the loss of critical technologies; and the illegal collection of private sector trade secrets and proprietary information" were considered threat issues. The result was the collection activities of many more countries were examined. It became apparent that the US's Cold War adversaries were not the only ones spying on America. Countries identified as aggressively pursuing espionage against America included old enemies such as the USSR, Cuba, and the PRC and newly identified collectors such as Taiwan and South Korea.

> "... there are friendly nations, but no friendly intelligence services."[1]

1. James M. Olson, "The Ten Commandments of Counterintelligence," Center for the Study of Intelligence, Central Intelligence Agency, https://www.cia.gov/library/center-for-the-study-of-intelligence/kent-csi/vol45no5/html/v45i5a08p.htm . Variations on this adage have been attributed to CIA counterintelligence chief James Jesus Angleton and to Gordon Bennett, UK Ministry of Defense, among others.

Recent History. Spy cases continued after the collapse of the Warsaw Pact and the Soviet Union between 1989 and 1991. CIA's most notorious case was CIA officer Aldridge Ames who betrayed numerous human assets, at least 10 of whom were executed.[15] Others – FBI Special Agent Earl Pitts (a Russian spy); CIA case officer Jim Nicholson (also a spy for the USSR); US Air Force NCO Jeffrey Carney (spy for East Germany); NSA employee Robert Lipka (spy for the USSR); Defense Intelligence Agency (DIA) employee Robert Kim (spy for South Korea); and Department of Defense employees Kurt Stand, Theresa Marie Squillacote, and James Clark (spies for East Germany) – were added to

15. Drawing from Ames' debriefings Sulick notes that Ames "was trapped in a vicious circle. The more he gave the KGB, the greater the risk that a Soviet asset could tell the CIA about a major leak. To protect himself, Ames decided that he would have to betray the Soviets who could endanger him." Sulick (2013), 192.

the list of many penetrations of the US Government.

In 2001, in the most damaging espionage case since Rick Ames in 1991 and the 1985 John Walker case, the FBI arrested one of its own: Supervisory Special Agent Robert Hanssen. An FBI counterintelligence expert, Hanssen revealed many US assets in Russia. Further, he revealed the complete national double agent program, names of personnel targeted for recruitment, a covert tunnel under the Soviet Embassy in Washington, DC, for SIGINT collection, the fact the US was reading Soviet communications satellite transmissions, many of NSA's limitations, and the US Government's continuity of government plans in the event of war, along with many other strategic and tactical secrets. "Thanks to Hanssen, the Russians owned the FBI's defensive playbook and knew in advance where the holes in the line were to run their offense."[16]

Cuba's Dirección General de Intelligencia (DGI, now known as the DI) — a KGB surrogate and aggressive intelligence service — had long-term highly placed agents in the national security community. Three of its spies in the US Government were uncovered by US CI. Ana Belen Montes, a senior DIA analyst and Cuban agent from 1984-2001, exposed the identities of US agents in Cuba, US technical collection programs, counternarcotics outposts in Central America, US IC assessments of Cuba, and US military contingency plans. Kendall and Gwendolyn Myers passed State Department secrets to Cuba from 1979 to 2006, and were arrested in 2009, three years after Kendall retired from State. In 1998, the FBI arrested five infiltrated Cuban intelligence agents (the "Wasp" network) in Florida who were targeted against Cuban-American groups and the US Southern Command. They were sentenced variously to 15 years to life for espionage, conspiracy to commit murder, and other charges.

"By the start of the 21st Century, Russian espionage threat was overshadowed by Chinese spying," with the majority of Chinese espionage cases involving theft of private sector technologies. However, a Chinese defector also revealed that most of the US's nuclear weapon secrets had been stolen by China. These included the W-78 warhead for the Minuteman ICBM, the W-76 for SLBMs, the W-87 for the MX Peacekeeper ICBM, the W-62 for the Minuteman III, the W-56 for the Minuteman II, the W-88 for the Trident D-5, and the W-70 neutron warhead.[17] Suspicion fell on two Chinese-Americans working in two nuclear weapons labs – Guo Bao Min at Lawrence Livermore National Laboratory (LLNL) and Wen Ho Lee at Los Alamos National Laboratory. The former was never prosecuted but fired. Lee was freed by a judge after an unsuccessful investigation, but also fired.

By the 21st century, economic espionage rose considerably. Sulick notes that "...revolutionary [technological] advances... changed spying against America. In the globalized economy, corporate information became as important

---

16. Sulick (2013), 214.
17. Wise, (2011), footnote 60, 254.

to a nation's security as military and political secrets."[18] In response, in 1996, the US enacted the Economic Espionage Act,[19] making the misappropriation of private sector proprietary information and trade secrets a federal crime.

Armed with this new law, US CI pursued the Chinese who targeted US private sector industries. The Mak family ring, when broken up in 2005, had been selling defense technologies to China for almost 30 years. When arrested, Dofung Chun, a Boeing engineer, had 250,000 pages of technical documents detailing the B-1 bomber, the Delta IV space launch vehicle, the C-17 cargo aircraft, the F-15 fighter, the Space Shuttle, and other systems ready to provide to China.

FIGURE 2. THIRTY SIGNIFICANT SPY CASES IMPACTING THE US SINCE 1960

William Martin & **Bernon Mitchell** National Security Agency	KGB 1960	Defected to USSR in June 1960. In public statements, divulged how NSA intercepted airborne communications and clandestine reconnaissance flights over foreign territory. Revealed US SIGINT efforts vs. Italy, France, UAE, Uruguay, and Indonesia. Debriefed extensively by the KGB about NSA codebreaking. Told Moscow US could not break its codes.
Nelson Drummond US Navy	GRU 1957-62	Handed over a great volume of classified information on naval combat systems, anti-submarine electronics, missile systems, and submarine support equipment. In 1963, sentenced to life.
Kim Philby UK Secret Intelligence Service	NKVD-MGB 1934-63	Passed UK and US CI information to USSR. Provided complete list of British agents worldwide to Moscow. Compromised Allies ULTRA secrets in WWII. Recruited other spies: Donald Maclean (UK Foreign Office), Guy Burgess (SIS & Foreign Office). With access to VENONA decrypts, he alerted Maclean to flee the UK.. Fled to USSR in 1963. Awarded the Order of Lenin and Red Banner of the KGB.
Robert Johnson US Army	MGB-KGB 1953-65	Compromised all materials (more than 1,600 documents) passing through classified distribution facility at Orly Airport, Paris, including codes, ciphers, operational plans, nuclear targets, intelligence reports, and SIGINT evidence of warning of attack. Convicted and sentenced to 25 years. His son murdered him in prison.
Andrew Dalton Lee & **Christopher Boyce** TRW (CIA contractor)	KGB 1975-77	Sold to the KGB information on the US's RHYOLITE SIGINT satellite, Defense Department top secret, and NSA cryptographic information, providing "the USSR with a unique window into America's ability to verify and monitor Soviet compliance with a treaty limiting the most lethal weapons aimed at the US heartland."[†] Boyce was sentenced to 40 years, with 27 more added after an escape. Lee received life; released in 1998. Boyce was released in 2002.
William Kampiles CIA	GRU 1978	Disgruntled CIA employee. Quit in 1977. Sold to the GRU the Top Secret manual for the US's newest spy satellite, the KH-11. Unfortunately sold the manual to a CIA asset in the GRU. Convicted and sentenced to 40 years; served 18 years.

† Sulick (2013), 66.

18. Sulick (2013), 184.
19. 18 USC § 1831.

Ronald Humphrey US Information Agency (USIA)	Vietnam 1976-78	Disclosed US negotiating positions to North Vietnam prior to peace talks in Paris. Sentenced to 15 years.
David Barnett CIA	KGB 1976-80	Identified CIA officers and sources in Indonesia. Also revealed a CIA operation (HABRINK) to exploit Soviet weaponry sold to Indonesia allowing the US to jam SA-2 missiles. Pled guilty, received 18 years, served 10.
William Holden Bell Hughes Aircraft Co.	Poland 1978-81	Revealed "quiet radar;" B-1 and B-2 electronics; F-15 look-down shoot-down radar; and Phoenix, Hawk, cruise, and anti-tank missiles information. Saved Soviet hundreds of millions of rubles in R&D. Sentenced to eight years. Bell's handler, Polish illegal Marian Zacharski, sentenced to life, was exchanged in a spy swap.
Larry Wu-Tai Chin CIA	MSP/MSS 1948-85	Gave Chinese names of POWs in Korea who provided information "who undoubtedly met untimely deaths once they were repatriated after the war."[†] For 30 years, leaked materials related to US intelligence and foreign policy toward China. Revealed Nixon's desire to open diplomatic relations two years before policy was implemented. Convicted in 1986. Committed suicide before sentencing.
Richard W. Miller FBI	KGB 1984	Provided classified FBI information to his "lover," KGB agent Svetlana Ogorodnikova, who passed it on to the KGB in San Francisco. Sentenced to 20 years in prison.
Karel (Karl) Koecher CIA	Czech Intel 1965-84	A Czechoslovakian illegal agent sent to the US. Hired as CIA translator, he provided Czech intelligence (and the KGB) identities of CIA officers and Russians being targeted for recruitment by the CIA. Provided information on Soviet diplomat recruited by the CIA, Alexander Dmitrievich Ogorodnik (Codename TRIGON), who committed suicide when arrested by the KGB. Traded for dissident Anatoly Shcharansky in 1986.
John Walker US Navy	KGB 1967-85	Provided codes and key lists allowing Soviets to read 80% of all naval communications. Provided USSR with "war winning" advantage. Revealed how US detected Soviet submarines by acoustics. Recruited three others including two family members. Sentenced to two life terms plus 10 years. Died in prison in 2014.
Ronald Pelton National Security Agency	KGB 1980-85	Recounted from memory how US decoded Soviet communications. Revealed IVY BELLS, highly secret undersea cable taps of Soviet communications. Sentenced to three life terms in 1986.
Jonathan Pollard US Naval Intelligence	LAKAM[††] 1984-85	Provided Israel more than 1 million pages of classified documents. Identified the location of PLO Headquarters in Tunisia, which the Israelis later bombed. Pled guilty and sentenced to life. Paroled in 2016.
Edward Lee Howard CIA	KGB 1984	Fired by CIA for drug use, minor theft, and lying in his training, defected to Moscow and betrayed Adolf Tolkachev, an extremely valuable CIA source, and GTTAW, a cable tap in Moscow providing valuable scientific intelligence.[†] Died of a broken neck in 2002.

† Sulick (2013), 160.
†† Israeli Office of Scientific Liaison (LAKAM) a specialized and little known spy unit established in 1957 with the mission to steal enough fissionable material from the US to enable Israel to build an atomic bomb while Israel built its own capability. Also stole plans for France's Mirage fighter.

Clayton Lonetree US Marine Corps	KGB 1985-86	As Marine security guard at the US Embassy in Moscow, involved in a love affair with a female KGB agent and recruited to provide the KGB with information about who were CIA officers and embassy security systems in Moscow and Vienna, Austria. Court-martialed. Served nine years of 30-year sentence due to cooperation.
Clyde Conrad US Army Europe	HMSIS 1974-88	Ran 11-member spy network for Hungary that betrayed NATO secrets, including war plans to defend Europe from the USSR, exact troop numbers, movements, and strategy in case of a Warsaw Pact attack. Germany arrested and sentenced him to life in prison. Died in prison in 1998.
Jeffrey M. Carney US Air Force	HVA 1982-91	Provided East Germany more than 100 classified documents on US SIGINT vs. Warsaw Pact and plans to dismantle Soviet communications in wartime. Damage was estimated at $14.5 billion. Defected to East Germany but arrested after reunification. Court martialed and sentenced to 38 years in prison; released after 11½ years for cooperating.
James Hall US Army Europe	KGB 1982-85 and HVA 1982-88	Betrayed US electronic surveillance capabilities vs. Warsaw Pact. Passed to both the Soviets and East Germans an overwhelming amount of material. Betrayed Project Trojan, a worldwide ability to pinpoint armored vehicles, missiles, and aircraft, negating a significant US military advantage. Sentenced to 40 years in military prison; released in 2011.
Aldridge Ames CIA	KGB-SVR 1985-94	Numerous assignments in the CIA including Chief of CIA's Soviet Division counterintelligence. Compromised every CIA and FBI source within Russia; at least 10 were executed. Pled guilty and sentenced to life in prison.
Edward Earl Pitts FBI	KGB-SVR 1987-96	Provided classified information about FBI CI investigation of KGB illegal operations in New York City and of FBI employees under reinvestigation while assigned to the FBI security office. Pled guilty and received 27-year sentence.
Robert Hanssen FBI	GRU 1979-81 KGB 1985-91 SVR 1999-2001	Compromised numerous FBI recruitments of Soviets; all aspects of FBI counterespionage technical and HUMINT activities; US worldwide double agent program; US Government's highly compartmented continuity of government plans; many aspects of highly compartmented HUMINT, SIGINT, imagery, & MASINT programs. Arrested 2001, sentenced to life.
Ana Montes Defense Intelligence Agency	DGI/DI 1984-2001	Compromised US agents in Cuba. Informed Cuba of Nicaraguan Contra efforts by US. Wrote, then compromised US national defense strategy relating to Cuba. Sentenced to 25 years in prison with no parole.
Katrina Leung FBI asset	MSS 1993-2002	Double agent working with the FBI in Los Angeles against the PRC. Provided to MSS classified FBI information. Pled guilty to tax evasion. Fined $100,000. Other charges dismissed

† See Milt Bearden & James Risen, *The Main Enemy: The Inside Story of the CIA's Final Showdown with the KGB* (New York: Random House, 2003).

Chi Mak Power Paragon (L3 Communications)	PRC 1970s-2005	PRC illegal send to the US. Stole technical documents, reports, schematics, and conference papers on naval technologies.[†] Five other co-conspirators involved. Found guilty of two counts of attempting to violate export control laws, failing to register as an agent of a foreign government, and making false statements to federal investigators. Sentenced to 24 years.
Dofung Chung Rockwell & Boeing	PRC 1979-2006	Provided technical information on many US military and space systems to PRC. Sentenced to 15 years and 8 months.
Kendall & Gwendolyn Myers Department of State	DGI/DI 1979-2009	Passed to Cuban intelligence US policy and some intelligence information related to Cuba. Kendall was sentenced to life in 2010; Gwendolyn to a minimum of six years.
Edward Snowden National Security Agency Contractor (previously, CIA)	Russia Unknown -2013	Leaked thousands of document related to NSA's surveillance capabilities worldwide, US military secrets, and secrets of "Five Eyes" nations to selected journalists. Defected to Russia in June 2013.

† "Chi Mak acknowledged that he had been placed in the United States more than 20 years earlier, in order to burrow into the defense-industrial establishment to steal secrets. It speaks of deep patience and is part of a pattern." Joel Brenner, *SpyPedia, http://www.spypedia/net*).

Examining Espionage. Analysis of the many espionage cases against the US provides some useful insights. From 1945 to October 2014, 748 individuals have been identified as involved in espionage-related activities. There has been a spike in the number of cases since 2002: 160 individuals associated with Soviet or Russian espionage, most involved in national security-related spying; individuals associated with China in the same period total 140, most involved in economic espionage against American (as well as other Western) companies. Iran is the nation most active in technology diversion with 126 individuals identified. These compare with only 49 domestic economic espionage cases – i.e., US company xyz illegally spying on its competitors.

Since WWII, a foreign intelligence service recruited less than half of the American spies . Forty-three percent were recruited by family members, friends, or co-workers.[20] Only 9.8% of compromises of classified information were by contractors; the majority (90.2%) were by government employees. Background investigations have never caught a spy, but serve as a deterrent.[21]

From a counterintelligence perspective, leaks of classified information to the press are akin to a spy stealing information. The only difference is that in a leak case, the US Government knows the information has been compromised and can take corrective actions, while in an espionage case, the government does not know information has been compromised until the spy is caught and prosecuted and submits to damage assessment interviews. And even then, not all compromised secrets are discovered.

---

20. This analysis of spy cases is based on the comprehensive case files in *SpyPedia*, a database maintained by the CI Centre and available under subscription.

21. For a discussion of the role of polygraphs in counterintelligence in the CIA see John F. Sullivan, "CIA and the Polygraph," *Guide to the Study of Intelligence*, Association of Former Intelligence Officers, http://www.afio.com/40_guide.htm.

Michael Sulick identifies the motivations of spies over the years. These motivations include "money, ego, revenge, romance, simple thrills, ideological sympathy, and dual loyalties." In the 1930's and 1940's, ideology played the major role. In later years, financial needs were more prevalent and too often downplayed after capture. In the vast majority of the cases, more than one motivation was in play.[22] A study of motivation revealed it is a complex problem with no simple answers. As Dr. David Charney states, the motivation to spy often relates to "a profound fear of failure as personally defined by that individual." History does confirm that individuals who decide to spy are usually going through a life crisis and are unhappy people when they make that irreversible decision.[23]

The Future. Russian spying against America today is at a level comparable to the height of the Cold War. Little, however, is conducted out of Russian embassies. As in the 1930's, the Russians appear to be relying on illegals, identified in the US, Canada, Portugal, Germany, and Estonia. In 2010, a SVR network of long-term illegals was broken up with the FBI arrest of 10 of its 12 members.[24] Illegals provide an advantage of being harder to uncover than embassy-based intelligence officers and their contacts; in cells more difficult to penetrate; and provide political distance for the sponsoring country.[25] Use of undercover paramilitary officers (Spetznaz) has been demonstrated in Russia's seizure of the Crimea and support of separatist rebels in eastern Ukraine. Several GRU officers have been identified as involved in these Russian provocations as were others in Russia's actions against its neighbors Georgia and Estonia, which continue today.

In recent years, Chinese spying has become very aggressive and economic-related. In 2012, five individuals, two of whom were former employees, were charged with economic espionage, theft of trade secrets, and other federal crimes for stealing DuPont's formula for titanium dioxide, an essential ingredient for paints and coatings, and providing it to a Chinese company seeking to compete in the $12-billion worldwide market.[26] Since 2003, 123 Chinese agents have been identified, which indicates that US CI is getting better at recognizing China's espionage methods,[27] which employ a long-term view of espionage. China collects 80% of its intelligence through open sources. Over 4,000 enti-

---

22. Sulick (2013), 7. See also David L. Charney, MD, and John A. Irvin, "A Guide to the Psychology of Espionage," *Guide to the Study of Intelligence*, Association of Former Intelligence Officers, *http://www.afio.com/40_guide.htm.*

23. See Charney and Irvin, "A Guide to the Psychology of Espionage.."

24. "FBI Breaks up alleged Russian spy ring in deep cover," *The Guardian*, 28 June 2010.

25. In the late 1980's Russian President Vladimir Putin was a KGB officer in Dresden (then East Germany) supporting the KGB Directorate S, responsible for identifying, training, and operating illegals in other countries.

26. "DuPont Hit by Chinese TiO2 Spy Ring," Paint and Coatings Industry News, February 16, 2012. *http://www.paintsquare.com/news/?fuseaction=view&id=7193.*

27. Former FBI China counterintelligence analyst Paul Moore described this historic Chinese approach to espionage as "a thousand grains of sand" (Wise, *Tiger Trap*, 9-10).

ties in China collect intelligence. "Chinese intelligence [has] flooded America with students, scientists, businesspeople, and émigrés from all walks of life to harvest America's political, military, economic, and scientific secrets."[28] They recruit young people who are encouraged to seek jobs, which will grow into positions lucrative for espionage. Universities are prime targets for these "seedling" recruitments. [29] In 2004, for example, there were 100,000 Chinese students in the US for higher education and 27,000 official delegations visiting US facilities. Chinese intelligence exploits the overseas Chinese population. "In Chinese culture, when people receive favors, they are expected to reciprocate, a deeply rooted tradition known as guanxi."[30] This method has been used to entrap ethnic Chinese into espionage, often under the motivation of helping the homeland.

The information age has made it easier to spy and to filch vast quantities of sensitive data. The threat comes from several directions: remotely through internet probing and phishing;[31] the insider who downloads sensitive data or installs malware that automatically exfiltrates data; and increasingly from embedded malware installed in the manufacturing process.

China, Russia, and Iran are aggressive cyber attackers. CI experts are learning how to exploit the digital trail left by today's digital exploitation spies.[32]

Based on an analysis of public records related to individuals indicted for espionage and related activities, 35% of all corporate economic espionage cases involving the theft of information technology is by company insiders, most of whom are foreign nationals (or have dual loyalties). Inside access is often coupled with external cyber attacks. Companies' failure to monitor access to sensitive information has allowed insiders to surreptitiously work for competitors or their home country. Refusal to recognize the danger has caused corporations to delay securing their networks or instituting counter-measures. China has gained access to vast amounts of proprietary information using these methods.[33]

Analysis of Justice Department information indicates that espionage is risky — spies get caught, although often not for many years. Long-running spies against America were Englishman Kim Philby (1934-1961), Larry Wu Tai Chin (1947-1985), Aldridge Ames (1985-1994), and Robert Hanssen (1979-

---

28. Sulick (2013), 270

29. Sulick, (2013), 264-265.

30. Wise, *Tiger Trap*, 56

31. Phishing is the attempt to steal sensitive information by masquerading as a trusted correspondent in an e-mail. (Zulfikar Ramzan, "Phishing Attacks and Countermeasures," in Mark Stamp and Peter Stavroulakis (eds.), *Handbook of Information and Communication Security* (New York: Springer, 2010).

32. For an explanation of the evolution of cyber intelligence and espionage, see Douglas R. Price, "A Guide to Cyber Intelligence," *Guide to the Study of Intelligence*, Association of Former Intelligence Officers, at *http://www.afio.com/40_guide.htm*.

33. Written testimony of David Major to the House Committee on Science, Space, and Technology, Subcommittee on Oversight, May 16, 2013. *http://fas.org/irp/congress/2013_hr/fedlab.pdf*.

2001). Thirty-two percent of spies are either intercepted before they can steal information or within a year of beginning. Another 25% are caught within five years, and an additional 20% within 10. American justice tends to treat spies harshly when compared to Western European countries (but not totalitarian nations). While only the Rosenbergs were executed, of the 217 apprehended spies who have compromised classified national defense information and been prosecuted, 25 received life sentences; 17 received 30-to-40 years; and 58 received 12 or more years.

Espionage is as old as human society and will be with us forever. Economic espionage will continue for the same reasons it has been around for so long: it is profitable. Why invent or invest when you can steal? Attempts to divert restricted technology to get around economic and trade sanctions will continue since the benefits outweigh the risks. The reality of espionage is that constant vigilance is essential. The US cannot afford to allow its CI capability to languish. History has taught us that in the "spy catching business" the old adage of "pay me now or pay me later" is very true because nations pay a high price when espionage is successful.

READINGS FOR INSTRUCTORS

Besides many of the citations in the footnotes the following are recommended as illuminating treatises on espionage.

Andrew, Christopher and Vasili Mitrokhin. *The Sword and the Shield: The Mitrokhin Archive and the Secret History of the KGB* (New York: Basic Books, 1999). (Soviet/ Russian intelligence).

Andrew, Christopher and Vasili Mitrokhin. *The World was Going Our Way: The KGB and the Battle for the Third World* (New York: Basic Books, 2005). (Soviet/ Russian intelligence).

Batvinis, Raymond. *The Origins of FBI Counterintelligence* (Lawrence, KS: University of Kansas Press, 2007).

Batvinis, Raymond. *Hoover's Secret War against Axis Spies: FBI Counterespionage during World War II* (Lawrence, KS: University of Kansas Press, 2014).

Bearden, Milt and James Risen. *The Main Enemy: The Inside Story of the CIA's Final Showdown with the KGB* (New York: Random House, 2003). (CIA operations).

Cave Brown, Anthony and Charles B. MacDonald. *On A Field of Red: The Communist International & the Coming of World War II* (New York: G. P. Putnam's Sons, 1981).

Cherkashin, Victor and Gregory Feifer. *Spy Handler, Memoir of a KGB Officer: The True Story of the Man Who Recruited Robert Hanssen & Aldrich Ames* (New York: Basic Books, 2005). (Soviet/Russian intelligence).

Dies, Martin. *The Trojan Horse in America* (New York: Dodd, Mead & Co., 1940).

Earley, Peter. *Confessions of a Spy: The Real Story of Aldrich Ames* (New York: G. P. Putnam's Sons, 1997). (Ames)

Klehr, Harvey, John Earl Haynes, and Fririkh Igorevich Firsov. *The Secret World of American Communism* (New Haven: Yale University Press, 1995).

Macintyre, Ben. *Double Cross: The True Story of the D-Day Spies* (New York: Crown Publishers, 2012).

Mangold, Tom. *Cold Warrior? James Jesus Angleton: The CIA's Master Spy Hunter* (New York: Simon and Schuster, 1991).

Powers, Richard Gid. *Not Without Honor: The History of American Anticommunism* (New York: The Free Press, 1995).

Riebling, Mark. *Wedge: The Secret War Between the FBI and CIA* (New York: Alfred A. Knopf, 1994). (CIA).

Sulick, Michael. *Spying in America: Espionage from the Revolutionary War to the Dawn of the Cold War* (Washington, DC: Georgetown University Press, 2012).

Sulick, Michael. *American Spies: Espionage Against the United States from the Cold War to the Present* (Washington, DC: Georgetown University Press, 2013).

Tanenhaus, Sam. *Whittaker Chambers: A Biography* (New York: Random House, Inc., 1997).

Wise, David. *Tiger Trap: America's Secret Spy War with China* (Boston: Houghton Mifflin Harcourt, 2011).

David Major, a graduate of Syracuse University, served for five years in the US Army before being appointed as an FBI Special Agent. During his 24-year FBI career, he served in numerous field offices as well as FBI Headquarters in the Sensitive Compartmented Information Security Office, the Counterintelligence Division, and the Inspection Division. He was the first FBI special agent detailed to the White House National Security Council under the Reagan administration. He worked foreign counterintelligence his entire career. Mr. Major has made a life-long commitment to the study of counterintelligence and counterterrorism, making him one of the nation's top experts on the subject. Upon retiring from the FBI, he founded the Centre for Counterintelligence and Security Studies, known as the CI Centre, which has provided counterintelligence, counterterrorism, and security training for over 100,000 people in both government and the corporate sector. He is a member of the AFIO board, a national board member for the Espionage Research Institute International (ERII), and a member of the Society of Former Special Agents of the FBI (SOCXFBI).

Peter Oleson is an associate professor in the graduate school of the University of Maryland University College. Formerly he was an assistant director of the Defense Intelligence Agency and senior intelligence policy advisor to the undersecretary of defense for policy. He was president of a consulting firm specializing in technology and program management for intelligence systems. He was a member of the AFIO board.

GUIDE TO THE STUDY OF INTELLIGENCE

Industrial Espionage

Edward M. Roche, PhD, JD

*No information I received was the result of spying.
Everything was given to me in casual conversations
without coercion.*

— Richard Sorge, interrogation at Sugamo
Prison.[1]

*Some persons argue that there is little harm from
industrial espionage because "technology inevitably
leaks out anyway."*

— Count Alexandre de Marenches[2]

Industrial espionage comes in many forms as illustrated from the following case studies:

- The head of an adhesives company's research and development (R&D), a naturalized US citizen, became involved with the daughter of a Taiwanese industrialist, and eventually started to supply the Taiwanese company with all the R&D technical information from his American company, resulting in competing imports at a much lower cost.

- An American with close ties to a Middle East country provided to them information on government contracts and technical information, which allowed companies there to develop new products ahead of the US companies from which the original technical information was stolen.

- A secretary in a major soft drink manufacturer in Atlanta, Georgia, got involved with an ex-con and was induced to steal product samples and technical details for the next new soft drink product, and an attempt was made to sell this information to a competitor.

---

1. Soviet spy in Tokyo before World War II, who warned Stalin of Operation Barbarosa, Hitler's intent to invade the USSR.
2. Former director of France's external intelligence service.

- A trained foreign agent, who had been in the United States for more than 20 years and had become a citizen, suddenly was "activated" by his controllers in Asia and given a "shopping list" of technical information to obtain, and then proceeded to steal massive amounts of technical information from his company on the next generation of nuclear submarines being constructed for the US Navy.

- An employee working for a large US manufacturing company decided to strike out and form his own company, but first stole all of the necessary technical information to manufacture competing high-technology products.

- A country that is an enemy (or "strategic competitor") to the United States sent a number of "illegals" into various companies to systematically report on all technical developments and strategies of the targeted US companies.

- A major hotel chain vice president decided that he was not being paid enough and took all of the records regarding the development of a new hotel concept to a competitor, where he got better pay and a substantial promotion.

These are many variations on the same theme: the theft of secret or proprietary information, usually for commercial purposes. The word "industrial" in "industrial espionage" has a specific reference to manufacturing companies, but in actuality, services industries (banking, hotels, R&D) are lucrative targets as well. Thus, the term "industrial" is an artifact.

Some industrial espionage is done by individuals out of greed, but other industrial espionage is done by organizations or even by governments. In most cases, there is a large financial component to industrial espionage, since at heart it is an operation involving business secrets and commercial gain. But there also are instances where industrial espionage is driven by the strategic competition (economic and military) between nation states.

There is an important distinction between classical and industrial espionage. Industrial espionage is a sub-set of espionage, but also has *sui generis* aspects; the term "espionage" refers to the taking of *government* secrets. Classical espionage would include stealing the US' negotiating position at the next Doha Trade round, or any information regarding troop movements, or the design of a stealth aircraft, or a sample of the surface paint or metallurgy of a stealth aircraft.

In the United States, the 1996 Economic Espionage Act divides industrial espionage into two classes: (1) industrial espionage committed against a corporation by anyone other than a foreign entity, and (2) industrial espionage committed by a foreign entity. The penalties are more severe for industrial espionage carried out by foreign entities. Unfortunately, there have been relatively few successful prosecutions under the 1996 Act.

Industrial espionage has a long history because, in a broader sense, it is part of the story of international technology diffusion.

American Industrial Espionage

In 1782, a young man named Samuel Slater was working in an English cotton mill. He memorized as much as he could about textile machinery, and then took his knowledge to the United States. At the time, England had strict laws against exporting such information.

Francis Cabot Lowell travelled to England in 1810, and learned enough so that, upon returning to the United States, he was able to set up a power loom that could turn raw cotton into finished cloth.[3]

TABLE 1. CHARACTERISTICS OF CLASSICAL ESPIONAGE AND INDUSTRIAL ESPIONAGE[1]

	Classical Espionage	Industrial Espionage	
	Government Information	Private Sector Information	
		Defense and Intelligence Contractors	Non-Government Business
Tangible	Equipment	Sample; Designs	Technology; Operations Manuals
Intangible (Intentions; plans)	Negotiating Position (Trade talks; arms control)	Plans; Software	Business Strategy (Pricing; negotiations; alliances; new products, R&D, etc.)

1. Note that espionage against "Defense and Intelligence Contractors," can be classified as either industrial espionage or as a type of classical espionage. Historically, classical espionage targeted only governments, and corporate contractors to the government were not included since contractors are private enterprises. Any theft of their technology or trade secrets is certainly a type of industrial espionage. In reality, espionage against defense and intelligence contractors can be called either classical espionage or industrial espionage.

The Soviet Union's Industrial Espionage

During the Stalin era (1922–1953), primarily prior to the World War II, the USSR operated a system of international industrial espionage targeting primarily Western Europe, but also the United States and Japan. Known as rabochy korrespondenti (рабочие корреспонденты, "people's correspondents"), these workers filed technical reports to Moscow. The program was expanded to include communist sympathizers working in factories throughout the West. "Engineers and experts of Russian war industries back home were asking a host of technical questions. The lists of questions from Russia were turned over by military intelligence headquarters to the military attachés, who had them translated at the embassies." These were then rewritten and distributed

3. For the astounding growth of United States manufacturing during this period, see Engerman & Sokoloff, "Technology and Industrialization, 1790 – 1914" in *The Cambridge Economic History of the United States*, Vols. 1 & 2 (Cambridge: Cambridge University Press, 1996, 2000).

to agents.[4] Unlike many types of espionage, these "correspondents" worked on a voluntary basis for ideological reasons. As the West opened up more to the Soviet Union, it became easier to conduct industrial espionage through organizations such as trade delegations. This type of state-supported system of international industrial espionage persisted until the fall of the Soviet Union. Industrial espionage for science and technology was operated under the KGB First Chief Directorate Directorate T.

> "Since 1970, Line X had obtained thousands of documents and sample products, in such quantity that it appeared that the Soviet military and civil sectors were in large measure running their research on that of the West, particularly the United States. Our science was supporting their national defense. Losses were in radar, computers, machine tools, and semiconductors. Line X had fulfilled two-thirds to three-fourths of its collection requirements – an impressive performance."[5]

Individuals become involved in industrial espionage for a variety of reasons:

Resentment: General Motors employee Shanshan Du became dissatisfied with his employer and decided to start his own business using GM trade secrets. He teamed with Yu Qin to create a company to manufacture advanced batteries for hybrid cars using GM proprietary information.[6]

Greed: In France, to make extra money on the side, three executives were investigated for selling the economic model of the Renault car to foreign interests rumored to be from China.[7]

Seduction and blackmail: Karl Heinrich Stohlze, working for the West German BND, seduced a senior secretary in a Boston defense company and sought to blackmail her into providing information on gene-splicing technology.[8]

Foreign spy: Chi Mak (real name: Dazhi Mai) had planned to enter into a position of trust specifically for the purpose of stealing confidential information. He was a long-term illegal from China who stole information on the quiet electric drive propulsion system for the next generation of US Navy Virginia Class nuclear submarines. It was more than 20 years before he was activated to begin stealing secrets.[9]

---

4. The work of the "people's correspondents" is detailed in David Dallin's book *Soviet Espionage* (New Haven: Yale University Press, 1955), 50-51.

5. Gus W. Weiss, "The Farewell Dossier," *Studies in Intelligence*, Washington, DC: Central Intelligence Agency, 39 (5), 1996.

6. U.S. v. YU QIN AND SHANSHAN DU, Opinion, United States Court of Appeals for Sixth Circuit, July 20, 2012.

7. Espionnage chez Renault – La piste chinoise privilégiée, *Le point.fr*, January 7, 2011.

8. Markus Wolf & Anne McElvoy. *Man Without a Face* (New York City: Times Books, 1997), 149.

9. U.S. v. CHI MAK ET AL., Second Superseding indictment, U.S. Dist. Court for Central Dist. of Calif.,

Divided loyalty: A variation on the above theme is someone who responds to an appeal to assist his native country. This is a common pitch to ethnic Chinese living in other countries. Dongfan Chung began to hand over massive amounts of space shuttle design and other aircraft secrets from Boeing to China out of a sense of duty to the homeland that had been carefully cultivated by his handlers.[10]

Fear: The German technology company Bosch inserted a paid mole into its increasingly successful market competitor, the British firm Dyson, to steal its new technology secrets. The spy never identified himself as being affiliated with Bosch.[11]

More than 80 percent of industrial espionage involves individuals operating *within* the target organization – an insider.

In some companies, industrial espionage, which is illegal, has been closely related to accepted business functions such as "competitive intelligence," "market research," or "planning." Industrial espionage has been used in instances where the amount of information available through public sources ("open sources") is insufficient, and the situation was seen as crucial. For example, when General Motors learned that a competitor had purchased property to construct a very large factory, but did not know for what purpose, it set up a "spy center" to determine what its competitor was doing.[12] The urgent need for information can arise from a number of business scenarios. In a takeover, one company may wish to know the salaries of top executives so it can better negotiate the deal. Any time an innovative and disruptive technology is introduced, competitors scramble to learn as much as possible. Companies regularly collect all the information they can regarding the new product pipeline of their competitors.

Most companies caught conducting industrial espionage had outsourced these activities to "consultants" or similar companies for a variety of reasons. For example, the company may not have had the internal capabilities to perform the service that is required. It is less expensive to outsource than to invest in developing one's own talent in-house. Management of companies often do not understand what needs to be done so that, even if it had internal resources, they would not be effective; therefore, management needs outside advice. In some cases the company wished to isolate itself from the actual industrial espionage because if caught it would face a scandal or worse.

Grand Jury, October 2005.

10. U.S. v. DONGFAN "GREG" CHUNG, Indictment, U.S. Dist. Court for Central Dist. of Calif., Grand Jury, October 2007.

11. Sean Poulter, Bosch "sent mole into British rival Dyson to steal details of its revolutionary digital motors," *MailOnline*, October 24, 2012.

12. John J. McGonagle & Carolyn M. Vella. *A New Archetype for Competitive Intelligence* (Westport: Quorum Books, 1996), 88-90.

A variety of companies have been associated with industrial espionage, including international law firms; consulting firms; persons retired from a career in government intelligence and now "free-lancing" their skills in the private market; and service firms, which act as intermediaries between a "legitimate" service provider (consultants or law firms) and sub-contractors, which have fewer scruples. Much of the utility in using sub-contractors is to reduce the legal vulnerability of the company, which usually works. For example, KPMG Financial Advisory Services Ltd. in Bermuda was penetrated via a false-flag recruitment of one of its accountants, Guy Enright. Enright thought he was working for British intelligence, but actually was being used by an agent of a US law firm that the Alpha Group, a Russian conglomerate, had retained. Alpha Group set up a differently named subsidiary, which hired the US firm Barbour Griffith & Rogers. In turn, Barbour hired the Diligence Corporation, which sub-contracted the operation to a retired British spy, going by the name of Nick Hamilton, who went to Bermuda and recruited the KPMG employee. These layers of hiring were designed to create an impenetrable barrier to hide Alpha's identity.[13]

The countries responsible for most industrial espionage against the United States have shifted over the years. The current "winner" (as of mid-2014) is the People's Republic of China (PRC). Other countries frequently mentioned include Israel, France, and Russia. Since it is difficult to account for most industrial espionage, knowing who is most responsible is problematical. Both allies and "enemies" (or to use a more polite term, "strategic competitors") appear equally responsible for industrial espionage. Intelligence on industrial espionage by US allies, such as Israel and France, to the extent it is known to the government, remains highly classified for fear of political backlash if discussed in public.

Industrial espionage reduces R&D costs for the entity that is able to exploit the stolen information. By stealing information, the recipient does not have to spend the resources or the time on R&D. In many cases, it would not be possible to discover how an innovation operates without industrial espionage. For example, the PRC stole all the relevant design information for various thermonuclear weapons from Los Alamos National Laboratory. These weapons were developed at substantial US cost. A Japanese mainframe computer company stole the design information and a sample for an IBM mainframe central processing unit (CPU) cluster, thus both saving time in R&D, but also learning crucial secrets about how the module operated.[14]

Another advantage of stealing information is that the recipient is

---

13. Eamon Javers, "Spies, Lies & KPMG," Bloomberg *Businessweek Magazine*, February 25, 2007. More details of the dispute are found in IPOC INTERNATIONAL GROWTH FUND, LTD. v. LEONID ROZHETSKIN, ET AL., Am. Compl., 06 Civ. 4338 (JVM) (S.D.N.Y. Feb. 7, 2007).
14. See Congressional Record, "The Japanese Conspiracy," House of Representatives, July 12, 1989, H3666.

able to produce the product much faster. It is estimated that the PRC created world-class supercomputers in approximately one-fifth of the time it should have taken if all of the R&D had been "home grown."[15] Similar stories apply across almost the entire Chinese defense sector. In a domestic case, when Hilton Hotels received the entire blueprint for Starwood's new line of boutique hotels, it saved years of work, and millions of dollars of consulting and market research costs to compete with its own. This case eventually was settled out of court with Hilton making a $75 million cash payment to Starwood.[16]

The broader effect of industrial espionage is to change the strategic balance of nations[17] and the *causal pattern is easy to recognize*: the theft of industrial secrets leads to the competitive weakening of companies. In turn, this leads to the competitive weakening of sectors and the reduction in economic value for the economy as a whole. This can reduce the resources available to exercise national power, such as military capabilities. The end result is a shift in power away from the weakened nation state.

The US' post-World War II dominance was so advantageous that the possibility of it slipping away has been inconceivable to many. Yet the US' continued technological dominance is a dangerous illusion. A shift in the "technology balance of power" can occur rapidly. Industrial espionage has substantially weakened the United States to the point that the US' *relative* economic dominance has declined drastically. While much of this decline in economic power has been due to the export from the United States of technologies that were a source of competitive advantage, industrial espionage accounts for an important part of the US' *relative* technology decline.

READINGS FOR INSTRUCTORS

Amaral, John. "Maximizing compliance and content protection," *Information Systems Security*, 2007. http://www.infosectoday.com/Articles/Content_Protection.htm

Dallin, David J. *Soviet Espionage* (New Haven: Yale University Press, 1955).

Engerman, Stanley L. and Robert E. Gallman (eds.), *The Cambridge Economic History of the United States*, Volume II, chapter on "Technology and Industrialization, 1790–1914," (Cambridge: Cambridge University Press, 2000), 367-402.

Fenwick & West LLP, *Trade secrets protection: A primer and desk reference for managers and in house counsel*, miscellaneous paper, (San Francisco, Fenwick & West LLP, 2001).

15. Commission on the Theft of American Intellectual Property, *The IP Commission Report*, (Seattle: National Bureau of Asian Research, 2013)
16. See STARWOOD V. HILTON, 09-03862, U.S. District Court, Southern District of New York (White Plains).
17. For a discussion of the components of national power see Ashley J. Tellis, Janice Bially, Christopher Layne, and Melissa McPherson. *Measuring National Power in the Postindustrial Age*. Number MR – 1110-A in Monograph Reports. RAND Corporation, Santa Monica, California, 2000.

Roche, Edward M. *Corporate Spy: Industrial Espionage and Counterintelligence in the Multinational Enterprise* (New York: Barraclough Ltd., 2009).

Roche, Edward M. *Snake Fish: The Chi Mak Spy Ring* (New York: Barraclough Ltd., 2009).

Tellis, Ashley J., Janice Bially, Christopher Layne, and Melissa McPherson. *Measuring National Power in the Postindustrial Age,* Number MR – 1110-A in Monograph Reports, (Santa Monica, CA: RAND Corporation, 2000).

Weiss, Gus W. "The Farewell Dossier," *Studies in Intelligence* 39 (5), 1996.

Edward M. Roche was educated at The Johns Hopkins School of Advanced International Studies in Washington, DC, Concord Law School, and Columbia University in New York City. In his overseas work, he has organized and run research projects on national technology policies for microelectronics, information technology, and telecommunications in Brazil, Japan, Korea, Russia, China, and Europe. He is the author of *Corporate Spy: Industrial Espionage and Counterintelligence in the Multinational Enterprise*, and *Snake Fish: The Chi Mak Spy Ring*. He teaches business intelligence, international law, and technology intelligence at the Grenoble École de Management, Grenoble, France.

GUIDE TO THE STUDY OF INTELLIGENCE

Counterintelligence, Homeland Security, and Domestic Intelligence

Gene Poteat

"Counterintelligence means information gathered and activities conducted to protect against espionage, other intelligence activities, sabotage, or assassinations conducted for or on behalf of foreign powers, organizations or persons, or international terrorist activities, but not including personnel, physical, document or communications security programs."

—EO-12333, 4 December 1981

Introduction[1]

T he stuff of great spy novels is not about the spy, it's about finding and catching the spy, which is counterintelligence, or more specifically, counterespionage. Interestingly, James Fennimore Cooper wrote The Spy: A Tale of the Neutral Ground (1821), the very first "great American novel," shortly after the Revolutionary War. His novel was based on the true exploits, trials, and tribulations of Enoch Crosby, one of George Washington's wartime counterespionage agents. The complexity of the plots in spy vs. spy thrillers tells us just how difficult, tricky, and controversial counterintelligence actually is. Sometimes it takes the smallest, seemingly insignificant detail—and even the right nose, hard work, or just plain dumb luck—to find and catch the spy.

---

1. It is impossible to adequately treat the history and importance of counterintelligence in such a brief article. A short bibliography is therefore included. For those more interested in the subject, a comprehensive graduate-level course in counterintelligence is taught at the Institute of World Politics (*http://www.iwp.edu*) in Washington, DC.

Counterintelligence doesn't end with uncovering and finally catching the foreign spy—or the American traitor. It ends only when there is enough hard evidence to arrest, successfully prosecute, and convict the spy—or to turn him (or her) into a double agent working against his foreign handlers. Counterintelligence in the US is, therefore, a law enforcement function and falls under the FBI's purview, which is empowered to arrest and prosecute American citizens. All too often, however, as with other serious crimes, prosecution can prove even more difficult than finding the spy, and any number have gone free.

The FBI is not the only player in the spy vs. spy game. The military has a strong role as well. EO-12333 states also that the secretary of defense shall "Conduct counterintelligence activities in support of Department of Defense components outside the United States in coordination with the CIA, and within the United States in coordination with the FBI pursuant to procedures agreed upon by the Secretary of Defense and the Attorney General."

In the broader sense, then, counterintelligence can readily be seen as just as difficult, and at times more frustrating and consequential, than conventional intelligence and espionage. Further, failing to catch the spy can be disastrous, even have war-winning consequences, under the right circumstances, as when Mikhail Gorbachev told President Ronald Reagan that had the US and the Soviet Union gone to war in 1980, the Soviets could easily have won. Gorbachev was basing his assessment on the advantage the Soviets had gained over the US—by knowing where all our ballistic missile submarines were at all times—from the US Naval codes provided by the traitor John Walker, a former Navy chief, over a period of 20 years. The Walkers, Aldrich Ames, and Robert Hansen were not only spies, they were traitors. A spy is a patriot who works for his own people and nation against a foreign adversary, whereas a traitor works against his own people and nation for a foreign power.

Counterintelligence in War

Historically, Americans have always had a problem with the "dirty business" of intelligence and counterintelligence. We forget, however, that George Washington was credited, by none other than Major George Beckwith, chief of British intelligence at the end of the Revolutionary War, with having won the war by simply having outspied, rather than outfought, the British. It was Washington's intelligence that told him when to fight, and when to avoid a fight, and it was his counterintelligence that kept British spying in check and helped him interdict Benedict Arnold's treachery by capturing the chief British spymaster, John André. The British made a serious counterintelligence mistake that could well have altered the outcome of the war—they never even considered turning Nathan Hale into a double agent rather than hanging him, which should always be a first consideration. By the time of the War of 1812, both intelligence and counterintelligence had been forgotten. The Civil War saw neither side with good military intelligence, which probably accounted for the heavy casualties on both sides. Alan Pinkerton, Lincoln's early chief of intelligence and a former railroad detective, did have a good sense of counterintelligence, however, and succeeded in jailing the first effective Confederate spy, Rose O'Neal Greenhow, and then went on to keep the city of Washington virtually free of Confederate spies.

A single intelligence operation is credited with the lop-sided win in the Spanish-American War when the Office of Naval Intelligence (ONI) tapped the undersea cables running into and out of Havana, enabling them to read the Spanish war planners' mail in real time. There was little need for counterintelligence during this war except during the brief period when Lieutenant Colonel Teddy Roosevelt's crack "rough riders" deployed to Tampa, Florida, heavily populated with Spanish immigrants working in the cigar factories. To keep his plans for the Cuban invasion secret, Major General William Shafter, commandant of the Cuban invasion forces, pulled off an unusual operation. Shafter employed Mabel Bean, the 16-year-old daughter of the local postmaster, to keep an eye out for any strangers circulating in the Cuban community. Mabel knew virtually everyone in Ybor City, the cigar manufacturing suburb of Tampa, spoke fluent Spanish, was well known and recognized as she bicycled and chatted with the locals. She had no trouble in keeping up with everyone and everything going on in the Cuban community and reporting back to Shafter. Mabel's successful counterespionage forays led Shafter to invite her to the many parties he arranged for his officers waiting to invade Cuba, where she was the belle of the ball.

World War I found America intelligence and counterintelligence capabilities again completely withered away; still with no laws on the books regarding espionage; and, when pressed by the US military to get back into the intelligence business, President Woodrow Wilson suggested that, if needed, the US could get its intelligence from our allies, the British and French. Meanwhile, British and German intelligence and counterintelligence activities against each other inside the US were rampant. The British were trying to get America into the war—on their side of course—and at the same time working against German intelligence efforts to keep us out of the war. The Germans focused on recruiting ethnic German-Americans to support their sabotage program.

The British very effectively used the Bohemian National Alliance, which included over 320,000 Czech and Slovak émigrés living throughout the US, and organized under the leadership of Emanuel "Victor" Voska, all of whom spoke flawless German and hated Germany, in highly successful counterintelligence and propaganda operations against the German spies in the US. Voska had placed his agents inside virtually every German diplomatic establishment, including the German Embassy, their covert sabotage organization, and their wireless station handling German diplomatic traffic. Voska even had one of his counterintelligence men on board a German ship that contained a bomb-making factory, interned in New York harbor. On their part, the Germans unsuccessfully tried to use Indian Sikh organizations, operating out of Berkeley, California, (where else?) and seeking independence from the detested Britain, in several covert political and paramilitary operations against the British. During this time, Wilson was concerned only with the plight of poor suffering Mexican peons during a series of Mexican revolutions and had sent the US Army off to chase after the elusive Pancho Villa.

One of the greatest British intelligence operations of the war was their placing their agent, Sir William Wiseman, into the heart of the Wilson White House. Sir William would become an incredibly effective agent of influence in the White House for the British intelligence that bypassed all normal diplomatic channels.

In 1916, the Germans finally made the fatal mistake of using ethnic Irish Americans—who intensely disliked the British—to sabotage a large depot stocked with American munitions, destined for England, at the Black Tom port in New Jersey just opposite the Statue of Liberty. The massive explosion killed three men and a child and blew out every window in Jersey City, with damages estimated at $14 million, and finally forced Wilson to go into the counterintelligence business, if not into intelligence. Britain's intelligence and counterintelligence in the US, along with the sinking of the Lusitania and Zimmerman's Telegram, finally dragged America into the war.

Once in the war, America quickly passed the Selective Service and Espionage Act of 1917. The Act defined espionage as the *unauthorized transmittal of national defense information to a foreign power or agent with intent to harm the U.S. or to aid a foreign power*. The problem for counterintelligence, however, was that there had to be two eyewitnesses and it was up to a jury to decide if there was any real intent to harm—and all 12 jurors had to agree that all four elements of the act were valid to convict and then expel an "alien." Little wonder there were no convictions or expulsions. The law prescribed penalties for: resisting the draft; insubordination in the armed forces; opposing the production of munitions; speaking, printing, or otherwise expressing contempt for the military; using language calculated to aid the enemy; using language favoring the enemy; and hampering the sale of war bonds. The Act also gave the government broad censorship powers over the press and the right to open mail. Wilson also used the earlier Alien and Sedition Acts to require all aliens, mostly recent immigrants, to register with the government. The American radical Left, which included anarchists, socialists, communists, and the International Workers of the World (IWW), called for "unyielding opposition" to the draft and identified itself with the Bolsheviks, who had removed Russia from the war.

It fell on the Justice Department's new Bureau of Investigation to not only enforce these laws; keep up with the aliens, the radical left, and German intelligence; but to protect the nation's war industry with security measures. In other words, American law enforcement began to back (perhaps stumble is a better word) into the business of counterintelligence. The Bureau was quickly in over its head, and an overzealous public, gripped by one of those periodic spy-frenzies that strike this and other nations when it suits their governments, seeing German spies behind every lamppost, formed volunteer amateur spy-chasing vigilante groups. Xenophobia led to hamburger becoming Salisbury steak, sauerkraut becoming liberty cabbage, and German fried potatoes became French fries, towns with German names were renamed, local orchestras stopped playing Beethoven, the Boy Scouts burned German newspapers and books, and a mob in Illinois lynched a German-American who had opposed the war—the ugly downside of spy hysteria. One group of volunteer counterintelligence amateurs, A. M. Brigg's American Protective League (APL), were issued tin badges and an ID card and had a quarter of a million members by the end of the war. At the attorney general's behest, the APL carried out a series of "slacker raids" against draft dodgers by emptying and searching theaters, restaurants, train stations, and arresting any draft-age man who couldn't produce a draft card—without finding a single German spy.

The Army found itself with only one experienced intelligence and counterintelligence officer, Major Ralph H. Van Deman, with experience in the Spanish-American War, the Philippines, in China during the Boxer Rebellion, and during the Japanese war scare of 1907-1908. Van Deman, now in the War College Division, wrote a staff study on what kind of intelligence and counterintelligence organization the Army needed, but Chief of Staff Major General Hugh Scott simply filed and forgot it. It seemed also that Van Deman had a long-standing liaison with the State Department, Voska's espionage organization, and Sir William Wiseman. Scott would later say that military intelligence was superfluous and parrot Wilson's view that intelligence could be provided by our British and French allies. When the paucity of American intelligence came to the attention of Sir William, he suggested to Van Deman that he speak with "Colonel" Edward M. House, Wilson's political crony and advisor. House helped Scott see the light and Van Deman was named head of the new Military Intelligence Section (MIS),starting with two officers and two clerks. Van Deman's British intelligence friend, Lieutenant Colonel Claude E. M. Dansey, offered considerable advice and help with a handbook on intelligence and counterintelligence, deception techniques and methods, and complete organizational details.

General John J. Pershing's intelligence chief, Colonel Dennis E. Nolan, seized the intelligence lead in Europe, forcing Van Deman to concentrate on counterintelligence and security in the Western Hemisphere. He formed MI-4G to deal with civilian subversion, and MI-10 to monitor and censor the mail, telephones, radio communications, books, newspapers, and motion pictures. Van Deman's was, therefore, the first true American counterintelligence organization. G-2 was finally separated from the War College Division and made a separate General Staff division, with a general officer placed in charge, and Van Deman assigned to Pershing's American Expeditionary Force headquarters in Europe in an uncertain job. Van Deman did eventually retire as a major general—having placed intelligence and counterintelligence on an equal footing with other staff functions.

ONI had a good head start in intelligence and counterintelligence, with a successful track record around the world. The Navy, apparently, as did the Army, set up separate intelligence operations in Europe to support the war. Admiral William S. Sims, who had run exceptionally effective intelligence operations in Europe during the Spanish-American War as a lieutenant in ONI, was now assigned to London, leaving ONI headquarters in charge of counterintelligence—and security at naval installations—in the Western Hemisphere. The Navy, with a history of successful intelligence operations and its Ivy League heritage, would, however, exhibit the same excessive zeal in counterintelligence during World War I, as did the Army. Their zeal would lead a naval officer to fire his "German-looking" housekeeper. Ethnicity, all too often the key to foreign intelligence penetrations in America, would always be a counterintelligence problem.

With the abdication of the Russian Czar on March 15, 1917, Sir William Wiseman's influence over Wilson was the means by which Britain secured American support in a failed effort to counter the German intelligence campaign to have the revolutionary Kerensky Government in Russia get out of the war against Germany. They succeeded with Kerensky, but failed with the Bolsheviks and Lenin. More interestingly, and after the failure to counter this German campaign, Sir William's intelligence back channel appears to have been the means by which Britain drew America into its scheme for an armed intervention in Russia from 1918 to 1920—a move that America would come to regret and Russia would never forget. This debacle could have been avoided if America had better intelligence—and counterintelligence—in respect to what was really going on in Russia.

By the end of World War I, the Army emerged with the world's greatest codebreakers, William Friedman and Herbert Yardley, a well-oiled and functioning G-2 organization that included a counterintelligence staff headed by Major Aristides Moreno. ONI would be the primary source for intelligence on Japan's moves, motives, and intentions from the beginning of the century to Pearl Harbor and beyond.

The inter-war period would see the rise of American military intelligence, especially its codebreaking expertise, to its zenith and in time to save the day in World War II, notably at the Battle of Midway. It would also see one of the greatest days in the annals of counterintelligence when the FBI arrested virtually every German spy and saboteur in the United States days before Hitler declared war on the US. On December 6, 1941, the FBI, after having penetrated a 33-member Nazi espionage ring with their double agent, Wilhelm Sebold, a loyal German-American, arrested and jailed Hitler's hope for espionage in America during the war. President Franklin Roosevelt had earlier placed the FBI in charge of all counterintelligence and foreign intelligence in the Western Hemisphere and ONI and MID assigned to cover the rest of the world. The FBI had equal success in Mexico, Central, and South America, where the Germans had hopes of drawing on the large and powerful business and industrial community of German émigrés—albeit with help from the Rockefellers and Pan American Airways, both with competing business interests in the region. The British would also arrange for another of their agents-in-place in America, William Stephenson, the self-anointed "Intrepid," to step into the shoes of Sir William Wiseman, and Roosevelt would agree to his assignment as Secret Intelligence Service (SIS, MI-6) counterintelligence liaison to the FBI during the war.

Enter the Red Menace

The rise of anarchy that spilled out of the 1917 Bolshevik coup quickly found its way to this country with the Communists taking advantage of the depression and unrest in the aftermath of World War I to spread their version of utopia by violent revolution. The engine driving the Communists' moves to expand their reach was their intelligence services, the Soviet General Staff Main Intelligence Directorate (GRU) and the NKVD.[2] They created and supported labor unrest, riots, the formation of the Civil Liberties Union, and established a spy network that would infiltrate the highest levels of government. Although the FBI well knew what was underway, Roosevelt and his left-leaning New Deal social experimenters didn't want to see or hear of any evil about the Soviet Union, so their hands were tied. Further, in 1937 Secretary of State Sumner Wells, dissolved the East European Affairs Division, the only effective intelligence group keeping an eye on Russia. State Department officials let it be known that the order to stop "spying" on Russia came directly from the White House. Secretary of State Henry L. Stimson will always be remembered for his 1929 closing down of Herbert Yardley's Black Chamber code breaking operation and his 1948 statement that "Gentlemen do not read each other's mail." Shortly after Roosevelt came into office, the Communications Act of 1934 was passed, which did not fix the Radio Act of 1927, which made it illegal to intercept any foreign diplomatic traffic, including that of an enemy. Fortunately, the Army and

---

2. The Communist-Party – controlled secret service changed its nomenclature many times: 1917 – Cheka; 1926 – OGPU; 1934 – NKVD; 1941 – NKGB; 1941 – NKVD (again); 1943 – NKGB/MGB; 1946 – MGB; 1954 – KGB (until the end of the USSR).

Navy ignored the law and quietly proceeded to hone their codebreaking skills.

The FBI got its first break, and insights, into the massive Soviet espionage campaign against the US with Whittaker Chambers' 1938 defection, although there was little that was done about it during the Roosevelt era. The FBI was, after that, neither blind nor deaf to what the GRU and NKVD were up to, but they were kept dumb, by having their hands tied. There were so many Soviet agents in high places in Roosevelt's Administration that they kept bumping into each other in Washington, creating their own security problem. There was: Lauchlin Currie and Harry Hopkins in the White House; Alger Hiss, Laurence Duggan, and Noel Field in State; Martha Dodd, the daughter of the US ambassador to Germany; Harry Dexter White and Harold Glasser at Treasury; Duncan Lee (descendant of Robert E. Lee and Donovan's administrative assistant), Donald Wheeler, and numerous others in the Office of Strategic Services (OSS); Judith Coplon in Justice; and no less than the paid Soviet agent, New York Congressman Samuel Dickstein. And then there was Michael Straight, with family connections to Roosevelt, friend to the Cambridge Five,[3] and later editor and publisher of the *New Republic*; and the infamous atomic traitors, the Rosenberg ring, scientists Klaus Fuchs and Theodore Hall, and hundreds of others never identified.

The FBI got its next real break with the 1945 defections of Elizabeth Bentley and Igor Gouzenko in Canada, which opened the window on atomic espionage. With President Roosevelt's death, the FBI was free to change its tactics, becoming more aggressive in pursuit of Soviet espionage. Had Roosevelt died four months earlier, Vice President Henry Wallace, a communist sympathizer who maintained close affiliation with Communist Party members, would have become President, instead of Harry Truman. Although Truman called it all a "red herring," he quickly changed his mind in 1949 when the Soviets exploded their atomic bomb. Counterintelligence moved back into high gear. McCarthyism in the 1950s, however, was a setback for counterintelligence. Senator Joseph McCarthy took a basically correct premise, the extraordinary degree to which the government, media, and entertainment industry harbored Soviet apologists, "fellow travelers," communists, and outright spies, but then expanded and distorted it with sweeping accusations that exceeded all bounds of credibility by including established patriots (e.g. General George Marshall), creating another public spy hysteria—thereby dealing legitimate anti-Communism a severe blow. The VENONA files of decrypted Soviet intelligence messages, released in the 1990s, however, would prove that McCarthy's basic premise was correct.

---

3. Soviet intelligence officer Arnold Deutsch recruited the Cambridge Five from Cambridge University, England. They were Kim Philby, Donald McLean, Guy Burgess, Anthony Blunt, and John Cairncross.

The Cold War

Inside the Soviet Union and Communist China, counterintelligence was more important than foreign intelligence. Their dictatorial leaderships came to power in coups, killing off their domestic rivals, and survived by keeping their own population under tight control—foreign intelligence, therefore, being of secondary importance. In other words, these regimes were counterintelligence states, where their own people were considered as much an enemy as foreign adversaries, and where the "means justified the end." In the US, intelligence and counterintelligence institutions and operations must operate more carefully, under the rule of law, and would never survive if using such means against the US citizenry in violation of the Constitution.

US counterintelligence during the Cold War was a series of disastrous failures and incredible successes. These failures and successes tell the true story of counterintelligence. More importantly, they clearly reveal what is required to maintain a healthy, effective, and lawful—and acceptable, accountable, and appreciated—American counterintelligence system. A few selected examples:

- **William Weisband** was a Soviet agent inside the Army's codebreaking operation in Arlington Hall during World War II. He tipped off the Soviets that their codes were being read. The failure to catch Weisband in time, and the resulting sudden change in Soviet codes contributed to US "blindness" on Chinese preparations to enter the Korean War.

- Operation SOLO: **Morris and Eva Childs** were FBI assets, with close connections at the highest levels in the Kremlin, providing the FBI with intelligence from the late 1950s onward. In 1987, President Reagan bestowed the National Security Medal for their lifetime work.

- CIA counterintelligence officer **Aldrich Ames** provided the Soviets the names of all CIA agents in the Soviet Union, resulting in their arrest and execution.

- Navy Petty Officer **John Walker**, and the ring of family and friends he recruited, provided the Soviets with critical Naval codes over a 20-year period, which had war-winning potential.

- Cuban intelligence infiltrated CIA intelligence agents throughout the Cuban community in Florida.

- In the 1970s, more than 200 Line X Soviet KGB officers worldwide targeted and stole US and Western technologies to support Soviet military developments and industries.

- **Jonathan Pollard**, a Naval intelligence analyst and Israeli agent, provided Israel with thousands of US secrets.

- **Robert Hanssen**, an FBI counterintelligence officer, armed with a license to probe into virtually every US secret, provided the Soviets with virtually every US secret and counterintelligence operation underway.

The Post Cold War Environment

In the present global economy, economic competition has been increasingly important in relation to military confrontations in world affairs. America's intellectual property, industrial and trade secrets are not only the basis of our strong economy and military, but also our economic competitiveness—and the loss of it through economic espionage to foreign governments poses a serious threat to the future of our nation. Economic espionage is a relatively-low risk enterprise with extremely high pay off—with little consequences even when caught at it. The technologically advanced strong US economy is a priority target for our competitors and the present economic espionage feeding frenzy taking place is now being carried out by both friend and foe alike, for both economic and defense reasons. This economic espionage is an entirely new challenge for counterintelligence and led to the passing of the Economic Intelligence Act of 1996. There is, nonetheless, a widely held perception that the end of the Cold War means that other than a few scattered terrorism and drug problems, we no longer face a truly serious foreign threat to our national security, and that these past threats have turned into nothing more than normal economic competition, or business as usual. The Economic Intelligence Act of 1996 thus far has failed to have much impact.[4]

The War on Terrorism

By any measure, the terrorist attacks of September 11, 2001 are rightly viewed as a counterintelligence failure, with the brunt of the criticism being leveled at the FBI, the legally constituted counterintelligence service. The reasons for the FBI's failures are clear. The FBI is a law enforcement agency, i.e., solving crimes after they have been committed, and not crime prevention, which is more of an intelligence and counterintelligence function requiring intelligence sources and methods. The FBI, therefore, had been preoccupied with obtaining post-crime evidence that could lead to an arrest, conviction, and prosecution before a jury in a court of law. Although the FBI was also primarily responsible for counterintelligence, their history in crime solving, along with legal constraints imposed against their collecting "preemptive" intelligence, i.e., collecting intelligence and information necessary, in advance, to prevent a crime—or terrorist attack—had left them culturally ill-equipped for this new threat environment.

In the immediate post-9/11 years, the questions were, "Is the FBI really be up to the job?" and "Can any counterintelligence agency, including the new Department of Homeland Security and other intelligence agencies, empowered by the Patriot Act, but hindered by those more concerned with civil liberties, be

---

4. Congress requires an annual report from the National Counterintelligence Executive on economic espionage by foreign countries. See *http://www.ncix.gov/publications/reports/index.php*.

able to protect America from the certain terrorists acts surely to come? Certainly military counterintelligence, which has historically been preoccupied with criminal investigations rather than real counterintelligence, and has failed to prevent the loss of the very weapons and technology that give our military its advantage, and now committed to tactical counterintelligence in the war zones, is inconsequential when it comes to counterterrorism and homeland defense.

These questions, along with the failures with respect to 9/11, the Wen Ho Lee and Robert Hanssen cases, led many to call for the creation of a new US domestic intelligence agency modeled on the British domestic intelligence agency, MI-5. Britain's Security Service Act of 1989 and 1996 read:

> "The function of MI-5 shall be the protection of national security and, in particular, its protection against threats from espionage, terrorism and sabotage, from the activities of agents of foreign powers and from action intended to overthrow or undermine parliamentary democracy by political, industrial or violent means. ... and to safeguard the economic well-being of the UK against threats posed by the actions or intentions of persons outside the UK ....and to support the activities of police forces and other law enforcement agencies in the prevention and detection of serious crime.... "

MI-5 has no executive powers, such as the authority to investigate individuals or organizations unless they fall within its statutory remit, nor can it arrest people. But Congress was doubtful that the American public would stand for MI-5's means and methods, things that would never be permitted here. Their deadly effectiveness is what led Parliament to give MI-5 the lead role over the military in countering the IRA in Northern Ireland. MI-5, for example, has access to all encryption codes used in Britain, and keys to virtually every house and apartment (flat). It is interesting to compare this authority with the far more limited allowances given the National Security Agency as has come to light in the aftermath of the leaks from defector Edward Snowden.

The Intelligence Reform and Terrorism Prevention Act (IRTPA) of 2004, which substantively changed the organization and management of the US Intelligence Community (IC), did not include provision for a new domestic counterintelligence agency. In the years since, the FBI has undergone a significant mission and cultural transformation. "Today's FBI is a threat-focused, intelligence-driven organization," new Director James B. Comey told Congress. "Counterterrorism remains our top priority."[5]

In the final analysis, counterintelligence must strive to know everything possible about an adversary's intelligence capabilities, including his sources and methods of collection, his covert actions, including terrorism, attempts at influencing and managing our actions and perceptions, and even his culture and thought processes. In other words, it must collect pre-emptive intelligence

---

5. Statement before the Senate Committee on Homeland Security and Governmental Affairs, November 14, 2013. *http://www.fbi.gov/news/testimony/homeland-threats-and-the-fbis-response.*

if it is to prevent the crime of terrorist attacks.

Counterintelligence is ultimately about protecting our core democratic values. It has done reasonably well so far, and is still improving. To be effective in the near-term, it will require continued coordination within the IC, continued funding and especially support from the American people. Counterintelligence cannot, however, no matter how effectively organized, coordinated, and implemented, completely eliminate terrorists bent on suicide attacks. The long-term solution will require our understanding the root causes of the hatred behind the suicidal attacks, and our attacking and correcting the basic problems and frustrations, perceived and real, behind this hatred of America and the West. And that may prove to be our mission impossible.

READINGS FOR INSTRUCTORS

The following is a selected list of informative readings useful for instructors:

Barron, John. *Operation SOLO: The FBI's Man in the Kremlin* (Washington, DC: Regnery Publishing, 1996).

Economic Intelligence Act of 1996 (Pub. L. 104-294, 110 Stat. 3488). *http://www.fas. org/irp/threat/handbook/act.pdf.*

EO-12333: United States Intelligence Activities, December 4, 1981, *http://www.archives. gov/federal-register/codification/executive-order/12333.html*

Mitchell, Marcia and Thomas. *The Spy Who Seduced America: Lies and Betrayal in the Heat of the Cold War: The Judith Coplon Story* (Chicago, IL: Independent Publishers Group, 2002).

O'Toole, G.J.A. *Honorable Treachery* (New York City: Atlantic Monthly Press, 1991).

Riebling, Mark, *Wedge: From Pearl Harbor to 9/11: How the Secret War Between the FBI and CIA Has Endangered National Security, Second Edition.* (New York City: Touchstone, 2002).

Romerstein, Herbert and Eric Breindel. *The Venona Secrets: Exposing Soviet Espionage and America's Traitors* (Washington, DC: Regnery Publishing, 2000).

Schecter, Jerrold and Peter Deriabin. *The Spy Who Saved the World: How a Soviet Colonel Changed the Course of the Cold War* (New York City: Scribner, 1992).

Weinstein, Allen & Alexander Vassiliev, *The Haunted Wood: Soviet Espionage in America – The Stalin Era* (New York City: Random House, 1998).

Wise, David. *Molehunt: The Secret Search for Traitors That Shattered the CIA* (New York City: Random House, 1992).

Wise, David. *Nightmover: How Aldrich Ames Sold the CIA to the KGB for $4.6 Million* (New York City: Harpercollins, 1995).

The National Counterintelligence Executive has on its website a CI Reader in three volumes at *http://www.ncix.gov/publications/ci_references/index.php.* Although spotty in places, it nonetheless is one of the more extensive histories of US counterintelligence.

Gene Poteat was president of the Association of Former Intelligence Officers (AFIO) and a senior career CIA science and technology intelligence officer. He teaches at the Institute of World Politics in Washington, DC.

GUIDE TO THE STUDY OF INTELLIGENCE

A Guide to the Psychology of Espionage

David L. Charney, M.D. and John A. Irvin

P eople are fascinated by espionage. The sheer volume of fiction and non-fiction books and movies dedicated to the subject of spying attests to this, as well as private citizens' enthusiasm for news reports on cases of espionage and their thirst for mere fragments of insight into those engaged in it. This is probably in no small part due to the fact that so much of what we consider espionage occurs in a world inaccessible to most people.

Even for those who have years of service in the Intelligence Community, however, one question remains difficult to fully explain: Why spy? History shows that most countries have at one time or another made the decision to seek out secret information regarding other countries, groups, or even their own people through clandestine means ... that is, to spy. Still, except for irrational behavior on the part of unaccountable dictators, the decision to spy is usually based on the consensus of a country's political leadership regarding national security goals and how to achieve them. This consensus decision may be complex but still more or less discernable to outsiders.

What is much more difficult to understand is why a particular individual would chose to engage in espionage. The psychology of espionage covers a number of areas and includes questions such as: Why does a particular individual choose a career in intelligence? What is the psychological profile of the clandestine officer who chooses a career spent largely in the shadows? How do individual psychological factors impact the collection and, especially, the analysis of intelligence?

Perhaps the most intriguing question is why a person who has been placed in a position of trust would then betray that trust and engage in espionage? Why harm his or her country or group? Why expose one's family to scandal ... or worse? This is the issue of the so-called "insider spy."

Definitions

For the purpose of this discussion, espionage will be defined in accordance with US Code Title 18 (Crimes and Criminal Procedure), Part I (Crimes), Chapter 37 (Espionage and Censorship), § 798 (Disclosure of classified information)[1] as knowingly and willfully communicating, furnishing, transmitting or otherwise making any classified information available to an unauthorized person, or publishing, or using it in any manner prejudicial to the safety or interest of the United States or for the benefit of any foreign government to the detriment of the United States. This definition does not include classified intelligence collected on behalf of the United States and in accordance with US law.

The word spy will refer to the "insider spy," that is, the individual who has been formally vetted, has obtained appropriate security clearances, is placed in a position of trust where he or she has access to classified information, and then chooses to betray that trust by committing espionage against the country or organization they serve. He or she may be a contractor or full-time employee of that organization. This is distinct from the person with whom the spy collaborates, traditionally a member of a foreign intelligence service, who serves as the spy's handler.

Why Spy?

Before the rise of the field of psychology in the late 19th century, human behavior was often explained based on moralistic or religious beliefs. Apart from the ancients (Hippocrates concluded that mental disorders arose from physical problems rather than demonic possession and Galen concluded that the brain and nervous system played a central role in thought and emotion),[2] the explanation for offensive or illegal behaviors, such as espionage, was often a moral judgment based on religious or social proscriptions rather than psychological motivation.

Moralistic approaches were based on what we might consider a black and white, good versus evil world view that portrayed transgressors as subject to external, often metaphysical influences that either destined them to be immoral or had the power to override their ability to control their own behavior. This remains an important point because, despite research demonstrating the complexity of individual motivation and behavior, this ostensibly common-sense view still influences our perception of those who commit espionage: the spy who is working for our side is "good," while the one working against us is "bad."

While a simple and emotionally satisfying explanation, viewing espionage

---

1. Cornell University Law School, Legal Information Institute website (http://www.law.cornell.edu/uscode/ text/18/798)
2. T. L. Brink. (2008) *Psychology: A Student Friendly Approach.* "Unit One: The Definition and History of Psychology."

in moralistic terms does little toward gaining the sort of insight that would assist in developing methods for prevention or early identification. An organization does not knowingly hire a traitor. Rather, on rare occasion an organization hires someone it believes it can trust who either successfully hides his or her intention to commit espionage or, more commonly, later finds themselves in circumstances that (for any number of complex personal reasons) present espionage as a reasonable, even attractive choice.[3] Like espionage itself, psychology presents us with a world where the certainties of black and white, moralistic approaches succumb to the reality of psychological nuance and complexity.

Of MICE and (Mostly) Men

In modern times, governments have instituted efforts to understand the psychological and social (psychosocial) factors that contribute to an individual's decision to spy. Initially, at least in the United States, conventional wisdom played a larger role than actual research.

Perhaps the most oft-cited explanation for espionage is the revealed knowledge known by the acronym MICE, as well as its many subsequent variations. While MICE presents a more or less common-sense view of general motivation that was likely popular before being presented to the public in print, it appears to have first been posited in a book by former KGB Major Stanislav Levchenko. After defecting to the United States in 1979, Levchenko wrote a memoir[4] in which he suggested there were four general motives for espionage: Money, Ideology, Compromise/Coercion, and Ego.

Money – This is a general category that would include such selfish motivation as avarice (extreme greed for wealth or material gain) as well as what might be considered more noble motives such as the need to pay for a family member's medical treatment or a child's education. In any event, the spy comes to the personal conclusion that espionage is the best or perhaps only means of obtaining the money desired. CIA research psychologist Terry Thompson suggests there are a number of additional factors that may contribute to the spy's vulnerability to the offer of money, to include a cultural tendency toward acquainting success with material gain, the social power and prestige that come with material success, the ego-gratification effect of receiving money, as well as the relief the spy in financial need feels upon receiving their pay. Thompson also makes the intriguing suggestion that a willingness to take risks, one of the personality traits that might attract an individual to a career as an intelligence collector, may also inadvertently contribute to poor financial decisions that place an individual in a state of financial need and to view espionage as a

---

3. K. Herbig, & M. Wiskoff. *Espionage against the United States by American Citizens. 1947-2001* (Monterey CA: Defense Personnel Security Research Center, 2002).

4. S. Levchenko. *On the Wrong Side: My life in the KGB* (New York: Pergamon, 1988).

plausible remedy.[5]

Ideology – An ideology is simply a shared set of beliefs about how the world is or ought to be. Psychiatrist and author Steven Pinker writes, "An ideology cannot be identified with a part of the brain or even with a whole brain, because it is distributed across the brains of many people."[6] Since it represents a shared belief system, an ideology is adopted by an individual to the degree that it reflects the individual's ego. In that sense, an ideology is like another motivation – money – in that it serves as a vehicle for the individual to express a personal value or belief; an ideology is chosen in order to confirm conscious or unconscious beliefs the individual has already internalized.[7] In the case of espionage, a particular ideology may serve as either the actual motivation for a spy to breach the trust placed in them or simply as a means of rationalizing that behavior. The so-called Cambridge Five[8] were likely "true believers" whose motivation for working with the Soviets against their native United Kingdom was based largely (but not exclusively) in a utopian belief in Communist ideology. Other examples of ideologically motivated US spies would include Cold War-era spies Julius and Ethel Rosenberg and, more recently, Defense Intelligence Agency (DIA) analyst and Cuban spy Ana Montes. Before the Cold War ended, however, ideology appeared to play a decreasing role in Soviet recruitment, forcing the KGB to seek other motives.[9] Nevertheless, Cold War-era political beliefs were only one form of ideology, and its demise certainly does not rule out the use of ideology as motivation in the present or future.

Compromise/Coercion – This is a negative rather than positive form of motivation and can be equated with what one might think of as "blackmail" or perhaps even torture. Unlike the other general forms of motivation offered in MICE, in this case, the spy does not act of his or her own free will but, rather, is effectively forced to commit espionage through fear of punishment, exposure of wrongdoing, or some other undesirable outcome. From a psychological perspective, it is the least reliable method of recruitment since the spy's primary motivation is to escape punishment rather than to please his or her handler. The spy is likely to cooperate only to the extent necessary and may attempt to break free of control as soon as practicable. An infamous example of compromise is the so-called "honey trap," in which a foreign intelligence service would direct a man or woman to seduce a targeted individual in order to obtain their cooperation through threat of exposure.

Ego – This could be considered the all-inclusive category, since an individ-

---

5. T. Thompson. *Why Espionage Happens* (Florence SC: Seaboard Press, 2009).

6. S. Pinker. *The Better Angels of Our Nature: Why Violence Has Declined* (New York: Viking, 2011)

7. M. Shermer. *The Believing Brain: From Ghosts and Gods to Politics and Conspiracies – How We Construct Beliefs and Reinforce Them as Truths* (New York: Times Books, 2011)

8. Kim Philby, Donald Maclean, Guy Burgess, Anthony Blunt, and John Cairncross were recruited while attending Cambridge University in the UK.

9. Herbig & Wiskoff (2002).

ual's opinion of him – or herself and the effort he or she puts into enhancing or defending that opinion is fundamental to their decision-making. Levchenko's use of the term was more focused and meant to highlight the potential spy's desire for challenge, adventure, and excitement.[10] Later efforts that went beyond MICE would identify personality traits such as narcissism or attitudes such as employee disgruntlement that are manifestly ego-related but perhaps more insightful than Levchenko's risk-taking behavior. In fact, with the exception of coercion, all of the MICE categories may fall under ego, inasmuch as money and ideology serve as vehicles for the expression of ego.

While still popular and oft-cited, MICE is of somewhat limited value in predicting who will or will not commit espionage. First, the categories are too general and lack nuance, so they fail to identify in a practical manner the myriad and complex motivation of individual spies. Furthermore, as limited, general categories, employing them runs the risk of making the behavior fit the category, resulting in ascribing oversimplified motivation such as "Ames was greedy" or "Hannsen was arrogant." Finally, being an expression of conventional wisdom or common sense, they are not based on any actual scientific research. The US Government would begin to address that problem in the wake of the enormous damage to national security wrought by Navy Chief Warrant Officer John Anthony Walker and his ring of spies.

The Stilwell Commission Report

Walker was arrested in May 1985, after his ex-wife informed the FBI about his spying on behalf of the Soviet Union. The New York Times later reported that Walker may have provided enough code-data information to significantly alter the balance of power between the US and the USSR.[11] In June of the same year, Defense Secretary Caspar W. Weinberger established the Department of Defense Security Review Commission to determine the effectiveness of security clearance procedures. Under the chairmanship of retired Army General Richard G. Stilwell, the commission produced a number of recommendations in what came to be known as The Stilwell Commission Report.[12]

Recognizing that up to that time security decisions were often subjective, the commission recommended that policies be grounded in hard evidence and scientific method.[13] This resulted in the establishment of two organizations that were given the mission of researching the psychology of those who had com-

---

10. K. ScheibeK. "The Temptations of Espionage: Self-Control and Social Control," In T. Sarbin, et al. (eds.). *Citizen Espionage: Studies in Trust and Betrayal* (Westport CT: Praeger, 1994).

11. John J. O'Connor. "American Spies in Pursuit of the American Dream," *NY Times,* February 4, 1990

12. Department of Defense Security Review Commission. *A Report to the Secretary of Defense by the Commission to Review DoD Security Policy and Practices* (Washington, DC: DoD Security Review Commission, 1995).

13. L. Fischer. *Espionage: Why Does it Happen?* (Washington, DC: Department of Defense Security Institute, 2014) [Kindle edition]. Retrieved from Amazon.com

mitted espionage against the United States: the Personnel Security Research Center (PERSEREC) in Monterey, California, and the Community Research Center in Newington, Virginia, whose research efforts would fall under the name "Project Slammer."

PERSEREC Collects the Data

PERSEREC's initial effort was to establish a database on all Americans involved in espionage against the US since World War II based on media reports, trial records, and unclassified official documents. The database would "ma[k]e it possible to systematically collect, quantitatively code, and statistically analyze basic information. This included such things as personal background, the methods and motivations of the offender, and pertinent facts about the crime itself—situational features, what was lost or compromised, and consequences for the subject."[14] Drawing from a database that included (at the time) 120 cases of espionage, PERSEREC issued a May 1992 report entitled, "Americans Who Spied Against Their Country Since World War II," which identified six key motivations. In addition to adding substance to the old MICE categories of money, ideology, and coercion, PERSEREC researchers suggested three additional motivations, disgruntlement/revenge, ingratiation, and thrills/self-importance, which were in effect more refined views of the MICE category ego.

Disgruntlement/Revenge – The spy is motivated by a non-ideological resentment or anger directed toward their country or their employer for some perceived injustice, such as a lack of recognition or inadequate appreciation, failure to achieve promotion, inadequate pay or other compensation, or any number of other perceived personal slights. As a result, the spy seeks revenge by engaging in espionage. A key point is that the injustice may or may not be real, but it is perceived by the spy as both real and personal. Thompson suggests that unrealistic expectations of workplace fulfillment, the depersonalization of large bureaucracies, overestimation of an individual's actual talent, and a culture of disgruntlement fostered by a constant stream of negative media reporting all contribute to disgruntlement.[15] Psychiatrist David Charney, who has interviewed several convicted spies, including Robert Hanssen, Earl Pitts, and Brian Patrick Regan, makes the counterintuitive observation that spies who act out of disgruntlement toward their own agency often continue to view themselves as patriotic citizens and claim it was never their intention to do damage to their country.[16]

Ingratiation – The spy is motivated by a desire to please another person.

---

14. Fischer (2013)

15. Thompson (2009).

16. D. Charney. "True Psychology of the Insider Spy," *The Intelligencer: Journal of U.S. Intelligence Studies* 18 (1), Fall-Winter 2010, 47-54. .

While it would seem unlikely that an individual would choose to spy simply to please another person, ingratiation may be a contributing factor in that decision. For example, if a spy is ideologically motivated, they may work especially hard to please their handler in an effort to demonstrate their commitment to the cause. Navy Seaman Michael Walker, son of John Anthony Walker and part of his father's spy ring, testified that he became a spy in 1983 "for the money and to please my father."[17] Ingratiation may also have played a role in the so-called "Romeo" operations conducted by the East German Stasi, in which a Stasi agent would establish a romantic relationship with a lonely, female secretary in a target West German organization. Unlike coercive "honey traps," the espionage was often based on genuine bonds of affection between the target and her "Romeo."[18]

Thrills/Self-Importance – This motivation is likely what Levchenko had in mind by the term ego. In its purest form, it might be considered the most egocentric of motivations, since it does not necessarily include a desire for personal gain or revenge against some perceived slight. In practice, it is likely a significant contributing factor but not necessarily the key motivation. The spy chooses espionage because of the feeling of excitement it brings, as well as the sense of superiority the spy derives from "putting one over" on their colleagues or their organization. Rather than a manifestation of high self-esteem, it may be the result of the low self-esteem experienced by the would-be-spy suffering some personal or professional setback. Ironically, the very desire for thrills that attracts some Intelligence Community (IC) employees to the profession may also make them particularly susceptible to the thrill of espionage. Likewise, the power and ego-enhancement that comes with keeping secrets from others may add to the feeling of superiority the spy obtains by keeping his or her espionage a secret from their co-workers and organization.

Project Slammer Interviews the Convicts

While PERSEREC focused on collecting as much data as possible from a variety of sources in order to build a database that might assist in identifying the personality traits of known spies, the CRC went directly to the source by conducting interviews with incarcerated US spies. Under the name "Project Slammer," the CRC initially interviewed 30 spies who agreed to undergo hours of psychological testing and in-depth discussion. CRC also interviewed individuals associated with the spy to obtain a better understanding of the spy's private life and how others perceived them at the time of their espionage. Although complementary, the two efforts were distinct in that PERSEREC's

---

17. Associated Press. "Member of spy ring released after 15 years." *The Topeka Capital-Journal*, February 17, 2000. *http://www.cjonline.com*, Accessed January 23, 2014.
18. M. Wolf. *Man Without a Face: The Autobiography of Communisms' Greatest Spymaster* (New York: Times Books, 1997).

findings were based on the statistical analysis of quantitative data on a large number of variables or indicators, while Project Slammer's were based on a qualitative, in-depth case study analysis of information on a smaller selection of offenders.[19]

In April 1990, Project Slammer issued its first, classified interim report, which has since been made available to the public, identifying general behavioral traits common to the subjects interviewed.[20] The report concluded that the spy perceives him – or herself as special, even unique, not a bad person, deserving yet dissatisfied with his or her situation, having no other (or easier) option than to engage in espionage and, at any rate, simply doing what others frequently do. The spy also believes security procedures do not apply to him or her, and that security programs have no meaning unless they connect to something with which he or she can personally identify.

The spy also isolates him or herself from the consequences of spying by rationalizing his or her behavior. A spy will interpret their behavior in a way that leaves espionage as the "only option" and an essentially victimless crime. Once the spy commits to espionage, he or she reinforces their rationalizations by belittling the security system and highlighting the ease with which they are able to fool others and bypass safeguards. After time, however, the initial excitement of their deception fades, while stress increases. Nevertheless, they are reluctant to attempt to break out of their situation because the risks of punishment are too high. Interestingly, spies do not consider themselves traitors, finding some self-justification for their actions, and do not display remorse until after they are apprehended. Finally, spies usually do not consider committing espionage until after they are in a position of trust.

Holes in the Screen

The PERSEREC and Project Slammer efforts stand out as the first serious attempts at understanding the psychology of espionage. Unfortunately, despite the insight gained, espionage cases continued. In 1994, Carson Eoyang, PhD, addressed this reality by examining what he considered models of espionage.[21] He postulated that there were effectively two models: p-models (p-psychology) that sought to identify the individual traits (personality, needs, emotions, mental health) that separated those who commit espionage from those who do not, and s-models (s-situational) that seek to identify the situations in which espionage is most likely to be committed and then to create mechanisms or procedures designed to prevent that possibility.

---

19. Fischer (2013).
20. Director of Central Intelligence. *Project SLAMMER Interim Report* (Washington, DC: Intelligence Community Staff, 1990).
21. C. Eoyang. "Models of Espionage" In Sarbin, et. al., *Citizen Espionage.*.

In comparing the two, he demonstrates that p-models will inevitably result in both false-positives and false-negatives, that is, they will screen out individuals as possessing traits that would indicate future espionage but who would, if placed in a position of trust, never actually commit espionage, while failing to screen out individuals who do not appear to possess those traits who do, under the right circumstances, commit espionage. For similar reasons, s-models fail in that once an individual is considered trustworthy they are frequently placed in a position that allows them the means of countering security measures.

Eoyang proposes a situational-dispositional model that acknowledges that "espionage agents and heroic patriots may share similar personal characteristics"[22] and seeks to match the unique individual and environmental factors that combine to create the possibility of espionage. However, he also writes that developing "a comprehensive and sophisticated program of countermeasures is by no means an easy or quick accomplishment."[23]

Recent research in the field of epigenetics[24] may suggest one reason why the task of identifying specific traits that would effectively screen out potential spies is an important but inevitably imperfect endeavor. Human behavior is almost infinitely complex, being the culmination of a unique lifetime of experience, belief, and conscious or unconscious bias. While screening for personality traits is effective in identifying the most overt and undesirable ones, a particular trait may, like a genetic predisposition, lie more or less dormant until activated by a specific set of circumstances. In this scenario, a benign trait may suddenly become cause for alarm, or an otherwise desirable trait may manifest itself in undesirable behavior.

Beyond Screening and Security

In a 2010 article, David Charney took a step beyond traditional screening models, proposing that regardless of motivation, once insider spies have crossed the line into espionage they tend to follow similar thought patterns that manifest in predictable behaviors.[25] Based on personal interviews with incarcerated spies, Charney postulated that the decision to spy is based on "an intolerable sense of personal failure, as privately defined by that person." Once the spy has made the decision to engage in espionage, Charney identifies what he calls The Ten Life Stages of the Insider Spy: 1) the sensitizing stage, 2) the stress/spiral stage, 3) the crisis/climax/resolution stage, 4) the post-recruitment stage, 5) the

---

22. Eoyang (1994).
23. Eoyang (1994).
24. Epigenetics involves genetic control by factors other than an individual's DNA sequence. Epigenetic changes can switch genes on or off and determine which proteins are transcribed. "What Is Epigenetics? How Do Epigenetic Changes Affect Genes?" Retrieved from *http://www.nature.com/scitable/ topicpage/ epigenetic-influences-and-disease-895*, May 8, 2014.
25. Charney (2010).

remorse-morning-after stage, 6) the active spy career stage, 7) the dormancy stage(s), 8) the pre-arrest stage, 9) the arrest and post-arrest stage, and 10) the brooding in jail stage. Each stage represents a development in the spy's effort to deal with their sense of personal failure by taking what they consider decisive action to boost their sense of worth. This is initially effective, but eventually the spy succumbs to second thoughts, feelings of regret, of being trapped, loneliness, and dependence on their handler. Charney's theory also postulates that certain stages present windows in which, given specific incentives, the spy may choose to reveal their activities to an appropriate authority.

Finally, while not specifically a work of psychology, security expert Nick Catrantzos offers a method of dealing with the insider threat based on group psychology that is essentially independent of the motivation of the insider spy.[26] While recognizing the necessary role of security professionals in any organization, Catrantzos offers a method that focuses on the group dynamics of an office in an effort to promote specific group behaviors and values. He postulates that the insider spy operates in the "dark corners" between the efforts of security professionals and the measures they institute and insider's fellow employees, who may not only feel security is not an issue they need be concerned with but may also be hostile to security practices they consider unnecessary or a hindrance. Catrantzos' offers ideas on how both groups can work together in an effort to close those security gaps and allow no space where the insider spy can comfortably operate.

Problems in Understanding the Psychology of Espionage

Despite the significant threat spies pose to national security, relatively little published material is available to the general public regarding the psychology of espionage. Naturally, some research is and should remain classified in order to protect sources and methods. Other information may be withheld for legal reasons. What is available, however, still suffers from one key problem: there are (fortunately) not that many spies accessible to psychology professionals on which to base research. Statistical conclusions (such as the traits that would identify a propensity toward espionage) are less valid when based on a small sample size. When compared to the hundreds of thousands of cleared individuals who never commit espionage, the fraction of those who do is almost infinitesimally small. This is compounded by the reality that research can only be done on those individuals who are both known to be spies and accessible to researchers. That translates to spies in prison and serving time for their crimes. Individual incarcerated spies may or may not be motivated to work with researchers.

The last and most intractable issue regarding understanding the psy-

---

26. N. Catrantzos. *Managing the Insider Threat: No Dark Corners* (Boca Raton, FL: CRC Press, 2012).

chology of espionage is the sheer complexity of personal motivation. Like the weather, behavior is predictable, but only to a certain degree. Measures can be enacted to screen out, secure from, or mitigate the actions of the insider spy, but it is unlikely they will ever prove universally and unerringly effective. The individual human mind is often an enigma and, as such, will continue to confound law enforcement, fascinate scientists and historians, and provide engaging storylines to writers of spy fiction.

Dr. David L. Charney is the founder and medical director of Roundhouse Square Psychiatric Center, Alexandria, Virginia. He has become familiar with the IC as a consultant and therapist to IC personnel for many years. He had the opportunity to join the defense team of his first spy case, Earl Pitts. Building on that foundation, Robert Hanssen's attorney, Plato Cacheris, invited Dr. Charney to join his defense team, which added a fascinating further dimension to his experience. With his third spy case, Brian Regan, Dr. Charney's in-depth knowledge of the psychological nuances of captured spies is unmatched. As a member of their defense teams, Dr. Charney was received by these spies as an understanding and supportive figure, which lowered their defensive mindsets, providing a truer picture of their inner lives. Many common assumptions of spy motivation have been brought into question by Dr. Charney's work. To further extend his findings, he has been working on a policy White Paper in which he will amplify his psychological findings and also propose new and perhaps controversial initiatives to better protect the country from spying.

John Alan Irvin has spent 14 years in the US Army and 10 with the Central Intelligence Agency. He has been an artillery, paratroop, and psychological operations officer. At the CIA, he served in the clandestine service as both a collection management and case officer as well as in managerial positions.

GUIDE TO THE STUDY OF INTELLIGENCE

CIA and the Polygraph

John F. Sullivan

For as long as the polygraph has been a part of the US Government's security apparatus, it has been an object of controversy and criticism. It is used in the Intelligence Community (IC) and by federal and state law enforcement entities. The controversy focuses on the lack of scientific evidence as to the polygraph's validity, and the criticism is rooted in the claims of those who believe they were treated unjustly during polygraph tests. The absence of a viable appeals process has exacerbated both the criticism and controversy.

The primary role of polygraph in the IC has been as a part of the applicant screening process, and was most often the deciding factor as to whether or not a security clearance was granted. One can pass a polygraph test and still be denied employment, due to medical, psychological, or other factors, but getting a clearance without successfully completing the polygraph process is extremely rare.

Within the CIA, there is a much more expanded role for polygraph. Included in that role is the support the clandestine service (CS) in its operations. That support consists of verifying the *bona fides* of recruited agents as well as the accuracy of the information they provide. The polygraph is also used as an interrogation aid in the debriefing of prisoners, defectors, and walk-ins offering supposedly valuable information. Other venues for CIA polygraph are as a tool in internal investigations to resolve allegations made against employees, as part of periodic re-investigations of employees, and the screening of contract employees. The polygraph also has a prophylactic role in that in many instances, knowing that there would be a polygraph in their futures, employees have refrained from misconduct; or so many have told me.

Because 99% of my polygraph experience is with the CIA, this article addresses the various roles of polygraph in the CIA.

A Little History

Historically, polygraph tests were used by law enforcement in connection with a specific crime. In considering the use of the polygraph, CIA decided that it needed to address a broader range of issues. To that end, in late 1947, G. Cleveland (Cleve) Backster, a former Army intelligence interrogator, was hired to come up with a test addressing lifestyle as well as counterintelligence issues. Lifestyle issues involved criminal activity, blackmail, drug use, homosexuality, alcohol problems, and involvement with communism. Among the counterintelligence issues addressed were the mishandling and unauthorized disclosure of classified information, contacts with foreign nationals, and unauthorized contacts with foreign intelligence services. Once a standard test was in place, Admiral Roscoe Hillenkoetter, the then director of central intelligence, authorized polygraph use on a voluntary and experimental basis.

The CIA's expanded application of the polygraph was contrary to polygraph practices espoused by the American Polygraph Association (APA) in that it diluted the process' validity. The Agency's program diverged from the mainstream of polygraph practice. Agency examiners were discouraged from joining the APA or participating in APA sponsored seminars, workshops, or conferences.

During the first year of use at CIA, more than 100 employees lost their clearances as a result of information developed during their polygraph tests. In the process, polygraph became an integral part of the CIA security apparatus. It didn't take long for the word to get out that volunteering to take a polygraph test might not be a good idea, and the pool of volunteers began to dry up. At some point, the testing of employees who volunteered to take polygraph tests expanded to the testing of applicants for CIA employment.

During my initial interview in 1968 with Mr. Bill Osborne, the then chief of the Office of Security (OS) Interrogation Research Division (IRD), as the Polygraph Division (PD) was formerly called, told me that 92% of applicants who took polygraph examinations "passed" or completed their tests and were offered positions. He also said that of the 8% who were denied employment, 92% were a direct result of polygraph-derived information. Mr. Osborne also noted that no applicant or employee had been denied employment or lost a clearance unless he or she admitted to disqualifying information, and closed out the interview by telling me, "We believe that it is better for 10 dishonest people to get through the process than to accuse an honest person of being dishonest."

The Early Years

Having demonstrated its utility with its early tests, and gained a modicum of acceptance in so doing, a proposal was made in 1951 to use the polygraph as part of the validation process of operational assets. To do this, the OS had to recruit examiners who spoke a foreign language, and to that end, examiners were recruited from the Directorate of Plans (DP).[1] As useful as polygraph had been up until that point, it became more so in the operational arena.

A defining moment for the Agency's DP polygraph program came during the Korean War, when polygraph examiners uncovered and neutralized a large double agent operation. The South Koreans had been sending teams of agents into North Korea to gather intelligence. When a new CIA chief arrived in Seoul in 1951, he ordered that returning members of these teams, as well as others involved in the operation be polygraphed. It turned out that the the Chinese had co-opted the operation, and many agents had been killed or doubled. One of the results of this success was that over the next several years, there was a dramatic increase in the use of polygraph in clandestine agent operations. To handle this increased workload, examiners were assigned overseas and teams of examiners would make periodic trips abroad to handle an overload of cases.

For the next two decades, there were few changes in the CIA polygraph program. There was no related research on methods or equipment.

While the primary focuses during this period were on applicant and operational testing, there was one other type of test employed, the Specific Issue Polygraph (SIP). This test was used when an allegation of misconduct was made against an employee. On these occasions, the accused employee was offered the opportunity to take a polygraph test to resolve the allegation.[2]

A Time of Change

Contained in the agreement that all applicants sign prior to being tested, is a clause advising the applicant that as an employee, they would be subject to periodic polygraph testing. Although authorized, periodic testing was rarely done. Operations and communications officers returning from overseas assignments were occasionally tested as they were seen as at greater risk for recruitment approaches.

In 1975, a policy of periodic retesting was formalized and called the Reinvestigation Polygraph Program (RIP). The main obstacle in establishing this program was an argument over the questions to be asked. One faction wanted lifestyle issues covered; the other, only counterintelligence questions. The latter faction prevailed, and since 1976, the RIP, using only counterintelligence questions, has been an integral part of the CIA's polygraph program.

---

1. The Directorate of Plans (DP) is an early name for the clandestine service, later called the Directorate of Operations and then the National Clandestine Service, the CIA organization that recruits and manages clandestine agents.

2. Of seven SIPs about which I have personal and specific knowledge, four were used to resolve allegations of homosexuality, one of child molestation, one of embezzlement, and one of theft. Five confessions were obtained and one individual was exonerated. Another individual refused to take a polygraph test, and was given a medical retirement. Two of the individuals who underwent SIPs committed suicide.

Employees were subject to testing at five-year intervals, but due to manpower issues, maintaining that schedule for all employees was not possible. The pool of employees who had been on duty for more than five years was huge, and growing every year. Selection of those to undergo RIP testing was done randomly, and many employees went through their entire career having taken only their entering on duty (EOD) test.

As was the case in the operational and applicant venues, the polygraph proved its utility in the RIP arena. The biggest "take" from the RIP tests were admissions of mishandling and making unauthorized disclosures of classified information. In 1977, an employee, during her RIP test, admitted to passing classified information to a foreign intelligence service member. This was the first employee to ever admit to espionage during a polygraph test.[3]

Often, something bad must happen before change occurs. That was how it was with the IRD's Industrial Polygraph Program. Prior to 1977, contractors working on Agency programs were polygraphed on a catch-as-catch-can basis. The Boyce-Lee case changed that. Christopher John Boyce was a clerk at the aerospace giant TRW. In January 1977, Boyce and his cohort, Dalton Lee, were arrested for passing classified information to the Soviets. Boyce would pass the information to Lee, who would travel to the Russian Embassy in Mexico City and turn the information over to the Russian handler. This case exposed the vulnerability of our industrial contractors, and as a result, an Industrial Branch was created in IRD to handle contractor polygraph examinations.[4]

In November 1977, William Kampiles stole the highly classified manual on the KH-11 satellite and sold it to the Soviets. Unfortunately for Kampiles, the Russian to whom he sold the manual was one of ours. Kampiles was arrested in 1978 and sentenced to 40 years in prison.[5] The upshot of this incident was the creation of a three-year probationary period for new employees. At the conclusion of the probationary period, a background investigation would be done, as well as a polygraph test that included both lifestyle and counterintelligence questions. Each question was prefaced with the phrase: "Since entering on duty, have you ......?"

In every aspect of CIA's polygraph testing — applicant, reinvestigation, probationary, industrial, operational, and specific issue — significant admissions have been obtained, to wit:

- Catching double agents is the Holy Grail for a CIA polygraph examiner, and in 1979 a CIA examiner caught a Czech double agent who had not only been working with the FBI for four years, but also had been trained to beat the polygraph. He and two of his colleagues were declared *persona non grata* and

---

3. Over FBI protests, the employee, who has never been named publically, was allowed to retire.
4. See Robert Lindsey, The Falcon and the Snowman: A True Story of Friendship and Espionage (New York City: Simon & Schuster, 1979).
5. On December 16, 1996, Kampiles was released from prison.

deported from the US. At the time, Czech intelligence was the only service that trained its agents to beat the polygraph.

- CIA operations officer Edward Lee Howard, was fired in 1983 after admitting to drug use and criminal activity during his RIP test. He subsequently defected to the Soviet Union.

- In 1985, during a routine RIP test, and after five days of testing and interrogation, Sharon Scranage confessed to engaging in espionage for Ghana and was sent to prison.

- During his applicant test in 1993, former New York State Trooper David Harding admitted falsifying evidence in a murder case. He was sentenced to prison.

- During his 1996 probationary test, an employee admitted to participating in a bank robbery between the time he passed his EOD test and entered on duty. He, too, was sent to prison.

In the operational arena, numerous double agents have been uncovered, phantom operations and fabricators exposed, and information affecting national policy decisions verified.

Out with the Old – In with the New

By the late 1970s, it became apparent that the in-house training of polygraph examiners was inadequate to meet the increasing demands. To address this issue, PD examiner candidates were sent to the John Reid and Associates polygraph school in Chicago for training. This outsourcing of examiner training led to participation in off-site seminars on polygraph, an increase in studies of human behavior as it related to polygraph, and a more academic approach to polygraph uses.

No more than four examiners at a time could be sent out for training, which was inadequate to meet demand. In 1984, CIA created its own polygraph school to replace its previous five-week, unstructured, one-on-one training program. CIA's polygraph course, certified by the American Polygraph Association, lasted nine months and was very structured and intensive. The graduates were the best trained examiners in the history of CIA's polygraph program and viewed as professional polygraph examiners, as opposed to being simply security officers, who, in many cases, through no fault or desire of their own, happened to be assigned to PD.

This new breed of examiners obtained admissions at a never before seen rate, but there was a price to pay. Complaints about polygraph skyrocketed. Single session polygraph tests became the exception to the rule and what had been skepticism about the polygraph morphed into open hostility. Polygraph tests, which had been perceived as mere inconveniences, were being seen as inquisitions.

CIA examiners were being told, "If you aren't getting complaints, you aren't doing your job," and "Everyone who comes in here is lying. It is our job to find out how much." More and more subjects were being called deceptive, with no admissions, and in the late 1980s, seven examiners were fired for rigging their tests to make sure their subjects passed.

With the Aldrich (Rick) Ames case, it got worse. In February 1994, CIA operations officer Ames was arrested for passing classified information to the Russians. While working for the Russians, he passed two polygraph tests, conducted by three graduates of CIA's school. Post Ames, the PD lost control of its school, additional levels of quality control were put in place, and the two examiners who had tested Ames were reassigned. The media excoriated the polygraph, PD morale descended even further, and there was a perception that the PD would not survive another miss on the scale of the Ames fiasco. CIA polygraphs were forever changed.

The New Polygraph

Polygraph Division management, and many of the examiners, became almost paranoid about making a bad call on another subject. Single session favorable determinations became rare. "Inconclusive" became the call of choice. One of PD's branch managers dictated that "Every subject, regardless of how good the charts are, will be brought back for additional testing." A senior CIA officer was quoted in *Newsweek*, saying, "They [the Polygraph Division] are treating us all like criminals."

PD was under constant attack, and a "circle the wagons," "us against them" attitude ensued. In that environment, polygraph subjects and their sponsors would no longer be given the results of their polygraph tests. This would give the examiners immunity from complaints, limit appeals, and take some of the pressure off them. Today, it is more difficult for unsuitable candidates and/ or malefactors to get through the polygraph process, and that is because an honest subject has no better chance than a dishonest subject of getting through the process. Honest subjects who did not get through the process were seen callously as collateral damage and a cost of doing business. Several have sued CIA over polygraph results.

A properly conducted polygraph test remains a valid, effective, and proven security screening technique. The polygraph test is usually the first interaction an applicant has with a CIA security officer. In too many cases applicants leave a polygraph session with a less than favorable impression. Polygraph testing is the most time consuming aspect of security processing and is unnecessarily long resulting in suitable candidates refusing to wait for the resolution of their tests and taking other employment. Most importantly, when an honest poly-graph subject fails to complete his or her polygraph test, the subject can draw two conclusions: either the instrument doesn't work or the examiner doesn't know what he is doing. In either case, the polygraph process' credibility suffers.

Ironically, as use increased, so did the number of false positives, complaints, and the number of subjects who were denied clearances without having made an admission. Polygraph lost much of its credibility, making it less effective. Over-reliance on the polygraph, while perhaps cost-effective from the government's perspective, has negative aspects from the perspective of fairness, ethics, and potential liability.

READINGS FOR INSTRUCTORS

The National Academy of Sciences and National Research Council, *The Polygraph and Lie Detection* (Washington, DC: National Academy of Sciences Press, 2003).

Reid, John and Fred Inbau. *Truth and Deception: The Polygraph (lie-detector) Technique*, (Baltimore, MD: Williams & Wilkins, 1977). This is the bible of polygraphy and essential reading.

Sullivan, John F. *Of Spies and Lies, A CIA Lie Detector Remembers Vietnam* (Lawrence, KS: University Press of Kansas, 2004).

Sullivan, John F. *GATEKEEPER: Memoirs of a CIA Polygraph Examiner* (Washington, DC: Potomac Press, 2007).

Additionally, much information on the polygraph can be found online at *http://www.antipolygraph.org*.

John F. Sullivan was a polygraph examiner with the CIA from 1968 to 1999. Since retiring in 1999, he has written two books about polygraph in the CIA, lectured extensively, and served as a consultant and expert witness in law suits involving polygraph issues.

GUIDE TO THE STUDY OF INTELLIGENCE

A Guide to the Teaching About Covert Action

Jon A. Wiant

There is no action but covert action.

— Alec T. Quinn, 1967
(Pseudonym)

Introduction

The post 9/11 fascination with intelligence issues and the consequent growth of academic interest in intelligence have led to a significant expansion of intelligence courses and seminars. Some focus almost exclusively on analytical issues while other syllabi suggest a rambling through all sorts of subjects that might fall loosely under the umbrella of intelligence studies. This Guide focuses on teaching about covert action. First, we need to define what it is, and what it is not.

There is little discipline in the language of intelligence. Existing literature and our media use the terms "intelligence" and "spying" interchangeably, and few editors seem to ponder whether intelligence is an adjective or a noun. Similarly words like "covert" and "clandestine" are used synonymously when in both modern law and operational doctrine these terms have distinctly different meanings. Clandestine is properly associated with the secret collection of information where primary operational attention is placed on ensuring that the target is unaware that the protected information has been taken. In the covert world, the actions are readily apparent but every effort is made to hide those who are responsible for the actions.[1]

---

1. This attempt at lexical clarity undoubtedly will provoke some letters to the editor questioning whether the author has ever heard of covert SIGINT, a doctrinal term used by SIGINT collectors to cover secret forms of close-in signals collection. Similarly we use covert communications (COVCOM)

These actions run the gamut from influence and propaganda operations, not dissimilar from advertising campaigns, to complex programs seeking to destabilize a government or oust a tyrannical regime. These activities may include sub-rosa political warfare, economic dislocations, and the fomenting of political violence from street demonstrations to a coup d'état. In recent years, covert action has been used to strengthen the counterterrorist capabilities of other countries, or allow us to use direct action to preempt a terrorist attack or to capture or kill terrorists.

In the "Readings for Instructors" section, we will look at each type of covert action, but first another cautionary note is warranted about confusing covert action with intelligence operations. Covert action has little do with intelligence in so far as we define the functions of intelligence as collection and analysis or, more broadly, as a function of the intelligence cycle. **Covert action is a policy tool used along with other instruments of national power to achieve a national security objective.** While covert action is often performed by intelligence organizations, it is not an intelligence function nor must it inherently be conducted by an intelligence organization. There are, however, characteristics of intelligence organizations as well as operational tradecraft that can facilitate covert operations. This fact and some peculiarities of history result in these two operationally distinct and often conflicted responsibilities sharing the same organizational bed, albeit without great comfort.

What Is Covert Action?

Most of the techniques, the stratagems, the "dirty tricks" that today we associate with covert action are not new. To the contrary, both early Western and Eastern history are rich with examples of these practices. What makes "covert action" a modern concept is not the novelty of the actions but rather the institutionalization of operational responsibilities, the integration of the tools of covert action into broader national security and foreign policy programs, and codification of rules governing its practice.

We can find many examples of covert activities in World War I. The Germans, for instance, ran a very robust program in the United States prior to the US entry in the war; T. E. Lawrence's Bedouin army was prototypical of paramilitary resistance programs; and British black propaganda designed to shift world opinion against the "brutal Hun" had many of the qualities of modern psychological warfare.

Nevertheless, it is World War II and the mobilization of all forms of national power, that provided the foundation for the modern covert action

---

for communicating secretly with agents. Elsewhere in the Anglo-Saxon world we will find practitioners of clandestine warfare, a term that could mean covert paramilitary operations or it could also mean military special operations. Words do mean something and I will endeavor at least to be consistent with the definitions of covert and clandestine in this article.

organization and also presaged the difficult divisions of labor that develop between or among intelligence and military organizations over responsibilities for these activities. The British created a separate Special Operations Executive as part of "political warfare" to do activities that the British Secret Intelligence Service (SIS, or MI-6) was either unable or unwilling to do. America entered the war with neither a national intelligence service nor a capability for covert operations. Neither the Army nor the Navy had developed such capabilities and were reluctant to invest in them. They also opposed the creation of an independent organization to do either clandestine or covert missions. With much lobbying from the British, President Roosevelt ordered the creation of the Office of Strategic Services (OSS). It was chartered to do secret intelligence but also paramilitary special operations and psychological operations, at that time called "morale operations."

Historians debate the contributions of OSS and the British services to the overall war effort, though all have their advocates as well as detractors. There is, however, no consensus in either the British or the US military and foreign affairs organizations of the need to keep a special operations and political or psychological warfare capability in peacetime. The militaries see such organizations as an erosion of their responsibilities, the foreign affairs communities view the peace time practice of covert operations as incompatible with diplomatic relations, and the secret intelligence organizations argue that the very presence of covert operators can jeopardize the security environment for successful clandestine collection, seen by both SIS and the CIA, an OSS precursor, as their primary mission.[2]

Why is CIA the principal agency for conducting covert actions? The missions of the CIA other than to conduct covert actions are to collect foreign intelligence; perform independent, all-source assessments; and conduct counterintelligence overseas. Covert actions require foreign intelligence collection, all-source analysis, and counterintelligence to ensure the operation's security. So the agency's other missions fit well with the covert action role. CIA is also focused overseas. All other government agencies have a domestic (and in some cases also an overseas) focus. CIA is prohibited by law from having any police powers in the US and by policy from influencing domestic activities. CIA maintains a worldwide, clandestine infrastructure. This includes bases; safe houses; land, air, and sea logistics capabilities; foreign equipment; and covert financial and communications capabilities, all of which are necessary for covert

---

2. Peter Grose explores this tension in some detail in his biography of Allen Dulles, *Gentleman Spy* (New York: Houghton Mifflin, 1994). The deep divisions within CIA over the wisdom of combining covert action with secret intelligence were echoed elsewhere in the West. In his *The Secret History of MI6: 1909-1949* (New York: The Penguin Press, 2010) Keith Jeffrey draws on declassified MI6 documents as well as those from the Foreign Office to explore the spirited debate at the end of World War II whether MI-6 should inherit the wartime covert capabilities of the Special Operations Executive. This debate remains active today.

operations. Most importantly, covert action is an integral part of clandestine human intelligence, which is CIA's principal method of intelligence collection.

The advent of the Cold War in the late 1940's and the evolution of grand strategy to contain, if not rollback, international communism or Soviet imperialism created rich opportunities for the reintroduction of psychological warfare, support to anti-communist resistance groups, and covert support to contemplated military operations. The term "covert action" had not yet become an umbrella under which all of these activities would fit, but the Cold War generated interest and advocacy for these capabilities.

Cold War history provides a good framework for studying the evolution of covert action. While the full range of psychological warfare was directed toward the Soviet Union and the Warsaw Pact in the West and China and North Korea in the East, nationalist or anti-colonial movements also provided rich targets for covert action. These included countering subversion or destabilizing hostile regimes, shoring up newly independent governments or funding paramilitary programs seeking to defeat anti-colonial or nationalist liberation struggles. In the sharp bi-polar divide of the Cold War, there was little middle ground for the non-aligned. Covert programs became the way of policing the divide and destabilizing countries whose strategic direction threatened the balance of power.

In the United States, Congress seemed content to fund these activities even though there was no precise definition of what they were or who could perform them. In the wake of hearings on need for intelligence oversight, Congress passed reporting requirements on some forms of covert action, and the President used an Executive Order to specify CIA's general responsibilities for covert action. The Hughes-Ryan Amendment to the 1961 Foreign Assistance Act established the first formal reporting requirements for the President on covert action. Through legislation and the series of Executive Orders culminating in 12333, they remain valid today though only with some creative interpretations of restrictions recognizing the challenges of active global counterterrorist programs of both the CIA and the military services. This legislation specifically reinforced the ambiguous language of the National Security Act of 1947, Article V that authorized CIA to perform "other activities as may be directed by the NSC," the most cited justification for CIA's role in covert action.

Finally, a Definition

In 1991, Congress amended the National Security Act to provide a legal definition of covert action:

> Covert action is an activity or activities of the United States government to influence political, economic or military conditions abroad, where it is intended that the role of the United States Government will not be apparent or acknowledged publicly.[3]

---

3. The Intelligence Oversight Act of 1980 adopted as part of the Intelligence Authorization Act of 1991

Students should focus on the key definitional attributes:

First is the expression "to influence...." This establishes covert action's role to affect the outcome of national security objectives. In this sense, covert action is a tool of national security rather than a policy. A plea to "do more covert action" is a hollow expression without relating it to the broader objectives that are being pursued.

Second is the admonition that though these are activities of the US Government, they are conducted in such ways that the US Government's role "will not be apparent or acknowledged publicly." This is an interesting construction. It raises the question of why you have a public law discussing creation of capabilities that are designed to be plausibly deniable. This is not quite as 'Lewis Carroll' as some have suggested but is a good recognition that government must sometimes do things that will not be stated parts of a US policy. As the late Director of Central Intelligence William Colby, himself a strong proponent of covert action, observed, if we do not acknowledge a program formally we do not compel our adversaries to acknowledge it formally and place them in a position where they must act directly to counter it.[4]

In addition to defining "covert action" both legislation and executive direction have mandated how covert action is to be authorized, defined the instruments for that authorization, the procedures for ensuring regular policy review, and the obligations for legislative oversight.[5]

The 1975 Senate inquiry (Church Committee) into allegations of illegal activities by CIA and other intelligence agencies initially created the impression that a "rogue CIA" was conducting covert operations of its own making irrespective of US policy. To the contrary, subsequent investigation strongly disputed the image of an out-of-control CIA engaged in this dark world of its own making. Rather, there was compelling evidence that all programs under investigation had been, in fact, ordered up by a President or his staff.[6]

Congress directed that, in the future, the President must find the need for

---

50 USC 413.

4. William Colby. *Honorable Men* (New York: Simon and Schuster, 1978), 194-195.

5. For a brief review of history of covert action legislation, see Alfred Cummings, Covert Action: Legislative Background and Possible Policy Questions (Congressional Research Service, April 6, 2011). Loch Johnson's America's Secret Power: The CIA in a Democratic Society (New York: Oxford University Press, 1990) offers among the best insights into the legislative debate over covert action.

6. President Truman was enthusiastic about covert political and influence operations to shore up pro-Western allies as a covert complement to the Marshall Plan's reconstruction program. President Eisenhower continued many of the Truman programs but also ushered in programs to refashion governments or overthrow hostile regimes through significant paramilitary programs. Historians debate President Kennedy's reluctant embrace of anti-Castro operations including the calamitous 1961 Bay of Pigs invasion, but elsewhere he was a vigorous proponent of covert nation building and special operations; he not only gave Special Forces the Green Beret, he did much to foster operational collaboration between Special Forces and CIA in ways that presage similar cooperation on Afghan battlefields today. President Johnson had some wariness of CIA operations though these activities were central to his Vietnam and Laos policies. President Nixon's use of covert action to destabilize the Allende regime in Chile as well as conducting an aggressive political action program in Vietnam were major factors contributing to the Congressional inquiries.

specific covert action and report his decision formally using a document referred to as a "Finding."[7] The congressional intelligence committees must authorize the funding for a specific covert action. The House Permanent Select Committee on Intelligence (HPSCI) is the authorizing committee for covert action funding though it shares some overlapping jurisdictional responsibilities with the House Armed Services Committee and the House Appropriations Committee. On the Senate side, the Senate Select Committee on Intelligence (SSCI) primarily holds these responsibilities. Daugherty notes that President Carter issued Omnibus Findings to provide authority for global propaganda and influence operations as well as legal justification for maintaining covert action infrastructure and capabilities.[8] Findings must be presented to the oversight committees within a timely fashion; though Congress has not legislated a time period, both the President and Congressional leadership have accepted the general practice that CIA will notify Congress within 48 hours of the President signing a finding directing CIA to engage in covert action.

While early Findings may have been very brief, they have become increasingly detailed particularly regarding limitations on actions. A Finding must specifically authorize CIA to engage in lethal activity whether that is in some direct action or developing the capability for a foreign group to use a level of violence that might lead to death. Regardless of having authority to use lethal action, CIA is still governed by Executive Order 12333 prohibiting engagement in assassination or supporting a group that might target political leadership. CIA's commitment to conduct a global campaign against terrorists has required very specific guidance on targeting, and under current practice, the President must approve specific actions such as the successful attack on Osama bin Laden or the use of unmanned aerial vehicles strikes against targets beyond the regular battlefield.

Readings for Instructors

The history of US covert action includes issues of ever-changing US national security and foreign policy strategies, the growth of the national security bureaucracy, the evolution of presidential and executive power, and shifting American popular perceptions about the place of covert action in the conduct of American policy. The following works provide a good appreciation for this complex interplay principally over the course of our post-World War II history including the Cold War and the post 9/11 shifts in national security policies:

Daugherty. William J. *Executive Secrets: Covert Action and the Presidency* (The University Press of Kentucky, 2004). This is a basic text on covert action

---

7. Executive Order 12333 and National Security Decision Directive 286 established the responsibilities for coordination within the Executive Branch prior to the notification of the Finding to Congress.
8. Daugherty, 184-185

that broadly ranges over both doctrine and practice. Some of his political observations and his defensiveness of some less successful operations occasionally detract from the overall excellent treatment of covert action.

Prados, John. *Safe for Democracy: The Secret Wars of the CIA* (Chicago: Ivan R. Dee, 2006). Prados' work spans the post-World War II period and treats both large programs and many smaller covert initiatives with careful scholarship, albeit offered up with a critical eye.

Ranelagh, John. *The Agency: The Rise and Decline of the CIA* (New York: Simon and Schuster, 1986). While now dated, this is a good, basic history of CIA that offers some "insiders' view" of covert action in the 1950s and 1960s. Several retired officers were interviewed in the work. Ranelagh's companion six-hour documentary film produced by BBC offers much commentary and illustration of early covert action program, a welcome classroom supplement to lectures. Among the teaching moments is William Sloane Coffin's reflections on his work on early Eastern European paramilitary programs, long before he became a noted theologian and sharp critic of the Vietnam War.

We have already noted that the covert action concept has been treated under a variety of names and euphemisms ranging from psychological warfare and dirty tricks to political warfare or special activities. Mark Lowenthal in his widely used textbook *From Secrets to Policy*, 5th Ed. (Washington: CQ Press, 2012) in Chapter 8 discusses covert action in terms of six analytically distinct activities:

Propaganda

This includes the covert development and placement of information in print and radio and television media as well as the use of agents of influence. Hugh Wilford's *The Mighty Wurlitzer: How the CIA Played America* (Cambridge: Harvard University Press, 2008) is among the best treatments of these activities during the Cold War. *Victory: The Reagan Administration's Secret Strategy that Hastened the Collapse of the Soviet Union* (New York: The Atlantic Monthly Press, 1966) by Peter Schweizer, explores many of the Reagan initiatives used to erode support within the Soviet Union and Eastern Europe. Milt Bearden and James Risen offer a compelling "last chapter" on the Cold War conflict in *The Main Enemy: The Inside Story of CIA's Final Showdown with the KGB* (New York: Random House, 2003).

Political activity

Covert work in the political realm can include everything from *sub rosa* financing of political and campaign consultants to "buying" elections by funneling large sums of money to candidates to purchase blocs of voting. Prados and Ranelagh, as well as many others, treat the 1948 Italian presidential election as a textbook case of covert political activity. A detailed examination of the policy discussions over the decision to influence an early 1960s Guyanese presidential election is an excellent case study of both costs and benefits of such operations (See Prados, 3-19). Since the 1980s, the openly funded National Endowment for Democracy (NED) has assisted many political activities that once would have been handled covertly. Congress has generally refused to fund covert activities that could or are being conducted by NED. "Arab Spring" has again raised questions whether we still need the flexibility to work covertly, as well as overtly, with helping resistance movements transform themselves into governing authorities.

Economic activity

President Kennedy authorized sabotage against Cuban sugar mills as a covert means for undermining the Cuban economy. President Nixon responded to Chilean President Allende's nationalization of American-owned industries with robust covert initiatives to forestall Allende's consolidation of the Chilean economy. This covert action grew into a more comprehensive covert campaign to overthrow Allende. The US Senate published an extraordinary collection of both policy documents and CIA operational traffic spanning 1970 to 1973, when the Chilean military overthrew Allende. (University Press of the Pacific, 1978).

The controversial covert mining of the Nicaraguan harbors in the mid-1980s was authorized as a way of blocking Nicaraguan exports and imports by creating the impression that the waterways around Nicaraguan were unsafe for navigation. It was hoped that this situation would lead the Lloyds of London insurance underwriters to raise insurance rates to the point where cost of maritime trade with Nicaragua would become prohibitively costly – thus creating a kind of trade embargo. Duane R. Clarridge, the architect of this operation, discusses its varied objectives in his memoir *A Spy for All Seasons* (New York, Scribner's, 1998).

Coups

The covert overthrow of a government can run the gamut of activities from subversion and the fomenting of violence that erodes the foundation of a government to the covert sponsorship of forces taking a government out by a coup d'état. The early cases cited in every CIA history are Iran in 1953 and Guatemala in 1954. Good history work has doggedly followed these situations so that 50 years later we have reasonably comprehensive histories of the covert actions. Steven Kinzer's *All the Shah's Men: An American Coup and the Roots of Middle East Terror* (New York: John Wiley and Sons, 2003) is excellent both on the history of the action and the longer term consequences. The best case study on Guatemala is Stephen Kinzer's *Bitter Fruit: The Story of the American Coup in Guatemala*, Revised and Expanded (New York: The David Rockefeller Series on Latin America Studies, 2003). A useful classroom supplement is *Secret History: The CIA Classified Account of its Operations in Guatemala 1952-1954* by Nick Cullather (Palo Alto, CA: Stanford University Press, 2006). Other covert involvement in coups include the 1963 overthrow of Vietnamese President Ngo Dinh Diem, the aforementioned 1973 Allende overthrow, and the killing of African leader Patrice Lumumba. Despite compelling evidence to the contrary, many authors and others treat these coups as examples of CIA engaging in assassination. Coups inevitably carry the prospect of the death of the overthrown leader, but, since 1975, the President has explicitly forbade by Executive Order for CIA either to conduct political assassination or to work with groups that may have that as their intent. The December 1989 military Operation Just Cause targeted against Panamanian strongman Manuel Noriega was developed as an alternative when Congressional oversight committees refused to fund

CIA's program to topple Noriega for fear that it involved Panamanians who might kill Noriega. (Daugherty, 93).

Paramilitary operations

Since its founding, CIA has had a paramilitary responsibility and capability, though not all Presidents have been enthusiastic about using it. The paramilitary responsibility spans a wide range of activities. It is most commonly used quietly to provide training assistance and material to countries that need assistance in leadership protection, countering narcotics traffickers or combatting terrorism. As an alternative to overt military assistance and training, CIA training offers the possibility of receiving training and material without the government having to acknowledge the assistance.

But CIA's paramilitary responsibilities also include the ability to raise, train, arm, and direct a covert paramilitary force to support some broader US national security objective. Over the last 65 years this has involved numerous programs.

Early in its history, CIA supported a number of unsuccessful anti-Communist resistance programs in the new Soviet Union and Eastern Bloc countries. These included operations in the Baltics, Ukraine, and Albania. All failed, though whether the reasons for failure were compromises by traitors within the ranks, or simply because the time had passed for such large-scale operations, remains debated. For study purposes a number of these programs are discussed in Ranelagh's *The Agency: The Rise and Decline of the CIA*.

CIA's involvement in the anti-Castro operation, codenamed Zapata, almost ended its paramilitary responsibilities. It is best remembered for the Bay of Pigs disaster and it serves as a case study for the problems of mounting a large-scale paramilitary overthrow program. Most of CIA's own inspector general's scathing review of the operation is available in redacted versions at CIA's website in the historical section. There are also numerous books looking at the campaign from a broad policy perspective down to individual accounts of both CIA and Cuban participants. The aftermath left CIA with a cadre of anti-Communist Cuban paramilitary specialists who subsequently served in operations in Africa, Southeast Asia, and Latin America.

CIA conducted a multitude of covert paramilitary operations in East Asia beginning with attempts to support anti-Communist guerillas on China's southern border in Thailand and Burma. This program was continuously complicated by allegations that the units were involved in narcotics trafficking. CIA also ran a long program of covert support for Tibetan rebels, but this terminated with the normalization of US-Chinese relations. CIA played a key psychological and paramilitary role in shoring up Philippine President Magsaysay in his counterinsurgency efforts against the Communist-supported Huk movement. CIA was much less successful with a 1958 covert program to support paramilitary opposition to Indonesian President Sukarno, and likewise failed in a modest effort to unseat Cambodian King Sihanouk in the same year.

CIA had an instrumental role in shaping South Vietnam from 1954 on, and it worked closely with US Army Special Forces with the mountain dwelling tribes along the Ho Chi Minh Trail. CIA also conducted deep penetrations into North Vietnam in an effort to organize resistance to the North Vietnam regime. While the US military increasingly transformed Vietnam into a more conventional military conflict, CIA did retain a key role in the pacification program. Critics have often characterized CIA's engagement in Operation Phoenix as an assassination campaign, but it was just one element of the pacification program and careful historical work has rebutted many of these allegations. Two works are especially commended here: Thomas Ahern's *Vietnam Declassified: The CIA and Counterinsurgency* (University Press of Kentucky, 2010) and William Colby's *Lost Victory: A Firsthand Account of America's Sixteen-Year Involvement in Vietnam* (Contemporary Books, 1989).

While Vietnam was something of a sideshow for CIA once the major US military commitment began in 1964, CIA's "war" in Laos was its largest paramilitary program during the Vietnam War. Kenneth Conboy's *Shadow War: The CIA's Secret War in Laos* (Paladin Press, 1995) is a useful work on this period because it includes a wealth of pictures provided by CIA veterans of the campaign. Also recommended is Roger Warner's *Shooting at the Moon: The Story of America's Clandestine War in Laos* (Steerforth Press, 1998). CIA's ability to create covertly infrastructure and capabilities became widely known during this period through accounts of Air America, a CIA proprietary firm. See William M. Leary's *Perilous Missions: Civil Air Transport and CIA Covert Operations in Asia* (The University of Alabama Press, 1984).

President Reagan ordered a number of major covert paramilitary operations, though President Carter signed the first Findings on a number of them. The program to block the Soviet occupation of Afghanistan was then considered among the most successful covert programs though much of it was openly discussed in the press. Reagan's Central America initiatives, however, were much more controversial and ended in the Iran-Contra affair where CIA and the administration were investigated for conducting covertly activities that had been prohibited by US law. Bob Woodward's *Veil: The Secret Wars of the CIA 1981-1987* (New York: Simon and Shuster, 1987) has a contemporary account of these programs though the book itself became controversial over the credibility of Woodward's account of death bed discussions with former DCI William Casey. The Reagan doctrine programs are also well discussed in both Daugherty and Prados.

Though CIA wound down its paramilitary capability at the end of the Cold War and dismantled much of its infrastructure for supporting paramilitary operations, the events of 9/11 and President George W. Bush's decision to pursue aggressively Al–Qa-ida and Osama bin Laden resulted in a substantial rebuilding of CIA's paramilitary capabilities over the next 10 years. Afghanistan became a major CIA theater. The man who led the initial CIA paramilitary team into Afghanistan a little more than a month after the attack of 9/11 wrote a revealing book about the operation. See Gary C. Schroen *First In: an Insider's Account of How the CIA Spearheaded the War on Terror in Afghanistan* (New York: Valentine Books, 2005). Also see Steve Coll *Ghost Wars: The Secret History of the CIA, Afghanistan, and Bin Laden, from the Soviet Invasion to September 10, 2001* (New York, Penguin Press, 2004). This is probably the best analysis of US policy, including covert actions, in the region to date.

To these traditional activities we should add another: "support to liaison." While we generally think of receiving intelligence information through liaison, we might also engage a liaison service to join us in the conduct of one or more of the other forms of covert action or we might covertly provide them technical assistance and training as discussed above.

Lowenthal notes that others have employed an additional activity – support to military operations, including covert preparations for overt military action. At the same time, the significant expansion of military special operations has sometimes blurred the distinction between covert action on the one hand, and secret operations, on the other. On the global battlefield of counterterrorism, a military "advanced clandestine support to military operations" (ACSMO) has many of the same definitional attributes of "covert action."

Finally, there are also significant questions about whether "information operations" can be a separate form of covert action. The expanding world of cyber warfare and information operations is another area the where division of labor and authorities for action remain ill defined. Covert attempts to disable computers engaged in weapons research and development may technically fall within the realm of peacetime covert action. Defense cyber warfare doctrine includes computer network attacks against command and control communications and denial of communications service. Both of these could be construed as overt acts of war.

One final word on the topic of covert action: For a secret subject, covert action has resulted in a voluminous bibliography. Works cited here have withstood considerable critical review. On the other hand, many authors confuse fact and fiction. Information has been leaked to cast favor on an initiative or to generate public opposition to the activity. Some is written with such flights of fancy that the writing has little tie to reality. On the other hand, critical and polemical attacks on covert action sometimes have some truth to them. Rigorous reading and spirited classroom discussions help to sort out the good from the bad.

Jon A. Wiant is a retired intelligence officer. During his 36 years with the government, Mr. Wiant served in senior positions at the Departments of State and Defense, Central Intelligence Agency, and the White House. He was twice deputy assistant secretary of state for intelligence and also was director for intelligence policy on the National Security Council. He graduated from the University of Colorado and was a Danforth Fellow at Cornell University. He was awarded the National Intelligence Distinguished Service Medal and is a decorated Vietnam combat veteran. In retirement, Mr. Wiant was professor of intelligence history at the National Defense Intelligence College and is currently an adjunct professor at George Washington University Elliott School of International Affairs.

Part V – Policy, Oversight, and Issues

Ye shall know the truth, and the truth shall make you free.

— John 8:32.
Inscription on wall in entry hall
of Central Intelligence Agency.

David Shedd, former Special Assistant to the President and Senior National Security Council Director for Intelligence Programs and Reform, in an interview with AFIO, discusses how intelligence is provided to, flows, and is used in the White House and the National Security Council.

Intelligence and diplomacy have an intimate relationship. But it is not always harmonious. As **Ambassador G. Philip Hughes** and **Peter Oleson** explain in their article, "Diplomacy & Intelligence: Strange Bedfellows," the two are mutually dependent, are beneficial for the nation when they work together, but often cause problems for each other.

Carl Ford, Secretary of State Colin Powell's intelligence officer, explains how the department's Bureau of Intelligence and Research (INR) focused its intelligence support on meeting the secretary's needs. He notes in his "Perspective on Intelligence Support to Foreign Policy" how the intelligence system is often not well geared to supporting policymakers.

University of Maryland Professor **Bill Nolte** was the first chancellor of the National Intelligence University and a career National Security Agency official. He reviews the never-ending efforts to "reform" intelligence that began soon after the enactment of the National Security Act in 1947 and the consequent reorganizations of the Intelligence Community.

While much study is focused on intelligence policies, policy implementation always requires dedicated resources. Many policy debates are contested in the resource allocation process – called programming and budgeting. Professor **Robert Mirabello**'s article, "Guide for the Study of Intelligence: Budget and Resource Management," explains the complex and sometimes arcane programming and budgeting process for the Intelligence Community. Understanding this oft-subterranean topic is essential to understanding intelligence policies.

Political scientist **Tobias Gibson** outlines in his article, "A Guide to Intelligence Oversight Design," the complex oversight that exists within the Executive, Legislative, and Judicial Branches of the US Government.

Jan Herring, a founding member of the Society of Competitive Intelligence Professionals (SCIP) and former National Intelligence Officer for Science and Technology, discusses the privatization of intelligence, the merger of public and private intelligence concerns, and the future environment for intelligence officers in his article "Educating the Next Generation of Intelligence Professionals."

While the 9/11 Commission of 2004 on the terrorist attacks on the US is well known, the 2005 WMD Commission is less well known. Yet the WMD Commission, officially the "Commission on the Intelligence Capabilities of the United States Regarding Weapons of Mass Destruction" and unofficially the "Silberman-Robb Commission," has had a significant impact on the Intelligence Community. More widely focused than on just the failure to understand the Iraqi WMD program, the WMD Commission made many recommendations to improve the collection, analysis, and dissemination of intelligence, putting meat on the bones of the 9/11 Commission recommendations. **Elbridge Colby** and **Stewart Baker**, both staff members of the WMD Commission, in their article provide considerable insight into this most significant commission.

How does international law govern intelligence collection or covert actions? Attorney **Ernesto Sanchez** explores many of the treaties, conventions, and International Court of Justice determinations in his article on international law and intelligence.

James Bruce, former chairman of the Intelligence Community's Foreign Denial and Deception Committee and Deputy National Intelligence Officer for Science and Technology, examines a continuing problem for the Intelligence Community in his piece "Keeping U.S. National Security Secrets: Why is it so Hard?" He addresses both spies and leaks to the press.

Thomas Spencer and **F.W. Rustmann, Jr.** in their article "The History of the States Secret Privilege" address the conflict between our open society and state secrets. They detail the conflicts that emerged early in our constitutional history and cases that have shaped today's secrecy policies.

Dr. Jan Goldman has focused on the ethical aspects of intelligence and is the editor of the International Journal of Intelligence and Ethics. His newly updated article on teaching about intelligence and ethics surveys the literature relevant to the debate over the ethics of intelligence that has evolved over the years. He presents a rich list of readings on the topic.

> *"What concerns me are the people who think they know what the future is going to look like. Our experience tells us we don't."*
>
> — General Joseph F. Dunford, Jr.,
> U.S. Marine Corps at his confirmation hearing
> to be Chairman of the Joint Chiefs of Staff
> before the Senate Armed Services Committee, July 9, 2015.

GUIDE TO THE STUDY OF INTELLIGENCE

Intelligence in the White House:

A Conversation With David R. Shedd

N. John MacGaffin and Peter C. Oleson

How intelligence is handled in the White House is little written about. Most references are in former officials' retrospectives that are largely anecdotal. To get a sense of how intelligence is handled in the White House, AFIO board members John MacGaffin and Peter Oleson sat down with David Shedd during the summer of 2015 to discuss the subject.

David Shedd served on the National Security Council (NSC) staff from February 2001 until May 2005, during the first term of President George W. Bush. Dr. Condoleezza Rice was the national security advisor. (She became secretary of state on January 26, 2005 and was succeeded as national security advisor by Stephen Hadley.)

Shedd was a career CIA official. Born in Bolivia in 1959 to missionary parents, he lived in Chile from 1962 to 1972 and finished his high school years in Uruguay. He recalls a home where discussions of world affairs figured prominently. In December 1971, he saw Cuban President Fidel Castro up close and personal when the Cuban revolutionary visited Chile, which had recognized Cuba diplomatically. This early exposure to often turbulent Latin American affairs and culture peaked his interest in international relations. While in graduate school at Georgetown University, he applied and was accepted into the Foreign Service.

In 1984, he served as a State Department Foreign Service political officer working at the US Embassy in Costa Rica. In 1988, he was posted to Mexico City and focused on a wide array of bilateral issues of importance to the United States, including the North American Free Trade Agreement (NAFTA). After five years, he returned to Washington, DC. After joining the CIA in the mid-1990s, he served as chief of operations for the Directorate of Operations Counterproliferation Division, where he was deeply involved in the unraveling of A. Q. Khan's international nuclear weapons technology proliferation network.[1]

After a stint in CIA's Congressional Affairs in 2000, Shedd joined the NSC staff in January 2001 serving in the Office of Intelligence Programs, becoming in 2004 the senior director and special assistant to the President for intelligence matters. Initially, he was responsible for overseeing at the beginning of the George W. Bush administration the NSC's covert action portfolio inherited from the Clinton Administration. The September 11, 2001 Al-Qa'ida attacks on the homeland changed the landscape as the President unleashed CIA and the military to use expanded authorities to address the threats posed by Al-Qa'ida and its leader, Osama bin Laden.

Shedd departed the NSC staff in May 2005 to go to the newly established Office of the Director of National Intelligence (DNI) to serve under the first DNI, Ambassador John Negroponte, and his deputy, US Air Force General Michael Hayden as chief of staff. Shedd had served under Negroponte when he was ambassador in Mexico. Later, Shedd became the deputy DNI for policy, plans, and requirements for Vice Admiral Michael McConnell (Ret.), the second DNI. He undertook the tasks to update Executive Order 12333, which governs all US intelligence activities, and the amendments to the Foreign Intelligence Surveillance Act (FISA) governing the National Security Agency's and the FBI's counterterrorism surveillance efforts.

Ready to retire in 2010, Shedd instead was tapped to be the deputy director of the Defense Intelligence Agency. With a son serving in the military in Iraq, he felt an obligation to continue his service. He became DIA acting director in August 2014 when the director, US Army Lieutenant General Michael Flynn, retired. Shedd retired from government service in February 2015, shortly after Marine Corps Lieutenant General Vincent R. Stewart was confirmed as DIA's 20th director.

AFIO: David, how would you describe your career?

Shedd: To this day, I consider myself to be among the most fortunate officers to serve in the US Government as a result of the enormous variety of challenging and equally exciting opportunities. The exposure to witness how and where intelligence informs (or can misguide) policy was an extraordinary privilege during the first decade of the 21st century. Other than my initial applications to each government agency or department I never applied for another job or position. For nearly 33 years, I always was asked to serve. I have no regrets.

AFIO: Let's discuss the policymaker's perspective. How do they get their

---

1. A. Q. Khan's international proliferation activities are described in William Langewiesche's two articles, "The Wrath of Khan: How A. Q. Khan made Pakistan a nuclear power – and showed that the spread of nuclear weapons can't be stopped," The Atlantic (November 2005), and "The Point of No Return," *The Atlantic* (January/February 2006); and by Gordon Corera, *Shopping for Bombs: Nuclear Proliferation, Global Insecurity, and the Rise and Fall of the A.Q. Khan Network* (Oxford: Oxford University Press, 2006).

intelligence? How do they determine what to focus on vice ignore?

Shedd: Presidents along with the top national security officials in any administration get their decision-making information – with intelligence being a subset to information – from a wide array of sources. Many of those sources are external to the Intelligence Community. Of course, every President since Truman gets an intelligence briefing. Some get this on a daily basis; others opt to get it on a more ad hoc schedule. President Bush relied heavily on his intelligence briefer who he saw usually six days a week. He also used his personal relationships around the globe, often meeting or calling world leaders. Intelligence was just one of the many feeds he relied upon to gain insights and better understand the world and presumably make his decisions.

Headline issues, of course, command the attention of the president and therefore much of the daily intelligence production. But the focus of intelligence support to the White House is set by the President's interests as well as his schedule to include travel, visits by foreign dignitaries, or planned telephone calls with foreign leaders or others. Concerns of congressmen and senators also affect the President's attention. Less urgent issues are of lower priority and await their turn. The time available limits what one can pay attention to.

It is important to note that intelligence is an educational tool for policy-makers.[2] The Intelligence Community provides much of the analysis affecting and even enabling national security decision-making. Presidents rely on the Intelligence Community for background information on various topics, as do Cabinet members and sub-cabinet members and staff of the National Security Council. The national security advisor, as was the case with Dr. Rice and Steve Hadley, were highly reliable conduits for understanding what the President requires by way of intelligence support. They each brought a long history of policy experience to the job.

AFIO: What are the principal intelligence concerns that a president has?

Shedd: First, no one likes surprises; the President is no exception to that rule. But, of course, surprises happen. The worst in recent history was 9/11 – undoubtedly the worst since December 7, 1941. But Presidents are resilient after campaigning for office. They seem to know how to react to surprises. But warning is at the top of the list of the intelligence delivery priorities. Every President wants the time to forestall adverse events and be able to plan and develop options on how to respond. Our U-2 photography of Cuba in 1962 gave President Kennedy the time he needed to respond effectively. That was intelligence at its best in a crisis.

Every President is torn between immediate problems and long-term concerns. Intelligence has to respond to both. President Bush learned to step

---

2. Jack Davis, a legendary CIA analyst, interviewed Ambassador Robert D. Blackwell in the early 1990s and wrote an article entitled "A Policymaker's Perspective on Intelligence Analysis," which expounds on how policymakers need and use intelligence. *https://www.cia.gov/library/center-for-the-study-of-intelligence/csi-publications/csi-studies/studies/95unclass/Davis.html* .

back from the immediate concerns to gain long-term strategic understanding of situations. As one example, he was particularly concerned with trying to understand the thinking of then North Korea's leader, Kim Jong-il. Obtaining a better understanding of Kim's motivations was critical given the aggressive North Korean reliance on pursuing nuclear weapons.[3] At the same time, President Bush's compassion for the North Korean people was evident in trying to understand why the despotic leader in P'yongyang was intent on starving many of his people. Things have not changed much under Kim Jong-un. The President began what we called "deep dives" into various subjects, getting in-depth briefings and analyses.

Rapid changes in world events most often dictate what become a president's intelligence needs. This is especially true for a global power such as the United States.

AFIO: The President's Daily Brief (PDB) is the principal Intelligence Community vehicle for informing the President of important matters. What was your involvement with it?

THE PRESIDENT'S DAILY BRIEF (PDB)

"Today, the PDB is an IC product coordinated by ODNI's PDB staff in partnership with the CIA Directorate of Intelligence (DI)'s President's Analytic Support Staff. It is still [the] all-source publication that the president relies upon heavily to inform his national security decisions, and CIA analysts remain primary contributors. The style, format and presentation of the PDB are based on the preferences of the current president. President Barack Obama, for example, asked CIA to explore a way to deliver the PDB electronically. On Feb. 15, 2014—68 years after the first Daily Summary was published—the final hard copy edition of the PDB was printed. President Obama and other key national security policymakers now receive the PDB, six days a week, in a tablet format."

"The Evolution of the President's Daily Brief," Central Intelligence Agency, https://www.cia.gov/news-information/featured-story-archive/2014-featured-story-archive/the-evolution-of-the-presidents-daily-brief.html.

Shedd: As the special assistant to the President for intelligence programs and reform, I would read the PDB daily. However, I did not attend the Oval Office meetings. The PDB briefer would come to my office and I would read it so I would know what was of concern to the President and the national security advisor. I was not involved in its preparation, of course; that was the responsibility of the director of central intelligence until a DNI came into existence in the spring of 2005. The PDB as a product served as a catalyst for instigating wide-ranging national security discussions in Oval Office.

AFIO: What other intelligence does a President receive that does not come via the PDB? For example, from the Department of Homeland Security, the Federal Bureau of Investigation, and others?

---

3. North Korea tested its first nuclear weapon in October 2006.

Shedd: The Department of Justice, the FBI, Homeland Security, and other departments and agencies provide information to the President. Some is presented orally face-to-face, such as FBI Director Mueller would do when briefing the president; other is via written product channeled through the national security advisor or, when I was at the NSC, the homeland security advisor.

As important as intelligence is as both a product and a service for the President and his national security cabinet, networking by President Bush and his senior White House officials with foreign counterparts, politicians, and experts were an important source of information. The President was a natural networker. He trusted some foreign leaders and spoke to them often. The national security advisors – Condi Rice and Steve Hadley – facilitated the President's discussions with relevant experts outside of government. He reportedly read a book a week. It was not unusual that when a topic interested or concerned him, he would ask for in-depth briefings from the Intelligence Community.

AFIO: How is the NSC process informed by intelligence?

Shedd: Intelligence for the NSC customers is often prepared for them based on specific policy issues or questions. As such, it can be a somewhat scattered process on a day-to-day basis. It is normal for the president's national security advisor to sit in the Oval Office for the PDB briefing and subsequent discussions. Dr. Rice or Steve Hadley would often review the PDB items before the Oval Office meeting to be prepared for the discussions that some of the items would engender. Below their level, the senior NSC staff developed contacts with CIA or others in the Intelligence Community to serve their specialized needs. Many of the senior NSC staff members had an IC briefer that they relied on keep them informed on specific topics germane to their geographic or transnational portfolio. The Intelligence Directorate on the NSC staff also served at times as a facilitator for other NSC Directorates in arranging for expert matter intelligence briefs or written products.

The intelligence support process becomes more focused and in-depth when the NSC itself is focused on an issue or a policy development. Specialized intelligence analyses, to include sometimes National Intelligence Estimates – NIEs – the most formal strategic-level assessments of the community, were commissioned at times to support the efforts of the Policy Coordination Committee [PCC] deliberations.[4] The PCC was made up of assistant – and undersecretary-level officials from the national security departments, ODNI – once established – and CIA. Additional intelligence support might be needed to support the Deputies Committee [comprising the deputy secretaries of the same departments], or the Principals Committee.[5] One of my responsibilities

---

4. In the Obama Administration, the PCC is renamed the Interagency Policy Committee (IPC). Presidential Policy Directive – 1, February 13, 2009.

5. Today, the NSC principals include the President, vice president, secretaries of state, treasury, de-

was to ensure the intelligence support needed by these convening bodies of the NSC process was provided. For matters pertaining to intelligence and counterintelligence of interagency interest, I chaired the PCC.

Over time in the Administration's timetable in office, as the national security principals become better informed and more comfortable with what intelligence can and cannot do for them, the requirements for intelligence contributions evolve to suit the customer's needs. While there was no way of getting away from the daily intelligence feed that addresses current issues via the PDB and other current intelligence products, national security policy customers from the President on down began to take an interest in obtaining more in-depth intelligence briefings on specific topics. President Bush, with the strong support from Dr. Rice and Steve Hadley, welcomed deep dives that brought intelligence subject matter experts on a specific topic into the Oval Office. These topics were often identified in advance to CIA and other Community elements so as to bring the best expertise together for the conversation with the principals, often times the President himself. For example, if a CIA Chief of Station was available on travel back from his/her overseas location, he/she often joined the "deep dive" since they could provide a unique perspective based on the location where they were stationed and the topic which was the subject for in-depth briefing and discussion. This type of focused and often intense review of a difficult topic would give the national security team members an opportunity to iterate themselves through various scenarios with variants on policy outcomes.

AFIO: What role does the White House Situation Room play in serving the President with intelligence?

Shedd: As it pertains to intelligence, the Situation Room — affectionately known as the Sit Room — is a 24/7 watch nerve center used to highlight fast breaking events to White House principals, including the President. It is tied to all of the various intelligence community operations centers, the National Military Command Center, and others, such as FEMA. A CRITIC message generated anywhere in the world would arrive in the Sit Room; the watch officers, mostly on loan from various agencies, delivered the intelligence to the national security advisor or her deputy immediately. Depending on the intelligence the president may be alerted immediately, including at night, or at the first convenient moment. The Sit Room staff would often task the PDB staff — or relay tasks from a White House principal — to address a fast breaking item that arrived in the night at the morning briefing.

President Bush would visit the Sit Room from time to time to talk to the staff. He was appreciative of their efforts.

---

fense, homeland security, and energy, the attorney general, the national security advisor, White House chief of staff, and the US representative to the United Nations. Statutory advisors include the DNI and chairman, Joint Chiefs of Staff. Others often attend too.

AFIO: How does the national security advisor and the NSC staff impact the intelligence provided to the president? The vice president?

Shedd: Personalities are important. The national security advisor is very influential in this regard. Condi Rice managed the intelligence going into the Oval Office. Condi — and Steve Hadley — were focused on creating a team atmosphere – and did so adroitly – in service the President. She would walk over to NSC staff member's offices to talk and asked for advice from her experts. I felt like an advisor, not just a staffer.

When Steve Hadley took over from Condi, he brought his personality to the job. He was meticulous about details. However, like Condi, Steve did not want to be a barrier to what he believed the President needed to know.

The NSC is a flat organization – or at least it was during my time on the NSC staff between 2001-2005. The environment is highly collaborative with directors having different portfolios that overlap, especially where transnational issues are concerned. So collaboration is essential. I would work with other NSC staff directors regarding their intelligence needs, making sure their needs were understood by the Intelligence Community and those needs were met.

The vice president had his own staff, including a national security advisor. While the NSC staff would support the vice president as tasked, he and his staff often pursued matters of interest independently. Vice President Chaney, who had been secretary of defense previously, was well familiar with the Intelligence Community, and knew how to leverage it for the intelligence support he was seeking.

At no time in my four plus years in the NSC did I feel pressured by any one on the NSC staff, White House policy officials, or by the vice president and/or his staff to alter a single intelligence judgment. It was important to know your subject thoroughly and stick to one's convictions based on the available intelligence on any given topic. I sensed there were some in the administration with strong pre-conceived notions about Iraq and what we should do. Non-intelligence decisions were made as a policy matter, such as the decision to pursue the removal of all Baathists from virtually all positions of any influence in Iraq.

AFIO: David, what was your experience serving the intelligence needs of the White House?

Shedd: When I first joined the NSC staff, I was the director of special programs, under the senior director and special assistant to the President for intelligence programs, Mary McCarthy. I focused on the presidential programs known as covert action. As you can imagine after 9/11, the President and his national security cabinet expanded significantly the focus on counterterrorism especially as it pertained to Al-Qa'ida as perpetrators of the 9/11 attacks on the homeland and on their presence in Afghanistan. I was responsible for helping address what additional authorities were needed for elements of the US Government to address potential additional threats from Al-Qa'ida. The President attached great urgency to responding to the attacks of 9/11 and determining what authorities were needed to combat Al-Qa'ida. That urgency was matched by a flurry of policy and legal support.

My job changed when I was named senior director and special assistant to the President for intelligence programs and reform — this was after the passage of the 2004 Intelligence Reform and Terrorism Prevention Act, IRTPA. My principal responsibility was to make sure that the national security advisor and her deputy alongside of the homeland security advisor, Fran Townsend, were kept informed of anything significant related to the Intelligence Community, intelligence operations, and the reform efforts recommended by the 9/11 Commission, the WMD Commission, or mandated in the IRTPA. I also had to stay informed of any recommendations to the president that came from the independent President's Intelligence Advisory Board (PIAB), made up of prominent individuals and experts outside of government.

One meeting that had a long and valuable tradition was the weekly meeting between the DCI and the NSC leadership. This meeting, hosted by the national security advisor, was subsequently expanded to include the homeland security advisor, the DNI — post IRTPA legislation — and the DCIA, when the title of DCI was overtaken by the 2004 IRTPA. The meeting provided a venue for candid exchanges on any intelligence topic that needed an airing by the one of the principals. I organized that agenda for Dr. Rice and/or Steve Hadley. The session often resulted in providing the requisite heads up on unfolding high impact intelligence issues or to impart guidance by the national security advisor.

The average day for me began at 7am and often did not end until 7 in the evening. The topics that one covered on any given day always seemed different from what was originally planned. As noted previously, fostering good relationships among the colleagues on the NSC staff was critical to managing the issues. No finger pointing, a willingness to always help a colleague, and integrity were all vital to making the NSC staff function properly.

AFIO: What makes a good intelligence officer working with and on policy matters?

Shedd: Supporting the decision makers, of which the policymaker is a key person, is the ultimate goal of intelligence. In the case of serving on the NSC staff, a good intelligence officer has to stay tethered to the policymaker to understand his or her needs. The intelligence officer has to anticipate what the policymaker is likely to need in terms of knowledge and understanding. But it is essential to keep any personal or institutional biases out of the intelligence or recommendations provided to a policymaker. Jack Webb, in the old TV drama, Dragnet, had it right: "Just the facts." A good intelligence officer needs constantly to be educating the policymaker as to what intelligence can and, as importantly, cannot do for them as a policymaker. This means, at times, delivering intelligence that is not necessarily welcome because the new information and/or assessments complicate life for the policymaker.

Long after I departed the NSC staff and was serving in the ODNI, I led the Intelligence Community's 2008 transition team for the Presidential succession. I did so from my position in the ODNI. I learned from that experience how different individuals receive intelligence in different ways. A good intelligence officer adjusts how intelligence is communicated to match how the recipient wants to receive it while never compromising the bottom line judgments made by the Intelligence Community. President Kennedy wanted his briefing in a form he could put in his pocket. President Johnson preferred a tabloid format. President George W. Bush liked being briefed orally. President Obama uses an electronic notepad. Everyone is different.

AFIO: Did you interact with the White House when you served at CIA and in the ODNI?

Shedd: Yes, I did. In my various senior positions in support of policy deliberations I was often at the White House — and Old Executive Office Building. As chief of staff for the DNI, I was also involved in keeping the NSC informed on the progress and issues related to the Intelligence Community reform efforts.

AFIO: When you went to the Defense Intelligence Agency was your White House interaction different?

Shedd: Note the D in DIA, it stands for Defense. While one of the major agencies in the Intelligence Community, DIA is nonetheless more focused on its customers within the Department of Defense and the combatant commands around the world. Most of the policy issues involving the White House were handled by the undersecretary of defense for intelligence, USD(I). For my tenure at DIA, this was Mike Vickers, who had previously been the assistant secretary of defense for special operations and low-intensity conflict — ASD/SOLIC. I did have to interact with the White House staff on issues related to the prisoners at Guantanamo Bay.

AFIO: David, any additional thoughts for us?

Shedd: It is critical that all intelligence professionals remind themselves that intelligence is a service that is highly customer driven and that the Intelligence Community produces both a product and service to those users of intelligence. Those customers extend from the White House to the Congress to the warfighter and the law enforcement community. Delivering on those user needs is directly proportional to the relevancy that an intelligence professional brings to a wide array of decisionmakers. Warning is a critical function in what gets delivered to the customer; providing the context for warning is also essential. A sound collection foundation to enable sharp intelligence judgments with well-articulated confidence levels ultimately leads to better decision-making. Understanding the process, which ultimately ends with giving the customer decision advantage over the adversary, is what I took away as a result of the privilege of serving in the White House and the NSC staff. The experience that combines policymaker interaction with the intelligence professional should be highly cherished. As a result, the perspective gained by an intelligence officer after living in a policy environment will ensure that officer's professional experience will be deeply enriched.

AFIO: Thank you for your time and willingness to share your insights.

GUIDE TO THE STUDY OF INTELLIGENCE

Diplomacy & Intelligence: Strange Bedfellows

G. Philip Hughes & Peter C. Oleson

"Women: can't live with 'em; can't live without 'em!"

— Kent Dorfman, Animal House (1978)

Spies and diplomats; diplomats and spies. Funnily enough, each could use precisely Dorfman's adage about the other.

Diplomacy – particularly effective diplomacy – depends on intelligence – particularly effective intelligence. For the purposes of this article, we use "diplomacy" to mean strategically purposeful official communication between and among governments intended to persuade other governments to cooperate with one's own position or course of action or to motivate collaboration on a collective solution to an international problem. By intelligence, we mean the collection by official governmental means of information on foreign parties and events/developments that is not otherwise publicly available, along with forecasts and analyses, which may combine this information with other openly collected or public-source information, to support policymakers' decision-making and/or military acquisition, deployment, or employment decisions.

But there's an interesting asymmetry here. Obviously, ineffective diplomacy – aimless, vacillating, irresolute, perhaps lacking strategic vision or clear goals, or a realistic grasp of the available leverage and resources – doesn't particularly need intelligence. In life, it's said, "If you don't know where you're going, any road will get you there." But in diplomacy, the problem is even more acute: if you don't know where you're going, even the most detailed and accurate "map," provided courtesy of your intelligence apparatus – even one that identifies every peril that lies down each available road – won't save you. In this sense, even the most effective intelligence can't redeem ineffective diplomacy. And, in diplomacy, taking just "any road" won't necessarily get you to your undetermined goals; more likely, it will just get you into deeper trouble.

By contrast, ineffective intelligence or assessments – too late, too vague, false, mistaken, or misleading – can destroy even the most craftily devised and executed diplomatic strategy. The most infamous recent example – Secretary of State Colin Powell's February 2003 briefing on the Iraqi weapons of mass destruction (WMD) to the UN Security Council – worked in the short-term, helping rally a "coalition of the willing" to join the US-led invasion of Iraq and equipping the Bush Administration with arguments that helped secure a substantial, bi-partisan Congressional authorization for the use of force. But, in the long run, failure to find the evidence of the WMD program that Secretary Powell described in such detail – and that Director of Central Intelligence George Tenet assured President Bush before the invasion decision would be a "slam dunk" to uncover – undermined confidence in the entire enterprise of the Iraq War, at home and abroad.

Diplomacy's Dependence on Intelligence

Diplomats are often reluctant to admit how much their "art" depends on the "craft" of intelligence. To anticipate looming international crises; to accurately assess adversaries' capabilities and intentions – and allies' strengths and degrees of steadfastness; to estimate the "limits of the possible" in enlisting/ aligning with allies and supporters, or in confronting international adversaries or miscreants; to understand and exploit sources of leverage provided by possibly peripheral or even unrelated issues, with allies or adversaries; to discover — if possible, in advance — diplomatic counterparts' negotiating positions and "bottom-lines"; even to verify adversaries' or allies' compliance with international obligations – all of these either require or are, at a minimum, facilitated by effective intelligence.

Here are three concrete 20th century illustrations – among the hundreds possible – of how intelligence helps diplomats. One is old; the others are of more recent vintage.

In 1921, the US intercepted and decrypted Japanese diplomatic communications during the Washington Naval Conference, providing foreknowledge of the Japanese negotiating positions, which allowed US diplomats to obtain an advantageous outcome.

More recently, the use of geospatial intelligence (GEOINT) during the 1995 Dayton Peace Accords provided detailed ground truth of the situation in that conflict area, which allowed the antagonists to negotiate having a common view of the terrain and who occupied what.[1]

---

1. See Gary Weir, "The Evolution of Geospatial Intelligence and The National Geospatial-Intelligence Agency," in the Guide to the Study of Intelligence, Association of Former Intelligence Officers, http://www.afio.com/40_guide.htm.

During the Cold War, the Reagan Administration regularly dispatched Defense Intelligence Agency Deputy Director for Intelligence John Hughes to allied capitals in Europe and Asia, sharing a detailed and comprehensive briefing on Soviet military capabilities and new weapons developments. These briefings made a major contribution to holding the NATO allies together in the face of enormous Soviet diplomatic and propaganda pressure through the Soviet boycott of the START nuclear arms reduction talks in Geneva. They bolstered the NATO allies in carrying through the decision to deploy intermediate-range nuclear forces (INF) in Europe to offset the Soviet SS-20 missile threat – leading ultimately to the negotiated elimination of INF weapons from Europe entirely.

Perhaps the most significant diplomatic achievements – bilateral and multilateral arms control and nonproliferation agreements – depend critically on intelligence. Verification of early Cold-War-era arms control agreements – the Atmospheric and Threshold Test-Ban Treaties, the Anti-Ballistic Missile (ABM) Treaty, the SALT I and START I nuclear weapons agreements – depended on "national technical means" – chiefly satellite reconnaissance.[2] Of course, other intelligence collection – human source collection (HUMINT), defectors, etc. – supplemented what could be discovered remotely about Soviet capabilities, new weapons developments and tests, and compliance or noncompliance. And at the end of the Cold War with the collapse of the Soviet Union, it became possible to agree to measures for continuous and periodic intrusive, on-site inspections – including on-the-ground monitoring of the output of missile production facilities – to provide robust and continuous verification.

Negotiated multilateral arms control/nuclear nonproliferation agreements similarly depend for their verification on the "national technical" intelligence capabilities of especially the United States and other Western nations, along with whatever insights can be gleaned from HUMINT, to bolster International Atomic Energy Agency (IAEA) on-site inspections. Compliance with multi-lateral nonproliferation agreements, like the Missile Technology Control Regime, the Chemical Weapons Treaty, the Nuclear Suppliers Group, and the Australia Group (which restricts international trade in chemical weapons-relevant technologies), relies on information and intelligence sharing and liaison among the participating countries, since these agreements lack a central agency responsible for surveilling compliance. And, rather obviously, the members with the most extensive and robust array of intelligence capabilities – like the United States – make the most critical contributions to compliance and enforcement efforts for such agreements

Without the contribution of intelligence to verification, both bilateral and multi-lateral arms control agreements – arguably the capstone achievements of the diplomat's "art" in pursuit of peace – would be worse than meaningless.

---

2. See Robert A. McDonald, "I Can See It From Afar: I Can Hear it From Afar," Guide to the Study of Intelligence at http://www.afio.com/40_guide.htm.

They would be dangerous, delusional traps, behind which nations bent on aggression would mask their military preparations.

Intelligence – particularly new or sudden discoveries or forecasts – often sets the diplomatic agenda. Presidents will direct diplomatic action when reading about specific threats or situations in their daily intelligence reports.[3] A threatened terrorist attack may lead to immediate cooperative international action against the terror group and its state sponsor, if it has one. Planned military actions always involve supportive diplomatic activity to gain acceptance or allay suspicions of what the US intends. Imagery intelligence of mass graves in Bosnia resulted in diplomatic pressure for the International Criminal Court to indict Serbian officials. Global warming data, gathered by both scientific earth observation satellites and intelligence sensors, has prompted diplomatic efforts to negotiate limits on greenhouse gas emissions.

Intelligence discoveries also help set the national strategy. For example, during the 1962 Cuban Missile Crisis, intelligence was important in allowing the President to choose diplomacy over immediate military action when he learned the readiness status of the missiles introduced to Cuba. A quarantine, coupled with intensive diplomatic action and public diplomacy, led to a successful – and peaceful – resolution of the crisis.

Furthermore, intelligence can serve as a check and balance for diplomats in their exchanges with others. Is a foreign representative lying? Or is he being only partially truthful? A well-placed human source can provide confirming or other intelligence.

Diplomacy's Contribution to Intelligence

Dependent as diplomacy is on effective intelligence, it is also a major contributor to the intelligence process and products. While military attachés in embassies abroad are ostensibly present to facilitate smoothly functioning military-to-military relations, they are also overt military intelligence collectors. In larger nations with sizeable militaries and in most NATO capitals, there would typically be an attaché representing each military service, with one – typically corresponding to that nation's "senior" military service – designated as the supervising defense attaché. These officers and their staffs are a primary source of intelligence on the host nation's military order of battle, the combat readiness of its units, the results of its military exercises, biographic intelligence on the host nation's military and national defense figures, etc. Military liaison personnel – typically implementing security assistance programs – although not generally considered intelligence collectors, certainly can be sources of insight into the readiness, logistical sustainment potential, and state of training

---

3. The President's Daily Brief (PDB) is shared with other senior national security policy officers, including the Secretaries of State and Defense.

and technological proficiency of host government armed forces.

Similarly, diplomatic reporting – although not in itself considered "intelligence," because host government counterparts are aware of the diplomatic interchanges and the information they yield – provide valuable background for intelligence analysts on the host country's leadership, politics, and political power struggles; on host government intentions and orientations; on trends and currents in the host country's society and culture; on its economic performance; and a range of other topics. Diplomatic reporting is also an invaluable source of biographic intelligence on leading personalities of the host country.

In addition to their reporting contributions, diplomatic establishments abroad also play host to important assets of the Intelligence Community (IC). While technically incompatible with their diplomatic status, it is an open secret that many nations use their diplomatic posts for intelligence purposes – placing intelligence operatives in "diplomatic cover" assignments and sometimes collecting communications intelligence. When the US stations such personnel under diplomatic cover abroad in allied or friendly capitals, these officers are declared to their counterpart agencies of the host government. Often they are the conduits of "liaison relationships" with the host country's intelligence services. These can involve varying degrees of intelligence cooperation – limited technical assistance; intelligence sharing of varying degrees – ranging from limited and specialized to extensive and wide ranging; the joint operation of collection facilities in the host government's territory; or mounting joint, cooperative intelligence operations.

As criminal enterprises – e.g., narcotics trafficking, money laundering, and human trafficking – have become major international problems, previously well-established lines between intelligence collected to support traditional national security functions and what was once considered law enforcement information to combat international criminality have blurred. Counterterrorism imperatives have contributed significantly to this blurring, with the Department of Homeland Security (DHS) now hosting its own integral Intelligence and Analysis Bureau. Justice Department legal ttachés (typically from the FBI) and Drug Enforcement Administration (DEA) agents have been posted for decades to selected US embassies around the world where their functions are most needed. Since the 9/11 attacks and the 2003 establishment of the DHS, representatives of that department have also deployed to select embassies worldwide. In addition to their work enforcing US laws and securing foreign government cooperation with their law-enforcement tasks, reporting by representatives of these agencies represents another important contribution to the intelligence product – emanating from these "tenants" of US overseas diplomatic posts.

Diplomats' Intelligence "Allergy"

Despite the importance of intelligence for effective diplomacy, many professional diplomats – certainly in the US – harbor an aversion to intelligence activities. Even if they appreciate the information that the IC can provide, many diplomats have distaste for intelligence operations and the operatives who mount and manage them. There are many sources for this attitude.

- First, many diplomats regard HUMINT as fundamentally immoral, involving, as it almost invariably does, suborning someone to betray his or her country for money or by exploiting some human appetite, vulnerability, or weakness.

- Second – and relatedly – diplomats often doubt the reliability of this type of human "intelligence" precisely because of the ways in which it is procured and the suspect motives of those who provide it. They not infrequently insist that there is little or nothing to be learned from such "intelligence" that can't be learned from a careful reading of open sources and from diplomatic reporting. In a relatively contemporary context, such diplomats might point to the "intelligence" of Saddam Hussein's weapons of mass destruction program in Iraq – and its source promoted by the Iraqi National Congress that several Western intelligence services unfortunately relied upon – as a prime example of this critique.

- Diplomats can be resentful of playing "landlord" for intelligence agency components residing within (and, technically, compromising) their diplomatic missions. This can be especially true if secrecy and mistrust leave the ambassador substantially in the dark about key aspects of intelligence activities underway in his country of accreditation – or if he/she is on the receiving end of nasty surprises, courtesy of their resident intelligence components.

- And, of course, intelligence operations gone awry can damage diplomatic relations with host governments. These can sometimes be exaggerated for effect by host government leaders or amplified by domestic politics – as in recent years' revelations of National Security Agency (NSA) "eavesdropping" on the cell phones of German Chancellor Angela Merkel and Brazilian President Dilma Roussef, or the recent expulsion of the CIA station chief in Berlin over revelations that the CIA had recruited an employee of Germany's Bundesnachrichtendienst (BND) in the Chancellery. Covert actions often cause diplomatic problems. Many are not so "covert" (e.g., the Bay of Pigs, the "secret war" in Laos, support for the mujahedeen in Afghanistan versus the Soviets, or the 1953 overthrow of Prime Minister Mossadegh in Iran). When they become known, covert actions can cause damaging waves of unwanted publicity and generate long-lasting enmity toward the US. A recent example is the revelation of non-judicial renditions and CIA-run "black sites" for holding and interrogating international terrorists, which has led to European Parliament and other nations' investigations. Such episodes disturb the smooth functioning of diplomatic relationships and leave "messes," large or small, that diplomats have to clean up.

All of these elements tend to make many diplomats skeptical and averse to intelligence operations, especially in their countries of accreditation or responsibility. And this aversion/caution need not apply only to human source activities or on-the-ground technical collections or covert operations. As the 2001 Chinese interception and forced landing of a US Navy P-3 surveillance aircraft underscored, even airborne technical intelligence collection – ostensibly out of the reach of hostile governments – can lead to prolonged, thorny, and delicate problems requiring diplomatic resolution – and under conditions of dramatically reversed leverage. The many earlier antecedents – the famous 1960 U-2 incident and the Soviet capture of pilot Francis Gary Powers, the (possibly mistaken) Israeli attack on the USS Liberty during the 1967 Arab-Israeli War, the North Korean capture of the USS Pueblo and its crew in 1968 – are reminders of the ever-present possibilities for a recurrence – particularly as US forces become more thinly spread and deployed in non-combat, support roles in theaters worldwide.

Diplomatic 'Successes'/Intelligence 'Headaches'

"Peace Is Our Profession" was the motto of the former US Air Force Strategic Air Command. Ask any diplomat, and he/she would probably consider that the Air Force stole their motto. Diplomats usually see themselves as constantly striving for peace – for the harmonious and agreeable working together of nations on the world's shared problems; for the peaceful resolution of international disputes; for the non-violent, eventual removal or replacement of the world's most inhumane and human-rights-abusing governments and leaders with more humane successors – all through patient diplomatic persuasion and perhaps some economic and public diplomacy pressure.

One area of diplomatic endeavor that has been associated in the popular imagination with "peace" efforts for well over a century has been the forging of arms control agreements – bilateral and multi-lateral – and of multi-lateral nonproliferation agreements, mentioned earlier. As discussed, these agreements depend critically on verification for their effectiveness – and this has been one of the key ways in which intelligence provides indispensable support to diplomacy. But by the same token, in this area, diplomacy can create some real "headaches" and challenges for the IC.

Diplomats like international consensus – and are usually prepared to engage internationally in the equivalent of legislative "log-rolling" that is often necessary to achieve it. Which is, in part, how projects for major international conventions get going and pick up steam. Sometimes these visionary projects, invented for the welfare of mankind and the peace and good order of the planet, actually achieve their targets. Numerous examples can be found – from the Geneva Conventions on the Law of War and the Treatment of Prisoners of War to the Vienna Conventions on Diplomatic and Consular Practices right down to the more recent UN Conventions Against Corruption and Against Narcotic Drugs and Psychotropic Substances, and the UN Convention on Civil and Political Rights, to name a few. Of course, it is not uncommon for new international convention projects to become freighted with ulterior and problematic agendas – particularly those whose effects would end up giving additional comfort and security to repressive regimes by, for instance, hobbling dissent or press freedoms, or weakening the economies of the Western democracies. A celebrated 1980s example of this was the New World Information Order promoted by UNESCO – an initiative that was fundamentally shot down during the Reagan Administration and prompted a roughly 20-year hiatus in US participation in that international body.

Sometimes, though, these visionary diplomatic projects can also have problematic implications for the IC. In years past, the UN Outer Space Treaty and Law of the Sea Treaty posed problems and challenges for some actual or potential US uses of these vast zones for assorted technologically advanced and imaginative intelligence collection efforts. The potential for adverse implications or (perhaps unintended) complications for intelligence collections efforts from international treaties has come into play most often in connection with efforts to define the limits of, access to, and "rules of the road" for "international commons" like the high seas or outer space. However, the progressive blurring of the lines between intelligence collection and law enforcement information, thanks to the growing and inter-linked threats of terrorism, narcotics (and even human) trafficking, and other criminality transcending national borders, means that such international initiatives as the 2002 establishment of the International Criminal Court can have repercussions for intelligence or even law enforcement agents abroad engaged in high-stakes, high-risk operations. Generally, the implications of these ambitious projects for the IC and its operations are among the last and least of diplomatic considerations. As often as not, these end up being illuminated in the course of addressing the Defense Department's larger concerns over their implications for military operations and personnel in the course of their duties on overseas deployments.

Obviously, once entered into, these international covenants – their restrictions, limitations, and requirements – are one more item that must be factored into intelligence plans and programs.

Bilateral and multi-lateral arms control and nonproliferation agreements, mentioned earlier, can also be a source of "headaches" for the IC in several ways.

- First, while such treaties' verification provisions are not defined in a vacuum, without IC input or advice – considering diplomacy as "the art of the possible" – at the end of the day, the IC is inevitably "on the hook" to devise ways and means of verifying such treaties' provisions to some reasonable level of confidence. That can be quite a challenge – one in which the IC is an advisor but not the designer or arbiter of the final outcome.

- Second, since ratification of such treaties – especially bilateral arms control agreements with Russia, but also such multi-lateral conventions as a Comprehensive Test Ban Treaty – is highly political, the IC is regularly put "on the spot" to "certify" the treaty's verifiability. This issue can become a political football. The administration responsible for negotiating the treaty expects the IC's "seal of approval" for its verifiability. Meanwhile, the administration's opposition in Congress can be quite adept at ferreting out dissenting or skeptical views within the IC, particularly if the treaty's verification provisions seem inadequate or rely excessively on trusting the "other side."

- Finally, there is the proverbial "hot potato" of evidence of the "other side" cheating on such agreements. When such evidence arises – birthed up by – yes – the IC – a flurry of politically charged questions arise – both within the community itself and between the community and the rest of the US national security apparatus that it serves. How strong and conclusive is the evidence? What action does it merit vis-à-vis the White House and the State and Defense Departments? How will it be handled in dealing with the violating party – diplomatically and otherwise? What if it is "leaked" by a source – within the administration or Congress –to "prove a point" either about the violator's perfidy and aggressiveness or about the weakness and timidity of the administration's response? Every such instance, in this verification context, constitutes a major potential "headache" for the Intelligence Community.

Beyond these canonical problems there are two fundamental dilemmas that lie at the root of the intelligence-policy (which is to say, also, diplomatic) nexus. As discussed, effective intelligence is essential for policymakers – and diplomats, who may be as much policy implementers as they are policymakers. Yet, in the face of policy reversals or failures, policymakers are constantly tempted – and often give in to the temptation – to blame those reversals and failures on the IC. Claims of being misled, of having inaccurate information, of "politicized" intelligence, etc. have repeatedly been deployed in modern American history to "explain" failed or counter-productive policies. And the policy failures regularly laid at the IC's doorstep often lead to sensational revelations – either by official leaks or self-appointed "watchdogs" – from Daniel Ellsberg to Edward Snowden – of intelligence programs supposedly "gone bad." Such revelations usually redound to the detriment of future access to information sources and channels that have been "blown" or lead to new legislative, judicially determined, regulatory or policy limitations on "what can be done" by US intelligence agencies. Yet, the IC is expected to accurately anticipate the next crisis, the next threat to national security, the next 9/11 attack, as if none of this self-justifying damage had occurred. And, rather like a whipped dog that nevertheless has no alternative but to remain loyal to his master, the IC will endeavor, despite the "feast and famine" budget oscillations of the last 40 years, to rise to the occasion of the next crisis – whatever it is.

Conclusion

Intelligence and diplomacy are locked in a marriage. Not a marriage of convenience. Rather the opposite: a marriage of necessity. Like all such marriages, it is not entirely comfortable for either party. There are significant frictions and differences of outlook that accompany the mutual dependency. Some of these "come with the territory"; others are generated, more or less regularly (though not necessarily consciously or purposely) as a natural by-product of that partner's normal work. Like all such marriages, patience, perseverance, a dedicated quest for mutual understanding, and a shared dedication to a common goal are necessary for the marriage to be fruitful and productive. And that's the imperative of intelligence professionals and diplomats working together to assure US national security.

<hr>

READINGS FOR INSTRUCTORS

The complex relationship between diplomacy and intelligence reflects some of the complexity that exists within the US Governmental agencies and processes related to national security. Recommended for instructors is Roger Z. George and Harvey Rishikof (eds.), *The National Security Enterprise: Navigating the Labyrinth* (Washington, DC: Georgetown University Press, 2011) with a foreword by former national security advisor, Lieutenant General Brent Scowcroft, USAF (Ret.).

G. Philip Hughes, currently senior director of the White House Writers Group (a Washington, DC, corporate communications consulting firm), has served as US ambassador to Barbados and the Eastern Caribbean; executive secretary (and, earlier, director for Latin American affairs) of the National Security Council; assistant secretary of commerce for export enforcement; deputy assistant secretary of state for politico-military affairs; and deputy assistant for national security affairs to Vice President George H. W. Bush. He currently serves as chairman of the Association for Diplomatic Studies and Training; as senior vice president and secretary of the Council of American Ambassadors; and as adjunct professor of diplomacy at the Institute of World Politics.

Peter C. Oleson is the editor of Association of Former Intelligence Officers' (AFIO's) Guide to the Study of Intelligence, a member of the AFIO board, and chairman of its academic outreach. Previously, he was the director for intelligence and space policy for the secretary of defense and assistant director for plans and policy of the Defense Intelligence Agency. He was CEO of Potomac Strategies & Analysis, Inc., a consulting firm on technology and intelligence and an associate professor in the graduate school of the University of Maryland University College.

GUIDE TO THE STUDY OF INTELLIGENCE

My Perspective on Intelligence Support of Foreign Policy

Carl Ford

The key to providing intelligence support to our foreign policymakers is delivering timely, relevant, and persuasive information. Sounds simple. Especially as we devote so many billions of dollars to the Intelligence Community (IC). In practice, however, the job of foreign intelligence analysts writing for the President's Daily Brief (PDB) and other assessments for senior officials is anything but straightforward. Foreign policy focused analysts must contend with a collection system geared primarily to military issues that produces little new information germane to the immediate requirements of policymakers including the President. Instead, reporters of current intelligence related to foreign policy matters depend largely for their insights on open sources, a few well-placed human assets, a smattering of signals intelligence, and bits and pieces of imagery. For the foreign policy focused analyst, squeezing as much as possible out of an imperfect collection system becomes the true measure of success.

Most of the intelligence budget goes to supporting the Defense Department and its combatant commands. This is not to suggest that foreign policy concerns are less important than military interests. The information the collection systems produce is often extremely detailed and designed specifically for military support purposes, not civilian foreign policy officials in Washington. As a result, most of the raw material available for foreign policy focused analysts is derivative and not specifically collected to support foreign policy.

The US' intelligence collection system has its own style, its own rhythm, and policymakers' priorities are not necessarily at the top of the list. The ability to target the vast collection system in a laser-like manner on a specific foreign policy related requirement is extremely limited. It is more appropriate to think of these systems in terms of having built a giant baseball catcher's mitt. One can point it where one thinks information may come from, but one has little control over when the balls are thrown and their exact direction of flight. As a result, we miss far more than we catch, and the timing of what we do catch rarely coincides with the publication schedule of the PDB.

Intelligence collection's scatter-shot nature also makes it easy for analysts to fall into the "connecting the dots" fallacy. Just because one has a dot does not mean it is, or can be, connected to other dots. It is the same story with the best human source reporting. It rarely, if ever, provides a complete picture. Sources are human. They make mistakes and are plagued with biases. The same is true for communications intercepts. Since when can a couple of telephone conversations and a few dozen e-mails be enough to tell much about someone, or what they stand for? This goes as well for overhead imagery. Although the US possesses the world's most capable system for collecting intelligence, it doesn't give analysts x-ray vision or an ability to see what someone is thinking.

It does not help that intelligence managers are prone to define success in terms of speed; the time it takes for a piece of newly collected information to reach a senior official. To speed up this process, very sensitive "eyes only" information is sometimes sent directly from collectors to the senior policy-makers, leaving all-source intelligence analysts out of the loop. The item might be important, but it also might be misleading or completely wrong. As if that were not enough, relevance, in the managers' minds, is often simply that the information is classified and comes from the IC.

This leads many IC managers to believe that policymakers consider the news delivered by the IC their highest priority, and the analysts' most important contribution. When, in fact, from my experience, it demonstrates how little contact most intelligence officers have with policymakers. Of course, news of fast-breaking events or new situations interests senior policymakers, includ-ing the President, but it is not all they want or need. Indeed, I do not think I have ever met a policymaker who was satisfied with the intelligence they were receiving — just the opposite. They complain loudly, especially when they think there are no intelligence officers around. The IC's overreliance on producing "news" only exacerbates the problem.

INR's Scheduled-Based Reporting

At the Department of State, analysts in the Bureau for Intelligence & Research (INR) attempt to take these factors into consideration by building their approach around the policymakers' schedule — not the collection cycle. INR has been, and always will be, a current events reporting agency, if only because of its small size — 150 or so analysts. Basic, long-term, and directed research is beyond its means. Only CIA and the Defense Intelligence Agency

(DIA) have the manpower resources necessary for this sort of heavy lifting. What INR was designed for, however, it does very well. Historically, its analysts have stayed focused on a region or issue much longer than those in other analytic offices, and the venerable INR Daily Brief they produce is widely admired for its style and substance. The people in INR are truly a national treasure; their level of expertise is something for other organizations to match.

During my time at INR, from May 2001 to October 2003, I was fortunate to work for Secretary Colin Powell.[1] He appreciated the value of intelligence and emphasized his support for INR to his top policy advisors. His instructions to me were clear. He looked to INR for more than the news. High on his list was the expectation that INR would provide more detailed answers to his most pressing concerns, usually a mirror image of the President's priorities. He also wanted to know when INR's views differed from those of other agencies, and, given his military background, he expressed a preference for us including a bit more from the military side of things in his daily briefing package.

From my perspective as INR director, I could see that the secretary already received more intelligence every day than he or any other top official could plow through in six weeks. It came in the form of the PDB, regular contact with senior US and foreign officials, INR's Daily Brief, and a fair amount of sensitive "eyes only" material from the National Security Agency (NSA). In addition, he regularly read news directly from the internet, received an oral briefing from INR at each morning's staff meeting, and received updates throughout the day from his senior policy officers. In short, he did not lack for news. It was clear to me that much of the material he received was duplicative and infringed on the little time he had to think.

Instead of always trying to match the PDB's coverage, INR emphasized topics especially relevant to the secretary. If another agency's product was as good, or better, than we could provide on a current event, it was added to our own material sent to the secretary. In cases where INR held a different opinion, we explained why and how in a note. We continued to supply INR's Daily Brief, and added a copy of the chairman of the Joint Chiefs' morning briefing courtesy of DIA's representative to INR.

For INR, scheduled-based reporting meant determining which questions to ask and making time for the answers needing the most attention. In both cases, better planning was key. The deputy assistants took responsibility for mapping out the secretary's schedule as best they could, and, whenever possible, sought advance notice of the President's upcoming events. At the same time, each INR office provided a list of priority questions they anticipated in their area of expertise. They also looked for opportunities to deliver their products at times that would maximize their relevance. This was especially important

---

1. Colin Powell served in the US Army from 1958 to 1993 retiring as a general and chairman, Joints Chiefs of Staff. He served as secretary of state from January 2001 to January 2005.

for matters not regularly making the headlines.

Managing such an approach required knowing a good deal about the policymaker's priorities and schedule. This type of information, admittedly, was not always easy to obtain. It started with INR taking the initiative to reach out to individual policymakers throughout the State Department each morning to provide a personalized intelligence briefing, and following up as necessary throughout the day. The policymaker's priorities — what was on the schedule — were addressed first, followed by new developments in their area of interest. INR's and the IC's full range of products was always available for the policymakers who liked to keep up with events outside of their immediate area of responsibility.

For the briefer, it was an opportunity to develop a face-to-face relationship with a policymaker and for gaining insights into priorities and upcoming events. INR analysts were instructed to leave policy formulation to the policymakers and concentrate on identifying the key questions — the things policymakers do not have the time or knowledge to do themselves. It is the policymakers' job to decide on the policy direction to take, and ideally the IC's analytical expertise helps them understand the problems and challenges they will face. When an analyst strays off course into recommending policy choices, however, his or her relevance and acceptance by policymakers suffers.

Adopting a schedule-based system requires more work. In-depth assessments are much harder to produce than reporting the news and do not lend themselves to the short timelines of the PDB and other daily reporting. Producing quality analyses takes time. Unless one can anticipate important questions sufficiently in advance, analysts do not have time to prepare a proper and useful answer. Thinking ahead is key.

Sometimes the valuable input to the policymaker can be as simple as preparing information in advance about the size and frequency of past anti-America demonstrations in the Middle East. This helps put new events into perspective as they happen. During the run up to the Iraq War, senior officials were particularly interested in the "Arab street's" reaction to US policy. Instead of just reporting an anti-American demonstration had happened somewhere in the region, INR wanted to provide a more useful answer. It asked: Was the event a regular occurrence or was it about average? Was it larger, or smaller in size, and what had prompted the event — Iraq, the Israel-Palestinian issue, or other complaints? In one instance, the lead article in most current IC reporting highlighted increased opposition in the region to the US policy on Iraq. The reports were based on evidence from two separate demonstrations. It turned out in both instances that the size of each demonstration was well below average levels for those cities. One of the demonstrations was focused on US support for Israel, the other on a local issue unrelated to anti-American activities. Judging strong opposition to US Iraq policy was a reasonable "guess" at the time, but using the demonstrations cited as evidence, was sloppy and wrong.

Another example of focused INR analysis involved a trip to Russia by the President and the secretary of state. Learning of the trip, a senior INR Russia analyst took the initiative to call on the services of a colleague outside INR for help. His friend, a Foreign Service Officer (FSO), had worked almost daily with the then more junior Vladimir Putin while both were stationed in St. Petersburg. Thinking that the FSO's recollections and impressions would help him in preparing for the upcoming trip, INR's analyst asked his friend to jot down his experiences on paper. He agreed. A few weeks later a lengthy report arrived, all 50 or 60 pages of it, so well written that we decided to send the entire manuscript to the secretary, adding only a note from INR summarizing the paper's findings. It turned out the secretary read the entire paper, not just the summary, and he decided to take the report with him on the trip. At some point, he shared the report with the President. The President's notes in the margin suggested he read most, if not all of the paper on the airplane. Moreover, the President's asking the secretary to pass on his thanks to the author suggests he liked what he read. "Atta boys" are rare in the intelligence business, making this one all the more special. For the report writer, my Russian analyst, and the entire Bureau, it was an unexpected, but gratefully accepted compliment.

The occurrence argues against the conventional wisdom in the IC that senior officials do not have time to read long, detailed pieces, and that it is better to provide them with just the highlights. True, we mostly send summaries to our consumers, but not necessarily because that is what they want from us. I have found that when policymakers are preoccupied with an issue, they are eager to receive anything we can give them. They read more, get quickly up to speed on what current reporting has to offer, and cast about for more details. Continuing to offer up short, summary, articles leaves them frustrated and unsatisfied.

What policymakers are looking for most is "good" intelligence, meaning intelligence that is timely and relevant to their top priority of the moment. Short and sweet may suffice in the early stages of a policy challenge, but as a problem wears on, the policymaker's requirements evolve. Details become more important. They start asking questions, wanting more in-depth answers. Opinions, even those of the IC's experts, are not what they expect to hear. Once they become engaged fully in an issue, only new evidence and the rationale for the conclusion suffices.

Even then, analysis may only serve to force them to question their own views, not buy another's ideas hook, line, and sinker. Actually influencing a policymaker's views — the intelligence officer's Holy Grail — depends almost entirely on the strength of the evidence. Even if one is the world's expert on a topic, don't expect the policymaker to take your word for it. Information is not useful intelligence until the policymaker is persuaded it makes sense.

Much of the persuasion must be done on paper, making the job all that much harder. Policymaker's face-to-face interactions with intelligence officers are usually brief, and often the information is presented by non-experts. A better approach, but difficult to implement, is giving the policymaker direct contact with analysts.

Deputy Secretary of State Richard Armitage was a good example of a policymaker who has learned the value of the face-to-face format. Knowing the President had tasked him to deliver an important message to a foreign leader, I once suggested he meet with INR analysts before his departure. Even though his trip was only days away, he agreed to a 15-minute meeting with the analysts, working the session into an already jam-packed schedule. I chose five or six true experts from various INR offices. The lead briefer, a political analyst considered by his peers to be a world-class expert, had met with the foreign leader on several occasions; rounding out the team were experienced analysts in military affairs, economic issues, nuclear weapons, and terrorism. Each was given a brief opportunity to introduce themselves and to share their expertise.

Secretary Armitage then began the back-and-forth with a question; followed by INR's responses; and then by a number of follow up questions. The session lasted almost an hour (despite repeated attempts by his administrative assistant to end it). Not long after he returned from his trip, he asked me to bring the team back for a debrief. Armitage included a summary of his mission, what information from the analysts had been most useful, and his personal assessment of the foreign leader. Although this sort of debrief is not always possible, the experience was an especially rewarding for the analysts. Ideally, this should be the norm, not the exception.

I believe INR's scheduled-based reporting — focusing on the policymaker's top priorities and daily schedule not just the daily collection intake – has paid dividends. The INR analysts' work was more relevant to the Department's work, without sacrificing the news cycle or becoming its slave. The guiding philosophy was to satisfy what the secretary and those supporting him most needed each day, not just report the serendipitous intelligence inherent in the collection cycle. For me that is what delivering timely, relevant, and persuasive information to the policymakers is all about.

READINGS FOR INSTRUCTORS

There are few studies specifically focusing on the IC's support for foreign policy. The voluminous works on analytical tradecraft contain much relevant material, and several of the best introductory texts dedicate whole chapters to the topic such as:

"The Analyst and the Customer," Chapter 15 in Robert M Clark's *Intelligence Analysis: A Target-Centric Approach*, (CQ Press, Washington, DC, 2007), 277-293.

Betts, Richard. "Analysis, War, and Decision: Why Intelligence Failures are Inevitable," *World Politics*, Brookings, October 1978, 61-80. http://journals.cambridge.org/action/displayAbstract?fromPage=online&aid=7629164&fulltextType=RA&fileId=S0043887100010182.

Lieberthal, Kenneth. "The U.S. Intelligence Community and Foreign Policy: Getting Analysis Right," a Brookings Foreign Policy Paper Series, Number 18, September 2009, monograph. http://www.brookings.edu/~/media/research/files/papers/2009/9/intelligence%20community%20lieberthal/09_intelligence_community_lieberthal.pdf.

"Part Two: The Policy-Analyst Relationship," in Roger Z. George and James B. Bruce (eds.), *Analyzing Intelligence: Origins, Obstacles, and Innovations*, 2nd edition. (Washington, DC: Georgetown University Press, 2008), 71-106.

For a behind the scenes look at the interaction of foreign policy and intelligence none are better than Bob Woodward's:

Bush at War (Simon & Schuster, New York, 2002).

Plan of Attack (Simon & Shuster, New York, 2004).

Covert action is one of the most complicated aspects of intelligence and foreign policy. The best explanations I have found is "Covert Action," Chapter 8 in Mark Lowenthal's *Intelligence: From Secrets to Policy* (Washington, DC: CQ Press, 2009), 165-179.

The CIA Center for the Study of Intelligence is the best source for how the IC covers foreign policy analysis:

"Analytic Professionalism and the Policymaking Process: Q&A on a Challenging Relationship." https://www.cia.gov/library/kent-center-occasional-papers/pdf/OPV2No2.pdf.

Davis Jack. The Sherman Kent Center for Intelligence Analysis, Occasional Papers: Volume 2, Number 3, *Sherman Kent's Final Thoughts on Analyst-Policymaker Relations*. https://www.cia.gov/library/kent-center-occasional-papers/pdf/OPV2No3.pdf.

Intelligence Community and Policymaker Integration, Intelligence Community and Policymaker Integration: A Studies in Intelligence Anthology, 2013. https://www.cia.gov/library/center-for-the-study-of-intelligence/csi-publications/books-and-monographs/intelligence-community-and-policymaker-integration/index.html.

Intelligence and Policy: The Evolving Relationship, Roundtable Report, June 2004, Center for the Study of Intelligence. https://www.cia.gov/library/center-for-the-study-of-intelligence/csi-publications/books-and-monographs/IntelandPolicyRelationship_Internet.pdf.

Intelligence, Policy, and Politics: The DCI, the White House, and Congress: a Symposium, 2013. https://www.cia.gov/library/publications/historical-collection-publications/intel-policy-and-politics/index.html.

President Nixon and the Role of Intelligence in the 1973 Arab-Israeli War. Center for the Study of Intelligence Presidential Series, 2013. https://www.cia.gov/library/publications/historical-collection-publications/arab-israeli-war/nixon-arab-isaeli-war.pdf.

Strategic Warning & The Role of Intelligence: Lessons Learned from the 1968 Soviet Invasion of Czechoslovakia, CIA Historical Collection Division. https://www.cia.gov/library/publications/historical-collection-publications/czech-invasion/soviet%20-czech-invasion.pdf.

The CIA Center for the Study of Intelligence is also the best source for studying the policymakers' perspective on intelligence:

"Insightful Interviews: A Policymaker's Perspective On Intelligence Analysis," Jack Davis, 1993. https://www.cia.gov/library/center-for-the-study-of-intelligence/kent-csi/vol38no5/pdf/v38i5a02p.pdf.

"A Policymaker's Perspective on Intelligence Analysis, CIA. https://www.cia.gov/library/center-for-the-study-of-intelligence/kentcsi/docs/v38i5a02p.htm.

Davis, Jack, "Intelligence Analysis and Policymaking: The Views of Ambassador Herman J. Cohen," *Studies in Intelligence*, 1995. https://www.cia.gov/library/center-for-the-study-of-intelligence/csi-publications/csi-studies/studies/davis-pdfs/the-views-of-ambassador-herman-j-cohen-davis-1995.pdf.

Davis, Jack. *The Challenge of Managing Uncertainty: Paul Wolfowitz on Intelligence Policy-Relations*, 1995. https://www.cia.gov/library/center-for-the-study-of-intelligence/kent-csi/vol39no5/pdf/v39i5a05p.pdf.

Mr. Ford has served for over 40 years in a variety of military, intelligence, policy, and academic positions. As an Army intelligence officer, he served two tours in Vietnam and another in the Defense Intelligence Agency as a China analyst. He joined CIA's Office of Strategic Research in 1974. In 1978, he was selected as a Congressional Foreign Affairs Fellow for Senator John Glenn focusing on arms control and foreign policy. The following year, he became a professional staff member of the Senate Foreign Relations Committee. He returned to CIA as the national intelligence officer for East Asia in 1985. From 1989 to 1993, he was seconded to the Department of Defense as principal deputy assistant secretary for international security affairs. Upon retiring from CIA that year, he consulted until the President appointed him in 2001 as assistant secretary of state for intelligence and research. He retired from the Department of State in October 2003. He has since taught at Georgetown University School of Foreign Service and George Mason University. He has a BA in Asian studies and an MA in East Asian studies from Florida State University.

GUIDE TO THE STUDY OF INTELLIGENCE

A Guide to the Reforming of American Intelligence

Past and Future[1]

William M. Nolte, PhD

In 1992, with the aftershocks of the Soviet Union's collapse still being felt, a small group of academicians and intelligence professionals, led by Roy Godson of Georgetown University and Ernest May of Harvard, formed the Working Group on Intelligence Reform. Three years later, the group produced its findings in U.S. Intelligence at the Crossroads: Agendas for Reform. The end of the Cold War notwithstanding, the contributors made clear their judgment that "intelligence still matters." If that sounds a bit self-evident, it was not fully so at the time. The primary focus of US intelligence after the Second World War – the only period in American history in which Americans had invested heavily intelligence during peacetime – had disappeared, leaving an enormous gap in the Intelligence Community's reason for being.

Noting the lessons of the 20th century, the then recent Persian Gulf War, and other issues, the Working Group judged "states cannot assume that intelligence will or will not play a significant role in the military and foreign affairs of the future." The question they saw at the time was not whether the US retained an intelligence capability "but whether the large intelligence bureaucracies spawned by World War II and the Cold War continued to suit US national security needs."[2]

---

1. Readers interested in more detailed accounts of the various efforts to reorganize or reform the intelligence establishment since 1947 should see: Michael J. Warner and J. Kenneth McDonald, *U.S. Intelligence Community Reform Studies Since 1947* (Washington, Center for the Study of Intelligence, 2005), and Richard A. Best, Jr., Proposals for Intelligence Reorganization, 1949-2004 (Washington, DC: Congressional Research Service, 2004).
2. Godson, May, & Schmitt (eds.), *U.S. Intelligence at the Crossroads: Agendas for Reform* (Washington, DC: Brassey's, 1995).

In the less than two decades since the Working Group completed its report, the United States has moved through a post-cold war era in intelligence, marked by deep budget cuts, some loss of focus, and an ever-shifting information environment. The events of September 2001 and their aftermath were marked by rapid increases in resources, a focus on counterterrorism, and the addition of domestic or homeland security concerns to the intelligence agenda.

We are now entering a post-post-9/11 era in which budgets are likely to decline, terrorism has not disappeared, but in which new issues, such as cyber security and turmoil in the Arab world, not only compete with terrorism for priority but link with it in uncertain and potentially dangerous ways. Add to this a public preoccupation with the nation's financial difficulties, an uncompromising political environment between political parties, and a general sense that the intelligence reforms of the post-9/11 have not taken root, and the questions from 1995 remain: How should the United States align its intelligence establishments with the operational, informational, political environments we face? Do the existing structures support that alignment or inhibit it? It is worth noting that a constant factor in all three of these environments has been the ongoing information revolution. A review of past efforts at alignment, a term I prefer over reform, may be useful.

The great post-World War II alignment in American intelligence was the National Security Act of 1947, creating the CIA. This reflected an historic policy realignment, as the Truman Administration shifted from a demobilization program to a recognition of the Soviet threat. The creation of the CIA marked two milestones: first, that some level of intelligence coordination beyond the departmental level was essential to deal with the anticipated security environment; and second, that the new agency would not just collect and coordinate intelligence. It would have an operational role that created tension in America's sense of itself as a nation that operated openly with the world, with a bare minimum of secret information, let alone secret or covert operations.

The ink was barely dry on the National Security Act of 1947 before additional "reforms" were suggested. This is not as unusual as it sounds. Growing out of the lessons from World War II, the CIA's creation started the job of building a modern intelligence establishment. It could hardly have completed it. Creation of the CIA did begin the process of creating some measure of national intelligence, coordinated across departmental lines, one of the major recommendations of the various commissions that had studied the Pearl Harbor attack and the conduct of the war.

At the same time, the National Security Act coincided with a larger effort to tidy up the messy bureaucratic creations of the New Deal. This effort, driven by the Republican-led 80th Congress, recommended the consolidation of many agencies that had been established independently with limited coordination among them.[3] As part of its work, the Hoover Commission conducted a separate classified annex on national security, which, in 1948, noted the need for improved structural and administrative controls in the new CIA. At almost the same time, the Truman Administration created the Armed Forces Security Agency (AFSA), a committee-led stopgap necessitated by the desire for greater coordination and the creation of an independent Air Force. The United States had worked through World War II with a naval cryptologic service that, put simply, had naval personnel performing the Navy's cryptologic mission, largely against the naval services of other countries. The Army's Army Security Agency handled military cryptology. The creation of the Air Force required something of a "property settlement" with the Army, including a division of cryptologic personnel and facilities. As historian Christopher Andrew has noted, the United States, which had suffered cryptologic failure with two agencies in 1941, entered the 1950s with four such agencies, three service-based and the emergent AFSA.

The cryptologic element is reflective of the evolution of US intelligence in another sense. Photographs of that period note the periodic meetings of the United States Intelligence Board, a largely powerless body, which brought together the various intelligence agencies. Other photographs record meetings of the United States Communications Intelligence Board, with some overlap of membership. Communications Intelligence was still seen as an extension of signals (as in Signal Corps) components, not true intelligence. Handling an ever larger, more powerful, and more expensive set of technical intelligence organizations would become a major issue in the evolution toward an intelligence community.

The next major organizational reform[4] came with the 1952 creation of the National Security Agency, replacing the ineffective AFSA. Over the next several years, two significant developments followed: first, a greater integration of the Army, Navy, and Air Force cryptologic components into a national system. Second, over time, communications intelligence gradually shifted from an extension of the signals community to a closer relationship to the emerging intelligence establishment.

By the late 1950s, imagery begun to increase in prominence. Photo reconnaissance had developed at a tactical level in the First World War.[5] It advanced dramatically in technology and importance in the Second World War. In the 1950s, it took two quantum leaps in response to the critical need to penetrate the vast Soviet landmass. The first was the historic U-2 project, which remains a landmark in both aviation and intelligence history. The second was CORONA,

---

3. One result of this was the creation of a Department of Health Education and Welfare, which itself lasted only into the Johnson Administration.
4. I am not addressing here internal structural, operational, and administrative improvements undertaken within agencies during this period.
5. See Finnegan, Terrence, *Shooting the Front: Allied Aerial Reconnaissance and Photographic Interpretation on the Western Front – World War I* (National Defense Intelligence College Press, 2006).

the imaginative use of satellites for photography. In the case of the latter, the trick was not taking pictures, but getting them back to earth for analysis.

In this as in other areas, friction between the CIA and the Air Force became an issue, one President Eisenhower attempted to resolve with the creation in 1960 of the National Reconnaissance Office (NRO). Within a very short time, Secretary of Defense Robert McNamara created the Defense Intelligence Agency, while leaving the services with individual, organic intelligence components.

Each of these actions responded to either technological or bureaucratic realities that could not have been envisioned with the 1947 creation of CIA. It was, after all, intended to be the centralizing component of US intelligence. But how was that to happen with the creation of new agencies, each addressing important and complex processes (or "ints"), and reporting to cabinet departments beyond the control of the CIA? These were easy questions to ask. They were harder to answer.

By the 1970s, the issues that had not been resolved or even anticipated in 1947 begged for answers. Several studies of the time delineated the fundamental dilemma, namely that the director of central intelligence (DCI) needed to have some responsibility for the entire community, but that he could not, within the structure of the executive branch, have control of all its components, at least not in the sense of direct, hierarchical authority.[6]

At precisely the same time, to complicate the issue, the nation was dealing with its most extensive public review of intelligence in the post-1945 era. And much of what it was learning was neither pleasant nor flattering. The public suspicions raised by the war in Southeast Asia and the Watergate affair had come down heavily on the intelligence community, leading at least one Senate member to describe the CIA as a "rogue elephant." Accurate or not, the public and Congress wanted to ensure that the American secret services were both under control and focused on foreign intelligence. The result was the creation of permanent oversight bodies in the House and the Senate and legislation, such as the Foreign Intelligence Surveillance Act. In the decade that followed, issues, such as the Iran-Contra scandal, arose from time to time, but the new arrangements largely succeeded in bringing about a sense that the intelligence services were under appropriate direction.

Then, in 1990, the Soviet Union, the *raison d'etre* for virtually everything the United States had done in national security since 1947, disappeared. One question for intelligence arising from this event was one of mission. And understanding of that took time. A second consideration was that with the Cold War over, politicians promised a "peace dividend." With most of the intelligence budget hidden within the defense budget, intelligence would escape the budget cuts. In fact, a powerful member of the House told a journalist at this time:

---

6. See Michael Warner and Kenneth McDonald, *US Intelligence Community Reform Studies Since 1947* (CIA: Center for the Study of Intelligence, 2005).

"There is a second peace dividend out there. It's called the intelligence budget."

For intelligence and the military, the 1991 Gulf War provided an opportunity to employ against a Soviet-equipped Iraq the instruments that had been built to operate against the Soviet Union. The success of that effort did not obscure the reality that in weaponry and the fields of information and communications systems, the world was in the midst of an enormous transformation. American intelligence was challenged by the implications of the information revolution.

Two congressionally mandated "reform" efforts followed: the Aspin-Brown Commission (1995-1996) and the House of Representatives' "IC21" review (1997). Congress authorized Aspin-Brown . The "Intelligence Community in the 21st Century" was pushed by a Republican majority in the House Permanent Select Committee on Intelligence clearly unhappy with Aspin-Brown's bipartisan nature. That aside, the studies agreed, at least in general terms, on the need to prepare American intelligence for a very different environment from that of the Cold War. The studies encouraged greater coordination of the intelligence community under the DCI, especially in planning, budgeting, and staffing. One of the more fundamental differences in the recommendations of the two groups concerned the management of defense intelligence. "IC 21" argued that strengthening the DCI's role in national intelligence needed a companion strengthening of overall intelligence within the Department of Defense, through creation of a single, powerful, high-level DOD intelligence official. This position had been advanced in several earlier studies, especially an effort undertaken in the 1971 review led by James Schlesinger, who shortly thereafter (and briefly) served as DCI. Aspin-Brown pointedly disagreed with this recommendation.

Aside from the creation of the new position of deputy DCI for community management, the reform efforts of the 1990s did not produce significant results. In the absence of a clear national strategy that went beyond the retrospective vision of a "post-Cold War" world, the decade produced little in the way of intelligence transformation. As others have noted, the Air Force during this same period shut down the nearly sacred Strategic Air Command, the Army commissioned studies of both a 21st century force and even an "army after next." But the Intelligence Community, lacking the long-term study and research capabilities of the military services, struggled to deal with a rapidly changing operational environment and an ongoing information revolution with organizations that were reduced in resources but continuations of their Cold War selves. Even such declarations as DCI George Tenet's 1998 "We are at war with Al–Qa'ida" memorandum seem to have had little impact. Later suggestions notwithstanding, the record suggests little urgent pressure from congressional overseers to face the question of whether intelligence was adequately realigned to deal with the world as it existed in the period before September 2001.

After 2001, of course, things changed. Roberta Wohlstetter's insight of the "signal to noise" problem as it pertained to the attack on Pearl Harbor remained valid, despite any number of critics who claimed to distinguish – with perfect clarity — meaningless noise to precise and timely signals of impending attack. Unfortunately, this precision was available only after.

Over the next several years, spurred by the 9/11 attacks and by the controversies surrounding the role of intelligence in building the case for the invasion of Iraq, public and congressional pressure for reform of intelligence ebbed and flowed. By the summer of 2004, when President George H. W. Bush nominated Porter Goss as DCI, it seemed to many that the surge for fundamental change, including the transferrence of Community leadership from the DCI to a new director of national intelligence (DNI), seemed unlikely, at least until after the election. But the release of the 9/11 Commission Report late in the summer changed that. Whatever one thinks of the report, on which disagreement remains, it created a tidal wave of pressure for change, promoted by the very public role of families of the 9/11 victims.

Almost immediately, both Senator John Kerry, the Democratic nominee, and President Bush issued statements endorsing the report and promising action. The result was the Intelligence Reform and Terrorism Prevention Act (IRTPA) of 2004. As readers will know, the IRTPA created a director of national intelligence, leaving the director of the Central Intelligence Agency with no Community control. Whether the Act gave the DNI such control remains, seven years (and now four DNIs) after passage, unclear. The IRTPA as passed significantly restricted the authority, especially budgetary authority that had been included in the Senate version of the bill. This limitation notwithstanding, the DNI has achieved significant and promising changes in important areas, especially in the requirement of joint assignments for intelligence officers seeking careers at senior levels and in major aspects of analytic standards. Whether such long-term changes are sufficient to warrant the creation of an additional layer of management remains to be seen.

Two additional challenges confront next stages in "intelligence reform." As noted above, the United States has moved from a post-9/11 national security environment to what could be called a "post-post-9/11" environment, with no clearer description yet provided. Terrorism remains an important issue, but no issue offers the prospect of the 40-year central adversary provided by the Soviet Union. Is China a strategic threat? Or a potential strategic partner? To what degree is cyber security a national security issue? Or a criminal issue? And within those lines, how much of the responsibility to deal with cyber issues rests with government versus the private sector organizations that "own" most of the cyber structure? Even a quick glance at the most recent DNI annual threat statements to Congress attest not just to the volatility of the security environment but to the degree that threats link together. How do the nation's security instruments, including intelligence, align themselves with this environment?

The second issue confronting – and complicating — further reform of intelligence is the near certainty that defense spending, after a decade of increases, will decline. In the American experience, as defense budgets go, so go intelligence budgets. Over time, because of the presence within the Defense Department of the service intelligence components but also the "national" agencies, i.e., the National Security Agency, the National Reconnaissance Organization, and the National Geospatial-Intelligence Agency, the percentage of defense spending dedicated to intelligence has increased slightly but by and large has remained remarkably constant. Periods of austerity have generally followed the same, largely parallel, direction. Is it possible this pattern could be broken? That is at least possible, but clearly not certain.

What impact will this next austerity period have on changes in the intelligence establishment? One could conclude from previous reform periods, that American intelligence since 1947 has accepted certain changes, certainly in the technology with which it performs its missions, but has been more resistant to changes or proposed changes that could affect its fundamental structure. Without question, the decade that followed the attacks of September 2001 has produced progress in information sharing across agencies and in the acknowledgment of the value of open source information, to cite two examples. The question remains, however, whether these changes have been sufficient to keep pace with changes in both the geopolitical world and the concurrent changes taking place in the information environment in which the world now functions. If the external environment moves at a rate of 2X over some period of time, it makes little sense to boast of internal change at the rate of 1X.

Perhaps the most significant unanswered question for the years immediately ahead is that of the DNI's role. Using the austerity of the 1990s as an example, it seems in retrospect that the budget cuts associated with the "peace dividend" that followed the Soviet Union's collapse did enormous damage to US intelligence capabilities. What may be less apparent is that reaction to those cuts, within Presidential administrations, the Congress, and the agencies themselves was as damaging as the reductions themselves. On the morning of September 11, 2001, American national security, including intelligence, was still looking for an overall strategy – even a defining metaphor that could guide its actions. In intelligence, the absence of such a strategy had left the initiative for dealing with the new budget realities to each agency, with little overall direction. In the next four to five years, it is at least possible that the DNI can emerge from a sometimes difficult birthing period to provide a greater sense of direction and purpose to a community dealing with difficult budgetary circumstances at a time of great complexity in its operating environment. If that should be the result, a report card from 2015 or 2020 on the Intelligence Reform Act of 2004 and its most important action could prove very positive.

William M. Nolte is a 30-year veteran of the US Intelligence Community. He is the former director of education and training in the office of the Director of National Intelligence and chancellor of the National Intelligence University. He is a former CIA deputy assistant director. He was director of training, chief of legislative affairs, and senior intelligence advisor at the National Security Agency. He also served as deputy national intelligence officer for the Near East and South Asia during the Gulf War. He has taught at several Washington area universities, is on the board of CIA's Studies in Intelligence, and directed the Intelligence Fellows Program. He holds a BA from La Salle University and a PhD from the University of Maryland.

GUIDE TO THE STUDY OF INTELLIGENCE

Budget and Resource Management

Robert A. Mirabello, Col., USAF (Ret)

Introduction

Budgeting is one of the core functions of management. Moreover, no grand strategic vision or policy has any basis in reality without sufficient financial resources. The Intelligence Community (IC) is not exempt from the fierce competition for always limited discretionary funding. So a working knowledge of the complex rules and processes of this bureaucratic warfare is an essential "staff survival skill" for IC managers, especially those at senior levels of responsibility. Budget battles are a reflection of the contest between alternative ways to meet requirements; the policy debate quantified in terms of dollars and personnel. It follows that some level of knowledge about budget and resource management is essential to a more complete understanding of how the IC really works ... or sometimes doesn't.

The Programs[1]

US intelligence is indeed a "big business." With about $75 billion dollars in appropriations to support both the National Intelligence Program (NIP) and the complementary defense activities of the Military Intelligence Program, the Intelligence Community, if it were a corporation, would rank approximately 24th on the Fortune 500 in terms of annual revenue.

The National Intelligence Program, the only interdepartmental/interagency operating budget in the Federal Government, is governed by US Code Title 50 and Executive Order 12333. With an FY 2012 $55 billion budget request

---

1. For a more detailed description of the various intelligence programs see Dan Elkins. *Managing Intelligence Resources* (Dewey, AZ: DWE Press, 2010), chapter 4.

the director of national intelligence (DNI) directs 14 distinct programs including:

- The Community Management Account (CMA) for the functions of the Office of the Director of National Intelligence (ODNI).
- Most CIA activities in the Central Intelligence Agency Program (CIAP).
- National reconnaissance satellites in the National Reconnaissance Program (NRP).
- The national signals collection effort in the Consolidated Cryptologic Program (CCP).
- The analysis of imagery and its amalgamation with geospatial data in the National Geospatial-Intelligence Program (NGP), and
- Department of Defense (DOD)-wide and combatant command-level collection, analysis, counterintelligence, and support activities in the General Defense Intelligence (GDIP) and the department's Foreign Counterintelligence (FCIP) Programs.

All of the above programs are embedded in the large defense budget for security purposes. The NIP also funds the national intelligence activities of the Federal Bureau of Investigation and Drug Enforcement Administration in the Department of Justice, as well as intelligence efforts in the Departments of State, Energy, Treasury, and Homeland Security, including the Coast Guard.

Other defense intelligence, counterintelligence, and related programs, projects, and activities that are not in the NIP are funded through the Military Intelligence Program (MIP). The MIP provides the "take it with you" intelligence organic to the deployable units in all services at all echelons of command, for example, the Navy's anti-submarine ships with the Surveillance Towed Array Sensor System (SURTASS), the Air Force's RC-135 Rivet Joint signals intelligence aircraft, the Army's and Marine Corps' tactical signals intelligence capabilities, and the Defense Intelligence Agency's analysts assigned to the theater joint intelligence operations centers. Governed by US Code Title 10 and EO 12333, and at $19.2 billion (FY 2013 request) less than half the size of the NIP, the MIP is more accurately described as an internal departmental management tool than a distinct set of programs. Senior managers assess the MIP programs within the budgets of Defense Department organizations to balance capabilities and ensure that those budgets adequately address defense-wide, operational and tactical intelligence requirements.

The sum of the NIP and MIP budgets does not reflect the total of US intelligence spending. For example, US Coast Guard Intelligence and the Office Intelligence and Analysis aside, the NIP does not fund domestic intelligence related activities of the various components of the Department of Homeland Security. Nor, except for liaison personnel, does NIP fund the intelligence-like activities of state, local, and tribal governments in the 72 domestic intelligence fusion centers or analogous functions in the private sector. Furthermore, the MIP does not include the E-3 Airborne Warning and Control System (AWACS) or the MQ-9 Reaper unmanned aerial vehicle (UAV) missile platform, even though those systems collect data that feed tactical intelligence systems. The MIP specifically excludes the inherent intelligence gathering capabilities of a weapons system whose primary mission is not intelligence.

The Players[2]

Overseen by the National Security Council, the DNI determines, develops, manages, oversees, and directs implementation of the NIP, setting objectives and priorities, approving requirements, all reprogramming[3] and transfers of funds during the fiscal year, and evaluating its execution. The DNI directs the apportionment of NIP funds through the White House Office of Management and Budget (OMB).[4] The NIP budgets are executed through the departments and agencies that are members of the Intelligence Community.

The DNI enlists the Intelligence Community leadership through the Deputies Executive Committee (DEXCOM), which functions as the Intelligence Requirements Board (IRB) to advise on the entire budgetary process. The DNI, assisted by his director of defense intelligence (DDI), also participates in the development of the DOD's MIP. The undersecretary of defense for intelligence (USD(I)) serves as the DNI's director of defense intelligence. The NIP program managers (PMs) are functionally oriented and act across organizational boundaries as agents of the DNI for their specific program, allocating resources, consolidating requirements, developing program and budget submissions, compiling justification materials for the Congress, and overseeing spending. One example of a DNI program manager is the director of the National Security Agency (NSA). He oversees the Consolidated Cryptologic Program that funds activities at NSA and the military services.

In contrast, as an integral part of the larger defense budget, the MIP, truly "belongs" to the secretary of defense. The DOD budget process is traditionally managed by the deputy secretary, assisted by the director, cost assessment & program evaluation (CAPE), and the DOD comptroller (USD(C)). The secretary's principal staff assistant for all intelligence and related matters is the USD(I), who exercises authority, direction and control over defense intelligence and related agencies. As such, the USD(I), who, as mentioned, is also the DNI's

---

2. See Elkins, chapter 3 for further details.
3. Reprogramming is the process of taking funds appropriated for one purpose and applying it to another, usually a new and higher priority effort.
4. Apportionment is the term used when OMB allocates congressionally appropriated funds to Executive Branch departments and agencies. Appropriated funds are apportioned periodically over the fiscal year, usually by fiscal year quarter. Some funds may be withheld to insure adequate monies are available late in the fiscal year for reprogramming to higher priority needs.

director of defense intelligence, coordinates the development and execution of both defense and national intelligence policy, plans and programs; leads all DOD actions involving the MIP as its program executive, including issuing guidance, coordinating its development and execution, and chairing groups to address programmatic issues; and monitors the broader Battle Space Awareness Portfolio to achieve balance and synergies from its panoply of intelligence, surveillance and reconnaissance, command and control and complementary capabilities.

Often underappreciated as a player, the OMB is deeply involved throughout the budgetary process involving the Intelligence Community as well as all other departments and agencies of the federal government. OMB issues policy, fiscal guidance, and working assumptions to initiate programming and budgeting; reviews and approves budget submissions to the President's budget; clears Executive Branch proposed legislation and issues Statements of Administrative Policy (SAPs); and apportions appropriated budget authority, orchestrates reprogrammings and assesses performance during budget execution.

The Process[5]

Both the NIP and the MIP (as an integral part of the defense budget) are managed through separate, though coordinated, processes: the Planning, Programming, Budgeting, and Execution (PPBE) process for the MIP; and the Intelligence Planning, Programming, Budgeting, and Evaluation (IPPBE) system for the NIP. Starting more than two years before the beginning of a fiscal year, both processes are used to plan, program, and budget updates to existing activities that project costs, manpower needs and required capabilities for five years into the future (a database known as the Future Year Defense Program, FYDP, in the DOD), and prepare portions of the annual President's budget.

Planning

The planning process determines the goals, objectives, and end-states that support the National Security and National Intelligence Strategies and derivative guidance. Within the DOD, the ongoing Joint Strategic Planning System (JSPS), managed by the chairman, Joint Chiefs of Staff (CJCS), provides an analysis of long-term trends, challenges, gaps, and shortfalls and identifies and prioritizes defense needs. A parallel NIP planning process is led by the DNI's assistant deputy DNI for systems and resource analysis. A full year before IPPBE program and budget submissions are due, the IC components, national intelligence managers, and functional managers participate in the strategic, needs, capabilities, and risk analyses to develop a Major Issues List (MIL) for further

---

5. See Elkins, chapters 5, 6, and 9, for details.

study and DNI priorities on guidance, milestones, metrics, etc. By mid-spring, based on further analysis and OMB fiscal and policy guidance, the secretary of defense issues Defense Planning and Programming Guidance (DPPG) and Integrated Program and Budget Guidance. Similarly, the DNI's programming phase, again led by the assistant deputy DNI for systems and resource analysis, incorporates the results of the MIL studies into enterprise wide assessments, studies, and evaluations to identify capabilities, gaps, shortfalls, duplications, and tradeoffs to facilitate the development of options; as well as independent cost estimates for major acquisitions. The resulting Overall Resource View informs DNI's decisions that are documented in the DNI's draft (December) and final (spring) Consolidated Intelligence Guidance (CIG). Interestingly, the CIG also contains the USD(I)'s guidance for all defense department components for developing their MIP, which illustrates the growing integration of intelligence across organizational boundaries.

Programming and Budgeting

Starting from a FYDP updated with the final data being used in the latest President's budget, and applying the latest programmatic, fiscal and procedural guidance, intelligence managers for the NIP and MIP propose changes or additions to their programs, which then compete as they percolate up the PPBE or IPPBE management chains. NIP activities that are hidden within the defense budget are assigned one or more program element (PE) designators as a "cover." Within the defense budget, every system, project, and activity is assigned a program element number, which are the building blocks for the FYDP. On or about July 30 each year, MIP proposals are submitted to the staff of the secretary of defense as part of a military service's or defense agency's combined Program Objectives Memorandum (POM)/ Budget Estimates Submission (BES), justifying the cost and manpower for the entire FYDP. At approximately the same time, NIP program managers submit a five year Intelligence Program Budget Submission (IPBS). The first year of both constitutes the proposed input to the upcoming president's budget.

Between August and December, an Integrated Program and Budget Review is conducted jointly by the staffs of the secretary of defense and DNI. Hearings are conducted; teams formed to research alternatives; with "crosswalks" between NIP components, or between NIP and MIP activities, to resolve redundancies or other issues. Results and recommendations are briefed to senior intelligence and defense advisory bodies. The OMB staff participates in these reviews and makes their own recommendations for the OMB Director's Review.[6] That review results in refined White House guidance and directs adjustments

---

6. The Director of OMB is the senior White House budget official who also oversees the management practices of the federal government.

to dollar and manpower data (called "passbacks") that must be reflected in the submission for the President's budget. The President's budget is due to the Congress by the first Monday in February and is followed by volumes of detailed justification materials (called Congressional Budget Justification Books, CBJB, for the NIP and Congressional Justification Books, CJB, for the MIP).

Budget Execution

After Congress passes and the President signs an Appropriation Act, that law provides budget authority (BA) to the departments and agencies of the Executive Branch. Once apportioned by OMB, managers can then buy goods and services. For the DOD, total obligation authority (TOA) is the sum of this new BA plus the residual authority from previous years' appropriations. By law, the DNI directs how the OMB director apportions NIP funds, an authority unique in the executive.[7] NIP funds are executed by the comptrollers of the departments in which the NIP program resides through the financial system of that department. Departmental comptrollers assist the DNI in ensuring compliance with guidance. This assumes that both MIP and NIP appropriated funds, IAW Section 504 of the National Security Act of 1947, as amended, were "specifically authorized by the Congress for use for such activities."

The Role of Congress[8]

Congressional "power of the purse," the essential constitutional check on the executive, is exercised in three phases. The Congressional Budget Act of 1974 devised a comprehensive, independent, and (supposedly) disciplined Congressional budget process. By mid-spring, the Budget Committees of both houses, supported by the Congressional Budget Office (CBO), respond to the President's proposal with a Concurrent Budget Resolution, which sets limits on discretionary spending.[9] Meanwhile, the authorizing committees' staffs review the President's budget line by line to determine which proposed activities ought to be permitted. Congress' approval of intelligence programs is contained in the Intelligence Authorization Bill for the NIP and in the National Defense Authorization Bill for the MIP.[10] Authorization for MIP activities involves the House Permanent Select Committee on Intelligence (HPSCI), the House Armed

---

7. This unique authority was contained in the *Intelligence Reform and Terrorism Prevention Act of 2004*.
8. See Elkins, chapters 7 and 8 for details.
9. Government spending is either mandatory or discretionary. Mandatory spending is that set by law. It includes Social Security, Medicare, interest on the national debt, and other automatic payments. Discretionary spending is that approved by the Congress each year and includes intelligence, defense, the space program, and foreign aid, for instance.
10. Congress failed to pass an Intelligence Authorization Bill from 2004 until 2010 due to political haggling. Intelligence activities and programs were "authorized" by including appropriate language in the annual Department of Defense Appropriations Act.

Services Committee (HASC) and the Senate Armed Services Committee (SASC), with the advice of the Senate Select Committee on Intelligence (SSCI). For the NIP, HPSCI has exclusive jurisdiction in the House of Representatives while the SSCI shares jurisdiction over DOD elements of the NIP with the Senate Armed Services Committee. The Foreign Affairs, Homeland Security, and Judiciary Committees of the House and Senate can become involved in intelligence matters related to the departments of State, Homeland Security, FBI, and DEA, respectively. Finally, the staffs of the Senate and House Appropriations Committees work on a series of Appropriation Bills that determine how many funds each authorized program should receive. The House Defense Subcommittee and Senate Appropriations Committee handle appropriations for the defense elements of the NIP and the CMA and CIA programs. Other appropriations subcommittees become involved in other departments' appropriations.

A report card on the effectiveness of the congressional budget reforms of the 1970s would have mixed grades. Formal, routine, documented, Congressional oversight of the Intelligence Community has become institutionalized, notwithstanding recurring disagreements on access to information. However, none of the recommendations in the 9/11 Commission Report to enhance the authority and effectiveness of the Intelligence Committees have been adopted by Congress. To the contrary, those committees' failure to produce timely intelligence authorization bills, and resultant problems resulting from authorization/appropriation mismatches, have further eroded their influence and relevance. More broadly, the breakdown of the budget resolution process, the weakening of constraints on spending, appropriating through omnibus continuing resolutions, the excessive reliance on urgent supplemental appropriations during the fiscal year, and the explosion of entitlements spending, suggest that the process is in need of serious reform.

Conclusion

The challenges facing IC resource managers may be analogous to those faced by their counterparts in industry, but government managers lack some key tools available to the private sector: e.g. a "hard" bottom line profit, or relevant and reliable performance metrics. Choosing among competing alternative programs is all the more challenging when issues of culture, secrecy, and compartmentalization; and often problematic relationships with policymakers, are added to the mix.[11] Finally, an "inconvenient truth" of the Budget Game is that its rigorous analysis using sophisticated decision support tools employs "data" largely derived from ambiguous estimates and imperfect assumptions. Decisions based on a poorly understood fiscal future of tax receipts, inflation, interest rates, the maturity of technology, global challenges, unidentified

---

11. See Elkins, chapters 1, 2, and 10.

adversaries, and a host of other "unknown unknowns" are inevitably flawed.[12] Along with the politics, and bureaucratic politics that are always in play, these uncertainties make the budgetary process as much art as science, with its effectiveness influenced to a great extent by the talents of the artists.

READINGS FOR INSTRUCTORS

The following are recommended readings for instructors on intelligence budgets and resource management:

Elkins, Dan. *Managing Intelligence Resources*, 3rd ed. (Dewey, AZ: DWE Press, 2010). For over 20 years, this privately published volume and its predecessors have been an essential text for "insider" study of the programs, participants, and the processes through which national and defense intelligence resources are acquired, managed, and overseen. *dwelkins2@cs.com.*

Hitch Charles. H. and Roland N. McKean. *The Economics of Defense in the Nuclear Age*, R-346 (Santa Monica: Rand Corporation, 1960). The book that "started it all": the original source for the program budgeting systems used by the intelligence community.

Lowenthal Mark M. *Intelligence: From Secrets to Policy*, 5th ed. (Washington, DC: CQ Press, 2011). An excellent introduction and comprehensive overview to the study of intelligence and policy, particularly the sections on the Intelligence Budget Process and Oversight and Accountability, pp 52-55 and 224-227.

Schick, Alan. *The Federal Budget: Politics, Policy and Process.* 3rd ed. (Washington, DC: The Brookings Institution, 2007). An examination of the federal budget processes and practices, an analysis of the underlying politics and the impact of the virtual collapse of Congressional discipline on the long-term budgetary outlook.

The Office of the Director of Intelligence Home Page <*http://www.dni.gov/index. html*> is an additional source of both current and historical information. It also has links to the entire IC. Useful references include:

An Overview of the United Sates Intelligence Community for the 111th Congress 2009

US National Intelligence: An Overview 2011

The National Intelligence Strategy of the United States of America August 2009

ODNI/Office of General Counsel, Intelligence Community Legal Reference Book

Budgeting for Intelligence Programs: Intelligence Community Directive (ICD) 104, May 17, 2006

Intelligence Planning, Programming, Budgeting, and Evaluation System: Intelligence Community directive (ICD) 116, September 14, 2011

Intelligence Community Strategic Enterprise Management Intelligence Community Directive (ICD) 106, May 20, 2008.

Other useful sources of current information on issues related to the manage-

---

12. See Charles. H Hitch and Roland N. McKean *The Economics of Defense in the Nuclear Age*, 182.

ment of Intelligence resources are reports of the General Accountability Office and the Congressional Research Service. Some examples include:

Best, Richard A. Jr, *Intelligence Issues for the Congress.* CRS RL33539, March 3, 2011. (This is a recurring publication of the Congressional Research Service)

Best, Richard A. Jr. and Alfred Cumming, *Director of National Intelligence Statutory Authorities: Status and Proposal,* RL34231. (CRS: May 26, 2010)

Daggett, Stephen. *The Intelligence Budget: A Basic Overview,* RS21945. (CRS: September 24, 2004).

GAO-11-465, Intelligence, Surveillance, and Reconnaissance: Actions Are Needed to Increase Integration and Efficiencies of DOD's ISR Enterprise, June 03, 2011

Colonel Robert A. Mirabello, USAF (Ret.), has 40 years of experience in military and national intelligence training and education. Currently a senior faculty member of the Intelligence and Security Academy, he is also an adjunct at the National Intelligence University and University of Maryland University College. From 1990 to 2007, he served at the National Intelligence University, including as dean of the School of Intelligence Studies. Since retiring from federal service, he has managed or advised professional development programs for the director of national intelligence and at the Department of Homeland Security.

GUIDE TO THE STUDY OF INTELLIGENCE

Intelligence Oversight Design

Tobias T. Gibson

Oversight of the US Intelligence Community (IC) is complex and involves many people and institutions across all three branches of the government. This essay introduces the major players, powers, roles, and jurisdictions of those charged with the oversight of our nation's intelligence agencies.

The President

Some of the President's powers are enumerated in the Constitution, for example those related to his role as commander-in-chief. Other powers may be only implied by the Constitution, such as the use of executive orders to direct Executive Branch bureaucracies. As the nation's chief executive, the President bears primary responsibility for directing the IC (a management task) and is also responsible for its oversight to ensure its adherence to laws and policies and its effectiveness.

As commander in chief, the President is charged with the nation's security. As such, he largely controls the nation's military capacity, which is a key influencer of the IC, partly because approximately 80 percent of the intelligence budget goes to the Department of Defense (DOD). Moreover, eight of sixteen intelligence agencies are subsets of Defense, including an intelligence group in each branch of the military, as well as the Defense Intelligence Agency, the National Security Agency, and others. Therefore, as commander in chief, especially when coupled with his duty to submit the initial budget to Congress each year, the President plays a major role in managing the IC.

The President has oversight power of intelligence agencies by virtue of his role in nominating the heads of these departments and agencies. For example, the President nominates the secretaries of defense, state, treasury, and homeland security. He also names the director of national intelligence and the heads of individual agencies such as CIA and FBI. These appointments are subject to Senate approval.

Executive orders (EOs) have historically had major impact on executive policy and national security. Three executive orders, 11905, 12036, and 12333, have played especially large roles in intelligence oversight. In 1976, President Ford issued EO 11905, implementing many changes in the wake of President Nixon's perceived intelligence abuses. According to 11905, the National Security Council (NSC) was to review intelligence activities twice a year, created the Committee for Foreign Intelligence (CFI), and was to have fiscal influence over the National Foreign Intelligence Program.[1] The CFI had only three members, the director of central intelligence (DCI), who was also the CFI chair, the deputy secretary of defense for intelligence; and the deputy assistant to the President for national security affairs. CFI reported to the NSC. The proposed intelligence budget was subject to Office of Management and Budget approval.

EO 12036, issued by President Carter, replaced 11905, and allowed the DCI to play a more central role in intelligence budget recommendations. This budgetary power of the DCI became a primary source of irritation with DCI Stansfield Turner, in particular from those agencies housed in the DOD.[2] EO 12036 also cut the NSC committees to two, and gave these committees broad oversight and review duties related to the quality of information the IC was providing.

EO 12333, issued by President Reagan in 1981, allowed the DCI to establish advisory boards as needed, and specifically named the DCI as the chair of these advising bodies. Reagan also sought to increase the "analytical competition" between IC agencies to improve the quality of the finished intelligence product.[3]

According to some, 12333 further granted the CIA power to covertly operate within the United States, though the Agency was prohibited from gathering intelligence on domestic activities of citizens and corporations. CIA was also allowed, with Presidential approval, to use covert actions domestically, as long as the intention was not undue influence of public opinion and the like. Similarly, FBI was granted permission to operate domestically in support of foreign intelligence collection.[4]

President George W. Bush amended EO 12333 to make the new director of national intelligence (DNI) the nation's chief intelligence officer. The DNI is the primary intelligence advisor to the President and the NSC; the director of central intelligence position and title were abolished.[5]

The President also manages the IC by more secret measures, including

---

1. Garthoff, 115-116. [See Bibliography for all references.]
2. Ibid, 143, 152.
3. EO 12333, Part 1.1A.
4. Richelson, 19, 153.
5. Ibid, 464.

National Security Directives (NSD). The nomenclature for National Security Directives can change from administration to administration. For example, Clinton called them Presidential Decision Directives, George W. Bush referred to them as National Security Presidential Directives, President Obama prefers Presidential Policy Directives.[6] NSDs are used as "...formal notification to the head of a department or other government agency informing him of a presidential decision in the field of national security affairs and generally requiring follow-up action by the department or agency addressed."[7] Although NSDs are similar to EOs, they often remain classified. They are not issued in the Federal Register and are often not acknowledged to exist by Presidential administrations.[8] NSDs have been used to impact intelligence agencies in several ways. For example, in an effort to limit information leaks, President Reagan required that intelligence employees with access to classified material be subject to polygraph tests and were monitored for their contacts with foreign nationals.[9]

Additional Oversight in the Executive Branch

The secretaries of defense, state, treasury, and homeland security oversee intelligence gathering by their departments. The secretary of defense, in particular, because of the number of agencies within, and the allotted funds to Defense, has a particularly important oversight role. State, treasury, and homeland security have intelligence capabilities, and are important players in the IC, making the secretary of each department important cogs in the oversight process. The secretary of state reviews intelligence activities consistency with US foreign policy.

The heads of individual agencies are essential in directing their individual agencies. The CIA director, for example, must direct the CIA to provide the best intelligence possible to the policymakers who depend on the information. Failure to do so can lead to questionable, or even horrendous, policy decisions.

The director of national intelligence is charged with directing the intelligence agencies. President Bush's amendment to EO 12333 directed the DNI to "oversee and direct implementation of the National Intelligence Program budget" and ordered the heads of individual intelligence agencies to "provide all programmatic and budgetary information necessary to support the Director in developing the National Intelligence Program."[10] This has proven to be a more difficult task than expected, however. For example, DNI Dennis Blair was let go by President Obama after controversy arose when he tried "to exert

---

6. Cooper, 144, http://www.fas.org/irp/offdocs/ppd/index.html).
7. President Lyndon Johnson, as quoted by Cooper, 144.
8. Ibid,145.
9. Ibid, 187.
10. As quoted in Richelson, 464.

too much operational control over CIA."[11]

This weakness seems to be in the design of the Office of the DNI (ODNI). Thomas Fingar describes the ODNI as "limited by ambiguity, ambivalence and animosity."[12] Indeed, DNI Mike McConnell spoke publicly about the DNI's inability to direct IC activities. When Congress considered giving the DNI more power "Secretary of Defense Donald Rumsfeld waged a successful campaign within the Executive Branch and with key members of Congress to preserve his (and other cabinet members') authorities."[13] Although the Intelligence Reform and Terrorism Prevention Act provided the DNI more power than the DCI possessed, the Act nonetheless limited the ODNI's power by requiring that it "must respect and not abrogate the statutory responsibilities of the heads of departments."[14]

The President's Intelligence Advisory Board (PIAB) and its Intelligence Oversight Board (IOB) reside in the Executive Office of the President (EOP). The PIAB provides the President with nonpartisan intelligence advice, and has served every President from Eisenhower to Obama, save Carter. The PIAB's recommendations to improve intelligence agency performance are reported to the president as needed, but at least twice a year. The Board, which does not exceed 16 members, has full access to intelligence data. The IOB, created by President Ford, is charged with ensuring the intelligence community's adherence to the Constitution, statutes and presidential fiats, and its members are also members of the PIAB.[15]

The Joint Intelligence Community Council (JICC) was created in 2004 to serve as an oversight body. The body is chaired by the DNI, and includes the heads of the Departments of State, Defense, Homeland Security, Treasury, Energy, and Justice. JICC was intended to advise the DNI on budget issues, and to support the performance of policies established by the DNI. It also was intended to help interagency cooperation, with advisory roles in matters of finance and budget, as well as oversight and evaluation of the IC. Some critics believe it is underutilized.[16]

The OMB, described by Gordon Adams as "one of the least understood, most influential, and sometimes most disliked institutions in the executive branch,"[17] has played an increased role in intelligence budgeting since the 1990s, including often being involved in discussions about covert actions. Moreover, because of the budgetary roles of ODNI, OMB is more active with IC budgeting. These activities include helping ODNI "develop an integrated budget

---

11. George, 165.
12. Fingar, p 139.
13. Ibid 142.
14. Ibid.
15. "About the PIAB."
16. Richelson, 470.
17. Adams, 57

planning system to examine the intelligence agencies' budget submissions, and ... participat[ing] in a joint intelligence budget review with ODNI."[18]

The Department of Justice Office of Legal Counsel (OLC) also plays a major, if understated, role in intelligence oversight. First, OLC is the original clearinghouse for executive orders, empowered to review EOs prior to issuance for "form and legality." Second, OLC serves as a primary legal advisor for the President and the Executive Branch as a whole.[19] The legal advice of OLC can have serious impact on the actions of the IC. For example, according to the Hughes-Ryan Amendment of 1974, the President should inform Congress of covert actions "in timely fashion." Reagan authorized a covert action connected with the Iran-Contra scandal, but required that Congress not be informed. In the wake of this unreported action, OLC determined that it was the duty of the President to interpret what constituted a timely report, and that he had "virtually unfettered discretion" to do so.[20] More recently, opinions issued by the OLC gave legal permission and protection to controversial interrogation methods, such as waterboarding, employed by CIA.

Congress

Unlike the Executive Branch, which has a singular head, Congress is comprised of 535 voting members, divided between two independent chambers and two parties and who represent 50 states and 435 congressional districts. Moreover, by organization and intent, the terms of office and rotating election of senators are designed to slow the course of legislation, and makes oversight, at least in some ways, more difficult by Congress than by the President. Despite Congress' comparative weakness, it has many oversight tools at its disposal.

Perhaps the most powerful tool that Congress has to ensure its role in the oversight process is that of appropriating funds. Although the President presents a recommended budget to Congress, constitutionally, the power of "the purse" belongs with Congress. If Congress is unhappy with an agency or department, or if an organization is non-responsive to Congress' preferences and attempts at oversight, Congress can reduce or restrict the budget in retaliation. Every bureaucrat, knowing this to be the case, has an incentive to stay within the particular bounds that Congress establishes.

While there are currently two congressional committees with primary jurisdiction over intelligence, the Senate Select Committee on Intelligence and the House Permanent Select Committee on Intelligence, there are other committees with indirect oversight ability. In particular, both the House and the Senate have Appropriations Subcommittees in charge of defense spend-

---

18. Ibid, 67
19. Gibson.
20. Crabb and Holt, 180.

ing, which play important oversight roles as well. Although the intelligence committees have primary jurisdiction, the House and Senate Armed Services Committees, and various committees in both chambers with jurisdictions over homeland security, energy, courts, and justice have overlapping jurisdictions with the select intelligence committees.

Hearings and investigations allow Congress to examine any agency. Although there are some protections offered to IC members, especially when testifying about policy, one should recall the hearings related to the Iran-Contra scandal and the acrimony and nation's eye on covert operations during the congressional hearings related to that scandal.

The Government Accountability Office (GAO) is a non-partisan body that assists Congress with its fiscal oversight. In May, 2011 DNI James Clapper, at Congress' behest in the 2010 Intelligence Authorization Act, ordered intelligence agencies to cooperate more fully when being reviewed by the GAO. Although some restrictions remain, the GAO has been able to play an increasingly active role in IC review. For example, GAO recently reviewed FBI counterterrorism activities after the FBI had balked at providing the information necessary for years.[21]

There are three particular caveats to the above discussion about congressional oversight that bear discussion. First, due to the classification and sensitivity of much of the information that intelligence agencies are asked to deliver to Congress, briefings to Congress often only include the leadership of both chambers and the chairs and ranking members of the chambers' intelligence committees.[22] Second, budget adjustments are difficult for Congress to make, especially with precision. Finally, there is literature, originating in political science, which suggests that Congress will often not take an active role in oversight. In particular, rather than embarking on continued, steady oversight actions, dubbed "police patrols," that account for much of its resources, Congress may prefer reacting to "fire alarms," or issues that arise sporadically and require congressional attention—but which do not require many oversight resources. A fire alarm system of oversight depends on "individuals and organized interest groups"[23] and other sources, such as whistleblowers and the media, to alert Congress to violations of law, policy, or congressionally directed preferences.

The fire alarm style of oversight seems reasonable, especially when the reader learns that many forms of active oversight attempts by Congress go unheeded by intelligence agencies.[24] For example, NSDs, discussed above, are often not revealed to Congress. Even during the Iran-Contra scandal, as Con-

---

21. Aftergood.
22. Lowenthal, 214.
23. McCubbins and Schwartz, 166.
24. Lowenthal, 211.

gress was seeking active oversight of the intelligence community, the Reagan Administration failed to reveal the full extent of its issued NSDs. Congressman Lee Hamilton (D-IN), who was chair of the select committee investigating the scandal, testified that NSDs are used "to create policy [that] infringes on Congress' constitutional prerogatives by inhibiting effective oversight and limiting Congress' policymaking role."[25]

Courts

The Supreme Court and other Article III federal courts rarely exercise direct oversight of intelligence operations. They do hear cases with ramifications for intelligence, however. Some of the more recent examples are the cases involving questions of *habeus corpus* stemming from the War on Terror. For example, Hamdi v. Rumsfeld, Hamdan v. Rumsfeld, and Rasul v. Bush all impacted the manner in which the United States could hold unlawful combatants who were suspected of terrorist activities.

A court with more direct oversight is the Foreign Intelligence Surveillance Court (FISC). Authorized by Congress in the Foreign Intelligence Surveillance Act (FISA), passed in the wake of revelations that the Johnson and Nixon administrations had participated in lawless domestic spying, the FISC is intended to provide intelligence agencies with a legal warrant while also retaining the secrecy necessary to a successful intelligence operation. The FISC judges are placed on the court by the chief justice of the United States. Via statute, and expanded by Executive Order, the FISC is charged with issuing warrants related to wiretapping, electronic surveillance and the collection of physical evidence.

FISC critics note that the warrant requests are rarely denied. Between 1979 and 2004, of the 18,748 warrant requests that were reviewed, only five were rejected,[26] others were altered significantly. Despite FISC's willingness to issue the requested warrants, the George W. Bush Administration chose to ignore the FISC and, under the Terrorist Surveillance Program, wiretap American citizens without telling the court.[27]

The federal judiciary, described by Alexander Hamilton as "the least dangerous branch," is even more dependent on Executive Branch cooperation with constitutional and statutory compliance regulations to exercise oversight than is Congress. When a President fails to comply, whatever the reason, the oversight capabilities of the judiciary are severely compromised.

---

25. As quoted in Cooper, 195.
26. Leonnig.
27. Ibid.

Conclusion

Oversight of the IC agencies is an exceptionally difficult, but decidedly important, task. On paper, the Executive, Legislative, and Judicial Branches seem to be designed with oversight in mind. With the changes in the oversight procedure in the wake of the attacks of September 11, 2001, hope remains that as the ODNI, as well as the political institutions with oversight capability and duty, matures on the job, that effective, consistent oversight can become a norm rather than a luxury.

This article is meant only to serve as an introduction to this material. Because of time and space constraints, this effort purposefully limits discussion of the history of the intelligence agencies founding, which the Executive and Legislative Branches, working in concert, are responsible for. There is little discussion of the ebb and flow, or the cyclical *laissez faire* and overcorrection models of oversight seemingly practiced by the elected and appointed officials who are responsible for overseeing the IC. There is very little history of the individual intelligence agencies, all of which play an important role in understanding the strengths and weaknesses of the models of oversight. Finally, there is very little said about the personalities which shape the intelligence community and those who oversee it, many of whom can have significant impact.

Readings for Instructors

"About the PIAB." http://www.whitehouse.gov/administration/eop/piab/about (accessed June 6, 2012).

Adams, Gordon."The Office of Management and Budget: The President's Policy Tool" in Roger Z. George and Harvey Rishikof, (eds.), *The National Security Enterprise: Navigating the Labyrinth*, (Washington, DC: Georgetown University Press, 2011)..

Aftergood, Steven. "GAO Expands Oversight of Intelligence," March 19, 2012, http://www.fas.org/blog/secrecy/2012/03/gao_expands.html (accessed June 7, 2012).

Cooper, Phillip J. *By Order of the President: The Use and Abuse of Executive Direct Action.*(Lawrence, KS: University of Kansas Press, 2002).

Crabb, Jr. Cecil V. and Pat M. Holt. *Invitation to Struggle: Congress, the President, and Foreign Policy*, 4th ed. (Washington, DC: CQ Press, 1992).

Fingar, Thomas."Office of the Director of National Intelligence: Promising Start Despite Ambiguity, Ambivalence, and Animosity," in Roger Z. George and Harvey Rishikof (eds.). *The National Security Enterprise: Navigating the Labyrinth*, (Washington, DC: Georgetown University Press, 2011).

George, Roger Z. "Central Intelligence Agency: The President's Own," in Roger Z. George and Harvey Rishikof, (eds.)., *The National Security Enterprise: Navigating the Labyrinth*, (Washington, DC: Georgetown University Press, 2011).

Gibson, Tobias T. "Office of Legal Counsel: Inner Workings and Impact" in *Law*

& *Courts* 18 (2), 2008, 7-12.

Garthoff, Douglas F. *Directors of Central Intelligence as Leaders of the U.S. Intelligence Community, 1946-2005* (Washington, DC: Potomac Press, 2007).

Leonnig, Carol D. "Secret Court's Judges Were Warned About NSA Spy Data." *Washington Post*, February 9, 2006, A01.

Lewis, Eugene. *Public Entrepreneurship: Toward a Theory of Bureaucratic Political Power.* (Bloomington, IN: Indiana University Press, 1980).

Lowenthal, Mark M. *Intelligence: From Secrets to Policy* (4th ed.).(Washington, DC: CQ Press, 2009).

"Presidential Policy Directives [PPDs]: Barack Obama Administration." *http:// www.fas.org/irp/offdocs/ppd/index.html* (accessed June 7, 2012).

Richelson, Jeffrey T. *The US Intelligence Community,* 6th ed. (Boulder, CO: Westview Press, 2012).

Dr. Tobias T. Gibson is an associate professor of political science and the Security Studies Program coordinator at Westminster College in Fulton, MO. His work appears in numerous books and other professional outlets. His areas of expertise include the American Executive and Judicial Branches, constitutional law, and security. Dr. Gibson earned his PhD at Washington University in St. Louis.

Guide to the Study of Intelligence

Educating the Next Generation of Intelligence Professionals

Jan P. Herring

Introduction: The Educational Challenge

The "future" that intelligence professionals will have to understand and work in will differ significantly from that of today. Educating and preparing students for that challenge requires intelligence educators both to be aware of how that future is likely to evolve and to begin developing new educational material and methods today.

The intelligence environment of 2020 and beyond will be shaped by many of the same issues we face today, i.e., geo-political differences, increasingly sophisticated military technology and weapons, international trade and monetary issues, a growing concern for the protection of critical infrastructure, and terrorism in all its multi-faceted forms; and, a host of new and emerging national policy issues that heretofore have mainly been the concern of the private sector, i.e., intellectual property (IP) protection, supply chain integrity, public health, and climate change. Preparing intelligence students to cope with both types of issues in an insightful and professional manner is a part of the challenge. Preparing them to work in either or both private-sector intelligence and government organizations is a new and emerging challenge for most educational institutions. We are probably better prepared to handle the former, but have much work to do to prepare today's students for intelligence work in the private-sector or to address private-sector issues within government intelligence organizations.

It is the private-sector challenge that we need to highlight. For the most part, both government and academic educational entities are well positioned to begin preparing government intelligence personnel for policy-related issues stemming from the private sector. Identifying the appropriate subject matter experts and bringing them into the current government and academic educational systems seems a rather straightforward approach to this challenge. And, possibly, enhancing such educational efforts through the assignment of government intelligence personnel in private-sector exchanges or hiring experienced business intelligence personnel for specific government intelligence work.

The private-sector intelligence situation is not so tractable. With the exception of a few universities and private-sector educational academies specializing in intelligence training, there is no formal or organized educational system producing intelligence professionals for the business community. As a result, both the quality and quantity of well-trained business intelligence professionals is woefully inadequate. For the most part, corporations either pay to have their employees trained for intelligence work or they are left to learn the "trade" on their own.

Some private-sector entities have hired former government intelligence officers for certain specialized needs such as communications security and counterintelligence work. But few government intelligence analysts or field collectors have been successful in finding equivalent jobs in the private sector. Their subject-matter expertise and associated skill sets are just not a good match for most business intelligence assignments. The few that have made a successful transition have either gone back to school to acquire appropriate business knowledge and occupational skills, or gone through some industry specific and/or business intelligence training. However, such occupational training is not easy to find and provides no guarantee of employment. Furthermore, most universities and other types of higher education have not seen this area of professional development as a part of their institutional responsibilities.

There is one additional problem that further complicates this educational challenge. The two intelligence "communities," public and private sector, currently have no formal way of communicating or working with each other on problems or issues of common concern. This is particularly true of contemporary issues such as cyber security or global supply chain protection. And while private-sector intelligence training is available to government employees, the reverse is not true. However, both communities are welcomed to participate in academically based education and training. So if universities and accredited private-sector training organizations were to develop appropriate "next generation" intelligence courses and materials, they could be the logical provider of such education services for both future public and private-sector intelligence professionals.

Two major forces-of-change appear to be shaping the future intelligence environment that both public and private sector intelligence professionals will be confronted with, and equally important, will be working in. The better we understand both, the better we as educators will be able to prepare today's students for their future assignments.

The Privatization of Intelligence

First, is an on-going trend, known as the Privatization of Intelligence. The concept of "privatizing intelligence" was defined by two former OSS officers and friends, Bill Colby and Stevan Dedijer.[1] Colby, a long-time CIA officer and one time Director of the CIA, and Dedijer, a Yugoslav that volunteered to serve in the U.S. military during WWII, subsequently becoming a university educator and the "godfather" of today's business intelligence discipline, were directly involved in the movement of professional intelligence operations from government auspices to private-sector entities such as corporations and financial institutions. This public to private sector migration during the 1970s and 80's, resembled that taking place in several countries where governments were divesting themselves of government-owned transportation, mining and other business enterprises. This governmental action was called "privatization." Thus, the creation and operation of organized intelligence functions by private sector entities was labeled the Privatization of Intelligence.

It began in the 1970s as business competition became more heated and international. Several multi-national corporations and their leaders recognized that they – like governments – would need formal, organized intelligence programs to compete successfully ... and possibly survive. In that vanguard were firms such as Motorola, Kodak, IBM, and corporate leaders in the chemical, communications, and pharmaceutical sectors.[2]

By the mid-1980s, the international business intelligence (BI) profession had grown to the size that it spawned its own professional society, i.e. the Society of Competitive Intelligence Professionals (SCIP, which was renamed Strategic and Competitive Intelligence Professionals).[3] Today, SCIP has members and chapters in some 50 countries. Its membership has varied over the years, from about 7,000 in the 1990s to around 3,000 today. An estimate of the total number of BI practitioners worldwide would probably be 10 to 100 times that number, which would include part-time as well as full-time employees. Furthermore, it has been estimated that up to 85% of all multinational corporations have some form of business or competitive intelligence function.[4]

---

1. See Jon Sigurdson and Yael Tågerud (eds.). *The Intelligent Corporation-The privatization of intelligence* (Taylor Graham, 1992).
2. See Jenny Fisher, "Competitive Intelligence: A Case Study of Motorola's Corporate Competitive Intelligence Group, 1983-2009" in the *Guide to the Study of Intelligence, http://www.afio.com/40_guide. htm.* See also John J. McGonagle's article, "Competitive Intelligence" in the Guide at http://www.afio. com/40_guide.htm.
3. *http://www.scip.org.*
4. Jan Herring, "Create an Intelligence Programs for Current and Future Business Needs," *Competitive Intelligence Magazine 8 (5)*, September-October 2005.

This growth in private-sector intelligence operations is worldwide. In some countries, their governments have encouraged and assisted them, China and France being prime examples. In most, however, it has been a business driven phenomenon.

The Merger of Private and Public Concerns

The second major force shaping the future of intelligence are governments worldwide focusing more on business or private-sector issues such as supply chain security, IP protection, and even climate change. Although this trend is rather late to the scene, it is clearly moving national intelligence communities into areas and disciplines that require government intelligence professionals to understand more about private-sector organizations and their operations. For the most part, government intelligence education and training has not yet begun to address these types of private-sector issues. And, except for a few universities, such as Mercyhurst, most academic educational institutions are not yet aware of these new government intelligence initiatives – and even fewer are currently capable of addressing them.

These two major forces-of-change will cause government intelligence professionals and private-sector intelligence practitioners to increasingly focus on similar issues and challenges. Both will use the same "open sources" of intelligence (OSINT) for collection and similar analytical methodologies – but will produce results for different types of customers with their specific public or private sector applications. Consequently, this future "intelligence world" will be both similar and different with new and unexpected intelligence challenges – of a different and increasingly complex nature. And, most likely, we will see an entirely new and disparate "Intelligence Community" – one including both government and business intelligence professionals.

What about this new "evolving" public/private-sector "Intelligence Community?" It is unlikely to be a formally combined public-private intelligence organization – for the most part, each sector will continue to operate separately, responding to its own priorities.

Both communities will work increasingly on similar problems, e.g., threats to company's IP and supply chains, cyber and financial security issues, threats to public health, including pharmaceutical production & supply chain integrity, and given the government's growing concerns about its security, the national infrastructure – which, for the most part, is owned by the private sector. These are just a few of the types of new security issues finding their way into national intelligence requirements in the US and worldwide.

Furthermore, as it becomes more and more evident that a country's national security in today's global marketplace is a combination of its military security and its economic wellbeing, the two intelligence communities' responsibilities will begin to converge. How and when is unsure. But they will – possibly sooner than expected. It would be in the best interest of all, for the two communities to work together on some aspects of these intelligence topics.

For intelligence professionals, it behooves us to begin thinking more constructively about that future intelligence environment. For educators, it is not too soon to begin considering how we will train future intelligence officers to work in that new intelligence world with over-lapping concerns and inter-dependent responsibilities.

"That Future" Intelligence Environment

Let me describe a possible scenario for "That Future" intelligence environment, at least one that seems reasonable for planning purposes in the near term:

- For the most part, governments will still view the world as made up of major geo-political blocs – North and South America; Europe, both separately and the Union; Russia, old and new; the Middle East – – both friendly and threatening; Southeast Asia, Northeast Asia, and China; and, a new and challenging Africa. Military and political affairs will continue to dominate their concerns – though energy and monetary issues will not be far behind. Global trade and commercial competition will become a national priority. International terrorism will continue to be a major national security concern – both domestically and abroad.

- The business world will increasingly be made up of "true" multi-national corporations (MNC's) including state-owned-enterprises (SOE's) ... all competing on a global basis ... with growing levels of government involvement and BI assistance. Such companies realize that to be successful, they will have to better understand the geo-political world they operate in ... and cope with the regional as well as global competitors they face in each chosen market... which in some cases, includes the local governments. They will need better BI and security capabilities than most currently possess if they are to survive and succeed.

- Both private sector and government entities will have growing interests in both geo-political and geo-economic affairs. MNC concerns about government activities affecting trade and monetary affairs have grown with their global operations – and will continue to do so. Joint interests in the new and emerging intelligence topics of cyber security, IP threats, and supply chain viability will grow internationally. And both communities will share a mutual concern for the threats posed by international terrorism ... and climate change related disasters and implications.

Preparing intelligence professionals for such a future world – with better skills, greater real world experience, and the ability to work together in public-private partnerships will be the challenge for both government and private-sector intelligence educators.

Preparing Professionals for "That Future"

What types of intelligence professionals will be needed to address this future intelligence world ... and what training they will need?

- Analysts – Both communities will require analysts. But each with new and different types of skills. Government analysts with business skills, enhanced by real world experience ... and, BI analysts with a greater understanding of international and geo-political affairs.

- Open Source Intelligence (OSINT) and Information Services Professionals. These are the new types of modern day librarians that are necessary to fully exploit the growing number of international databases and syndicated information services. These professionals are a combination of library science and information services experts. Some of the best have come from the ranks of the Special Library Association (SLA) membership. But they too require "intelligence" training before they can become BI practitioners.

- Knowledge Technologists. Peter Drucker's "blue collar" workers of the knowledge-worker age. The tech-savvy, computer science experts that both Intelligence Communities will need to fully exploit the internet world and apply all the advanced collection and analytical software that will be available. They will be needed for both intelligence production and counterintelligence purposes. Cyber security will be one of their specialties.

- Human Source Intelligence (HUMINT) Collectors. This profession will continue to play its critical role in government intelligence operations – and, will increase in importance in business intelligence, where it has played only a limited role up to now.[5] The private sector needs to increase substantially its professional development in the HUMINT collection field.

- Counterintelligence Professionals. This group of intelligence officers will play an increasingly important role in both the government and business worlds. As a country's national security becomes more dependent upon its economic wellbeing, the protection of both industrial and financial resources from foreign government intelligence and criminal threats will become national intelligence priorities. Government counterintelligence officers are better prepared for this new challenge, but will need education about the private sector's current capabilities and limitations to better assist corporations protect their IP including trade secrets. And, although business professionals are fairly good at traditional security and patent protection tasks, few have the counterintelligence training necessary to protect their IP and key personnel from sophisticated hackers or hostile intelligence services.

- Intelligence Managers. Management training for intelligence professionals is an area that has largely been overlooked. Promotion to management in government primarily has been governed by the "Peter Principle" – pro-

---

5. A CI Foundation survey in 2006 revealed that less than 3% of BI professionals work in this field full time. "State of the Art: Competitive Intelligence," A Competitive Intelligence Foundation Research Report 2005-2006.

moted to your level of incompetence. There have been some leadership courses and senior-level seminars provided as one rose in rank, and possibly an academic sabbatical. Recently, both government and one or two academic institutions have begun to address this short-coming; however, much more is needed. The University of Maryland University College (UMUC) is the only institution to offer a graduate degree in intelligence management.[6] The BI community has very little to offer as far as formal intelligence management training. Corporations would benefit greatly from such education.

- The Intelligence Customers. Lastly, the users of intelligence – both government officials and business executives – need formal intelligence education, basically "what it is – and how to use it." The private sector probably needs it more because there are fewer good role models or experienced users around to learn from. For the business community, it is pretty much what they can learn from "spy novels & movies." Intelligence is not taught as a management discipline in any of the leading business schools.

The education and training of these intelligence professionals – both business and government –will be a challenge. Preparing them for "that future" world described, along with our current, traditional educational offerings, will require thinking more creatively and new materials and innovative methods to educate:

- Government intelligence officers how to address those new and emerging policy subjects stemming from private-sector activities;
- Business intelligence professionals how to handle both the geopolitical challenges confronting MNC's and the threats posed by foreign intelligence services; and,
- Both communities, jointly how to deal more effectively with intelligence issues affecting both our economic and national security.

It is not too early to start thinking and preparing for this challenging educational task.

Jan P. Herring, a well-recognized expert in the business intelligence field, is a charter member of the Society of Competitive Intelligence Professionals, a SCIP Fellow, and 1993 recipient of the Society's Meritorious Award. His professional experience includes developing Motorola's highly acclaimed intelligence program, co-founding the Academy of Competitive Intelligence, and setting up the US Government's first business intelligence program. Before his BI career, Mr. Herring served 20 years with the CIA as an analyst, field collector, and a manager. His assignments covered a wide range of intelligence activities, including: weapons systems and threat analysis for the national reconnaissance program; managing the IC's National Technical Assessment program for the Defense Department; and leading IC efforts in a wide variety of international affairs,

---

6. http://www.umuc.edu/academic-programs/masters-degrees/management-with-intelligence-management-specialization.cfm.

including strategic arms limitation negotiations; export control implementation; and the opening of US-China trade relations. During his government career, he served as chairman of the Director of Central Intelligence's Scientific & Technical Intelligence Committee and as the first chairman of the Inter-Agency Technology Transfer Intelligence Committee. Mr. Herring's last government assignment was as the first national intelligence officer (NIO) for science & technology. Upon leaving CIA, he was awarded the Agency's highest honor, the Medal of Distinction, and received letters of commendation from President Ronald Reagan, Attorney General William F. Smith, and FBI Director William H. Webster, for his contributions to national security and federal law enforcement. He is the author of numerous articles and several book chapters on intelligence in the private-sector and co-edited a two-volume series entitled The Art and Science of Business Intelligence Analysis (Greenwich, CT: JAI Press, 1996.) Mr. Herring has a bachelor's degree in physics from the University of Missouri.

This article was based on a keynote presentation given by the author at the 10th annual conference of the International Association for Intelligence Education (IAFIE) at Mercyhurst University in Erie, Pennsylvania, July 14, 2014.

GUIDE TO THE STUDY OF INTELLIGENCE

Commission on the Intelligence Capabilities of the United States

Regarding Weapons of Mass Destruction

Elbridge Colby and Stewart Baker

B y 2002, the President George W. Bush administration was persuaded that Saddam Hussein's Iraq constituted a major threat to US and international security and that, in the atmosphere following the 9/11 attacks, the threat needed to be addressed. The Bush administration was particularly concerned that Baghdad was beginning to restart its weapons of mass destruction (WMD) programs and that it would use any WMD it acquired in intolerably menacing and possibly irrational ways.[1] Over the course of 2002, the administration launched a major political initiative to build domestic and international support for undertaking decisive action against Iraq; by the fall of 2002, most of the focus of this initiative centered on the assessment, grounded in the estimates of the US and allied intelligence services, that Iraq was reinitiating its WMD programs. Most notably, the administration pointed to the findings of a 2002 National Intelligence Estimate – the US Intelligence Community's (IC's) flagship medium for communicating its consensus views – entitled "Iraq's Continuing Programs for Weapons of Mass Destruction."[2] This Estimate formed an important part of the baseline of the Congress' contentious vote in October 2002 to authorize the use of force against Iraq.

Based in part on that authorization, in March 2003, the United States and a

---

1. Following the American-led ejection of Iraqi forces from Kuwait in 1990-1991 and the discovery that Baghdad had advanced nuclear and other weapons of mass destruction (WMD) programs underway, Iraq was placed under United Nations sanctions designed to prevent it from reinitiating its WMD efforts. These sanctions were strengthened after the revelation in 1994 that Hussein had restarted covert WMD programs.
2. A declassified redacted version is available at *http://www2.gwu.edu/~nsarchiv/NSAEBB/NSAEBB129/nie.pdf*.

coalition of allied nations launched an invasion of Iraq. Coalition forces swiftly reached Baghdad and deposed the Saddam Hussein-led Ba'ath Government. Over the course of 2003, however, as the American-led occupation came under attack from a growing insurgency in Iraq, it also became clear that the WMD assessments that provided the primary public justification for the attack were at the very least seriously exaggerated and in many respects wrong. Following months of careful investigation, in January 2004, David Kay, the head of the Iraq Survey Group (originally chartered to document evidence of Hussein's WMD programs), announced to Congress and an increasingly skeptical American public that his group had found no evidence that Iraq had in fact stockpiled WMD.[3] The Iraq Survey Group continued its work following Kay's resignation under the directorship of Charles Duelfer, but likewise found no evidence of a significant WMD program in pre-war Iraq, "though it did suggest that Hussein was maintaining the option to do so once sanctions were removed and Iraq's economy stabilized."[4]

Kay's announcement and others like it generated a firestorm of criticism that the American people and their representatives had been misled. This in turn created intense political pressure to determine just what had happened to lead American intelligence so far astray. Why had the US IC, the most formidable and well resourced in the world, been so far off the mark in its estimates of Iraq's WMD programs? Had the American people been deliberately misled? How could such an enormous intelligence failure be averted in the future?

The Commission and its Findings

Responding to this rising political tide and hoping to head off the appointment of a congressional panel, President Bush decided to create a commission of distinguished national leaders on his own authority to investigate the matter. Given the raw political sensitivities surrounding the role of intelligence in the lead-up to the Iraq War, the fact that the Commission was appointed by the President stirred controversy, as did the fact that the White House limited the Commission's scope of investigation to examining the IC's failures rather than to probing the actions and decisions of the policymaker consumers who had decided policy on Iraq.[5] For instance, the Commission did not look at the advisability, propriety, or legality of the attack on Iraq but rather solely on the IC's performance in assessing Iraq's WMD programs. Many commentators asserted that this was not the central issue – rather, they contended that the Bush Administration had "stretched" or gone beyond the IC's assessments

---

3. http://www.cnn.com/2004/WORLD/meast/01/25/sprj.nirq.kay/.
4. Comprehensive Report of the Special Advisor to the DCI on Iraq's WMD. September 30, 2004, available at https://www.cia.gov/library/reports/general-reports-1/iraq_wmd_2004.
5. Richard K. Betts, *Enemies of Intelligence; Knowledge and Power in American National Security* (New York: Columbia University Press, 2009), 136.

and/or had used the IC's WMD assessments as a convenient public rationale for a war undertaken for different reasons. The Commission did not in fact investigate the policy uses or rationales for the war, but focused solely on the performance of the IC.[6] For these reasons, some voices had urged that Congress should charter the Commission and be given subpoena power, like the earlier 9/11 Commission, to ensure independence from the Executive Branch and the willingness to take on the administration. This political dynamic formed the background in which the Commission undertook its work.[7]

To lead the commission, Bush appointed Appellate Court Judge and former Ambassador Laurence H. Silberman, an experienced hand in intelligence and foreign policy issues; and former Virginia Senator and Governor Charles S. Robb, one of the most prominent contemporary congressmen on national security issues, as co-chairmen. The other members were: Senator John McCain, Yale President Richard Levin, former National Security Agency Director and Deputy Director of Central Intelligence (DDCI) Admiral William Studeman, former Undersecretary of Defense Walter Slocombe, retired Appellate Court Judge Patricia Wald, former Pentagon and National Intelligence Council official Henry Rowen, and former Massachusetts Institute of Technology President Charles Vest. Former White House Counsel Lloyd Cutler was to be a serving member of the Commission but was compelled to bow out of active participation due to illness. The commissioners were balanced between Republicans and Democrats. As a Presidential creation, the Commission was chartered by Executive Order 13328 of February 2004 and conducted its work supported by the Executive Office of the President, the administrative arm of the White House.

To address concerns about independence and subpoena power, Judge Silberman promised other members of the Commission that he would resign if any of the Commission's requests for information were denied – a promise that he would later invoke.

Beginning preliminary operations (largely administrative and legal) in the spring of 2004, the Commission began bringing on staff, mostly current or former intelligence professionals along with a number of lawyers with military or security experience, over the course of the summer and began work in earnest in the late summer of 2004. In the following nine months, the Commission conducted an in-depth investigation of how the IC came to its assessments regarding Hussein's WMD programs. Commissioners and staff pored over thousands of intelligence cables and reports; interviewed hundreds of officials and experts, senior and working-level, serving and retired; and hashed out consensus positions in lengthy and detailed meetings of the Commissioners.

---

6. For a typical reaction, see Ellen Laipson, "The Robb-Silberman Report, Intelligence, and Nonproliferation," Arms Control Association, June 2005, *http://www.armscontrol.org/act/2005_06/Laipson*.
7. For a discussion of the background of the creation and appointment of the Commission, see Bob Woodward, *State of Denial* (New York: Simon & Schuster, 2006), 283-287.

Commissioners conducted often probing and even contentious interviews of key figures such as former DCI George Tenet, DDCI John McLaughlin, Secretary of Defense Donald Rumsfeld, Secretary of State Colin Powell, other serving officials, and distinguished former officials such as Henry Kissinger. Staff members also conducted extensive interviews with relevant CIA and other IC officials.

The Commission operated essentially wholly autonomously. Although the co-chairs talked regularly to White House and intelligence officials, and the Commission adopted a "responsible" rather than "muckraking" modus operandi, the Commission conducted its work independently and, in the view of most observers, objectively.

The commissioners personal and political stature, as well as their divergent political backgrounds, allowed the Commission to operate from a position of political strength and independence. Two early efforts to restrict the Commission's inquiry or staffing authority were turned back by Judge Silberman. In one instance, the Commission sought to review the President's Daily Brief (PDB) on Iraq WMD issues. Access to the PDB had been a matter of bitter contention with the 9/11 Commission, and it looked as though the WMD Commission might go down the same road until Judge Silberman said that denying access to the PDB would require him to resign as promised. Shortly thereafter, the Executive Branch agreed to let a small group of commissioners review the PDBs. Judge Silberman used similar leverage to turn aside Department of Justice (DOJ) objections to the Commission's hiring of a Democrat and former Supreme Court clerk for the General Counsel's Office. The attorney, Mike Leiter, went on to have a brilliant career in government under Democratic and Republican Presidents, most recently as head of the National Counterterrorism Center.

Iraq

In its May 31, 2005 report (with the basic findings released March 31 of the same year), the Commission unanimously found that the IC was "dead wrong in almost all of its pre-war judgments about Iraq's weapons of mass destruction," which constituted "a major intelligence failure." The Commission attributed this failure to "the Intelligence Community's inability to collect good information about Iraq's WMD programs, serious errors in analyzing what information it could gather, and a failure to make clear just how much of its analysis was based on assumptions, rather than good evidence." The Commission also found no evidence of politicization and "no indication that the Intelligence Community distorted the evidence regarding Iraq's weapons of mass destruction."[8]

While the Commission was quite stern in its basic judgments concerning the IC's performance on Iraq's WMD programs, it did note that obtaining

---

8. Cover letter, Commission report.

accurate and relevant intelligence on hard targets such as Iraq's unconventional weapons programs "is no easy task" and that, on such targets, "failure is more common than success." The Commission observed that it did "not fault the Intelligence Community for formulating the hypothesis, based on Saddam Hussein's conduct, that Iraq had retained an unconventional weapons capability and was working to augment this capability ... [n]or ... for failing to uncover what few Iraqis knew [as] ... only a handful of Saddam Hussein's closest advisors were aware of some of his decisions [on WMD issues]."[9]

Despite these balancing considerations, however, the Commission "conclude[d] that the Intelligence Community could and should have come much closer to assessing the true state of Iraq's weapons programs than it did. It should have been less wrong – and, more importantly, it should have been more candid about what it did know."[10] The Commission chastised the IC for allowing uncertain and, in some cases, known bad information to exercise a high degree of influence over its assessments, and to obscure this evidentiary weakness from policymakers and, in many cases, from the Community's own senior leadership.[11]

More broadly, the Commission criticized the Community for allowing a reasonable and intuitive judgment – that Saddam Hussein would again try to covertly restart his WMD program – to harden into a near certainty that was essentially impervious to disproof. As the Commission observed, "The failure to conclude that Saddam had abandoned his weapons program was...an understandable one.... [But t]he Intelligence Community did not even evaluate the possibility that Saddam would destroy his stockpiles and halt his work on his nuclear program.... Rather than thinking imaginatively, and considering seemingly unlikely and unpopular possibilities, the Intelligence Community instead found itself wedded to a set of assumptions about Iraq, focusing on intelligence reporting that appeared to confirm those assumptions."[12] As Co-Chairman Silberman explained in the press conference announcing the report's findings, "[T]he bottom line is the Intelligence Community operated on presumptions or assumptions based on what they had seen in 1991.... [A]lthough it was perfectly reasonable for them to speculate or assume [based on this], what the Intelligence Community should have done is said, 'Look, we ... have ... very little evidence of this [the IC's assessments]; we really don't know.'" [13]

---

9. Commission report, 46-47.
10. Commission report, 47.
11. See, for instance, the report's discussion of the failure to convey clearly the inadequacy of the reporting and the unreliability of the source codenamed Curveball, Commission report, 87-105.
12. Commission report, 155.
13. *http://www.washingtonpost.com/wp-dyn/articles/A15908-2005Mar31.html.*

Intelligence Reform

Though the Commission's genesis and most prominent focus lay in the controversies surrounding the erroneous IC assessments regarding Iraq's WMD, the breadth of the Commission's mandate (and the IC's failures), required a much more wide-ranging report. Thus, a good part of the Commission's work and much of the final report's substance dealt with the IC's reform and management. Under the Executive Order's terms, the Commission was tasked with investigating broadly whether the IC was adequately and appropriately authorized, organized, and resourced to respond to the challenges posed by the proliferation of WMD "and other related threats." The Commission was specifically given the writ to examine the IC's ability to collect on and analyze the doings of the fullest range of WMD and related threats.[14] The Commissioners took this writ seriously and focused much of their and the staff's efforts on developing a blueprint for intelligence reform.

In light of this, the Commission report, in addition to its Iraq findings, delivered 74 recommendations for improving the IC's performance. These recommendations were particularly appropriate because of the uncertainty about how to implement changes in the IC's structure that had been recommended by the 9/11 Commission and largely passed into law by the Congress in the Intelligence Reform and Terrorism Prevention Act of 2004 (IRTPA). This law created a director of national intelligence (DNI) and a supporting office (ODNI) to oversee the IC, established National Counterterrorism and Counterproliferation Centers (NCTC and NCPC, respectively), and provided a broad template for what became the "intelligence reform" effort.[15]

The Commission's recommendations emphasized four main themes: endowing the new position of DNI with the authorities needed to carry out his responsibilities, integrating the Federal Bureau of Investigation (FBI) and DOJ more fully into the IC, demanding more of and creating a culture of accountability in the Community, and rethinking the PDB.

More concretely, the Commission called for a variety of concrete steps to focus, systematize, and generally improve the IC's collection, analysis, and dissemination of intelligence, such as: the creation of mission managers to integrate collection and analysis against key intelligence targets such as Iran and North Korea, providing blueprints for designing the IRTPA-formed NCTC and NCPC, recommending oversight mechanisms such as a strengthened President's Intelligence Advisory Board, and urging focused action on the better sharing of information within the Community. In the crucial and sensitive

---

14. Executive Order 13328 available at: *http://www.fas.org/irp/offdocs/eo/eo-13328.htm*.

15. For background on the formulation of the IRTPA law, see Michael Allen, *Blinking Red: Crisis and Compromise in American Intelligence After 9/11*, Dulles, Virginia: Potomac Books, 2013. On the history of reform efforts since 1947, see Dr. Bill Nolte's article, "A Guide to the Reforming of American Intelligence," *Intelligencer 19 (1)*, Winter/Spring 2012, 57-61.

matter of the role of the FBI and DOJ in domestic intelligence, the Commission recommended creation of a National Security Division at Justice and organizational and other changes designed to foster a culture within the Bureau more oriented to intelligence collection in the post-9/11 era rather than traditional counterespionage and prosecution alone.

Reception and Influence

The Commission's report received an initial flurry of news attention, but, in part due to its length and detail, quickly fell off the news pages. Within the IC and at the White House, however, the Commission's recommendations received significant and lasting attention and achieved considerable influence.

In late June 2005, President Bush endorsed 70 of the Commission's 74 recommendations and issued directives that they be implemented, giving the Commission's recommendations the imprimatur and, to some degree, the White House's political support.[16] The newly formed ODNI, and particularly the new DNI, John Negroponte (who came from outside the IC and thus had a natural tendency to look for ideas and inspiration to a body such as the Commission), also sought to implement the Commission's reforms.[17] Key staff from the Commission moved into the IC and other relevant parts of the US Government, where they were able to influence intelligence policy along the lines recommended by the Commission; other senior ODNI staff in particular had also been intimately involved in the development of IRTPA and were supportive of the Commission's recommendations.[18] The DOJ and FBI were more resistant to some of the organizational changes the Commission proposed, but eventually adopted the bulk of them.

Overall, the Commission exercised its most substantial influence on the implementation of the often general and even vague IRTPA law, fleshing out the skeletal provisions contained within the legislation.[19]

---

16. http://iipdigital.usembassy.gov/st/english/texttrans/2005/06/20050629184054esnamfuak0.538479.html#axzz2ngEpkuJA
17. See, for instance, the ODNI effort to track its implementation of the Commission's approved recommendations: https://www.fas.org/irp/dni/prog072706.pdf.
18. For instance, Commission Executive Director, Scott Redd, was appointed the first director of the National Counterterrorism Center; Commission General Counsel Stewart Baker became Department of Homeland Security assistant secretary for policy; Deputy General Counsel Brett Gerry joined the White House Counsel's office before becoming chief of staff to Attorney General Michael Mukasey; and Deputy General Counsel Michael Leiter became ODNI deputy chief of staff and subsequently deputy director and then director of the NCTC. Several commissioners also remained involved in public advocacy and commentary on intelligence issues, such as Charles Robb and William Studeman. David Shedd, who had been the senior National Security Council official for intelligence and had been intimately involved in the formulation of the IRTPA legislation, became chief of staff to DNI Negroponte and was a key figure in the ODNI pushing intelligence reform for several years before becoming deputy director of the Defense Intelligence Agency.
19. See, for instance, M. Kent Bolton, U.S. National Security and Foreign Policymaking After 9/11: Present at the Re-Creation (Lanham: Rowman & Littlefield, 2008), 286.

READINGS FOR INSTRUCTORS

Besides the references in the footnotes the following are recommended readings for instructors:

Betts, Richard K. *Enemies of Intelligence: Knowledge and Power in American National Security* (New York: Columbia University Press, 2007). Professor Betts examines the complexities, and sometimes unintended consequences, of intelligence reform efforts.

Jervis, Robert L. *Why Intelligence Fails: Lessons from the Iranian Revolution and the Iraq War* (Ithaca, NY: Cornell University Press, 2010). Professor Jervis examined the failure to anticipate the 1979 Iranian revolution for CIA. He compares the reasons for that failure with the reasons for the Iraq WMD intelligence failure.

Posner, Richard A. *Uncertain Shield: The U.S. Intelligence System in the Throes of Reform* (Stanford: The Hoover Institution, 2006). US Court of Appeals Judge Posner opines that the intelligence reforms following 9/11 have created a top-heavy intelligence bureaucracy with all its attendant challenges.

Woodward, Bob. *State of Denial* (New York: Simon & Schuster, 2006). Woodward addresses the policy conflicts within the George W. Bush Administration as the Iraq War continued in a fashion not envisioned before the 2003 invasion.

Finally, recommended is the Comprehensive Report of the Special Advisor to the DCI on Iraq's WMD (30 September 2004), available on the CIA website at https://www.cia.gov/library/reports/general-reports-1/iraq_wmd_2004.

Elbridge Colby is a fellow at the Center for a New American Security, where he focuses on issues of strategy, nuclear weapons, and intelligence and serves as a consultant or advisor to a number of US Government entities. He previously served for over five years in the US Government in a number of intelligence and nuclear policy positions, including on the Silberman-Robb WMD Commission and with the ODNI. He is a graduate of Harvard College and Yale Law School.

Stewart Baker is a partner in the law firm of Steptoe & Johnson in Washington, DC, with a law practice that covers homeland security, international trade, cyber security, data protection, and travel and foreign investment regulation. He was general counsel of the Silberman-Robb WMD Commission in 2004-2005. From 2005 to 2009, he was the first Department of Homeland Security assistant secretary for policy. Mr. Baker has also been general counsel of the National Security Agency and is the author of *Skating on Stilts* (Stanford: Hoover Institution Press, 2010), a book (and blog) on terrorism, cyber security, and other technology issues.

GUIDE TO THE STUDY OF INTELLIGENCE

Intelligence Collection, Covert Operations, and International Law

Ernesto J. Sanchez

Introduction

U S intelligence officers are trained to abide by the law – American law. But does that mean that they or, for that matter, other countries' intelligence officers trained to follow their countries' laws can otherwise just do whatever they need or want to accomplish their missions?

Intelligence is the process by which specific types of information important to national security are requested, collected, analyzed, and provided to policymakers. This process entails safeguarding such information by counterintelligence activities and carrying out related operations as requested by lawful authorities.[1]

There are five main ways of collecting intelligence that are often collectively referred to as "intelligence collection disciplines" or the "INTs."[2]

- Human intelligence (HUMINT) is the collection of information from human sources. The collection may occur openly, as when FBI agents interview witnesses or suspects, or it may be done through clandestine means (espionage), such as when CIA officers interview human assets.

- Signals intelligence (SIGINT) refers to electronic transmissions collected by ships, planes, ground sites, or satellites. Communications intelligence (COMINT) is a type of SIGINT entailing the interception of communications between two parties.

---

1. Mark Lowenthal, *Intelligence: From Secrets To Policy, 4th ed.* (Washington, DC: CQ Press, 2008), 7-8.
2. For a detailed discussion of the various intelligence collection disciplines see Robert M. Clark, "Perspectives on Intelligence Collection," *The Intelligencer 20 (2)*, Fall/Winter 2013; also on the web at *http://www.afio.com/40_guide.htm*.

- Imagery intelligence (IMINT) is sometimes also referred to as photo intelligence (PHOTINT) and can also be collected by ships, planes, ground sites, or satellites.

- Measurement and signatures intelligence (MASINT) is a relatively little-known collection discipline that concerns weapons capabilities and industrial activities. MASINT includes the advanced processing and use of data gathered from overhead and airborne IMINT and SIGINT collection systems. Telemetry intelligence (TELINT) is sometimes used to indicate data relayed by weapons during tests, while electronic intelligence (ELINT) can indicate electronic emissions picked up from modern weapons and tracking systems. Both TELINT and ELINT can qualify as SIGINT and contribute to MASINT.

- Open source intelligence (OSINT) refers to a broad array of information and sources that are publicly available, including information obtained from the media (newspapers, radio, television, etc.), professional and academic records (papers, conferences, professional associations, etc.), and public data (government reports, demographics, hearings, speeches, etc.).[3]

All these collection disciplines have potential implications for international law – the rules and principles of general application, defined by treaties and international custom, dealing with the conduct of states and international organizations and with their relations among themselves, as well as states' relations with individual persons.[4]

For example, how can intelligence collection or other operations comply with international law? Do certain operational methods violate international law? What safeguards have policymakers put into place to ensure intelligence operations comply with international law? How do policymakers balance the risks of violating international law with national security priorities?

These questions evidence how policymakers worry about whether international law prohibits particular intelligence operations or aspects thereof. How these concerns apply also has much to do with the type of activities an intelligence operation entails, where that operation actually takes place, and the surrounding circumstances. This article describes some of the major international law issues surrounding intelligence collection and a more controversial function of intelligence agencies – covert actions.

Intelligence Collection

Intelligence collection implicates six aspects of international law: (1) norms of nonintervention, (2) principles surrounding diplomatic and consular relations, (3) human rights obligations governing the interrogation of human

---

3. Ibid.
4. Restatement of the Law, The Foreign Relations Law of the United States, § 101 (1987).

assets or criminal suspects under hostile circumstances, (4) law surrounding the clandestine surveillance of communication or conduct by electronic or other means, (5) arms control treaties, and (6) intelligence-sharing agreements.

Sovereignty and nonintervention. Article 2(4) of the UN Charter mandates that all member states "shall refrain in their international relations from the threat or use of force against the territorial integrity or political independence of any state..."[5] Article 51 of the UN Charter, however, mandates that nothing "shall impair the inherent right of individual or collective self-defense if an armed attack occurs."[6] In that respect, espionage and accompanying operations conducted as preparation for an armed attack likely qualify as part of an unlawful threat or use of force, as well as a breach of obligations to not intervene in the affairs of other states. But espionage and accompanying operations conducted in self-defense, or with the permission of an affected state, probably does not.

Diplomatic and consular relations. Most espionage in the form of HUMINT collection abroad is conducted by intelligence officers working under diplomatic cover in their countries' embassies. Arguably, the clandestine collection of human or electronic intelligence (e.g., an National Security Agency listening post at an embassy) falls outside of traditional diplomatic functions as defined by the Vienna Convention on Diplomatic Relations (VCDR).[7] But, as Professor Craig Forcese of Canada's University of Ottawa has noted, "[t]here is ... no need for precise definition of proper diplomatic functions where states retain the discretion to, in essence, define these functions according to their own standards," as well as expel individuals with diplomatic immunity who violate those standards.[8] As a result, international law governing diplomatic relations implicitly acknowledges the tradition of intelligence collection by individuals operating under diplomatic cover.

Human intelligence and interrogation. The interrogation of hostile individuals has figured prominently in the post-9/11 debate over how far counter-terrorism measures should go. In this respect, Article 9 of the International Covenant on Civil and Political Rights (ICCPR) prohibits arbitrary arrest and detention – any person "deprived of his liberty by arrest or detention shall be entitled to take proceedings before a court, in order that that court may decide without delay on the lawfulness of his detention and order his release if the detention is not lawful."[9] Moreover, Article 7 of the ICCPR mandates that "no one shall be subjected to torture or to cruel, inhuman, or degrading treatment or punishment."[10]

---

5. UN Charter art. 2(4).
6. UN Charter art. 51.
7. See generally Vienna Convention on Diplomatic Relations, Apr. 18, 1961, 500 U.N.T.S. 95, art. 29.
8. Craig Forcese, "Spies Without Borders: International Law and Intelligence Collection" 5, *Journal of National Security Law and Policy*, 2011, 179, 201.
9. International Covenant on Civil and Political Rights art. 9, Dec. 16, 1966, 999 U.N.T.S. 171.
10. *Ibid.* art. 7.

According to Article 1 of the UN Convention Against Torture and Other Cruel, Inhuman, or Degrading Treatment or Punishment (UN Torture Convention), torture constitutes any act "by which severe pain or suffering, whether physical or mental, is intentionally inflicted on a person" for specified purposes. These purposes are (1) obtaining from a person or a third person information or a confession, (2) punishing the person for an action s/he or a third person have committed or are suspected of having committed, (3) intimidating or coercing the person or a third person, or (4) discrimination of any kind.[11] In turn, decisions of international tribunals and national courts have concluded that, for ICCPR purposes, individuals may come within a state's jurisdiction when those individuals are within the effective control of the state, even if not on the state's actual territory.[12] The ICCPR and the UN Torture Convention are thus the reason why so much debate has taken place ever since the 9/11 attacks in the media and in the courts about what exactly constitutes torture or cruel, inhuman, or degrading treatment or punishment (e.g., waterboarding), especially in regard to CIA renditions of terrorism suspects to "black sites" abroad for "enhanced interrogation."[13]

Surveillance. Article 17 of the ICCPR mandates: "No one shall be subjected to arbitrary or unlawful interference with his privacy, family, home, or correspondence, nor to unlawful attacks on his honor or reputation...."[14] As Forcese notes, then, "electronic surveillance of communications or surveillance that amounts to intrusions into the 'home' (including the place of work) must be authorized by law and by the appropriate official, on a case-by-case basis, and be reasonable under the circumstances."[15] For domestic intelligence collection, those circumstances are usually determined by domestic law (e.g., the Fourth Amendment to the US Constitution and surrounding jurisprudence, European privacy law for domestic intelligence collection by European security services).

But with regard to surveillance, whether the ICCPR protects human targets abroad remains a subject of debate.[16] Indeed, the UN Convention on the Law of the Sea does not prohibit intelligence collection by ships operating outside states' territorial waters (i.e., beyond twelve nautical miles from a state's coast-

---

11. Convention Against Torture and Other Cruel, Inhuman or Degrading Treatment or Punishment art. 1, Dec. 10, 1984, S. Treaty No. Doc. 100-20 (1988), 1465 U.N.T.S. 85.

12. See, e.g., Legal Consequences of the Construction of a Wall in the Occupied Palestinian Territory, Advisory Opinion, I.C.J. 136, para. 111, July 9, 2004. "[T]he Court considers that the International Covenant on Civil and Political Rights is applicable in respect of acts done by a State in the exercise of its jurisdiction outside its own territory."

13. See generally Jane Mayer, *The Dark Side: The Inside Story Of How The War On Terror Turned Into A War On American Ideals.* (New York City: Anchor Books, 2009) .

14. Supra note 8, art. 17.

15. Forcese, supra note 6, at 196.

16. See Ryan Goodman, "UN Human Rights Committee Says ICCPR Applies to Extraterritorial Surveillance: But is that so novel?," *Just Security*, March 27, 2014, available at *http://justsecurity.org/8620/human-rights-committee-iccpr-applies-extraterritorial-surveillance-novel/*.

line).[17] Neither does the Outer Space Treaty prohibit intelligence collection by orbiting satellites.[18] Nor does the International Telecommunications Convention explicitly prohibit the interception of electronic communications.[19] The issues surrounding the National Security Agency's controversial eavesdropping on German Chancellor Angela Merkel's phone calls could consequently be more political than legal.

Arms control and intelligence sharing. President Ronald Reagan adopted as a signature phrase the Russian proverb "trust, but verify" when discussing arms control issues with the Soviet Union. One might consequently argue that intelligence collection amounts to investigating whether international law has been violated. For example, the Anti-Ballistic Missile Treaty and SALT I Agreement, providing for "national technical means of [treaty compliance] verification" and in conjunction with other arms control accords, "effectively establish a right to collect intelligence, at least with respect to assessing compliance with the arms control obligations."[20] Such intelligence-sharing arrangements as the "five eyes" relationship between the signals intelligence agencies of the US, UK, Canada, Australia, and New Zealand may also "evidence customary norms for what constitute acceptable forms of espionage."[21]

Covert Action

What intelligence agencies are probably best known for – covert action – can entail intelligence collection. But covert action usually involves much more as a policy tool used to pursue a geopolitical and national security goal or as "an activity...to influence political, economic, or military conditions abroad, where it is intended that the role of the [sponsoring government] will not be apparent or acknowledged publicly."[22] Covert action may include:

- Covert support of friendly governments. In the wake of open or secret alliances with foreign governments that share common policy objectives, covert action can be limited to such measures as sharing intelligence with the government's own security service on groups in the government's country who would foment political unrest.

---

17. See United Nations Convention on the Law of the Sea arts. 3, 19(2)(c), opened for signature Dec. 10, 1982, 1833 U.N.T.S. 397.

18. Treaty on Principles Governing the Activities of States in the Exploration and Use of Outer Space, Including the Moon and Other Celestial Bodies art. II, done Jan. 27, 1967, 18 U.S.T. 2410, 610 U.N.T.S. 205 ("("Outer space, including the moon and other celestial bodies, is not subject to national appropriation by claim of sovereignty, by means of use or occupation, or by any other means.").

19. International Telecommunication Convention art. 22, done Oct. 25, 1973, 28 U.S.T. 2495, 1209 U.N.T.S. 255 (providing that states "reserve the right to communicate [international telecommunications] correspondence to the competent authorities in order to ensure the application of their internal laws or the execution of international conventions to which they are parties").

20. Simon Chesterman, "The Spy Who Came In from the Cold War: Intelligence and International Law," 27 *Michigan Journal of International Law 27*, 2006, 1071-1091.

21. Ibid. at 1093-98.

22. 50 U.S.C. 2093(e).

- Covertly influencing the perceptions of a foreign government or population regarding U.S. policy goals. The "simplest and most direct method" of affecting a foreign government's actions is to use agents of influence – well-placed individuals who persuade colleagues to adopt policies "congenial to another government's interests." Moreover, intelligence agencies can disseminate information (or disinformation) to enhance a foreign population's backing for a policy objective.

- Covert support of non-governmental forces or organizations. If a government wishes to weaken one of its hostile counterparts, material support can be provided to opposing political parties, civic groups, labor unions, media, and even armed insurgent groups.

- Support for coups. Support can also be extended to groups seeking to outright overthrow a hostile government. For example, in 1953, the US, in partnership with the UK and the shah of Iran, orchestrated a coup to overthrow of Mohammed Mossadegh, Iran's democratically elected prime minister, who had nationalized his country's oil industry, doing great harm to British economic interests. And, in 1954, the US orchestrated the military overthrow of the Guatemalan Government to prevent the establishment of a perceived "Soviet beachhead" in Central America and to protect US economic interests in the country.

- Paramilitary operations. Governments can also train irregular forces to launch insurgencies against hostile governments, though, in practice, these types of operations are unlikely to remain secret. US support in the 1980s for the mujahedeen struggle against Afghanistan's Soviet-backed government and the contra rebels' efforts against Nicaragua's Soviet-backed Government best exemplify this type of covert action.

- Lethal actions. Covert action can also take the form of acts of violence directed against specific individuals, such as the assassination of key foreign political figures or property. Sustained lethal action operations in armed conflicts, such as the US unmanned aerial vehicle ("drone") strikes against terrorism suspects in Pakistan, Yemen, and Somalia, can also be carried out in partnership with special forces personnel.[23]

The more aggressive a covert action conducted without the affected state's consent is, the greater the likelihood that it will, if made public, raise charges that international law has been violated.

Sovereignty and covert action. The 1986 International Court of Justice (ICJ) decision in the case of Military and Paramilitary Activities in and against Nicaragua thus bears much significance due to its implications for covert actions conducted to destabilize affected states' governments. The court decided that the US had breached Nicaraguan sovereignty by (1) training, arming, equipping, and financing the contra rebel movement in the conduct of activities against the

---

23. See generally Abram Shulsky and Gary Schmitt, *Silent Warfare: Understanding the World of Intelligence*, 75-98 (2002).

Nicaraguan Government; (2) coordinating specified paramilitary attacks on Nicaraguan territory; (3) directing certain over flights of Nicaraguan territory; and (4) laying mines in Nicaraguan territorial waters.[24] While ICJ decisions have no binding effect in a *stare decisis* (i.e., precedent governs) sense,[25] the Nicaragua decision arguably has the effect of prohibiting the type of covert action the US conducted in similar circumstances.[26]

Still, no consensus has arisen among the global intelligence and policy community as to what makes a proactive covert operation a violation of international law, especially because such compliance questions are inevitably very fact-specific. In this regard, Yale University Law School Professor W. Michael Reisman and Chief Judge James Baker of the US Court of Appeals for the Armed Forces have proposed the following test: (1) whether a covert action promotes such basic UN Charter policy objectives as self-determination; (2) whether it adds to or detracts from minimum world order; (3) whether it is consistent with contingencies authorizing the overt use of force; (4) whether covert coercion was implemented only after plausibly less coercive measures were tried; and (5) whether the covert action complied with such international humanitarian law requirements as necessity, proportionality, and distinction.[27]

The latter inquiry, which concerns the law of armed conflict, has been especially significant with regard to such lethal actions as the previously mentioned drone strikes in Pakistan, Yemen, and Somalia and the 2011 raid in Pakistan resulting in the killing of Osama bin Laden. An intelligence agency like the CIA can team up with military personnel (i.e., special forces) to plan and execute such missions where, for example, a host government does not wish to acknowledge receiving assistance from the US.[28] The planning of such missions must take into account their necessity for attaining a greater policy goal, whether the harm caused to civilians or civilian property is proportional and not excessive in relation to the concrete and direct military advantage anticipated by the operation, as well as distinguish between combatants and civilians.[29]

Lethal actions or assassination. Readers may question whether such lethal operations conducted by the US comport with the executive prohibition on

---

24. 1986 I.C.J. 14, paras. 75-125, 172-269 (June 27).

25. Statute of the International Court of Justice art. 59.

26. See Robert Williams, "(Spy) Game Change: Cyber Networks, Intelligence Collection, and Covert Action," 79 *George Washington University Law Review* 103, 2011, 1162-1179. "To the extent the state claiming self-defense is invoking it as a collective right, the decision of the International Court of Justice in NICARAGUA V. UNITED STATES may have limited the availability of such claims to cases of force used in response to an armed attack."

27. W. Michael Reisman & James E. Baker, *Regulating Covert Action: Practices, Contexts, and Policies of Covert Coercion Abroad in International and American Law* 77, 1992.

28. See Robert Chesney, "Military-Intelligence Convergence and the Law of the Title 10/Title 50 Debate," *Journal of National Security Law and Policy* 5 (539), 2012, 539-629.

29. See Harold H. Koh, Legal Adviser, U.S. Department of State, "The Obama Administration and International Law, Remarks at the Annual Meeting of the American Society of International Law," March 25, 2010, available at *http://www.state.gov/s/l/releases/remarks/139119.htm.*

assassinations, enacted in 1981 following scandals over past CIA connections – actual and alleged – to assassination attempts against such anti-US world leaders as Cuba's Fidel Castro.[30] As one well-known government memorandum concludes, peacetime assassination encompasses, without more, the murder of a private individual or public figure for political purposes. Assassination is unlawful killing, and would be prohibited by international law even if there was no executive order proscribing it. But "the clandestine, low visibility or overt use of military force against legitimate targets in time of war, or against similar targets in time of peace where such individuals or groups pose an immediate threat to United States citizens or the national security of the United States, as determined by competent authority, does not constitute assassination or conspiracy to engage in assassination."[31] In other words, the killing of Saddam Hussein, if one believes that the invasion Iraq was not a continuation of the 1991 Persian Gulf War, would have constituted an unlawful assassination. But the killing of Saddam Hussein as supreme commander of the Iraqi armed forces during the invasion of Iraq, to the extent that he even wore a military uniform, probably would have been lawful.

Conclusion

So why do states continue to conduct intelligence collection and covert operations that arguably violate international law? These operations need not violate international law and can take place legally, albeit secretly. But the reality remains that the international legal system is largely decentralized, lacking the sorts of integrated enforcement mechanisms inherent in national legal systems. There is no global executive, legislature, judiciary, police, military, or paramilitary force that can take action against states that violate treaty obligations or other international law.

The US and the four other permanent members of the UN especially find themselves in advantageous positions with regard to this situation because of their ability to veto measures like diplomatic or economic sanctions or multilateral military force that could otherwise "enforce" against international law violations. But a country that respects the rule of law will do its best to make attempts at ensuring its intelligence efforts comply with international law, even though there is a relative paucity of such law to govern such efforts.

---

30. See Executive Order No. 12,333, 3 C.F.R. 200 (1982).
31. Memorandum from W. Hays Parks, Special Assistant to The Judge Advocate Gen. of the Army for Law of War Matters, to The Judge Advocate Gen. of the Army, "Executive Order 12333 and Assassination (Dec. 4, 1989)" reprinted in *Army Lawyer*, December 1989, at 4, available at *http://www.loc.gov/rr/frd/Military_Law/pdf/12-1989.pdf*.

READINGS FOR INSTRUCTORS

Anderson, Kenneth. *Targeted Killing in U.S. Counterterrorism Strategy and Law* 24–25 (Brookings Institution, Georgetown University Law Center, & Hoover Institution, Working Paper of the Series on Counterterrorism and American Statutory Law, 2009), available at *http://papers.ssrn.com/sol3/papers.cfm?abstract_id=1415070.*

Baker, Christopher D. "Tolerance of International Espionage: A Functional Approach," 19 *American University International Law Review* 1091, 2004.

Chesney, Robert M. "Military-Intelligence Convergence and the Law of the Title 10/Title 50 Debate," *Journal of National Security Law and Policy* 5 (539), 2012.

Chesney, Robert M. "Leaving Guantanamo: The Law of International Detainee Transfers," *University of Richmond Law Review* 40, 2006, 657-752.

Chesterman, Simon. "The Spy Who Came In from the Cold War: Intelligence and International Law," 27 *Michigan Journal of International Law* 1071, 1091 (2006).

Demarest, Geoffrey B. "Espionage in International Law," *Denver Journal of International Law & Policy* 24, 1996.

Forcese, Craig. "Spies Without Borders: International Law and Intelligence Collection," *Journal of National Security Law and Policy* 5, 2011.

Goldsmith, Jack. *The Terror Presidency: Law and Judgment Insider the Bush Administration.* (New York City: Norton, 2007).

HCJ 769/02 Public Committee Against Torture in Israel v. Government of Israel (Targeted Killings Case) [2005], available at *http://elyon1.court.gov.il/Files_ENG/02/690/007/a34/02007690.a34.pdf.*

Koh, Harold H. Legal Adviser, U.S. Department of State, "The Obama Administration and International Law," Remarks at the Annual Meeting of the American Society of International Law, March 25, 2010, available at *http://www.state.gov/s/l/releases/remarks/139119.htm.*

Mayer, Jane. *The Dark Side: The Inside Story Of How The War On Terror Turned Into A War On American Ideals.* (New York City: Doubleday, 2009) .

Memorandum from W. Hays Parks, Special Assistant to The Judge Advocate Gen. of the Army for Law of War Matters, to The Judge Advocate Gen. of the Army, "Executive Order 12333 and Assassination (Dec. 4, 1989)" reprinted in *Army Lawyer,* Dec. 1989, at 4, available at *http://www.loc.gov/rr/frd/Military_Law/pdf/12-1-1989.pdf.*

Preston, Stephen W. Remarks by CIA General Counsel Stephen W. Preston as prepared for delivery at Harvard Law School, April 10, 2012, available at *https://www.cia.gov/news-information/speeches-testimony/2012-speeches-testimony/cia-general-counsel-harvard.html.*

Reisman, W. Michael & James E. Baker, *Regulating Covert Action: Practices, Contexts, and Policies of Covert Coercion Abroad in International and American Law* (New Haven: Yale University Press, 1992).

Silver, Daniel B. (updated and revised by Frederick P. Hitz & J.E. Shreve Ariail). "Intelligence and Counterintelligence," in John Norton Moore & Robert Turner (eds.), *National Security Law* 935, 2005.

Smith, Jeffrey H. Keynote Address, "State Intelligence Gathering and International Law," 28 *Michigan Journal of International Law* 543, 544, 2007.

Sofaer, Abraham D. Sixth Annual Waldemar A. Solf Lecture in International Law: "Terrorism, the Law, and the National Defense," 126 *Military Law Review* 89, 119 (1989).

Special Rapporteur on Extrajudicial, Summary or Arbitrary Executions, Report of the Special Rapporteur on Extrajudicial, Summary or Arbitrary Execution: Study on Targeted Killings, delivered to the Human Rights Council, U.N. Doc. A/HRC/14/24/Add.6 (May 28, 2010), available at *http://www2.ohchr.org/ english/bodies/hrcouncil/docs/14session/A.HRC.14.24.Add6.pdf.*

Sulmasy, Glenn & John Yoo. "Counterintuitive: Intelligence Operations and International Law," *Michigan Journal of International Law* 28, 2007.

Williams, Robert. "(Spy) Game Change: Cyber Networks, Intelligence Collection, and Covert Action," *George Washington University Law Review* 79 (103), 2011, 1162-1179.

Yoo, John. "Transferring Terrorists," *Notre Dame Law Review* 79, 2004.

Yoo, John. *War by Other Means: An Insider's Account of the War on Terror* (New York City: Grove/Atlantic, 2006).

Ernesto J. Sanchez is an attorney, who focuses his practice on international law, and senior analyst at Wikistrat, Inc. The American Bar Association has just published his book, *The Foreign Sovereign Immunities Act Deskbook*, on the law governing lawsuits against foreign governments in US courts.

GUIDE TO THE STUDY OF INTELLIGENCE

The History of the State Secrets Privilege

Thomas R. Spencer and F.W. Rustmann, Jr.

No nation can function without secrets. It is a fundamental characteristic of sovereignty that information vital to the conduct of a nation's business be kept confidential. The history of civilization is peppered with tales of secret intelligence, codes, covert correspondence, and closely held military inventions used to vanquish enemies.[1] The control of these secrets is universally the prerogative of the sovereign leader.

In the United States today, the state secrets[2] privilege is an almost unassailable privilege of the Executive Branch to refuse to disclose secret information to anyone. Moreover, a lawsuit against the government, which is based on state secrets is almost always dismissed by the courts. The privilege is intertwined with the political history of our country and the contest over the balance of power and liberty.

The American colonists were steeped in the history of civilization and schooled in the prerogatives of the English Crown — the arbitrary exercise of which spawned economic and political disputes leading to the American Revolution. Crown Privilege, which included the "state secrets privilege" was a self-proclaimed and indisputable power of the Crown beyond the reach of the law. The Crown refused to permit its courts or Parliament to bridle its unilateral right to withhold information from its subjects. The justification for this royal privilege was the centuries-old belief, binding the social fabric, that the Crown always operated in the interests of its subjects, and that state secrets served the proper administration of the Crown's responsibilities to the people. Since the Crown was the sole determiner of what was in the public interest, neither

---

1. See Simon Singh, *The Code Book: The Secret History of Codes and Code Breaking* (Anchor Books, 2000).
2. "Secrets" can be facts, inventions, policies, correspondence, procedures, views—anything the government may decide should be secret. At the end of Fiscal Year 2008, there were 4,109 offices of original classification in the federal government. See *http://www.fas.org* "*Secrecy News.*"

a court nor Parliament could overturn or debate that determination.[3]

In the discussions and arguments over the construction of America's new form of government — unknown and untested in history — the drafters were wary of concentration of power. Checks and balances on each branch of government were demanded as a reaction to the autocratic sovereignty just overthrown. Yet the framers knew that secrecy was fundamental to government. They assumed that the Executive Branch, as the administrative branch, would house the new nation's secrets privilege and saw no need to specify its existence, its exercise or fashion its limits.[4] After all, in their view, the Legislative Branch, itself divided into two parts, was the premiere, most powerful branch — it resided in Article I of the Constitution. The Executive Branch was deemed secondary (hence Article II) and the Judicial Branch the weakest (Article III).

Bitter political arguments over the power of the new government festered in the elections following the adoption of the new Constitution in 1787. Partisan feuds smoldered in a second political revolution, bursting into the election of 1800 — Thomas Jefferson versus then President John Adams. Jefferson[5] barely won the nasty election, and John Adams paid him back by packing the courts and commissions, prior to the end of his term. This led to the 1803 case of Marbury v. Madison,[6] in which Justice John Marshall declared that the Constitution, despite the absence of specific language, implied that the courts had the final power to review actions of the Executive Branch for legality. It was a bold and gigantic grasp of political power. But so delicate and incendiary was the political balance at the time, that neither Jefferson nor Congress challenged Marshall's opinioin. In a second Constitutional crisis in 1807, President Jefferson charged Aaron Burr with treason concerning Burr's activities in the Louisiana Territory, a territory Burr allegedly tried to grab for himself. The judge who assigned himself to the treason case was Jefferson's cousin but political enemy, Justice Marshall. Burr requested to subpoena secret documents from President Jefferson. Marshall issued the subpoena. President Jefferson, still burning from the Marbury decision, refused to comply with the subpoena as a matter of principle, raising, in effect, the state secrets privilege,[7] which he said was implied as a necessary component of the Executive Branch functions. Justice Marshall was wary of pushing the issue. Moreover, Jefferson avoided the crisis by producing some of the requested documents voluntarily

---

3. See Weaver and Escontrias, "Origins of the State Secrets Privilege" at the Social Science Research Network, SSRN: *http://ssrn.com/abstract=1079364*, February 10, 2008.

4. See Gabriel Schoenfeld, *Necessary Secrets* (Norton, 2010), Chapter 2 "Secrets of the Founders."

5. Thomas Jefferson was intrigued with intrigue and secrecy. In fact, he invented and frequently used a secret code machine, the Wheel Cipher, still admired today. See David Kahn, *The Story of Secret Writing*. (Scribner, 1966).

6. 5 U.S. (1 Cranch) 137 (1803). See Sloan and McKean, *The Great Decision: Jefferson, Adams and Marshall, the Battle for the Supreme Court* (Public Affairs, 2009).

7. See Hoffer, *The Treason Trials of Aaron Burr* (University Press of Kansas, 2008). See UNITED STATES V. BURR, 25 Fed Cas.30 (D.C.D.Va.1807).

"for the justice of the situation." Marshall exonerated Burr thereby avoiding a collision with Jefferson and the state secrets privilege.

Almost 70 years after the trial of Aaron Burr, President Lincoln personally retained the services of a spy during the Civil War. He promised the spy compensation for information on certain Confederate military operations. After Lincoln was assassinated and the spy had died, his family made a claim for compensation, which the government denied. The family sued and the case, Totten v. United States, made its way to the Supreme Court in 1875.[8] The Court turned down the claim, deciding that any claim in court which relies on the disclosure of state secrets, may not be maintained and must be dismissed. This Precedent is still the law today.[9]

In 1953, the state secrets privilege faced its third challenge. An Air Force B-29 aircraft crashed in Georgia killing the entire crew. The families of the crew sued the government, claiming negligence in the maintenance of the aircraft. The Air Force refused to produce any of its records or recovered materials, even after a court order required it, claiming that the Executive Branch could refuse even the courts based on the state secrets privilege. The Supreme Court sustained the government and its privilege in Reynolds v. United States,[10] holding that the privilege must be raised in court and that a judge has the right only to determine whether the privilege has been properly raised. The Court ruled that courts should not force disclosure to review the propriety of the privilege; else the purpose of secrecy would be lost. This decision has never been modified or vitiated by any court.

State Secrets are classified by the President based on the level of possible harm to the nation's security:

Top Secret: "Disclosure would cause exceptionally grave danger to national security."

Secret: "Disclosure would cause grave damage to national security."

Confidential: "Disclosure would cause damage or prejudice to national security."

FIGURE 1. DEFINITIONS OF CATEGORIES OF CLASSIFIED INFORMATION[1]

1. See Executive Order 13526, Classified National Security Information. Available at www.fas.org .

Today, the President categorizes secret information, classifying it into a hierarchy of the damage to the nation if disclosed. "Confidential information" is the lowest category of state secrets and "Top Secret" is the highest (see Figure

8. TOTTEN V. UNITED STATES, 92 U.S. 105 (1875).
9. See TENET V. DOE, 544 U.S. 1 (2005).
10. 345 U.S. 1 (1953). Recently, all of the classified information and the facts were inadvertently spilled out on the internet. The facts showed absolute negligence in maintenance of the aircraft. But in HERRING V. UNITED STATES, 424 F.3d 384 (3rd Cir. 2005), the Circuit Court held that the government was right in withholding the evidence, due the fact that secret equipment was onboard.

1). In reality, there are many levels within the "Top Secret" category, but those levels and who has access are frequently considered state secrets themselves!

The state secrets privilege frequently collides with other concepts, which are equally important to American values. Personal liberties and freedom of the press are just two collision points frequently debated and sometimes litigated. Citizens, media, politicians, and courts historically have been concerned over the validity of the use of the privilege.[11] After all, the privilege could easily be used to cover up crimes, unethical or corrupt conduct.

Lawsuits are filed often against the President seeking disclosure of secret information. Congress has attempted many times, especially in recent years, to legislate limitations and procedures on the President in his use of the privilege. Thus far, all attempts have failed.[12]

However, the Department of Justice has recently announced a new policy of only withholding secret information in cases if the disclosure would "significantly harm" national security, such as intelligence information. Now, the attorney general personally will make the final decision on the use of the privilege in court. Recent court decisions demonstrate that the sanctity of the privilege, first used by Thomas Jefferson in 1807, is very much intact today. The courts are extremely reluctant to force disclosure when the President has decided that the nation's security could be compromised.[13]

READINGS FOR INSTRUCTORS

For an exhaustive study of the origins of the State Secrets Privilege, read "Origins of the State Secrets Privilege," by William G. Weaver and Danielle Escontrias, available at the Social Science Research Network, SSRN: http://ssrn.com/abstract=1079364 (February 10, 2008).

Also see W. Weaver and R. Pallito, "State Secrets and Executive Power," 120 Pol.Sci. Q.85,101 – 02(2005); R. Chesney, "State Secrets and the Limits of National Security Litigation," 75 Geo.W. L.R. 1249 (2007).

For an understanding of the importance of the Aaron Burr trial, see Peter Charles Hoffer, *The Treason Trials of Aaron Burr* (University Press of Kansas, 2008); and Buckner F. Melton, Jr., *Conspiracy to Treason* (John Wiley& Sons, Inc., 2002).

The original letters of Thomas Jefferson concerning the Burr subpoena are contained in Doug Linder, "The Treason Trial of Aaron Burr "(2001) available at http://www.law.umkc.edu./faculty/projects/f.trials/burr/burr.

For an analysis of Reynolds vs. United States and its present implications, see Louis Fischer, *In the name of National Security: Unchecked Presidential Power*

---

11. See the Pentagon Papers Case, New York Times Co. v. United States, 403 U.S. 713 (1971).

12. The 111th Congress attempted to pass the State Secrets Protection Act, S. Bill 417; H.R. 984, without success.

13. See Mohammed v. Jeppesen DataPlan, The *en banc* opinion of the 9th Circuit Court of Appeals is reported at 614 F.3d 1070 (9thCir. 2010). An appeal to the Supreme Court was denied on May 15, 2011.

and the *Reynolds Case* (University Press of Kansas, 2006). See also, Barry Siegel, *Claim of Privilege: A Mysterious Plane Crash, a Landmark Supreme Court Case, and the Rise of State Secrets* (Harper Perennial, 2009).

The Federation of American Scientists collects information on state secrets law and policy. See, *http://www.fas.org* "*Secrecy News.*"

For the impact of the state secrets privilege on the media, see Gabriel Schoenfeld, *Necessary Secrets—National Security, the Media and the Rule of Law* (Norton, 2010). Also worth reading is Abram N. Shulsky and Gary J. Schmitt, *Silent Warfare, Understanding the World of Intelligence Third Edition*, (Potomac Books, 2002).

For an excellent review of the law in the context of the War on Terror, it is recommended that review of the case of Mohamed et al. v. Jeppesen Dataplan, Inc., decided by the 9th Circuit Court of Appeals on September 8, 2010 would be extremely helpful. In a 6-5 en banc ruling, the Court narrowly dismissed a suit based on the state secrets privilege. The plaintiffs requested that the Supreme Court review the decision. The Supreme Court refused the appeal on May 15, 2011.

The State Secrets Privilege is the centerpiece of a debate today over the power of the President. Compare Gary Wills, *Bomb Power: The Modern Presidency and the National Security State* (Penguin Press, 2009) with Steven G. Calabresi, Christopher Yoo, *The Unitary Executive: Presidential Power From Washington To Bush* (Yale University Press, 2008).

Thomas R. Spencer is a Miami lawyer. He concentrates on international business, commercial litigation, governmental litigation, and international arbitration. He regularly represents intelligence officers of the National Clandestine Service.

F. W. Rustmann, Jr. is a 24-year veteran of the National Clandestine Service, retiring as a member of the Senior Intelligence Service. He is the founder and chairman of CTC International Group, Inc. of West Palm Beach, Florida, a leading provider of business intelligence, legal support and analysis . Among other assignments, Rustmann was an instructor at the CIA's covert training facility known as "The Farm." He is the author of CIA, Inc.: Espionage and the Craft of Business Intelligence (Brassey's 2002).

GUIDE TO THE STUDY OF INTELLIGENCE

The Protection of Intelligence Sources and Methods

Dr. Robert M. Clark

I have grown to love secrecy ... the commonest thing
is delightful if one only hides it

— Oscar Wilde

To the new initiate, the US Intelligence Community's system of security protections is a confusing maze, and its compartmentation system for protecting highly sensitive information is sometimes overwhelming. The protection system is loosely called the compartmentation system. It is a system that is sometimes misused, frustrating to understand, but it all really makes sense. To understand why it makes sense, one must go back to the system's origins. It helps to understand how the system evolved, and what it is protecting. Also, it has a lot of colorful history.

The system of protecting sources and methods can be better understood by answering one key question: *If this information were revealed to an opponent, how much damage would we suffer?* The answer to this question determines the nature of the protection. To understand how we have answered that question over the years, let's start with some history.

Historical Development

Until about 1960, the US (and British Commonwealth) control systems for protecting sources, methods, and the intelligence product was as described below. Most other countries had similar systems for protection of their intelligence resources.

HUMINT

The clandestine collection of intelligence through human sources (HUMINT) goes back at least to biblical times, when the Israelites spied out the land of Canaan. This first attempt, incidentally, was a disaster (its direct result was 40 more years of Israelite wandering in the wilderness) for reasons familiar to any intelligence analyst: unreliable sources.

HUMINT was developed to a fine art by Sir Francis Walsingham, Queen Elizabeth I's skilled spymaster, who established many of the basic principles of a clandestine service.[1] The two levels of protection that exist today date from his time (at least). The distinction is between the *product* of HUMINT and the *sources and methods*, and the key to the distinction is need-to-know.

The highest level of protection is placed on information that might allow someone to determine the identity of the source (the agent). Loss of this information usually results in someone being imprisoned or killed, loses the source permanently, and discourages others from volunteering to become agents. Therefore, a high level of protection of the source is necessary. The protection for this information was called the Bigot list.[2] The term "Bigot" is not used here in a pejorative sense, but merely in the sense of narrow, or restricted in access. The term originated when the allies were preparing for the Normandy invasion during World War II. Everyone with knowledge of the invasion plans, codenamed Operation Overlord, received security clearances and was listed on what was known as the BIGOT list – BIGOT being short for "British Invasion of German Occupied Territory."

Many such lists have been created since to protect HUMINT sources. Each list contains the names of individuals who need to know, for example, the true name of a specific agent. The lists are tightly controlled, but are not a formal control system.

The lower level of protection is on the content of information provided by a source. Such information, if lost, only reveals what you know, but not how you know it. This level of information is included in HUMINT reports that are sent to the intelligence analysis community. It is typically classified SECRET or below, though TOP SECRET reports are used to protect especially sensitive information. Codewords are not normally used.

The US State Department produces HUMINT reporting, though the department eschews the use of the term HUMINT (officially, Foreign Service officers do not engage in intelligence activities). So diplomatic reporting may be classified, but State also uses terms such as Limited Dissemination (LIMDIS) Exclusive Dissemination (EXDIS) and No Dissemination (NODIS) markings to protect sources and methods.[3]

---

1. Allen Dulles (1977), *The Craft of intelligence*, Greenwood Press edition, p. 18.
2. U.S. Senate. Final Report, *Book I: Foreign and Military Intelligence*, Final Report of the Select Committee to Study Governmental Operations, 94th Congress, 2nd session, Report no. 94-755, April 26, 1976.
3. Office of the Director of National Intelligence [ODNI], *Intelligence Community Classification and Control Markings Implementation Manual*, Vol. 4, Ed. 2, 31 May 2011, https://www.fas.org/sgp/othergov/intel/capco_imp.pdf .

COMINT

Communications intelligence (COMINT) – the interception and analysis of communications — predates the use of radio. Any follower of old Western movies is familiar with the frequently repeated scene where a US Cavalry scout deciphers Indian smoke signals. Military units were deciphering messages sent by their opponent's flag signaling systems immediately after the systems were invented. COMINT began to expand markedly after radio was introduced. The Russians lost their first major battle of World War I, at Tannenberg, primarily because the Germans intercepted Russian high frequency radio communications and thereby knew the exact deployment of Russian field armies. COMINT during World War I included both radio intercept and the tapping of telephone lines laid by armies in the field; it expanded after World War I to include information obtained from wiretaps and hidden microphones (bugs). Encryption came into wide use to protect against COMINT, and cryptanalysis came into wide use as countries attempted to break each other's diplomatic codes and encrypted military communications. (Encryption and cryptanalysis, of course, predate both electronic communications and COMINT).

The original protection of COMINT information was basically the same as for the Bigot system used in HUMINT: lists of persons approved for access. This approach was found to be unsatisfactory as a result of the Pearl Harbor surprise attack. US cryptanalysts had broken the codes that provided warning of the attack, but compartmentation contributed to keeping the information from those who could have benefited.

It was clear that a Bigot system would not work for COMINT; too many people had to have the COMINT product. Though the loss of COMINT information would not directly cost human lives, it could cause loss of the source (the opponent would develop a new encryption system). COMINT organizations would lose valuable information if a compromise occurred, and it was expensive to break new encryption systems.

The result was the beginning of the COMINT compartmentation system during World War II. Under this system, only cleared and briefed people (usually senior government officials and military commanders) had access to the product information.

The codeword system has evolved into the present Special Intelligence (SI) control system, which uses two classes of compartments and associated security systems.

- One class protects the sources and methods: access is usually granted only to SIGINT collectors and processors. It functions much like the Bigot list. A large number of compartments exist in this set.

- The second class protects the product, and access is granted to a wide range of people.

The SI control system's extensive use of SIGINT-only compartments leads to some amusing exchanges. In one case, a senior US military officer found out that his National Security Agency (NSA) contact was providing sensitive material to the Government Communications Headquarters (GCHQ, the British SIGINT organization). In response to his question "How can you give it to the British, but not to me?" the NSA man replied "Well, they're SIGINT, you're not."

IMINT

Imagery intelligence (IMINT) originally was called photographic intelligence (PHOTINT), and was conducted by reconnaissance aircraft. Aerial photography matured as an intelligence discipline during World War II, and photo interpreters (PIs) became common in all military services. There were no special controls on imagery, because the information needed to be made available quickly to field commanders. Very little protection of sources and methods was needed anyway, because when a reconnaissance aircraft flew overhead, it was obvious to the enemy that you were taking their pictures. Most aerial photography was classified secret or below.

The term IMINT became standard during the Cold War because it included, in addition to standard photography, infrared photography, multispectral imagery, and radar imagery. With the 1996 establishment of the National Imagery and Mapping Agency (NIMA), the geospatial intelligence concept was born, combining imagery with geographical information. When NIMA changed its name to the National Geospatial-Intelligence Agency (NGA) in 2003, GEOINT became a standard intelligence discipline similar to SIGINT and HUMINT.

ELINT

Electronic intelligence, or ELINT, is a SIGINT sub-discipline. It refers primarily to the collection and processing of the signals emitted by radars. It dates back to the first use of radars in combat. Like IMINT, ELINT was not tightly protected during World War II, and most ELINT today continues to be classified secret or below. Little protection of sources and methods was needed because, when an opponent uses radar, he has to assume that you will intercept it; and denying ELINT collection is very difficult.

FISINT

Foreign Instrumentation Signals Intelligence (FISINT) refers to the collection and processing of signals collected from a missile, aircraft, or satellite platform – primarily telemetry. Telemetry signals give status and performance characteristics of the platform. Telemetry signals are useful for predicting the performance of weapons systems that are in testing phase, and for assessing the operations of satellites. In FISINT, our ability to break out the telemetry channels and determine the meaning of each channel signal is the important method to protect. FISINT therefore resembles COMINT – the processing part needs a very high level of protection.

Open Source

Little or no special protection is given to the open source "INT," and since the source material is unclassified, it seems difficult to justify any protection. However, the techniques for exploiting open source material, and the specific material of interest for exploitation, can tell an opponent much about an intelligence service's targets. For this reason, NSA has for years marked its translations of open source as "Official Use Only." A restrictive marking also allows a government to ignore copyright laws while limiting use of the material. Corporations make use of similar restrictive markings on material that is translated or reproduced for in-house use, for the same reasons — concealment of interest and avoidance of copyright problems.

A more serious reason for protecting open source exploitation methods is that, if your opponent knows what your target materials are, it is easier for him to carry off a successful deception. The US has long been aware that many intelligence services translate and avidly read *Aviation Week and Space Technology* (AW&ST). Within the intelligence community, *Aviation Week* was often referred to as "aviation leak." When the Defense Department wishes to mislead or deceive another country about US capabilities and intentions, AW&ST is the natural place to attempt to "plant" the misleading story.

The Modern Compartmentation System

Since about 1960, an extensive new control system has developed for protecting sensitive intelligence information. It had its origins in the US decision to conduct peacetime photoreconnaissance over the USSR using the U-2. Because such flights violated international law, the consequences of their exposure were expected to be severe (and in fact, their exposure subsequent to the U-2 shootdown did cause severe consequences). Therefore, the compartmentation on both the sources and methods and on the imagery product (since the product revealed the fact of such reconnaissance) was very tight.

Clearly, the US was not protecting the "fact of" reconnaissance from the Soviets; they were well aware of the overflights. So long as the US did not publicize the overflights, however, the Soviets found it expedient not to do so themselves — at least, until they could shoot one of the U-2s down.

By the time of the 1960 U-2 shoot down and the termination of all aircraft reconnaissance overflights over the USSR, the US was already building the first reconnaissance satellites. Satellite reconnaissance, however, posed several unique security concerns.

- By necessity, satellites overfly many international boundaries. The USSR launch of Sputnik I established the principle that satellites could legally overfly other countries. In the 1960s, however, it was not clear whether satellites could legally conduct reconnaissance during such overflights, and the right of another country to shoot down a "spy satellite" over its territory was in dispute.

- If a US airplane deliberately overflies a hostile country's territory, the opponent can assume its mission was intelligence collection. In contrast, an opponent could not easily determine whether a satellite was an intelligence collector.

- Satellites are very expensive to build, launch, and support. The more opponents know about a reconnaissance satellite, the easier it is for them to counter its mission. The high cost of any disclosure of sources and methods argued for a stringent security system.

The Kampiles case illustrates the importance of protecting the details of satellite reconnaissance. The US lost a significant advantage in intelligence collection when former CIA employee William Kampiles, who had resigned after failing to qualify as an overseas operations officer, sold the technical manual for the new KH-11 satellite to the Soviets for $3,000 in 1977. The KH-11 was the first imagery satellite that could transmit its images to earth in near real time. Because it did not downlink directly to a ground station, the Soviets did not intercept any signals from the satellite, leading them to believe that it was a system failure. Therefore, they took no security measures when the satellite passed overhead. The National Reconnaissance Office (NRO) collected valuable imagery of new Soviet weapons systems being tested in the open until the Soviets realized that the satellite was a new system that transmitted its imagery away from the earth to a relay satellite in higher orbit. The surprise factor was lost. Knowing its capabilities the Soviets took measures to conceal sensitive activities and deny the US valuable intelligence.[4]

The Sensitive Compartmented Information (SCI) protection system, which originated in US peacetime aircraft and satellite reconnaissance, provides two levels of protection, much like the COMINT control system. An extensive set of compartments was developed to protect collection sources and methods, and another set was developed to protect the product.

Since the 1960s, a number of separate compartmentation systems have evolved within the SCI system. Three examples illustrate the nature of these

---

4. Defense Security Service Security Research Center, *Recent Espionage Cases, 1975-1999*, (Monterey, CA: Defense Department, 1999), 41; George C. Wilson, "Soviets learned of spy satellite from U.S. manual," *Washington Post*, November 23, 1978 at http://www.jonathanpollard. org/7890/112378.htm.

compartments.

The BYEMAN and RESERVE Systems

After the NRO was created in 1960, it adopted a compartmentation system to protect its system development process as well as its operations. Under the BYEMAN compartmentation system, an extensive set of sub-compartments, with codewords assigned to each, was created to protect specific systems and studies. Persons having access to the system development for a specific overhead system might not, for example, be permitted access to the operations part, and would not automatically be permitted to know anything about other overhead systems.

A number of efforts were made to shrink the number of compartments within the BYEMAN system. Criticisms of the NRO security system came from both outside and inside the organization. An NRO inspector general report noted that there are "numerous examples of over classification and use" of the BYEMAN compartment. The NRO security system, the report noted, is often used as the excuse to bypass or mitigate established procedures and controls. A special panel review (the Jeremiah Panel review) noted that the practice of using the NRO security system as something more than a security compartment existed within the NRO. It also noted the perception by many outsiders that the NRO uses its security system selectively and arbitrarily to restrict what is seen as legitimate access to NRO information.[5]

The BYEMAN control system was retired on 20 May 2005; the system became unwieldy, as more and more defense officials needed knowledge of satellite systems and their capabilities. However, the principles of compartmentation were retained and sensitive operational details and system vulnerabilities continued to be protected from general knowledge. The most sensitive of such material is now protected in compartments within a new NRO control system called RESERVE.[6]

The HUMINT Control System

A formal compartmentation system now exists for the control of human source intelligence, entitled the HUMINT Control System (HCS). HCS covers both source identity and sensitive reporting.

---

5. Report of the Jeremiah Panel on Defining the Future of the NRO for the 21st Century, Chapter IX, Security, 26 August 1996 (Unclassified Extract).
6. ODNI, *Intelligence Community Classification and Control Markings Implementation Manual*, Vol. 4, Ed. 2, 31 May 2011, 146, *https://www.fas.org/sgp/othergov/intel/capco_imp.pdf*.

The GEOINT Control System

The National Geospatial-Intelligence Agency (NGA) uses the KLONDIKE control system as an SCI control system to protect sensitive geospatial intelligence (GEOINT).[7]

A Note on Codewords

Those whose job involves working with the military or intelligence communities soon learn about codewords. They are endemic to both, and most of them, in the military at least, have little or nothing to do with intelligence.

But the intelligence compartmentation system does rely heavily on codewords in protecting sources and methods. Today, codewords are an essential part of the intelligence information management process. Codewords and compartmentation, though, are two separate things. Compartmentation is the system for controlling access to classified information. Codewords are short names used to identify the control systems.

Codewords, in both military and intelligence, serve several purposes, though not all of the purposes served are legitimate. If properly chosen, they are useful in protecting programs from hostile intelligence efforts. This is, in fact, their main legitimate purpose.

- Codewords are a convenient way to define something — a concept, a collection program, a software project — in a brief word. They allow quick identification of security access to a specific compartment.
- Codewords are more easily remembered, especially at budget time. A project with a code name acquires special stature, especially if the code name is protected by compartmentation.
- Codewords, when protected by compartmentation, can shield programs from scrutiny, especially from auditors and budget-cutters.

Codewords have been used in industry for years, and the computer industry is particularly fond of them. Apple Computer executives have consistently followed the prudent course of choosing codewords that "evoke inappropriate images."[8] Names like "Lisa" provide no clue as to the project nature, and "Macintosh" provides only a slight clue; whereas, when your current product is named iPhone 6, a codename such as iPhone 7 could tell a great deal to an industrial spy.

Fortunately for intelligence analysts, a powerful temptation exists for military officers to choose codewords that have some meaning, often ones that represent an insider joke. The Germans during World War II were particularly vulnerable to this temptation:

---

7. Ibid.
8. John A. Barry, *Technobabble* (Cambridge, MA: MIT Press, 1992), 142.

One of the more inappropriate codewords was the one the Germans chose during World War II for their air raid of 14-15 November 1940, which devastated the British city of Coventry. The name, "Moonlight Sonata," correctly suggested to British Intelligence that the raid would be conducted at night, near the time of the full moon.[9]

The British did not act effectively on the intelligence, and Coventry suffered; but that is another story. Intelligence has its limits, and it does not make operational decisions.

Another time, the Germans chose the nickname "Freya" for a new aircraft detection system. The name provoked R.V. Jones, while waiting for photography of the new system, to do some research on mythology. Freya, the Nordic goddess of Beauty, Love, and Fertility, had a prized necklace called Brisingamen. Its guardian, the watchman of the gods, was Heimdal; and Heimdal could see one hundred miles in every direction, day or night. Jones cautiously (but correctly) reported that the system was probably a radar, and gave an estimate of its range performance based on the nickname.[10]

The US still uses codewords that evoke appropriate images. In the days leading up to the Gulf War, the US adopted the codeword "Desert Shield" for its preparations – evoking a fairly clear image of a defensive deployment in the Saudi Arabian desert; and once the opponent understands the meaning of this codeword, then the codeword "Desert Storm" conveys a very clear image of what is to happen next.

In contrast, the Russians and British have been able to resist the temptation to assign nicknames or codewords that have meaning, and even in some cases to choose codewords that were carefully designed to mislead intelligence analysts. A famous example is the British use of "tank" during World War I for machines that, when enclosed in canvas for transport to the front, looked like fuel storage receptacles of the same name. The Russians learned this lesson well, and they consistently rely on neutral codewords, heavily oriented to names of natural objects — rivers and bodies of water, rocks or minerals. It once seemed that every third Soviet program was nicknamed "Almaz" (Russian for "diamond"). The use of the same codeword for different programs, in fact, makes the intelligence analyst's life much more difficult because separating fragments of information into the proper program becomes harder. The British tend to rely more on names of man-made objects; for example, "window" was the British codename in World War II for reflecting chaff that is dropped from aircraft to confuse enemy radar. In contrast to the US codeword approach to Gulf War preparations, the British adopted the unevocative codeword GRANBY for its RAF deployment to the theatre; a Defense Ministry computer randomly

9. N. E. Evans, "Air Intelligence and the Coventry Raid," RUSI/RMAS Research Centre Bulletin 121 (3), September 1976.
10. Alfred Price, *Instruments of Darkness: The History of Electronic Warfare, 1939-1945* (London: William Kimber, 2006) 78.

selected GRANBY .[11]

All countries, however, tend to fall into the consistency trap in assigning codenames, as the British and Russian examples above suggest. NATO designators for Soviet aircraft always began with "B" if the aircraft was a bomber and "F" if it was a fighter; one-syllable names indicated propeller-driven, two syllables indicated a jet. Thus BEAR would be a prop-driven bomber, FOXBAT a jet fighter. For a long time, one could tell that a program originated in the US Air Force, and which USAF group originated it, by the first word of the two-word nicknames that USAF selected. Codenames such as "HAVE xxxx" or "PAVE xxxx or "RIVET xxxx" were part of a series, for example, and conveyed specific information about the associated program. (The "xxxx" refers to a specific program name, e.g. RIVET JOINT, RIVET BRASS.) Codenames such as "CLASSIC xxxx," "SENIOR xxxx," or "COMPASS xxxx" had similar patterns. The temptation to choose codewords in such series is understandable, since a codenamethat fits into a familiar pattern has more legitimacy with budgeteers. However, such patterns are a gift to hostile intelligence analysts. Over time, this has become less of a problem, as many codewords (especially within the US Intelligence Community) now are randomly generated.

In Conclusion...

The US compartmentation system has frustrated, amazed, and confused most of us on occasion. Furthermore, the continuing proliferation of special compartments seems counter to the stated missions of the director of national intelligence (DNI): to lead intelligence integration and forge an Intelligence Community that delivers the most insightful intelligence possible. But one of the DNI goals is to "drive responsible and *secure* information-sharing"[12] [emphasis added]. For all of its flaws, the compartmentation system continues to serve us well in that regard.

Robert M. Clark, Ph.D., J.D., is a consultant for the US Intelligence Community, a faculty member of the Intelligence and Security Academy, and adjunct professor of intelligence studies at the University of Maryland University College and Johns Hopkins University. Dr. Clark served in the United States Air Force as an electronics warfare officer and intelligence officer. At CIA, he was a senior analyst and group chief managing analytic methodologies. He subsequently was President and CEO of the Scientific and Technical Analysis Corporation. Dr. Clark has published three books: *Intelligence Analysis: A Target-centric Approach*, now in its fourth edition; *The Technical Collection of Intelligence*, published in 2010; and Intelligence Collection, published in 2013. He is co-author of *Target-Centric Network Modeling*, and co-editor of *The 5 Disciplines of Intelligence Collection*, both published in 2015.

---

11. Mark Urban, *UK Eyes Alpha* (London, Faber and Faber Ltd., 1996), 155.
12. DNI Mission, Vision, and Goals, *http://www.dni.gov/index.php/about/mission*.

GUIDE TO THE STUDY OF INTELLIGENCE

Keeping U.S. National Security Secrets

Why Is This So Hard?

James B. Bruce

If someone wants to protect a personal secret, he or she only needs to exercise restraint and tell no one. If no one else is told, the secret is safe. If the US Government wants to protect a national security secret, restraint is not enough. The government is huge, so keeping secrets requires rules, regulations, and laws; added safeguards, such as classifying information; physical, personnel, information, and operational security for the secure use, dissemination, storage, and retrieval of protected information; and a counterintelligence capability to thwart spies.

Despite an elaborate edifice of protection, the government is not good at keeping secrets.[1] As a consequence, foreign governments and terrorist groups exploit disclosed secrets: They thus expand their abilities to neutralize, defeat, or deceive US intelligence. Diminished intelligence results in diminished military and diplomatic capabilities. The net result of poor secret-keeping is the diminution of American power.

There are many threats to government secrets. Leakers and spies represent the greatest threats. What leakers have demonstrated over time—and dramatically of late—is that for all its power and resources, the US Government is unable to stop the leaking. The most notable recent disclosures are those of Edward Snowden, a contractor for the National Security Agency.[2] In

---

1. James B. Bruce and W. George Jameson, *Fixing Leaks: Assessing the Department of Defense's Approach to Preventing and Deterring Unauthorized Disclosures* (Santa Monica: The RAND Corporation, 2013), 11-16.

2. See Peter C. Oleson, "Assessing Edward Snowden—Whistleblower, Traitor, or Spy?" *The Intelligencer 21* (2), Spring/Summer, 2015, 15-24; David V. Gioe, "Tinker, Tailor, Leaker, Spy: The Future Costs of Mass Leaks," *The National Interest*, Jan-Feb 2014; Edward Jay Epstein, "Was Snowden's Heist a Foreign Espionage Operation?" *Wall Street Journal*, May 9, 2014. Views sympathetic to Snowden are in James Bamford, "The Most Wanted Man in the World," *Wired Magazine*, Sep 2014, 78-85; and Glenn

mid-2013, he stole 1.5 million files of classified information—nearly all of it highly classified. Possibly 200,000 of these documents have been leaked to the press so far; and all those taken are presumed to be now in the possession of Russia and China.

The staggering scale of Snowden's theft is unprecedented. But the means of doing this, i.e., massive electronic downloading to thumb drives and small portable media, had only one precedent—Army Private First Class Bradley (now Chelsea) Manning. Manning provided roughly 750,000 classified documents to WikiLeaks, run by fugitive Julian Assange whose avowed mission is the large-scale exposure of classified information.[3] Today, Manning is serving a 35-year sentence in a federal prison. Snowden defected to Russia. And as of July 2016, Assange has been holed-up more than four years in the Ecuadorian Embassy in London where he took refuge in 2012 to evade criminal charges in Sweden, Britain, Australia, and the United States.

Yet much of the publicity surrounding mega-leakers Snowden and Manning, and WikiLeaks founder Assange, portrays them as heroes and whistleblowers, press-freedom fighters combating governments' excessive secrecy practices to reveal alleged wrongdoing. Their declared aim is to expose US intelligence, military, and diplomatic secrets.

The favorable press coverage afforded these leakers demonstrates the power of the one-sided argument. While the government has, for the most part, taken a low profile and constrained its public commentary, supporters of Snowden in particular, and those of Manning and Assange, have succeeded in controlling the public narrative. And their polemic plays well to sympathetic press elements that tout unrestrained First Amendment freedoms and often encourage leakers to circumvent government rules.[4] For example, the *Washington Post* editorial board explains: "As a newspaper, *The Post* thrives on revelatory journalism and often benefits from leaks, sometimes inspired by dissent and other times by spin."[5] Bill Keller of *The New York Times* has written frequently of the *Times's* putative right to publish leaked classified information. And *Washington Times* writer Bill Gertz often publicly trolls his readers for classified leaks as grist for his articles and books. Quite apart from the supportive public narrative, their successes highlight numerous vulnerabilities in the US Government framework for information protection. When seen against the long history

---

Greenwald, *No Place to Hide: Edward Snowden, The NSA, and the US Surveillance State* (New York: Holt & Co., 2014). Official views in the Intelligence Community are in Office of the Director of National Intelligence, IC [Intelligence Community] on the Record, at *http://icontherecord.tumblr.com/tagged/ statement; and http://icontherecord.tumblr.com.*

3. For Manning and WikiLeaks coverage, see Steve Fishman, "Bradley Manning's Army of One," *New York Magazine*, July 31, 2011; and articles by Nakashima, Tate, and Londono in the *Washington Post*, May 4, 2011 and July 30, 2013.

4. See Paul Pillar, "Leaks and an Irresponsible Press," *The National Interest*, December 26, 2013.

5. Washington Post Editorial Board, "Not Every Leak Is Tantamount to Treason," *Washington Post*, August 1, 2013.

of successful leaking of secrets, these vulnerabilities reveal a fundamentally flawed system of preserving secrets, suggesting the need for a new paradigm for secrecy protection, or at least a significantly more effective one.

Why Is Secrecy Important?

In general, the US Government classifies information it wishes to protect from disclosure at three levels: Confidential, Secret, and Top Secret. These ascending levels of classification assign relative importance and increased protection to discrete pieces of information. Executive Order (EO) 12356 states that compromised Confidential information would cause *damage* to US national security; if information is Secret, its compromise would cause *serious damage*; if Top Secret, *exceptionally grave damage*.[6] Additionally, some information of great sensitivity may be further categorized as "sensitive compartmented information" (SCI—usually identified by a codeword), and afforded greater protection from disclosure than other classification levels.

The secrets that the government wishes to protect can involve the following organizations and topics:

Department of Defense:

- Military plans, weapons capabilities, and operations;
- Military intentions and capabilities, including tactics, techniques, and procedures (TTPs) for special operations forces as well as those for strategic and conventional conflict;
- US security and military weaknesses and vulnerabilities; and
- Sensitive military technologies.

Intelligence Community (IC):

- Collection sources and methods, including identities of intelligence officers; recruited agents; and technical characteristics of collection sensors, platforms, systems, and architectures; and
- Operational activities such as covert action.

Department of State:

- Diplomatic discussions and protected communications; and
- Foreign policy deliberations and initiatives.

Department of Energy:

- The safeguarding of nuclear materials, facilities and sensitive technologies; and

---

6. Whether these distinctions remain useful or are merely archaic is beyond the scope of this article but might be worth examining in a research project or classroom exercise given today's Information Age.

- Weapons design data.

   Other departments and agencies: this includes many governmental organizations who must protect sensitive information related to homeland security, law enforcement investigations, proprietary intellectual property, individual's private data, or other information that is restricted by law.

The rationale for such secrets is not to keep the American public in the dark or to hide official wrongdoing. It is rather to deny sensitive information to foreign enemies and adversaries and, in cases of privacy data, protect individual citizen's rights.

Threats to Secrecy and Why That Matters

Disclosures of classified information can be authorized or unauthorized.[7] Authorized disclosures entail foreign intelligence sharing; use of sensitive intelligence to support a diplomatic démarche that asks a foreign government to do or stop doing something (such as to stop underground nuclear testing); the major government declassification program in support of greater transparency;[8] and official release of classified information through the Freedom of Information Act (FOIA) process. Disclosures from these authorized procedures, while fully legal, can still be potentially damaging.

Unauthorized disclosures can be diverse, but the two most serious — foreign espionage and leaks of classified information — are considered here.[9] Both can be seriously damaging and diminish American power.

Espionage

The United States has long been a high priority target of foreign intelligence services. And too many Americans have either volunteered or have been recruited to help them spy against their country. Since the end of World War II, as many as 217 Americans have been identified and prosecuted for committing espionage. Three-fourths have been volunteers, reaching out on their own initiative to offer their services to foreign intelligence.[10]

---

7. See discussion in the Commission on the Intelligence Capabilities of the United States Regarding Weapons of Mass Destruction, *Report to the President of the United States, March 31, 2005* (Washington, DC: US Government Printing Office, 2005), 380-384.

8. DNI Clapper's recent initiative on implementing transparency, *Principles of Intelligence Transparency for the Intelligence Community*, is described in ODNI Press Release Number 22-15, October 27, 2015, and can be downloaded from *http://www.dni.gov*.

9. Other examples of unauthorized disclosures can include verbal comments involving classified information with persons who do not have clearances or a need-to-know, or inadvertently leaving classified materials on a bus.

10. Discussion here draws from the PERSEREC study, *Espionage and Other Compromises of National Security: Case Summaries from 1975 to 2008* (Monterey, CA: Defense Personnel Security Research Center, 2009); and from David Major and Peter C. Oleson, "Espionage in America," *The Intelligencer*, in printed version of *The Guide to the Study of Intelligence* [Falls Church, VA: AFIO, 2016] and also online at *http://www.afio.com/40_guide.htm*, who cite the 217 prosecutions.

American spies have provided, or tried to provide, US classified information to 26 foreign countries and to Al–Qa'ida. Russia has enjoyed the greatest success with roughly 86 penetrations from 1947 to 2007. Counting the former Warsaw Pact countries (East Germany, Hungary, Czechoslovakia, and Poland) having run another 29 American spies, China 13, and Cuba 9 more, the loss of US classified information to Cold War adversaries from their combined 137 penetrations can be described as a hemorrhage. As many as 10 friendly or allied countries can also claim espionage successes against the United States, and several have run more than one American spy (Philippines, 5; Israel, 4; and Taiwan, 2).[11] America stands tall as the target of choice, and a lucrative one to adversaries who have defeated underperforming US counterintelligence

Understanding these penetrations would be better appreciated when the full damage is assessed. But it never has been. Although damage assessments have been conducted of most individual cases, a comprehensive damage assessment compiling the results and implications of multiple spy cases — even across the major ones — has never been done. Lacking that, assessing overall espionage losses is impossible.

Military Spies. In the tradition of the Soviet atomic spies who penetrated the Manhattan Project (Klaus Fuchs and the Rosenbergs are the most well-known), some Cold War spies, such as the Navy's John Walker and the Army's Clyde Lee Conrad, provided the Soviets with significant military secrets. According to the Defense Personnel Security Research Center (PERSEREC) 2009 study, *Espionage and Other Compromises of National Security*,[12] the Walker spy ring compromised key cards used for enciphering messages, information about encryption devices themselves, and at least a million classified messages of the US military and intelligence. This study notes that a defector said that the KGB considered the Walker operation as the most important in its history. Some believe that the third leg of the US strategic triad, the submarine force that carries long-range nuclear missiles, could have been rendered impotent in a nuclear war as a result of Walker's treachery.

The Conrad spy ring compromised secrets regarding the planned use of tactical nuclear weapons, manuals on military communications, and documents concerning NATO's war plans against the Warsaw Pact. These included detailed descriptions of nuclear weapons and plans for the movement of troops, tanks and aircraft.[13]

Intelligence Community Spies. For all the espionage damage to US military capabilities during the Cold War, the damage to intelligence was almost

---

11. Data presented for the period 1947 to 2007 are based on conservative, open source information in the PERSEREC study of documented cases of passing classified information to a foreign intelligence service. Espionage can also be more broadly defined, and data supporting a more expansive definition are in the Major and Oleson study, which also notes a spike in cases since 2002.
12. PERSEREC, *Espionage*, 58-59.
13. PERSEREC, *Espionage*, 10.

certainly worse. It entailed many more spies, and their reach into classified repositories was stunning. The two showstopper cases — it is arguable which was worse — were the CIA's Aldrich Ames and the FBI's Robert Hanssen. But there were many others.

Undetected for nine years, Ames provided Moscow the identities of perhaps a dozen clandestine US penetrations (of whom 10 were executed); the identities of other US double agents run against the Russians; tradecraft of agent operations and communications; identities of CIA officers under cover and other US intelligence personnel; on-going technical collection operations, sensitive analytic techniques; and hundreds of intelligence reports including National intelligence Estimates, arms control studies—some analyzing scenarios of how the Russians could cheat on treaties — and the cable traffic of several federal departments.[14]

Hanssen was almost as prolific, though perhaps more damaging because of his special compartmented accesses, well beyond Ames'. Hanssen's espionage went undetected for 22 years, more than twice as long as Ames. Highlights of his compromises include over 6,000 pages of classified documents, the identities of seven US penetrations (three were executed), details on many US counterintelligence operations, information on some of the most sensitive and highly compartmented projects in the US Intelligence Community, and even details on otherwise well-protected and sensitive US nuclear war defenses.[15]

The voluminous materials provided by these two spies will serve as playbooks for Russia to neutralize US intelligence effectiveness in many important areas, and provide the basis for future deception operations to hoodwink American leaders. As exemplars of damaging cases, the measure of harm Hanssen and Ames wrought to US security may be incalculable, but must also be assessed in the context of other serious foreign penetrations of US intelligence.

Foreign knowledge of US intelligence is the bedrock foundation of foreign denial and deception. It begins with an understanding of how the major collection disciplines work. Since intelligence capabilities are best defeated—that is, denied, deceived, or otherwise neutralized—by attacking individual collection disciplines, we can array the major spy cases against them. Spies damage classified collection capabilities by exposing secrets to adversaries about how classified collection techniques work. Sometimes referred to as intelligence "sources and methods," the better that adversaries understand them, the better they can counter them.

The spies in Table 1 represent the most damaging from a long list. The

---

14. See Pete Early, *Confessions of a Spy: The Real Story of Aldrich Ames* (New York: Putnam, 1997); and PERSEREC, *Espionage*, 2-3.
15. David Wise, *Spy: The Inside Story of How the FBI's Robert Hanssen Betrayed America* (New York: Random House, 2003); PERSEREC, *Espionage*, 19-20; and Victor Cherkashin with Gregory Feifer, *Spy Handler: The True Story of the Man Who Recruited Robert Hanssen and Aldrich Ames* (New York: Basic Books, 2004), 246-147.

TABLE 1. MAJOR SPIES WHO DAMAGED US COLLECTION DISCIPLINES

SPY	HUMINT	SIGINT	IMINT/ GEOINT	MASINT
Aldrich Ames, CIA	X	X	X	X
Robert Hanssen, FBI	X	X	X	X
Ana Montes, DIA	X	X	X	X
David Barnett, CIA	X			
Edward Howard, CIA	X			
Harold Nicholson, CIA	X			
Earl Pitts, FBI	X			
Richard Miller, FBI	X			
Jonathan Pollard, Navy		X	X	
James Hall III, Army		X	X	
David Boone, Army		X	X	
Christopher Boyce, Contractor		X		
Ronald Pelton, NSA		X		
Jeffrey Carney, Air Force		X		
Ronald Kampiles, CIA			X	
Glenn Souther, Navy			X	

worst of these— Hanssen, Ames, and Ana Montes (a Defense Intelligence Agency, DIA, all-source analyst who spied for Cuba for 16 years) — passed highly damaging information pertaining to multiple disciplines. Much of what these spies passed was in the form of analytical reports descriptive of classified collection capabilities and limitations. Others, such as Pollard, Hall, Boone, and Boyce, caused significant damage to technical collection capabilities. Some spies only damaged a single discipline, such as Nicholson for human intelligence (HUMINT), Pelton for signals intelligence (SIGINT), and Kampiles for imagery intelligence (IMINT), but the sensitive information they provided was highly detailed and especially destructive.

Intelligence is sometimes described as collecting secret information by secret means. When classified collection capabilities are compromised, adversaries can develop countermeasures, including *denial*—hiding the targets of collection. Commonly used denial techniques include better-informed counterintelligence against HUMINT, encryption against SIGINT, and camouflage and concealment against IMINT. Adversaries are also better able to conduct *deception* against US collection by manipulating information that they allow to be collected or that they make available (including disinformation) through compromised channels. Unless such collected information is recognized as deceptive, it can influence analytical judgments provided to policymakers. "Collected" information of this kind—i.e., deceptive information—serves the purposes of the deceiving country, and damages the unwitting country.

Given that no comprehensive effort has yet been made to synthesize and aggregate assessed damage done by multiple spies compromising separate collection disciplines, it is probably fair to say that the US IC lacks a good understanding of the effects of foreign espionage on the performance of its various collection capabilities. Lacking such understanding, impairments in current collection are difficult to overcome, analysts are unable to assess the effects of these breaches on their analyses, research and development may build on compromised concepts and technologies, and users of intelligence may never receive critical intelligence because our collection capabilities can no longer produce high-value intelligence where espionage did the most damage to them.

Press Leaks

As damaging as espionage has been, leaks to the press are arguably as bad or even worse. As former Director of Central Intelligence (DCI) George Tenet explained to the House intelligence oversight committee:

> I'm appalled by the sheer number of leaks and the number of government officials who apparently have no concern whatsoever for the harm their disclosures cause, nor any feeling that they may get caught. It is indefensible, inexcusable, and highly damaging. *The damage caused by leakers can be every bit as great as damage caused by espionage...* It is impossible to measure the total damage done to U.S. intelligence through these leaks, but knowledgeable specialists assess the cumulative impact as truly significant.[16]

He later added in an interview that press leaks "have become one of the biggest threats to the survival of US Intelligence."[17] The volume and seriousness of leaks have not let up since these gloomy characterizations. Rather with the massive Manning and Snowden disclosures, Tenet's alarming view has become understatement.

The government cannot publicly present evidence to substantiate Tenet's argument because such evidence is necessarily classified. Government is hamstrung, unable to make a detailed public case as further publicity can only cause further harm. Thus, markedly different understandings emerge of the damage that press leaks cause between the government on one side, and journalistic and general public opinion on the other that cannot grasp why leaks are so damaging to intelligence. This is not a level playing field.

A few cases have been made public—the tip of a huge iceberg—that illustrate the harm that press leaks can cause: [18]

---

16. George Tenet, Testimony to the House Select Committee on Intelligence on "The Impact of Unauthorized Disclosures on Intelligence," November 3, 1999; italics added.
17. *USA Today*, October 11, 2000, 15A.
18. Except for the first cited human source case (note 19 below), and the Snowden damage to counterterrorism (note 21), the remainder of the leaks cases cited here are discussed more fully in James B. Bruce, "Laws and Leaks of Classified Intelligence: The Consequences of Permissive Neglect," *Studies in Intelligence* 47 (1), March 2003, 40-43.

- **HUMINT: A CIA asset killed through press exposure.**[19] Although his body has never been found, a CIA terrorist source was certainly killed when a front-page article by Tim Weiner in the *New York Times* on August 21, 1995— despite strenuous efforts by the Agency to prevent it — revealed enough identifying details that he disappeared shortly after he was exposed. The press leak occurred within 24 hours of briefing Congress about the agent, a so-called "unsavory asset" who had earlier participated in a terrorist attack that injured Americans, but whose subsequent intelligence reporting on terrorism was judged to be of incalculable value.

- **HUMINT: Liaison Relationships.** Effective intelligence depends on cooperative relationships with friendly governments and individuals who trust the United States to protect their confidences, sources, and sensitive intelligence. Liaison relationships are conducted through HUMINT cooperation. Press disclosures can—and sometimes do—undermine these relationships, making both governments and individuals reluctant to share information, thereby inhibiting intelligence sharing. Foreign countries are increasingly reluctant to trust the United States to protect their human and technical sources. The Snowden and Manning disclosures elevated this problem to a new level, exacerbating diplomatic relationships with close allies and intelligence partners on whom we depend for shared intelligence especially in counterterrorism, and with partners in industry as well.[20]

- **SIGINT: Al–Qa'ida and Osama bin Laden.** After the 9/11 attacks, US intelligence was criticized about why it did not have better warning intelligence on Al–Qa'ida. White House Press Secretary Ari Fleisher provided part of the answer in a press conference: "In 1998, for example, as a result of an inappropriate leak of NSA information, it was revealed about NSA being able to listen to Osama bin Laden on his satellite phone. As a result of the disclosure, he stopped using it. As a result of the public disclosure, the United States was denied the opportunity to monitor and gain information that could have been very valuable for protecting our country."[21] Uniquely valuable intelligence on the Al–Qa'ida leadership and operations was lost, much impairing the Intelligence Community's ability to warn of terrorism attacks.

- **SIGINT: Counterterrorism.** In 2014, former National Counterterrorism Center Director Matt Olsen described Snowden's damaging impact on US collection against terrorists:[22]

  We've lost ability to intercept the communications of the key terrorist operatives and leaders. Look, we know these groups monitor the press, we know they're suspicious of our ability to collect.... [It] is not news to them that the NSA and the United States Government Intelligence Agencies around the world are trying

---

19. For elaboration of this tragic case, see the former CIA acting general counsel's account in John Rizzo, *Company Man: Thirty Years of Controversy and Crisis in the CIA* (New York: Scribner, 2014), 148-151.
20. Oleson, "Assessing Edward Snowden," 2015.
21. White House press statement, 20 June 2002.
22. Matt Olsen, Comments made at the American Political Science Association meeting, August 28, 2014.

to collect their communications.

But [what] this information did was essentially confirmed in excruciating detail to scale and scope of our capabilities. And in many ways, it revealed information that had nothing to do with the privacy of civil liberties of Americans; it was purely information about the capabilities, the technical capabilities of US Intelligence agencies.

We have specific examples of terrorists who have adopted greater security measures in the last year including various types of encryption. They change Internet service providers. They drop their changed e-mail addresses and they had otherwise in some cases just ceased communicating in ways they had before and drop out of our ability to see what they were doing.

- **SIGINT: Soviet Leaders' Conversations.** In the September 16, 1971 *Washington Post*, Jack Anderson disclosed that US intelligence was intercepting the radiotelephone conversations from the limousines of top Soviet leaders in Moscow. British historian Christopher Andrew explained that this extraordinary US collection program (codeword: Gamma Gupy), ended abruptly after Anderson's revelations.[23]

- **SIGINT and Imagery: Soviet ICBM Testing.** A January 31, 1958 *New York Times* story reported that the United States was able to monitor the eight-hour countdown broadcasts for Soviet missile launches from Kazakhstan, providing enough time for US aircraft to observe the splashdowns and collect data to estimate the intercontinental ballistic missiles' accuracy. Following publication, Moscow reduced the countdown broadcasts to four hours—too little time for US aircraft to react. Occurring in the midst of the missile-gap controversy, the press item left President Eisenhower livid. Reportedly, some intelligence was lost forever, and, to recoup the remainder, the US Air Force had to rebuild an Alaskan airfield at a cost of many millions of dollars.[24]

- **Imagery: Surprise Indian Nuclear Tests.** Both authorized and unauthorized disclosures about intelligence techniques can be damaging. In this case, classified imagery had been used to support a diplomatic démarche asking India to stand down from its plans to test nuclear weapons in 1995, and was also the topic press of coverage based on leaked intelligence. The 1995 intelligence and diplomatic success backfired in May 1998 when the Indians employed countermeasures learned from these earlier disclosures. They prevented satellite imagery from detecting the signatures of their nuclear test preparations, which caught the United States by surprise.[25]

- **Imagery—Missile Tests in Pakistan.** In the mid-1990s, dozens of press articles covered whether Chinese M-11 missiles had been covertly transferred to Pakistan. If such missiles had been acquired, Pakistan could be

---

23. Christopher Andrew, *For the President's Eyes Only* (New York: Harper Perennial, 1966), 359.

24. Wayne Jackson, *Allen Welch Dulles, Director of Central Intelligence* (July 1973, declassified history, National Archives, Volume 4, 29-31, record group 263).

25. For a fascinating Indian account of how India converted its newfound knowledge of US imagery collection to countermeasures to defeat it, see Raj Chengappa, *Weapons of Peace: The Secret Story of India's Quest To Be a Nuclear Power* (New Delhi: HarperCollinsIndia, 2000), 403, 413-414, 419-420, 425-428.

found in violation of the Missile Technology Control Regime (MTCR) to which it was a signatory. Under the National Defense Authorization Act, US law mandated sanctions against proven MTCR violators. Press reports claimed that US intelligence had found missiles in Pakistan but "spy satellites" were unable to "confirm" such missiles. Readers of both the *Washington Times* and the *Washington Post* learned that intelligence had failed to convince the Department of State of the missiles' presence in Pakistan. The message from the press coverage was, in effect, that any nation could avert US sanctions if they neutralized intelligence by shielding missiles from satellite observation. These articles not only suggested to Pakistan and China that some key denial measures were succeeding, but also spelled out specific countermeasures that other potential violators could take to prevent US intelligence from satisfying the standards needed for sanctions under the MTCR.

- **Technical Recovery Operation: The Glomar Explorer.** *The Los Angeles Times* published a story on February 7, 1975 that the CIA had mounted an operation to recover a sunken Soviet submarine, its nuclear weapons and cryptographic equipment, from three miles deep on the Pacific Ocean floor. *The New York Times* ran its own version of the story the next day. Jack Anderson further publicized the secret operation on national television on March 18. In his memoir, former DCI William Colby wrote: "There was not a chance that we could send the Glomar [Explorer] out again on an intelligence project without risking the lives of our crew and inciting a major international incident.... The Glomar project stopped because it was exposed."[26]

Unlike spies, most of whom are eventually caught; leakers of classified information are infrequently identified. The dramatic cases of Snowden (who identified himself) and Manning are notable exceptions. Most leakers remain hidden, and only a handful has ever been prosecuted. The record is dismal. During the four-year period 2009-2013, intelligence agencies filed 153 crimes reports about classified leaks to the press with the Department of Justice. But only 24 were investigated; only half of these were identified, and not a single indictment was issued.[27] The scorecard reads: Leakers 153; Intelligence Community 0. In general, our legal system is ill equipped to deal with leakers.[28] And the culture that strongly supports First Amendment press freedoms often seems conflicted about whether leakers are really law-breakers and is skeptical that press leaks of intelligence actually do much damage. Perhaps the greatest damage to national security from press leaks, as with espionage, is opportu-

---

26. William Colby, *Honorable Men: My Life in the CIA* (London: Hutchinson, 1978), 413-418.

27. Sharon LaFraniere, "Math Behind the Leak Crackdown: 153 Cases, 4 Years, 0 Indictments," *The New York Times*, July 20, 2013.

28. See Bruce, "Laws and Leaks of Classified Intelligence" in *Studies in Intelligence*, 43-48; and W. George Jameson, "Holding Leakers Accountable: Considering a Comprehensive Leaks Approach," in Paul Rosenzweig, Timothy J. McNulty, and Ellen Shearer (eds.), *Whistleblowers, Leaks, and the Media: The First Amendment and National Security* (Chicago: American Bar Association, 2014), 207-234.

nity costs: The intelligence that will never be collected or used for the nation's decision advantage because of the damage to or even the loss of classified collection sources and methods compromised by press leaks.

Conclusions

Importantly, American spies and government employees who leak classified information to the press have recently become a national priority for a concerted program to counter the threats they pose to national security. On November 21, 2012, the White House issued a Presidential Memorandum establishing a new Insider Threat Program. It aims to deter, detect, and mitigate such actions by government employees as espionage and unauthorized disclosures of classified information, including "vast amounts of classified data available on interconnected United States Government computer networks and systems."[29] While a notably important initiative, it falls dramatically short of the comprehensive steps really needed.

Until the United States makes game-changing improvements in the way it protects its sensitive and classified information, it cannot expect a fully performing intelligence community, military, or diplomatic corps. Poor performance in keeping secrets correlates directly with diminished capabilities of the major instruments of national power—and thus, a diminution of American power. The relationship is causal. A comprehensive, zero-based, review of how the nation keeps its secrets—and how to get better at it—is long overdue.

There is compelling evidence that the classified information protection (or secrecy) paradigm, created in the mid-twentieth century long before the modern digital age was even imagined, is woefully outdated and does not meet present day national security demands. This broken paradigm requires disciplined scrutiny that will determine whether it is so broken that it must be replaced. If repairable, we should identify what needs to be fixed and fix it without further delay. If we determine that the secrecy paradigm is beyond repair, then we should work to develop a new one. Continued failure should not be an option, and doing little or nothing about severe impairments in keeping state secrets is a prescription for failure.

READINGS FOR INSTRUCTORS

Bowman, M. E. "Dysfunctional Information Restrictions," The Intelligencer 15 (2), Fall/Winter, 2006-2007, 29-37.

Bruce, James B. "Laws and Leaks of Classified Intelligence: The Consequences of Permissive Neglect," Studies in Intelligence 47 (1), March, 2003, 39-49.

---

29. https://www.whitehouse.gov/the-press-office/2012/11/21/presidential-memorandum-national-insider-threat-policy-and-minimum-standards-for-executive-branch-insider-threat-programs.

Bruce, James B. "The Impact on Foreign Denial and Deception of Increased Availability of Public Information about U.S. Intelligence," in Roy Godson and James J. Wirtz (eds.), *Strategic Denial and Deception: The Twenty-First Century Challenge* (New Brunswick, NJ: Transaction Pub. Co., 2001), 229–240.

Gioe, David V. "Tinker, Tailor, Leaker, Spy: The Future Costs of Mass Leaks," *The National Interest*, Jan-Feb 2014.

Kramer, Lisa A. and Richards J. Heuer, Jr. "America's Increased Vulnerability to Insider Espionage," *International Journal of Intelligence and Counterintelligence* 20 (1), 2007, 50-64.

Office of the Director of National Intelligence, IC on the Record, at *http://icontherecord.tumblr.com/tagged/statement*.

Rosenzweig, Paul S., Timothy J. McNulty, and Ellen Shearer (eds.). *Whistleblowers, Leaks and the Media: The First Amendment and National Security* (Washington, DC: American Bar Association, 2014).

Schoenfeld, Gabriel. *Necessary Secrets: National Security, the Media, and the Rule of Law* (New York: W. W. Norton, 2010).

Sulick, Michael. *American Spies: Espionage Against The United States from the Cold War to the Present* (Washington, DC: Georgetown University Press, 2013).

James B. Bruce is a senior political scientist at the RAND Corporation. He retired from the CIA in 2005 as a senior executive officer after nearly 24 years. He held management positions in CIA's Directorates of Analysis and Operations, and served as deputy national intelligence officer for science and technology in the National Intelligence Council. His unclassified publications have appeared in *Studies in Intelligence, American Intelligence Journal, Journal of Strategic Security, Defense Intelligence Journal, World Politics*, and several anthologies. He co-edited, with Roger George, *Analyzing Intelligence: National Security Practitioners' Perspectives*, 2nd ed. (Georgetown University Press, 2014). He is an adjunct professor at Georgetown University and previously an adjunct at Columbia and American Universities. He is a member of the board of directors of the Association of Former Intelligence Officers.

The author thanks Peter Oleson for his keen editorial skills and uncommon patience in improving the clarity of the original draft and making it shorter at the same time.

This article has been reviewed by CIA's Publication Review Board to ensure it contains no classified information. The views expressed here are solely those of the author.

GUIDE TO THE STUDY OF INTELLIGENCE

Teaching About Intelligence and Ethics

Jan Goldman, Ed.D.

Introduction

George Smiley clearly felt the moral ambiguity of his profession. His ambivalence is well described in John Le Carré's novels. The fundamental question is, "Is spying ethical?" To some idealists, the answer is an unequivocal "no." In referring to his 1929 shutting down of the department's cryptologic effort in his 1948 memoirs, Secretary of State Simpson declared: Gentlemen do not read each others' mail. Idealism aside, since antiquity, virtually all major powers have maintained intelligence services for the basic purpose of ensuring their security and existence.[1] Given the fundamental covenant between governments and their citizens to provide for the common security; those activities that promote security – defense, law enforcement, and intelligence – are necessary and ethical. This is not to say that intelligence work is always ethical. Note, for example, the repressive actions of some governments. Most notable being Nazi Germany and Soviet Russia.

Ethics related to spying has been a topic of examination for many years. In 1977, the Central Intelligence Agency (CIA) compiled a bibliography, "Morality and Ethics: Intelligence and Security in Our Democracy." This bibliography contained 99 entries[2] from academic journals and magazines, to

---

1. See other articles in AFIO's "Guide to the Study of Intelligence" series on intelligence history, especially those of Colonel Rose Mary Sheldon and Professor Douglas Wheeler.
2. The list can be obtained from the Federation of American Scientists, *http://www.fas.org/irp/cia/product/morality.pdf*.

include *The Atlantic Monthly*,[3] *George Washington Law Review*,[4] and *Playboy*.[5] Early articles usually focused on foreign policy and the United States' role in world affairs, positing questions such as, "Should the US intervene or participate in particular actions overseas?" There are only 29 books on this list. The earliest were published in 1905,[6] 1922,[7] and 1949.[8] Common themes were the tension between a democratic society and the use of espionage or power, and whether the government had a right to keep secrets from its citizens.

Considering Intelligence and Ethics

To teach about intelligence and ethics, it is important to remember three things: (1) ethics are not the same as the law, (2) the ethics of intelligence work are not necessarily synonymous with a person's personal ethics, and (3) given its fundamental mission, working in the intelligence community (IC) should be considered ethical.

Most government ethics training focuses on an individual's knowledge of rules, regulations, policy, and law. In the mid-1970s, CIA's misdeeds became public. These included the Agency's involvement in drug experimentation on American citizens. Further, CIA and other intelligence agencies aggressively collected information about US citizens who were involved in the civil rights movement or opposed the Vietnam War. Consequently, Congress began taking a more active role in oversight, including examining what was permissible for intelligence operations. Since then, most ethics training has been developed and is administered by legal offices within each intelligence agency. Every organization wants to ensure its workforce understands and follows the rules. For lack of a better term, this is what may be referred to as "rules-based" ethics.

Loch Johnson, a former staff member on the Senate's Church Committee during the 1970s, has written about "rules-based ethics" (i.e., intelligence oversight).[9] He has also co-edited an excellent introduction to how the United States and other democratic societies seek accountability among their intelligence agencies.[10] Amy Zegart's most recent book questions whether Congressional

---

3. I.I. Rabi, "The Cost of Secrecy," *The Atlantic Monthly*, 1960.
4. Wallace Park, "The Open Government Principle: Applying the Right to Know Under the Constitution; Secrecy and Public Internets in Military Affairs," *Georgetown Washington Law Review*, October 1957.
5. Stephen Young, "Curbing America's Invisible Government: The CIA" *Playboy*, May 1967.
6. Horace E. Warner, *The Ethics of Force* (Boston: Ginn & Co., 1905).
7. Paul Reinsch, *Secret Diplomacy: How Far Can It Be Eliminated?* (Harcourt Brace, 1922).
8. Martin J. Hillenbrand, *Power and Morals* (New York City: Columbia University Press, 1949).
9. Two of the best books by the author on this topic are *America's Secret Power: The CIA in a Democratic Society* (Oxford University Press, 1991) and *Secret Agencies: U.S. Intelligence in a Hostile World* (Yale University, 1998).
10. The other co-authors, Hans Born and Ian Leigh are both international scholars on the subject of intelligence oversight, which provide further credibility to their book, *Who's Watching the Spies: Establishing Intelligence Service Accountability* (Potomac Books, 2005). The other countries considered include, *inter alia*, Argentina, Canada, Germany, Norway, Poland, South Africa, South Korea, and the United Kingdom.

oversight capability (or the lack thereof) is effective.[11] One of the best books on intelligence oversight, which provides basic historical knowledge, is by Frank Smist Jr. entitled *Congress Oversees the United States Intelligence Community: 1947-1994.*[12]

At the other end of the spectrum is personal ethics. Typically, a person's history of moral and ethical conduct will determine if he or she can receive a security clearance. Most people strive to have high moral and ethical standards, and behavior can be modified with some direction and support. There are countless self-help books on how to be a better person. The hypothesis for these publications is that if you are a good person, you will be a good worker (i.e., including an intelligence analyst or collector). Popular books include those by self-help icons Stephen Covey[13] and Rushworth Kidder.[14] While Covey does an effective job in providing assistance in achieving personal and professional goals in a safe, efficient, and successful approach; Kidder's books focus more on assisting people with "tough choices" and developing "moral courage," the titles of two of his most popular books. Without a doubt, working in the IC requires all these traits. More philosophically focused are Sissela Bok's books. A noted philosopher and ethicist, she wrote two books that can be used as the backbone for any ethics course. Bok discusses ethics and morals from a theoretical, yet practical, approach in understanding the inherent forces on anyone performing intelligence work, as suggested by one of her book's titles: *Lying and Secrets.*[15]

It should be assumed that intelligence work is a profession. In an article written by this author, a key component of professionalism is to have a code of ethics.

To be a professional includes other things, too, although there is a debate as to what exactly these attributes are. If we (intelligence personnel) want to think of ourselves as more than merely intelligence "workers," then becoming a professional and defining intelligence as a profession is probably what is needed. The concept "profession" has a moderately complicated sociological definition with the following seven factors: extensive training or education, a significant intellectual component, a service that is deemed important, credentialing, an organization, autonomy of work, and a code of ethics. Although,

---

11. See, *Eyes on Spies: Congress and the United States Intelligence Community* (Hoover Press, 2011); and her *Spying Blind: The CIA, the FBI, and the Origins of the 9/11* (Princeton University Press, 2009).

12. *Congress Oversees the United States Intelligence Community: 1947-1994* (University of Tennessee Press, 1994). Copies of this book are rare.

13. There are many books by Stephen Covey, but, his most influential is *The 7 Habits of Highly Effective People: Powerful Lessons in Personal Change* (Free Press, 2004).

14. See *How Good People Make Tough Choices* (Harper Perennial, 2009) and *Moral Courage* (William Morrow Paperbacks, 2006).

15. *Lying: Moral Choice in Public and Private Life* (Pantheon Books, 1978; Vintage paperback editions, 1979, 1989, 1999); *Secrets: on the Ethics of Concealment and Revelation* (Pantheon Books, 1982; Vintage paperback editions, 1984, 1989).

no single factor is regarded as a necessary condition, a low score in one factor can be compensated by high scores in other factors.[16]

In an article in *Studies in Intelligence* (1984), George Allen[17] uses Samuel Huntington's model of associating warfare with tradecraft. He views the intelligence vocation as a process reaching its developmental stage, and this requires serious attention. Allen's article advocating intelligence as a profession is in sharp contrast to a memo that appeared over 40 years earlier. In a memorandum from February 3, 1941, a US Naval officer provides the rationale for creating a special intelligence section to conduct intelligence operations. In the memorandum, the officer writes, "In order to develop an organization capable of carrying through the mission ... there are certain self evident, fundamental facts which must be faced: Espionage is by its very nature not to be considered as 'honorable or clean' or 'fair' or 'decent.' It is suggested that for the Navy to conduct proper intelligence activities, they will have to find employees from "the petty criminal class, malcontents, revolutionaries, refugees, or psychopaths."[18]

Although, this type of thinking may seem out-of-date today, some citizens and those in the intelligence community are concerned that ethics will constrain the ability to perform required tasks. According to a former CIA operations officer, "Depending on where you're coming from, the whole business of espionage is unethical.... It's not an issue, it never was and never will be, not if you want a real spy service."[19] The former agency employee goes on to say that spies operate under false names, lie about their jobs, and bribe or blackmail foreigners to betray their countries.

It is difficult to argue that a country has no right to operate an intelligence service. As argued earlier, every country has an obligation to protect its citizens. Coming out of World War II, however, the international community agreed that although "war is hell," there is a notion of a "war crime" (the Geneva Conventions and Hague Protocols). Professional soldiers, therefore, must adhere to a code of conduct. In recent years, there has been debate over whether intelligence officers also must adhere to a code of conduct.

Teaching Intelligence and Ethics

To appreciate intelligence and ethics, one can study any novel or movie by John Le Carré that stars master spy George Smiley. Although fiction, these are excellent tools for examining this subject. Of note is Myron Aronoff's *The*

---

16. Jan Goldman, "Ethics of Spying" *Defense Intelligence Journal* 14 (2), 2005, 45-52.
17. George Allen was a 30-year veteran of US military intelligence and the CIA, and is the author of *None So Blind: A Personal Account of the Intelligence Failure in Vietnam* (Ivan R. Dee Publisher, 2001).
18. Both Allen's and Goldman's articles are reprinted in this author's *Ethics of Spying: A Reader for the Intelligence Professional*, Vol. 2 (Rowman and Littlefield, 2010).
19. *New York Times*, "An Exotic Tool For Espionage: Moral Compass," January 28, 2006, A1. Quote comes from Duane R. Clarridge, who retired in 1988 after 33 years in the CIA.

Spy Novels of John LeCarre: Balancing Ethics and Politics (Palgrave Macmillan, 1998). Aronoff, a professor of anthropology and political science, clearly is an avid reader of all of Le Carré's novels, and his discussion of espionage in a democratic society has a lot of historical depth.

Until the United States became involved in the "War on Terrorism," most of the literature on professional ethics in intelligence was scattered in journals and book chapters, if mentioned at all. The first books specifically focusing on this topic appeared in 2006. That year, the first international conference on intelligence and ethics was held just outside of Washington, DC, and *Ethics of Spying: A Reader for the Intelligence Professional* (Scarecrow Press, 2006) was published. A second volume was published four years later (Scarecrow Press, 2010). Both books include articles from historical, practical and theoretical perspective on ethics written by practitioners and academics. In the back of the books are appendices that list codes of ethics from various members of the intelligence community, as well as 20 case studies. Also that year, CIA veteran James Olson's *Fair Play: The Moral Dilemmas of Spying* (Potomac Books, 2006) was published. This contains 50 scenarios, which form the majority of the book, in which he provides some excellent ethical dilemmas. Olsen provides comments and in some instances, the answers to each dilemma. Unfortunately, most of the case studies are not ethical dilemmas, but rather situations that have a procedural or legislative answer, which the author provides.

For anyone interested in how other countries treat intelligence and ethics, see Michael Andregg's *Intelligence Ethics: The Definitive Work of 2007.*[20] Andregg brings together authors who have years of practical and academic experience from Sweden, Israel, the United Kingdom, and other countries, to discuss their views of how ethics supports their country's intelligence service.[21]

As the role of domestic spying appears to be debated today, the timing of Ross Bellaby's *Intelligence and Ethics Collection: A New Framework* (Routledge, 2014) argues that the most appropriate ethical framework for intelligence collection does create harm to society, but that it also is sometimes necessary to protect the "greater good." Once the harm is understood, however, he relies on what he calls "Just Intelligence Principles" to consider when the harm caused is justified. David Perry, previously an ethics professor at the Army War College, is the author of *Partly Cloudy: Ethics in War, Espionage, Covert Action, and Interrogation* (Lanham, MD: Scarecrow Press, 2009). Perry explores ethical issues in war and intelligence operations, and applies careful reasoning to issues to include secrecy and democratic accountability, employing espionage to penetrate hostile regimes and terrorist cells, covert political influence, coups, and targeted

---

20. Michael Andregg. *Intelligence Ethics: The Definitive Work of 2007* (St. Paul, MN: Center for the Study of Intelligence and Wisdom). A free copy of this booklet can be found at *http://conservancy.umn.edu/bitstream/46979/1/Intelligence%20Ethics%202007.pdf.*
21. An abridged version of Andregg's book appears in "A Symposium on Intelligence Ethics." *Intelligence and National Security* 24 (3), June 2009, 366-386.

killings, and the question of torture in interrogating detainees.

Since 9/11 and the ensuing counterterrorism efforts, many books have emerged on the topics of torture, human and civil rights, law, and politics. One of the most widely discussed is Jane Mayer's, *The Dark Side: The Inside Story of How the War on Terror Turned Into a War on American Ideals* (Anchor, 2009). Less well known may be Michael Skerker's *An Ethics of Interrogation* (University of Chicago Press, 2012) on the subject of interrogation and torture. Skerker focuses on the act of interrogation from both a philosophical and legal perspective raising questions about the morality of keeping secrets and the rights of suspected terrorists and insurgents. Other less familiar books are Paul Lauritzen's *The Ethics of Interrogation: Professional Responsibility in an Age of Terror* (Georgetown University Press, 2013); Fritz Allhof's *Terrorism, Ticking Time-Bombs, and Torture: A Philosophical Analysis* (University of Chicago Press, 2012); Michael L Gross, *Moral Dilemmas of Modern War: Torture, Assassination, and Blackmail in an Age of Asymmetric Conflict* (Cambridge University Press, 2010); and J. Jeremy Wisnewski, and R.D. Emerick, *The Ethics of Torture* (Continuum Publishing, 2009). All of these books examine the ethics of obtaining intelligence by causing harm to an individual and are germane to today's political debate on counterterrorism policies.

To step slightly outside of the realm of the intelligence profession, there are two books that highlight the tension between being a medical professional and having moral responsibility. The first is Steven H. Miles' *Oath Betrayed: Torture, Medical Complicity, and the War on Terror* (New York City: Random House, 2010). Miles clearly believes the medical profession has no business in supporting interrogation that causes harm. The other book is Ryan Goodman and Minday J. Rosemann's *Interrogations, Forced Feedings and the Role of Health Professionals: New Perspectives on International Human Rights, Humanitarian Law and Ethics* (Harvard Law School Human Rights Program, 2009). Other professions face ethical dilemmas that can be related to intelligence work. This would include George Lucas' *Anthropologists in Arms: The Ethics of Military Anthropology* (Altamira Press, 2009), which highlights the tension of engaging anthropologists with combat units as cultural intelligence advisors.

Finally, one should not ignore the ethics of intelligence analysis, or in other words, the politicization of intelligence analysis (i.e., intelligence analysts providing subjective assessments). Some people have argued that it was the politicization of intelligence that led to the incorrect assessment that Saddam had weapons of mass destruction and ultimately led to the 2003 US invasion of Iraq. Joshua Rovner's *Fixing the Facts: National Security and the Politics of Intelligence* (Cornell University Press, 2011) does an excellent job of explaining whether intelligence shapes policy or policy and politics shape intelligence. Intelligence analysis should be objective, but, as Rovner points out, politicization occurs in many forms (often subtle and indirect).

Ethics are an important ingredient of politics. Studying intelligence and ethics is fundamental to appreciating how intelligence can operate in a democratic system.

READINGS FOR INSTRUCTORS

Any of these books cited above can be used in any course on intelligence and ethics. Of course, they can be easily supplemented with the numerous articles that appear frequently in many publications. Besides those books and articles in the footnotes, the following are recommended:

J.E. Drexel Godfrey's article, "Ethics and Intelligence" in the well-regarded *Foreign Affairs* (April 1978) is often credited as the first article to focus on the juxtaposition of espionage and morals. The author brings out the need to accept intelligence work as a profession.

John Langan, in "Moral Damage and the Justification of Intelligence Collection from Covert Political Action" in *Studies in Intelligence* (Summer, 1981) assesses claims that immoral activity damages the perpetrator. Langan, a professor and Jesuit priest, believes preserving national security is regarded as a morally worthy goal, when the nation observes standards of internal and external justice in persevering a just political community.

Written after the Iran-Contra Affair, Lincoln Bloomfield's article "Legitimacy of Covert Action: Sorting Out the Moral Responsibilities" in the *International Journal of Intelligence and CounterIntelligence* (1990) makes the argument that intelligence is not involved in morals, rather it's political. He believes that if citizens do not like how intelligence is conducted, they need to replace their elected officials.

Allison Shelton's "Framing the Oxymoron: A New Paradigm for Intelligence Ethics" (*Intelligence and National Security*, February 2011) proposes that ethical justifications should be considered along a moral psychological spectrum. Students will find extremely interesting the example of targeted political assassination, although, they will have to pass through some philosophical terminology.

As the editor of the *International Journal of Intelligence Ethics* (Roman and Littlefield Publishers), every issue has at least three or four articles on different aspects of the intelligence cycle. However, articles of particular interest for students would be "Rights of Irregular Combatants" by Michael Skerker (Spring/Summer 2011), "Privatized Information Gathering: Just War Theory and Morality" by Christopher Caldwell, and "Using Private Corporations to Conduct Intelligence Activities for National Security Purposes: An Ethical Appraisal by James Roper" (both appear in the Fall/Winter 2011 issue). All three of these articles discuss the new realities of tradecraft against the backdrop of counterterrorism and the free enterprise of intelligence operations.

Ethics in intelligence has come a long way from the days of Cold War novels and an identifiable enemy on the battlefield. However, ethics is "doing the right thing, for the right reason," and that has not changed over time.

Dr. Jan Goldman, the founding editor of the *International Journal of Intelligence and Ethics*, has studied the intelligence profession for over 25 years. He has co-chaired six international conferences on intelligence and ethics. His books include *The Central Intelligence Agency: An Encyclopedia of Covert Operations, Intelligence Gathering, and Spies*, 2 vols, (Praeger, 2014); *War on Terror Encyclopedia: From the Rise of Al Qaeda to 9/11 and Beyond*, (ABC-CLIO, 2015); and as series editor of *The Handbook of European Intelligence Cultures* by Bob DeGraaff and James M. Nyce (Rowman & Littlefield, 2016).

Part VI – Intelligence Abroad

C anada and the United States share a long border and many of the same security concerns. Canadian scholars **Stéphane Lefebvre** and **Jeremy Littlewood, Ph.D.,** in their "Guide to Canadian Intelligence Issues" explain the Canadian intelligence system. Readers in the US will note some similarities and distinct differences in the approach to intelligence taken in Canada. The authors present a rich menu for further reading. The US and Mexico also share a long border. There is little written about Mexico's intelligence. **Professor José Medina González Dávila** writes about the evolution of the Mexican intelligence and security services since the Mexican Revolution of 1920-1921. He outlines the various intelligence organizations and discusses the relationships between them and their challenges.

The British have a rich history in intelligence from the era of Elizabeth I to the present. **Drs. Huw Dylan** and **Michael S. Goodman** of King's College, London, explain the "British way of Intelligence" in their article that covers the history, organization, functioning and oversight of the British intelligence establishment.

The history, structure, and political environment for French intelligence differ markedly from that of the US or even other western countries' services. French intelligence has gone through a significant transformation in recent years. **Philippe Hayez** and **Hedwige Regnault de Maulmin** explain the evolution of French intelligence and the recent push for a national intelligence community.

Dr. Eleni C. Braat of the University of Leiden in the Netherlands writes of the dysfunction of Dutch intelligence prior to and during World War II and its many transitions during and following the Cold War.

Historian **Michael Fredholm** recounts the long history of Swedish intelligence and the significant role it played in World War II and the Cold War.

Dr. Robert W. Pringle is an expert on the Russian intelligence services. His article, "Guide to Soviet and Russian Intelligence Services," addresses their long history from the time of Tsars to today's *Sluzhba Vneshney Razvedki* (SVR), the foreign intelligence service, and *Federal'naya sluzhba bezopasnosti Rossiyskoy Federatsii* (FSB), the internal federal security service.

Much in the news for its cyber activities, Chinese intelligence practices differ significantly from others. Italian scholar **Dr. Stefania Paladini** of Coventry University outlines the structure of the PRC's intelligence services and their approach with some case studies.

Since the 1979 revolution Iran's supreme leaders have created a complex and overlapping intelligence and covert action structure. The various organizations have the dual missions of protecting the mullahs' revolutionary government and promoting Iran's international goals. **Professor Carl Wege** explains the unique and complex structure in his article "Iran's Intelligence Establishment."

Many foreign intelligence services are not covered in the *Guide*. There are several recent publications that address different foreign intelligence organizations.

The Australian intelligence community is described on the official website of the Office of National Assessments (*http://www.ona.gov.au/about-ona/ overview*). ONA coordinates the activities of Australia's intelligence community comprised of the all-source analysis Defence Intelligence Organization (DIO); the Australian Secret Intelligence Service (ASIS), which focused on HUMINT; the Australian Signals Directorate (ASD), its SIGINT element; the Australian Geospatial-Intelligence Organization (AGO); and the Australian Security Intelligence Organization (ASIO), its domestic security element. Links from the ONA site address the coordination and oversight of the Australian community and the history of its development following the 1974-1977 Royal Commission on Intelligence and Security. **Aaron Phillip Waddell** has also written an examination of Australia's "whole-of-government" approach to national security that describes how the intelligence and security services fit within the broader context.[1]

Jonathan Haslam and **Karina Urbach** of Cambridge University have edited and contributed to an interesting volume entitled *Secret Intelligence in the European States System, 1918 – 1989* (Stanford: Stanford University Press, 2014). Its chapters address the early evolution, subsequent disasters and significant success of Soviet intelligence; the tribulations of French intelligence, including about the Far East after World War II; British intelligence in the Cold War, described as "impecunious" by chapter author **Richard J. Aldrich**; and German intelligence, from both the Stasi and West German services perspectives.

Philip H. J. Davies and **Kristian C. Gustafson** have edited another volume, *Intelligence Elsewhere: Spies and Espionage Outside the Anglosphere* (Washington, DC: Georgetown University Press, 2013) that addresses intelligence in Pakistan, Iran, Indonesia, Japan, China, Argentina, Sweden, and Finland.

Of course, Internet searches can produce volumes of information about various intelligence services. The necessary caution, however, is that many entries returned by searches are anonymous. Therefore, *caveat emptor*.

---

1. Aaron Phillip Waddell, "Cooperation and Integration among Australia's National Security Community," Central Intelligence Agency, *Studies in Intelligence*, Vol. 59, No. 3 (September 2015).

GUIDE TO THE STUDY OF INTELLIGENCE

Guide to Canadian Intelligence Issues

Stéphane Lefebvre and Jeremy Littlewood, PhD

For most of the Cold War period, Canadian intelligence activities were largely conducted in secrecy, and the monopoly of the Executive Branch. The security intelligence function was the responsibility of Canada's national police, the Royal Canadian Mounted Police (RCMP). Foreign intelligence was also an area of intense activity throughout the Cold War and after. Besides the military intelligence activities, which fall under the purview of the Canadian armed forces, and are focused on the intentions and capabilities of foreign militaries, Canada also has a signals intelligence organization (Communications Security Establishment Canada, CSEC), but its very existence was not publicly acknowledged until 1983.

A seminal event in the history of Canadian intelligence occurred in 1981 when the Commission of Inquiry Concerning Certain Activities of the Royal Canadian Mounted Police (the McDonald Commission) recommended that a civilian service replace the RCMP Security Service along with robust review and accountability mechanisms. Having agreed with the thrust of the Commission's report, government enacted legislation in 1984 creating the Canadian Security Intelligence Service (CSIS) and a review body, the Security Intelligence Review Committee (SIRC).[1]

In December 2001, Parliament's adoption of the *Anti-Terrorism Act* represented another seminal event. By amending the *National Defence Act*, it provided CSEC[2] with its first-ever legislated mandate as well as instituting a distinct review mechanism in the form of a commissioner's office.[3] Beyond the core agencies (CSIS, CSEC, and chief of Defence Intelligence) Canada's Intelligence Community encompasses a wide array of organizations that are part of federal

---

1. See CSIS; *http://www.csis-scrs.gc.ca/* and SIRC; *http://www.sirc-csars.gc.ca/*, respectively.
2. *http://www.cse-cst.gc.ca/*
3. *http://ocsec-bccst.gc.ca/*

departments or agencies, including the RCMP-National Security Criminal Investigations program, an Integrated Terrorism Assessment Centre (ITAC, originally called the Integrated Threat Assessment Centre upon its 2004 establishment), as well as an independent agency—the Financial Transactions and Reports Analysis Centre (FINTRAC)—Canada's financial intelligence organization, which reports to the finance minister.[4] The mandate and legislation applicable to each are detailed in the 2006 report of the Commission of Inquiry into the Actions of Canadian Officials in Relation to Maher Arar, titled *A New Review Mechanism for the RCMP's National Security Activities*.[5]

To study the seminal events that have affected the origin, evolution, and effectiveness of the Canadian Intelligence Community and its constituent parts, American scholars, students, and practitioners would not be well served by recently edited volumes and anthologies on the subject of intelligence and its study because of their overwhelming emphasis on the Anglo-American experience. Relying on them, a reader would be hard pressed to discern how that experience differs from the Canadian one. Yet, it does. While American students and practitioners are well served by these volumes, Canadians, unfortunately, have no single volume to point to that captures the breadth and detail of their own nation's intelligence experience.[6]

Yet, as a distinct field of enquiry, intelligence studies in Canada are vibrant today. Twenty years ago, the field was nascent and limited to a select few academics. It expanded in slow increments until the events of 9/11, whereupon it developed significantly with an influx of new scholars and distinctive scholarly activities, fuelled in part by the impact of particular government decisions affecting the rights of individuals and for which intelligence played a significant role. The Canadian Association for Security and Intelligence Studies (CASIS),[7] established in 1985, played a part in increasing the legitimacy and popularity of studying intelligence. Intelligence analysts themselves within the Canadian Government have paid attention proactively to the professionalization and improvement of the intelligence field of study and have organized into a

---

4. See http://www.cdi-crd.forces.gc.ca/, *http://www.rcmp-grc.gc.ca/nsci-ecsn/index-eng.htm, http://www. itac-ciem.gc.ca/,* and *http://www.fintrac.gc.ca/.*

5. *A New Review Mechanism for the RCMP's National Security Activities* (Ottawa: Public Works and Government Services Canada, 2006).

6. Since 2007, Routledge, Oxford University Press, and Praeger Security International have published major anthologies on all aspects of intelligence. This reflects the fact that the study of intelligence has gained not only in popularity but also as a legitimate field of research. These volumes have included: *Intelligence: Critical Concepts in Military, Strategic & Security Studies,* 4 Volumes, edited by Loch K. Johnson (London: Routledge, 2011); *Intelligence and National Security. The Secret World of Spies: An Anthology,* Third Edition, edited by Loch K. Johnson and James J. Wirtz (New York: Oxford University Press, 2011); *The Oxford Handbook of National Security Intelligence,* edited by Loch K. Johnson, (Oxford: Oxford University Press, 2010); *Secret Intelligence: A Reader,* edited by Christopher Andrew, Richard J. Aldrich, and Wesley K. Wark (London and New York, Routledge, 2009); *Strategic Intelligence,* 5 Volumes, edited by Loch K. Johnson (Westport: Praeger Security International, 2007); and the *Handbook of Intelligence Studies,* edited by Loch K. Johnson (London: Routledge, 2007).

7. *http://www.casis.ca/*

Canadian Association of Professional Intelligence Analysts (CAPIA) to further promote professional development, training, and education of intelligence analysts. CAPIA, supported by the Privy Council Office (the Prime Minister's Department), was "created to promote training and high analytical standards with the Canadian intelligence community and foster networks and information sharing."[8]

However, an epistemic community intending to grow and move the research yardstick forward needs more than good motivation. It also needs access to key material from which to take stock of past and current research and findings and to draw research agendas for the future. It is in this context that this short article brings together a set of readings for the study of Canadian intelligence. The readings we propose concerning Canadian intelligence issues include authoritative chapters, books, and articles that have appeared over the past 20 years critically analyzing some key issues: the legal framework for intelligence, intelligence culture, security intelligence, foreign intelligence, signals intelligence, military intelligence, and accountability and review. The introductory material we identify covers the progress and achievements of the Canadian literature on intelligence from 1990 to 2010 (state of the discipline's scholarship) in a manner reminiscent of Geoffrey Weller's 2001 *International Journal of Intelligence and CounterIntelligence* article and of Stuart Farson's 1989 *Conflict Quarterly* article.[9]

In our view, these major texts in Canadian intelligence studies represent key reference points for those—students, professors, intelligence and national security professionals, and the general public—seeking (a) to understand how the Canadian Intelligence Community has evolved since the end of the Cold War and (b) to better comprehend how it did so and under what conditions. These texts should also be of interest for students beyond intelligence studies, including security studies and international relations. Dependent on their availability outside of Canada, they should also help educate the public about the role, place, and importance of intelligence in Canada, and motivate scholars in Canada and abroad to further study the Canadian Intelligence Community.

We have organized our suggested reading material around the key issues outlined above, which also reflects the major topics of study within Canadian intelligence studies. Following the introduction, the first section situates the Canadian Intelligence Community within the wider frameworks within which it operates, including the global, legal, cultural, and change-management

8. Paul Martin, *Privy Council Office 2004-2005 Departmental Performance Report* (Ottawa: Privy Council Office, 2005), 37. Also noted in Natalia Derbentseva, Lianne McLellan, and David R. Mandel, "Issues in Intelligence Production: Summary of Interviews with Canadian Managers of Intelligence Analysts," *DRDC Toronto Technical Report 2010-144* (Toronto: Defence R&D Canada Toronto, December 2010), 63-64.
9. Geoffrey R. Weller, "Assessing Canadian Intelligence Literature: 1980-2000," *International Journal of Intelligence and CounterIntelligence* 14 (1), 2001, 49-61; Stuart Farson, "Schools of Thought: National Perceptions of Intelligence," *Conflict Quarterly* 2 (2), Spring 1989, 52-104.

contexts. This is important, as each of these contexts influences, through constraints and opportunities, the practice of intelligence and the performance of each agency, each being a government bureaucracy of its own. The second section proposes material that examines the evolution of security intelligence in Canada and the broadening of its mandate post-9/11. The following sections respectively look at foreign intelligence, signals intelligence, and military intelligence. The last section examines accountability and review by identifying its major features (such as the role of the legislative branch, the media, special inquiries and independent review bodies), all recognized as essential to the proper functioning of an intelligence community within a democratic system.

Some caveats, however, are in order:

To fully comprehend and understand the practice and evolution of intelligence in Canada, instructors will need to access and go through a sizeable amount of government material. In particular, reports of major government inquiries and landmark court decisions (the latter are accessible through the Canadian Legal Information Institute[10]) will represent key primary sources. The former include:

- Report of the Royal Commission on Security (Ottawa: The Queen's Printer, June 1969).

- Freedom and Security Under the Law, several volumes (Ottawa: Commission of Inquiry Concerning Certain Activities of the Royal Canadian Mounted Police, August 1981).

- A New Review Mechanism for the RCMP's National Security Activities, Report of the Commission of Inquiry into the Actions of Canadian Officials in Relation to Maher Arar (Ottawa: Public Works and Government Services Canada, 2006).

- Internal Inquiry into the Actions of Canadian Officials in Relation to Abdullah Almalki, Ahmad Abou Elmaati and Muayyed Nureddin (Ottawa: Her Majesty the Queen in Right of Canada, represented by the Minister of Public Works and Government Services, 2008).

- Air India Flight 182: A Canadian Tragedy, Report of the Commission of Inquiry into the Investigation of the Bombing of Air India Flight 182, several volumes (Ottawa: Minister of Public Works and Government Services, 2010).

In addition to these major inquiries' reports, instructors will require familiarity with a variety of annual or public reports produced by the agencies themselves. These include the annual CSIS Public Report, the annual Security Intelligence Review Committee operational audit, and the CSCE commissioner's annual report.[11]

Contrary to what one can find in the United States or the United Kingdom,

---

10. *http://www.canlii.org/en/index.php*
11. See *http://www.csis-scrs.gc.ca/pblctns/nnlrprt/index-eng.asp, http://www.sirc-csars.gc.ca/anrran/index-eng.html*, and *http://www.ocsec-bccst.gc.ca/ann-rpt/index_e.php*, respectively.

there is no major history of the intelligence community available in Canada. A history of the Canadian Intelligence Community in the first decades of the Cold War was prepared several years ago by University of Toronto Professor Wesley Wark with support and access to archival documentation provided by the Privy Council Office, but no consensus on the declassification of Dr. Wark's study could be reached after its completion.[12]

Canadian and other scholars have paid more attention to the oversight and review mechanisms—either in place or lacking—than the effectiveness and practices of the community and its constituent parts. This is reflected in the paucity of material on operational effectiveness, performance management, and organizational issues. For instance, no scholarly work has ever been done on the intelligence components of the Departments of Transport and Environment, the Canada Border Services Agency, and others.

READINGS FOR INSTRUCTORS

Overview

Brodeur, Jean-Paul. "The Globalisation of Security and Intelligence Agencies: A Report on the Canadian Intelligence Community," in Jean-Paul Brodeur, Peter Gill, and Dennis Töllborg (eds.), *Democracy, Law and Security: Internal Security Services in Contemporary Europe* (Burlington, VT: Ashgate, 2003), 210-261.

Farson, Stuart and Reg Whitaker. "Canada," in Stuart Farson, Peter Gill, Mark Phythian, and Shlomo Shpiro (eds), *PSI Handbook of Global Security and Intelligence: National Approaches*. Volume One: The Americas and Asia (Westport: Praeger Security International, 2008), 21-51.

Lefebvre, Stéphane. "Canada's Legal Framework for Intelligence," *International Journal of Intelligence and CounterIntelligence* 23 (2), 2010, 247-295.

Lefebvre, Stéphane. "Canada's Intelligence Culture: An Evaluation," in Russell G. Swenson and Susana C. Lemozy (Eds.), *Democratization of Intelligence: Melding Strategic Intelligence and National Discourse* (Washington, D.C.: National Defense Intelligence College Press, 2009), 7998.

Wark, Wesley K. "Canada and the Intelligence Revolution," in Heike Bungert, Jan G. Heitman and Michael Wala (eds.), *Secret Intelligence in the Twentieth Century* (London: Frank Cass, 2003), 176-192.

Security Intelligence

Kislenko, Arne. "Guarding the Border: Intelligence and Law Enforcement in Canada's Immigration System," in Loch K. Johnson (ed.). *The Oxford Handbook of National Security Intelligence* (Oxford: Oxford University Press, 2010), 310-327.

Potter, Evan H. "The System of Economic Intelligence-Gathering in Canada,"

---

12. The authors are grateful to Dr. Wark for verifying and confirming this information.

in Evan H. Potter (Ed.). *Economic Intelligence & National Security* (Ottawa: Carleton University Press, 1998), 21-78.

Rudner, Martin. "Protecting North America's Energy Infrastructure Against Terrorism," *International Journal of Intelligence and CounterIntelligence* 19 (3), 2006, 424-442.

Wark, Wesley K. "Security Intelligence in Canada, 1864-1945: The History of a 'National Insecurity State'," in Keith Neilson and B.J.C. McKercher (Eds.), *Go Spy the Land: Military Intelligence in History* (Westport: Praeger, 1992), 153-178.

Whitaker, Reg. "Origins of the Canadian Government's Internal Security System, 1946-1952," *The Canadian Historical Review LXV* (2), 1984, 154-183.

Whitaker, Reg. "Cold War Alchemy: How America, Britain and Canada Transformed Espionage into Subversion," *Intelligence and National Security* 15 (2), 2000, 177-210.

Whitaker, Reg. "Made in Canada? The New Public Safety Paradigm," in G. Bruce Doern (ed.). *How Ottawa Spends 2005-2006: Managing the Minority* (Montreal and Kingston: McGill-Queen's University Press, 2005), 77-95.

Foreign Intelligence

Cooper, Barry. *CFIS: A Foreign Intelligence Service for Canada* (Calgary: Canadian Defence & Foreign Affairs Institute, 2007). http://www.cdfai.org/PDF/CFIS.pdf.

Jensen, Kurt F. *Canadian Foreign Intelligence 1939-1951: Cautious Beginnings* (Vancouver: UBC Press, 2008).

Livermore, Dan. "Does Canada Need a Foreign Intelligence Agency?" *CIPS Policy Brief No. 3* (Ottawa: University of Ottawa, Centre for International Policy Studies, 2009).

Munton, Don. "Intelligence Cooperation Meets International Studies Theory: Explaining Canadian Operations in Castro's Cuba," *Intelligence and National Security* 24 (1), 2009, 119-138.

Signals Intelligence

Farson, Stuart. "So you don't like our Cover Story—Well we have Others: The Development of Canada's Signals Intelligence Capacity through Administrative Sleight of Hand, 1941-2000," in Bob Menzies, Dorothy Chunn and Susan Boyd (eds.), (Ab) *Using Power: The Canadian Experience* (Halifax: Fernwood Press, 2001), 78-94.

Robinson, Bill. "The Fall and Rise of Cryptanalysis in Canada" *Cryptologia XVI* (1), 1992, 23–38.

Rudner, Martin. "Canada's Communications Security Establishment from Cold War to Globalization," *Intelligence and National Security* 16 (1), 2001, 97-128.

Rudner, Martin. "Canada's Communications Security Establishment, Signals Intelligence and Counter-Terrorism," *Intelligence and National Security* 22 (4), 2007, 473-490.

Military Intelligence

Breede, Captain H. Christian. "Intelligence Lessons and the Emerging Canadian Counter-Insurgency Doctrine," *Canadian Army Journal* 9 (3), 2006, 24-40.

Rudner, Martin. "The Future of Canada's Defence Intelligence," *International Journal of Intelligence and CounterIntelligence* 15 (4), 2002-2003, 540-564.

Rudner, Martin. "Canada, the UN, NATO, and Peacekeeping Intelligence," in Ben de Jong, Wies Platje, and Robert David Steele (eds.), *Peacekeeping Intelligence: Emerging Concepts for the Future* (Oakton, Va.: OSS International Press, 2003),. 371-378.

Villeneuve, Lieutenant Colonel Daniel. "A Study of the Changing Face of Canada's Army Intelligence," *Canadian Army Journal* 9 (2), 2006, 18-36.

Wark, Wesley K. "The Evolution of Military Intelligence in Canada," *Armed Forces & Society* 16 (1), 1989, 77-98.

Accountability and Review

Campbell, Anthony. "Bedmates or Sparring Partners? Canadian Perspectives on the Media-Intelligence Relationship in 'The New Propaganda Age'," in Robert Dover and Michael S. Goodman (eds.). *Spinning Intelligence: Why Intelligence Needs the Media, Why the Media Needs Intelligence* (New York: Columbia University Press, 2009), 165-183.

Faragone, Joe. "Assessing the Performance of the Canadian Intelligence Community Through an Integrated Results-Based Management Method," paper presented at the International Studies Association 2009 Annual Convention, New York City, February 15-18, 2009

Farson, Stuart. "Restructuring Control in Canada: The McDonald Commission of Inquiry and its Legacy," in Glenn P. Hastedt (ed.) *Controlling Intelligence* (Abingdon: Frank Cass, 1991), 157-188.

Farson, Stuart and Reg Whitaker. "Accounting for the Future or the Past? Developing Accountability and Oversight Systems to Meet Future Intelligence Needs," in Loch K. Johnson (ed.), *The Oxford Handbook of National Security Intelligence* (Oxford: Oxford University Press, 2010), 673-698.

Littlewood, Jez. "Accountability of the Canadian Security and Intelligence Community post 9/11: Still a Long and Winding Road?" in Daniel Baldino (ed.), *Democratic Oversight of Intelligence Services* (Sydney: The Federation Press, 2010), 83-107.

Rempel, Roy. "Canada's Parliamentary Oversight of Security and Intelligence," *International Journal of Intelligence and CounterIntelligence* 17 (4), 2004-2005, 634-654.

Shore, Jacques. "Intelligence Review and Oversight in Post-9/11 Canada," *International Journal of Intelligence and CounterIntelligence* 19 (3), 2006, 456-479.

Mr. Stéphane Lefebvre has worked for three Canadian intelligence organizations. When this article was written, he was defence scientist-in-residence at the Canadian Centre for Intelligence and Security Studies, Carleton University Norman Paterson School of International Affairs. He is now pursuing a PhD in the Department of Law at Carleton University. *slefebv3@carleton.connect.ca*

Jeremy (Jez) Littlewood, PhD is the director, Canadian Centre for Intelligence and Security Studies and an assistant professor at the Carleton University Norman Paterson School of International Affairs. He previously worked at the University of Southampton (UK), and has served on secondment to the UK Foreign & Commonwealth Office, at the UN Department for Disarmament Affairs in Geneva, and with HM Forces (Army) in the UK. *jeremy_littlewood@carleton.ca*

GUIDE TO THE STUDY OF INTELLIGENCE

Mexican Intelligence[1]

José Medina González Dávila

Over the last 15 years, several members of the Mexican Government, opinion leaders, mass media, and academics have stated that the Mexican intelligence services are in a deep state of "crisis."[2] While their perceptions can be interpreted differently, an important fact is that very little is publicly known or acknowledged regarding the Mexican security and intelligence services. While secrecy is required for any intelligence organization to operate and contribute to the government's decision-making, in the case of Mexico, the lack of public information has created an impression of a lack of accountability and fostered doubt, a general perception of corruption, and distrust in such government entities.

While there are many elements of the Mexican state and its federal government that are acknowledged formally, there are many that are not. Secrecy has been such that the citizens and academic specialists do not know of the existence of all elements. This prevents observers, including the academic community, from studying intelligence organizations and limits one's analytic perspective.

The Origins of Mexican Intelligence[3]

During the 11 years of the Mexican Revolution (1910-1921), most of the

---

1. This article is one of the first academic looks at the subject of the Mexican intelligence services. Because of that, much of the discussion regarding specific organizations, their activities, roles, and functions in the top-level decision-making process are excluded.
2. These general comments have been shared with the author in private conversations on several occasions between 2004 and 2015.
3. The historical information presented in this paper is a brief synthesis of Sergio Aguayo, *La Charola* and information published by the Mexican Secretariat of the Interior (SEGOB), Secretariat of National Defense (SEDENA), and Secretariat of the Navy (SEMAR).

country was disorganized, lacked leadership, and was in a state of constant chaos and turmoil. The nation lacked any degree of economic, political, social, or diplomatic cohesion. There were 11 presidents during that period, but there was no effective public administration in the country. Most regions of Mexico were governed by "caudillos," regional political and military leaders that ruled through the use of indiscriminate violence. The ineffective central government during that period of time also was wracked by several "cloak and dagger" political conflicts at its highest levels.

On 1 December 1924, General Plutarco Elías Calles took office as president of Mexico, succeeding his mentor, Alvaro Obregón, a former general and commander of the Mexican Army, and president from 1920 to 1924. One of Calles' first priorities was to establish political and security measures to protect his administration. Obregón had conducted a series of political assassinations and/or negotiations with the caudillos to subdue them and gain control of the entire Mexican national territory, which helped him maintain his authority and power as president. However, Calles searched for institutional mechanisms to protect the Office of the Presidency against political intrigues and internal threats. He appointed a hand-picked group of Mexican Army officers for that task, whose sole purpose was to protect the president by providing physical security and information to support his political decisions. Such was the humble inception of the Mexican intelligence service.

In 1929, President Emilio Portes Gil created the "Confidential Department" (Departamento Confidencial) as part of the Secretariat of the Interior (Secretaría de Gobernación). Its purpose was to provide political information and analysis and to serve as an "administrative police force." The Confidential Department was Mexico's secret police, and its primary role was strictly political. Military and defense matters were relegated to the Army. However, the Mexican Government's main focus was internal policy and public domestic administration. In 1939, President Lázaro Cárdenas re-named the Confidential Department the "Office of Political Information" (Oficina de Información Política), maintaining the focus on political and social themes.

In 1942, in the context of World War II, the Office of Political Information was transformed into the "Social and Political Investigations Department" (Departamento de Investigaciones Políticas y Sociales), whose purpose was to maintain information regarding political and social movements, the activities of foreigners in Mexican territory, and any potential conflicts and subversion within the country. Its agents were oriented towards physical law enforcement and information gathering, and there is little evidence of analytical processes that turned such information into our current concept of "finished intelligence." This would change in 1947.

Recognizing the potential threats that Mexico could experience in the context of the Cold War, President Miguel Alemán Valdés created the Federal

Security Directorate (*Dirección Federal de Seguridad*, DFS), appointing Army Lieutenant Colonel Marcelino Inurreta de la Fuente as its first director. DFS was organized based on the previous Mexican secret police forces and with the assistance of several US agencies. The Central Intelligence Agency and the Federal Bureau of Investigations were among the "role models" for DFS, as were their doctrine and operative roles.[4]

DFS focused almost exclusively on domestic matters; political espionage; counterinsurgency; law enforcement; and to provide "confidential" services for top Mexican Government officials, including illegal activities, political coercion, violence against political enemies, and cooperation with Mexican organized crime. At the same time, DFS was a "power tool" to the Mexican political leadership for operations against communism. During the 1950s and 1960s, DFS consolidated its position as a government institution, augmented the number of agents and operatives, created informant networks, and developed specific analytical capabilities. The main consumers of its "intelligence" were the Office of the Presidency, the Secretariat of the Interior, and the American CIA.[5]

However, by the mid-1970s, the DFS was totally infiltrated by Mexican and transnational drug cartels and other criminal organizations, and corruption permeated the entire institution. DFS agents and leadership were involved in numerous international scandals and conflicts involving drug trafficking, abuse of authority, illegal activities, clandestine political espionage, violation of human rights, and other crimes. Most notorious of all was DFS participation in the assassination of Mexican journalist Manuel Buendía and US Drug Enforcement Agency (DEA) Agent Enrique Camarena Salazar in 1985.[6]

Because of these scandals and resulting foreign pressure, President Miguel de la Madrid disbanded the DFS and created the General Directorate of Investigations and National Security (*Dirección General de Investigaciones y Seguridad Nacional*), which President Carlos Salinas de Gortari re-named in 1989 as the National Security and Investigations Center (*Centro de Investigación y Seguridad Nacional*, CISEN), under the leadership of General Jorge Carrillo Olea, as part of the Secretariat of the Interior.

CISEN's main role and purpose was to become "the maximum house of intelligence in Mexico," to consolidate all intelligence to support top-level decision making, and to provide the necessary analytical support for the Mexican Federal Government.[7] Its focus was strictly internal, related to domestic

---

4. This statement has been made to the author on several occasions by top-level Mexican intelligence officials, and is also referred to in numerous historical sources, for example, Sergio Aguayo Quezada, *La Charola: Una historia de los Servicios de Inteligencia en México* (Mexico: Grijavlo Editorial Group, 2001).
5. This also has been told to the author by several sources.
6. For further discussion on this matter, see Esquivel, Jesús, *La CIA, Camarena y Caro Quintero* (Grijalbo, Mexico, 2010).
7. Different senior Mexican intelligence officials have made this statement to the author on several

political, social, and economic matters. However, from its creation in 1989 to 2005, there was a lack of legal authorities — a "vacuum" that was not to be corrected until the presidency of Vicente Fox Quesada almost 15 years later.

National Security Law and the Contemporary Structure of Mexican Intelligence

During the 1990s, CISEN gained a reputation as the "Mexican Central Intelligence Agency."[8] It played an important role during the Zapatista insurgency movement that erupted in southern Mexico in 1994-1995 and other political and social crises. With the inclusion of Mexico in the North American Free Trade Agreement (NAFTA) in 1994, new diplomatic, regional, and global pressures and commitments were exerted on the Mexican Government, on its security and defense capabilities, and on general public policy and administration. The need for legal and institutional resources to provide adequate levels of security and international exchange of information became critical, and CISEN was the only civilian intelligence organism tasked with such responsibilities.

The Mexican Economic Crisis of the late 1990s created an even more complex environment for its Intelligence Community, not only because it limited resources but also because of the emergence of new social movements and potential threats to domestic security. While officially CISEN spearheaded the efforts to provide actionable analysis and intelligence to top policymakers, the Army and Navy intelligence organizations obtained new resources and capabilities as well.

At the beginning of the presidency of Vicente Fox Quezada (2000-2006),[9] there was a public and political discussion on the role, scope, and potential limits of Mexican intelligence and national security. While these topics were discussed in academic circles and there were varying definitions used in Mexican military and public policy doctrine since the 1980s, there was no legal definition for them. In 2005, the Federal Government adopted the National Security Law (Ley de Seguridad Nacional), focused on establishing the legal fundamentals for the management and conduct of the nation's intelligence elements.

However, the bill by itself is limited in several aspects. First of all, "National Security" is defined in the law as a "set of actions" (Article 3), not as a necessary condition and/or a prerequisite for the adequate development of national economic, social, and political activities. This limits to a high degree the actions of the Federal Government and its institutions, and places strict boundaries

---

occasions, and it is a common expression used by CISEN members in official and academic environments.

8. This perception is common among many Mexican citizens, several academics and scholars, and by CISEN personnel themselves. However, other intelligence organizations do not agree with such a reputation.

9. Modern Mexican presidents serve six-year terms of office.

on the information gathering, intelligence analysis, and dissemination of intelligence to support top-level, strategic decisions.[10]

The National Security Law also stipulates clearly that the main focus of the Mexican intelligence agencies and services is to be focused *within the national territory*. This excludes developing foreign intelligence capabilities, adequate measures to exchange information with other countries and organizations, and leaves a void in all aspects related to transnational threats and intelligence processes. It is understood that international cooperation is mandatory in the globalized world; however, the bill does not mention it *per se*.[11] All Mexican Intelligence efforts are limited to the inside of the country.

The National Security Bill of 2005 creates the National Security Council with the president of Mexico as its head and the secretary of the interior as second-in-command. CISEN is recognized as the "primary" intelligence agency, and the bill grants it authority to coordinate intelligence and operational efforts related to national security. This places CISEN in a central role in Mexico's intelligence networks and in national security matters; however presidential political decisions suggest otherwise.

Conflicts and Tensions Within Mexico's Intelligence Services

Several official and unofficial sources have revealed that during Vicente Fox Quesada's presidency, despite the National Security Law of 2005, there was an intention to disband CISEN because of political reasons. Because of CISEN's background as a political espionage organization, numerous scandals and conflicts of interest, and systematic abuses of authority, President Fox considered it necessary to disband CISEN and create new intelligence organizations.[12] However, by the end of his administration, he had not done so. His need for CISEN impeded such an action. However, other government agencies, both civilian and military, deeply distrusted the "Center."[13]

CISEN gained a reputation as a "gatherer and concentrator of all the intelligence, but shared none with anyone," a situation that deeply irritated other government organizations.[14] While secrecy and compartmentalization of information is required in any intelligence organization, as the Americans have learned after the attacks of September 11, 2001, sharing information horizontally among different national agencies promotes efficient results and is an operational requirement. CISEN's reputation motivated other government

---

10. These perceptions are shared by several top-level intelligence officials in Mexico, which have shared their opinions with the author.
11. For further information, see Cámara de Diputados, *Ley de Seguridad Nacional*, Mexico, 2005.
12. This perception is common knowledge in the Mexican Intelligence Community, and several specialists and officials agree that this was the President's intention at the time.
13. Several military and civilian intelligence officers have shared this perception with the author.
14. Ibid.

organizations to create and/or strengthen their own intelligence gathering and analysis capabilities.

In the civilian sector, the Attorney General's Office (*Procuraduria General de la República*, PGR) and the Federal Police (*Policía Federal*, PF) created their own intelligence departments. Focused on law enforcement and combating transnational organized crime, the PGR created the Criminal Investigations Agency and strengthened the "Under-office for the Investigations of Organized Crime" (*Subprocuraduría de Investigación en Delincuencia Organizada*, SIEDO). The PF first created Section 2 (*Sección Segunda-Inteligencia*) and then the Mexico Center (*Centro México*) tasked with gathering information related to drug trafficking, organized crime, and to monitor potential threats to public safety and internal security.

At the same time, the PGR also funded the inception of the National Center for the Planning, Analysis, and Information to Combat Delinquency (*Centro Nacional de Planeación, Análisis, e Información para el Combate a la Delincuencia*, CENAPI), intended as an agency to integrate all crime information and to serve as a "center" of all criminal investigations and a national liaison with international organizations such as INTERPOL, the DEA, FBI, and the US Marshalls Service.[15]

Despite the efforts of the PGR and the PF to strengthen their intelligence capabilities, the military possessed far superior intelligence resources. The Mexican Army had its S-2 (*Sección Segunda*) within their Secretary of Defense's Staff (*Estado Mayor de la Defensa Nacional*), with a corresponding section in the Air Force (*Sección Segunda del Estado Mayor de la Fuerza Aérea*).[16] During the administration of President Felipe Calderón Hinojosa (2006-2012), the Mexican Federal Government decided to counteract drug trafficking and transnational organized crime. Mislabeled the "Mexican War on Drugs" by the media, such efforts prompted all Mexican security organizations to develop greater intelligence capabilities and to organize specialized criminal intelligence organizations.

The Mexican Army, in addition of their S-2 and the Air Force S-2, created the Antinarcotics Information Center (*Centro de Información Antinarcóticos*, CIAN), which later evolved into the S-7 and then the S-10 of the National Defense Staff (*Sección Séptima y Sección Décima del Estado Mayor de la Defensa Nacional*). The primary mission of these military organizations is to develop intelligence to counter drug trafficking and other manifestations of organized crime. The S-2 now focuses on broad subjects related to national defense and security.

The Mexican Navy also has an S-2 in the Naval General Staff (*Estado Mayor de la Armada de México*), whose functions and missions are similar to the Army's. The Navy has developed the Naval Intelligence Unit (*Unidad de Inteligencia Naval*,

---

15. For further information, see Procuraduría General de la República (Mexico), *http://www.pgr.gob.mx*.

16. In Mexico, the administrative entity for defense is the Secretariat of National Defense (*Secretaría de la Defensa Nacional, SEDENA*), and its armed-operational components are the Mexican Army and the Mexican Air Force as separate entities.

UIN), whose purpose is to develop strategic intelligence, develop tactical intelligence to counteract transnational maritime crime and drug trafficking, and to generate "special intelligence" to the high command. By "special intelligence," it is understood specific communications interceptions, special reconnaissance, infiltration of specific cells of organized crime, and (sometimes) political intelligence; which Naval High Command and Staff consider critical. The UIN integrates the efforts of their Army counterparts as well as develops special reconnaissance and analysis related to maritime intelligence.

The S-2s in both the Army and Navy have similar structures and roles, to include (but not limited to) counterintelligence, security of information, protection of sensitive material, secure communications, and management of Mexican military attachés abroad.

Other Intelligence Organizations in Mexico

In broad terms, the organizations mentioned in the previous section represent the major players of the Mexican Intelligence Community. It should be noted that while the leadership of these organizations has made important efforts at cooperation, there remains a high level of distrust and tension among their personnel. Tensions between the Army and Navy can be considered traditional; but over the last several years, a high level of competition has emerged between the military and civilian organizations.[17]

Within the military and civilian organizations there are other more discrete agencies. Both the Army and Navy have their "Sensitive Information Groups" (*Grupos de Información Sensible, GIS*), whose purpose is to manage and process critical intelligence for the secretary of Defense and the secretary of the Navy respectively. Furthermore, the Presidential Staff (*Estado Mayor Presidencial, EMP*) – a separate military organization under the president, trusted with his personal security — has its own intelligence section. The Office of the President also has an intelligence department, in charge of collecting, processing, and supplying the commander in chief with critical political, social, economic, and military information.

The Secretariat of the Treasury (*Secretaría de Hacienda y Crédito Público*), the Secretariat of Foreign Relations (*Secretaría de Relaciones Exteriores*), and the Secretariat of Economics (*Secretaría de Economía*) have their own information and analysis departments. However, as with the rest of the Mexican Federal Government, their interests and focus are largely domestic, inside Mexican boundaries. In the case of the Secretariat of Foreign Relations, their activities are limited to obtaining and analyzing information only if it pertains to Mexican citizens, corporations and/or Mexican government entities.

---

17. Numerous military and naval intelligence officers in Mexico have shared these perceptions with the author.

For much of its international information, Mexico relies on other countries, such as the United States, Canada, Germany, and Israel. Using well-established international cooperation mechanisms, Mexico relies on foreign agencies for certain information directly related to Mexican national security. Such cooperation binds specific agencies in the United States with specific organizations in Mexico. During the presidency of Felipe Calderón (2006-2012), the Mexican Federal Government established several international agreements to share information with other countries, such as the famous *"Merida Plan"* with the United States.[18] Administrative and management conflicts regarding such information are still a problem within Mexican intelligence services and are likely to continue in the future.

With the new administration of President Enrique Peña Nieto (2012-2018), there was a high level of expectations regarding the efficient operation of Mexican security services – and their intelligence organizations – based on his statements during his political campaign. At the same time, since President Peña's party is the Institutional Revolutionary Party (*Partido Revolucionario Institucional*, PRI), which ruled Mexico for over 70 years and is considered by many citizens as a very corrupt party, general perception of the security services' efficiency and integrity remains low. While there has been significant Intelligence Community successes – such as the arrest of several leaders of drug cartels and other organized crime structures[19] – their integrity and efforts are still questioned by the media, the academic world, and other political parties.

The Future of Mexican Intelligence

As described, there are many intelligence organizations across the Mexican Federal Government. Given their backgrounds and histories, their roles and missions overlap. This results in a less than optimal efficiency, mostly because of the distrust and lack of sharing among the security services. In terms of public administration and management, this represents the main challenge in future years. International cooperation, while helpful, also causes tension inside Mexican intelligence: not because it is deficient, but because different organizations and agencies compete for exclusivity of the information received from abroad.

Like all complex systems, any Intelligence Community benefits from a good and healthy degree of competition, especially in analysis. However, in the case of the Mexican services, such competition has led to a lack of trust and a less than efficient cooperation. This represents a major challenge toward

---

18. For further information, refer to the "Merida Initiative" document available on the US Embassy in Mexico's website *http://mexico.usembassy.gov/eng/ataglance/merida-initiative.html*
19. Some of the drug cartel "leaders" that have been captured during Peña's administration are Joaquin "El Chapo" Guzmán of the Sinaloa Cartel in 2014, and Servando "La Tuta" Gómez of the Knights Templar Cartel of Michoacán in early 2015.

the future.

Based on this brief description of the Mexican intelligence services, and recognizing the challenges they face in the new millennium, it would be appropriate to discern if there is a "real" crisis of Mexican intelligence, or it is only a "perception." While it is undeniable that Mexican intelligence services, both civilian and military, have come a long way since their humble beginnings in the first quarter of the last century, it is also undeniable that high levels of corruption, inefficiency, tensions and conflicts between services, private and political interests, and even less-than-adequate leadership are constant factors within the Mexican Intelligence Community. These are challenges that must be faced both as government entities and as intelligence and information organizations.

At the same time, the scope, reach, and focus of Mexican intelligence is mainly within its national borders, and lacks sufficient and efficient resources to cooperate effectively with international organizations and to develop foreign intelligence. Furthermore, there are no adequate means or measures to develop "strategic intelligence" as other countries do. This places important limitations on the Mexican intelligence services, its value for strategic decision-making, and its support of public policy and administration.

In this regard, the "real crisis" of Mexican intelligence is not based on the internal problems of the various services, but in the relatively limited concept that shapes the Mexican Intelligence Community. This represents a major challenge to Mexico's Government, since the 21st century brings new conditions to the international community, its security and development. Mexico cannot isolate itself from its responsibility on these matters as a member of the global community; and because of this the Mexican State must adapt its security organizations to meet such challenges. To do so will represent a major national and international advancement; not to do so will represent a major setback for the Mexican State and its society.

READINGS FOR INSTRUCTORS

Little is published in English about Mexican intelligence except for references in American newspaper articles, usually associated with an operation against a drug cartel leader. For those proficient in Spanish the following are relevant resources:

Aguayo Quezada, Sergio. *La Charola: Una historia de los Servicios de Inteligencia en México* (Grijavlo Editorial Group, Mexico, 2001).

Cámara de Diputados. *Ley de Seguridad Nacional* (Mexico" Mexico's Legislative Power, 2005.

Centro de Estudios Superiores Navales. *Inteligencia Estratégica* (Mexico: Naval Superior Studies Center, Secretariat of the Navy, 2014).

José Medina González Dávila has a BA in international relations from the Monterrey Superior Studies Institute of Technology, an MA in international studies from the Graduate School of Public Policy and Public Administration of the Monterrey Superior Studies Institute of Technology (ITESM), and a PhD in social anthropology from the Universidad Iberoamericana. His fields of study are strategic and international intelligence, military anthropology, and national security. E-mail: *yaocoatl@gmail.com*

GUIDE TO STUDY OF INTELLIGENCE

British Intelligence[1]

Dr. Huw Dylan and Dr. Michael S. Goodman

For centuries, British kings and queens have utilised their spies and spy-masters to safeguard their grip on power. Today's intelligence officers can trace their professional lineage to the sixteenth century. They can look to a long tradition of foreign spying during the age of empire, and the exploits of the officers who, for the defence of India, surveyed and spied in the badlands of Afghanistan – the adventures that inspired possibly the greatest spy story, Rudyard Kipling's Kim.[2] And they can examine how British intelligence per-formed, often with distinction, in the great wars of the twentieth century. They have an historic legacy. Today, in the United Kingdom, intelligence remains a vital component of statecraft. This article introduces British intelligence and offers an insight into 'the British way' in intelligence.

The rich history has been obscured by official secrecy until fairly recently. In 1985, the great historian of war, Professor Sir Michael Howard, lamented that "so far as official government policy is concerned, the British security and intelligence services do not exist. Enemy agents are found under gooseberry bushes and intelligence is brought in by the storks."[3] This is no longer the case. Over the final decades of the twentieth century a small revolution occurred in official attitudes towards secrecy. Wartime intelligence veterans published their memoirs; official histories were published; and the 1993 Waldegrave Open Government initiative increased the volume of intelligence papers in the British National Archives, leading to a boom in popular and academic writing. This trend towards limited (although unprecedented) openness has

---

1. Editor's Note: AFIO has retained the original UK spellings of these two British scholars.
2. See Peter Hopkirk. *The Great Game: On Secret Service in High Asia* (London: John Murray, 2006); Matthew Grant (ed.), *The British Way in Cold Warfare: Intelligence, Diplomacy and the Bomb, 1945-75.* (London: Continuum, 2011).
3. Christopher Andrew, "Intelligence, International Relations and Under-theorisation," *Intelligence and National Security* 19 (2), 2004, 71.

continued, most notably through the publication of official histories of the Security Service (MI-5), the Secret Intelligence Service (SIS/MI-6), and the Joint Intelligence Committee (JIC).[4] It has also been supplemented by authoritative inquiries into the intelligence community, most notably the Butler Report into pre-war intelligence on Iraqi weapons of mass destruction.[5] Combined, these sources provide students and scholars with outstanding insight into the role of intelligence in British statecraft.

Establishing the British Way in Intelligence

As early as the sixteenth century, Sir Francis Walsingham and his predecessor, Sir William Cecil, ran a network of "intelligencers," gathering intelligence on Catholic plots against Queen Elizabeth.[6] Throughout the seventeenth century Britain gathered intelligence on restive plotters by intercepting their post, and by the eighteenth century there was an official decipherer targeting the codes of foreign powers.[7] These activities were funded by a national secret service fund, administered by the secretary of state for foreign affairs. However, before the twentieth century, intelligence gathering was not professionalised in the same manner as diplomacy; it was viewed as a distinctly ungentlemanly activity. It was the armed forces who developed and formalised intelligence, operating, as they were, on the sharp end of imperial expansion. Britain boasted a naval intelligence department in 1887 and the War Office established its intelligence branch in 1873.[8] These organisations pioneered modern intelligence in Britain, gathering, processing, and disseminating intelligence, based on all sources. But it took many more years to develop a true British Intelligence Community.

The catalyst for the creation of the modern intelligence machinery was the rise of Germany. British military organisations and the Foreign Office proved unable to deliver the intelligence demanded by anxious ministers, so, in 1909, the Committee of Imperial Defence created the Secret Service Bureau (SSB). The SSB domestic or "home" section would eventually become the Security Service and was headed by Army Captain Vernon Kell. The foreign section, MI-1c, would eventually become SIS; it was headed by the redoubtable Royal Navy Commander Mansfield Cumming, who signed his letters in green ink

---

4. Christopher Andrew, *Defence of the Realm: The Authorised History of MI5* (London: Allen Lane, 2009); K. Jeffery, *MI6: The History of the Secret Intelligence Service, 1909-1949* (London: Bloomsbury, 2010); M. S. Goodman, *The Official History of the Joint Intelligence Committee: From the Approach of the Second World War to the Suez Crisis* (London: Routledge, 2014).

5. Butler, the Lord of Brockwell, HC898. *Review of Intelligence on Weapons of Mass Destruction* (London: TSO, 2004).

6. See Stephen Alford, *The Early Elizabethan Polity: William Cecil and the British Succession Crisis, 1558-1569* (Cambridge: Cambridge University Press, 1998).

7. Stephen Twigge, Edward Hampshire, Graham Macklin, *British Intelligence: Secrets, Spies and Sources,* (London: The National Archives, 2008), 10 –11.

8. Ibid, 11.

with the single letter, "C" – a tradition followed by all SIS chiefs to this day.[9]

Establishing the SSB began the long process that yielded a functional Intelligence Community. As befitted its imperial heritage, until the Second World War, the military largely dominated intelligence. MI-5 and SIS were civilian agencies, but heavily staffed by former military men, and their concern was largely (although by no means entirely) with enemy capabilities. After 1923, communications intelligence was the purview of the SIS-controlled Government Code and Cypher School (GC&CS), which after World War I amalgamated the Admiralty and the Army's wartime signals intelligence (SIGINT) outfits, Room 40 and MI-1b.[10] The Army and Navy maintained their own intelligence branches.[11] But the level of coordination was questionable. The Foreign Office remained rather aloof from the agencies, considering itself the sole authority on foreign and diplomatic developments. Duplication was rife, with one commentator after the war noting how he witnessed "junior officers in the intelligence divisions of the Air Ministry, War Office, and the Admiralty all doing the same job, writing the same things, gathering the same information, most of it not secret in any way."[12]

In 1936, with war clouds once again on the horizon, the secretary to the Cabinet and the Committee of Imperial Defence, Sir Maurice Hankey proposed reforms to ensure that the medley of organisations generated useful intelligence to meet the needs of the Chiefs of Staff and the government. They created the Joint Intelligence Committee, which established itself at the apex of Britain's intelligence machinery, and remained there.[13] This development was significant for the way Britain managed its intelligence affairs. After some teething troubles, the JIC secured the Foreign Office's active engagement, and its members included relevant policy departments, the armed forces, and the intelligence agencies, all of which would contribute and agree to the Committee's proceedings. This ensured that direction and collection were more focused; that JIC reports were truly "national," consensus reports, rather than departmental ones; that intelligence and policy were coordinated; and that no single department could dominate. Today these characteristics remain: the British way in intelligence is characterised by the committee approach to management, an intelligence community working jointly rather than competitively, a (general) drive for consensus, and the view that intelligence is valuable to all facets of national business.

---

9. Alan Judd, *The Quest for 'C': Mansfield Cumming and the Founding of the Secret Service* (Harper Collins: London, 1999), 100; Andrew, *The Defence of the Realm*; Keith Jeffery, *MI6*.

10. Twigge, Hampshire, Macklin, *British Intelligence*, 297.

11. M. S. Goodman, "Learning to Walk: The Origins of the UK's Joint Intelligence Committee," *International Journal of Intelligence and Counterintelligence* 21 (1), 2008, 40-56.

12. Patrick Howarth, *Intelligence Chief Extraordinary* (London: Bodley Head, 1986), 199.

13. Michael S. Goodman, *The Official History of the Joint Intelligence Committee*.

British Intelligence Today

The core institutions of British intelligence have proven resilient. They have survived withering criticism following spectacular failures and have weathered economic boom and bust. This is due to several factors: the legacy of intelligence support for policy making during the Second World War; the Cold War, and the Soviet nuclear threat; the centrality of intelligence to the Anglo-American relationship – valued and nurtured by British politicians from Churchill to Tony Blair; the importance of good intelligence in the small wars of the end of empire; and because of the consistent threat the UK has faced from terrorists. Britain has fought very hard to maintain its intelligence power, even as other aspects of its global influence diminished.

Two notable features differentiate the contemporary machinery from its Cold War incarnation. Firstly, today, the services have reasonably prominent public profiles. They recruit openly, (some of) their records are available, they have published official histories, and the leaders have appeared in public before the parliamentary Intelligence and Security Community (ISC). The second feature is the ISC itself, and oversight of the British intelligence Community. Although the JIC and ministers exercised internal oversight throughout the twentieth century, the services were not subject to robust parliamentary oversight. This changed in 1994 with the Intelligence Services Act and the ISC's establishment. Recently reformed with the 2013 Justice and Security Act, the ISC is now a Committee of Parliament, reporting directly to that institution on the policy, administration, expenditure, and aspects of operational activity of the agencies.[14]

Setting Intelligence Requirements in Britain

The British Intelligence Community is comparatively small, therefore setting defined requirements has been vital. For the Cold War and the early years of the twenty-first century, this was the responsibility of the JIC. In 2010, this changed when the coalition government established a National Security Council (NSC).[15] Chaired by the prime minister, the NSC works to "coordinate and deliver the Government's international security agenda," and decide upon the strategic direction of British foreign, defence, and security policy.[16] Soon after its establishment, the NSC published Britain's first national security

14. See the ISC's informative website: http://isc.independent.gov.uk/ (accessed 12 June 2014).
15. Some have argued that this led to a downgrading of the JIC, see P. H. J. Davies, "Twilight of Britain's Joint Intelligence Committee," International Journal of Intelligence and Counterintelligence 24 (3), 2011, 427-446.
16. See the UK Government's statement at: https://www.gov.uk/government/news/establishment-of-a-national-security-council (accessed 11 June 2014). See the list of priorities in the National Security Strategy at the UK Government website: https://www.gov.uk/government/publications/the-national-security-strategy-a-strong-britain-in-an-age-of-uncertainty (accessed 11 June 2014).

strategy, which identified 15 "priority risk types."[17] These national priorities guide the more detailed priorities the JIC sets for the intelligence machinery annually. The Security Service remains somewhat anomalous in that it retains more capacity than the other agencies to set its own requirements within the broad guidance set by the Security Service act of 1989.[18] The system is based on similar principles to those upon which the JIC was established: Firstly, of utilising the committee approach to achieve coordination, consensus, and efficiency. Secondly, ensuring that intelligence departments and policy departments are closely linked.

Collection

For the past century, Britain's intelligence agencies have existed in a paradoxical state: their existence was officially denied, and yet their exploits and presence in popular culture ensured their fame. It is rumoured that London bus conductors would announce that it was time for spies to alight when commuter buses stopped near the Security Service's nominally secret headquarters. And despite not being officially acknowledged until 1992, and not being put on a statutory basis until the 1994 Intelligence Services Act, MI-6 had been a global brand for decades. Prior to being established on a statutory basis in 1994, the foreign secretary could, theoretically, have unilaterally disbanded the agency. Today, Britain openly acknowledges its three main intelligence agencies. MI-5 and SIS work closely with their extremely secretive sister agency, the Government Communications Headquarters (GCHQ). All are funded centrally through the Single Intelligence Account, overseen by the ISC. They are sometimes known as the SIA agencies and represent the core of British intelligence collection. They are not the sole collection agencies, the Defence Ministry retains a capacity in Defence Intelligence (DI), which works with the core national agencies. DI is funded separately through the Defence Vote.

Based in Vauxhall Cross on the south bank of the River Thames in London, SIS is Britain's foreign intelligence agency. Although its contemporary activities are secret, its role is clear: it collects "secret intelligence and mounts covert operations overseas in support of British Government objectives." This includes a wide range of activities relating to national, international, and economic security, and serious crime. SIS "uses human and technical sources" and maintains "liaison with a wide range of foreign intelligence and security services."[19] The foreign secretary remains the government minister responsible for it and its activities. Guided broadly by JIC requirements, SIS can also be tasked by its

---

17. Ibid.
18. See the Security Service's website: *https://www.mi5.gov.uk/home/the-threats/espionage/how-does-mi5-tackle-espionage.html* (accessed 11 June 2014).
19. See SIS's website *https://www.sis.gov.uk/about-us/what-we-do.html* (accessed 11 June 2014).

customer departments, for example the Foreign Office.

SIS's domestic counterpart is the Security Service, known as MI-5. Based in Thames House on the north bank of the Thames, belatedly it was given a statutory basis by the 1989 Security Service Act and is responsible for "protecting the UK against threats to national security from *espionage, terrorism* and *sabotage*, from the activities of agents of foreign powers, and from actions intended to *overthrow or undermine parliamentary democracy* by political, industrial or violent means."[20] As of 2014, the Service's main areas of work are currently international and domestic counterterrorism, counterespionage, protective security, and counterproliferation. To fulfil its functions, it collects intelligence through human sources, surveillance, cooperation with foreign and domestic partners, interception of communications, and intrusive surveillance (bugging). The Security Service is answerable to the home secretary, who authorises intrusive operations under the authority granted by the 2000 Regulation of Investigatory Powers Act (RIPA). It has no powers of arrest, being primarily an investigative and analytical organisation, a factor that mandates close cooperation with the police.

Both agencies are dwarfed in terms of personnel and budget by GCHQ, Britain's SIGINT agency. Based in Cheltenham, in a building commonly known as "the doughnut," it is an extremely secretive agency; in contrast with SIS and MI-5, GCHQ has not published an authorised, official history. It is, however, an agency built on a rich tradition of code breaking. Today, GCHQ is the responsibility of the foreign secretary, and notes that it "plays a part in the fight against terrorism, drug trafficking, and other forms of serious crime, as well as supporting military operations across the world."[21] Broadly, its work is based on intercepting and breaking the communications of targets. But the agency's remit is expansive. It remains responsible for "information assurance," securing British communications from eavesdropping enemies, which is managed by the Communications Electronics Security Group.[22] A major and growing component of its work is related to the cyber realm, a first order British security priority in the 2010 National Security Strategy.[23] This is primarily a defensive function, and there are myriad organisations that aid it in identifying, understanding, and countering the threat. They are managed by the Office of Cyber Security and Information Assurance, which is based in the Cabinet Office.[24] But GCHQ also houses an offensive element. Defence

---

20. See the Security Service's website: *https://www.mi5.gov.uk/home/about-us/who-we-are.html* (accessed 11 June 2014).

21. See GCHQ's website: *http://www.gchq.gov.uk/what_we_do/Pages/index.aspx* (accessed 11 June 2014).

22. *https://www.gov.uk/government/organisations/cesg* (accessed 11 June 2014).

23. *http://www.gchq.gov.uk/what_we_do/the-threats-we-face/Pages/The-cyber-threat.aspx* (accessed 11 June 2014).

24. See *https://www.gov.uk/government/groups/office-of-cyber-security-and-information-assurance* (accessed 11 June 2014), and the Parliamentary Note on 'Cyber Security in the UK', 2001, available at

Secretary Philip Hammond noted in 2013 that Britain was "developing a full spectrum military cyber capability, including a strike capability."[25]

Analysis

The JIC has gained a degree of notoriety as "the anvil" of British intelligence assessment. However, the JIC members are extremely senior (and, therefore, busy) officials and politicians, and they are supported by a comparatively small Assessments Staff (the drafters). Although they may be responsible for the most exalted intelligence assessment products, they are by no means alone in performing the task. Indeed, the processing of intelligence in Britain involves more than a common-sense understanding of the word "analysis" suggests.

As Lord Butler noted in his 2004 report, the processing of intelligence can refer to validation, analysis, and assessment.[26] Validation is a process that usually occurs within the relevant agency. It is a process of ensuring that the means by which the information was gathered is sound. This process is generally conducted within the collecting agency.[27]

Analysis follows validation. This is the process of examining the information, generally by subject matter experts. The expert "assembles individual intelligence reports into meaningful strands, whether weapons programmes, military operations or diplomatic policies. Intelligence reports take on meaning as they are put into context."[28] According to Butler, the main cohort of analysts in Britain is to be found in DI. DI's parent department, the Defence Ministry, is the largest recipient of intelligence. But the Security Service, GCHQ, and law enforcement organisations, like the National Crime Agency, all house a number of analysts.[29]

Finally, assessment is the process of fitting the often diffuse intelligence into a broader pattern or trend. In Britain, this process is usually – but not always, or necessarily – all source. It can be conducted departmentally, in DI for military trends, for example, or interdepartmentally, for example, at the Joint Terrorism Analysis Centre (JTAC) for short – and medium-term assessments of the terror threat. JTAC was created in 2003 and analyses and assesses all intelligence relating to international terrorism, at home and overseas.[30] But the main thrust of national analysis is performed by the Cabinet Office Assess-

---

http://www.parliament.uk/documents/post/postpn389_cyber-security-in-the-UK.pdf

25. https://www.gov.uk/government/news/reserves-head-up-new-cyber-unit (accessed 11 June 2014).

26. Butler, The Lord of Brockwell. HC898. *Review of Intelligence on Weapons of Mass Destruction* (London: TSO, 2004).

27. Butler, *Review of Intelligence on Weapons of Mass Destruction*, 9.

28. Butler, *Review of Intelligence on Weapons of Mass Destruction*, 10.

29. A browse through the jobs advertised on their websites offers a glimpse into the kind of analytical work they conduct.

30. See https://www.mi5.gov.uk/home/about-us/who-we-are/organisation/joint-terrorism-analysis-centre.html (accessed 11 June 2014).

ments Staff, which consists of roughly 30 officials. They are assigned topics and assess incoming intelligence in consultation with relevant departments. The papers they produce are "subject to formal inter-departmental scrutiny and challenge" in subject or area specific Current Intelligence Groups (CIG), which bring together experts from across government.[31] Once agreed, the paper is forwarded to the JIC for discussion, approval, and dissemination to relevant customers.

Dissemination

Given the number of channels that exist between the policy departments, the armed forces, and the intelligence agencies, generalising about the process of dissemination is problematic. Intelligence can be passed directly to departments in raw form, from SIS to the Foreign Office for example. If it is actionable and time-sensitive, it may be passed to enforcement agencies or to the military. Processed intelligence like JTAC reports are disseminated widely to a range of relevant customers, as are DI reports on issues like weapons of mass destruction. At the highest level of government, the JIC remains the mechanism of dissemination, reflecting the "national" character of its reporting. Since 2013, it has produced three specific types of reports: JIC assessments, broader papers approved by the Committee; shorter Joint Intelligence Organisation (JIO) Intelligence Briefs, short notice assessments in response to received intelligence, approved by the JIC chair or a delegated authority; and JIO Intelligence Summaries, assessments produced periodically in response to streams of intelligence or other information.[32] The process is designed to ensure that at-the-top-of-government assessments are the product of consensus and a robust all-source process, agreed upon by a wide range of government departments.

This final point underlines what might be described as "the British way" in intelligence. In contrast to the larger American Intelligence Community, there is a drive to provide customers at the highest level with a single, all-source, and community-agreed national product. Working to a consensus is key. This reflects the British Cabinet system of government; the British intelligence community is indeed a product of its environment. In the future, the machinery will continue to adapt. The central assessment machinery has undergone several reforms since the Butler Review; individual agencies will adapt to meet developing threats. Like all intelligence communities, the British must struggle with the question of how to deal with the volume of information available from open sources, and the question of how to identify the needles of threat information in the haystacks of communications data. This will continue to

---

31. *National Intelligence Machinery* (London: HMSO, 2011), 24
32. Intelligence and Security Committee: Annual Report. 33. Available at *http://isc.independent.gov.uk/committee-reports/annual-reports*

provoke controversy, as the Snowden revelations have recently shown. But two things can be said for sure: intelligence will continue to be a vital component of British statecraft, its legacy will serve it well in this regard. And secondly, the services are unlikely to be able to retreat from the public eye.

Readings for Instructors

Overview

Aldrich, Richard J. Rory Cormac, & Michael S. Goodman (eds.), Spying on the World: The Declassified Documents of the Joint Intelligence Committee, 1936-2013 (Edinburgh: Edinburgh University Press, 2014).

Scott, Len. "British Intelligence and the Cold War" in Loch K. Johnson (ed.), The Oxford Handbook of National Security Intelligence (Oxford: Oxford University Press, 2010).

National Intelligence Machinery (London: HMSO, 2010) available online at https://www.gov.uk/government/uploads/system/uploads/attachment_data/file/61808/nim-november2010.pdf

Twigge, Stephen, Edward Hampshire, & Graham Macklin, British Intelligence: Secrets, Spies and Sources (London: The National Archives, 2008).

Security Intelligence

Andrew, Christopher. The Defence of the Realm: The Authorized History of MI5 (London: Allen Lane, 2009).

Hewitt, Steve. The British War on Terror: Terrorism and Counter-Terrorism on the Home Front Since 9/11 (London: Continium, 2010).

Rimington, Stella. Open Secret: The Autobiography of the Former Director-General of MI5 (London: Arrow, 2002).

Foreign Intelligence

Corera, Gordon. MI6: Life and Death in the British Secret Service (London: Phoenix, 2012).

Jeffery, Keith. MI6: the History of the Secret Intelligence Service, 1909-1949. (London: Bloomsbury, 2010).

Aldrich, Richard J. The Hidden Hand: Britain, America and Cold War Secret Intelligence (London: John Murray, 2009).

Signals Intelligence

Aldrich, Richard J. GCHQ: The Uncensored Story of Britain's Most Secret Agency (London: HarperPress, 2010).

Ferris, John. "The Road to Bletchley Park: The British Experience with Signals Intelligence 1892–1945,." Intelligence and National Security 17 (1), 2002.

Ferris, John. "Before 'Room 40': The British Empire and Signals Intelligence, 1898-1914," Journal of Strategic Studies 12 (4), 1989.

Military Intelligence

Davies, Philip H. J. "Defence Intelligence in the UK after the Mountbatten Reforms: Organisational and inter-organisational Dilemmas of Joint Military Intelligence," *Public Policy and Administration* 28 (2), 2012.

Dylan, Huw. "The Joint Intelligence Bureau: (Not so)Secret Intelligence for the Post War World," *Intelligence and National Security* 27 (1), 2012.

Urban, Mark. *Task Force Black: The Explosive True Story of the SAS and the Secret War in Iraq* (London: Little, Brown, 2010).

Accountability

The Intelligence and Security Committee publishes annual and special reports at: http://isc.independent.gov.uk/

Gill, Peter and Mark Phythian. *Intelligence in an Insecure World* (Cambridge: Polity, 2009) – particularly chapter 8, "Can Intelligence be Democratic?"

Gill, Peter. "Evaluating Intelligence Oversight Committees: The UK Intelligence and Security Committee and the 'War on Terror," *Intelligence and National Security* 22 (1), 2007.

Huw Dylan is lecturer in intelligence and international security at the Department of War Studies, King's College London, where he leads a wide variety of courses related to British and American intelligence. He received his PhD from the University of Aberystwyth in 2010. A regular commentator on intelligence and security issues on the BBC, his research is focused on British intelligence in the early Cold War and the relationship between intelligence and deception. His book *Defence Intelligence and the Cold War* is published by Oxford University Press.

Michael S. Goodman is a reader in intelligence and international affairs in the Department of War Studies, King's College London. He has published widely in the field of intelligence history, including *Spying on the Nuclear Bear: Anglo-American Intelligence and the Soviet Bomb* (Stanford University Press, 2008); *Spinning Intelligence: Why Intelligence Needs the Media, Why the Media Needs Intelligence* (Columbia: Columbia University Press, 2009); *Learning from the Secret Past: Cases in British Intelligence History* (Georgetown University Press, 2011); *The Routledge Companion to Intelligence Studies* (Routledge, 2014); *Spying on the World: The Declassified Documents of the Joint Intelligence Committee, 1936-2013* (Edinburgh University Press, 2014); and *The Official History of the Joint Intelligence Committee, Volume I: From the Approach of the Second World War to the Suez Crisis* (Routledge, 2014).

French Intelligence

Philippe Hayez and Hedwige Regnault de Maulmin

Today's dialectic between transparency and secrecy regarding intelligence issues questions the very existence of secret services. Indeed, the idea that government prerogatives should be hidden from the citizens to serve the *raison d'Etat* is paradoxical in an era where transparency is encouraged and seen as a characteristic of an ideal democracy.

However, as *realpolitik* has evolved to international relations with more embedded cultural, economic, and financial interests, where the economic competition is a transposition for war, and where the international social culture approaches that of community, international leaders have faced diffused, non-static threats that have multiplied.[1] Therefore, in a labyrinthine environment, the activities of secret services have shifted to a more defensive posture, adjusting to the threats.[2] This evolution is illustrated by changes in the French intelligence and security services.

While considered by the US historian Douglas Porch[3] as only marginal to the development of French foreign and security policy and lacking a national intelligence culture, the French services underwent an "Intelligence Springtime"[4] between 1989 and 1992. In the decade between the fall of the Berlin Wall and the 9/11 attack on the twin towers of the World Trade Center, their budgets and staffs increased, contrary to the trend in other NATO countries. Having surmounted the main crises of the last decade (Afghanistan, Iraq, Africa)

---

1. B. Bajolet, "La DGSE, outil de réduction de l'incertitude?" *Revue Défense Nationale* No. 766, January 2014, 27-31.

2. Ibid.

3. Douglas Porch, *The French Secret Services: From the Dreyfus Affair to the Gulf War* (New York: Farrar, Strauss & Giroux, 1995).

4. J.-M. Pennetier, "The Springtime of French Intelligence," *Intelligence and National Security* 11 (4), October 1996.

and prevented any terrorist attack on its territory,[5] France has modernized its Intelligence Community since 2008.

The original 2008 White Paper on Defense and National Security, confirmed by that of 2013,[6] aimed at filling the gap between the country's strategic interests and the capabilities of the French services to fulfill them. The 2008 White Paper gave them a strategic function named "Knowledge and Anticipation" and, thereby, propelled the services from obscurity to a central role. According to the present head of the French foreign agency General Directorate for External Security (*Direction générale de la sécurité extérieure*, DGSE), Bernard Bajolet, intelligence is now seen as necessary in supporting national security decisions and anticipating and assessing risks.

Some peculiarities make French intelligence quite difficult to handle. France remains an exception within the democracies since its intelligence services are not ruled by any parliamentary law, but by a simple regulation (*règlement*). Another characteristic of French intelligence is a paucity of intelligence-related research. French universities have not included intelligence as a field of study, with the notable exception of Sciences Paris.[7]

This paper provides a brief history, and outlines the structure and oversight of French intelligence services in the light of the counterterrorism paradigm that dominates today's politics.

Brief History of French Intelligence Services

Heirs to post-World War II organizations, such as the External Documentation and Counter-Espionage Service (*Service de documentation extérieure et de contre-espionnage*, SDECE) and the Directorate for the Surveillance of the Territory (*Direction de la surveillance du territoire*, DST), the French intelligence services have gone through a tremendous, although belated, series of reforms. Over the last quarter of the 20th century, they have emerged from murkiness to greater openness as a consequence of their institutionalization, structuring, and with a new relation to the public. French intelligence services have been brought into the public sphere, becoming "public secret services," and integrated to the government's "common welfare" strategy.

As Frederic Coste notes,[8] contrary to the Anglo-Saxon notion of security,

---

5. Editor's note: This article was written in 2014 before the Paris terrorist attacks of January 2015 (Charlie Hebdo magazine and a kosher supermarket) or of November 2015 (Bataclan theater and elsewhere) or the Nice attack in 2016.

6. French White Paper on Defense and National Security – June 2013, *http://www.rpfrance-otan.org/ IMG/pdf/ White_paper_on_defense_2013.pdf*.

7. See O. Chopin, et. al., "Étudier le renseignement en France," Hérodote No. 140, 2011, 91-102; and O. Forcade, "Objets, approches et problématiques d'une histoire française du renseignement : un champ historiographique en construction," *Histoire, économie & société,* / 31ème année, 2012, 99-110.

8. Frederic Coste, "L'adoption du concept de sécurité nationale: une révolution conceptuelle qui peine à s'exprimer," *Recherche & documents, Fondation pour la recherche stratégique* No. 3, 2011.

the concepts of defense and security (i.e. domestic security) have long been divided in France. Domestic security (involving the police, justice system, and domestic intelligence) were distinct from the measures supporting diplomacy and foreign military operations. This separation reflected a lack of a clear national security policy. A very important paradigmatic shift occurred with the 2002 Law on Domestic Security, which defined security as a state of stability in which the fundamental interests of the nation (i.e. public order, functioning of the institutions, and the administration's freedom of action) are preserved. The two notions were addressed in the 2008 White Paper on Defense and National Security, the former name of which was simply White Paper on Defense.

One explanation for this comparatively late change in approach has to be found in the political attitude toward intelligence. The Dreyfus Affair (1894 to 1906) was an important and long-enduring trauma for French politicians, and their trust *vis à vis* intelligence was not increased by several incidents, such as the July 1985 sinking of Greenpeace's *Rainbow Warrior* in Auckland harbor, New Zealand.

Nevertheless, French intelligence services have evolved quietly. After François Mitterrand's 1981 election, the replacement of the reviled SDECE by DGSE was merely a face change. But, since 1991 and the end of the Cold War, a *ministerial circulaire* mentioned that the General Intelligence Directorate (*Direction centrale des Renseignements généraux*, DCRG) — one of the two existing security services — should focus only on predicting events via multiple sources of information and not any more on the covert surveillance of political opponents. French involvement in the 1991 Gulf War revealed the weaknesses of military intelligence and led to the creation in 1992 of a dedicated and unified service, the Military Intelligence Directorate (*Direction du renseignement militaire*, DRM), whose director assists and advises the defense minister on military intelligence.

After the 9/11 attacks, the French intelligence services focused much more on Islamic terrorism. President Jacques Chirac created a Homeland Security Council (*Conseil de Sécurité intérieure*, CSI) responsible for defining internal security policy. In 2006, a White Paper on Internal Security sponsored by then Interior Minister Nicolas Sarkozy started an "intelligence-led policy" process that he pursued and enforced under his presidential term. To promote efficiency in domestic intelligence, the General Intelligence Directorate (*Renseignements généraux*, RG) and the DST were merged in 2008 in a new security service, the Domestic Intelligence Directorate (*Direction centrale du renseignement intérieur*, DCRI), which became the most powerful French domestic intelligence service ever. However, the DCRI's weaknesses after the 2012 Mohammed Merah Affair (a lone-wolf jihadist killing several people near Toulouse) led to a rethinking of the domestic security, and in 2014 the DCRI became the General Directorate for Domestic Intelligence (*Direction générale du renseignement intérieur*, DGSI), symbolically bringing this service on a par with the foreign intelligence service DGSE.

From "Tribes" to a "Community":
A Look at the Structure of the French Intelligence Services

Historically, as the different French intelligence services operated under different authorities and were under different ministries, cooperation between them was always an issue. French intelligence services have undergone recent reforms to better coordinate their efforts to resemble a "community." This notion is relatively new since its appearance in the 2000's and is outlined in the 2008 and 2013 White Papers on defense and national security, which brought to light for French citizens the importance of intelligence and the perception of the intelligence services as a strategic tool for the nation.

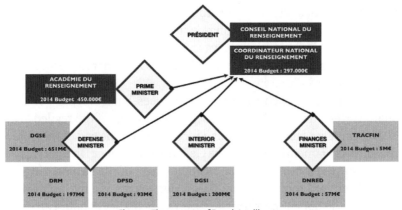

Figure 1: The structure of French Intelligence.

As described in the 2008 White Paper, the French intelligence community is structured as several complementary services within the Ministries of Defense (DGSE, DRM, and Directorate for the Protection and Security of the defense — *Direction de la protection et de la sécurité de défense*, DPSD), Interior (DGSI), and Finance (National Directorate for Customs Intelligence — *Direction nationale des enquêtes douanières*, DNRED, and Intelligence Processing and Action Against Clandestine Financial Circuits — *Traitement du renseignement et action contre les circuits financiers clandestins*, TRACFIN) ."

There are two general services (DGSE and DGSI) and four specialized ones (DRM, DPSD, DRED, and TRACFIN). The heads of these six services sit in the National Intelligence Council (*Conseil National du Renseignement*, CNR), chaired by the president. There is no separate technical agency, such as the US' National Security Agency or the British Government Communications Headquarters; the DGSE is the service in charge of most signal (SIGINT) and digital intelligence capabilities for the benefit of the entire community.

DGSE is responsible for the collection and analysis of intelligence outside of national territory. Since 1966, DGSE has been under the defense minister's direct supervision. Within the Defense Ministry, the DGSE is responsible for foreign intelligence. Its organization, processes and intelligence analysis are continuously adapted to cope with the evolving threats. As a global service, DGSE retains all means of collection (HUMINT, SIGINT) and has had since its creation its own clandestine action capacity (*Service Action*). Its analysts work closely with French diplomats concerning international crises. For the past decade, this service has benefited from regular increases in its budget and staff. To remain relevant and meet the challenges of performance, the DGSE must remain adaptable, which also means that it must reconcile intellectual plasticity and moral rigor.[9]

The **DGSI** is responsible for the collection, centralization, and analysis of all intelligence involving domestic security or the "fundamental interests of the nation." It, as its predecessors DST and DCRI were, is under the interior minister's authority. The DGSI replaced the DCRI in May 2014. It maintains the same attributions of its predecessor, but has formally improved in autonomy. The DGSI is intended to match symmetrically to the DGSE's structure with its new Intelligence Directorate (*direction du renseignement*) and Technical Directorate (*direction technique*). In May 2013, a parliamentary report on the intelligence services criticized the DCRI and its treatment of the March 2012 Merah killings. The DGSI is no longer under the General Directorate of the National Police's supervision, but remains under the interior minister. Its staff is mostly from police superintendants (*commissaires*) and officers (*officiers*) from the National Police, but is seeking diversification. Unlike their British counterparts, DGSI officers have a judiciary capability (*officiers de police judiciaire*), which enhances their abilities, especially in counterterrorism and counterintelligence affairs.

Of the four specialized agencies under the Defense Ministry's supervision are the DRM and the DPSD, making this ministry one of the most involved in intelligence with NATO countries.

For its part, the **DRM**, which reports to the chief of Defense Staff, has the mission to meet the intelligence requirements of "military interest" (*renseignement d'intérêt militaire*, a notion coined in 1992) and those of the military's operational and organic commands. It is responsible for centralizing, analyzing, exploiting, and disseminating military intelligence among the authorities and bodies concerned. DRM is committed on all overseas theaters of operations in support of French forces.

The **DPSD** is the service available to the defense minister for the protection of its personnel, information, equipment, sensitive installations, and industrial infrastructures. Structured around permanent entities in the defense areas, overseas and abroad, the DPSD's territorial coverage ensures permanent operational cooperation with the armed forces. It is supplemented by a presence among the forces deployed in theaters of operations. Essentially acting in a preventive manner, DPSD collects, analyzes, and disseminates information

---

9. B. Bajolet, "La DGSE, outil de réduction de l'incertitude?," *Revue Défense Nationale* No. 766, janvier 2014, 27-31.

relating to potential threats against the interests of the defense establishment in the broadest sense.

The Finances Ministry hosts the DNRED and TRACFIN. The **DNRED** is attached to the General Directorate of Customs and is responsible for implementing the policy of intelligence, oversight, and fight against fraud. It's the less publicized service but has a strong reputation of efficiency. **TRACFIN** is an intelligence service associated with the financial departments, analogous to the US Treasury Department's Financial Crimes Enforcement Network (FinCEN). It fights illegal financial networks, money laundering, and terrorist financing. The service is responsible for collating and analyzing suspicious transaction reports that some institutions are required by law to report (the banks being amongst them). It does not have its own collection capability; rather it relies mostly on the compulsory collaboration of economic organizations.

Toward an Intelligence Community

In accordance with the White Paper, governance of these services has been strengthened with the establishment of the CNR and of a national intelligence coordinator (*coordonnateur national du renseignement*). This community approach, clearly inspired by foreign examples, reflected the top-level political decisions to respond to the international terrorist threat. In addition, a National Academy for Intelligence (*Académie du renseignement*) has been established.

The CNR, established on 23 July 2008, acts as the steering committee of the French intelligence services. It took over the responsibilities of the Interdepartmental Intelligence Committee (*Comité interministériel du renseignement*, CIR), a body established in 1959 under the responsibility of the prime minister's General Secretariat of National Defense (*Secrétariat général de la défense et de la sécurité nationale*, SGDSN), that, according to some commentators, never properly exercised its coordination function. Incidentally, the new organization has transferred the political responsibility across the Seine River, from the prime minister to the president. The previous CIR met infrequently at the principals' level. Placing the CNR under the president gave the chief of state the means to control intelligence more directly.[10] The CNR is now a specialized function of the Defense Council (*Conseil de défense*), established with the Fifth Republic by its founder, Charles de Gaulle. The CNR acts as a US National Security Council committee where the principals are the prime minister, the relevant ministers, the directors of the intelligence and security services, and the national intelligence coordinator. Its role is to provide strategic direction and priorities for intelligence through a National Intelligence Policy Plan (*Plan national d'orientation du renseignement*, PNOR) every three years, which is more or less a roadmap shared by all.

---

10. Bajolet, B., op.cit.

The synergy between those services is also pursued through the supervising of the equipment programs (especially informatics and electronics) so that they can be mutualized.

The council's creation has been accompanied by the creation of a **national intelligence coordinator** whose task is to ensure the CNR's good functioning. He participates in setting the political administrations' policies and priorities, especially through the PNOR and supervises the *mutualisation* of the main capacities. Through regular meetings with the directors of the different services, he facilitates, with his staff, exchanges between those services that have different cultures. The national intelligence coordinator advises the president of the Republic in the field of intelligence and conveys his instructions to the various services. The coordinator also prepares a daily intelligence summary for the president. The coordinator reports to the CNR and oversees the implementation of council decisions.

The 2008 White Paper states that the national intelligence coordinator is the "intelligence's entry point for the President of the Republic" but it does not prevent the president from direct contact with the chiefs of the main intelligence and security services. The coordinator is supported by a "light support structure" of experts drawn from relevant ministries (Foreign Affairs, Defense, Interior, Finance) or from the services themselves.

To foster a community, with shared interests, goals, affinities, beliefs and culture, and develop a common French intelligence "culture," a **National Academy for Intelligence** (*Académie du renseignement*) was established in 2008. It is responsible for training personnel of the intelligence services under the authorities of the ministers of internal security, defense, economy, and budget, to strengthen links within the French Intelligence Community as well as "disseminating a French intelligence culture." It designs, organizes, and implements initial and ongoing training activities for the services, and helps raise the general awareness of intelligence. It does not aim to substitute for the different services' internal training, but it promotes "mutual understanding and executive mobility between different services."[11] This institutional evolution matches recent doctrinal and conceptual changes. With the adoption of the "national security" notion and the affirmation of a continuum between defense and domestic security, the Academy reflects a common effort even if the various services stay distinct from each other.[12]

Improved Oversight of the Intelligence Services

France has devised a rather unique oversight system, which is in the pro-

---

11. Lucile Dromer-North, in J.-F. Dumont, *L'Académie du renseignement*, http://european-security.com/n_index.php?id=5873.
12. Coste, op.cit.

cess of being overhauled. The intelligence services are subject to the scrutiny of both administrative and judiciary judges. They are also overseen by the Audit Court (*Cour des comptes*) — the equivalent of the US' Government Accountability Office (GAO), which acts as a financial watchdog. And they are obviously subjected to internal oversights. For instance, within the Defense Ministry, intelligence services (strictly military) are subject to the ministry's internal audit bodies and inspections such as the General Inspection of the Armed Forces (*Contrôle général des armées*). An exception is the DGSE, which, while being administratively attached to the Defense Ministry since 1966, is under the *de facto* authority of the president of the Republic and the prime minister. Very recently, an Intelligence Inspection has also been established (July 2014) to exercise oversight duties over the services. It is placed under the prime minister's authority and its tasks consist in monitoring, auditing, consulting, and evaluating the French intelligence services.

But, what is more unique and specific to both French history and culture are the oversight by some autonomous administrative entities (*autorités administratives indépendantes*, AAI) not placed under a minister's direct authority and the intrinsic weakness of parliamentary oversight. AAI are state institutions in charge of ensuring the regulation of some sectors considered as essential, for which the government doesn't want to intervene directly. Although they are budgetarily linked to a ministry, the AAI are not subordinated to its authority. Two kinds of those exist, serving two different purposes: protecting citizens or regulating an economic activity. They take no orders, instructions, or advice from the government and their members are not revocable. Their existence is an exception to Article 20 of the French Constitution according to which "the government exercises its authority of administration."

Among the AAI, two main ones oversee the intelligence services' activities: the National Commission for the Oversight of Security Interceptions (*Commission nationale de contrôle des interceptions de sécurité*, CNCIS) and the National Commission on Informatics and Liberties (*Commission nationale de l'informatique et des libertés*, CNIL).

Established in 1991, the **CNCIS** supervises the legality of security interceptions. Chaired by a retired judge or senior civil servant, the Commission expresses its opinion on proposals for all non-judiciary telecommunications interceptions before the prime minister gives his approval. Once approved by the prime minister, these interceptions are permitted to obtain "information relating to national security; safeguard of the essential elements of scientific and economic potential of France; or prevention of terrorism, crime, and delinquency" according to the 1991 law. When CNCIS finds a violation of the law, it has the power to send to the prime minister a recommendation to stop an interception. It also has the power and duty to report to the judicial authority any breach of the law. It exerts two kinds of oversight: an *a priori* one and *a* *posteriori* one. Exercising *a priori* oversight, the CNCIS must verify the legality of requests for interception security, but this oversight is not very strict since the CNCIS must just check whether the tapping has been authorized by competent ministers, and if it complies with the quotas (maximum simultaneous interceptions ordered) and its intended purpose. The *a posteriori* oversight concerns the execution of intercepts. It reviews the recording, transcription and duration of interceptions; reviews the services' capacities; and examines individual complaints and denunciations to any judicial authority.

The **CNIL** is another AAI created in 1978. It is responsible for ensuring that information technology is serving the interests of the citizens and is not impairing human identity, human rights, private life, or individual or public liberties. Its reach is far broader than only oversight of intelligence services, but this AAI participates in the citizen's protection when it comes to intelligence issues, although it faces some limitations regarding questions involving defense and national security.

For a long time, relations between Parliament and intelligence services in France have been either complex or non-existent. Mutual trust is the primary factor. The services resisted parliamentary inquiries, being unsure that the top secrets (*secret défense*) would be protected. When the first attempts under the Fifth Republic in 1945 came up to exert oversight over the intelligence services, General de Gaulle stressed that parliamentary oversight over the intelligence services "should better be avoided." After several aborted attempts (in 1971, 1985, 1988, and in 1999 especially) — many following public intelligence abuses or failures[13] — legislation proposed by the government established a Parliamentary Delegation on Intelligence (*Délégation Parlementaire au Renseignement,* DPR) in 2007. Previously, France was the only Occidental democratic country, apart from Portugal, not to have a parliamentary oversight mechanism over its services.

The **DPR** is a joint body of the National Assembly and the Senate, the two chambers of the French Parliament. It represents progress by giving "a clear and solid legal framework concerning the protection of secrecy, regarding the dialogue between Parliament and the intelligence services" and allows "an overview of the organization and activity of the intelligence services."

The DPR's creation paved the way for parliamentary oversight of intelligence, but its prerogatives were so limited compared to its mission that it received serious criticisms. Owing to this, and a more general concern for having a legal framework for the intelligence services, a special ad hoc commit-

13. In 1971 after the "Delouette Affair," when a SDECE agent was caught convoying 44kg of heroin by the US Customs in New Jersey and alleged he was acting on the orders of his service. In 1985 and 1988, after the "Rainbow Warrior" episode and in 1999 after a possible involvement of the French services in Rwanda's genocide. J.-J. Urvoas and P. Verchere, "Rapport d'information sur l'évaluation du cadre juridique applicable aux services de renseignement," *Assemblée nationale,* May 2013, 77, http://www.assemblee-nationale.fr/14/pdf/rap-info/i1022.pdf.

tee of the National Assembly proposed in 2013 to reform the DPR, promoting an expansion of its powers and capabilities. In 2013, following the publication of the French White Paper on defense and national security, which promised an expansion of the powers of the DPR, the *Loi de Programmation Militaire* (Defense Programming Law) for 2014-2019 charged the DPR with "exercising parliamentary oversight over the government action on intelligence and evaluates public policy in this area." This reform diluted the Committee for Auditing Special Funds (*Commission de vérification des fonds spéciaux*, CVFS). This AAI, established in 2001, is responsible for ensuring that the special funds, unvouched expenses voted for the services' operational needs and spent through a special procedure, are used according to the Finance Law (*Loi de Finances*). It checks the regularity of special funds expenditures by ensuring the accuracy of their accounting. It has the responsibility to verify that these funds were used to finance activities, which, because of their special nature, could not be funded through other means. Although the DPR reform extended the powers of this parliamentarian body, it came with a limited scope regarding what could have been expected and does not have equivalent authority as other countries' parliaments, such as the German *Bundestag*.

Thus, the French intelligence and security services have gone through various reforms aiming at building a trustworthy and cooperative intelligence community. Those reforms are embedded in the redefinition of the concept of national security, where domestic security is considered more and more relevant, and are a response to the protean nature of today's threats. With a budget of €2.1 billion (about US $2.8 billion) and a consolidated staff of about 13,000 people, the French services seem able to cope with the many challenges facing *la Grande Nation*.

READINGS FOR INSTRUCTORS

Becker, A. "The Spy Who Couldn't Possibly Be French: Espionage (and) Culture in France," *Journal of Intelligence History No. 1*, Summer 2001.

Chopin, O. et al. "Étudier le renseignement en France," *Hérodote No. 140*, 2011, 91-102.

Coste, F. "L'adoption du concept de sécurité nationale: une révolution conceptuelle qui peine à s'exprimer," Recherche & documents, *Fondation pour la recherche stratégique No. 3*, 2011.

Denece E. and G. Arboit. "Intelligence Studies in France," *International Journal of Intelligence and Counterintelligence 23 (4)*, August 2010.

Forcade, O. "Considérations sur le renseignement, la défense nationale et l'Etat secret en France aux XIXème et XXème siècles," *Revue historique des armées 247*, 2007. http://rha.revues.org/2013.

French White Paper on National Defense and Security – June 2008, http://www.ambafrance-ca.org/IMG/pdf/Livre_blanc_Press_kit_english_version.pdf.

French White Paper on Defense and National Security – June 2013, *http://www. rpfranceotan.org/IMG/pdf/White_paper_on_defense_2013.pdf*.

Forcade, O. "Objets, approches et problématiques d'une histoire française du renseignement: un champ historiographique en construction," *Histoire, économie & société, 31ème année*, 2012, 99-110.

Hayez P., "'Renseignement': The new French intelligence policy," *International Journal of Intelligence and Counterintelligence 23 (3)*, June 2010.

Laurent, S. "Is there something wrong with intelligence in France? The birth of the modern secret state," *Intelligence and National Security 28 (3)*, June 2013.

Lepri C. "Parliamentary and specialized oversight of security and intelligence agencies in France" in European Parliament's study Parliamentary oversight of intelligence and security agencies in the European Union – 2011, 207-217, *http://www.europarl.europa.eu/document/activities/cont/201109/20110927ATT27674/20110927ATT27674EN.pdf*

Pautrat R. "Le renseignement aujourd'hui ou les nouveaux moyens de la puissance," *Le Débat*, February 1992.

Pennetier J.-M. "The Springtime of French Intelligence," *Intelligence and National Security 11 (4)*, October 1996.

Porch D. *The French Secret Services: From the Dreyfus Affair to the Gulf War* (New York: Farrar, Strauss & Giroux, 1995).

Sueur, J.-P. "Rapport relatif à l'activité de la délégation parlementaire au renseignement pour l'année 2013," *Sénat – April 2014*, *http://www.senat.fr/rap/r13-462/r13-4621.pdf*.

Urvoas J.-J. and P. Verchere, "Rapport d'information sur l'évaluation du cadre juridique applicable aux services de renseignement," *Assemblée nationale*, May 2013, *http://www.assemblee-nationale.fr/14/pdf/rap-info/i1022.pdf*.

Urvoas J.-J., and F. Vadillo. "Réformer les services de renseignement français," note *Fondation Jean Jaurès*, April 2011, *http://www.jean-jaures.org/Publications/Essais/Reformer-les-services-de-renseignement-francais*.

Philippe Hayez, a graduate of Sciences-Po Paris and Ecole nationale d'administration, is an adjunct professor at the Paris School of International Affairs, Sciences-Po Paris. As a civil servant, he was a member of the French Defense Ministry's Policy Planning Staff (Délégation aux Affaires stratégiques) and took managing positions in the French DGSE between 2000 and 2006. He publishes occasional papers on intelligence and security. *philippe.hayez@sciencespo.fr*

Hedwige Regnault de Maulmin, a 2013 master's in international law graduate from Jean Moulin Lyon III University, is now a master's student at the Paris School of International Affairs, Sciences-Po Paris. *hedwige.regnaultdemaulmin@sciencespo.fr*

GUIDE TO THE STUDY OF INTELLIGENCE

Dutch Intelligence and Security Services

Eleni Braat

The Dutch Government institutionalised the gathering of intelligence prior to the First World War in 1913. Since then, the Dutch intelligence services have evolved through five stages. In the first, between 1913 and 1940, when the Netherlands adhered to a policy of neutrality, intelligence was small-scale, centralised, and institutionally clearly demarcated. In the second stage, during the Second World War and the years immediately afterward, Dutch intelligence was chaotic, decentralised, and generally malfunctioning, characterized by blurred objectives and personal disputes over areas of responsibility. At the height of the Cold War in the fifties, sixties, and seventies, the third stage, the five various services stabilized institutionally, facing well-defined areas of interest. They remained decentralized and did not excel in efficient collaboration. The fourth stage, between the end of the 1980s and 2002, was characterized by attempts to respond to diffuse threats and political calls for greater efficiency and transparency. Finally, since 2002, Dutch intelligence has been centralised and clearly demarcated, as it was between 1913 and 1940, though not small-scale. The surprise of the 9/11 terrorist attacks led to a significant growth in the civil intelligence and security service and blurred the differences between civil and military intelligence.

Intelligence During Neutrality, 1913-1940

At the beginning of the 20th century the Netherlands was as affluent as its neighbouring countries. It possessed a colonial empire that clearly outsized its European territory, which it had conquered largely in the 17th century. The years of conquest were followed by a period of passiveness: the government did not aspire to new territory and did not have enemies. All it wished was for things to remain as they were. A policy of armed neutrality suited this purpose best. To remain neutral, however, the government needed to be well informed of the strategic ambitions of others. With this aim, the General Staff Third Section (GSIII) was founded in 1913. GSIII, was a military intelligence service, headed and manned by a single person, Hendrik A. C. Fabius. During the war, the staff increased to 10 persons and in 1918 to 25.[1] It acquired most of its intelligence through open source material, like foreign newspapers and journals. The police supplied it with counterespionage intelligence. After the war, Bolshevik revolutionaries, albeit limited in the Netherlands, led to the formation of a security service, the Central Intelligence Service (CID). The separation from GSIII suggests more than the CID represented in practice: GSIII and CID personnel were the same, but occasionally operated under a different name. This vague distinction between military and civil intelligence continued throughout the interwar years.[2] In addition to GSIII, another intelligence service, GSIV, was concerned with, among others, censorship and code breaking, in which it was rather successful.[3]

Ever since GSIII was dissolved in 1940, it has had a bad reputation. This was mainly due to the November 1939 Venlo incident, when the German *Sicherheitsdienst* (Security Service, SD) kidnapped two British MI-6 (Secret Intelligence Service, SIS) officers in the Netherlands, with whom GSIII was closely collaborating.[4] The collaboration with MI-6 was sensitive. Despite this, the government remained very keen on maintaining neutrality and "normal" relationships with Nazi Germany. A second reason for GSIII's bad reputation was that the service failed to foresee the war and that, accordingly, it had not made any preparations to manage the agency in case of governmental exile. Hence, when the government cabinet and Dutch Queen Wilhelmina fled to London on the day after the German invasion on May 10, 1940, they found themselves with little intelligence capacity in the occupied Netherlands, needing to establish intelligence networks from scratch.

---

1. Frans Kluiters, *De Nederlandse inlichtingen – en veiligheidsdiensten* (The Hague: Sdu, 1993), 192-193. Edwin Ruis, *Spionnennest 1914-1918. Spionage vanuit Nederland, in België, Duitsland en Engeland* (Meppel, NL: Just Publishers, 2012), 37.
2. J.A. van Reijn, "De wordingsgeschiedenis van de MIVD," in B.A. de Graaf, E.R. Muller, J.A. van Reijn (eds.), *Inlichtingen – en veiligheidsdiensten* (Alphen aan den Rijn, NL: Kluwer, 2010), 74.
3. Ruis, *Spionnennest*: 39.
4. Unreliable informants managed to convince GSIII and MI-6 representatives of the existence of an opposition group within the German Wehrmacht that was seeking support against Hitler. They fell into the trap when in November 1939 they agreed to meet the leader of this non-existent group by the Dutch-German border near Venlo. See B.G.J. de Graaff, "Trefpunt Venlo. Amerikaans-Belgisch-Brits-Frans-Nederlandse spionagesamenwerking ten aanzien van nazi-Duitsland in 1939," in *Mededelingen van de Sectie Militaire Geschiedenis*, deel 15, 1993.

Intelligence, Power Struggles, and Personal Loyalty, 1940-1948

During the Second World War, when the Dutch Government was in exile and officially allied with the British Government, numerous Dutch intelligence and subversive services succeeded one another, overlapping each other's work. A striking characteristic of Dutch wartime intelligence was that former GSIII personnel were not part of the intelligence community until 1944 and that, consequently, there was very little intelligence experience. Dutch services often competed with each other, especially for establishing relationships with British intelligence agencies. And their continued existence greatly depended on personal sympathies between Dutch and British intelligence officials, and the loyalty of their leaders vis-a-vis Queen Wilhelmina. The Queen had made Dutch wartime intelligence a matter of personal concern, in which she was keen to interfere. She considered the services the most important of all government institutions-in-exile.[5] Willing or not, the Dutch depended on their British counterparts for the recruitment and training of their agents, the dropping of agents into the Netherlands and communications between London and the Netherlands.[6]

Dutch intelligence during the war suffered from a long period (May 1940-mid 1943) of critical instability and a subsequent gradual period of recovery until the end of the war. During the period of instability, in November 1942 until the end of the war, the CID was succeeded by three services with the same name, when the Bureau of Intelligence (BI) took over. Part of the blame for this rather chaotic period was the presence of the unbreakable quartet of the unfathomable Francois van 't Sant as head of the first CID, SIS Dutch section head C. E. C. Rabagliati, their adventurous and confident agent Erik Hazel-hoff Roelfzema, and their personal ties with Queen Wilhelmina. This quartet derived its powerful position from the key positions of its members within the Dutch Government — Dutch ministers were generally afraid to contradict Queen Wilhelmina, a rather dominant personality — and within the Dutch and British intelligence communities. Moreover, Van 't Sant, Hazelhoff Roelfzema, Rabagliati, and Queen Wilhelmina all had in common their rather outspoken preferences with whom they wished, or absolutely refused, to collaborate. They thereby monopolized the gathering of intelligence in the Netherlands by refusing to work with others than themselves.

On the subversive side, which included active measures of sabotage and covert actions against Nazi Germany, the period of crisis lasted longer with the Bureau for the Preparation for the Return to the Netherlands (BVT); its military

---

5. According to Van 't Sant. Loe de Jong, *Het Koninkrijk der Nederlanden tijdens de Tweede Wereldoorlog* (The Hague: Staatsuitgeverij, 1969-1994), 843, 973. http://www.niod.nl/nl/koninkrijk.

6. Eleni Braat, "Secrecy, power struggles and personal loyalty. Dutch secret services-in-exile and relationships to their British counterparts," paper prepared for presentation at the conference *Secret Services-in-Exile. The Secret War Fought From London 1939-1945*, London, September 26-27, 2013.

successor, the Office for the Preperation for Military Reoccupation (MVT); and the Military Intelligence Service (MID). They all spent quite some time on power struggles with the British services over control of operations, until the Bureau Special Assignments (BBO) took over initiating a more harmonious period in March 1944.

In the Dutch East Indies, the government gathered intelligence through the Netherlands Forces Intelligence Service (NEFIS). Established in 1943 and operating from Melbourne, Australia, until the end of the war, it moved to Batavia (now Jakarta) in 1945. Whereas NEFIS concentrated on military intelligence during the war, it moved its main focus to (underground) political organisations when resistance to Dutch colonial rule grew after the war. In 1948, NEFIS was reorganised and renamed Central Military Intelligence Service (CMI). When Indonesia gained independence the next year, the CMI was dissolved.[7]

In the Netherlands, the postwar situation proved to be just as tumultuous as the early forties. An influential figure during this period until 1961 was Louis Einthoven.[8] In May 1945, he became head of the newly founded Bureau of National Security (BNV), which was tasked to remove the remaining pro-Nazi espionage and sabotage networks in the Netherlands. In his memoirs, Einthoven describes how difficult it was to recruit reliable personnel while lacking the time to check their often shady and violent wartime backgrounds. The service's fast and uncontrolled growth to about 1,360 people[9] was the principal reason for its dissolution in December 1946. In the meantime, Einthoven had prepared secretly for the BNV's successor, the Central Security Service (CVD). Contrary to the BNV, it was supposed to have a more permanent character; that is, it was to resemble the British Security Service (MI-5) organisationally, and focus on communism rather than on Nazi collaborators and sympathizers. In 1949, the CVD continued under the Interior Ministry as the National Security Service (BVD).

Stabilisation During the Cold War, 1949-1987

During the Cold War, the Netherlands had five main services whose existence, despite their occasionally overlapping operational foci, remained stable from the end of the 1940's until the end of the 1980s. Civil and military intelligence, moreover, was more clearly delineated than during the preceding years. From 1952, Parliament had strengthened its monitoring of the BVD through the Standing Committee on the BVD, which later extended to all security and intelligence services. Despite its *de jure* authority, the Committee provided only

---

7. Kluiters, *Inlichtingen – en veiligheidsdiensten*, 129-136, 259-270.
8. For more information on Louis Einthoven, see Dick Engelen, *Geschiedenis van de Binnenlandse Veiligheidsdienst* (The Hague: Sdu, 1995), 60-81. See Einthoven's memoirs for a personal account of this specific period, *Tegen de stroom* (Apeldoorn: Semper Agendo, 1974).
9. Engelen, *Veiligheidsdienst*: 83.

minor *de facto* parliamentary control of the services.[10]

The BVD grew considerably in the 1950s because of two anti-communist measures that required substantial data collection on communist political activities and individual preferences. Members of the Communist Party and related organizations were excluded from working in government organisations. And, in case of an imminent revolution or conflict, the government was allowed to intern persons suspected of being supportive of a (communist) revolution or a foreign (Soviet) power.[11] Through these measures, the BVD developed a strong focus on the Communist Party, which characterized the service until the beginning of the 1980s. By then, infiltration in the Communist Party was so successful that the BVD had at least one agent in every section of the party and that it managed to found a successful rival, the Marxist-Leninist party.[12] This fixed focus on communism led to some operational ossification,[13] even when other threats arose in the 1970s. In the 1980s, parliamentary criticism on the persistent focus on communism made the BVD finally loosen its grip on the Communist Party.[14]

After the Second World War, the government also founded the External Intelligence Service (BID, later IDB).[15] It was in many respects a continuation of the wartime BI. The BID/IDB had a difficult start until the 1960s and an abrupt ending in 1994. During these years, it never earned much respect within (or outside) government ministries. It never employed more than 70 officials, it had almost no operational knowledge of Eastern Europe, and did not foresee major political events like the Hungarian uprising or the building of the Berlin Wall.[16] The IDB's history was characterized by lamentable working relationships, operational failure, and poor political support. An exception was the recruitment of an important source in Indonesia and the ensuing long-term successful Operation Virgil.[17] When some of its personnel publicly voiced their

---

10. Eleni Braat, "Recurring tensions between secrecy and democracy: Arguments about the Security Service in Dutch Parliament, 1975-1995," paper prepared for presentation at the International Intelligence History Association conference, *Intelligence, Democracy and Transparency*, 2-4 May 2014. Tutzing. Constant Hijzen is preparing a PhD dissertation at Leiden University entitled *Publiek geheim: de Nederlandse veiligheidsdiensten tussen 1912 en 1992*, in which he also addresses the Standing Committee's shortcomings.

11. Dick Engelen, 'Beknopte geschiedenis van de AIVD', B.A. de Graaf, E.R. Muller, J.A. van Reijn (eds.), *Inlichtingen – en veiligheidsdiensten*, Alphen aan den Rijn: Kluwer, 2010: 64. Chris Vos, Rens Broekhuis, Lies Janssen & Barbara Mounier, *De geheime dienst. Verhalen over de BVD* (Amsterdam: Boom, 2005), 102-125.

12. Dick Engelen, *Frontdienst. De BVD in de Koude Oorlog* (Amsterdam: Boom, 2007), 83-105.

13. Eleni Braat, *Van oude jongens, de dingen die voorbij gaan... Een sociale geschiedenis van de Binnenlandse Veiligheidsdienst, 1945-1998* (Zoetermeer: AIVD, 2012), 153.

14. Engelen, *Frontdienst* (De BVD), 230-236.

15. The IDB's highly secretive nature and the disappearance or inaccessibility of an important part of its archive have seriously hampered historical research. A significant and engaging account of the IDB is Bob de Graaff & Cees Wiebes, *Villa Maarheeze. De geschiedenis van de Inlichtingendienst Buitenland* (The Hague: Sdu, 1998).

16. De Graaff & Wiebes *Villa Maarheeze*, 105-106, 412.

17. Operation Virgil concerned the valuable information an important Indonesian source provided to

dissatisfaction at the end of the 1980s, its dissolution was only one step away.

During the Cold War, military intelligence remained divided along three services: the Naval Intelligence Service (MARID); the Army Intelligence Service (MID, later LAMID), both founded in 1949; and the Air Force Intelligence Service (LUID), founded in 1951. Embedded in the MARID was the signals intelligence (SIGINT) organisation Mathematical Center (WKC), renamed Technical Information Collection Center (TIVC) after 1982. It provided the government with valuable information, for example, by decoding Indonesian communications traffic on Dutch New Guinea in the early 1960s and by intercepting European and Middle Eastern diplomatic correspondence during the oil crisis in October 1973.[18] The Cold War and the NATO alliance determined the separate, internationally embedded tasks of the three military intelligence services and their respective branch. The army and air force had to defend the North German Plain by land and air, and were under effective operational command of NATO. The naval tasks were targeted against hostile submarines and mines in the English Channel. Consequently, the international orientation of the three military intelligence services did not converge with a possible centralisation or nationalisation of their tasks. Rather than cooperating, the three services had a tendency to compete for resources and, sometimes, in operations.[19] This competition, painfully visible through a number of incidents, led to increased parliamentary criticism and, in 1987, to the creation of a single military intelligence service. Interestingly, the foundation of this centralised Military Intelligence Service (MID) was not a consequence of the Cold War's nearing end.

Post-Cold War Transitions, 1987-2002

In the 1990s, the external civil intelligence service (IDB) was dissolved, the MID painstakingly moved from a centralized service in theory, to one in practice; and the BVD underwent drastic changes to address post-Cold War operational and political demands. This latter "revolution" deserves some extra attention.

In 1988, Arthur Docters van Leeuwen (1988-1995) became head of the BVD and ushered in a series of drastic changes that prepared the service for the post-Cold War period. He was eager to transform the service into a more

---

the IDB. This information concerned, for example, Indonesian strategic plans regarding the possible take-over of Dutch New Guinea, a Dutch colony until 1962. De Graaff and Wiebes argue that the agent in question was H. Ruslan Abdulgani, Indonesian high-level diplomat and close collaborator of President Sukarno. Abdulgani denied he was ever an IDB agent. De Graaff & Wiebes, *Villa Maarheeze,* 121-182.

18. Cees Wiebes, "Dutch Sigint during the Cold War, 1945-1994"; in Matthew M. Aid & Cees Wiebes, *Secrets of Signals Intelligence during the Cold War and Beyond* (Frank Cass & Co, 2001), 243; Kluiters, *Inlichtingen – en veiligheidsdiensten,* 239.

19. J. A. van Reijn, "MIVD," 79-80.

politically responsive, flexible, and transparent organization, as he deemed fit for the coming international changes. Under his lead, the BVD went through a major internal reorganisation to make the service responsive to more diffuse and unexpected threats. Docters van Leeuwen appeared on television, rendering public accounts of an unprecedented amount of organisational and even operational information. The service started issuing annual reports on its interests and goals. And a historian was commissioned to write an official history of the service, disclosing a remarkable amount of information about its operational past.[20] As the stable Cold War threats had disappeared, the BVD's operational future proved rather unclear in the 1990s. At the end of the decade, however, the BVD started to pay increasing attention to so-called "integrative problems" in society and radicalism within migrant communities, anticipating its operational foci after 9/11.

Civil and Military Intelligence Since 2002

A 2002 law on the intelligence and security services and the 9/11 attacks in the US prompted significant changes that characterize the most recent stage for Dutch intelligence. The new law replaced the MID with the Military Intelligence and Security Service (MIVD) and the BVD with the General Intelligence and Security Service (AIVD). This meant that civil intelligence was again institutionalized, this time under the same roof as the security service. The law also created the independent Review Committee on the Intelligence and Security Services (CTIVD). It issues public supervision reports and it advises the responsible ministers, both when asked and on its own initiative. This oversight committee complemented the parliamentary Standing Committee, which had been for a long-time subject of criticism for its passiveness and inertia.

The 9/11 attacks led to a major increase in AIVD personnel, from about 580 at the end of the 1990s to about 1,600 in 2014; whereas the MIVD grew less. With the blurring differences between civil and military intelligence, the AIVD and MIVD overlapped each other more than before. Since 2004, coordination has occurred largely through the National Coordinator for Security and Counterterrorism (NCTV). This is a counterterrorism unit analyzing terrorist threats by coordinating assessments of, among others, the AIVD and MIVD. Also, the increased use of signals intelligence by both the AIVD and MIVD resulted in the National Signals Intelligence Organisation (NSO, established in 2003) merging in 2014 into a joint AIVD-MIVD project, the Joint SIGINT Cyber Unit (JSCU).

This collaboration between the AIVD and MIVD is characteristic of a trend of the last few years. Since 2008, the economic crisis and the associ-

---

20. Dick Engelen's key publications include his PhD dissertation *Geschiedenis van de Binnenlandse Veiligheidsdienst*, (The Hague: Sdu, 1995) and *Frontdienst* (Amsterdam: Boom, 2007).

ated government financial constraints halted the AIVD's growth and led to a number of reorganisations within the service. Most importantly, budget cuts have been minor, but Parliament seems to be more concerned about efficiency and collaboration than in the past. Some parliamentarians even contemplate an AIVD-MIVD merger. The combination of the blurring of civil and military intelligence on the one hand, and the economic crisis on the other, will probably shape the principal challenges for the years to come.

Conclusions

From a historical perspective, the present-day situation is remarkable in four respects. First, the Netherlands has only two main services, compared to the multiple (competing and overlapping) services from the past. Second, the two services have now been centralised, whereas this has not happened for both civil and military intelligence since the beginning of the Second World War. Third, the need for external intelligence now seems politically more accepted than during the Cold War, and between 1994 and 2002, when the government had no external intelligence service at all. Fourth, the distinct security and intelligence activities are now being carried out under the same roof, on both the military and the civil side. Such monolithic services were common in the Soviet Union and Eastern Europe during the Cold War, while they have become particularly uncommon after the Cold War in Russia, the US, and Eastern and Western European countries.[21] The Netherlands, in this respect, is a notable exception.

READINGS FOR INSTRUCTORS

The field of intelligence studies in the Netherlands is a small but growing area of research. The majority of the literature in this field has been written in Dutch and is, therefore, largely inaccessible to non-Dutch speakers. For example, indispensable overviews by Dick Engelen on the BVD and Bob de Graaff and Cees Wiebes on the IDB are in Dutch. This severely restricts comparisons between Dutch and foreign intelligence services, as foreign scholars find it difficult to include a "Dutch" case. Research on Dutch intelligence, moreover, risks parochialism when focusing on the Dutch environment uniquely. Another factor that hampers the scope of research on Dutch intelligence is the limited access to secret services' archives. This is due to an exemption in the Dutch freedom of information act for security and intelligence services, the painstakingly long process to make parts of the BVD archive publicly accessible in the National Archives, and the AIVD's more general lack of transparency regarding publications on its past. The AIVD also refuses to cooperate in the publication of memoirs of its retired officials

---

21. This last point is made by Engelen, "Beknopte geschiedenis van de AIVD," 69.

(for example, Frits Hoekstra), in contrast, for example, to the CIA.[22]

Nevertheless, interested non-Dutch speakers may have a look at various AIVD publications on the service's topics of interest and, more interesting, the service's annual reports since 2001 in English.[23] Despite the lack of an English-language survey publication on the Dutch services, there are a small number of interesting publications, primarily on the BVD/AIVD. These are:

Graaf, B.A., "The Netherlands," in Stuart Farson, Peter Gill, Mark Phythian, Shlomo Shpiro, PSI Handbook of Global Security and Intelligence: National Approaches (Westport, CT: Praeger Security International, 2008), 339-360.

Graaff, B. de & C. Wiebes, "Intelligence and the Cold War behind the Dikes: The relationship between the American and Dutch intelligence communities, 1946-1994" in Intelligence and National Security 12, 1997, 41-58.

Graaff, B. de, "Dutch-American intelligence relations," in H. Krabbendam, C. van Minnen, & G. Scott-Smith (eds.). Four Centuries of Dutch-American Relations 1609-2009 (Amsterdam: Boom, 2009), 674-682.

Graaff, B. de, "From security threat to perception of vital interest. The changing perceptions of the Dutch security service, 1945-1991," Conflict Quarterly 12, 1992, 9-35.

Hijzen, C.W. & Graaf, B.A. de, "Bound by silver cords. The Dutch intelligence community in a transatlantic context," in G. Scott-Smith (ed.), Obama, US Politics and Transatlantic Relations: Change or Continuity (New York: Peter Lang, 2012), 201-217.

Hijzen, C.W., "The perpetual adversary. How Dutch security services perceived communism (1918-1989), Historical Social Research 38 (1), 2013, 166-199.

Hijzen, C.W., "More than a ritual dance. The Dutch practice of parliamentary oversight and control in the intelligence community," Security and Human Rights 24 (3-4), 2014, 227-238.

Platje, W., "Dutch Sigint and the conflict with Indonesia, 1950-1962," in Matthew M. Aid & Cees Wiebes (eds.), Secrets of Signals Intelligence During the Cold War and Beyond (Frank Cass & Co, 2001), 285-312.

Wiebes, C., "Dutch Sigint during the Cold War, 1945-1994," in Matthew M. Aid & Cees Wiebes (eds.), Secrets of Signals Intelligence During the Cold War and Beyond (Frank Cass & Co, 2001), 243-284

Eleni Braat is a lecturer at the Leiden University Institute for History, Holland, The Netherlands. Her research interests include 20th century administrative, international, and intelligence history. Braat's most recent book is: Van oude jongens, de dingen die voorbij gaan. Een sociale geschiedenis van de Binnenlandse Veiligheidsdienst, 1945-1998 (Old boys and the Things That Pass. A Social History of the Dutch Security Service, 1945-1998).[24] It focuses on the Dutch Security Service's

22. Bob de Graaff, "Accessibility of secret service archives in the Netherlands," Intelligence and National Security 12 (2), 1997, 154-160. Ben de Jong, "Hoe transparant is de AIVD?," Liberaal Reveil 50 (3), 2009, 133-139. Ben de Jong, "De AIVD houdt zijn verleden binnenskamers," Socialisme & Democratie, 29 September 2014.
23. https://www.aivd.nl/english/publications-press/aivd-publications/ (last visited on 20 December 2014)
24. http://www.inlichtingendiensten.nl/literatuur/oudejongens.pdf

organizational culture. This book was published in her capacity as the official historian of the Dutch General Intelligence and Security Service (AIVD) (2008-2014). She received her PhD in history from the European University Institute, Florence, in 2008.

GUIDE TO THE STUDY OF INTELLIGENCE

Sweden's Intelligence Services

Michael Fredholm

For much of the twentieth century, Sweden has adhered to a policy of neutrality. It declined to participate in either of the world wars and avoided being a target of any of the belligerent powers. Its intelligence and security services played a major role supporting Sweden's foreign policy in both the First and particularly the Second World War. However, since details of these successes remained highly classified throughout the subsequent Cold War, this fact was little appreciated by later governments, which may have concluded that righteousness, not effective use of intelligence, had kept Sweden safe.

It was not by pure chance that Sweden's intelligence system functioned well during the world wars. Although Sweden opted out of foreign adventures after the Napoleonic wars, its armed forces possessed an intelligence tradition no less rich than those of the great European powers of long standing. Sweden's intelligence services operate today in an environment largely formed during the Second World War, but which originated far earlier.

Origins of the Swedish Intelligence System

An intelligence system existed very early in Sweden, although it was neither well organized nor formalized. In the late Viking Age, the Swedish king appointed bailiffs in the border regions. One of them, Eilif, among his other duties, was responsible for keeping an eye on developments on the Norwegian side of the border. In c. 1017, Norway's King Olaf moved with his army toward the border. Eilif sent out spies to monitor the Norwegian activities. However, King Olaf had already sent men to infiltrate Eilif's retinue, and these agents had Eilif assassinated.

While there existed a foreign intelligence system, there was no security service, at least not until Jöran Persson, the secretary and prosecutor for the mentally unstable King Erik XIV, established one in 1560. Persson's mission was to track down rivals among the nobility. In a ruthless and often deceitful manner, he produced a large number of death sentences, until eventually he himself was sentenced and executed by his own court. Persson's security organization was limited to a purely domestic role; the king controlled his own agents abroad. A document from 1566-1567 lists the names of agents in neighboring countries and as far away as at the courts of France, England, Spain, and several German states including the Imperial capital of Vienna. The king also ran agents in Poland, Russia, and in what had been the Kazan Khanate on the Volga.[1]

The Swedish intelligence system developed substantially during the Thirty Years War (1618-1648). A military engineering corps was established in 1613. Its responsibilities included producing reliable maps in all theaters of operations. In the field army, select cavalry patrols gathered tactical intelligence. Meanwhile, a strategic intelligence system was introduced. Swedish officers responsible for intelligence collection, referred to as "residents," were positioned in major European cities and were augmented by "correspondents" elsewhere throughout Europe, who sent intelligence reports back to Sweden. Correspondents were recruited in Vienna, the German states, and the Netherlands, France, Switzerland, and Italy. Ciphers of various kinds were used to maintain communications security, and records suggest (but do not prove) that the Swedes also broke foreign cipher systems.

Surviving documents show that sound principles of intelligence work were already understood, including those of intelligence planning and verification. When Johan Salvius was appointed resident in Hamburg, Lars Grubbe, who then ran the intelligence system, was dissatisfied at first with his reports. Grubbe accordingly directed the new resident to report more frequently on specifically Danish activities. In addition, Grubbe emphasized the need also to report the source of the information. "Distinguish between such intelligence that seems reliable and such information the correctness of which cannot be verified,"[2] he instructed the newly appointed resident. In a similar manner, within the field army, cavalry patrols were regularly dispatched to verify the information in tactical intelligence reports.

Military mapping became the responsibility of the Fortification Office. In 1673, a fortification officer was sent with a diplomatic mission to Moscow. On the way, he produced a manual on Russian fortifications, garrisons, artillery, and military organization, including details on the individual colonels, uniforms, and standards of each regiment. He also mapped and described the roads and waterways *en route* to Moscow.

---

1. A successor state of the Mongol Golden Horde located near the confluence of the Volga and Kama rivers in present central Russia, west of the Urals, Russia conquered it in 1552.
2. Generalstaben, *Sveriges krig 1611-1632: Bilagsband 1* (Stockholm: Generalstaben, 1937), 323.

In 1715, the Swedish diplomatic representative in London, Count Carl Gyllenborg, organized an intelligence network in the city and English ports to provide forewarning of Russia-bound ships, which carried strategic products and volunteers for the Russian Army. The intelligence reports were dispatched via small ships that would rendezvous with Swedish warships in the North Sea. The British arrested Gyllenborg in 1717.

Although Sweden's power and international standing eventually declined, military mapping remained an important task. In 1805, the Field Survey Corps was established for this purpose. In 1873, a Department of Military Statistics was created within the General Staff to process and analyze military attaché reports and published information. Around 1900, code breaking was the responsibility of Room 100 within the General Staff, headed by R. Torpadie, who previously had studied the cryptographic systems of the Thirty Years War. The Navy formed its own integral intelligence department, and in 1901, within a year of the first Swedish naval experiments in radiotelegraphy, it began to take an interest in signals intelligence (SIGINT).

Sweden remained at peace after the Napoleonic Wars. Its first national emergency in almost a century came in the Union Crisis of 1905, which resulted in the dissolution of the union between Sweden and Norway. As a result, that same year, Sweden established a clandestine Intelligence Bureau (Upplysningsbyrån, UB) within the General Staff tasked with both foreign and domestic intelligence. This was a new departure, as counterespionage and the suppression of political crimes traditionally had been the role of the police department in Stockholm; a secret police had been established in Stockholm as early as 1776. Although the Stockholm police continued to be responsible for domestic security, in 1908, the police began to cooperate with the General Staff, particularly in the monitoring of suspicious foreigners.

The First World War

Naval SIGINT may have been first to report the outbreak of war, and within a week had broken Russian encoded telegrams. At the time, Russian telegraphic communications with the West passed through Stockholm. This was too good an opportunity to ignore. In 1914, Sweden and Germany agreed to cooperate against Russian diplomatic communications. A special section was formed within the General Staff, consisting of Russian-speaking intelligence officers. They intercepted Russian telegrams and handed them over to the Germans. In return, they received the deciphered messages. In time, the Swedes began to engage in code breaking of its own, especially after the wife of the Swedish liaison officer in Germany smuggled particulars of the ciphers back to Sweden hidden in her corset. Among important Russian state telegrams intercepted was one in 1918 that reported the execution of the imperial family. During the war, naval SIGINT focused on the Russian Baltic Fleet, although it also made some efforts against the German Navy.

Even before the outbreak of war in 1914, it was decided to establish a common security service, as the *ad hoc* cooperation between the Stockholm police and the General Staff was regarded as insufficient. A special organization within the General Staff, known as the Police Bureau, consisting primarily of police detectives, was responsible for counterespionage and domestic security until early 1918, when both the Police Bureau and its mission were returned to the Stockholm police.

Between the Wars

In 1931, the new Air Force formed its own intelligence unit.[3] In 1937, the Defense Staff was formed as a joint services staff with an intelligence section that included both a foreign and a domestic department. Military attachés were subordinated to the intelligence section.

The Navy continued its SIGINT work. With the formation of the Defense Staff, a signals section was established, which was tasked with SIGINT intercepts and traffic analysis. A cryptography section, referred to as Unit IV, was also formed. In 1938, a joint services SIGINT collection unit was set up in the naval base of Karlskrona. It was named the Defense Staff Radio Establishment (*Försvarsstabens radioanstalt*, FRA).

The Stockholm Police Bureau continued to be responsible for counterespionage, in particular against foreigners, until 1933, when the National Police (*Statspolisen*) was established, in a first modest attempt to create a national police force. The counterespionage mission was then transferred to the new organization.

The Second World War

In 1942, the Defense Staff intelligence section was renamed Section II but with little substantive change. Far greater change took place with regard to intelligence collection. As a result of the 1939 Soviet attack on Finland, a clandestine human intelligence (HUMINT) unit was established, known as the Border Bureau (*Gränsbyrån*), and later renamed G Section (*G-sektionen*). The clandestine organization grew rapidly, hiring a considerable number of civilians. In 1942, it was placed under the head of Section II and renamed the C Bureau (*C-byrån*).

The most successful intelligence effort was SIGINT within Unit IV. A number of Soviet ciphers were broken; however, far more important to Swedish interests was the fact that, following the April 1940 German invasions of

---

3. The military services retained integral intelligence units until as late as 1981.

Norway and Denmark and the deployment of German troops to Finland, key German telegraphic communication lines passed through Sweden. While in the First World War, Germany had benefited from the fact that Russian telegraphic communications passed through Stockholm, this time Germany had to rely on Swedish landlines. And Sweden was not averse to tapping them. Germany relied on an advanced crypto-machine known as the Geheimschreiber ("secret writer"), a non-morse teleprinter system that was believed to be secure. However, in a masterful act of code breaking, Professor Arne Beurling broke the Geheimschreiber system and, from June 1940 until May 1943, the Swedes could read virtually all German military and diplomatic communications passing through their country. Even the results of German code-breaking efforts against Soviet ciphers were transmitted by Geheimschreiber, so copies of German intelligence reports on the Soviet Union could be read as well. Among valuable intelligence gained by the Swedes was information on the German plan to attack the Soviet Union in June 1941. This information was passed to the British through diplomatic channels. Most importantly, Sweden learned that the German troop movements would not result in an attack on Swedish territory, a keen concern after the invasions of Denmark and Norway. Swedish intelligence corroborated US SIGINT on Japanese diplomatic reporting from Berlin, thus influencing the British Joint Intelligence Committee assessment that Germany would likely attack the Soviet Union later in the month.

The Swedes broke the German teleprinter codes before the British did. The British first broke one of them, collectively referred to as "Fish," by hand in January 1942. By early 1943, assisted by an early computer, called Colossus, the British Government Code and Cipher School at Bletchley Park was reading Fish materials regularly. However, the most important teleprinter system read by the Swedes, called "Sturgeon" in Britain, Bletchley Park only broke later and never read regularly. In June 1942, the Germans learned via a leak that the Swedes had broken its Geheimschreiber code and changed it, gradually denying the Swedes this source of intelligence.[4]

The large volume of intercepts in 1942 prompted the move of the SIGINT service to a new location, outside Stockholm. Reconstituted as an independent authority, known as the National Defense Radio Establishment (Försvarets radio-anstalt, FRA), under the Defense Ministry, it continued to report to the Defense Staff. The new setup meant changes in the priorities of SIGINT tasking: the primary effort focused on German traffic. Soviet Navy traffic, important as it was to Swedish security, was a second-priority target. The Western Allies' traffic was assigned considerably less priority, merely "some monitoring of certain British traffic," Which was presumably related to British clandestine

---

4. See the suggested readings, below, or the earlier but more easily obtainable Lars Ulfving and Frode Weierud, "The Geheimschreiber Secret: Arne Beurling and the Success of Swedish Signals Intelligence," at https://cryptocellar.web.cern.ch/ cryptocellar/pubs/ulfving_weierud_secret. pdf+&cd=6&hl=en&ct=clnk&gl=us .

activities in Sweden[5]

The tide of war may have played a role in the establishment of the FRA. Sweden had charted a fairly neutral course between the Axis and the Allies. Sweden supported its neighbor Finland against the Soviet Union, so there was little reason to favor the Allies, except to the extent that Germany posed a potential threat to Sweden as well. Such a threat arose with the 1940 German invasions of Denmark and Norway. Sweden suddenly was surrounded by German armies, and the war was not going well for the Allies. In mid-1942, Colonel Count Carl Björnstjerna, of the Defense Staff intelligence section, began to supply the British naval attaché, Captain Henry Denham, with the results of Swedish SIGINT, including information on the German Navy in Norway. Denham had little to offer in return, and the information transfer was presumably not authorized, since later in the year Björnstjerna was removed from his post. However, by then, the Foreign Ministry was advocating an end to intelligence exchanges with Axis military attachés and a new focus on those of the Allied powers.

One could argue that the contacts with British intelligence and the establishment of the FRA as an organization separate from the Defense Staff was an indication that Swedish intelligence professionals and diplomats realized that the tide of war was changing. Within the Defense Staff, some officers were sympathetic to Germany, which was not surprising in light of the long relationship between the two militaries. Perhaps it was believed that a new intelligence organization, largely staffed by civilians, might be more inclined to see the Allies as potential partners.

From 1944, the first experiments in electronic intelligence (ELINT) took place with some cooperation with Britain. The Swedes allowed the Royal Air Force to establish a special duty ELINT unit in southern Sweden.

International intelligence cooperation during the war took place with Finland and Germany on one side and Britain and the United States on the other. Swedish intelligence also maintained links with Denmark and Norway and the resistance movements in these countries. SIGINT played a major role in international cooperation. In 1939-1940, the Swedes broke the Soviet air force cipher. Soviet bombers targeting Finland only received encrypted targeting data after take-off. The Swedes intercepted, broke, and forwarded the targeting data in real time to Finland, thus forewarning Finnish air defenses.

In December 1943, the C Bureau began a substantial effort to introduce a HUMINT network into the occupied Baltic States.[6] With the help of Baltic refugees and with FRA radio support, the mission was to collect intelligence on

---

5. C. G. McKay och Bengt Beckman, *Swedish Signal Intelligence, 1900-1945* (London: Frank Cass, 2003), 176. .
6. The Soviet Union occupied the Baltic States in 1940 and incorporated them into the USSR. The German army overran them in 1941. The Soviet Army recaptured them in 1944.

conditions under first German, then Soviet occupation. The operation largely failed, with the loss of most or all agents.

In September 1944, the Finnish intelligence service evacuated to Sweden. The motivation was to continue intelligence operations against Soviet targets in the event of a Soviet occupation. The plan to continue operations failed, but some 20 Finns were given Swedish identities and were employed by the FRA, where many of them remained until retirement.

Already in 1937, the Defense Staff intelligence section proposed the establishment of a new, secret security service. In 1938, the General Security Service (*Allmänna säkerhetstjänsten*) was established, led by District Police Commissioner Eric Hallgren, who was subordinated to the social affairs minister, and incidentally also had led the old Police Bureau from 1918. The counterespionage and domestic security mission was transferred from the National Police to the General Security Service, which received a broad mandate including letter censorship and telephone monitoring. Among those recruited to carry out these tasks was Astrid Lindgren, later a well-known writer of children's stories such as the Pippi Longstocking books.

Swedish Intelligence in the Cold War

Defense Staff Section II continued operations after the Second World War as did the SIGINT service, FRA. Changes took place in the clandestine HUMINT C Bureau, reorganized in 1946 as the T Office (*T-kontoret*). Much of the work focused on the Soviet threat. The Polish people's referendum on 30 June 1946 and parliamentary elections on 19 January 1947 had a particular impact on the Swedish Government. The Swedish press trusted the Soviet newspaper *Pravda*, so news reporting presented a rosy picture of the situation. However, SIGINT reporting, based on broken Polish ciphers, confirmed the widespread manipulation of the election results and voter intimidation. The FRA reporting enabled Prime Minister Tage Erlander to assess the real situation in Soviet-controlled Poland and base Sweden's policies on fact, not newspaper reporting. Erlander noted: "The election methods were exposed with terrible exactness—'investigate so that they do not hide an opposition ballot up their shirtsleeves.' So this is the nice election, which even our press has been duped into believing in."[7] The FRA reporting greatly influenced the Swedish Government's understanding of events in Poland and elsewhere in Soviet-held Europe, pushing it further toward the West.

The SIGINT effort was not free from loss of life. On 13 June 1952, a Soviet fighter shot down with no survivors the DC-3 Dakota ELINT aircraft, with an

---

7. Tage Erlander, *Dagböcker 1945-1949* (Hedemora: Gidlunds, 2001), 160-161. The prime minister's diaries, subsequently published.

FRA crew, while on a mission over the Baltic Sea.[8]

Because of the threat from Soviet agents, Section II in 1957 formed a secret counterespionage unit, the B Bureau (B-byrån). Technical intelligence organizations were also established which used technical experts from institutions such as the Royal Institute of Technology (Kungliga tekniska högskolan, KTH) when, for instance, foreign military materiel had been acquired. In 1945, the Defense Research Establishment (Försvarets forskningsanstalt, FOA) was created. The FOA combined the Defense Chemical Establishment (Försvarsväsendets kemiska anstalt, FKA), the Institute of Military Physics (Militärfysiska institutet, MFI), and a component of the Swedish Board of Inventions (Statens uppfinnarnämnd, SUN). The SUN echo radar unit, formed in 1942, was involved in advanced ELINT efforts in addition to research in radar technology. In 1958, at the initiative of Section II, intelligence units were formed in the FOA and the service administrations. The latter were reorganized as the Defense Matériel Administration (Försvarets materielverk, FMV) in 1968, but retained technical intelligence units.

In 1959, the Eastern Economic Bureau (Östekonomiska byrån) was formed with the task to carry out research on the economies of the Soviet bloc. At first a function within the Defense Staff, it was established as a non-state foundation, funded in part from private sources.

The General Security Service was dissolved in 1945, and the National Police resumed responsibility for counterespionage. At the same time, the government severely cut security service funding and staff. It took until the early 1947 Polish elections before the government fully realized that a cold war had begun. Because of the lack of resources and coordination, Colonel Stig Wennerström, the spy for the Soviets who perhaps caused most damage to Swedish interests, operated from at least 1948 until his arrest in 1963. For years, the police and military did not share their suspicions of him.[9]

In 1965, the Swedish police system was finally put under national control. This led to reorganizations also within military intelligence. The T Office (foreign intelligence) and the B Bureau (counterespionage) were combined, called the IB, and subordinated to the head of the Defense Staff. The police were subordinated to a new organization, called the National Police Board (Rikspolisstyrelsen, RPS), which had two departments: the Police and Security Departments. The Police Department eventually became the National Bureau of Investigation (Rikskriminalpolisen, RKP), tasked primarily with organized

---

8. The Soviets demonstrated a great sensitivity to any foreign intelligence gathering. "... [A]s many as thirteen intelligence gathering American aircraft were shot down around and over the Soviet periphery between 1947 and 1960..." Michael Herman, "Intelligence as Threats and Reassurance," in Michael Herman & Gwilyn Hughes (Editors), Intelligence in the Cold War: What Difference Did It Make? (New York: Routledge, 2013): 42.

9. See Alexander Mull, Notes on the Wennerström Case (CIA Historical Review Program, 22 September 1993; at https://www.cia.gov/library/center-for-the-study-of-intelligence/kent-csi/vol10no3/html/v10i3a07p_0001.htm); and Thomas Whiteside, An Agent in Place: The Wennerström Affair (New York: The Viking Press, 1966).

and transnational crime. The Security Department (*säkerhetsavdelningen*, SÄK) became responsible for counterespionage.

In 1969, new legislation to safeguard the freedom of opinion outlawed government registration of political sympathies. The RPS claimed sole jurisdiction with regard to domestic security. As a result, the IB's domestic intelligence activities, primarily counterespionage and the registration of political extremists, ceased in 1970. However, the IB resumed these activities in 1971. The media exposed this in 1973, which also exposed for the first time key organizations and personnel in the intelligence community. The IB's domestic collection ceased, and, in 1974, the first public review of the intelligence community was initiated, a year before the establishment in the US of congressional committees to investigate intelligence community transgressions revealed by the press. All foreign intelligence activities were also put under direct government and parliamentary oversight with the establishment of the Defense Intelligence Committee (*Försvarets Underrättelsenämnd*, FUN).

No longer permitted to engage in domestic intelligence activities, the IB was reorganized in 1973 and renamed the Joint Intelligence Bureau (*Gemensamma byrån för underrättelser*, GBU). In 1982, the GBU was renamed the Special Collection Section (*Sektionen for särskild inhämtning*, SSI) and, subsequently, in 1989, the Special Collection Office (*Kontoret för särskild inhämtning*, KSI), the designation which the military clandestine foreign intelligence organization has since retained.

Domestic security and intelligence activities in the late 1960s and 1970s were characterized by considerable rivalry between different organizations and their respective supporters, with the ruling Social Democratic Party, the Armed Forces, and various groupings within the police often opposed to each other. Journalists took advantage of the persistent rivalry, and leaks of sensitive information were commonplace. Domestic politics trumped national security issues. From the mid-1960s, successive Swedish Governments, led by a new generation of political leaders, championed a variety of foreign national liberation movements while promising firm and unshakeable international neutrality. Simultaneously, Swedish Governments maintained close (but often secret) links with NATO member states and regarded the Soviet bloc as a common opponent.

In 1981, the Defense Staff reorganized, and Section II became Operations Section 5 (Op 5), which for the first time combined the services' intelligence units into one integrated military intelligence service.

Swedish Intelligence From 1989 to the Present

From 1989, further reorganizations of the Defense Staff took place. From 1989 to 1994, Op 5 was called the Intelligence and Security Office (*Underrät-*

telse – och säkerhetskontoret, Underrättelse – och säkerhetsledningen, USK/USL). In 1994, intelligence was named the Military Intelligence and Security Service (*Militära underrättelse – och säkerhetstjänsten,* MUST), its current designation. Colloquially known as the security police (*Säkerhetspolisen,* Säpo), the RPS Security Department in 1989 attained a more autonomous position, under its own director general. Soon afterwards, the National Bureau of Investigation (RKP) developed its own integral intelligence function. The security police focused on counterespionage and domestic security investigations; the RKP, in addition to investigations, grew its intelligence as part of its crime prevention mandate, establishing an analytic intelligence unit to report on trends, causes, and patterns of crime. Focus lay on prospective, intelligence-led policing (unlike investigations, which are retrospective and focus on events that already have occurred). The RKP was also tasked with international police cooperation, including with Europol as a joint intelligence organization for the European Union (EU) member states.

In 2001, a new Defense Research Agency (*Totalförsvarets forskningsinstitut,* FOI) was created by combining the Defense Research Establishment (FOA) with the Institute for Aeronautic Research (*Flygtekniska försöksanstalten,* FFA).

An Intelligence Secretariat (*Samordningssekretariatet för säkerhetspolitiska underrättelsefrågor,* SUND) was formed in 2000 within the Defense Ministry to coordinate the intelligence services. This did not change oversight and control. The MUST, FRA, and FOI remained under the Defense Ministry control of, while the RPS remained under Justice Ministry controlof. Legislation and supervision of the intelligence services were enhanced, though. In 2000, for the first time, legislation regulated military intelligence activities. Legislation was also introduced to regulate SIGINT activities. The Social Democratic Party, which prepared the legislation, lost the parliamentary election before the new proposed law could be put before parliament. Ironically, the party, in opposition, sharply criticized the legislation when the succeeding government introduced it in 2007. This resulted in a vicious political debate, with intelligence often denounced in principle on moral grounds. While the law eventually came into force, it included a range of privacy safeguards and a battery of newly formed oversight institutions. New legislation also followed for the RPS, including further regulation in 2010 to protect the personal data of those suspected of criminal activities.

On January 1, 2015, the police system was again reorganized. The RPS and all police departments were combined into one police authority. All intelligence activities would henceforth be led by a new organization, the National Operations Department (*Nationella operativa avdelningen,* NOA). At the same time, the security police (Säpo) became an independent authority, under the Justice Ministry, with the exclusive mission to handle counterespionage and the protection of the national government and the democratic system. For the first time since 1945, and during a period not at risk of war for the first time since 1560, Sweden again had an independent security service.

In retrospect, the years following the end of the Cold War suggest a sense of loss of mission for the Swedish intelligence community. The Soviet threat was gone; what would come in its place? At the same time, Sweden joined the EU, so many in government believed that Sweden no longer needed foreign intelligence. The disappearance of the Soviet threat also led to a widespread feeling that there was little need for armed forces. It followed that there was also little need for military intelligence. The intelligence services increasingly came to be seen as political liabilities, and regulation became far more important than intelligence results. This would perhaps have been understandable had there been any major abuse of intelligence powers. However, none had taken place since the registration of political extremists back in the early 1970s. Perhaps it was simply the rhetoric of righteousness in combination with the lack of obvious foreign threats to national security that persuaded a new generation of political leaders that intelligence was, like war itself, something that ought to be confined to museums.

Readings For Instructors

There are few books in English on the Swedish intelligence services. Notable exceptions are:

Beckman, Bengt. *Codebreakers: Arne Beurling and the Swedish Crypto Program During World War II* (Providence, Rhode Island: American Mathematical Society, 2002).

McKay, C. G. *From Information to Intrigue: Studies in Secret Service Based on the Swedish Experience, 1939-1945* (London: Frank Cass, 1993).

McKay, C. G. and Bengt Beckman. *Swedish Signal Intelligence, 1900-1945* (London: Frank Cass, 2003).

While reputable scholars such as Wilhelm Agrell, Matthew M. Aid, and Cees Wiebes have carried out research, few papers on the Swedish intelligence services by knowledgeable researchers were published in English.

Michael Fredholm is an historian who has written extensively on the history, defense strategies, security policies, intelligence services, and energy sector developments of Eurasia. He is currently affiliated with the Stockholm International Program for Central Asian Studies (SIPCAS), originated at Stockholm University and since 2012 at the Swedish Research Institute in Istanbul. At SIPCAS, he has made a special study of Central Asian geopolitics, Afghanistan, Islamic extremism, and the causes of and defense strategies against terrorism. He has worked as an independent academic advisor to governmental, inter-governmental, and non-governmental bodies for more than two decades. Michael Fredholm has also lectured, during conferences or as visiting professor, at numerous institutions and universities in cities around the world including Ankara, Istanbul, Madrid, New Delhi, Oslo, Shanghai, Tashkent, Vienna, and Vilnius.

GUIDE TO THE STUDY OF INTELLIGENCE

Soviet and Russian Intelligence Services

Robert W. Pringle

Intelligence and security services have played a critical role in Russian domestic and foreign policy for more than a century. The tsars, general secretaries of the Communist Party of the Soviet Union, and post-Soviet leaders have viewed the services as crucial in coping with dissenters, punishing enemies at home and abroad, gathering intelligence, and serving as a signaling channel with foreign governments and terrorist organizations.

The Tsarist Legacy

The Okhrana was created in 1882 after the assassination of Tsar Aleksandr II to penetrate opposition political movements at home and abroad, and conduct pogroms against the empire's Jewish minority. The Okhrana recruited hundreds of informers and penetrated revolutionary movements, including the Social Revolutionaries and the Bolsheviks. The Bolshevik leader of the Russian Duma, Roman Malinovskiy, was an Okhrana agent who fooled the Bolshevik leader Vladimir Lenin for more than a decade.

Yet, despite successes, the Okhrana was as feckless an organization as the empire it served. Many Okhrana agents continued to work as terrorists. One agent masterminded the killing of tsarist ministers, another assassinated a prime minister. Most infamously, an Okhrana agent, Father Gapon led a march on the Winter Palace in St. Petersburg in 1905 that was met with gunfire. More than 100 once loyal workers and their families died. Widely feared inside and outside Russia, the Okhrana could not prevent the collapse of the monarchy in the revolution of 1917.

From the Cheka to the KGB

Vladimir Lenin, leader of the Bolsheviks, believed that a revolution without a firing squad was doomed to failure. He asked Polish revolutionary Feliks Dzerzhinsky to head the Extraordinary Commission for Combating Counter-revolution and Sabotage (CHEKA) in 1918. The CHEKA crushed all opposition to the new regime, executing more than 143,000 men and women, intellectuals, capitalists, and priests between 1918 and 1921 (compared to less than 12,000 executions between 1881 and 1917). Dzerzhinsky grew the CHEKA into a security empire with more than 250,000 employees (Chekists) with responsibility for foreign intelligence, counterintelligence, domestic security, and border control. The CHEKA oversaw the Gulag system of forced labor camps. One of his great achievements was the creation of the Trust, a fabricated anti-Bolshevik underground used as a deception against White Russian émigrés and foreign intelligence services, which operated from 1921 until 1926.

Lenin's successor and disciple, Josef Stalin, gradually took over the security services between 1924 and 1937. Its leaders, Genrikh Yagoda and later Nikolai Yezhov, used the services against insurgents in Central Asia, peasants resisting collectivization, political opponents, and ultimately some of Stalin's comrades within the Communist Party. Stalin had most of Lenin's remaining deputies executed. In mass show trials, some confessed to treason and even the attempted assassination of Lenin. At the same time, the police purged the Red Army,

		EVOLUTION OF SOVIET AND POST-SOVIET INTELLIGENCE AND SECURITY SERVICES
1917	Cheka	All-Russian Extraordinary Committee to Combat Counterrevolution and Sabotage
1922	NKVD – GPU	People's Commissariat for Internal Affairs – State Political Directorate
1923	OGPU	All Union State Political Directorate
1934	GUGB	Main Directorate for State Security
1941	NKGB	People's Commissariat for State Security
1946	MGB	Ministry for State Security
1953	MVD	Ministry of Internal Affairs
1954	KGB	Committee for State Security
1991	SVR	Foreign Intelligence Service
	FSB	Federal Security Service of the Russian Federation
	FSO	Federal Protective Service

arresting and executing over 650 general officers and more than 30,000 others. During the Yezhovshchina, the time of Yezhov, more than 1,500,000 were arrested and at least 750,000 were shot, died under interrogation, or perished in the Gulag. In late 1938, Stalin restored some order, replacing Yezhov with Lavrenty Beria, a competent and cruel Georgian Chekist. Yezhov was executed in 1940.

Both the NKVD and the GRU (the Soviet General Staff military intelligence service) provided foreign intelligence for the Soviet leadership. Case officers from both services, many serving under non-official cover ("illegals") ran spies in the British, French, German, American, and Japanese Governments. Most spied for ideological reasons. Spies provided the Soviet Union with critical military, scientific, and industrial technologies and targeted enemies of the regime. In 1940, an NKVD assassin murdered Leon Trotsky, Stalin's last living rival in Mexico.

Before Germany invaded the USSR in June 1941, Soviet spies penetrated both the German military and Nazi political bureaucracy. Stalin received more than 100 warnings from these agents of German plans to invade the mother-land—information he largely rejected. However, following this spectacular error, Stalin became a sophisticated consumer of intelligence. Soviet spy rings, such as the *Rote Kapelle* (Red Orchestra) operating in France, Belgium, and Germany, provided detailed information on German strategy and weapons. Spies in London and Washington also provided detailed information about the allies' plans.

In one of the greatest successes in history, the NKGB and GRU stole critical information about the first atom bomb, accelerating the Soviets nuclear capabilities by years. Soviet spies in London, Washington, Los Alamos, and Oak Ridge provided details about many aspects of the bomb. According to declassified US intelligence reports, the Soviets had six agents in Los Alamos—only three of whom were ever identified.

By the end of World War II, Stalin had more than 600 agents in the United States, London, and Ottawa. They had penetrated the White House, State and War Departments, and both the British and American intelligence services. (By contrast the West had no agents inside the Soviet Union.) Yet, much of this apparatus disintegrated when a key agent confessed to the FBI and a GRU code clerk defected in Canada. Western counterintelligence got better. By the late 1940's, the United Stated has decrypted and analyzed more than 2,400 coded NKGB messages (codenamed VENONA), leading to the arrest of spies such as Julius and Ethel Rosenberg.

In his last years, Stalin was increasingly paranoid. By early 1953, there were more than 5,000,000 people in the Gulag or internal exile. In 1950, several of the Party's young stars were purged, and in 1952-1953, Stalin turned against the country's Jews. The MVD concocted the Doctors' Plot to implicate thousands of leading Jews as Anglo-American spies. Stalin's death on March 1, 1953, saved many of these people.

Stalin's successors faced a vexing question, how to disengage from the Stalinist system without losing power. They agreed that Beria had to go. He was arrested in July 1953 and shot with some of his closest associates five months later. Nikita Khrushchev, the new Communist Party general secretary, attempted to cut the Gordian knot. More than a million were released from the camps and exile, Stalin's crimes were denounced; and the security police were renamed the Committee of State Security (KGB) and placed under Party control.

The KGB and the Last Years of the Soviet Union

The KGB evolved into an extensive intelligence community, which incorporated the functions of the American CIA, FBI, National Security Agency, and military intelligence. By 1989, the KGB was the largest intelligence/security service in the world with a staff of more than 480,000. This included approximately 250,000 border guards, which had armor fighting vehicles and helicopters. The other important components of the KGB were:

The First Chief Directorate, responsible for foreign intelligence.
The Second Chief Directorate, responsible for internal security and counterintelligence.
The Fifth Directorate, responsible for surveillance of churches and dissidents.
The Eighth and Sixteenth Chief Directorates, responsible for communications security and codebreaking.

During the last decades of the Soviet Union, the KGB became infamous for spying on foreign governments, stealing Western technology, propaganda operations ("active measures"), and the suppression of dissent. While the KGB recruited sources in the 1930s and 1940's based on ideological sympathies, following World War II, recruits were well paid for their treachery. For example:

- US Navy Petty Officer John Walker provided the Soviets the keys to decrypt US military codes over more than 10 years. He was paid over one million dollars.

- CIA officer Aldrich Ames, who betrayed a number of American agents within the KGB (10 of whom were executed), was paid more than two million dollars. Like Walker, he is serving a life-term in federal prison.

- Agents within the West German Government and security services allowed Moscow to track NATO war plans.

The Communist Party expected the KGB to destroy political dissent. During the 1970s and 1980s, thousands of dissident Protestant, Catholic, and Russian Orthodox believers were arrested, as well as nationalists from the Ukraine and Central Asia. Famous dissidents harassed by the KGB were the writers Aleksandr Solzhenitsyn and Nobel Laureate Andrei Sakharov. Solzhenitsyn was exiled from the USSR, and returned more than two decades later. Sakharov spent more than five years in internal exile. The persecution of these two, and their supporters, seriously damaged the Soviet Union's international reputation. While an organized opposition never emerged in the USSR, KGB actions actually hurt the regime far more than any opposition was capable of.

Communist Party General Secretary Mikhail Gorbachev tried to curb the KGB in the last years of Soviet power. Key elements of the KGB turned against Gorbachev and took part in the failed August 1991 putsch that marked the end of the Soviet Union. The KGB proved that – like the Okhrana – an omnipotent and all-seeing intelligence service could not save an inefficient and corrupt regime.

Post-Soviet Services and the Future

The post-communist Russian Government broke the KGB into several services. The most important were the Foreign Intelligence Service of Russia (SVR) and the Federal Security Service (FSB), the former internal component of the service. Former President Vladimir Putin served in the KGB's foreign intelligence arm and remains a proud veteran of it.

Western counterintelligence services indicate that the level of Russian spying has returned to the levels seen during the Cold War. Since 2006, Russian-British relations have been hurt seriously by the poisoning in London of Alexandr Litvinenko, a former KGB/FSB defector. The suspected assassin is a member of Russia's Federal Protective Service (FSO).

Russian intelligence has an older pedigree than that of the United States or the United Kingdom. America's first civilian intelligence service, the Central Intelligence Agency, was only formed in 1947. The British internal and external services date from the first decade of the twentieth century. Neither the British or American services have been as well supported politically as the Okhrana or the KGB.

READINGS FOR INSTRUCTORS

The following are recommended readings for instructors on Soviet and Russian Intelligence Services

A good account of Soviet repression is Aleksandr Solzhenitsyn's novella, *One Day in the Life of Ivan Denisovich* (London, Penguin Books, 1991). His three-volume history of the forced labor camp system, *Gulag Archipelago* (New York, Harper Row, 1973) has been condensed in later printings into one book.

For more advanced students, Anne Applebaum, *GULAG: A History* (New York, Doubleday, 2003), is highly recommended. The website http://www.memoria. ru has an English and Russian language section about the years of Stalinist repression.

Two good accounts of KGB foreign operations are Victor Cherkashin, *Spy Handler: Memoirs of a KGB Officer* (New York, Basic Books, 2005) and Oleg Kalugin, *Spy Master: My Thirty-two Years in Intelligence and Espionage Against the West* (New York, Basic Books, 2009; originally published as The First

Directorate, St. Martin's Press, 1994).

An account of the Walker spy case from the perspective of the FBI is by Robert W. Hunter, *Spy Hunter: Inside the FBI Investigation into the Walker Espionage Case* (Annapolis, Naval Institute Press, 1999).

Again for strong and interested students, a good read is Christopher Andrew and Vasili Mitrokhin's *The Sword and the Shield: The Mitrokhin Archive and the Secret History of the KGB* (New York, Perseus Books, 1999).

For CIA operations against the KGB, a good book is Robert Wallace and H. Keith Melton's *Spy Craft: The Secret History of the CIA's Spytechs from Communism to Al-Qaeda* (New York, Basic Books, 2005).

Robert W. Pringle received a PhD in Russian history from the University of Virginia. After service as an Army intelligence officer in Vietnam, he was a Foreign Service Officer from 1974 to 1983 in southern Africa and Moscow. He joined the CIA in 1983 as an intelligence analyst and manager. Following his retirement, he taught at the University of Kentucky, Georgetown College (KY), and Virginia Military Institute. He is the author of *The Historical Dictionary of the Russian Intelligence* and several articles.

GUIDE TO THE STUDY OF INTELLIGENCE

Chinese Intelligence

Dr. Stefania Paladini

Intelligence With Chinese Characteristics

Comparing systems and concepts like the Chinese and the Anglo-American is challenging, and intelligence studies are no exception. It is even more difficult, considering that there is not a perfect translation in Chinese for the word "intelligence." In fact, the term used by the Chinese is *qingbao*, which can be translated as "information," as much as "intelligence." The Western distinction that intelligence is information that has been analyzed does not completely apply to Chinese doctrine. However, what is clear from Chinese terminology is the action-enabling purpose of intelligence – expressed with the terms *jihuo zhishi* – "activating knowledge."[1]

Albeit this terminology-related question, China has a long tradition in this subject, and every cultivated Chinese, let alone politicians and intelligence experts, knows about Sun Zi, the scholar from 300 BC who first theorized the use of intelligence, more specifically espionage, for warfare purposes.[2]

This article presents a brief overview of the intelligence organizations in the People's Republic of China (PRC) and a few notes to understand intelligence with Chinese characteristics.[3]

---

1. There is also another term used, *ziliao*, which refers to data, and often is put in comparison with *qingbao*, which generally involves an element of secrecy. For more about this linguistic debate, see Huo & Wang, 1991, and Mattis, 2013 in the "Readings for Instructors" section.
2. Sun Zi is often Romanized as Sun Tzu.
3. This article does not address Taiwan, Hong Kong, or Macao. While considered part of Chinese territory by the PRC Government, the first is labeled a "renegade province" and the other two go under the term of "one-country, two systems."

Current Structure of PRC Intelligence Services

There are several intelligence and security organizations in the PRC, some part of larger organizations. None is in charge overall. Only the ones exclusively devoted to intelligence are presented here, and the list is not exhaustive.[4] Furthermore, a section intentionally missing here regards the important area of intelligence oversight. This is because intelligence activities in China lack parliament oversight for the basic reasons that China is not a democracy (apart from direct elections at township and local level) and there are not transparent rules to how security, internal and external, is ensured.

The obvious starting point is the **Ministry of State Security (Guójiā Ānquánbù, 国家安全部, MSS)**. It is the main agency, responsible for intelligence and state security, in charge of counterintelligence and foreign intelligence (but not military intelligence). It was established in 1983, with Ling Yun as his first chief, after the reform of the predecessor Central Investigation Department (*Diaochabu*) that was established at the creation of PRC in 1949 and first headed by Kang Sheng and later by Li Kenong. Before there was no intelligence service separate from the Communist Party, even though there were organized intelligence activities since at least 1927.

According to the Federation of American Scientists,[5] the MSS is organized – unsurprisingly – on the model of the old KGB, with a First Bureau dealing with domestic security, the Second with foreign services and counterintelligence. Other sections deal with signals intelligence (SIGINT) and countersurveillance, or focus on outer territories like Taiwan. According to some sources, the 17th Bureau is in charge of economic intelligence, the collection of which is one of the characteristics of Chinese services, which have targeted specifically the United States and European countries, France among them.

French sources[6] in 2005 estimated the MSS had around 7,000 employees, but some 50,000 undercover operatives.[7] The chief of the service since early 2015 is Geng Huichang. According to many observers, he is President Xi Jinping's man and not a holder of autonomous power, as often has been the case with former chiefs.

The MSS should not to be confused with the **Ministry of Public Security (Gōng'ānbù, 公安部, MPS)** that looks after police bureau and internal/ordinary

---

4. One of the best open sources is the French intelligence service website: *http://servicederenseigne-ments.e-monsite.com/pages/grandes-agences/republique-populaire-de-chine.html*. French sources are especially good concerning Chinese intelligence, starting with Faligot & Remi (1990), which is a recommended reading.

5. FAS' own source here is: "Spy Headquarters Behind the Shrubs — Supplement to `Secrets About CPC Spies'" No. 233, by Tan Po Cheng Ming [Hong Kong], March 1, 1997, 34-37; Cheng Ming on Chinese Spy Headquarters, FBIS-CHI-97-047, March 1, 1997. Source no longer retrievable.

6. French intelligence website, accessed on March 2015.

7. In MSS slang, the often dormant, long-term operatives are called "fish at the bottom of the ocean" (*Chen di yu*). Eftimiades, 1999, 35.

security,[8] but has no intelligence gathering mission.[9]

Military intelligence is the prerogatives of the People's Liberation Army (PLA). Two PLA departments specifically deal with it:

One is the **PLA General Staff Headquarters Second Department** (Qingbaobu, **2PLA**), which is more specifically responsible for collecting and disseminating military information, via human sources (HUMINT), signals intelligence (SIGINT), and imagery intelligence (IMINT). Officers are dispatched to China's embassies and consulates overseas, and also to big Chinese state-owned enterprises (SOEs), banks, and think tanks. On the other hand, the **Third Department (3PLA)** is in charge of the direct monitoring of foreign armies and their SIGINT, and with dissemination of collected intelligence. It should be mentioned that Chinese SIGINT is quite impressive and is considered the most extensive of all Asian countries.

2PLA also has a military counterintelligence service called *Chi Pao Ko*,[10] which exercises a degree of influence on think tanks and research institutes connected with intelligence studies in China, such as the China Institutes of Contemporary International Relations (CICIR, primarily connected to the MSS) and the China Institute for International Strategic Studies (CIISS).[11]

There are other bodies in China performing specific kinds of intelligence activities, but they are less prominent than the ones presented here.

Worth mentioning are a couple of historical notes on Chinese intelligence. Sun Zi's *Art of War*, the classical text about military strategy from the fifth century BC, devotes the last chapter to intelligence and is still a most common reference about the practice and doctrine of espionage and its political uses.[12] Intelligence operations in Communist China started long before 1949 and are linked to Kang Sheng,[13] Mao Zedong's spymaster and a central figure in China's foreign policy for decades. Among other achievements, Kang Sheng played a substantial role in obtaining nuclear technology for developing a national atomic program.

Another figure to be mentioned for importance is the second MSS chief. Soon after the removal of its first chief, Lin Yun, in 1985 over the defection of

---

8. An important exception here is riot control, which is not under MPS domain but is taken care of by the Chinese People's Armed Police Force (中国人民武装警察部队, CAPF) at the provincial level.

9. The two services are located near each other at 14, Dongchang'an (East Chang'an Street), Beijng.

10. Belonging to PLA Intelligence is Xiong Guangkai, considered by many the most important intelligence figure of the last two decades (Mulvenon, 2008).

11. See Gates & Mulvenon, 2002

12. "What enables the wise sovereign and the good general to strike and conquer, and achieve things beyond the reach of ordinary men, is foreknowledge. Now this foreknowledge cannot be elicited from spirits; it cannot be obtained inductively from experience, nor by any deductive calculation. Knowledge of the enemy's dispositions can only be obtained from other men" (Sun Zi, *The Art of War*, Chapter 13).

13. Given that this brief outline excludes Taiwan, all references to Chiang Kai-shek (Jiang Jieshi) and his formidable intelligence apparatus have been omitted. However, it is worth noting that Tai Li (Dai Li), his intelligence chief, was for many years a valid adversary to Kang Sheng. For more about Dai Li, see the recommended readings.

Yu Qiangsheng, head of the Counterespionage Bureau, to the US, Jia Chunwang rose to power and held tenure until 1998; until today the longest serving MSS chief and one of the most influential. Jia's tenure was fundamental in expanding the scope and grasp of the MSS[14]. The MSS began as a central-level ministry with only a handful of provincial departments. By the end of Jia's tenure, the MSS covered every province, provincial-level city, and a countless number of municipalities.

Chinese Methods and Approach to Intelligence

The methods used by Chinese intelligence often differ from the more easily understood methods of other nations. Not only does the collection of intelligence present some peculiarities, as outlined below, but Chinese methods have evolved considerably over the years.

In the 1950s and 1960s, every Chinese diplomatic post overseas had an Investigation and Research Office with staff from the Central Investigation Department – the so-called Institute of Contemporary International Relations. However, from Deng Xiaoping (in office from 1981 to 1989) onward, non-intelligence personnel, from newsmen to businessmen to academic researchers, started to be charged with intelligence collection tasks. Only a few career officers were left in embassies.

In general, Western perceptions of Chinese intelligence have been long biased due to the fact that China is essentially an inward-focused country. When it comes to security, its approach to intelligence gathering has been often regarded as "unsophisticated and risk-averse, particularly when you consider the bureaucratic inefficiencies inherent in the Communist Party of China's (CPC) administrative structure. But it is an approach that takes a long and wide view, and it is more effective than it may seem at first glance."[15] There are at least the three main Chinese intelligence-gathering characteristics, which often overlap, and that make China's approach to intelligence and espionage different.

Most important is the so-called mosaic-approach, where low-grade and generally unclassified, but massive in scope, information is collected by thousands of assets. According to the open-source intelligence company Stratfor, this approach is particularly successful because it is designed to "overload foreign counterintelligence agencies by the painstaking collection of many small pieces of intelligence that make sense only in the aggregate. This is a slow and tedious process, and it reflects the traditional Chinese hallmarks of patience and persistence as well as the centuries-old Chinese custom of guanxi, the cultivation and use of personal networks to influence events and engage

14. Mattis, 2011.
15. Stratfor, 2010.

in various ventures."[16]

Another important characteristic is related to the identity of the intelligence collectors. Most of the time, they are not professionals, but amateurs recruited among Chinese-born residents in other countries or students and researchers who are abroad for study and research.[17]

The third method is the long-term cultivation of foreign assets, often via blackmail, honey-pots,[18] corruption, or other expedients, once useful pressure points of the targets are identified.

Surprisingly enough given this highly specific approach, Chinese doctrine is more similar to Western approaches than one might imagine. This is evident looking at scholarly articles on the subject, especially recent ones. This is due to the fact that Chinese doctrine has evolved considerably over the years, mirroring the progressive opening of China to the Western world and the increasing amount of knowledge available. As one of the most prominent scholars of Chinese intelligence has written, "Chinese writings on intelligence bear remarkable similarity to familiar US definitions of intelligence functions and goals."[19]

Finally, in the last 20 years, new methods for intelligence collection have emerged in the cyber world.

Some Case Studies

Since 2003, 123 Chinese agents have been identified in the US.[20] It is impossible to present here, even briefly, all instances of Chinese espionage over the decades. Some cases, however, stand out.

One of the most damaging was Larry Wu-Tai Chin who worked for the US Army as a translator beginning in 1944. After becoming an American citizen, he worked for the Central Intelligence Agency's Foreign Broadcast Information Service (FBIS). For decades until his apprehension in 1985, he spied on the US and "revealed President Nixon's desire to open diplomatic relations two years

---

16. *Guanxi* is a typical feature of the Chinese culture, and it can be translated as "network." (*Stratfor*, 2010, 2). But *guanxi* also means "relationships" and is "a system of interpersonal relationships that has long historical and cultural roots," constituting an essential feature of Chinese society. "*Guanxi* itself works as an important power base that represents saved favors, faces, and special relationships with powerful people. When relational norms and Confucian values are considerably eroded, *guanxi* could bring out further egoism, opportunism, and instrumentality" (Y. Luo, "The changing Chinese culture and business behavior: The perspective of intertwinement between *guanxi* and corruption," *International Business Review 17 (2)*, 2008, 188-193.

17. The closest equivalent practice is by Israel's Mossad, which employs the *Sayanim*, volunteers in the Jewish diaspora not directly connected with the intelligence services but willing to help and provide various services.

18. A few instances have been recorded, one of the most famous was the Bernard Boursicot case, a French diplomat caught in Kang Sheng's net in the 1970s when he became enamored of a Beijing transgender opera singer, Shi Peipu.

19. Mattis, 2012:3.

20. Ibid. This number is as of April 2015.

before the policy was implemented."[21]

A substantial focus of Chinese activities targeted US military secrets, especially nuclear technology. A most important analysis is the 1988 *Report of the Select Committee on US National Security and Military/Commercial Concerns with the People's Republic of China*, US House of Representatives (Cox Report), released in redacted form during the Clinton Administration in the 1990s. While some parts of the report remain classified, the report stated that China had managed to obtain sensitive information about thermonuclear weapons, including deployment details and reentry vehicles. An FBI investigation, code-named Kindred Spirit, took place when "U.S. intelligence discovered in 1995 that secrets about the W88, the most advanced miniature nuclear warhead (deployed on the Trident II SLBM), may have leaked from Los Alamos National Laboratory to China between 1984 and 1988. U.S. intelligence reportedly was handed a secret PRC document from 1988 containing designs similar to that of the W88."[22] The Cox Report warned that "elements of the stolen information on U.S. thermonuclear warhead designs will assist the PRC in building its next generation of mobile ICBMs" and, more worryingly, that "despite repeated PRC thefts of the most sophisticated U.S. nuclear weapons technology, security at our national nuclear weapons laboratories does not meet even minimal standards."[23] Subsequent investigations focused on three Chinese-Americans, Guo Bao Min, employed at Lawrence Livermore National Laboratory; Wen Ho Lee, on the staff of Los Alamos National Laboratory where the W-88 warhead was designed; and Peter Lee, also at Los Alamos and TRW Corporation.

Another famous case was Chi Mak, an "illegal" sleeper agent sent to the US to gain access over the long term to US military technologies, and the object of one of the FBI's biggest counterintelligence operations. He managed to send to China information on sensitive electric drive technology for submarines. On May 10, 2007, a jury convicted Mak on charges of conspiring to export US military technology to China and acting as an unregistered agent of a foreign government. [24]

But Chinese intelligence activities have not just targeted military objectives. For instance, a lot of press attention has been given to Katrina Leung, the lover of two FBI counterintelligence special agents focused on Chinese intelligence activities who had initially recruited her as an asset. She was in reality

---

21. David Major & Peter Oleson, "Espionage Against America," *Guide to the Study of Intelligence*, Association of Former Intelligence Officers, *http://www.afio.com/40_guide.htm*.

22. Kan, 2006, 5.

23. The tone, if not the conclusions of the Cox Report, has been criticized by a group of scholars from Stanford University, which observed in a note that "The language of the report, particularly its Overview, was inflammatory and some allegations did not seem to be well supported." The details of the Stanford note have been provided in the reference list for documentation, while the debate about the report remains open.

24. Yudhijit Bhattacharjee, 2014 "How the F.B.I. Cracked a Chinese Spy Ring," *The New Yorker*. May 12, 2014. Available at: *http://www.newyorker.com/news/news-desk/how-the-f-b-i-cracked-a-chinese-spy-ring*. [Accessed 15 Jun. 2015].

an MSS double agent and managed since 1991 to pass classified information to the Chinese Government.[25]

A growing number of cases are concerned with industrial espionage. According to FBI data, since 2006,[26] there have been federal investigations and criminal prosecutions of about 44 individuals in 26 separate investigations.

An example is the case of Dongfan Chung, a Chinese-born naturalized American and an engineer working at Rockwell International and Boeing. As a result of his activities, an impressive amount of technological details was revealed regarding the B-1 bomber, Delta IV space launch vehicle, the C-17 cargo plane, the F-15 fighter, and, last but not least, the Space Shuttle. He was sentenced to 15 years in prison for economic espionage.

The outlook will not be complete without briefly mentioning the so-called 863 Program sponsored since 1986 by the PRC's State High Technology R&D Organization, i.e. a specific kind of approach where companies steal US commercial technologies to advance the Chinese economy.[27]

Chinese Cyber Activities.

Chinese cyber espionage represents a substantial threat to Western countries. It long has been known that China uses state-sponsored "hackers." Also, the PLA has a military espionage unit specifically devoted to cyber operations, the Chengdu Province First Technical Reconnaissance Bureau (TRB).[28]

According to the Cyber Intelligence Sharing and Protection Act (CISPA), "China is the world's most active and persistent perpetrator of cyber economic espionage. U.S. companies have reported an onslaught of Chinese cyber intrusions that steal sensitive information like client lists, merger and acquisition data, pricing information, and the results of research and development. This illegally-acquired information gives Chinese companies an unfair competitive advantage against the companies from which it was stolen."[29]

The most famous instance to date has been the 2010 attack on Google servers, which were attacked in "a concerted political and corporate espionage effort that exploited security flaws in e-mail attachments to sneak into the networks of major financial, defense and technology companies and research institutions in the United States."[30] With Google, about 20 other companies,

25. Lloyd Vries, "Real-Life 'Spy Who Loved Me' Scandal," CBS News, April 16, 2003. Available at: http://www.cbsnews.com/news/real-life-spy-who-loved-me-scandal/ [Accessed 15 Jun. 2015].
26. I. C. Smith & Nigel West, Historical Dictionary of Chinese Intelligence (Lanham, MD: The Scarecrow Press, 2012).
27. Among the most-sought after sectors are biotechnologies, space, IT, and energy; while, geographically speaking, California's Silicon Valley is the main target.
28. Wise, 2011.
29. CISPA, 2012.
30. Ariana Eunjung Cha and Ellen Nakashima, "Google China cyberattack part of vast espionage campaign," Washington Post, January 14, 2010. http://www.washingtonpost.com/wp-dyn/content/arti-

such as Yahoo, Symantec, Adobe, and Northrop Grumman, have found that Chinese hackers targeted them, in what has been dubbed "Operation Aurora."[31]

However, it would be incorrect to believe that only government-sponsored espionage exists. As the Cox Report clarified, a plethora of Chinese actors – public and private – have been involved in technology theft and economic espionage. There have been, for example, cases involving Chinese corporations as well – with the result that some of them have been denied the acquisition of American companies and their technologies, for example Huawei and ZTE. In both cases, the companies have been excluded in the US (and Huawei later in Canada) from public works on the basis of national security. The companies, on the other hand, have always maintained they were private corporations, with no links or instructions from the Chinese Government to illegally acquire Western technology.[32]

Recent Developments

Another important point is how the system regulates itself from within. What is evident is that every change in CPC leadership – at this moment with the fifth generation leaders at the helm since the November 2012 18th Party Congress – is normally carried along with some purges at the top of those services. This is what has happened with the new leader, Xi Jinping, CPC general secretary and PRC president, and the procedures still appear to be ongoing at the moment.

As a matter of fact, since 2013, Xi has been waging an anti-corruption campaign that is considered by many observers as a way to get rid of political adversaries, in the biggest purge since the Cultural Revolution (around 15,000 people to be investigated). One of the latest victims has been, in January 2015, Vice Minister Ma Jiang,[33] MSS chief, implicated in the Founder Group's investigation.[34] Ma was a high-profile official, in charge of China's counterespionage operations, and the highest-ranking security official investigated after Zhu

cle/2010/01/13/AR2010011300359.html?sid=ST2010011300360.

31. Ibid.

32. Ellen Messmer, "A House Intelligence Committee report blasts Huawei and ZTE as threats to U.S. national security," NetworkWorld, October 8, 2012. Available at: *http://www.networkworld.com/ article/2160516/data-center/house-intelligence-committee-report-blasts-huawei—zte-as-threats-to-u-s—na-tional-secur.html*.

33. Jamil Anderlini, "Chinese spymaster Ma Jian detained in corruption purge," *Financial Times*, January 12, 2015. *http://www.ft.com/cms/s/0/84707fd8-9a37-11e4-8426-00144feabdc0.html#axzz3Od8O0tbm*

34. Founder Group is a Beijing University-owned technology company, under investigation since 2012 over corruption claims. "Founder has been involved in a high-profile spat with Beijing Zenith, a property developer with a mysterious background, but which is also the second-biggest shareholder in the conglomerate's Founder Securities unit. Beijing Zenith publicly accused Founder executives of insider trading and misappropriating company assets to the tune of several billion yuan." (2015). "Chinese spy chief Ma Jian detained as corruption crackdown widens." *South China Morning Post*, January 11, 2015. Available at: *http://www.scmp.com/news/article/1678537/chinese-spy-chief-ma-jian-detained-corruption-crackdown* [Accessed 15 Jun. 2015].

Yongkang, MPS chief between 2002-2007.[35] Zhu was demoted in July 2014. He was the first member of the Politburo's Standing Committee to be involved in an official investigation in the PRC's history. While the official charges, which were formalized in April 2015, talk of "bribes, abuse of power and intentionally leaking state secrets" that cover a period since 1988, thus most of Zhu's three-decade political career, the outlook seems more complex than that. As related by the South China Morning Post "The Supreme People's Court said last month that Zhou had "undermined the party's solidarity and engaged in political activities not approved by the authorities," a rare accusation that some analysts suggested was an indication that Zhou would face charges for political offences." The trial, held in Tianjin No. 1 Intermediate People's Court in spring 2015, where Zhou risked a death penalty, concluded in June 2015 with the former security tzar pleading guilty and receiving a sentence of life imprisonment.[36]

READINGS FOR INSTRUCTORS

There are a few important on-line references for Chinese intelligence services, although some are not up-to-date. They still represent a useful starting point for instructors. The main three to be consulted are:

http://www.globalsecurity.org/intell/world/china/mss.htm .

http://fas.org/irp/world/china/mss/index.html .

http://servicederenseignements.e-monsite.com/pages/grandes-agences/republique-populaire-de-chine.html.

Also, there are the websites of Chinese think tanks devoted to, among other subjects, intelligence studies, some of them only available in Chinese. For an updated list of the most prominent of them and a brief description, see: http://libguides.gwu.edu/content.php?pid=77975&sid=591628.

Recommended books and journal articles include:

Bates, G. and J. Mulvenon, "Chinese Military-Related Think Tanks and Research Institutions," The China Quarterly 171, September 2002.

Byron, J. and R. Pack. The Claws of the Dragon: Kang Sheng-the Evil Genius Behind Mao and His Legacy of Terror in People's China (New York: Simon and Schuster, 1992).

---

35. Li Jing, "China's ex-security chief Zhou Yongkang charged with corruption, leaking secrets," *South China Morning Post*, April 3, 2015 http://www.scmp.com/news/china/article/1755037/chinas-ex-security-tsar-zhou-yongkang-indicted-after-graft probe?utm_source=edm&utm_medium=edm&utm_content=20150403&utm_ campaign=breaking_news.

36. Alvin Yibanez, "Ex-Security Chief Zhou Yongkang Sentenced to Life in Prison," Yibada [online]. Available at: *http://en.yibada.com/articles/38175/20150613/ex-security-chief-zhou-yongkang-sentenced-life-prison.htm.* [Accessed 15 Jun. 2015]. Yet, "with the arrest of a major leader in a continuing, and massive, purge, and constant reminders that the stakes of the struggle against corruption are nothing less than the survival of the party, Xi and his colleagues have sought to generate a period of crisis in which major changes are possible. The question to remain is whether this political window is wide enough—and will stay open long enough—to allow systemic change to take root" (Cohen, 2014).

Eftimiades, Nicholas. *Chinese Intelligence Operations* (Annapolis, MD: Naval Institute Press, 1994).

Faligot, R., and K. Remi, *The Chinese Secret Service* (New York: William Morrow & Co., 1990).

Huo, Z. & and Z. Wang. *Techniques of Obtaining National Defense Science and Technology Intelligence.* [Guofang Keji Qingbaoyuan ji Huoqu Jishu] Kexue Jishu] (Wenxuan Publishing Co., Beijing, 1991), available at: *http://fas.org/ irp/world/china/docs/sources.html* .

Lin, Q. *Kan Sheng Waizhuan* [An Unofficial Biography of Kang Sheng] (Beijing: Zhongguo Qingnian, 1988).

Kan, Zhongguo, "Intelligence Agencies Exist in Great Numbers, Spies Are Present Everywhere; China's Major Intelligence Departments Fully Exposed," *Chien Shao* (Hong Kong, 1 January 2006).

Kan, S. *China: Suspected Acquisition of U.S. Nuclear Weapon Secrets,* CRS Report for Congress, RL30143, 2006, online at: *https://www.fas.org/sgp/crs/nuke/ RL30143.pdf* .

Li, Mingyang, (ed.). *Sunzi Bingfa* [SunTzu's Art of War] (Hefei, Anhui: Huangshan Shushe, 2001).

Mattis, P., "Assessing the Foreign Policy Influence of the Ministry of State Security," *China Brief* 11 (1), January 14, 2011.

Mattis P., "The Analytic Challenge of Understanding Chinese Intelligence Service," *Studies in Intelligence* 56 (3), September 2012. Available at: *https:// www.cia.gov/library/center-for-the-study-of-intelligence/csi-publications/csi-stud-ies/studies/vol.-56-no.-3/pdfs/Mattis-Understanding%20Chinese%20Intel.pdf* .

Roche, E. M. *Corporate spy: Industrial espionage and counterintelligence in the multinational enterprise* (New York: Barraclough, 2008).

Smith, I. C. and Nigel West, *Historical Dictionary of Chinese Intelligence* (Lanham, MD: The Scarecrow Press, 2012).

Stokes, M., J. Lin, and L.C. Russell Hsiao, "The Chinese People's Liberation Army Signals Intelligence and Cyber Reconnaissance Infrastructure," Occasional Paper, Project 2049 Institute, 11 November 2011.

Sun Zi, *The Art of War*, online at: *http://ctext.org/art-of-war.*

Trulock, Notra. *Code Name Kindred Spirit: Inside the Chinese Nuclear Espionage Scandal* (San Francisco: Encounter Books, 2004).

Wakeman, F. *Spymaster: Dai Li and the Chinese Secret Services* (Berkeley: University of California Press, 2003).

Wise, David. *Tiger Trap: America's Secret Spy War With China* (Boston: Houghton Mifflin Harcourt, 2011).

Zhang, Shaojun, et al. *Junshi Qingbao Xue* [The Science of Military Intelligence] (Beijing: Junshi kexue chubanshe [Academy of Military Science Press], 2001), 6, 10–12.

Newsclippings and other media sources consulted for the writing of this article:

Cohen, D., "Zhou's Fall About Institutions, Not Personalities," China Brief 14 (15), July 31, 2014. *http://www.jamestown.org/programs/chinabrief/single/?tx_ ttnews%5Btt_news%5D=42688&tx_ttnews%5BbackPid%5D=758&no_*

cache=1#.VVJCldpVikp .

De Graffenreid, Kenneth (ed.). The Unanimous and Bipartisan Report of the House Select Committee on U.S. National Security and Military Commercial Concerns With the People's Republic of China ("The Cox Report"). (Washington, DC: Regnery, 1999). A copy of the declassified sections of the Cox Report is accessible at: http://www.house.gov/coxreport/chapfs/over.html

Johnston, A. et al, "The Cox Committee Report: An Assessment," 1999, online at: http://iis-db.stanford.edu/pubs/10331/cox.pdf .

Mattis, Peter, "Five Ways China Spies. Not as different as you might think," National Interest, March 6, 2014 at http://nationalinterest.org/commentary/five-ways-china-spies-10008.

Lo, Ping, "Secrets About CPC Spies — Tens of Thousands of Them Scattered Over 170-Odd Cities Worldwide," Hong Kong Cheng Ming No. 231, 1 January 1997, 6-9 ["Journal Discloses `Secrets' About PRC Spy Network," FBIS-CHI-97-016, 1 Jan 1997]

Dr. Stefania Paladini is an associate professor at Coventry University, UK, where she is also in charge of a EU-FP7 project researching Chinese investments in Europe. Before joining academia, she worked several years for the Italian government, seven of which were spent in East Asia as trade commissioner. She obtained her PhD in international relations and security studies from City University of Hong Kong.

GUIDE TO THE STUDY OF INTELLIGENCE

Iran's Intelligence Establishment

Carl Anthony Wege

Introduction

Iran's 1979 revolution, one of the major events of the twentieth century led by Grand Ayatolla Ruhollah Mostafavi Moosavi Khomeini, established a new form of government — the *Vilayat-e Faqih* or "Guardianship of the Islamic Jurists." Built on the Twelver (Ithna-Ashari) Shi'a claim that any government outside that of the hidden Imam was illegitimate,[1] the innovation of Khomeini's revolution was that Shi'a religious authorities began, for the first time in Iranian history, to govern directly through the *Vilayat-e Faqih*.[2]

Iran, or Persia as it was historically known, is a multiethnic country of 80 million people whose Farsi-speaking Persian (and Azeri) populations dominate the government and are geographically concentrated in the central Iranian plateau. Modern Iran incorporates additional ethnic groups, including Turks, Kurds, Lurs, and Arabs who constitute a significant portion of the population and mostly live around the periphery of that central plateau. This center-periphery division, generally along ethnic lines, is the most significant cultural

---

1. As Shi'as believe, the twelfth Imam, Muhammad al-Mahdi, was hidden from the world by divine intervention in 874 AD and his return will usher in the day of Judgment. The Shi'a community also includes Fivers (*Zaydis*), who claim five true Imams and Seveners (*Ismailis*), who now live primarily in an arc from Central Asia and Afghanistan to western China. Iran's 16th century Safavid Dynasty disguised tensions between historic Persian ideas of divine kingship and Twelver Shi'a concepts of legitimate governance, solely through the hidden Imam, by asserting that the Shah and associated institutions derived their authority from Allah during the time of the Imam's hiding. The 17th century creation of the office of Mullabashi (chief mullah) precipitated ongoing contention between religious and secular power in Iran. See Roger M. Savory, "The Problem of Sovereignty in an Ithna Ashari ("Twelver") Shi'i State," in *Religion and Politics in the Middle East*. Michael Curtis ed., Boulder, Colorado: Westview Press, 1981, p 135-7 and Heinz Halm, *Shi'ism*, New York: Comubia University Press, 1987, p 81.
2. Azar Tabari, "The Role of the Clergy in Modern Iranian Politics," in Nikki R. Keddie (ed.), *Religion and Politics In Iran* (New Haven and London: Yale University Press, 1983), 72.

feature characterizing modern Iran's national state.[3] The potential for these minorities living along the periphery of the country to be exploited by Iran's enemies is one of the major concerns of the country's security services.

The objectives of Iran's security services are not dissimilar from those of neighboring states. Many of the Arab dictatorships in the Middle East have been called *mukhābarāt* states to convey the idea that they are built on multiple security agencies whose primary purpose is to protect the regime from internal dissent. A multiplicity of agencies prevents any concentration of power that could precipitate an anti-regime coup. Iran, while not an Arab state, has engaged its many security agencies for the same objective. Politically, Tehran's *Vilayat-e Faqih* government incorporates a complex intra-Iranian matrix of relationships between clerics, the economic power centers (*bonyad*), the Revolutionary Guard (IRGC, *Pasdaran* or *Pasdan-e Inqilal-e Islami*) and other Iranian security organs, which compete for influence in an ever-changing constellation of conflicting interactions. The various nodes of this matrix, all carefully watched by the security organs, make a successful coup unlikely.

Iran's National Security Establishment

The apex of Iran's national security establishment is the *Supreme National Security Council* (SNSC), roughly similar in concept to the US National Security Council in that the organizational intent is to aggregate policymakers with the heads of the security organs and the armed forces. Iran's SNSC then brings together the heads of the regular military, foreign affairs, and political leadership and includes the heads of the Interior Ministry, the Intelligence and Security Ministry, and the Islamic Revolutionary Guards Corps (IRGC).

Like all governments, Iran is adapting to the increasing importance of national information infrastructures. Tehran has established a variety of bodies to manage various security aspects of this emergent cyber domain. The evolving security organs have nodes spread across multiple institutions. For example, two "cyber war" centers exist in Tehran and operate under the tutelage of the Revolutionary Guards. Offensively, the Revolutionary Guards support a variety of Iranian "hacker" organizations like the *Iran Cyber Army* that are little more than unofficial affiliates of the Guards. These unofficial affiliates coordinate operations with *Cyber Hizballah* and the *Syrian Electronic Army*, generally targeting dissident groups as well as the information infrastructure of enemy countries.[4] There is a *Basiji Cyber Council* with minimal security responsibilities,

---

3. "Iran's lurking enemy within," *Asia Times*, January 8, 2006.
4. Olivier Danino,"Cyber Capabilities of Israel and Iran: Clash Seen in a new Light," Institute for European Research February 26, 2013. *http://www.medea.be/2013/02/les-capacites-cybernetiques-disrael-et-de-liran-un-affrontement-vu-sous-un-nouvel-angle/*. The assassination of Mojtaba Ahmadi, commander of the IRGC cyber war centers in Tehran in 2013, indicates that regional powers now take seriously Iran's cyber war capacity.

but more than a thousand personnel who create and post regime-friendly content across multiple public cyberspace venues.[5] Iran created a *Cyber Defense Command* (*Gharargah-e Defa-e Saiberi*) in 2010 under the armed forces (*Artesh*) Passive Defense Organization. This is a kind of Iranian civil defense program with responsibility to help defend the nation in wartime. The Cyber Defense Command, as part of that Passive Defense, was tasked with defending Iran's information infrastructure. A cyber police organization (FATA) began in 2011 to target internet crime and suppress online dissent. Within a couple of years, FATA had established a presence in all 31 provinces and 56 cities across Iran. FATA is distinct from the National Police Organization (NAJA), and one of FATA's primary objectives is to reduce or eliminate anonymous access to the internet. In furthering that objective, the FATA are promoting a new biometric ID card that Iranians would need to access the internet. In 2012, a *Supreme Council of Cyberspace* (*Shora-ye Ali-ye Fazo-ye Majazl*) was decreed by Iran's second supreme leader, Ali Khamenei, to coordinate Iranian governmental agencies with security-related cyber responsibilities.[6]

Iran's Interior Ministry plays a somewhat ancillary role in Tehran's security architecture controlling ordinary crime as well as suppressing political dissent. It includes Iran's *Law Enforcement Forces* (*Niruha-ye Entezami-ye Jomhuri-ye Islami*) created in 1991 to incorporate urban police, the rural gendarmerie, and various revolutionary committees. This includes the national police force called the *Islamic Republic Police Force* (*Niruyih Intizamiyih Jumhuriyih Islamiyih Iran*, NAJA). A decade ago, a number of informal groups made up of personnel from multiple security organizations were aggregated into *ad hoc* security bodies that operated during the presidency of Mohammad Khatami (1997 – 2004). These organizations were referred to as a *Parallel Intelligence Apparatus* (*Nahad-hayih ittia'tiyih muvazi*). They were anchored in an "off the books" conspiracy between the Revolutionary Guards and the judiciary. These *ad hoc* entities were usually described as plainclothes police who operated at the behest of political conservatives opposed to Khatami's reformist ideas. They apparently acted with the approval of Supreme Leader Khamenei and established a limited system of secret prisons to detain reformist intellectuals.[7] With the presidency of Mahmoud Ahmadinejad in 2005, these *ad hoc* secret police forces devolved back into their formal parent organizations. However, such *ad hoc* secret police forces could, no doubt, be reconstituted to work with the Islamic Republic Police Forces if conditions warranted.

---

5. The *Basiji* are defined as "Mobilization of the Oppressed" (*Basij-e Mostaz'afin* or *Basiji*) discussed later.

6. LTC Eric K. Shafa, "Iran's Emergence as a Cyber Power," *Strategic Studies Institute*, August 20, 2014. *http://www.strategicstudiesinstitute.army.mil/index.cfm/articles/Irans-emergence-as-cyber-power/2014/08/20n.*

7. "Covert Terror: Iran's Parallel Intelligence Apparatus," *Human Rights Documentation Center*, New Haven, Connecticut, April 2009.

Iran's post-revolutionary intelligence establishment developed on the foundation of both the Ministry of Intelligence and Security (MOIS, sometimes called Vezarat-e Ettela'at va Amniyat-e Keshvar, VAVAK) and the Revolutionary Guard Corps. In keeping with the vision of the Vilayat-e Faqih, every intelligence minister since the revolution has been a religious authority rather than a technocrat.[8] The MOIS functions more as an executive body than a traditional ministry reporting directly to the supreme leader of the Islamic Republic, 'Ali Hosseini Khamenei.[9]

Security Organizations

The strength of Iran's intelligence and security organizations is built on the twin pillars of the Ministry of Intelligence and Security and the Revolutionary Guard.

MOIS was created in 1984 as the successor organization to the Ministry of Intelligence and National Security (Sazman-e Ettela'at Va Amniat-e Melli-e, SAVAMA).[10] One of VAVAK's first actions was to institute a system of regional centers across Iran in the 1980s as the Khomeini government consolidated the Revolution.[11] Iran's intelligence services, maturing in the 1990s, established relationships with foreign services, and most importantly with the Russian Foreign Intelligence Service (Sluzhba Vneshnei Razvedki, or SVR). The SVR trained hundreds of Iranian intelligence personnel and were allowed to station Russian personnel on Iranian soil. In addition to the traditional intelligence skill sets, the SVR trained MOIS personnel in the old KGB methods of disinformation, which the MOIS calls Nefaq (an Arabic, not Farsi, word for "discord" or "hypocrisy").[12] The French Centre for Research on Intelligence estimates the MOIS staff numbers roughly 15,000, with several thousand deployed outside the country covertly or under cover of official Iranian organizations, including charities and cultural centers, in addition to the local embassy.[13] VAVAK officers who are assigned to a local Iranian embassy typically serve three – to five-year terms.[14] In

---

8. "Iran's Clerical Spymasters," *Asia Times*, July 21, 2007. Likewise there is what amounts to a "commissar system" of clergy in every entity of governance who report directly to the supreme leader. It is also relevant that much of the MOIS leadership have attended the *Madrase-ye Haqqani* theological school in Qom. See also Wilfred Buchta, *Who Rules Iran* (Washington, DC: Washington Institute of Near East Policy and Konrad Adenauer Stifung, 2000), 166. The Haqqani school itself was founded by the Hojjatieh, a semi-secret anti-Sunni society that technically rejects the *Velayat-e Faqih* of post-revolutionary Iran. See "Shi'ite Supremacists Emerge from Iran's Shadows," *AsiaTimes* September 9, 2005.

9. Khamenei appears to be coming to the end of his life, which will likely place the security organizations in the position of refereeing the transition to a new Supreme Leader.

10. SAVAMA was a transitional organization between the SAVAK secret police organization of the pre-revolutionary government of the Shah of Iran and the MOIS.

11. *Intelligence Newsletter* 286, April 18, 1996.

12. "Special Report: Iranian Intelligence Regime Preservation," *Stratfor*, June 21, 2010, 7.

13. "The Iranian Intelligence Services," *Centre for Research on Intelligence* Note for News No. 200, 5 January 2010, Paris http://www.cf2r.org.

14. Precision in this sort of thing is always problematic due to everything from definitional differences respecting what constitutes a ministry employee to active disinformation efforts on the ministry's part.

the early 21st century, the major VAVAK training sites in Tehran and Qom were supported by recruitment at noted academic institutions such as Imam Mohammed Bagher University in Tehran. Structurally, VAVAK was not dissimilar to many intelligence agencies; it contained about a dozen separate directorates, although VAVAK had three with direct responsibility for terrorist operations. A Directorate of Overseas Affairs was responsible for MOIS branches abroad with special emphasis on operations against the Peoples Mujahidin Organization, a Marxist organization founded in 1965 and dedicated to the overthrow of the Islamic Republic. Although considered a terrorist organization by the United States, it has nonetheless provided apparently accurate information on Iran's nuclear program. A Directorate of Foreign Intelligence and Liberation Movements participated in typical foreign espionage operations. A Directorate for Security ostensibly engaged in internal security, but was primarily responsible for overseas assassinations of regime opponents.[15] VAVAK's organizational matrix also incorporated entities with focus on: analysis and strategy, homeland security (protecting state institutions), national security (responsible for monitoring overseas opposition movements), counterintelligence, and foreign intelligence (with analytical departments and geographic regional divisions).[16] Domestically, MOIS has responsibility to monitor Iran's ethnic minorities, particularly on the country's periphery; and, externally, MOIS is tasked to neutralize Iranian expatriate dissident organizations.[17] Several distinct MOIS bodies recruit candidates for operations in the Gulf, Yemen and Sudan, Lebanon and Palestine, North Africa, Europe, South Asia and the Far East, North America, and Latin America.[18] A competition of sorts has developed between MOIS and the Revolutionary Guard with the Guards slowly becoming the more dominant organization.

The second pillar of Iran's intelligence and security organizations is the Revolutionary Guard, which first attained the status of an independent ministry in 1982 and has evolved into a Praetorian Guard constituting the backbone of the Islamic Republic. The IRGC is now essentially a state within a state, responsible for Iran's nuclear weapons and ballistic missile programs as well as maintaining a military structure that parallels the regular armed forces (Artesh). Like the Chinese People's Liberation Army (PLA), the IRGC now also controls large swaths of Iran's economy. A lesser-known responsibility of the IRGC is to manage a suspected biological weapons program including the *Revolutionary Guards Baqiyatollah Research Center* and the Queshm Island Persian

---

15. *Intelligence Newsletter* No. 286, April 18, 1996; "MOIS Structure," February 28, 2006 *http://www. iranterror.com/content/view/176/66.*)

16. "The Iranian Intelligence Services," Note for News No. 200, 5 January 2010 .

17. "Special Report: Iranian Intelligence Regime Preservation" *Stratfor,* June 21, 2010, 7.

18. See "Insight: Iran-MOIS/IRGC structure and operations," *Global Intelligence Files,* Wikileaks, March 17, 2010, *https://wikileaks.org/gifiles/docs/96/96828_insight-iran-mois-irgc-structure-and-operations-.html.*

Gulf Marine Biotechnology Research Center.[19]

In 2005, the Eagle 2 (*Oghab* 2) organization, headed by Ahmad Wahidi, was created under the Revolutionary Guards to defend Iran's nuclear program. While under the IRGC, *Oghab* 2 appears to report to the MOIS Counterintelligence Directorate and has several thousand employees tasked with protecting various aspects of the nuclear program.[20] This kind of lateral reporting line, where a subsidiary agency of one organization reports to a subsidiary agency of another organization, occurs with some regularity in Iran's security enterprise. The operational scope of *Oghab* 2 is fairly wide given the need to protect senior scientists and engineers, industrial equipment across the nuclear program and now the cyber domain of information networks supporting the program.

The IRGC Quds (the Holy, Jerusalem) Force, now commanded by Hossein Hamadani, incorporates its own security apparatus with responsibilities for both intelligence gathering and covert actions outside Iran.[21] Following the near uprising over Iran's fraudulent elections in 2009, the Khamenei government reorganized a number of security organizations including several associated with the IRGC. Khamenei decreed creation of a new organization, called the Intelligence Organization of the Islamic Revolutionary Guard Corps. Since the only immediate source of qualified intelligence officers would be from the management of sister organizations, there is a certain amount of "hat changing" mitigating the new agency's significance. The IRGC Intelligence Organization is now headed by Hojjatoleslam Hossein Taeb, with Hojjatoleslam Gholamhossein Ramezani as his counterintelligence chief.[22] Taeb's organization is headquartered at Qasr-e Firouzeh in Kamali, near Tehran. Taeb's IRGC Intelligence Organization also commands the MOIS Internal Security Directorate and the security apparatus of the *Basiji*. It has authority over Khamenei's Department 101, which acts as a special intelligence unit within MOIS and is tasked with coordinating some intelligence activities between MOIS and the IRGC Intelligence Organization.[23] Taeb's role illustrates a characteristic of Iran's intelligence architecture, with reporting lines sometimes laterally crossing agency jurisdiction. This obscures the observer's view of the functional relationships between Iranian intelligence bodies and thereby enhances their security. It also facilitates those bodies watching each other, mitigating the

---

19. See "Revolutionary Guards Baqiyatollah Research Center," *Iran Watch,* January 26, 2004. http://www.iranwatch.org/iranian-entities/revolutionary-guards-baqiyatollah-research-center See also "Mapping Iran's Biological Warfare Complex" *The Biological Warfare Blog: Black Six, http://bio-defencewarfare-analyst.blogspot.com/2014/05/mapping-irans-biological-warfare-complex.html.* May 12, 2014.

20. "Iran's Ministry of Intelligence and Security: A Profile," Library of Congress under an Interagency Agreement with the Combating Terrorism Technical Support Office's Irregular Warfare Support Program, December 2012, 34.

21. Wilfred Buchta, *Who Rules Iran?* (Washington, DC: Washington Institute for Near East Policy, 2000), 69. From 1998 until 2014, Qassem Suleimani commanded the Quds Force .

22. Taeb studied jurisprudence in Qom and Mashhad and was on the faculty at Imam Hossein University. He also briefly served as MOIS espionage chief.

23. "Iran exile group: Khamenei tightens intelligence grip," *Reuters,* November 12, 2009.

risk of a coup against the state.

Separately, the larger Quds Special Operations Forces, numbering several thousand, serves in Lebanon, Iraq, Syria, Bosnia, Sudan, and elsewhere. The infrastructure the Guard creates for these operations can last for years. A decade ago, for example, Quds Ramazan (Ramadan) Corps (subdivided into Nasr, Zafar, and Fajr commands) operated against US and coalition forces in Iraq, but now that infrastructure can be enhanced to fight the Islamic State that has emerged under Caliph Ibrahim and which threatens both Iran and its interests in Shi'a dominated Iraq.[24]

Iran's national ambition to dominate the Middle East has also led the IRGC Quds Special Operations Forces to cooperate with a variety of Sunni extremist organizations that further that ambition. Part of this cooperation involves utilizing an IRGC-controlled system of terrorist training camps within Iran to train and influence proxy organizations that can be deployed in Iran's cause. This system of camps was fashioned quite early in the Islamic Republic and has trained both Sunni and Shi'a fighters who support Iran's foreign policy goals and continues to this day. Regular groups of Sunni Hamas activists from the Gaza Strip, for example, continue to cycle through the Iranian camp system.[25] Iran's camp system was configured to support different terrorist organizations and has been developed to focus on differentiated skill sets. In Qom, for example, the Fatah Ghani Husseini Camp was used primarily by Turkish Islamists; while in Qasvim, the Abyek Camp was used for terrorist training in political assassination. Thousands of trainees have now passed through this system with about ten percent selected for more extensive training.[26] Additional camps have included the Nahavand Camp in Hamadan for Lebanon's Hizballah; and the Imam 'Ali Camp in east Tehran, which is the largest camp, used by Saudi opposition groups. Iranian exile groups have also named Bahonar Barracks, Mostafa Kohomeini Barracks, Ghayoor Asli Barracks, Imam Sadegh Camp, Korreit Camp, Lavizan and Abyek training centers, etc.[27] Virtually all of these foreign terrorist trainees should be considered potential proxy actors for the IRGC. These camps are considerably more substantial than the Western image of terrorist training camps, such as those that various Palestinian factions had maintained in Lebanon or what had been available in Libya or Syria 30 years ago. Externally, the Revolutionary Guard tries to exploit Yemen's rebel Houthi Clan, and runs networks in Venezuela and Bolivia as well as throughout sub-Saharan Africa, where it typically relies on Hizballah to influence the local expatriate

24. Bill Roggio, "Iran's Ramazan Corps and the ratlines into Iraq," *The Long War Journal*, December 5, 2007. *http://www.longwarjournal.org/archives/2007/12/irans_ramazan_corps.php*.

25. "Iran's al-Quds Octopus Spreads Its Arms," *Jerusalem Post*, October 27, 2008.

26. "Iran builds up network of terror schools," *Electronic Telegraph*, July 8, 1996.

27. See "Terrorist Training by The Quds Force and the VEVAK," February 28, 2006, *http://www.iranterror.com*.

Lebanese community.[28] This gives the IRGC an international network, separate from that of VAVAK, for operations and to project Iran's power.

Ancillary organizations under IRGC command and used to protect the Khameini regime from domestic dissent includes the Mobilization of the Oppressed (*Basij-e Mostaz'afin or Basiji*) militias. The *Basiji* militia were placed under command of the IRGC after 2008, and are generally poorly educated and uniformly drawn from rural areas. The three main branches of the *Basiji* include the Ashoura and Al-Zahra Brigades, which function as glorified neighborhood watches; the Imam Hossein Brigade, which can handle more serious matters as most of its members are war veterans; and the Imam 'Ali Brigades, which can also be used for more serious security threats.[29] A similar organization, the Helpers of God (*Ansar e-Hizballah*), sometimes cooperates with the *Basiji*. These became the blunt instrument of suppression used on the streets in large numbers and physically beat anti-government protesters in Iran's urban centers and ultimately crushed opponents of the 2009 election results.

Conclusions

Internally, both VAVAK and the IRGC are most active on the periphery of Iran's national borders. For example, both have developed a deep understanding of Salafi terrorist networks that have engaged in Afghanistan and Pakistan over the last two decades.[30] Likewise, both have extensive networks in Iraq and Syria, where the flames of civil war are burning hot enough to threaten Khamenei's house. VAVAK also operates a large station in Amman, Jordan, which, along with Dubai, is becoming the Vienna of the Near East.

The Revolutionary Guard and VAVAK now appear to be sharing parallel intelligence and security functions, with the Revolutionary Guard shouldering a greater share of responsibility. These parallel responsibilities allow the Khamenei regime to create a lattice tying these agencies together while using each organization to check the other, lessening the chance of a successful coup against the *Vilayat-e Faqih*. This veil of unknowing obscures the organizational structure and function of Iran's intelligence agencies from outside observers, shielding the regime's enforcers with a cloak of anonymity.

In the long run, it is post-18th century European Enlightenment-style modernity itself that is the real threat to Iran and other Islamist governments. The ability to isolate a creative and educated population from the larger world and new ideas inevitably crashes on the shoals of reality. Economic and social globalization is not moving toward a worldwide Islamic revolution, it

---

28. "Iran's Special Services Under Fire," January 9, 2012 Note For News No. 284, *French Centre for Research on Intelligence*, Paris, http://www.cf2r.org.

29. See 'Ali Alfoneh "The Basij Resistance Force," *Iran Primer*, U.S. Institute of Peace, undated, http://iranprimer.usip.org/resource/basij-resistance-force.

30. "The Iranian Intelligence Services and the War on Terror," *Terrorism Monitor* 2 (10), May 19, 2004.

is moving decisively away from it. Khomeini's majestic vision of an unfolding Shi'a revolution has now deteriorated into the merely profane. Iran's security organs can protect the *Vilayat-e Faqih* for a while. They cannot, however, halt a progressively unifying world.

READINGS FOR INSTRUCTORS

Bill, James A. and Carl Leiden. *Politics Middle East* (Boston and Toronto: Little, Brown, and Company, 1984).

Buchta, Wilfred. *Who Rules Iran?* (Washington, DC: Washington Institute of Near East Policy and Konrad Adenauer Stifung, 2000).

Fuller, Graham E. *The Center of the Universe: The Geopolitics of Iran* (Boulder, San Francisco, Oxford: Westview Press, 1991).

Katzman. Kenneth. *Warriors of Islam: Iran's Revolutionary Guard* (Boulder and London: Westview Press, 1993).

Keddie, Nikki R. (ed.). *Religion and Politics in Iran* (New Haven and London: Yale University Press, 1983).

Library of Congress. *Iran's Ministry of Intelligence and Security: A Profile.* under an Interagency Agreement with the Combating Terrorism Technical Support Office's Irregular Warfare Support Program, December 2012. Available at *http://fas.org/irp/world/iran/mois-loc.pdf*.

Thaler, David E., Nader Alirez, Shahram Chubin, Jerrold D. Green, Charlotte Lynch, and Frederic Wehrey. *Mullahs, Guards, and Bonyads: An Exploration of Iranian Leadership Dynamics* (RAND National Defense Research Institute Intelligence Policy Center, 2010).

Wehrey, Frederic, Jerold D. Green, Brian Nichiporuk, Alireza Nader, Lydia Hansell, Rasool Nafisi, and S. R. Bohandy. *The Rise of the Pasdaran* (RAND National Defense Research Institute Intelligence Policy Center, 2010).

Wege, Carl A. "Iranian Intelligence Organizations" in Philip H. Davies and Kristian C. Gustafson (eds)., *Intelligence Elsewhere* (Washington, DC: Georgetown University Press, 2013).

Carl A. Wege is a professor of political science at the College of Coastal Georgia. He has traveled in Asia, Latin America, Africa, and Israel and published a variety of articles discussing terrorism and security relationships involving Hizballah, Syria, and Iran. His full publication record is available on LinkedIn. *twege@ccga.edu*

Part VII – Miscellany

The information age and the Worldwide Web have made it challenging to keep up with what is published about the intelligence field. **Professor Peter Oleson** in his article, "Staying Informed," focuses on resources that are generally reliable for educators and others to maintain currency on topics of particular interest.

Dr. Edward Mickolus previously was a CIA recruiter. His article on popular books that have shaped students' opinions of intelligence provides a unique perspective for teachers and instructors.

Finally, **Professor Douglas Wheeler**, who has read extensively about intelligence, traces the evolution of intelligence-related literature over the past century. He shares his recommendations in "The Literature of Intelligence: Another Kind of Need to Know."

GUIDE TO THE STUDY OF INTELLIGENCE

Staying Informed

Information Sources on the Web
Intelligence Bibliographies, Newsletters, Blogs, and Webliographies

Peter C. Oleson

For those educators and interested parties who try to keep up with the world of intelligence the flood of information can be daunting. Newspaper articles, new books, scholarly journals, and web blogs that address intelligence are numerous. Many are politically motivated, none is comprehensive. Unclassified sources lack much of the primary material. Classified sources, unless leaked, are not available. Nevertheless, the following are useful resources, presented in alphabetical order.

> **AFCEA International** (Armed Forces Communications and Electronics Association) publishes *Signal* magazine monthly, which contains numerous intelligence-related articles and news. AFCEA also publishes via its website webinars and white papers related to intelligence, *http://www.afcea.org*. AFCEA also has a monthly intelligence-related blog, the MAZZINT Blog.

> **Air University** has an excellent compilation of intelligence-related materials with many links to articles and relevant websites at its "Gateway to Intelligence." *http://www.au.af.mil/au/awc/awcgate/awc-ntel.htm*.

> The **American Enterprise Institute**'s Critical Threats project tracks and provides analysis of key and emerging threats to national security. *http://www.aei.org/feature/critical-threats-project/*.

> The **Association of Former Intelligence Officers** (AFIO) is an education-oriented national association and has two major recurring publications. The *Weekly Intelligence Notes* (WIN), available to paid members, provides synopses and links to major intelligence-related news stories. The WINs also have a comprehensive calendar of intelligence-related events, including for the International Spy Museum in Washington, DC. AFIO's journal,

Intelligencer, carries articles, opinion pieces, book reviews, and association news. It is published three times a year. AFIO's website contains a plethora of information and links to official government websites. Articles for AFIO's *Guide to the Study of Intelligence*, aimed at educators, appear on its website (http://www.afio.com). AFIO is non-partisan. Most of its members are former intelligence officers.

The Central Intelligence Agency's **Center for the Study of Intelligence** contains rich resources for educators including Agency-related news, reports, a FOIA electronic reading room, topical papers from CIA University's Kent School, and a selected bibliography of books. Unclassified articles from its in-house magazine, *Studies in Intelligence*, are published on its website. https://www. cia.gov and *https://www.cia.gov/library/center-for-the-study-of-intelligence.*

The **CiCentre** is a private counterintelligence training firm that maintains a comprehensive database on international espionage cases, terrorism and cyber security incidents, and other related counterintelligence events. Its on-line database, *Spypedia*, is available via subscription. *http://www. cicentre.com.*

Both the **US House** and **Senate** intelligence committees maintain informative websites. The House site is *http://intelligence.house.gov/.* The Senate site is *http://www.intelligence.senate.gov/.* Both sites now include archival as well as current materials.

The **Council on Foreign Relations** publishes *Foreign Affairs* magazine and includes analytical articles on its website. *http://www.foreignaffairs.com.*

The **Defense Intelligence Alumni Association** (DIAA) provides subscribed members with the *Early Bird*, the Department of Defense's daily summary of news. Founded in 1998, membership is limited to those who have served in the Defense Intelligence Agency. *http://www.diaalumni.org/.*

The **Federation of American Scientists** (FAS) is a national organization. It publishes a free electronic blog, *Secrecy News*, (*http://fas.org/blogs/secrecy/*) that often addresses intelligence and related issues. *Secrecy News* is archived at *http://www.fas.org/sgp/news/secrecy/index.html.* FAS maintains an extensive electronic library on national security related topics, including intelligence (*http://www.fas.org*) and many research reports from the non-partisan Congressional Research Service (CRS) that are not readily available to the public.

Foreign Policy magazine provides excellent daily analysis of world events. Subscription required. *http://foreignpolicy.com*

For items of interest related to China see *RedStarRising@googlegroups.com.*

H-Net Network on Intelligence History and Studies is a donation-supported web service that covers intelligence items of historical significance. Members receive three to five e-mails per week on intelligence history related topics. The network also provides a forum for historians to query one another and collaborate on-line. *Hnet@h-net.msu.edu.*

The **Intelligence and National Security Alliance** (INSA) was established as the Security Affairs Support Association (SASA) in 1979 to bring together professionals in the intelligence field, primarily employees of the National Security Agency; and to help members keep abreast of intelligence and national security community issues and facilitate cooperation, information sharing, and innovation within the Intelligence Community. INSA provides its members with periodic e-mails on current events and working group white papers on current issues of intelligence and industry interest. *http:// www.insaonline.org/.*

IntelNews.org is a daily email of items related to intelligence. It is valuable for its coverage of intelligence issues worldwide. *http://www.intelnews.org.*

International Association for Intelligence Education (IAFIE). An international networking organization for university educators teaching about intelligence, IAFIE has a ListServ via which members can discuss various topics. Its website lists both government and private sector intelligence-related journals. *http://www.iafie.org/.*

Lawfare is a blog published by the Lawfare Institute in cooperation with the Brookings Institution. It covers many issues related to national security and intelligence. *https://www.lawfareblog.com/.* A more liberal point of view comes from **Just Security**. *https://www.justsecurity.org/.*

Loyola University Maryland's Department of Political Science maintains the **Loyola Homepage on Strategic Intelligence**, which provides links to many web sites, journals, articles, documents, laws, and congressional hearing transcripts related to intelligence. http://www.loyola.edu/departments/academics/political-science/strategicintelligence/index.html.

Mercyhurst University's Professor Kristan Wheaton maintains a blog site, *Sources and Methods* at *http://sourcesandmethods.blogspot.com/.* One posting addresses "What Should You be Reading!" *http://sourcesandmethods.blogspot. com/2015/ 03/what-you-should-be-reading-blog-list.html.*

The **Military Intelligence Corps Association** has published *The Vanguard* magazine for its members since 2005. *The Vanguard* contains historical and other articles on military intelligence. Its archived articles are available at *http://www.micastore.com/Vanguard.html.*

One of the most useful and comprehensive bibliographies of intelligence related books and articles was begun in 1998 by Professor J. Ransom Clark at **Muskingum College**, New Concord, Ohio. The *Literature of Intelligence: A Bibliography of Materials with Essays, Review, and Comments* is a free resource. *http://intellit.muskingum.edu/*

The **Director of National Intelligence** website (http://www.dni.gov) provides extensive information on the Intelligence Community, including reports, transcripts of speeches by senior officials, interviews, testimony before Congress, and links to all Intelligence Community organizations' home pages.

The **National Military Intelligence Association** (NMIA), founded in 1974, publishes an on-line *American Intelligence Journal* once every year or two. It contains articles on military and national intelligence topics. Membership in NMIA also enables members to receive a thrice-weekly news summary, *ZGram,* that covers national security and intelligence related news reports from around the world. *CableGram* is another e-mail summary that is available and covers foreign and domestic homeland security matters. *http:// www.nmia.org.*

George Washington University's **National Security Archive** was founded in 1985 by journalists and scholars to check rising government secrecy and expand public access to government information. It is an advocate of open government and indexer and publisher of former secrets. Its research institute maintains an extensive archive of declassified US documents. Its *Digital National Security Archive* contains well-indexed collections on major national security topics including intelligence. *http://www2.gwu.edu/~nsarchiv/*.

The **National Security Institute** in Medway, Massachusetts, produces a weekly e-newsletter, *Security NewsWatch*. It addresses security threats including cyber threats and is complimentary. To subscribe, visit http://nsi.org/newsletter.html. NSI provides a variety of professional information and security awareness services to defense contractors and US Government security practitioners.

Naval Intelligence Professionals (NIP) was founded in 1985 for present and former Naval intelligence professionals to stay informed of developments in the Naval intelligence community and of the activities and whereabouts of past shipmates. It publishes an on-line quarterly journal with articles and news about naval intelligence personnel. *http://www.navintpro.org/*.

NightWatch is a daily analysis of hot spots and crises around the world. Written by a former senior intelligence analyst, it is particularly valuable for coverage of events on the Korean peninsula and Africa. By subscription. *KGSNightWatch@kgsnightwatch.com*.

The **Strategic and Competitive Intelligence Professionals** (SCIP) is a business intelligence-oriented association (formerly known as the Society of Competitive Intelligence Professionals). Its *Competitive Intelligence*™ magazine is published four times a year. *http://www.scip.org/*.

StratFor is a subscription private intelligence service that alerts its subscribers to terror events and other international happenings. It also provides analysis of incipient situations that could pose a national security problem. *https://www.stratfor.com/*.

Since March 2012, the **University of Maryland University College** library has compiled a weekly e-newsletter on cyber security issues and cyber incidents. It provides links to the full articles from many sources. Some links are restricted to university-affiliated personnel due to copyright agreements. Issues are available at *http://cybersecurityupdate.wordpress.com*

WIRED magazine includes a section entitled "Threat Level," which addresses issues of privacy, on-line crime, and security. *http://www.wired.com/category/security*.

Many of the association-related journals include book reviews, as do some subscription journals. The best sources for book reviews include CIA's *Studies in Intelligence*, AFIO's *Intelligencer*, NMIA's *American Intelligence Journal*, *Intelligence and National Security*, and the *International Journal of Intelligence and Counterintelligence*, the latter two published by Taylor and Francis Group, an international academic publisher.

The original 2013 draft of this article was crowd-sourced for additional recommendations. Thanks are due to Dr. Robert Clark, Joseph Fitsanakis, Kristan Wheaton, Joe Mazzafro, and Steven Aftergood for many valuable additions. Due to the dynamic nature of information sources in today's world, readers need to be alert for new sources, but also careful as many sources have a specific political motivation, which should be understood.

Peter Oleson was previously on the board of AFIO, and still serves as the director of its academic exchange program, and editor of the *Guide to the Study of Intelligence*. He is a former associate professor in the Graduate School of the University of Maryland University College and senior intelligence official in the Office of the Secretary of Defense and Defense Intelligence Agency.

GUIDE TO THE STUDY OF INTELLIGENCE

A Guide to Popular Student Books on Intelligence

What do students think they know about intelligence before they walk into the classroom?

Edward F. Mickolus, PhD

During my decades with the Central Intelligence Agency, I had the opportunity to chat with thousands of students and applicants to the Intelligence Community. They bring with them points of view that are shaped by the news media, entertainment industry, blogs, wikis, social networks, and on occasion, even books. Professors routinely provide their charges with lists of books that are designed to give students a handle on what the intelligence business is all about.

Whatever a list of suggested readings includes, readers' opinions will be shaped by a host of books, accurate and inaccurate, balanced and rabidly pro – or anti-intelligence. The following is a sample of what students are reading; some of these books will appear on your recommended list, and some you would not recommend under any circumstances. This list is not complete, nor an endorsement of any particular book. It rather gives an idea of what has shaped the attitudes an instructor can expect to find in the classroom and is organized by the types of questions the books address. Many of these books were written by CIA alumni and/or regarding the CIA, but are applicable to the rest of the Intelligence Community as well.

What's it like to work in the Intelligence Community?

Lowenthal, Mark M. *Intelligence: From Secrets to Policy*, 6th edition (Washington, DC: CQ Press, 2014), 560 pp. A straightforward account of the role of the Intelligence Community in national security affairs by the former assistant director of central intelligence for analysis and production and vice chairman of the National Intelligence Council for evaluation. [Editor's note: Lowenthal was recommended as the one book to read if one was to read only one in "Getting Started: Initial Readings for Instructors of Intelligence," *Intelligencer* 18 (2), Winter/Spring 2011.]

What was it like to run the CIA?

Colby, William and Peter Forbath. *Honorable Men: My Life in the CIA* (New York: Simon and Schuster, 1978), 493 pp. Colby conducted behind the lines operations as one of the World War II Office of Strategic Service (OSS) Jedburghs before engaging in a sterling career with the Agency, which included stints as chief of the East Asia Division, director of operations, and director of central intelligence (DCI).

Dulles, Allen. *The Craft of Intelligence* (New York: Harper and Row, 1963), 277 pp. This was the first memoir by a major Agency officer, providing an excellent historical background, particularly on key counterespionage issues.

Gates, Robert. *From the Shadows: The Ultimate Insider's Story of Five Presidents and How They Won the Cold War* (New York: Simon and Schuster, 1996), 604 pp. Gates is the only DCI to come up through the analytical ranks.

Helms, Richard with William Hood. *A Look Over My Shoulder: A Life in the Central Intelligence Agency* (New York: Random House, 2003), 478 pp. The author has a wonderful flair for the *bon mot*. The memoir gives the reader a good grasp for the high politics of running the Directorate of Operations (DO) and the Agency. He was not in the field for much of his career, but rather ran large organizations with integrity.

Tenet, George J. with William Harlow. *At the Center of the Storm: My Years at the CIA* (New York: HarperCollins, 2007), 549 pp. Unlike other DCI memoirs, which tend to cover entire careers, Tenet concentrates on the big issues of policymakers, mostly during the Bush years, rather than dwelling on what it was like to run the Agency.

What's it like to work in the National Clandestine Service? — Memoirs by Operations Officers

Baer, Robert. *See No Evil: The True Story of a Ground Soldier in the CIA's War on Terrorism* (New York: Crown, 2002), 284 pp. Baer's other books are similarly popular among students. Also see Robert Baer and Dayna Baer, *The Company We Keep: A Husband-and-Wife True-Life Spy Story* (New York: Crown, 2011), 320 pp., their memoir on how home life is affected by balancing Agency careers.

Bearden, Milt and James Risen, *The Main Enemy: The Inside Story of the CIA's Final Showdown with the KGB* (New York: Random House, 2003), 506 pp. Unlike most memoirs, this one has an overarching theme of how the Cold War played out. While Bearden includes personal reminiscences, he focuses on how the Agency's operations affected global geopolitics. He covers "sticks and bricks" tradecraft in the Soviet Bloc, and paramilitary operational discussion regarding the Soviet invasion of Afghanistan.

Clarridge, Duane R. *A Spy for All Seasons: My Life in the CIA* (New York: Scribner, 1996), 430 pp. Clarridge's discussions of his first tours give a flavor of the level responsibility that even young officers have overseas.

Gilligan, Tom. *CIA Life: 10,000 Days with the Agency* (Guilford, Connecticut: Foreign Intelligence Press, 1991), 285 pp. In addition to details of an operational career, Gilligan includes life as a recruiter on campuses.

Holm, Richard. *The American Agent: My Life in the CIA* (London: St. Ermin's Press, 2003), 462 pp., updated as *The Craft We Chose: My Life in the CIA* (Mountain Lake Press, 2011), 568 pp. Holm is a great role model for his courage, operational savvy, and just plain decency. He gives a feeling for how one's life experiences are shaped by an overseas career, and how that career influences family life.

Olson, James. *Fair Play: The Moral Dilemmas of Spying* (Washington, DC: Potomac, 2006), 291 pp. If you have time to read only one book about the CIA, this is the one. Olson poses 50 scenarios, covering false flags, renditions, cover, human rights, covert actions, etc., to scholars, practitioners, journalists, activists, and others from a variety of political inclinations and experiences, asking for their views on the issues. He also includes an Intelligence 101 introduction to espionage tradecraft.

Paseman, Floyd L. *A Spy's Journey: A CIA Memoir* (St. Paul: Zenith Press, 2004), 287 pp. The book tends to be episodic, but covers a sterling career that included positions as chief of station, division chief, and professor.

Rodriquez, Jr., Jose A. with Bill Harlow. *Hard Measures: How Aggressive CIA Actions After 9/11 Saved American Lives.* (New York: Threshold Editions, 2012). Rodriguez, former Director of the National Clandestine Service, assisted by Bill Harlow, former CIA director of public affairs, describe how hard measures – including the controversial Enhanced Interrogation Techniques – derailed terrorist activity targeting the U.S. and saved American lives.

Shackley, Ted with Richard A. Finney. *Spymaster: My Life in the CIA* (Dulles, Virginia: Potomac Books, 2005), 309 pp. Shackley gives one of the most readable accounts of covert influence strategy and techniques available anywhere outside the classified realm.

What's it like to work in the National Clandestine Service? — Journalist/Academic Accounts

Ashley, Clarence. *CIA Spymaster* (Gretna, Louisiana: Pelican Publishing Company, 2004), 350 pp. A former Directorate of Intelligence analyst examines the career of Russian immigrant George Kisevalter, a legendary Agency officer who ran the Popov and Penkovskiy cases.

Gup, Ted. *The Book of Honor: Covert Lives and Classified Deaths at the CIA* (New York: Doubleday, 2000), 390 pp. Gup tracked down the stories of several deceased Agency officers whose names were not officially listed in the Book because of cover or family preference.

Kessler, Ronald. *CIA at War: Inside the Secret Campaign Against Terror* (New York: St. Martin's Griffin, 2003), 378 pp.; and *Inside the CIA* (New York: Pocket, 1994), 400 pp. *CIA at War* updates his earlier word, *Inside the CIA* (1992). Kessler describes the Agency's overall mission and structure and some of its key leaders in the 1990s. It also offers a rare look at the work of collection management officers (then called reports and requirements officers).

Persico, Joseph. *Casey: The Lives and Secrets of William J. Casey: From the OSS to the CIA* (New York: Viking, 1909), 601 pp. Students are also attracted to Bob

Woodward, *Veil: The Secret Wars of the CIA 1981-1987* (New York: Simon and Schuster, 1987), 543 pp. Persico offers a more classical biography of Casey, and spends some time debunking Woodward's deathbed story.

Schecter, Jerrold L. and Peter Deriabin. *The Spy Who Saved the World: How a Soviet Colonel Changed the Course of the Cold War* (New York: Charles Scribner's Sons, 1992), 488 pp. This is the definitive study of the Penkovskiy case delving into the initial concerns about his *bona fides*.

Weiser, Benjamin. *A Secret Life: The Polish Officer, His Covert Mission, and the Price He Paid to Save His Country* (New York: Public Affairs, 2004), 383 pp. A companion definitive study of Ryszard Kuklinski, who spied for CIA for 11 years, and how collection management officers prepare very detailed questions for assets and protect sources.

What's it like to be a female case officer?

Boyle Mahle, Melissa. *Denial and Deception: An Insider's View of the CIA from Iran-Contra to 9/11* (New York: Nation Books, 2004), 352 pp. Her's is a balanced look at a short 15-year career that included a tour as a recruiter.

Plame Wilson, Valerie with an afterword by Laura Rozen. *Fair Game: My Life as a Spy, My Betrayal by the White House* (New York: Simon and Schuster, 2007), 411 pp. The book later became a motion picture. The subtitle mirrors the coverage and tone of the book. The first 100 pages cover her operational training and overseas and headquarters assignments.

What's it like to work in Paramilitary/Covert Action?

Coll, Steve. *Ghost Wars: The Secret History of the CIA, Afghanistan, and bin Laden, From the Soviet Invasion to September 10, 2001* (New York: Penguin, 2004), 712 pp. The former managing editor of the *Washington Post* offers a balanced account of agency activities, beginning where the Bearden book ends and ending where Schroen begins.

Schroen, Gary. *First In: An Insider's Account of How the CIA Spearheaded the War on Terror in Afghanistan* (New York: Ballantine, 2005), 379 pp. While going out the door to retirement, Schroen was invited to lead the Agency's efforts to re-contact and reconstitute the Northern Alliance after 9/11. He and a small team of Agency officers funded Alliance contacts, provided targeting information for US military operations, and began the Afghan portion of the War on Terror.

Berntsen, Gary and Ralph Pezzullo. *Jawbreaker: The Attack on Bin Laden and al Qaeda: A Personal Account by the CIA's Key Field Commander* (New York: Crown, 2005), 328 pp. Berntsten followed Schroen as chief of the Agency's Afghan operations; students often read these books in sequence.

Crile, George. *Charlie Wilson's War: The Extraordinary Story of the Largest Covert Operation in History* (New York: Atlantic Monthly Press, 2003), 550 pp. A rollicking look at heroes in the halls of Congress and halls of the Agency, later made into a major motion picture starring Tom Hanks.

What's it like to be a CIA intelligence analyst?

Andrew, Christopher. *For the President's Eyes Only: Secret Intelligence and the Amer-*

ican Presidency from Washington to Bush (New York: Harper Perennial, 1995), 688 pp. A scholarly examination of the roller coaster of relations between Presidents and the CIA.

Anonymous (Michael Scheuer). *Imperial Hubris: Why the West is Losing the War on Terror* (Washington, DC: Potomac Books, 2004), 314 pp. Scheuer served in the Agency for two decades including running Alec Station, the CIA Counterterrorism Center's unit focused on Osama bin Laden. This gives an example of how analytical tradecraft can be used in targeting terrorists.

George, Roger Z. and James Bruce (eds.). *Analyzing Intelligence: Origins, Obstacles, and Innovations* (Washington, DC: Georgetown University Press, 2008), 340 pp. Essays by practitioners on the craft of analysis.

Hasler, Susan. *Intelligence: A Novel of the CIA* (Thomas Dunne Books, 2010), 320 pp. A former Directorate of Intelligence analyst and DCI speechwriter offers a dead-on satire of life as an analyst.

Heuer, Richards J. Jr. *The Psychology of Intelligence Analysis* (Washington, DC: Center for the Study of Intelligence, 2007), 210 pp. A classic in the field of how mindsets and biases filter data.

What's it like to work in the Directorate of Science and Technology?

Mendez, Antonio J. with Malcolm McConnell. *The Master of Disguise: My Secret Life in the CIA* (New York: Perennial, 1999), 351 pp. How members of the disguise team operate, including the story of rescuing six Americans trapped during the 1979 takeover of the US Embassy in Tehran. Readers also consult Antonio and Jonna Mendez with Bruce Henderson, *Spy Dust: Two Masters of Disguise Reveal the Tools and Operations That Helped Win the Cold War* (New York: Atria Books, 2002), 306 pp., in which Tony and his wife, Jonna, provide more accomplishments of the Office of Technical Services.

Richelson, Jeffrey T. *The Wizards of Langley: Inside the CIA's Directorate of Science and Technology* (Boulder: Westview, 2001), 416 pp. This is a balanced history of the Directorate, ranging from micro-technology to large satellite systems.

Wallace, Robert and H. Keith Melton with Henry R. Schlesinger. *Spycraft: The Secret History of the CIA's Spytechs, from Communism to Al-Qaeda* (New York: Plume, 2009), 576 pp. Wallace served as director of the Office of Technical Services in the Agency's Directorate of Science and Technology. Melton is a well-known espionage historian and collector of espionage paraphernalia. This is the definitive history of Agency gadgetry.

What's it like to work in the Directorate of Support?

Irwin, Richard G. *KH601: And Ye Shall Know the Truth and the Truth Shall Make You Free: My Life in the Central Intelligence Agency* (Virginia: Fortis, 2010), 372 pp. Irwin chronicles his path from a junior security officer to a senior executive in the Intelligence Community.

Sullivan, John F. *Of Spies and Lies: A CIA Lie Detector Remembers Vietnam* (Lawrence: University Press of Kansas, 2002), 250 pp.; and *Gatekeeper: Memoirs of a CIA Polygraph Examiner* (Washington, DC: Potomac, 2007), 273 pp. These books go a long way in humanizing the person on the other side of the box and demystifying the polygraph process.

What kind of training will I get?

Moran, Lindsay. *Blowing My Cover: My Life as a CIA Spy* (New York: GP Putnam's, 2005), 297 pp. A breezy tale, entertainingly told, but ultimately readers tend to ignore it as not serious-minded.

Berlinski, Claire. *Loose Lips: A Novel* (New York: Ballantine, 2004), 272 pp. Another entertaining bit of humor, told in the form of a novel. She spends more time than Moran on non-paramilitary aspects of the training. She also says she never served in the Agency.

Waters, T. J. *Class 11: Inside the CIA's First Post-9/11 Spy Class* (New York: Dutton, 2006), 320 pp. Despite a wealth of factual errors, this is the best of the three recent books on Agency training.

What are the counterintelligence issues?

Andrew, Christopher and Vasili Mitrokhin. *The Sword and the Shield: The Mitrokhin Archive and the Secret History of the KGB* (New York: Basic Books, 2000), 700 pp. and its second volume, Christopher Andrew and Vasili Mitrokhin, *The World Was Going Our Way: The KGB and the Battle for The Third World* (New York: Basic Books, 2005), 678 pp. Mitrokhin was a KGB archivist who smuggled out extensive files on hundreds of Soviet spy cases.

Bagley, Tennent H. *Spy Wars: Moles, Mysteries, and Deadly Games* (New Haven: Yale University Press, 2007), 313 pp. A survey of cases from the Cold War, including a detailed defense of the "Nosenko was a plant" position of legendary CIA counterintelligence chief, James Angleton.

Are any works of fiction accurate?

Ignatius, David. *Blood Money: A Novel of Espionage* (New York: WW Norton, 2011), 372 pp; *The Increment* (New York: WW Norton, 2010), 390 pp.; *Body of Lies* (New York: WW Norton, 2007), 349 pp.; *Agents of Innocence* (New York: WW Norton, 1987), 444 pp.; *SIRO* (New York: Farrar, Straus and Giroux, 1991), 464 pp.; and *A Firing Offense* (New York: Ivy, 1997), 366 pp. Ignatius, former foreign editor and now frequent Middle East op-ed writer for *The Washington Post*, has written a series of widely praised spy thrillers. *Body of Lies* became a major 2008 motion picture, starring Leonardo DiCaprio and Russell Crowe.

Littell, Robert. *The Company: A Novel of the CIA* (New York: Overlook, 2002), 894 pp. A multigenerational CIA spy thriller, set principally in the Cold War, which became a TNT television miniseries in 2007.

Mathews, Francine. *Blown* (New York: Bantam, 2005), 325 pp.; and *Cutout* (New York: Bantam, 2001), 511 pp. Mathews is a former CIA intelligence analyst whose DO heroine battles terrorists while trying to save her case officer husband.

Are there any humorous treatments of intelligence?

Hall, Roger. *You're Stepping on My Cloak and Dagger* (Naval Institute Press reprint, 2004), 220 pp. A look at espionage during World War II.

Sileo, Thomas. *CIA Humor* (Alexandria, Virginia: Washington House, 2004), 101 pp. A former senior Agency officer offers amusing anecdotes from his career.

Mickolus, Ed. *The Secret Book of CIA Humor* (Gretna, Louisiana: Pelican, 2011), 240 pp. A collection of jokes, practical jokes, pranks, and urban legends from throughout the Intelligence Community, but mostly from the CIA.

Edward F. Mickolus, PhD, served for 33 years with CIA as an analyst, operations officer, manager, recruiter, and public affairs officer. He is the author of 21 books and scores of scholarly journal articles on intelligence, international terrorism, international organizations, African politics, psychology, law, education, and humor.

GUIDE TO THE STUDY OF INTELLIGENCE

The Literature of Intelligence

"Another Kind of Need to Know"

Douglas L. Wheeler, PhD

".....What does he next prepare?
Whence will he move to attack?
By water, earth or air?-
How can we head him back?...."

— Rudyard Kipling, *The Spies' March*, 1913[1]

Introduction

Today, few would dispute the notion that there is a literature of intelligence. In 1955, however, Dr. Sherman Kent, the father of contemporary American intelligence analysis, argued that there really was no literature of intelligence and that American intelligence services required a literature.[2] While such a literature is a relatively recent phenomenon, one should ask: Was there a literature of intelligence in 1955 and, if so, what was it? And today how might one define, classify and assess what is now a much larger body of literature?

The literature of intelligence and studies related thereto, including analyses about this literature, is now a vast, multi-disciplinary body of work in many languages. It includes not only printed books and articles but also a growing

---

1. From Hugh & Graham Greene (eds.), *The Spy's Bedside Book* (London: Rupert Hart-Davis, 1957) 133; and from 2nd edition, with an introduction by Dame Stella Rimington, former MI-5 director (London: Hutchinson, 2007), 120-121.
2. Sherman Kent, "The Need for an Intelligence Literature," *Studies In Intelligence* 1 (1) (originally classified), Sept. 1955.

online presence, which can be perishable.

Unlike better established and larger bodies of literature on other topics (for example, military studies), the literature of intelligence studies is more recent, and its quality and reliability more uneven. Authoritative, critical scholarly commentary on it is a recent phenomenon. Some of it remains more contentious than aspects of military studies, and an unknown part of it remains classified. Besides the two questions above, this article provides background and answer to other questions: Why does such literature matter and why should students in intelligence studies, whatever their specialty, have a need to know essential components?

The Literature of Intelligence in 1955
— A Brief Review —

When Sherman Kent wrote his article in *Studies In Intelligence*, he was correct that his profession needed a literature but was mistaken that there was no literature of intelligence of any sort. There was little on that topic that most concerned Kent — the theory and practice of intelligence analysis – six years before he had published a book on the topic.[3] By the mid-1950s, there was a growing body of intelligence-related books and articles in a variety of subjects.

In fact, a major turning point in the history of this literature was World War I. In the decade or two following, a small flood of publications about secret aspects of the war came out in Britain, continental Europe, and North America. Literature about international espionage won a growing readership, according to publishers tracking of book sales and ranking their popularity. An example was a 1933 memoir by a former British diplomat involved in spying in Bolshevik Russia that hit the top of the non-fiction book sales charts in the United States.[4] It is worth noting that events described in many of these books contained revelations about several Soviet intelligence services.[5]

Before 1955, the taxonomy of intelligence literature was not as complex as today. There were still relatively few categories, including spy fiction with spy novels and stories; as well as non-fiction works with the memoirs of former spies or spymasters, anthologies of recollections of former spies, surveys of spy history, and historical accounts of spying in World War I, including well-doc-

---

3. Sherman Kent, *Strategic Intelligence for American World Policy* (Princeton, NJ: Princeton University Press, 1949).

4. Robert Bruce Lockhart's *British Agent* (New York: Putnam, 1933) was one of several books by former secret agents published between 1933 and 1952, which achieved best-selling status in the United States as well as in Britain. A British feature film, based in part on Lockhart's account, starred Leslie Howard and was released in 1934.

5. Concerning non-fiction best-sellers, see Alice Payne Hackett and James Henry Burke, *80 Years of Best Sellers. 1895-1975* (New York: R.R. Bowker, 1977), 115, 131, 158. A 1941 bestseller was Jan Valtin's sensational memoir of a German communist secret agent for the Soviets who defected in 1938 to the United States, *Out of the Night* (Garden City, NY: Garden City Publishing, 1941/1942). A 1952 top seller was Whittaker Chambers, *Witness* (New York: Random House, 1952).

umented warnings of American vulnerability to foreign spying in the 1930s[6]; and memoirs of the early Soviet defectors (1928-1939).

While a few German and French scholars, and one German spymaster, published accounts of espionage history, as early as the 1880's and 1890's, it was not until after World War I that a handful of British, American, French, and German scholars, journalists, and spymasters began to probe systematically the history of spying in international affairs.[7] In the footsteps of British spy fiction writers Oppenheim, Le Queux, and Buchan, a new generation began to publish spy novels in the 1930s.[8]

In the late 1940's, dozens of books and many newspaper stories were published in the United States, Britain, and France on World War II Allied secret operations and stories of Office of Strategic Services actions. Many were sensationalized personal accounts. In addition, a new genre of serious intelligence literature started to emerge. This was intelligence history in a popular form. An early example was Richard Rowan's intriguing, but eccentric historical romp of 1937, on spying from pre-biblical times to 1936, *The Story of Secret Service*,[9] which sold well but was soon out of print. Published in 1941 before Pearl Harbor, *Terror in Our Time: The Secret Service of Surprise Attack*, was Rowan's sensational expose of pre-December 7, 1941 Japanese spying and potential sabotage activities, and although it was not the best seller that his 1937 book was, it did arouse the interest of the FBI readers who began surveillance of his

---

6. A former British intelligence officer in World War I warned about the United States' vulnerability to German spies in the late 1930s. See Captain Henry Landau, *The Enemy Within: The Inside Story of German Sabotage in America* (New York: Putnam's, 1937).

7. The 1882 memoir (edited by J. Auerbach) of Prussian spymaster Wilhelm Stieber was probably the first published memoir of a European state's secret intelligence service, and was finally translated to English in a 1980 edition, Wilhelm Stieber, *The Chancellor's Spy*. The memoir of Walther Nicolai, chief of Germany's military intelligence service in World War I, was translated into English and published as *The German Secret Service* (London, 1924). There was also the general study of the subject by W. N. Klembowski, *L'espionnage militaire en temps de guerre* (Paris, 1895) and an account by F. Routier, *L'espionnage et la trahison en temps de paix et en temps de guerre* (Paris, 1911). A pioneering scholar of intelligence studies was French historian-archivist George Bourgin, at France's Archives Nationales, Paris, the author of "Espionage," in Volume 8 (Edwa-Extract) *Encyclopaedia Britannica* (Chicago, IL: University of Chicago, 1929 edition; 1944 reprinting), 712-714.

8. E. Phillips Oppenheim (1860-1946) wrote *The Avenger* in 1908. William LeQueux (1864-1927) wrote the popular anti-German story, *The Invasion of 1910 and the Tsar's Spy*. John Buchan (1875-1940) wrote the spy thriller *The Thirty-Nine Steps* in 1915. Later, following Somerset Maugham's *Ashendon* (New York: Random House, 1928), Graham Greene and Eric Ambler began to publish international thrillers, most notably, Eric Ambler's *Epitaph for a Spy* (New York: Vintage, 1937).

9. Rowan's 1937 classic of 732 pages sold well as a Literary Guild of America book and though the book soon went out of print, it had an afterlife. A British edition was published, as well editions in French and other European languages. There may also have been a Japanese edition. The author later claimed on the public speaking circuit in New York that Japanese intelligence used *The Story of Secret Service* to instruct their spies. A revised, expanded edition, which carried espionage history up to 1964 but deleted some early history, was published in 1967 and included a laudatory preface from former Director of Central Intelligence Allen Dulles. See Richard Wilmer Rowan with Robert G Deindorfer, *Secret Service: Thirty-Three Centuries of Espionage* (New York: Hawthorn Books, 1967); also Douglas L. Wheeler, "Fiftieth Anniversary of Richard Wilmer Rowan's *The Story of Secret Service*," *Foreign Intelligence Literary Scene* 6 (6), Nov-Dec 1987, 1-5. A collection of Rowan's papers is in the Milne Special Collections and Archives, Dimond Library, University of New Hampshire, Durham, New Hampshire.

public lectures, opened an investigation on him, and questioned him as to where he got his information on sabotage of US targets.[10]

A major milestone came with Kent's key 1955 article, "The Need for an Intelligence Literature." Sherman Kent, a former history professor from Yale University who joined the CIA's Board of National Estimates, became, in effect, the father of contemporary intelligence assessment. He had suggested in 1941 the US intelligence capability was at a low point[11] but that, 14 years later in 1955, the profession of intelligence in the United States had come of age and now required its own literature. For Kent, intelligence was not only a "profession" but a distinct "discipline." He argued that like all disciplines it too needed a literature so that however secret the work of intelligence was there could be publications that would allow the public to study the discipline's "methodology." A literature of intelligence, too, served a more subtle purpose — as a hedge against budget cutbacks or post-war demobilization of intelligence services, as had happened after the end of both World War I and World War II. Additionally, Kent saw a practical reason for such a literature at a nervous moment in the new nuclear age. That was to leave a printed legacy for readers who might survive a war with the Soviet Union. From the 1948-1949 Berlin airlift crisis, to the August 1949 Soviet test of its first atomic bomb, to the 1950 beginning of the Korean War, and to other war and spy scares, Americans were fearful of a nuclear catastrophe.[12]

After the May 1960 U-2 incident and the April 1961 Bay of Pigs debacle, and the consequent greater public awareness of previously secret American intelligence activities, scholars and journalists began to examine the intelligence profession and the literature of intelligence began to expand.

Characterizing the Literature of Intelligence Studies

Like "classics" in any field, notable works in the literature of intelligence are of enduring value and contain a notability beyond a simple tally of sales at any point in time. Classics embody high standards in written expression,

---

10. Richard W. Rowan, *Terror in Our Time: The Secret Service of Surprise Attack* (New York: Longmans, 1941). Information on the FBI file on Rowan was obtained in the late 1980s by this writer from a Freedom of Information Act request to the FBI. The file in question was from an "Internal Security" investigation of historian Rowan, which began in late 1940 and was closed in 1943. The file was listed as "Richard Wilmer Rowan," File 100-7688. Information on case described in my unpublished conference paper, "Testing 'The Great Spy Theory of History,' and Other Problems in Historical Methodology of Intelligence Studies," prepared for a panel on Comparative Methodologies in the Study of Intelligence, chaired by Professor David Charters, 32nd Annual Meeting, International Studies Association, Vancouver, BC, Canada, March 20-23, 1991.

11. Kent, "The Need for an Intelligence Literature," op cit. See also an important biographical source on Kent, a brief monograph by Jack Davis, "Sherman Kent and the Profession of Intelligence Analysis," The Sherman Kent Center for Intelligence Analysis, Central Intelligence Agency/Library, Occasional Papers 1 (5), Nov. 2002. Accessed on the CIA Library/Kent Center website, January 25, 2014.

12. Perhaps it was no coincidence that a popular hit song of 1949 had a lyric that advised radio listeners to "Enjoy yourself, it's later than you think."

authenticity of sources, unique stories, and original thought.

Some works have had an important impact on historical events by influencing leaders, helping change government policy, and alerting and inspiring public opinion. I have selected the following five books and a collection of leaked secret documents published in scores of newspapers and magazines that appeared between 1903 and 2013. They were made available to the public by British, Irish, and American authors and, however controversial the materials they presented, they inspired later generations of students in the field of intelligence studies and also had an impact on both public opinion and government policy. Some of the material, such as the Snowden leaks, which began to appear in 2013, appear online as digital literature that can be ephemeral and incomplete.

Erskine Childers' 1903 spy thriller, The Riddle of the Sands was a best seller in Britain and has never gone out of print. It is centered in the North Sea and Frisian Islands, in which young English yachtsmen discover a German plot to invade England. It was also an early warning to the British Government of a future menace. The book aroused anxiety that the country was unprepared for a naval conflict with Germany. Within a year or two, the Royal Navy established a naval reserve force to use the sailing skills and knowledge of amateur sailors. The Balfour Government arranged for the establishment of more fleet ports in Scotland. Seldom has a single book had such an unexpected, vital impact. [13]

Some books have influenced later spy novelists and presented a more realistic portrayal of spying. Some have been used to teach about secret work in intelligence schools. Such is the case of the celebrated British novelist Somerset Maugham's spy stories collected in the 1928 book, Ashenden. It is a memoir only lightly disguised as fiction. Maugham, who was trained as a medical doctor but became a celebrated playwright and novelist, served in British secret intelligence in Switzerland and Russia in World War I. Despite Maugham's view that the intelligence work was not only tediously boring but also amoral and futile, it was said that British intelligence recommended that newly recruited agents-in–training read Ashenden. Like The Riddle of the Sands, the slim volume has long remained in print. [14]

An important book on secret writing or cryptology was Herbert O. Yardley's 1931 memoir, The American Black Chamber, [15] two years after Yardley lost his job as a codebreaker with the State Department – and Navy-sponsored unit in New

---

13. David Stafford, The Silent Game: The Real World of Imaginary Spies (Toronto: Lester&Orpen Dennys, 1988), 31-35.

14. Stafford, The Silent Game, pp. 80-83.

15. David Kahn, The Codebreakers: The Story of Secret Writing, 2nd ed. (New York: Scribners, 1996), 350-369. For Kahn's comment on how his reading of Yardley's 1931 book as a boy of 13 helped inspire Kahn's career interest in pursuing the history of codebreaking, see David Kahn, "Introduction" to the 1981 paperback reprint of Yardley's The American Black Chamber (New York: Balantine, 1981, part of its Espionage/Intelligence Library), ix-xvi. See also Yardley, The American Black Chamber (Indianapolis: Bobbs-Merrill, 1931). And see Kahn's definitive biography of Yardley, The Reader of Gentlemen's Mail: Herbert O. Yardley and the Birth of American Codebreaking (New Haven: Yale University Press, 2004).

York. Unemployed and in need of funds, he wrote the book simply for money. The author's motives are much less complex than the consequences of its publication. Its wide readership, including in Japan, influenced American and Japanese cryptography and adversely impacted American capabilities before World War II. *The American Black Chamber* was an early example of a government employee "leaking" diplomatic and military secrets, and led to the government rapidly passing a law to prevent him from publishing another book along the same lines. The impact of Yardley's sensational book has become clothed in myth and half-truth. Only recently have historians determined the actual effects of the book's publication. The Japanese did not alter their code system and move to mechanical coding just because of Yardley's book; this evolution was already underway before mid-1931. The fears of damage to American intelligence work were overblown, according to historian David Kahn; rather, the long-term effects of the book during World War II were positive for American codebreaking.[16]

In 1964, a best-selling book by two Washington-based journalists, David Wise and Thomas Ross, *The Invisible Government*, revealed much about American intelligence services that was new to the public. Until this book, American writers had discussed intelligence-related incidents such as the U-2 affair and the Bay of Pigs fiasco largely as news stories, but had not ventured to offer a full picture of our intelligence system. Wise and Ross' book focused mainly on the CIA but it was also one of the first works to reveal basic information on the most secret and newest of America's intelligence services, the National Security Agency (NSA), established in 1952.[17]

What came to be called "Pentagon Papers" gained public attention in 1970-1971 when a senior, high-level Federal government employee leaked copies of secret materials about the Vietnam war to several American Senators and the press.[18] What began as controversy over American policies in the expanding Vietnam war, assumed crisis proportions when secret Pentagon documents were leaked by senior RAND Corporation policy consultant and researcher who was a Vietnam expert, Daniel Ellsberg. Some of the material reached *The New York Times*, which in June 1971 began to publish extracts. This provoked a constitutional crisis when President Nixon's administration's sought to prevent that newspaper from publishing them. In its scale, contents, and consequences, this was no ordinary small leak of information by a disgruntled government employee; the material in question, 7,000 pages in 47 volumes, was a Pentagon

---

16. Kahn, *The Reader of Gentlemen's Mail*, chapter 12, "The Best Seller"; and Chapter 13, "The Critics, the Effects."

17. David Wise and Thomas B. Ross, *The Invisible Government* (New York: Ballantine, 1964), 218-225.

18. On the Pentagon Papers, see Daniel Ellsberg, *Secrets. A Memoir of Vietnam and the Pentagon Papers* (New York: Viking, 2002); *The New York Times, The Pentagon Papers. The Secret History of the Vietnam War* (New York: Bantam, 1971 ed.); a longer published edition of the documents derived from what Ellsberg leaked to Senator Mike Gravel of Alaska: *The Pentagon Papers: The Defense Department History of the United States' Decision-making on Vietnam* (4 vols: Boston: Beacon Press, 1971).

commissioned, in-house secret history of US-Vietnamese relations from World War II to 1967. For 10 days, by court order, *The New York Times* was prevented from publishing extracts of the material Ellsberg had given them before the Supreme Court allowed publication. When President Nixon sought to persecute and discredit Ellsberg by means of obtaining and revealing Ellsberg's psychiatrist's records, the affair became part of the Watergate scandals, ending with President Nixon's resignation in August 1974.

A final example of an influential and controversial leak about intelligence is the still unfolding story surrounding Edward Snowden's leaks of National Security Agency documents. Unlike our earlier examples, what Snowden obtained and has leaked in segments has not been collected or published in book form. So far, it remains dispersed in thousands of newspaper and magazines stories or online in websites and blogs. Significant portions of Snowden's leaked documents, extracts and summaries are found scattered in several biographical accounts of Snowden's life and activities, and extracts have been published by many newspapers all over the world, including most prominently the first newspapers which published Snowden materials in June 2013: in UK and the US, *The Guardian* (previously known as *The Manchester Guardian*), *The Washington Post*, *The New York Times*, and in Germany, *Der Spiegel*. But scores of other periodicals as well as online websites published extracts as well. The newspaper response was truly global. There is a breathless, poorly sourced, hagiographic account by *The Guardian* journalist Luke Harding, *The Snowden Files: The Inside Story of the World's Most Wanted Man* (New York: Vintage, 2014). Glenn Greenwald, the American lawyer, journalist, and blogger who was one of the first to work with Snowden and is based in Brazil, has a forthcoming biography, *No Place To Hide: Snowden, NSA and...*, slated to be published in the US in late April 2014. Some of Snowden's materials are published in spurts in Greenwald's online blog, The Intercept.

Snowden's main focus was NSA, but there were also significant revelations about the signal intelligence services of the other so-called "Five Eyes" (UK, Canada, Australia, and New Zealand). Snowden's leaks have provoked a vigorous, if nervous, national and global debate on surveillance and privacy in the United States and abroad. The scale of his leaks is unprecedented, dwarfing those of previous large-scale leakers such as Julian Assange's "Wikileaks" and Bradley Manning. Current best estimates of the size of Snowden's leaks range from approximately 1.8 to 2 million files, and this is a conservative, early count as the story further enfolds.[19]

The National Security Agency's surveillance capabilities has a literature of its own, beginning with important books by Dan Brown (a spy novel) and

---

19. These estimates are cited in Daniel Soar, "Incendiary Devices," a review of Luke Harding's book on Snowden, cited above, published in *London Review of Books* 36 (4), February 20, 2014, 9; and an *Associated Press* wire report, "Obama fuels reform on some but not all NSA spying," published in many American papers, including Foster's *Daily Democrat* (Dover, NH: January 19, 2014), A3.

James Bamford and Frank Donner published between 1980 and 2004,[20] as well as many related articles.

Conclusion

Trends in the post-1955 patterns of intelligence literature are worth summarizing. The decade of the 1960s saw literature stimulated in part by the sensational intelligence-related news stories of 1960 and 1962 from the USSR to Cuba, including the Cuban Missile Crisis. As the public fascination with spy stories was exploited by popular television series about spies from the early 1960s to the early 1970s, the literature grew after 1972-1974 with the publication of memoirs and reports of British intelligence officers recounting once closely held "ULTRA" secret and "the Double-Cross system." In the late 1970s, scholarly books began to be published that documented how secret intelligence had been a hidden dimension of diplomatic history. Finally, in the 1980s, British and American scholars began to publish capsule histories of their intelligence services, and a respectable early encyclopedia of intelligence history was published.[21] In conclusion, the first two scholarly, refereed journals devoted entirely to intelligence studies began publishing in the late 1980s. *International Journal of Intelligence and Counterintelligence* in the US and *Intelligence and National Security* in the UK.

Humor in the Literature of Intelligence

Humor and satire in the literature of intelligence are not included in the bibliography that follows. But it should be noted that there is a modest body of literature with or about humor in intelligence. It is not limited to the American humor books by former CIA officers cited in a note below. There are also such works in Britain, including satirical cartoons on intelligence subjects in magazines. It is interesting to note and may be significant that much of the humor material this writer has discovered focuses more on foreign rather than domestic intelligence services. This aspect of the field is experiencing only a modest growth.[22]

---

20. See Dan Brown, *Digital Fortress* (New York: St. Martin's, 1998); Frank J. Donner, *The Age of Surveillance. The Aims and Methods of America's Political Intelligence System* (New York: Knopf, 1980); and books by James Bamford: *The Puzzle Palace: A Report on America's Most Secret Agency* (New York: Penguin, 1982 and later eds.); *Body of Secrets: Anatomy of the Ultra-Secret National Security Agency* (New York: Doubleday, 2001); and *A Pretext for War: 9/11, Iraq, and the Abuse of America's Intelligence Agencies* (New York: Doubleday, 2004).

21. Vincent and Nan Buranelli, *Spy/Counterspy: An Encyclopedia Of Espionage* (New York: McGraw-Hill, 1982).

22. A brief list includes sections of the anthology of Graham Greene and Hugh Greene, *The Spy's Bedside Book* (London: Rupert-Hart Davis, 1957); a recent work by a former CIA officer, Ed Mickolus, *The Secret Book of CIA Humor* (Gretna: LA: Pelican, 2011), which has a suggestive bibliography, and could include a satirical novel by Scottish-American writer, Compton Mackenzie, *Water on the Brain* (1933)

Nearly 60 years after Kent's prescient article, there is not only a literature of intelligence of considerable dimensions, but it is larger, more diverse, and more exotic than Kent might have imagined. To the benefit of many, it includes many scholarly disciplines from the sciences to the arts. It has also provided resources for academic approaches to intelligence studies at many institutions of higher education in various colleges and departments. Besides courses in law schools, there are also relevant courses of study in many colleges of arts and sciences in departments such as government and politics, national security, history, sociology, and international relations.[23] There are also intelligence-related courses taught in the Armed Services' academies and universities, which offer various graduate degrees. Intelligence studies are no longer at the margins of academia but have an increasingly important and central place in the classroom, in the electronic media, and in the publishing world.

READINGS FOR INSTRUCTORS

Listed below is a selection of the outstanding, well-written, and enduring examples of American and British intelligence literature. Though some of the foreign language literature has been translated into English, a significant quantity remains untranslated and only in the original languages.[24]

Intelligence Textbooks

Andrew, Christopher, Richard J. Aldrich, and Wesley K. Wark (eds.). *Secret Intelligence: A Reader* (London and New York: Routledge, 2009/2010).

Lowenthal, Mark. *Intelligence: From Secrets to Policy* 5th edition, (Washington, DC: CQ Press, 2011).

Histories

Andrew, Christopher. *Defend the Realm. The Authorized History of MI5* (New York: Knopf, 2009). This was an official history of the Security Service.

Andrew, Christopher. *Her Majesty's Secret Service: The Making of the British Intelligence Community* (New York: Viking, 1986). This covers the period up to 1950.

---

and Graham Greene's classic send-up of both MI-6 and early James Bond novels: *Our Man In Havana* (1958). Unlike many other such publications in Britain, beginning in World War I and extending into the 1960s, there were a number of humorous cartoons related to the subject of espionage in London's *Punch* magazine and less frequently in the American magazine, *The New Yorker*, especially during the mid-Cold War years.

23. AFIO lists colleges and universities with intelligence-related courses on its website *http://www.afio. com/12_academic.htm*.

24. One of the most useful bibliographies related to intelligence is the *Literature of Intelligence: A Bibliography of Materials with Essays, Review, and Comments* by Professor J. Ransom Clark available at http://intel-lit.muskingum.edu, cited in Peter Oleson, "Staying Informed: Information Sources on the Web, Intelligence Bibliographies, Newsletter and Webliographies," *The Guide to the Study of Intelligence*, http://www.afio. com/40_guide.htm.

Brugioni, Dino A. *Eyeball To Eyeball: The Inside Story of the Cuban Missile Crisis* (New York: 1990/1991). Brugioni was a pioneer in photo interpretation.

Budiansky, Stephen. *Battle of Wits: The Complete Story of Code-Breaking in World War II* (New York: Free Press, 2000).

Collier, Basil. *Hidden Weapons: Allied Secret or Undercover Services in World War II* (Barnsley, UK: Pen & Sword Military Classics, 2006; 1st ed., London: Hamish Hamilton, 1982).

Felix, Christopher. *The Spy and His Masters: A Short Course in the Secret War* (London: Secker & Warburg, 1963; 2nd rev. edition, with new introduction by the author, New York: Ballantine, 1987). Felix was a US Foreign Service officer whose real name was James McCargar.

Fishel, Edwin C. *The Secret War for the Union: The Untold Story of Military Intelligence in the Civil War* (Boston and New York: Houghton-Mifflin, 1996).

Fishel, Edwin C. "Myths That Never Die," *International Journal of Intelligence and Counterintelligence* 2 (1), Spring 1988. Also about the Civil War.

Hinsley, F. H. et. al. *British Intelligence in the Second World War* (London: Her Majesty's Stationery Office, 1979-1990). In six volumes.

Jeffrey, Keith. *The Secret History of MI6 —1909-1949*, (London: Penguin, 2010). This was an official authorized history of the Secret Intelligence Service.

Jones, R. V. *The Wizard War: British Scientific Intelligence 1939-1945* (New York: Coward, McCann, 1978). Jones headed British scientific intelligence.

Kahn, David. *The Codebreakers: The Story of Secret Writing* (New York: Scribner, 1967, 1st ed.; 2nd ed., 1996). A classic.

Masterman, J.C. *The Double-Cross System in the War of 1939 to 1945.* (New Haven, CT: Yale University Press, 1972).

O'Toole, G.J.A. *Honorable Treachery: A History of U.S. Intelligence, Espionage, and Covert Action From the American Revolution to the CIA* (New York: Atlantic Monthly Press, 1991). Covers the period up to 1962.

Ranelagh, John. *The Agency: The Rise and Decline of the CIA from Wild Bill Donovan to William Casey* (New York: Simon & Schuster, 1986).

Ransom, Harry Howe. *Central Intelligence and National Security* (Cambridge, MA: Harvard University Press, 1958).

Richelson, Jeffrey. *A Century of Spies: Intelligence in the Twentieth Century* (New York: Oxford University Press, 1995).

Richelson, Jeffrey. *The Wizards of Langley: Inside the CIA's Directorate of Science and Technology* (Boulder, CO: Westview, 2001).

Tuchman, Barbara W. *The Zimmermann Telegram* (New York: Ballantine: 1958, 1966).

Winterbotham, F.W. *The Ultra Secret* (New York: Dell, 1974).

Yardley, Herbert O. *The American Black Chamber* (1931; 2nd ed. with introduction by David Kahn, New York: Ballantine, 1981).

Biographies and Memoirs

Baer, Robert. *See No Evil: The True Story of a Ground Soldier in the CIA's War on Terrorism* (New York: Three Rivers, 2002).

Carter, Miranda. *Anthony Blunt: His Lives* (New York: Farrar, Straus & Giroux, 2001).

Helms, Richard with William Hood, *A Look Over My Shoulder: A Life in the Central Intelligence Agency* (New York: Random House, 2003).

Hornblum, Allen M. *The Invisible Harry Gold: The Man Who Gave the Soviets the Atom Bomb* (New Haven: Yale University Press, 2010).

Knightley, Phillip, Bruce Page, and David Leitch. *The Philby Affair* (London: 1967): US ed. title, *The Philby Conspiracy* (1968).

Knightley, Phillip. *Philby: The Life and Views of the K.G.B. Masterspy* (London: Andre Deutsch, 1988).

Meier, Andrew. *The Lost Spy: An American in Stalin's Secret Service* (New York: Norton, 2008). The life of Isaiah Oggins (1898-1947).

Meyer, Cord. *Facing Reality: From World Federalism To The CIA* (New York: Harper & Row, 1980).

Phillips, David L. *The Night Watch: 25 Years of Peculiar Service* (New York: Atheneum, 1977). UK ed. (London: Robert Hale, 1978).

Powers, Thomas. *The Man Who Kept the Secrets: Richard Helms and the C.I.A.* (New York: Knopf, 1979). Presidio Press issued a paperback edition in 1982.

Pujol, Juan and Nigel West. *Operation Garbo* (New York: Random House, 1986).

Schecter, Jerrold L. and Peter S. Deriabin. *The Spy Who Saved the World: How a Soviet Colonel Changed the Course of the Cold War* (New York: Scribner, 1992). The story of Oleg Penkovsky.

West, Nigel and Roberts Madoc. *Snow: The Double Life of a World War II Spy* (London: Biteback, 2011).

Assessments of Intelligence
(including of spies)

Andrew, Christopher. *For The Presidents' Eyes Only: Secret Intelligence and the American Presidency from Washington to Bush* (New York: HarperCollins, 1995).

Burn, Michael. *The Debatable Land: A Study of the Motives of Spies in Two Ages* (London: Hamish Hamilton, 1970). Elizabethan England and Cold War Britain.

Dulles, Allen. *The Craft of Intelligence* (New York: Harper & Row, 1963).

Farago, Ladislas. *War of Wits: The Anatomy of Espionage and Intelligence* (New York: Funk & Wagnalls, 1954; Popular Library, 1962; Greenwood, 1976).

Kahn, David. "The Intelligence Failure of Pearl Harbor," *Foreign Affairs* 70 (5), Winter 1991/1992, 138-152.

Kahn, David. "An Historical Theory of Intelligence," *Intelligence and National Security* 16 (3), Autumn, 2001, 79-92.

Katz, Barry M. *Foreign Intelligence: Research and Analysis in the Office of Strategic Services 1942-1945* (Cambridge, MA and London: Harvard University Press, 1989).

Keegan, John. *Intelligence in War: The Value and Limitations of What the Military Can Learn About the Enemy* (New York: Vintage, 2002).

Kent, Sherman. *Strategic Intelligence for American World Policy* (Princeton, NJ: Princeton University Press, 1949; 1966).

Lindsay, Robert. *The Falcon and the Snowman: A True Story of Friendship and Espionage* (New York: Simon & Schuster, 1979).

May, Ernest R. (ed.). *Knowing One's Enemies: Intelligence Assessment Before the Two World Wars* (Princeton, NJ: Princeton University Press, 1984).

May, Ernest R. and Richard E. Neustadt. *Thinking in Time: The Uses of History for Decision Makers* (New York: Free Press, 1986).

Moorehead, Alan. *The Traitors* (London: Hamish Hamilton, 1952).

O'Toole, George J.A. "Kahn's Law: A Universal Principal of Intelligence?" *International Journal of Intelligence and Counterintelligence* 4 (1), 1989, 39-45.

West, Rebecca. *The New Meaning of Treason* (New York: Viking, 1964; later eds, including London: Penguin, 1985).

Wise, David. *Spy: The Inside Story of How the FBI's Robert Hanssen Betrayed America* (New York: Random House, 2002).

Wohlstetter, Roberta. *Pearl Harbor: Warning and Decision* (Stanford: Stanford University Press, 1962). A classic.

Wohlstetter, Roberta. "Cuba and Pearl Harbor: Hindsight and Foresight," *Foreign Affairs* 43 (4), July 1965, 691-707.

Zegart, Amy B. *Spying Blind: The CIA, the FBI, and the Origins of 9/11* (Princeton, NJ: Princeton University Press, 2007).

Fiction
(including interpretations of spy fiction)

Ambler, Eric. *Epitaph for a Spy* (1st ed., London, 1938; 2nd ed. London: Dent, 1984).

Barzun, Jacques. "Meditations on the Literature of Spying," *The American Scholar* 34 (2), Spring 1965,168. Slightly abbreviated, reprinted in collection, Jacques Barzun, *A Jacques Barzun Reader: Selections From His Works* (New York: HarperCollins, 2002), 581-587.

Buchan, John. *The Thirty-Nine Steps* (New York: Curtis, 1915. Many later editions, including: London: Penguin, 2000).

Cawelti, John G. and Bruce A. Rosenberg. *The Spy Story* (Chicago: Chicago University Press, 1987).

Childers, Erskine. *The Riddle of the Sands* (London: 1903;later editions, including London: Dent, 1984).

Conrad, Joseph. *The Secret Agent: A Simple Tale* (London, 1907;and later editions, including London: Penguin, 1982).

Furst, Alan. *Spies of the Balkans* (New York: Random House, 2010).

Greene, Graham. *Our Man in Havana* (London: Heinemann, 1958).

Greene, Graham. *The Human Factor* (New York: Simon & Schuster, 1978).

Hood, William. *Spy Wednesday* (New York: Norton, 1986).

Kipling, Rudyard. *Kim* (London, 1901; later editions, including Penguin, 2007).

Le Carre, John. *The Spy Who Came in From the Cold* (London: Gollancz, 1963).

Le Carre, John. *Tinker, Tailor, Soldier, Spy* (New York: Knopf, 1974).

Littell, Robert. *The Company: A Novel of the CIA* (New York: Overlook, 2002).

Maugham, Somerset. *Ashenden* (London, 1928; later editions including, Penguin, 2007). This is a memoir disguised as fiction.

McCarry, Charles. *The Miernik Dossier* (New York: E.P. Dutton, 1973).

Masters, Anthony. *Literary Agents: The Novelist as Spy* (London: Blackwell, 1987).

Stafford, David. *The Silent Game: The Real World of Imaginary Spies* (Toronto: Lester & Orpen Dennys, 1988).

Wark, Wesley (ed.). "Spy Fiction, Spy Films and Real Intelligence," *Intelligence and National Security* 5 (4), October 1990.

Douglas L. Wheeler is professor emeritus of history at the University of New Hampshire and a frequent contributor to AFIO's *Guide to the Study of Intelligence*.

End Note

If you are reading the printed version of this Guide, and are looking for an index with which to quickly search the contents, that is available online at *http://www.afio.com/40_guide.htm* using the PDF version of The Guide which has a full electronic index incorporated.

The Association of Former Intelligence Officers (AFIO) welcomes comments and suggestions from readers. Please email *guide@afio.com*.

The Association of Former Intelligence Officers® (AFIO®) was incorporated in 1975 as a §501(c)3 non-profit, non-political, educational association for current and former intelligence, security, military, and homeland security professionals and supporters of the US intelligence community, be they from business, academia, or the media. The Association is based in Falls Church, Virginia, has over 4500 members, with 18 active chapters across the United States. Despite its formal name, AFIO is open to all U.S. citizens who support its mission. It encourages professors teaching in the field, and students considering or studying for careers in the IC, to become members.

When AFIO was created in 1975 during heated national debates regarding the nature and purpose of US Intelligence, the organization defined its mission to try to present a clearer understanding of the function of intelligence and what intelligence officers can and cannot do. From the very beginning it sought to reach out to teachers and students across the country, as well as to the media, through publications, and periodic luncheons and conferences. These early efforts have grown into the robust outreach and support programs present today, including scholarships, a Speakers Bureau, academic and civic outreach, a variety of print and online publications, including the Intelligencer; the *Weekly Intelligence Notes*; *Careers in Intelligence* – our student guidebook; the online *Guide to the Study of Intelligence*, and this bound, 788-page printed version of the *Guide*; an annual symposium co-hosted with one of the top six Intelligence Community agencies; support to CIA and other IC conferences; as well as quarterly luncheons featuring senior officials from the Intelligence and Policy Communities, authors, academics, and the media.

AFIO is more than a professional or fraternal organization. Its educational mission is to build a public constituency for a sound, healthy, responsible, and capable US intelligence system. Its focus on education fosters an understanding of the important role of intelligence in national security, in privacy and encryption that is responsive to counterterrorism/counterintelligence needs, and a nurturing of interest by students in the many exciting and challenging careers to be found in the wide variety of fields offered by US Intelligence Agencies. This includes the role of supporting intelligence activities in US policy, diplomacy, strategy, security, and homeland defense.
In addition, AFIO focuses on understanding the critical need for effective counterintelligence and security against foreign, political, technological, or economic espionage, as well as covert, clandestine, and overt counter-terrorist or criminal operations threatening US security, the national infrastructure, or corporate and individual safety. In many ways, AFIO is the public face of the Intelligence Community.
For membership information or to subscribe to our publications, or explore academic, scholarship, and career opportunities, visit our website or email us.

Association of Former Intelligence Officers
7700 Leesburg Pike, Suite 324
Falls Church, VA 22043-2618
www.afio.com / afio@afio.com / 703-790-0320